MONEY AND CAPITAL MARKETS

THE IRWIN SERIES IN FINANCE

FINANCIAL MANAGEMENT

Block and Hirt
Foundations of Financial Management
Seventh Edition

Brooks
Fingame: The Financial Management Decision Game
Third Edition

Bruner
Case Studies in Finance: Managing for Corporate Value Creation
Second Edition

Fruhan, Kester, Mason, Piper, and Ruback
Case Problems in Finance
Tenth Edition

Harrington
Corporate Financial Analysis: Decisions in a Global Environment
Fourth Edition

Helfert
Techniques of Financial Analysis
Eighth Edition

Higgins
Analysis for Financial Management
Third Edition

Jones
Introduction to Financial Management
First Edition

Kallberg, Parkinson
Corporate Liquidity: Management and Measurement
First Edition

Ross, Westerfield, and Jaffe
Corporate Finance
Third Edition

Ross, Westerfield, and Jordan
Fundamentals of Corporate Finance
Second Edition

Schary
Cases in Financial Management
First Edition

Stonehill and Eiteman
Finance: An International Perspective
First Edition

White
Financial Calculator Applications
First Edition

INVESTMENTS

Bodie, Kane, and Marcus
Essentials of Investments
First Edition

Bodie, Kane, and Marcus
Investments
Second Edition

Bolster
The Wall Street Journal: Applications in Finance
1994 Edition

Cohen, Zinbarg, Zeikel
Investment Analysis and Portfolio Management
Fifth Edition

Hirt and Block
Fundamentals of Investment Management
Fourth Edition

Lorie, Dodd, and Kimpton
The Stock Market: Theories & Evidence
Second Edition

MarketBase, Inc.
MarketBase^{SM}-E
First Edition

Shimko
The Innovative Investor, Version 2.0
First Edition

FINANCIAL INSTITUTIONS AND MARKETS

Rose
Readings on Financial Institutions and Markets
Eighth Edition

Rose
Money and Capital Markets: Financial Institutions and Instruments in a Global Marketplace
Sixth Edition

Rose
Commercial Bank Management: Producing and Selling Financial Services
Third Edition

Rose and Kolari
Financial Institutions: Understanding & Managing Financial Services
Fifth Edition

Saunders
Financial Institutions Management: A Modern Approach
First Edition

REAL ESTATE

Berston
California Real Estate Practice
Sixth Edition

Berston
California Real Estate Principles
Sixth Edition

Brueggeman and Fisher
Real Estate Finance and Investments
Ninth Edition

Smith and Corgel
Real Estate Perspectives: An Introduction to Real Estate
Second Edition

Shenkel
Real Estate Finance
First Edition

FINANCIAL PLANNING AND INSURANCE

Allen, Melone, Rosenbloom, and VanDerhei
Pension Planning: Pensions, Profit-Sharing, and Other Deferred Compensation Plans
Seventh Edition

Crawford and Beadles
Life Insurance Law
Seventh Edition

MONEY AND CAPITAL MARKETS

Financial Institutions and Instruments in a Global Marketplace

Sixth Edition

Peter S. Rose
Texas A&M University

IRWIN

Chicago • Bogotá • Boston • Buenos Aires • Caracas
London • Madrid • Mexico City • Sydney • Toronto

Irwin Book Team

Publisher:	*Michael W. Junior*
Associate editor:	*Maureen M. Harrington*
Editorial coordinator:	*Wendi Sweetland*
Marketing manager:	*Katie Rose*
Senior project supervisor:	*Rebecca Dodson*
Production supervisor:	*Pat Frederickson*
Designer:	*Larry J. Cope*
Cover design:	*Annette Rapier/A.M. Design*
Cover illustration:	*George Schill*
Prepress buyer:	*Charlene R. Perez*
Assistant manager, graphics:	*Charlene R. Perez*
Compositor:	*Weimer Graphics, Inc., Division of Shepard Poorman Communications Corp.*
Typeface:	*10/12 Times Roman*
Printer:	*Times Mirror Higher Education Group, Inc., Print Group*

Times Mirror
Higher Education Group

Library of Congress Cataloging-in-Publication Data

Rose, Peter S.
   Money and capital markets : financial institutions and instruments
in a global marketplace / Peter S. Rose. — 6th ed.
     p. cm. — (Irwin series in finance
   Includes index.
   ISBN 0-256-15239-X
   1. Finance — United States. 2. Money market — United States.
3. Capital market — United States. I. Title. II. Series.
HG181.R66 1997
332'.0973 — dc20   96–8515

To My Family

Preface

THE STUDY OF MONEY AND CAPITAL MARKETS

As teachers and practitioners of financial decision making are well aware, it would be difficult to find a subject for study of greater importance than the financial system and its markets. The *money and capital markets* are the mechanism in our society for converting the public's savings into investments — buildings, machinery and equipment, airports and highways, and inventories of goods and raw materials — so the economy can grow, new jobs can be created, and living standards can rise. It is the system of money and capital markets that handles most of the payments made each day for purchases of food, clothing, shelter, and tens of thousands of other goods and services. The financial system generates credit to sustain the public's spending and standard of living and stores future purchasing power (wealth) in the form of stocks, bonds, and other securities. The system of financial markets also makes possible the liquidation of those securities whenever the public needs cash for immediate spending.

The money and capital markets offer risk protection to businesses and individuals through sales of insurance policies and hedging instruments (such as options and futures contracts). And both domestic and international financial markets carry the great burden of public policy, serving as the conduit for government actions designed to promote economic growth, reduce unemployment, and avoid inflation. A central theme of this book, in all its editions, has been to highlight these essential contributions of the financial system to today's economy and society. This book's primary goal is to leave its readers with a clear picture of how money and capital markets around the globe work to fulfill these varied, yet vital, roles of facilitating savings and investment, making payments, supplying credit, accumulating wealth, supplying liquidity, protecting against risk, and supporting public policy.

THE FINANCIAL SYSTEM OF MARKETS BESET BY CHANGE

Clearly, today's financial system is of great importance to every one of us. Student and teacher, businessman and businesswoman, consumer and investor, government policy-maker, and private citizen — all depend on the speed, efficiency, and quality of services that the system of money and capital markets provides. But, as this book tries to convey in each of its nine sections, that system of financial markets and institutions is today beset by sweeping change and serious problems — challenges whose dimensions and solutions are not easily grasped, and whose consequences will affect every individual and institution in the global economy for years to come.

As we will discover in the pages of this book, the financial system of money and capital markets is *not* independent of the economy and society that surrounds it. Economic booms and recessions, government budget deficits and taxes, technological innovations, political upheavals, wars, and social change — all impact the decisions made in the financial marketplace and often have devastating financial consequences. Consider the enormous political and social changes we have seen recently — the collapse of the Warsaw Pact and the ending of the cold war, the opening of Eastern Europe and the republics once a part of the Soviet Union to investment and financial aid from the West, the growth of private market systems in economies formerly dominated by government control, the growing financial and political integration of Europe, the movement toward free trade zones in North and South America, war and then reconstruction in the Middle East, and the search for personal freedom and economic security in Africa, Asia, and Eastern Europe. At the same time, new financial service needs are emerging as the earth's population ages, people living alone or in smaller families become the norm, and good-paying jobs, financial security at retirement, and affordable health care seem more elusive than ever. These economic, political, and social changes have set in motion powerful forces reshaping financial systems around the globe.

There is a powerful trend toward increasingly intense worldwide competition for financial services as improvements in communications technology have brought widely separated banks and other financial institutions into direct competition with one another. National financial systems are merging into one vast, global financial services marketplace where national borders mean less and less. Deregulation of the financial sector by governments in Australia, Canada, Great Britain, Japan, the United States, and many other nations has further stimulated the global spreading of competition for financial services. This unfolding of worldwide financial services competition may well be benefiting us as consumers of financial services with lower prices and better quality, but it has also brought enormous problems that desperately await new solutions.

For one thing, intense financial services competition and rapid economic, social, and technological change have led to more failures among banks and other financial institutions, with even the largest and most venerable of financial institutions vulnerable to collapse. At the same time, in the decade of the 90s scandals rocked some popular financial markets, such as the market for U.S. government securities and the over-the-counter market in corporate stock, making investors question whether the system of money and capital markets is as efficient, equitable, and sound as we once thought it was. The result is a serious threat to public confidence in the soundness of banks and other financial institutions and the safety of the public's savings. How can we reassure the public about risk in the financial system and help them deal with that risk? Clearly, if we are to do so in the future, we must learn as much as we can about how the system of money and capital markets works and where it is headed.

A related problem centers on the huge volume of debt carried by many nations in both industrially developed regions of the globe and among lesser-developed countries of the Third World. In the United States, government debt has reached unprecedented levels, so that the interest and good will of foreign investors, who buy a substantial portion of that debt, has come to have a potent impact on economic and financial conditions inside the U.S. and in other countries as well. And what is true of nations has also been true of businesses and individuals, who, in some cases, built up unprecedented amounts of indebtedness over the past decade and now face the painful task of managing that debt in an era of slower and more uncertain growth. When is debt a useful financial tool and when is it harmful to us? What forms of debt are issued in the money and capital markets today and why? What might happen to the economy and the financial system if government could reduce its huge deficits and begin to pay down some of its enormous debt? These and other issues surrounding debt are addressed in numerous chapters throughout this book.

One of the factors that makes the rapid rise of debt in the financial markets such a problem is the volatility of the world economy. Recent decades have brought wide and unprecedented swings in the prices of crude oil and natural gas, gold, industrial raw materials, food, and fiber. Key industries, such as agriculture, construction, autos, and energy fuels, have fluctuated from unparalleled prosperity to the depths of depression. Not surprisingly, because of the close links between the economy and the financial system, the money and capital markets and financial institutions have mirrored the ups and downs of these volatile industries. For example, stock prices on exchanges in London, New York, Tokyo, and other global financial centers rose to unprecedented heights, only to come tumbling down, and then rise again toward new record levels. Interest rates rose as fears of business bankruptcies and government defaults increased and then fell to the lowest levels in decades. The economy once again has responded to fluctuations in the financial system — lower interest rates and higher security prices have stimulated construction and investment, although growth in new jobs remains disappointingly low.

FINANCIAL RISK MANAGEMENT

As we will see in this new edition, the result today is a financial system of markets and institutions both more sensitive and more alert to *risk* in all of its forms. *Risk management* has become a cornerstone of modern business decision making, and the financial markets have responded with a rapidly widening array of innovative new risk-management services, including security options, financial futures contracts, portfolio immunization, interest-rate and currency swaps, and balanced-funds management. This new edition of *Money and Capital Markets* contains an expanded discussion of today's risk management tools (especially in Chapters 7, 12, 13, 25, 27, 28, and 30) and integrates them more fully into the material in all of the relevant chapters. The discussion of futures, options, and swaps, in particular, has been significantly expanded.

ABOUT THIS BOOK

As *Money and Capital Markets* enters its sixth edition, its goals remain much the same as in earlier editions:

- To present a comprehensive, yet interesting, analysis of the entire financial system — both domestic and international — and its component parts, with an expanded discussion in nearly every chapter of the trend toward globalization of financial markets and institutions.

- To acquaint the reader with all the major types of financial instruments, including bonds, stocks, mortgages, bills, notes, deposits, and other financial assets, and their uses, principal buyers and sellers, and trading characteristics.

- To provide a clear view of all the major types of financial institutions that operate within the global financial system, with a strong new emphasis in this edition on the many management tools available to financial institutions today.

- To provide a thorough discussion of how interest rates and security prices are determined and what causes security prices and interest rates to change under conditions of market efficiency or in a world characterized by the asymmetric distribution of information.

- To promote a better understanding of public policy issues in the financial marketplace and how government policymakers, working through the financial system, can influence financial and economic conditions and the welfare of businesses, individuals, and families.

- To explore the many important roles played by government regulation in shaping the character and health of the financial system (including the Basle Agreement on international capital standards for depository institutions and the new rules guiding the spread of interstate banking in the United States).

- To identify and understand the current and future trends — economic, demographic, social, and financial — that are reshaping the global financial system in order to respond to tomorrow's financial service needs.

FEATURES OF THIS BOOK

These objectives are pursued by creating a variety of educational tools:

- Each chapter begins with a clear statement of its *learning objectives* to alert the reader to what is most important in the pages that follow.

- Numerous *illustrations, tables,* and *examples* appear throughout the book to help emphasize and clarify key points, equations, and ideas, and there is significantly expanded use of information boxes, including numerous *management insights* that focus upon the modern tools used by managers of financial institutions and an *international focus* series of boxes that add a global dimension to numerous topics throughout the text.

- A list of *key terms and concepts* appears at the end of each chapter and inside the text these key terms and concepts are marked in boldface so the reader can quickly see how each term is defined.

- *Problems to solve* are included at the end of most of the chapters (and there are more problems in this new edition) accompanied by extensive references for readers interested in achieving mastery of the subject.

- A *Money and Capital Markets Dictionary* appears at the end of the book to provide immediate access to brief definitions of each of the key terms presented in the chapters.

- The last chapter of the book, entitled *The Future of the Financial System*, attempts to tie together the various economic, demographic, and financial trends that are reshaping the money and capital markets into a global, intensely competitive, and risk-laden environment. This chapter and several that precede it look at the impact of new legislation (such as the 1994 Riegle-Neal Interstate Banking Act in the United States), new regulations (such as the Basle Agreement on international capital standards for banks), and historic trade agreements such as NAFTA and the Maastricht Treaty for European unity.

This new edition also addresses numerous topics of current concern around the world, including the impact of asymmetric information in the financial marketplace (discussed principally in Chapter 3), standby credit arrangements (presented principally in Chapters 4 and 17), the changing character of regulations surrounding financial institutions (which are now concentrated in a completely new chapter for this edition, Chapter 7), new research findings on inflation, interest rates, and stock prices (Chapter 10), expanded coverage of the Black-Scholes model and new types of futures, options (Chapter 13), and interest-rate swaps (Chapter 12), the changing rules for auctioning government securities (Chapters 15 and 22), recent innovations in money market instruments (Chapters 16 and 17), new household financial services and new government laws to protect the consumer of financial services (principally in Chapters 24 and 25), new regulations surrounding the entry of foreign banks into the United States (principally Chapters 4 and 29), and recent reform of the deposit insurance system (found principally in the new Chapter 7).

ACKNOWLEDGMENTS

As in earlier editions of this book, the author has benefited from the ideas, criticisms, and data provided by many economists, financial analysts, government agencies, trade associations, and private groups. The author wishes to extend special appreciation to James C. Baker of Kent State University, Ivan T. Call of Brigham Young University, Eugene F. Drzycinski of the University of Wisconsin, Mona J. Gardner of Illinois State University, Timothy Koch of the University of South Carolina, David Mills of Illinois State University, John P. Olienyh of Colorado State University, Colleen C. Pantalone of Northeastern University, Richard Rivard of the University of South Florida, Paul Bolster of Northeastern University, Robert M. Crowe formerly with the American College at Bryn Mawr, Joseph P. Ogden of the University of Tennessee-Knoxville, Donald A. Smith of Pierce College, Oliver G. Wood, Jr., of the University of South Carolina, Larry Lang of the University of Wisconsin-Oshkosh, Jeffrey A. Clark of Florida State University, James F. Gatti of the University of Vermont, Gioia P. Bales of Hofstra University, Ahmad Sohrabian of California State Polytechnic University-Pomona, and Thomas A. Fetherston of the University of Alabama-Birmingham for their helpful and insightful reviews and criticisms of the various editions through which this book has passed. In addition, numerous associations and institutions gave their permission to reprint important data or other pieces of information in various editions, including the American Council of Life Insurance, the *Canadian Banker* (official publication of the Canadian Bankers' Association), the Chicago Board of Trade, the Credit Union National Association, Dow Jones Reprints, Dun & Bradstreet, Inc., the First Boston Corporation, the Insurance Information Institute, Moody's Investor Service, Standard & Poor's Corporation, and the United States League of Savings Associations. The author also gratefully acknowledges the support, patience, and understanding of his family, which made completion of this sixth edition possible. Nevertheless, any shortcomings that remain belong to the author.

A NOTE TO THE STUDENT

The money and capital markets are a fascinating field of study. What happens in those markets affects the quality of our lives every day in many different ways. The financial markets are dynamic institutions continually "putting on a new face" in the form of new services, new instruments, and new methods. This text is only an *introduction* to these vast, ever-changing institutions — one that you will want to build on throughout your career through continued reading and personal involvement.

As you begin each chapter of this new book, aim for mastery of the material, for making the most of an important opportunity to learn. How can you do that?

Let me suggest that you start with the short list of *learning objectives* that begin each chapter. These are guideposts, a brief description of what I hope you will come away with after you have closed the book. It is a good idea to go over this list of learning objectives as you start to read and then again when you have finished each chapter. If you are still unsure whether you have received any help with any one of these learning objectives, go back and review the portion of the chapter which deals with that particular objective. Ask yourself if the goal makes sense to you and if you now feel better informed about it than before.

Next note the *key terms and concepts* at the end of each chapter. Let me suggest that you make a pencil list of these key terms on a sheet of notebook paper or list them in your PC or programmable calculator and then be on the lookout for them as you read each chapter. (All key terms are shown in boldface type where they appear within a chapter so they will stand out.) Consider writing a definition of each of the key terms in your own words. Then double check your definitions with those given in each chapter or in the *Money and Capital Markets Dictionary* that appears at the end of the book.

Also, at the conclusion of each chapter is a list of *Study Questions and Problems.* Your instructor may assign some of these, but even if that doesn't happen, try to answer them for yourself. If you have the time, writing or typing out an answer to each question and problem (perhaps saving your answers in a PC file) is the best approach for mastering the subject. Or you can try to answer each question orally or discuss them in a group study session with other members of the class. If you don't feel comfortable with your answer to a particular problem or question, go through the chapter until you find the right section and review that portion of the reading material again.

Keep in mind that this text is designed with *two* fundamental purposes in mind: (1) to arm you with analytical tools to help you understand why the financial marketplace behaves as it does and how we should make financial decisions and (2) to describe how today's money and capital markets operate and where they appear to be headed, so that you can more easily "speak the language" of the markets and comfortably find your way around in them. Chapters 1 through 13 are aimed mainly at the first of these purposes, developing a good set of analytical tools. Chapters 14 through 30 mainly aim at the second purpose, to see how each financial market operates today and to be able to "speak their language." A successful course in money and capital markets will give you *both* the tools and the language of the financial markets.

Reading this book and successfully completing this course should help you in meeting your long-range career goals and in successfully completing your degree or professional certification program. *Money and Capital Markets* provides essential background for those taking subsequent course work in investments, capital budgeting, business finance, money and banking, macroeconomics, international finance, and government policy. Moreover, this book sensitizes you to the key problems and issues faced today by business managers and government policymakers on a daily basis, especially in those problem areas related to borrowing and lending money and to government regulation of the financial marketplace. However, just as with every other course you will take, your future success in using this new knowledge will depend on the energy and enthusiasm, the commitment to excellence and hard work that you bring to the subject. It is a challenge worthy of your best efforts. Good luck!

Peter S. Rose

Contents in Brief

Contents

Contents

The Role of the Financial System in the Global Economy

LEARNING OBJECTIVES IN THIS CHAPTER

- To explain the functions and roles played by the system of financial markets in the global economy and in our daily living.
- To define key terms and concepts about the money and capital markets that will be used throughout the course.

This book is devoted to a study of the **financial system** — the collection of markets, institutions, laws, regulations, and techniques through which bonds, stocks, and other securities are traded, interest rates are determined, and financial services are produced and delivered around the world. The financial system is one of the most important inventions of modern society. Its primary task is to move scarce loanable funds from those who save to those who borrow to buy goods and services and to make investments in new equipment and facilities so that the global economy can grow and increase the standard of living enjoyed by its citizens. Without the financial system and the funds it supplies, each of us would lead a much less enjoyable existence.

The financial system determines both the cost of credit and how much credit will be available to pay for the thousands of different goods and services we purchase daily. Equally important, what happens in this system has a powerful impact on the health of the global economy. When credit becomes more costly and less available, total spending for goods and services falls. As a result, unemployment rises and the economy's growth slows down as businesses cut back their production and lay off workers. In contrast, when the cost of credit declines and loanable funds become more readily available, total spending in the economy increases, more jobs are created, and the economy's growth accelerates. In truth, the financial system is an integral part of the economic system. We cannot really understand one system without understanding the other.

THE ECONOMY AND THE FINANCIAL SYSTEM
Flows within the Economic System

To better understand the role played by the financial system in our daily lives, we begin by examining its position within the global economy.

The basic function of any economy is to allocate scarce resources — land, labor, management skill, and capital — to produce the goods and services needed by society. The high standard of living most of us enjoy today depends on the ability of the global economy to turn out each day an enormous volume of food, shelter, and other essentials of modern living. This is an exceedingly complex task because scarce resources must be procured in just the right amounts to provide the raw materials of production and combined at just the right time with labor, management, and capital to generate the products and services demanded by consumers. In short, any economic system must combine inputs — land and other natural resources, labor and management skill, and capital equipment — to produce output: goods and services. The economy generates a flow of production in return for a flow of payments (see Exhibit 1–1).

We may also depict the flows of payments and production within the economic system as a *circular flow* between producing units (mainly businesses and governments) and consuming units (principally households). (See Exhibit 1–2.) In modern economies, households provide labor, management skill, and natural resources to business firms and governments in return for income in the form of wages and other payments. Most of the income received by households is spent to purchase goods and services from businesses and governments. In 1995, for example, about 96 percent of the $6 trillion in total personal income received by individuals and families in the United States was spent on the consumption of goods and services or paid out in taxes to purchase government services. (The remainder of personal income — about 4 percent — was set aside as *savings*.) The result of this spending is a flow of funds back to producing units as income, which stimulates them to produce more goods and services in the future. The circular flow of production and income is interdependent and never ending.

The Role of Markets in the Economic System

In most economies around the world, markets are used to carry out this complex task of allocating resources and producing goods and services. What is a **market**? It is an institution set up by society to allocate resources that are scarce relative to the demand for them. Markets are the channel through which buyers and sellers meet to exchange goods, services, and resources.

The marketplace determines what goods and services will be produced and in what quantity. This is accomplished through changes in the prices of goods and services offered

Exhibit 1–1   **The Economic System**

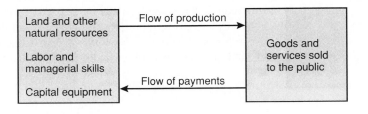

Exhibit 1–2   **Circular Flow of Income, Payments, and Production in the Economic System**

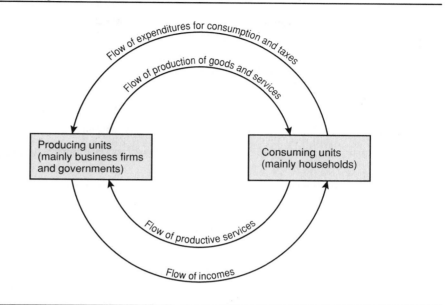

in the market. If the price of an item rises, for example, this stimulates business firms to produce and supply more of it to consumers. In the long run, new firms may enter the market to produce those goods and services experiencing increased demand and rising prices. A decline in price, on the other hand, usually leads to reduced production of a good or service, and in the long run some firms may leave the marketplace.

Markets also distribute *income*. In a pure market system, the income of an individual or business firm is determined solely by the contributions each makes to producing goods and services demanded by consumers. Markets reward superior productivity and sensitivity to consumer demands with increased profits, higher wages, and other economic benefits.

Types of Markets

There are essentially three types of markets at work within the economic system: (1) factor markets, (2) product markets, and (3) financial markets (see Exhibit 1–3). In factor markets, consuming units sell their labor and other resources to those producing units offering the highest prices. The *factor markets* allocate factors of production — land, labor, and capital — and distribute income — wages, rental payments, and so on — to the owners of productive resources.

Consuming units use most of their income from factor markets to purchase goods and services in *product markets*. Food, shelter, automobiles, theater tickets, and swimming pools are among the many goods and services sold in product markets.

The Financial Markets and the Financial System: Channel for Savings and Investment

Of course, not all factor income is consumed. A substantial proportion of after-tax income received by households each year — more than $200 billion in 1995 — is earmarked for *personal saving*. In addition, business firms save billions of dollars each year to build up

Exhibit 1–3   **Types of Markets in the Economic System**

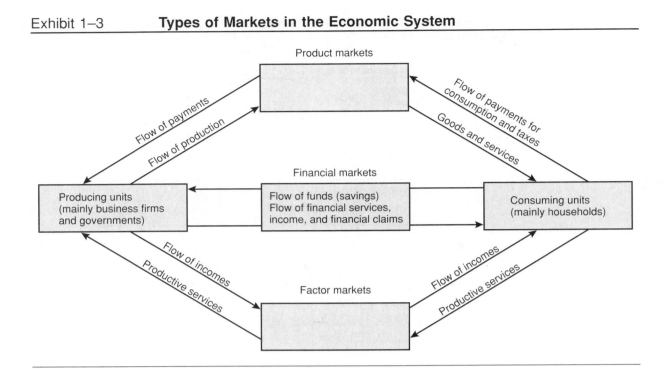

their reserves for future contingencies and for long-term investment. For example, in 1995 U. S. corporations earned about $560 billion in after-tax profits, of which about $120 billion was set aside (undistributed) for possible future needs as *business savings*. It is here that the third kind of market, the **financial market**, performs a vital function within the economic system. The financial markets channel savings to those individuals and institutions needing more funds for spending than are provided by their current incomes. The financial markets are the heart of the financial system, attracting and allocating savings and setting interest rates and security prices.

Nature of Savings. As we will see more fully in Chapter 8, the definition of **savings** differs depending on what type of unit in the economy is doing the saving. For households, savings are what is left from current income after current consumption expenditures are made. In the business sector, savings include current earnings retained inside business firms after payment of taxes, stockholder dividends, and other cash expenses. Government savings arise when there is a surplus of current revenues over current expenditures.

Nature of Investment. Most of the funds set aside as savings flow through the financial markets to support **investment** by business firms, governments, and households. Investment generally refers to the acquisition of capital goods, such as buildings and equipment, and the purchase of inventories of raw materials and goods to sell. The makeup of investment varies with the particular unit doing the investing. For a business firm, expenditures on *capital goods* (fixed assets, such as buildings and equipment) and for *inventories* (consisting of raw materials and goods offered for sale) are investment expenditures. Households invest (that is, make expenditures on capital account) when they buy a new home or purchase furniture, automobiles, and other durable goods, while their purchases of food, clothing, and fuel are considered to be consumption spending (i.e., expenditures on current account), not investments. Government spending to build and maintain public facilities is another form of investment.

Modern economies require enormous amounts of investment to produce the goods and services demanded by consumers. Investment in new equipment increases the productivity of labor and leads to a higher standard of living. However, investment often requires huge amounts of funds, far beyond the resources available to a single firm or government. By selling financial claims (such as stocks and bonds) in the financial markets, large amounts of funds can be raised quickly from the pool of savings accumulated by households, businesses, and governments. The business firm or government carrying out the investment then hopes to repay its loans from the financial marketplace by drawing on future income. Indeed, the financial markets operating within the financial system make possible the *exchange of current income for future income* and the *transformation of savings into investment* so that production and income can grow.

Those who supply funds to the financial markets receive only *promises* in return for the loan of their money. These promises are packaged in the form of attractive financial claims and financial services, such as stocks, bonds, deposits, and insurance polices (see Exhibit 1–4). Financial claims promise the supplier of funds a future flow of income in the form of dividends, interest, or other returns. But there is no guarantee that the expected income will ever materialize. However, suppliers of funds to the financial system expect not only to recover their original funds but also to earn additional income as a reward for waiting and assuming risk.

The role of the financial markets in channeling savings into investment is absolutely essential to the health and vitality of the economy. For example, if households set aside savings and those funds are not returned to the spending stream through investment by businesses and governments, the economy will begin to contract. The amount of income paid out by business firms and governments will *not* be matched by funds paid back to those same sectors by households. As a result, future income payments will decline, leading, in turn, to reduced consumption spending. The public's standard of living will fall. Moreover, with less spending going on, the need for labor will be curtailed, resulting in fewer jobs and rising unemployment.

FUNCTIONS PERFORMED BY THE FINANCIAL SYSTEM AND THE FINANCIAL MARKETS

The great importance of the financial system in our daily lives can be illustrated by reviewing its different functions. The financial system in a modern economy has seven basic functions. (See Exhibit 1–5.)

Exhibit 1–4   **The Financial System**

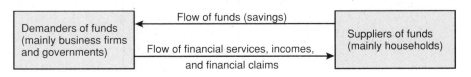

Exhibit 1–5   **Functions of the Financial System**

Savings function
   Providing a potentially profitable, low-risk outlet for the public's savings
Liquidity function
   Providing a means of raising funds by converting securities and other financial assets into cash balances
Payments function
   Providing a mechanism for making payments to purchase goods and services
Policy function
   Providing a channel for government policy to achieve society's goals of high employment, low inflation, and sustainable economic growth

Wealth function
   Providing a means to store purchasing power until needed for future spending on goods and services
Credit function
   Providing a supply of credit to support both consumption and investment spending in the economy
Risk function
   Providing a means to protect businesses, consumers, and governments against risks to people, property, and income

Savings Function

As we noted earlier, the system of financial markets and institutions provides a *conduit for the public's savings*. Bonds, stocks, and other financial claims sold in the money and capital markets provide a profitable, relatively low-risk outlet for the public's savings, which flow through the financial markets into investment so that more goods and services can be produced, increasing society's standard of living. When savings flows decline, investment and living standards begin to fall.

Wealth Function

For those businesses and individuals choosing to save, the financial instruments sold in the money and capital markets provide an excellent way to *store wealth* (i.e., preserve the value of assets we hold) until funds are needed for spending. Although we might choose to store our wealth in "things" (e.g., automobiles), such items are subject to depreciation and often carry great risk of loss. However, bonds, stocks, and other financial instruments do *not* wear out over time and usually generate income; moreover, their risk of loss often is much less than for other forms of stored wealth.

Incidentally, what is **wealth**? For any individual, business firm, or government, wealth is the sum of the values of all assets held. Some authorities prefer a concept called *net wealth* that equals all the assets held by an economic unit minus the debts (liabilities) it owes. Both wealth and net wealth are built up by a combination of current savings plus income earned on previously accumulated wealth. In symbols,

$$\Delta W_t = S_t + r_t \cdot W_{t-1}$$

where ΔW_t represents the change in wealth in the current period, S_t is the volume of current savings, r_t is the current average rate of return on accumulated assets, and W_{t-1} is the initial value of all accumulated wealth (assets) held.

The portion of wealth held by society in the form of stocks, bonds, and other financial instruments is substantial. For example, in 1995 more than $40 trillion in securities, deposits, and other financial instruments were held by business, households, and governments in the U.S., and foreign investors held nearly $2.9 trillion in financial instruments issued originally inside the United States. Individuals and families alone held more than $18 trillion in stocks, bonds, and other financial instruments. These forms of wealth (financial assets) broke down as follows for the various segments making up the U.S. economy in 1995:

Holders of Financial Assets	Wealth Holdings ($ Billions)
Individuals and families (households)	$18,550
Nonfinancial business firms	3,461
Banks and other financial institutions	17,204
Federal, state, and local governments and government agencies	1,811
Foreign businesses and individuals involved in U.S. domestic markets	2,872
Total holdings of wealth in financial assets in the United States	$43,898

Even if we subtract total debts owed by the above U.S. businesses, households, and governments, which amounted to $13,129 billion in 1995, the total *net* wealth held in financial assets by U.S. individuals and institutions was an impressive $30,769 billion. Wealth holdings represent stored purchasing power that will be used in future periods to finance purchases of goods and services and to increase society's standard of living.

Liquidity Function

For wealth stored in financial instruments, the financial marketplace provides a means of converting those instruments into cash with little risk of loss. Thus, the financial markets provide *liquidity* for savers who hold financial instruments but are in need of money. In modern societies, money consists mainly of deposits held in banks and is the only financial instrument possessing perfect liquidity. Money can be spent as it is without the necessity of converting it into some other form. However, money generally earns the lowest rate of return of all assets traded in the financial system, and its purchasing power is seriously eroded by inflation. That is why savers generally minimize their holdings of money and hold other financial instruments until they really need spendable funds.

Credit Function

In addition to providing liquidity and facilitating the flow of savings into investment to build wealth, the financial markets furnish **credit** to finance consumption and investment spending. Credit consists of a loan of funds in return for a promise of future payment. Consumers need credit to purchase a home, buy groceries, repair the family automobile, and retire outstanding debts. Businesses draw on their lines of credit to stock their shelves, construct new buildings, meet payrolls, and grant dividends to their stockholders. State, local, and federal governments borrow to construct buildings and other public facilities and to cover daily cash expenses until tax revenues flow in.

The volume of credit extended by the money and capital markets today is huge and growing. In the United States alone, as shown in Exhibit 1–6, total net credit funds raised in U.S. financial markets in 1995 (including issues of corporate stock) amounted to well over $1 trillion, compared to less than half that figure only a decade before. Growth of the economy, inflation, and the tax deductibility of some interest payments all appear to have fueled this rapid growth in credit usage by businesses, households, and governments.

Payments Function

The financial system also provides a *mechanism for making payments for goods and services*. Certain financial assets, mainly checking accounts and negotiable order of withdrawal (NOW) accounts, serve as a medium of exchange in making payments. Plastic credit cards issued by banks, credit unions, and retail stores give the customer instant access to short-term credit but are also widely accepted as a convenient means of payment.

Exhibit 1–6   **Net Funds Raised in U.S. Financial Markets
by Major Sectors of the U.S. Economy, 1995***

Sector and Funding Source		Amount of Funds Raised ($ Billions)	Percentage of Total Net Funds Raised†
Net borrowing by sector:			
Households		$ 304.7	24.3%
Nonfinancial business firms:			
Farms	0.5		
Nonfinancial corporations	234.3		
Other businesses	68.8		
Total for all business firms		303.6	24.1
Private financial institutions		157.1	12.5
Governments:			
U.S. government	271.8		
Federally sponsored agencies	125.4		
State and local governments	−63.1		
Total for all governments		334.1	26.6
Foreign borrowers in the United States, net		55.7	4.4
Total net borrowings		$1,154.8	92.0
Net funds raised by issuing new corporate stock (equities)		100.9	8.0
Total net borrowings and equity funds raised in U.S. financial markets		$1,255.7	100.0%

†Column does not add to exactly 100 percent due to rounding of figures.
*Figures are for first quarter of 1995.

Source: Board of Governors of the Federal Reserve System, *Flow of Funds Accountants: Flows and Outstandings*, First Quarter 1995.

Plastic cards and electronic means of payment, including computer terminals in homes, offices, and stores, will eventually displace checks and other pieces of paper as the principal means of payment in the future.

Risk Function

The financial markets offer businesses, consumers, and governments *protection against life, health, property, and income risks*. This is accomplished, first of all, by the sale of insurance policies. Policies marketed by life insurance companies indemnify a family against possible loss of income following the death of a loved one. Property-casualty insurers protect their policyholders against an incredibly wide array of personal and property risks, ranging from ill health, crime, and storm damage to negligence on the highways. In addition to making possible the sale of insurance policies, the money and capital markets have been used by businesses and consumers to "self-insure" against risk; that is, holdings of wealth are built up as a precaution against future loss.

Policy Function

Finally, in recent decades, the financial markets have been *the principal channel through which government has carried out its policy of attempting to stabilize the economy and avoid inflation*. By manipulating interest rates and the availability of credit, government can affect the borrowing and spending plans of the public, which, in turn, influence the growth of jobs,

---

MANAGEMENT INSIGHT:

The Financial System of Money and Capital Markets
Viewed as a Supplier of Financial Services to the Public

The financial system can also be viewed simply as a collection of financial service firms (FSFs) that produce, distribute, and sell those financial services most in demand by the public. Among the financial services most widely sought by the public and supplied by the money and capital markets are:

- *Payments services*, providing payments accounts against which the customer can write checks or wire funds to pay for purchases of goods and services.

- *Thrift services*, providing attractive financial instruments with adequate safety and yield to encourage people, businesses, and governments to save for their future financial needs.

- *Insurance services*, providing protection from loss of income or property in the event of death, disability, negligence, or other adverse developments.

- *Credit services*, providing loanable funds to supplement current income in order to sustain current living standards.

- *Hedging services*, providing protection against loss due to unfavorable movements in market prices or interest rates through such devices as futures, options, and other hedging instruments.

- *Agency services*, providing services by acting as agent for a customer in managing retirement funds or other property (as a bank trust department, insurance company, pension fund, or security broker/dealer might do).

---

production, and prices. As we will see later on, this task of economic stabilization has been given largely to central banks, such as the Federal Reserve System in the United States, the Bundesbank and the Bank of England in Europe, and the Bank of Japan.

TYPES OF FINANCIAL MARKETS WITHIN THE FINANCIAL SYSTEM

Charged with many different functions, the financial system fulfills its various roles through *markets* where financial claims and financial services are traded. These markets may be viewed as *channels* through which moves a vast flow of funds that is continually being drawn upon by demanders of funds and continually being replenished by suppliers of funds.

The Money Market versus the Capital Market

The flow of funds through the financial markets may be divided into different segments, depending on the characteristics of financial claims being traded and the needs of different investors. One of the most important divisions in the financial system is between the money market and the capital market.

The Most Important Function of the Financial System of Money and Capital Markets: To Facilitate the Transformation of Savings into Real (Nonfinancial) Investment So the Economy Can Grow and Living Standards Increase

---

Savings vary with the unit in the economy doing the saving:

1. Current savings for business firms = Total sales receipts − Operating expenses (including business taxes) = Current retained (undistributed) earnings + Noncash expenses (especially depreciation).

2. Current savings for households = Personal income − Current consumption spending (including taxes).

3. Current savings for governments = Receipts from the current budget (including tax collections and user fees) − Current budgetary expenditures.

Real (nonfinancial) investment varies with the unit doing the investing:

1. Current real investment for business firms = Purchases of equipment + Purchases of inventory + Construction of new business facilities.

2. Current real investment for households = Purchases of durable household goods and construction of homes, apartments, and other residences.

3. Real investment for governments = Construction of new public facilities.

---

a. The financial system operates to bring planned savings by businesses, households, and governments into balance with planned real investment by businesses, households, and governments.

b. The financial system also makes possible the supplementing of savings with borrowing so that both real investment in capital goods and inventories and financial investment in stocks, bonds, and other financial assets can occur at the level the public wishes.

The **money market** is designed for the making of short-term loans. It is the institution through which individuals and institutions with *temporary* surpluses of funds meet the needs of borrowers who have *temporary* funds shortages. Thus, the money market enables economic units to manage their liquidity positions. By convention, a security or loan maturing within one year or less is considered to be a money market instrument. One of the principal functions of the money market is to finance the working capital needs of corporations and to provide governments with short-term funds in lieu of tax collections. The money market also supplies funds for speculative buying of securities and commodities.

In contrast, the **capital market** is designed to finance long-term investments by businesses, governments, and households. Trading of funds in the capital market makes possible the construction of factories, highways, schools, and homes. Financial instruments in the capital market have original maturities of *more than one year* and range in size from small loans to multimillion dollar credits.

Who are the principal suppliers and demanders of funds in the money market and the capital market? In the money market, commercial banks are the most important institutional supplier of funds (lender) to both business firms and governments. Nonfinancial business corporations with temporary cash surpluses also provide substantial short-term funds to the money market. On the demand-for-funds side, the largest borrower in the money market is the U.S. Treasury, which borrows billions of dollars weekly. The largest and best-known corporations and securities dealers are also active borrowers in the money market. Due to the large size and strong financial standing of these well-known money market borrowers and lenders, money market instruments are considered to be high-quality, "near money" IOUs.

The principal suppliers and demanders of funds in the capital market are more varied than in the money market. Families and individuals, for example, tap the capital market when they borrow to finance a new home. Governments rely on the capital market for funds to build schools and highways and provide essential services to the public. The most important borrowers in the capital market are businesses of all sizes that issue long-term IOUs to cover the purchase of equipment and the construction of new facilities. Ranged against these many borrowers in the capital market are financial institutions, such as insurance companies and pension funds, that supply the bulk of long-term funds.

Divisions of the Money and Capital Markets

The money market and the capital market may be further subdivided into smaller markets, each important to selected groups of demanders and suppliers of funds. Within the money market, for example, is the huge *Treasury bill* market. Treasury bills — short-term government IOUs — are a safe and popular investment medium for financial institutions and corporations of all sizes.

Nearly as large in total dollar volume is the market for *negotiable certificates of deposit* (CDs) issued by the best-known banks and other depository institutions to raise funds in order to carry on their lending activities. Two other important money market instruments that arise from large corporations borrowing money are *bankers' acceptances* and *commercial paper*. In another corner of the money market, *federal funds* — the reserve balances of banks plus other immediately transferable monies — are traded daily in huge volume. Another segment of the money market reaches around the globe to encompass suppliers and demanders of short-term funds in Europe, Asia, and the Middle East. This is the vast, largely unregulated *Eurocurrency* market, in which bank deposits denominated in the world's major trading currencies — the dollar, the franc, the pound, the yen, and the mark — are loaned to corporations and governments around the globe.

The capital market, too, is divided into several sectors, each having special characteristics. For example, the largest segment of the capital market is devoted to residential and commercial *mortgage loans* to support the building of homes and business structures, such as factories and shopping centers. In the United States, state and local governments sell their *tax-exempt (municipal) bonds* in another sector of the capital market. Households borrow in yet another segment, using *consumer loans* to make purchases ranging from automobiles to home appliances. There is also an international capital market represented by *Eurobonds* and *Euronotes*.

Probably the best-known segment of the capital market is the market for *corporate stock* represented by the major exchanges, such as the New York Stock Exchange (NYSE) and the Tokyo Exchange, and a vast over-the-counter (OTC) market. No matter where it is sold, however, each share of stock (equity) represents a certificate of ownership in a corporation, entitling the holder to receive any dividends paid out of current earnings.

Exhibit 1–7   **Principal Financial Instruments Traded in the U.S. Money and Capital Markets, 1995* ($ Billions)**

Instruments	Amount Outstanding
Principal money market instruments:	
U.S. Treasury bills	$ 756.5
Bank and thrift large certificates of deposit ($100,000+)	435.0
Small time and savings deposits at banks and thrifts	2,206.3
Securities issued by federal and federally sponsored agencies	2,219.2
Federal funds sold and repurchase agreements	593.6
Eurodollar deposits**	299.7
Commercial paper	612.6
Bankers' dollar acceptances	29.8
Total for Money Market	$ 7,152.7
Principal capital market instruments:	
Mortgages	$ 4,467.0
Common stocks	6,573.6
Corporate and foreign bonds	2,462.2
U.S. Treasury notes and bonds	2,455.9
State and local government bonds and notes	917.4
Consumer loans	983.8
Total for Capital Market	$17,859.9

*Figures are for the first quarter of 1995.
**U.S. bank deposits held in foreign countries.

Source: Board of Governors of the Federal Reserve System.

Corporations also sell a huge quantity of *corporate notes* and *bonds* in the capital market each year to raise long-term funds. These securities, unlike shares of stock, are pure IOUs, evidencing a debt owed by the issuing company. A list of the principal financial instruments traded in the U.S. money and capital markets is shown in Exhibit 1–7.

Open versus Negotiated Markets

Another distinction between markets in the financial system that is often useful focuses on **open markets** versus **negotiated markets**. For example, some corporate bonds are sold in the open market to the highest bidder and bought and sold any number of times before they mature and are paid off. In contrast, in the negotiated market for corporate bonds, securities generally are sold to one or a few buyers under private contract.

An individual who goes to his or her local banker to secure a loan for a new car enters the negotiated market for auto loans. In the market for corporate stocks there are the major stock exchanges, which represent the open market. Operating at the same time, however, is the negotiated market for stock, in which a corporation may sell its entire stock issue to one or a handful of buyers.

Primary versus Secondary Markets

The financial markets may also be divided into **primary markets** and **secondary markets**. The primary market is for the trading of *new* securities never before issued. Its principal function is raising financial capital to support new investment in buildings, equipment, and

Declining Savings Rate in the U.S. Economy

As we have seen earlier in this chapter, saving is vital to support the growth of investment in new capital equipment and new technologies so that an economy can grow and increase the standard of living of its citizens. Although the national savings rate of the United States — its gross savings, including business depreciation reserves as a percent of the U.S. gross national product — has remained remarkably stable for most of the nation's history, the United States today posts one of the lowest savings rates in the world, with a savings-to-gross national product ratio less than half that of Japan and Germany, for example. Among the world's leading industrialized nations, only the United Kingdom has a lower gross savings rate than the United States. In terms of net savings (defined as gross savings by households, businesses, and governmental units less business depreciation), the United States generally ranks dead last among industrialized nations.

The causes of the low U.S. savings rate are many. First, throughout much of the 1970s, 80s, and 90s, the number of young adults entering the U.S. workforce increased rapidly as the baby boom generation established families of their own. According to the "life cycle theory of consumption," younger adults tend to borrow and spend more and save less than older adults in order to achieve a desired level of living standard. Younger individuals are willing to do this because they expect to work for many years and achieve higher incomes in the future to pay off any debts they incur today. In contrast, older people, who have fewer working years ahead and, therefore, a shorter stream of expected future income, tend to save more and spend less.

A second reason for declining savings rates may simply be changing public attitudes toward saving itself. Older generations remember the Great Depression, with millions of people out of work. Younger savers, however, are more likely to have experienced periods of prosperity and low unemployment. Thus, many younger individuals see less reason to make strenuous efforts to save based on their own life experiences.

Another reason for the relatively low U.S. savings rate may be the huge government budget deficits that have made the U.S. government a net "dissaver" rather than a net saver, gobbling up the savings of the private sector through government borrowing and higher taxes. These deficits force the United States to rely heavily on foreign savers to supplement domestic savings so that sufficient credit is available. Thus, the current U.S. tax structure and government policy appear to favor consumption and borrowing over saving.

Moreover, when inflation rises many consumers prefer to buy now rather than to save. At the same time, fears about the safety of key financial institutions that hold the public's savings — banks, savings and loans, and insurance companies — have discouraged some savers from committing their funds to traditional savings accounts.

The consequences of a low rate of savings in the United States include higher interest rates, which make it more expensive for business firms to invest, and result in fewer new jobs being created. As a result, the United States is among the lowest-ranked nations not only in its rate of personal (household) savings but also in investment spending to boost future production and employment among leading industrialized countries.

(continued)

A relatively low savings rate coupled with a relatively low investment rate make the economy more prone to inflation because, with less investment in new equipment, fewer goods and services can be produced as demands for goods and services increase. Living standards of individuals and families are likely to grow more slowly in the future.

Among the possible cures for a low national savings rate are lower taxes on personal income and business profits, smaller government deficits, greater stability in the economy, the avoidance of inflation, and a regulatory policy that promotes safety among banks and other financial institutions. In addition, some economists believe that the U.S. personal savings rate will begin to rise in the future as the population ages because there will be more Americans concerned about building their savings for retirement. Let's hope they are right!

inventories. You engage in a primary-market transaction when you purchase shares of stock just issued by a company or borrow money through a new mortgage to purchase a home.

In contrast, the secondary market deals in securities previously issued. Its chief function is to provide *liquidity* to security investors — that is, provide an avenue for converting financial instruments into ready cash. If you sell shares of stock or bonds you have been holding for some time to a friend or call a broker to place an order for shares currently being traded on the American Stock Exchange or the Tokyo Stock Exchange, you are participating in a secondary-market transaction.

The volume of trading in the secondary market is far larger than trading in the primary market. However, the secondary market does *not* support new investment. Nevertheless, the primary and secondary markets are closely intertwined. For example, a rise in security prices in the secondary market usually leads to a similar rise in prices on primary-market securities and vice versa. This happens because some investors will switch from one market to another in response to differences in price and yield.

Spot versus Futures, Forward, and Option Markets

We may also distinguish between *spot markets, futures* or *forward markets,* and *option markets.* A spot market is one in which securities or financial services are traded for immediate delivery (usually within one or two business days). If you pick up the telephone and instruct your broker to purchase Telecon Corporation shares at today's price, this is a spot market transaction. You expect to acquire ownership of Telecon shares within a matter of minutes or hours.

A *futures* or *forward market*, on the other hand, is designed to trade contracts calling for the *future delivery* of financial instruments. For example, you may call your broker and ask to purchase a contract from another investor calling for delivery to you of $1 million in Treasury bonds six months from today. The purpose of such a contract would be to reduce risk by agreeing on a price today rather than waiting six months, when Treasury bond prices might have risen.

Finally, *options markets* also offer investors in the money and capital markets an opportunity to reduce risk. These markets make possible the trading of options on selected stocks and bonds, which are agreements (contracts) that give an investor the right to either buy from or sell designated securities to the writer of the option at a guaranteed price at any time during the life of the contract. We will see more clearly how and why such transactions take place when we explore the financial futures and options markets in Chapter 13 and the forward markets for foreign currencies in Chapter 28.

Factors Tying All Financial Markets Together

Each corner of the financial system represents a market segment with its own special characteristics. Each segment is insulated from the others to some degree by investor preferences and by rules and regulations. Yet when interest rates and security prices change in one corner of the financial system, *all* of the financial markets will be affected eventually. This implies that, even though the financial system is split up into many different markets, there must be forces at work to tie all the financial markets together.

Credit, the Common Commodity. One unifying factor is the fact that the basic commodity being traded in most financial markets is *credit*. Borrowers can switch from one market to another, seeking the most favorable credit terms wherever they can be found. It is not uncommon, for example, for an oil company to finance the construction of a drilling rig through short-term loans from the money market, because interest rates in the capital market today are unusually high, but to seek long-term financing of the project later on when capital market conditions are more favorable. The shifting of borrowers between markets helps to weld the parts of the financial system together and to bring credit costs in different markets into balance with one another.

Speculation and Arbitrage. Another unifying element is profit seeking by demanders and suppliers of funds. *Speculators* in securities are continually on the lookout for opportunities to profit from their forecasts of future market developments. The speculator in the financial marketplace gambles that security prices or interest rates will move in a direction that will result in quick gains due to his or her ability to outguess the market's collective judgment. Many speculators are risk seekers, willing to gamble their funds even when the probability of success is low. Speculators perform an important function in the financial markets by leveling out the prices of securities, buying those they believe are underpriced and selling securities thought to be overpriced.

Still another unifying force in the financial markets comes from investors who watch for profitable opportunities to **arbitrage** funds — transferring funds from one market to another whenever the prices of securities in different markets appear to be out of line with each other. *Arbitrageurs* help to maintain consistent prices *between* markets, aiding other security buyers in finding the best prices with minimal effort.

Perfect and Efficient Markets. There is considerable research evidence today suggesting that all financial markets are closely tied to one another due to their perfection and efficiency. What is a **perfect market**? It is one in which the cost of carrying out transactions is zero or nearly so and all market participants are *price takers* (rather than being able to dictate prices to the market). In such a market, there are no significant government restrictions on trading and the movement of funds; rather, competition among buyers and sellers sets the terms of trade.

Some financial markets may also have another very desirable characteristic: *The prices of financial instruments may accurately reflect their inherent value and fully reflect all available information.* Moreover, any new information supplied to the market may quickly be impounded in a new set of prices. A market in which prices fully reflect the latest available information is an **efficient market**. In an efficient market, no information

---

INTERNATIONAL FOCUS:
The Globalization of the Money and Capital Markets

Today, trading in financial instruments spans the globe. Literally, the sun never sets on the financial markets. For example, as the sun comes up in London, security traders leave early for their posts on London's exchanges and for their offices at the world's largest banks and security dealers represented in London's financial district. They trade daily not only securities issued by British firms and governmental units but also loans and securities coming from U.S., European, and Japanese corporations as well.

As London approaches the noon hour, security dealers are stirring in New York and Chicago. On and off the major exchanges there, loans, securities, and currencies are bought and sold in huge volume. And as the daylight hours draw to a close in the United States, traders continue to follow the sun westward, preparing to transfer their "book" (computer files showing dealer and customer security positions and instructions) to traders in Tokyo, Singapore, Sydney, and other security markets surrounding the Pacific Rim. For example, trading usually begins in Tokyo when it is about 7:00 P.M. on the East Coast of the United States. In this eastern corner of the world, too, U.S. and European banks and dealers have offices so that trading continues almost without letup.

We are moving toward a world in which the sun will never go down on the financial markets and in which any buyer or seller can carry out transactions at any time, day or night. Nevertheless, there remain important barriers to 24-hour trading of securities worldwide. For one thing, few companies or governments have the prestige that would cause investors throughout the world to want to trade their securities; as a result, the set of worldwide tradable assets is likely to remain relatively small for some time. For example, less than 100 U.S. corporations have their securities listed for trading in Tokyo. One of the few such worldwide instruments is U.S. government bonds, which are widely recognized around the globe for their quality and salability.

What will be needed eventually is multiple listing of the same securities on all major exchanges in Europe, Asia, and the United States. But this will require common operating rules, open access to membership on all exchanges for foreign as well as domestic investors, and compatible electronic systems to speed price and volume information to all investors.

Even more significant, it still takes at least 24 hours to verify the terms of a security trade (known as *clearing*) and then to effect payment for and delivery of securities to distant parts of the globe (known as *settlement*). Clearing and settlement risks are among the most significant risks confronting international traders today. Steps must be taken to speed up clearing and settlement of worldwide security trades without sacrificing accuracy and reliability. This is no small task, but it will happen eventually, resulting in a true global financial marketplace.

---

that might affect security prices or interest rates is wasted. Thus, no buyer or seller can expect to reap excess profits from collecting information and then trading on the basis of that information. As we will see in Chapters 3 and 27, numerous studies of the financial markets spanning decades suggest that they approach fairly closely the ideal of a perfect and an efficient marketplace.

Financial Markets in the Real World: Imperfection and Asymmetry. Unfortunately, as we will see in subsequent chapters, as nearly perfect and efficient as many financial markets are, there is still a great deal that is *imperfect* in our financial system. Not all financial service markets are fully competitive, and collusion to fix prices and interest rates does occur. Recent scandals involving the trading of new U.S. government securities in which a handful of traders attempted to control that market and the funding of criminal activities worldwide through the ill-fated Bank of Credit and Commerce International (BCCI) remind us that the functioning and regulation of our financial marketplace still leaves substantial room for improvement.

Moreover, we now realize that not all the information needed by purchasers of financial services is readily or cheaply available. Increasingly, we are coming to an awareness of the importance of **asymmetric information** in our financial system — that is, different participants in the financial markets often operate with different sets of information, some possessing special or inside information that others do not possess. The result is that some market players may be able to earn excess profits by taking advantage of the special information they possess. Moreover, as we will see in Chapter 3, high-quality financial assets and services may be driven from the market when the asymmetrical distribution of information is particularly severe.

The Dynamic Financial System

There is an old saying: "You cannot step into the same river twice, for rivers are ever flowing onward." That statement can be applied with equal force to the financial system — it is rapidly changing into a *new* financial system. As shown in Exhibit 1–8, powerful trends are underway to convert national financial systems into an integrated global system, at work 24 hours a day to attract savings, extend credit, and fulfill other vital roles. Satellites, computers, and other automated systems now tie together financial-service businesses and trading centers as widely dispersed as London, New York, Tokyo, Singapore, and Sydney. This process of integrating financial systems has been aided by gradual deregulation of financial institutions and services on the part of leading industrialized nations (such as Australia, the United States, Japan, Canada, and members of the European Common Market). Many of these countries have also begun to "harmonize" their regulations so that financial-service firms operate under similar rules no matter where they are located. The results have been increasingly intense competition for customers, the development of many new financial services, increased risk to financial-service firms and their customers, and a wave of mergers and failures among financial institutions. One of the purposes of this book is to help us understand why these trends are occurring and what they are likely to mean for all of us in the future.

THE PLAN OF THIS BOOK

This text is divided into eight sections, each devoted to a particular segment of the financial system. Part One provides an overview of the financial system — its role in the economy and its basic characteristics. The vital processes of saving and investing, lending and borrowing, and creating and destroying financial assets are described. Part One concludes with a survey of the principal sources of information available today on the workings of the global financial marketplace.

In Part Two, the spotlight turns to financial institutions — commercial banks, credit unions, savings and loan associations, money market funds, insurance companies, pension funds, mutual funds, and other financial service firms. The reader is presented with an

Exhibit 1–8   Key Trends in the Financial System for Today and Tomorrow

- Increasing competition among suppliers of financial services in all countries and growing competition among domestic markets for a greater share of global trading volume.

- Broadening financial markets to circle the globe with trading 24 hours a day and with many foreign institutions entering domestic markets.

- Growing risks faced by financial-service firms, with more failures.

- Increasing consolidation of financial firms through mergers into larger companies (to reduce risk, expand markets, and offset rising costs).

- Increasing emphasis on financial innovation (i.e., the development of many new financial services).

- Continuing spread of new technologies to produce and deliver financial services (faster and more efficient methods to store and transfer financial information).

- Deregulating financial-service firms by governments and liberalizing restrictions against cross-border capital flows (letting the free market operate to allocate resources and price services).

- Growing volume of debt issued by businesses, households, and governments, with more loan defaults and bankruptcies.

- Increasing sophistication among borrowers and lenders about sources of financial services (including increased borrowing by business firms in the open market instead of through traditional lenders) and a growing sensitivity of lenders to risk.

- Increasing harmonization of regulation by leading nations so that financial services and financial institutions are increasingly coming under a similar set of rules regardless of their country of origin.

overview of their financial characteristics, regulation, current problems, and management tools designed to deal with many of those problems.

Part Three examines the forces that shape interest rates and the prices of financial instruments. Because the rate of interest is the key price in the financial system, this section begins in Chapter 8 with a review of theories of interest rate determination. Subsequent chapters address such important topics as the measurement of interest rates and security prices, yield curves, duration, inflation, the risk of default, and taxes. Part Three concludes with a review of methods for forecasting and hedging against interest rate changes, including swaps, futures, and options.

Part Four draws our attention to the money market and its principal institutions and instruments. Chapters in this section examine the characteristics of U.S. Treasury bills, federal funds, repurchase agreements, bank certificates of deposit, commercial paper, federal agency securities, bankers' acceptances, and Eurodollars.

Part Five presents a thorough examination of the many roles and functions of the central bank within the financial system. It contains an in-depth look at the history, organizational structure, and policy tools of the Federal Reserve System as well as the policy tools used by other central banks around the world. The section concludes with a review of the goals and problems of implementation of monetary policy.

Part Six turns to the role of governments — federal, state, and local — within the global financial system. The opening chapter explores the fiscal policy and debt management policy activities of the U.S. government. This chapter explains how U.S. Treasury financing operations impact the economy, interest rates, and the supply of credit, and looks at the pros and cons of having a large and growing government debt. This section concludes with an overview of state and local government financial activities, including state and local government borrowing, spending, and taxation.

The financial characteristics of consumers, both families and individuals, are considered in Part Seven. Chapter 24 examines the types of consumer debt and savings instruments available today and reviews current laws that affect the consumer of financial services. Chapter 25 takes a detailed look at the largest of all consumer debt markets — residential mortgages — in which recent innovations have created many new options for financing home purchases.

Part Eight focuses our attention on the financial activities of nonfinancial business firms. Chapter 26 explores business borrowing, especially the pricing and marketing of corporate bonds, and Chapter 27 looks at recent developments in the stock market and the growing volume of research on the efficiency of trading in equities.

Finally, Part Nine is devoted to the international financial system and future trends in global finance. Topics covered include international trade and the balance of payments, the markets for foreign currencies, hedging against currency risk, and international banking. Chapter 30 concludes this section with an examination of current and future trends that are likely to reshape the financial system for years to come.

Throughout this text, there is a strong emphasis on the innovative character of modern financial systems and institutions. A veritable explosion of new instruments and trading techniques has occurred within the financial system in recent years. Moreover, the pace of innovation in financial services appears to be accelerating under the combined pressure of increased competition, rising costs, and growing risks. As we will see in the pages that follow, these forces of innovation, competition, rising costs, and growing risk are profoundly reshaping the structure and operations of our whole financial system today.

KEY TERMS AND CONCEPTS IN THIS CHAPTER

financial system	credit	secondary markets
market	money market	arbitrage
financial market	capital market	perfect market
savings	open markets	efficient market
investment	negotiated markets	asymmetric information
wealth	primary markets	

STUDY QUESTIONS

1. Why is it important to understand how the financial system operates? In what ways is the financial system linked to the economy as a whole?

2. What are the principal functions of the financial system? How do the financial markets fulfill those functions?

3.   Explain what is meant by *saving* and by *investment*. Why are they important to economic growth and our standard of living?

4.   Distinguish between money market and capital market; open and negotiated markets; primary and secondary markets; and spot, forward, and futures markets. What are the principal divisions of each?

5.   Why do interest rates and security prices in the various segments of the financial system tend to move in the same direction? What forces seem to bind the various parts of the financial system together?

6.   What is a *perfect* market? An *efficient* market? Identify some features of real-world markets that in your judgment limit their efficiency and perfection. What is *asymmetric information*?

PROBLEMS

1.   Please *classify* the following financial transactions as to whether they fit in (a) the money market or the capital market, (b) the primary or the secondary market, (c) the open or negotiated market, and (d) the spot or futures/forward market. (*Note:* The transactions below may fit in more than one of the above categories of markets. Be sure to include all the appropriate types of markets that each transaction fits.)

Financial Transactions to Classify:

a.   You visit a local bank today and secure a three-year loan to finance the purchase of a new car and some furniture.

b.   You purchase a new U.S. Treasury bill for $9,800 through the Federal Reserve bank in a neighboring city for delivery today.

c.   Responding to a rise in the price of Texaco common stock, you have just purchased 100 shares of that company's stock through a phone call to your broker, who is linked to a major stock exchange.

d.   Concerned about recent trends in the price of the Mexican peso, you contact a large money center bank in the region and purchase 10,000 pesos at today's dollar/peso exchange rate for delivery in six months, when you plan to fly to Mexico City.

e.   Receiving an unexpected windfall, you contact a local savings and loan association and purchase a $15,000 two-year CD bearing an interest rate on which you and the association's officer have agreed.

f.   The corporation you represent needs to raise $25 million immediately to purchase raw materials. You contact a securities dealer who agrees to advertise the sale of $25 million in commercial paper, maturing in 90 days, this afternoon. The dealer expects to sell all the notes within 24 hours.

2.   What *functions of the financial system* do the following transactions illustrate or represent? (*Note:* Some transactions may involve more than one function. Be sure to identify *all* the financial system functions involved in each transaction.)

a.   James Rhodes purchases health and accident insurance policies through the company where he works.

b.   Sharon MacArthur uses her credit card to purchase wallpaper for a home remodeling project.

c.   Fearing a slowdown in the nation's rate of economic growth and increasing joblessness, the Federal Reserve System moves to lower interest rates.

d.   Dynamic Corporation places some of its current earnings in a bank CD, anticipating a need for funds in about a year to build a new warehouse.

e.   The U.S. Treasury sells new bonds in the open market to cover a large deficit.

f.   Cal and Jane Lewis hope to put their three young children through college someday. Accordingly, they begin buying U.S. savings bonds.

g.   Needing immediate spending power, Hillcrest Corporation sells its holdings of Denton County bonds through a security broker.

3.   From the information presented below on the U.S. economy, please calculate (a) the volume of current savings for all U.S. households, business firms, and governments and (b) the volume of current investment for households and businesses. (*Hint:* Not all of the information below needs to be used to answer this question.)

Total personal income........ $4,677.7 billion	Undistributed business profits .... 42.1 billion
Personal tax and nontax payments .... 709.0 billion	U.S. government budget outlays ....424.5 billion
Personal consumption expenditures...................3,697.6 billion	State and local government budget outlays ....677.3 billion
Change in business inventories ....9.6 billion	U.S. government budget surplus (or deficit) .... −143.0 billion
Expenditures on nonresidential plant and equipment .... 532.4 billion	State and local governments' budget surplus ....39.2 billion
Residential construction .... 218.2 billion	
Capital consumption on business plant and equipment .... 500.0 billion	Purchases of durable goods .....481.9 billion

4.   In a recent year, the following amounts of money market and capital market instruments — loans and securities — were issued and outstanding in the United States:

Business inventory loans ....$185 billion	Treasury bills ....540 billion
Treasury notes and bonds .... 1,650 billion	Eurodollar deposits ....390 billion
Commercial mortgages for the construction of factories and equipment .... 740 billion	School and highway construction bonds .... 75 billion
Foreign bonds .... 295 billion	State and local government (municipal) notes and bonds....................601 billion
Bank certificates of deposit .... 442 billion	Commercial paper ....545 billion
Corporate stock (equities) .... 4,158 billion	Federal agency securities..........398 billion
Federal funds and repurchase agreements .... 187 billion	Farm mortgages .... 80 billion
Corporate notes and bonds ..... 1,491 billion	Bankers' acceptances............... 41 billion
4-year and 5-year automobile loans to consumers .... 285 billion	Eurobonds ....137 billion
Loans to security dealers .... 87 billion	
Residential mortgages to support the construction of homes and apartments.......................3,137 billion	

Based on the discussion in this chapter, *classify* each of the above instruments as to whether they usually qualify as (a) a money market instrument or (b) a capital market instrument. If the above instruments represent all money and capital market instruments outstanding, what was the total dollar size of the money market? the total size of the capital market?

5.   The household sector (individuals and families) of the U.S. economy recorded current income of approximately $3.35 trillion in a recent year and total consumption expenditures (including taxes) of $2.89 trillion in that same year. The household sector held about $24.36 trillion in the total value of its wealth (including stocks, bonds, bank deposits, accumulated retirement savings, houses, etc.) at the beginning of the year and earned an

average rate of return of 4.5 percent on its wealth holdings during the year. Calculate the change (growth) in wealth for the household sector that occurred during the year.

6. The Wilkins family held total assets, including a home, stocks, bonds, and other accumulated assets, of $175,000 at the beginning of the year. If the family's accumulated wealth increased by $4,400 this year and its income and consumption spending amounted to $36,000 and $34,800, respectively, what was the average rate of return on the family's accumulated wealth during the year?

7. Suppose that U.S. banks held total financial assets (loans, securities, and other financial instruments) of $3,786 billion, while the banking sector's total liabilities amounted to $3,631 billion. What is the U.S. banking system's *net* financial wealth? If the banking system began the year with total financial assets of $3,639 billion and saved $53 billion during the year, how much income was earned on previously accumulated assets? What was the U.S. banking system's *net* financial wealth at year-end?

SELECTED REFERENCES

Fama, Eugene F., and Merton H. Miller. *The Theory of Finance*. New York: Holt, Rinehart & Winston, 1972.

Sanford, Charles S., Jr. "Financial Markets in 2020." *Economic Review*. Federal Reserve Bank of Kansas City, First Quarter 1994, pp. 19–28.

Scarlata, Jodi G. "Institutional Developments in the Globalization of Securities and Futures Markets." *Review*. Federal Reserve of St. Louis, January/February 1992, pp. 17–30.

Webb, Roy H. "Personal Saving Behavior and Real Economic Activity." *Economic Quarterly*. Federal Reserve Bank of Richmond, Vol. 79, No. 2 (Spring 1993), pp. 68–94.

Chapter 2

Financial Assets, Money, and Financial Transactions

LEARNING OBJECTIVES IN THIS CHAPTER

- To examine the different ways in which funds flow from lenders to borrowers within the financial system.
- To explore the nature and characteristics of *financial assets* — how they are created and destroyed in the money and capital markets.
- To examine the critical roles played by financial intermediaries and other financial institutions in lending and borrowing, creating and destroying financial assets within the financial system.

The financial system is the mechanism through which loanable funds reach borrowers. Through the operation of the financial markets, money is exchanged for financial claims in the form of stocks, bonds, and other securities. And through the exchange of money for financial claims, the economy's capacity to produce goods and services is increased. This happens because the money and capital markets provide the financial resources needed for real investment. Although it is true that the financial markets deal mainly in the exchange of paper claims and bookkeeping entries, these markets provide an indispensable conduit for the transformation of savings into real investment, accelerating the economy's growth and developing new businesses and jobs.

This chapter looks closely at the essential role played by the financial markets in converting savings into investment and how that role has changed over time. We begin by observing that nearly all financial transactions between buyers and sellers involve the creation or destruction of a special kind of asset: a financial asset. Moreover, financial assets possess a number of characteristics that make them unique among all assets held by individuals and institutions. In the next section, we consider the nature of financial assets and how they are created and destroyed through the workings of the financial system.

THE CREATION OF FINANCIAL ASSETS

What is a **financial asset**? It is a claim against the income or wealth of a business firm, household, or unit of government, represented usually by a certificate, receipt, or other legal document, and usually created by the lending of money. Familiar examples include stocks, bonds, insurance policies, and deposits held in a bank.

CHARACTERISTICS OF FINANCIAL ASSETS

Financial assets do *not* provide a continuing stream of services to their owners as a home, an automobile, or a washing machine would do. These assets are sought after because they promise *future* returns to their owners and serve as a store of value (purchasing power).

A number of other features make financial assets unique. They cannot be depreciated because they do not wear out like physical goods. Moreover, their physical condition or form usually is *not* relevant in determining their market value (price). A stock certificate is not more or less valuable, for example, because of the size or quality of paper it is printed on or whether it is frayed around the edges. Because financial assets are generally represented by a piece of paper (certificate or contract) or by information stored in a computer file, they have little or no value as a commodity, and their cost of transportation and storage is low. Finally, financial assets are *fungible* — they can easily be changed in form and substituted for other assets. Thus, a bond or share of stock usually can be quickly converted into any other asset the holder desires.

Different Kinds of Financial Assets

Although there are thousands of different financial assets, they generally fall into three categories: money, equities, and debt securities.

Any financial asset that is generally accepted in payment for purchases of goods and services is **money**. Thus, checking accounts, currency and coin, are financial assets serving as payment media and, therefore, are forms of money. **Equities** (more commonly known as *stock*) represent ownership shares in a business firm and, as such, are claims against the firm's profits and against proceeds from the sale of its assets. We usually further subdivide equities into *common stock*, which entitles its holder to vote for the members of a firm's board of directors and, therefore, determine company policy, and *preferred stock*, which normally carries no voting privileges but does entitle its holder to a fixed share of the firm's net earnings ahead of its common stockholders.

Debt securities include such familiar financial claims as *bonds, notes, accounts payable*, and *savings deposits*. Legally, these financial assets entitle their holders to a priority claim over the holders of equities to the assets and income of an individual, business firm, or unit of government. Usually, that claim is fixed in amount and time (maturity) and, depending on the terms of the *indenture* (contract) that accompanies most debt securities, may be backed up by the pledge of specific assets as collateral. Financial analysts usually divide debt securities into two broad classes: (1) *negotiable*, which can easily be transferred from holder to holder as a marketable security and (2) *nonnegotiable*, which cannot legally be transferred to another party. Passbook savings accounts and U.S. savings bonds are good examples of nonnegotiable debt securities. In this book, our primary but not exclusive focus is on negotiable (marketable) debt instruments such as Treasury bonds and corporate notes and bonds.

The Creation Process for Financial Assets

How are financial assets created? We may illustrate this process using a rudimentary financial system in which there are only two economic units: a household and a business firm.

Assume that this financial system is *closed*, so no external transactions with other units are possible. Each unit holds certain assets accumulated over the years as a result of its saving out of current income. The household, for example, may have accumulated furniture, an automobile, clothes, and other items needed to provide entertainment, food, shelter, and transportation. The business firm holds inventories of goods to be sold, raw materials, machinery and equipment, and other assets required to produce its product and sell it to the public.

The financial position of these two economic units is presented in the form of balance sheets, shown in Exhibit 2–1. A balance sheet, of course, is a financial statement prepared as of a certain date, showing a particular unit's assets, liabilities, and net worth. Assets represent accumulated uses of funds made by an economic unit; liabilities and net worth represent the accumulated sources of funds that an economic unit has drawn upon to acquire the assets it now holds. The net worth (equity) account reflects total savings accumulated over time by each economic unit. A balance sheet must always balance; total assets (accumulated uses of funds) must equal total liabilities plus net worth (accumulated sources of funds).

The household in our example holds total assets valued at $20,000, including an automobile, clothes, furniture, and cash. Because the household's financial statement must balance, total liabilities and net worth also add up to $20,000, all of which in this instance happens to come from net worth (accumulated savings). The business firm holds total assets amounting to $100,000, including a building housing the firm's offices, equipment, and inventory. The firm's only source of funds currently is net worth (accumulated savings), also valued at $100,000.

Exhibit 2–1   **Balance Sheets of Units in a Simple Financial System**

HOUSEHOLD
Balance Sheet

Assets		Liabilities and Net Worth	
Accumulated uses of funds:		Accumulated sources of funds:	
Cash	$ 13,000	Net worth (accumulated savings)	$ 20,000
Furniture	1,000		
Clothes	1,500		
Automobile	4,000		
Other assets	500		
Total assets	$ 20,000	Total liabilities and net worth	$ 20,000

BUSINESS FIRM
Balance Sheet

Assets		Liabilities and Net Worth	
Accumulated uses of funds:		Accumulated sources of funds:	
Inventories of goods	$ 10,000	Net worth (accumulated savings)	$100,000
Machinery and equipment	25,000		
Building	60,000		
Other assets	5,000		
Total assets	$100,000	Total liabilities and net worth	$100,000

By today's standards, the two balance sheets shown in Exhibit 2–1 look very strange. Neither the household nor the business firm has any outstanding debt (liabilities). Each unit is entirely self-financed, because each has acquired its assets by saving and by spending within its current income, not by borrowing. In the terminology of finance, both the household and the business firm have engaged in **internal financing**: the use of current income and accumulated savings to acquire assets. In the case of the household, savings have been accumulated by taking some portion of each period's income and setting money aside rather than spending all of its income on current consumption. The business firm has abstained from paying out all of its current revenues in the form of expenses (including stockholder dividends), retaining some of its current earnings in its net worth account.

For most businesses and households, internally generated funds are still the most important resources for acquiring assets. For example, in the U.S. economy, half or more of all investment in plant, equipment, and inventories carried out by business firms each year is financed internally rather than by borrowing. Households as a group save substantially more than they borrow each year, with the savings flowing into purchases of real assets (such as homes and automobiles) and into sizable purchases of stocks, bonds, and other financial assets.

Suppose that the business firm in our rudimentary financial system wishes to purchase new equipment in the form of a drill press. Due to inflation and shortages of key raw materials, however, the cost of the new drill press has been increasing rapidly. Internal sources of funds are not sufficient to cover the equipment's full cost. What can be done? There are four likely alternatives: (1) postpone the purchase of the new equipment until sufficient savings can be accumulated, (2) sell off some existing assets to raise the necessary funds, (3) borrow all or a portion of the needed funds, or (4) issue new stock (equity).

Time is frequently a determining factor here. Postponement of the equipment purchase probably will result in lost sales and lost profits. A competing company may rush ahead to expand its operations and capture some share of this firm's market. Moreover, in an environment of inflation, the new drill press surely will cost even more in the future than it does now. Selling some existing assets to raise the necessary funds is a distinct possibility, but this may take time, and there is risk of substantial loss, especially if fixed assets must be sold. The third alternative — borrowing — has the advantage of raising funds quickly, and the interest cost on the loan is tax deductible.[1] The firm could sell additional stock if it hesitated to take on debt, but equity financing is usually more expensive than borrowing and requires more time to arrange.

If the business firm decides to borrow, who will lend the funds it needs? Obviously, in this two-unit financial system, the household must provide the needed funds. The firm must engage in external financing by issuing to the household securities evidencing a loan of money. In general, if any economic unit wishes to add to its holdings of assets but lacks the necessary resources to do so, it can raise additional funds by issuing financial liabilities (borrowing) — provided that a buyer of those IOUs can be found. The buyer will regard the IOUs as an asset — a financial asset — that may earn income unless the borrower goes out of business and defaults on the loan.

---

[1] An added advantage associated with issuing debt is the *leverage effect*. If the firm can earn more from purchasing and using the new equipment than the cost of borrowing funds, the surplus return will flow to the firm's owners in the form of increased earnings, increasing the value of the company's stock. The result is positive financial leverage. Unfortunately, leverage is a two-edged sword. If the firm earns less than the cost of borrowed funds, the owners' losses will be magnified as a result of unfavorable (negative) financial leverage.

Exhibit 2–2   **Unit Balance Sheets following the Purchase of Equipment and the Issuance of a Financial Asset**

HOUSEHOLD
Balance Sheet

Assets		Liabilities and Net Worth	
Cash	$ 3,000	Net worth (accumulated savings)	$ 20,000
Financial asset	10,000		
Furniture	1,000		
Clothes	1,500		
Automobile	4,000		
Other assets	500		
Total assets	$ 20,000	Total liabilities and net worth	$ 20,000

BUSINESS FIRM
Balance Sheet

Assets		Liabilities and Net Worth	
Inventories of goods	$ 10,000	Liabilities	$ 10,000
Machinery and equipment	35,000	Net worth	100,000
Building	60,000		
Other assets	5,000		
Total assets	$110,000	Total liabilities and net worth	$110,000

Suppose that the business firm decides to borrow by issuing a liability (debt security) in the amount of $10,000 to pay for its new drill press. Because the firm is promising an attractive interest rate on the new IOU, the household willingly acquires it as a financial asset. This asset is *intangible*: a mere promise to pay $10,000 at maturity plus a promised stream of interest payments over time. The borrowing and creation of this financial asset will impact the balance sheets of these two economic units. As shown in Exhibit 2–2, the household has purchased the firm's IOU by using up some of its accumulated cash. Its total assets are unchanged. Instead of holding $13,000 in non-interest-bearing cash, the household now holds an interest-bearing financial asset in the form of a $10,000 security. The firm's total assets and total liabilities *increase* due to the combined effect of borrowing and the acquisition of a productive real asset.

FINANCIAL ASSETS AND THE FINANCIAL SYSTEM

This simple example illustrates several important points concerning the operation and role of the financial system in the economy. First, the act of borrowing simultaneously gives rise to the creation of an equal volume of financial assets. In the foregoing example, the $10,000 financial asset held by the household lending money is exactly matched by the $10,000 liability of the business firm borrowing money. This suggests another way of defining a financial asset: *Any asset held by a business firm, government, or household that is also recorded as a liability or claim on some other economic unit's balance sheet is a financial asset.* As we have seen, many different kinds of assets satisfy this definition, including stocks, bonds, bank loans, and deposits held with a financial institution.

For the entire financial system, the sum of all financial assets held must equal the total of all financial liabilities (claims) outstanding. In contrast, real assets, such as automobiles and buildings, are not necessarily matched by liabilities (claims) somewhere in the financial system.

This distinction between *financial assets* and *liabilities*, on the one hand, and *real assets*, on the other, is worth pursuing with an example. Suppose that you borrow $4,000 from the bank to purchase an automobile. Your balance sheet will now contain a liability in the amount of $4,000. The bank from which you borrowed the funds will record the transaction as a loan — an interest-bearing financial asset — appearing on the asset side of its balance sheet in the like amount of $4,000. On the asset side of your balance sheet appears the market value of the automobile — a real asset. The value of the real asset probably exceeds $4,000, since most banks expect a borrower to supply some of his or her own funds rather than borrowing the full purchase price. Let's say the automobile was sold to you for $5,000, with $1,000 of the cost coming out of your savings account and $4,000 from the bank loan. Then, your balance sheet will contain a new real asset (automobile) valued at $5,000, a liability (bank loan) of $4,000, and your savings account (a financial asset) will decline by $1,000.

Clearly, there are two equalities that hold not only for this transaction but whenever funds are loaned and borrowed in the financial system. First,

$$\begin{array}{l} \text{Volume of financial} \\ \text{assets created for} \\ \text{lenders} \end{array} = \begin{array}{l} \text{Volume of liabilities} \\ \text{issued by borrowers} \end{array} \tag{2-1}$$

$$\begin{array}{l} \text{In this case, a bank} \\ \text{loan of \$4,000} \end{array} = \begin{array}{l} \text{A borrower's IOU} \\ \text{of \$4,000} \end{array}$$

Second,

$$\text{Total uses of funds} = \begin{array}{l} \text{Total sources of} \\ \text{funds} \end{array}$$

$$\begin{array}{l} \text{Purchase of \$5,000} \\ \text{automobile} \end{array} = \begin{array}{l} \text{Issuance of a} \\ \text{\$4,000 borrower} \\ \text{IOU} + \$1,000 \\ \text{drawn from a} \\ \text{savings account} \end{array} \tag{2-2}$$

Every financial asset in existence represents the lending or investing of funds transferred from one economic unit to another.

Because the sum of all financial assets created must always equal the amount of all liabilities (claims) outstanding, the amount of lending in the financial system must always equal the amount of borrowing going on. In effect, *financial assets and liabilities (claims) cancel each other out across the whole financial system.* We can illustrate this fact by reference to the balance sheet of any unit in the economy — business firm, household, or government. The following must be true for all balance sheets:

$$\text{Total assets} = \text{Total liabilities} + \text{Net worth} \tag{2-3}$$

Then, because all assets may be classified as either real assets or financial assets, it follows that

$$\text{Real assets} + \text{Financial assets} = \text{Total liabilities} + \text{Net worth} \tag{2-4}$$

Because the volume of financial assets outstanding must always equal the volume of liabilities (claims) in existence, it follows that the aggregate volume of real assets held in the economy must equal the total amount of net worth. Therefore, for the economy and financial system *as a whole,*

$$\text{Total financial assets} = \text{Total liabilities} \tag{2-5}$$

$$\text{Total real assets} = \text{Net worth (i.e., accumulated savings)} \tag{2-6}$$

This means that the value of all buildings, machinery, and other real assets in existence matches the total amount of *savings* carried out by all businesses, households, and units of government. We are *not* made better off in real terms by the mere creation of financial assets and liabilities. These are only pieces of paper or blips on a computer screen evidencing a loan or the investment of funds. Rather, society increases its wealth only by saving and increasing the quantity of its real assets, for these assets enable the economy to produce more goods and services in the future.

Does this suggest that the creation of financial assets and liabilities — one of the basic functions of the financial system — is a useless exercise? Not at all. The mere act of saving by one economic unit does not guarantee that those savings will be used to build or purchase real assets that add to society's stock of wealth. In modern economies, saving and investment usually are carried out by different groups of people. For example, most saving is usually carried out by households (individuals and families), and business firms account for the majority of investments in productive real assets. Some mechanism is needed to ensure that savings flow from those who save to those who wish to invest in real assets, and the financial system of money and capital markets is that mechanism.

The *financial system* provides the essential channel necessary for the creation and exchange of financial assets between savers and borrowers so that real assets can be acquired. Without that channel for savings, the total volume of investment in the economy surely would be reduced. All investment by individual economic units would have to depend on the ability of those same units to save (i.e., engage in internal financing). Many promising investment opportunities would have to be foregone or postponed due to insufficient savings. Society's scarce resources would be allocated less efficiently than is possible with a system of financial markets. Growth in society's income, employment, and standard of living would be seriously impaired without a vibrant financial system at work.

LENDING AND BORROWING IN THE FINANCIAL SYSTEM

Business firms, households, and governments play a wide variety of roles in modern financial systems. It is quite common for an individual or institution to be a lender of funds in one period and a borrower in the next, or to do both simultaneously. Indeed, financial intermediaries, such as banks and insurance companies, operate on both sides of the financial markets, borrowing funds from customers by issuing attractive financial claims and simultaneously making loans available to other customers. Virtually all of us at one point or another in our lifetimes will be involved in the financial system as both a borrower and a lender of funds.

A number of years ago, two economists, John Gurley and Edward Shaw (1960), pointed out that each business firm, household, or unit of government active in the financial system must conform to the following identity:

$$R - E = \Delta FA - \Delta D \tag{2-7}$$

Current income receipts − Expenditures out of current income	=	Change in holdings of financial assets − Change in debt and equity outstanding

If our current expenditures (E) exceed our current receipts (R), we usually make up the difference by (1) reducing our holdings of financial assets ($-\Delta FA$), for example, by drawing money out of a savings account; (2) issuing debt or stock ($+\Delta D$); or (3) using some combination of both. On the other hand, if our receipts (R) in the current period are larger than our current expenditures (E), we can (1) build up our holdings of financial assets ($+\Delta FA$), for example, by placing money in a savings account or buying a few shares of stock; (2) pay off some outstanding debt or retire stock previously issued by our business firm ($-\Delta D$); or (3) do some combination of both of these steps.

It follows that for any given period of time (e.g., day, week, month, or year), the individual economic unit must fall into one of three groups:

Deficit-budget unit (net borrower of funds)	$E > R$; and so $\Delta D > \Delta FA$
Surplus-budget unit (net lender of funds)	$R > E$; and thus $\Delta FA > \Delta D$
Balanced-budget unit (neither net lender nor net borrower)	$R = E$; and, therefore, $\Delta D = \Delta FA$

A *net lender of funds is really a net supplier of funds to the financial system*. He or she accomplishes this function by purchasing financial assets, paying off debt, or retiring equity (stock). In contrast, a *net borrower of funds is a net demander of funds from the financial system*, selling financial assets, issuing new debt, or selling new stock. The business and government sectors of the economy tend to be net borrowers (demanders) of funds in most periods; the household sector, composed of all families and individuals, tends to be a net lender (supplier) of funds.

This pattern for the U.S. economy is revealed by the data on purchases of financial assets and increases in liabilities compiled each year by the Federal Reserve System. For example, as Exhibit 2–3 shows, in 1995, households acquired almost $560 billion in financial assets and issued about $295 billion in liabilities, making this sector of the U.S. economy a net lender of funds to the financial markets in the amount of more than $260 billion. Business firms, in contrast, normally are net borrowers from the money and capital markets. In 1995, for example, the business sector borrowed almost $123 billion net from the financial marketplace, as its liabilities rose by $385 billion and its acquisition of financial assets increased by only $262 billion. The federal government borrowed even

Exhibit 2–3

Net Acquisitions of Financial Assets and Liabilities by Major Sectors of the U.S. Economy, 1995* ($ Billions)

Sectors	Net Acquisitions of Financial Assets During the Year	Net Increase in Liabilities During the Year	Net Lender (+) or Net Borrower (-) of Funds
Households	$ 556.6	$295.0	$ 261.6
Nonfinancial business firms	262.2	385.1	-122.9
State and local governments	-91.8	-62.4	-28.7
Federal government	26.2	279.5	-253.3
Foreign investors and borrowers	301.8	137.0	+164.8

*1995 figures are annualized figures for the first quarter of the year.

Source: Board of Governors of the Federal Reserve System, *Flow of Funds Accounts*, 1995.

more, with just over $250 billion in net borrowing during the year, while state and local governments posted net borrowings of more than $28 billion.

If we add together all the net borrowings by governments and businesses in 1995, they totaled almost $405 billion; yet U.S. households managed to lend these sectors, net, only about $260 billion. Who supplied the extra funds to meet the huge net credit needs of U.S. governments and businesses? Most of these required funds came from foreign investors, who supplied, net, more than $164 billion to other borrowing sectors of the U.S. economy in 1995.

Of course, over any given period of time, any one household, business firm, or unit of government may be a deficit-, surplus-, or balanced-budget unit. In fact, from day to day and week to week, many households, businesses, and governments fluctuate from being deficit-budget units to surplus-budget units and back again. Consider a large corporation such as Ford or Exxon. Such a firm may be a net lender one week, supplying monies to deficit-budget units in the financial system for short periods of time through purchases of U.S. Treasury bills, bank CDs, and other financial assets. The following week, a dividend payment may be due company stockholders, bonds must be refunded, or purchases must be made to increase inventories and expand plant and equipment. At this point, the firm may become a net borrower of funds, drawing down its holdings of financial assets, securing loans by issuing financial liabilities, or selling equity (stock). Most of the large institutions that interact in the global financial marketplace continually fluctuate from one side of the market to the other. This is also true of most households today. *One of the most important contributions of the financial system to our daily lives is in permitting businesses, households, and governments to adjust their financial position from that of net borrower to net lender and back again, smoothly and efficiently.*

MONEY AS A FINANCIAL ASSET

What Is Money?

The most important financial asset in the economy is *money*. All financial assets are valued in terms of money, and flows of funds between lenders and borrowers occur through the medium of money. Money itself is a true financial asset, because all forms of money in use today are claims against some institution, public or private. For example, one of the largest components of the money supply today is the checking account, which is the debt of a commercial bank. Another important component of the money supply is currency and coin — the pocket money held by the public. The bulk of currency in use today in the United States, for example, consists of Federal Reserve notes, representing debt obligations of the 12 Federal Reserve banks. In fact, if the Federal Reserve ever closed its doors (a highly unlikely event!), Federal Reserve notes held by the public would be a first claim against the assets of the Federal Reserve banks. As we will see in the accompanying box on alternative definitions of the money supply, some concepts of what money is today include savings accounts at banks, credit unions, and money market funds — all forms of debt, giving rise to financial assets.

The Functions of Money

Money performs a wide variety of important services. It serves as a *standard of value (or unit of account)* for all the goods and services we might wish to trade. Without money, the price of every good or service would have to be expressed in terms of exchange ratios with all other goods and services — an enormous information burden for both buyers and sellers. We would need to know, for example, how many loaves of bread would be required to purchase a quart of milk or what quantity of firewood might exchange for a suit of clothes. To trade just 12 different goods and services, we would have to remember 66 different exchange ratios! In contrast, the existence of money as a common standard of value permits us to express the prices of all goods and services in terms of only one good — the *monetary unit*. In the United States and Canada, that unit is the dollar; in France and Switzerland, the franc; in Japan, the yen. But whatever the monetary unit is called, it always has a constant price in terms of itself (i.e., a dollar always exchanges for a dollar). The prices of all other goods and services are expressed in multiples of the monetary unit.

Money also serves as a *medium of exchange*. It is usually the only financial asset that virtually every business, household, and unit of government will accept in payment for goods and services. By itself, money typically has little or no use as a commodity (except when gold or silver, for example, is used as the medium of exchange). People accept money only because they know they can exchange it at a later date for goods and services. This is why modern governments have been able to separate the monetary unit from precious metals such as gold and silver bullion and successfully issue *fiat money* (i.e., pieces of paper or data stored in a computer file) not tied to any particular commodity. Money's service as a medium of exchange frees us from the terrible constraints of barter, allowing us to separate the act of selling goods and services from the act of buying goods and services. With a medium of exchange, buyers and sellers no longer need to have an exact coincidence of wants in terms of quality, quantity, time, and location.

Money serves also as a *store of value* — a reserve of future purchasing power. Purchasing power can be stored in currency or in a checking account until the time is right to buy. Of course, money is not always a good store of value. The value of money, measured by its purchasing power, can experience marked fluctuations. For example, the prices of consumer goods represented in the U.S. cost-of-living index more than tripled between the 1960s and the 1990s. If individuals or families had purchased in each of these years the identical market basket of goods and services represented in the cost-of-living index, they would have found that the purchasing power of each unit of their money had decreased by more than two thirds during this period.

Money functions as the *only perfectly liquid asset* in the financial system. An asset is liquid if it can be converted into cash quickly with little or no loss in value. A liquid asset possesses three essential characteristics: price stability, ready marketability, and reversibility. An asset must be considered liquid if its price tends to be reasonably stable over time, if it has an active resale market, and if it is reversible so that investors can recover their original investment without loss.

All assets — real and financial — differ in their degrees of liquidity. Generally, financial assets, especially bank deposits and stocks and bonds issued by major corporations, tend to be highly liquid; on the other hand, real assets, such as a home or an automobile, may be extremely difficult to sell in a hurry without taking a substantial loss. Money is the most liquid of all assets because it need not be converted into any other form to be spent. Unfortunately, the most liquid assets, including money, tend to carry the lowest rates of return. One measure of the "cost" of holding money is the income forgone by the owner who fails to convert his or her money balances into more profitable investments in real or financial assets. The *rate of interest* determined by the financial system is a measure of the penalty suffered by an investor for not converting money into income-earning assets.

Alternative Definitions of Money

As discussed in this chapter, money performs several important functions in the financial system, serving as a medium of exchange, a store of value (purchasing power), a standard for valuing goods and services (unit of account), and as a source of liquidity (spending power). These different functions of money in the financial system have given rise to a variety of different definitions of the actual money supply available to the public, with each definition reflecting a different role or function that money performs for those who hold it. For example, in the United States the principal definitions of money in use today are:

M1 = The sum of all U.S. currency and coin held by the public (outside the cash in the vaults of the U.S. Treasury, the Federal Reserve banks, and depository institutions), travelers checks issued by nonbank financial institutions, and checking accounts (demand deposits), NOW accounts, and Automatic Transfer Services at all commercial banks, credit unions, and thrift institutions (except for interbank, U.S. government, and foreign bank deposits and Federal Reserve float). (In 1996 M1 totaled just over $1 trillion.)

M2 = The sum of M1 plus small savings and time deposits (under $100,000 each in amount), balances held in general-purpose and broker-dealer money market fund accounts, short-term repurchase agreements (bearing overnight maturities and continuing contracts that can be canceled with a 24-hour notice) issued by depository institutions, and overnight foreign U.S. dollar deposits (Eurodollars) issued to U.S. residents by foreign branches of U.S. banks worldwide. (In 1996 M2 amounted to just over $3.6 trillion.)

M3 = The sum of M2 plus large time deposits (each over $100,000 in amount) and longer-term repurchase agreements issued by all depository institutions, longer-term foreign U.S. dollar deposits (Eurodollars) held by U.S. residents at foreign branches of U.S. banks worldwide and at all banking offices in the United Kingdom and Canada, and balances in institution-only money market funds. (In 1996 M3 was about $4.4 trillion.)

L = The sum of the components of M3 plus the nonbank public's holdings of U.S. savings bonds, short-term U.S. Treasury securities, commercial paper, and bankers' acceptances net of money market fund holdings of these assets. (L totaled about $5.5 trillion in 1996.)

Note that M1, the narrowest definition of the supply of money or money stock, focuses mainly upon immediately spendable money (such as pocket change and checking accounts) and, therefore, views money primarily as a *medium of exchange*. In contrast, M2 and M3 reflect mainly money's *store of value* role as captured by savings accounts, money market fund shares, and short-term borrowing in the money market by depository institutions. The L (liquidity) definition of the money stock reflects both the store of value idea and the near-money assets held by the public that can be quickly converted (liquidated) into spendable cash, such as U.S. savings bonds and other shorter-term negotiable securities. No single definition of money is necessarily "right" or "wrong." Each reflects a different dimension of money's function as an important financial asset in the economy.

THE EVOLUTION OF FINANCIAL TRANSACTIONS

Financial systems are never static. They change constantly in response to shifting demands from the public, the development of new technology, and changes in laws and regulations. Competition in the financial marketplace forces financial institutions to respond to public need by developing better and more convenient financial services. Over time, the system of financial markets has evolved from simple to more complex ways of carrying out financial transactions. The growth of industrial centers with enormous capital investment needs and the emergence of a huge middle class of savers have played major roles in the gradual evolution of the financial system.

Whether simple or complex, all financial systems perform at least one basic function. They move scarce funds from those who save and lend (surplus-budget units) to those who wish to borrow and invest (deficit-budget units). In the process, money is exchanged for financial assets. However, the transfer of funds from savers to borrowers can be accomplished in at least three different ways. We label these methods of funds transfer: (1) direct finance, (2) semidirect finance, and (3) indirect finance. Most financial systems have evolved gradually over time toward greater reliance on indirect finance.

Direct Finance

With the direct financing technique, borrower and lender meet each other and exchange funds in return for financial assets. You engage in **direct finance** when you borrow money from a friend and give him or her your IOU, or when you purchase stocks or bonds directly from the company issuing them. We usually call the claims arising from direct finance *primary securities* because they flow directly from the borrower to the ultimate lender of funds. (Exhibit 2–4 illustrates the process of direct financing between borrowers and lenders.)

Direct finance is the simplest method of carrying out financial transactions. However, it has a number of serious limitations. For one thing, both borrower and lender must desire to exchange the same amount of funds at the same time. More important, the lender must be willing to accept the borrower's IOU, which may be quite risky or slow to mature. Clearly, there must be a coincidence of wants between surplus- and deficit-budget units in terms of the amount and form of a loan. Without that fundamental coincidence, direct finance breaks down.

Another problem is that both lender and borrower must frequently incur substantial *information costs* simply to find each other. The borrower may have to contact many lenders before finding the one surplus-budget unit with just the right amount of funds and a willing-

Exhibit 2–4   **Direct Finance** (Direct Lending Gives Rise to Direct Claims against Borrowers)

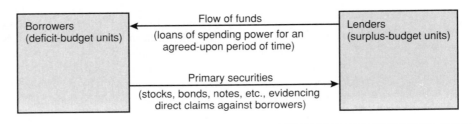

Exhibit 2–5   **Semidirect Finance** (Direct Lending with the Aid of Market Makers Who Assist in the Sale of Direct Claims against Borrowers)

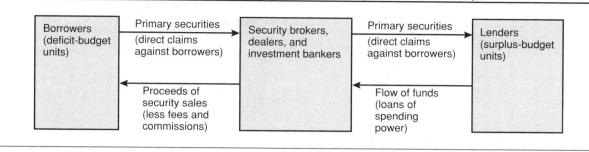

ness to take on the borrower's IOU. Not surprisingly, direct finance soon gives way to other methods of carrying out financial transactions as money and capital markets develop.

Semidirect Finance

Early in the history of most financial systems, a new form of financial transaction called **semidirect finance** appears. Some individuals and business firms become securities brokers and dealers whose essential function is to bring surplus- and deficit-budget units together, thereby reducing information costs (see Exhibit 2–5).

We must distinguish here between a broker and a dealer in securities. A *broker* is merely an individual or financial institution who provides information concerning possible purchases and sales of securities. Either a buyer or a seller of securities may contact a broker, whose job is simply to bring buyers and sellers together. A *dealer* also serves as an intermediary between buyers and sellers, but the dealer actually acquires the seller's securities in the hope of marketing them at a later time at a favorable price. Dealers take a "position of risk" because, by purchasing securities outright for their own portfolios, they are subject to losses if those securities decline in value.

Semidirect finance is an improvement over direct finance in a number of ways. It lowers the search (information) costs for participants in the financial markets. Frequently, a dealer will split up a large issue of primary securities into smaller units affordable by even buyers of modest means and, thereby, expand the flow of savings into investment. In addition, brokers and dealers facilitate the development of secondary markets in which securities can be offered for resale.

Despite the important contribution of brokers and dealers to the functioning of the financial system, the semidirect finance approach is not without its limitations. The ultimate lender still winds up holding the borrower's securities, and, therefore, the lender must be willing to accept the risk and maturity characteristics of the borrower's IOU. There still must be a fundamental coincidence of wants and needs between surplus- and deficit-budgeted units for semidirect financial transactions to take place.

Indirect Finance

The limitations of both direct and semidirect finance stimulated the development of **indirect finance** carried out with the help of *financial intermediaries*. Financial intermediaries active in today's financial markets include commercial banks, insurance companies, credit unions, finance companies, savings and loan associations, savings banks, pension funds,

Exhibit 2–6

Major Financial Institutions Active in the Money and Capital Markets

Financial Intermediaries

Depository institutions:
  Commercial banks
  Nonbank thrifts:
    Savings and loan associations
    Savings banks
    Credit unions
    Money market funds
  Other financial intermediaries:
    Finance companies
    Government credit agencies

Contractual institutions:
  Life insurance companies
  Property-casualty insurers
  Pension funds
Investment institutions:
  Investment companies (mutual funds)
  Real estate investment trusts

Other Financial Institutions

Investment bankers
Mortgage bankers

Security dealers
Security brokers

mutual funds, and similar organizations. (See Exhibit 2–6.) Their fundamental role in the financial system is to serve both ultimate lenders and borrowers but in a much more complete way than brokers and dealers do. Financial intermediaries issue securities of their own — **secondary securities** — to ultimate lenders and at the same time accept IOUs from borrowers — **primary securities** (see Exhibit 2–7).

The secondary securities issued by financial intermediaries include such familiar financial instruments as checking and savings accounts, life insurance policies, and shares in a mutual fund. For the most part, these securities share several common characteristics. They generally carry *low risk of default*. For example, most deposits held in U.S. banks and credit unions are insured by an agency of the federal government for amounts up to $100,000. Moreover, the majority of secondary securities can be acquired in *small denominations*, affordable by savers of limited means. For the most part, secondary securities are liquid and, therefore, can be converted quickly into cash with little risk of significant loss. Financial intermediaries in recent years have tried to make savings as convenient as possible through the mail and by plastic card, computer terminal, and telephone in order to reduce transactions costs to the saver.

Exhibit 2–7   **Indirect Finance** (The Financial Intermediation of Funds)

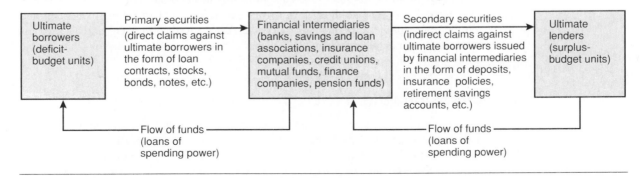

Financial intermediaries accept primary securities from those who need credit and, in doing so, take on financial assets that many savers, especially those with limited funds and limited knowledge of the market, would find unacceptable. For example, many large corporations require billions of dollars in credit financing each year — sums that would make it impractical to deal directly with thousands of small savers. By pooling the resources of scores of small savings accounts, however, a large bank or other intermediary frequently can service the credit needs of several large firms simultaneously. In addition, many primary securities, even those issued by some of the largest borrowers, are not readily marketable and carry sizable risk of borrower default — a situation usually not acceptable to the small saver. By issuing its own securities, attractive to ultimate lenders (savers), and accepting primary securities from ultimate borrowers, the financial intermediary acts to satisfy the financial needs of both surplus- and deficit-budget units in the economy.

One of the benefits of the development of efficient financial intermediation (indirect finance) has been to smooth out consumption spending by households and investment spending by businesses over time, despite variations in income, because intermediation makes saving and borrowing easier and safer. Financial intermediation permits a given amount of saving in the economy to finance a greater amount of investment than would have occurred without intermediation.

RELATIVE SIZE AND IMPORTANCE OF MAJOR FINANCIAL INSTITUTIONS

Financial intermediaries and other financial institutions differ greatly in their relative importance within the U.S. financial system. Measured by total financial assets, *commercial banks* dominate the financial system, as shown in Exhibit 2–8. The more than $4 trillion in financial assets held by U.S. banks represent about one-quarter of the total resources of all U.S. financial institutions. By some measures banks appear to have lost some of their market share to nonbank financial institutions (such as mutual funds), who are often less regulated and offer more flexible service options. Lagging well behind banks are *savings and loan associations* — another deposit-type financial intermediary active in the mortgage market but facing serious problems today and an uncertain future.

Very similar in sources and uses of funds to savings and loans are *savings banks* (headquartered mainly along the Atlantic coast), which attract small savings deposits from individuals and families. The fourth major kind of deposit-type financial intermediary, the *credit union*, was also created to attract small savings deposits from individuals and families and make loans to credit union members.

When the assets of all four deposit-type intermediaries — commercial banks, savings and loans, savings banks, and credit unions — are combined, they make up just under 40 percent of the total financial assets of all U.S. financial institutions. The remainder of the sector's financial assets are held by a highly diverse group of nondeposit financial institutions. *Life insurance companies*, which protect policyholders against the risks of premature death and disability, are among the most important nondeposit institutions and rank third to commercial banks in total assets. The other type of insurance firm — *property-casualty insurers* — offers a far wider array of policies to reduce the risk of loss associated with crime, weather damage, and personal negligence. Among the fastest-growing financial institutions are *pension funds*, which protect their customers against the risk of outliving their sources of income in the retirement years. Private pensions now rank second behind commercial banks in total assets held (see again Exhibit 2–8).

Exhibit 2–8   **Total Financial Assets Held by U.S. Financial Institutions, Selected Years** ($ Billions at Year-End)

Financial Institutions	1960	1970	1980	1990	1995*
Financial intermediaries:					
Commercial banks	$224	$489	$1,248	$3,340	$4,261
Savings and loan associations and savings banks	111	252	794	1,358	1,017
Life insurance companies	116	201	464	1,367	1,919
Private pension funds	38	110	413	1,629	2,491
Investment companies (mutual funds)	17	47	64	602	1,656
State and local government and pension funds	20	60	198	820	1,236
Finance companies	28	63	199	611	759
Property-casualty insurance companies	26	50	174	534	686
Money market funds	—	—	74	498	633
Credit unions	6	18	72	202	299
Mortgage companies	—	—	16	49	39
Real estate investment trusts	—	4	6	13	24
Other financial institutions:					
Security brokers and dealers	7	16	36	262	455

*1995 figures are annualized numbers from the first quarter of the year.

Source: Board of Governors of the Federal Reserve System, *Flow of Funds Accounts: Financial Assets and Liabilities*, selected years.

Other important financial institutions include finance companies, investment companies, money market funds, and real estate investment trusts. *Finance companies* lend money to businesses and consumers to meet short-term working capital and long-term investment needs. *Investment companies* (or mutual funds) pool the funds contributed by thousands of savers by selling shares and then investing in securities sold in the open market. A specialized type of investment company is the *money market fund*, which accepts savings (share) accounts from businesses and individuals and places those funds in high-quality money market securities. Also related to investment companies are *real estate investment trusts*, the smallest member of the financial institutions sector, which invest mainly in commercial and residential properties.

CLASSIFICATION OF FINANCIAL INSTITUTIONS

Financial institutions may be grouped in a variety of different ways. One of the most important distinctions is between **depository institutions** (commercial banks, savings and loan associations, savings banks, and credit unions); **contractual institutions** (insurance companies and pension funds); and **investment institutions** (investment companies, money market funds, and real estate investment trusts). Depository institutions derive the bulk of their loanable funds from deposit accounts sold to the public; contractual institutions attract funds by offering legal contracts to protect the saver against risk (such as an insurance policy or retirement account). Investment institutions sell shares to the public and invest the proceeds in stocks, bonds, and other assets.

PORTFOLIO DECISIONS BY FINANCIAL INTERMEDIARIES AND OTHER FINANCIAL INSTITUTIONS

The management of a financial institution is called on daily to make *portfolio decisions* — that is, deciding what financial assets to buy or sell. A number of factors affect these critical decisions. For example, the *relative rate of return and risk* attached to different financial assets will affect the composition of the institution's portfolio. Obviously, if management is interested in maximizing profits and has minimal aversion to risk, it will tend to pursue the highest yielding financial assets available, such as corporate bonds and stocks. A more risk-averse institution, on the other hand, is likely to surrender some yield in return for the greater safety available from acquiring government bonds and high-quality money market instruments.

The *cost, volatility, and maturity of incoming funds* provided by surplus-budget units also has a significant impact on the financial assets acquired by financial institutions. Commercial banks, for example, derive a substantial portion of their funds from checking accounts, which are relatively inexpensive but highly volatile. Such an institution will tend to concentrate its lending activities in short- and medium-term loans to avoid an embarrassing shortage of cash (liquidity). On the other hand, a financial institution such as a pension fund, which receives a stable and predictable inflow of savings, is largely freed from concern over short-term liquidity needs. It is able to invest heavily in long-term financial assets. Thus, the *hedging principle* — the approximate matching of the maturity of financial assets held with liabilities taken on — is an important guide for choosing those financial assets that a financial institution will hold in its portfolio.

Decisions on what financial assets to acquire and what sources of funds to draw upon are also influenced by the *size* of the individual financial institution. Larger institutions frequently can take advantage of greater diversification in their sources and uses of funds. This means that the overall risk of a portfolio of securities can be reduced by acquiring securities from many different borrowers. Similarly, a larger financial institution can contact a broader range of savers and achieve greater stability in its incoming flows of funds. At the same time, through economies of scale (size), larger financial institutions can often sell financial services at lower cost per unit and pass those cost savings along to their customers.

Finally, *regulations and competition*, two external forces, play major roles in shaping the sources and uses of funds for a financial institution. Because they hold the bulk of the public's savings and are so crucial to economic growth and investment activity, financial intermediaries are among the most heavily regulated of all business firms. Commercial banks are prohibited from investing directly in corporate stock. Insurance companies and pension funds must restrict any security purchases to those a "prudent person" would most likely choose. Most regulations in this sector pertain to the assets than can be acquired, the adequacy of net worth, and the services that can be offered to the public. Such regulations are designed to promote competition and ensure the safety of the public's funds.

DISINTERMEDIATION OF FUNDS

One factor that in recent years has influenced the financial assets selected by financial institutions for their portfolios is the phenomenon of **disintermediation**. Exactly opposite from the intermediation of funds, disintermediation means the withdrawal of funds from a financial intermediary by ultimate lenders (savers) and the lending of those funds directly

Exhibit 2–9   **Financial Disintermediation**

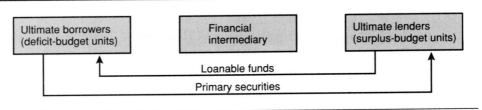

to ultimate borrowers. In other words, disintermediation involves the shifting of funds from indirect finance to direct and semidirect finance (see Exhibit 2–9).

You engage in disintermediation when you remove funds from a savings account at the local bank or savings and loan association and purchase common stock or Treasury bills through a broker. The phenomenon is more likely to occur during periods of high and rapidly rising interest rates, when the higher returns demanded by savers may outpace the interest rates offered by financial intermediaries. Disintermediation forces a financial institution to surrender funds and, if severe, may lead to losses of its assets and ultimate failure. A good example is provided by savings and loan associations which, during the 1980s and early 1990s, lost billions of dollars in assets due to massive withdrawals of funds by worried depositors who feared the loss of their savings.

Although intermediaries are forced to be more liquid and reduce their credit-granting activities during periods of disintermediation, there is no evidence that the *total* flow of credit through the financial system is reduced during such periods. Moreover, disintermediation need not be as stressful for financial intermediaries now that regulatory interest rate ceilings on deposits have been phased out in the United States, Japan, and in several other countries, allowing most intermediaries to respond more freely to movements in market interest rates. Correspondingly, however, financial intermediaries today are faced with greater uncertainty about the sources and cost of their funds than ever before.

New Types of Disintermediation

Some authorities argue that new forms of disintermediation have recently appeared, some initiated by financial intermediaries themselves and some by their borrowing customers. For example, some banks and savings and loan associations in recent years have begun to sell off their loans because of difficulties in raising capital. At the same time, some of the largest borrowing customers of these intermediaries have learned how to raise funds directly from the open market (i.e., through direct and semidirect finance) rather than borrowing from a bank or other institutional lender. For example, many corporations have learned how to pool the credit receivables or other assets they hold and use those assets as collateral for the sale of bonds in the open market to raise new money. Recently, many borrowing firms have issued lower-quality ("junk") bonds, which are much longer-term than most bank loans, represent less of a drain against a business's cash account, and often give a business more freedom in how it can use borrowed funds. A substantial portion of these borrowed funds has been used to pay off loans from banks and other financial intermediaries.

These new forms of disintermediation have tended not only to shrink the size of some banks and other intermediaries but also to gradually reduce the importance of banks — still the most important financial intermediary — within the global financial system. An increasing volume of funds today flow through the financial system via direct and semidirect finance rather than through indirect finance. In the next section of the book, we will explore the role of financial institutions in the money and capital markets. We will discover that their activities have been changing significantly in recent years in response to the changing needs of savers; the massive credit demands of businesses, consumers, and governments; and the new forms of disintermediation that are revolutionizing the financial system today.

SUMMARY

The financial system of money and capital markets performs the important function of channeling savings into investment, creating a unique kind of asset — the financial asset — in the process. Financial assets represent claims against the income and assets of the individuals and institutions issuing those claims and generally fall into three categories — money, debt, and equity. Money is among the most important of all financial assets in the economy because it serves as a medium of exchange to facilitate purchases of goods and services, a standard for valuing all items bought and sold, a store of value or purchasing power, and a reserve of liquidity (instant purchasing power).

The creation of financial assets generally occurs within the financial system through three different channels — direct, semidirect, or indirect finance. Direct finance involves the direct exchange of financial assets for money between a borrower and a lender. Semidirect finance involves the use of a broker or dealer to bring borrower and lender together and, thereby, reduce information costs. Indirect finance refers to the creation of financial assets by financial intermediaries who accept primary securities from ultimate borrowers and issue secondary securities to ultimate savers to raise funds. Financial intermediaries have generally grown to dominate most financial systems today due to their greater expertise, efficiency, and ability to diversify away some of the risks of lending money. However, intermediaries have faced many new forms of disintermediation — that is, loss of funds to direct or semidirect finance — in recent years, as innovation has occurred within the financial system and borrowers (issuers of financial assets) have found new ways to obtain the funds that they need.

KEY TERMS AND CONCEPTS IN THIS CHAPTER

financial asset	surplus-budget unit	primary securities
money	direct finance	depository institutions
equities	semidirect finance	contractual institutions
debt securities	indirect finance	investment institutions
internal financing	secondary securities	disintermediation
deficit-budget unit		

STUDY QUESTIONS

1. What is a *financial asset*? How does it arise within the workings of the financial system? Why must the volume of financial assets outstanding equal the volume of liabilities issued?

2. Explain the difference between *internal* and *external finance*. When an economic unit, such as a business, household, or government, needs funds, what are its principal alternatives? What factors enter into the choice among different sources of funds?

3. How is the creation of financial assets and liabilities linked to saving and investment activity in the economy?

4. Define the terms *deficit-budget unit, surplus-budget unit*, and *balanced-budget unit*. Which were you last month? Why?

5. What is *money*? What are its principal functions within the financial system? Its principal limitations?

6. Distinguish among *direct finance, semidirect finance*, and *indirect finance*. Which is most important today in the financial system? Explain why.

7. What are *primary securities? Secondary securities*? Give examples of each. What are the principal characteristics of each?

8. List the major kinds of financial intermediaries in the U.S. economy. Which ones can be classified as *depository intermediaries? Contractual intermediaries? Investment intermediaries?*

9. What is *disintermediation*? What are its principal causes and possible cures? What new forms of disintermediation have appeared in recent years?

PROBLEMS

1. In a recent year, the sectors of the U.S. economy listed below reported the following *net* changes in their financial assets and liabilities (measured in billions of dollars):

	Net Acquisitions of Financial Assets	Net Increase in Liabilities
Households	$434.6	$292.0
Farm businesses	2.7	-2.5
Nonfarm noncorporate businesses	8.7	35.0
Nonfinancial corporations	84.9	127.8
State and local governments	74.8	60.6
U.S. government	13.0	236.3
Foreign individuals and institutions	150.7	29.0
Federal Reserve System	32.0	31.2
Commercial banking	256.0	245.7
Private nonbank financial institutions	556.9	590.7

Using these figures, indicate which sectors were deficit-budget sectors and which were surplus-budget for the year under study. Were there any balanced-budget sectors? For all these sectors *combined*, were more funds loaned or more funds borrowed? Why do you think there is a discrepancy between total funds loaned and total funds borrowed?

2. Consider the balance sheets shown on page 43 for a household (individual or family), business firm, and government — the only units present in a *closed* economy. Which economic units above are completely self-financed? Which economic units above are deficit-budget units? Surplus-budget units? Balanced-budget units? Referring to Equations 2–4, 2–5, and 2–6 in this chapter, do these equations hold for the units depicted below? Please demonstrate.

Household			Business Firm			Government		
Assets		**Liabilities and Net Worth**	**Assets**		**Liabilities and Net Worth**	**Assets**		**Liabilities and Net Worth**
Cash	$15	Notes payable $20	Cash	$10	Bonds $60	Loans	$20	Securities $50
Securities	65	Taxes payable 15	Securities	45	Taxes payable 40	Buildings	85	Money 25
Automobile	5	Net worth 135	Truck	25	Net worth 90	Equipment	30	
Home	75		Plant	60		Tax receivables	55	Net worth 140
			Equipment	20				
Other real assets	10		Other real assets	30		Other real assets	25	
Total assets	$170	Total liabilities and net worth $170	Total assets	$190	Total liabilities and net worth $190	Total assets	$215	Total liabilities and net worth $215

3. In this chapter, a number of different types of financial transactions were discussed: direct finance, semidirect finance, indirect finance (intermediation), and disintermediation. Examine each of the following financial transactions and indicate which type it is. (*Note:* Some of the transactions described below involve more than one type of financial transaction. Be sure to identify *all* types of transactions involved.)

    a. Borrowing money from a bank.

    b. Purchasing a life insurance policy.

    c. Selling shares of stock through a broker.

    d. Withdrawing money from a savings deposit account and lending it to a friend.

    e. Selling shares of stock to a colleague at work.

    f. Your corporation's contracting an investment banker to help sell its bonds.

    g. Writing a bank check to purchase stock from your broker.

4. ITT Corporation in the most recent period reported current sales receipts of $542 million, current operating expenditures of $577 million, and net new debt issued of $5 million. What change in holdings of financial assets must have occurred over the period? Was ITT a deficit-, surplus-, or balanced-budget unit in the most recent period? Explain why.

5. Demonstrate that, for any given time period for any economic unit, current receipts plus additions (positive or negative) to debt and equities outstanding must equal current expenditures plus additions (positive or negative) to holdings of financial assets. Please explain exactly what this statement means.

SELECTED REFERENCES

Diamond, Douglas W. "Monitoring and Reputation: The Choice Between Bank Loans and Directly Placed Debt." *Journal of Political Economy* 99, no. 4 (1991), pp. 689–721.

Gurley, John, and Edward S. Shaw. *Money in a Theory of Finance.* Washington, D.C.: Brookings Institution, 1960.

Napoli, Janet, and Herbert L. Baer. "Disintermediation Marches On." *Chicago Fed Letter*, Federal Reserve Bank of Chicago (January 1991), pp. 1–3.

Chapter 3

Sources of Information for Financial Decision Making in the Money and Capital Markets

LEARNING OBJECTIVES IN THIS CHAPTER

- To identify the most important sources of data and information on the money and capital markets and the financial system.
- To learn why the efficient distribution of information in the financial system is important and what can happen when relevant financial information is not readily available to all market participants.
- To see how a participant in the financial marketplace can follow the prices of securities and changes in interest rates.
- To explore the concept and content of social accounting as represented by the Flow of Funds Accounts of the United States.

Every day in the money and capital markets, individuals and institutions must make important financial decisions. For those who plan to borrow, for example, key decisions must be made concerning the timing of a request for credit and exactly where the necessary funds should be raised. Lenders of funds must make decisions on when and where to invest their limited resources, considering such factors as the risk, marketability, and expected return on loans and securities available in the financial marketplace. Government policymakers also are intimately involved in the financial decision-making process. It is the responsibility of government to ensure that the financial markets function smoothly in channeling savings into investment and in creating a volume of credit sufficient to support business and commerce.

Sound financial decisions require adequate and accurate *financial information*. Borrowers, lenders, and those who make financial policy require data on the prices and yields attached to individual loans and securities today and the prices and yields likely to prevail in the future. A borrower, for example, may decide to postpone taking out a loan if it appears that the cost of credit will be significantly lower six months from now than it is today. Those who wish to forecast future interest rates and security prices need information concerning the expected supply of new securities brought to market and the expected demand for those securities. Because economic conditions exert a profound impact on the money and capital markets, the financial decision maker must also be aware of economic data series that reflect trends in employment, prices, and related types of information.

What are the principal sources of financial information? Where do financial decision makers go to find the data they need? We may divide the sources of information relied on by financial decision makers into five broad groups: (1) debt security prices and yields, (2) stock prices and dividend yields, (3) information on security issuers, (4) general economic and financial conditions, and (5) social accounting data. In this chapter, we will discuss the most important sources of each of these different kinds of information.

EFFICIENT MARKETS AND ASYMMETRIC INFORMATION

Before we examine the principal sources of information available to financial market participants, however, we need to be aware of a great debate going on in the fields of finance and economics today concerning the availability and cost of information. One view, referred to as the **efficient markets hypothesis**, contends that information relevant to the pricing (valuation) of loans, securities, and other financial assets is readily available to *all* borrowers and lenders at *negligible cost*. The other view, called **asymmetry** or the concept of asymmetric information, argues that the financial marketplace contains pockets of inefficiency in the availability and use of information. Some market players — for example, professional lenders of funds, auditors, attorneys, journalists, or members of management and the boards of directors of corporations — may possess special information that enables them to get a more accurate picture of the value and risk of certain assets. These "insiders" allegedly can earn excess returns by selectively trading financial and other assets based on the special information they have been able to acquire — information that would be costly for others to obtain.

As a prelude to this chapter, we briefly sketch out these two contrasting views — efficient markets and asymmetric information — of the cost and availability of relevant information to participants and decision makers in the financial marketplace.

The Efficient Markets Hypothesis

The efficient markets hypothesis (hereafter EMH) suggests that *all* information that has a bearing on the value of stocks, bonds, and other financial assets will be used to value (price) those assets. *An efficient market simply does not waste information.* Under the terms of the EMH, money and capital markets will not consistently ignore information that can earn profits, so there won't be any profitable trades that are not made (at least not for very long).

For example, if an individual has savings to invest in stocks and bonds, he or she will seek out information on the financial conditions of the business firms issuing those securities, the quality of their management and products, the strength of each firm's industry, and the condition of the economy in which each firm operates. Each individual investor will rationally use *all* the available information relevant to valuing the stocks and bonds he or she might wish to buy. Because all other investors are likely to be seeking the same information for the same reasons, the current market price of any financial asset will reflect all relevant information that investors as a group have been able to obtain regarding that asset's true value. Because all of

Exhibit 3–1   **The Security Market Line (SML) —** A Schedule of Expected Returns
for All Assets and Portfolios of Assets

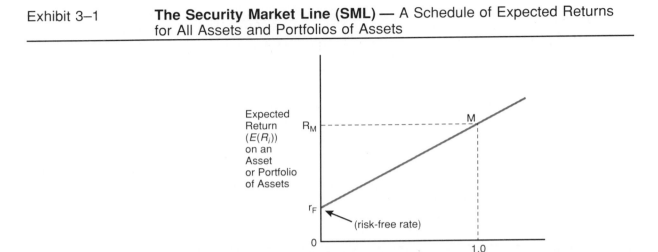

Beta (β) as an Index of Risk

the information available has been used to establish the value of financial instruments, no
single user of that same information can earn "excess returns" by trading on information
available to all. Rather, in an efficient marketplace, each financial asset will generate an
"ordinary" or "normal" rate of return commensurate with its level of risk.[1]

Under the terms of the capital asset pricing model (CAPM) the *expected return* on a
financial asset will be equal to:

$$E(R_i) = r_f + \beta_i[E(R_M) - r_f] \tag{3–1}$$

where *E(R_i)* measures the expected return on the *i*th asset, *E(R_M)* is the expected return on
the market's entire collection of financial assets (i.e., the market portfolio), and *r_f* is the
risk-free interest rate (often approximated by the return on government bonds). The term
$\beta_i[E(R_M)-r_f]$ measures the *risk premium* — reward for risk taking — that will be demanded by investors in the money and capital markets before they are willing to buy and
hold a risky asset (such as a corporate bond or stock). This risk premium is the product of
the financial marketplace's reward for each unit of risk accepted by an investor holding the
market portfolio (*M*) times the individual asset's own risk level, measured by β_i. (Note that
the market's entire portfolio of assets has a beta (β) of 1.0 and a return of R_M.)

The line or curve described by the above equation in the CAPM is usually called the
security market line (SML), as illustrated in Exhibit 3–1. Under the terms of the EMH, any
deviation of an asset's actual return (*AR_i*) from its expected return (*E(R_i)*) results in a
positive or negative excess return (*EXR*) that must be random with an expected value of
zero. Thus, the yields on all financial assets should lie along the SML, and if the EMH is
correct, any deviation of actual returns from the expected returns lying along the SML (i.e.,
excess returns) should be quickly eliminated as investors react to temporary underpricing
(when an asset's actual return rises *above* its expected return along the SML) or temporary

---

[1]By "excess returns" we mean the excess amount of actual returns earned on an asset above its "expected"
"ordinary," or "normal" return, based on the amount of risk the asset carries. Thus, if AR_i represents the actual
return (including interest or dividends and any price gains) and *E(R_i)* equals the "normal" return (or the return
expected on the asset given its level of risk), then the excess return (*EXR*) must be *EXR_i = AR_i − E(R_i)*.

overpricing (when an asset's actual return falls *below* its expected return on the SML) of assets by reshuffling the assets they hold. In short, the discovery of a financial asset whose expected return is above or below the SML (that is, carrying a positive or negative excess return) would be a signal of market inefficiency, inconsistent with the EMH. This would be true because, according to the EMH, rational market participants use *all* relevant information available to value assets all the time. Because all asset prices instantaneously impound all relevant information concerning asset values in an efficient market, no asset trades that generate consistent excess returns will be available.

Moreover, only when *new* information reaches the marketplace will the prices (value) of financial assets change, and according to the EMH, they will change quickly as investors possessing new information move rapidly to seize any profitable opportunities, bidding up the prices of some assets and lowering the prices of others. And, because market prices respond only to *new* information, which by its nature is unpredictable, the value of financial assets and services cannot be predicted consistently. If we could consistently predict asset values, this would be evidence of an inefficient market in which not all information is being fully utilized. Thus, the prices of financial assets in an efficient market will appear to behave *randomly* over time.

The essential contribution that the EMH makes to our understanding of the money and capital markets is to suggest that the current prices of all financial assets represent the *optimal use* of all available information. And, each asset's price, determined by demand-and-supply forces in the financial marketplace, is an optimal forecast of each asset's fundamental value. Thus, if the current market price of a financial asset is P_t, if the set of all available information in the current time period (t) is Ω_t, and if P_t^* is the asset's expected fundamental or "true" value, then, according to the EMH,

$$P_t = E\ (P_t^* | \Omega_t) \tag{3-2}$$

meaning that an asset's current market price is the *best estimate* of that asset's expected fundamental value. However, each asset's fundamental value will vary with the state of the world (e.g., the condition of the economy and the current concerns of asset buyers about risk) prevailing at the time the asset is being traded. If we designate the state of the world that prevails at any moment in time (t) as S, and if the probability that any particular state of the world (S) will prevail at time t is $Prob(S/\Omega_t)$, then the asset's current price (market value) must be:

$$P_t = \Sigma P_S^* \cdot Prob(S|\Omega_t) \tag{3-3}$$

In words, the current price of a financial asset (P_t) equals its expected fundamental value given all possible states of the world recognized by buyers and sellers actively trading in the market. Under the terms of the EMH, the price of an asset must already encompass all of the information relevant to the valuation of that asset, including all present and past information. Moreover, the optimal forecast of next period's market value (price) for an asset, P_{t+1}, when we know only this period's information (Ω_t), must be the asset's *current price* (P_t), because any new information that appears in the next period, Ω_{t+1}, is, by definition, unpredictable. Therefore, any financial asset's *future price* will be simply a random fluctuation around the asset's *current price*.

Different Forms of the EMH. In recent years, the EMH has been split into three different versions based on what each assumes to be true about the availability and cost of information. These three versions of the EMH are:

1. *Weak form of the EMH*, which argues that the current prices of financial assets contain all information that buyers and sellers have been able to obtain on the past trading of

those assets: their *price history and past volume of trading*. Moreover, this past price and trading information is publicly available and of negligible cost to obtain. No one buyer or seller of stocks, bonds, or other financial assets can earn excess profits beyond those that are normal for the amount of risk taken on from trading on this historical price and volume information. If this were not true, investors would have figured out long ago how to profit from such historical data and asset prices would have been adjusted accordingly, eliminating further opportunities for exceptional returns.

2. *Semistrong form of the EMH*, which contends that the current prices of stocks, bonds, and other financial assets already reflect *all publicly available information* affecting the value of these financial instruments, including information about past prices and volume, the financial condition and credit rating of each issuer, any published forecasts, the condition of the economy, and all other relevant information. All buyers and sellers are rational and use all publicly available information to help them value financial assets. No one buyer or seller will, therefore, find opportunities for exceptional profits by trading on any publicly available information.

3. *Strong form of the EMH*, which argues that the current prices of financial assets capture all the information — *both public and private* — that is relevant to the value of those financial instruments. This includes the information possessed by "insiders," such as the officers, directors, and principal owners of a corporation issuing stocks and bonds or even accountants, attorneys, or journalists who work with the company and have access to its privileged information.

Under current U.S. law (specifically, the Securities Act, Rule 106–5), if an insider decides to trade the securities of a firm for whom he or she works or does business, that individual must report such trades to the Securities and Exchange Commission, which makes the information available to the public. Anyone who has a fiduciary relationship with a corporation, such as an accountant, consultant, or attorney, and who has access to privileged information about the firm is restrained under U.S. law from using that privileged information to trade in the firm's securities for profit.

Repeated research studies (several of which we will review in Chapter 27) have essentially confirmed the weak and semistrong forms of the EMH. Few opportunities for exceptional profits flowing from trading on past or present publicly available information appear to exist. The strong form of the EMH, however, has aroused the most controversy and resulted in mixed research findings. A more current view of the possible existence of pockets of special information scattered throughout the financial system has emerged to challenge the validity of the strong-form EMH.

The Concept of Asymmetric Information

What if *all* relevant information about the true value of financial assets is *not* readily available or costless to obtain? What would happen if some important information pertinent to decision making were distributed *asymmetrically* so that deep pockets of special knowledge existed in the financial marketplace?

The asymmetric view says that there *are* pockets of special information — a "lumpiness" in the supply of relevant information about financial assets. These pockets may include corporate insiders, journalists, security dealers, and financial analysts who possess unique analytical skills in spotting profitable trades. These possessors of special knowledge need not be operating illegally. Indeed, they may come by their unique talents in assessing value and risk through rigorous schooling and on-the-job training or by virtue of the special location they occupy within the financial system. Every year hundreds of corporations flock to college campuses to hire graduates whom they believe have the potential to become expert judges of the quality of financial assets.

Attempts by those armed with special information to exploit asymmetries in information could have great consequences for the financial marketplace as a whole. For example, if the asymmetric distribution of relevant information exists, there will be differences of opinion (heterogeneous expectations) among buyers and sellers of assets. This is particularly true of any estimates of future asset returns (that is, the probability distribution of expected returns from stocks, bonds, and other financial instruments). With differing estimates of value and risk, the prices of financial assets will tend to settle at a "consensus" price, reflecting the average expectation currently prevailing in the marketplace.

Moreover, with asymmetrically distributed information, there will be variations in both the quantity and the quality of information available. Unfortunately, most users of financial information cannot easily assess its quality at the time they must pay for it. Thus, considerable incentive exists in the money and capital markets for sellers of information to make wild claims about the quality and value of the information they are selling. It is not clear that the financial markets have yet developed an effective mechanism for policing the quality and truthfulness of information, although, over time, those who provide false or misleading information may suffer a loss of reputation and eventually exit the industry due to lack of demand for their services.

The asymmetric information theory does not necessarily contradict the weak and semistrong forms of the EMH. It concedes that the value of financial assets will capture all publicly available information. Where it departs from the EMH is in believing that some market participants have sufficient access to special or costly information and that they can, at times, profit from that special information, earning excess returns. Moreover, in instances where asymmetries are very strong, a financial market can misfire, misallocate resources, and even collapse.

Problems Informational Asymmetries Can Create: Lemons and Plums

Asymmetries can create many difficulties in the availability and distribution of information. One of the most familiar — often called the *lemons problem* — has confronted used car buyers ever since the automobile was invented. Everyone who has ever purchased a used car is aware of the risks involved in the process. The buyer does not know for sure whether the used automobile he or she is looking at is a real "lemon," a continuing source of trouble and grief as repair bills mount, or if the car is a "plum," a solid piece of transportation that runs and runs with few problems. The seller, in hopes of getting a higher price, has a strong incentive to misrepresent the car as a plum. Unless he or she is convinced this is true, the buyer will probably be unwilling to pay the full price for a plum due to the risk that the car will ultimately turn out to be a lemon. The seller possesses special ("inside") information built up by personal experience with the vehicle; the buyer cannot obtain this information except at considerable cost (such as by hiring a mechanic to do a bumper-to-bumper inspection of the vehicle).

A similar problem confronts the loan officer of a bank or credit union. Dozens of customers come in every day asking for loans and claiming they will use the requested funds for a good (hopefully, profitable and legal) purpose that meets the lending institution's credit standards and promising that they will repay their loans on time. Clearly, the loan officer can't be sure without expending considerable resources and incurring substantial costs which of his or her customers is a lemon or a plum. Equally frustrating, some customers who were plums when they took out their first loan may now be lemons due to changing circumstances, such as the loss of a job or the failure of a business. Only by spending resources to gain access to inside information can any lending institution fully evaluate its borrowing customers. This is especially the case with consumers and small businesses, who usually do not present financial statements that have been attested to by an independent auditor. This asymmetry problem helps us explain why credit bureaus and credit rating agencies have become so important to lending institutions that willingly pay the added expense required to have someone accumulate and evaluate the credit histories of borrowing businesses and consumers.

One more observation concerning the lemons problem is worth noting. Given the right circumstances, it can be shown that a market divided between lemons and plums can eventually become largely a market in which only lemons are offered for sale. This can happen because buyers will generally be unwilling to pay a premium price for plums if there is a substantial probability that they will, in fact, be purchasing lemons. However, the seller, possessed of inside information, knows whether he or she owns a plum and will usually be unwilling to sell a plum for the price of a lemon. If there is no low cost way around this asymmetry problem, the ultimate result over time is that the plums will be driven from the market and only lemons will remain to be sold. That is, in the extreme case where this asymmetry problem can't be overcome, lower-value assets will drive away higher-value assets.

What can happen to used cars also can happen to financial assets, such as loans made by banks and other lending institutions. Unless significant informational asymmetries can be overcome, lower-quality borrowers can drive away higher-quality borrowers who are unwilling to borrow at the higher interest rates that lower-quality borrowers must pay. Instead, higher-quality borrowers may turn to other markets for funds in which informational asymmetries are less of a problem. As we noted in the previous chapter, a new form of *disintermediation* has occurred in recent years in which top-quality borrowers have gone around traditional lenders such as banks and have gone instead directly to the open market, selling their bonds and stocks to larger and wealthier investors who may be more knowledgeable about the true quality of high-quality borrowers' IOUs. In short, the existence of information asymmetries has helped to restructure some of our most important financial markets.

Problems Asymmetries Can Create: The Problem of Adverse Selection

A related problem that the presence of informational asymmetries can create revolves around differences in the risk presented by different groups of customers who enter into contracts with financial institutions. When an asymmetrical distribution of information is present, it can drastically alter the nature of contracts that a business firm is willing to write in order to serve its customers.

For example, banks face an adverse selection problem with one of their most important services, checking accounts. To a banker, there are two principal categories of checking account customers: (1) those who hold high deposit balances and write few checks, giving the bank more money to lend while the low level of account activity keeps bank costs down, and (2) those customers who keep low balances in their account but write lots of checks, giving the bank few funds to invest while heavy account activity runs up bank costs. When a customer walks in to open a new account, the banker doesn't know what kind of checking account customer he or she will be. Only the customer has the "inside" information on what kind of checking account user he or she is.

If the banker sets *one price* for all checking account customers in such an asymmetric situation, the bank runs the risk of being *adversely selected against* by its potentially most profitable customers. The preferred high-balance, low-activity customers will leave because the one price set by the bank is likely to be too high for them, but that price may be too low to cover the bank's operating costs in servicing the less preferred low-balance, high-activity checking account customers. Another bank could simply enter the market with a checking account service that is cheaper and more attractive to high-balance customers and attract away the most profitable accounts. The first bank would be adversely selected against by those customers it most wanted to attract.

How does the first bank escape, or at least mitigate, this problem of adverse selection? The most common technique today is to set up a *price schedule* in which the prices charged vary based on how much money each customer keeps on deposit each month and how many checks are written and to let the customer pick which checking account plan to sign up for. Such a price schedule based on customer usage and deposit balances helps a bank to ensure that low-balance, high-activity deposit customers will pay higher service fees and that low-activity, high-balance customers will pay lower fees. In effect, the customer "self-selects" his or her own checking account plan according to the "inside" information he or she possesses. Moreover, the customer's own choice of deposit plan signals to the banker what kind of customer he or she is likely to be.

Thus, one way to deal with the problem of asymmetrical information is through *signaling*: letting the participants in the marketplace who possess special or inside information take an action that reveals the nature of the unique information they possess. In the case of checking accounts, the more costly customer to the bank signals this fact by choosing a checking account plan that allows low account balances but assesses higher service fees. In much the same way, an insider in a corporation who knows that his or her company is in trouble can signal the problem to the public by selling the company's stock. If the public sees insiders selling out, they too may begin to sell, driving the value of the company's stock lower in the market.

Asymmetry, Efficiency, and Real-World Markets. No market in the real world in which we live is either completely efficient or completely asymmetric. Rather, all real-world markets have elements of *both* efficiency and asymmetry.

As Peter Fortune (1991) observes, recent research has found some evidence that appears to be inconsistent with the pure efficient markets hypothesis. For example, there is evidence that some investors earn excess returns from trading the stock of small firms or from buying shares in certain types of mutual funds (known as closed-end funds). Moreover, some market anomalies seem inconsistent with a truly efficient market, such as unusually high stock returns on Fridays and unusually low stock returns on Mondays (known as the *weekend effect*) and exceptional returns in the month of January (known as the *January effect*). Stock prices also appear to display exceptionally high volatility in the short run, with some traders apparently buying on the basis of a stock's past performance rather than on its fundamental value, temporarily driving its price higher, and then, subsequently, selling the stock as its price returns to its former level (a phenomenon called *mean reversion*, which is inconsistent with the efficient markets hypothesis). Perhaps real-world markets are split into two segments: (1) a highly efficient segment, in which well-informed individual investors and financial institutions (the "smart money") trade, and (2) a market segment in which less-well-informed small investors and small businesses trade, where information is asymmetrically distributed and much of the information that becomes public is of poorer quality.

We will see in the following chapters of this book how financial market participants have moved to counter informational asymmetries by developing special kinds of expertise, forming special kinds of organizations (such as credit bureaus and credit rating agencies), writing unique contractual agreements (such as detailed insurance and loan contracts), and by striving continually to become more efficient and reduce their operating costs. It is also useful to bear in mind that the possession of special or inside information does not always result in an advantage for its possessor. Recent research has suggested that, at times, there is a "curse of knowledge": more information is not always better. For example, better-informed market participants often find it impossible to ignore private information even if it would be advantageous for them to do so.[2]

Possible Remedies for Informational Asymmetries.   One way to deal with market asymmetries is to pass laws and regulations designed to improve the flow of information between buyers and sellers and to protect the public against lying and deception in trading and valuing financial assets. For example, in 1933 the United States passed the Securities Act, requiring companies selling securities across state lines to submit a *prospectus* to a federal agency, the Securities and Exchange Commission (SEC), giving detailed economic and financial information on the firm's condition and prospects. Once the prospectus is approved, the SEC requires that the security issuer supply a prospectus to any investor interested in buying those securities. Misrepresentation or fraud in a prospectus can trigger lawsuits by the SEC and by investors against a business firm selling securities, its directors, any public accounting firms involved, and even security dealers handling the sale of those securities.

In 1934 the Securities Exchange Act was passed, requiring corporate insiders — the officers and directors of a company — to follow guidelines in trading the securities of firms with which they are affiliated in order to avoid excessive profit taking from privileged information. This law also moved to outlaw fraud and misrepresentation in trading securities already issued, requiring securities traded on exchanges and trading firms themselves to register with the SEC and to provide detailed annual reports to the SEC and to their own shareholders. Shortly thereafter, the Maloney Act was passed, requiring trade associations, such as the National Association of Securities Dealers (NASD), to register with the SEC. Today NASD tries to discourage cheating and deception of investors by enforcing an ethics code and by licensing security dealers.

The Investment Company Act, passed in 1940, required mutual funds (investment companies) to register with the SEC and provide the shareholding public with reports on their activities and performance. The Investment Advisers Act, passed in the same year, required the registration of professional investment advisers, who also must report their procedures for analyzing and recommending investments. Finally, in 1970, the Securities Investor Protection Act set up the Securities Investor Protection Corporation (SIPC) to insure an investor from loss of up to $500,000 on securities and up to $100,000 in lost cash should his or her brokerage firm fail. The SIPC agrees to replace any securities lost due to the collapse of a brokerage firm, although it does not guarantee the value of those securities.

These rules help to protect the public by giving them easier access to pertinent information as an aid to sound decision making. They do not, however, eliminate all, or even most, market asymmetries. The individual saver and borrower must remain constantly on guard regarding the quality, cost, and availability of financial information that emanates from the money and capital markets each day. We turn now to look at some of the most important sources of financial information currently available to the public.

---

[2]A study by Camerer, Lowenstein, and Weber (1989) of corporate earnings forecasts found that better-informed forecasters predicted the judgments of less-well-informed forecasters, but with a bias because they couldn't ignore the special information they possessed. Better-informed individuals often think their knowledge is shared by others and act accordingly, helping to reduce potential damage from informational asymmetries.

DEBT SECURITY PRICES AND YIELDS

Bonds and Notes. Among the most important securities traded in the financial system are bonds and notes. Bonds and notes are debt obligations issued by governments and corporations, usually in units (par values) of $1,000. A **note** is a short-term written promissory obligation, usually not exceeding 5 years to maturity; a **bond** is a long-term promissory note, usually at least 5 to 10 years to maturity and often much longer. Although bonds and notes generally pay a fixed rate of return to the investor in the form of coupon income, their prices fluctuate daily as interest rates change. Therefore, although bonds and notes are often referred to as *fixed-income securities*, the investor may experience significant gains or losses on these securities as their prices change. Bonds and notes generally carry a set maturity date, at which time the issuer must pay the holder the security's par value. These securities are generally identified by the name of the issuing company or governmental unit, their coupon (fixed interest) rate, and their maturity date.

Bid and Ask Prices of Bonds and Notes. Both bid and asked prices for bonds and notes are posted by dealers, who will purchase securities at the **bid price** but sell to customers at the **asked price**. Yields are computed against the asked price and are generally figured to maturity when the security is selling at a discount from its par value. When the security is selling at a premium over its par value and has various possible maturity dates, the yield is generally figured to the nearest maturity date. New prices and yields must be posted continually by dealers because demand and supply factors continually alter the price and return on individual securities.

Price Information. Today traders require information regarding the prices and availability of securities on an up-to-the-minute basis. Computer networks report instant prices and quotations on the most actively traded bonds and other securities. Most daily newspapers contain a list of prices for bonds traded on the New York and American stock exchanges as of the close of business the previous day. One of the most complete listings of daily price and yield quotations appears in *The Wall Street Journal (WSJ)* published by Dow Jones. *WSJ* reports the prices of securities traded on the major securities exchanges and also the prices of issues sold over the counter (OTC). Exhibit 3–2 shows the prices of corporate bonds traded on the New York Stock Exchange on March 21, 1996, as reported in the *WSJ*. In these quotations, bonds are priced in dollars and fractions of a dollar (in this case, down to one eighth of a dollar, or $0.125), assuming a $100 face (par) value bond.

For example, we note that bonds issued by American Telephone and Telegraph (AT&T) carrying a coupon rate of $7\frac{1}{2}$ percent and due to mature in the year 2006 traded the previous business day at a price of 105. This means that, when trading ended on the date indicated, these AT&T bonds were selling for $1,050. This closing price was unchanged from the price established at the market's close on the previous day. The current yield (Cur Yld) is also shown for each bond except for convertible bonds, which are designated with a "cv."[3] The current yield is simply the ratio of the annual interest income each bond promises divided by its current price.

Many of the bond trades on the major securities exchanges are small-volume, odd-lot transactions. Purchases and sales of large quantities of bonds (known as *round lots*) between dealers and major institutional investors generally take place off the major exchanges through direct negotiation or with the aid of security brokers.

---

[3]See Chapter 11 for a description of convertible bonds.

Exhibit 3–2 **Bond Price and Yield Quotations from *The Wall Street Journal***

NEW YORK EXCHANGE BONDS

CORPORATION BONDS
Volume, $20,155,000

Bonds	Cur Yld	Vol	Close	Net Chg
ADT Op zr10	...	5	49	− 1½
AMR 8.10s98	7.8	47	104	+ ⅛
AMR 6⅛24	cv	30	116	...
ATT 4⅜99	4.6	53	95¼	+ ⅛
ATT 6s00	6.0	105	100	+ ¼
ATT 5⅛01	5.4	80	94¾	...
ATT 7⅛02	6.9	10	103½	+ ⅞
ATT 7½06	7.1	86	105	...
ATT 8⅛22	7.8	82	103⅞	+ ⅝
ATT 8⅛24	7.7	21	105	+ 1
ATT 8⅝31	8.0	28	108½	− ¼
Advst 9s08	cv	5	101	...
AirbF 6¾01	cv	50	101	+ ¼
AlskAr 6½05	cv	1	136	− ⅛
AlskAr 6⅞14	cv	222	94½	− 1
AlldC zr97	...	40	91⅞	...
AlldC zr2000	...	9	75¾	− ⅛
AlldC zr09	...	25	37⅞	+ ¼
Allwst 7¼14	cv	1	85	+ 1
Alza zr14	...	40	45	...
AmBrnd 7½99	7.3	99	102½	+ ⅜
AMedia 11⅝04	11.0	30	105½	...
Amresco 03	...	1	101	− ¼
AnnTaylr 8¾00	9.6	319	91⅜	+ ⅞
Arvin 7½14	cv	31	101	− ½
Ashlnd 6¾14	cv	17	101½	+ ½
ARch 10⅞05	8.6	10	126⅝	− 5⅛

Quotations as of 4 p.m. Eastern Time
Thursday, March 21, 1996

Volume $20,995,000

SALES SINCE JANUARY 1
(000 omitted)

1996	1995	1994
$1,516,446	$1,699,120	$1,949,224

	Domestic Thu.	Domestic Wed.	All Issues Thu.	All Issues Wed.
Issues traded	307	318	317	324
Advances	135	144	140	146
Declines	108	110	111	112
Unchanged	64	64	66	66
New highs	7	6	7	6
New lows	4	4	5	4

Dow Jones Bond Averages

−1995− High	−1995− Low	−1996− High	−1996− Low		−1996− Close	−1996− Chg.	−1996− %Yld	−1995− Close	−1995− Chg.
105.34	93.63	106.09	103.37	20 Bonds	103.68	unch	7.01	97.78	− 0.05
102.30	89.08	102.43	99.74	10 Utilities	100.06	+ 0.13	7.20	93.56	+ 0.01
108.96	98.08	109.94	106.98	10 Industrials	107.30	− 0.14	6.83	102.00	− 0.12

Source: *The Wall Street Journal*, Southwest edition, March 22, 1996, p. C16. Reprinted by permission of *The Wall Street Journal*, © 1995 Dow Jones & Company, Inc. All Rights Reserved Worldwide.

Several other sources of information on bond yields and prices are readily available to investors in published form. *The Daily Bond Buyer*, for example, gives a detailed breakdown of daily prices and yields for a large number of actively traded bond issues. Moreover, a number of *bond yield indexes* have been compiled in recent years; these pool several bond issues of similar quality and report the average rate of return (yield) to the investor for the entire pool of bonds. With bond yield indexes, investors and companies planning to issue new bonds can see the trend of recent price and yield changes and decide whether their plans need to be altered to reflect the latest developments.

Bond Yield Indexes. Among the most popular bond yield indexes are those compiled by Moody's Investor Service and the *Bond Buyer* newspaper for both corporate and state and local government bonds. In addition, the U.S. Treasury makes available estimated average yields for its notes and bonds, arrayed by maturity. Dow Jones publishes a daily index of prices for some of the most actively traded corporate bonds.

These various bond yield indicators appear in numerous publications, including both private and governmental sources. The *Federal Reserve Bulletin*, published by the Board of Governors of the Federal Reserve System, and the *Survey of Current Business*, published by the U.S. Department of Commerce, report weekly, monthly, and annual average bond yields. Recent changes in various bond yield indexes as reported in the *Federal Reserve Bulletin* are shown in Exhibit 3–3. We note the marked fluctuations in bond yields between 1985 and 1996, reflecting significant changes in economic conditions and credit demands during this period.

Buyers of bonds are often called "contrarions," because they usually react positively to bad economic news (such as declining economic growth or rising unemployment). The

Exhibit 3–3

Indicators of Average Bond Yields (Average Annual Yields in Percent)

Yield Series	1985	1990	1992	1994	1995*	1996**
State and local government notes and bonds:						
Aaa-Moody's Series	8.60%	6.96%	6.09%	5.77%	6.45%	5.80%
Bond buyer Series	9.11	7.29	6.48	6.18	6.44	5.95
Corporate bonds:						
Seasoned issues, all industries	12.05	9.77	8.55	8.26	8.73	7.83
Moody's corporate bond indices classified by rating:						
Aaa	11.37	9.32	8.14	7.97	8.49	7.59
Aa	11.82	9.56	8.46	8.15	8.62	7.72
A	12.28	9.82	8.62	8.28	8.72	7.83
Baa	12.72	19.36	8.98	8.63	9.10	8.20

*Average for the month of January 1995.
**Averages for the month of January 1996.

Source: Board of Governors of the Federal Reserve System, *Federal Reserve Bulletin*, selected issued.

reason is that a slower growing economy usually means less inflation and lower interest rates, which push bond prices higher. This is why bond buyers pay a great deal of attention to announcements each week of new economic data, such as the release of new information on auto sales, factory orders, industrial production, money supply growth, or the construction of new homes. Each week *The Wall Street Journal* publishes newly released statistics on the economy's performance, and the *Journal* lets investors know what new economic data is about to be released (see Exhibit 3–4 for an example). Any hint of softening in the economy often results in a short-term bond market price rally.

Exhibit 3–4

Announcing New Data on the Economy's Performance to Interested Investors

Tracking the Economy   June 26, 1995

Key statistics scheduled to be released this week:

ECONOMIC INDICATOR	PERIOD	RELEASE DATE	PREVIOUS ACTUAL	TECHNICAL DATA CONSENSUS FORECAST
Consumer Confidence	June	Tuesday	101.6	101.5
Initial Jobless Claims	Week to June 24	Thursday	395,000	390,000
Money Supply: M2	Week to June 19	Thursday	+$9.2 billion	+$10.0 billion
Factory Orders	May	Friday	−1.9%	+1.3%
Real GDP (ann. rate)	1st qtr., 2d rev.	Friday	+2.7%*	+2.7%
GDP Deflator (ann. rate)	1st qtr., 2d rev.	Friday	+3.3%*	+3.3%

* Previous estimate of 1st quarter   *Source: Technical Data*

Source: *The Wall Street Journal,* Southwest Edition, June 26, 1995, p. A4. Reprinted by permission of *The Wall Street Journal,* © 1995 Dow Jones & Company, Inc. All Rights Reserved Worldwide.

STOCK PRICES AND DIVIDEND YIELDS

Of all securities traded in the money and capital markets, **stocks** are among the most popular with investors. Stock prices can be extremely volatile, offering the prospect of substantial capital gains if prices rise but also significant capital losses if prices fall. Many corporations issuing stocks pay dividends regularly, thus giving the investor a reasonably steady source of income as well as the opportunity to achieve "windfall" gains if the value of the stock rises. Unlike a bond, however, a share of stock is a certificate of ownership in a corporation, not a debt obligation. No corporation need pay dividends to its stockholders, and some never do, preferring to retain all after-tax earnings in the business or simply failing and disappearing from the industry.

Price and Yield Information. As in the case of bonds, price and yield data on the most actively traded stocks are reported daily in the financial press. Most daily newspapers list current stock prices. *The Wall Street Journal* contains an extensive list of the daily prices and dividend yields of major stocks sold over the counter and on the major securities exchanges, including the New York, American, Midwest, Pacific, Philadelphia, Boston, and Cincinnati stock exchanges in the United States, and the London, Tokyo, Frankfurt, and other major exchanges abroad. An example of *WSJ* stock price quotations is shown in Exhibit 3–5.

We note that each stock price quotation is identified by the abbreviated name of the company issuing it. High and low prices at which the stock has been traded during the past year and the most recent annual dividend declared by the issuing company are given.[4] The dividend yield, or ratio of dividends to current price, appears next, along with the ratio of the stock's current price to the past 12 months of company earnings (the P-E ratio). All remaining entries provide a summary of the previous business day's transactions in the markets on which that particular stock is bought and sold. The one-day sales volume, expressed in hundreds of shares, is shown, as well as the highest and lowest prices at which the stock was exchanged that day. The closing price for which the stock was traded in the last sale of the day is reported, expressed in dollars and fractions of a dollar down to eighths. The final entry gives the net change between the day's closing price and the closing price one day earlier.

Stock prices for individual companies, covering a period of several years, are provided by *The Value Line Investment Survey*, published weekly by Arnold Bernhard & Company of New York. Each company's business is described and basic financial information, such as sales, net earnings, and long-term indebtedness, is provided for at least a decade. Stock prices and basic financial data for individual companies are also presented in comprehensive reports compiled by Standard & Poor's Corporation (S&P) and published in *Stock Reports*. This monthly S&P series covers shares traded on the New York and American stock exchanges and over the counter. Information is provided to subscribers on dividends paid by each company and its principal products, as well as an analysis of its performance. Daily and weekly stock price movements are also reported in S&P's quarterly publication, the *Daily Stock Price Record*, and in the monthly publication *Trendline's Current Market Perspectives*. The performance of the shares issued by mutual funds is tracked in Weisenberger's *Survey of Investment Companies.*

---

[4]The occasional letters that appear beside certain stocks in the list of quotations refer to footnotes that give special information. All stocks shown are common equity shares unless the symbol *pf* appears, indicating an issue of preferred stock. The symbol *u*, when it appears, indicates a 52-week high in price, and the symbol *d* reflects a new 52-week low. The letter *s* refers to a stock split or stock dividend of 25 percent or more in the past 52 weeks, and *n* refers to securities newly issued within the past 52 weeks. The symbol *x* reflects a stock currently being traded without dividends or shareholder rights attached.

Exhibit 3–5 Stock Price Quotations from *The Wall Street Journal*

NYSE COMPOSITE TRANSACTIONS

Quotations as of 5 p.m. Eastern Time
Tuesday, March 19, 1996

	52 Weeks Hi	52 Weeks Lo	Stock	Sym	Div	Yld %	PE	Vol 100s	Hi	Lo	Close	Net Chg
			-A-A-A-									
	22⅛	12⅛	AAR	AIR	.48	2.4	22	158	20⅜	20⅛	20⅜	...
	31⅛	21	ABM Indus	ABM	.70f	2.3	16	27	31	30⅞	31	...
	9⅞	8	ACM Gvt Fd	ACG	.90	9.4	...	579	9⅝	9½	9⅝	+ ⅛
	7⅞	6⅝	ACM OppFd	AOF	.66	9.1	...	449	7⅜	7¼	7¼	– ⅛
	9⅛	7¼	ACM SecFd	GSF	.90	10.3	...	1492	8¾	8⅝	8¾	+ ⅛
	7¼	6	ACM SpctmFd	SI	.75	11.0	...	646	7	6¾	6 13/16	– ⅛
	11⅝	8	ACM MgmdInc	ADF	1.26	11.7	...	690	10⅞	10¾	10¾	– ⅛
	9⅝	7⅝	ACM MgdIncFd	AMF	.90	9.6	...	586	9⅜	9¼	9⅜	+ ⅛
	13¼	11⅛	ACM MuniSec	AMU	.90	6.9	...	129	13	12⅞	13	...
s	31⅜	13¾	♣ ACX Tch A	ACX		...	20	937	18	17⅛	17¼	...
	18	10⅛	ADT	ADT		...	45	6871	17⅝	17⅜	17⅜	– ¼
s	33	24¼	♣ AFLAC	AFL	.35	1.1	14	2504	32⅛	31	31¾	– ½
s	28⅝	14 13/16	AGCO Cp	AG	.04	.2	10	2109	27¼	26¼	26⅝	+ ⅛
s	20⅜	16⅝	AGL Res	ATG	1.06i	5.8	16	415	18¼	18	18¼	+ ⅛
n	22	18½	AJL PepsTr	AJP	.34p	...	...	412	20⅞	20¼	20⅞	+ ⅝
	21⅜	17	♣ AMLI Resdntl	AML	1.72	8.6	17	240	20¼	19¾	20	+ ¼
	46¼	35⅝	♣ AMP	AMP	1.00f	2.3	22	4492	43⅝	42½	43¼	+ ⅛
	93⅜	61⅝	AMR	AMR		...	38	10995	92½	91¼	91¾	+ ¾
	52⅞	43¼	ARCO Chm	RCM	2.80	5.3	10	223	52⅝	52⅜	52⅜	...
	50½	36⅜	ASA	ASA	2.00	4.6	...	1013	44¼	43⅝	43¾	...
	44½	23⅝	♣ ATT Cap	TCC	.44	1.0	16	471	42⅝	42⅛	42½	+ ½
	68⅞	47⅞	AT&T Cp	T	1.32	2.1	cc	33285	62¾	61⅞	61⅞	...
	37⅞	11¾	AamesFnl	AAM	.30	.9	16	338	35½	34⅞	34⅞	– ⅝
	44¾	35⅝	AbbotLab	ABT	.96f	2.3	20	22969	41⅜	40⅛	41⅜	+ ⅞
	19	13⅜	Abitibi g	ABY	.40e	...	...	798	14⅞	14⅝	14⅝	– ¼
	17½	13⅛	♣ AcceptIns	AIF		...	52	507	14¾	14⅝	14⅝	...
	50⅜	23⅝	ACE Ltd	ACL	.56	1.3	6	3039	43¾	43¼	43¾	– ¼
	31¼	14⅛	AcmeCleve	AMT	.52f	1.7	7	406	30½	30⅜	30⅜	...
	38¾	6	AcmeElec	ACE		...	dd	120	6¾	6⅝	6⅝	...
	33⅛	23½	♣ Acordia	ACO	.80	2.6	19	13	31½	31¼	31¼	...
	15¾	10⅛	Acuson	ACN		...	56	486	14⅝	14½	14½	– ¼
	19⅝	16⅛	♣ AdamsExp	ADX	1.66e	8.7	...	216	19¼	19⅛	19⅛	+ ⅛
	39¼	16⅛	♣ AdvMicro	AMD		...	6	7296	18⅜	17⅞	18⅛	...
	10¼	5½	Advest	ADV		...	10	68	9⅝	9⅝	9⅝	...
	20⅛	16⅝	AtlanEngy	ATE	1.54	8.8	11	928	17⅝	17⅜	17½	...
	118⅞	104¼	AtlanRich	ARC	5.50	4.7	14	5955	117	115⅞	116⅛	+ ⅜
	280½	249⅛	AtlanRich pfC		2.80	1.0	...	2	278⅜	278⅜	278⅜	+ 10⅜
	30	22⅛	AtlanRich97	LYX	2.23	7.4	...	6989	30	29⅜	30	+ ⅛
	2¼	1⅛	AtlasCp	AZ		...	dd	149	1½	1⅜	1½	...
	23	17½	♣ ATMOS Eng	ATO	.96	4.3	16	59	22⅜	22⅛	22⅜	+ ⅛
	24½	15	Augat	AUG	.16	.9	46	516	17⅞	17⅛	17⅞	+ ¾
	26⅜	17⅛	Aus&NZ Bk	ANZ	1.20e	5.0	...	27	24⅝	24⅛	24⅛	– ¼
	28¼	24⅞	Aus&NZ Bk pf		2.28	8.3	...	34	27½	27⅛	27⅜	– ⅛
	19⅛	13½	AustStkIdx	SPJ		...	...	133	19	18⅞	19	+ ⅛
	9⅜	7½	AustriaFd	OST		...	...	246	8¾	8½	8⅝	...
	29	13¾	AuthenticFit	ASM	.04e	.1	29	256	27⅞	27⅜	27½	– ½
	2¼	½	AutoSec	ASI		...	...	597	1	15/16	1	+ 1/16
s	43⅜	30¼	AutoDataProc	AUD	.40	1.0	27	4795	41½	39¾	40⅜	– ⅝
▲	31⅞	22	AutoZone	AZO		...	32	12659	32½	31⅝	32⅜	+ ¾
	23¼	18⅝	AvalonProp	AVN	1.48	6.8	19	277	22⅛	21⅞	21⅞	– ⅛
n	25	24⅛	AvalonProp pfA			...	...	44	25	24¾	24⅞	...
	18¼	14⅝	AVEMCO	AVE	.48	3.3	16	74	14⅞	14¾	14¾	– ⅛
▲	57⅛	38⅞	AveryDensn	AVY	1.20	2.1	21	1810	57¼	56⅝	57	+ ¼
	10⅛	5⅜	♣ Aviall	AVL	j	...	dd	338	8⅜	8⅛	8⅜	+ ⅛
	55⅝	38	Avnet	AVT	.60	1.2	13	1808	50⅞	49⅝	49⅞	+ ¼
	88⅝	56¾	AvonPdts	AVP	2.32f	2.7	23	1952	87⅜	85⅞	86¼	– ⅜
n	38	21⅛	AVX Cp	AVX	.10e	.4	...	1065	24	23⅝	24	+ ¼
	19⅜	12⅞	Aydin	AYD		...	19	31	15	15	15	– ⅛
	10½	6⅞	AztarCp	AZR		...	dd	2109	8¼	8	8¼	+ ⅛

Source: *The Wall Street Journal*, Southwest edition, March 20, 1996, p. C3. Reprinted by permission of *The Wall Street Journal*, © 1996 Dow Jones & Company, Inc. All Rights Reserved Worldwide.

The stock market is watched closely by investors as a barometer of expectations in the business community. A rising trend in stock prices generally signals an optimistic assessment of future business prospects and expectations of higher corporate earnings. A declining market, on the other hand, is often a harbinger of adverse economic news and may signal a cutback in business investment and lower corporate earnings. Among the most important factors watched by stock buyers are reports of corporate earnings, merger and dividend announcements, changes in corporate management, announcements of new products being introduced, changes in government policy that might affect interest rates (with the prospect of lower interest rates generally favorable for stocks), and apparent changes in the strength of the economy (as reflected in such data series as new orders to manufacturers of durable goods, new housing construction, the growth of consumer and business investment expenditures, changes in the level of business inventories, and measures of inflation) that impact the outlook for sales of goods and services.

Stock Price Indexes. Many students of the financial markets follow several broad stock price indexes that reflect price movements in groups of similar quality securities. One of the most popular indexes is the Dow Jones Industrial Average of 30 stocks, including such major companies as American Telephone & Telegraph, General Motors, and Exxon. Dow Jones also reports a transportation average of 20 stocks (including such industry leaders as American Airlines) and a utility average of the shares of 15 leading utility companies (such as Consolidated Edison and Pacific Gas and Electric). The utility average is of special importance to many investors because it appears to be highly sensitive to interest rate fluctuations, and some analysts regard it as a barometer of interest rate expectations. Recent movements in the Dow Jones Industrial Average reported in *The Wall Street Journal* are shown in Exhibit 3–6. Daily reports of the performance of all the Dow series also may be found in local newspapers, as well as in Standard & Poor's *Daily Stock Price Record*.[5]

Two of the most comprehensive stock market indicators available are Standard & Poor's 400 Industrial Stock Price Index and 500 Composite Stock Price Index, both including the most actively traded U.S. corporate equity shares. The S&P 500 includes the shares of 40 utility companies, 20 transportation firms, and 40 financial stocks not present in the S&P 400 industrial index. All five S&P stock series — the 400 Index, Utility Index, Transportation Index, Financial Stock Index, and the 500 Composite Index — are widely followed and regarded as sensitive barometers of general stock price movements in the United States. An even broader price index than the S&P 500 Composite is the New York Stock Exchange Composite Index, which gives greatest weight to stocks having the highest market values. Considered a useful indicator of total market performance, the NYSE composite is often used to compare the performance of major institutional investors, such as investment companies and pension funds, against the market as a whole. Two other broad market indicators are the AMEX Index, which is a weighted average of all stocks traded on the American Stock Exchange, and the NASDAQ OTC composite, which measures price movements in stocks sold over the counter rather than on the major exchanges.

Many newspapers, including *The Wall Street Journal*, and financially oriented magazines contain daily stock market diaries or summaries similar to that shown in Exhibit 3–6. Such summaries of recent market developments indicate both price movements and the volume of trading on the major exchanges. Examples may be found in *Barrons, The Wall Street Transcript, Forbes, Fortune, Money*, and *Financial World*. Market diaries or summaries usually report the total number of shares traded on a given day or week, the number of stocks advancing or declining in price, and those whose price remains unchanged after recent trading.

Foreign Stock Prices. With the spreading globalization of the financial markets, more and more savers and borrowers are turning to foreign markets to invest their savings and raise needed funds. Therefore, key financial information sources increasingly are reporting daily changes in security prices and interest rates in foreign trading centers. A good example is Exhibit 3–7, which reports the prices of selected corporate stock as of the preceding day in London, Frankfurt, Hong Kong, Amsterdam, and other important financial centers around the globe (all denominated in their respective home currencies). To help foreign investors who deal predominantly in their own home currencies, there is also a listing of currency exchange rates (shown at the bottom of Exhibit 3–7) so that they can translate a security's current price from one currency into another. It also reports the previous day's movements

---

[5]The Dow industrial, transportation, and utility averages are combined to form a fourth market indicator — the 65-stock composite average. Probably the most widely followed stock market index in the world, the Dow industrials are constructed by adding up the current prices of 30 industrial stocks and dividing by an adjustment factor designed to account for stock splits and changes in the list of the 30 companies represented in the average.

Exhibit 3–6   **Daily Stock Market Diary**

STOCK MARKET DATA BANK   3/21/96

MAJOR INDEXES

— †365 DAY — HIGH	LOW		DAILY HIGH	DAILY LOW	CLOSE	NET CHG	% CHG	†365 DAY CHG	% CHG	FROM 12/31	% CHG
DOW JONES AVERAGES											
5683.60	4087.83	30 Industrials	5668.79	5613.87	x5626.88	− 28.54	− 0.50	+ 1539.05	+ 37.65	+ 509.76	+ 9.96
2215.21	1574.26	20 Transportation	2203.27	2177.93	2188.90	− 5.60	− 0.26	+ 614.64	+ 39.04	+ 207.90	+ 10.49
234.00	185.67	15 Utilities	214.43	213.11	214.02	− 0.06	− 0.03	+ 28.35	+ 15.27	− 11.38	− 5.05
1847.58	1356.99	65 Composite	1843.43	1828.47	x1832.65	− 6.84	− 0.37	+ 475.66	+ 35.05	+ 139.44	+ 8.24
623.15	467.17	Equity Mkt. Index	616.00	612.86	613.98	− 0.62	− 0.10	+ 146.81	+ 31.43	+ 32.55	+ 5.60
NEW YORK STOCK EXCHANGE											
351.70	267.92	Composite	348.71	347.64	348.06	− 0.14	− 0.04	+ 80.14	+ 29.91	+ 18.55	+ 5.63
443.68	340.36	Industrials	442.24	440.97	441.47	unch	....	+ 101.11	+ 29.71	+ 28.18	+ 6.82
266.69	203.66	Utilities	247.42	246.56	247.27	+ 0.97	+ 0.39	+ 43.61	+ 21.41	− 5.63	− 2.23
333.59	243.93	Transportation	328.41	326.19	328.41	− 1.35	− 0.41	+ 84.48	+ 34.63	+ 26.45	+ 8.76
298.31	212.58	Finance	291.51	290.25	290.25	− 1.32	− 0.45	+ 77.67	+ 36.54	+ 16.00	+ 5.83
STANDARD & POOR'S INDEXES											
661.45	495.95	500 Index	651.54	648.10	649.19	− 0.79	− 0.12	+ 153.24	+ 30.90	+ 33.26	+ 5.40
776.23	591.34	Industrials	769.80	765.82	767.19	− 0.65	− 0.08	+ 175.85	+ 29.74	+ 46.00	+ 6.38
213.83	157.68	Utilities	194.75	193.16	194.11	+ 0.77	+ 0.40	+ 36.43	+ 23.10	− 8.47	− 4.18
232.53	179.91	400 MidCap	230.67	229.85	229.99	− 0.29	− 0.13	+ 50.08	+ 27.84	+ 12.15	+ 5.58
126.48	97.02	600 SmallCap	126.55	126.12	126.19	− 0.12	− 0.10	+ 29.17	+ 30.07	+ 5.09	+ 4.20
142.35	107.56	1500 Index	140.87	140.19	140.39	− 0.17	− 0.12	+ 32.83	+ 30.52	+ 7.15	+ 5.37
NASDAQ											
1117.79	811.39	Composite	1104.36	1098.58	1099.79	− 2.03	− 0.18	+ 288.40	+ 35.54	+ 47.66	+ 4.53
1026.46	791.75	Industrials	1021.86	1017.53	1019.66	+ 1.74	+ 0.17	+ 227.70	+ 28.75	+ 54.98	+ 5.70
1344.70	999.36	Insurance	1308.57	1300.30	1303.70	+ 2.05	+ 0.16	+ 304.34	+ 30.45	+ 11.06	+ 0.86
1050.72	768.89	Banks	1042.08	1039.80	1040.71	+ 0.51	+ 0.05	+ 271.53	+ 35.30	+ 31.30	+ 3.10
500.28	362.63	Nat. Mkt. Comp.	494.23	491.56	492.08	− 0.99	− 0.20	+ 129.45	+ 35.70	+ 20.91	+ 4.44
417.86	321.61	Nat. Mkt. Indus.	415.90	414.12	414.93	+ 0.60	+ 0.14	+ 92.46	+ 28.67	+ 21.63	+ 5.50
OTHERS											
570.31	458.52	Amex	568.76	566.63	568.32	+ 1.05	+ 0.19	+ 109.80	+ 23.95	+ 20.09	+ 3.66
351.81	263.52	Russell 1000	347.66	345.98	346.45	− 0.37	− 0.11	+ 82.93	+ 31.47	+ 17.56	+ 5.34
328.93	257.53	Russell 2000	329.06	328.31	328.67	+ 0.33	+ 0.10	+ 71.14	+ 27.62	+ 12.70	+ 4.02
374.89	282.46	Russell 3000	371.40	369.80	370.26	− 0.30	− 0.08	+ 87.80	+ 31.08	+ 18.35	+ 5.21
344.93	286.95	Value-Line(geom.)	344.30	343.48	343.81	− 0.01	− 0.00	+ 56.86	+ 19.82	+ 12.77	+ 3.86
6449.34	4865.05	Wilshire 5000	...	...	6383.31	− 5.93	− 0.09	+ 1518.26	+ 31.21	+ 326.10	+ 5.38

†-Based on comparable trading day in preceding year.

Source: *The Wall Street Journal*, Southwest edition, March 22, 1996, p. C2. Reprinted by permission of *The Wall Street Journal*, © 1995 Dow Jones & Company, Inc. All Rights Reserved Worldwide.

in broad stock price indexes at the major securities exchanges in the Americas, Western Europe, Canada, South Africa, and around the Pacific Rim. (See Exhibit 3–8.)

INFORMATION ON SECURITY ISSUERS

Moody's and Standard & Poor's. Lenders of funds have a pressing need to secure accurate financial information on those individuals and institutions that seek to borrow funds or to sell their stock. Fortunately, financial information on many individual companies and other security issuers, particularly for the largest institutions, is available from a wide variety of published sources.

Exhibit 3–7   **Stock and Currency Price Movements in Selected Countries**

FOREIGN MARKETS

Tuesday, March 19, 1996

	Close	Prev. Close
Tsugami	550	+ 7
Uny	1850	+ 20
Ushio	1140	+ 20
Wacoal	1270	+ 40
Yamaha	1850	....
Yamaichi Sec	771	+ 11
Yamanouchi Phm	2300	− 10
Yamatake-Hnywl	1740	+ 30
Yamato Transport	1210	+30
Yamazaki Baking	1900	....
Yasuda Fire	760	+ 23
Yokogawa Elec	1120	+ 20

LONDON
(in pound/pence)

	Close	Net Chg.
Abbey National	5.61	+ 0.11
Allied-Domecq	4.91	....
Argyll Group	3.14	+ 0.05
Arjo Wiggins	2.05	+ 0.03
Assoc Brit Fds	4.08	+ 0.04
BAA PLC	5.29	+ 0.09
Barclays	7.25	+ 0.12
Bass	7.43	+ 0.01
BAT Indus	4.87	− 0.01
Blue Circle	3.38	+ 0.01
BOC Group	9.06	+ 0.02
Body Shop	1.48	− 0.02
Boots	5.99	+ 0.04
BPB Indus	3.20	+ 0.04
British Aero	8.74	....
British Airwys	5.28	+ 0.02
British Gas	2.32	+ 0.02
British Pete	5.75	+ 0.15
British Steel	1.96	+ 0.02
British Telcom	3.52	+ 0.01
BTR	3.33	− 0.03
Burmah Castrol	10.28	− 0.02
Cable&Wireless	4.83	− 0.02
Cadbury Schwp	5.10	+ 0.09
Caradon	2.15	+ 0.01
Charter plc	8.66	....
Coats Vivella	2.00	....
Commercial Un	5.79	+ 0.07
Cookson Group	3.09	+ 0.02
Courtaulds	4.39	+ 0.02
Eng Ch Clay	3.17	+ 0.04
Enterprise Oil	4.31	+ 0.06
Euro Tunnel	0.78	....
Forte	3.51	+ 0.01
GEC	3.60	....
Genrl Accidnt	6.31	+ 0.09
GKN	9.15	+ 0.02
Glaxo	8.08	+ 0.09

	Close	Prev. Close
Smith&Nephew	1.84	....
Smithkln Bchm	6.59	− 0.14
Std Chartrd	6.12	+ 0.02
Sun Alliance	3.61	+ 0.05
Tarmac	1.18	....
Tate & Lyle	4.82	+ 0.05
Tesco	2.78	+ 0.06
Thorn EMI	16.22	− 0.08
TI Group	4.87	+ 0.11
Tomkins	2.56	+ 0.04
Trafalgar Hse	0.49	....
Unilever	12.47	+ 0.11
Utd Biscuits	2.49	+ 0.03
Vodafone	2.52	+ 0.01
Williams Hldgs	3.15	....
WPP Group	1.90	+ 0.02

South African Mines
(in U.S. dollars)

	Close	Net Chg.
Bracken	0.21	....
Deelkraal	1.17	....
Durban Deep	8.50	....
E. Rand Gold	2.38	− 0.06
E. Rand Prop	0.72	....
Elandsrand	6.38	....
Grootvlei	2.84	....
Harmony	13.13	− 0.10
Hartebstftn	3.69	− 0.06
Impala Pltm	16.88	− 0.50
Kinross	11.50	....
Leslie	1.20	....
Loraine	3.33	....
Randfontein	8.25	+ 0.13
Rustenburg	16.88	− 0.25
Southvaal	36.50	− 1.25
Stilfontein	1.13	+ 0.06
Unisel	4.50	....
Winkelhaak	9.50	....

HONG KONG
(in Hong Kong dollars)

	Close	Net Chg.
Bank E Asia	26.50	+ 0.40
Cathay Pacific	13.15	− 0.05
Cheung Kong	54.00	+ 2.00
China L & P	34.50	+ 0.60
Hang Seng Bk	79.00	+ 2.75
HK Electric	25.40	+ 0.15
HK Telecom	15.30	+ 0.25
HSBC Hldgs	117.00	+ 2.00
Hutchsn Whmp	45.80	+ 1.00
Hysan Develop	23.80	+ 1.05

FRANKFURT
(in marks)

	Close	Net Chg.
AEG	165.50	+ 2.00
Allianz	2728.00	+ 54.00
Asko	940.00	+ 17.00
BASF	401.00	+ 1.00
Bayer	502.30	+ 9.80
BMW	818.00	+ 9.00
Byr Vereinsbk	43.30	+ 0.05
Commerzbank	332.50	+ 3.50
Continental	26.03	+ 0.26
Daimler Benz	822.30	+ 9.80
Degussa	543.50	+ 2.00
Deutsche Bank	73.95	+ 1.30
Dresdner Bank	38.05	+ 0.08
Heidlbg Zemnt	970.00	− 5.00
Henkel	556.00	+ 4.00
Hochtief	622.00	+ 3.00
Hoechst	503.00	....
Karstadt	563.50	+ 6.00
Kaufhof	485.00	+ 3.00
Linde	868.50	+ 6.50
Lufthansa	229.50	+ 3.50
MAN	417.00	+ 6.50
Mannesmnn	530.00	+ 14.00
Metallges	31.84	+ 0.44
Munchen Ruck	3024.00	+ 10.00
Porsche	783.00	+ 3.00
RWE	59.50	+ 1.25
SAP	212.00	− 0.50
SAP Pfd	213.80	+ 0.30
Schering	116.95	− 1.35
Siemens	835.80	+ 8.80
Thyssen	290.30	+ 6.00
Veba	69.98	+ 0.63
VEW	492.00	+ 4.00
Volkswagen	544.50	+ 10.00

MEXICO
(in pesos)

	Close	Net Chg.
Alfa A	96.40	+ 2.40
Apasco A	36.75	+ 1.65
Banacci B	15.32	+ 0.32
Bimbo A	32.00	+ 0.40
Cemex B	29.00	+ 1.40
Cifra B	9.74	+ 0.34
Cifra C	9.54	+ 0.24
Femsa B	22.00	+ 0.85
Gcarso A1	51.70	+ 1.75
Kimber A	145.50	+ 11.40
Maseca B	6.52	+ 0.38
Tamsa	60.50	− 0.10
Televisa	98.00	+ 8.00
Tolmex B2	34.55	....
Vitro	13.56	+ 0.58

	Close	Prev. Close
Electrolux	340.00	− 6.00
Ericsson	154.50	+ 5.00
SE Bank	49.50	+ 0.30
Skanska	206.00	− 1.00
SKF	160.00	− 1.50
Volvo	154.50	− 2.00

AMSTERDAM
(in guilders)

	Close	Net Chg.
ABN Amro	80.00	....
Aegon	73.00	+ 1.00
Ahold	77.10	+ 1.10
Akzo Nobel	181.90	+ 1.00
AMEV	113.00	− 1.30
Bols Wessanen	33.10	....
DSM	154.70	+ 0.50
Elsevier	24.40	+ 0.10
Fokker	0.35	....
Gist-Brocades	52.90	− 0.50
Heineken	333.90	+ 3.90
Hoogovens	62.80	− 0.30
Hunter Douglas	102.00	....
ING Groep N.V.	114.80	− 0.10
KLM	57.00	+ 0.40
KNP BT	46.00	....
Nedlloyd	36.50	....
Oce-van Grntn	138.50	+ 3.20
Pakhoed Hldg	44.60	− 0.20
Philips	67.40	+ 0.70
Robeco	122.20	+ 0.70
Rodamco	46.50	+ 0.30
Rolinco	130.20	+ 1.60
Rorento	94.20	+ 0.40
Royal Dutch	233.50	+ 2.90
Royal PTT	68.10	+ 0.10
Unilever	228.70	+ 3.20
VNU	26.60	....
VOC	56.10	− 0.20
Wolters Kluwer	178.30	+ 1.10

BRUSSELS
(in Belgian francs)

	Close	Net Chg.
Arbed	3260	− 80
BBL	5660	+ 50
Bekaert	28600	+ 450
CBR	12225	+ 125
Delhaize	1312	....
Electrabel	6850	+ 30
Gen de Bnque	10925	+ 100
Gevaert	1845	+ 10
GIB	1484	+ 30
Petrofina	8540	+ 30
Soc Gen Belg	2475	+ 30
Solvay	17900	+ 100

Source: *The Wall Street Journal*, Southwest Edition, March 20, 1996, p. C16. Reprinted by permission of *The Wall Street Journal*, © 1995 Dow Jones & Company, Inc. All Rights Reserved Worldwide.

Key Currency Cross Rates   Late New York Trading Mar 21, 1996

	Dollar	Pound	SFranc	Guilder	Peso	Yen	Lira	D-Mark	FFranc	CdnDlr
Canada	1.3621	2.0929	1.1384	.82233	.18053	.01274	.00087	.92034	.26821	
France	5.0785	7.8031	4.2445	3.0660	.67309	.04751	.00325	3.4314		3.7284
Germany	1.4800	2.2740	1.2369	.89350	.19616	.01385	.00095		.29142	1.0866
Italy	1564.5	2403.9	1307.6	944.52	207.36	14.637		1057.1	308.06	1148.6
Japan	106.89	164.24	89.336	64.532	14.167		.06832	72.223	21.048	78.474
Mexico	7.5450	11.593	6.3059	4.5551		.07059	.00482	5.0980	1.4857	5.5392
Netherlands	1.6564	2.5451	1.3844		.21954	.01550	.00106	1.1192	.32616	1.2161
Switzerland	1.1965	1.8384		.72235	.15858	.01119	.00076	.80845	.23560	.87842
U.K.	.65083		.54394	.39292	.08626	.00609	.00042	.43975	.12815	.47781
U.S.		1.5365	.83577	.60372	.13254	.00936	.00064	.67568	.19691	.73416

Source: Dow Jones Telerate Inc.

Source: *The Wall Street Journal*, Southwest Edition, March 22, 1996, p. C11. Reprinted by permission of *The Wall Street Journal*, © 1995 Dow Jones & Company, Inc. All Rights Reserved Worldwide.

Exhibit 3–8   **Stock Indexes around the Globe**

DOW JONES WORLD INDUSTRY GROUPS

Tuesday, March 19, 1996

REGION/ COUNTRY	DJ EQUITY MARKET INDEX, LOCAL CURRENCY	PCT. CHG.	CLOSING INDEX	CHG.	PCT. CHG.	12-MO HIGH	12-MO LOW	12-MO CHG.	PCT. CHG.	FROM 12/31	PCT. CHG.
Americas			152.18	− 0.18	− 0.12	153.90	115.55	+ 36.64	+ 31.71	+ 8.58	+ 5.97
Canada	133.14 + 0.10		113.24	+ 0.15	+ 0.13	115.26	96.33	+ 16.79	+ 17.41	+ 4.99	+ 4.61
Mexico	212.29 + 4.48		86.86	+ 4.01	+ 4.84	91.88	51.61	+ 35.13	+ 67.91	+ 8.89	+11.41
U.S.	616.17 − 0.18		616.17	− 1.08	− 0.18	623.15	466.54	+149.63	+ 32.07	+34.74	+ 5.98
Europe/Africa			141.22	+ 1.12	+ 0.80	141.34	118.05	+ 22.61	+ 19.06	+ 4.21	+ 3.07
Austria	103.48 + 1.26		106.42	+ 1.17	+ 1.11	113.71	96.56	+ 0.10	+ 0.09	+ 5.13	+ 5.07
Belgium	138.12 + 0.94		142.94	+ 1.55	+ 1.10	148.48	117.76	+ 23.28	+ 19.45	+ 0.39	+ 0.27
Denmark	109.44 − 0.74		113.59	− 0.77	− 0.67	118.94	97.96	+ 13.06	+ 12.99	+ 1.17	+ 1.04
Finland	231.44 + 1.45		207.97	+ 3.04	+ 1.48	303.04	186.32	+ 5.23	+ 2.58	+ 5.09	+ 2.51
France	121.92 + 0.07		125.44	+ 0.40	+ 0.32	127.26	111.60	+ 12.64	+ 11.21	+ 5.42	+ 4.51
Germany	143.03 + 1.07		147.04	+ 1.88	+ 1.30	147.49	121.19	+ 21.56	+ 17.19	+ 8.80	+ 6.37
Ireland	191.33 + 0.84		157.02	+ 1.45	+ 0.93	157.63	123.84	+ 33.10	+ 26.71	+ 4.19	+ 2.74
Italy	130.23 + 0.42		103.34	+ 0.74	+ 0.72	121.02	94.98	+ 2.63	+ 2.61	− 0.16	− 0.16
Netherlands	172.36 + 0.80		176.06	+ 1.70	+ 0.98	176.06	138.96	+ 35.69	+ 25.43	+ 8.75	+ 5.23
Norway	143.31 + 0.28		133.69	+ 0.56	+ 0.42	140.54	116.12	+ 15.38	+ 13.00	+ 4.48	+ 3.47
South Africa	204.21 − 0.07		142.73	− 0.05	− 0.04	160.95	122.07	+ 18.77	+ 15.14	+ 0.02	+ 0.02
Spain	149.29 + 0.80		116.85	+ 1.08	+ 0.93	122.25	84.41	+ 31.53	+ 36.96	+ 2.54	+ 2.22
Sweden	219.62 + 1.05		182.47	+ 2.97	+ 1.66	182.47	120.08	+ 58.97	+ 47.75	+19.32	+11.84
Switzerland	214.99 + 0.70		245.08	+ 2.04	+ 0.84	245.08	173.64	+ 71.42	+ 41.13	+12.46	+ 5.36
United Kingdom	151.83 + 0.65		124.60	+ 0.92	+ 0.74	127.62	110.53	+ 14.07	+ 12.73	+ 0.11	+ 0.09
Europe/Africa (ex. South Africa)			140.96	+ 1.17	+ 0.84	141.07	118.05	+ 22.35	+ 18.84	+ 4.43	+ 3.24
Europe/Africa (ex. U.K. & S. Africa)			153.41	+ 1.36	+ 0.89	153.41	123.97	+ 27.87	+ 22.20	+ 7.19	+ 4.91
Asia/Pacific			118.31	+ 0.93	+ 0.79	124.04	108.03	+ 7.55	+ 6.82	− 1.49	− 1.25
Australia	132.69 + 1.01		134.98	+ 1.13	+ 0.84	136.79	106.89	+ 26.52	+ 24.45	+ 7.08	+ 5.53
Hong Kong	241.99 + 1.97		243.21	+ 4.70	+ 1.97	260.15	185.19	+ 51.25	+ 26.70	+19.54	+ 8.74
Indonesia	217.24 + 1.49		185.23	+ 2.49	+ 1.36	200.27	150.13	+ 28.02	+ 17.82	+12.75	+ 7.39
Japan	93.68 + 0.74		110.12	+ 0.73	+ 0.67	121.30	102.27	+ 3.60	+ 3.38	− 3.96	− 3.47
Malaysia	229.97 + 0.45		246.11	+ 0.74	+ 0.30	255.72	198.20	+ 29.53	+ 13.63	+23.03	+10.32
New Zealand	142.98 − 0.08		180.29	− 0.04	− 0.02	189.29	161.30	+ 17.28	+ 10.60	+ 4.12	+ 2.34
Philippines	315.37 + 0.76		312.89	+ 2.36	+ 0.76	328.15	239.18	+ 60.78	+ 24.11	+31.41	+11.16
Singapore	184.54 + 2.08		212.63	+ 4.33	+ 2.08	224.73	170.17	+ 39.74	+ 22.98	+16.71	+ 8.53
South Korea	145.24 + 0.79		140.88	+ 1.10	+ 0.79	167.89	135.98	− 13.81	− 8.93	− 4.69	− 3.22
Thailand	215.40 + 0.85		201.29	+ 1.63	+ 0.82	227.64	171.02	+ 25.41	+ 14.45	+ 4.53	+ 2.30
Asia/Pacific (ex. Japan)			186.03	+ 2.29	+ 1.25	191.66	152.69	+ 32.01	+ 20.78	+12.58	+ 7.25
World (ex. U.S.)			126.20	+ 1.00	+ 0.80	127.99	110.60	+ 13.99	+ 12.47	+ 1.08	+ 0.87
DJ WORLD STOCK INDEX			137.41	+ 0.53	+ 0.39	138.49	113.98	+ 22.95	+ 20.05	+ 3.95	+ 2.96

Indexes based on 6/30/82=100 for U.S., 12/31/91=100 for World.   ©1996 Dow Jones & Co. Inc., All Rights Reserved.

Source: *The Wall Street Journal*, Southwest edition, March 20, 1996, p. C16. Reprinted by permission of *The Wall Street Journal*, © 1995 Dow Jones & Company, Inc. All Rights Reserved Worldwide.

Two of the most respected sources of information on major security issuers are Moody's Investors Service, Inc., and Standard and Poor's Corporation, both headquartered in New York City. In a series of annual volumes, Moody's provides financial data on industrial corporations, commercial banks and other financial institutions, utilities, and state and local units of government. The most widely known of Moody's annual volumes include the *Industrial Manual, Bank and Finance Manual, Public Utility Manual, Transportation Manual*, and *Municipal and Government Manual*. In the case of individual corporations, Moody's provides information on the history of each firm, including any recent acquisitions, the names of key officers, and recent financial statements. In addition, Moody's assigns credit ratings to selected issuers of corporate and municipal bonds, commercial paper, and preferred stock as a guide for investors. These ratings are published monthly in Moody's *Bond Record*. Standard & Poor's provides similar credit ratings for corporate and municipal bonds, assessing the likelihood of default on a security issue and the degree of protection afforded the investor. The S&P *Bond Guide*, containing information on more than 6,000 bond issues, appears once a month.

SEC Reports. Even more extensive financial data are provided by the reports and registration statements that corporations must file with the Securities and Exchange Commission (SEC). These SEC reports and statements are available in many libraries on microfiche or microfilm. One company, Disclosure Incorporated, provides its subscribers with microfiche copies of more than 100,000 corporate documents filed each year by approximately 11,000 companies. The most important of these corporate documents is the SEC's 10-K report, an annual report that must be filed by most companies within 90 days after their fiscal year-end. These 10-K reports identify the principal products or services of each firm, provide a summary of its operations for the past five years, note any securities outstanding, and list the names of key officers.

Dun & Bradstreet. Another useful source of data on business firms seeking credit is the Business Information Report prepared by Dun & Bradstreet, Inc. (D&B). This credit rating company collects information on approximately 3 million firms, making detailed financial reports available to its subscribers. A sample page from a Dun & Bradstreet Business Information Report is presented in Exhibit 3–9. Dun & Bradstreet also provides industrywide financial data so that the financial condition of an individual business borrower can be compared with that of other firms in the same industry. D&B's Key Business Ratios series includes key operating and financial ratios for more than 800 lines of business. Similar industrywide performance indicators are prepared and published in *Troy's Almanac*, in Robert Morris & Associates' *Annual Statement Studies*, and in Standard & Poor's *Industry Surveys* and the *Analysts Handbook*. This information can be supplemented with news about individual industries and firms by checking *The Wall Street Journal Index*, the *New York Times Index*, the *Business Periodicals Index*, and *Barron's Index*.

Financial Institutions. Information on banks and other financial institutions is available from a wide variety of sources, including trade associations in each industry and federal and state regulatory agencies. For example, the American Bankers Association, Life Insurance Association of America, League of U.S. Savings Associations, and Credit Union National Association frequently provide annual reports or pamphlets describing recent industry trends. Studies of financial institutions' problems are found in specialized journals and magazines, such as the *Journal of Commercial Bank Lending, Bankers Magazine, Financial Analysts Journal, Euromoney, The Economist, Forbes, Barron's, Fortune*, and the *Journal of Portfolio Management*.

Among key government agencies that provide annual reports and special studies of financial institutions' trends and problems are the Federal Deposit Insurance Corporation, Federal Reserve Board and Federal Reserve Banks, the Federal Home Loan Banks, and the Comptroller of the Currency. For example, the Federal Deposit Insurance Corporation provides periodic reports on bank financial conditions and bank failures. Many government reports are available in university libraries or through the Superintendent of Documents in Washington, D.C.

Exhibit 3–9   **The Dun & Bradstreet Business Information Report**

BE SURE NAME, BUSINESS AND ADDRESS MATCH YOUR FILE	ANSWERING INQUIRY	SUBSCRIBER: 008-001042

CONSOLIDATED REPORT		{FULL REVISION}

```
DUNS:  06-647-3261              DATE PRINTED              SUMMARY
RETTINGER PAINT CORP.          AUG 13, 197-          RATING      CC2

727 WHITMAN WAY                WHOL PAINTS &         STARTED     1950
BENSON, MI  48232              VARNISHES            PAYMENTS    DISC-PPT
       TEL 313 961-0720                              SALES     $ 424,612
                               SIC NO.              WORTH     $ 101,867
CARL RETTINGER, PRES.          51 98                EMPLOYS     5
                                                    HISTORY     CLEAR
                                                    CONDITION   GOOD
                                                    TREND       STEADY

SPECIAL EVENTS   Business burglarized July 3 but $18,000 loss is fully insured.

PAYMENTS    {Amounts may be rounded to nearest figure in prescribed ranges}
REPORTED    PAYING      HIGH      NOW     PAST      SELLING       LAST SALE
            RECORD     CREDIT    OWES     DUE        TERMS         WITHIN
07/7-       Disc       30000     17000    -0-       2 10 30       1-2 mos.
            Disc       27000     14000    -0-       1 10 30       2-3 mos.
            Disc-Ppt   12000      4400    200       2 10 30       1 mo.
            Ppt         9000      8000    -0-       30            1 mo.
06/7-       Disc       16000      7500    -0-       2 10 30       2-3 mos.
05/7-       Disc        9000      3800    -0-       2 10 30       1 mo.
            Ppt         1500       -0-    -0-       30            1-2 mos.

FINANCE
06/22/7-         Fiscal statement dated May 31, 197-:
            Cash          $   20,623     Accts Payable        $   47,246
            Accts Rec         55,777     Owing Bank               34,000
            Merchandise       92,103     Notes Pay {Trucks}        7,020
                          ---------                           ---------
            Current          168,503     Current                  88,266
            Fixts. & Equip.   13,630     Common Stock             35,000
            Trucks             8,000     Earned Surplus           66,867
                          -------                             -------
            Total Assets     190,133     Total                   190,133
            SALES {Yr}: $424,612.  Net profit $17,105.  Fire ins. mdse $95,000;
            equipt $20,000.  Mo. rent: $3500.  Prepared by Steige Co., CPAs, Detroit, MI.
                                    --0--
            06/22/7- Lawson defined monthly payments: $3000 to bank, $400 on notes.
            Admitted collections slow but losses insignificant.  Said inventory will drop
            to $60,000 by December.  Expects 5% sales increase this year.
PUBLIC FILINGS
03/25/7-         March 17, 197- financing statement #741170 named subject as debtor and
            NCR Corp., Dayton, O. as secured party.  Collateral: equipment.
05/28/7-         May 21, 197- suit for $200 entered by Henry Assoc., Atlanta, Ga. Docket
            #27519.  Involves merchandise which Lawson says was defective.
BANKING
06/25/7-         Account, long maintained, carries average balances low to moderate five
            figures.  Unsecured loans to moderate five extended and now open.
HISTORY
06/22/7-    CARL RETTINGER, PRES.                    JOHN J. LAWSON, V PRES.
            DIRECTORS:  The Officers
                 Incorporated Michigan February 2, 1950.  Authorized capital 3500 shares,
            no par common.  Paid in capital $35,000, officers sharing equally.
                 RETTINGER, born 1920, married.  Employed by E-Z Paints, Detroit 12 yrs,
            five as manager until starting subject early 1950.
                 LAWSON, born 1925, married.  Obtained accounting degree 1946 and then
            employed by Union Carbide, Chicago until joining Rettinger at inception.
OPERATION
06/22/7-         Wholesales paints and varnishes {85%}, wallpaper and supplies.  500
            local accounts include retailers {75%} and contractors.  Terms: 2 10 30.  Peak
            season spring thru summer.  EMPLOYEES:  Officers active with three others.
            LOCATION: Rents 7500 sq ft. one-story block structure, good repair.
```

Source: Dun & Bradstreet.

Credit Bureaus. Information on individuals and families who seek credit is assembled and disseminated to institutional lenders by nearly 2,000 credit bureaus in the United States. The files of these bureaus include such information as the individual's place of residence and occupation, debts owed, and the promptness with which an individual pays his or her bills. Most credit bureaus maintain files on an individual's bill-paying record for up to seven years and may release that information only to lenders, employers, or licensing agencies who have a legitimate right to know the individual's credit standing. Individuals also have a right to see their credit files and verify their accuracy.

GENERAL ECONOMIC AND FINANCIAL CONDITIONS

A number of different sources provide market participants with information on developments in the economy, prevailing trends in the money and capital markets, and actions by the government that may affect economic and financial conditions (for a summary, see Exhibit 3–10). For example, many of the world's major commercial banks publish monthly newsletters for the benefit of their customers. These newsletters frequently contain discussions of recent changes in employment, industrial output, and interest rates.

The Federal Reserve. The Federal Reserve System releases large quantities of financial information to the public on request. Statistical releases available on a weekly or monthly basis cover such items as interest rates, money supply measures, industrial output, and international transactions. Information of this sort is summarized each month in the *Federal Reserve Bulletin*, published by the Board of Governors of the Federal Reserve System in Washington, D.C. The Board also publishes the results of internal staff studies that examine recent financial trends or address major issues of public policy.

Within the Federal Reserve System, the Federal Reserve Bank of St. Louis publishes large quantities of financial data in its news releases. One of the most popular is *U.S. Financial Data*, which contains a summary of week-to-week changes in interest rates and in the components of the nation's money supply. Another regular St. Louis Fed publication is *Monetary Trends*, which summarizes monthly changes in the money supply and bank reserves. These data series are watched closely by many investors because they often foreshadow broad movements in interest rates, security prices, and national economic conditions. Addresses for the Federal Reserve Board and all the Federal Reserve banks appear at the back of each monthly *Federal Reserve Bulletin*.

Other Domestic Sources. A number of published sources regularly report on the status of the economy. Daily financial newspapers, such as *The Wall Street Journal*, nearly always include important economic data. The Federal Reserve Bank of St. Louis publishes a monthly news release, *National Economic Trends*, which tracks changes in U.S. employment, consumer and wholesale prices, and industrial production. *The Survey of Current Business*, a monthly magazine published by the U.S. Department of Commerce (USDC), contains one of the most comprehensive collections of U.S. economic data available anywhere, including the latest statistics on consumer, government, and business spending, and on exports and imports. The USDC also publishes several other convenient compilations of business data, including monthly editions of *Business Conditions Digest* and *Economic Indictors*, the annual *Statistical Abstract of the United States*, the *U.S. Industrial Outlook*, and the biennial *Business Statistics*.[6]

---

[6]Many government documents, including some of those published by the U.S. Department of Commerce, are sold by the Superintendent of Documents, U.S. Government Printing Office, Washington, D.C. 20402. The Board of Governors of the Federal Reserve System can be reached for information on its publications through its Division of Publications Services, Washington, D.C. 20551.

Exhibit 3–10   **Summary of Key Sources of Information on the Financial Markets and Market Participants**

Information on Securities and Security Prices and Interest Rates (Bonds, Notes, Other Forms of Debt, and Stock)

The Wall Street Journal
Barron's
The Wall Street Journal Transcript
Forbes
Financial World
Fortune
Money
Daily Bond Buyer
New York Times
Dealer quotations
Broker reports
Financial sections of daily newspapers
Value Line Investment Survey
U.S. Financial Data (Federal Reserve Bank of St. Louis) and other data releases of the Federal Reserve Banks and the Federal Reserve Board
Survey of Current Business (U.S. Department of Commerce)
Federal Reserve Bulletin (Federal Reserve Board)
The Treasury Bulletin (U.S. Treasury Department)
Moody's Investors Service (various publications)
Standard & Poor's Corporation (various publications)
Journal of Portfolio Management
Financial Analysts Journal

Information on Individual Borrowers and Security Issuers

The Wall Street Journal (news stories and journal index)
Barron's
The Wall Street Transcript
Fortune
Forbes
The New York Times (news stories and index)
Dun & Bradstreet (business information reports and key business ratios)
Moody's Banking and Industrial Manuals
Standard & Poor's Reports, Industry Surveys, and Analysts Handbook
Securities and Exchange Commission Reports (annual reports, 10-Ks, etc.)
Business Periodicals Index
Trade associations
Credit bureaus

Information on Domestic and Financial Conditions

The Wall Street Journal
Federal Reserve Bank of St. Louis, *National Economic Trends, Monetary Trends*
Newsletters issued by large commercial banks
Economic consulting firms
Flow of Funds Accounts
Statistical Abstract of the United States (USDC)
U.S. Industrial Outlook

Federal Reserve Bulletin (Federal Reserve Board)
Survey of Current Business (USDC)
Business Conditions Digest (USDC)
Economic Indicators (USDC)
Business Statistics (USDC)
Industry and government forecasts
National Income Accounts

Information on International Economic and Financial Conditions

The Economist (London)
Asiaweek (Hong Kong)
Euromoney (London)
Euroweek (London)
Business Mexico (Mexico City)
The International Economy (Washington D.C.)
Far Eastern Economic Review (New York)

International Economic Trends (Federal Reserve Bank of St. Louis)
The Financial Times (London)
The Wall Street Journal/Europe (Brussels)
The Columbia Journal of World Business (New York)
The Journal of International Money and Finance
Asiamoney (New York)

Forecasts of *future* economic and financial developments are available from a wide variety of sources. For example, Salomon Brothers, a leading investment banking firm, provides annual estimates of the supply and demand for credit and a forecast of interest rates for the ensuing year. Other major investment/brokerage houses usually make economic and financial forecasts available on request. The Federal Reserve Bank of Philadelphia publishes *The Livingston Survey*, which compiles a summary of the forecasts of leading economists twice each year. Forecasts of annual capital spending based on repeated industry surveys are prepared by the U.S. Department of Commerce and McGraw-Hill Publication Company. Businesses often subscribe to the services of one or more of a number of economic consulting firms that prepare detailed forecasts of the nation's income and interest rates. Among the more prominent of these forecasting firms are Chase Econometrics and Data Resources, Inc.

International Sources. The growing internationalization of the financial markets has led to dramatic increases in new sources of information regarding foreign markets and institutions. For example, the Federal Reserve Bank of St. Louis publishes *International Economic Trends*, a compilation of data on foreign currency prices, production, income, and inflation. Up-to-date security price and interest rate data are published in *The Wall Street Journal/Europe* from Brussels, and a corresponding *Asian Wall Street Journal* is issued from Hong Kong. *The Financial Times* of London is considered one of the finest daily newspapers in the world. *The Economist*, also published in London, deals with foreign business and political developments throughout the world. Of comparable quality is the monthly *Euromoney* (London), which monitors Europe's ongoing economic integration. For businesspersons interested in Asia and the Pacific Rim, such magazines as *Asiaweek*, the *Far Eastern Economic Review*, and *Asiamoney* offer greater understanding of Pacific economies and institutions.

Finally, two nations of growing importance to businesses in the United States, Europe, and Asia are Canada and Mexico, due to recent growth inside these countries and their progress toward stronger links to the United States through the recently adopted North American Free Trade Agreement (NAFTA). Key sources of financial market and business opportunities in Canada and Mexico include *Business Mexico, The Statistical Abstract of Latin America, The Canadian Journal of Economics*, and *The Canadian Banker*, published in Toronto by the Canadian Bankers Association.

SOCIAL ACCOUNTING DATA

Students of the economy and the financial markets also make use of social accounting systems to keep track of broad trends in economic and financial conditions. **Social accounting** refers to a system of record keeping that reports transactions between the principal sectors of the economy, such as households, financial institutions, corporations, and units of government. The two most closely followed social accounting systems in the United States are the National Income Accounts and the Flow of Funds Accounts.

National Income Accounts

The **National Income Accounts** (NIA) system is compiled and released quarterly by the U.S. Department of Commerce. It presents data on the nation's production of goods and services, income flows, investment spending, consumption, and savings. Probably the best-known account in the NIA series is gross national product (GNP), a measure of the market value of all goods and services produced by U.S.-resident institutions and individuals (regardless of their location) within a year's time. Recently, the gross domestic product (GDP), a closely related, but slightly smaller measure of production in the U.S. economy that includes only goods and services produced within the geographical boundaries of the United States, was introduced. GDP may be broken down into the uses to which the nation's output of goods and services is put. For example, Exhibit 3–11, drawn from the

Exhibit 3–11   **National Income and Product Accounts: The Components of U.S. Gross Domestic Product (GDP) in 1995* ($ Billions, Current)**

Personal Consumption expenditures:		$4,782.1
Durable goods	$ 615.2	
Nondurable goods	1,432.2	
Services	2,734.8	
Gross private domestic investment:		1,107.8
Fixed investment	1,053.3	
Change in business inventories	54.5	
Net exports of goods and services:		−111.1
Exports	778.8	
Imports	889.9	
Governmental purchases of goods and services:		1,198.7
Federal	434.4	
State and local	764.3	
Gross domestic product of the United States (GDP)		$6,977.4

*Figures are for first quarter of the year.

Source: U.S. Department of Commerce, *Survey of Current Business* and Board of Governors of the Federal Reserve System, *Federal Reserve Bulletin*, September 1995, Table 2.16.

Survey of Current Business and *Federal Reserve Bulletin*, indicates the size of the U.S. GDP and its major components during 1995.

The National Income Accounts system provides valuable information on the level and growth of the nation's economic activity, which has a profound impact on conditions in the money and capital markets. However, the NIA accounts provide little or no information on financial transactions themselves. For example, one component of the NIA system reports the annual amount of personal savings, but it does *not* show how those savings are allocated among purchases of bonds, stocks, and other financial assets. This task is left to the **Flow of Funds Accounts** prepared by the Board of Governors of the Federal Reserve System.

The Flow of Funds Accounts

Flow of funds data have been prepared and published quarterly by the Federal Reserve System since 1955. Monthly issues of the *Federal Reserve Bulletin* contain the latest summary reports of flow of funds transactions, and detailed breakdowns of financial transactions among major sectors of the economy are readily available on both a quarterly and an annual basis from the Federal Reserve Board in Washington, D.C.

Purposes of the Flow of Funds Accounts. The basic purpose of the Flow of Funds Accounts are to (1) trace the flow of savings by businesses, households, and governments into purchases of financial assets; (2) show how the various parts of the financial system interact with each other; and (3) highlight the interconnections between the financial sector and the rest of the economy.

Construction of the Flow of Funds Accounts takes place in four basic steps.

Sectoring the Economy. The first step is to divide the economy into several broad *sectors*, each consisting of economic units (transactors) with similar balance sheets. The 12 major sectors in the current account series include the following:

- Households, including personal trusts, foundations, private schools and hospitals, labor unions, churches, and charitable organizations.
- Farm businesses.
- Nonfarm noncorporate businesses, including partnerships and proprietorships engaged in nonfinancial activities.
- Nonfinancial corporations
- State and local governments.
- U.S. government, including government-owned agencies.
- Federally sponsored credit agencies, such as the Federal Land Banks and Federal National Mortgage Association.
- Monetary authorities, including the Federal Reserve System and certain monetary accounts of the U.S. Treasury.
- Commercial banks.
- Foreign banking agencies.
- Savings institutions, including savings and loans, insurance companies, and pension funds.
- Other financial institutions, such as finance companies, investment companies, and security brokers and dealers.

Constructing Sector Balance Sheets. The second step in assembling the Flow of Funds Accounts is to construct *balance sheets* for each of the sectors listed above at the end of each quarter. Like any balance sheet for a business firm or household, sector balance sheets contain estimates of the total assets, liabilities, and net worth held by each sector at a single point in time. The assets held by each sector are divided into financial assets and real (nonfinancial) assets.

An example of such a partial balance sheet containing financial assets and liabilities for the household sector for the years 1980, 1990, and 1995 is shown in Exhibit 3–12. We note, for example, that U.S. households held total financial assets of more than $18.5 trillion in 1995 (shown in line 1), nearly triple their financial asset holdings only 15 years before. A substantial part of this total was represented by holdings of deposits — checking (demand) accounts and time and savings deposits at commercial banks and savings institutions. These liquid financial assets totaled just over $3 trillion in 1995 (line 2). An even larger financial asset held by households was pension fund reserves (line 20), accumulated to prepare for the retirement years, which amounted to more than $5 trillion, followed by corporate stock (equities), totaling more than $3 trillion in 1995 (line 18). Holdings of debt securities (credit market instruments), including Treasury notes and bonds, federal agency securities, state and local government bonds, mortgages, and similar assets, amounted to nearly $1.9 trillion (line 7) in 1995.

It is interesting that the total indebtedness of individuals and families in the United States is far less than their holdings of financial assets. Exhibit 3–12 indicates that the household sector's liabilities totaled almost $4.9 trillion in 1995 (line 25), roughly one fourth of its total financial assets. Most household indebtedness was in the form of home mortgages (line 27) and installment debt (line 28).

Sources of Balance Sheet Data. Data needed to construct sector balance sheets in the Flow of Funds Accounts come from a wide variety of public and private sources. For example, information on lending, borrowing, and acquisition of securities by nonfinancial

Exhibit 3–12   **Statement of Financial Assets and Liabilities for the Household Sector, 1980, 1990, and 1995** ($ Billions, Outstanding at Year-End)

Asset and Liability Items	1980	1990	1995*
1. Total financial assets	$6,398.5	$13,901.1	$18,550.0
2. Deposits	1,562.6	3,248.3	3,129.8
3. Checkable Deposits and Currency	258.6	527.1	700.3
4. Small Time and Savings Deposit	1,088.2	2,056.1	1,906.8
5. Large Time Deposits	152.9	252.4	149.3
6. Money Market Fund Shares	63.0	412.7	373.4
7. Credit Market Instruments	476.9	1,454.6	1,872.4
8. U.S. Government Securities	216.8	550.9	1,092.9
9. Treasury Issues	182.3	298.4	686.6
10. Savings Bonds	72.5	126.2	181.4
11. Other Treasury Securities	109.8	172.2	505.3
12. Federal Agency Securities	34.4	252.6	406.3
13. Tax-Exempt Securities	80.0	468.9	370.3
14. Corporate and Foreign Bonds	35.2	94.9	191.4
15. Mortgages	112.0	170.4	191.9
16. Open Market Paper	33.0	169.5	26.0
17. Mutual Fund Shares	45.6	451.7	1,102.6
18. Corporate Equities	975.4	1,758.7	3,144.8
19. Life Insurance Reserves	216.4	380.0	494.7
20. Pension Fund Reserves	949.3	3,400.3	5,228.1
21. Investment in Bank Personal Trusts	218.7	509.9	707.2
22. Equity in Noncorporate Businesses	1,863.6	2,440.6	2,474.6
23. Security Credit	16.2	62.4	108.1
24. Miscellaneous Assets	73.5	214.6	287.7
25. Total Liabilities	1,450.9	3,706.2	4,864.3
26. Credit Market Instruments	1,392.1	3,594.8	4,686.6
27. Home Mortgages	904.9	2,419.4	3,194.6
28. Consumer Credit	302.1	812.4	983.8
29. Tax-Exempt Debt	16.7	84.0	135.7
30. Commercial Mortgages	31.5	133.5	196.4
31. Bank Loans (not elsewhere classified)	27.8	33.1	34.2
32. Other Loans	54.7	109.8	141.8
33. Security Credit	24.7	38.8	68.9
34. Trade Credit	22.1	56.2	91.1
35. Deferred and Unpaid Life Insurance Reserves	12.9	16.5	17.8

Note: The definition of "households" includes personal trusts and nonprofit organizations as well as individuals and families. It excludes corporate equities.
*1995 figures are for the first quarter of the year.

Source: Board of Governors of the Federal Reserve System, *Flow of Funds Accounts: Flows and Outstandings*, selected issues.

businesses is derived from such sources as the Securities and Exchange Commission and the U.S. Department of Commerce. Various trade groups provide financial data on their respective industries, and the Securities Industry Association provides selected information on gross offerings of securities. Inevitably, inconsistencies arise in classifying financial transactions due to differences in accounting procedures among the groups contributing data to the accounts. Moreover, in an economy as vast and complex as that of the United States, some financial transactions fall between the cracks. To deal with problems in data consistency and coverage, the Federal Reserve includes a statistical discrepancy account that brings each sector into balance.

Preparing Sources and Uses of Funds Statements. After balance sheets are constructed for each sector of the economy, the third step in the construction of the Flow of Funds Accounts is to prepare a **sources and uses of funds statement** for each sector. This statement shows changes in net worth and changes in holdings of financial assets and liabilities taken from each sector's balance sheet at the beginning and end of a calendar quarter or year. The basic structure of a sources and uses statement is given below:

Sources and Uses of Funds Statement

Uses of Funds	Sources of Funds
Change in real assets (or net real investment) Change in financial assets (or net financial investment)	Change in liabilities outstanding (or net borrowing) Change in net worth (or net current savings)
Change in total assets = Total uses of funds	Change in liabilities and net worth = Total sources of funds

An example of such a statement for the U.S. commercial banking sector for 1995 is shown in Exhibit 3–13. The first portion of the sources and uses statement (lines 1–20) shows changes in the banking sector's net worth (current surplus), real assets (net investments in plant and equipment), and net acquisitions of financial assets. The second portion of the statement (lines 21–36) reflects net borrowing as reflected in an increase in the liabilities carried by U.S. commercial banks and their affiliates.[7]

We note, for example, that U.S.-chartered commercial banks increased their holdings of financial assets by $321 billion during 1995 (line 3). Bank loans to consumers, businesses, and other borrowers rose by $243 billion (line 10), as the U.S. economy enjoyed a period of recovery after a recession at the beginning of the decade. With faster growth in the economy, more individuals and businesses were demanding bank credit to increase their standard of living and expand production. Commercial bank holdings of U.S. government securities and federal agency securities (including issues of mortgage-backed securities guaranteed by a federal government agency) declined by almost $53 billion (line 5). Commercial banks also reduced their holdings of state and local government (tax-exempt) securities by nearly $9 billion (line 8) in 1995. And bank holdings of vault cash and reserves held at the central bank (the Federal Reserve banks inside the U.S.) fell by $6 billion (line 19) in 1995, reflecting changing economic conditions and new regulations allowing banks to hold fewer reserves. U.S.-chartered commercial banks invested almost $30 billion (line 2) in plant and equipment during the year.

Where did the banking sector get the funds it needed to make new loans and increase its investments in new plant and equipment in 1995? The necessary funds came principally from sales of checking accounts (checkable deposits), which climbed by $68 billion (line 22), small time and savings deposits (line 23), and large time deposits, which rose by more than $70 billion (line 24), as well as massive sales of government-issued securities mentioned in the preceding paragraph. Close behind the growth of deposits were bank borrowings in the money market (using federal funds and Security RPs), which climbed more than $70 billion (line 25). U.S.-chartered banks also managed to save (in the current surplus

[7]All changes on a sources and uses of funds statement are shown *net* of purchases and sales. When purchases of an asset exceed sales of that asset, the resulting figure is reported as a *positive* increase in the asset. When sales exceed purchases, an asset item will carry a *negative* sign. A nonnegative liability item on the sources and uses statement indicates that net borrowing (i.e., total borrowings larger than debt repayments) has occurred during the period under study. If a liability item is negative, debt repayments exceed new borrowings during the period covered by the statement.

Exhibit 3–13

Sources and Uses of Funds Statement for the U.S. Banking Sector, 1981, 1990, and 1995* ($ Billions)

Asset and Liability Items

1. Current Surplus (Saving)	38.9	19. Vault Cash and Reserves at the Federal Reserve Banks	−6.1
2. Fixed Nonresidential Investment (plant and equipment)	29.7	20. Miscellaneous Assets	151.4
3. Net Acquisitions of Financial Assets	321.3	21. Net Increase in Liabilities	236.2
4. Total Bank Credit	169.8	22. Checkable Deposits	68.2
5. U.S. Government Securities	−52.5	23. Small Time and Savings Deposits	26.8
6. Treasury Issues	−43.1	24. Large ($100,000+) Time Deposits	71.6
7. Agency Issues (including mortgage pool securities)	−11.8	25. Federal Funds and Security RPs, Net	70.3
8. Tax-Exempt Obligations	−8.9	26. Net Interbank Claims	−77.9
9. Corporate and Foreign Bonds (including privately issued mortgage-backed securities)	−13.5	27. Federal Reserve Float	3.1
10. Total Loans	243.0	28. Borrowing at the Federal Reserve Banks	−0.6
11. Mortgages	107.9	29. Claims Owed to Domestic Banks	−63.0
12. Consumer Credit	29.0	30. Claims Owed to Foreign Banks	−17.4
13. Bank Loans Not Elsewhere Classified (NEC)	110.0	31. Corporate Equities	6.7
14. Open-Market Paper	−1.0	32. Corporate Bonds	0.7
15. Security Credit	−2.8	33. Acceptance Liabilities	6.0
16. Mutual Fund Shares	0.5	34. Federal Home Loan Bank Loans	−1.3
17. Corporate Equities	1.2	35. Taxes Payable	0.8
18. Customers' Liabilities on Acceptances	6.2	36. Miscellaneous Liabilities	64.4
		37. Statistical Discrepancy	−75.9

*Figures are as of the first quarter of 1995 for all U.S.-chartered commercial banks.

Sources: Board of Governors of the Federal Reserve System, *Flow of Funds Accounts*, selected quarterly issues.

account) nearly $39 billion (line 1) out of current earnings in 1995 to help fund their growing assets.

Balancing Out a Sources and Uses of Funds Statement. As we have seen, sources and uses of funds statements in the Flow of Funds Accounts are derived from the aggregated balance sheets of each sector of the economy. Because balance sheets must always balance, we would also expect a sources and uses of funds statement to balance (except, of course, for discrepancies in the underlying data). In a sources and uses statement,

$$\begin{matrix} \text{Net investment} \\ \text{in plant} \\ \text{and equipment} \end{matrix} + \begin{matrix} \text{Net acquisitions} \\ \text{of financial} \\ \text{assets} \end{matrix} = \begin{matrix} \text{Net increase in} \\ \text{liabilities} + \text{Change in} \\ \text{current surplus} \\ \text{account} \end{matrix} \qquad (3\text{--}4)$$

Net acquisitions of financial assets are frequently referred to as **financial investment**; net purchases of plant and equipment may be labeled **real investment**. Both are *uses of funds* for a sector or economic unit. Net increases in liabilities represent **borrowing** in the current period, while changes in the current surplus account reflect **current saving**. These latter two items are *sources of funds*. Therefore, the relationship shown above may be written as follows:

$$\begin{matrix} \text{Net real investment} + \text{Net financial investment} \\ = \text{Net borrowing} + \text{Net current saving} \end{matrix} \qquad (3\text{--}5)$$

or

$$\text{Total uses of funds} = \text{Total sources of funds} \qquad (3\text{--}6)$$

For each unit — business, household, or government — and for each sector of the economy, the above statement *must* be true. For example, in the commercial banking sector in 1995 we have, as shown in Exhibit 3–13:

Uses of Funds ($ Billions)		Sources of Funds ($ Billions)	
Net investment in plant and equipment (line 2)	$29.7	Net borrowing (net increase in liabilities) (line 21)	$236.2
Net financial investment (acquisitions of financial assets) (line 3)	321.3	Net current saving (change in net worth) (line 1)	38.9
Statistical discrepancy (line 37)	−75.9		
Total uses of funds	$275.1	Total sources of funds	$275.1

Once the statistical discrepancy is considered, total uses and sources of funds should be equal for this and all other sectors in the economy.

Constructing a Flow of Funds Matrix for the Economy as a Whole. The final step in the construction of the Flow of Funds Account is to combine the sources and uses of funds statement for each sector into a flow of funds matrix for the entire U.S. economy. An example of such a matrix is shown in Exhibit 3–14, which shows borrowings by each major sector of the economy and total borrowings by all sectors combined. Another example appears in Exhibit 3–15, which shows funds loaned by each major sector to domestic nonfinancial borrowers and total credit extended by all sectors. The majority of funds sought by businesses, consumers, and governments in the financial markets clearly were raised by issuing debt instruments, as shown in Exhibit 3–14. The sum total of all debt instruments outstanding rose by over $1150 billion (line 1 in the third panel of Exhibit 3–14) in 1995 (first quarter of the year annualized). The U.S. Treasury and various federal agencies were among the heaviest borrowers of funds, issuing more than $397 billion in debt instruments (line 2). Next in line for the most borrowed funds were issuers of mortgages (both home and commercial mortgage loans), who borrowed $218 billion (line 5 in the third panel of Exhibit 3–14). Borrowings from banks ranked third in volume in 1995 at more than $176 billion (line 7). Of course, borrowing — issuing debt — is not the only possible source of funds from the money and capital markets. Substantial funds can be raised by issuing stock (corporate equities), which, in 1995, totaled just over $100 billion (line 1 in the lower half of the third panel of Exhibit 3–14).

Exhibit 3–15 looks at borrowing in the economy from both the lenders' and borrowers' points of view. From Chapter 2 we know that what is borrowed by one sector must equal the credit extended to that sector by other sectors. For example, line 24 in Exhibit 3–15 shows that total funds loaned in U.S. credit markets during 1995 amounted to just over $1,154 billion. This amount exactly matches the total net borrowings by all sectors reported in line 1 of Exhibit 3–15 for 1995 and the total borrowings figures given in line 1 of the third panel of Exhibit 3–14. *The flow of funds matrix reminds us that, for all sectors of the economy combined into one, the amount of saving must equal the total amount of real investment in the economy, and the amount of borrowing in total must equal total financial investment* (i.e., the total amount of financial assets acquired by all sectors).

Exhibit 3–14   **Funds Raised in Credit and Equity Markets** ($ Billions, Quarterly Data at Seasonally Adjusted Annual Rates)

	1992 II	1992 III	1992 IV	1993 I	1993 II	1993 III	1993 IV	1994 I	1994 II	1994 III	1994 IV	1995* I	Instrument or Sector	
	— Credit Market Borrowing by Nonfinancial Sectors													
505.1	564.8	456.0	485.7	729.4	613.8	659.6	634.7	530.2	580.2	634.4	816.0	Domestic	1
347.4	294.6	242.7	240.5	336.4	173.4	274.2	210.5	122.9	135.0	133.0	271.8	U.S. government	2
347.0	285.5	240.0	237.4	232.3	157.2	266.5	211.8	118.2	130.7	162.1	273.0	Treasury securities	3
0.4	9.0	2.7	3.2	4.1	16.2	7.7	-1.3	4.7	4.3	-7.1	-1.2	Budget agency secur. & mtgs.	4
157.7	270.3	213.3	245.1	393.0	440.4	385.5	424.1	407.3	445.8	479.4	544.2	Private, by transaction	5
52.1	45.6	-15.8	88.6	121.0	65.2	27.3	2.6	-25.4	-63.2	-50.4	-65.6	Tax-exempt securities	6
77.8	61.7	54.0	85.7	75.7	72.0	67.4	35.4	35.9	14.2	2.7	41.4	Corporate bonds	7
52.5	160.7	86.6	99.8	152.2	222.1	148.5	62.8	170.4	221.2	191.6	213.0	Mortgages	8
92.6	227.4	164.9	120.9	193.5	236.5	184.6	198.5	164.5	220.8	200.7	188.3	Home	9
-16.9	-11.5	-26.5	-5.5	-11.4	-4.9	-2.3	-1.0	4.6	6.5	-4.3	2.6	Multifamily	10
-25.9	-58.0	-51.4	-15.7	-30.9	-9.9	-33.9	-34.9	-.9	-7.7	-5.8	21.5	Commercial	11
2.7	2.8	-.5	0.2	1.0	0.4	0.2	0.3	2.3	1.7	1.0	0.7	Farm	12
-15.0	12.0	29.6	20.3	41.6	76.2	111.3	72.7	121.9	125.9	149.4	83.4	Consumer credit	13
-20.5	-23.0	19.1	-16.2	-.2	7.8	28.5	65.8	55.5	86.8	88.0	156.7	Bank loans n.e.c.	14
-2.0	4.0	22.3	-14.1	33.2	17.2	3.8	8.2	16.4	33.8	27.2	1.1	Commercial paper	15
12.8	9.3	17.5	-19.0	-30.4	-20.2	-1.3	76.6	32.7	27.1	70.9	114.3	Other loans	16
157.7	270.3	213.3	245.1	393.0	440.4	385.5	424.1	407.3	445.8	479.4	544.2	Private, by sector	17
121.0	261.6	249.6	167.5	264.1	368.5	337.7	310.3	307.3	381.9	407.0	304.7	Household sector	18
2.2	-25.4	1.9	-7.4	25.0	25.6	30.8	127.3	144.3	134.0	137.5	302.7	Nonfinancial business	19
5.2	1.6	-2.4	-2.3	2.7	4.1	3.6	2.6	8.1	1.6	-2.8	-.5	Farm	20
-45.3	-54.3	-53.9	-28.6	-31.4	-23.2	-15.6	5.4	12.5	17.9	18.2	68.8	Nonfarm noncorporate	21
42.4	27.4	58.2	23.6	53.7	44.8	42.7	119.3	134.7	114.5	122.1	234.3	Corporate	22
34.5	34.1	-38.1	85.0	103.9	46.3	17.0	-13.4	-44.3	-70.2	-65.1	-63.1	State and local govts.	23
55.0	30.6	3.6	58.9	42.8	83.1	22.9	-66.3	-10.1	8.3	29.0	55.7	Foreign borrowing in U.S.	24
18.7	12.1	26.0	66.5	45.3	84.5	41.4	29.0	9.4	8.6	23.4	11.0	Bonds	25
14.1	3.9	-10.3	1.5	6.6	1.0	-6.3	6.0	-4.5	4.7	-.5	8.3	Bank loans n.e.c.	26
27.8	13.1	-12.1	-21.7	-.6	-1.6	-12.0	-101.8	-5.2	-8.1	5.9	37.9	Commercial paper	27
-5.6	1.4	-.**	-7.5	-8.4	-.8	-.1	0.5	-9.8	3.2	0.2	-1.5	U.S. govt. and other loans	28
560.1	595.4	459.6	524.6	772.2	696.9	682.6	568.3	520.1	589.1	663.3	871.7	Domestic and foreign	29

Exhibit 3–14 (continued) **Funds Raised in Credit and Equity Markets** ($ Billions, Quarterly Data at Seasonally Adjusted Annual Rates)

Credit Market Borrowing by Financial Sectors

	1992 II	1992 III	1992 IV	1993 I	1993 II	1993 III	1993 IV	1994 I	1994 II	1994 III	1994 IV	1995* I	Instrument or Sector	
1	251.7	306.1	198.8	180.4	175.5	438.9	361.6	518.7	366.7	403.1	518.5	282.5	By transaction	1
2	188.2	171.9	132.6	169.4	56.6	287.3	143.3	336.8	254.7	243.1	302.4	125.4	U.S. government-related	2
3	48.3	67.7	33.6	32.2	68.8	167.8	53.4	160.9	146.6	152.1	249.0	62.9	GSE securities	3
4	139.9	104.3	99.2	137.2	-12.2	119.5	89.9	196.0	108.1	91.0	33.4	62.5	Mortgage pool securities	4
5	—	—	—	—	—	—	—	—	—	—	—	—	Loans from U.S. government	5
6	63.5	134.1	66.1	11.0	118.9	151.6	218.4	182.0	112.0	160.0	216.1	157.1	Private financial sectors	6
7	80.5	84.5	97.0	99.0	92.4	143.4	138.1	156.3	91.4	86.9	87.9	115.2	Corporate bonds	7
8	0.1	0.4	0.9	1.4	1.4	6.2	5.5	9.8	12.4	12.0	4.9	5.1	Mortgages	8
9	-5.7	18.0	-6.5	-75.1	-16.2	-9.4	76.0	36.6	3.6	42.3	84.0	11.6	Bank loans n.e.c.	9
10	-13.8	18.0	-6.5	-75.1	-16.2	-9.4	76.0	36.6	3.6	42.3	84.0	48.9	Open market paper	10
11	2.3	13.2	-1.1	20.4	28.4	27.4	16.8	-10.8	32.3	30.7	38.8	-23.6	Fed. Home Loan Bank loans	11
12	251.7	306.1	198.8	180.4	175.5	438.9	361.6	518.7	366.7	403.1	518.5	282.5	By sector	12
13	48.3	67.7	33.5	32.2	68.8	167.8	53.4	140.8	146.6	152.1	249.0	62.9	Govt.-spons. enterprises	13
14	139.9	104.3	99.2	137.2	-12.2	119.5	89.9	196.0	108.1	91.0	53.4	62.5	Fed. related mortgage pools	14
15	63.5	134.1	66.1	11.0	118.9	151.6	218.4	182.0	112.0	160.9	216.1	157.1	Private financial sectors	15
16	6.5	12.6	14.5	3.5	11.3	6.5	1.2	2.0	12.4	22.8	2.9	9.6	Commercial banks	16
17	-9.2	6.6	0.8	21.1	1.3	0.5	12.2	3.5	10.1	11.5	16.0	9.5	Bank holding companies	17
18	16.3	14.0	3.6	-31.4	-1.6	7.9	36.7	48.8	-17.2	47.2	17.9	62.9	Funding corporations	18
19	-8.8	6.3	-5.4	9.7	12.6	13.5	8.8	-5.6	5.8	14.8	36.1	-21.7	Savings institutions	19
20	**	**	-0.1	**	0.3	0.3	0.1	0.1	0.2	0.5	0.2	-.5	Credit unions	20
21	**	0.2	-.2	0.1	0.6	-.1	0.4	**	**	**	1.3	**	Life insurance companies	21
22	-3.5	15.2	1.0	-19.6	-13.6	17.5	16.3	63.3	67.0	16.9	62.6	72.5	Finance companies	22
23	-3.3	14.4	-5.4	-25.2	32.4	-.8	-10.4	-21.6	-18.2	-7.0	1.0	2.0	Mortgage companies	23
24	1.3	2.3	-5.6	1.3	1.3	6.0	6.1	14.5	15.3	18.8	6.3	6.9	REITs	24
25	13.5	-1.6	-4.0	-9.5	13.7	14.6	29.3	-9.9	0.3	-7.6	19.3	-29.6	Brokers and dealers	25
26	50.7	64.0	67.7	62.0	60.5	85.8	117.6	86.9	36.5	42.1	52.5	45.3	ABS issuers	26

Exhibit 3–14 (continued)

Funds Raised in Credit and Equity Markets ($ Billions, Quarterly Data at Seasonally Adjusted Annual Rates)

	1992			1993				1994				1995*	Instrument or Sector	
	II	III	IV	I	II	III	IV	I	II	III	IV	I		
Credit Market Borrowing, All Sectors, by Transaction														
	811.8	901.5	658.4	705.0	747.6	1135.8	1044.2	1087.1	886.8	992.2	1181.9	1154.2	Total	1
	535.6	466.5	375.5	409.9	393.0	460.7	417.5	566.5	377.6	378.1	457.4	397.2	U.S. government securities	2
	52.1	45.6	−15.8	88.6	121.0	65.2	27.3	2.6	−25.4	−63.2	−50.4	−65.6	Tax-exempt securities	3
	177.0	158.3	177.0	251.2	213.4	299.9	246.9	220.6	136.6	109.7	114.0	167.5	Corporate and foreign bonds	4
	52.6	161.2	87.4	101.2	153.5	228.3	154.0	172.6	182.8	233.2	196.5	218.1	Mortgages	5
	−15.0	12.0	29.6	20.3	41.6	76.2	111.3	72.7	121.9	125.9	149.4	83.4	Consumer credit	6
	−12.0	−1.1	−15.3	−49.2	19.2	−7.3	4.2	61.9	23.3	79.5	88.0	176.6	Bank loans n.e.c.	7
	11.9	35.1	3.7	−110.9	16.4	6.3	67.7	−57.0	14.8	48.0	117.1	87.9	Open market paper	8
	9.6	23.9	16.3	−6.1	−10.5	6.4	15.4	47.1	55.2	61.1	109.9	89.2	Other loans	9
Funds Raised Through Mutual Funds and Corporate Equities														
	274.5	315.2	294.8	381.6	435.6	513.0	430.1	344.4	213.1	162.9	−44.1	100.9	Total net issues	1
	200.4	243.4	205.4	306.6	321.8	363.9	187.7	236.2	144.0	165.4	7.7	113.9	Mutual funds	2
	74.0	69.7	89.4	75.0	113.9	149.1	142.4	108.1	69.1	−2.5	−51.8	−13.0	Corporate equities	3
	36.0	12.0	14.0	8.2	23.2	32.3	21.5	−9.6	−2.0	−50.0	−102.0	−46.8	Nonfinancial	4
	26.9	22.9	27.7	35.2	38.6	38.2	40.9	48.3	24.4	23.7	17.9	15.9	Financial	5
	11.1	34.8	47.8	31.6	52.1	78.6	80.0	69.4	46.7	23.8	32.2	17.9	Foreign shares purchased by U.S. residents	6

*Figures for 1995 are for the First quarter of the year.
**Less than $0.1 billion dollars.

Source: Board of Governors of the Federal Reserve System, *Flow of Funds Accounts*, First Quarter 1995.

Exhibit 3–15   Total Claims of Lenders Against Borrowers ($ Billions, Quarterly Data at Seasonally Adjusted Annual Rates)

	1992 II	1992 III	1992 IV	1993 I	1993 II	1993 III	1993 IV	1994 I	1994 II	1994 III	1994 IV	1995* I	Transactions Category or Sector	
													Total Net Borrowing and Lending in Credit Markets†	
1	811.8	901.5	458.4	705.0	947.6	1135.8	1044.2	1087.1	856.8	992.2	1181.9	1154.2	Total net borrowing	1
2	505.1	564.8	456.0	485.7	729.4	613.8	659.6	634.7	530.2	580.8	634.4	816.0	Domestic nonfinan. sectors	2
3	347.4	294.6	242.7	240.5	336.4	173.4	274.2	210.5	122.9	135.0	155.0	271.8	U.S. government	3
4	157.7	270.3	213.3	245.1	393.0	440.4	385.5	424.1	407.3	445.8	479.4	544.2	Private domestic	4
5	121.0	261.6	249.6	147.5	264.1	368.5	337.7	310.3	307.3	381.9	407.0	304.7	Household sector	5
6	5.1	1.6	-2.4	-2.3	2.7	4.1	3.6	2.6	8.1	1.6	-2.8	-.5	Farm business	6
7	-45.3	-54.5	-53.9	-28.6	-31.4	-23.2	-15.6	5.4	12.5	17.9	18.2	68.8	Nonfarm noncorp. bus.	7
8	42.4	27.4	58.0	23.6	53.7	44.8	42.7	119.3	123.7	114.5	122.1	234.3	Nonfin. corporate bus.	8
9	34.5	34.1	-38.0	85.0	103.9	46.3	17.0	-13.4	-44.3	-70.2	-65.1	-63.1	State and local govts.	9
10	55.0	30.6	3.6	38.9	42.8	83.1	22.9	-66.3	-10.1	8.3	29.0	55.7	Rest of the world	10
11	251.7	306.1	198.8	180.4	175.5	438.9	361.6	518.7	366.7	403.1	518.5	282.5	Financial sectors	11
12	48.3	67.7	33.5	32.2	68.8	167.8	53.4	140.8	146.6	152.1	249.0	62.9	Govt.-spons. enterprises	12
13	139.9	104.3	99.2	137.2	-12.2	119.5	89.9	196.0	108.1	91.0	53.4	62.5	Fed. related mtg. pools	13
14	6.5	12.6	14.5	3.5	11.3	6.5	1.2	2.0	12.4	22.8	2.9	9.6	Commercial banks	14
15	-9.2	6.6	0.8	21.1	1.3	0.5	12.2	3.5	10.1	11.5	16.0	9.5	Bank holding companies	15
16	16.3	14.0	3.6	-31.4	-1.6	7.9	36.7	48.8	-17.2	47.2	17.9	62.9	Funding corporations	16
17	-8.8	6.4	-5.3	9.7	12.9	13.8	8.9	-5.5	5.9	15.3	36.3	-22.0	Thrift institutions	17
18	.8	0.2	-.2	0.1	0.6	-.1	0.4	**	**	**	1.3	**	Life insurance companies	18
19	-3.5	15.2	1.0	-19.6	-13.6	17.5	16.3	63.3	67.0	16.9	62.6	72.5	Finance companies	19
20	-3.3	14.4	-6.4	-25.2	32.4	-.8	-10.4	-21.6	-18.2	-7.0	1.0	2.0	Mortgage companies	20
21	1.3	2.3	-5.6	0.4	1.3	6.0	6.1	14.5	15.3	18.8	6.3	6.9	REITs	21
22	13.5	-1.6	-4.0	-9.5	13.7	14.6	29.3	-9.9	0.3	-7.6	19.3	-29.6	Brokers and dealers	22
23	50.7	64.0	67.7	62.0	60.5	85.8	117.6	86.9	36.5	42.1	52.5	45.3	ABS issuers	23
24	811.8	901.5	658.4	705.0	947.6	1135.8	1044.2	1087.1	886.8	992.2	1181.9	1154.2	Total net lending	24
25	83.1	-72.8	104.3	-64.0	17.3	-52.8	85.8	295.0	299.1	109.5	239.7	-26.0	Private dom. nonfin. sectors	25
26	43.7	-54.7	112.0	-115.6	-54.5	-83.0	174.3	350.1	400.0	183.5	344.0	81.1	Household sector	26
27	-1.0	-1.0	-1.3	-3.0	-3.2	-3.3	-3.5	-3.6	-1.8	-1.9	-.5	-.1	Nonfarm noncorp. business	27
28	30.7	29.9	31.8	-2.4	14.3	41.2	16.0	23.0	16.8	25.5	366.0	15.4	Nonfin. corporate business	28
29	9.6	-47.1	-38.3	57.0	57.7	-7.7	-101.0	-74.4	-115.9	-97.6	-140.5	-122.3	State & local governments	29
30	-21.7	-26.3	-16.0	-23.2	-27.1	-15.4	-7.9	-46.5	-16.2	-9.4	-24.3	-19.2	U.S. government	30
31	152.5	65.4	98.3	70.2	91.6	125.0	203.7	127.7	65.1	124.1	216.1	267.9	Rest of the world	31
32	597.9	935.2	471.9	721.9	865.8	1079.0	762.5	710.9	538.8	768.0	750.4	931.5	Financial sectors	32

Exhibit 3–15 (continued) **Total Claims of Lenders Against Borrowers** ($ Billions, Quarterly Data at Seasonally Adjusted Annual Rates)

Total Net Borrowing and Lending in Credit Markets†

	1992 II	1992 III	1992 IV	1993 I	1993 II	1993 III	1993 IV	1994 I	1994 II	1994 III	1994 IV	1995* I	Transactions Category or Sector	
33	34.4	68.7	80.7	16.7	128.0	144.8	71.2	92.4	101.1	125.6	174.3	12.2	Govt.-spons. enterprises	33
34	139.9	104.3	99.2	137.2	-12.2	119.5	89.9	196.0	108.1	91.0	53.4	62.5	Fed. related mtg. pools	34
35	20.9	16.1	48.2	62.5	35.7	28.2	38.5	48.8	17.9	24.0	35.4	24.8	Monetary authority	35
36	57.4	158.8	63.8	100.5	133.4	146.7	188.1	184.7	109.1	191.3	163.0	337.1	Commercial banking	36
37	10.1	133.3	53.4	103.4	137.4	160.3	197.3	120.6	128.4	164.6	178.7	177.2		37
38	44.9	4.0	6.5	-1.4	-14.3	-16.9	-6.5	59.0	-21.5	22.1	-15.0	157.8	Fgn. banking ofc. in U.S.	38
39	-1.9	17.4	0.2	-4.5	7.9	1.2	-4.8	3.1	0.2	2.7	-2.4	0.4	Bank holding companies	39
40	-4.3	4.1	3.6	3.0	2.4	2.2	2.1	2.2	1.9	1.9	1.8	1.7	Banks in U.S.-aff. areas	40
41	-17.3	69.9	11.4	-3.8	1.1	32.4	42.6	19.5	33.5	25.1	-23.0	11.3	Funding corporations	41
42	-75.3	-41.6	-22.6	-30.7	16.1	21.0	-13.3	13.6	42.6	50.9	33.5	36.2	Thrift institutions	42
43	69.6	80.4	100.8	113.0	109.4	111.8	86.4	53.7	6.1	83.4	101.1	72.3	Life insurance cos.	43
44	15.8	-.2	11.9	27.3	36.0	37.6	32.1	27.9	20.8	16.0	19.7	13.0	Other insurance cos.	44
45	74.1	99.9	8.4	118.0	11.1	91.9	-60.1	-97.7	-30.7	-17.6	-23.6	97.6	Private pension funds	45
46	33.9	46.8	16.7	-9.8	47.5	27.4	36.9	72.9	69.3	26.3	74.6	67.4	St. & loc. govt. rtr. funds	46
47	-13.9	-2.0	22.3	-33.3	-34.7	9.4	22.6	72.1	49.8	58.9	91.8	95.7	Finance companies	47
48	-38.5	28.9	-12.8	-50.4	65.1	-1.6	-13.3	-43.5	-36.3	-14.0	2.1	4.0	Mortgage companies	48
49	125.7	160.1	96.1	189.4	163.0	186.9	138.9	61.5	9.3	24.3	-64.7	-5.3	Mutual funds	49
50	15.8	15.2	17.3	16.7	10.5	5.9	7.7	8.3	3.2	1.4	1.0	0.8	Closed-end funds	50
51	-12.2	21.3	-29.4	-57.3	33.3	25.3	56.9	-45.0	32.3	50.9	76.7	26.5	Money mkt. mutual funds	51
52	2.6	-.3	2.6	0.2	0.8	1.0	0.2	6.6	6.6	5.5	0.2	2.5	REITs	52
53	107.6	40.6	-113.1	75.2	52.5	-7.8	-82.8	-55.7	-52.6	-19.3	-8.6	32.2	Brokers and dealers	53
54	50.9	61.7	62.1	61.5	59.4	88.6	111.1	86.0	38.7	37.3	42.1	38.9	ABS Issuers	54
55	7.6	7.5	8.3	9.1	10.0	9.9	8.9	8.9	10.2	7.7	1.4	1.6	Bank personal trusts	55

†Excludes corporate equities and mutual fund shares.
*Figures for 1995 are for first quarter.
**Less than $0.1 billion.

Source: Board of Governors of the Federal Reserve System, *Flow of Funds Accounts*, First Quarter 1995.

Limitations and Uses of the Flow of Funds Accounts. It should be clear by now that the Flow of Funds Accounts provide a vast amount of information on trends in the financial system. These accounts provide indispensable aid in tracing the flow of savings through the money and capital markets. As we will see in Chapter 12, estimates of flow of funds data can be used to make forecasts of lending, borrowing, and interest rates. However, these social accounts have a number of limitations that must be kept firmly in mind.

First, the Flow of Funds Accounts present no information on transactions among economic units *within* each sector. If a household sells stock to another household, this transaction will *not* be picked up in the accounts, because both units are in the same sector. However, if a household sells stock to a business firm, this transaction *will* be captured by the flow of funds bookkeeping system. The accounts show only *net* flows between one point in time and another point, not the changes that occur between the beginning and ending points of the period at which we are looking.

Finally, all flow of funds data are expressed in terms of current market values. Therefore, these accounts measure not only the flow of savings in the economy but also capital gains and losses. This market-value bias distorts estimates of the amount of actual savings and investment activity that occur from year to year.

Despite these limitations, however, the Flow of Funds Accounts are among the most comprehensive sources of information available to students of the financial system. These accounts provide vital clues on the demand and supply forces that shape movements in interest rates and security prices. The Flow of Funds Accounts indicate which types of securities are growing or declining in volume and which sectors finance other sectors. One of the principal uses of Flow of Funds data today is to forecast interest rates and build econometric models to simulate future conditions in the credit markets. Combined with other sources of information, flow of funds accounting provides us with the raw material from which to make financial decisions.

SUMMARY

An unimpeded flow of relevant information is vital to the functioning of the financial system. If the scarce resource of credit is to be allocated efficiently and an ample flow of savings made available for investment, financial information must be readily available to all market participants. There are really two types of markets within the financial system: an information market and a market for financial assets. The two markets must work together in a coordinated fashion to accomplish the desired end result, directing a smooth flow of scarce loanable funds toward their most profitable and beneficial uses.

If the information market is truly efficient, so that all relevant information for valuing financial assets is readily available at negligible cost, financial instruments will be correctly priced based on their expected return and risk, and scarce resources will flow to those uses carrying the highest expected returns. When asymmetries exist in information flow and availability, however, the financial marketplace will operate imperfectly, and some market participants, blessed with special information, will generate excess profits (exceeding the *normal* rate of return for the amount of risk assumed). Scarce resources will then be allocated less efficiently than otherwise might be the case. Research evidence to date suggests that most financial markets are efficient but that important asymmetries still remain.

In this chapter, we have examined the information market in some detail. Our principal focus has been on five broad categories of financial information available today: debt security prices and yields, stock prices and dividend yields, the financial condition of security issuers, general conditions in the economy and financial system, and social accounting data. The purpose of this chapter has been to give the student of the financial system a broad overview of the kinds and quality of information currently available to the public. Knowing where to find relevant, up-to-date information is an essential ingredient in the process of solving economic and financial problems.

KEY TERMS AND CONCEPTS IN THIS CHAPTER

efficient markets hypothesis (EMH)	asked price	sources and uses of funds statement
asymmetry	stocks	financial investment
bond	social accounting	real investment
note	National Income Accounts (NIA)	borrowing
bid price	Flow of Funds Accounts	current savings

STUDY QUESTIONS

1. Why is the availability of financial information important to borrowers and lenders of funds? Government policymakers?

2. What is an *efficient market*? And what are the different forms of market efficiency? What are *informational asymmetries*? What are some of the problems that the presence of asymmetric information can create in the marketplace?

3. List several major sources of financial information and discuss which types of information each contains.

4. If you need to gather information for a possible stock or bond purchase, where would you look? What information is available on the financial condition of major U.S. companies?

5. What is *social accounting*? Compare and contrast the Flow of Funds Accounts with the National Income Accounts. What types of information does each provide that might be useful for making financial decisions?

6. Explain how the Flow of Funds Accounts system is constructed. What is a sources and uses of funds statement?

7. Discuss the principal limitations of Flow of Funds data and the implications of those limitations.

PROBLEMS

1. For each of the following or data items, cite at least two sources (where possible) from which this information could be obtained:

    a. Stock prices of a corporation whose shares are publicly traded.

    b. Credit ratings of the bonds and notes issued by U.S. corporations.

    c. Interest rates (yields) on government bonds and notes.

    d. Financial statements of corporations.

e. Volume of savings generated by U.S. households, businesses, and units of government.

f. The allocation of current savings by businesses, households, and governments among various types of financial assets.

g. Volume of investment in real assets by businesses and households.

h. Size and rate of growth in the money supply.

i. Current rate of inflation in consumer and producer prices.

j. Volume of credit extended by banks and other financial institutions.

k. Recent rate of growth in the economy's income, output, and employment.

2. Construct sources and uses of funds statements for each sector of the economy and for the whole economy using the following information:

	Households ($ Billion)	Business Firms ($ Billion)	Banks and Other Financial Institutions ($ Billion)	Governmental Units ($ Billion)
Current saving	$428.8	$280.0	$35.0	-$35.0
Current real investment	332.5	350.0	17.5	—
Current financial investment	306.3	78.8	43.8	8.8
Current borrowing	210.0	148.8	26.3	43.8

Assume that the four sectors listed above are the only sectors in the economy and that there are no international transactions. Is there a statistical discrepancy? Where? Referring back to the discussion in Chapter 2, which sectors are deficit-budget and which are surplus-budget?

3. Suppose that you are given the data listed below for the household sector of the economy. From this information, please construct a statement of financial assets and liabilities for the household sector.

($ Billion)			($ Billion)
Deposits in banks and savings institutions	$540	U.S. government securities	$110
Home mortgages	290	Credit extended by nonbank lending institutions	40
Installment loans extended by banks	110	Trade credit	5
Holdings of currency and coin	120	Corporate and foreign bonds	30
Security credit owed	10	Corporate equities	680
State and local government bonds	50	Life insurance reserves	130
Deferred and unpaid life insurance premiums	10	Pension fund reserves	420
Holdings of miscellaneous financial assets	50	Miscellaneous liabilities	35

4. Construct a sources and uses of funds statement for the commercial banking sector for the year immediately concluded. A check of the Federal Reserve's Flow of Funds Accounts indicates that U.S. banks reported a current earnings surplus (after paying stockholder dividends) of $12 billion and made investments in plant and equipment of $11 billion. They acquired net $120 billion in loans to their customers and purchased $4 billion in corporate bonds, $13 billion in state and local government bonds, and $25 billion in U.S. governmental securities. Miscellaneous financial assets rose $10 billion. There was a statistical discrepancy in the Flow of Funds Accounts of $8 billion in the banking sector's sources of funds.

5. At year-end 19X1, the corporate business sector posted net worth of $60 billion, total investment in plant and equipment of $75 billion, total holdings of financial assets of $131

billion and total debt outstanding of $146 billion. The following year-end, 19X2, total corporate indebtedness climbed to $167 billion, holdings of financial assets fell to $120 billion, and net worth increased to $63 billion due to retained profits. Construct a sources and uses of funds statement for the corporate sector for 19X2.

SELECTED REFERENCES

Board of Governors of the Federal Reserve System. *Introduction to the Flow of Funds.* Washington, D.C., February 1975.

Camerer, Colin; George Lowenstein; and Martin Weber. "The Cause of Knowledge in Economic Settings: An Experimental Analysis." *Journal of Political Economy* XGVII, no. 5 (1989), pp. 1232–1354.

Fortune, Peter. "Stock Market Efficiency: An Autopsy." *New England Economic Review*, Federal Reserve Bank of Boston (March/April 1991), pp. 17–40.

Webb, Roy H. *Macroeconomic Data: A User's Guide.* Federal Reserve Bank of Richmond, 1990, pp. 7–48.

Chapter 4

The Commercial Banking Industry

LEARNING OBJECTIVES IN THIS CHAPTER

- To understand how important commercial banks are in the functioning of a modern economy and financial system.
- To examine the makeup (structure) of the U.S. banking industry.
- To see how and why banks are regulated and to explore the recent trend toward deregulation of this important industry.
- To be able to read and understand bank financial statements and grasp how banks create and destroy money.

The dominant privately owned financial institution in the United States and in the economies of most major countries is the *commercial bank*. This institution offers the public both deposit and credit services, as well as a growing list of newer and more innovative services, such as investment advice, security underwriting, and financial planning. The name *commercial* implies that banks devote most of their resources to meeting the financial needs of business firms. In recent years, however, commercial banks have significantly expanded their offerings of financial services to consumers and units of government. The result is the emergence of a financial institution that has been called a *financial department store* because it satisfies the broadest range of financial service needs in the economy.

The importance of commercial banks may be measured in a number of ways. They hold more than a third of the total assets of all financial institutions headquartered in the United States as well as a major share of financial assets abroad. Banks are still the principal means of making payments, through the checking accounts (demand deposits) and electronic funds transfer services they offer. And banks are important because of their ability to create money from excess reserves made available from the public's deposits. The banking system can take a given volume of excess cash reserves and, by making loans and investments, generate a multiple amount of credit — a process explored later in this chapter.

Banks today are the principal channel for government monetary policy. In the United States, the Federal Reserve System implements policies to affect interest rates and the availability of credit mainly through altering the level and growth of reserves held by banks and other depository institutions. The same is true in Canada, Great Britain, Germany, Japan, and many other nations. Today, commercial banks are the most important source of consumer credit and one of the major sources of loans to small businesses. Recent research evidence suggests that fluctuations in bank-supplied credit account for a substantial proportion of observed changes in national income and employment. Banks are major buyers of debt securities issued by federal, state, and local governments. For all these reasons, commercial banks play a dominant role in the money and capital markets and are worthy of detailed study if we are to understand more fully how the financial system works.

THE STRUCTURE OF U.S. COMMERCIAL BANKING

The structure of U.S. banking is unique in comparison with other banking systems around the globe. The term **banking structure** focuses on the number and different sizes of commercial banks operating in thousands of local communities across the nation. Although the banking systems of most other nations consist of a few large banking organizations operating hundreds or thousands of branch offices, the U.S. system is dominated by thousands of small commercial banks. For example, at year-end 1995, about 8,000 independently owned commercial banking institutions were headquartered in the United States, compared to less than a dozen domestically chartered banks in Canada and less than three dozen domestically owned banks in the United Kingdom and Mexico.

Not surprisingly, most U.S. banks are modest in size compared to banks in other countries. About 70 percent of all U.S. commercial banks hold total assets of under $100 million each, although only about 4 percent hold assets of a billion dollars or more and actively compete in global markets for loans and deposits. Smaller banks predominate in numbers, but the larger banks have a disproportionate share of the industry's assets. For example, the roughly 3 percent of all U.S. banks with $1 billion or more in total assets hold about three fourths of all assets in the industry.

Most commercial banks in the United States are chartered by the states rather than by the federal government. As shown in Exhibit 4-1, of the roughly 10,000 U.S. commercial banks in operation in 1994, about 7,300 were **state-chartered banks.** The remaining one third, classified as **national banks,** were chartered by the federal government. National banks, on average, are larger and include nearly all of the nation's billion-dollar banking institutions. All national banks must be insured by the Federal Deposit Insurance Corporation (FDIC) and be members of the Federal Reserve System ("the Fed"). State-chartered banks may elect to become members of the Fed and also seek FDIC deposit insurance if they are willing to conform to the regulations of these two federal agencies. The vast

Exhibit 4-1

Number of Operating Commercial Banks and Branches in the United States, Year-End 1994

Type of Bank	Number of Banks	Number of Branch Offices
National banks	3,025	28,558
State-chartered member banks	975	8,390
Total members of the Federal Reserve System	4,050	36,948
Nonmember state-chartered banks	6,400	18,196
Total of all insured banks	10,450	55,144

Source: Federal Deposit Insurance Corporation, *Statistics on Banking,* 1994.

majority of U.S. banks (more than 98 percent) are FDIC insured, but only a minority have elected to join the Fed. Nevertheless, Fed member banks hold more than two thirds of all bank deposits and assets in the United States. (We will have more to say about the roles of the Fed, the FDIC, and other bank regulatory agencies in Chapter 7 of this book.)

A Trend toward Consolidation

A number of structural changes have affected the banking industry in recent years. One of the most important is the drive toward **consolidation** of industry assets into fewer, but larger, banking organizations.

The United States is still essentially a nation of small banks. But great pressures are operating to form larger banking organizations in order to make more efficient use of resources. Research studies by Benston, Hanweck, and Humphrey (1982), and others suggest that, as banks grow, their costs increase more slowly than output, resulting in cost savings. For example, a 100 percent rise in deposit and loan accounts may result in only a 92 percent increase in the cost of bank operations. When automated bookkeeping and computer processing of accounts are used, substantial economies of scale characterize bank lending and the offering of checking accounts. Under pressure from a cost squeeze, declining profit margins, and increased competition from other financial institutions, many U.S. bankers view the strategy of growing into larger-sized banking organizations as a competitive response to these pressures.

We hasten to add, however, that scale economies resulting from bank growth appear to be modest — once a bank reaches perhaps $500 million or so in total assets, its unit production costs appear to level out. In fact, some analysts argue that production costs begin rising when banks approach $1 billion in size because of the tendency of larger banks to multiply their service offerings. Others argue, however, that large banks enjoy lower costs of raising capital and risk-reducing benefits from diversification across many different services and geographic areas, which give them a significant advantage over smaller banks.

BRANCH BANKING

The drive toward consolidation of banks into larger organizations is most evident in the long-term historical shift toward branch banking. Until the 1940s and 1950s, the United States was basically a nation of unit banks, each housed in only a single office. For example, in 1900 there were 12,427 banks, but only 87 of these had any branches. By 1995, however, there were only about 8,000 independently owned U.S. commercial banks, the majority of which were branch banking organizations. The number of branch offices has increased dramatically in recent years: in 1950 there were approximately 4,700 branch banking offices in operation; by 1996, the number of total U.S. full-service branches had climbed to more than 55,000 offices.

The growth of branching has been aided by the liberalization of many state laws to permit greater use of branch offices as a means of bank growth. As we will see more fully in Chapter 7, interstate bank expansion should become more common in future years due to the passage of a new interstate banking bill by the U.S. Congress in 1994. The spread of branching across the United States has also been aided by a massive population shift over the last three decades to suburban and rural areas and to the sunbelt states. Many of the nation's largest banks have followed their customers to distant markets through branching and mergers to protect their sources of funds and their earnings.

INTERNATIONAL FOCUS:

Banking and the North American Free Trade Agreement (NAFTA)

One factor that is likely to reshape the future of banking in the United States as well as in neighboring Canada and Mexico is the North American Free Trade Agreement (NAFTA) adopted in November 1993. NAFTA calls for the gradual reduction of the barriers to trade in goods and services, including banking and financial services. Trade quotas were eliminated immediately, and tariffs levied against NAFTA-member countries are being phased out over a 10-year period. Canadian and U.S. investors are able to own banks and other financial-service firms operating inside Mexico. However, Canadian and U.S. banking organizations cannot branch directly into Mexico. Instead, they must establish subsidiary companies in Mexico. Once established, however, such a company can control not only banks but also securities firms, insurance companies, and other financial firms and set up branch offices throughout Mexico.

In fact, U.S. and Canadian banks will be able to operate under the same rules as apply to Mexican banks (known as *national treatment*). However, foreign investment is limited over a transition period ending in the year 2000. Even after the transition period, U.S. and Canadian financial firms will continue to face capital and market-share restrictions designed to protect domestic financial firms and to give Mexico's financial system time to adjust. Mexico looks attractive to Canadian and U.S. banks today because the Mexican economy has good long-term growth prospects. But, following a sharp decline in the value of the peso in 1994 and early 1995, Mexico has struggled with inflation, high interest rates, and substantial unemployment. Mexico needs to stabilize its economy, improve the efficiency of its banking and nonbanking industries, and bring inflation under control in order to attract more foreign investment.

Banks have also pursued greater geographic expansion through the establishment of branch offices because of the strong competitive challenge they face from a host of nonbank financial service firms, including security brokers and dealers, mutual funds, credit unions, and dozens of other financial institutions. Many of these nonbank financial institutions appear to have gained market share at the expense of commercial banks, often by offering better returns and more flexible savings. The rise of this form of outside competition for commercial banks has brought strong protests from the banking community for faster government deregulation of the industry and for permission to offer many new services.

Bank Holding Companies

Paralleling the rapid growth of branch banking has been the growth of bank holding companies, which originated in the nineteenth century. A **bank holding company** is a corporation organized to acquire and hold the stock of one or more banks. The company may also hold stock in certain nonbank business ventures. Holding companies have become popular as vehicles to avoid laws prohibiting the extension of branch banking and as a way to offer services that banks themselves cannot offer.

Bank holding companies have grown rapidly in the United States. In 1960 there were just 47 registered holding company organizations controlling only about 8 percent of the total assets of U.S.-insured banks. By the 1990s, holding companies numbered more than

6,000 and held over 90 percent of U.S. bank assets. The growth of nonbank business activities of holding companies also has been rapid. Insurance agencies, finance companies, mortgage companies, consulting firms, and other financially related businesses have been started or acquired in large numbers by bank holding companies in recent years. These ventures represent an attempt to diversify banking operations to reduce risk and gain access to a broader market. Unfortunately, many bankers have found that they cannot effectively manage a diverse set of nonbank businesses. Toward the end of the 1980s and into the 1990s, several large holding companies sold off some of their nonbank business ventures in an effort to cut costs and raise more capital for their banks.

International Banking

The growth of banking organizations at home has been paralleled by substantial growth of banks reaching for business abroad. This expansion overseas has not been confined to the largest institutions in such established money centers as New York, Chicago, and San Francisco but includes leading banks in regional financial centers such as Atlanta, Dallas, and Miami. Several of the largest U.S. banks receive half or more of their net income from foreign sources, although many U.S. banks have reduced their overseas activity recently due to poorly performing international loans and high costs.

While branch banks and bank holding companies have dominated the expansion of banking inside the United States, bank expansion into international markets has taken place through a wide variety of unique organizational forms. *Representative offices,* the simplest form, represent the "eyes and ears" of a bank in foreign markets, helping to market each bank's services to both old and new customers, but these limited-service facilities cannot take deposits or book loans. In contrast, a *branch office* offers all or most of the services the home office provides, including the taking of deposits and the booking of loans. International banks sometimes find it less expensive to acquire an existing bank overseas with an established clientele than to set up their own branch office. The acquired institution becomes a *subsidiary* of the international bank, retaining its own charter and capital stock.

Alternatively, a bank may establish a *joint venture* with a foreign firm, sharing expenses but gaining access to the expertise and customer contracts already made by the foreign company. Moreover, U.S. and foreign banks with international operations based inside the United States frequently set up both *Edge Acts* and *international banking facilities* (IBFs). The former institutions can be located anywhere in the U.S., but most devote the majority of their transactions to international accounts; IBFs are simply computerized account records related to international commerce that are exempt from many U.S. banking regulations (such as deposit insurance fees).

Banks today penetrate overseas markets for a wide variety of reasons. In many cases, their corporate customers expanding abroad demand access to multinational banking facilities. The huge Eurodollar market, which spans the globe, also offers an attractive source of bank funds when domestic funding sources are less available or more costly. Foreign markets frequently offer fewer regulatory barriers and less competition than may be found at home.

Foreign banks have grown rapidly in the United States, with many of the largest Canadian, European, and Asian banks viewing the 50 states as a huge economically and politically stable common market. Moreover, foreign banks are able to offer some services, such as underwriting corporate securities or selling insurance, that U.S. banking organizations currently are prohibited from offering in the domestic market or can offer in only a limited way after receiving permission from the Federal Reserve Board. The Japanese banks, in particular, have grown into global dominance and include a majority of the largest banks in the world (see Exhibit 4–2). Congress responded to this invasion by

Exhibit 4–2   **The Growing Global Competition Faced by All Banks Today — A List of the Largest Banks and Other Financial Institutions in the World**

1. Nomura Securities, Japan	26. Deutsche Bank, Germany
2. Sumitomo Bank, Japan	27. American International Group, United States
3. Dai-Ichi Kangyo Bank, Japan	28. Nippon Credit Bank, Japan
4. Fuji Bank, Japan	29. Swiss Bank Corporation, Switzerland
5. Mitsubishi Bank, Japan	30. Asahi Bank, Japan
6. Industrial Bank of Japan, Japan	31. Bank of Yokohama, Japan
7. Sanwa Bank, Japan	32. J.P. Morgan, United States
8. Sumitomo Trust & Banking Company, Japan	33. National Westmister Bank, United Kingdom
9. Mitsubishi Trust, Japan	34. Citicorp, United States
10. Long-Term Credit Bank of Japan	35. Aetna Life and Casualty Co., United States
11. Daiwa Securities, Japan	36. Münchner Ruckversicherungsgesellschaft, Germany
12. Nikko Securities, Japan	37. Credit Suisse, Switzerland
13. Sakura Bank, Japan	38. Yasuda Fire & Marine, Japan
14. Tokai Bank, Japan	39. General Reinsurance, United States
15. Tokoi Marine and Fire, Japan	40. Barclays Bank, United Kingdom
16. Mitsui Trust and Banking Company, Japan	41. Credit Agricole Mutuel, France
17. Assicurazioni Generali, Italy	42. Bank of China, China
18. Bank of Tokyo, Japan	43. Banque Nationale de Paris, France
19. Yamaichi Securities, Japan	44. Midland Bank, Great Britain
20. American Express, United States	45. Hong Kong Bank, Hong Kong
21. Daiwa Bank, Japan	46. Credit Lyonnais, France
22. Merrill Lynch and Company, United States	47. Dresdner Bank, Germany
23. Yasuda Trust and Banking Co., Japan	48. Royal Bank of Canada, Canada
24. Union Bank of Switzerland	49. Canadian Imperial Bank, Canada
25. Allianz A. G. Holding, Germany	

passing the International Banking Act of 1978, bringing foreign banks under federal regulation for the first time. Passage of the FDIC Improvement Act in 1991 gave the Federal Reserve Board authority to close the U.S. offices of foreign banks if they are operated in an unsafe manner.[1]

Perhaps the most common characteristic of all international banks today is their striving to offer a full line of services to all customers. Thus, *commercial banks,* which specialize predominantly in lending and deposit taking, are combining with *investment banks,* which deal in securities issued by their customers. Many banks in Canada, Great Britain, and Western Europe long ago took an additional step to become *universal* or *merchant banks.* Universal banks, like Germany's Deutsche Bank, France's Credit Agricole, Canada's Royal Bank, and Britain's Barclays Bank, provide not only deposit, loan, and security underwriting services but also consulting, insurance, and real estate sales. Merchant banks invest some of their owners' capital in their customers' projects, thus becoming principals as well as creditors in business investment projects. As a result, merchant and universal banks tend to make longer-term investments than traditional banks and are active in both the money market and the capital market simultaneously.

Bank Failures

One undesirable side effect of all these recent changes in banking is a relatively high bank failure rate. For most of its history, the banking industry experienced an extremely low failure rate (only about 1 or 2 percent of the banking population each year failed) due to

[1]The provisions of the International Banking Act and the recent growth of international banking are discussed more fully in Chapter 29.

extensive regulation and conservative management. However, the number of bank failures and the average size of failing banks advanced sharply in the 1980s, though the failure rate slowed down in the 1990s. For example, a postwar record number of failures in a single year was set in 1988 and again in 1989, when more than 200 U.S. banks closed their doors. In addition, several money center banks got into deep financial trouble and had to be merged with healthy institutions or backstopped by government loans. Most notable in this case were Continental Illinois Bank of Chicago, which in 1984 was propped up by approximately $6.5 billion in federal insurance funds, and First Republic Bank of Dallas, which required nearly $4 billion in federal support and was ultimately acquired by an affiliate of NationsBank.

The reasons behind recent bank failures are numerous. Many bankers today are willing to accept greater risk in their operations, in part because of intensified competition and government insurance of bank deposits. Moreover, a worldwide movement toward banking **deregulation** (which we will discuss more fully in Chapter 7) has given banks greater opportunities to market new services and expand geographically without such strict controls, but it has also increased their opportunities for failure. Some analysts argue that even more important is the *increased volatility of economic and financial conditions,* especially interest rates and the prices of foreign currencies. This volatility has made bank earnings and stock prices more unstable and forced bankers to devote more time to the control and management of risk.

Changing Technology

Banking today is passing through a technological revolution. Computer terminals and high-speed information processing are transforming the industry, stressing convenience and speed in handling such routine transactions as making deposits and cashing checks. Most of the new technology is designed to reduce labor and paper costs, making the industry less labor intensive and more capital intensive.

Among the most important pieces of technology in the industry are automated teller machines (ATMs). ATMs accept deposits, dispense cash, and accept payments on loans and other bills owed by customers. For many banking transactions, they perform as well as human tellers do, with the added advantage of 24-hour availability. Initially, ATMs were placed on bank premises, but their growth has extended to shopping centers, airports, and train terminals. In these locations, they are known as *remote service units* (RSUs). Most ATMs promote lower transactions costs for the customer and reduce the need for conventional branch banking offices.

Related to ATMs are point-of-sale (POS) terminals located in retail stores and other commercial establishments. Connected on-line to the bank's computer, POS terminals accept plastic credit and debit cards, permitting the customer to pay instantly for a purchase without the necessity of cashing a check. Customers have not accepted POS terminals as enthusiastically as they have ATMs, however. Part of the problem is the customer's loss of checkbook float because payments are made instantly.

Another important new piece of machinery is the automated clearinghouse (ACH). An ACH transfers information from one financial institution to another and from account to account via computer tape. More than 10,000 banks and other institutions are members of about three dozen ACHs serving the United States. They are used principally for handling business payrolls and processing federal government transactions. Check truncation systems are being used alongside the ACH. Such a system transmits images of checks electronically from one financial institution to another, eliminating the need to transfer paper.

The future will bring increased emphasis on in-home and at-work banking via TV and computer screen and by telephone, coupled with retail shopping information and other convenient services. Using a keyboard and a variety of electronic pathways, including the Internet, the customer can enter requests for information or conduct financial transactions. Credit cards with built-in microprocessors have appeared that allow customers to transfer funds or get account information on the spot. Fax machines permit customers to send money drafts or apply for loans from virtually any location on the globe. Recently some banks began experimenting with automated loan machines (ALMs) that allow a customer to apply for a loan and receive an answer in minutes. Such systems make every customer a branch and cut down on the expensive use of paper.

These recent technological changes have profound implications for bank costs, employment, and profitability. In the future, customers will have less need to enter a bank building, and the need for brick-and-mortar branches will decline. Indeed, many branch offices have recently been closed, suggesting that future needs will be met mainly by electronically transferring information rather than by requiring people to move from one location to another. The banker's principal function will be one of providing the necessary equipment and letting customers conduct their own transactions. This development implies fewer but more highly skilled bank employees and more equipment per dollar of deposits. Heavy investment in computers and money machines will result in substantial fixed costs, requiring a large volume of transactions and favoring the largest banking organizations. The new technology of banking should further intensify pressures for consolidation of the industry into banks smaller in number but much larger in size.

PORTFOLIO CHARACTERISTICS OF COMMERCIAL BANKS

Commercial banks are the financial department stores of the financial system. They offer a wider array of financial services than any other financial institution, meeting the credit, payments, and savings needs of individuals, businesses, and governments. This characteristic of financial diversity is reflected in the basic financial statement of the industry, its balance sheet (or statement of condition). Exhibit 4–3 provides a list of the principal uses of funds (assets) and the major sources of funds (liabilities and equity capital) for all FDIC-insured U.S. commercial banks.

Cash and Due from Banks (Primary Reserves)

All commercial banks hold a substantial part of their assets in **primary reserves,** consisting of cash and deposits held with other banks. These reserves are the banker's first line of defense against withdrawals by depositors and customer demand for loans. Banks generally hold no more cash than is absolutely required to meet short-term contingencies, however, because the yield on cash assets is minimal. The deposits held with other banks do provide an implicit return, however, because they are a means of "paying" for correspondent banking services. In return for the deposits of smaller banks, larger U.S. correspondent banks provide such important services as clearing checks and processing records by computer. Thousands of smaller banks across the United States invest their excess cash reserves in loans to other banks (called *federal funds*) with the help of their larger correspondents.[2]

---

[2]A more complete discussion of the operations of the federal funds market is presented in Chapter 16. Primary reserves also include reserves held behind deposits as required by Federal Reserve System.

Exhibit 4–3   **Bank Report of Condition (Balance Sheet): Assets, Liabilities, and Capital of Insured Commercial Banks in the United States ($ Billions, Year-End Figures)**

	1980		1990		1994	
	Millions of Dollars	Percent of Total Assets	Millions of Dollars	Percent of Total Assets	Millions of Dollars	Percent of Total Assets
Assets:						
Cash and Deposits Due From Banks	$ 331.9	17.9%	$ 318.0	9.4%	$ 303.6	7.6%
Investment Securities:						
U.S. Treasury Securities	104.5	5.6	150.8	4.4	243.6	6.1
Federal Agency Securities	59.1	3.2	275.6	8.2	400.1	10.0
State and Local Govt. Securities	146.3	7.9	83.5	2.5	77.3	1.9
Corporate Bonds	13.4	0.7	85.9	2.5	86.4	2.5
Corporate Stock	1.8	0.1	8.8	0.3	15.6	0.4
Totals	$ 325.0	17.5%	$ 604.6	17.8%	$ 823.0	20.5%
Total Loans and Leases, Gross	1,016.5	54.8	2,110.2	62.3	2,364.5	59.0
Real Estate Loans	269.1	14.5	829.8	24.5	997.7	24.9
Commercial and Industrial Loans	391.0	21.1	615.0	18.1	589.1	14.7
Loans to Individuals	187.4	10.1	403.5	11.9	487.2	12.1
Agricultural Loans	32.3	3.2	33.3	1.0	39.2	1.0
Loans to Depository Institutions	81.2	8.1	51.2	1.5	68.1	1.7
All Other Loans and Leases	55.5	5.5	177.4	5.2	183.3	4.6
Less: Unearned Income	−21.0	−2.1	−13.7	−0.4	−6.4	−0.2
Allowance for Loan and Lease Losses	−10.1	−0.5	−55.5	−1.6	−52.6	−1.3
Net Loans and Leases	1,006.4	54.2	2,054.6	60.6	2,306.1	57.5
Bank Premises and Equipment	26.7	1.4	51.4	1.5	58.9	1.5
Other Real Estate Owned	2.2	0.1	21.6	0.6	10.2	0.3
Intangible Assets	NA	NA	10.6	0.3	24.0	0.6
All Other Assets	163.4	8.8	328.5	9.7	484.9	12.1
Total Assets	$1,855.7	100.0%	$3,389.5	100.0%	$4,010.7	100.0%
Liabilities:						
Total Deposits	$1,481.2	79.8%	$2,650.1	78.2%	$2,874.4	71.7%
Demand Deposits	431.5	23.3	463.9	13.7	977.5	24.4
Savings Deposits	200.9	10.8	798.1	23.5	1,047.8	26.1
Time Deposits	554.7	29.9	1,094.7	32.3	849.1	21.2
Borrowings in the Money Market	177.7	9.6	385.3	11.4	545.1	13.6
Subordinated Capital Notes and Debentures	6.5	0.4	23.9	0.7	40.7	1.0
Other Liabilities	82.7	4.5	111.5	3.3	238.3	5.9
Total Liabilities	$1,748.1	94.2%	$3,170.8	93.5%	$3,698.5	92.2%
Equity Capital:						
Preferred Stock	$ 0.1	0.0*	$ 1.7	0.1	$ 1.5	0.0*
Common Stock	21.7	1.2	30.9	0.9	34.6	0.9
Surplus	37.8	2.0	92.4	2.7	136.0	3.4
Undivided Profits	48.0	2.6	93.7	2.8	140.1	3.5
Total Equity Capital	107.6	5.8	218.6	6.4	312.2	7.8
Total Liabilities and Capital	$1,855.7	100.0%	$3,389.5	100.0%	$4,010.7	100.0%

*Less than $50 million.

Source: Federal Deposit Insurance Corporation, *Historical Statistics on Banking*, 1934–1992, and *Statistics on Banking*, 1994.

MANAGEMENT INSIGHT:

Making Loans and Managing a Financial Institution's Loan Portfolio

One of the most challenging areas for the management of a financial institution comes in making new loans and in properly managing those loans already on the books. This challenge arises because for many financial institutions (such as banks and finance companies) loans are their number one asset and principal revenue source. Moreover, most of the risk is concentrated in the loan portfolio.

Many lending institutions today have a written loan policy to guide individual loan decisions and shape their whole loan portfolio. A good written loan policy will contain a statement of the institution's goals for its loan portfolio, spell out who has authority to make loans, describe what procedure is to be followed in soliciting and evaluating each loan request, and specify what documents must accompany a loan application before and after it is approved. Written loan policies help to train new loan officers and help a financial institution see how well its loan policies are being followed.

Most loan policies require a customer to submit a financial statement, often detailing at least three years' worth of information on assets, liabilities, revenues, and expenses. In the case of a corporate borrower, a board of directors' resolution authorizing the company to negotiate a loan will be requested. For households borrowing money, the customer will usually be asked for written permission to access the loan applicant's credit bureau file (showing past credit history) and to contact his or her employer (to verify employment and income).

Most lending decisions made by financial institutions focus upon three key issues:

1. Is the borrower worthy of credit as indicated by his or her character (including past payment record), cash flow or income (when measured against debts and expenses), collateral (in the form of assets that might be pledged to help secure the loan), and conditions (including the health of the economy and industry involved)?

2. Can a loan agreement be crafted (in terms of maturity, repayment schedule, and other terms) in such a way that it protects the lender and meets the customer's credit needs?

3. Where collateral is offered or demanded, can the lender perfect its claim to that collateral (so that the collateral can be seized legally and sold with minimal cost)?

Among the most popular forms of loan collateral in use today are accounts receivable and inventory of a business firm, real and personal property (including land, buildings, securities, and vehicles), and some type of personal or institutional guarantee. Most loan officers like to write into a loan agreement two or three different sources of repayment of a loan (including borrower cash flow or income, assets, and guarantees).

While different loan officers review different facets of a loan application, most examine closely the borrower's income or cash flow, ability to control expenses, operating efficiency (as reflected in such measures as inventory and accounts receiv-

(continued)

able turnover), marketability of product or service (as reflected in sales or income growth), liquidity (as reflected, for example, in the borrower's ratio of current assets to current liabilities), leverage (such as the borrower's ratio of liabilities to equity), and any contingent liabilities (such as lawsuits against the customer or unpaid taxes). If approved, a loan today will generally be priced off of some base or reference rate, such as the prime bank rate, Eurodollar interest rate (known as LIBOR), or domestic money market interest rate, with more risky borrowers paying the highest rate spreads above the reference or base loan rate.

Security Holdings and Secondary Reserves

Commercial banks hold securities acquired in the open market as a long-term investment and as a secondary reserve to help meet short-term cash needs. Many banks still hold sizable quantities of municipal securities — bonds and notes issued by state, city, and other local governments — because their interest income is tax exempt, although recent tax reform legislation has substantially limited the tax advantages of municipal notes and bonds for banks. However, holdings of U.S. Treasury obligations and debt obligations of federal agencies (such as the Federal National Mortgage Association ("Fannie Mae") or the Farm Credit System) make up the largest item in the security portfolios of U.S. banks. Banks generally favor shorter-term government securities because these securities can be marketed readily to cover short-term cash needs and are free of default risk.

A related type of security purchased in large volume by banks are loan-backed securities (such as collateralized mortgage obligations, or CMOs), each representing an interest in a pool of previously made loans, which pay interest and principal to investors as the loans are paid out. Most loan-backed securities held by banks are backed by government-guaranteed real estate mortgages or credit-card receivables.

Commercial banks also hold small amounts of corporate bonds and notes, although they generally prefer to make direct loans to businesses as opposed to purchasing their securities in the open market. Under existing regulations, U.S. commercial banks are forbidden to purchase corporate stock. However, banks do hold small amounts of corporate stock as collateral for some of their loans.

Recently, American banks have been under strong regulatory pressure to value their security holdings and other assets at current market value rather than at book value on the day they were acquired. The long-range goal is to make bank balance sheets reflect more accurately the true condition of a bank so that capital-market investors and depositors can make a more informed judgment about the bank's true financial standing. To date, banks have only been required to value those investment securities they plan to sell prior to maturity at market value, with all other assets and liabilities valued at book value. Unfortunately, this step has done little, thus far, to improve the quality of information stemming from bank financial reports.

Loans

The principal business of commercial banks is to make *loans* to qualified borrowers. Loans are among the highest yielding assets a bank can add to its portfolio, and they provide the largest portion of most banks' operating revenue.

Banks make loans of reserves to other banks through the federal funds market and to securities dealers through repurchase agreements. Far more important in dollar volume, however, are direct loans to businesses and individuals. These loans arise from negotiation between the bank and its customer and result in a written agreement designed to meet the specific credit needs of the customer and the requirements of the bank for adequate security and income.

As shown in Exhibit 4–3, a substantial portion of bank credit (nearly 15 percent of all bank assets) is extended to commercial and industrial customers in the form of direct loans. Historically, commercial banks have preferred to make *short-term loans* to businesses, principally to support purchases of inventory. In recent years, however, banks have lengthened the maturity of their business loans to include *term loans* (which have maturities over one year) to finance the purchase of buildings, machinery, and equipment. Moreover, longer-term loans to business firms have been supplanted to some extent in recent years by equipment leasing plans. These leases are the functional equivalent of a loan — that is, the customer not only makes the required lease payments while using the equipment but is also responsible for repairs and maintenance and for any taxes due. Lease financing carries not only significant cost and tax advantages for the customer but also substantial tax advantages for a bank, because it can depreciate leased equipment.

Commercial banks are also important lenders in the real estate field, supporting the construction of residential and commercial structures. In fact, real estate loans are, by volume, the most important bank loan category. Major types of loans in the real estate category include farm and real estate credit, conventional government-guaranteed (FHA and VA) single-family residential loans, conventional and government-guaranteed loans on multifamily residences (such as apartments), and mortgage loans on nonfarm commercial properties. Today, commercial banks are the most important source of construction funding in the economy.

One of the most dynamic areas in bank lending today is the making of installment loans to individuals and families, particularly loans secured by a property owner's equity in his or her home (i.e., *home equity loans,* the interest costs of which may be tax deductible to the home owner and borrower). Home equity loans can be used to finance a college education or to cover a variety of other financial needs not related to housing. Banks also finance the purchase of automobiles, home furnishings, and appliances and provide funds to modernize homes and other properties and to pay for education and travel. There is a growing concern today that consumer loans, particularly of the credit-card variety, have become more risky for banks due to higher default rates. Unemployment and a slowly growing economy account for part of this trend, but probably as important is the growing competition for quality customers from nonbank firms, such as American Telephone and Telegraph Co. (AT&T) and Ford Motor Company. This intense competition has encouraged many banks to give credit cards to customers who may have little or no credit history, some of whom turn out to be poor credit risks.

Deposits

To carry out their extensive lending and investing operations, banks draw on a wide variety of deposit and nondeposit sources of funds. The bulk of commercial bank funds — almost three fourths of the total — comes from deposits. There are three main types of deposits: demand, savings, and time. *Demand deposits,* more commonly known as *checking accounts,* are the principal means of making payments because they are safer than cash and are widely accepted. *Savings deposits* generally are in small dollar amounts; they bear a relatively low interest rate but may be withdrawn by the depositor with no notice. *Time deposits* carry a fixed maturity and usually offer the highest interest rates a bank can pay. Time deposits may be divided into nonnegotiable certificates of deposit (CDs), which are usually small, consumer-type accounts, and negotiable CDs that may be traded in the open market in million-dollar amounts and are purchased mainly by corporations.

During the 1970s and 1980s, new forms of checkable (demand) deposits appeared, combining the essential features of both demand and savings deposits. These **transaction accounts** include negotiable orders of withdrawal (NOWs) and automatic transfer services (ATS). NOW accounts may be drafted to pay bills but also earn interest, while ATS is a preauthorized payment service in which the bank transfers funds from an interest-bearing savings account to a checking account as necessary to cover checks written by the customer. Two relatively new transaction accounts — money market deposit accounts (MMDAs) and Super NOWs — are designed to compete directly with the high-yielding share accounts offered by money market mutual funds, carry prevailing market rates on short-term funds, and can be drafted via check, automatic withdrawal, or telephone transfer.

In recent years banks have experienced a shift in their deposits toward more costly interest-bearing accounts, such as MMDAs. These newer deposits are generally *market-linked accounts*, the returns of which are tied to movements in interest rates and security prices, reflecting prevailing credit conditions in the financial system. This shift toward more expensive, market-responsive deposits reflects the growing sophistication of bank customers, who have developed efficient cash management practices and insist on maximum returns on their funds.

Moreover, the cost of attracting customer funds has been further increased in recent years by the tendency of bankers to expand their services in an effort to offer their customers "one-stop" financial convenience. Thus, to retain old deposits and attract new ones, many banks have developed or are working through franchise agreements to offer (1) security brokerage services so that customers can purchase stocks, bonds, and shares in mutual funds and pay by charging their deposit accounts; (2) insurance counters to make life, health, and property-casualty insurance coverage available (usually through joint ventures with cooperating nonbank firms); (3) networking agreements with other banks so that customers can access their deposit accounts while traveling; (4) account relocation services and real estate brokerage of homes and other properties for customers who move; (5) financial and tax counseling centers to aid customers with important personal and business decisions; and (6) merchant banking services that aid major corporations with mergers and long-term financing requirements. Bankers are also pushing Congress and the regulatory agencies for permission to offer a broader range of *investment banking* services — purchasing corporate securities issued by their business customers and reselling them to investors. Although generally prohibited by federal law, a few leading U.S. and foreign bank holding companies have received permission to underwrite corporate securities through subsidiary firms, provided the revenues generated by corporate security underwriting activities do not exceed 10 percent of all revenues flowing through the bank's underwriting subsidiary. These new services may have opened up new markets for banks, but they have also created new complexities for bank management and demanded greater efficiency in bank operations.

Nondeposit Sources of Funds

One of the most marked trends in banking in recent years is greater use of **nondeposit funds** (borrowings), especially as competition for deposits increases. Principal nondeposit sources of funds for banks today include purchases of reserves (federal funds) from other banks, security repurchase agreements (when securities are sold temporarily by a bank and then bought back later), and the issuance of capital notes. Capital notes are of particular interest because many of these securities may be counted under current

Exhibit 4–4   **Securitizations of Bank Loans to Raise Funds**

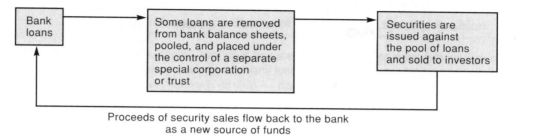

regulations as capital for purposes of determining a bank's loan limit. Both state and federal laws limit the amount of money a commercial bank can lend to any one borrower to a fraction of the bank's capital. To be counted as capital, however, capital notes must be subordinated to deposits, so that if a bank is liquidated, the depositors have first claim on its assets.

Recently banks have turned to new nondeposit funds sources, including floating-rate CDs and notes sold in international markets, sales of blocks of loans, securitizations of selected assets, and standby credit guarantees. The floating-rate securities tend to be longer-term borrowings of funds, stretching out beyond one year, with an interest rate that is adjusted periodically to reflect changing conditions in international markets. Larger banks (such as Chase Manhattan and Citicorp) have expanded their sales of short-term business loans from their books, usually selling these credits in million-dollar blocks to raise new funds. Better-quality loans have been packaged into asset pools and *securitized* — that is, used as collateral for bank security issues that are sold to investors through a broker or dealer. (See Exhibit 4–4.) The bank secures additional funds to make new loans and investments from these **securitized assets,** which have included packages of auto, credit-card, and home mortgage loans. The packaged loans generate interest and principal payments, which are passed through to investors who purchased the securities backed by these loans.

Finally, many large banks today are issuing **standby credit letters** on behalf of their customers who borrow from another lender or sell securities in the open market. As illustrated in Exhibit 4–5, standbys contain the bank's pledge to pay (guarantee) if its customer cannot pay a third party. They generate fee income for the bank without using up scarce funds or booking more assets that would require a bank to pledge more capital behind them.

Equity Capital

Equity capital (or net worth) supplied by a bank's stockholders provides only a minor portion (less than 8 percent, on average) of total funds for most banks today. In fact, while the ratio of equity capital to bank loans and deposits has risen recently, it previously had been in a decline for several decades due to falling profit margins, inflation, and efforts by bank managers to employ greater financial leverage. This concerned many financial experts because one of the most important functions of equity capital is to keep a bank open in the face of operating losses until management can correct its problems. Recently, federal law has mandated minimum capital-to-asset ratios for banks, and many banks have re-

Exhibit 4–5   **Bank Standby Letters of Credit Issued on Behalf of Their Customers**

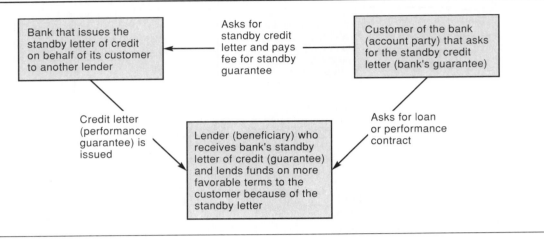

cently expanded their equity capital positions. There is also a move toward cooperative international capital regulation for major banks by the United States, Great Britain, Japan, and the nations of Western Europe. The Basle Agreement, reached in 1988, now imposes common minimum capital requirements on all banks in leading industrialized countries based on the risk contained in the assets they hold.[3]

Revenues and Expenses

The majority of bank revenues come from interest and fees on loans, as shown by the industry's statement of earnings and expenses presented in Exhibit 4–6. Interest and dividends on security holdings are the second most important source of bank revenues after loans. Other minor sources of income include earnings from trust (fiduciary) activities and service charges on deposit accounts.

Bank expenses have risen rapidly in recent years, threatening to squeeze the industry's operating income. Greater competition from bank and nonbank financial institutions has resulted in dramatic increases in the real cost of raising funds. Interest on deposits and other borrowed funds is the principal expense item for commercial banks, followed by the salaries and wages of their employees.

A careful perusal of the statement of earnings and expenses (Report of Income) for all U.S. insured banks in Exhibit 4–6 shows an interesting arrangement of revenue and expense accounts. First, bankers record all of their bank's interest income from loans and security investments. Then the total interest paid out on borrowed funds is subtracted to derive each bank's net interest income or *interest margin.* The interest margin measures how efficiently a bank is performing its function of borrowing and lending funds. For many banks the interest margin is the principal determinant of their profitability.

---

[3]See Chapter 7 for a fuller discussion of the Basle Agreement on bank capital requirements.

Exhibit 4–6

Bank Report of Income (Earnings and Expense Statement): Income and Expenses of Insured Commercial Banks in the United States, 1980, 1990, and 1994

	1980		1990		1994	
	Billions of Dollars	Percent of Total Operating Income	Billions of Dollars	Percent of Total Operating Income	Billions of Dollars	Percent of Total Operating Income
Total Interest Income:	$176.4	92.5%	$320.5	85.4%	$257.8	77.2%
Interest and Fees on Loans	127.0	66.7	234.4	62.4	187.1	56.0
Lease Income	1.4	0.7	4.4	1.2	3.1	0.9
Income from Investment Securities	23.1	12.1	51.1	13.6	48.6	14.6
Trading Account Income	NA	NA	5.4	1.4	7.5	2.2
Income from Federal Funds Loans and Security RPs	8.8	4.6	12.5	3.3	6.4	1.9
Other Interest Income	16.3	8.5	12.7	3.4	5.1	1.5
Total Interest Expense:	$120.1	63.0%	$205.0	54.6%	$111.3	33.3%
Interest on Deposits	34.9	18.3	161.5	43.0	79.4	23.8
Interest on Federal Funds and Security RPs	16.8	8.8	22.7	6.0	12.6	3.8
Interest on Subordinated Capital Notes and Debentures	0.5	0.3	1.8	0.5	2.5	0.7
Interest on Other Borrowed Funds	4.4	2.3	18.9	5.0	16.8	5.0
Net Interest Income	$ 56.3	29.5%	$715.5	30.8%	$146.5	43.9%
Total Noninterest Income:	14.3	7.5	54.9	14.6	76.2	22.8
Service Charges on Deposits	3.2	1.7	11.4	3.0	15.3	4.6
Other Noninterest Income	11.2	5.9	43.4	11.6	60.9	18.2
Total Noninterest Expense	46.7	24.5	115.8	30.8	144.2	43.2
Employee Salaries and Benefits	24.7	13.0	51.8	13.8	60.6	18.1
Occupancy Expenses	7.4	3.9	17.4	4.6	18.9	5.7
All Other Noninterest Expenses	14.6	7.7	46.6	12.4	64.7	19.4
Net Noninterest Income	−32.4	−17.0	−60.9	−16.2	−68.0	−20.4
Provision for Loan and Lease Losses	4.5	2.4	−32.1	8.6	10.9	3.3
Pre-Tax Net Operating Income	19.5	10.2	22.6	6.0	67.6	20.2
Securities Gains (or Losses)	(0.9)	(0.5)	0.5	0.1	(0.6)	0.2
Applicable Income Taxes	4.7	2.5	7.7	2.1	22.4	6.7
Net Extraordinary Items	0.0*	0.0**	0.6	0.2	0.0**	0.0**
Net Income After Taxes	$ 14.0	7.3%	$ 16.0	4.3%	$ 44.6	13.4%

*Less than $50 Million.
**Less than 0.05 percent.

Source: Federal Deposit Insurance Corporation.

Of increasing importance in the industry, however, is the *noninterest margin,* which is the difference between total noninterest income (such as service fees on deposits) and noninterest expenses (such as employee salaries and wages). The noninterest margin is growing in importance as a determinant of bank profits because commercial banks are developing more and more new services that generate noninterest fees, such as security underwriting services, guaranteeing the credit a customer has gotten from another lender, managing pension plans for corporations, and so forth. Because bankers face stiff

Exhibit 4–7   **Worldwide Trends in the Banking Industry**

1. Deregulation of banking in the United States, Canada, Great Britain, Japan, and in many other nations around the globe, permitting private markets to determine prices and services instead of governments.
2. Increased penetration of foreign markets by major banks, securities firms, and other financial institutions in most countries, so that banking and financial services are increasingly becoming a global industry with few territorial boundaries.
3. Growing proliferation of services (i.e., financial innovation) as bankers respond to increased competition, including the spread of securities underwriting, insurance services, and real estate development and brokerage services.
4. A spreading technological revolution with more banking transactions carried out via teller machines, satellites, "smart" cards, fax machines, and other innovative devices instead of through human labor, transforming banking into an increasingly automated, fixed-cost, capital-intensive industry.
5. Changing sources and uses of bank funds as banking's customer base changes toward older, more financially sophisticated, and more interest-sensitive depositors. New sources of bank funds include loan sales, securitized loans, and market-linked accounts (where yields to the depositor fluctuate with market conditions). In addition, banks are doing more "off-balance-sheet" financing of their customers' credit needs, providing guarantees behind customer borrowings. These devices usually earn fee income for banks but avoid draining scarce bank capital.
6. Growing international cooperation between governments and regulatory agencies from different countries to promote uniform regulation and supervision of banks, regardless of country.

competition for funding, they have little influence over the interest expenses on their borrowed funds. Accordingly, they work especially hard to minimize their *noninterest expenses*, particularly employee costs, by substituting automated equipment for labor.

In summary, bankers today must contend with increasing competition from both foreign and domestic financial institutions; a shifting customer base of older, higher-income, and better-educated consumers; the ever-changing technology of service production and delivery; and greater risk of failure in a more competitive and volatile environment (as Exhibit 4–7 reminds us). To be a successful banker today demands a unique combination of technical and social skills and the capacity to learn new methods in a dynamic financial marketplace.

MONEY CREATION AND DESTRUCTION BY BANKS

Commercial banks differ from many other financial institutions in one critical respect: *Banks have the power to create money in the form of new checkable deposits.* The banking system creates and destroys billions of dollars in money each year at the stroke of a pen or merely by posting amounts in a computer file. Of course, an individual bank cannot create any more money in the form of checkable deposits than the volume of excess reserves that it holds. However, the banking system as a whole can create a volume of money equal to a *multiple* of any excess reserves deposited with it simply by making loans and purchasing securities.

Reserve Requirements and Excess Reserves

Money creation by banks is made possible because the public readily accepts claims on bank deposits (mainly checks and computer debits) in payment for goods and services. In addition, the law requires individual banks to hold only a fraction of the amount of

INTERNATIONAL FOCUS:

Banking and the Drive Toward a Unified Europe

The international market for banking services is likely to feel a significant impact in the years ahead as Europe, with more than 340 million consumers, moves toward economic unity. A giant step toward European unity was taken in December 1991 when leaders of the European Community (EC) signed the Maastricht Treaty, which sets forth a three-stage process to achieve one economy with a single currency and a unified financial system by the turn of the century. Specifically, the Maastricht Treaty calls for deregulation of capital movements and the integration of all Eurocurrencies into the European Monetary System with each individual nation's currency kept within a narrow band vis-à-vis other European currencies.

In the final phases of European integration, the Maastricht Treaty requires eventual coordination of monetary policies among member countries, with the European System of Central Banks to begin coordinated operations under one European central bank (known as the European Monetary Institute, or EMI) and the European Currency Unit (ECU) to become a tradable currency in its own right at the turn of the century.

Foreign banks, including those from the United States, hope that the new trade freedom in Europe will allow them greater opportunity to expand without restrictions throughout Europe. However, there is the threat that the EC will put restrictions on the licensing of foreign banks and other firms, granting them less freedom to operate than it gives to EC firms. Moreover, economic integration means more competition for all banks operating in Europe, setting in motion a wave of mergers. In fact, a massive consolidation of European banks is now underway so they can more easily fend off competition. They are also combining with European securities and insurance firms to offer more services than many U.S. and other foreign banks can offer.

The road to complete European economic and financial unity will not be an easy journey, however. In June 1992, Danish voters rejected the terms of the Maastricht Treaty in a national referendum. Later, several nations cut their currencies loose from agreed-upon parities with other European currencies due to massive speculative flows of funds and concern over a serious recession. Complete integration of the European banking and financial system will require costly retooling of the accounting and computer systems of European-based financial institutions. Considerable advance planning will be required if European financial and economic integration is to succeed.

deposits received from the public as cash reserves, thus freeing up a majority of incoming funds for making loans and purchasing securities. We need to look more closely at the reserve requirements banks must meet, because they play a key role in money creation.

Under current federal law, U.S. banks and other depository institutions must hold reserves in cash or in deposit form behind selected types of deposits. These reserve requirements are linked to the size of the depository institution and require that a specified percentage (ranging from 3 to 10 percent) of reservable deposits must be placed in either an account at the regional Federal Reserve bank or as cash in the bank's vault. Vault cash and deposits at the Fed constitute a bank's holdings of **legal reserves** — those assets acceptable for meeting legal reserve requirements behind the public's deposits.

Each bank's legal reserves may be divided into two categories: required reserves and excess reserves. *Required reserves* are equal to the legal reserve requirement ratio times the volume of deposits subject to reserve requirements. For example, if a bank holds $50 million in checkable (transaction) deposits and the law requires it to hold 3 percent of its transaction accounts in legal reserves, the reserve requirement for this bank would be $50 million × 3%, or $1.5 million.

Excess reserves equal the difference between the total legal reserves actually held by a bank and the amount of its required reserves. For example, if a bank is required to hold legal reserves equal to $1.5 million but finds on a given date that it has $500,000 in cash on the premises and $1.5 million on deposit with the Federal Reserve bank in its region, this bank holds $500,000 in excess reserves. Because legal reserves earn little or no interest income, most banks try to keep their holdings of excess reserves as close to zero as possible.

The Creation of Money and Credit

The distinction between excess and required reserves is important because it plays a key role in the growth of credit in the economy and the creation of money by the banking system. To understand why, we need to make certain assumptions concerning how banks behave and the regulations they face. To simplify the arithmetic, assume that the Federal Reserve has set a basic reserve requirement of 20 percent behind the public's deposits.[4] Therefore, for every dollar that the public deposits in the banking system, each bank must put aside in either vault cash or deposits at the Federal Reserve 20 cents as required reserves. Assume also that, initially, the banking system is "loaned up" — that is, bankers have loaned out all excess legal reserves available to them. In addition, assume that all bankers are profit maximizers and attempt to loan out immediately any excess funds available to earn the most interest income possible.

Suppose that a deposit of $1,000 is made from some source outside the banking system. For example, the public may decide to convert a portion of its currency and coin holdings ("pocket money") into bank deposits for greater convenience and safety. Suppose a deposit of $1,000 appears at Bank A as shown in Exhibit 4–8. This exhibit contains an abbreviated balance sheet (T account) for Bank A with changes in its assets shown on the left-hand side and changes in its liabilities and net worth shown on the right-hand side.

Under the assumed Federal Reserve regulations, Bank A is required to place $200 aside as required reserves (i.e., 20 percent of the $1,000 deposit), leaving excess legal reserves of $800. Because the $800 in cash earns no interest income, the banker will immediately try to loan out these excess reserves. Banks make loans today by simple bookkeeping entry. The borrower signs a note indicating how much is borrowed, at what

[4]Commercial banks' current reserve requirements and the role that they play in government monetary policy are discussed in Chapter 20.

Exhibit 4–8   **The Creation of Credit and Deposits by the Banking System**

1. Bank A Receives New Deposit			
Assets		*Liabilities*	
Required reserves	200	Deposits	1,000
Cash	800		

4. Loan Made by Bank B			
Assets		*Liabilities*	
Required reserves	160	Deposits	800
Loans	640		

2. Loan Made by Bank A			
Assets		*Liabilities*	
Required reserves	200	Deposits	1,000
Loans	800		

5. Deposit of Loan Funds in Bank C			
Assets		*Liabilities*	
Required reserves	128	Deposits from Bank B	640
Cash	512		

3. Deposit of Loan Funds in Bank B			
Assets		*Liabilities*	
Required reserves	160	Deposits from Bank A	800
Cash	640		

6. Loan Made by Bank C			
Assets		*Liabilities*	
Required reserves	128	Deposits	640
Loans	512		

By making loans whenever there are excess reserves, the banking system will ultimately generate a volume of deposits several times larger than the amount of the initial deposit received by Bank A.

Transactions within the Banking System

Name of Bank	Deposits Received	Loans Made	Required Reserves
A	$1,000	$ 800	$ 200
B	800	640	160
C	640	512	128
D	512	410	102
—	—	—	—
—	—	—	—
Final amounts of all banks in the system	$5,000	$4,000	$1,000

rate of interest, and when the note will come due. In return, the banker creates a checking account in the borrower's name. In our example, assume that Bank A has received a loan request from one of its customers and decides to grant the customer a loan of $800 — exactly the amount of excess reserves it holds.

Banks find that, when they make loans, the borrowed funds are withdrawn rapidly as borrowers spend the proceeds of their loans. Moreover, it is likely that most of the borrowed funds will wind up as deposits in other banks as borrowing customers write checks against their loan balances. For this reason, Bank A will not loan out any more than the $800 in excess reserves it currently holds. This way, when a borrower spends his or her funds and the money flows to other banks, Bank A will have sufficient funds in reserve to cover the cash letters demanding payment it will receive from other banks.

Assume that the $800 loaned by Bank A eventually winds up as a deposit in Bank B. As indicated in Exhibit 4–9, Bank B must place $160 (20 percent) of this deposit in required reserves; it then has excess reserves of $640, which are quickly loaned out. As the new borrowers spend their funds, the $640 in loans will find its way into deposits at Bank

Exhibit 4–9   **Deposit and Credit Destruction in the Banking System**

Depositor withdraws funds

Federal Reserve Bank		Bank A	
Assets	Liabilities	Assets	Liabilities
	Member bank reserves −1000	Required reserves −1000	Deposits −1000

If Bank A was loaded up when the withdrawal occurred, it will now have a reserve deficiency of $800 as indicated below:

Total reserves lost at Bank A when depositor withdrew funds	$1000
Required reserves no longer needed due to deposit withdrawals	−200
Total reserve deficit at Bank A	$ 800

Bank A		Bank B	
Assets	Liabilities	Assets	Liabilities
Securities −800		Required reserves −800	Deposits −800
Required reserves +800 from Bank B			

The sale of securities in the amount of $800 enables Bank A to cover its reserve deficit. However, customers of Bank B bought those securities and that bank was already loaned up. Therefore, Bank B now has a reserve deficiency of $640. Thus:

Total reserves lost at Bank B after deposit withdrawals to purchase Bank A's securities	$800
Required reserves no longer needed due to deposit withdrawal	−160
Total reserve deficit at Bank B	$640

C. After setting aside required reserves of $128, Bank C has excess reserves of $512. It too will move rapidly to loan out these funds if suitable borrowers can be found.

The pattern of these changes in deposits, loans, and required reserves should now be fairly clear. The results are summarized in the bottom portion of Exhibit 4–8. Note that the total volume of bank deposits has been considerably expanded by the time it reaches the third or fourth bank. Similarly, the total volume of new loans grows rapidly as funds flow from bank to bank within the system. If the credit-creation process works through the entire banking system with no leakages, then with a new $1,000 deposit and a 20 percent reserve requirement, the banking system ultimately will hold $5,000 in deposits and will have created $4,000 in new loans. By making loans whenever excess reserves appear, the banking system eventually creates total deposits and total loans several times larger than the original volume of new funds received.

In the foregoing example, each dollar of required reserves supports $5 in deposits, due to the fact that the legal reserve requirement is 20 percent. Total deposits created by the banking system are equal to the initial amount of legal reserves deposited in the system times the reciprocal of the reserve requirement ratio, in this case 1/0.20, or 5. The reciprocal of the reserve requirement ratio is known as the *deposit multiplier,* a concept we will discuss more fully in Chapter 20. In the real world, leakages from the banking system greatly reduce the size of the deposit multiplier, probably to no more than 2. Among the most important leakages are the public's desire to convert some portion of new demand deposits into currency and coin (pocket money) and the presence of unutilized lending capacity.

MANAGEMENT INSIGHT

Managing the Legal Reserve (Money) Position of a Depository Institution

As we have seen in this chapter, banks along with other depository institutions must hold a small percentage of their deposits in the form of *legal reserves* — vault cash plus deposits at the central bank. In the United States each depository institution's total required holdings of legal reserves are determined from the formula:

$$\begin{array}{c} \text{Total required} \\ \text{legal reserves} \end{array} = \begin{array}{c} \text{Reserve} \\ \text{requirement} \\ \text{on transaction} \\ \text{deposits} \\ \text{(such as} \\ \text{checking} \\ \text{accounts)} \end{array} \times \begin{array}{c} \text{Daily} \\ \text{average} \\ \text{amount of} \\ \text{net transaction} \\ \text{deposits held} \\ \text{over a designated} \\ \text{time period} \end{array} + \begin{array}{c} \text{Reserve} \\ \text{requirement on} \\ \text{nontransaction} \\ \text{reservable} \\ \text{liabilities} \\ \text{(such as savings} \\ \text{accounts or bank CDs)} \end{array} \times \begin{array}{c} \text{Daily} \\ \text{average} \\ \text{amount of} \\ \text{nontransaction} \\ \text{reservable} \\ \text{liabilities held over} \\ \text{a designated} \\ \text{period} \end{array}$$

The daily average amount of deposits held is figured over a two-week period called the *reserve computation period.* For example, suppose a bank held a daily average of $10 million in transaction (checkable) deposits and $20 million in nontransaction reservable liabilities over the period that it must figure its required legal reserve. Suppose the reserve requirement on transaction deposits is currently 3 percent and nontransaction liabilities (such as savings accounts) carry *no* reserve requirement. Therefore, this bank's total required legal reserves would be:

$$\begin{array}{c} \text{Total required} \\ \text{legal reserves} \end{array} = 0.03 \times \$10 \text{ million} + 0.00 \times \$20 \text{ million} = \$300,000$$

Federal law in the United States allows banks and other depository institutions to count the daily average amount of cash held in their vaults over a two-week period to help satisfy their reserve requirements. The remainder of the reserve requirement must be held in a deposit at the Federal Reserve bank located in the depository institution's district. For example, suppose the depository institution mentioned above held a daily average of $100,000 in vault cash. Then, it must hold on deposit with the Federal Reserve bank in its district:

$$\begin{array}{c} \text{Daily Average Amount of} \\ \text{required legal reserves} \\ \text{that must be held in a} \\ \text{deposit at the Federal} \\ \text{Reserve} \end{array} = \begin{array}{c} \text{Total} \\ \text{required} \\ \text{legal} \\ \text{reserves} \end{array} - \begin{array}{c} \text{Daily average} \\ \text{vault cash} \\ \text{holdings} \end{array} = \$300,000 - \$100,000 = \$200,000$$

In this case the depository institution must make sure it averages $200,000 a day in an account at the Federal Reserve bank in its district over a two-week period known as the *reserve maintenance period.* If the institution falls more than 4 percent below this required daily-average legal reserve amount, the Federal Reserve can impose a penalty fee based on the size of the deficit. On the other hand, if the institution holds *more* than is required, there is no legal penalty, but there will be an *opportunity cost* in the form of excess cash that should have been profitably invested. This is why the

(continued)

manager of a depository institution's legal reserve position tries to hit the required legal reserve target as closely as possible, running neither a substantial reserve deficit nor a surplus.

The manager of legal reserves faces a real challenge because a depository institution's reserve account at the central bank changes daily in response to multiple factors. These include check clearings for and against the institution, purchases and sales of government securities (which in the U.S. are handled through debits and credits to a depository's legal reserve account), and any borrowing or lending in the money market. Reserve position managers must continually check the balance in their institution's legal reserve account to make sure the daily average amount held matches the planned amount as closely as possible.

When the reserve account falls into a deficit, the reserve (money) position manager must weigh several factors in deciding how to eliminate the deficit. These factors include how quickly the deficit must be covered (e.g., in the next few minutes or not for several days), the length of time funds will be needed (e.g., a few hours or several days), the relative costs of different sources of funds, expected changes in government economic policy, and any applicable regulations. For example, a bank facing a legal reserve deficit may decide to borrow from the Federal Reserve bank where it holds its reserve account, paying the discount rate the Reserve bank is currently charging for borrowed legal reserves. However, the Federal Reserve limits the amount and frequency of such borrowing, sometimes forcing the borrowing institution to find the money it needs somewhere else. On the other hand, if a reserve surplus appears, the liquidity manager must move quickly (usually within minutes) to invest the surplus funds and generate income for his or her institution.

Destruction of Deposits and Reserves

Not only can the money supply expand by a multiple amount as a result of the injection of new reserves, but it can also *contract* by a multiple amount when reserves are withdrawn from the banking system. This is illustrated in Exhibit 4–9, in which a depositor has decided to withdraw $1,000 from a transaction account at Bank A. Recall that behind the $1,000 deposit, Bank A holds only $200 in required reserves. This means that when the deposit is withdrawn, that bank will have a deficiency of $800. If Bank A is loaned up and has used all of its cash to make loans and investments, it will have to raise the necessary funds through the sale of securities or through borrowing.

Suppose that Bank A decides to sell securities in the amount of $800. As indicated in Exhibit 4–9, the sale of securities increases Bank A's legal reserves by the necessary amount. However, the individuals and institutions that purchase those securities pay for them by writing checks against their deposits in other banks, reducing the legal reserves of those institutions.

For example, assume that Bank B loses deposits of $800 and required reserves of $800 as Bank A gains these funds. Considering Bank A and Bank B together, total deposits have fallen by $1,800. This deposit contraction has freed up $360 ($200 + $160) in required reserves. However, if Bank B is also loaned up and has a net reserve deficiency of $640, further contraction of deposits will occur as Bank B attempts to cover its reserve deficiency by drawing reserves from other banks. In fact, with a 20 percent reserve requirement and no other leakages from the banking system, deposits will contract by a full $5,000 as banks try to cover their reserve deficits by raising funds at the expense of other banks.

Implications of Money Creation and Destruction

This capacity of banks to create and destroy money has a number of important implications for the financial system and for the economy. Creation of money by banks is one of the most important sources of credit funds in the global economy — an important supplement to the supply of savings in providing funds for investment so the economy can grow faster. Money created by banks is instantly available for spending and, therefore, unless carefully controlled by government action, can fuel inflation. That is why the Federal Reserve System and other central banks around the globe regulate the growth of the money supply principally through controlling the growth of bank reserves, a subject dealt with at length in Chapters 20 and 21.

SUMMARY

It is clear that the banking industry has undergone significant financial and structural changes in recent years. The drive toward larger banking organizations centered around branch banks and holding companies appears to be a continuing trend for the future, as is the spread of interstate banking in the United States. These changes have been brought about by strong economic and financial pressures. Volatile interest rates, soaring operating costs, and intense competition have propelled bankers into a new scenario in which the character of their loans, investments, and sources of funds has changed markedly. More-over, there is no end in sight to many of these trends. Costs of labor and raising funds remain at relatively high levels, placing great pressure on bankers to find higher yielding uses for their funds. A key factor in the industry's response to these demand and cost pressures will be the willingness of governments to permit banks to respond freely to new and changing public demands for quality financial services. ∎

KEY TERMS AND CONCEPTS IN THIS CHAPTER

banking structure	bank holding company	securitized assets
deregulation	money creation	consolidation
transaction accounts	legal reserves	branch banking

STUDY QUESTIONS

1. In what ways are commercial banks of special importance to the functioning of the money and capital markets and the economy?

2. What are the principal uses of commercial bank funds? Major sources of funds? What *new* sources and uses of funds have been developed in recent years?

3. Three dominant movements in the structure of U.S. banking in recent years have been the spread of branch banking, the growth of holding companies, and the rise of interstate banking. Explain what has happened in these areas and why.

4. Explain how the securitization of loans helps to raise new funds for a bank.

5. What benefits do standby credit letters provide for banks and their customers?

6. What are a bank's principal revenue and expense items?

7. What is the net interest margin? The noninterest margin? Why are they important to banks?

8. Why and how are banks able to create money? Does the ability of banks to create money have important implications for public policy?

PROBLEMS

1. Given the following information on the revenues and expenses of First National Bank, determine the bank's net income after taxes for the year just concluded:

Salaries and employee benefits	$80,000	Applicable income taxes	$50,000
Interest on deposits	170,000	Occupancy costs	11,000
Interest on loans	320,000	Provision for loan losses	22,000
Income from U.S. Treasury securities	75,000	Miscellaneous expenses	8,000
		Interest on municipal securities	86,000
Extraordinary items, net	-0-	Service charges on deposits	10,000
Interest on nondeposit borrowings	30,000	Miscellaneous operating revenues	13,000
Net securities gains	-0-		

2. Construct the report of condition (balance sheet) for First National Bank for December 31 of the year just ended from the following information:

Equity capital	$50 million	Real estate loans	$60 million
Demand deposits	100 million	U.S. Treasury securities	25 million
Savings deposits	150 million	Commercial and industrial loans	300 million
Time deposits	200 million	Other liabilities	38 million
Federal funds borrowings	12 million	Municipal securities	55 million
Cash and due from banks	20 million	Loans to individuals	40 million
Other assets	50 million		

3. A commercial bank holds $120 million in transaction deposits and $240 million in nontransaction reservable liabilities. Suppose that reserve requirements set by the Federal Reserve Board stipulate that 3 percent of the first $30 million in transaction deposits and 12 percent of any excess transaction deposits over $30 million must be held in a legal reserve account. Similarly, suppose 3 percent of nontransaction liabilities must be placed in the legal reserve account. What is the bank's total reserve requirement based on the above deposit totals? Suppose the bank's legal reserve account has a current average balance of $20 million. Does the bank have any excess reserves? If so, how much?

4. See if you can fill in correctly the missing items from the balance sheet (report of condition) and the statement of earnings and expenses (report of income) of the bank whose financial accounts are listed below:

Balance Sheet		Statement of Earnings and Expenses	
Cash and interbank deposits	$11	Revenue sources:	
Investment securities	?	Domestic loan interest and fees	$?
Federal funds sold	8	Foreign loan interest and fees	6
Loans, gross	81	Income from security investments	4
Allowance for loan losses	(6)	Miscellaneous revenues	1
Unearned discount on loans	(1)	Total revenues	?
Net loans	?	Expenses:	
Premises and fixed assets	2	Interest on deposits	?
Miscellaneous assets	5	Interest on nondeposit borrowings	1
Total assets	$110	Salaries and wages	2
Demand deposits	?	Occupancy costs	1
Savings deposits	20	Provision for loan losses	1
Time deposits	65	Miscellaneous expenses	2
Nondeposit borrowings	12	Total expenses	15
Total liabilities	?	Net operating income	3
Stockholder's equity capital	4	Income taxes	?
		Net income (or loss) after taxes	1

5. Suppose you have been given the financial information below for a commercial bank:

Income taxes owed	$13	Interest paid to depositors	$64
Noninterest revenues from service fees	70	Interest on nondeposit borrowings	8
Interest revenues from loans	129	Salaries and wages of bank employees	27
Interest and dividends from investments in securities	26	Overhead costs	3
		Loan-loss provision	2
Dividends paid to stockholders	4		

a. Please calculate this bank's net interest income, net noninterest income, net income before taxes, net income after taxes, undivided profits (or retained earnings), total revenues, and total expenses.

b. Suppose the above bank's return on assets — the ratio of its net income after taxes to total assets — is 0.85 percent. What is the total of the bank's assets in dollars?

c. Suppose this bank's return on stockholder's equity capital — the ratio of its net income after taxes to total equity capital — is 12 percent. What is the bank's total equity capital in dollars?

d. Suppose the above bank's total deposits equal 75 percent of its total liabilities. How many deposits in total dollar volume does the bank hold?

SELECTED REFERENCES

Bentson, George J.; Gerald A. Hanweck; and David Humphrey. "Scale Economies in Banking: A Restructuring and Reassessment." *Journal of Money, Credit and Banking* 14 (November 1982), Part I, pp. 435–56.

Mester, Loretta J. "Curing Our Ailing Deposit Insurance System." *Business Review.* Federal Reserve Bank of Philadelphia (September/October 1990), pp. 13–24.

Rose, Peter S. "The Quest for Bank Funds: New Directions in a New Market." *The Canadian Banker* (December 1987), pp. 56–61.

Nonbank Thrift Institutions: Credit Unions, Savings and Loan Associations, Savings Banks, and Money Market Mutual Funds

LEARNING OBJECTIVES IN THIS CHAPTER

• To understand how important nonbank depository institutions (thrifts) — credit unions, savings and loan associations, savings banks, and money market funds — are in the functioning of a modern economy and financial system.

• To examine the financial services offered by nonbank thrift institutions.

• To see how nonbank thrift institutions are similar and how they differ from one another.

There is a tendency in discussions of the financial system to minimize the role of nonbank financial institutions and emphasize the part played by commercial banks in the flow of money and credit. For many years, financial experts did not consider the liabilities of nonbank financial institutions, including deposits in savings and loan associations, savings banks, and credit unions, as really close substitutes for bank deposits. It was argued that interindustry competition between commercial banks and other financial institutions was slight and, for all practical purposes, could be ignored. Today, however, an entirely different view has emerged concerning the relative importance of nonbank financial institutions. We now recognize that these institutions play a vital role in the flow of money and credit within the financial system and are particularly important in selected markets, such as the mortgage market and the market for personal savings.

In truth, many nonbank financial institutions are becoming increasingly like commercial banks and are competing for many of the same customers. Moreover, banks themselves are offering many of the services traditionally offered by nonbank financial firms, such as brokering securities and selling insurance (often through joint ventures with nonbank firms). This is why financial analysts today stress the importance of studying the *whole* financial institutions' sector to understand how the financial system works. In this chapter and the next, we examine the major types of nonbank financial institutions that channel the public's savings into loans and investments.

CREDIT UNIONS

The characteristics and operations of **credit unions** have been a neglected area of research in the financial system. Recently, however, there has been a revival of interest in credit union behavior. One reason has been the rapid growth of this financial intermediary. For example, credit union assets have more than tripled since 1980 (see Exhibit 5–1), though a combination of failures and mergers among smaller credit unions has recently slowed credit union growth. Overall, U.S. credit unions are the third largest institutional supplier of installment credit to individuals and families, trailing only commercial banks and finance companies, and account for about one eighth of all consumer installment loans in the United States. These institutions are household-oriented intermediaries, offering deposit and credit services to individuals and families. Their long-run survival stems mainly from being able to offer low loan rates and high deposit interest rates to their customers.

Credit unions are cooperative, self-help associations of individuals rather than profit-motivated financial institutions. Savings deposits and loans are offered only to members of each association, and the members are technically the *owners,* receiving dividends and sharing in any losses that occur. Each member gets one vote regardless of the size of his or her account. Credit unions began early in the 20th century to serve low-income individuals and families by providing inexpensive credit and an outlet for their savings. Early growth

Exhibit 5–1	**Credit Unions in the United States and Worldwide**		
Year	Number of U.S. Credit Unions	Number of U.S. Credit Union Members	Total U.S. Assets ($ Millions)
1940	9,023	2,826,612	$253
1950	10,586	4,617,086	1,005
1960	20,094	12,025,393	5,651
1970	23,687	22,775,511	17,872
1980	21,465	43,930,569	68,974
1990	14,549	61,610,957	221,759
1994	11,425	62,221,247	274,683

Credit unions worldwide in 1994: 88 million members with total assets of $418 billion in 55,000 credit unions.

Source: Credit Union National Association, Inc., *Credit Union Report,* 1994; and World Council of Credit Unions, *1994 Annual Statistical Report.*

was modest until the 1950s, when these institutions broadened their appeal to middle-income individuals by offering many new financial services.

The credit union sector remains small compared to other major financial institutions, accounting for less than 10 percent of all consumer savings in the United States placed with depository institutions. However, worldwide the industry's potential for future growth appears promising due to its innovative character and solid public acceptance. For both savings deposits and consumer installment loans, the credit union has become an aggressive competitor of banks and savings associations. Beginning in 1978, credit unions were authorized to offer money market certificates, which can carry the same terms as the money market deposit plans sold by banks. In addition, many credit unions offer payroll savings plans by which employees can automatically set aside a portion of their salary in a savings account.

Credit union loans have kept pace with the growth of their deposits and today account for nearly 15 percent of all consumer installment loans in the United States and a substantial portion of these loans worldwide. Consumer loan rates charged by credit unions are fully competitive with loan rates charged by most other major consumer lenders. Moreover, credit unions frequently grant their borrowing members interest refunds up to 20 percent of the amount of a loan. Many credit unions provide life insurance free to their customers, a service charged for by most other lending institutions. Thus, credit unions accept a smaller spread between their loan and deposit interest rates. This is possible because their operating costs are usually so low. Frequently, the sponsoring employer or association provides free office facilities, and credit union members elect officers and directors who frequently serve with no compensation at all.

Credit Union Membership

Credit unions are organized around a common affiliation or common bond among their members. Most members work for the same employer or for one of a group of related employers. Moreover, if one family member belongs to a credit union, other family members are eligible as well. Occupation-related credit unions account for about three quarters of all U.S. credit unions; about one sixth are organized around nonprofit associations, such as a labor union, a church, or a fraternal or social organization. Common area of residence, such as a city or state, and age (e.g., an association for retired persons) have also been used to get credit unions started.

Size of Credit Unions

There is a strong shift today toward fewer, but larger, credit unions. For example, the number of associations reached an all-time high in 1969 at almost 24,000 but now totals less than 12,000 in the United States, the decline due primarily to mergers, failures, and a structural shift in the U.S. economy away from manufacturing industries (where credit unions have concentrated historically) toward more service industries (where credit union activity tends to be more subdued). With declining numbers of credit unions but continued industry growth, the average size of credit unions has risen substantially in recent years.

For example, although only about one sixth of credit unions held more than $1 million in assets in 1970, today more than 90 percent of all U.S. credit unions exceed $2 million in total assets. Although the average size of credit unions still remains very small compared to other types of depository institutions, worldwide membership in credit unions has not stopped its upward climb. Around the globe more than 88 million people belong to one or more of about 55,000 credit unions scattered in more than 80 countries. Inside the United

States credit union members have grown from fewer than 5 million in 1950 to more than 60 million in the 1990s.

New Services Offered

Credit unions are expanding the number of services they offer. Some sell life insurance; others act as brokers for group insurance plans when state law permits. Many credit unions are active in offering 24-hour automated or telephone teller services, travelers checks, financial planning services, retirement savings, credit cards, home equity and first mortgage loans, and money orders. Larger credit unions compete directly with banks for transaction accounts by offering **share drafts** — interest-bearing checkbook deposits. A substantial proportion of U.S. credit unions also offers credit cards and automated teller machines (many of which are linked nationwide through an electronic exchange network in order to accommodate members who travel). Several have recently begun to take loan applications via fax and personal computers and offer preauthorized drafts as well as telephone bill paying.

U.S. credit unions are under intense pressure to develop new services and penetrate new markets due to increasing competition from other financial institutions and a decline in the demand for their historically most important credit service — automobile loans — where they face fierce competition from banks and finance companies (such as GMAC and Ford Motor Credit). In addition, because a larger proportion of family income today is spent on food, fuel, education, and other necessities, credit unions have begun shifting their loans into these areas. First-mortgage loans to purchase new homes and second-mortgage loans to repair or improve existing homes, as well as home equity credit to fund a wide variety of household purchases, have grown rapidly and now account for nearly a third of all credit union loans. (See Exhibit 5–2.) Finally, loans to small businesses (not exceeding

Exhibit 5–2   **Financial Assets and Liabilities Held by U.S. Credit Unions, 1980–95**
($ Billions)

Item	1980	1985	1990	1995*
Financial Assets:				
Checkable deposits and currency	$ 1.2	$ 3.3	$ 4.8	$ 7.3
Time deposits	7.1	20.0	21.7	16.3
Federal funds loans and security RPs	0.7	8.4	14.6	9.2
U.S. government and federal agency securities	4.3	13.1	23.0	61.2
Home mortgage and equity loans	4.7	12.4	48.2	62.2
Consumer installment loans	44.0	72.7	93.1	122.9
Open-market paper	—	0.2	2.3	1.7
Miscellaneous assets	5.7	4.4	9.3	18.6
Total financial assets	$67.6	$134.5	$217.0	$299.3
Liabilities:				
Checkable deposits/shares	$ 3.3	$ 12.6	$ 22.2	$ 29.6
Small time and savings deposits/shares	57.9	111.7	175.3	233.4
Large ($100,000+) deposits/shares	0.5	1.2	3.3	7.5
Loans from the Federal Home Loan banks	—	—	—	0.4
Miscellaneous liabilities	3.1	2.8	3.9	4.9
Total liabilities	$64.8	$128.3	$204.7	$275.7

*Figures for 1995 are as of the first quarter.

Source: Board of Governors of the Federal Reserve System, *Flow of Funds Accounts,* selected issues.

20 percent of a credit union's capital) have recently been added to many credit union service menus, along with auto and equipment leases.

Under current federal government rules in the United States, credit unions are permitted to make unsecured loans to members (including credit card loans) not exceeding 5 years to maturity and to grant secured loans out to 30 years. Their permissible investments in securities are limited to a list prescribed by either state or federal regulations. In the main, credit unions are permitted to acquire U.S. government securities, to hold savings deposits at banks, savings and loan associations, and federally insured credit unions; and to purchase selected federal agency securities. They rely heavily on U.S. government securities and on savings deposits to provide liquidity to meet deposit withdrawals and accommodate member credit needs. Credit unions pay dividends to their members but are considered *nonprofit* associations, doing business only with their owners and, therefore, are classified as *tax-exempt* mutual organizations.

A Strong Competitive Force

Credit unions represent stiff competition for commercial banks, savings banks, and other financial institutions serving consumers. Today, one of every five Americans belongs to a credit union — roughly double the proportion of a decade earlier. True, the number of credit unions is declining in some areas, such as in the United States; however, this industry has repeatedly demonstrated its capacity for service innovation and its ability to compete successfully for both consumer loans and savings accounts against some of the largest financial service competitors in the world.

SAVINGS AND LOAN ASSOCIATIONS

Savings and loan associations are similar to credit unions because they extend financial services primarily to households. They differ from credit unions, however, in their heavy emphasis on long-term rather than short-term lending. In particular, **savings and loans** are a major source in the United States of mortgage loans to finance the purchase of single-family homes and multifamily dwellings. And like credit unions, savings and loans today are developing many new financial services to attract customers and protect their earnings. However, these associations today face the most serious challenge to their survival in half a century. Hundreds of S&Ls have failed, and many have converted to bank charters or have been absorbed by bank holding companies. We will discuss some of the causes of the recent S&L debacle in the sections that follow.

Origins

The first savings and loans were started early in the 19th century as building and loan associations. Money was solicited from individuals and families so that certain members of the group could finance the building of new homes. The same individuals and families who provided loanable funds were also borrowers from the association. Today, however, savers and borrowers are frequently different individuals.

Savings and loan associations began as a *single-product industry,* accepting savings deposits from middle-income individuals and families and lending those funds to home buyers. More recently, however, competition from commercial banks and credit unions, coupled with unstable interest rates and many failures, have forced savings and loans to diversify their operations and aggressively solicit new customers.

Many savings and loans are **mutuals** and therefore have no stockholders. Technically, they are owned by their depositors. However, a growing number of associations are converting to stock form. Stockholder-owned S&Ls can issue capital stock to increase their net worth, a privilege that is particularly important when a savings and loan is growing rapidly and needs an additional source of long-term capital. Stockholder-owned associations, on average, are much larger in size than mutuals, holding more than half of the industry's assets.

How Funds Are Raised and Allocated

Savings and loans, like credit unions, are gradually broadening their role, with many choosing to offer a full line of financial services for individuals and families. Other S&Ls are branching out into business credit and commercial real estate lending.

Asset Portfolios. Residential mortgage loans dominate the asset side of the savings and loan business. Exhibit 5–3 shows the combined financial assets and liabilities of both savings and loans, and savings banks (which we will discuss next in this chapter). As

Exhibit 5–3   **Combined Financial Balance Sheet of Savings and Loans and Savings Banks, 1995*** ($ Billions)

Item	Amount	Percentage of Total
Assets:		
Checkable deposits and currency	$ 12.3	1.2%
Reserves held at the Federal Reserve banks	2.5	0.2
Time deposits	1.1	0.1
Federal funds loans and security RPs	8.8	0.9
Corporate equities	11.3	1.1
U.S. government and federal agency securities	187.0	18.4
State and local government (tax-exempt) securities	2.0	0.2
Corporate and foreign bonds	84.9	8.4
Mortgage loans	601.6	59.2
Consumer credit	39.5	3.9
Loans to business firms	11.9	1.2
Purchases of open-market paper	0.1	0.0
Miscellaneous assets	77.9	7.7
Total financial assets	$1,016.7	100.0%
Liabilities:		
Checkable deposits	$ 81.8	8.2%
Small time and savings deposits	583.4	58.3
Large ($100,000 +) time deposits	74.1	7.4
Borrowings through security repurchase agreements	44.6	4.5
Corporate bonds	2.5	0.3
Borrowings from banks (not elsewhere classified)	10.0	1.0
Borrowings from the Federal Home Loan banks	93.8	9.4
Investments by parent companies	4.4	0.4
Taxes payable	1.3	0.1
Miscellaneous liabilities	104.0	10.4
Total liabilities	$1,000.0	100.0%

*Figures are as of the first quarter of 1995.

Source: Board of Governors of the Federal Reserve System, *Flow of Funds Accounts,* selected issues.

revealed in the exhibit, direct mortgage credit (predominantly loans to purchase new homes) account for more than half of all industry assets. But the current era has brought rapid growth in other housing-related investments, such as mortgage-backed securities, mobile home loans, and home equity loans. Mortgage-backed securities include pass-throughs issued by the Government National Mortgage Association, participation certificates (PCs) issued by the Federal Home Loan Mortgage Corporation, and collateralized mortgage obligations (CMOs). Pass-throughs, PCs, and CMOs are investor shares in pools of mortgage loans backed by the issuing government agency or put together by a private lender. CMOs are a little more flexible than other types of mortgage-related securities because they can be found in short, medium, or long maturities, helping S&Ls minimize their risk exposure from changing interest rates and from mortgage loans being paid off too early.

As we will see in Chapter 7, the savings and loan industry was first deregulated in the early 1980s and given broad new service powers, including credit cards and other consumer lending powers, trust services, investments in mutual funds, and the power to invest in riskier corporate and government bonds. Predictably, many S&Ls went overboard, bought too many "junk" bonds, and launched into new services with very little preparation. Hundreds collapsed, so that by the beginning of the 1990s new legislation pushed S&Ls back heavily into the home mortgage market, where they reside today.

Liabilities of S&Ls. Savings deposits provide the bulk of funds available to the savings and loan industry. However, there has been a significant shift in deposit mix in recent years from those savings accounts earning the lowest interest rate to deposits earning higher and more flexible returns. Particularly important among the newer higher-yield savings deposit plans offered by the industry are money market deposit accounts, CDs, NOW and Super NOW accounts, and Keogh and IRA retirement accounts. **Money market deposit accounts (MMDAs)** and Super NOWs were authorized for banks and S&Ls in 1982. Both of these new deposit accounts are draftable by check and carry interest rates that change with market conditions. One unfortunate side effect of these newer deposits is that savings and loans today are faced with a costlier and more volatile deposit base.

Savings and loans also rely on several nondeposit sources of funds to support their loans and investments. One of the most important consists of advances (loans) from the Federal Home Loan Bank System, which provides extra liquidity in periods when deposit withdrawals are heavy or when loan demand exceeds incoming deposits. Another rapidly growing source of funds is securitized assets, when mortgages or other S&L loans are packaged together into a pool of loans (often backed by the guarantee of a government agency), and debt securities are issued against these pooled assets and sold to investors to raise longer-term, lower-cost funds. Thrift institutions are making widespread use of securitized assets, issued against a growing list of home mortgage and consumer installment loans, to supplement their deposit flows and keep funding costs down. Many of these securitized assets are removed from an S&L's balance sheet, which lowers its total assets and improves its ratio of capital to assets, lessening regulatory pressure on the institution to raise more capital.

Another popular nondeposit funds source is *loan sales* — sales of mortgages and other loans to investors in the secondary market. These sales of S&L assets tend to be heaviest in periods when loan demand is high and deposit growth is sluggish, and they give savings and loans the opportunity to invest in new, higher-yielding loans. They also help S&Ls better diversify their assets and avoid an increased regulatory burden (such as demands for more owners' capital). One danger, however, is that S&Ls and other financial institutions will sell their best-quality loans, leaving them with a riskier loan portfolio.

Equity capital or net worth (i.e., the retained earnings and reserves held by individual associations) presently makes up only about 3 to 4 percent of total S&L funds sources but is very important to the public. The net worth account absorbs losses and keeps the doors open until management can correct any problems. Some S&Ls, particularly in those regions of the nation hit hard by an overbuilt real estate market, have a net worth that is close to zero and have relied heavily on continued government support and patience (forbearance) to keep them afloat. As we will see in Chapter 7 on regulation, the U.S. government has taken strong steps in recent years to reduce or eliminate regulatory forbearance and in the early 1990s received the power to close banks and thrifts even if their net worth had not quite reached zero.

Trends in Revenues and Costs

Recently, savings and loans have experienced one of the darkest periods in their long history. Many savings associations remain unprofitable or have very little net worth. Dozens of ailing associations have been helped into mergers by the **Federal Deposit Insurance Corporation (FDIC),** which has purchased sizable amounts of questionable industry assets. The industry's former deposit insurance agency (the FSLIC) went bankrupt during the 1980s, to be replaced at the beginning of the 1990s by the Savings Association Insurance Fund (SAIF) managed by the FDIC. At the same time, Congress moved to authorize agency-assisted mergers in which a troubled S&L could be merged with a stronger association (even one in another state if suitable in-state associations are in short supply) or with another depository institution (such as a commercial bank) through its holding company.

One indication of the industry's problems is the situation regarding its assets, deposits, and net earnings in recent years:

Year	Total Financial Assets of U.S. Savings & Loans at Year-End ($ Billions)	Total Deposits of U.S. Savings & Loans at Year-End ($ Billions)	Net Income After Taxes ($ Millions)
1980	$792	$665	$781
1984	1,180	1,172	1,013
1988	1,641	1,605	−12,057
1990	1,358	1,342	1,800e
1992	1,071	853	5,100e
1994	1,014	734	4,200e
1995	1,030	736	4,720e

e=Estimate for the year indicated.

Source: Board of Governors of the Federal Reserve System, *Flow of Funds Accounts,* selected quarterly issues; and Office of Thrift Supervision.

As the preceding figures suggest, the industry's overall size peaked in 1988 and then began to contract, the result of massive numbers of failures and the conversion of some S&Ls into other kinds of financial institutions (most notably commercial and savings banks). By 1995 S&Ls were earning an average return on equity capital of just over 8 percent and more than 90 percent of the industry was profitable — a much better performance record than in earlier years, but not yet really competitive with most other financial service industries.

What circumstances got the industry into such a troubled state? One cause is the fact that S&Ls historically have issued mortgage loans with fixed interest rates while accepting deposits whose interest rates are sensitive to changing market conditions. In short, *many S&L assets are rate insensitive, while a growing portion of their liabilities are highly rate sensitive.* In periods of rapidly rising interest rates, the industry's net interest

MANAGEMENT INSIGHT:

The Thrifts' Principal Problem: Portfolio Maturity Mismatch

Savings and loan associations, savings banks, and credit unions face a common problem that, at several times in the past, has caused many of them to fail. *The maturities* (and, therefore, the expected streams of future cash payments) *of many of their assets and their liabilities do not match.* In particular, asset maturities are usually considerably longer than the maturities attached to liabilities. For example, the bulk of savings and loans' assets are long-term home mortgage loans, which usually take years to pay out, while the bulk of their liabilities are savings deposits and checking accounts that are often turned into cash by a thrift's depositors in a matter of hours, days, or weeks. This means that thrifts must be prepared to pay out large amounts of cash on short notice. Moreover, the interest costs on their borrowed funds (including interest owed on deposits) tend to change faster, up or down, than the interest revenues from their assets.

If we use what has become conventional terminology when talking about thrift institutions, their volume of *interest-rate-sensitive liabilities (ISL)* (consisting largely of short-term savings and checkable deposits) exceeds their volume of *interest-rate-sensitive assets (ISA)* (such as floating-rate loans or short-term loans about to mature). That is, for most thrift institutions, ISA<ISL.

A liability or an asset is interest sensitive if its rate of return changes with market conditions. For example, a loan carrying a floating interest rate is considered interest sensitive because the lender can change the loan rate in sympathy with changes in market rates of interest and, therefore, keep the lender's expected rate of return from the loan in line with rates of return currently available on newly issued financial instruments. Similarly, a loan or deposit that matures today or within a few days would be considered interest sensitive because, if the customer applies to renew the maturing loan or deposit, its interest rate can then be changed to reflect the latest market conditions. Most deposits are interest sensitive, but most of the thrifts' number one asset — home mortgages — are *not.* This difference in the thrifts' volume of interest-rate-sensitive assets and liabilities is usually called the GAP:

$$GAP = ISA - ISL$$

If the volume of rate-sensitive assets exceeds the volume of rate-sensitive liabilities, the GAP is considered to be *positive.* On the other hand, if rate-sensitive liabilities are larger than the volume of rate-sensitive assets, the GAP is *negative,* which is the usual situation for most thrift institutions.

The GAP concept tells us that a thrift with a negative GAP will lose interest income if interest rates rise. This happens because interest costs attached to the thrifts' rate-sensitive liabilities will move upward faster than the revenues derived from rate-sensitive assets as market interest rates rise. The thrifts' net interest income (i.e., their interest revenues less interest expenses) will fall.

For example, suppose a thrift, which we will call Metro City Savings, reports total assets of $300 million, of which $150 million are rate-sensitive assets, and holds rate-sensitive liabilities totaling $250 million (largely short-term deposits) plus $50 million in non-rate-sensitive liabilities and equity. Thus, its balance sheet looks like this:

(continued)

Metro City Savings and Loan Association

Assets		Liabilities	
Interest-rate-sensitive assets (ISA)	$150 million	Interest-rate-sensitive liabilities (ISL)	$250 million
Non-rate-sensitive assets	$150 million	Non-rate-sensitive liabilities and equity capital	$50 million
Total assets	$300 million	Total liabilities and equity capital	$300 million

Suppose market interest rates are expected to rise by one-half percentage point from 5.50 percent to 6.00 percent. We can determine how much net interest income this thrift institution will lose if interest rates rise by the expected one-half point (0.50 percent) from the formula:

$$\text{Change in Net Interest Income } (\Delta NII) = ISA \cdot E(\Delta i) - ISL \cdot E(\Delta i) = GAP \cdot E(\Delta i)$$

where $E(\Delta i)$ represents the expected change in interest rates. Using the figures given above we see that the expected loss in net interest income for Metro City Savings if interest rates rise by half a percentage point to 6 percent must be:

$$\text{Change in Net Interest Income} = \$150 \text{ million} \cdot (.055 - .06) - \$250 \text{ million} \cdot (.055 - .06)$$

$$= -\$100 \text{ million} \cdot (.005) = -\$0.5 \text{ million or } -\$500,000$$

Clearly, a rise in interest rates of just half a percentage point causes a sizable loss of income for this thrift institution.

We can represent this classic maturity mismatch problem faced by thrift institutions also by means of a diagram like that shown below, which measures the interest rates attached to a thrift's loans and the interest rate it must pay to attract deposits from the public. Deposit rates, like most other short-term interest rates, change rapidly and move over a wide range, rising as the economy expands and inflation increases and falling as the economy slows down or inflation weakens.

The Maturity Mismatch Problem for a Thrift Institution

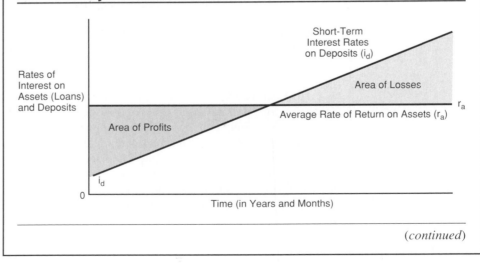

(continued)

The short-term deposit rate (i_d in the diagram) eventually may rise higher than the average interest rate attached to long-term loans and other thrift assets (r_a in the diagram), resulting in a *negative* spread ($r_a - i_d$) between the average rate of return on a thrift's assets and the short-term deposit rate it pays to attract funds. During these periods thrift institutions usually lose money, as their borrowing costs exceed their returns from earning assets. To be sure, the average rate of return on long-term assets also rises somewhat as the economy expands into a period of prosperity and new loans are being made at higher interest rates. However, average loan rates usually do not rise as fast as short-term deposit interest rates because the thrift's portfolio is dominated by long-term loans made in earlier years when interest rates may have been much lower than they are today.

As long as market interest rates remain moderate (and inflation is not rapid), thrift institutions can earn profits due to a positive spread between average returns on their loans and short-term deposit rates. In the later stages of an economic expansion (often a period of rapid inflation and high interest rates), however, a negative spread may develop between loan rates and deposit rates and losses will be sustained until the economy moves on to another phase. During such adverse periods many thrifts will fail or be forced into drastic action (such as a merger with a healthier financial institution).

If the management of a thrift could forecast when short-term interest rates are likely to rise, it might be able to head off big losses by planning ahead and shifting its assets and funds sources appropriately. Due to the difficulties involved in consistently forecasting interest rates, however, most thrifts have adopted interest-rate hedging techniques (such as using financial futures and options) to minimize losses from the risks associated with changing interest rates. We will examine the various interest-rate-hedging tools available to thrifts and other financial institutions in Chapters 12 and 13 of this book.

margin — the difference between its interest earnings on assets and its interest costs on borrowed funds — has been severely squeezed. Indeed, in several recent periods, short-term interest rates paid on deposits exceeded interest rates earned on long-term loans, and the industry's net interest margin turned *negative.*

Other recent trends have also hurt S&L profitability. The individuals and families whose savings provide the bulk of association funds have become more financially sophisticated, withdrawing deposits whenever high returns are available elsewhere or whenever there is even a hint of trouble in the thrift industry. Unquestionably, the savings and loan industry was damaged severely in the 1970s and 1980s by the growth of money market mutual funds — aggressive institutions that offered small savers higher and more flexible yields. At the same time, government rules prevented S&Ls from introducing more flexibility into their investments so their revenues could grow as fast as their rising operating costs.

The pressure of rising costs and the resulting squeeze on earnings and net worth have caused many savings and loans to merge or be absorbed by larger institutions. As a result, the number of associations in the United States has been declining since 1960. The S&L population decreased from about 6,300 in 1960 to only about 1,600 by the 1990s. More savings and loans are likely to be absorbed into larger financial institutions (especially bank holding companies) in the future.

Possible Remedies for the Industry's Problems

If savings and loans are to be viable institutions in the future, they will need help from at least four sources: (1) sound decision making by S&L management to further diversify their activities by geographic areas and by services offered, (2) careful management of the loan portfolio to put good loans on the books and minimize future loan losses, (3) better use of risk management tools (such as financial futures and options), and (4) a further relaxation of government regulations to permit the offering of new services and the merging of smaller associations into larger ones. The classic savings and loan association — investing the bulk of its assets in long-term fixed-rate mortgages and offering relatively low-yielding savings accounts to the public — probably cannot survive in today's volatile economic environment unless it operates in a market with few competitors.

More aggressive S&Ls today are branching out in at least three different directions. Some have followed a *real estate model,* literally becoming mortgage banking firms. These savings associations are selling off their long-term mortgages and converting into real estate service organizations, managing and developing property, and brokering mortgages. Many have become *family financial centers,* offering a full range of retail banking services to the consumer. Home mortgages continue to dominate their asset portfolios, but most S&Ls today offer adjustable-rate mortgages (ARMs), whose yield adjusts more readily to changing market conditions, and a wide variety of other loans. Other S&Ls have adopted a *diversified model,* becoming holding company organizations with ownership and control over retail-oriented consumer banks, mortgage banking firms, and commercial credit affiliates. Only time will tell which of these models can adapt successfully to the changing character of the financial system. One hopeful sign recently has been the return to profitability of many S&Ls that survived the debacle of the 1980s and early 1990s and managed to direct their assets into better-quality investments.

SAVINGS BANKS

Savings banks actually began in Scotland early in the 19th century and then took root in the United States approximately 150 years ago to meet the financial needs of the small saver. These institutions play an active role in the residential mortgage market, as do savings and loans, but are more diversified in their investments, purchasing corporate bonds and common stock, making consumer loans, and investing in commercial mortgages.

In 1982 the U.S. Congress voted to allow savings and loan associations to convert readily into federally chartered savings banks, and savings banks to convert readily into S&Ls if they wished to do so. In 1989 Congress decided to allow S&Ls that qualify to become commercial banks. Recently, substantial numbers of S&Ls have converted to savings banks (along with a more modest number of conversions to commercial bank charters) in an effort to lower their regulatory costs. For this reason, the distinction between savings and loans, savings banks, and commercial banks is becoming very blurred. The public often cannot tell these depository institutions apart.

From their earliest origins, savings banks have designed their financial services to appeal to individuals and families. Deposit accounts can be opened for amounts as small as $1, with transactions carried out by mail or, in many instances, at 24-hour automated tellers in convenient locations. Savings banks in Massachusetts and New Hampshire were the first to develop the interest-bearing and checkable NOW account, perhaps the most important new consumer financial service of the past two decades. Many savings banks advertise the availability of family financial counseling services, home equity loans, and travel planning, as well as a wide variety of savings instruments.

Number and Distribution of Savings Banks

The number of savings banks operating today is small, at around 600. Through most of this century, the savings bank population has been declining. However, the U.S. Congress authorized the chartering of federal savings banks (FSBs) in 1978, which led to an increase in the savings bank population. Unfortunately, many of these institutions failed in the economic dislocations of the late 1980s and early 1990s, particularly in New England, where some savings banks made excessive investments in residential and commercial real estate that subsequently plunged in value.

Savings banks today are scattered throughout the United States, though they are most prominent in the New England and Middle Atlantic states. Massachusetts leads the list, followed by New York. Other states in which savings banks are particularly important include Connecticut, Maine, New Hampshire, New Jersey, Pennsylvania, Rhode Island, Vermont, and Wisconsin.

How Funds Are Raised and Allocated

Technically, savings banks are owned by their depositors. All earnings available after funds are set aside to provide adequate reserves must be paid to the depositors as owners' dividends. The industry's role in the financial system can be seen by looking at its financial balance sheet, which is shown for both savings and loans and savings banks combined in Exhibit 5–3. On the asset side, the key instruments are mortgages and mortgage-related instruments, which account for almost three fifths of the industry's total assets.

Most of the mortgage total represents direct mortgage loans to build single-family homes, apartments, shopping centers, and other commercial and residential structures. The remainder of the mortgage asset total is devoted to mortgage-backed securities, such as Government National Mortgage Association (GNMA) pass-through securities (also known as Ginnie Maes) and similar mortgage-related securities backed by a pool of mortgages.[1]

A distant second in importance to mortgages are savings bank investments in nonmortgage loans (mainly consumer installment credit), corporate bonds, corporate stock, and government bonds. The volume of corporate bonds held by the industry slightly outnumbers its investments in corporate stock, which have been growing rapidly in recent years. Due to the pressures of inflation and higher deposit costs, many states have liberalized their regulations to allow savings banks to make increased purchases of common and preferred stock. Another factor favoring investments in stock has been the industry's growing federal tax burden. Because most of their stock dividend income is exempt from federal taxation, savings banks have taken greater interest in the stock market. State law and tradition, however, limit the growth of savings bank investments in the stock market. Savings banks also make loans for the support of education, to fund home improvements, and to cover household expenses.

The principal source of funds for savings banks is *deposits,* representing about 90 percent of total funds available. Savings deposits have no specific maturity but may be

---

[1]See Chapter 25 for a discussion of GNMA pass-through and other mortgage-related securities.

withdrawn at any time by the customer and they carry the lowest rate of interest. Time deposits, on the other hand, have fixed maturities, and savings banks pay higher interest rates on these deposit accounts, depending on their maturity date.

Industry deposits have grown rapidly over the past three decades, reflecting the ability of savings banks to appeal to the financial needs of individuals and families. The larger savings banks have established extensive branch office systems and have been highly innovative in offering new services. Nearly all savings banks today offer checkable NOW accounts, money orders, loans against savings accounts, and home equity and home improvement loans. Many savings banks also offer life insurance policies to their customers when permitted by state law.

Like savings and loan associations, savings banks have discovered that the customers they serve have become more financially sophisticated in recent years. The highest-yielding deposit accounts have grown much faster than lower-yielding savings plans. The most pronounced shift has been from regular passbook savings accounts to fixed-maturity time deposits and money market accounts that carry contract rates that float with conditions in the money market. The net result of all these changes has been to push interest costs higher, put pressure on savings bank earnings, and increase the volatility of their funds flows. Savings banks today must be more concerned with their liquidity (cash) position than has been true in the past.

Current Trends and Future Problems

The savings bank industry faces a number of problems that will significantly affect its future as a conduit for savings and investment. One factor is increasing competition with savings and loan associations and commercial banks offering similar services. Because of the heavy concentration of savings bank assets in mortgage-related investments, savings banks are less flexible than commercial banks in adjusting to changing financial conditions and to the changing service needs of their customers. Many have severe earnings problems due to inflexible asset structures and numerous bad real estate loans, coupled with higher deposit interest costs. On the other hand, many savings banks have countered this relative inflexibility in their asset structures with aggressive competition for funds and innovative new services. The future growth of this industry, like that of most other financial institutions, will depend heavily on the ability of savings banks to gain the necessary changes in government regulations to allow them to respond to changing financial market conditions.

MONEY MARKET FUNDS

A fourth major nonbank thrift institution appeared on the scene as recently as 1972. In that year, the first **money market mutual fund** — a financial intermediary pooling the savings of thousands of individuals and businesses and investing those monies in short-term, high-quality money market instruments — opened for business. Taking advantage of the fact that interest rates on most deposits offered by commercial and savings banks were then restrained by government regulation, the money fund offered share accounts whose yields reflected prevailing interest rates in the money market. Thus, the money fund represents the classic case of profit-seeking entrepreneurs finding a loophole around ill-conceived government regulations.

MANAGEMENT INSIGHT:

Raising Funds for a Financial Institution

As we have seen in these chapters on financial institutions, different financial institutions rely upon different sources of funds. For banks and thrifts, for example, the principal sources of funds are deposits, money market borrowings, and equity capital provided by their owners; for insurance companies, policyholder premiums usually provide a steady inflow of funds. Whatever the sources of funds a financial institution relies upon, several common problems are faced by *all* financial institutions attempting to raise funds. Each institution must decide which of multiple sources of funds to draw upon, how to measure the cost of those funds, and how to price its services to cover its funding costs.

Among the most important factors the managers of the fund-raising departments of a financial institution must consider are:

1. The relative cost of raising funds from each source.

2. The risk (volatility or dependability) of each fund's source.

3. The length of time (maturity or term) for which a source of funds will be needed.

4. The size and market access of the financial institution attempting to raise funds.

5. Laws and regulations that may limit a financial institution's access to any particular source of funds.

The *relative cost* factor is particularly important because, other factors held equal, a financial institution would prefer to borrow from the cheapest sources of funds available. Moreover, if an institution is to maintain consistent profitability, its cost of fund-raising must somehow be kept below the returns earned on the sales of its services. One common method for assessing a financial institution's costs is called the *pooled-funds approach*. For example, suppose a financial institution plans to draw upon the following funds sources to make new loans and investments:

Sources of New Funds	Volume of New Funds Generated	Interest Costs and Other Expenses Involved in Raising the New Funds
Deposits	$200	$20
Money market borrowings	50	5
Equity capital	50	5
Total new funds raised	$300	Total cost of fund-raising $30

Then the estimated overall cost of funds for this financial institution would be:

$$\text{Pooled fund-raising expense} = \frac{\text{All expected fund-raising costs}}{\text{Total new funds raised}} = \frac{\$30}{\$300} = 0.10 \text{ or } 10 \text{ percent}$$

However, suppose that only $250 of the $300 in funds raised can be used to invest in new loans and investments (earning assets), with the remaining $50 going into the

(continued)

cash account. We can get an estimate of the minimum amount this financial institution must earn on its earning assets (loans and investments) just to cover its cost of raising funds. In this case:

$$\begin{array}{l}\text{Minimum rate of}\\\text{return required on a}\\\text{financial institution's}\\\text{earning assets to}\\\text{cover its fund-}\\\text{raising costs}\end{array} = \frac{\begin{array}{c}\text{All expected}\\\text{fund-raising costs}\end{array}}{\begin{array}{c}\text{Amount of funds}\\\text{available to invest}\\\text{in earning assets}\end{array}} = \frac{\$30}{\$250} = 0.12 \text{ or } 12\%$$

This financial institution will have to earn at least a 12 percent return on its loans, securities, and other earning assets just to cover its fund-raising costs.

In addition to fund-raising costs, financial institutions must weigh the *risk of changing interest rates,* since the interest cost on borrowed funds may change very quickly. A source of funding that carries a low interest rate today may become very expensive the next day. Financial institutions that borrow interest-rate-sensitive funds in large volume must expect considerable volatility in their operating costs and, therefore, in their net earnings. There is also the *risk of funds availability,* because some markets may be closed to a financial institution, especially if it appears to be excessively risky or is simply too small to be able to gain access to a particular funds market. Financial institution managers must also consider the timing and length of a funds need — for example: Will new funds be required immediately or next week? Will the money be needed for just 24 hours or for several days or weeks?

Finally, *laws and regulations* often limit access to or raise the cost of a financial institution's funds sources. For example, banks, savings and loans, and credit unions selling insured deposits must pay an insurance fee to the government to protect their depositors and must set aside a small fraction of each deposit in a cash reserve. These regulations increase the cost of this particular funding source and may make it somewhat less attractive than other funds sources upon which the institution might draw.

The growth of money market funds was explosive. As of year-end 1973, there were only four in existence, with assets totaling just $100 million. Money funds appeared to peak in 1982, when more than 200 of them held over $200 billion in assets (see Exhibit 5–4). Beginning in late 1982 and 1983, a decline in their assets set in as banks and other depository institutions fought back with Super NOWs and Money Market Deposit Accounts (MMDAs), both authorized by the U.S. government in 1982 to carry unregulated interest rates. Subsequently, however, money market funds resumed their rapid growth, making sharp gains late in the 1980s and in the 1990s.

What factors explain the initial rapid growth and continuing viability of this newest nonbank thrift institution? One is the comparative absence of regulatory restrictions. There are no legal interest rate ceilings and, unless the money funds themselves impose it, no mandatory penalties for early withdrawal, as is required by law with many deposit plans offered by banks and thrifts. However, this important advantage of money market funds may be fading. Some of these institutions reached out for riskier, but higher-yielding, issues of commercial paper (i.e., short-term corporate notes) so they could offer higher yields to savers. Unfortunately, massive losses occurred for some of the money funds when, in 1989, Integrated Resources, Inc., failed, defaulting on almost $1 billion in

Exhibit 5–4 | **Money Market Funds: Assets Held and Total Shares Outstanding, 1974–1995** ($ Billions)

Item	1974	1980	1990	1995*
Financial Assets:				
Demand deposits and currency	$—	$ 0.2	$ 11.4	$ −6.7
Time deposits	1.6	21.0	21.0	32.6
Loans made through security RPs	0.1	5.6	59.0	74.0
Foreign deposits	—	6.8	27.1	15.1
U.S. government and federal agency securities	0.1	8.2	82.4	143.6
State and local government (tax-exempt) securities	—	1.9	83.6	116.5
Open-market paper	0.6	31.6	206.7	208.1
Miscellaneous assets	−0.1	1.2	7.3	49.7
Total assets	$2.4	$76.4	$498.4	$632.9
Total shares outstanding	2.4	76.4	498.4	632.9

Note: Columns may not add to totals because of rounding.
*1995 figures are for first quarter of the year.

Source: Board of Governors of the Federal Reserve System, *Flow of Funds Accounts; Financial Assets and Liabilities,* selected issues.

commercial paper. This and other losses on investments in commercial paper led the U.S. Securities and Exchange Commission (SEC) in February 1991 to impose limits on money market fund investments in less than top-quality securities, restricting their investments in lower-quality financial instruments to no more than 5 percent of total assets. No more than 1 percent of a money fund's assets may be placed in securities coming from a single corporate issuer.

Moreover, future money market fund investments were restricted to securities that are rated in one of the two highest rating categories by at least two nationally recognized credit-rating companies (such as Moody's and Standard & Poor's). In the same year, the SEC allowed money funds to reach for somewhat longer maturity financial instruments, allowing them to buy securities with maturities up to 13 months compared to a 12-month maximum under previous rules. However, the SEC reduced the permissible average maturity of a money fund's investment portfolio from a maximum of 120 days to a maximum of only 90 days. In 1996 the SEC tightened restrictions on money funds investing in risky derivative securities to reduce the risk that changing interest rates might threaten a money fund's stability and solvency. These new restrictions were accompanied by widely publicized reminders from the SEC to the general public that savings left with money market funds are *not* protected by federal insurance.

On the whole, however, money market funds hold high-quality assets — primarily U.S. Treasury bills, bank certificates of deposit, bankers' acceptances, commercial paper, and securities issued by federal government agencies[2] — which helps explain why money market funds remain so popular with millions of investors. The interest-bearing securities they acquire generally carry low risk of borrower default and limited fluctuations in price. Contributing to the low-risk character of money fund investments is their short average maturity of only a few weeks or months. The short maturity of fund investments results in a highly liquid security portfolio that can be adjusted quickly to changing market conditions. Many funds declare dividends on a daily basis, crediting their earnings to customer

[2]These various money market securities are discussed in depth in Part Four.

Exhibit 5–5   **Money Market Fund Yields as Reported in The Wall Street Journal**

MONEY MARKET MUTUAL FUNDS

The following quotations, collected by the National Association of Securities Dealers Inc., represent the average of annualized yields and dollar-weighted portfolio maturities ending Wednesday, June 21, 1995. Yields don't include capital gains or losses.

Fund	Mat.	Yld.	Assets	Fund	Mat.	Yld.	Assets	Fund	Mat.	Yld.	Assets	Fund	Mat.	Yld.	Assets
AALMny	47	4.61	76	GrtHallPr	47	5.36	1474	RegisDSI	12	5.48	145	FidCapRsMu	46	3.18	121
AARP HQ	56	4.98	387	Griffin	67	5.65	75	RemTreasTr	31	5.30	106	FidInTxEx	42	3.90	1923
AFD ExRsv A	45	4.81	42	GrdCsFd	15	5.53	361	RemGovtTr	41	5.58	188	FidCA	42	3.35	742
AFD ExResB	45	4.30	69	GrdCsMg	15	5.20	69	RembMMTr	29	5.65	437	FidCT	24	3.45	322
AIM MM C	31	5.00	227	HanvCsh	68	5.53	1186	ResrveFd Gvt	5	5.05	739	FidDlyTE	45	3.44	485
AIM MMA	31	5.02	154	HanvGov	24	5.43	1479	ReserveFd	9	5.13	1677	FidMA	35	3.22	753
AVESTA Tr	84	5.60	57	HanvUSTr	7	5.53	1461	RimcoTrs	67	5.51	86	FidMI	28	3.46	216
AccUSGov	77	5.38	17	HanvTreas	54	5.23	1028	RIMCOPrm	58	5.67	284	FidNJ	61	3.40	427
ActAsGv	72	5.41	559	Harbor	66	5.44	63	RiversdeCap	30	5.21	174	FidNY	43	3.39	737
ActAsMny	72	5.72	5721	HarrisCashA	37	5.57	449	RdSqMM	51	5.62	738	FidOH	71	3.51	277
Advantus a	45	5.14	31	HarrisCashC	37	5.84	142	RdSqUS	36	5.53	331	FidSpCA	40	3.76	1261
AetnaAdvs	49	5.98	56	HTInsgtGv p	49	5.48	296	RshFGI	45	5.03	557	FidSpCT	23	3.51	173
Aetna Sel	49	5.98	229	HtgCshA	43	5.26	1265	Rshmre	13	5.28	21	FidSpNJ	62	3.75	455
AlexBwn	52	5.54	1660	HIMrkUSFld	50	5.30	176	RydexUSGv	1	5.52	276	FidSpNY	42	3.57	604
AlxBTr	46	5.22	558	HIMrkTrsFid	62	5.06	256	SBSF MM	69	5.35	28	FidSpPA	42	3.60	222
AlgerMM	48	5.86	164	HIMrkDvFid	56	5.37	366	SEICshTrea	19	5.92	48	FidTxEx	39	3.57	3606
Aiii TrResv	42	5.10	435	HIlrdGovt	34	5.26	297	SEI CsPrB	42	5.62	23	FidSpFL	47	3.58	355
AlliaCpRs	61	5.14	2939	HmestdDiv	43	5.36	46	SEI CshGvll	35	5.83	837	FidSpMA	38	3.32	426
								SEI CsMM	59	5.98	215	FidSpMu	47	3.77	2217
								SEI CsPr	42	5.92	2240	FtInvTax	34	3.34	23
								SEI DlvInGvC	47	5.38	429	FLMuniCash	50	3.66	131
								SEI LqGv	42	5.61	201	FrkCal	36	3.21	650
								SEI LqPr	44	5.68	985	FrkNYTE	13	3.33	60
								SEI LqTr	27	5.71	1215	FrkTx c	25	3.32	170

Source: *The Wall Street Journal,* Southwest edition, June 22, 1995, C13. Reprinted by permission of *The Wall Street Journal,* © 1995 Dow Jones & Company, Inc. All Rights Reserved Worldwide.

accounts and often notifying the customer by mail monthly of any additional shares purchased with the dividends earned. Most are "no load" funds that do not charge their customers commissions for opening an account, purchasing additional shares, or redeeming shares for cash.

Another outstanding advantage of the money funds for many investors is the ease with which their accounts can be accessed. Most funds allow the customer to write checks to redeem shares, provided the amount of each check exceeds a designated minimum ($500 is common). The customer is issued a book of checks and can write and deposit checks in his or her local bank account, often receiving credit for the deposited check from the local bank the same day, even though it may take several days for the money fund check to be collected. Meantime, daily interest is still being earned on the monies waiting in the customer's share account. Most money funds also offer customers the option of purchasing or redeeming shares by wire or by telephone.

The Wall Street Journal has recently made it easier for money market fund customers to compare the yields and average maturities of different money market funds before reaching a decision on where they want to invest their funds. As Exhibit 5–5 shows, the *Journal* reports daily the average maturity, 7-day yield (assuming no capital gains or losses), and total assets held by each fund. While Exhibit 5–5 shows only selected taxable money funds, *The Wall Street Journal* contains a separate listing of tax-exempt money funds for investors faced with high tax exposure.

Despite their numerous advantages for customers interested in professional management of their short-term funds, money market funds today possess some competitive disadvantages that must be overcome if their rapid growth is to continue. Their share accounts are not government insured, although many of the funds have attempted to deal with this problem by arranging for private insurance or by creating funds invested solely in default-free government securities, which attracted thousands of small investors in the late 1980s and early 1990s as concerns about risk in the banking system mounted. Moreover, the yield differential between posted yields on money market fund share accounts and

MANAGEMENT INSIGHTS:

Managing a Financial Institution's Liquidity Position

Banks, thrifts, and other financial institutions face more serious *liquidity problems* — that is, making sure they have sufficient cash available at reasonable cost to meet all cash demands on time — than almost any other business firm. One reason is that financial institutions rarely can perfectly match the maturities of their assets and the maturities of their liabilities. Therefore, the volume of cash flowing in rarely matches exactly the volume of cash flowing out. Moreover, some of a financial institution's liabilities (such as checkable deposits) are payable immediately upon demand, requiring the outflow of cash with little or no notice. Financial institutions are especially sensitive to interest-rate movements, which affect both the flow of savings they attract from the public and the earnings from the loans and securities they acquire.

Liquidity managers usually meet their institutions' cash needs through two different methods: (a) asset conversion or (b) liability management. *Asset conversion* refers to selling selected assets (preferably those that are closest to cash, such as deposits or government securities) that a financial institution holds in order to cover a pending cash need. Unfortunately, asset conversion results in a financial institution losing future earnings from the assets it must sell. Moreover, conversion requires a financial institution to "store" liquidity in low-yielding assets that can easily be liquidated, generating an *opportunity cost* in the form of reduced earnings. As a result, liquidity managers try to sell those assets carrying the least profit potential.

Liability management, on the other hand, calls for borrowing enough liquidity to cover a financial institution's cash demands as they arise. The borrowing institution simply uses interest rates to bid in the financial marketplace for the cash it needs, and it borrows only as needed. Among the most popular sources of borrowed liquidity are selling deposits, borrowing in the money market, or, in the case of depository institutions, borrowing from the central bank. Most financial institutions today use a combination of asset conversion and liability management, known as a *balanced* liquidity management approach.

How does a liquidity manager estimate a financial institution's future liquidity needs? The *sources and uses of funds* method calls for estimating the sources of liquidity (such as sales of deposits or borrowing in the money market) and the uses of liquidity (such as making loans) over each planning interval. Then the institution's estimated liquidity deficit or surplus equals the estimated change in liquidity sources minus the estimated change in liquidity uses. For example, suppose a bank made the following sources and uses of funds estimates for the next two days:

Planning Interval	Estimated Change In Funds Sources	Estimated Change in Funds Uses	Estimated Liquidity Surplus (+) or Deficit (−)
Tomorrow	+$25 Million	+$20 Million	+$5 Million
The Next Day	−$10 Million	+$10 Million	−$20 Million

Clearly, the bank is expecting a $5 million liquidity surplus tomorrow, because estimated funds sources grow by $5 million more than estimated funds uses (that is, +$25 million − (+$20)million = $5 million). However, it faces a projected $20

(*continued*)

million liquidity deficit the next day, as funds sources are expected to decline and funds uses are projected to rise (that is, − $10 million − (+ $10 million) = −$20 million). The liquidity manager must plan to invest tomorrow's $5 million surplus in an overnight money market loan in order to earn some interest income and then, the next day, must borrow $20 million from some other institution.

The *structure of funds* method, on the other hand, calls for dividing a financial institution's liabilities into categories based on their estimated probability of leaving the institution. For example, some funds received may be "hot money" that are highly sensitive to changing interest rates and could be withdrawn by the customer on a moment's notice. These funds should be covered 90 percent or more with holdings of liquid assets or borrowings because they might disappear within minutes if another financial institution offers the customer a better return. On the other hand, if a financial institution holds substantial "core" funds — highly stable funds from customers who are loyal to the institution — very little liquidity (perhaps 10 percent of the amount of these funds) needs to be held in readiness to back "core" funds. As an example, suppose a financial institution expects to have $60 million in "hot money" and $100 million in loyal "core" funds next week. In addition, it is expecting its customers to demand new loans amounting to $36 million next week. Its estimated need for liquidity would be:

Estimated liquidity need = 0.90 × ["Hot money" funds] + 0.10 × ["core" funds]
+ Estimated new loan demand from customers
= 0.90 × [$60 million] + 0.10 × [$100 million] + $36 million
= $100 million

In this case the liquidity manager would want to check to be sure that $100 million was available in some combination of holdings of liquid assets (i.e., asset conversion) and borrowing capacity (i.e., liability management).

Some financial institutions use *liquidity indicators* to supply them with tell-tale signs that a liquidity problem is developing. Examples of familiar liquidity indicators include the ratio of cash to total assets, the ratio of hot-money assets to hot-money liabilities, or, for a bank, the ratio of its checkable (demand) deposits (which are often unstable) to its time and savings deposits (which are often more stable). Other, market-based liquidity indicators include the stock price of a financial institution and the risk premiums it must pay to attract funds (for example, if the institution must pay higher interest rates to borrow liquidity than other financial institutions of comparable size and location are currently paying).

Liquidity managers of financial institutions must pay special attention to their institutions' largest customers, trying to find out in advance what these biggest customers plan to do with their money (for example, if a large depositor is planning to withdraw his or her deposit any time soon). By knowing ahead of time when the institution's liquidity position is likely to change, the liquidity manager can make a good decision on when and where to raise new cash in order to cover a liquidity deficit or invest wisely the cash made available by a liquidity surplus.

money market deposits at banks has narrowed in recent years. Certainly, the money market funds are not likely to go away; they are a potent competitor for both small individual savings accounts and businesses' liquid funds. However, barring further restrictive federal regulation of bank and thrift deposits, all bank and nonbank thrift institutions, including money market funds, will continue to compete for savings and transaction accounts on relatively equal terms, leading to intense competition and more failures among competing financial institutions.

SUMMARY

Nonbank thrift institutions — credit unions, savings and loans, savings banks, and money market funds — have faced a period of intense turmoil. These institutions began primarily to reach small savers and help these customers achieve home ownership and other personal goals. Over time thrifts have diversified their services and attempted to reach out to many different kinds of financial service customers. For some of these institutions, especially money market funds, there has been rapid growth, while others, especially savings and loans, have experienced slow or even negative growth and many failures. The volatility in funds flows experienced by nonbank thrifts in recent years may be accentuated in the years ahead by another powerful force: competition. An intense competitive battle for savings deposits, transaction accounts, and consumer loans is now under way between commercial banks, nonbank thrifts, and other financial service providers in thousands of local markets around the world.

This fierce competitive battle is not likely to end in the near future; in fact, it should intensify as electronic systems are developed further for the automated transfer of funds. Savings and loans, savings banks, credit unions, and money market funds are determined to be a part of the growing "electronic money" network that moves funds almost instantly at relatively low cost. Continuing innovation in new electronic delivery systems should open up markets for a wide variety of new consumer-oriented financial services necessary for the thrifts' future survival.

Moreover, the thrift industry will continue its ongoing trend toward consolidation — smaller numbers of, but larger, thrifts — well into the next century. Thus, there will be less need for thousands of small financial intermediaries, especially for specialized thrifts that can offer only the most basic savings and credit services. Surviving thrift institutions will have to be larger firms that are strongly capitalized, with effective expense-control programs that stress efficiency in operations, skill in hedging against various operating risks, and innovation in developing and introducing new services. ■

KEY TERMS AND CONCEPTS IN THIS CHAPTER

credit unions

share drafts

savings and loans

mutuals

money market deposit accounts (MMDAs)

Federal Deposit Insurance Corporation (FDIC)

savings banks

money market mutual funds

STUDY QUESTIONS

1. Credit unions are one of the fastest-growing financial intermediaries in the United States. What factors have contributed to this rapid growth?

2. What are the principal differences between savings and loan associations and savings banks? How are these institutions similar to each other?

3. How and why did money market funds begin in the 1970s? What factors have contributed to their rapid growth?

4. Competition between commercial banks, credit unions, savings banks, money market funds, and savings and loan associations is increasing rapidly, especially in the markets for savings deposits, payments accounts, and consumer credit. Explain the reasons for this trend toward increasing competition. What are the probable consequences for the consumer?

5. Why is the savings and loan industry in trouble? What solutions have been offered to deal with its problems?

PROBLEMS

1. Westfield Savings Association holds $56 million in interest-rate-sensitive assets and $135 million in interest-rate-sensitive deposits and other liabilities. If its non-rate-sensitive liabilities and equity capital total $62 million, what is Westfield's total volume of non-rate-sensitive assets? What is the size of Westfield's interest-sensitive GAP? Please calculate the ratio of ISA to ISL for this savings institution.

   If market interest rates *rise* from 6 percent to 6.25 percent, how much net interest income will Westfield lose? What would you recommend that this thrift's management do? What will happen to this thrift's net interest income if market rates *decline* from 6 percent to 5.75 percent?

2. Sunset Savings Bank holds $1,370 million in total assets, and its equity capital currently amounts to $124 million. Sunset's non-rate-sensitive liabilities currently stand at $196 million, while its non-rate-sensitive assets total $282 million. How large is Sunset's interest-sensitive GAP? Market interest rates are expected to increase from their current average level of about 7.30 percent to 7.75 percent. Will Sunset Savings lose net interest income if interest rates rise as expected? What will be the magnitude of its loss, if any? Suppose interest rates decline, rather than increase, to 7 percent from 7.30 percent. What will happen to Sunset Savings' net interest income in this instance?

3. Axtell Credit Union elects to draw upon the following new sources of funds to support the $40 million in new automobile loan requests it is expecting from its customers next week:

Expected Sources of New Funds	Interest and Noninterest Costs Incurred in Raising New Funds ($ million)	Amount of New Funds Raised ($ million)
Member share-draft deposits	$0.6	$10
Member savings deposits	1.4	20
Member time deposits	1.6	20

   If only 80 percent of the total of new funds raised will actually be available for making new auto loans, what is the minimum rate of return Axtell must earn in order to at least break even on these new loans?

4. A thrift institution's liquidity manager estimates that funds sources will grow by $85 million in the coming week, while the thrift's funds uses will increase by $104 million. The following week the thrift's funds sources are expected to increase by $112 million and its funds uses will grow a projected $68 million. What liquidity deficits or surpluses will the thrift face? What must the liquidity manager be prepared to do? What sources of liquidity might the manager draw upon?

5. Exeter National Bank reports that its total "core" funds currently stand at $836 million, while its current holdings of "hot money" total $297 million. Loan demand during the coming month is expected to rise by $540 million. If the bank's liquidity manager decides

to hold a reserve plus additional borrowing capacity equal to 85 percent of the bank's "hot money" holdings and 20 percent of its "core" funds, what is the bank's total estimated liquidity need? Do you have any recommendations on how management should respond to this liquidity need?

SELECTED REFERENCES

Aguilar, Linda. "Still Toe-to-Toe: Banks and Nonbanks at the End of the 80's." *Economic Perspectives.* Federal Reserve Bank of Chicago (January–February 1990), pp. 12–23.

Osterberg, William P., and James B. Thomson. "SAIF Policy Options." *Economic Commentary.* Federal Reserve Bank of Cleveland, June 1995.

Pavel, Christine, and Harvey Rosenblum. "Banks and Nonbanks: The Horse Race Continues." *Economic Perspectives.* Federal Reserve Bank of Chicago (May–June 1985), pp. 3–17.

Chapter 6

Insurance Companies, Pension Funds, and Other Financial Institutions

LEARNING OBJECTIVES IN THIS CHAPTER

- To examine the roles played and the financial services offered by a variety of financial institutions ranging from life and property-casualty insurance companies to pension funds, finance companies, security dealers, mortgage banks, and investment companies.
- To explore the principal sources of funds and principal uses of funds for these financial institutions.
- To understand the problems faced by financial institutions operating in the money and capital markets today.

W e now turn to a highly diverse group of financial institutions that attract savings mainly from individuals and families and, for the most part, make long-term loans in the capital market. Included in this group are life insurance companies, pension funds, and property-casualty insurance companies, which today are leading institutional buyers of bonds and stocks. Finance companies, another member of the group, are active lenders to both business firms and consumers and borrow heavily in the money market. As we will soon see, the majority of these financial institutions provide important services to participants in the markets for both business and consumer credit.

LIFE INSURANCE COMPANIES

Life insurance companies have been operating for centuries in Europe and were one of the first financial institutions founded in the American colonies. The Corporation for Relief of Poor and Distressed Presbyterian Ministers, established in 1759, was the first life insur-

Exhibit 6–1   **Life Insurance in Force in the United States, 1983 and 1993**
($ Billions)

Category	1983	1993
Total Amount:		
Ordinary	$ 2,544	$ 6,428
Group	2,220	4,456
Industrial	31	20
Credit	171	200
	$ 4,966	$ 11,105
Average Amount:		
Per family	$56,300	$111,600
Per insured family	69,500	143,100

Note: Columns may not add to totals due to rounding.

Source: American Council of Life Insurance, *1994 Life Insurance Fact Book* (Washington, D.C., 1994).

ance company in the United States. Life insurance companies offer their customers a hedge against the risk of earnings losses that often follow death, disability, or retirement. Policy holders receive risk protection in return for the payment of policy premiums that are set high enough to cover estimated benefit claims against the company, all operating expenses, and a target profit margin. Additional funds to cover claims and expenses are provided by the earnings from investments made by life insurance companies in bonds, stocks, mortgages, and other assets approved by law and government regulation. Figures on the volume of insurance in force in the United States are shown in Exhibit 6–1, and the principal kinds of insurance policies sold by U.S. life insurers are listed in Exhibit 6–2.

The Insurance Principle

The insurance business is founded upon the *law of large numbers*. This mathematical principle states that a risk that is not predictable for one person can be forecast accurately for a sufficiently large group of people with similar characteristics. No insurance company can accurately forecast when any one person will die, but its actuarial estimates of the total number of policy holders who will die in any given year are usually quite accurate.

Life insurance companies today insure policy holders against three basic kinds of risk: premature death, the danger of living too long and outlasting one's accumulated assets, and serious illness or accident. Many policies combine financial protection against death, disability, and retirement with savings plans to help the policy holder prepare for some important future financial need, such as the purchase of a home or meeting the costs of a college education. Actually, most benefit payments are made to living, rather than deceased, policy holders, who receive annuities, disability checks, and other health insurance benefits. Life insurance companies are among the leading sources of retirement (pension) benefit payments for older citizens, and today more than 50 million U.S. citizens are enrolled in pension programs managed by life insurers.

Investments of Life Insurance Companies

Life insurers invest the bulk of their funds in long-term securities such as bonds, stocks, and mortgages, thus helping to fund real capital investment by businesses and governments. They are inclined to commit their funds long term due to the high predictability of

Exhibit 6–2   **The Principal Kinds of Insurance Policies Sold by Life Insurance Companies**

Ordinary or whole life insurance	Insurance protection that covers the entire lifetime of the policy holder whose designated beneficiaries are paid when the policy holder dies. Premiums build up cash values that may be borrowed by the policy holder.
Term life insurance	Insurance coverage for a certain number of years so that the policy holder's beneficiaries receive benefit payments only if death occurs within the period of coverage.
Endowment policy	A policy with benefits payable to the living policy holder on a specified future date or to the policy holder's beneficiaries if death occurs before the date specified in the policy.
Group life insurance	Master insurance policy covering a group of people, usually all working for the same employer or members of the same organization.
Industrial life insurance	Small-denomination life policies with premium payments collected monthly or weekly by a company agent calling at the insured's residence.
Universal life insurance	Insurance protection with premium payments whose amount and timing can be changed by the policy holder and including a savings account with a flexible rate of return.
Variable life insurance	Insurance protection whose benefits vary in amount with the value of assets pledged behind the policy contract.
Adjustable life insurance	A flexible form of insurance protection that permits the policy holder to alter some of the policy's terms, period of coverage, or face value.
Credit life insurance	A policy pledged to pay off a loan in the event the borrower dies or becomes disabled before the debt is retired.

their cash inflows and outflows. This predictability normally would permit a life insurance company to accept considerable risk in the securities it acquires. However, both law and tradition require a life insurer to act as a "prudent person." This restriction is imposed to ensure that sufficient funds are available to meet all legitimate claims from policy holders or their beneficiaries at precisely the time those claims mature.

Life insurance companies generally pursue *income certainty* and *safety of principal* in their investments. The majority of corporate securities they purchase are in the top four credit-rating categories.[1] Life insurers frequently follow a "buy and hold" strategy, acting as long-term holders of securities rather than rapidly turning over their portfolios. This investment approach reduces the risk of fluctuations in income and avoids having to rely on forecasting interest rates. We should note, however, that in recent years some life insurers have become more active traders in securities. Emphasizing performance more than permanence in their investments, larger life insurance companies have set up trading rooms to more closely monitor the performance of their investment holdings, selling out and reinvesting in higher yielding alternatives when circumstances warrant. Because this new investment strategy creates additional risk, some larger insurers now use financial futures contracts and other risk-hedging tools and more closely match asset and liability maturities to protect themselves against losses from fluctuating interest rates.[2]

Exhibits 6–3 and 6–4 show the kinds of investments held by U.S. life insurance companies in the early 1990s. The primary investment is in *corporate bonds* issued by both domestic and foreign companies. Several companies have run into trouble recently from heavy purchases of high-risk ("junk") corporate bonds as well as poorly performing real estate investments. In

---

[1]See Chapter 11 for an explanation of security ratings.

[2]See Chapters 12 and 13 for a detailed discussion of various interest rate hedging methods.

Exhibit 6–3   **Financial Assets and Liabilities of Life Insurance Companies, 1995***

Asset and Liability Items	Amount ($ Billions)	Percent of Total
Assets:		
Checkable deposits and currency	$ 5.3	0.3%
Shares held in money market funds	46.3	2.4
Shares held in mutual funds (investment companies)	144.4	7.5
Corporate stock (equities)	141.7	7.4
U.S. Treasury securities	121.0	6.3
Federal agency securities	235.2	12.3
State and local government (tax-exempt) securities	17.0	0.9
Corporate and foreign bonds	785.6	40.9
Mortgage loans	212.7	11.1
Open-market paper	13.4	0.7
Loans to policyholders	85.4	4.5
Miscellaneous assets	110.8	5.8
Total assets	$1,918.9	100.0%
Liabilities:		
Life insurance reserves	$ 484.0	26.6%
Pension fund reserves	1,146.9	63.0
Borrowings from the Federal Home Loan banks	0.6	0.0**
Taxes payable	1.3	0.1
Miscellaneous liabilities	188.3	10.3
Total liabilities	$1,821.1	100.0%

Note: Columns may not add to totals due to rounding.
*Figures as of the end of the first quarter of 1995.
**Less than 0.05 percent.

Source: Board of Governors of the Federal Reserve System, *Flow of Funds Accounts: Flows and Outstandings,* First Quarter 1995.

1991, Mutual Benefit Life Insurance Company and Executive Life Insurance Company were taken over by state regulators, both firms among the largest U.S. insurers ever to fail. Several state regulators have restricted further purchases of junk bonds. Holdings of common and preferred stock, although smaller, have become significant in recent years. Life insurance companies have shown renewed interest in corporate stock due to the growing importance of variable annuity and variable life insurance policies in their sales programs.

Another important asset held by life insurance companies is *mortgage loans* on farm, residential, and commercial properties. Substantial changes have occurred in life insurer mortgage investments in recent years. The industry has reduced its holdings of farm and residential mortgages on one- to four-family homes and increased its holdings of commercial mortgages, including loans on retail stores, shopping centers, office buildings, apartments, hospitals, and factories. The higher yields and shorter maturities of the latter loans explain much of the recent growth of commercial mortgage lending by the life insurance industry.[3] However, life insurers continue to provide indirect support to the residential

---

[3]In granting mortgage credit, life insurance companies often employ *advance commitments.* These consist of promises to provide long-term mortgage funds to a real estate developer before a residential or commercial construction project begins. The developer will use that financing commitment as an aid in obtaining short-term cash (usually from banks) to complete construction. Later, when the project is completed, the insurance company will loan the funds promised, and the proceeds of the long-term loan will be used to repay any short-term borrowings. Advance commitments are less common today than in the past due to the impact of inflation and volatile interest rates.

Exhibit 6–4   **Total Assets of U.S. Life Insurance Companies, 1993**

Item	Dollar Amount ($ Billions)	Percent of Total Assets
Government securities:		
U.S. Treasury obligations	$ 88.5	
Federal agency securities	203.4	
State and local debt obligations	14.4	
Debt of foreign governments and international agencies	33.5	
Total government securities	$ 339.8	19.5%
Corporate securities:		
Bonds and notes	681.2	
Common stocks	241.2	
Preferred stocks	10.7	
Total corporate securities	$ 933.1	53.4
Mortgages:		
Farm	$ 9.5	
Nonfarm	219.6	
Total mortgages	$ 229.1	13.1
Loans to policy holders	77.7	4.4
Real estate owned	54.2	3.1
Miscellaneous assets	112.4	6.4
Total assets	$1,746.3	100.0%

Note: Columns may not add to totals due to rounding.

Source: American Council of Life Insurance, *1994 Life Insurance Fact Book* (Washington, D.C., 1994).

mortgage market by making heavy purchases of federal agency securities, most of which come from government agencies aiding the home mortgage market.

Government securities play a secondary but still important role in the portfolios of life insurance companies. These securities serve the important function of providing a reservoir of *liquidity* because they may be sold with little difficulty when funds are required. Recently, investments in government securities have been rising as industry cash flows have become more volatile, increasing demands for liquid reserves. U.S. life insurers buy mostly federal government securities rather than state and local government obligations. The industry has only a limited need for the tax-exempt income provided by state and local bonds because its tax rate is relatively low.

One asset whose importance increased dramatically during the 1970s and early 1980s is *loans to policy holders*. The holder of an ordinary (whole life) insurance policy can borrow against the accumulated cash value of that policy, which increases each year. The interest rate on policy loans is stated in the policy contract and in some policies is quite low. Policy loans tend to follow the business cycle, rising in periods when economic activity and interest rates are increasing, and declining when the economy or interest rates are headed down. Because of this cyclical characteristic, policy loans are a volatile claim on the industry's resources. When policy loan demand is high, life insurance companies frequently are forced to reduce their purchases of bonds and stocks. In recent years, however, most new whole life policies have had floating loan rates tied to an index of corporate bond yields, and policy holder borrowing has declined relative to other industry assets.

Sources of Life Insurance Company Funds

The primary income source for life insurers comes from premium receipts from sales of insurance policies. Premiums from sales of annuity plans and health insurance policies have actually grown faster than sales of traditional life insurance policies. Annual net income from investments in bonds, stocks, and other assets averages only about a third of premium receipts. The industry's net earnings after expenses roughly equal its investment income each year, because virtually all premiums from the sale of policies are ultimately returned to policy holders or their beneficiaries. This means that, on balance, the industry hopes to break even from its insurance underwriting operations (with premiums flowing in balanced by benefits paid out) while earning profits from its investment income.

Structure and Growth of the Life Insurance Industry

The majority (more than 90 percent) of the more than 1800 U.S. life insurance companies are corporations owned by their stockholders. The rest are *mutuals*, which issue ownership shares to their policy holders. However, mutuals are much bigger, on average, typically were established much earlier than stockholder-owned companies, and hold almost 40 percent of the industry's assets. Most new insurance companies in recent years have been stockholder owned, and a few mutuals have converted to *stock* companies to gain greater financial flexibility and open up new sources of capital.

Many new life insurance companies were formed in the 1970s and 1980s to meet special local insurance needs, leaving older and larger companies to cover the national and international market for insurance. At the same time a substantial number of foreign companies, such as Britain's Royal Insurance, have been buying out some U.S. companies, as millions of Americans from the post–World War II baby boom have now reached middle age, the time at which most life insurance and retirement plan purchases are made. As the 1990s began, however, there were signs of a *consolidation* trend in the industry, with larger companies absorbing smaller ones. Life insurers have been forced by deregulation and the appearance of new competitors to offer market-sensitive rates of return to customers on most of their services, which has reduced profits and driven out smaller and less-efficient firms. The U.S. life insurance industry's population reached a high of almost 2,350 in 1988 and has been falling since that time.

New Services

Life insurers are under increasing pressure to develop new services due to a long-term decline in their share of household savings and pressure on their earnings caused by new high-cost, more automated service delivery systems. Many analysts argue that life insurance is becoming less attractive as a product as the population ages, while retirement planning and retirement savings instruments are likely to grow in importance. Increasing competition from other financial intermediaries has also played a major role in encouraging the development of new services. Among the most important recent developments are the creation of separate accounts and the offering of such innovative services as universal and adjustable life insurance, variable premium and variable life insurance, mutual funds, tax shelters, venture capital loans, corporate cash management systems, and deferred annuities.

A *separate account* is a portfolio of assets that a life insurance company holds on behalf of one of its customers (usually a pension fund) and is kept apart from its other assets. Separate accounts have enabled life companies to compete successfully for the growing volume of pension savings from an aging population. Funds stored in these accounts are subject to more liberal investment rules, permitting a larger portion of these monies to be placed in common stock and other riskier investments.

Begun in 1979, *universal life insurance* allows the customer to change the face amount of his or her policy and the size and timing of premium payments, as well as earn higher investment returns from any premiums paid in. Premium payments on a universal life insurance policy usually are invested in a money market fund. Another example of the newer and more flexible life insurance products emerging in recent years is *adjustable life insurance*, which permits the policy holder to change periodically from a whole life policy to term insurance (which offers protection only for a designated period) and back again to deal with changing circumstances. Adjustable policies allow the policy holder to increase or decrease the face value of a policy, the period of insurance protection, and the size of premium payments within limits spelled out in the policy contract. A variation of this idea is *variable premium life insurance*, which grants the policy holder lower premium payments when investments made by the life insurer earn a greater return. *Variable life insurance* pays benefits according to the value of assets pledged behind the policy rather than paying a fixed amount of money. There is normally a guaranteed minimum benefit for the policy holder's beneficiary, however. It is a form of inflation-hedged life insurance now authorized all over the United States.

Life insurers have also been active in loans to help start new businesses and in offering professional funds management services to many businesses that have neither the time nor the experience to manage their own cash accounts. These insurers have also found success in attracting *deferred annuity* accounts in which an individual will deposit funds with the insurer under an agreement to receive a future stream of income flowing from those deposited funds beginning on a stipulated future date. The insurer agrees to invest the funds in earning assets that will grow over time and escape any taxation until the customer actually begins receiving income.

In recent years, insurance companies have found a way to supplement their cash inflows from insurance premiums by selling *guaranteed investment contracts* (GICs) to large institutional investors such as pension funds and state and local governments. Similar to deposits, GICs promise investors a fixed rate of return for a stipulated period. Many corporations and governmental units that have sold bonds in the open market have in turn purchased GICs with the proceeds of those bond issues. These instruments have increased insurance company risk because of their relatively high fixed cost in an era of volatile interest rates.

One area of growing insurance needs is coverage for small businesses. New businesses are being formed today in record numbers, with more than 30 million uninsured persons currently working for them in the United States alone. The provision of life and health insurance for owners and employees of small firms has become a promising service area for those insurers able to correctly price the coverages they provide. Another area of need for the future is health and life insurance for individuals, such as retired citizens, who are no longer members of group insurance plans. Without question, the new services offered by life insurers in future years will depend heavily upon favorable changes in government laws and regulations. One prominent example is the possibility of expanded entry into Japan and China, two of the largest insurance and pension plan markets in the world, but this opportunity is heavily dependent upon the willingness of the Japanese and Chinese governments to let more foreign financial firms come in. Life insurers must also find lower-cost ways to market and deliver their services, such as increased use of automation, more skilled investment professionals, and joint-venture sales of policies through banks and stockbrokers. Correspondingly, the industry recently has made major cuts in its traditional vehicle for the delivery of its services — local insurance agencies.

MANAGEMENT INSIGHT:

How the Premiums Charged by Insurance Companies Are Computed

When insurance companies agree to provide risk protection services to their customers, how do they decide how much to charge policy holders?

Let's consider an example from the life insurance industry. Suppose a life insurer has 100,000 policy holders who are each 40 years of age. Each customer has requested a $1 million life insurance policy. The company must set an annual premium rate to charge these customers so it will have sufficient cash to pay off the beneficiaries of any customers who die this year.

The first thing the insurer must do is to determine the expected number of deaths from the group of 100,000 policy holders this year. Actuarial science has produced mortality tables that predict how many individuals of any age are expected to die each year out of every 1,000 persons. Let's say the expected death rate for 40-year olds is 4 per 1,000. Then the expected number of deaths in the coming year from this group of 100,000 policy holders is

$$\begin{matrix} \text{Expected} \\ \text{deaths} \end{matrix} = \begin{matrix} \text{Number of} \\ \text{policy} \\ \text{holders in} \\ \text{age group} \end{matrix} \times \begin{matrix} \text{Expected} \\ \text{mortality} \\ \text{rate} \end{matrix} = \begin{matrix} 100 \\ \text{thousand} \end{matrix} \times \begin{matrix} 4 \text{ per} \\ \text{thousand} \end{matrix} = \begin{matrix} 400 \\ \text{deaths} \\ \text{expected} \end{matrix}$$

If each policy holder has a $1 million dollar policy, the insurance company must prepare for expected claims of:

$$\begin{matrix} \text{Expected} \\ \text{claims} \end{matrix} = \begin{matrix} \text{Expected} \\ \text{deaths} \end{matrix} \times \begin{matrix} \text{Policy} \\ \text{amounts} \\ \text{promised} \end{matrix} = 400 \times \$1 \text{ million} = \$400 \text{ million}$$

How much should the insurance company charge each policy holder in premiums? Suppose the 400 deaths expected will occur toward the end of this year. We want to determine how much to charge all policy holders at the beginning of this year to be ready for $400 million in claims near year's end. We need to estimate how much the insurance company will earn when it invests the premiums paid by its policy holders in stocks, bonds, and other financial assets. Let's suppose the company's analysts have estimated it will earn an average of 8 percent on its portfolio of investments in the coming year. Thus, to have $400 million available at year's end, the company needs the following amount from its policy holders at the beginning of the policy period:

$$\begin{matrix} \text{Present value} \\ \text{of expected} \\ \text{claims} \end{matrix} = \left[\frac{\begin{matrix} \text{Dollar volume of} \\ \text{expected claims} \end{matrix}}{\begin{matrix} \text{Expected} \\ \text{1+ investment} \\ \text{rate of return} \end{matrix}} \right]^t = \frac{\$400 \text{ million}}{[1+0.08]^t} = \$370.4 \text{ million}$$

If all policy holders fall in the same risk class, the *pure* or *net premium* to charge each policy holder would be

(continued)

$$\begin{array}{l}\text{Estimated net} \\ \text{premium per} \\ \text{policy holder}\end{array} = \dfrac{\begin{array}{c}\text{Present value} \\ \text{of claims expected}\end{array}}{\begin{array}{c}\text{number of policy} \\ \text{holders}\end{array}} = \dfrac{\$370.4 \text{ million}}{100,000} = \begin{array}{l}\$3704 \text{ per} \\ \text{policyholder.}\end{array}$$

However, this calculation does not include the insurer's operating costs (salaries of sales personnel, etc.), including the need to earn a normal profit for the company's stockholders. Suppose it will cost $2.6 million to service the insurance needs of these 100,000 policy holders this year. This cost is called the *loading*, which must be added to the net premium to drive the *gross premium* charged policy holders:

$$\begin{array}{l}\text{Gross} \\ \text{premium}\end{array} = \dfrac{\begin{array}{c}\text{Present value} \\ \text{of claims} \\ \text{expected}\end{array} + \begin{array}{c}\text{Total} \\ \text{operating} \\ \text{costs}\end{array}}{\text{number of policy holders}} = \dfrac{\$370.4 \text{ million} + \$2.6 \text{ million}}{100,000}$$

$$= \dfrac{\$373 \text{ million}}{100,000} = \begin{array}{l}\$3730 \text{ per} \\ \text{policy holder}\end{array}$$

The insurance premium rates actually charged are also shaped by competition, which tends to hold premium rates down and encourages insurance companies to be more efficient in controlling their operating costs.

PROPERTY-CASUALTY INSURANCE COMPANIES

Property-casualty (P/C) insurers offer protection against fire, theft, bad weather, negligence, and other acts and events that result in injury to persons or property. So broad is the range of risk for which these companies provide protection that P/C insurers are sometimes referred to as *insurance supermarkets*. In addition to their traditional insurance lines — automobile, fire, marine, personal liability, and property coverage — many of these firms have branched into the health and medical insurance fields, clashing head-on with life insurers offering the same services. (See Exhibit 6–5 for a list of the major types of policies written by P/C insurers.)

Makeup of the Property-Casualty (P/C) Insurance Industry

The property-casualty insurance business has grown rapidly in recent years due to the effects of inflation, rising crime rates, and an increasing number of lawsuits arising from product liability and professional negligence claims. There were about 3,900 P/C companies in the United States in 1992, holding more than $600 billion in total assets. Stockholder-owned companies are dominant, holding about three fourths of the industry's total resources. Mutual companies — owned by their policy holders — command roughly one fourth of all industry resources.

Changing Risk Patterns in Property/Liability Coverage

Property-casualty insurance is a riskier business than life insurance. The risk of policy holder claims arising from crime, fire, personal negligence, and similar causes is much less predictable than is the risk of death. Inflation has had a potent impact on the cost of

Exhibit 6–5   **Principal Lines of Insurance Coverage Provided by U.S. Property-Casualty (P/C) Companies, 1991** ($ Millions)

Insurance Lines	Net Premiums Written by U.S. P/C Companies*	Insurance Lines	Net Premiums Written by U.S. P/C Companies*
Auto liability	$63,318	Accident and health	$5,147
Auto physical damage	35,999	Inland marine	4,317
Medical malpractice	4,068	Ocean marine	1,165
Other nonauto liability insurance	16,851	Surety and fidelity	2,790
Fire insurance and allied lines†	7,189	Boilers and machinery	656
Homeowners' multiple peril insurance	19,303	Aircraft insurance	437
Commercial multiple peril insurance	17,032	Burglary and theft	105
Farmowners' multiple peril insurance	1,036	Glass insurance	18
Workers compensation	31,258	Financial guaranty coverage	690
Other property-casualty insurance lines	11,612		

*Net premiums written represent premium income earned by insurance companies, direct or through reinsurance, less payments made for business reinsurance.
†Allied lines include crop-hail insurance premiums

Source: Insurance Information Institute, *The Fact Book 1993* (New York City, 1993).

property and services for which this form of insurance pays. For example, the cost of medical care and repair of automobiles has more than doubled over the past decade.

Equally important, basic changes now seem to be under way in the risk patterns of many large insurance programs, creating problems in forecasting policy holder claims and in setting new premium rates. Examples include a rapid rise in medical malpractice suits; a virtual explosion in product liability claims against manufacturers of automobiles, home appliances, and other goods; and the emergence of billions of dollars in claims from so-called *toxic torts*, arising from individuals suffering from illness or injury caused by exposure to asbestos, nuclear radiation, and other hazardous substances. To reduce risk, more P/C insurers have become *multiple-line companies*, diversifying into many different lines of insurance. Another risk-reducing device of growing importance is the *reinsurance* market, in which an insurer contracts with other companies to share some of the risks of its insurance underwriting in return for a share of the insurer's premium income.

It is interesting to compare the distribution of assets held by life insurance companies and by P/C companies. The net cash flows of the two industries — their annual premium income — are roughly comparable. Yet life insurers hold about three times the assets of P/C insurers. Much of the difference is explained by the fact that life insurance is a highly predictable business, whereas property and personal injury risks are not. Most life insurance policies are long-term contracts, and claims against the insurer are not normally expected for several years. In contrast, P/C claims are payable from the day a policy is written because an accident or injury may occur at any time. Therefore, although life insurers can stay almost fully invested, P/C insurers must be ready at all times to meet the claims of their policy holders. In addition, claims against P/C companies are directly affected by inflation, which drives up repair costs. Most life insurance policies, in contrast, pay the policy holder or beneficiary a fixed sum of money.

Investments by Property-Casualty (P/C) Companies

The majority of funds received by P/C companies are invested in state and local government bonds and common stock. P/C insurers, unlike most financial institutions, are subject to the full federal corporate income tax rate (except that policy holder dividends are tax deductible

Exhibit 6–6   **Financial Assets and Liabilities of U.S. Property-Casualty Insurance Companies, 1995***

Asset and Liability Items	Dollar Amounts ($ Billions)	Percent of Total Assets or Liabilities
Checkable deposits and currency	$5.2	0.8%
Security repurchase agreements	36.3	5.3
Corporate stock (equities)	115.7	16.8
U.S. Treasury securities	138.0	20.1
Federal agency securities	46.7	6.8
State and local government (tax-exempt) securities	154.0	22.4
Corporate and foreign bonds	104.6	15.2
Commercial mortgages	3.7	0.5
Trade credit	51.9	7.6
Miscellaneous assets	30.8	4.5
Total financial assets	686.4	100.0%
Taxes payable	1.3	0.3
Miscellaneous liabilities	482.6	99.7
Total liabilities	$484.0	100.0%

Note: Columns may not add to totals due to rounding.
*Data for through the first quarter of 1995.

Source: Board of Governors of the Federal Reserve System, *Flow of Funds Accounts: Flows and Outstandings*, First Quarter 1995.

for the issuing company). Faced with a potentially heavy tax burden, these companies find tax-exempt state and local government bonds an attractive investment. As shown in Exhibit 6–6, industry holdings of state and local bonds represented almost a quarter of its total financial assets, although property-casualty insurers have placed less emphasis on purchases of municipal bonds in recent years, due in part to their sluggish earnings and recent changes in tax laws. Another important asset — corporate stock — is intended to protect industry earnings and net worth against inflation. Other significant investments include U.S. government securities, federal agency securities, and corporate bonds. P/C insurers have stepped up their purchases of federal government securities and corporate bonds in recent years due to their higher yields and, in the case of government bonds, their greater safety and liquidity.

Sources of Income

Like life insurance firms, P/C insurers plan to break even on their insurance product lines and earn most of their net return from their investments. Achieving the break-even point in insurance underwriting has been difficult in recent years, however, due to rising costs, increased litigation, and new forms of risk. For example, in 1991 the industry ran a net underwriting loss of almost $20 billion. It was the ninth consecutive year of record underwriting losses. While investment income usually offsets underwriting losses, industry profits are highly volatile from year to year due to unexpected losses and to the refusal of many state insurance commissions to adjust premiums as fast as industry expenses change.

Business Cycles, Inflation, and Competition

Property-casualty insurance is an industry whose earnings and sales revenue reflect the ups and downs of the business cycle. This cyclical sensitivity, coupled with the vulnerability of P/C insurers to inflation, has created a difficult environment for insurance managers. Inflation has pushed up the cost of claims, while intense competition has held premium rates

INTERNATIONAL FOCUS:
The Troubled Lloyds of London

One of the best examples of the struggles insurance companies have faced in recent years to preserve their profitability and capital is Lloyds of London — the three-century-old insurance market in which individual investors (called "names"), who are banded together in syndicates, underwrite the risks taken on by their clients in return for premium and investment income. Lloyds has insured some unusual risks, including actress Elizabeth Taylor's eyes while also underwriting the reward for corralling the Loch Ness monster! But what is equally unusual about Lloyds is that their "names" (underwriters) pledge their entire net worth, if necessary, to cover their share of any losses that may occur.

Unfortunately for Lloyds, the risks associated with a volatile economy, political upheaval and war, as well as extremes in weather, environmental damage (such as the Alaska Valdez oil spill), and other sources of loss, have resulted in burgeoning claims — so huge, in fact, that many of the "names" (about 10,000 strong) have simply refused to pay their share of expected losses. By 1996 these projected claims totaled about $2 billion. To date, Lloyds has never reneged on paying an insurance claim, but is dangerously close to doing so unless other sources of capital can be found.

One point in Lloyds' favor is that it requires full (100 percent) setting aside of reserves behind any possible future claims, whereas most regular insurance companies set aside fewer reserves and count on other income (mainly investment earnings and policy holder premiums) to help cover policy holder claims. Moreover, Lloyds has imposed special levies on its members and, for the first time in its history, allowed corporate capital to come in. The venerable insurer has also turned more heavily to the reinsurance market (where policies are written to back up any excess risk presented by conventional insurance policy contracts). These recent steps by Lloyds illustrate how creative the managers of insurance companies must be to deal with the risks and the intense global competition that confront the insurance industry today.

down. Among U.S. P/C companies, a key challenge today is the rapid growth of foreign insurance underwriters who have entered the United States in large numbers. Moreover, many U.S. corporations have started their own captive insurance companies.

To improve their situation for the future, P/C insurers must become more innovative in developing new services and more determined to eliminate those services that result in underwriting losses. This will not be easy due to extensive regulations and public pressure for lower insurance rates. Moreover, the insurance industry in the United States has been exempted from antitrust prosecution (and therefore has been relatively free to exchange information between companies) under the McCarran–Ferguson Act for many years, but recently numerous Congressional proposals have been put forward to modify or repeal that law and the special protection it gives this industry.

PENSION FUNDS

Pension funds protect individuals and families against loss of income in their retirement years by allowing workers to set aside and invest a portion of their current income. A pension plan places current savings in a portfolio of stocks, bonds, and other assets in the

Exhibit 6–7   **Total Assets of Private and Public Pension Funds, Selected Years**
($ Billions)

Type of Pension Plan or Program	1940	1950	1960	1970	1980	1990	1993
Private pension programs:	$2.0	$12.1	$52.0	$138.2	$422.7	$2,324.8	$3,167.5
Insured plans	0.6	5.6	18.8	41.2	165.8	695.7	825.4
Noninsured plans	1.4	6.5	33.2	97.0	286.8	1,629.1	2,342.1
Government pension programs:	$4.3	$25.8	$56.1	$125.9	$289.8	$1,203.5	$1,579.8
State/local retirement systems	1.6	5.3	19.3	60.3	185.2	720.8	858.8*
Federal civilian systems	0.6	4.2	10.5	23.1	75.8	247.5	330.7
Railroad retirement program	0.1	2.6	3.7	4.4	2.1	9.9	12.0
Social security program (OASDI)	2.0	13.7	22.6	38.1	26.5	225.3	378.3
Total assets of all funds	$6.3	$37.9	$108.2	$262.0	$712.3	$3,528.3	$4,747.3

Note: Columns may not add to totals due to rounding.
*Figure for state and local government pension programs is for 1992.

Source: Securities and Exchange Commission; Railroad Retirement Board; U.S. Department of Health and Human Services; and the American Council of Life Insurance, *1994 Life Insurance Fact Book*, p. 55.

expectation of building an even larger pool of funds in the future. In this way, the pension plan member can balance planned consumption after retirement with the amount of savings set aside today.

Growth of Pension Funds

Pension funds have been among the most rapidly growing of all financial intermediaries. Between 1980 and 1990, the assets of all private and public pension funds more than tripled, reaching almost $5 trillion in the United States alone in 1993. (See Exhibit 6–7.) Approximately half of all full-time workers in private businesses and three quarters of all civilian government employees are protected by pension plans other than the U.S. social security program (OASDI). More than 180 million persons are insured under the U.S. social security program.

Pension fund growth in the past has been spurred on by the relatively few retirees drawing pensions compared to the number of people working and contributing to a pension program. That situation is changing rapidly, however; individuals over 65 years of age now represent one of the fastest growing segments of the world's population. The growing proportion of retired individuals will threaten the solvency of many private pension funds and has already created major funding problems for various government programs (such as the U.S. medicare program) designed primarily to aid the elderly.[4]

Competition among employers for skilled management personnel has also spurred pension fund growth as firms have tried to attract top-notch employees by offering attractive fringe benefits. This growth factor is likely to persist in the 1990s and beyond due to a possible shortage of skilled entry-level workers as the population ages. Some experts foresee a real problem in this area, stemming from the recent difficulties pension plans have had in keeping up with inflation and with the increasing number of retirees. Workers

---

[4]The present ratio of working adults to retired persons in the U.S. population is about 3:1. This ratio is projected to shrink to about 2:1 during the next century. When the U.S. Social Security Act was passed in 1935, there were 11 working adults for each retired individual.

MANAGEMENT INSIGHT:

Managing a Financial Institution's Investment Portfolio

In addition to making direct loans to customers, most financial institutions, including insurance companies, pension funds, and banks, actively buy securities sold through brokers and dealers in the money and capital markets. Examples include purchases of common and preferred stock, corporate and government bonds, Treasury bills, commercial paper, and other marketable securities.

The purpose of adding security-type assets to a financial institution's portfolio varies from institution to institution but generally includes a desire to (a) add new sources of income; (b) stabilize a financial institution's income flow (for example, when loan revenues decline, security income may be increasing); (c) offset the risks presented by riskier assets (such as from direct loans and real estate holdings); (d) provide additional liquidity (with securities that can be readily sold for cash with little risk of loss); and (e) reduce tax exposure (such as by purchasing tax-exempt securities). Most financial institutions today have written investment policies describing the goals they expect to achieve with their security investments, the quality or risk exposure they are willing to accept in their investment portfolio, and the maturities and other terms that they consider most desirable on any securities they may wish to add to their asset portfolios.

Different types of financial institutions often hold very different kinds of investment securities. Banks, for example, tend to favor short-term and medium-term government securities, while insurance companies tend to buy large quantities of longer-term corporate bonds and stock. Among the principal factors that affect which types of investment securities a financial institution will buy are:

1. The *expected rate of return* on the security and how that return correlates with the returns from other assets that the financial institution already holds (because a negative or low positive correlation will help to stabilize an institution's overall flow of income). Most financial institutions estimate the before- or after-tax yield to maturity or holding-period yield on any securities they are thinking of acquiring (see Chapter 9 for a description on how to calculate these particular yield measures).

2. *Degree of tax exposure*, with heavily taxed financial institutions (such as banks and insurance companies) generally preferring those securities that are tax exempt or have low tax exposure.

3. *Exposure to credit or default risk* [with regulations often limiting such institutions as banks and insurance companies to higher-quality (investment-grade) financial investments].

4. *Exposure to interest rate risk* (indicating how strongly the market price of a security reacts to changes in interest rates).

5. *Exposure to liquidity risk* (indicating how much of a loss the institution might be forced to take if a security must be sold quickly).

6. *Exposure to call risk* (or the danger the issuer might call in and retire a security before it reaches maturity, lowering the holder's expected return).

(continued)

7. *Exposure to prepayment risk* (on load-backed securities, where some loans in the pool of loans backing the securities are paid off early, lowering the investing institution's expected yield).

8. *Exposure to inflation risk* (with some securities, such as common stock, perhaps rising in value when inflation threatens, while others, such as bonds, may tumble in price with rising inflation).

9. *Desired maturity range* (with financial institutions holding relatively short-term liabilities generally preferring to match these with shorter-term security investments).

Clearly, the choice of what types of investment securities to hold is not an easy one for the manager of a financial institution. Expected return, risk exposure, and regulations must all be weighed before a decision is made to add a new security to or sell off a security already held in a financial institution's investment portfolio.

in the future are likely to demand better performance from their plans and greater control over how their long-term savings are invested.

Investment Strategies of Pension Funds

Pension funds are long-term investors with limited need for liquidity. Their incoming cash receipts are known with considerable accuracy because a fixed percentage of each employee's salary is usually contributed to the fund. At the same time, cash outflows are not difficult to forecast, because the formula for figuring benefit payments is stipulated in the contract between the fund and its members. This situation encourages pensions to purchase common stock, long-term bonds, and real estate and hold these assets on a permanent basis. In addition, interest income and capital gains from investments are exempt from federal income taxes, and pension plan members are not taxed on their contributions unless cash benefits are actually paid out.

Although favorable taxation and predictable cash flows favor longer-term, somewhat riskier investments, the pension fund industry is closely regulated in all its activities. The Employee Retirement Income Security Act (ERISA) requires all U.S. private plans to be *funded*, which means that any assets held plus investment income must be adequate to cover all promised benefits. ERISA also requires that investments must be made in a "prudent" manner, which is usually interpreted to mean that they be invested in highly diversified holdings of high-grade common stock, corporate bonds, and government securities and only limited real estate investments.

Although existing regulations emphasize conservatism in pension investments, private pensions have been under intense pressure in recent years by management and employees of sponsoring companies to be more liberal in their investment policies. The sponsoring employer has a strong incentive to encourage its affiliated pension plan to reduce operating expenses and earn the highest possible returns on its investments. This permits the company to minimize its contributions to the plan. However, in 1985 the Financial Accounting Standards Board issued SFAS 87, which calls upon *defined-benefit pension plans* (that is, those promising specific retirement benefits to their members) to more fully disclose their funding status, asking businesses to make projections of their future pension obligations, publish estimates of how much in pension benefits employees will receive, and report any *unfunded* portion of pension benefits (that is, total obligations to pension plan members less the fair value of plan assets) on each business's balance sheet as a liability. These accounting requirements make some business firms offering pension plans look weaker and, along with stricter government regulations, have caused many businesses to abandon their pension programs, leaving it to their employees to develop and manage their own retirement plans.

Sponsoring employers and employees both have a keen interest in seeing that their pension plan earns a high enough return on its investments to at least keep pace with inflation. Otherwise, the employees will tend to seek other jobs whose pension programs offer more lucrative returns. One result of these pressures has been a significant rise in pension fund purchases of "junk" (low credit-quality) bonds. By the beginning of the 1990s, the pension fund industry held about 15 percent of all junk bonds. State regulatory agencies, however, have acted recently to limit pension fund exposure to the high risks inherent in these debt instruments.

Pension Fund Assets

The particular assets held as investments by pension funds depend heavily on whether the fund is government controlled or a private venture. As shown in Exhibit 6–8, private funds emphasize investments in corporate stock, which represent almost half of their assets. Corporate bonds rank a distant second, accounting for about one eighth of all private pensions' assets. A growing volume of these securities is purchased overseas, where both risk and rates of return are generally higher. With few liquidity needs, private pension funds held relatively small amounts of cash and bank deposits, although their holdings of U.S. government and federal agency securities have remained substantial (about 15 percent of their total assets) due to the relatively high yields and safety of these financial instruments. Many of the largest pension plans also hold substantial real estate investments for asset diversification and as a hedge against inflation.

Corporate stock is less important in the portfolios of government pensions than among private pension plans. As Exhibit 6–8 shows, state and local government pension programs hold only about two fifths of their assets in corporate stock. Stock investments are followed in government pension plans by holdings of corporate bonds, which represent just over one fifth of their assets. The pressure of regulation falls more heavily upon government (public) pension plans rather than on private plans. As a result, the investments of government pensions tend to be somewhat more conservative.

Factors Affecting the Future Growth of Pension Funds

Most experts believe that pension fund growth is likely to slow significantly in future years. One reason is the rising proportion of pension beneficiaries to working contributors, related to the aging of the population. At the same time, the cost of maintaining pension programs has increased dramatically. The full funding of a plan to cover all promised benefits may place extreme pressure on corporate profits, particularly if declining security markets or falling interest rates diminish investment returns.

Even more significant is the rising cost of government regulation, which has imposed costly reporting requirements on the industry, granted employees the right to join pension programs soon after they are hired, and allowed pension plan members to acquire ownership and control more quickly of monies contributed on their behalf.

The new government regulations have forced many private pension plans to close. The control of others has been turned over to a financial institution — typically a bank trust department or life insurance company — better able to deal with the current rules. Many

Exhibit 6–8

Financial Assets Held by Private, Noninsured Pension Funds and State and Local Government Employee Pension Funds, 1995*
($ Billions)

Assets Held by Private Pension Plans	Private Noninsured Pension Funds	
	Amount	Percent
Checkable deposits and currency	$ 3.4	0.1%
Small time and savings deposits	166.9	6.7
Large ($100,000+) time deposits	55.0	2.2
Money market fund shares	26.1	1.0
Mutual fund shares	163.2	6.6
Corporate stock (equities)	1,128.6	45.3
U.S. Treasury securities	282.7	11.3
Federal agency securities	108.9	4.4
State and local government (tax-exempt) securities	1.8	0.1
Corporate and foreign bonds	303.1	12.2
Mortgages	40.8	1.6
Open market paper	15.4	0.6
Miscellaneous assets	195.6	7.9
Total financial assets	$2,491.4	100.0%

Assets Held by State and Local Government Employee Retirement Plans	State and Local Government Retirement Plans	
	Amount	Percent
Checkable deposits and currency	$ 6.1	0.5%
Time deposits	4.4	0.4
Corporate stock (equities)	553.0	44.7
U.S. Treasury securities	181.7	14.7
Federal agency securities	88.4	7.2
State and local government (tax-exempt) securities	0.3	0.0**
Corporate and foreign bonds	276.0	22.3
Mortgages	15.4	1.2
Open market paper	58.5	4.7
Miscellaneous assets	52.7	4.3
Total financial assets	$1,236.3	100.0%

Note: Columns may not add to totals due to rounding.
*Figures are for first quarter 1995 at annualized rates.
**Less than 0.05 percent.

Source: Board of Governors of the Federal Reserve System, Flow of Funds Accounts.

private pension plans are in weak financial condition, especially those connected to corporations that are in serious trouble. Another group of troubled pensions consists of those that invested heavily in so-called open-end real estate pools, which placed their funds in office buildings, shopping malls, and other real estate projects that now are bankrupt. In addition, some of the best pension plans have been terminated because their sponsoring employers are trying to recapture their assets, the value of which has risen substantially in recent years.

In short, the pension fund sector faces some serious problems that will require creative solutions in the future, including a redefining of the role of public and private institutions in assuring an equitable and adequate distribution of retirement monies to those who have earned them.

MANAGEMENT INSIGHT:

How Pension Funds Work

Pension funds set aside current savings in a pool of earning assets (stocks, bonds, etc.) in the hope of accumulating a larger amount of savings that will provide a stream of income in the retirement years. For example, suppose an employee of a company with a pension plan who is scheduled to retire in five years has $2,500 deposited in her retirement account this year. If the pension plan promises her a 6 percent annual yield on each dollar set aside for retirement, the $2,500 she sets aside today in five years will be worth

$$\begin{matrix} \text{Value of funds} \\ \text{contributed today} \\ \text{at retirement} \end{matrix} = \begin{matrix} \text{Amount set} \\ \text{aside today} \end{matrix} \left(1+ \begin{matrix} \text{Promised} \\ \text{rate of return} \end{matrix} \right)^{\begin{matrix}\text{Years}\\\text{invested}\end{matrix}}$$

$$= \$2,500(1+.06)^5 = \$3,345.57$$

Suppose this same employee who plans to retire in five years has $2,500 contributed every year between now and retirement and earns 6 percent on each dollar saved for each year. Then her total savings pool at retirement will be:

$$\begin{matrix} \text{Total funds} \\ \text{available at} = \\ \text{retirement} \end{matrix} \begin{matrix} \text{Amount of} \\ \text{savings} \\ \text{contributed} \\ \text{each year} \end{matrix} \times \begin{matrix} \text{Sum of compound} \\ \text{interest factors for} \\ \text{savings contributed} \\ \text{each year up to} \\ \text{retirement at} \\ \text{interest rate } i \end{matrix}$$

$$= \$2,500[(1+.06)^5 + (1+.06)^4 + \ldots + (1.06)^1]$$

$$= \$14,937.50$$

How much in annual income can this employee look forward to in retirement from this one pension plan? The answer depends on the annual annuity rate promised in the contract between the pension plan and the employee and whether the employee has access to (i.e., is vested with) all funds contributed in her name. Suppose this employee is vested with the full amount shown above (i.e., a vesting ratio of 1.00 or 100 percent) and is promised an annual annuity (income) rate of 5.5 percent based on her life expectancy. Then her expected annual retirement income from this pension plan will be:

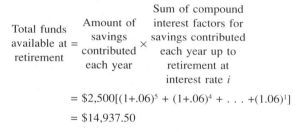

$$\begin{matrix} \text{Expected} \\ \text{annual} \\ \text{retirement} \\ \text{income} \end{matrix} = \begin{matrix} \text{Annual} \\ \text{annuity} \\ \text{rate} \end{matrix} \times \begin{matrix} \text{Total funds} \\ \text{available to} \\ \text{employee at} \\ \text{retirement} \end{matrix} \times \text{Vesting Ratio} = 0.055 \times \$14,937.50 \times 1.0 = \$821.56$$

(*Note:* To verify the preceding figures please see Chapter 9 and the compound interest table at the back of this book.)

FINANCE COMPANIES

Finance companies are sometimes called *department stores of consumer and business credit.* These institutions grant credit to businesses and consumers for a wide variety of purposes, including the purchase of business equipment, automobiles, vacations, and home appliances. Most authorities divide firms in the industry into one of three groups: consumer finance companies, sales finance companies, and commercial finance companies.

Different Finance Companies for Different Purposes

Consumer finance companies (such as Beneficial Finance) make personal cash loans to individuals. The majority of their loans support the purchase of passenger cars, home appliances, and mobile homes. However, a growing proportion of consumer-finance-company loans centers on aiding customers with medical and hospital expenses, educational costs, vacations, home repair, and energy bills. Loans made by consumer finance companies are considered to be riskier than other consumer installment loans and, therefore, generally carry steeper finance charges than those assessed by most other lending institutions.

Sales finance companies (such as GMAC) make indirect loans to consumers by purchasing installment paper from dealers selling automobiles and other consumer durables. Many of these firms are captive finance companies controlled by a dealer or manufacturer. Their principal function is to promote sales of the sponsoring firm's products by providing credit. Companies having captive finance affiliates include such industry leaders as General Motors, General Electric, and Motorola. Generally, sales finance companies will specify in advance to retail dealers the terms of installment contracts they are willing to accept. Frequently they will give the retail dealer a supply of contract forms, which the dealer fills out when a sale is made. The contract is then sold to the finance company.

Commercial finance companies (such as CIT) focus principally on extending credit to business firms. Most of these companies provide accounts receivable financing or factoring services to small- or medium-sized manufacturers and wholesalers. With accounts receivable financing, the commercial finance company may extend credit against the borrower's receivables in the form of a direct cash loan. Alternatively, a factoring arrangement may be used in which the finance company acquires the borrowing firm's credit accounts at an appropriate discount rate to cover the risk of loss. Most commercial finance companies today do not confine their credit-granting activities to the financing of receivables but also make loans secured by business inventories and fixed assets. In addition, they offer lease financing for the purchase of capital equipment and rolling stock (such as airplanes and railroad cars) and make short-term unsecured cash loans.

We should not overdramatize the differences among these three types of finance companies. The larger companies are active in all three areas. In addition, most finance companies today are extremely diversified in their credit-granting activities, offering a wide range of installment and working capital loans, leasing plans, and long-term credit to support capital investment. Exhibit 6–9 shows that business loans are the most important financial assets held by finance companies, accounting for almost half of their assets, followed by loans to individuals and families (consumers), accounting for about a sixth of industry assets. Real estate mortgage loans are also significant, representing one of the fastest growing finance company assets in recent years. Smaller amounts of funds are held in cash to provide liquidity.

Growth of Finance Companies

Finance companies have been profoundly affected by recent changes in the character of competition among all financial intermediaries. The lack of an extensive network of branch offices has put many finance companies at a disadvantage in reaching the household

Exhibit 6–9   **Financial Assets and Liabilities Held by Finance Companies, 1995***

Asset and Liability Items	Amount ($ Billions)	Percent of Total
Checkable deposits and currency	$12.8	1.79%
Real estate (mortgage) loans	80.8	10.6
Consumer credit (loans to individuals)	135.8	17.9
Business loans	351.9	46.4
Miscellaneous assets	177.7	23.4
Total financial assets	$759.0	100.0%
Corporate bonds	$252.1	37.19%
Bank loans (not elsewhere classified)	21.0	3.1
Open market paper	183.3	26.9
Taxes payable	1.0	0.1
Foreign direct investment in the U.S.	36.1	5.3
Investments in finance companies by their parent companies	52.9	7.8
Other liabilities	134.0	19.7
Total liabilities	$680.3	100.0%

Note: Columns may not add to totals due to rounding
*Figures through the first quarter of 1995.

Source: Board of Governors of the Federal Reserve System, *Flow of Funds Accounts: Flows and Outstandings*, First Quarter 1995.

borrower who values convenience. As a result, both banks and nonbank thrifts have been able to capture a larger share of the consumer loan market at the expense of finance companies. For example, data compiled by the Federal Reserve Board show that finance companies held about 45 percent of consumer installment loans extended by financial institutions in 1950, but only about 15 percent in 1995, although captive finance companies of the automobile firms (such as Ford Motor Credit) have done well vis-à-vis their competitors by offering discount-rate auto loans. Over the same time interval, however, credit unions tripled their share of the consumer installment loan market.

Many experts now believe that the fastest growing market for finance companies in future years will be in business-oriented, not consumer-oriented, financial services. Revolving credit, second mortgages on real property, working capital loans, merger and acquisition loans, and equipment leasing are among the fastest growing forms of credit extended by finance companies today. Recently, finance companies have expanded their lending programs to include small- and medium-sized businesses, making loans to and accepting some of the stock of these firms.

Methods of Industry Financing

Finance companies are heavy users of *debt* in financing their operations. Principal sources of borrowed funds include bank loans, commercial paper, and debentures (bonds) sold primarily to banks, insurance companies, and nonfinancial corporations. (See Exhibit 6–9.) Which source of funds these companies emphasize most heavily at any given time depends on the structure of interest rates. When long-term rates are high, these companies tend to emphasize commercial paper and short-term bank loans as sources of funds. In years when long-term rates are relatively low, bonds will be drawn on more heavily. The only source of industry funds that has declined significantly in recent years is borrowings from parent companies, as finance companies have come to borrow more heavily in the open market rather than relying as much on internally generated capital.

Recent Changes in the Character of the Finance Company Industry

The structure of the finance industry has changed markedly in recent years. As in the case of credit unions and savings and loans, the number of finance companies has been trending downward, although the average size of such companies has grown considerably. A survey by the Federal Reserve Board revealed that in 1960 there were more than 6,400 finance companies operating in the United States, but by 1980 only about 2,000 independent companies could be found. A modest rise in the number of new firms occurred during the 1970s, however, as bank holding companies, centered around some of the nation's largest banks, organized new finance company subsidiaries.

This long-term downtrend in the industry's total population of firms reflects a number of powerful economic forces at work. Rising cost pressures, the broadening of markets, the need to innovate, and intensified competition have encouraged finance companies to strive for larger size and greater efficiency. Many smaller companies have sold out to larger conglomerates. Despite their declining numbers, however, finance companies continue to be a potent force in the markets for business and consumer credit.

INVESTMENT COMPANIES

Investment companies provide an outlet for the savings of thousands of individual investors, directing their funds into bonds, stocks, and money market securities. These companies are especially attractive to the small investor, to whom they offer continuous management services for a large and varied security portfolio. By purchasing shares offered by an investment company, the small saver gains greater price stability and reduced risk, opportunities for capital gains, and indirect access to higher yielding securities that can be purchased only in large blocks. In addition, most investment company stock is highly liquid, because many companies stand ready at all times to repurchase their outstanding shares at current market prices.

The Background of Investment Companies

Investment companies made their appearance in the United States after World War I as a vehicle for buying and monitoring subsidiary corporations. Many were unsuccessful in the early years, and the Great Depression of the 1930s forced scores of these firms into bankruptcy. New life was breathed into the industry after World War II, however, when investment companies appealed to a rapidly growing middle class of savers. They were also buoyed by rising stock prices that attracted millions of investors, most of whom had only modest amounts to invest and little knowledge of how the financial markets work. The industry launched an aggressive advertising campaign that attracted more than 40 million shareholders during the 1960s.

Then the roof fell in as the long postwar bull market in stocks collapsed in the late 1960s and again in the 1970s. Small investors began to pull out of the stock market in droves. Many investment companies disappeared in this shakeout period; most of them were consolidated into larger firms.

The future of the industry seemed in doubt until a new element appeared: *innovation.* Owners and managers began to develop new types of investment companies designed to appeal to groups of investors with specialized financial needs. By tradition, investment companies had stressed investments in common stock, offering investors capital appreciation as well as current income. With the stock market performing poorly, these firms turned their focus increasingly to bonds and money market instruments. New *bond funds* directed the majority of their funds into corporate debt obligations or tax-exempt municipal bonds. Their principal objectives in recent years have been to generate current income and, in the case of the municipal bond fund, a higher after-tax rate of return for the investor. Capital appreciation is normally a secondary consideration to these companies.

Money market funds, discussed in Chapter 5, began in 1972 with the announced intent of holding money market securities, mainly bank certificates of deposit (CDs), commercial paper, and government bills. They were created in response to record-high interest rates and the desire of the small investor to skirt federal interest rate ceilings on time and savings deposits offered by banks and thrift institutions. In addition, the money funds have offered investors professional management of their liquid funds and reduced risk through diversification.

Interestingly enough, the traditional stock-investing mutual funds began to grow rapidly again in the 1980s and 1990s. Although money market funds rescued the investment companies during the turbulent 1970s, the equity funds have frequently outpaced the money market funds more recently, with money flowing in from individual retirement accounts (IRAs) and from investors enamored of "bargain" stock prices. Moreover, several stock funds outperformed the market as a whole (as measured by the Standard & Poor's 500 Stock Index) by purchasing stocks from smaller, rapidly growing firms dealing in high-tech products or specialty items. Nevertheless, many stock funds did *not* outperform the market, which increased the popularity of so-called *index funds* that invest in a portfolio of stocks and bonds reflective of the whole market and tend to move synchronously with that market.[5]

Even more important in the 1980s and 1990s has been the rapid growth of *global funds*. These are stock and bond funds whose income-earning securities come from all over the world. These funds have access to security trading 24 hours a day through active exchanges in London, Tokyo, Singapore, Hong Kong, and other financial centers around the globe. Managers of these funds believe that higher returns are achievable with a balanced international portfolio, rather than from just holding domestic securities. Another innovative investment company developed recently is the *vulture fund*, which purchases securities from firms in trouble in the hope of scoring exceptional returns should these firms recover or when their more valuable assets are liquidated.

Finally, during the 1990s so-called *hedge funds* became prominent. These mutual funds are really private partnerships that sell shares to only a limited number of investors in the hope of reaping large returns from pursuing high-risk investments. In this case the word "hedge" refers to an investment strategy that splits the money being invested between those assets expected to increase in value if the market goes up and those assets believed to benefit if the market goes down. Many hedge funds gamble on the market's direction by betting that they know better than the market as a whole which way interest rates and security prices are likely to go. The high risk posed by these funds gave rise in the 1990s to public calls for closer regulation of investment company behavior, though many oppose such regulation because it might limit the options currently available to investors.

---

[5]*Index funds* are based on the theory of efficient markets, which argues that in the long run, active money managers cannot beat the market as a whole. Thus, index funds tend to hold their investments longer and charge lower brokerage and service fees than do investment companies that turn over their security portfolios more rapidly. See Chapters 3 and 27 for further discussion of market efficiency.

Tax Status of the Industry

Investment companies have a highly favorable tax situation. As long as they conform to certain rules to qualify as an investment company, they pay no federal taxes on income generated by their security holdings. However, no less than half their resources must be devoted to securities and cash assets. Investment companies must maintain a highly diversified portfolio: a maximum of one quarter of their total resources can be devoted to securities issued by any one business firm. Only a small portion of net income (no more than 10 percent) can be retained in the company. The rest must be distributed to shareholders.

Open-End and Closed-End Investment Companies

There are two basic kinds of investment companies. *Open-end companies* — often called *mutual funds* — buy back (redeem) their shares any time the customer wishes and sell shares in any quantity demanded. Thus, the amount of their outstanding shares changes continually in response to public demand. The price of each open-end company share is equal to the *net asset value* of the fund, that is, the difference between the values of its assets and liabilities divided by the volume of shares issued.

Open-end companies may be either *load* or *no-load* funds. Load funds offer shares to the public at net asset value plus a commission to brokers marketing their shares. No-load funds sell shares purely at net asset value. The investor must contact the no-load company directly, however. Whether load or no-load, open-end investment companies are heavily invested in common stock, with corporate bonds running a distant second. As Exhibit 6–10 shows, corporate stock represents just over half of the industry's assets, with government bonds and corporate bonds accounting for most of the remaining assets.

Closed-end investment companies sell only a specific number of ownership shares, which usually trade on an exchange like many other stocks. An investor wanting to acquire closed-end shares must find another investor who wishes to sell; the investment company itself does not take part in the transaction. These funds often attract investors by offering "double discounts," which consist of discounted prices on the stocks they hold and discounted share prices to buy into the fund itself. Closed-end companies issue a variety of

Exhibit 6–10   **Financial Assets Held by Mutual Funds (Investment Companies) 1995* (Open-End Investment Companies)**

Asset Items	Amount ($ Billions)	Percent of Total
Checkable deposits and currency	$24.7	1.5%
Corporate stock (equities)	881.7	53.2
U.S. Treasury securities	207.3	12.5
Federal agency securities	85.3	5.1
State and local government (tax-exempt) securities	211.0	12.7
Corporate and foreign bonds	175.6	10.6
Open-market paper	70.8	4.3
Total financial assets	$1,656.4	100.0%
Total shares of stock in mutual funds outstanding	1,656.4	

Note: Columns may not add to totals due to rounding.
*Figures through the first quarter of 1995.

Source: Board of Governors of the Federal Reserve System, *Flow of Funds Accounts: Flows and Outstandings,* First Quarter 1995.

securities to raise funds, including preferred stock, regular and convertible bonds, and stock warrants. In contrast, open-end companies rely almost exclusively on the sale of equity shares to the public in order to raise the funds they need.

Goals and Earnings of Investment Companies

Investment companies adopt many different goals. *Growth funds* are interested primarily in long-term capital appreciation and tend to invest mainly in common stocks offering strong growth potential. *Income funds* stress current income in their portfolio choices rather than growth of capital, and they typically purchase stocks and bonds paying high dividends and interest. *Balanced funds* attempt to bridge the gap between growth and income, acquiring bonds, preferred stock, and common stock that offer both capital gains (growth) and adequate current income.

The majority of investment companies give priority to capital growth over current income. However, the industry's growth in recent years has centered primarily on funds that stress current income. Prominent examples include bond funds, money market funds, and option funds (which issue options against a portfolio of common stocks). Although most investment companies hold a highly diversified portfolio of securities, a few specialize in stocks and bonds from a single industry or sector (such as precious metals or oil and natural gas).

Policies and goals for investing funds are determined by an investment company's board of directors, elected by its shareholders. Its assets, however, are managed by an *investment advisory service* in return for an annual fee (usually 1 to 2 percent of a fund's assets). The contract between investment advisor and mutual fund must generally be approved by the fund's stockholders.

The rapid growth of investor interest in mutual funds led *The Wall Street Journal* to publish a significantly expanded section called "Mutual Fund Quotations" beginning in 1995. A sample report from that newly expanded section is shown in Exhibit 6–11. In this sample report we look at one of the larger groupings of funds, the AIM family of funds. We note, for example, that the AIM Aggressive Growth Fund (Agrsv) had an NAV (net asset value after deducting all debt obligations from the fund's total assets) of $42.77 per share, which was an increase of 2 cents from the previous trading day. The third column of figures (YTD) shows the year-to-date percentage change in yield assuming that all distributions of income are reinvested and annual expenses are deducted. The symbol *r* appears if there is a redemption charge that investors might have to pay if they sell some of their fund shares. By presenting return data and net asset values for several hundred mutual funds, *The Wall Street Journal* provides investors with an opportunity to compare the fund in which they are interested with other mutual funds and with the returns earned by the market as a whole.

It is not at all clear that mutual funds hold a significant advantage over other investors in seeking the highest returns available in the financial marketplace. Moreover, there is evidence that these companies may roll over their portfolios too rapidly, which runs up the cost of managing the fund and reduces earnings. Less frequent trading activity on the part of investment companies might well result in greater long-term benefits for the saver. Research evidence has been mounting for a number of years that security markets are highly efficient. Overvaluation or undervaluation of securities is, at most, a temporary phenomenon. In this kind of environment, it is doubtful that investment companies are of significant benefit to the large investor, though they may aid the small investor in reducing information and transactions costs and opening up investment opportunities not otherwise available.

Finally, several mutual funds have recently run up serious financial losses due to excessive risk taking by purchasing large quantities of so-called "derivatives" (such as

Exhibit 6–11   **Mutual Fund Quotations in *The Wall Street Journal***

MUTUAL FUND QUOTATIONS

Name	NAV	Net Chg	YTD %ret
AAL Mutual:			
Bond p	9.72	+0.01	- 2.9
CaGr p	18.49	-0.04	+ 5.0
Intl p	10.53	+0.07	+ 4.1
MuBd p	10.91	+0.02	- 2.7
SmCoStk p	15.95	-0.09	+ 6.8
Util p	11.04	...	-2.4
AARP Invst:			
BalS&B	17.33	-0.01	+ 2.8
CaGr	41.36	-0.17	+ 7.5
GiniM	15.02	+0.01	- 0.8
GthInc	42.47	-0.02	+ 6.8
HQ Bd	15.87	+0.01	- 2.5
TxFBd	17.76	+0.03	- 1.9
AHA Funds:			
Balan	13.06	+0.02	+ 4.6
DivrEq	17.11	+0.02	+ 7.2
Full	9.73	+0.01	- 3.3
Lim	10.16	...	- 0.4
AIM Funds:			
Agrsv p	42.77	+0.02	+ 8.1
BalA p	19.80	+0.02	+ 3.6
BalB †	19.80	+0.02	+ 3.4
ChartA p	10.36	...	+ 4.5
ChartB	10.36	...	+ 4.3
Const p	24.22	-0.07	+ 7.6
GlAgGrA	14.30	+0.07	+ 7.8
GlAgGrB	14.19	+0.07	+ 7.7
GlGrA p	13.06	+0.09	+ 4.6
GlGrB p	12.97	+0.09	+ 4.6
GlUtilA p	14.47	+0.05	-0.1k
GlUtilB †	14.48	+0.05	-0.3k
GrthA p	13.94	-0.04	+ 6.8
GrthB †	13.62	-0.04	+ 6.7
HYldA p	9.45	...	+2.4k
HYldB †	9.45	...	+2.3k

Name	NAV	Net Chg	YTD %ret
Gwth p	32.15	-0.18	+ 5.3
HiInMuni	14.95	+0.01	-2.1k
HI Tr p	14.61	+0.02	+3.3k
Inco p	16.31	-0.01	+ 2.8
IntBd p	13.44	+0.01	-0.9k
LtdTEBd p	14.36	+0.02	-0.3k
NEco p	17.21	...	+ 6.4
N Per p	17.19	+0.03	+ 4.9
SmCp p	25.31	+0.04	+ 7.7
TxEx p	11.85	+0.01	-2.0k
TECA p	15.68	+0.02	-2.4k
TEMd p	15.30	+0.02	-2.3k
TEVA p	15.69	+0.03	-2.1k
Wsh p	22.87	+0.01	+ 4.1
A GthD	9.49	+0.09	+ 7.2
A Heritg	0.71	...	+20.3
A HeritgGr	1.67	...	+ 9.2
Amer Natl Funds:			
Grth	4.59	...	+ 4.6
Inco	23.84	+0.05	+ 5.5
Triflex	17.38	...	+ 3.1
Am Perform:			
AggGro	16.92	+0.06	+12.6
Bond	9.20	+0.01	- 3.2
Equity	13.60	-0.02	+ 6.6
IntBd	10.15	+0.01	- 1.9
IntmTxF	10.61	+0.01	- 0.9
AmSouth Funds:			
Balance	13.30	+0.01	+ 3.0
Bond	10.67	+0.01	- 2.7
Equity	18.14	-0.01	+ 7.7
FlaTxF	10.27	+0.01	- 0.7
Gvtin	9.51	+0.01	- 1.6
LtdMat	10.37	...	- 0.6
RegEq	21.33	-0.01	+ 6.6

Name	NAV	Net Chg	YTD %ret
Tg2005	56.85	+0.19	- 7.0
Tg2010	41.86	+0.15	- 10.7
Tg2015	NA	NA	NA
Tg2020	NA	NA	NA
TNote	10.22	...	- 1.3
UtilIn	11.07	+0.04	- 2.5
Berger Group:			
GrInc p	13.57	+0.02	+ 3.7
100 p	19.31	+0.01	+ 6.7
SmCoGr p	4.01	+0.01	+ 5.5
Bernstein Fds:			
GvSh	12.51	...	- 0.1
ShtDur	12.45	...	- 0.2
ShCAMu	12.54	...	+ 0.3
ShDivMu	12.53	...	+ 0.3
ShNYMu	12.55	...	+ 0.5
IntDur	13.11	+0.02	- 2.5
Ca Mu	13.53	+0.02	- 1.2
DivMu	13.41	+0.02	- 1.1
NYMu	13.32	+0.02	- 1.3
IntlVal	16.93	+0.11	+ 4.2
EmMkts	22.45	+0.18	NA
BerwynFd	20.57	+0.05	+ 5.8
BerwynInc	12.39	+0.03	+ 3.7
BhirudMcPGr	9.47	-0.07	+ 3.3
Biltmore Funds:			
Balanced	11.95x	-0.11	+ 2.9
EmgMkt	11.55	+0.08	+ 7.3
Equity	12.92x	-0.07	+ 5.5
EqIndex	13.73x	-0.10	+ 6.2
FixedInc	9.59x	-0.04	- 2.5
QuantEq	13.59x	-0.03	+ 6.4
SpecVal	12.80	+0.05	+ 8.4
STFixInc	9.71x	-0.04	+ 1.2
SCMuni	10.72	+0.02	-2.2k
Blanchard Funds:			
AmerEq	11.97	-0.03	+ 6.6

Name	NAV	Net Chg	YTD %ret
TxFInc	10.65	+0.02	- 2.0
ValueEqS	14.53	...	+ 5.2
Composite Group:			
BdStkA p	14.23	-0.02	+ 3.1
Gr&IncA p	16.11	...	+ 6.8
InFdA p	9.01	+0.02	- 3.3
NWFdA p	18.64	+0.09	+ 5.9
TxExA p	7.70	+0.01	- 3.0
USGvA p	10.37	...	- 3.1
Conestoga Funds:			
BalncB	10.95	-0.01	+ 3.0
Bond	10.29	...	- 2.5
Equity	18.44	-0.05	+ 9.6
Int Inc	10.55	+0.01	- 1.3
ShTInl	10.00	...	+ 0.2
SpcEq	10.84	-0.03	+ 7.7
Conn Mutual:			
Govt	10.30	+0.01	- 3.0
Grwth	18.81	+0.02	+ 5.4
Income	9.41	...	- 0.1
LifeBal	11.39	...	+ 3.1
LifeCap	11.94	...	+ 4.8
TotRet	15.75	+0.02	+ 1.9
Copley	24.27	-0.02	- 2.3
CoreFunds:			
BalanA	12.40	-0.01	+ 2.1
EqIdx	27.74	-0.04	+ 6.2
GIBdA	9.91	+0.01	+ 0.1
GrEqA	12.93	-0.03	+ 4.5
IntBdA	9.82	+0.01	- 0.4
IntlGrA	13.33	+0.14	+ 2.3
ValEqA	14.38	+0.04	+11.4
ValEqB p	14.39	+0.04	+11.4
Cowen Funds:			
IFxInA p	9.39	...	- 1.6
InGrA p	13.01x	-0.12	- 0.4
OpptA p	13.78	+0.05	+ 2.3

Name	NAV	Net Chg	YTD %ret
Inv A	22.10	-0.07	+ 6.6
Inv B	21.72	-0.07	+ 6.4
LtdGvA p	12.54	...	- 1.5
LtdInR	10.66	+0.01	- 2.0
LtdMuA p	11.93	+0.01	- 1.2
MgdIA p	10.65	...	- 2.5
MN MuB †	15.04	+0.02	- 2.3
CTMuB †	11.91	+0.02	- 2.2
FLMuB	14.49	+0.02	- 3.0
MAMuA	11.50	+0.02	- 3.0
MdMuA	12.71	+0.02	- 1.8
MdMuB †	12.71	+0.02	- 1.9
MIMuA	15.18	+0.03	- 3.2
MNMuA	15.02	+0.03	- 2.1
MuBdA	14.02	+0.02	- 3.0
MuBdB †	14.02	+0.02	- 3.1
NYMuA	14.45	+0.03	- 2.8
NYMuB †	14.45	+0.02	- 3.0
NCMuA	12.91	+0.03	- 3.4
NCMuB †	12.90	+0.03	- 3.5
OHMuA	12.62	+0.03	- 2.4
OHMuB †	12.62	+0.02	- 2.6
PAMuA	16.19	+0.03	- 2.5
PAMuB †	16.18	+0.03	- 2.6
SmCoStR	14.24	+0.01	+ 6.5
StraGrA p	42.59	-0.15	+13.4
TXMuA	20.87	+0.04	- 2.5
VAMuA	16.28	+0.04	- 3.6
VAMuB †	16.28	+0.04	- 3.7
Dreyfus Strategic:			
Income	14.09	+0.01	- 1.6
DuffPEnhRes	10.00	...	+ 0.4
Dupree Mutual Fds:			
IntGov	9.98	+0.01	-2.0k
KYTF	7.39	+0.01	-1.9k
KYSM	5.17	...	-0.7k
EAI Select	10.50	-0.02	NS

Source: *The Wall Street Journal*, Southwest edition, March 20, 1996, p. 21. Reprinted by permission of *The Wall Street Journal*, © 1996 Dow Jones & Company, Inc. All Rights Reserved Worldwide.

bonds and notes backed by pools of mortgage loans), whose prices usually plummet in the wake of rising interest rates. These risky purchases appear to have been motivated by strong competition (including the rapid rise of bank-offered mutual funds and the development of many new mutual funds), which has pressured mutual fund managers to reach for higher rates of return by taking on more risk. When several funds posted millions of dollars in losses in the mid-1990s, the U.S. Congress held hearings in an effort to determine if additional regulations might be needed to protect their customers' money. Another direct result of today's intense competition among mutual funds is an ongoing "price war" among many leading funds, reducing management fees and lowering sales charges in an effort to attract more business.

OTHER FINANCIAL INSTITUTIONS

In addition to the foregoing, a number of other financial institutions have developed over the years to meet the specialized financial needs of their customers. For example, **security dealers** provide a conduit for buyers and sellers of marketable securities to adjust their holdings of those securities. These dealer houses stand ready at all times to buy selected private and government securities or sell from a list of securities to their customers at posted "bid" and "asked" prices. The best known of the dealers are the roughly three dozen primary government securities dealers that aid the U.S. Treasury in selling new issues of federal debt and trade securities regularly with the Federal Reserve System.

MANAGEMENT INSIGHT:

Measuring and Evaluating the Performance of a Financial Institution

Finance institutions today are closely watched by their customers, by regulators, and by the financial markets. The performance of a financial institution is evaluated not only relative to the institution's own goals but also relative to the performance of other businesses competing for capital and other productive resources in the global marketplace.

What measures of a financial institution's performance are the most widely used? Most performance measures employed focus upon four different dimensions of a financial institution's behavior:

1. The *stock price* (market value) of a stockholder-owned financial institution.

2. The *rate of return* or *profitability* of a financial institution.

3. The *risk exposure* of a financial institution, which encompasses multiple aspects of its financial condition and behavior.

4. The *operating efficiency* of a financial institution, measuring how well the institution uses the resources at its command to produce and sell its services.

For stockholder-owned institutions, the current *stock price* of the institution is a key barometer of the capital market's assessment of the adequacy of a financial institution's current and expected earnings and its ability to control risk exposure. Management tries to enhance its financial institution's prospects for greater future earnings (often by such overt moves as announcing the introduction of new services, entering new markets, or pursuing mergers and acquisitions) and to reduce the market's perception of the institution's risk exposure (such as by strengthening capital or diversifying sources of revenue). In a market-driven economy, stock price is usually the single best indicator of how well a stockholder-owned financial institution is performing. However, many financial institutions (such as mutual savings banks, credit unions, and mutual insurance companies) do *not* have stockholders; for these institutions, other measures are needed to evaluate how well these financial service firms are performing.

Widely used indicators of a financial institution's profitability or rate of return include:

$$\text{Return on assets (ROA)} = \frac{\text{Net after-tax income}}{\text{Total assets}} \qquad \text{Return on equity capital (ROE)} = \frac{\text{Net after-tax income}}{\text{Total equity capital}}$$

$$\text{Net operating margin (NOM)} = \frac{[\text{Total operating income less total operating expenses}]}{\text{Total assets}} \qquad \text{Net interest margin (NIM)} = \frac{[\text{Interest revenues from earning assets less interest costs on borrowed funds}]}{\text{Total earning assets}}$$

Return on assets and return on equity capital are the most comprehensive measures of a financial service firm's profitability. Return on assets is a measure of overall efficiency because it indicates how much net income the management of a financial institution has been able to generate from all the resources (assets) placed

(continued)

under the institution's control. Return on equity capital, on the other hand, shows the rate of return flowing to the institution's owners (its stockholders). The net operating margin is a good measure of how well a financial institution runs its daily operations of producing and delivering financial services, while the net interest margin measures the net return from the act of borrowing and lending money.

Among the most widely used indicators of a financial institution's risk exposure are:

$$\frac{\text{Solvency}}{\text{risk measure}} = \frac{\text{Total equity capital/}}{\text{Total risky assets}} \qquad \frac{\text{Credit risk}}{\text{measure}} = \frac{\text{Allowance for loan losses}}{\text{Total equity capital}}$$

$$\frac{\text{Liquidity risk}}{\text{measure}} = \frac{\text{Cash and government securities/Total assets}}{} \qquad \frac{\text{Interest rate}}{\text{risk measure}} = \frac{\text{Interest-sensitive assets/Interest-sensitive liabilities}}{}$$

As the above ratios illustrate, financial institutions are subject to *multiple* types of risk, including risk to the solvency (and survival) of the institution as reflected in how much long-term capital the owners have placed in the institution relative to its risk-exposed assets. If an institution's risky assets decline in value by more than the volume of its owners' capital (net worth), it will become *insolvent*. Similarly, financial institutions that make loans may face serious trouble if a substantial proportion of their loans must be written off as uncollectible. If loan losses come to exceed equity capital, the institution's credit risk will overwhelm the owners' stake in the firm and it will collapse.

As we saw earlier, financial institutions face significant *liquidity risks* in the form of "cash outs." One indicator of how well a financial institution has prepared for liquidity risk is the volume of liquid assets (particularly in the form of cash and government securities) that it holds relative to its total assets. Finally, financial institutions are exposed to *interest rate risk* — the danger of loss due to changing market interest rates. Any financial institution will suffer loss if its assets and liabilities cannot be adjusted to a new interest rate environment. One popular measure of a financial institution's sensitivity to interest rate risk is its ratio of the volume of assets held whose rates of return can be changed as market interest rates change (usually called interest-sensitive assets) to the volume of liabilities the institution has taken on whose cost rate changes as market interest rates change (usually called interest-sensitive liabilities).

Popular measures of the *operating efficiency* of a financial institution include:

$$\frac{\text{Operating}}{\text{expense ratio}} = \frac{\text{Total operating expenses}}{\text{Total operating revenues}} \qquad \frac{\text{Income productivity}}{\text{ratio}} = \frac{\text{Net after-tax income}}{\text{Number of employees}}$$

$$\frac{\text{Noninterest}}{\text{operating ratio}} = \frac{\text{Noninterest revenues}}{\text{Noninterest expenses}}$$

Intense competition in recent years has pressured financial institutions into watching their expenses very closely to ensure that operating expenses don't completely eat away the revenues generated from service sales. Many institutions have recently reduced their staff sizes in the hope that the remaining employees will be highly productive and able to generate maximum levels of net income after all

(continued)

expenses are met. Finally, increased emphasis has been placed in recent years on generating *noninterest* fee income from services not directly tied to the borrowing and lending of money (including fees for managing a customer's asset portfolio or from providing checking account services). Managers of financial institutions recently have attempted to minimize the amount by which their noninterest expenses (including salaries, wages, and overhead costs) exceed their noninterest (fee) income.

Many of these dealers also serve as **investment bankers**, who market large amounts of new securities on behalf of governments, governmental agencies, and corporations. These specialized "banks" are especially prominent in the offering of *new* corporate securities, state and local government bonds and notes, and securities issued by federal government agencies such as the Federal National Mortgage Association (Fannie Mae). They *underwrite* new offerings of these securities, purchasing them from the original issuer and placing them in the hands of investors at a higher price. When a new issue of securities involves substantial risk, several investment banking firms band together to form a *syndicate* to bid for and market the issue, thus spreading the risk. Investment banks also give advice on the best terms and times to sell new securities and on how to finance corporate mergers and acquisitions. These firms are among the best-known names in the financial world and include such prominent companies as Morgan Stanley, Nomura Securities, Salomon Brothers, First Boston-Credit Suisse, Merrill Lynch Capital Markets, and E. F. Hutton. Competition between these investment firms has become intense, as capital markets have become global and investment bankers must be prepared to market new securities worldwide.

A related type of dealer firm is the **mortgage bank**. Mortgage bankers commit themselves to take on new mortgage loans used to fund the construction of homes, office buildings, and other structures. They carry these loans for a short time until the mortgages can be sold to a long-term (permanent) lender such as an insurance company or savings bank. As in the case with other dealer operations, the financial risks to the mortgage banker are substantial. A rise in interest rates sharply reduces the market value of existing fixed-rate mortgage loans, presenting the mortgage banker with a loss when it sells the loans out of its portfolio. The risk of rising interest rates and falling mortgage prices encourages mortgage banks to turn over their portfolios rapidly and to arrange lines of credit from commercial banks to backstop their operations. These firms also service the mortgage loans they sell to other lenders, collecting loan payments and inspecting mortgaged property.

Authorized by federal law in 1960, **real estate investment trusts (REITs)** are publicly held, tax-exempt corporations that must receive at least three quarters of their gross income from real estate transactions (such as rental income, mortgage interest, and sales of property). They also must devote at least three quarters of their assets to real estate property or loans, cash, and government securities. REITs raise funds by selling stock and debt securities and invest most of their available funds in mortgage loans to finance the building of apartments, housing tracts, office buildings, shopping centers, and other commercial ventures.

Leasing companies represent still another kind of specialized financial institution that provides customers with access to productive assets, such as airplanes, automobiles, and equipment through the writing of leases. These leases allow a business or household to use assets sometimes at a lower cost than borrowing and owning those same assets. The leasing company, on the other hand, benefits from the stream of lease payments and gains substantial tax benefits from depreciating the leased assets. Competition is intense in this industry because of the entry of scores of banks and bank holding companies, insurance companies, and manufacturing firms that have either opened leasing departments or formed subsidiary leasing companies.

A unique financial institution that emerged in the 1970s and 1980s combined several different institutions under the same corporate umbrella. This dynamic financial institution is the **symbiotic**, a conglomerate financial firm that frequently merges insurance sales, security and real estate brokerage, financial counseling, and credit services under the same roof in an effort to become a "financial department store." Usually, each unit within the symbiotic attempts to sell its customers not only its own services but also the services offered by other units in the conglomerate. The same top management team may oversee all parts of the conglomerate organization. Prominent examples include Sears, Roebuck & Company, which in 1981 acquired control of Coldwell Banker, the leading U.S. real estate brokerage firm; Prudential Insurance Company, which acquired Bache Group, Inc., a leading security broker; and the well-known credit card company, American Express, which acquired broker Shearson Loeb Rhodes. We could add to this list of prominent financial conglomerates General Motors, General Electric, Ford Motor Company, and J.C. Penney, all of which control major finance companies designed to help finance and sell their manufactured products and gain a share of the rapidly expanding market for financial services.

The symbiotics possess an advantage over banks and other financial institutions with which they compete because at least some aspects of their business are *unregulated*. However, a major uncertainty that surrounds their operations is whether their managements can successfully control and market such a diverse range of products and services. Several symbiotics have spun off some of their affiliated firms in recent years because of huge losses and control problems that top management seemed unable to deal with. It is now evident that many consumers of financial services do not prefer necessarily to buy all of their services from one supplier — an ideal on which many symbiotics were founded — but willingly shop around for the best terms and best quality available for each significant financial service they need.

TRENDS AFFECTING ALL FINANCIAL INSTITUTIONS TODAY

The emergence of the symbiotics is but a reflection of the major trends that affect all financial institutions today. One of these trends is *increasing cost pressures*, due to the considerable expense associated with raising funds for lending and investing and burgeoning labor and equipment costs that have narrowed profit margins. Another trend is *consolidation*, in which each financial institution tries to expand its size to improve efficiency and ease its growing cost burden. Certainly the new symbiotics represent a move to consolidate financial resources into a large conglomerate organization and utilize existing managerial talent, labor, and physical facilities more efficiently. A key result of the consolidation movement is declining numbers of independent financial institutions, while the remaining institutions average much larger in size and organizational complexity.

Still a third trend is *service diversification*, as all major financial institutions have invaded each other's traditional markets with new services in an effort to offset rising costs and protect thinning profit margins. Service diversification has led to a blurring of functions among the different institutions to such an extent that it is becoming increasingly difficult to distinguish between different financial institutions. The symbiotics are a good example of this trend toward diversification, but so are banks, insurance companies, mutual funds, and many other financial institutions today.

The offering of many new services over wider market areas has been made possible by another trend in the financial institutions' sector: a *technological revolution*, particularly in the growing adoption of automated electronic equipment for making payments and transferring financial information. Soon there may be little need to walk into the offices of a financial institution, because many transactions will be handled more efficiently via home and office computers linked on-line to each financial institution's computer network. The technological revolution has made possible a global financial system and unleashed a trend toward *global competition* in which all financial institutions find themselves increasingly in a common market, competing for many of the same customers. Distance and geography no longer shelter and insulate financial institutions from the forces of demand and supply in the financial system as they once did. Accompanying the rise of global competition is a drive toward *regulatory cooperation*, so that financial institutions headquartered in different countries face essentially the *same* regulatory rules. There is a trend toward harmonizing laws and regulations so that no one country's financial institutions operate at a competitive disadvantage vis-à-vis those of another country.

Many of the new services, technological innovations, and the development of global competition have come into existence because of a seventh trend, *deregulation*, in which the content and prices of financial services increasingly are being determined by the marketplace rather than by government rules. Most of the deregulation movement, thus far, has centered in banking and among nonbank depository institutions as well as leading security dealers and brokers in Canada, the United States, Japan, Great Britain, Australia, and Western Europe. However, as depository institutions and securities firms continue to receive new service powers and expand their markets, it is quite likely that the whole panoply of financial institutions will seek to loosen the regulatory rules that bind them today. It is hoped that the public will be the ultimate beneficiary in terms of more and better financial services at lower cost.

SUMMARY

This chapter examined the services offered by and the portfolio characteristics of a variety of different financial institutions, including life and property-casualty insurance companies, pension funds, finance companies, investment companies, and financial conglomerates (symbiotics). Many of these institutions provide risk protection for their customers against death, ill health, negligence, loss of property, and the danger of outliving one's savings in retirement. They also make loans in the money and capital markets to businesses, individuals, and governments.

All of these financial institutions are undergoing major changes in the form of consolidation of smaller companies into larger companies, rising production costs, proliferation and diversification of services offered so that each financial institution tends to invade the markets served by many other financial institutions, a technological revolution as new forms of electronic information equipment allow financial institutions to serve their customers with great accuracy and speed over wide geographic areas, global competition as financial service providers reach across national borders and continents with their services, greater cooperation among regulators of financial institutions in different nations so that different institutions face a more level playing field with their competitors, and, in many countries, deregulation of the financial sector so that government plays a less prominent role in the operations of privately owned financial institutions. These changes make the financial institutions' sector one of the most dynamic industries in the global economy today. ∎

KEY TERMS AND CONCEPTS IN THIS CHAPTER

life insurance companies

property-casualty (p/c) insurers

pension funds

finance companies

investment companies

security dealers

investment bankers

mortgage bank

real estate investment trusts (REITs)

leasing companies

symbiotic

STUDY QUESTIONS

1. Against what kinds of risk do life insurance companies protect their policy holders? How about property-casualty insurers?

2. Compare and contrast the asset portfolios of life insurance companies and property-casualty insurers. Try to explain any differences you observe.

3. What is the principal function of pension funds? Explain why these institutions have been among the most rapidly growing financial institutions in recent years. Do you expect their growth to be faster or slower in the future? Why?

4. What are the principal assets acquired by pension funds? What factors guide their selection of securities?

5. What role do finance companies play in providing funds to the financial markets? How many different kinds of finance companies are there?

6. What advantages do investment companies offer the small saver? Why has their growth been so erratic in recent years?

7. Define the following terms:
   a. *Open-end company*
   b. *Closed-end company*
   c. *Bond fund*
   d. *Money market fund*
   e. *Growth funds*
   f. *Balanced funds*
   g. *Global funds*
   h. *Index funds*

8. What is a REIT? A mortgage bank? A leasing company? Why do you think these specialized financial institutions came into being?

9. How do symbiotics differ from more traditional financial institutions? What advantages do they have in the race for customer financial accounts? What disadvantages do they face?

10. In the concluding section of this chapter, seven major trends affecting all financial institutions today are discussed. Identify these trends. Which ones do you expect to continue over the next decade, and which do you think might be short lived? Explain your reasoning.

PROBLEMS

1. The manager of a life insurance company is trying to decide what annual premium to charge a group of policy holders, each of whom has just reached his or her 40th birthday. A check of mortality tables indicates that, for every million persons born 40 years ago, 3 percent die, on average, sometime during their 40th year. If the company has 10,000 policy holders in this age bracket and each has taken out a $50,000 life insurance policy, estimate the probable amount of death benefit claims against the company. How much must be

charged in premiums from each policy holder just to cover these expected claims? Suppose the company has operating expenses (plus a target profit) on sales to these policy holders of $500,000. What annual premium must be charged each policy holder to recover expenses and meet expected benefit claims?

2.   A pension fund has accumulated $1 million in a retirement plan for James B. Smith, who retires this month at age 65. If Mr. Smith has a life expectancy of 75 years, what is the minimum size of annual annuity check the pension plan will be able to send him each year (assuming that the value of the pension fund's investments remain stable)? Should he insist on receiving that size payment each year? Why or why not? What other kinds of information would be helpful in analyzing Mr. Smith's financial situation at retirement? (*Note:* If you're not sure about how annuity plans are supposed to work, see Chapter 9 for a discussion of annuity payments.)

3.   An employee has just joined SONY Corporation and a pension plan is set up in her name under which the company will contribute $5,000 per year and the employee herself will contribute $1,000 per year. How much will this year's contributed funds be worth in 10 years if the pension plan pledges a 7 percent annual return on each dollar saved? Suppose the employee plans to retire in 10 years. How much will be available in total at retirement if the company and the employee contribute the amounts noted above each year for the next 10 years and this employee owns (is vested with) the full amount of savings contributed to the pension plan? If the pension promises an annual annuity rate of 6 percent given this employee's life expectancy, what annual retirement income can she expect?

4.   Delbert Ray is planning to retire this year and draw upon the accumulated savings in his pension plan, which amount to $205,800. Mr. Ray is vested with 80 percent of the accumulated funds and, based on his life expectancy, has been promised an annual annuity (income) rate of 3.5 percent. What is Delbert Ray's expected annual retirement income from his pension plan?

5.   A financial institution reports the following figures in its latest annual report:

Net after-tax income	$15 million	Equity capital	$145 million
Total assets	$996 million	Interest revenues	$42 million
Earning assets	$775 million	Interest expenses	$28 million
Risky assets	$685 million	Noninterest sources of revenue	$5 million
Allowance for Loan losses	$38 million	Noninterest expenses	$19 million
Cash and government securities	$250 million	Interest-sensitive liabilities	$493 million
Interest-sensitive assets	$382 million		
Number of employees	185		

Drawing upon the discussion in this chapter on measuring and evaluating the performance of a financial institution, please calculate as many measures of this firm's performance as you can. Do you notice any performance measures that the management of this institution might wish to investigate for possible problems.

SELECTED REFERENCES

Abken, Peter A. "Corporate Pensions and Government Insurance: Déjá Vu All Over Again?" *Economic Review*. Federal Reserve Bank of Atlanta (March/April 1992), pp. 1–16.

Insurance Information Institute. *1992 Property-Casualty Insurance Facts*. New York City, 1992.

Light, Larry. "Why Life Insurers Are Suddenly to Die For." *Business Week*, May 21, 1990, pp. 140–41.

Rose, Peter S. "Symbiotics: Financial Supermarkets in the Making." *The Canadian Banker & ICB Review*, April 1982, pp. 77–84.

Chapter 7

The Regulation of Financial Institutions

LEARNING OBJECTIVES IN THIS CHAPTER

- To explore the reasons why financial institutions are one of the most regulated sectors of most modern economies.
- To examine and understand the many types of regulations affecting the behavior and growth of financial institutions.
- To understand how regulation has shaped the structure of the financial services industry.
- To explore the recent global trend toward deregulation of financial institutions and what its effects are likely to be.

Financial institutions are one of the most heavily regulated of all businesses in the world. Around the globe these financial service firms face stringent government rules limiting the services they can offer, the territories they can enter or not enter, the makeup of their portfolios of assets, liabilities, and capital, and even how they price and deliver their services to the public. As we will see in this chapter, over the centuries a variety of reasons have been offered for heavy government intrusion into the financial institutions' sector, including protecting the public's savings and ensuring that consumers receive an adequate quantity and quality of financial services that are reasonably priced.

Many economists, financial analysts, and financial institutions have argued over the years that government **regulation** has done more harm than good for both financial institutions themselves and for the public they serve. In particular, government restrictions allegedly have allowed nonregulated or less regulated financial service firms to invade the markets and capture many of the customers of regulated financial institutions, who are not sufficiently free to compete effectively. Moreover, regulations are often backward looking, addressing problems which have long since disappeared, and they may compound this problem of "relevancy" by changing much more slowly than the free marketplace, inhibiting the ability of regulated financial institutions to stay abreast of new technologies and changing customer tastes. Other observers, however, argue that government regulations have achieved some positive results in the financial institutions' sector, reducing the number of failed financial service firms, promoting more stable financial markets, and reducing the incidence of racial, age, and sex discrimination in public access to financial services.

In this chapter we explore these and many other issues as we examine the variety of government regulations and regulatory agencies that oversee financial institutions today, assess the reasons for and the effectiveness of existing regulations, and explore recent attempts to deregulate the financial institutions' sector.

THE REASONS BEHIND THE REGULATION OF FINANCIAL INSTITUTIONS

Elaborate government rules controlling what financial institutions can and cannot do arise from multiple causes. One is a concern about the *safety* of the public's funds, especially the savings of millions of individuals and families. The reckless management and ultimate loss of personal savings can have devastating consequences for a family's future èconomic well-being and lifestyle, particularly at retirement. While savers have a responsibility to carefully evaluate the quality and stability of a financial institution before committing their funds to it, governments have long expressed a special concern for small savers who may lack the financial expertise and access to quality information necessary to be able to correctly judge the true condition of a financial institution. Moreover, many of the reasons that cause financial institutions to fail — such as fraud, embezzlement, deteriorating loans, or manipulation of the books by insiders — are often concealed from the public.

Related to the desire for safety is a government's goal of *promoting public confidence* in the financial system. Unless the public is confident enough in the safety and security of their funds placed under the management of financial institutions, they will withdraw their savings and thereby reduce the volume of funds available for productive investment to construct new buildings, purchase new equipment, set up new businesses, and create new jobs. The economy's growth will slow and, over time, the public's standard of living will fall.

Government rules are also aimed at ensuring *equal opportunity* and *fairness* in the public's access to financial services. For example, in an earlier era many groups of customers — women, members of racial minority groups, the elderly, and those of foreign birth — found that their ability to borrow money on convenient terms was often severely restricted. Consumers of financial services were not well organized then, and the discriminatory policies of lending institutions seemed to change very slowly, particularly in markets where competition was less intense. While many economists believed that the potent force of competition generated by both domestic and foreign service suppliers would eventually kill off the vestiges of discrimination, other observers argued that such an event might take a very long time, particularly in those markets where financial firms colluded with each other and agreed not to compete.

Many regulations in the financial institutions sector spring from the ability of some financial institutions to create money in the form of credit cards, checkable deposits, and other accounts that can be used to make payments for purchases of goods and services. History has shown that the creation of money is closely associated with inflation. If uncontrolled money growth outstrips growth in the economy's production of goods and services, prices will begin to rise, damaging especially those consumers on fixed incomes, as their money balances can buy fewer and fewer goods and services. Thus, the regulation of *money creation* has become a key objective of government activity in the financial sector.

Regulation is often justified as the most direct way to aid so-called "disadvantaged" sectors in the economy — those groups that appear to need special help in the competition for scarce funds. Examples include new home buyers, farmers, small businesses, and low-income families. Governments often place high social value on subsidizing or guaranteeing loans made to these sectors and supporting through beneficial regulations those financial institutions that lend money to these sectors of the economy.

Finally, the enforcement of government rules for financial institutions has arisen because governments depend upon these institutions for many important services. Governments borrow money and depend upon financial institutions to buy a substantial proportion of government IOUs. Financial institutions also aid governments in the collection and dispersal of tax revenues and in the pursuit of economic policy through the manipulation of interest rates and the money supply. Thus, governments frequently regulate financial institutions simply to ensure that these important financial services will continue to be provided at a reasonable cost and in a reliable manner.

What are we to make of these reasons so often posed for the extensive government regulations applied to many financial institutions? Few of them can go unchallenged. For example, while safety is important for many savers, no government can completely remove risk for savers. Indeed, in the long run, it may be more efficient and far less costly for governments to promote full disclosure of the financial conditions of individual financial institutions and let competition in a free marketplace discipline poorly managed, excessively risky financial service firms. Similarly, there is no question that discrimination on the basis of sex, race, religious affiliation, or other irrelevant factors is repugnant, but can we be more effective in eliminating discrimination by some method other than by writing and struggling to enforce complicated rule books and by requiring endless compliance reports? Perhaps the same ends could be achieved by lowering the regulatory barriers to competition and by making it easier for customers hurt by discrimination to recover their damages in court.

Certainly the ability of financial institutions to create money needs to be monitored carefully, because excessive money growth can easily generate inflation and weaken the economy. But, aren't there already enough tools available to control money growth? For example, when money grows too fast, a central bank like the Federal Reserve System can use its powerful tools (like deposit reserve requirements or open market operations) to slow money growth. And wouldn't it be more efficient to pay direct money subsidies to disadvantaged groups (such as new home buyers) rather than to indirectly reach these groups by regulating financial institutions and interfering with the free operation of the financial services markets? As for providing a reliable stream of financial services to governments, wouldn't profit-motivated financial institutions be likely to provide these services if it were profitable to do so?

In brief, there are no absolutely irrefutable arguments justifying the regulation of financial institutions. Much depends on your personal political philosophy regarding society's goals and whether those goals are each more likely to be achieved by an unfettered marketplace or by collective action through government laws and regulations. As we shall see shortly, there is a trend today toward gradually allowing private markets to discipline risk taking by financial institutions and minimize the role of government. Progress toward **deregulation** of the financial sector is slow, however, and can easily be derailed if financial institutions abuse the new liberties that may soon come their way.

Does Regulation Benefit or Harm Financial Institutions?

For many years a controversy has been brewing as to whether government regulations help or hurt financial institutions. One of the earliest arguments on the positive side was propounded by economist George Stigler (1971), who suggested that regulated industries, far from dreading regulation, actually *invite* government intrusion, expecting to benefit from it. In the early history of the United States, for example, the railroads often prospered because government subsidized their growth and protected them from competition. Because regulators may prevent or restrict entry into an industry, the firms involved may earn excess profits ("monopoly rents") due to the absence of strong competitors. Therefore, the lifting of regulatory rules (deregulation) may bring about decreased profits for financial institutions.

A more balanced view of the benefits and the costs of regulation has been offered by Edward Kane (1983). He suggests that, on the positive side, regulation tends to increase public confidence in the regulated industry. Thus, customers may trust their banks' stability and reliability more because they are regulated, increasing customer loyalty to regulated firms and helping to shelter them from risk. Moreover, regulation may lead to a curious form of "innovation," which Kane labels the *regulatory dialectic*. He believes that regulated firms are constantly searching for ways around government rules in order to increase the market value of their business. Once they find a regulatory loophole that attracts the regulators' attention, new rules are imposed to close the gap. But this leads to still more "innovation" by regulated businesses in order to escape the new restrictions. The result is a continuing chain reaction: regulations spawn innovative escapes that, in turn, give rise to new rules in a never-ending struggle between the regulators and the regulated. Many observers of the banking industry in recent years see clear evidence of this dialectic process — bankers finding ways to offer prohibited services, like security underwriting and sales of insurance, spawning still more restrictive rules.

Notice, too, that the so-called "innovation" brought on by the regulatory dialectic is not the most productive and efficient form of innovation from society's point of view. Instead of developing ways to lower costs and deliver financial services more efficiently to the public, financial institutions are spending their time and energy looking for regulatory loopholes — something they wouldn't do if the regulations weren't there in the first place. This "wasted" time and energy, Kane believes, places regulated firms at a disadvantage vis-à-vis their unregulated competitors. Other factors held equal, the market share of regulated firms begins to fall. Many economists believe that this has happened to banks and other depository institutions in recent years, as security dealers and mutual funds, facing fewer regulations, have captured many of the banking industry's biggest and most profitable customers, reducing the share of the financial services marketplace controlled by depository institutions.

On balance, then, regulation of financial institutions may be a "tale of two cities," delivering both the best of times and the worst of times. Regulation may increase regulated institutions' profitability and shelter them from risk, resulting in fewer failures, but perhaps at the price of costlier services and less efficient financial firms. In return for greater stability and greater public confidence in financial institutions, customers must expect to be less well served in terms of prices charged and quality of services delivered.

THE REGULATION OF COMMERCIAL BANKS

Due to their importance in the financial system, *commercial banks* are typically the most regulated of all financial institutions. Moreover, in the United States, banking is more heavily regulated than in most other industrialized countries. From earliest history, there has been a fear of concentrated power in banking because bank credit is so vital to the well-being of businesses and households. During colonial times, several banks were burned to the ground due to public mistrust. During the 19th century and again in this century, severe restrictions were placed on the growth of U.S. banks through branching and holding companies in an effort to prevent banks from becoming so large they could intimidate their customers.

Responsibility for regulating U.S. banks today is divided among three federal banking agencies and 50 state banking commissions. These regulatory agencies have overlapping responsibilities, so most banks are subject to multiple jurisdictions. The regulatory agencies responsible for enforcing banking's ground rules include the Federal Reserve System, the Comptroller of the Currency, and the Federal Deposit Insurance Corporation — all at the federal level — and the state banking commissions of the 50 states. Exhibit 7–1 provides a summary of the principal regulatory powers exercised by these federal and state agencies in the United States.

The Federal Reserve System

The **Federal Reserve System** is responsible for examining and supervising the activities of all its member banks. When a member bank wishes to merge with another bank or establish a branch office, it must notify the Fed. The Fed must review and approve the acquisition of nonbank businesses by bank holding companies. The Federal Reserve is responsible for supervising U.S.-based international banking corporations, for supervising the operations of member banks in foreign countries, and for regulating foreign-bank activities inside the United States. The Fed also sets reserve requirements on deposits for all depository institutions.

The Comptroller of the Currency

The **Comptroller of the Currency** — also known as the Administrator of National Banks — is a division of the U.S. Treasury established under the National Banking Act of 1963. The Comptroller has the power to issue federal charters for the creation of new *national banks*. These banks, once chartered, are subject to an impressive array of regulations, most of which pertain to the kinds of loans and investments that may be made and the amount and types of capital each bank must hold. All national banks are examined periodically by the Comptroller's staff and may be liquidated or consolidated with another financial institution if deemed to be in the public interest.

Federal Deposit Insurance Corporation

The **Federal Deposit Insurance Corporation** (FDIC) insures deposits of commercial banks, savings banks, and savings and loans that meet its regulations. As a result of passage of the Financial Institutions Reform, Recovery, and Enforcement Act of 1989, the FDIC's insurance reserves are divided between the Bank Insurance Fund (BIF), backing commercial bank deposits; and the Savings Association Insurance Fund (SAIF) for the deposits of savings and loans and savings banks. With passage of the FDIC Improvement Act of 1991, each depositor is limited to a maximum of $100,000 in insurance coverage of ordinary deposits and to $100,000 to cover retirement accounts per insured depository institution should a bank or savings institution fail. Each participating bank is assessed a fee equal to a fraction of its eligible deposits to build and maintain the national insurance fund.

Exhibit 7–1   **Principal Bank Regulatory Agencies**

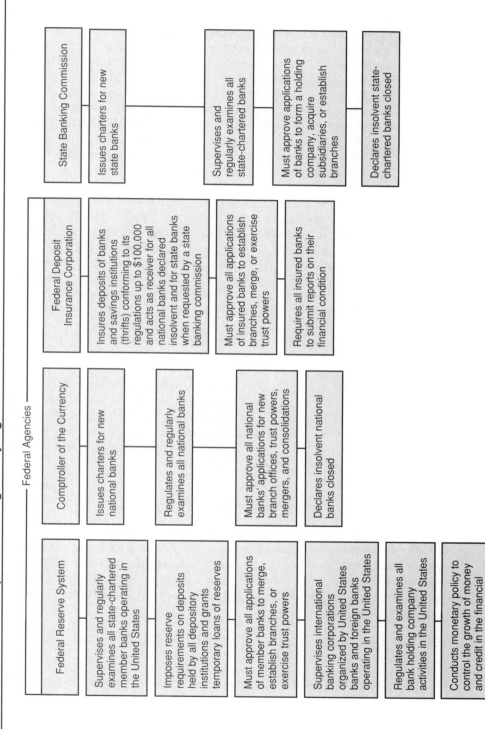

— Federal Agencies —

Federal Reserve System

Supervises and regularly examines all state-chartered member banks operating in the United States

Imposes reserve requirements on deposits held by all depository institutions and grants temporary loans of reserves

Must approve all applications of member banks to merge, establish branches, or exercise trust powers

Supervises international banking corporations organized by United States banks and foreign banks operating in the United States

Regulates and examines all bank holding company activities in the United States

Conducts monetary policy to control the growth of money and credit in the financial system

Comptroller of the Currency

Issues charters for new national banks

Regulates and regularly examines all national banks

Must approve all national banks' applications for new branch offices, trust powers, mergers, and consolidations

Declares insolvent national banks closed

Federal Deposit Insurance Corporation

Insures deposits of banks and savings institutions (thrifts) conforming to its regulations up to $100,000 and acts as receiver for all national banks declared insolvent and for state banks when requested by a state banking commission

Must approve all applications of insured banks to establish branches, merge, or exercise trust powers

Requires all insured banks to submit reports on their financial condition

State Banking Commission

Issues charters for new state banks

Supervises and regularly examines all state-chartered banks

Must approve applications of banks to form a holding company, acquire subsidiaries, or establish branches

Declares insolvent state-chartered banks closed

One of the most important functions of the FDIC is to act as a check on state banking commissions, because few banks today — even those with state charters — open their doors without FDIC deposit insurance. The FDIC reviews the adequacy of capital, earnings prospects, the character of management, and the public convenience and needs aspects of each application before granting deposit insurance. This agency is also charged with examining insured banks that are *not* members of the Federal Reserve System. The FDIC acts as receiver for all failed national banks and for failed state-chartered banks when requested by a state banking commission. In most cases, an insolvent bank will be merged with or absorbed by a healthy one. The FDIC often purchases some of the bankrupt institution's weaker assets to support such a merger. As a result of passage of the Competitive Equality Banking Act of 1987, the FDIC received the authority to set up "bridge banks" — newly chartered banking firms created to manage the assets of a failed depository institution until a suitable buyer could be found.

The savings and loan debacle of the 1980s, coupled with the failure of hundreds of banks in recent years, has led to the realization that the federal deposit insurance system as originally created was flawed. Until the mid-1990s, each bank, no matter how risky, paid the *same* insurance premium per dollar of the public's deposits. Moreover, until passage of the Financial Institutions Reform, Recovery, and Enforcement Act (FIRREA) of 1989, there was lax enforcement of federal capital standards, which led to excessive risk exposure to the federal insurance fund. The result was the appearance of a "moral hazard" problem in which banks and savings and loans could attract low-cost deposits (due to the benefit of deposit insurance coverage) and then invest in highly risky assets, knowing the government would, in effect, underwrite their gamble. Because the FDIC's reserves accumulated to pay off depositors in failed banks began declining in the 1980s, numerous proposals were brought forward to strengthen the deposit insurance system. Finally, with the deposit insurance fund almost drained, the FDIC Improvement Act of 1991 put Congress on record in favor of risk-adjusted deposit insurance premiums. The FDIC was ordered to charge riskier banks higher deposit insurance fees by no later than January 1, 1994. Moreover, the FDIC was given authority to borrow additional funds through the U.S. Treasury and authorized to raise insurance fees until the government's pool of insurance reserves reached at least 1.25 percent of all insured deposits — something that was accomplished for the bank insurance fund (BIF) in 1995.

State Banking Commissions

The regulatory powers of the federal banking agencies overlap with those of the **state banking commissions** that regularly examine all state-chartered banks. The states also have rules prescribing the minimum amount of equity capital for individual state-chartered banks and issue charters for new banks. As we shall see in the next section, the states have historically played a major role in the geographic and services expansion of banks.

Regulations Controlling the Geographic Expansion of Banks

One of the areas where state and federal regulators have exercised the most influence over banking is in controlling what new geographic markets banks can enter with their offices. Until the beginning of this century, few U.S. banks operated branch offices and most authorities believed that banks chartered by the federal government (that is, national banks) couldn't branch at all under the terms of the National Bank Act of

1863–64. (See Exhibit 7–2.) In the 1920s Congress passed the McFadden Act, which allowed national banks to branch within cities provided banks chartered by the states operating in those same areas possessed similar branching powers. Later, in the Banking Act of 1933 (Glass-Steagall), national banks could set up branch offices throughout their home state if state law permitted state-chartered banks to do the same. However, branching across state lines was forbidden unless the states involved expressly permitted interstate branching.

Exhibit 7–2	**Key Federal Laws That Have Affected the Structure and Regulation of the U.S. Banking Industry and Foreign Banks Operating in the United States**

National Bank Act (1863–1964)	Authorized federal chartering and supervision of banks by the Comptroller of the Currency.
Federal Reserve Act (1913)	Created the Federal Reserve System as central bank and guarantor of the banking system's liquidity.
McFadden Act (1927)	Vested the states with authority to limit branch banking and prohibit interstate branching if they wished.
Banking Act of 1933 (Glass-Steagall Act)	Created the FDIC to insure the public's deposits and denied banks the power to underwrite corporate securities.
Bank Holding Company Act (1956)	Required holding companies controlling two or more banks to register with the Federal Reserve Board; prohibited control by out-of-state holding companies of banks within a given state without the express permission of that state.
Bank Merger Act (1960)	Required mergers involving federally supervised banks to have the approval of their principal federal regulatory agency.
Bank Merger Act and Bank Holding Company Act Amendments (1966)	Allowed mergers and holding-company acquisitions to be approved by federal banking agencies if their anticompetitive effects are outweighed by public benefits, such as offering more convenient services.
Bank Holding Company Act Amendments (1970)	Made holding companies controlling only one bank subject to Federal Reserve regulation; confined nonbank business ventures of holding companies to bank-related services.
International Banking Act (1978)	Brought foreign banks operating in the United States under federal regulation for the first time.
Depository Institutions Deregulation and Monetary Control Act (1980)	Granted nonbank thrift institutions broader deposit and credit powers like those possessed by banks, began the phaseout of federal deposit rate ceilings, and imposed uniform deposit reserve requirements on banks and thrifts.
Garn–St Germain Depository Institutions Act (1982)	Authorized banks and savings and loans to offer money market deposit accounts, granted savings and loans additional commercial and consumer lending powers, and granted federal regulators new powers to deal with troubled depository institutions.
Competitive Banking Equality Act (1987)	Placed a moratorium on banks offering new services and required depositories to make any funds deposited by check available more quickly for spending by the public; allowed interstate emergency acquisitions of banks and permitted the FDIC to operate a failed bank as a "bridge bank" until a suitable buyer could be found.
Financial Institutions Reform, Recovery, and Enforcement Act (1989)	Restructured the federal supervisory agencies responsible for monitoring savings and loan associations, allowed bank holding companies to acquire savings and loans, and created two deposit insurance funds, one for banks (BIF) and the other for savings and loans (SAIF) under the FDIC.
Federal Deposit Insurance Corporation Improvement Act (1991)	Provided additional funding and borrowing authority for the federal deposit insurance fund (FDIC); gave federal regulatory agencies the power to close an undercapitalized bank or thrift; required the FDIC to set deposit insurance fees based on a bank's risk exposure; and imposed new regulations on foreign bank expansion in the United States.
Riegle-Neal Interstate Banking and Branching Efficiency Act (1994)	Allowed bank holding companies to acquire banks in any state and to branch across state lines beginning in 1997 if the states do not "opt out" of interstate branching.

As the years rolled by, especially after World War II, more and more states voted to allow branch banking within their borders. By the 1970s about a third of the states were *unit banking* states, allowing no full-service branch banking at all; roughly another third granted their banks *limited branching* powers, allowing branch offices only within certain cities, counties, or special districts; the remaining third were *statewide branching* states, permitting branch offices anywhere within the home state. However, by the 1990s all U.S. states allowed full-service branching of one form or another within their borders, reflecting the combined influence of a wave of bank mergers, bank failures, and a more mobile population.

When bank branching was prohibited or restricted by many states, bank holding companies — corporations controlling the stock of one or more banks — were developed in order to tie together groups of banks serving different geographic markets. Each holding company could issue debt or stock and use the proceeds to buy up a network of banks in a single state or even make acquisitions across state lines. In response to a chorus of complaints from bankers and state legislatures, the U.S. Congress passed the Bank Holding Company Act in 1956. Thereafter, bank holding company activities could be prohibited or restricted by state law if individual states chose to do so, though few states elected to outlaw this form of banking organization. Moreover, Congress stipulated in the Douglas Amendment that no bank holding company could acquire more than 5 percent of the voting stock of a bank located outside its home state without express permission from the state entered.

When the Bank Holding Company Act effectively blocked bank expansion across state lines, bankers soon found important loopholes in the law. The original Bank Holding Company Act left an unregulated opening for holding companies that held stock in only one bank. As a result, many of the largest banks formed one-bank holding companies during the late 1950s and began to acquire nonbank businesses far removed from the business of banking, including steel mills and meatpacking plants. Congress closed this loophole with passage of the 1970 amendments to the Bank Holding Company Act. From this point on, all holding companies seeking to acquire even a single bank had to register with the Federal Reserve Board and gain approval before purchasing any new bank or nonbank business. Nonbank business ventures acquired must now be "closely related" to banking, but they retain the advantage of being able to branch across state lines without significant restrictions.

What business activities are closely related to banking and, therefore, legal for bank holding companies to acquire or start? To date, the Federal Reserve Board has approved holding company acquisitions of those businesses engaged in such activities as making loans (such as finance, mortgage, or credit-card companies); writing property leases (e.g., equipment leasing companies); insuring credit repayments (such as firms selling credit life insurance); recording financial information (such as data processing firms); giving financial advice (i.e., through a trust company, consulting firm, or investment adviser); executing security trades (such as discount brokerage services); and, with Federal Reserve approval on a case-by-case basis, underwriting corporate stocks and bonds (i.e., buying these securities from their issuers and reselling them). Passage of the Financial Institutions Reform, Recovery, and Enforcement Act of 1989 permitted holding company acquisitions of savings and loan associations and savings banks as well, thus making it possible for bank holding companies to purchase nonbank thrifts and their deposits across state lines.

Banks also sought to expand their market territory by outright *mergers* with other institutions. When the industry seemed on the verge of being transformed by a tidal wave of merger activity, the U.S. Congress stepped in once again and, in the Bank Merger Act of 1960, required each bank involved in a merger to receive the approval of its principal federal regulatory agency. For national banks this means that the Comptroller of the Currency must approve the merger transaction, while state-chartered banks who are members of the Federal Reserve System must secure the approval of the Fed and state-chartered nonmember banks must get approval from the Federal Deposit Insurance Corporation. The Department of Justice must review each proposed merger and can sue in federal court to block it if competition would be damaged significantly. Amendments to the Bank Merger Act in 1966 allowed U.S. bank regulatory agencies to approve mergers even if competition were slightly damaged provided there were other benefits stemming from a merger, such as expanding the quality or quantity of services or rescuing a troubled bank. Recently, as consolidation gathers momentum, the U.S. banking industry has experienced a wave of mega-mergers, including such leading banks as Chase Manhatten Bank, NationsBank, Chemical Bank, First Union Corp., First Fidelity, and First Chicago Corp.

Few states granted out-of-state bank holding companies permission to enter their territory through mergers or acquisitions until the 1980s. However, a massive wave of bank failures coupled with pressures from bankers' associations soon led to state after state voting to permit interstate holding company acquisitions. By the 1990s, 49 of the 50 states (excepting Hawaii) had voted to permit interstate bank holding companies to come in, but under a wide variety of entry conditions. For example, most states, at least in the beginning, would only permit entry from neighboring states (so-called *regional* interstate banking) and insisted that their own banks be given reciprocal entry privileges by other states (so-called *reciprocity* laws). However, gradually over time more and more states expanded their regional entry laws, many allowing entry from any other state in the nation, and several states with serious economic problems (such as Louisiana, Oklahoma, and Texas) dropped the requirement of reciprocal entry privileges for their own banks in the hope that more out-of-state banks would enter and prop up their ailing banks.

Clearly, holding company banking had opened the door to the interstate expansion of banks, but this approach proved to be an expensive way for a banking organization to reach into new markets. Every bank acquired by a holding company had to be kept open as a separate corporation with its own capital, management, and board of directors. Establishing branch offices might be considerably less expensive because of less duplication of personnel and resources, but both the McFadden and Glass-Steagall Acts prohibited interstate branch banking.

The final step at the federal government level toward interstate branching was finally taken in August 1994 when the U.S. Congress passed the Riegle-Neal Interstate Banking and Branching Efficiency Act. (See Exhibit 7–3.) This law arose out of concern for the roughly 60 million Americans who commute to work or shop across state lines each day but usually find that their bank account relationships are not as easily transportable. It also sprang from the long-standing complaint among the largest banks that using holding companies as a vehicle to cross state lines was inefficient and expensive. The Riegle-Neal Act permits bank holding companies to acquire banks in any of the remaining 49 states, thus rendering ineffective those state laws limiting entry to regions or requiring reciprocal entry privileges. The new law took an additional important step, however, in allowing banks acquired across state lines to be converted into branch offices unless the states involved voted before June 1, 1997 to "opt out" of interstate branching. However, should certain states vote to remove themselves from the interstate branching network, their own banks would not be allowed to participate in interstate banking.

Finally, in order to guard against an excessive concentration of banking industry resources in the hands of a few banks, the Riegle-Neal law held that no one banking organization would be allowed to control more than 10 percent of nationwide deposits nor more than 30 percent of all deposits in a single state (unless the state involved chooses to waive this latter upper limit). And, to ensure against the draining away of local deposits by

| Exhibit 7–3 | **The Riegle-Neal Interstate Banking and Branching Efficiency Act of 1994** |

President Bill Clinton signed this nationwide bank holding company and interstate branching law on September 29, 1994. This sweeping banking structure law included the following provisions:

Nationwide Holding-Company Banking
1. Beginning September 30, 1995 bank holding companies can acquire banks in any state even if state law prohibits such acquisitions.
2. However, no one banking organization can control more than 10 percent of nationwide deposits or more than 30 percent of the deposits in a single state unless a state chooses to waive this latter limit.

Interstate Branch Banking
1. Beginning June 1, 1997 a banking organization can merge with banks in other states and convert those acquired banks into branch offices unless the state or states involved choose to "opt out" of the interstate branching portions of the new law.
2. A state may enact legislation that exempts that state from interstate branching. However, its own banks cannot participate in further interstate banking acquisitions.
3. States can vote to permit *de novo* interstate branching, allowing a bank to branch into their territory without having previously acquired any banks there.

Community Reinvestment Requirements
Branch offices established by national banks must conform to local laws requiring consumer protection, fair lending, intrastate branching, and investments in local communities. Federal regulatory agencies must consider the views of local community organizations prior to closing an interstate banking organization's branch office situated in a low-income neighborhood.

Foreign Banking Provisions
1. If a foreign-owned bank has established a subsidiary corporation based in the United States, it can acquire banks and branch across state lines to the same extent as U.S. banks.
2. Foreign-owned banks acquiring domestic U.S. banks subject to the Community Reinvestment Act must conform to all the provisions of that Act.

a large interstate company, banks expanding across state lines were required to commit a minimum percentage of their incoming funds to locally based loans.

Regulation of the Services Banks Can Offer

Even as banks have sought greater freedom to expand geographically, they have also fought for, but only occasionally won, new service powers in order to retain their existing customers and attract new ones. Unfortunately, regulations have been tight and sometimes unyielding in this area out of concern for bank safety (as service innovation can be highly risky) and because of a desire to protect certain nonbank financial institutions, such as credit unions, savings and loans, and insurance companies, from tough bank competition.

Probably the most influential law in American history in defining bank service powers was the **Glass-Steagall Act** (or Banking Act) of 1933. This sweeping law confined bank service powers essentially to the making of loans and the taking of deposits, while insurance services were largely relegated to insurance companies, and home lending was centered in savings and loan associations and savings banks. U.S. bankers also lost an important service power they possessed in the decades before Glass-Steagall — the power to assist their largest corporate customers by purchasing corporate stock and then reselling it in the open market. Foreign banks have continued to offer corporate bond and stock *underwriting services* to American companies, and U.S. banks are active in the security underwriting business overseas through a variety of affiliated organizations, but they have clearly lost customers to security dealers and foreign banks (principally from Canada and Western Europe) in domestic underwriting, except for underwriting those types of securities where exceptions have been granted from federal restrictions. Bankers have avidly sought security underwriting powers because this business can be highly profitable and it complements traditional lending services.

Beginning in the late 1980s the Federal Reserve Board began to permit individual banking organizations on a case-by-case basis to underwrite selected types of securities through separate subsidiaries. For example, individual institutions such as Bankers Trust of New York, Citicorp, and Security Pacific Corporation (now part of Bank America) were granted authority to underwrite certain loan-backed securities and some forms of corporate debt. Finally, in September 1990, J.P. Morgan was extended the power to underwrite new corporate stock issues. By 1995, nearly 30 U.S. and foreign banking corporations had been approved by the Federal Reserve Board to offer selected debt security underwriting services, while close to a dozen banking companies had received approval to underwrite corporate stock. Companies approved by the Federal Reserve Board to underwrite stock issues included such industry leaders as Bankers Trust Company, Chemical Bank, Dauphin Deposit, J.P. Morgan, Bank of Montreal, Bank of Nova Scotia, Canadian Imperial Bank of Commerce, Deutsche Bank, and the Royal Bank of Canada. However, tight restrictions were imposed upon all participating banks. For example, the underwriting of previously forbidden types of securities had to be carried out through a special subsidiary, not by the bank itself, and revenue generated from these previously forbidden underwriting activities could represent no more than 10 percent of the total revenues of the underwriting subsidiary.

Despite these restrictions, however, U.S. banks' share of all corporate security underwriting activities has recently grown quite rapidly and many bankers are asking for further expansion of their underwriting powers. The U.S. Congress debated a bill in the middle and late 1990s to repeal Glass-Steagall's restrictions against bank expansion into security underwriting, insurance underwriting and sales, and other new service activities. However, the proposed changes in the law faced stiff opposition from trade groups, representing the industries that banks wished to enter, and from public interest groups concerned about the proposed repeal of consumer rights' legislation.

Bankers have had more success at entering other service fields directly or indirectly. For example, beginning in the 1980s several large banks (led by Security Pacific National Bank of Los Angeles) began to offer security brokerage services through special subsidiary firms. In 1987 the U.S. Supreme Court voted to allow national banks and bank holding companies to operate discount security brokerage offices anywhere in the nation, and subsequently the Federal Reserve Board voted to permit bank holding companies to offer full-service security brokerage (including providing customers with investment advice) through a separate subsidiary. Numerous joint ventures between security brokerage companies and banking organizations have appeared recently in an effort to give bank customers full access to the stock and bond markets.

A related service involves trading of shares in *mutual funds*, which banks began to offer in significant volume during the 1990s in an effort to keep their depositors from leaving in order to pursue higher yielding stock and bond investments. Sales of these shares in stock and bond funds has been held not to violate the Glass-Steagall Act provided that a business firm not affiliated with a U.S. bank underwrites and distributes the mutual funds' shares. However, new regulations stipulate that depositors must be given written statements explaining the risks involved in buying mutual fund shares and explicitly stating that these funds are *not* insured by the federal government or even guaranteed by the offering bank.

Within the field of insurance, bankers have managed to convince certain states (for example, Delaware and Indiana) to allow the offering of insurance policies through affiliated companies. Despite a strong challenge from the insurance industry, the U.S. Supreme Court in January 1995 affirmed an earlier ruling by the Comptroller of the Currency that national banks could legally sell *annuities* — funds invested in a pool of securities that eventually pay out a stream of income to the annuity holder. The Comptroller argued that annuities are not "insurance products" but "investment products" similar to bank CDs and retirement accounts and, therefore, banks offering annuities are not violating the half-century-old federal restrictions against banks selling insurance products. Some banks would also like to engage in underwriting insurance risks, but both federal and state governments have stoutly resisted this step because of the unusually high risks involved.

The recent debate over banks being allowed to sell insurance policies, along with other new services, is a reminder of the difficulties the banking industry has always faced when it tries to develop and offer new services. Bankers have argued that many new services would actually *reduce* bank risk, because the earnings generated by these new services have a low positive, or even a negative, correlation with the earnings from traditional bank services. Moreover, they argue, unless banks can keep up with shifting public demand for financial services they are in danger of becoming irrelevant in the workings of the financial system. Regulators, however, generally adopt a "go slow" approach in order to assess the risks involved for depositor safety. Bankers that wish to retain federal deposit insurance coverage must expect that regulations are likely to continue to be a significant hurdle to bank service innovation for the foreseeable future.

The Rise of Disclosure Laws in Banking

One of the most rapidly expanding areas of U.S. banking regulation today centers around *disclosure rules* — regulations requiring financial institutions to reveal certain information to customers (in an effort to encourage shopping around and avoid deception) and to regulators (to improve supervision of the banking industry). Among the most prominent examples are the Truth in Lending Act (1968) and the Truth in Savings Act (1991), which require disclosure of all the interest and fees associated with selling loans and deposits to individuals who are bank customers. Similarly, the Home Mortgage Disclosure Act (1975) requires banks to report to the public and to regulators the locations of both their approved and rejected applications for loans to purchase or improve homes as a check on possible discrimination in lending. The FDIC Improvement Act (1991) requires banks and other depositories to notify customers and regulators in advance when branch offices are to be closed. Finally, the Community Reinvestment Act (1977) stipulates that bankers must make an affirmative effort to serve *all* segments of their trade territory, including low-income neighborhoods, and disclose to the public their community service performance ratings. Community reinvestment rules require bankers to document all of their community-support activities.

These and other disclosure rules have aroused a storm of controversy. For most such rules it is not clear that the benefits of greater disclosure outweigh the costs involved. For example, the U.S. Office of Management and Budget has estimated that U.S. bankers commit an average of 7.5 million hours each year just to comply with the Truth in Lending Act. Nor is it clear that the public pays much attention to these disclosure requirements; regulators, not customers, seem to be the audience that most closely watches the behavior and performance of banks and other financial institutions.

The Growing Importance of Capital Regulation in Banking

In addition to the spread of interstate banking and the explosion in branching activity by banks, another major trend reshaping the regulation of banks and other financial institutions today centers upon their capital — the long-term funds invested in a financial institution, mainly by its owners. For example, when stockholders buy ownership shares in a bank, they have a claim against the bank's earnings and assets. However, a bank's stockholders bear all the risks of ownership. If the bank fails to generate sufficient earnings, the stockholders may receive no dividend income and, if the bank fails, they could lose everything.

Beginning in the 1980s, bank regulators in the leading industrialized countries (including the United States, Canada, Japan, and the nations of Western Europe) came to the conclusion that control of risk taking by banks is best centered upon a bank's *owners*. When a bank chooses to take on more risk, its owners should be asked to increase their financial commitment to the bank by supplying more capital. Because stockholder capital is expensive to raise and could be lost completely if the bank fails, the owners of the bank are likely to monitor the bank's risk taking more closely, pressuring management to be more prudent in taking on additional risk.

This concept of making a bank's owners more responsible for the consequences of risk taking by their banks led in June of 1988 to the adoption of *minimum capital standards* for all banks by the leading countries of Western Europe, Canada, Japan, and the United States. The so-called **Basle Agreement** (named for Basle, Switzerland, where it was adopted) stipulates that banks in all the participating nations must have a minimum ratio of total capital to risk-weighted assets and other related risk-exposed items of 8 percent. Risk-weighted assets are to be determined by classifying each of a bank's assets listed on its balance sheet into categories based on each asset's degree of risk exposure and then multiplying the volume of assets in each risk category by a fractional risk weight ranging from 0 for cash and government securities to 1.00 for commercial loans and other high-risk assets. Thus:

$$
\begin{array}{l}
\text{Total risk-weighted assets on} \\
\text{a bank's balance sheet}
\end{array}
=
\begin{array}{l}
0 \times (\text{cash and U.S. government securities}) + 0.20 \times (\text{other types} \\
\text{of government securities and interbank deposits}) + 0.50 \times \\
(\text{residential mortgage loans, government revenue bonds, and} \\
\text{selected types of mortgage-backed securities}) + 1.00 \times \\
(\text{commercial and consumer loans and other assets of the highest} \\
\text{risk exposure})
\end{array}
$$

The Basle Agreement was unique in also including off-balance-sheet commitments that banks often make to their largest customers and to hedge themselves against risk, including standby credit letters, credit commitments to grant future loans, loans sold with recourse, and futures, options, and swap contracts. The amount of each off-balance-sheet item is multiplied by a fractional amount known as its "credit-equivalent" value, which is, in turn, multiplied by a fractional risk weight based on its assumed degree of risk exposure. The volume of risk-weighted off-balance-sheet items is then added to a bank's total risk-weighted on-balance-sheet assets. Thus:

$$
\begin{array}{l}
\text{Total risk-weighted} \\
\text{on- and off-balance} \\
\text{sheet items}
\end{array}
=
\begin{array}{l}
\text{Total risk-weighted} \\
\text{assets on a bank's} \\
\text{balance sheet}
\end{array}
+
\begin{array}{l}
\text{Total risk-weighted} \\
\text{off-balance-sheet} \\
\text{items}
\end{array}
$$

To determine a bank's total capital, its longer-maturity liabilities and its equity (owners') capital are classified into two broad categories:

$$
\begin{array}{l}
\text{Tier-one or permanent} \\
\text{(core) bank capital}
\end{array}
=
\begin{array}{l}
\text{Tangible equity including common stock} \\
+ \text{Perpetual preferred stock} + \text{Surplus} + \\
\text{Retained earnings} + \text{Capital reserves less} \\
\text{Intangibles}
\end{array}
$$

$$
\begin{array}{l}
\text{Tier-two or} \\
\text{supplemental capital}
\end{array}
=
\begin{array}{l}
\text{Subordinated capital notes and} \\
\text{debentures over 5 years to maturity} \\
+ \text{Limited-life preferred stock} + \\
\text{Loan-loss reserves}
\end{array}
$$

The Basle Agreement requires each bank in all participating countries to achieve and hold the following capital minimums:

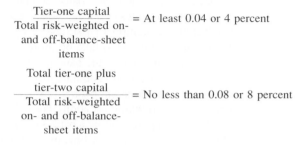

$$\frac{\text{Tier-one capital}}{\substack{\text{Total risk-weighted on-} \\ \text{and off-balance-sheet} \\ \text{items}}} = \text{At least } 0.04 \text{ or } 4 \text{ percent}$$

$$\frac{\substack{\text{Total tier-one plus} \\ \text{tier-two capital}}}{\substack{\text{Total risk-weighted} \\ \text{on- and off-balance-} \\ \text{sheet items}}} = \text{No less than } 0.08 \text{ or } 8 \text{ percent}$$

Thus, a bank with a 4 percent tier-one capital ratio and a 5 percent tier-two capital ratio would have a ratio of total capital to risk-weighted on- and off-balance-sheet items of 9 percent, one percent above the minimum required. However, if a bank had only a 3 percent tier-one capital ratio and a tier-two capital ratio of 5 percent, it would actually fall *below* the minimum 8 percent total capital ratio. This is because it must have at least a 4 percent tier-one capital ratio and can count toward meeting the Basle capital requirements only an amount of tier-two capital up to the amount of its tier-one capital. Thus, this last bank is short 1 percent in tier-one capital and must work out a plan with its principal regulatory agency to raise the additional amount of required tier-one capital.

In the United States and selected other countries, a bank that holds more than the required minimum amounts of capital is allowed to expand its services and service facilities with few or no regulatory restrictions imposed. However, if bank capital drops below the minimum percentage of risk-exposed assets, regulatory restrictions become increasingly stiff, restraining the bank's growth and subjecting its operations to greater control and supervision. This new regulatory policy, called *prompt corrective action*, was adopted in the United States with passage of the FDIC Improvement Act of 1991. In addition, the FDIC Improvement Act required riskier, inadequately capitalized U.S. banks to pay higher fees for government deposit insurance. Worldwide, as banks have become more involved in the markets for derivative securities, such as futures and options, regulatory agencies have acted to impose capital requirements on bank investments in derivative instruments.

The Unfinished Agenda for Banking Regulation

The tremendous changes in banking regulation in recent years — including the adoption of nationwide banking in the United States and the spreading internationalization of bank regulation as evidenced by the Basle Agreement on bank capital — might lead us to think that there is little left to do in reshaping the future structure of bank regulation. Nothing could be further from the truth! Banking in the United States (and in most other countries of the world) remains heavily burdened by constraining government rules. Slowly, and along a zig-zag path, banking is experiencing an era of *deregulation*, as legal constraints are being lifted on a few banking activities.

Nevertheless, many important bank regulatory barriers remain. In the United States the Glass-Steagall Act passed in 1933, along with several other Depression-inspired laws, defined the legal scope of services banks could offer vis-à-vis other financial institutions. The net effect was to wall off banking activities from the markets served by security brokers and dealers, mutual funds, insurance companies, and thrift institutions. Lawmakers and regulators reasoned that by isolating each financial institution in its own special niche, all would be safer and less damaged by competition, thus bringing greater stability to the financial system.

MANAGEMENT INSIGHT:

Managing a Financial Institution's Capital Position

Financial institutions have struggled greatly in recent years to build up their capital in order to restore public confidence and avoid regulatory penalties. *Capital* for a financial institution generally refers to its long-term sources of funding — monies that are raised through the issue of stocks and long-term debt and from earnings retained in the business. For most financial institutions today, capital includes owners' equity — common and preferred stock, surplus, retained earnings (or undivided profits), and equity reserves — plus long-term bonds or debentures.

Capital performs several essential roles in the life of a financial institution. It provides the start-up funds to acquire facilities and hire staff in order to get the institution organized and running. Capital provides a cushion against the risk of failure, absorbing operating losses until management can work to make the firm profitable again. Capital is the base upon which a financial institution grows and develops new services. Capital promotes public confidence in the long-run stability of a financial institution and limits how fast each financial institution can grow. Among the telltale indicators of how well capitalized a financial institution is are such financial ratios as:

$$\frac{\text{Total capital}}{\text{Total assets}}, \quad \frac{\text{Total capital}}{\text{Total risk assets*}}, \quad \text{and} \quad \frac{\text{Total capital}}{\text{Total liabilities}}$$

When a financial institution's capital ratios fall significantly below those of comparable institutions, its stock price may begin to fall and its cost of borrowed funds may rise as investors in the money and capital markets become more sensitive to its risk exposure.

Therefore, one indicator of how much capital a financial institution needs is the financial marketplace itself, which sends out signals if it believes any particular financial institution is under-capitalized. Another indicator is *regulation*, where regulators spell out the minimum amount of institutional capital required.

---

*Risk assets usually include all assets held by a financial institution except cash and fully-guaranteed government securities.

As we saw earlier, the U.S. Congress has debated several times the wisdom of repealing Glass-Steagall's prohibition against the underwriting of corporate securities and even considered loosening the bonds on banks' insurance activities. However, each time strong opposition has emerged from the various financial service industries who would be most affected by banking deregulation. Several states (such as Delaware, Indiana, and South Dakota) have moved to allow the banks they charter to offer insurance and other services. The U.S. Congress, however, seems mired down by contending lobbyists in its efforts to deregulate the service activities of the U.S. banking industry. Clearly, much remains to be done to give U.S. bankers the tools to compete with both domestic nonbank financial firms and foreign financial service competitors.

There is also much more work to be done in the international dimension of financial institutions' regulation. The 1988 Basle Agreement on international capital standards represented a major step forward in recognizing the unfairness of different national regulations to bankers trying to compete in international markets. If banks are to achieve a "level playing field" around the globe, there must not only be similar capital requirements from country to country but also similar tax rules, service powers, examination standards, etc. In the absence of greater balance in the scope and depth of banking regulation worldwide, bankers striving to maximize the value of their banks will seek out those global markets where regulation poses a lower cost burden for them.

THE REGULATION OF NONBANK THRIFT INSTITUTIONS

As we saw in Chapter 5, nonbank thrift institutions include credit unions, savings and loan associations, savings banks, and money market mutual funds. Each of these institutions also faces an impressive array of federal or state regulations or both.

Credit Unions

In the United States, credit unions are chartered and regulated at both state and federal levels (see Exhibit 7–4). Today about three fifths of all credit unions are chartered by the federal government; the remainder are chartered by the states. Federal credit unions have been regulated since 1970 by the **National Credit Union Administration** (NCUA), an

Exhibit 7–4   Government Agencies That Regulate the Nonbank Thrifts (Federal and State Agencies That Control)

Nonbank Thrift Institution	Chartering and Licensing of Thrifts	Setting Up New Branches	Mergers and Acquisitions	Deposit Insurance	Supervision and Examination
Credit unions	National Credit Union Administration (NCUA)/state credit union or banking departments	No approval required	NCUA/state credit union or banking departments	NCUA Share Insurance Fund/state deposit insurance departments	NCUA/state credit union or banking departments
Savings and loan associations	Office of Thrift Supervision/state banking or savings and loan departments	Office of Thrift Supervision/Federal Deposit Insurance Corporation (FDIC)/state banking or savings and loan departments	Office of Thrift Supervision/FDIC/state banking or savings and loan departments	FDIC's Savings Association Insurance Fund/state insurance departments	Office of Thrift Supervision/state banking or savings and loan departments
Savings banks	Office of Thrift Supervision/state banking departments	Office of Thrift Supervision/state banking departments	Office of Thrift Supervision/FDIC/state banking departments	FDIC/state insurance funds	FDIC/state banking departments
Money market funds	Securities and Exchange Commission (SEC)	No approval required	No approval required	No government insurance; some funds have private insurance	SEC for selected activities

Source: Federal Reserve Bank of New York and the author.

independent agency within the federal government. Deposits are insured by the National Credit Union Share Insurance Fund (NCUSIF) up to $100,000. State-chartered credit unions may qualify for federal insurance if they conform to NCUA's regulations.

Credit unions, like banks, are closely regulated in the services they can offer the public, the investments they can make with their depositors' money, and the types of deposits they can sell. Fortunately for the industry, regulations have been liberalized in recent years through such federal deregulation laws as the Depository Institutions Deregulation and Monetary Control Act (1980) and the Garn–St Germain Depository Institutions Act (1982), which gave U.S. credit unions the power to offer checkable deposits (share drafts) and home mortgage (real estate) loans in order to be able to compete effectively against commercial banks. (See Exhibits 7–5 and 7–6.)

Savings and Loans

Savings and loan associations are also regulated and can receive their charter of incorporation from either state or federal government agencies. About half have charters from state authorities who supervise their activities and regularly examine their books while the remainder have federal charters. Federal savings and loans are insured (up to a maximum of $100,000 per depositor) by the Savings Association Insurance Fund (SAIF) managed by the Federal Deposit Insurance Corporation (FDIC). (See Exhibit 7–7.)

S&Ls chartered by the states also may qualify for insurance coverage from the FDIC. Both federally chartered and federally insured state associations are supervised and examined by the **Office of Thrift Supervision** of the U.S. Treasury Department, and the FDIC also has certain S&L supervisory powers, such as regulating the capital positions of these savings associations. Qualified S&Ls can borrow emergency funds from the Federal Home Loan banks and from the discount windows of the Federal Reserve banks.

Regulation of the savings and loan industry over the past two decades has resembled a roller coaster, with wide swings from deregulating the industry to imposing much tougher restrictions. For example, as Exhibits 7–5 and 7–6 illustrate, two major laws passed in the

Exhibit 7–5

Provisions of the Depository Institutions Deregulation and Monetary Control Act (DIDMCA) of 1980 Applying to Credit Unions, Savings and Loan Associations, and Savings Banks

New Deposit Powers
1. Interest-rate ceilings on deposits were to be phased out, permitting interest yields offered the public to respond to competition and market forces.
2. NOW accounts, which bear interest and can be used to make payments, could be offered to individuals and nonprofit organizations by all federally insured depository institutions.
3. Federally insured credit unions were authorized to offer share drafts (interest-bearing checking accounts) to their members.
4. Savings banks were empowered to offer demand deposits to business customers.

New Loan and Investment Powers
1. Federally insured credit unions were approved to offer real estate loans.
2. Federally chartered savings and loan associations could issue credit cards, offer trust services, and make investments in consumer loans, commercial paper, and corporate bonds up to 20 percent of their assets.
3. Savings banks with federal charters could invest up to 5 percent of their total assets in commercial, corporate, and business loans within their home state or within 75 miles of their home office.

Exhibit 7–6

Provisions of the Garn–St Germain Depository Institutions Act of 1982 (Garn bill; HR-6267) Applying to Credit Unions, Savings and Loan Associations, and Savings Banks

New Deposit Powers
1. Depository Institutions Deregulation Commission (DIDC) was authorized to develop a deposit account for banks and nonbank thrifts competitive with shares in money market funds.
2. Federally chartered savings associations could accept regular checkbook deposits from businesses having a long-term relationship to a savings association or could serve as a repository for business payments.
3. All deposit-type institutions are permitted to offer NOW accounts to governmental units.

New Loan and Investment Powers
1. Federal savings associations may make secured or unsecured loans to businesses totaling up to 10 percent of their assets.
2. Commercial real estate loans may be increased from 20 to 40 percent of the total assets at federal savings associations and required loan-value minimum ratios are eliminated. Federal credit unions are granted broader real estate loan powers.
3. Federal savings associations may purchase municipal revenue bonds (up to 10 percent of their capital) as well as general-obligation municipal bonds and invest in insured time deposits.
4. Federal savings associations may invest in consumer loans up to 30 percent of their total assets.
5. Federal savings associations may lease or lend against personal property up to 10 percent of their total assets.
6. State laws and court decisions restricting enforcement of due-on-sale clauses in real property loans are preempted so that when a mortgaged home is sold, the outstanding mortgage loan becomes due and payable.

Other Provisions
Depository institutions could freely change organizational form from mutual to stockholder owned and change their federal or state supervisory agency.

early 1980s — the Depository Institutions Deregulation and Monetary Control Act of 1980 and the Garn–St Germain Depository Institutions Act of 1982 — granted federally supervised savings and loans major new service powers (such as credit cards, corporate bonds, and consumer installment loans) so they could compete directly with commercial banks. Then, after hundreds of S&Ls failed in the mid-1980s, in part because they sometimes moved too quickly to offer new services, the federal government substantially tightened the rules surrounding savings and loan operations with passage of the Financial Institutions Reform, Recovery and Enforcement Act of 1989. No longer could S&Ls buy low-quality (junk) bonds, and the majority of their lending had to be focused on the housing industry. Designed to restore public confidence in savings and loans, this new law stipulated that to be a "qualified thrift lender" (QTL), eligible for tax benefits and to borrow funds at low cost from the Federal Home Loan banks — a lender of last resort for the industry, S&Ls must hold a minimum of 70 percent of their total assets in real estate mortgage loans or mortgage-backed securities.

This latter provision of the Financial Institutions Reform, Recovery, and Enforcement Act proved to be severely constraining on S&Ls that chose to remain in the thrift industry. Many converted to commercial or savings banks to have more freedom and flexibility. In November 1991, these restrictive rules limiting S&L asset diversification were eased somewhat with passage of the FDIC Improvement Act, allowing savings associations to qualify as thrift lenders (QTLs) if a minimum of 65 percent of their total assets were in mortgage-related investments or other qualified assets. Moreover, a portion of consumer

Exhibit 7–7

Provisions of the Financial Institutions Reform, Recovery, and Enforcement Act of 1989 Applying to Savings and Loan Associations, Other Thrifts, and Banks (Passed on August 9, 1989)

A New Insurance and Regulatory Plan for Depository Institutions

1. The Federal Savings and Loan Insurance Corporation, created originally to insure S&L deposits, is replaced by the Savings Association Insurance Fund (SAIF) to insure the public's deposits up to $100,000. SAIF is placed under the management of the Federal Deposit Insurance Corporation (FDIC), which also manages the Bank Insurance Fund (BIF) to insure commercial banks' deposits.
2. Supervisory powers over the U.S. savings and loan industry are transferred from the Federal Home Loan Bank (FHLB) Board to the Office of Thrift Supervision (OTS), a division of the U.S. Treasury Department, and the FDIC. The OTS can limit the growth of thrift institutions that are inadequately capitalized and prevent these institutions from accepting deposits brokered by security dealers, thus reducing possible future drains on federal insurance reserves.
3. The FDIC is empowered to increase deposit insurance assessments against thrifts until federal insurance reserves rise to at least 1.25 percent of all insured deposits.
4. Federal regulators were given greater power to restrict risky investments by savings and loans and greater flexibility in closing insolvent depository institutions. The FDIC can become a conservator (operating a depository institution as a going concern) or a receiver (closing and liquidating a depository institution) for any insured depository chartered under either federal or state law that has been declared insolvent or can suspend insurance coverage for a risky depository institution.
5. Responsibility for disposing of the assets of closed depository institutions is given to the Resolution Trust Corporation (RTC), which has authority to borrow in the financial markets.

Changes in Capital, Investment, and Service Powers

1. To promote greater safety among depository institutions, new minimum capital standards are imposed on depository institutions so that core capital provided by their owners equals at least 3 percent of their total assets and tangible capital must amount to at least 1.5 percent of their assets.
2. Thrift institutions are prohibited from purchasing junk bonds.
3. Depository institutions desiring to be "qualified thrift lenders" (and, therefore, receive tax benefits and FHLB low interest loans) must increase the proportion of their assets placed in mortgage-related investments up to at least 70 percent of their total assets.

---

loans and mortgage loans previously sold could be counted toward meeting the new requirements to qualify for federal tax benefits as a QTL. (See Exhibit 7–8.)

The savings and loan industry was further jolted by tough new *regulatory forbearance* rules when the Financial Institutions Reform, Recovery, and Enforcement Act was passed in 1989 and when the FDIC Improvement Act (FDICIA) appeared in 1991. Prior to these laws, regulatory agencies often allowed insolvent S&Ls, banks, and other depository institutions to keep their doors open and permitted them to pay higher and higher interest rates in an effort to keep the public's deposits invested in these troubled institutions. This form of regulatory forbearance drove up deposit costs for *all* depository institutions and, on occasion, drove some healthy banks and S&Ls to the point of failure. Moreover, if the regulators were eventually forced to close the insolvent institutions, the delay in taking action made it difficult, if not impossible, to sell the failed institutions to healthy companies for enough money to recover all the costs involved. While regulatory forbearance was originally designed to save deposit insurance money, it often wound up costing the government's insurance fund *more* in the long run.

Congress put a stop to regulatory forbearance when the FDIC Improvement Act was passed. Under the new law, a bank or thrift could be closed if its ratio of tangible equity capital to total assets fell below two percent for more than 90 days. The troubled institution must be closed down or sold to a healthy firm if its undercapitalized condition lasts for more

Exhibit 7–8

Provisions of the Federal Deposit Insurance Corporation Improvement Act of 1991 Applying to Savings and Loan Associations, Other Thrifts, and Banks (Passed in November 1991)

Recapitalization of the FDIC and Protecting Federal Insurance Reserves

1. The Federal Deposit Insurance Corporation (FDIC) is empowered to borrow an additional $30 billion from the U.S. Treasury to be repaid from future insurance premiums. The FDIC may also borrow using the assets of the failed institutions it has taken over as collateral.
2. Federal regulators may close an undercapitalized bank or thrift institution that is not yet insolvent. Critically undercapitalized institutions (with capital/asset ratios below 2 percent) may be placed in receivership. Regulations become increasingly strict as a depository institution's capital position weakens and may include requiring a merger, placing prohibitions on interest paid to depositors, restricting growth, replacing management, or prohibiting stockholder dividends.
3. Riskier depository institutions will be assessed higher insurance fees. The FDIC must assess sufficient fees to bring federal insurance reserves up to at least 1.25 percent of all insured deposits by the year 2006.
4. The FDIC may prohibit undercapitalized depository institutions or those with no more than average capital from accepting deposits placed with them by brokers unless the FDIC finds that this activity is not unsafe.
5. Deposit insurance coverage of personal retirement accounts is limited to a maximum of $100,000 for any one retirement account holder in any one insured depository institution.

Restrictions on Services Offered

1. State-chartered branches and agency offices operated by insured depository institutions cannot engage in activities that federally chartered depository institutions cannot legally offer unless approved by the Federal Reserve or the FDIC.
2. State-chartered banks are subject to the same lending limits as federally chartered banks and cannot offer insurance underwriting services or make equity investments if national banks are not permitted to do so.
3. Depository institutions must retain a licensed or certified appraiser to evaluate real estate for large investments or loans. Federal regulators must adopt uniform standards for real estate lending.
4. Misleading advertising of deposits is prohibited and any adverse change in deposit terms must be communicated to depositors 30 days prior to the change. Moreover, any insured depository institution must notify its customers and its principal regulator at least 90 days before closing any branch office.
5. Savings and loans may qualify for special benefits (e.g., tax benefits and borrowing from the Federal Home Loan banks at low cost) if at least 65 percent of their total assets are in mortgage-related assets or other qualified assets. Qualified assets can include securities issued by government agencies as well as 10 percent of all consumer loans outstanding and 20 percent of all originated residential mortgage loans sold within 90 days.

New Restrictions on Foreign Banks

The Federal Reserve Board must approve new offices and service activities of foreign banks and can revoke a foreign bank's license to operate in the United States if it is pursuing unsafe or illegal activities or is not adequately supervised by regulators in its home country.

Other Provisions

1. Federal savings associations can loan up to 35 percent of their total assets to individuals and families.
2. Savings associations and banks can merge with each other, subject to regulatory approval.

than 270 days. Thus, bank and thrift regulators do not have to wait until a depository has zero capital (i.e., is technically bankrupt) to close it, permitting the regulators to sell the troubled institution while it still retains enough value to interest potential buyers.

One final regulatory problem facing the savings and loan industry centers upon SAIF — the Federal Savings Association Insurance Fund administered by the FDIC. When Congress passed the Financial Institutions Reform, Recovery, and Enforcement Act of 1989, it mandated that all federal deposit insurance pools must be built up to a point where $1.25 in insurance reserves are available to cover each $100 in insured deposits by no later than 2006. The Bank Insurance Fund (BIF) reached the mandated insurance coverage goal in 1995, and bankers were told that their federal insurance fees would be reduced from about 24 cents per $100 of insured deposits to about 4 cents per $100. (Subsequently, adequately capitalized banks with acceptable examiner ratings had their insurance fees set at zero.) SAIF, on the other hand, is far away from the minimum-coverage goal, meaning savings and loans and other thrifts insured by SAIF will have to pay much larger federal insurance fees than commercial banks must pay unless the U.S. Congress chooses to change the rules. If not, savings and loans and other thrifts will operate under a real competitive disadvantage with banks in selling their deposits and turning a profit.

Savings Banks

Savings banks, like savings and loans, can be chartered by either the states or the federal government. State and federal governments also share responsibility for insuring savings bank deposits (see again Exhibit 7–4). However, most savings banks have deposits insured by the Federal Deposit Insurance Corporation up to $100,000. Regulations are designed to insure maximum safety of deposits. This is accomplished principally through close control over the types of assets a savings bank is permitted to acquire. For example, state law and the "prudent person" rule enforced by the courts generally limit savings bank investments to first-mortgage loans, U.S. government and federal agency securities, high-grade corporate bonds and stocks, and municipal bonds. Investment powers are heavily restricted in this industry, because it focuses upon small depositors who may not be able to evaluate the riskiness of these institutions. On the negative side, however, these strict regulations limit the flexibility of savings banks in responding to shifting customer service needs.

One regulatory issue involving savings banks that has rocketed into public prominence recently concerns the recent trend toward converting mutuals into stockholder-owned savings associations. As we saw in Chapter 5, the purpose of these mutual-to-stock conversions is to infuse new capital into these organizations and force them to become more profit and cost conscious and act in the interest of their owners. Unfortunately, these conversions have sometimes led to multimillion-dollar windfalls for the managements and boards of directors of mutuals with few gains for the depositors, who, legally at least, own a mutual savings bank. Employees and trustees of these associations sometimes award themselves options to buy a major proportion of the converted savings banks' new stock. The management of the converting bank may pick an appraisal firm that underprices the initial stock offering. When trading begins in the new stock, its price rises rapidly to its true market value and insiders score capital gains sometimes in the tens of millions of dollars.

Recently, U.S. regulators have begun to clamp down on these mutual-to-stock conversions of thrift institutions. In the case of savings banks, the FDIC requires the submission of a conversion plan, which that agency can approve or disapprove in an effort to make sure that depositors are not cheated and that "insiders" in a mutual are not "unjustly enriched."

Money Market Funds

The final type of nonbank thrift institution is the *money market mutual fund*. Because this financial intermediary sells shares in pools of securities, it is primarily regulated by the U.S. Securities and Exchange Commission (SEC), which limits money market fund investments primarily (95 percent or more) to top-quality securities and restricts the maximum and average maturity of money market fund security holdings. The SEC requires money funds to issue a prospectus to any potential buyer of their shares detailing the objectives of the fund, describing its recent performance, and revealing in what assets the shareholders' money has been invested. Today, in an effort to protect the small individual saver, money funds must remind their customers that their shares are *not* government insured and may not be able to maintain their par (usually $1.00) value.

THE REGULATION OF INSURANCE COMPANIES

While not quite as heavily regulated as commercial banks, insurance intermediaries face tough rules that are imposed primarily by state governments, which create insurance commissions to regulate the industry. The fundamental purpose of insurance company regulation is to ensure that the public is not overcharged or poorly served and to guarantee adequate compensation to insurance companies themselves. A new company must be chartered under the rules of a particular home state (with most selecting states that have more lenient rules, such as Arizona or Delaware). Once chartered, each company must submit periodic reports to state commissions, its agents must be licensed by the states, and the terms of its policies (including the premium rates it charges policyholders) must be approved by state insurance commissions. Both the courts and state commissions insist that any investments of incoming policyholder premiums must conform to the common law standard of a "prudent person." While, as we saw in Chapter 6, speculative investments by insurance companies rose considerably in the 1980s, the 1990s ushered in a more conservative standard, with state insurance commissions inside the United States and regulators in other countries putting great pressure on insurance companies to significantly increase the quality of their asset portfolios.

THE REGULATION OF PENSION FUNDS

Because pension funds have risen rapidly to hold the bulk of the retirement savings of millions of workers, they have been subject to much heavier regulation by the courts and government agencies in recent years. Because employers — the principal creators and managers of pension plans — have an incentive to take on considerable risk in an effort to minimize the cost burden they must carry, many pension plans even today remain only *partially funded* — that is, the market value of their assets plus expected investment income does *not* fully cover all the benefits promised to pension plan members. While English common law requires pension plans to be "prudent" managers of their members' retirement savings, many pensions have branched out into riskier investments, including real estate development projects and derivative securities contracts.

Responding to these concerns, the U.S. Congress in 1974 passed the Employee Retirement Income Security Act (ERISA), which requires full funding of all private pensions and prudent investment policies. ERISA granted employees the right to join a pension program, in most cases, after only one year on the job. More rapid *vesting* of accumulated benefits was also required so that employees can recover a higher proportion of their past contributions should they decide to retire early or move to another job. Trying to eliminate the danger that pensions may not have adequate funds to pay future claims against them, Congress now requires employers eventually to cover any past liabilities not fully funded at present. In addition, a federal agency, the Pension Benefit Guaranty Corporation (PBGC or "Penny Benny"), was created in 1974 to insure some vested employee benefits. Currently, Penny Benny insures the pension benefits of approximately 40 million U.S. workers who belong to about 85,000 defined-benefit pension programs.

Penny Benny was expected to be self-supporting, receiving inflows of cash from insurance premiums, from its own investments, and from the assets received from companies turning their pension plans over to Penny Benny. By the early 1990s, however, Penny Benny had taken over more than 1,600 pension plans and its liabilities were larger than its assets. By the mid-1990s Penny Benny reported a deficit of more than $2 billion and unfunded liabilities totaling over $50 billion. Some experts fear a savings and loan type financial debacle in the future as the number of retired persons continues to increase, demanding a rapidly increasing volume of pension benefits.

Under the law, Penny Benny must insure all *defined-benefit plans* (that is, those promising a fixed amount of income at retirement and representing about three quarters of all private pensions in the United States). Penny Benny assesses a flat insurance premium for each pension plan member and does not charge riskier pension plans a higher insurance fee. This creates a "moral hazard," with riskier pensions being subsidized by safer ones. Moreover, Penny Benny currently has no legal authority to regulate pension funds, nor does it receive any financial support from the government, having only a small line of credit with the U.S. Treasury. Clearly, there is a pressing need for pension plan reform so that all pension plan members can have reasonable assurance of receiving their benefits. Recently proposed reforms include charging higher insurance premiums and placing a freeze on additional Penny Benny guarantees for those corporate pension plans that have been severely underfunded for a long period of time.

THE REGULATION OF FINANCE COMPANIES

As we saw in Chapter 6, finance companies rank among the most important lenders to consumers and businesses in recent years. The bulk of regulation of this industry is at the *state* level and focuses principally on the making of consumer loans. Several states impose maximum loan rates so that finance companies are limited in the amount of interest they can charge consumers, which tends to limit the volume of credit extended to riskier households. The states, trying to protect consumers, also usually spell out the rules for installment loan contracts and the conditions under which automobiles, furniture, home appliances, or other household assets can be repossessed for nonpayment of a loan extended by a finance company.

THE REGULATION OF INVESTMENT COMPANIES

Investment companies or mutual funds, which invest in pools of stocks or bonds on behalf of individuals and institutional customers, are regulated predominantly by the federal government in the United States. Among the most important laws are the Investment Company Act and Investment Advisers Act, passed by the U.S. Congress in 1940. Registration of investment company ownership shares and the submission of periodic reports to the Securities and Exchange Commission (SEC) are mandatory under American law. The SEC requires investment companies to provide their customers with a *prospectus* that describes each company's goals, performance, and financial condition. It is the SEC's duty to make sure the rights of investment company shareholders are fully protected, including the shareholders' right to elect at least two third's of an investment company's board of directors and the right to approve the choice of an investment advisory service that will manage the investment company's asset portfolio and make buy/sell decisions.

AN OVERVIEW OF TRENDS IN THE REGULATION OF FINANCIAL INSTITUTIONS

In this chapter we have tried to convey at least a sense of the great complexity of regulations that surround the financial institutions' sector and the rationale for those regulations. We have seen that regulation is rooted in the belief that financial institutions occupy a special place in the economy and that the behavior and performance of financial institutions can profoundly affect the welfare of businesses, governments, and institutions. Thus, regulation seeks to promote the safety and stability of financial institutions in order to preserve the confidence of the public and avoid institutional failures.

Unfortunately, the regulation of financial institutions has not proceeded at a measured pace over time. New regulations have been piled on top of old regulations, in many cases set up to deal with problems that are no longer important in today's economy. Thus, regulations can become a costly burden that significantly increases financial institutions' operating costs and limits the cleansing effects of failure and competition. The research evidence suggests that the ultimate impact of regulation is to restrict the entry of new competitors, raising financial service prices but also reducing the likelihood of institutional failures.

The thrust of regulation is changing. It is seeking a lower profile as governments around the world seek to pull back from the financial marketplace somewhat and allow the management and owners of financial institutions to face more fully the competition of the marketplace and respond more directly to customer needs. Rather than seeking to wall off and protect one type of financial institution from another, there is growing recognition that the distinctions between financial institutions are blurring and that, eventually, all financial firms must learn how to compete with one another and learn how to be efficient enough to survive.

As financial service industries are gradually being deregulated, the focus of regulation is moving away from control over services offered and geographic expansion to *controlling risk taking* and to *promoting full disclosure* of the prices and other terms of sale on the services the public buys. As we have seen in this chapter, more regulatory attention has recently been focused upon the amount of capital contributed by a financial institution's owners relative to the amount of risk accepted in a financial institution's assets and in its off-balance-sheet activities. Regulators increasingly are insisting that financial institutions have in place written plans describing their polices and procedures for managing exposure to a wide variety of risks, especially credit risk, interest rate risk, and currency risk.

At the same time there is increasing attention to *public disclosure* — making sure the public is fully informed on the prices, service fees, risk exposures, and possible penalties they are paying for loans, deposits, and other key financial services. The fundamental idea is that an informed consumer will make better decisions regarding the use of financial services. Fuller disclosure stimulates competition as informed consumers shop around for the best terms available.

Finally, for the first time in more than a century the future of government regulation of the financial services sector is in doubt. We are beginning to question seriously the benefits and the costs of letting governments set rules for financial institutions. We are asking more frequently: What purpose is served by both old and proposed new rules? Do the costs of both old and new regulations outweigh their benefits? How will market forces be distorted, and what will society gain or lose as a result of government interference with market forces? It is answers to these particular questions that will form the guideposts to the future of financial institutions' regulation around the world.

A Key Regulatory Agency for Financial Institutions Selling Securities: The SEC

One of the most important regulators of mutual funds and other financial institutions in the United States is the **Securities and Exchange Commission** (SEC), created by the Securities Act of 1933 and the Securities Exchange Act of 1934. The SEC requires that a mutual fund or other business firm selling new securities to the public provide a potential investor with a *prospectus* that truthfully describes the nature of the operations of the offering company, its management and financial condition, the purpose of the new security offering, and any legal actions pending that involve the offering firms. All mutual funds and other security issuers must also file a *registration statement* with the SEC. Any false or misleading information in an SEC registration statement may subject the offending security issuer to criminal penalties and lawsuits from investors who may have relied on such statements and lost money in the process.

Beginning in 1982 the SEC adopted Rule 415, its so-called *shelf registration* rule, which allows a financial institution or other security-issuing firm to file a statement of intention to sell new securities up to two years before those securities are actually brought to market. Designed to reduce costs and other barriers to businesses trying to raise new capital, shelf registrations give a security issuer greater flexibility in deciding both when to market new securities and how many securities to issue. The SEC's Rule 415 appears to have increased competition among investment bankers seeking to offer their underwriting services to companies trying to raise new capital, helping to further lower the cost of new-fund raising.

The SEC also sets rules for the operation of securities exchanges, such as the New York Stock Exchange and the American Stock Exchange. Each security exchange must set its own rules consistent with SEC guidelines and enforce those rules to ensure fair practices, including rules to discipline or expel exchange members who break the exchange's rules. If any exchange fails to effectively regulate itself, the SEC may step in to enforce federal securities laws. Passage of the Maloney Act of 1939 extended the SEC's regulatory power to regulate the over-the-counter securities market as well as the securities exchanges. The over-the-counter securities markets are self-regulated by the National Association of Securities Dealers (NASD), whose rules must be approved by the SEC. The SEC limits the amount of debt a securities dealer can take on in an effort to protect the public against losses on security trading resulting from the failure of a dealer firm.

The SEC is a leader in promoting tough accounting standards for U.S. firms so the public can find out as much as possible about each company's true financial condition. Until recently, the SEC stoutly resisted approving more lenient accounting rules from overseas, which would allow more foreign companies to issue and trade their securities inside the United States. However, the SEC has begun to sanction at least some foreign accounting standards, allowing a growing number of foreign-owned businesses to sell their securities inside U.S. borders. Today, more than 20 foreign firms have their stock listed on the New York Stock Exchange, for example. Recently, the SEC has pushed hard to require financial institutions active in

(*continued*)

U.S. markets to value a greater share of their asset portfolios at market values rather than book values in order to give investors a more accurate picture of the financial strengths and weaknesses of these firms.

With passage of the Investment Advisors and Investment Company Acts of 1940, the SEC was granted power to regulate both those who give investment advice for pay — so-called investment advisors — and investment companies or mutual funds. This law prohibits fraud and the intentional deception of investors through advertising and other means and demands that investment advisors keep records subject to SEC inspection. A professional advisor must register with the SEC, which only means that the advisor must file registration forms; the SEC doesn't usually investigate to determine if an investment adviser is competent or competitive.

For mutual funds, the Investment Company Act requires that these intermediaries invest no more than 5 percent of their assets in securities issued by any one firm, nor may they hold more than 10 percent of the voting shares of a single company (though these restrictions apply to only three quarters of an investment company's portfolio, with the remaining 25 percent not subject to the foregoing rules in an effort to stimulate mutual funds' investments in small businesses). The SEC's Rule 126-1 (adopted in 1980) requires mutual funds to disclose to investors how they account for advertising and sales expenses and what impact brokerage commissions and other investment company operating expenses can have on an investor's expected return.

The SEC is governed by five commissioners, each appointed by the President of the United States for 5-year terms, and has a staff of well over a thousand employees. One of its most highly publicized activities is control over corporate *insider trading* activity, where officers or employees of a firm who have special (asymmetric) knowledge of the firm's activities or outsiders (such as accountants or attorneys) who are privileged to receive material nonpublic information about a company use that information to trade in the firm's securities for personal benefit. When insider trading activity places outside investors at a disadvantage, the SEC may move in to stop illegal trading under the terms of the Insider Trading Act of 1988. Securities firms must develop written policies and internal procedures to prevent illegal use of inside material information. Moreover, every stockholder that holds more than 10 percent of a corporation's outstanding shares and any officers and directors of that company must report their transactions in the firm's stock. This information is released to the public through the SEC's "Report of Insider Activity."

KEY TERMS IN THIS CHAPTER

Regulation

Deregulation

Federal Reserve System

Federal Deposit Insurance Corporation

Comptroller of the Currency

State banking commissions

Securities and Exchange Commission

Basle Agreement

Glass-Steagall Act

Office of Thrift Supervision

National Credit Union Administration

STUDY QUESTIONS

1. What are the principle purposes or goals of financial institutions' regulation?

2. What impact does regulation appear to have upon the availability and cost of financial services to the public? Upon financial institutions themselves?

3. What are the principal regulatory agencies affecting the behavior and performance of U.S. commercial banks? What aspects of banking does each agency regulate?

4. Who are the principal government agencies that regulate:
    a. credit unions
    b. savings and loan associations
    c. savings banks
    d. insurance companies
    e. finance companies
    f. investment companies
    g. pension funds
    h. security brokers and dealers

5. What major trends are reshaping the character of regulation today? Why has capital regulation become so important? What new disclosure rules have recently appeared?

PROBLEMS

1. A commercial bank has the following components in its capital account:

Common Stock	$110	Undivided Profits	$160
Perpetual Preferred Stock	15	Surplus	35
10-year Subordinated Debt	25	Loan-Loss Reserves	280
Equity Reserves	50	Limited-Life Preferred Stock	5

    How much tier-one (or core) capital does this bank have? Tier-two capital?

2. First National Bank of Wimbley reports tier-one capital of $60 million and tier-two capital of $70 million. First National has assets of $10 million with a risk weight of zero, assets of $350 million with a 0.2 risk weight, assets of $680 million with a 0.5 risk weight, and assets of $1,010 million with a risk weight of 1.00. What is First National's total risk-weighted assets? Does the bank have enough tier-one capital? Enough total capital? Why or why not?

SELECTED REFERENCES

Abken, Peter A. "Corporate Pensions and Government Insurance: Deja Vu All Over Again?" *Economic Review*. Federal Reserve Bank of Atlanta, March/April 1992, pp. 1–16.

Mester, Loretta J. "Curing Our Ailing Deposit Insurance System." *Business Review*. Federal Reserve Bank of Philadelphia, September/October 1990, pp. 13–24.

Osterberg, William P., and James B. Thomson. "SAIF Policy Options." *Economic Commentary*. Federal Reserve Bank of Cleveland, June 1995.

Shaffer, Sherrill. "Rethinking Disclosure Requirements." *Business Review*. Federal Reserve Bank of Philadelphia, May/June 1995, pp. 15–29.

Chapter 8

Interest Rates in the Financial System

LEARNING OBJECTIVES IN THIS CHAPTER

- To determine the roles that interest rates play in the economy and financial system.
- To explore the most important explanations (theories) of what determines the level of and changes in interest rates.

In the opening chapter of this book, we described the money and capital markets as one vast pool of funds, depleted by the borrowing activities of households, businesses, and governments and replenished by the savings these sectors supply to the financial system. The money and capital markets make saving possible by offering the individual saver a wide menu of choices where funds may be placed at attractive rates of return. By committing funds to one or more financial instruments, the saver, in effect, becomes a lender of funds. The financial markets also make borrowing possible by giving the borrower a channel through which securities (IOUs) can be issued to lenders. And the money and capital markets make investment and economic growth possible by providing the funds needed for the purchase of machinery and equipment and the construction of buildings, highways, and other productive facilities.

Clearly, then, the acts of saving and lending, borrowing and investing are intimately linked through the financial system. And one factor that significantly influences and ties all of them together is the **rate of interest**. The rate of interest is the price a borrower must pay to secure scarce loanable funds from a lender for an agreed-upon period. It is the **price of credit.** But unlike other prices in the economy, the rate of interest is really a *ratio* of two quantities: the money cost of borrowing divided by the amount of money actually borrowed, usually expressed on an annual percentage basis.

Interest rates send *price signals* to borrowers, lenders, savers, and investors. For example, higher interest rates generally bring forth a greater volume of savings and stimulate the lending of funds. Lower rates of interest, on the other hand, tend to dampen the flow of savings and reduce lending activity. Higher interest rates tend to reduce the volume of borrowing and capital investment, and lower rates stimulate borrowing and investment spending. In this chapter, we will discuss in more detail the forces that are believed by economists and financial analysts to determine prevailing rates of interest in the financial system.

FUNCTIONS OF THE RATE OF INTEREST IN THE ECONOMY

The rate of interest performs several important roles or functions in the economy:

- It helps guarantee that current savings will flow into investment to promote economic growth.

- It rations the available supply of credit, generally providing loanable funds to those investment projects with the highest expected returns.

- It brings into balance the supply of money with the public's demand for money.

- It is also an important tool of government policy through its influence on the volume of saving and investment. If the economy is growing too slowly and unemployment is rising, the government can use its policy tools to lower interest rates in order to stimulate borrowing and investment. On the other hand, an economy experiencing rapid inflation has traditionally called for a government policy of higher interest rates to slow both borrowing and spending.

In the pages of the financial press, the phrase "the interest rate" is frequently used. In truth, there is no such thing as "the interest rate," for there are thousands of different interest rates in the financial system. Even securities issued by the same borrower often carry a variety of interest rates. In Chapters 10 and 11 the most important factors that cause rates to vary among different loans and securities and over time are examined in detail. In this chapter, we focus upon those basic forces that influence the level of *all* interest rates.

To uncover these basic rate-determining forces, however, we must make a simplifying assumption. We assume in this chapter that there is one fundamental interest rate in the economy known as the **pure** or **risk-free rate of interest,** which is a component of *all* interest rates. The closest approximation to this pure rate in the real world is the market yield on government bonds. It is a rate of return presenting little or no risk of financial loss to the investor and representing the opportunity cost of holding idle cash, because the investor can always invest in low-risk bonds and earn this minimum rate of return.

Once the pure rate of interest is determined, all other interest rates may be determined from it by examining the special characteristics of the securities issued by individual borrowers. For example, only the government can borrow at approximately the pure or risk-free interest rate; other borrowers pay higher rates than this due in part to the greater risk of loss attached to their securities. Differences in liquidity, marketability, and maturity are other important factors causing interest rates to differ from the pure or risk-free rate. First, however, we must examine the forces that determine the pure or risk-free interest rate itself.

THE CLASSICAL THEORY OF INTEREST RATES

One of the oldest theories concerning the determinants of the pure or risk-free interest rate is the **classical theory of interest rates,** developed during the 18th and 19th centuries by a number of British economists and elaborated by Irving Fisher (1930) earlier in this century. The classical theory argues that the rate of interest is determined by two forces: (1) the supply of savings, derived mainly from households, and (2) the demand for investment capital, coming mainly from the business sector. Let us examine these rate-determining forces of savings and investment demand in detail.

Saving by Households

What is the relationship between the rate of interest and the volume of savings in the economy? Most saving in modern industrialized economies is carried out by individuals and families. For these households, saving is simply abstinence from consumption spending. *Current savings, therefore, are equal to the difference between current income and current consumption expenditures.*

In making the decision on the timing and amount of saving to be done, households typically consider several factors: the size of current and long-term income, the desired savings target, and the desired proportion of income to be set aside in the form of savings (i.e., the propensity to save). Generally, the volume of household savings rises with income. Higher-income families and individuals tend to save more and consume less relative to their total income than families with lower incomes.

Although income levels probably dominate saving decisions, interest rates also play an important role. Interest rates affect an individual's choice between current consumption and saving for future consumption. The classical theory of interest assumes that individuals have a definite *time preference* for current over future consumption. A rational individual, it is assumed, will always prefer current enjoyment of goods and services over future enjoyment. Therefore, the only way to encourage an individual or family to consume less now and save more is to offer a higher rate of interest on current savings. If more were saved in the current period at a higher rate of return, future consumption and future enjoyment would be increased. For example, if the current rate of interest is 10 percent and a household saves $100 instead of spending it on current consumption, it will be able to consume $110 in goods and services a year from now.

The classical theory considers the payment of interest a reward for *waiting* — the postponement of current consumption in favor of greater future consumption. Higher interest rates increase the attractiveness of saving relative to consumption spending, encouraging more individuals to substitute current saving (and future consumption) for some quantity of current consumption. This so-called **substitution effect** calls for a *positive* relationship between interest rates and the volume of savings. Higher interest rates bring forth a greater current volume of savings. Exhibit 8–1 illustrates the substitution effect: If the rate of interest in the financial markets rises from 5 to 10 percent, the volume of current savings by households is assumed to increase from $100 to $200 billion.

Saving by Business Firms

Not only households, but also businesses, save and direct a portion of their savings into the financial markets to purchase securities and make loans. Most businesses hold savings balances in the form of retained earnings (as reflected in their equity or net worth accounts). In fact, the increase in retained earnings reported by businesses each year is a key measure of the volume of current business saving. And these retained earnings supply most of the money for annual investment spending by business firms.

The volume of business saving depends on two key factors: the level of business profits and the dividend policies of corporations. These two factors are summarized in the *retention ratio,* the ratio of retained earnings to net income after taxes. This ratio indicates the proportion of business profits retained in the business for investment purposes rather than paid out as dividends to the owners. Experience has shown that dividend policies of major corporations do not change very often. Many corporations prefer to keep their dividend payments level or increase them slightly each year, regardless of their current earnings. Any shortfalls in earnings needed for dividend payments are made up through

Exhibit 8–1 **The Substitution Effect Relating Savings and Interest Rates**

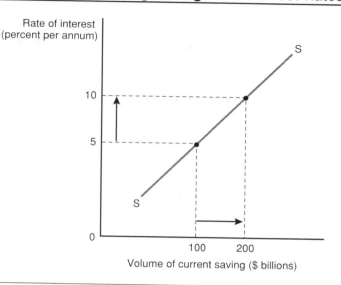

borrowing. The critical element in determining the amount of business savings is, then, the level of business profits.

If profits are expected to rise, businesses will be able to draw more heavily on earnings retained in the firm and less heavily on the money and capital markets for funds. The result is a reduction in the demand for credit and a tendency toward lower interest rates. On the other hand, when profits fall but firms do not cut back on their investment plans, they are forced to make heavier use of the money and capital markets for investment funds. The demand for credit rises, and interest rates may rise as well.

Although the principal determinant of business saving is profits, interest rates also play a role in the decision of what proportion of current operating costs and long-term investment expenditures should be financed internally and what proportion externally. Higher interest rates in the money and capital markets typically encourage firms to use internally generated funds more heavily in financing projects. Conversely, lower interest rates encourage greater use of external funds from the money and capital markets.

Saving by Government

Governments also save, though less frequently than households and businesses. In fact, most government saving (i.e., a budget surplus) appears to be unintended saving that arises when government receipts unexpectedly exceed the actual amount of expenditures. Income flows in the economy (out of which government tax revenues arise) and the pacing of government spending programs are the dominant factors affecting government savings. Interest rates are probably *not* a key factor here.

The Demand for Investment Funds

Business, household, and government savings are important determinants of interest rates according to the classical theory of interest, but not the only ones. The other critical rate-determining factor is *investment spending by business firms.*

Businesses require huge amounts of funds each year to purchase equipment, machinery, and inventories and to support the construction of new buildings and other physical facilities. The majority of business expenditures for these purposes consists of what economists call *replacement investment,* that is, expenditures to replace equipment and facilities that are wearing out or are technologically obsolete. A smaller but more dynamic form of business capital spending is labeled *net investment:* expenditures to acquire additional (new) equipment and facilities in order to increase output. The sum of replacement investment plus net investment equals *gross investment.*

Replacement investment usually is more predictable and grows at a more even rate than net investment. This is due to the fact that such expenditures are financed almost exclusively from inside the firm and frequently follow a routine pattern based on depreciation formulas. Expenditures for new equipment and facilities (net investment), on the other hand, depend on the business community's outlook for future sales, changes in technology, industrial capacity, and the cost of raising funds. Because these factors are subject to frequent changes, it is not surprising that net investment is highly volatile.

Net investment, because of its size and volatility, is a driving force in the economy. Changes in net investment are closely linked to fluctuations in the nation's output of goods and services, employment, and prices. A significant decline in net investment frequently leads to a business recession, a decline in productivity, and a rise in unemployment unless offset by increased consumer or government spending. In fact, substantial cutbacks in new inventory investment and long-term capital spending seem to occur, on average, every three to five years in the United States, usually precipitating a recession. Two recent examples occurred in 1982 and 1991, when high interest rates and other factors combined to slow the pace of net investment, leading to a sharp rise in unemployment in the United States and several other nations.

The Investment Decision-Making Process. The process of investment decision making by business firms is complex and depends on a host of qualitative and quantitative factors. The firm must compare its current level of production with the capacity of its existing facilities and decide whether it has sufficient capacity to handle anticipated demand for its product. If expected future demand will strain the firm's existing facilities, it will consider expanding its operating capacity through net investment.

Most business firms have several investment projects under consideration at any one time. Although the investment decision-making process varies from firm to firm, each business generally makes some estimate of net cash flows (i.e., revenues minus all expenses including taxes) that each project will generate over its useful life. From this information plus knowledge of each investment project's acquisition cost, management can calculate its expected rate of return and compare that expected return with anticipated returns from alternative projects.

One of the more popular methods for performing this calculation is the *internal rate of return method,* which equates the total cost of an investment project with the future net cash flows (NCF) expected from that project discounted back to their present values. Thus,

$$\text{Cost of project} = \frac{NCF_1}{(1+r)^1} + \frac{NCF_2}{(1+r)^2} + \ldots + \frac{NCF_n}{(1+r)^n} \qquad (8\text{–}1)$$

where each *NCF* represents the expected annual net cash flow from the project and r is its expected internal rate of return. The internal rate performs two functions: (1) it measures the annual yield the firm expects from an investment project and (2) it reduces the value of all future cash flows expected over the economic life of the project down to their present value to the firm. In general, if the firm must choose among several mutually exclusive projects, it will choose the one with the *highest* expected internal rate of return.

Although the internal rate of return provides a yardstick for selecting potentially profitable investment projects, how does a business executive decide how much to spend on investment at any point in time? How many projects should be chosen? It is here that the financial markets play a key role in the investment decision-making process.

Suppose a business firm is considering the following projects with their associated expected internal rates of return:

Project	Expected Internal Rate of Return (annualized)
A	15%
B	12
C	10
D	9
E	8

How many of these projects will be adopted? The firm must compare each project's expected internal return with the cost of raising capital — the interest rate — in the money and capital markets to finance the project.

Assume that funds must be borrowed in the financial marketplace to complete any of the above projects and the current cost of borrowing — the rate of interest — is 10 percent. Which projects are acceptable from an economic standpoint? As shown in Exhibit 8–2, projects A and B clearly are acceptable because their expected returns exceed the current cost of borrowing capital (10 percent) to finance them. The firm would be indifferent about project C because its expected return is no more than the cost of borrowed funds (i.e., the current interest rate). Projects D and E, on the other hand, are unprofitable at this time.

It is through changes in the cost of raising funds that the financial markets can exert a powerful influence on the investment decisions of business firms. As credit becomes scarcer and more expensive, the cost of borrowed capital rises, eliminating some investment projects from consideration. For example, if the cost of borrowed funds rises

Exhibit 8–2   **The Cost of Capital and the Investment Decision**

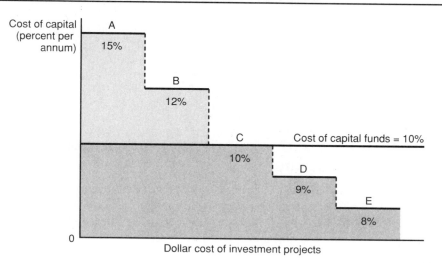

Exhibit 8–3   **The Investment Demand Schedule in the Classical Theory of Interest Rates**

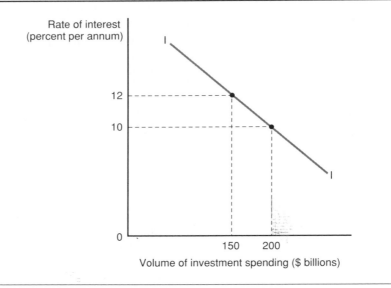

Volume of investment spending ($ billions)

from 10 to 13 percent, it is obvious that only project A in our earlier example would then be economically viable. On the other hand, if credit becomes more abundant and less costly, the cost of capital for the individual firm will tend to decline and more projects will become profitable. In our example, a decline in the cost of borrowed funds from 10 to 8½ percent would make all but project E economically viable and probably acceptable to the firm.

Investment Demand and the Rate of Interest. This reasoning explains, in part, why the demand for investment capital by business firms was regarded by the classical economists as *negatively* related to the rate of interest. Exhibit 8–3 depicts the business investment demand schedule as drawn in the classical theory. This demand schedule slopes downward and to the right. At low rates of interest, more investment projects become economically viable and firms require more funds to finance a longer list of projects. On the other hand, if the rate of interest rises to high levels, fewer investment projects will be pursued and fewer funds will be required from the financial markets. For example, at a 12 percent rate of interest, only $150 billion in funds for investment spending might be demanded by business firms in the economy. If the rate of interest drops to 10 percent, however, the volume of desired investment by firms might rise to $200 billion.

The Equilibrium Rate of Interest in the Classical Theory of Interest

The classical economists believed that interest rates in the financial markets were determined by the interplay of the supply of saving and the demand for investment. Specifically, the equilibrium rate of interest is determined at the point where the quantity of savings supplied to the market is exactly equal to the quantity of funds demanded for investment. As shown in Exhibit 8–4, this occurs at point E, where the equilibrium rate of interest is i_E and the equilibrium quantity of capital funds traded in the financial markets is Q_E.

Exhibit 8–4   **The Equilibrium Rate of Interest in the Classical Theory**

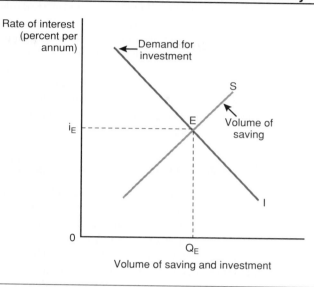

To illustrate, suppose the total volume of savings supplied by businesses, households, and governments in the economy at an interest rate of 10 percent is $200 billion. Moreover, at this same 10 percent rate, businesses would also demand $200 billion in funds for investment purposes. Then 10 percent must be the equilibrium rate of interest, and $200 billion is the equilibrium quantity of funds that would be traded in the money and capital markets.

The market rate of interest moves toward its equilibrium level. However, supply and demand forces change so fast that the interest rate rarely has an opportunity to settle in at a specific equilibrium level. At any given time, the rate is probably above or below its true equilibrium level but moving *toward* that equilibrium. If the market rate is temporarily above equilibrium, the volume of savings exceeds the demand for investment capital, creating an excess supply of savings. Savers will offer their funds at lower and lower rates until the market interest rate approaches equilibrium. Similarly, if the market rate lies temporarily below equilibrium, investment demand exceeds the quantity of savings available. Business firms will bid up the interest rate until it approaches the level at which the quantity saved equals the quantity of funds demanded for investment purposes.

The classical theory of interest rates helps us to understand some of the *long-term forces* driving interest rates. For example, several economists (e.g., Bryan and Byrne, 1990) have argued that, in the future, interest rates should average lower than today's interest rates. This may be true because the populations of the United States, Japan, and most other nations are aging, shifting heavily toward those age groups in which individuals spend less of their current income and save more (in part to prepare for retirement). This viewpoint assumes that people's consumption and savings habits tend to follow a predictable *life cycle,* with younger workers borrowing heavily in anticipation of higher incomes in the future and older workers, who have reached their maximum annual earnings, saving heavily in anticipation of lower incomes in the future and retirement. The money and capital markets make a vital contribution to this process, directing the savings of older individuals into the hands of younger people who desire to improve their current standard of living by borrowing.

With the ongoing decline in the number of younger workers and the rise in the proportion of retirees, the United States and several other leading economies *may* have passed the maximum projected level of expected per capita real income. If so, more of their citizens are likely to scale back current consumption spending and save more for the long run. In terms of the diagram given in Exhibit 8–4, the supply of savings curve may move outward and to the right as a flood of new savings reaches the financial marketplace. With demand for savings unchanged, interest rates may average *lower* in the future, making it cheaper, on average, for many people to borrow funds. Note, too, that if domestic savings rise, this implies less dependence on foreign savers to supply the funds necessary to support domestic living standards.

Limitations of the Classical Theory of Interest

The classical theory sheds considerable light on the factors affecting interest rates. However, it has serious limitations. The central problem is that the theory ignores factors other than saving and investment that affect interest rates. For example, many financial institutions have the power to create money today by making loans to the public. When borrowers repay their loans, money is destroyed. The volume of money created or destroyed affects the total amount of credit available in the financial system and therefore must be considered in any explanation of the factors determining interest rates.

In addition, the classical theory assumes that interest rates are the principal determinant of the quantity of savings available. Today economists recognize that *income* is more important in determining the volume of saving. Finally, the classical theory contends that the demand for borrowed funds comes principally from the business sector. Today, however, both consumers and governments are important borrowers, significantly affecting credit availability and cost. As we will see in the rest of this chapter, more recent theories of interest rates address a number of these limitations of the classical theory.

THE LIQUIDITY PREFERENCE THEORY

The classical theory of interest has been called a *long-term* explanation of interest rates because it focuses on the public's thrift habits and the productivity of capital — factors that tend to change slowly. During the 1930s, British economist John Maynard Keynes (1936) developed a short-term theory of the rate of interest that, he argued, was more relevant for policymakers and for explaining near-term changes in interest rates. This theory is known as the **liquidity preference theory of interest rates.**

The Demand for Liquidity

Keynes argued that the rate of interest is really a payment for the use of a scarce resource, *money.* Businesses and individuals prefer to hold money for carrying out daily transactions and also as a precaution against future cash needs even though its yield is low or nonexistent. Investors in fixed-income securities, such as corporate and government bonds, frequently desire to hold money as a haven against declining security prices. Interest rates, therefore, are the price that must be paid to induce money holders to surrender a perfectly liquid asset and hold other assets that carry more risk. At times the preference for liquidity grows very strong. Unless the government expands the money supply, interest rates will rise.

In the theory of liquidity preference, only two outlets for investor funds are considered: bonds and money (including bank deposits). Money provides perfect liquidity (instant spending power); bonds pay interest but cannot be spent until converted into cash.

If interest rates rise, the market value of bonds paying a fixed rate of interest falls; the investor would suffer a capital loss if those bonds were converted into cash. On the other hand, a fall in interest rates results in higher bond prices; the bondholder will experience a capital gain if his or her bonds are sold for cash. To the classical theorists, it was irrational to hold money because it provided little or no return. To Keynes, however, the holding of money could be a perfectly rational act if interest rates were expected to rise, because rising rates can result in substantial losses for investors in bonds.

Motives for Holding Money. Keynes observed that the public demands money for three different purposes (motives). The *transactions motive* represents the demand for money to purchase goods and services. Because inflows and outflows of money are not perfectly synchronized in either timing or amount and because it is costly to shift back and forth between money and other assets, businesses, households, and governments must keep some cash in the till or in demand accounts simply to meet daily expenses. Some money also must be held as a reserve for future emergencies and to cover extraordinary expenses. This *precautionary motive* arises because we live in a world of uncertainty and cannot predict exactly what expenses or opportunities will arise in the future.

Keynes assumed that money demanded for transactions and precautionary purposes is dependent on the level of national income, business sales, and prices. Reflecting money's role as a medium of exchange, higher levels of income, sales, or prices increase the need for money to carry out transactions and to respond to future opportunities. However, neither the precautionary nor the transactions demand for money was assumed to be affected by changes in interest rates. In fact, Keynes assumed money demand for precautionary and transactions purposes to be fixed in the short term. In the longer term, however, transactions and precautionary demands change as income changes.

Short-term changes in interest rates were attributed by Keynes to a third motive for holding money — the *speculative motive* — that stems from uncertainty about the future prices of bonds. To illustrate, suppose an investor has recently purchased a corporate bond for $1,000. The company issuing the bond promises to pay $100 a year in interest income. To simplify matters, assume the bond is a *perpetual security.* This means the investor will receive $100 a year for as long as the security is held. The annual rate of return (or yield) on the bond, then, is 10 percent ($100/$1,000). Suppose now that the interest rate on bonds of similar quality rises to 12 percent. What happens to the price of the 10 percent bond? Its price in the marketplace will fall because its annual promised yield at a price of $1,000 is *less* than 12 percent. The 10 percent bond's price will approach $833 because at this price the bond's $100 annual interest payment gives the investor an approximate annual yield of 12 percent ($100/$833). In the reverse situation, if interest rates were to decline — say, to 9 percent — the 10 percent bond would experience a rise in its market price.[1]

If investors expect rising interest rates, many of them will demand money or near-money assets instead of bonds because they believe bond prices will fall. As the expectation that interest rates will rise grows strong in the marketplace, the demand for money as a secure store of value increases. We may represent this speculative demand for money by a line or curve that slopes downward and to the right, as shown in Exhibit 8–5, reflecting a *negative* relationship between the speculative demand for money and the level of interest rates. At low

---

[1] The price of a perpetual bond (P) is related to its market interest rate (r) by the formula

$$P = R/r$$

where R is the annual income in dollars paid by the security. Clearly, as interest rate r increases, market price P falls. As we will see in Chapter 9, the same *inverse* relationship between the price and interest yield on a fixed-income security holds even if we assume the security is not perpetual but has a finite maturity.

Exhibit 8–5   **Speculative Demand for Money**

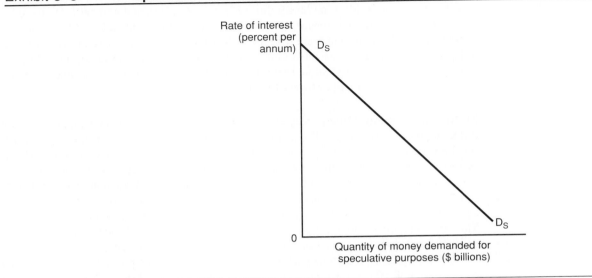

rates of interest, many investors believe that interest rates are soon to rise (i.e., bond prices are going to fall), and therefore more money is demanded. At high rates of interest, on the other hand, many investors will conclude that interest rates soon will fall and bond prices rise, so the demand for money decreases while the demand for bonds increases.

From another vantage point, when interest rates are high, the opportunity cost (loss) from holding idle cash increases. Thus, high interest rates encourage investors to reduce their cash balances and buy bonds. In contrast, when interest rates are low, the opportunity cost of holding idle cash is also low, but the expected capital loss from holding bonds is high should interest rates rise. Thus, there is more incentive to hold money rather than bonds when interest rates are low.

Total Demand for Money. The total demand for money in the economy is simply the sum of transactions, precautionary, and speculative demands. Because the principal determinant of transactions and precautionary demand is income, not interest rates, these money demands are fixed at a certain level of national income. Let this demand be represented by the quantity OK shown along the horizontal axis in Exhibit 8–6. Then, any amount of money demanded in excess of OK represents speculative demand. The total demand for money is represented along curve D_T. Therefore, if the rate of interest lies at the moment at i, Exhibit 8–6 shows that the speculative demand for money will be KJ and the total demand for money will be OJ.

The Supply of Money

The other major element determining interest rates in liquidity preference theory is the supply of money. In modern economies, the money supply is controlled, or at least closely regulated, by government. Because government decisions concerning the size of the money supply presumably are guided by the public welfare, not by the level of interest rates, we assume that the supply of money is *inelastic* with respect to the rate of interest. Such a money supply curve is represented in Exhibit 8–7 by the vertical line M_S.

Exhibit 8–6   **The Total Demand for Money in the Economy**

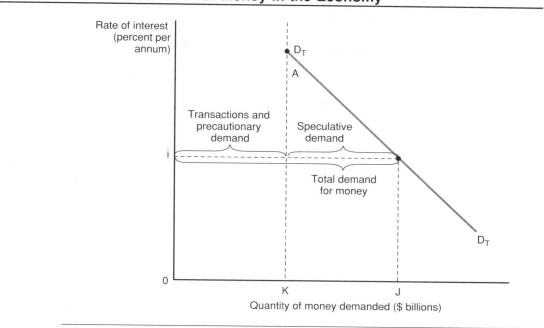

Exhibit 8–7   **The Equilibrium Rate of Interest in the Liquidity Preference Theory**

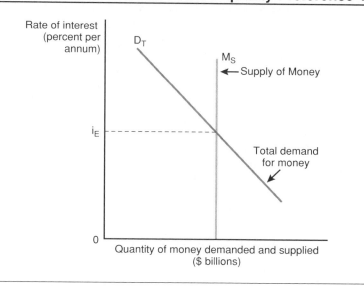

The Equilibrium Rate of Interest in Liquidity Preference Theory

The interplay of the total demand for and the supply of money determines the equilibrium rate of interest in the short run. As shown in Exhibit 8–7, the equilibrium rate is found at point i_E, where the quantity of money demanded by the public equals the quantity of money supplied. Above this equilibrium rate, the supply of money exceeds the quantity demanded, and some businesses, households, and units of government will try to dispose of their unwanted money balances by purchasing bonds. The prices of bonds will rise, driving interest rates down toward equilibrium at i_E. On the other hand, at rates below equilibrium, the quantity of money demanded exceeds the supply. Some decision makers in the economy will sell their bonds to raise additional cash, driving bond prices down and interest rates up toward equilibrium.

Liquidity preference theory provides some useful insights into investor behavior and the influence of government policy on the economy and financial system. For example, the theory suggests that it is rational at certain times for the public to hoard money (cash balances) and at other times to "dishoard" (spend away) unwanted cash. If the public disposes of some of its cash by purchasing securities, this action increases the quantity of loanable funds available from the financial markets. Other things being equal, interest rates will fall. On the other hand, if the public tries to "hoard" more money, (expanding its cash balances by selling securities), less money will be available for loans. Interest rates will rise, *ceteris paribus*.

Liquidity preference theory illustrates how central banks such as the Federal Reserve System can influence interest rates in the financial markets, at least in the short term. For example, if higher interest rates are desired, the central bank can contract the size of the money supply and interest rates will tend to rise (assuming the demand for money is unchanged). If the demand for money is increasing, the central bank can bring about higher interest rates by ensuring that the money supply grows more slowly than money demand. In contrast, if the central bank expands the money supply, interest rates will decline in the short term (provided the demand for money does not increase).

Subsequent research by Friedman (1968), Cagan (1972), and others suggests that three dynamic effects on the equilibrium interest rate follow when the money supply changes: (1) an initial *money-supply liquidity effect,* (2) a subsequent *money-supply income effect,* and, over a longer time horizon, (3) a *money-supply price expectations effect.* For example, an increase in the money supply creates excess liquidity, at least temporarily, and interest rates fall. However, the excess liquidity will generate additional spending in the economy, driving up income and increasing the demand for money. Unless the money supply expands further, interest rates will begin rising. Finally, an increasing money supply coupled with rising incomes may generate inflationary expectations. Businesses and consumers will come to expect rising prices, as will lenders of funds, who therefore will raise interest rates on their loans. Thus, given sufficient time, the liquidity effect of money supply changes will be offset by income and price-expectations effects. Interest rates may end up higher or lower than their initial level after a money-supply change, depending on the relative strengths of these three effects.

Limitations of the Liquidity Preference Theory

Like the classical theory of interest, liquidity preference theory has limitations. It is a short-term approach to interest rate determination unless modified because it assumes that income remains stable. In the longer term, interest rates are affected by changes in the level of income and inflationary expectations. Indeed, it is impossible to have a stable equilibrium interest rate without also reaching an equilibrium level of income, saving, and investment in the economy. Also, liquidity preference considers only the supply and demand for the stock of money, whereas business, consumer, and government demands for credit clearly have an impact on the cost of credit. A more comprehensive view of interest rates is needed that considers the important roles played by *all* actors in the financial system: businesses, households, and governments.

THE LOANABLE FUNDS THEORY

A view that overcomes many of the limitations of earlier theories is the **loanable funds theory of interest rates.** This view argues that the risk-free interest rate is determined by the interplay of two forces: the demand for and supply of credit (loanable funds). The demand for loanable funds consists of credit demands from domestic businesses, consumers, and governments and also borrowing in the domestic market by foreigners. The supply of loanable funds stems from four sources: domestic savings, hoarding demand for money, money creation by the banking system, and lending in the domestic market by foreign individuals and institutions. We consider each of these demand and supply factors in turn.

Consumer Demand for Loanable Funds

Domestic consumers demand loanable funds to purchase a wide variety of goods and services on credit. Recent research indicates that consumers are not particularly responsive to the rate of interest when they seek credit but focus instead principally on the nonprice terms of a loan, such as the down payment, maturity, and size of installment payments. This implies that consumer demand for credit is relatively *inelastic* with respect to the rate of interest. Certainly a rise in interest rates leads to some reduction in the quantity of consumer demand for loanable funds (particularly when home mortgage credit is involved), whereas a decline in interest rates stimulates some additional consumer borrowing. However, along the consumer's relatively inelastic demand schedule, a substantial change in the rate of interest must occur before the quantity of consumer demand for funds changes significantly.

Domestic Business Demand for Loanable Funds

The credit demands of domestic businesses generally are more responsive to changes in the rate of interest than is consumer borrowing. Most business credit is for such investment purposes as the purchase of inventories and new plant and equipment. As noted earlier in our discussion of the classical theory of interest, a high interest rate eliminates some business investment projects from consideration because their expected rate of return is lower than the cost of funds. On the other hand, at lower rates of interest, many investment projects look profitable, with their expected returns exceeding the cost of funds. Therefore, the quantity of loanable funds demanded by the business sector increases as the rate of interest falls.

Government Demand for Loanable Funds

Government demand for loanable funds is a growing factor in the financial markets but does not depend significantly on the level of interest rates. This is especially true of borrowing by the federal government. Federal decisions on spending and borrowing are made by Congress in response to social needs and the public welfare, not the rate of interest. Moreover, the federal government has the power both to tax and to create money to pay its debts. State and local government demand, on the other hand, is slightly interest-elastic because many local governments are limited in their borrowing activities by legal interest rate ceilings. When open market rates rise above these legal ceilings, some state and local governments are prevented from offering their securities to the public.

Foreign Demand for Loanable Funds

In recent years, foreign banks and corporations, as well as foreign governments, have increasingly entered the huge U.S. financial marketplace to borrow billions of dollars. This huge foreign credit demand is sensitive to the spread between domestic lending rates and interest rates in foreign markets. If U.S. interest rates decline relative to foreign rates, foreign borrowers will be inclined to borrow more in the United States and less abroad. At the same time, with higher foreign interest rates, U.S. lending institutions will increase their foreign lending and reduce the availability of loanable funds to domestic borrowers. The net result, then, is a *negative* or *inverse relationship* between foreign borrowing and domestic interest rates relative to foreign interest rates.

Total Demand for Loanable Funds

The total demand for loanable funds is the sum of domestic consumer, business, and government credit demands plus foreign credit demands. This demand curve slopes downward and to the right with respect to the rate of interest, as shown in Exhibit 8–8. Higher rates of interest lead some businesses, consumers, and governments to curtail their borrowing plans; lower rates bring forth more credit demand. However, the demand for loanable funds does not determine the rate of interest by itself. The supply of loanable funds must be added to complete the picture.

The Supply of Loanable Funds

Loanable funds flow into the money and capital markets from at least four different sources: (1) domestic saving by businesses, consumers, and governments; (2) dishoarding (spending down) of excess money balances held by the public; (3) creation of money by the

Exhibit 8–8   **Total Demand for Loanable Funds**

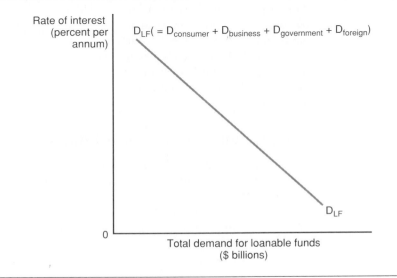

domestic banking system; and (4) lending to domestic borrowers by foreigners. We consider each of these sources of funds in turn.

Domestic Saving. The supply of domestic savings is the principal source of loanable funds. As noted earlier, most saving is done by households and is simply the difference between current income and current consumption. Businesses, however, also save, by retaining a portion of current earnings and by adding to their depreciation reserves. Government saving, while relatively rare, occurs when current revenues exceed current expenditures.

Most economists today believe that income levels, rather than interest rates, are the dominant factor in the decision of how much and when to save.[2] But there is evidence that business and household saving may be goal oriented: the so-called **income effect.** For example, suppose an individual wishes to accumulate $100,000 in anticipation of retirement. Interest rates subsequently rise from 5 to 10 percent. Will this individual save more out of each period's income or less? Probably *less,* because the higher interest rates will enable the saver to reach the $100,000 goal with less sacrifice of current income. At higher interest rates, savings accumulate faster. On the other hand, a lower interest rate might lead to a greater volume of saving because a business firm or household then must accumulate savings at a faster rate to achieve its savings goal.

Clearly, then, the income effect would have the opposite result on the volume of saving than the substitution effect described earlier in our discussion of the classical theory of interest. The substitution effect argues for a *positive* relationship between the rate of interest and the volume of savings, while the income effect suggests a *negative* relationship between interest rates and savings volume. Thus, these two effects pull aggregate saving in opposite directions as interest rates change. It should not be surprising, therefore, that the annual volume of saving in the economy is difficult to forecast.

Recent research using econometric models has suggested the importance of another factor — the **wealth effect** — in influencing savings decisions.[3] Individuals accumulate wealth in many different forms: real assets (automobiles, houses, land) and financial assets (stocks, bonds). What happens to the value of financial assets as interest rates change? If rates rise, for example, the market value of many financial assets will fall until their yield approaches market-determined levels. Therefore, a rise in interest rates will result in decreases in the value of wealth held in financial assets, forcing the individual to save more to protect his or her wealth position. Conversely, a decrease in interest rates will increase the value of many financial assets, increasing wealth and necessitating a lower volume of current saving.

For businesses and individuals heavily in debt, however, the *opposite* effects may ensue. When interest rates rise, debt contracted in earlier periods when interest rates were lower seems less of a burden. For example, a home mortgage taken by a family when interest rates in the mortgage market were 10 percent seems a less burdensome drain on income when rates on new mortgages have risen to 15 percent. Therefore, a rise in interest rates tends to make those economic units carrying a large volume of debt relative to their financial assets feel better off. They may tend to save *less* as a result. A decrease in interest rates, on the other hand, may result in *more* savings due to the wealth effect.

The *net* effect of the income, substitution, and wealth effects leads to a relatively *interest-inelastic* supply of savings curve. Substantial changes in interest rates usually are

---

[2]There is, however, considerable controversy as to just what measure of income determines the annual volume of savings. Some economists argue that current saving is determined not by current income levels but by a *long-term* view of income, perhaps adjusted for the stage in the life cycle of each income recipient. See, for example, Ando and Modigliani (1963).

[3]See especially Boskin (1978) and Justen and Taylor (1975).

required to bring about significant changes in the volume of aggregate saving in the economy.

Dishoarding of Money Balances. Still another source of loanable funds is centered on the public's demand for money relative to the available supply of money. As noted earlier, the public's demand for money (cash balances) varies with interest rates and income levels. The supply of money, on the other hand, is closely controlled by the government. Clearly the two — money demand and money supply — need not be the same. The difference between the public's total demand for money and the money supply is known as *hoarding*. When the public's demand for cash balances exceeds the supply, *positive hoarding* of money takes place as some individuals and businesses attempt to increase their cash balances at the expense of others. Hoarding *reduces* the volume of loanable funds available in the financial markets. On the other hand, when the public's demand for money is less than the supply available, *negative hoarding (dishoarding)* occurs. Some individuals and businesses will dispose of their excess cash holdings, *increasing* the supply of loanable funds available in the financial system.

Creation of Credit by the Domestic Banking System. Commercial banks and nonbank thrift institutions offering payments accounts have the unique ability to create credit by lending and investing their excess reserves (a process described earlier in Chapter 4). Credit created by the domestic banking system represents an additional source of loanable funds, which must be added to the amount of savings and the dishoarding of money balances (or minus the amount of hoarding demand) to derive the total supply of loanable funds in the economy.

Foreign Lending to the Domestic Funds Market. Finally, foreign lenders provide large amounts of credit to domestic borrowers in the United States. These inflowing loanable funds are particularly sensitive to the difference between U.S. interest rates and interest rates overseas. If domestic rates rise relative to interest rates offered abroad, the supply of foreign funds to domestic markets will tend to rise. Foreign lenders will find it more attractive to make loans to domestic borrowers. At the same time, domestic borrowers will turn more to foreign markets for loanable funds as domestic interest rates climb relative to foreign rates. The combined result is to make the net foreign supply of loanable funds to the domestic credit market *positively* related to the spread between domestic and foreign rates of interest.

Total Supply of Loanable Funds

The total supply of loanable funds, including domestic saving, foreign lending, dishoarding of money, and new credit created by the domestic banking system, is depicted in Exhibit 8–9. The curve rises with higher rates of interest, indicating that a greater supply of loanable funds will flow into the money and capital markets when the returns from lending increase.

The Equilibrium Rate of Interest in the Loanable Funds Theory

The two forces of supply and demand for loanable funds determine not only the volume of lending and borrowing going on in the economy but also the rate of interest. *The interest rate tends toward the equilibrium point at which the supply of loanable funds equals the demand for loanable funds.* This point of equilibrium is shown in Exhibit 8–10 at i_E.

Exhibit 8–9   **The Supply of Loanable Funds**

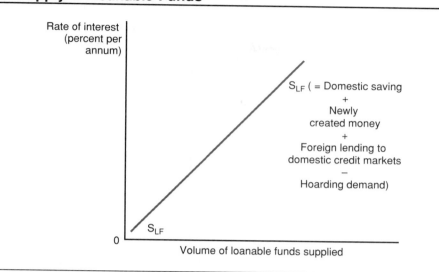

If the interest rate is temporarily *above* equilibrium, the quantity of loanable funds supplied by domestic savers and foreign lenders, by the banking system, and from the dishoarding of money (or minus hoarding demand) exceeds the total demand for loanable funds, and the rate of interest will be bid down. On the other hand, if the interest rate is temporarily *below* equilibrium, loanable funds demand will exceed the supply. The interest rate will be bid up by borrowers until it settles at equilibrium once again.

The equilibrium depicted in Exhibit 8–10 is only a *partial* equilibrium position, however. This is due to the fact that interest rates are affected by conditions in *both* the domestic and

Exhibit 8–10   **The Equilibrium Rate of Interest in the Loanable Funds Theory**

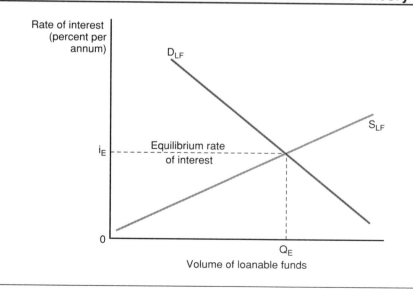

Exhibit 8–11   **Changes in the Demand for and Supply of Loanable Funds**

A. Effects of increased supply of loanable funds with demand unchanged

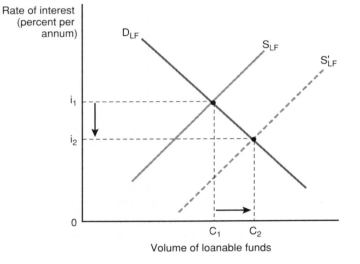

Volume of loanable funds

B. Effects of increased demand for loanable funds with supply unchanged

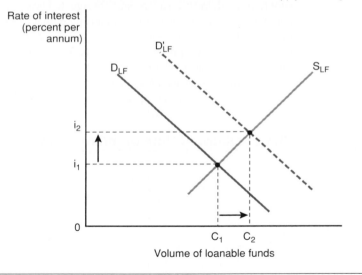

Volume of loanable funds

world economies. For the economy to be in equilibrium, planned saving must equal planned investment across the whole economic system. For example, if planned investment exceeds planned saving at the equilibrium rate shown in Exhibit 8–10, investment demands will push interest rates higher in the short term. However, as additional investment spending occurs, incomes will rise, generating a greater volume of savings. Eventually, interest rates will fall. Similarly, if exchange rates between dollars, yen, and other world currencies are not in equilibrium with each other, there will be further opportunities for profit available to foreign and domestic lenders by moving loanable funds from one country to another.

Only when the economy, the money market, the loanable funds market, and foreign currency markets are *simultaneously* in equilibrium will interest rates remain stable. Thus, a *stable* equilibrium interest rate will be characterized by the following:

1. Planned saving = Planned investment (including business, household, and government investment) across the whole economic system (i.e., equilibrium in the economy).

2. Money supply = Money demand (i.e., equilibrium in the money market).

3. Quantity of loanable funds supplied = Quantity of loanable funds demanded (i.e., equilibrium in the loanable funds market).

4. The difference between foreign demand for loanable funds and the volume of loanable funds supplied by foreigners to the domestic economy = The difference between current exports from and imports into the domestic economy (i.e., equilibrium in the balance of payments and foreign currency markets).

This simple demand-supply framework is useful for analyzing broad movements in interest rates. For example, if the total supply of loanable funds is increasing and the total demand for loanable funds remains unchanged or rises more slowly, the volume of credit extended in the financial markets must increase. Interest rates will fall. This is illustrated in Exhibit 8–11A, which shows the supply schedule sliding outward and to the right when S_{LF} increases to S'_{LF}, resulting in a decline in the equilibrium rate of interest from i_1 to i_2. The equilibrium quantity of loanable funds traded in the financial system increases from C_1 to C_2.

What happens when the demand for loanable funds increases with no change in the total supply of funds available? In this instance, the volume of credit extended will increase, but loans will be made at higher interest rates. Exhibit 8–11B illustrates this. The loanable funds demand curve rises from D_{LF} to D'_{LF}, driving the interest rate upward from i_1 to i_2.

THE RATIONAL EXPECTATIONS THEORY

In recent years, a fourth major theory about the forces determining interest rates has appeared and now appears to be gaining supporters. This is the **rational expectations theory of interest rates.** It builds on a growing body of research evidence that the money and capital markets are highly efficient institutions in digesting *new information* affecting interest rates and security prices.

For example, when new information appears about investment, saving, or the money supply, investors begin immediately to translate that new information into decisions to borrow or lend funds. In a short space of time — perhaps in minutes or seconds — security prices and interest rates change to reflect the new information. So rapid is this process of the market digesting new information that security prices and interest rates presumably impound the new data from virtually the moment they appear. As we saw in Chapter 3, in a perfectly efficient market, it is impossible to win excess returns consistently by trading on publicly available information.

The important assumptions and conclusions of the rational expectations theory are that (1) the prices of securities and interest rates should reflect all available information and the market uses all of this information to establish a probability distribution of expected future prices and interest rates; (2) changes in rates and security prices are correlated only with unanticipated, not anticipated, information; (3) the correlation between rates of return in successive time periods is zero; (4) no unexploited opportunities for profit (above a normal

INTERNATIONAL FOCUS:
Comparative Interest Rates Between Countries

Recent research studies suggest that interest rates in different countries tend to behave in similar fashion, generally rising or falling at approximately the same time. For example, a recent study of real (inflation-adjusted) interest rates in Japan and the United States by Hutchison (1993) finds these rates moving closely together, particularly since 1980.

Moreover, both research and casual observation reveal that U.S. interest rates profoundly affect capital flows all over the world. When U.S. interest rates decline relative to foreign interest rates, capital flows out of the United States to seek the higher rates available abroad. Domestic and foreign investors may dump hundreds of millions of dollars of U.S. securities, the prices of which usually plummet with fewer interested buyers around. In contrast, when U.S. interest rates rise relative to interest rates prevailing overseas, a large-scale sell off of foreign bonds and stocks often occurs, as both U.S. and foreign investors buy American securities in greater volume. Eventually, domestic and foreign interest rates will achieve a relatively stable relationship with each other and capital flows will moderate. However, no longer can interest rates in one country be viewed as separate and independent from interest rates in other countries.

The broad similarities in interest-rate movements from country to country appear to reflect common rate-determining forces at work. Among the most prominent of these rate-determining forces in recent years have been changes in savings rates, government budget deficits, wide fluctuations in borrowing and new issues of stock by corporations and other major borrowers, deregulation of the financial sector, and concern over risk on the part of international capital-market investors. Of course, not all countries experience the same changes in these rate-determining forces. For example, the ratio of government debt to national income generally has risen and personal savings rates have fallen in the United States over the past two decades, while the government's debt-to-income ratio has remained relatively level or fallen in such countries as Germany, France, and Japan, where personal savings rates have been relatively high. Differences in the speed with which these rate-determining factors have changed from country to country means that interest rates themselves usually do not move at the same rate of speed in each nation. Thus, attempting to predict interest rates in one nation from rates prevailing in another nation is a treacherous exercise.

However, with falling trade barriers all over the world, capital should flow more freely between nations, resulting in stronger linkages between real interest rates in different countries as time passes. This closer tracking of one country's interest rates with those of another will require more active cooperation between economic policymakers in different nations. For example, higher interest rates in Japan might lead to higher interest rates in the United States, which could slow the U.S. economy and create more unemployment. Mutual respect and understanding of each country's economic problems and institutional framework will be more important than ever in the years ahead.

Source: See, for example, Howard Howe and Charles Pigott, "Determinants of Long-Term Interest Rates: An Empirical Study of Several Industrial Countries," *Quarterly Review,* Federal Reserve Bank of New York, Winter 1991–92, pp. 12–28; and Michael M. Hutchison, "Interdependence: U.S. and Japanese Real Interest Rates," *FRBSF Weekly Letter,* Federal Reserve Bank of San Francisco, June 18, 1993.

return) can be found in the securities' markets; (5) transactions and storage costs for securities are negligible and information costs are small relative to the value of securities traded; and (6) expectations concerning future security prices and interest rates are formed rationally and efficiently.

This last observation means that businesses and individuals are assumed to be *rational agents* who form expectations about the distribution of future security prices and interest rates that do not differ significantly from optimal forecasts made from using all the available information the marketplace provides. Rational agents attempt to make optimal use of the resources at their disposal to maximize their returns. Moreover, a rational agent will tend to make *unbiased* forecasts of future security prices, interest rates, and other variables. That is, he or she will make no systematic forecasting errors and will easily spot past patterns in forecast errors and correct them quickly.

If the money and capital markets are highly efficient in the way we have described, this implies that interest rates will always be at or very near their equilibrium levels. Any deviation from the equilibrium rate dictated by demand and supply forces will be almost instantly eliminated. Security traders who hope to *consistently* earn windfall profits from correctly guessing whether interest rates are "too high" (and therefore will probably fall) or are "too low" (and therefore will probably rise) are unlikely to be successful in the long term. Interest rate fluctuations around equilibrium are likely to be random and momentary. Moreover, knowledge of *past* interest rates — for example, those that prevailed yesterday or last month — will *not* be a reliable forecast of where those rates are likely to be in the future. Indeed, the rational expectations theory suggests that, in the absence of new information, the *optimal forecast* of next period's interest rate would probably be equal to the current period's interest rate (i.e., $E(r_{t+1}) = r_t$) because there is no particular reason for next period's interest rate to be either higher or lower than today's interest rate until new information causes market participants to revise their expectations.

Old news will *not* affect today's interest rates because those rates already have impounded the old news. Interest rates will change only if entirely *new and unexpected* information appears. For example, if the federal government announces for several weeks running that it must borrow an additional $10 billion next month, interest rates probably reacted to that information the first time it appeared. In fact, interest rates probably *increased* at that time, because many investors would view the government's additional need for credit as adding to other demands for credit in the economy and, with the supply of funds unchanged, interest rates would be expected to rise. However, if the government merely repeated that same announcement again, interest rates probably would *not* change a second time; it would be old information already reflected in today's interest rates.

Imagine a new scenario, however. The government suddenly reveals that, contrary to expectations, tax revenues are now being collected in greater amounts than first forecast and therefore no new borrowing will be needed. Interest rates probably will fall immediately as market participants are forced to revise their borrowing and lending plans to deal with a new situation. How do we know which *direction* rates will move? Clearly, the path interest rates take depends on *what market participants expected to begin with.* Thus, if market participants were expecting increased demand for credit (with supply unchanged), an unexpected announcement of reduced credit demand implies lower interest rates in the future. Similarly, a market expectation of less credit demand in the future (supply unchanged), when confronted with an unexpected announcement of higher credit demand, implies that interest rates will rise.

We can illustrate the foregoing points about the rational expectations theory of interest by modifying the loanable funds theory of interest so that its demand and supply schedules reflect not just actual demand and supply but also the *expected* demand for and supply of loanable funds. For example, referring to Exhibit 8–12, suppose D_0 and S_0 reflect the *actual*

Exhibit 8–12   **Expected Demand for and Supply of Loanable Funds under the Rational Expectations Theory**

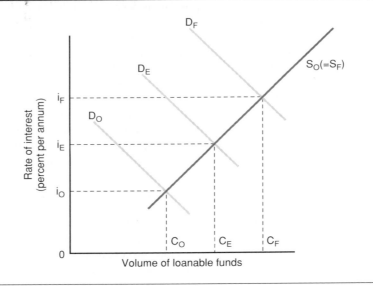

supply and demand for loanable funds in the current period, while D_F reflects the *actual* demand for loanable funds that will prevail in the next (future) time period. The supply of loanable funds is assumed to be the same in both time periods ($S_0 = S_F$).

Now imagine that during the current period, the government makes an unexpected announcement of its increased need to borrow more money in future period F due to an unusually large budget deficit. The result is a new expected demand for loanable funds curve D_E, projected to prevail in the next (future) period F but as viewed by borrowers and lenders today in time period 0. In this case, the equilibrium interest rate in the current period will not be i_0, but rather i_E, where the expected demand curve (D_E) intersects the actual supply curve S_0. The equilibrium quantity of loanable funds traded in the current period then will be C_E not C_0. This is because, according to the rational expectations theory, borrowers and lenders will act as rational agents, using all the information they possess (including expected events, such as the government announcing it will need to borrow more money in a future period) to price financial assets *today*. When the future period arrives, the equilibrium interest rate will rise to rate i_F and the quantity of loanable funds traded then will be C_F. The equilibrium rate moves upward because the demand for loanable funds in period F is more than the expected future loanable-funds demand as seen by market participants in period 0.

Suppose, on the other hand, that actual loanable-funds demand in period F increases upward and beyond D_0 but by a smaller amount than was anticipated by investors in the market in period 0. Demand schedule D_F would then fall somewhere between D_0 and D_E. The equilibrium interest rate (with the supply curve unchanged) would be *lower* than i_E, lying somewhere between i_0 and i_E.

But this is a startling conclusion! Actual demand *increased* (above D_0, but not to D_E) in the next period with supply held constant; still, the equilibrium interest rate *fell*! How could this be? Clearly, it makes sense only when we assume that the real world works the way the rational expectations theory says it should. *To know which way interest rates will go, we must know what the market expects to begin with.* In this example, demand for loanable funds rose but not as high as the market expected. Therefore, interest rates will *decline*, other factors held constant.

The rational expectations view argues that forecasting interest rates requires knowledge of the public's *current set of expectations*. If new information is sufficient to alter those expectations, interest rates *must* change. If correct, this portion of the rational expectations theory creates significant problems for government policymakers. It implies that policymakers cannot cause interest rates to move in any particular direction without knowing what the public already expects to happen and, indeed, cannot change interest rates at all unless government officials can convince the public that a new set of expectations is warranted. Moreover, because guessing what the public's expectations are is treacherous at best, rational expectations theorists suggest that *rate hedging* — using various tools to reduce the risk of loss from changing interest rates — is preferable to rate forecasting. Indeed, to be a consistently correct interest rate forecaster under the rational expectations theory you must know (a) what market participants expect to happen and (b) what new information will arrive in the market before that information actually arrives. That's a tall order!

A growing number of studies today imply that at least some elements of the rational expectations/efficient markets view *do* show up in actual market behavior. For example, studies by Mishkin (1978) and Phillips and Pippenger (1976) find that past interest rate movements are *not* significantly related to current rates of return on bonds or stock, as the theory predicts. Other studies (e.g., Rozeff, 1974) find that past information on economic conditions and money supply movements also appears to bear little correlation to today's interest rate levels or to observed changes in current interest rates. However, *unanticipated* growth in the money supply, income, and the price level *do* appear to be correlated with bond and stock returns, especially with short-term interest rates (as noted by Engel and Frankel, 1984). Moreover, adjustments in interest rates and security prices to *new* information appear to be very rapid.

Nevertheless, the rational expectations view is still in the development stage. One key problem is that we do not know very much about how the public forms its expectations — what data are used, what weights are applied to individual bits of data, and how fast people learn from their forecasting mistakes. As Bullard (1991) notes, because the rational expectations theory is not well defined, empirical tests of the theory are *not* yet very convincing.

Several characteristics of real-world markets seem at odds with the assumptions of the expectations theory. For example, the cost of gathering and analyzing information relevant to the pricing of loans and securities is not always negligible, as assumed by the theory, tempting many lenders and borrowers of funds to form their expectations by rules of thumb (trading rules) that are *not* fully rational. Although rationally formed expectations appear to exist in large auction markets (such as the markets for government securities or listed common stock), it is not clear that such is the case for other financial markets, such as those for consumer loans. Finally, some current interest rates — for example, those on short-term securities — do exhibit significant correlations with past interest rate movements. Thus, not all interest rates and security prices appear to display the kind of behavior implied by the rational expectations theory. A great deal of research work remains to be done about how people learn and especially on how systematic forecasting errors are corrected by market participants.

SUMMARY

Each theory of the determinants of interest rates reviewed in this chapter offers insights into the functioning of the financial system. The classical theory of interest emphasizes saving and investment demand as interest rate determinants, while the liquidity preference theory points to the demand and supply of cash balances. The loanable funds theory views interest rates as determined by the total demand for and total supply of credit, while the rational expectations theory emphasizes the roles played by public expectations regarding interest rates and the economy and by the impact of *new* information in moving interest rates to a new equilibrium.

Collectively, the different theories of interest rate determination examined in this chapter point us toward those forces in the economy and financial system — saving, investment demand, money supply growth, and the demand for cash balances — that should be studied carefully if we are to understand current trends in interest rates and anticipate future trends. In the chapters that follow, we consider various factors that cause the interest rate on one security or loan to be different from the rate on another security or loan. These factors include expectations of inflation, the maturity or length of a security or loan, the risk of borrower default, the risk of calling in a security in advance of its maturity, taxes, and security convertibility. We will find that a thorough understanding of the entire structure of interest rates in the economy requires us to be aware of all these factors as well as the interest rate theories we have reviewed in this chapter.

KEY TERMS AND CONCEPTS IN THIS CHAPTER

rate of interest	substitution effect	income effect
price of credit	liquidity preference theory of interest rates	wealth effect
pure or risk-free rate of interest	loanable funds theory of interest rates	rational expectations theory of interest rates
classical theory of interest rates		

STUDY QUESTIONS

1. What are the different roles of the rate of interest in the economy?

2. What is the risk-free, or pure, interest rate? Explain its relationship to other interest rates in the economy.

3. What factors determine the rate of interest in the classical theory? Explain why the supply of savings curve has a positive slope. What determines the shape of the demand curve in this theory?

4. Define the following: *transactions motive, precautionary motive,* and *speculative motive.* How is the total demand for money determined in the liquidity preference theory?

5. What is the liquidity effect associated with changes in the money supply? The money-supply income effect? The money-supply price expectations effect? Explain how these effects cause interest rates to change when the money supply expands (demand for money unchanged).

6. What factors make up the demand for loanable funds? The supply of loanable funds? How is the equilibrium rate of interest determined in the loanable funds theory?

7. Trace through what happens to the equilibrium rate of interest when the demand for loanable funds increases with supply unchanged. What happens to the equilibrium rate if the supply of loanable funds expands with demand unchanged?

8. Describe the rational expectations theory of interest rate determination. What is assumed in this theory? Can you see any problems in trying to use this theory to anticipate future trends in rates?

PROBLEMS

1. Construct a supply of savings schedule (with all schedules and axes correctly labeled) that illustrates the *income effect*. Do the same to illustrate the *wealth effect* and the *substitution effect*. Explain the differences you observe.

2. Suppose the going market rate of interest on high-quality (AAA rated) corporate bonds is 12 percent. FORTRAN Corporation is considering an investment project that will last 10 years and requires an initial cash outlay of $1.5 million but will generate estimated revenues of $500,000 per year for 10 years. Would you recommend that this project be adopted? Explain why.

3. A government securities dealer has purchased a 10-year bond bearing a coupon rate of 9 percent. The bond was purchased at par ($1,000). Interest rates on *new* bonds with comparable terms rise to 11 percent. What will happen to the 9 percent bond's market price? What price will it approach? Answer these same questions in the case in which bond rates decline to 7 percent. Explain the price changes you have calculated.

4. The statements listed below were gathered from recent issues of financial news sheets. Read each statement carefully and then (*a*) identify which theory or theories of interest rate determination is implicit in each statement and (*b*) indicate which *direction* interest rates should move if the statement is a correct analysis of the current market situation. Use appropriate supply-demand diagrams, where possible, to show the reasoning behind your answers to part *b*.

    a. The factor which is likely to dominate interest rate changes in the weeks ahead is a tighter credit policy at the Federal Reserve.

    b. The White House unexpectedly disclosed today that budget negotiations with Capitol Hill have broken down. Market analysts are fearful of the effects on the bond and stock markets when trading begins tomorrow morning.

    c. Corporate profits have declined significantly in the quarter just concluded, following a year of substantial growth. Financial experts expect this negative trend to continue for at least the next six months.

    d. Personal consumption expenditures are rising rapidly, fueled by an unprecedented level of borrowing. Personal savings are up in real dollar terms, but the national savings rate dropped significantly this past year and further declines are expected. Economists believe this recent change in the savings rate explains the current trend in interest rates — a trend likely to continue into next autumn.

5. Suppose that total savings and business investment demand in the economy behaves as follows (dollars are in billions):

Total Business Investment Demand	Volume of Total Savings Expected	Alternative Market Interest Rates
$170	$ 80	5%
155	96	6
142	103	7
135	135	8
128	178	9
111	207	10
92	249	11
86	285	12

According to the classical theory of interest, what equilibrium interest rate will prevail given the above schedules of planned saving and investment? What could cause the equilibrium rate to change?

6. Suppose the total demand for money is described by the following equation:

$$MD = 30 - 2i$$

where i is the prevailing market interest rate. The total supply of money is described by the following equation:

$$MS = 3 + 7i$$

According to the liquidity preference theory of interest rates, what is the prevailing equilibrium rate of interest?

SELECTED REFERENCES

Ando, A., and Franco Modigliani. "The Life Cycle Hypothesis of Saving." *American Economic Review,* March 1963, pp. 55–84.

Boskin, M.J. "Taxation, Savings, and the Rate of Interest." *Journal of Political Economy,* April 1978, pp. S3–S27.

Bryan, Michael F., and Susan Byrne. "Don't Worry, We'll Grow Out of It: An Analysis of Demographics, Consumer Spending, and Foreign Debt." *Economic Commentary.* Federal Reserve Bank of Cleveland, October 1, 1990, pp. 1–4.

Bullard, James B. "Learning, Rational Expectations, and Policy: A Summary of Recent Research." *Review.* Federal Reserve Bank of St. Louis, January/February 1991, pp. 50–60.

Cagan, Phillip. *The Causes of Monetary Effects on Interest Rates.* New York: National Bureau of Economic Research, 1972.

Engel, Charles M., and Jeffrey A. Frankel. "Why Interest Rates React to Money Announcements: An Explanation from the Foreign Exchange Markets." *Journal of Monetary Economics* 13 (January 1984), pp. 31–39.

Fisher, Irving. *The Theory of Interest.* New York: Macmillan, 1930.

Friedman, Milton. "Factors Affecting the Level of Interest Rates." *Proceedings of the Conference on Savings and Residential Financing.* U.S. League of Savings Associations, 1968, pp. 11–27.

Justen, F.T., and L.D. Taylor. "Towards a Theory of Saving Behavior." *American Economic Review,* May 1975, pp. 203–9.

Keynes, John M. *The General Theory of Employment, Interest and Money.* New York: Harcourt Brace Jovanovich, 1936.

Mishkin, Frederick. "Efficient-Markets Theory: Implications for Monetary Policy." *Brookings Papers on Economic Activity* 3 (1978), pp. 707–52.

Phillips, Llad, and John Pippenger. "Preferred Habitat vs. Efficient Markets: A Test of Alternative Hypotheses." *Review.* Federal Reserve Bank of St. Louis, May 1976, pp. 11–39.

Rozeff, Michael S. "Money and Stock Prices: Market Efficiency and the Lag in Effect of Monetary Policy." *Journal of Financial Economics* 1 (September 1974), pp. 245–302.

Chapter 9

Relationships between Interest Rates and Security Prices

LEARNING OBJECTIVES IN THIS CHAPTER

- To examine the methods used today to measure and calculate interest rates and the prices of securities and other financial assets.
- To understand the relationship between the interest rate on a bond or other debt security and its market price.
- To see how banks and other lending institutions calculate the interest rates they charge borrowers for loans and the interest rates they pay on deposits.

Theories of the rate of interest, such as those we sketched out in the preceding chapter, help us to understand the forces that cause interest rates and the prices of securities to change. However, these theories provide little or no information on how interest rates should be *measured* in the real world. As a result, many different measures of interest rates on securities and loans have been developed, leading to some confusion, especially for small borrowers and savers. In this chapter, the methods most frequently used to measure interest rates and security prices in today's financial markets are examined. We also consider the relationship between security prices and interest rates and how they impact each other.

UNITS OF MEASUREMENT FOR INTEREST RATES AND SECURITY PRICES

Definition of Interest Rates

The **interest rate** is the price charged a borrower for the loan of money. This price is unique because it is really a *ratio* of two quantities: the total required fee a borrower must pay a lender to obtain the use of credit for a stipulated period divided by the amount of credit actually made available to the borrower. By convention, the interest rate is usually expressed in *percent per annum*. Thus,

$$\begin{matrix} \text{Annual} \\ \text{rate of} \\ \text{interest on} \\ \text{loanable} \\ \text{funds (in} \\ \text{percent)} \end{matrix} = \frac{\begin{matrix}\text{Fee required by the} \\ \text{lender for the} \\ \text{borrower to obtain credit}\end{matrix}}{\begin{matrix}\text{Amount of credit made} \\ \text{available to the} \\ \text{borrower}\end{matrix}} \times 100 \qquad (9\text{--}1)$$

For example, an interest rate of 10 percent per annum on a $1,000 one-year car loan implies that the lender of funds has received a borrower's promise to pay a fee of $100 (10 percent of $1,000) in return for the use of $1,000 in credit for a year. The promised fee of $100 is in addition to the repayment of the loan principal ($1,000), which must occur sometime during the year.

Interest rates are usually expressed as *annualized percentages* even for loans and investments shorter than a year. For example, in the federal funds market, commercial banks frequently loan reserves to each other overnight, with the loan being repaid the next day. Even in this market, the interest rate quoted daily by lenders is expressed in percent per annum, as though the loan were for a year's time. As we will soon see, however, various types of loans and securities display important differences in how interest fees and amounts borrowed are valued or accounted for, leading to several different methods for determining interest rates. Some interest rate measures use a 360-day year and others, a 365-day year. Some employ compound rates of return, with interest income earned on accumulated interest, and some do not use compounding.[1]

Basis Points

Interest rates on securities traded in the open market rarely are quoted in whole percentage points, such as 5 percent or 8 percent. The typical case is a rate expressed in hundredths of a percent: for example, 5.36 percent or 7.62 percent. Moreover, most interest rates change by only fractions of a whole percentage point in a single day or week. To deal with this situation, the concept of the basis point was developed. A *basis point* equals $1/100$ of a percentage point. Thus, an interest rate of 10.5 percent may be expressed as 10 percent plus 50 basis points, or 1,050 basis points. Similarly, an increase in a loan or security rate from 5.25 percent to 5.30 percent represents an increase of 5 basis points.

Security Prices

The prices of common and preferred stock in the United States are measured in dollars and eighths of a dollar. Thus, a stock price of 5⅛ is a quote of $5.125 (because one eighth of a dollar is $0.125), and 40¼ means each share of a particular stock is selling for $40.25.

Bond prices are expressed in points and fractions of a point, with each point equal to $1 on a $100 basis. Thus, a U.S. government bond with a price quotation of 97 points is selling for $97 for each $100 in par (face) value. A $1,000 par value bond, therefore, would be selling for $970. Fractions of points are typically measured in 32nds, eighths, quarters,

---

[1]Interest rates on U.S. Treasury bills, commercial paper, and a few other short-term financial instruments are based on a 360-day year and do not compound interest. See Part Four (especially Chapter 15) for a discussion of these instruments and the basis for calculating their rates of return to the investor, known as the *bank discount method*.

or halves, and occasionally even 64ths. Note that one-half point equals $0.50, and $1/_{32}$ equals $0.03125 on a $100 basis. Thus, a price quote on a bond of $97^{4}/_{32}$ (sometimes expressed as 97.4 or 97–4) is $97.125 for each $100, or $971.25 for a $1,000 bond. Quotations expressed in 64ths usually are indicated by a plus (+) sign added to the nearest 32nd. Thus, 100.4+ means $100^{9}/_{64}$.

As we noted in Chapter 3, security dealers quote *two* prices for a security rather than one. The higher of the two is the *asked* price, which indicates what the dealer will *sell* the security for. The *bid* price is the price at which the dealer is willing to *purchase* the security. The difference between bid and asked prices — known as the *spread* — provides the dealer's return for creating a market for the security. Generally, the longer the maturity of a security, the greater the spread between its bid and asked prices. This is due, at least in part, to the added risks associated with trading in long-term securities. Short-term securities may trade with a spread as low as $1/_{32}$ (equal to $312.50 for a sale of $1 million in securities). Purchases and sales of intermediate maturities may carry spreads of $4/_{32}$ (equal to $1,250 on a $1 million trade), and long-term bonds may be trading on spreads of $8/_{32}$ (or about $2,500 for every $1 million sold). For small transactions, a commission fee is usually added to cover the cost of executing the transaction. On large sales, however, dealers often forgo commissions and quote a *net* price.

MEASURES OF THE RATE OF RETURN, OR YIELD, ON A LOAN OR SECURITY

The interest rate on a loan is the annual rate of return promised by the borrower to the lender as a condition for obtaining the loan. However, that rate is not necessarily a true reflection of the yield or rate of return actually earned by the lender during the life of the loan. Some borrowers will default on all or a portion of their promised payments. The market value of the security evidencing the loan may rise or fall, adding to or subtracting from the lender's total rate of return (yield) on the transaction. Thus, the interest rate measures the "price" the borrower has promised to pay for a loan, but the actual *yield*, or rate of return, on the loan from the lender's viewpoint may be quite different. In this section, a number of the most widely used measures of the yield or rate of return on a loan or security are discussed.

Coupon Rate

One of the best-known measures of the rate of return on a debt security is the **coupon rate**, which appears on corporate and government bonds and notes. The coupon rate is the contracted rate that the security issuer agrees to pay at the time a security is issued. If, for example, a company issues a bond with a coupon rate printed on its face of 9 percent, the borrower has promised the lender an annual interest payment of 9 percent of the bond's par value. Most bonds are issued with $1,000 par values, and interest payments are semiannual.

The amount of promised annual interest income paid by a bond is called its *coupon*. The annual coupon may be determined from the formula

$$\text{Coupon rate} \times \text{Par value} = \text{Coupon} \tag{9–2}$$

Thus, a bond with par value of $1,000 bearing a coupon rate of 9 percent pays an annual coupon of $90.

The coupon rate is *not* an adequate measure of the return on a bond or other debt security unless the investor purchases the security at a price equal to its par value, the borrower makes all of the promised payments on time, and the investor sells or redeems the bond at its par value. However, the prices of bonds fluctuate with market conditions; rarely does a bond trade exactly at par.

Current Yield

Another popular measure of the return on a loan or security is its **current yield**. This is simply the ratio of the annual income (dividends or interest) generated by the loan or security to its current market value. Thus, a share of common stock selling in the market for $30 and paying an annual dividend to the shareholder of $3 would have a current yield calculated as follows:

$$\text{Current yield} = \frac{\text{Annual income}}{\text{Market price of security}} = \frac{\$3}{\$30} = 0.10, \text{ or } 10\% \tag{9-3}$$

Frequently, the yields reported on stocks and bonds in the financial press are current yields. Like the coupon rate, the current yield is usually a poor reflection of the rate of return actually received by the lender or investor. It ignores the stream of actual and anticipated payments associated with a loan or security and the price at which the investor will be able to sell or redeem it.

Yield to Maturity

The most widely accepted measure of the rate of return on a loan or security is its **yield to maturity**. It is the rate of interest the market is prepared to pay for a financial asset to exchange present dollars for future dollars. Specifically, the yield to maturity is the rate that equates the purchase price of a security or other financial asset (P) with the present value of *all* its expected annual net cash inflows (income). In general terms,

$$P = \frac{I_1}{(1 + y)^1} + \frac{I_2}{(1 + y)^2} + \ldots + \frac{I_n}{(1 + y)^n} \tag{9-4}$$

where y is the yield to maturity and each I represents the expected annual income from the security, presumed to last for n years and terminate when the financial asset is retired. The I terms in the formula include both receipts of income and repayments of principal.

To illustrate the use of this formula, assume that the investor is considering the purchase of a bond due to mature in 20 years, carrying a 10 percent coupon rate. This security is available for purchase at a current market price of $850. If the bond has a par value of $1,000, which will be paid to the investor when the security reaches maturity, the bond's yield to maturity, y, may be found by solving the equation:

$$\$850 = \frac{\$100}{(1 + y)^1} + \frac{\$100}{(1 + y)^2} + \ldots + \frac{\$100}{(1 + y)^{20}} + \frac{\$1,000}{(1 + y)^{20}} \tag{9-5}$$

In this instance, y equals 12 percent, a rate higher than its 10 percent coupon rate, because the bond is currently selling at a *discount* from par.

Suppose this same $1,000, 10 percent coupon bond were selling at a *premium* over par. For example, if this 20-year security has a current market price of $1,200, its yield to maturity could be found from the following equation:

$$\$1,200 = \frac{\$100}{(1 + y)^1} + \cdots + \frac{\$100}{(1 + y)^{20}} + \frac{\$1,000}{(1 + y)^{20}} \qquad (9\text{--}6)$$

In this case, y equals 8 percent. Because the investor must pay a higher current market price than par value (the amount the investor will receive back when the bond matures), this bond's yield to maturity must be *less* than its coupon rate.

From these two examples, it should be clear that the *value of a debt security depends on the size of its promised rate of return (coupon rate) relative to prevailing market interest rates on securities of comparable quality and terms*. If a security's coupon rate equals the current market interest rate on comparable securities, that security will trade at par. If the security's coupon rate is less than the prevailing market rate, it will sell at a *discount* from par. Finally, if the security's coupon rate exceeds the current interest rate in the market, it will sell at a *premium* above its par value.

The yield to maturity has a number of significant advantages as a measure of the rate of return or yield on a financial asset. In fact, security dealers typically use the yield to maturity in quoting rates of return to investors. Unlike the current yield, this return measure considers the time distribution of expected cash flows from a financial asset. Of course, the yield-to-maturity measure does assume that the investor will hold a security until it reaches final maturity. Moreover, yield to maturity is *not* an appropriate measure for most stocks, the majority of which are perpetual instruments, or even for some bonds, because the investor may sell them prior to their termination date or the bonds may pay a variable return each year that is unpredictable. Another problem is that this measure assumes that all cash flowing to the investor can be reinvested at the computed yield to maturity.[2] And we have not yet considered the impact of taxes on the investor's true return, a subject taken up in Chapter 11.

Holding-Period Yield

A slight modification of the yield-to-maturity formula results in a return measure for those situations in which an investor holds a financial asset for a time and then sells it to another investor in advance of the asset's maturity. This so-called **holding-period yield** is simply

$$P = \frac{I_1}{(1 + h)^1} + \frac{I_2}{(1 + h)^2} + \cdots + \frac{I_m}{(1 + h)^m} + \frac{P_m}{(1 + h)^m} \qquad (9\text{--}7)$$

where h is the holding-period yield and the investor's holding period covers m time periods. Thus, the holding-period yield is simply the rate of discount (h) equalizing the market price of a financial asset (P) with all net cash flows between the time the asset is purchased and the time it is sold (including the selling price, P_m). If the asset is held to maturity, its holding-period yield equals its yield to maturity.

---

[2]The examples shown assume that interest is paid once a year; however, most bonds pay interest semiannually and some even more frequently. In this instance, the yield-to-maturity formula needs to be modified to include the parameter k, the number of times during the year that interest is paid to the bondholder. The formula then becomes:

$$\text{Purchase price} = \frac{I_1/k}{(1 + y/k)^1} + \frac{I_2/k}{(1 + y/k)^2} + \cdots + \frac{I_{nk}/k}{(1 + y/k)^{nk}} + \frac{\text{Final price}}{(1 + y/k)^{nk}}$$

Thus, for a 10-year government bond paying $50 interest twice each year, $k = 2$ and there would be 20 periods ($n \times k = 10 \times 2$) in which the investor receives $50 in interest income. Solution of the yield-to-maturity formula proceeds the same way as before except that you need to look up y/k percent in the present value and annuity tables (instead of y) and discount over $n \times k$ rather than n time periods.

Calculating Yields to Maturity and Holding-Period Yields

Holding-period yields and yields to maturity can be calculated in several different ways. One method is to employ present value tables identical to those presented in most finance and accounting texts.

Suppose, for example, that an investor is contemplating the purchase of a corporate bond, $1,000 par value, with a coupon rate of 10 percent. To simplify the problem, assume that the bond pays interest of $100 just once each year. Currently, the bond is selling for $900. The investor plans to hold the bond to maturity in five years. We have

$$\$900 = \frac{\$100}{(1+y)^1} + \frac{\$100}{(1+y)^2} + \frac{\$100}{(1+y)^3} + \frac{\$100}{(1+y)^4} + \frac{\$100}{(1+y)^5} + \frac{\$1,000}{(1+y)^5} \qquad (9\text{--}8)$$

It is useful at this point to consider what each term in Equation 9–8 means. Both the yield-to-maturity and holding-period yield formulas are based on the concept of *present value*: Funds to be received in the future are worth less than funds received today. Present dollars may be used to purchase and enjoy goods and services today, but future dollars are only *promises* to pay and force us to postpone consumption until the funds actually are received. Equation 9–8 indicates that a bond promising to pay $100 for five successive years in the future plus a lump sum of $1,000 at maturity is worth only $900 in present value dollars. The yield, y, serves as a rate of discount reducing each payment of future dollars back to its present value in today's market. The further into the future the payment is to be made, the larger the discount factor, $(1 + y)^n$, becomes.

Turning the concept around, the purchase of a security in today's market represents the investment of present dollars in the expectation of a higher return in the form of future dollars. The familiar *compound interest formula* (discussed later in this chapter) applies here. This formula

$$FV = P(1 + y)^t \qquad (9\text{--}9)$$

indicates that the amount of funds accumulated t years from now (FV) depends on the principal originally invested (P), the investor's expected rate of return or yield (y), and the number of years the principal is invested (t). Thus, a principal of $1,000 invested today at a 10 percent annual rate will amount to $1,100 a year from now [i.e., $\$1,000 \times (1 + 0.10)^1$]. Rearrangement of the compound interest formula gives

$$P = \frac{FV}{(1 + y)^t} \qquad (9\text{--}10)$$

Equation 9–10 states that the present value of FV dollars to be received in the future is P if the promised interest rate is y. If we expect to receive $1,100 one year from now and the promised interest rate is 10 percent, the present value of that $1,100 must be $1,000.

Each term on the right-hand side of the yield-to-maturity and holding-period yield formulas is a form of Equation 9–10. Solving Equation 9–8 for the yield to maturity of a bond simply means finding a value for y, which brings both right- and left-hand sides of the yield formula into balance, equating the current price (P) of a financial asset with the stream of future dollars it will generate for the investor. When all expected cash flows are not the same in amount, trial and error may be used to find the solution. Fortunately, in the case of the bond represented in Equation 9–8, the solution is not complicated. Rewrite Equation 9–8 in the following form:

$$\$900 = \$100\left[\frac{1}{(1+y)^1} + \frac{1}{(1+y)^2} + \ldots + \frac{1}{(1+y)^5}\right] + \$1,000\left[\frac{1}{(1+y)^5}\right] \qquad (9\text{--}11)$$

This indicates that the bond will pay an annuity of $1 per year (multiplied by $100) for five years, plus a lump-sum payment of $1 (multiplied by $1,000) at the end of the fifth year.

Use of Present Value Tables. What is the yield on this bond? A reasonable initial guess is 10 percent. To determine how accurate a guess it is, we need to consult the present value and annuity tables in the appendix at the back of this book. The annuity table indicates the present value of $1 received annually for five years at a discount yield of 10 percent is $3.791. The present value table shows that the present value of $1 to be received five years from today at 10 percent is $0.621. Inserting these figures into Equation 9–11 yields

$$\$100\ [3.791] + \$1,000\ [0.621] = \$1,000.1 > \$900 \tag{9-12}$$

An annual yield of 10 percent is obviously too small because it results in a present value for the bond far in excess of its current price of $900. A 12 percent yield gives a present value of $927.50, and a 14 percent yield results in a present value for the bond of $862.30. Clearly, the true yield to maturity of this $900 bond lies between 12 percent and 14 percent, but closer to 12 percent. Linear interpolation fixes this yield at 12.84 percent.[3] The investor interested in maximizing return would compare this yield to maturity with the yields to maturity available on other assets of comparable risk.

Present value tables may also be used to calculate the holding-period yield on corporate stock. To illustrate, suppose an investor is considering the purchase of common stock issued by Gulf Oil Corporation currently selling for $40 per share. He plans to hold the stock for two years and sell out at an expected price of $50 per share. If dividends of $2 per share are expected each year, what holding-period yield does the investor expect to earn? Following the form of Equation 9–6, we have

$$\$40 = \frac{\$2}{(1 + h)^1} + \frac{\$2}{(1 + h)^2} + \frac{\$50}{(1 + h)^2} \tag{9-13}$$

The reader may wish to verify from the present value and annuity tables in the appendix at the back of this book that the holding period yield on Gulf Oil's stock is 16.54 percent.

Bond Yield Tables. Present value tables provide a reasonably accurate method for calculating maturity and holding-period yields. However, use of the tables is a trial and error process and can be time consuming. To save time, securities dealers and experienced investors use bond yield tables, which give the appropriate yield for bonds of a given

---

[3]The present value and annuity tables provide the following information for the bond described above:

Difference in Yield to Maturity	Difference in Present Value of Bond
14%	$862.3
12	927.5
2%	$−65.2

There is a difference of $27.5 between the current $900 price of the bond and its present value at a yield of 12 percent, which is $927.50. Therefore, the bond's approximate actual yield to maturity may be found from

$$12\% + \frac{\$27.5}{\$65.2} \times 2\% = 12\% + 0.8436\% \approx 12.84\%$$

Linear interpolation of this sort must be used with care, especially when yield differentials are substantial, because the yield-price relationship is *not* linear.

Exhibit 9–1   **Bond Yield Table** (Prices of a Bond with a 10 Percent Coupon Rate)

Yield to Maturity in Percent	Maturity of a Bond in Years				
	5	10	15	20	25
5%	121.88	138.97	152.33	162.76	170.91
6	117.06	129.75	139.20	146.23	151.46
7	112.47	121.32	127.59	132.03	135.18
8	108.11	113.59	117.29	119.79	121.48
9	103.96	106.50	108.14	109.20	109.88
10	100.00	100.00	100.00	100.00	100.00
11	96.23	94.02	92.73	91.98	91.53
12	92.64	88.53	86.24	84.95	84.24
13	89.22	83.47	80.41	78.78	77.91
14	85.95	78.81	75.18	73.34	72.40
15	82.84	74.51	70.47	68.51	67.56

Note: Prices expressed on the basis of $100 par value.

coupon rate, maturity, and price. An example of a page from a bond yield table is shown in Exhibit 9–1.

To illustrate, suppose that the investor holds a corporate bond, bearing a 10 percent coupon rate, with 10 years remaining until maturity. The bond's purchase price may be found in the table under the correct number of years (or, for more detailed bond yield tables, number of months and years) to maturity. The correct yield to maturity will be found along the same line as the price in the extreme left-hand column of the table. For example, if the 10-year bond's purchase price were $88.53 (on a $100 basis), then its yield to maturity would be 12 percent, as shown in the table (Exhibit 9–1).

The Yield Approximation Formula. When tables or computer programs are unavailable, the yield approximation formula can be used to estimate the rate of return on a security. This formula assumes that

$$
\begin{array}{c}
\text{Approximate} \\
\text{average} \\
\text{annual} \\
\text{yield on a security}
\end{array}
=
\frac{
\begin{array}{c}
\text{Average annual income} \\
\text{from the security}
\end{array}
}{
\begin{array}{c}
\text{Average amount of funds} \\
\text{invested in the security}
\end{array}
}
\qquad (9\text{–}14)
$$

In the case of a bond, the approximate yield would be composed of annual interest income plus the average amount of price appreciation (or minus the average price depreciation) that occurs each year. The average amount of funds invested can be represented by the simple arithmetic average of the purchase price and the expected selling price of the security. That is,

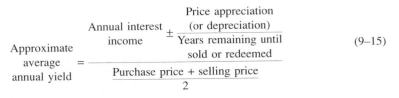

$$
\begin{array}{c}
\text{Approximate} \\
\text{average} \\
\text{annual yield}
\end{array}
=
\frac{
\text{Annual interest income}
\pm
\dfrac{
\begin{array}{c}
\text{Price appreciation} \\
\text{(or depreciation)}
\end{array}
}{
\begin{array}{c}
\text{Years remaining until} \\
\text{sold or redeemed}
\end{array}
}
}{
\dfrac{\text{Purchase price} + \text{selling price}}{2}
}
\qquad (9\text{–}15)
$$

To illustrate the use of this formula, suppose an investor is considering the purchase of a bond with a current market price of $900 and a coupon rate of 10 percent, and that the bond will be sold or redeemed in 10 years at an expected price of $1,000. The approximate expected yield would be:

$$\text{Approximate average annual yield on bond} = \frac{\$100 + \dfrac{(\$1,000 - \$900)}{10}}{\dfrac{\$900 + \$1,000}{2}} = \frac{\$110}{\$950} = 11.58\% \qquad (9\text{--}16)$$

Note that the investor expects price appreciation of $100 over the remaining life of this bond because it sells currently for $900 and will be redeemed in 10 years for $1,000. The average gain in price, therefore, is $10 per year.

The same formula may be used for an asset that is expected to experience a depreciation in price between time of purchase and time of sale or redemption. Suppose, for example, the investor wishes to purchase a $1,000 par value bond currently selling for $1,200 with a coupon rate of 10 percent. If the bond matures in 10 years and is held to maturity, then

$$\text{Approximate average annual yield on bond} = \frac{\$100 + \dfrac{(\$1,000 - \$1,200)}{10}}{\dfrac{\$1,200 + \$1,000}{2}} = 7.27\% \qquad (9\text{--}17)$$

The expected price depreciation of the bond partially offsets the annual interest income it will pay, thus reducing the investor's average yield.

YIELD-PRICE RELATIONSHIPS

The foregoing yield-to-maturity and holding-period yield formulas illustrate a number of important relationships between security prices and yields or interest rates that prevail in the financial system. One of these important relationships is expressed as follows:

> The price of a security and its yield or rate of return are *inversely* related — a rise in yield implies a decline in price; conversely, a fall in yield is associated with a rise in the security's price.

Recall that investing funds in financial assets can be viewed from two different perspectives, the borrowing and lending of money or the buying and selling of securities. As noted in Chapter 8, the equilibrium rate of interest from the lending of funds can be determined by the interaction of the supply of loanable funds and the demand for loanable funds. Demanders of loanable funds (borrowers) supply securities to the financial marketplace, and suppliers of loanable funds (lenders) demand securities as an investment. Therefore, the equilibrium rate of return or yield on a security and the equilibrium price of that security are determined at one and the same instant and are simply different aspects of the same phenomenon, the borrowing and lending of loanable funds.

This point is depicted in Exhibit 9–2, which shows demand and supply curves for both the rate of interest (yield) and the price of securities. The supply of loanable funds curve (representing lending) in the interest rate diagram (Exhibit 9–2A) is analogous to the demand for securities curve (also representing lending) in the price of securities diagram (Exhibit 9–2B). Similarly, the demand for loanable funds curve (representing borrowing) in the interest rate diagram is analogous to the supply of securities curve (also representing borrowing) in the price of securities diagram.

Exhibit 9–2   **Equilibrium Security Prices and Interest Rates (Yields)**

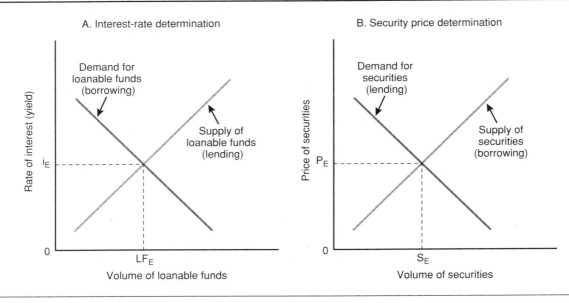

We note in Exhibit 9–2B that borrowers are assumed to issue a larger volume of securities at a higher price and that lenders will demand more securities at a lower price. In Exhibit 9–2A, on the other hand, borrowers demand a smaller quantity of loanable funds at a higher interest rate, while lenders supply fewer loanable funds at a lower interest rate (yield). The *equilibrium interest rate* (yield) in Exhibit 9–2A is determined at point i_E, where the demand for loanable funds equals the supply of loanable funds. Similarly, in Exhibit 9–2B, the *equilibrium price* for securities lies at point P_E, where the demand for and supply of securities are equal. Only at the equilibrium interest rate and equilibrium security price will *both* borrowers and lenders be content with the volume of lending and borrowing taking place within the financial system.

The *inverse* relationship between interest rates and security prices can be seen quite clearly when we allow the supply and demand curves depicted in Exhibit 9–2 to change. This is illustrated in Exhibit 9–3. For example, suppose that, in the face of continuing inflation, consumers and business firms accelerate their borrowings, increasing the demand for loanable funds. As shown in the upper left-hand portion of Exhibit 9–3, the demand for loanable funds curve slides upward and to the right with the supply of loanable funds unchanged. This increasing demand for loanable funds also means that the supply of securities must expand, as shown in the upper right-hand portion of Exhibit 9–3 by a shift in the supply curve from S to S'. Both a new *lower* equilibrium price for securities and a *higher* equilibrium interest rate for loanable funds result.

Conversely, suppose that consumers decide to save more, expanding the supply of loanable funds. As shown in the lower left-hand panel of Exhibit 9–3, the supply of loanable funds curve slides downward and to the right from S to S'. But with more savings, the demand for securities curve must rise, sliding upward and to the right from D to D' as those added savings are invested in securities. The result is a *rise* in the equilibrium price of securities and a *decline* in the equilibrium interest rate.

Exhibit 9–3   **Effects of Changing Supply and Demand on Security Rates (Yields) and Prices**

A. Effects of an increase in the demand for loanable funds: higher interest rates and lower security prices

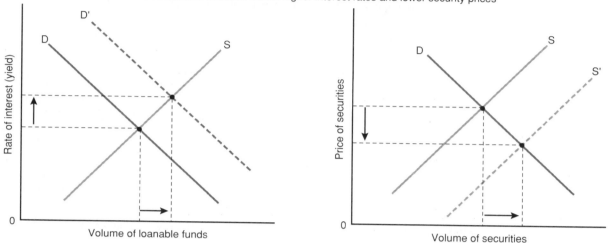

B. Effects of an increase in the supply of loanable funds: lower interest rates and higher security prices

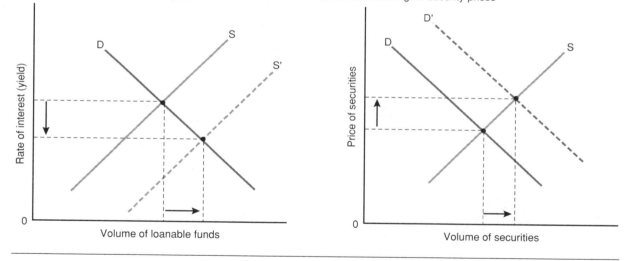

INTEREST RATES CHARGED BY INSTITUTIONAL LENDERS

In this chapter, we have examined several different measures of the rate of return, or yield, on financial assets. Our list is not complete, however, for institutional lenders of funds — banks, credit unions, insurance companies, and finance companies, to name the most important — often employ very different methods to calculate the rate of interest charged on their loans. Six commonly used methods for calculating institutional loan rates are discussed on the following pages.

The Simple Interest Method

The widely used **simple interest method** assesses interest charges on a loan for only the period of time the borrower actually has use of borrowed funds. The total interest bill *decreases* the more frequently a borrower must make payments on a loan.

For example, suppose you borrow $1,000 for a year at simple interest. If the interest rate is 10 percent, your interest bill will be $100 for the year. This figure is derived from the formula

$$I = P \times r \times t \qquad (9\text{--}18)$$

where I represents the interest charge (in dollars), P is the principal amount of the loan, r is the annual rate of interest, and t is the term (maturity) of the loan expressed in years or fractions of a year. (In this example, $1,000 \times 0.10 \times 1 = $100.)

If the $1,000 loan is repaid in one lump sum at the end of the year, you will pay a total of

Principal + Interest =	Total payment
$1,000 + $100 =	$1,100

Suppose, however, that this loan principal is paid off in two equal installments of $500 each, every six months. Then you will pay

	Principal + Interest	= Total payment
First installment:	$500 + $50 (i.e., 6 months' interest on $1,000 at 10%)	= $ 550
Second installment:	$500 + $25 (i.e., 6 months' interest on $500 at 10%)	= $ 525
		$1,075

Clearly, you pay a lower interest bill ($75 versus $100) with two installment payments instead of one. This happens because with two installment payments you effectively have use of the full $1,000 for only six months. For the remaining six months of the year you have use of only $500. A shorthand formula for determining the total payment (interest plus principal) on a simple interest loan is

$$\text{Total payment due} = P + P \times r \times t = P(1 + r \times t) \qquad (9\text{--}19)$$

The simple interest method is still popular with many mortgage lenders, credit unions, and banks.

Add-On Rate of Interest

A method for calculating loan interest rates often used by finance companies and banks is the **add-on rate** approach. In this instance, interest is calculated on the full principal of the loan, and the sum of interest and principal payments is divided by the number of payments to determine the dollar amount of each payment. For example, suppose you borrow $1,000 for one year at an interest rate of 10 percent. You agree to make two equal installment payments six months apart. The total amount to be repaid is $1,100 ($1,000 principal + $100 interest). At the end of the first six months, you will pay half ($550), and the remaining half will be paid at the end of the year.

If money is borrowed and repaid in one lump sum (a single payment loan), the simple interest and add-on methods give the same interest rate. However, as the number of installment payments increases, the borrower pays a higher effective interest rate under the add-on method. This happens because the average amount of money borrowed declines with the greater frequency of installment payments, yet the borrower pays the *same* total interest bill. In fact, the effective rate of interest nearly doubles when monthly installment payments are required. For example, if you borrow $1,000 for a year at 10 percent simple interest but repay the loan in 12 equal monthly installments, you have only about $500 available for use, on average, over the year. Because the total interest bill is $100, the interest rate exceeds 18 percent.

Discount Method

Many commercial loans, especially those used to raise working capital, are extended on a discount basis. This so-called **discount method** for calculating loan rates determines the total interest charge to the customer on the basis of the amount to be repaid. However, the borrower receives as proceeds of the loan only the *difference* between the total amount owed and the interest bill. For example, suppose you borrow $1,000 for one year at 10 percent, for a total interest bill of $100. Using the discount method, you actually receive for your use only $900 (i.e., $1,000 − $100) in net loan proceeds. The effective interest rate, then, is

$$\frac{\text{Interest paid}}{\text{Net loan proceeds}} = \frac{\$100}{\$900} \times 100 = 11.11\% \qquad (9\text{--}20)$$

Some lenders grant the borrower the full amount of money required but add the amount of discount to the face amount of the borrower's note. For example, if you need the full $1,000, the lender under this method will multiply the effective interest rate (11.11 percent) times $1,000 to derive a total interest bill of $111.11. The face value of the borrower's note and, therefore, the amount that must be repaid becomes $1,111.11. However, the borrower receives only $1,000 for use during the year. Most discount loans are for terms of one year or less and usually do not require installment payments. Instead, these loans generally are settled in a lump sum when the note comes due.

Home Mortgage Interest Rate

One of the most confusing of all rates charged by lenders is the interest rate on a home mortgage loan. Many home buyers have heard that under the terms of most mortgage loans, their monthly payments early in the life of the loan go almost entirely to pay the interest on the loan. Only later is a substantial part of each monthly payment devoted to reducing the principal amount of a home loan. Is this true?

Yes, and we can illustrate it quite easily. Suppose that you find a new home you want to buy and borrow $100,000 to close the deal. The mortgage lender quotes you an annual interest rate of 12 percent on the loan. If we divide this annual interest rate by 12 months, we derive a monthly mortgage loan rate of 1 percent. The lender tells you that your monthly payment will be $1,100 each month (to cover property taxes, insurance, interest, and principal on the loan). This means that the first month's payment of $1,100 will be divided by the lender as follows: (1) $1,000 for the interest payment(or 1% per month × $100,000); and (2) $100 to be applied to the principal of the loan, insurance premiums, taxes, and so forth. For simplicity, let's assume the $100 left over after the $1,000 interest payment goes entirely to help repay the $100,000 loan principal. This means that next month your loan now totals just $99,900 (or $100,000 − $100). When you send in that next monthly payment of $1,000, the interest payment will drop to $999, and, therefore, $101 will now be left over to help reduce the loan principal. Gradually, the monthly interest payment will fall and the amount left over to help retire the loan's principal will rise. After several years, as the mortgage loan's maturity date gets near, each monthly payment will consist mostly of repaying the loan principal itself.

How do mortgage lenders figure the amount of the monthly payment new home buyers must make on their home loan? The usual formula is

$$\text{Total amount borrowed} \times \frac{\left[\dfrac{\text{Loan interest rate}}{12}\right] \times \left[1 + \dfrac{\text{Loan interest rate}}{12}\right]^{t \times 12}}{\left[1 + \left(\dfrac{\text{Loan interest rate}}{12}\right)\right]^{t \times 12} - 1} \tag{9-21}$$

where t stands for the number of years the money is borrowed by the home buyer and the annual interest rate charged on the mortgage loan is divided by 12 to restate that interest rate on a monthly basis.

To see how this formula works, suppose a family takes out a $50,000 loan for 25 years at an interest rate of 12 percent to buy its new home. In this case, the required payment on the loan each month would be

$$\$50,000 \times \frac{\left[\dfrac{0.12}{12}\right] \times \left[1 + \dfrac{0.12}{12}\right]^{25 \times 12}}{\left[1 + \dfrac{0.12}{12}\right]^{25 \times 12} - 1} = \frac{\$9,894.23}{18.7885} = \$526.62$$

Actually, there is an easier way to calculate the required monthly payment on a home mortgage using the annual percentage rate (APR) table given in the appendix at the back of this book. With an annual loan rate of 12 percent and 25 years multiplied by 12, or 300 monthly payments, the APR table gives us the following information:

Total finance charge per $100 financed = $215.97

$$\text{Total finance charge on a \$50,000 loan} = \frac{\$50,000}{\$100} \times \$215.97 = \$107,985$$

Then the monthly home mortgage payment will be as follows:

$$\frac{\text{Total finance charge + Loan amount}}{\text{Number of loan payments}} = \frac{\$107,985 + \$50,000}{300} = \$526.62$$

Note that the borrower in this case pays a total amount of interest ($107,985) that is more than *double* the amount of money borrowed ($50,000)!

Annual Percentage Rate (APR)

The wide diversity of rates quoted by lenders is often confusing and discourages shopping around for credit. With this in mind, Congress passed the Consumer Credit Protection Act in 1968. More popularly known as *Truth in Lending*, this law requires institutions regularly extending credit to consumers to tell the borrower what interest rate he or she is actually paying and to use a prescribed method for calculating that rate.[4] Specifically, banks, credit unions, and other lending institutions are required to calculate an **annual percentage rate (APR)** and inform the loan customer what this rate is before the loan contract is signed. The actuarial method is used to determine the APR, and loan officers usually have tables at hand to translate a simple interest or add-on rate into the APR.

The constant ratio formula, shown below, usually gives a close approximation to the true APR:

$$APR = \frac{\begin{array}{c} 2 \times \text{Number of payment periods in a year} \\ \times \text{ Annual interest cost in dollars} \end{array}}{\begin{array}{c}(\text{Total number of loan payments} + 1) \\ \times \text{ Principal of the loan}\end{array}} \times 100 \qquad (9\text{--}22)$$

To illustrate, suppose you borrow $1,000 at 10 percent simple interest but must repay your loan in 12 equal monthly installments. The APR for this loan is approximately:

$$APR = \frac{2(12)(\$100)}{(12 + 1)(\$1,000)} \times 100 = 18.46\%$$

Regulatory agencies have developed APR tables, such as the one shown in the appendix at the back of this book, to aid lenders in figuring a borrower's required monthly payment and total finance charge on an installment loan. For example, consider the loan described above. The borrower is asked to pay a 10 percent simple interest rate on a loan of $1,000, or $100 in annual interest. The APR table shows that an annual percentage rate of 18 percent (last column in the APR table) comes closest to the true annual interest rate for this loan. At an 18 percent APR, the borrower must pay $10.02 per $100 loaned if repayment is to be made in 12 equal monthly payments. On a $1,000 loan, this means the total finance charge will be $10.02 × $1,000 ÷ $100 = $10.02 × 10 = $100.20. Therefore, the borrower's required monthly payment will be the sum of the total finance charge plus the total amount of the loan divided by the required number of payments:

$$Monthly\ payment = \frac{\$100.02 + \$1,000}{12} = \$91.67$$

Congress hoped that introduction of the APR would encourage consumers to exercise greater care in the use of credit and to shop around to obtain the best terms on a loan. It is not at all clear that either goal has been realized, however. Most consumers appear to give primary weight to the size of installment payments in deciding how much, when, and where to borrow. If their budget can afford principal and interest charges on a loan, most consumers seem little influenced by the reported size of the APR and are often not inclined to ask other lenders for their rates on the same loan. Consumer education is vital to intelligent financial decision making, but progress in that direction has been slow.

Compound Interest

Some lenders and loan situations require the borrower to pay **compound interest** on a loan. In addition, most interest-bearing deposits at banks, credit unions, savings and loans, and money market funds pay compound interest on the balance in the account as of a

---

[4]See Chapter 24 for a discussion of consumer credit laws.

certain date. The compounding of interest simply means that the lender or depositor earns interest income on both the principal amount and on any accumulated interest. Thus, the longer the period over which interest earnings are compounded, the more rapidly does interest earned on interest and interest earned on principal grow.

The conventional formula for calculating the future value of a financial asset earning compound interest is simply

$$FV = P(1 + r)^t \qquad (9\text{--}23)$$

where FV is the sum of principal plus all accumulated interest over the life of the loan or deposit, P is the asset's principal value, r is the annual rate of interest, and t is the time expressed in years. For example, suppose $1,000 is borrowed for three years at 10 percent a year, compounded annually. Using an electronic calculator or a compound interest table (see the appendix tables at the back of this book) to find the compounding factor, $(1 + r)^t$, gives

$$FV = \$1,000(1 + 0.10)^3 = \$1,000(1.331) = \$1,331$$

which is the lump-sum amount the borrower must pay back at the end of three years.[5] The amount of accumulated compound interest on this loan must be

$$Compound\ interest = FV - P = \$1,331 - \$1,000 = \$331 \qquad (9\text{--}24)$$

Increased competition in the financial institutions sector has encouraged most deposit-type institutions to offer their depositors interest compounded more frequently than annually, as assumed in the formula above. To determine the future value of accumulated interest from such a deposit, two changes must be made in the formula: (1) the quoted annual interest rate (r) must be divided by the number of periods during the year for which interest is compounded and (2) the number of years involved (t) must be multiplied by the number of compounding periods within a year. For example, suppose you hold a $1,000 deposit, earning a 12 percent annual rate of interest, with interest compounded monthly and you plan to hold the deposit for three years. At the end of three years, you will receive back the lump sum of

$$FV = P(1 + r/12)^{t \times 12} = \$1,000(1 + 0.12/12)^{3 \times 12}$$
$$= \$1,000(1.431) = \$1,431 \qquad (9\text{--}25)$$

Total interest earned clearly will be $1,431 − $1,000, or $431. Compounding on a more frequent basis increases the depositor's accumulated interest and therefore the deposit's future value.[6]

---

[5]The compound interest table may be used to derive the compound interest factor in this problem. Simply check along the top row of the table for the appropriate annual percentage rate (10 percent in the above problem) and then check the number of time periods (in this case, three years) in the extreme left-hand column. The figures in the body of the compound interest table indicate the total future value (FV) — principal plus interest — repaid or earned per $1 of principal at alternative annual rates and time periods.

[6]The reader can look up the 1.431 compounding factor in the compound interest table simply by checking under the 1 percent (i.e., 12%/12 months) annual percentage rate column and checking the rows for 36 (3×12 months) payment periods. Many financial institutions quote deposit rates compounded *daily*. In this case, the annual interest rate (r) is divided by 360 for simplicity and the number of years (t) in the formula is multiplied by 365. Thus, the formula for *daily* interest rate by compounding is

$$FV = P(1 + r/360)^{t \times 365}$$

See the table of compounding factors in the appendix at the back of this book for daily interest rate compounding.

The Annual Percentage Yield (APY)

In 1991 the U.S. Congress passed the Truth in Savings Act in response to customer complaints about the way some depository institutions were calculating their customers' interest returns on deposits. Instead of giving customers credit for the average balance in their deposit accounts, some depository institutions were figuring a customer's interest return on the amount of the *lowest* balance in their account. The U.S. Congress responded to this practice by requiring depository institutions to calculate the *daily average* balance in a customer's deposit over each interest-crediting period and to use that daily average balance to determine the customer's **annual percentage yield** (or APY) from the deposit account.

For example, suppose a customer deposits $2,000 in a one-year bank savings account for 6 months (180 days) but then withdraws $1,000 to help meet personal expenses, leaving $1,000 for the remainder of the year (185 days). Then the customer's daily average balance would be:

$$\text{Daily average balance} = \frac{\$2,000 \times 180 \text{ days} + \$1,000 \times 185 \text{ days}}{365 \text{ days}} = \$1,493.15$$

Suppose the bank credits the customer's account with $100 in interest. If the account has a term of 365 days (a full year) or has no stated maturity, then the customer's annual percentage yield can be calculated from the simple formula:

$$\text{APY} = 100 \text{ [Annual interest earned/Daily average balance]} \qquad (9\text{--}26)$$

In this case,

$$\text{APY} = 100 \text{ [\$100/\$1493.15]} = 6.70 \text{ percent}$$

On the other hand, if the deposit account runs for *less* than a year, a depository institution subject to the provisions of the Truth in Savings Act must use the formula:

$$\text{APY} = 100 \left[\left(1 + \frac{\text{Amount of interest earned/Daily average balance}}{} \right)^{365/\text{days in term}} - 1 \right] \qquad (9\text{--}27)$$

For example, suppose that a customer opens a savings account with a maturity of 182 days (6 months) and leaves $1,000 in the account for the whole period. Suppose too that at the end of the deposit's term the bank credits the customer with $30.37 in interest earned. Then, the annual percentage yield (APY) that must be reported to the customer under the Truth in Savings Act would be:

$$\text{APY} = 100 \text{ [}(1 + \$30.37/\$1,000)^{365/182} - 1] \approx 6.18 \text{ percent.}$$

Whenever a customer opens a new deposit account in the United States, he or she must be informed about how interest will be computed on his or her account, what fees will be charged that could reduce the customer's interest earnings, and what must be done to earn the full APY promised on the deposit.

SUMMARY

Interest rates and security prices are among the most important ingredients of financial decisions. Over the years, a number of methods have been developed for measuring interest rates and security prices. The intelligent investor must learn to distinguish one method from another. From a conceptual point of view, the yield-to-maturity and holding-period yield methods are among the best for measuring the true return from lending and investing funds because both consider the time value of money. From the borrower's point of view, the annual percentage rate (APR) is an effective technique for measuring the true cost of credit.

In this chapter, we have highlighted one of the fundamental principles of finance. This is the mandatory inverse relationship between the prices of debt securities and interest rates. Falling bond prices, for example, are associated with rising interest rates; rising bond prices imply falling interest rates. We also frequently observe stock prices falling during a period of rising interest rates, although this is not always the case, because stock prices are also sensitive to other factors such as the size of corporate earnings. In the next two chapters, various factors that significantly influence the interest rate attached to a loan or security are reviewed. These factors — inflation, maturity, marketability, default risk, taxation, and other influences — have a significant impact on the price of credit in the money and capital markets. ∎

KEY TERMS AND CONCEPTS IN THIS CHAPTER

interest rate	holding-period yield	annual percentage rate (APR)
coupon rate	simple interest method	
current yield	add-on rate	compound interest
yield to maturity	discount method	

STUDY QUESTIONS

1. What is a *basis point?* How are stock and bond prices measured?

2. Do you think the coupon rate and the current yield are good measures of the true rate of return on a bond? Why?

3. What is the difference between yield to maturity and holding-period yield? Why are bond yields typically quoted on a yield-to-maturity basis, while stock yields are usually expressed as current yields?

4. Explain why debt security prices and interest rates are inversely related. Illustrate with a diagram.

5. Explain the meaning of the following terms:
   a. *Simple interest*   d. *APR*
   b. *Add-on interest*   e. *Compounding of interest*
   c. *Discount method*   f. *APY*

6. How are home mortgage loan payments determined? Explain why most of the payments made early in the life of a home mortgage loan go to pay interest rather than the principal amount of the loan.

PROBLEMS

1.   Suppose a 10-year bond is issued with a coupon rate of 8 percent when the market rate of interest is also 8 percent. If the market rate rises to 9 percent, what happens to the price of this bond? What happens to the bond's price if the market rate falls to 6 percent? Explain why.

2.   Preferred stock for XYZ corporation is issued at par for $50 per share. If stockholders are promised an 8 percent annual dividend, what was the stock's current yield at time of issue? If the stock's market price has risen to $60 per share, what is its new current yield?

3.   An AAA-rated corporate bond has a current market price of $800 and will pay $100 in interest for 10 years. If its par value is $1,000, what is its yield to maturity? Suppose the investor plans to sell it in five years for $900. What would his or her holding period yield be?

4.   Using the yield approximation formula, calculate the average yield on a $1,000 bond six years from final maturity with a 12 percent coupon rate, selling today for $1,100. What would the bond's yield be if it were selling for $940?

5.   You plan to borrow $2,000 to take a vacation and want to repay the loan in a year. The banker offers you a simple interest rate of 12 percent with repayment of principal in two equal installments, 6 months and 12 months from now. What is your total interest bill? What is the APR? Would you prefer an add-on interest rate with one payment at the end of the year? If the bank applied the discount method to your loan, what are the net proceeds of the loan? What is your effective rate of interest?

6.   An investor is interested in purchasing a new 20-year government bond carrying a 10 percent coupon rate. The bond's current market price is $875 for a $1,000 par value instrument. If the investor buys the bond at the going price and holds to maturity, what will be his or her yield to maturity? Suppose the investor sells the bond at the end of 10 years for $950. What is the investor's holding period yield?

7.   You discover a $1,000 par value bond just issued by XYZ corporation that pays interest semiannually at a coupon rate of 12 percent. The bond will mature in 10 years and can be purchased today at a price of $900 including the broker's commission. What is the bond's yield to maturity if all interest payments are made on time?

8.   You borrow $2,500 for five years at a rate of 12 percent per annum, compounded annually. What is the lump-sum amount due at the end of five years? What is the total amount of interest owed?

9.   In Problem 8, if interest were compounded monthly instead of annually, what lump-sum amount would be due in five years and how much total interest must be paid?

10.   You have just placed $1,500 in a bank savings deposit and plan to hold that deposit for eight years, earning 5½ percent per annum. If the bank compounds interest daily, what will be the total value of the deposit in eight years? How does your answer change if the bank switches to monthly compounding? Quarterly compounding?

11.   You decide to take out a 30-year mortgage loan to buy the home of your dreams. The home's purchase price is $120,000. You manage to scrape together a $20,000 down payment and plan to borrow the balance of the purchase price. Hardy Savings and Loan Association quotes you a fixed annual loan rate of 12 percent. What will your monthly payment be? How much total interest will you have paid at the end of 30 years?

12.   A home mortgage loan for $60,000 is available from the neighboring bank at an interest rate of 1 percent per month. The loan will mature in 25 years. What payment must the borrower make each month under the terms of this loan agreement?

13.   A depositor leaves her funds in the amount of $5,000 in a credit union deposit account for a full year but then withdraws $1,000 after 270 days. At the end of the year the credit union pays her $300 in interest. What is this depositor's daily average balance and APY?

14.   A bank customer takes out a CD from his principal bank for 90 days in the amount of $2500 and earns $99 in interest for the 90-day period. What is the depositor's APY?

SELECTED REFERENCES

The First Boston Corporation. *Handbook of Securities of the U.S. Government and Federal Agencies.* 33rd ed. New York: The First Boston Corporation, 1988.

Trainer, Richard D.C. *The Arithmetic of Interest Rates.* New York: Federal Reserve Bank of New York, 1980.

Chapter 10

Inflation, Yield Curves, and Duration

LEARNING OBJECTIVES IN THIS CHAPTER

- To understand what inflation is and how it can affect interest rates and the prices of loans and securities in the financial markets.
- To see how yield curves are created and understand the forces at work in the financial markets that determine the shape (slope) of yield curves.
- To see how yield curves can be a useful tool for investors.
- To explore the concept of duration as a measure of the length of maturity of a loan or security and show how it can be used to aid in making investment choices.

In Chapter 8, we examined the demand and supply forces believed to determine the rate of interest on a loan or security. We know, however, that there is not just one interest rate in the economy, but thousands. And many of these rates differ substantially from one another. For example, early in 1996 the going market rate (yield) on one-year U.S. Treasury bills averaged less than 5 percent, while the market rate (yield) on seasoned corporate bonds was about 7.25 percent. At the same time, major banks were quoting average loan rates to their largest and most financially sound (prime) customers of about 8.25 percent. Meanwhile, investors in the market for state and local government bonds were receiving an annual rate of return of about 5.50 percent.

Why are all these rates so different from one another? Are these rate differences purely random, or can we attribute them to a limited number of factors that can be studied and perhaps predicted? Understanding the factors that cause interest rates to differ among themselves is an indispensable aid to the investor in choosing financial assets for a portfolio. It is not always advisable, for example, to reach for the highest rate available in the financial marketplace. The investor who does so may assume an unacceptable level of risk, have his or her securities called in by the issuer in advance of maturity, pay an unacceptably high tax bill, accept a rate of return whose value is seriously eroded by inflation, or suffer other undesirable consequences. Without question, the intelligent investor must have a working knowledge of the factors affecting interest rates and be able to anticipate future changes in those factors.

For example, what role does inflation play in accounting for differences between one interest rate and another? What influence do changes in the maturity (term) of a loan or security have on the rate of return that a financial instrument pays to the investor? Why are default risk and marketability important determinants of relative interest rates? What is call risk and how does it influence the interest rate (yield) on callable securities? What role do taxes and convertibility play in accounting for rate differences? In this chapter and the next, we address each of these important questions.

INFLATION AND INTEREST RATES

One of the most serious problems confronting economies around the globe in recent years is **inflation**. Inflation is defined as *a rise in the average level of prices for all goods and services*. Some prices of individual goods and services are always rising while others are declining. However, inflation occurs when the *average* level of all prices in the economy rises.[1] Interest rates represent the "price" of credit. Are they also affected by inflation? The answer is *yes*, though there is considerable debate as to exactly *how* and by *how much* inflation affects interest rates.

The Correlation between Inflation and Interest Rates

To be sure, the apparent correlation in recent years between the rate of inflation in the United States and both long- and short-term interest rates is high. Exhibit 10–1, which reports two popular measures of the rate of inflation — the consumer price index and the GNP deflator — and a money market interest rate — the yield on six-month prime commercial paper — suggests a close association between inflation and interest rates, especially during the 1970s and 1980s. Note, for example, the sharp run-up in the rate of inflation between 1971 and 1974 and the parallel upward surge in the commercial paper rate, which reached an average yield of nearly 10 percent in 1974. Similarly, between 1974 and 1980, the inflation rate soared into double digits before falling back in the early 1980s, and interest rates did the same. Between 1980 and 1995, both inflation and U.S. interest rates generally declined.

In reality, however, the correlation between these two data series has not always been so high. During the 1950s and early 1960s, for example, a relatively calm economic environment prevailed, with modest annual price increases. Interest rates, too, were more stable, and the simple correlation between inflation and interest rates was not statistically significant. More recently, interest rates and inflation have tended to become more closely correlated.

The Nominal and Real Interest Rates

To explore the relationship between inflation and interest rates, several key terms must be defined. First, we must distinguish between nominal and real interest rates. The **nominal rate** is the published or quoted interest rate on a security or loan. For example, an announcement in the financial press that major commercial banks have raised their prime lending rate to 10 percent per annum indicates what nominal interest rate is now being quoted by banks to their best customers. In contrast, the **real interest rate** is the return to the lender or investor measured in terms of its actual purchasing power. In a period of

---

[1]See Chapter 21 for a discussion of the nature, causes, and recent public policy responses to inflation.

Exhibit 10–1   **Inflation and Interest Rates** (Annual Rates, Percent)

Year	Rate of Inflation Measured by Percentage Change in		Interest Rate on Prime Commercial Paper (Six-Month Maturities)
	Consumer Price Index	**GNP Deflator**	
1960	1.6%	1.7%	3.85%
1965	1.7	2.2	4.38
1970	5.9	5.4	7.72
1975	9.4	9.5	6.32
1980	13.5	8.8	12.29
1985	3.6	3.1	8.01
1990	6.2	4.0	7.83
1995*	3.1	3.0	6.40

*Consumer price index is for the year ended April 1995, the GNP deflator is for the first quarter of 1995, and the commercial paper rate is the average for the first four months of 1995.

Source: U.S. Department of Commerce and Board of Governors of the Federal Reserve System.

inflation, of course, the real rate will be lower than the nominal rate. Another important concept is the **inflation premium**, which measures the rate of inflation expected by investors in the marketplace during the life of a particular financial instrument.

These three concepts are related. Obviously, a lender of funds is most interested in the *real rate of return* on a loan; that is, the purchasing power of any interest earned. For example, suppose you loan $1,000 to a business firm for a year and expect the prices of goods and services to rise 10 percent during the year. If you charge a nominal interest rate of 12 percent on the loan, your *real* rate of return on the $1,000 loan is only 2 percent, or $20. However, if the actual rate of inflation during the period of the loan turns out to be 13 percent, you have actually suffered a real decline in the purchasing power of the monies loaned. In general, lenders will attempt to charge nominal rates of interest that give them desired *real* rates of return on their loanable funds. Nominal interest rates will change as frequently as lenders alter their expectations regarding inflation.

The Fisher Effect

In a classic article written just before the turn of the century, economist Irving Fisher (1896) argued that the nominal interest rate was related to the real rate by the following equation:

$$\text{Nominal interest rate} = \text{Expected real rate} + \text{Inflation premium} + \text{Expected real rate} \times \text{Inflation premium} \qquad (10\text{--}1)$$

Clearly, if the expected real interest rate is held fixed, changes in nominal rates will reflect shifting inflation premiums (i.e., changes in the public's views on expected inflation). The cross-product term in the above equation (expected real rate × inflation premium) is often eliminated because it is usually quite small except in countries experiencing severe inflation.[2]

---

[2]For example, if inflation is running 5 percent a year and the real rate of interest is 3 percent, the cross-product term in Equation 10–1 is only 0.05×0.03, or 0.0015. Equation 10–1 is derived from the relationship (1 + nominal rate) = (1 + real rate) × (1 + inflation premium).

Does Equation 10–1 suggest that an increase in expected inflation *automatically* increases nominal interest rates? Not necessarily. There are several different views on the matter. Fisher argued that the expected real rate of return tends to be relatively stable over time because it depends on such long-term factors as the productivity of capital and the volume of savings in the economy. Therefore, a change in the inflation premium is likely to influence only the nominal interest rate, at least in the short run. The nominal rate will rise by the full amount of the expected increase in the rate of inflation. For example, suppose the expected real rate is 3 percent and the expected rate of inflation is 10 percent. Then the nominal rate would be:

$$\text{Nominal interest rate} = 3\% + 10\% = 13\% \tag{10–2}$$

According to Fisher's hypothesis, if the expected rate of inflation now rises to 12 percent, the expected real rate will remain unchanged at 3 percent, but the nominal rate will rise to 15 percent.

If this view, known today as the **Fisher effect**, is correct, it suggests a method of judging the *direction* of future interest rate changes. To the extent that a rise in the actual rate of inflation causes investors to expect greater inflation in the future, higher nominal interest rates will soon result. Conversely, a decline in the actual rate of inflation may cause investors to revise downward their expectations of future inflation, leading to lower nominal rates. This will happen because, in an efficient market, investors will be compensated for the risk of expected changes in the purchasing power of their money.

The Harrod-Keynes Effect of Inflation

The Fisher effect conflicts directly with another view of the inflation/interest rate phenomenon, developed originally by British economist Sir Roy Harrod.[3] It is based upon the Keynesian liquidity preference theory of interest discussed in Chapter 8. Harrod argues that the *real* rate *will* be affected by inflation, but the nominal rate need not be. Following the liquidity preference theory, the nominal interest rate is determined by the demand for and supply of money. Therefore, unless inflation affects either the demand for or supply of money, the nominal rate must remain unchanged regardless of what happens to inflationary expectations.

What, then, is the link between inflation and interest rates according to this view? Harrod argues that a rise in inflationary expectations will lower the *real* rate of interest. In liquidity preference theory, the real rate measures the inflation-adjusted return on bonds. However, conventional bonds, like money, are not a hedge against inflation, because their rate of return is fixed by contract. Therefore, a rise in the expected rate of inflation lowers investors' expected real return from holding bonds. If the nominal rate of return on bonds remains unchanged, the expected real rate must be squeezed by expectations of rising prices.

This so-called *Harrod-Keynes effect* does not stop with bonds, however. There are two other groups of assets in the economy that, unlike bonds, may provide a hedge against inflation: common stocks and real estate. Inflationary expectations often lead to rising prices for homes, farmland, and commercial structures and occasionally to rallies in the stock market. Proponents of the Harrod-Keynes view argue that an increase in the rate of inflation causes the demand for these inflation-hedged assets to increase as well. Real

---

[3]The Harrod view of inflation and interest rates is outlined by Mundell (1963).

estate and stock prices rise and their nominal rates of return fall until an equilibrium set of returns on stocks, bonds, real estate, and other assets is achieved.

Alternative Views on Inflation and Interest Rates

The simple one-to-one relationship between the expected inflation rate and the nominal rate of interest proposed by Irving Fisher was the majority view for decades until researchers began to find problems with it. For example, the Fisher effect assumes that inflation is *fully anticipated*. As an example, let us imagine that both borrowers and lenders of funds expect an inflation rate for the next year of 10 percent and the real interest rate is 3 percent. We can illustrate this using Exhibit 10–2, which shows two sets of demand and supply curves for loanable funds — a set of *real* demand and supply curves intersecting at a 3 percent real interest rate and a set of *nominal* demand and supply curves intersecting at a point just high enough to fully reflect the expected inflation rate (in this example, 10 percentage points higher than the real rate). The supply and demand curves for loanable funds both shift upward just enough to ensure that the going nominal interest rate on a one-year loan is 3 percent plus 10 percent, or 13 percent. Lenders will be unwilling to lend money at any rate lower than 13 percent because they expect the prices of the goods and services they plan to purchase to increase by 10 percent during the life span of the loan.

Suppose, however, that all or a portion of the increase in inflation is *unanticipated*. In this case, there is no way to be certain about what the equilibrium nominal interest rate will be, for the nominal rate may not fully reflect the amount of inflation expected. The simple one-for-one change in the nominal rate in response to changing inflationary expectations breaks down.

Exhibit 10–2   **The Impact of Fully Anticipated Inflation on Real and Nominal Interest Rates**

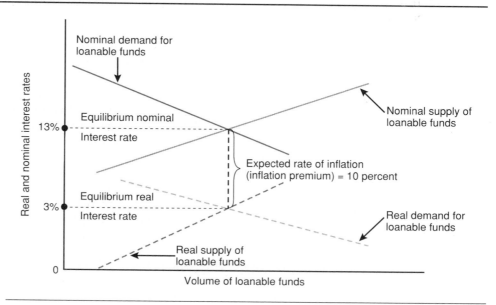

The Inflation-Caused Wealth Effect. Another problem with the Fisher effect centers on its assumption that people will borrow and lend the *same* amount of funds at any expected real interest rate, regardless of the expected inflation rate. However, inflation can affect incomes, wealth holdings, the attractiveness or unattractiveness of business investment, the burden of taxes, and so on. Suppose, for example, that people come to expect a higher inflation rate and they perceive this change as lowering the value of their inflation-adjusted (real) wealth. In response to this inflation-caused wealth effect, people may decide to save more, lowering the equilibrium expected real rate of interest. Therefore, the nominal interest rate will rise *less* than the expected increase in inflation because of the offsetting decline in the expected real rate. Similarly, a decrease in expected inflation might lead to a perceived increase in the real value of wealth holdings, reduce current saving, and cause the real interest rate to rise. Thus, the nominal interest rate will fall by less than the decrease in expected inflation. Clearly, with the **inflation-caused wealth effect**, there is *less* than a one-to-one relationship between changes in expected inflation and nominal interest rates.

The Inflation-Caused Income Effect. The wealth effect of changing inflation may be joined by an **inflation-caused income effect**. A rise in expected inflation, for example, may lead to an increase in real (inflation-adjusted) income. This may happen because a declining real interest rate associated with the reduced value of wealth may cause consumers to reduce their supply of savings to the financial markets and to step up their current spending on goods and services. In response, businesses will borrow more to increase production and stock their shelves with additional goods to sell. The expanded consumption and production will increase employment, and both businesses and consumers will experience a rise in their incomes. Out of that higher income more savings will eventually flow into the financial system, expanding the supply of loanable funds. Other factors held equal, borrowing and lending will take place at a lower real rate of interest, and the nominal rate will again rise by *less* than the increase in expected inflation.

Similarly, a decrease in expected inflation may stimulate more saving and less consumption, reducing business investment and incomes. Eventually, savings flowing into the financial markets will begin to fall with the decline in incomes, and the real interest rate will rise even as nominal rates fall due to lower expected inflation. As before, there is *less* than a one-to-one relationship between changes in expected inflation and the nominal interest rate.

Both the inflation-caused income effect and wealth effect take *time* to exert their influence on real and nominal rates, and this time factor can distort the inflation-interest rate linkage. Unless we adopt a pure rational expectations-efficient markets approach to explaining interest rates (as discussed in Chapter 8), nominal interest rates will reach equilibrium only after a series of rate-determining adjustments have been made. For example, suppose the central bank increases the nation's money supply. The liquidity preference theory of interest discussed in Chapter 8 suggests that nominal rates will fall at first due to the expansion in the available money stock relative to the public's money demands. However, the growing money stock may kindle both expectations of inflation and rising incomes, eventually putting upward pressure on nominal rates. Thus, the nominal interest rate we observe at any single point in time may not fully reflect the public's inflationary expectations because it is being buffeted by several other forces in its journey toward equilibrium.

The Inflation-Caused Depreciation Effect. Still another factor to consider in the inflation/interest rate story is the **inflation-caused depreciation effect**. Inflation drives up the cost of new capital goods — buildings and machinery — that must be purchased to replace old capital items that are wearing out. However, old capital must be depreciated by formulas (such as the straight-line method) dictated by federal and state tax laws. In periods of rapid inflation, the true cost of using up existing capital equipment is understated, so that taxable business income is inflated. As a result, *after-tax* income from business investment projects is less than would be true with lower or no inflation. With less income after taxes, businesses will cut back on their plans to purchase new capital goods, and the resulting fall in the demand for loanable funds will decrease the equilibrium real interest rate. Clearly, then, if the expected rate of inflation rises and the real rate falls at the same time, the nominal interest rate is likely to rise by *less* than the increase in expected inflation. The opposite effects ensue if expected inflation declines, with nominal rates dropping by less than the decrease in expected inflation.

The Inflation-Caused Income Tax Effect. The depreciation effect brings taxes into the picture. Recent research suggests that the tax impact may work in both directions; that is, while the depreciation effect tends to dampen changes in the nominal interest rate, the **inflation-caused income tax effect** may widen movements in the nominal rate so that it changes by *more* than any given change in inflation. The heart of this argument is that lenders and investors not exempt from federal and state income taxes make lending and investing decisions on the basis of their expected real rate of return *after* taxes. If an investor desires to protect (i.e., hold constant) his or her expected real after-tax rate of return, then the nominal rate has to increase by a *greater* amount than any rise in the expected inflation rate because otherwise real after-tax returns will decline when inflation increases.

To see the validity of this argument, we observe that

$$\begin{matrix} \text{Expected after-tax} \\ \text{real rate of return} \\ \text{earned by a} \\ \text{taxpaying} \\ \text{investor} \end{matrix} = \begin{matrix} \text{Nominal} \\ \text{rate} \end{matrix} - \left[\begin{matrix} \text{Nominal} \\ \text{rate} \end{matrix} \times \begin{matrix} \text{Taxpayer's income} \\ \text{tax bracket rate} \end{matrix} \right] - \text{Inflation premium} \qquad (10\text{--}3)$$

Suppose an investor is in the 28 percent income tax bracket, so that a little more than a quarter of any additional income he or she earns is taxed. Moreover, suppose the current nominal interest rate on a one-year taxable security this investor is interested in buying is 12 percent, and the inflation premium (expected inflation rate) over the coming year is 5 percent. Then this investor's expected real after-tax return from the security must be

$$\begin{matrix} \text{Expected after-tax} \\ \text{real rate of return} \\ \text{earned by a tax-} \\ \text{paying investor} \end{matrix} = 12\% - [12\% \, (0.28)] - 5\% = 3.64\% \qquad (10\text{--}4)$$

Now suppose the expected rate of inflation rises from 5 to 6 percent. By how much must the *nominal rate* on the taxable security rise to yield this investor the *same* expected real return after taxes? The answer must be 13.39 percent, for

$$\begin{matrix} \text{Expected after-tax} \\ \text{real rate of return} \\ \text{earned by a tax-} \\ \text{paying investor} \end{matrix} = 13.39\% - [13.39\% \, (0.28)] - 6\% = 3.64\% \qquad (10\text{--}5)$$

INTERNATIONAL FOCUS:

The Relationship Between Inflation and Interest Rates Across Countries

The positive association between inflation and interest rates spelled out in the *Fisher effect* seems to hold up pretty well across countries. As the table below shows, nations with faster rates of price inflation generally experience higher interest rates, consistent with the idea that lenders of funds seek to be compensated for their expected loss of purchasing power by receiving a higher rate of interest on their loans.

Country	Inflation Index (Annual Increase in Consumer Prices, 1993)	Interest Rate on Short-Term Government Bills (3-Month Maturities, 1993)
Canada	1.8%	4.84%
France	2.1	8.38
Belgium	2.8	8.52
Germany	4.1	6.25
Italy	4.5	10.58
Spain	4.6	10.53
South Africa	9.8	11.32
Mexico	9.8	14.93
Greece	14.4	18.20

We note, however, that the inflation/interest rate relationship is not perfect. For example, in the table above we see that Germany experienced a higher inflation rate in consumer prices than France and Belgium but recorded a lower government interest rate than either of these two countries. Similarly, South Africa and Mexico experienced similar inflation rates, but market interest rates were much higher in Mexico. Some of the discrepancies arise because the consumer price index is constructed somewhat differently from country to country (e.g., different kinds of goods and services are included with varying weights). Then, too, the Fisher effect is stated in terms of *expected values* — the expected rate of inflation and the expected rate of interest — rather than the actual rate of inflation and the actual level of interest rates as cited in the table above. Nevertheless, the overall *positive* relationship between inflation and market rates of interest shows up even in fairly crude international data.

Source: International Monetary Fund, *International Financial Statistics Yearbook*, 1994.

Thus, a change of 1 percent in expected inflation required a 1.39 percent change in the nominal rate to leave this taxed investor in the same place in terms of a real (purchasing-power) return from his or her investment.

The arithmetic shown above works both ways: a *reduction* in expected inflation by 1 percent requires a 1.39 percent *decline* in the nominal rate to leave the real after-tax return where it is. While investors in lower tax brackets would not require as numerically large a change in nominal rates to leave after-tax real returns unaltered, inflation tends to force most investors into higher and higher tax brackets as both prices and nominal incomes rise, unless government tax schedules are indexed to change with inflation, something the federal government mandated for U.S. taxpayers beginning in 1985.

Conclusions from Recent Research. With all the foregoing possible effects from inflation, what actually happens to nominal rates when the expected rate of inflation shifts? The bulk of recent research suggests *nominal rates rise by less than any given increase in the expected inflation rate and decline by less than any given decrease in the expected inflation rate*. In essence, the inflation-caused income, wealth, and depreciation effects appear to outweigh influences pulling in the opposite direction, such as the income tax effect. Estimates vary but generally suggest that nominal rates change by 60 to perhaps 90 percent of the calculated change in the expected inflation rate.

When it comes to the Harrod-Keynes effect, the research evidence is mixed. As LeRoy (1973) observes, during the 1950s and early 1960s the correlation between the inflation rate and nominal interest rates was positive but very low, providing some support for the Harrod-Keynes effect. During the 1970s and early 1980s, however, there was a relatively high positive correlation between the inflation rate and nominal rates of return, tending to support Fisher's view. At the same time, there has been a tendency for the prices of inflation-hedged assets, including common stocks and real estate, to respond to changes in inflationary expectations, as Harrod suggested might happen. It seems likely that a combination of the two views is needed to help us get closer to the true impact of inflation on interest rates.

Thanks to recent studies by Walsh (1985) and others, we now know that real interest rates are *not* constant. During the 1970s real rates were negative (measured ex post) at times but then rose to high levels in the 1980s and 1990s as the rate of inflation fell. Recent research by Fama and Gibbons (1990) and Mishkin (1990) suggests that expected real interest rates may behave as a *random walk*, similar to stock prices. The Fisher effect, if it exists, apparently is *not stable*.

For their part, nominal interest rates appear to change in response to changes in *both* real interest rates and inflationary expectations. Indeed, some recent studies (e.g., Carmichael and Stebbing, 1983; and Groenewold, 1989) find that the real rate responds even more to inflation than the nominal interest rate. And McNees (1989) has observed a relatively strong relationship between the future inflation rate and the slope of the yield curve (discussed later in this chapter). Accelerating inflation appears to be associated with a flattening yield curve as short-term interest rates rise relative to long-term interest rates, while weakening inflation seems to go along with a more steeply sloped yield curve as short-term interest rates fall. Similarly, Mishkin (1990) finds evidence that at least some portions of the yield curve contain information about the future path of inflation.

The response of interest rates to inflation seems to depend crucially on whether inflation is anticipated or unanticipated by the public. Hayford (1990), for example, finds that if an increase in inflation was *not* expected by the marketplace, the value of investor wealth will decline and total spending in the economy will fall, which subsequently will lead to *lower* real interest rates. This linkage suggests that those, such as Harrod, who have argued that nominal interest rates do *not* change point-for-point with changes in inflation are probably right. However, the reader should retain a healthy skepticism about research in this field. The topic of inflation and interest rates is plagued by numerous measurement problems.

For example, there are no direct, widely accepted measures of two key actors in the drama — the expected real rate and the expected rate of inflation. Because the underlying theory speaks of *expected* inflation and the *expected* real interest rate, there is the obvious problem of measuring people's expectations. We cannot, as a practical matter, survey all investors, and the results of such a survey would soon be irrelevant anyway, because expectations change. Note, too, that we cannot automatically derive the expected real interest rate merely by subtracting the current inflation rate from the current nominal rate; this gives us a measure of the actual (ex post) real rate at a single point in time, not necessarily the *expected* real rate. Moreover, none of these approaches takes into account *time lags* as interest rates, buffeted by numerous forces, strive to reach long-run equilibrium.

Inflation and Stock Prices

The discussion so far has centered on the public's inflationary expectations and their possible impact on interest rates attached to bonds, bank loans, and other debt securities. However, another interesting question centers on the relationship between expectations of inflation and stock prices. Does inflation cause the prices of corporate stock (equities) to rise? The conventional wisdom says *yes*. Common stock, for example, is widely viewed as a hedge against inflation — a place to park your money if you want to preserve the purchasing power of your savings over the long haul.

Unfortunately, the facts often contradict what everybody "knows." For example, the stock market rose to unprecedented highs in the mid-1980s and again in the mid-1990s, yet the U.S. inflation rate *fell* during these periods. One useful way to view this issue is to decide what factors determine the prices of corporate stock and see if those factors are likely to be affected by inflation.

In basic terms, the stock price of any corporation is positively related to the dividends investors expect the company to pay to shareholders in future periods and is negatively related to the risk attached to that stream of expected dividends. That is,

$$\text{Price per share of corporate stock } (P_S) = \sum_{t=0}^{\infty} \frac{E(D_t)}{(1 + r)^t}$$

where $E(D_t)$ are expected dividend payments in each period t, and r is the rate of discount applied to those expected dividends to express them in terms of their present value. The riskier the corporation's dividend stream, the higher the required rate of discount, r, because investors demand a higher rate of return to compensate them for the added risk of holding the stock.

Clearly, if a rise in expected inflation raises stock prices, it must increase the amount of dividends shareholders expect each company to pay them [$E(D)$], or lower the perceived risk of holding stock (r), or both. On the other hand, stock prices will tend to fall if more inflation causes investors to lower their dividend expectations, increases the perceived risk to stockholders, or both. Is there any research evidence on which way the relationship goes?

There are several conflicting views. One line of argument says that if inflation is fully expected by all investors, nominal (published) stock prices may rise but *real* stock prices will not change at all. This is because company revenues and expenses will grow equally fast and the size of the firm's net income and dividend payments probably will *not* be affected (assuming the company's board of directors does not change the dividend rate). On the other hand, if inflation is only partly expected, the amount of unexpected inflation may be captured by company shareholders, as opposed to debt holders, in the form of increased earnings, and real stock prices will rise. Conversely, if the company's depreciation expenses on worn-out equipment are inadequate to offset the rising cost of new equipment in a period of inflation, current before-tax corporate income will be overstated, resulting in higher taxes against the firm, lowering its after-tax income and reducing stockholder dividend payments. In this instance, more rapid inflation would tend to lower stock prices. Indeed, studies by Ammer (1994), Solnik (1983), and others find a *negative* relationship between stock prices and inflation (whether expected or unexpected) for several countries.

Recently the concept of *nominal contracts* has emerged to explain the inflation/stock price connection. What are nominal contracts? They are agreements between parties, such

---

The Nominal Contracts Hypothesis for Explaining the Links between Inflation and Stock Prices

---

Nominal contracts are formal agreements that *fix* the time and terms in current dollars under which a business firm will compensate its employees, creditors, and other suppliers of productive resources and the prices at which it will deliver its product or service to customers. Examples include business contracts with labor unions that fix wage rates or wage increases, the issue of bonds at a fixed interest cost, or the valuing of business inventories and the depreciation of capital equipment using prespecified, unchanging formulas. A business firm can be hurt by inflation, experiencing a fall in its stock price, if actual inflation turns out to be different from what it expected when it agreed to a nominal contract. However, some nominal contracts can benefit a firm experiencing inflation, particularly if the company correctly anticipated future price changes or, by using well-structured nominal contracts, managed to hold down its expenses or enhance its revenues. For example:

If a business firm enters into nominal contracts that:	Then, if inflation turns out to be *greater than expected*:	However, suppose inflation turns out to be *less than expected.* Then:
A. Fix its expenses at a constant level or constant rate of growth (e.g., borrowing money at a fixed rate or paying employees a guaranteed wage) based on its current expectations for inflation.	Business revenues may grow faster than expenses, increasing profits; the firm's stock price may *rise*.	Business expenses may increase faster than revenues, reducing profits; the firm's stock price may *fall*.
B. Fix its revenues at a constant level or constant rate of growth (e.g., selling to customers at a guaranteed price for the coming year) based on its current inflationary expectations.	Business expenses may grow faster than revenues, reducing profits; the firm's stock price may *fall*.	Business revenues may grow faster than expenses, increasing profits; the firm's stock price may *rise*.

as a company and its workers or customers, that fix prices or costs in terms of current dollar (nominal) values for a stipulated time period. For example, corporations and labor unions may agree to increase wages 10 percent a year until current labor-management contracts expire or pledge to deliver their products to customers at a fixed price during the coming year. Corporate rules for valuing inventories or calculating depreciation expenses are other examples of nominal contracts. If inflation subsequently rises faster or slower than a company expected when it entered into its current nominal contracts, its profits may be squeezed or enhanced and its stock price may decrease or increase depending upon the circumstances. Thus, *the impact of inflation on stock prices may vary from firm to firm and from industry to industry depending upon the actual rate of inflation and the terms of existing nominal contracts.*

An alternative view — called the *proxy effect* — argues for a *negative* relationship between inflation and stock prices but claims that relationship is *spurious*, not real. Fama (1981) and Geske and Roll (1983) contend, for example, that changes in inflation are inversely related to fluctuations in expected output in the economy. If the public comes to believe that living costs will rise and the nation's economic output will decline at about the same time, then real stock prices may fall due to a more pessimistic outlook for business profits. However, it is the expected decrease in the economy's output, not the expected change in living costs (inflation), that leads to a decline in stock prices. Similarly, inflation and stock prices may have a spurious relationship due to monetary policy. If the economy's output falls and the central bank expands the nation's money supply to fight the output decline, inflation may accelerate because more money is in circulation. However, if stock prices subsequently fall, the public may blame inflation for the decline, when, in fact, the cause was the economy's declining production. Research evidence on these new views is decidedly mixed (as evidenced by the studies by Kaul (1987) and DeFina (1991)) but seems to favor the nominal contracts approach. Either way, the issue of stock prices and inflation remains in doubt, awaiting further research to find the right answers.

THE MATURITY OF A LOAN

One of the most important factors causing interest rates to differ from one another is differences in the **maturity** (or term) of securities and loans. Financial assets traded today in the world's financial markets have a wide variety of maturities. In the federal funds and U.S. government securities markets, for example, some loans are overnight or over-the-weekend transactions, with the borrower repaying the loan in a matter of hours. At the other end of the spectrum, mortgages used to finance the purchase of new homes often stretch out 25 to 30 years. Between these extremes lie thousands of securities issued by large and small borrowers with a tremendous variety of maturities.

The Yield Curve and the Term Structure of Interest Rates

The relationship between the rates of return (yields) on financial instruments and their maturity is called the *term structure of interest rates*. This term structure may be represented visually by drawing a **yield curve** for all securities having the same credit quality. An example of a yield curve for U.S. government securities as it appeared in a recent issue of the *Treasury Bulletin* is shown in Exhibit 10–3. We note that yield to maturity (measured by the annual percentage rate of return) is plotted along the vertical axis, and the horizontal scale shows the length of time (term) to final maturity (measured in months and years).

The yield curve considers only the relationship between the maturity or term of a loan or security and its yield at one moment in time (all other influential factors held constant). For example, we cannot draw a yield curve for securities bearing different degrees of credit risk or subject to different tax laws because both risk and tax laws affect relative yields along with maturity. We may, however, draw a yield curve for U.S. government securities of varying maturity because they all have minimal credit risk, the same tax status, and so on. Similarly, yield curves could be constructed for all corporate bonds or for all municipal bonds having the same credit rating.

Types of Yield Curves

Several different shapes of yield curve have been observed, but most may be described as upward sloping, downward sloping, or horizontal (flat). An upward-sloping yield curve indicates that borrowers must pay higher interest rates for longer-term loans than for shorter-term loans. A downward-sloping yield curve means that longer-term loans and securities presently carry lower interest rates than shorter-term financial assets. Exhibit 10–3 illustrates a downward-sloping yield curve, Exhibit 10–4 depicts a recent horizontal or

Exhibit 10–3   Yields on Treasury Securities, March 31, 1980
(Based on Closing Bid Quotations)

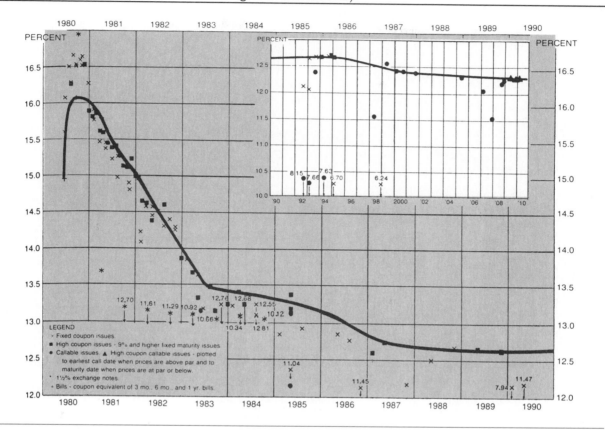

Source: *U.S. Treasury Department.*

flat yield curve, and Exhibit 10–5 pictures an upward-sloping curve. Each shape of the yield curve has important implications for lenders, borrowers, and the financial institutions that serve them.

The Unbiased Expectations Hypothesis

What determines the shape or slope of the yield curve? One view is the **unbiased expectations hypothesis**, which argues that investor expectations regarding future changes in short-term interest rates determine the shape of the curve. For example, a rising yield curve is presumed to be an indication that investors expect short-term interest rates to rise above their current levels in the future. A declining yield curve suggests declining short-term interest rates in the future. Finally, a horizontal yield curve implies that investors in the market expect interest rates to remain essentially unchanged from their present levels. If the unbiased expectations hypothesis is true, the yield curve becomes an important forecasting tool, because it suggests the direction of future movements in short-term interest rates as viewed by the financial marketplace today.

The unbiased expectations hypothesis assumes that investors act as *profit maximizers* over their planned holding periods and have no maturity preferences. All securities in a given risk class, regardless of maturity, are perfect substitutes for each other in the minds of

Exhibit 10–4

Yields on Treasury Securities, June 29, 1990
(Based on Closing Bid Quotations)

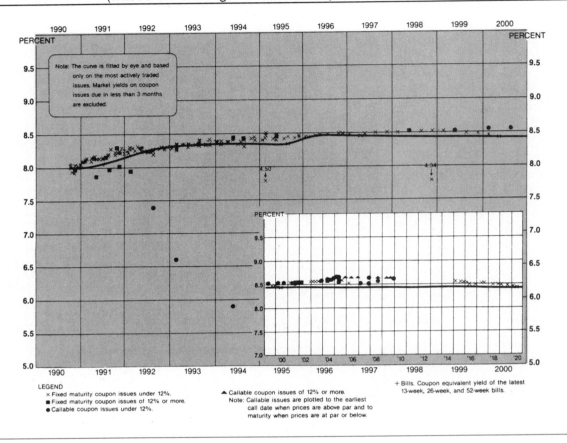

Source: *U.S. Treasury Department.*

investors. Under this theory, all investors are *risk neutral*. That is, they do not care about the character of the distribution of possible returns from a security, only about its expected (mean) return. Each investor will seek those individual securities or combinations of securities offering the highest expected (mean) rates of return. For example, it is immaterial to investors with a planned 10-year investment horizon whether they buy a 10-year security, two 5-year securities, or a series of 1-year securities until the 10-year holding period terminates. Each investor will pursue that investment strategy that offers the highest expected rate of return or yield over the length of his planned holding period.

Profit-maximizing behavior on the part of thousands of investors interacting in the marketplace ensures that holding-period yields on all securities move toward equality. Once equilibrium is achieved, and assuming no transactions costs, the investor should earn the *same* yield from buying a long-term security as from purchasing a series of short-term securities whose combined maturities equal that of the long-term security. If the rate of return on long-term securities rises above or falls below the return the investor expects to receive from buying and selling several short-term securities, forces are quickly set in motion to restore equilibrium. Investors at the margin will practice *arbitrage* (moving funds from one security market to another) until long-term yields once again are brought into balance with short-term yields.

Exhibit 10–5   **Yields of Treasury Securities, December 31, 1994** Based on Closing Bid Quotations (in percentages)

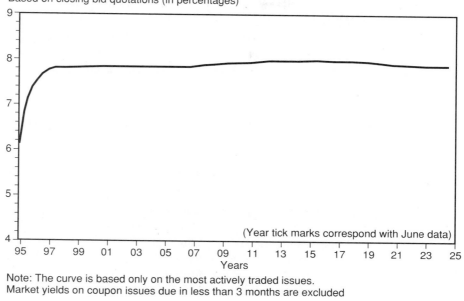

Based on closing bid quotations (in percentages)

(Year tick marks correspond with June data)

Years

Note: The curve is based only on the most actively traded issues.
Market yields on coupon issues due in less than 3 months are excluded

Source: *U.S. Treasury Bulletin*, March 1995, p. 67.

The Role of Expectations in Shaping the Yield Curve

How can a factor as intangible as expectations determine the shape of the yield curve? Expectations are a potent force in the financial marketplace because *investors act on their expectations.* For example, if interest rates are expected to rise in the future, this is disturbing news to investors in long-term bonds. As we noted in Chapter 9, rising interest rates mean falling prices for bonds and other debt securities. Moreover, the longer the term of a bond, the more sensitive its price is to changes in interest rates. Faced with the possibility of falling bond prices, many investors will sell their long-term bonds and buy short-term securities or hold cash. As a result, the prices of long-term bonds will plummet, driving their rates (yields) higher. At the same time, increased investor purchases of short-term securities will send the prices of these securities higher and their yields lower. With rising long-term interest rates and falling short-term interest rates, the yield curve will gradually assume an upward slope. The yield curve's prophecy of rising interest rates will have come true simply because investors responded to their expectations by making changes in their security portfolios.

Relative Changes in Long-Term Interest Rates

One assumption of the expectations theory does help to explain an interesting phenomenon in the financial markets. Long-term rates tend to change gradually over time, while short-term interest rates are highly volatile and often move over wide ranges. The expectations hypothesis presumes that the expected long-term interest rate may be represented as a *geometric* average of a series of interest rates on current and future (forward) short-term loans whose combined maturities equal that of the long-term loan. In terms of conventional symbols

$$(1 + {}_tR_n)^n = (1 + {}_tR_1)(1 + {}_{t+1}r_{1t}) \ldots (1 + {}_{t+n-1}r_{1t}) \tag{10–6}$$

where

$_tR_n$ = The rate of interest prevailing at time t on a long-term loan covering n periods of time

$_tR_1$ = The one-period loan rate prevailing at time period t

$_{t+1}r_{1t}$ = Forward interest rate as quoted at time t on a one-period loan to start in time period $t+1$

$_{t+2}r_{1t}$ = Forward interest rate as quoted at time t on a one-period loan to start in time period $t+2$

$\vdots$

$_{t+n-1}r_{1t}$ = Forward interest rate as quoted at time t on a one-period loan to start in time period $t+n-1$

The unbiased expectations hypothesis presumes that each of the forward rates — $_{t+1}r_{1t}$, $_{t+2}r_{1t}$, . . . , $_{t+n-1}r_{1t}$ — is equal to the future interest rate the market expects to exist in each future time period from $t+1$ through $t+n-1$. Equation 10–6 illustrates a fundamental principle in the expectations theory: *An investor expects the same holding period yield regardless of whether he or she purchases one long-term security or a series of short-term securities whose combined maturities make up the maturity of the long-term security. This is true because all markets are presumed to be perfectly competitive without significant barriers between them and all securities, whatever their maturity, are presumed to be perfect substitutes for each other in the minds of investors.*

According to the expectations theory, the rate of interest on a 20-year bond, for example, may be viewed as equivalent to the geometric average of the interest rate on a current 1-year loan plus the rates expected to be attached in future periods to a series of 19 separate 1-year loans, together adding up to 20 years. Experience teaches us that an *average* changes much more slowly than the individual components making up that average. If the long-term interest rate is really a geometric average of current and expected future short-term rates, then this helps to explain why, in real-world markets, long-term interest rates tend to lag behind short-term interest rates and are less volatile. As we will see in Chapter 12, the assumption that the long-term interest rate embodies the market's expectation regarding expected future short-term interest rates suggests an important clue for forecasting future interest rate movements.

Policy Implications of the Unbiased Expectations Hypothesis

The unbiased expectations hypothesis has important implications for public policy. The theory implies that changes in the relative amounts of long-term versus short-term securities do *not* influence the shape of the yield curve *unless* investor expectations also are affected. For example, suppose the U.S. Treasury decided to refinance $100 billion of its maturing short-term IOUs by issuing $100 billion in long-term bonds. Would this government action affect the shape of the yield curve? Certainly, the supply of long-term bonds would be significantly increased, while the supply of short-term securities would be reduced. However, according to the expectations theory, the yield curve itself would not be changed unless investors altered their expectations about the future course of short-term interest rates.

To cite one more example, the Federal Reserve System buys and sells government securities almost daily in the money and capital markets to promote the economic goals of the United States. Can the Fed influence the shape of the yield curve by buying one maturity of securities and selling another? Once again, the answer is no *unless* the Federal Reserve can influence the interest rate expectations of investors. Why? The reason lies in the underlying assumption of the unbiased expectations hypothesis: *Investors regard all securities, whatever their maturity, as perfect substitutes.* Therefore, the relative amounts of long-term bonds versus short-term securities simply should *not* matter.

The Liquidity Premium View of the Yield Curve

The strong assumptions underlying the unbiased expectations hypothesis coupled with the real-world behavior of investors have caused many financial analysts to question that theory's veracity. Securities dealers who trade actively in the financial markets frequently argue that other factors besides interest rate expectations also exert a significant impact on the character and shape of the yield curve.

For example, in recent years, most yield curves have sloped *upward*. Is there a built-in bias toward positively sloped yield curves due to factors other than interest rate expectations? The liquidity premium view of the yield curve suggests that such a bias exists.

Long-term securities tend to have more volatile market prices than short-term securities. Therefore, the investor faces greater risk of capital loss when buying long-term financial instruments. This greater risk of loss will be important to an investor who is *risk averse* (not risk neutral as in the expectations theory). To overcome the risk of capital loss, investors must be paid an extra return in the form of an interest rate (term) premium to encourage them to purchase long-term financial instruments. This additional rate or yield premium for giving up liquidity — known as the **liquidity premium** — would tend to give yield curves a bias toward a positive slope.

Why then do some yield curves slope downward? In such instances, expectations of declining interest rates plus other factors simply overcome the liquidity premium effect. The liquidity premium view does not preclude the important role of interest rate expectations in influencing the shape of the yield curve. Rather, it argues that other factors, such as liquidity, play an important role as well.

The liquidity argument may help explain why yield curves tend to flatten out at the longest maturities. (Note that this flattening out at the long-term end of the maturity spectrum is characteristic of all three yield curves shown in Exhibits 10–3, 10–4, and 10–5.) There are obvious differences in liquidity between a 1-year and a 10-year bond, but it is not clear that major differences in liquidity exist between a 10-year bond and a 20-year bond, for example. Therefore, the size of the required liquidity (or term) premium may decrease for securities bearing longer maturities.

The Segmented-Markets or Hedging-Pressure Argument

A strong challenge to the expectations theory appeared in the 1950s and 1960s in the form of the **market segmentation argument** or *hedging-pressure theory* of the term structure of interest rates. The underlying assumption is that all securities are *not* perfect substitutes in the minds of investors. Maturity preferences exist among some investor groups, and these investors will not stray from their desired maturity range unless induced to do so by higher yields or other favorable terms on longer- or shorter-term securities.

Why would some investors *prefer* one maturity of security over another? Market segmentation theorists find the answer in a fundamental assumption concerning investor behavior, especially the investment behavior of financial intermediaries, such as investment companies, pension funds, and banks. These investor groups, it is argued, often act as *risk minimizers* rather than profit maximizers as assumed under the expectations hypothesis. They prefer to *hedge* against the risk of fluctuations in the prices and yields of securities by balancing the maturity structure of their assets with the maturity structure of their liabilities.

For example, pension funds have stable and predictable long-term liabilities. Therefore, these intermediaries prefer to invest in bonds, stocks, and other long-term assets. Commercial banks, on the other hand, with volatile deposits and money market liabilities, prefer to confine the majority of their investments to short-term loans and securities. These investor groups use the *hedging principle* of portfolio management: correlating the maturities of their liabilities with the maturities of their assets to ensure the ready availability of liquid funds when those funds are needed. This portfolio strategy reduces the risks of fluctuating income and loss of principal.

The existence of maturity preferences among investor groups implies that the financial markets are *not* one large pool of loanable funds but rather are segmented into a series of submarkets. Thus, the market for securities of medium maturity (5- to 10-year securities) attracts different investor groups than the market for long-term (over 10-year) securities. Demand and supply curves within each maturity range are held to be the dominant factors shaping the level and structure of interest rates within that maturity range. However, interest rates prevailing in one maturity range are little influenced by demand and supply forces at work in other maturity ranges.

The segmented-markets or hedging pressure theory does *not* rule out the possible influence of expectations in shaping the term structure of interest rates, but it argues that other factors related to maturity-specific demand and supply forces are also important.

Policy Implications of the Segmented-Markets Theory

The segmented-markets theory, like the expectations theory, has significant implications for public policy. If markets along the maturity spectrum are relatively isolated from each other due to investor preferences, government policymakers can alter the shape of the yield curve merely by influencing supply and demand in one or more market segments.

For example, if a positively sloped yield curve were desired, the government could flood the market with long-term bonds. Simultaneously, the government could purchase large quantities of short-term securities. The expanded supply of bonds would drive long-term interest rates higher, while government purchases of short-term securities would push short-term interest rates down, other factors held equal. Therefore, the government could alter the shape of the yield curve merely by shifting the supplies available of different maturities of securities relative to the demand for those securities. This conclusion directly contradicts the expectations hypothesis.

> ## INTERNATIONAL FOCUS:
> ### Yield Curves Across Different Countries
>
> Do yield curves tend to look the same in different countries, and do they change in the same way? Evidence is beginning to accumulate that the term structure of interest rates in major industrialized countries tends to change over time in roughly the same way. For example, a recent research study at the Federal Reserve Board by Helen Popper (1990) finds that term premia in the United States, Germany, and Japan (based upon on-shore interest returns) display similar movements and, therefore, behave as if these nations were part of a single market for capital. Similarly, a study by Campbell and Clarida (1987) finds parallel movements in term premia among the nations of Western Europe.
>
> This should not surprise us, because these nations actively trade both goods and capital with each other. Where resources, including capital, can flow freely across national borders in response to temporary differences in interest rates, any major differences in the term structure of interest rates among trading partners are likely to be significantly and quickly reduced. However, few international studies to date provide convincing support for any of the yield curve theories mentioned in this chapter, though the expectations hypothesis supplemented by liquidity (or term) premiums seems to be the most popular view today.
>
> Source: See, for example, Helen Popper, "The Term Structure of Interest Rates in the Onshore Markets of the United States, Germany, and Japan," *International Finance Discussion Paper No. 382*, Board of Governors of the Federal Reserve System, June 1990; and J. Campbell and N. Clarida, "The Term Structure of Euromarket Interest Rates: An Empirical Investigation," *Journal of Monetary Economics*, 19 (1987), pp. 25–44.

The Preferred Habitat or Composite Theory of the Yield Curve

During the 1960s and 1970s, an expanded model of the determinants of the yield curve appeared that attempted to combine the expectations, liquidity premium, and market segmentation arguments into a single theory. This composite view argues that investors seek out their **preferred habitat** along the scale of varying maturities of securities that matches their risk preferences, tax exposure, liquidity needs, regulatory requirements, and planned holding periods. Normally, an investor will not stray from her preferred habitat unless rates of return on longer- or shorter-term securities are high enough to overcome each investor's preferences. The result is that security markets are divided into distinct submarkets by these multifaceted investor preferences. Thus, according to the preferred habitat theory, factors other than expectations alone play a role in shaping the character of the yield curve.

Proponents of preferred habitat argue that investors derive their expectations about future interest rates on the basis of *historical experience* — the recent trend of interest rates and what history suggests is a "normal" range for rates. In the short term, the majority of investors expect current interest rate trends to persist into the future; thus, rising interest rates in recent weeks often lead to the expectation that rates will continue to rise in the near term. However, investors generally expect that, given sufficient time (months or years), interest rates will return to their historical averages. An important research implication here is that more recent movements in interest rates are linked to *past* interest rate behavior — a conclusion that tends to contradict the expectations and efficient markets theories of how the financial markets operate.

Research Evidence on Yield-Curve Theories

Which view of the yield curve is correct? A number of recent studies (e.g., Shiller, Campbell, and Schoenholtz, 1983; Campbell, 1986; and Mankiw, 1986) seem to reject the unbiased expectations hypothesis and find that the yield curve does *not* have significant predictive power in forecasting interest rates. However, these findings are contradicted by other studies (e.g., Froot, 1989; Longstaff, 1990; Fama and Bliss, 1987; and Sargent, 1982) that find evidence consistent with the unbiased expectations hypothesis. Some of these studies find significant forecasting power from the yield curve over certain time periods.

For example, Froot (1989) finds that the expectations hypothesis does *not* seem to work for interest rates on short-term securities, but for long maturities of bonds the yield curve appears to move, point for point, with changes in expected future rates. Also consistent with the unbiased expectations hypothesis, long-term interest rates appear to "underreact" to changes in short-term interest rates. Fama (1984) observes that the term structure of rates can be used to forecast one-month interest rates one month ahead; and Fama and Bliss (1987) found that one-year forward interest rates could forecast changes in the one-year interest rate two to four years in advance. Moreover, as Abken (1993) notes, there is some evidence that yield curves provide useful forecasts of inflation over periods of one year or longer.

This longer-term forecasting power of the yield curve may be due to the tendency of interest rates to move back toward their historic mean levels over a sufficiently long period of time (known as *mean reversion*). Although all investors clearly do not regard all maturities of securities as perfect substitutes, there are sufficient numbers of traders in the financial marketplace who do *not* have specific maturity preferences. These investors are guided principally by the relative expected returns on different securities. Their beliefs and actions can bring about the results generally predicted by the expectations theory.

Nevertheless, there is evidence that nonexpectations factors, especially the demand for liquidity, do affect the shape of the yield curve. Studies by Van Horne (1965) and others point to the existence of a liquidity premium attached to the yields on longer-term securities, compensating investors for added risk. Moreover, liquidity premiums appear to get smaller as we move toward longer maturities of securities. In fact, Fama and Bliss (1987) have found that liquidity premiums (or, more generally, *term premiums*) are *not* constant. Rather, term premiums seem to vary with business conditions. Fama and French (1989), for example, find that term premiums move opposite to business conditions, rising in recessions and falling in expansions. Term premiums do *not* appear to increase or decrease *uniformly* as maturity increases or decreases. Starz (1982) observes substantial variation in the size of liquidity or term premiums, making it more difficult to forecast future short-term interest rates using the yield curve's shape.

More recently, Kiely, Kolari, and Rose (1994) confirmed that liquidity premiums vary over time, rising and falling with the business cycle. They suggest that these premiums may arise from two opposing forces: the *price-risk hypothesis* and the *money-substitutes hypothesis*. The price-risk hypothesis claims that liquidity premiums are *inversely*

YIELD CURVES AND GOVERNMENT POLICY:
The U.S. Government Proposes to Borrow Short-Term to Save on Interest Costs

In 1993, the administration of President Bill Clinton announced a plan to reduce the huge borrowing costs faced by the United States' government. U.S. Treasury debt managers proposed to reduce the amount of long-term bonds they would sell, while boosting sales of short-term Treasury IOUs, which, at the time, carried much lower interest rates. The Clinton administration estimated that this policy of *short-term borrowing* could save the U.S. government as much as $11.5 billion over a four-year period because the yield curve at the time was steeply positively-sloped. For example, the gap between the interest rate on three-month Treasury securities and 30-year Treasury bonds was about four percentage points.

Several strong objections were raised to the government's proposed borrowing strategy. One problem cited by many economists was the government's assumption that short-term interest rates would remain stable and relatively low — that is, it was assumed that the yield curve would remain positively sloped throughout the period that this policy remained in force. This means that the proposed borrowing strategy assumed the public's expectations regarding long- versus short-term interest rates would *not* change significantly as a result of the new policy.

For example, if the launching of the government's new short-term borrowing strategy led investors in the money and capital markets to believe that short-term security prices would be driven lower (i.e., short-term yields would rise) and long-term security prices would rise (i.e., long-term yields would fall), then the yield curve would become less steep or might even become negatively sloped. If the yield curve adopted a negative slope, the government would wind up paying higher borrowing costs for short-term borrowings than it would pay for long-term borrowings. On the other hand, if the public's expectation about future interest rates did *not* change, the expectations hypothesis discussed in this chapter suggests that simply issuing more short-term and fewer long-term securities should *not* change the yield curve's overall shape.

Many economists argued that, instead of shortening the average maturity of the government's debt by emphasizing short-term borrowings, the U.S. Treasury should emphasize *long-term borrowings*. The reasoning here centered on the fact that, by the mid-1990s, long-term interest rates were at the lowest point in about 20 years. Indeed, when the U.S. Treasury announced its proposed short-term borrowing plan, many businesses were doing the exact opposite — issuing *long-term* IOUs in order to "lock in" the historically low long-term debt costs before interest rates on bonds moved higher. By extending the maturity of the government's debt the Treasury would not have to enter the financial marketplace as often to borrow new money.

(negatively) related to the level of market interest rates. For example, when interest rates fall below the level investors regard as normal, the public will come to expect rising interest rates and, therefore, anticipate greater losses on long-term bonds, which carry greater price risk. In this instance, investors will demand larger liquidity premiums on longer-term securities to compensate them for the expected losses. If interest rates rise above "normal," however, investors will come to expect an eventual decline in the level of interest rates and capital gains on the bonds they hold. The public will settle for lower liquidity premiums in this case.

The *money-substitutes hypothesis* suggests that a *direct* (positive) relationship exists between liquidity premiums and the level of interest rates. This is because interest rates represent the opportunity cost of holding money (cash balances). The more cash investors hold as opposed to investing their money in interest-bearing securities, the more potential income they give up. However, because the longest-term securities carry the greatest price risk, risk-averse investors normally prefer to place their idle cash in *short-term securities*, which can be converted into cash more easily when the need arises. Therefore, as market interest rates rise, many investors will shift a portion of their cash balances into short-term securities to avoid suffering the higher opportunity costs of holding idle cash. Because short-term securities are usually better substitutes for money than longer-term securities, the added demand for short-term securities generates a more positively sloped yield curve — that is, liquidity premiums on long-term securities become larger relative to liquidity premiums on short-term securities. Thus, a rising level of interest rates can lead to higher liquidity premiums and a more steeply sloped yield curve, while falling interest rates lead to smaller liquidity premiums and a flatter or downward-sloping yield curve, according to the money-substitutes hypothesis. Kiely et al. (1994) find that the price-risk hypothesis tends to be more significant in low interest-rate periods, but the money-substitutes hypothesis seems to be more important when interest rates are relatively high.

There is also evidence provided by Elliot and Echols (1976) and Terrell and Frazier (1972), among others, that changes in the supply of securities in any particular maturity range can, at least temporarily, alter the shape of the yield curve, offering some support for the segmented-markets theory. For example, at certain phases of the business cycle, banks become heavy sellers of medium-term government securities to raise cash and make more loans. The yield curve may take a bowed or humped shape at those times. In this instance, a sudden massive increase in the supply of medium-term bonds seems to briefly alter the yield curve's shape.

Traditional models of the yield curve are giving way today to *new* term-structure models. These newer models are being created in response to recent developments in financial theory centered around the Black-Scholes option pricing formula (see Chapter 13) and the rational expectations theory (see Chapter 8). Traditional yield-curve theories do not appear to explain easily the more volatile movements in stock and bond prices observed in recent years or to help in valuing some of the newest financial instruments, such as securitized assets and swap agreements (see Chapter 12). Newer models of the term structure incorporate the presence of *uncertainty* in the financial markets about future movements in interest rates. In effect, some of the newest models assume that interest rates move randomly, an idea that many recent studies seem to support. Recent modeling has brought measures of economic activity into the process of determining the yield curve's shape, arguing that the term structure of interest rates is influenced by the economy and cannot be fully explained without including measures of the economy's performance.

Uses of the Yield Curve

The controversy surrounding the determinants of the yield curve should not obscure the fact that this curve can be an extremely useful tool for borrowers and lenders.

Forecasting Interest Rates. If the expectations hypothesis is correct, the yield curve gives the investor a clue concerning the future course of interest rates. If the curve has an upward slope, for example, the investor may be well advised to look for opportunities to move away from long-term securities into investments whose market price is less sensitive to interest rate changes. A downward-sloping yield curve, on the other hand, suggests the likelihood of near-term declines in interest rates and a rally in bond prices if the market's forecast of lower rates turns out to be true. Under the terms of the unbiased expectations hypothesis, the current yield curve generates a very precise forecast of what the market expects interest rates to be in any future period. We will see exactly how in Chapter 12.

Uses for Financial Intermediaries. The slope of the yield curve is critical for financial intermediaries, especially banks, credit unions, and savings and loan associations. A rising yield curve is generally favorable for these institutions because they borrow most of their funds by selling short-term deposits and lend a major portion of those funds long term. The more steeply the yield curve slopes upward, the wider the spread between borrowing and lending rates and the greater the potential profit for a financial intermediary. However, if the yield curve begins to flatten out or slopes downward, this should serve as a warning signal to managers of these institutions.

A flattening or downward-sloping yield curve squeezes the earnings of financial intermediaries and calls for an entirely different portfolio management strategy than an upward-sloping curve. For example, if an upward-sloping yield curve starts to flatten out, portfolio managers of financial institutions might try to lock in relatively cheap sources of funds by getting long-term commitments from depositors and other funds-supplying customers. Borrowers, on the other hand, might be encouraged to take out long-term loans at fixed rates of interest. Of course, the institution's customers also may be aware of impending changes in the yield curve and resist accepting loans or deposits with terms heavily favoring the offering institution.

Detecting Overpriced and Underpriced Securities. Yield curves can be used as an aid to investors in deciding which securities are temporarily overpriced or underpriced. This use of the curve derives from the fact that, in equilibrium, the yields on all securities of comparable risk should come to rest along the yield curve at their appropriate maturity level. In an efficiently functioning market, however, any deviations of individual securities from the yield curve will be short lived, so the investor must act quickly.

If a security's rate of return lies *above* the yield curve, this sends a signal to investors: the security is temporarily *underpriced* relative to other securities of the same maturity. Other things equal, this is a *buy* signal some investors will take advantage of, driving the price of the purchased security upward and its yield back down toward the curve. On the other hand, if a security's rate of return is temporarily *below* the yield curve, this indicates a temporarily *overpriced* financial instrument, because its yield is below that of securities bearing the same maturity. Some investors holding this security will *sell*, pushing its price down and its yield back up toward the curve.

Indicating Trade-Offs between Maturity and Yield. Still another use of the yield curve is to indicate the current trade-off between maturity and yield confronting the investor. If an investor wishes to alter the maturity of her portfolio, the yield curve indicates what gain or loss in rate of return may be expected for each change in the portfolio's average maturity.

With an upward-sloping yield curve, for example, an investor may be able to increase a bond portfolio's expected annual yield from 7 percent to 9 percent by extending the portfolio's average maturity from 1 to 10 years. However, the prices of longer-term bonds are more volatile, creating greater risk of capital loss. Longer-term securities tend to be less liquid than short-term securities. Therefore, the investor must weigh the gain in yield from extending the maturity of his or her portfolio against added price and liquidity risk. Because yield curves tend to flatten out for the longest maturities, the investor bent on lengthening the maturity of a portfolio eventually discovers that gains in yield get smaller for each additional unit of maturity. At some point along the yield curve, it no longer pays to further extend the maturity of an investor's portfolio.

Riding the Yield Curve. Finally, some active security investors, especially dealers in government securities, have learned to "ride" the yield curve for profit. If the curve is positively sloped, with a slope steep enough to offset transactions costs, the investor may gain by timely portfolio switching.

For example, if a security dealer purchases U.S. Treasury bills six months from maturity, holds them for three months and converts the bills into cash, and then buys new six-month bills, he can profit in two ways from a positively sloped yield curve. Because the yield is lower (and the price higher) on the three-month than the six-month bills, the dealer experiences a capital gain on the sale. The purchase of new six-month bills replaces a lower-yielding security with a higher-yielding one at a lower price. Riding the yield curve can be risky, however, because yield curves are constantly changing their shape. If the curve gets flatter or turns down, a potential gain can be turned into a realized loss. In this case, riding the yield curve may be less profitable than a simple "buy and hold" strategy. Experience and good judgment are indispensable in using the yield curve for profitable investment decision making.

DURATION: A DIFFERENT APPROACH TO MATURITY
The Price Elasticity of a Debt Security

Theories of the yield curve remind us that longer-maturity securities tend to be more volatile in price. That is, for the same change in interest rates, the price of a longer-term bond generally changes more than the price of a shorter-term bond. A popular measure of how responsive a security's price is to changes in interest rates is its **price elasticity**, thus:

$$\text{Price elasticity of a debt security } (E) = \frac{\text{Percentage change over time in a security's price}}{\text{Percentage change over time in a security's yield}} = \frac{\dfrac{P_1 - P_0}{P_0}}{\dfrac{y_1 - y_0}{y_0}} \tag{10-7}$$

where P_0 and y_0 represent a security's price and yield at some initial point in time, while P_1 and y_1 represent the security's price and yield at a subsequent point in time. Price elasticity is generally measured from the security's par value and coupon rate and is larger for downward price movements than for upward price movements.[4] Security price elasticity must be negative, because rising interest rates (yields) result in falling security prices, and conversely.

For example, suppose we are interested in purchasing a 10-year bond, par value of $1,000, promising its holder a 10 percent annual coupon rate ($100 a year in interest). Information in a bond yield table (see Chapter 9) tells us that if interest rates on comparable securities sold in the open market are at 10 percent, this bond will sell for exactly $1,000. If interest rates fall to 5 percent, this 10 percent bond will have a price of $1,389.70, and if rates climb to 15 percent, the bond's price will drop to just $745.10. What is the price elasticity of this bond, measured from par? From Equation 10–7, we have for the *downward* movement in interest rates from 10 to 5 percent:

$$\begin{array}{c}\text{Price elasticity}\\ \text{of 10 percent}\\ \text{bond } (E)\end{array} = \dfrac{\dfrac{(\$1,389.70 - \$1,000)}{\$1,000}}{\dfrac{5\% - 10\%}{10\%}} = \dfrac{0.3897}{-0.5} = -0.779 \qquad (10\text{--}8)$$

On the other hand, for an upward movement in rates from 10 to 15 percent, this bond's elasticity is −0.510. (The reader should verify this.) Clearly, E is greater in absolute terms for the downward movement in interest rates (from 10 to 5 percent) than it is for the rise in interest rates (from 10 to 15 percent).

Greater price elasticity means that a security goes through a greater price change for a given change in market rates of interest. And, as we noted above, longer-term securities generally carry greater price risk (their price elasticity, E, is larger) than shorter-term securities. However, this relationship between maturity and price elasticity is *not* linear (i.e., not strictly proportional). It is *not* true, for example, that 10-year bonds are twice as price elastic (and price volatile) as 5-year bonds. One important reason for this nonlinear relationship is that the price volatility and elasticity of a security depend upon the size of its *coupon rate* — the annual rate promised by the borrower — as well as its maturity.

The Impact of Varying Coupon Rates

The lower a security's annual coupon rate, the more volatile (and elastic) its price tends to be. Investors buying lower coupon securities generally take on greater risk of price fluctuations. In effect, a security promising lower annual coupon payments behaves as though it has a longer maturity even if it is due to mature on the same date as a security carrying a higher coupon rate. With a low coupon (promised) rate, the investor must wait longer for a substantial return on her funds because a greater proportion of the low-coupon security's total dollar return lies in the final payment at maturity, when the bond's face value is returned to the investor. And the further in the future cash payments are to be received, the more sensitive is the present value of that stream of payments to changes in interest rates.

---

[4]That is, for the same change in yield, capital gains generally are larger than capital losses on the same security.

The relationship we have been describing is called the **coupon effect**. It says simply that the prices of low coupon securities tend to rise *faster* than the prices of high-coupon securities when market interest rates decline. Similarly, a period of rising interest rates will cause the prices of low-coupon securities to fall *faster* than the prices of high-coupon securities. Thus, the potential for capital gains and capital losses is greater for low coupon than for high coupon securities.

An Alternative Maturity Index for a Security: Duration

Knowledge of the impact of varying coupon rates on security price volatility and elasticity resulted in the search for a new index of maturity other than straight calendar time (years and months) — the maturity measure used in conventional yield curves. What was needed was a measure of the term of a bond that would allow financial analysts to construct a *linear* (strictly proportional) relationship between maturity and security price volatility or elasticity, regardless of differing coupon rates. Such a measure would have the property, for example, that a doubling of maturity would mean a doubling of a security's price elasticity, thereby giving us a direct measure of the price risk faced by an investor. This maturity measure is known as **duration** (D):

$$D = \frac{\text{Present value of interest and principal payments from a security weighted by the timing of those payments}}{\text{Present value of the security's promised stream of interest and principal payments}} = \frac{\sum\limits_{t=1}^{n} \dfrac{I_t(t)}{(1+y)^t}}{\sum\limits_{t=1}^{n} \dfrac{I_t}{(1+y)^t}} \qquad (10\text{--}9)$$

In the duration formula above, I represents each expected payment of principal and interest income from the security and t represents the time period in which each payment is to be received. The discount factor, y, is the security's yield to maturity, with final maturity reached at the end of n periods. Duration reflects the price elasticity of a debt instrument with respect to changes in the instrument's yield to maturity. As the formula indicates, D is a *weighted average* measure of maturity in which each payment of interest and principal is multiplied by the time period in which it is expected to be received by the investor.

We can explain the use of duration through an example. Let us imagine that an investor is interested in purchasing a $1,000 par value bond that has a term to maturity of 10 years, a 10 percent annual coupon rate (with interest paid once a year), and a 12 percent yield to maturity based on its current price of $887.10. Then its duration must be

$$\text{Duration } (D) = \frac{\dfrac{\$100(1)}{(1.12)^1} + \dfrac{\$100(2)}{(1.12)^2} + \ldots + \dfrac{\$100(10)}{(1.12)^{10}} + \dfrac{\$1,000(10)}{(1.12)^{10}}}{\dfrac{\$100}{(1.12)^1} + \dfrac{\$100}{(1.12)^2} + \ldots + \dfrac{\$100}{(1.12)^{10}} + \dfrac{\$1,000}{(1.12)^{10}}} \qquad (10\text{--}10)$$

or

$$D = \frac{\$5810.90}{\$887.10} = 6.55 \text{ years}$$

There is a simple way to calculate D that has the added value of making it easy to check your figures. Using the example above of the 10-year bond with a 12 percent yield to maturity, we can set up the following table:

Period	Expected Cash Flows from Security	Present Values of Expected Cash Flows (at 12% Rate of Discount)	Time Period Cash Is to Be Received (t)	Present Values of Expected Cash Flows × t
1	$ 100	$ 89.30	1	$ 89.30
2	100	79.70	2	159.40
3	100	71.20	3	213.60
4	100	63.60	4	254.40
5	100	56.70	5	283.50
6	100	50.70	6	304.20
7	100	45.20	7	316.40
8	100	40.40	8	323.20
9	100	36.10	9	324.90
10	100	32.20	10	322.00
10	1,000	322.00	10	3,220.00
		$887.10		$5,810.90

Then, as above, the duration of this bond must be

$$D = \frac{\text{Sum of present values of cash flows} \times t}{\text{Sum of present values of cash flows}} = \frac{\$5810.90}{\$887.10} = 6.55 \text{ years}$$

Note that the denominator of the ratio above ($887.10) is the same value as the bond's current price.

A number of duration's features are evident from this example. For example, duration is always *less* than the time to maturity for a coupon-paying security.[5] Duration increases with a longer stream of future payments, but the rate of increase in D decreases as time to maturity increases. The larger a security's yield to maturity, y, the lower its duration.

Duration reflects the amount and timing of *all* payments expected during the life of a security, unlike the conventional measure of maturity — calendar time — which shows only the length of time until the final cash payment. In simplest terms, duration is an index of the average amount of time required for the investor to recover the original cash outlay used to buy the security. Securities with higher values of D are more volatile in price and, therefore, carry increased price risk. Low-coupon bonds have longer durations and, therefore, display more price risk than high-coupon bonds.

Uses of Duration

Because duration is related in linear fashion to the price volatility of a security, there is a useful approximate relationship between changes in interest rates and percentage changes in security prices. This relationship may be written:

$$\begin{array}{c} \text{Percent change in the price} \\ \text{of a debt security} \end{array} \approx -D \left[\frac{\Delta r}{1 + r} \right] \times 100 \qquad (10\text{--}11)$$

where D is duration and Δr is the change in interest rates. For example, consider the bond whose duration was calculated above to be 6.55 years. The bond's price at the coupon rate of 10 percent is $1,000; and at an r of 12 percent, its price is $887.10. Thus, if the interest

---

[5]See Chapter 9 for a discussion of yield to maturity and calculating discounted present values such as required in the above duration formula. Any security carrying installment payments of principal and/or interest will have a duration shorter than its calendar maturity. Only for zero coupon bonds or for any loan in which principal and accumulated interest are paid in a lump sum at maturity will duration and maturity be the same.

rate changes from 10 to 12 percent, the bond's approximate percentage decline in price would be

$$\text{Percent change in bond's price} \approx -6.55 \times \left[\frac{.02}{1 + 0.10}\right] \times 100 = -11.91\% \qquad (10\text{--}12)$$

In this instance, if interest rates rise by two percentage points, the bond's price declines by almost 12 percent (measured from the bond's par value and coupon rate). An investor who expects interest rates to rise would find this information helpful in deciding whether to continue holding this bond. In general, investors concerned about the risk of loss due to rising interest rates tend to move toward securities of shorter duration, while falling interest rates usually lead investors toward securities of longer duration.

Today, duration has aroused great interest among portfolio managers. The reason is its possible usefulness as a device to insulate (or, in the terminology of finance, immunize) security portfolios against the risk of changing interest rates. In theory, **portfolio immunization** against interest rate changes can be achieved by simply acquiring a portfolio of securities whose average duration equals the investor's desired holding period. If this is done, the effect is to hold the investor's total return *constant* regardless of whether interest rates rise or fall. In the absence of borrower default, the investor's realized return can be no less than the return he has been promised by the borrower. Only if the future course of interest rates is known for certain would portfolio immunization be a less than optimal strategy.

Let's consider an example of how portfolio immunization with duration works. Suppose we are interested in purchasing a bond with a $1,000 par value that will mature in two years. The bond has a coupon rate of 8 percent, paying $80 in interest at the end of each year. Interest rates on comparable bonds also are currently at 8 percent but may fall to as low as 6 percent or rise as high as 10 percent. The buyer knows he will receive $1,000 at maturity, but in the meantime he must face the uncertainty of having to reinvest the annual $80 in interest earnings from this bond at 6 percent, 8 percent, or 10 percent, depending on whether interest rates rise or fall.

Suppose interest rates decline to 6 percent. This bond will earn $80 in interest payments for year one, $80 for year two, but only $4.80 (or $80 × 0.06) when the $80 interest income received the first year is reinvested at 6 percent during year 2. With interest rates falling to 6 percent, the investor will earn only $1,164.80 in total over the two-year period:

First year's interest earnings		Second year's interest earnings		Interest earned reinvesting the first year's interest earnings at a 6 percent interest rate		Par value of security returned to investor at maturity		Total return
$80	+	$80	+	$4.80	+	$1,000	=	$1,164.80

On the other hand, what if interest rates rise to 10 percent after the first year? Again, the investor holding this bond earns $80 interest in each of the next two years but will also earn $8 in interest when he reinvests the $80 in interest income received at the end of the first year at the new rate of 10 percent ($80 × .10). In this second case, the investor's total return from the bond will be $1,168 after two years:

First year's interest earnings		Second year's interest earnings		Interest earned reinvesting the first year's interest earnings at a 10 percent interest rate		Par value of security returned to investor at maturity		Total return
$80	+	$80	+	$8.00	+	$1,000	=	$1,168.00

Clearly, the bond buyer's earnings could drop as low as $1,164.80 (with a 6 percent interest rate) or rise as high as $1,168 (with a 10 percent interest rate). Is there a way to avoid this kind of fluctuation in earnings and stabilize the total return received regardless of what happens to interest rates? Yes, if the buyer finds a bond whose *duration matches his or her planned holding period.* For example, suppose the buyer finds a $1,000 bond that also carries an 8 percent coupon rate whose maturity exceeds two years but whose duration is exactly two years, matching the buyer's planned holding period. This means that, at the end of two years, the buyer will have to *sell* the bond at the price then prevailing in the market, because it will not yet have reached maturity.

What will happen to the buyer's total earnings with a bond whose duration is exactly two years? First, if interest rates fall to 6 percent, the bond will earn $80 interest at the end of year 1 and another $80 at the end of year 2, but as before, only $4.80 will be earned when the first year's interest income is invested during the second year at the low rate of 6 percent ($80 × 0.06). However, the bond's market price will *rise* to $1,001.60 due to the drop in interest rates. Therefore, the investor will receive in two years a total of $1,166.40 in cash:

$$\frac{\text{First year's}}{\substack{\text{interest} \\ \text{earnings} \\ \$80}} + \frac{\text{Second year's}}{\substack{\text{interest} \\ \text{earnings} \\ \$80}} + \frac{\substack{\text{Interest earned on} \\ \text{reinvesting the first} \\ \text{year's interest} \\ \text{earnings at a} \\ \text{6 percent interest rate}}}{\$4.80} + \frac{\substack{\text{Market price received} \\ \text{when selling bond} \\ \text{at the end of the} \\ \text{investor's planned} \\ \text{holding period}}}{\$1,001.60} = \frac{\text{Total}}{\substack{\text{return} \\ \$1,166.40}}$$

Suppose instead that interest rates rise to 10 percent. Clearly, interest earnings will go up, but the bond's market price will be lower because of the rise in interest rates. In this case, the investor also receives a total return of $1,166.40:

$$\frac{\text{First year's}}{\substack{\text{interest} \\ \text{earnings} \\ \$80}} + \frac{\text{Second year's}}{\substack{\text{interest} \\ \text{earnings} \\ \$80}} + \frac{\substack{\text{Interest earned on} \\ \text{reinvesting the first} \\ \text{year's interest} \\ \text{earnings at 10 percent}}}{\$8} + \frac{\substack{\text{Market price received} \\ \text{when selling bond at the} \\ \text{end of the investor's} \\ \text{planned holding period}}}{\$998.40} = \frac{\text{Total}}{\substack{\text{return} \\ \$1,166.40}}$$

In the foregoing example, *the buyer earns identical total earnings whether interest rates go up or down!* This happens because, with duration set equal to the buyer's planned holding period, a fall in the reinvestment rate (in this case, down to 6 percent) is completely offset by an increase in the bond's price (in this instance, the bond's market value climbs from $1,000 to $1,001.60). Conversely, a rise in the reinvestment rate (up to 10 percent in the second case) is counterbalanced by a fall in the bond's market price (down to $998.40). The bond buyer's total return is fully protected regardless of the future path followed by interest rates.

Of course, there is a price to be paid for reducing risk exposure. Duration, like any interest rate hedging tool, is *not* free. Suppose in the example above that the bond buyer had chosen not to worry about duration and just purchased a bond with a calendar maturity of two years. Suppose also that interest rates rose to 10 percent during the second year. Clearly, this investor would have earned a larger total return ($1,168) without using portfolio immunization. The cost of immunization is a lower, but more stable, expected return.

Limitations of Duration

All this sounds easy: *To protect the return from a portfolio of securities against changes in interest rates, merely select a portfolio whose duration equals the time remaining in your planned holding period*. In practice, it does not work out quite this easily. For example, it is often difficult to find a collection of securities whose average portfolio duration exactly matches the investor's planned holding period. As time passes, the investor's planned holding period grows shorter, as does the average duration of the investor's portfolio. However, these two items — the remaining holding period and the duration of the investor's portfolio — are not likely to decline at the same speed. Therefore, an investor must constantly make portfolio adjustments to ensure that duration still equals the remaining length of the investor's planned holding period. And because many bonds are callable in advance of their maturity, bondholders may find themselves with a sudden and unexpected change in their portfolio's average duration.

Another problem with duration matching arises if the slope of the yield curve changes during the investor's planned holding period. In general, different patterns of interest rate movements require somewhat different measures of duration — a complex problem. Because the future path of interest rates cannot be perfectly forecast, immunization with duration cannot be perfect without developing a complicated model that takes account of a wide range of factors. Thus, there is always some risk associated with the use of conventional measures of duration due to uncertainty about future interest rate movements: a type of risk called *stochastic process risk*.[6] However, there is evidence that investors can achieve reasonably effective immunization by *approximately* matching the duration of their portfolios with their planned holding periods. The duration model, in other words, seems to be quite robust under a variety of market conditions.

SUMMARY

Although theories of interest rate determination typically assume there is a single interest rate in the economy, there are in fact thousands of different interest rates confronting investors. This chapter has focused upon two major factors: (1) the maturity, term, or duration of a loan and (2) inflationary expectations, which cause interest rates on different types of securities to vary. Knowledge of these factors is of critical importance in making intelligent portfolio decisions.

One key factor affecting interest rates considered in this chapter is *inflation*. If lenders expect a higher rate of inflation during the life of a credit contract, they will adjust upward the nominal interest rate on a loan to achieve their desired real rate of return. Financial theory argues that the nominal (published) rate on a financial asset equals the sum of the expected real rate of return (measured in terms of the real purchasing power of any income earned) and the inflation premium (or expected rate of inflation). According to the *Fisher effect*, if the expected inflation rate rises, the nominal interest rate on a financial asset must also rise by exactly the same amount, point for point.

Lesser-known views referred to as the *inflation-caused wealth, income*, and *depreciation effects* contend that a rise in expected inflation reduces the real rate of return to lenders as well as pushing nominal rates higher. However, because of the offsetting decline in the real rate, nominal interest rates rise by less than the increase in expected inflation. A contrasting view argues that taxation of interest income forces the nominal interest rate to rise by more than expected inflation so that investors can protect their expected after-tax real rate of return. Dispute over the true direction and magnitude of the inflation effect points to the need for further research.

---

[6]For a discussion of stochastic process risk see, for example, Bierwag, Kaufman, and Toevs (1983).

This chapter also emphasizes the usefulness of the *yield curve* in explaining and predicting interest rate movements. The yield curve expresses the relationship between the annual rate of return on a financial instrument and its term to maturity when all other factors are held constant. One theory traced in this chapter — the unbiased expectations hypothesis — argues that yield curves reflect the interest rate *expectations* of the marketplace and hint at the direction, if not the magnitude, of future rate movements. Contending theories, such as the liquidity premium view, the preferred habitat theory, and the segmented markets argument, contend that other factors in addition to expectations influence the yield curve. Regardless of which theory is valid, yield curves can play a key role in the management of financial institutions, which borrow a substantial portion of their funds at the short end of the maturity spectrum and lend heavily at longer maturities.

In recent years financial analysts have become somewhat dissatisfied with one of the two key variables making up the yield curve relationship: the term to maturity, or number of months and years until a security is retired. After all, the term to maturity of a security conveys no information on the timing or size of payments received by an investor over the life of a security but gives only the date of the final payment. An alternative measure called *duration* has become popular in recent years because it is a weighted average capturing both the size and timing of all cash payments from an individual asset or portfolio of assets. Duration has grown in popularity among portfolio managers because it can be used to at least partially immunize an asset portfolio against changing interest rates. ■

KEY TERMS AND CONCEPTS IN THIS CHAPTER

inflation

nominal interest rate

real interest rate

inflation premium

Fisher effect

inflation-caused wealth
    effect

inflation-caused income
    effect

inflation-caused
    depreciation effect

inflation-caused income
    tax effect

maturity

yield curve

unbiased expectations
    hypothesis

liquidity premium

market segmentation
    argument

preferred habitat

price elasticity

coupon effect

duration

portfolio immunization

STUDY QUESTIONS

1. Explain how *inflation* affects interest rates. What is the Fisher effect? The inflation-caused income effect? Wealth effect? Depreciation effect? Tax effect? The Harrod-Keynes effect?

2. How are stock prices affected by inflation?

3. Explain the meaning of the phrase "term structure of interest rates." What is a yield curve? What assumptions are necessary to construct a yield curve?

4. Explain the difference between the expectations, market segmentation, preferred habitat, and liquidity-premium views of the yield curve. Depending on which of these views is correct, what are the implications of each for investors? For public policy?

5. What *uses* does the yield curve have? Why is each possible use of value to borrowers and lenders of funds?

6. What is the *coupon effect*? How does it relate to the concept of *security price elasticity*? What is the relationship between the coupon rate on a security and the volatility of its price as interest rates change?

7. Explain the meaning and importance of the concept of *duration*.

8. What is *portfolio immunization*? How does it work? What are its limitations?

PROBLEMS

1. According to the Fisher effect, if the real interest rate is currently 3 percent and the nominal interest rate is 8 percent, what rate of inflation is the financial marketplace predicting? Explain the reasoning behind your answer. If the nominal rate rises to 11 percent and follows the assumptions of the Fisher effect, what would you conclude about the expected inflation rate? The real rate?

2. Suppose the real interest rate in the economy is 4 percent and the nominal interest rate is 9 percent. Now investors in the financial marketplace expect a sudden doubling in the rate of inflation. According to the Fisher effect, what new rate of inflation is expected? If the depreciation, income, or wealth effects are at work, what do you conclude is the new expected rate of inflation?

3. Calculate the expected after-tax rate of return for an investor in the 28 percent marginal income tax bracket if she purchases a bond whose nominal rate is 12 percent and the expected rate of inflation is 4 percent.

4. An investor buys a U.S Treasury bond whose current yield to maturity as reported in the daily newspaper is 10 percent. The investor is subject to a 33 percent federal income tax rate on any new income received. His real after-tax return from this bond is 2 percent. What is the expected inflation rate in the financial marketplace?

5. Calculate the price elasticity of a 15-year bond around its $1,000 par value and 10 percent coupon rate if market interest rates on comparable securities drop to 6 percent. The market price of the bond at a 6 percent yield to maturity is $1,392. Suppose now that the yield to maturity climbs to 14 percent. If the bond's price falls to $751.80, what is the bond's price elasticity?

6. Calculate the value of duration for a 4-year, $1,000 par value U.S. government bond purchased today at a yield to maturity of 15 percent. The bond's coupon rate is 12 percent, and it pays interest once a year at year's end. Now suppose the market interest rate on comparable securities falls to 14 percent. What percentage change in this bond's price will result?

7. A government bond is scheduled to mature in five years. Its coupon rate is 10 percent, with interest paid to holders of record at the conclusion of each year. This $1,000 par value carries a current yield to maturity of 10 percent. What is its duration?

8. For the bond described in Problem 7, calculate the percentage change in its price if interest rates on comparable securities in the market decline to 9 percent. What percentage change will occur if interest rates jump to 11 percent?

9. A bank buying bonds is concerned about possible fluctuations in earnings due to changes in interest rates. Currently the bank's investment officer is looking at a $1,000 par value

bond that matures in four years and carries a coupon rate of 12 percent. Market interest rates are also currently at 12 percent, but the bank's officer believes there is a significant probability that interest rates could drop to 10 percent or rise to 14 percent during the first year and stay there until the bond matures. What would be this bond's total earnings for the bank over the next four years if interest rates rise to 14 percent? Fall to 10 percent? Remain at 12 percent? What will happen to total earnings if the bank's investment officer finds another bond whose maturity is reached in five years but whose duration is four years, the same as the bank's planned holding period?

10. A bank grants a loan to AXTEL Corporation for three years to cover repairs at one of its production units. The terms of this $10 million loan call for the accrual of interest by the bank at a compound interest rate of 9 percent. However, the interest and the principal owed on this loan are due and payable when the loan matures at the end of the third year. What is the duration of this loan?

SELECTED REFERENCES

Abken, Peter A. "Inflation and the Yield Curve." *Economic Review*. Federal Reserve Bank of Atlanta, May/June 1993, pp. 13–31.

Ammer, John. "Inflation, Inflation Risk, and Stock Returns." *International Finance Discussion Paper 464*. Board of Governors of the Federal Reserve System, April 1994.

Bierwag, G.O.; George G. Kaufman; and Alden Toevs. "Duration: Its Development and Use in Bond Portfolio Management." *Financial Analysts Journal*, July–August 1983, pp. 15–35.

Campbell, J.Y. "A Defense of Traditional Hypotheses about the Term Structure of Interest Rates." *Journal of Finance* 41 (1986), pp. 183–93.

Carmichael, J., and P.W. Stebbing. "Fisher's Paradox and the Theory of Interest." *American Economic Review* 73 (1983), pp. 619–30.

De Fina, Robert H. "Does Inflation Depress the Stock Market?" *Business Review*. Federal Reserve Bank of Philadelphia, November/December 1991, pp. 3–12.

Elliot, J.W., and M.E. Echols. "Market Segmentation, Speculative Behavior, and the Term Structure of Interest Rates." *Review of Economics and Statistics*, February 1976, pp. 40–49.

Fama, Eugene F. "Stock Returns, Real Activity, Inflation and Money." *American Economic Review*, September 1981, pp. 545–65.

———. "The Information in the Term Structure." *Journal of Financial Economics* 13 (December 1984), pp. 509–28.

———, and R.R. Bliss. "The Information in Long-Maturity Forward Rates." *American Economic Review* 72 (1987), pp. 680–92.

———, and Kenneth R. French, "Business Conditions and Expected Returns on Stocks and Bonds." *Journal of Financial Economics* 25 (November 1989), pp. 23–49.

———, and M.R. Gibbons, "Inflation, Real Returns, and Capital Investment." *Journal of Monetary Economics* 9 (May 1990), pp. 297–324.

Fisher, Irving. "Appreciation and Interest." *Publication of the American Economics Association*, August 1896.

Froot, R.A. "New Hope for the Expectations Hypothesis of the Term Structure of Interest Rates." *Journal of Finance* 44 (1989), pp. 283–305.

Geske, Robert, and Richard Roll. "The Fiscal and Monetary Linkages between Stock Returns and Inflation." *Journal of Finance*, March 1983, pp. 1–33.

Groenewold, Nicolaas. "The Adjustment of the Real Interest Rate to Inflation." *Applied Economics* 21 (1989), pp. 947–56.

Hayford, Marc. "Real Interest Rates and the Distribution Effects of Unanticipated Inflation." *Journal of Macroeconomics* 12, no. 1 (Winter 1990), pp. 1–22.

Kaul, Gautam. "Stock Returns and Inflation: The Role of the Monetary Sector." *Journal of Financial Economics*, June 1987, pp. 253–76.

Kiely, Joseph K.; James W. Kolari; and Peter S. Rose. "A Re-examination of the Relationship between Liquidity Premiums and the Level of Interest Rates." *Journal of Business Research*, 1994.

LeRoy, Stephen F. "Inflation and Interest Rates." *Monthly Review*. Federal Reserve Bank of Kansas City, May 1973, pp. 11–18.

Longstaff, Francis A. "Time Varying Term Premia and Traditional Hypotheses about the Term Structure." *The Journal of Finance* 41, no. 4 (September 1990), pp. 1307–14.

McNees, Stephen K. "How Well Do Financial Markets Predict the Inflation Rate?" *New England Economic Review*. Federal Reserve Bank of Boston, September/October 1989, pp. 31–46.

Mankiw, N.G. "The Term Structure of Interest Rates Revisited." *Brookings Papers on Economic Activity*, 1986, pp. 61–96.

Mishkin, F.S. "What Does the Term Structure Tell Us about Future Inflation?" *Journal of Monetary Economics* 25 (1990), pp. 77–95.

Mundell, Robert. "Inflation and Real Interest." *Journal of Political Economy*, June 1963, pp. 280–83.

Sargent, Thomas J. "Anticipated Inflation and Nominal Interest." *Quarterly Journal of Economics*, May 1982, pp. 161–73.

Shiller, R.J.; J.Y. Campbell; and R.K. Schoenholtz. "Forward Rates and Future Policy: Interpreting the Term Structure of Interest Rates." *Brookings Papers on Economic Activity*, 1983, pp. 173–217.

Solnik, Bruno. "The Relation Between Stock Prices and Inflationary Expectations: The International Evidence." *Journal of Finance* 38 (1983), pp. 35–48.

Startz, Richard. "Do Forecast Errors or Term Premia Really Make the Difference Between Long and Short Rates?" *Journal of Financial Economics* 10 (November 1982), pp. 323–29.

Terrell, William T., and William J. Frazier, Jr. "Interest Rates, Portfolio Behavior, and Marketable Government Securities." *Journal of Finance*, March 1972, pp. 1–35.

Van Horne, James. "Interest-Rate Risk and the Term Structure of Interest Rates." *Journal of Political Economy*, August 1965, pp. 344–51.

Walsh, Carl E. "A Rational Expectations Model of Term Premia with Some Implications for Empirical Asset Demand Equations." *Journal of Finance* 60, no. 1 (March 1985), pp. 63–83.

Chapter 11

Default Risk, Taxes, and Other Factors Affecting Interest Rates

LEARNING OBJECTIVES IN THIS CHAPTER

- To explore the impact of several different characteristics of loans and securities — marketability, liquidity, default risk, call privileges, prepayment risk, convertibility, and taxability — on their attached interest rates or yields.

- To learn why not one but, in fact, thousands of different interest rates exist in the economy.

In the preceding chapter, we examined two factors that cause the interest rate or yield on one security to be different from the interest rate or yield on another. These factors included the maturity or term of a loan and expected inflation. In this chapter, our focus is upon a different set of elements influencing relative interest rates: (1) marketability, (2) default risk, (3) call privileges, (4) taxation of security income, and (5) convertibility. The impact of each of these factors is analyzed separately, but it should be noted that yields on securities are influenced by several factors acting *simultaneously*. For example, the market yield on a 20-year corporate bond may be 12 percent, while the yield on a 10-year municipal bond may be 8 percent. The difference in yield between these two securities reflects not only the difference in their maturities but also any differences in their degree of default risk, marketability, callability, and tax status. To analyze yield differentials between securities, therefore, we must understand thoroughly *all* the factors that shape interest rates in the money and capital markets.

MARKETABILITY

One of the most important considerations for an investor is *whether a market exists for those assets he would like to acquire*. Can an asset be sold quickly, or must the investor wait some time before suitable buyers can be found? This is the question of **marketability**, and financial instruments vary widely in terms of the ease and speed with which they can be converted into cash.

For example, U.S. Treasury bills, notes, and bonds have one of the most active and deep markets in the world. Large lots of marketable Treasury securities in multiples of a million dollars are bought and sold daily, with the trades taking place in a matter of minutes. Small lots (under $1 million) of these same securities are more difficult to sell. However, there is usually no difficulty in marketing even a handful of Treasury securities provided the seller can wait a few hours. Similarly, common stock actively traded on the New York, London, or Tokyo exchanges typically can be moved in minutes or hours, depending on the number of shares being sold. In active markets like these, negotiations are usually conducted by telephone and confirmed by wire; frequently payment for any securities purchased is made the same day by wire or within one or two days by check.

For thousands of lesser-known securities not actively traded each day, however, marketability can be a problem. Stocks and bonds issued by smaller companies usually have a narrow market, often confined to the local community or region. Trades occur infrequently, and it is difficult to establish a consistent market price. A seller may have to wait months to secure a desired price or, if the security must be sold immediately, its price may have to be discounted substantially.

Marketability is positively related to the *size* (total sales or total assets) and *reputation* of the institution issuing the securities and to the number of similar securities outstanding. Not surprisingly, stocks and bonds issued in large blocks by the largest corporations and governmental units tend to find acceptance more readily in the market. With a larger number of similar securities available, buy-sell transactions are more frequent, and a consistent market price can be established.

Marketability is a decided advantage to the security purchaser (lender of funds). In contrast, the issuer of securities is not particularly concerned about any difficulties the purchaser may encounter in the resale (secondary) market unless lack of marketability significantly influences security sales in the primary market. And where marketability is a problem, it does influence the yield the issuer must pay in the primary market. In fact, there is a *negative* relationship between marketability and yield. More marketable securities generally carry *lower* expected returns than less marketable securities, other things being equal. Purchasers of securities that can be sold in the secondary market only with difficulty must be compensated for this inconvenience by a higher promised rate of return.

LIQUIDITY

Marketability is closely related to another feature of financial assets that influences their interest rate or yield: their degree of **liquidity**. A liquid financial asset is *readily marketable*. In addition, its price tends to be *stable* over time and it is *reversible*, meaning the holder of the asset can usually recover her funds upon resale with little risk of loss. Because the liquidity feature of financial assets lowers their risk, liquid assets carry lower interest rates than illiquid assets. Investors strongly interested in maximum profitability try to minimize their holdings of liquid assets.

DEFAULT RISK AND INTEREST RATES

Another important factor causing one interest rate to differ from another is the degree of default risk carried by individual securities. Investors in securities face many different kinds of risk, but one of the most important is **default risk** — the risk that a borrower will not make all promised payments at the agreed-upon times. All securities except government securities are subject to varying degrees of default risk. If you purchase a 10-year corporate bond with $1,000 par value and a coupon rate of 9 percent, the issuing company promises in the indenture (bond contract) to pay you $90 a year (or more commonly, $45 every six months) for 10 years plus $1,000 at the end of the 10-year period. Failure to meet *any* of these promised payments on time puts the borrower in default, and the investor may have to go to court to recover the monies owed.

The Premium for Default Risk

The yield on a risky security is positively related to the risk of borrower default as perceived by investors. Specifically, the yield on a risky security is composed of at least two elements:

$$\text{Yield on risky security} = \text{Risk-free interest rate} + \text{Default risk premium} \qquad (11\text{--}1)$$

where:

$$\text{Default risk premium} = \text{Promised yield on a risky security} - \text{Risk-free interest rate} \quad (11\text{--}2)$$

The *promised yield* on a risky security is the yield to maturity that will be earned by the investor if the borrower makes all promised payments when they are due. As Exhibit 11–1 illustrates, the higher the degree of default risk associated with a risky security, the higher the default risk premium on that security and the greater the required rate of return (yield) that must be attached to that security as demanded by investors in the marketplace. Any adverse development, such as a downturn in the economy or serious financial difficulties,

Exhibit 11–1   **The Relationship between Default Risk and the Yield on Risky Securities**

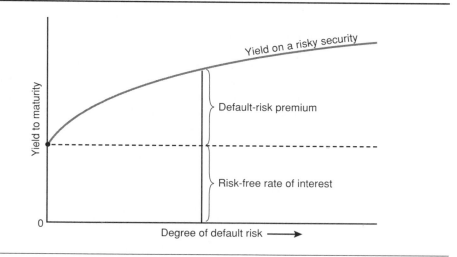

that makes a borrower appear riskier will lead the market to assign a higher default risk premium to his security. And if the risk-free rate remains unchanged, the security's risky yield must rise and its price must decline.

The Expected Rate of Return or Yield on a Risky Security

Increasingly in recent years, some of the largest firms (such as Circle K, Western Union, and Resorts International) and even some local government units (such as Orange County, California) have been forced into bankruptcy and into default on their bonds. Others, like Chrysler Corporation and Continental Illinois Corporation, have experienced highly publicized financial problems and have required government help to survive. Volatile changes in business and consumer spending, interest rates, and commodity prices frequently have led to serious miscalculations by both large and small firms with sometimes fatal results. For this reason, many investors today have learned to look at the *expected* rate of return, or yield, on a security as well as its *promised* yield.

The **expected yield** is the weighted average of all possible yields to maturity from a risky security. Each possible yield is weighted by the probability that it will occur. Thus, if there are m possible yields from a risky security:

$$\text{Expected yield} = \sum_{i=1}^{m} p_i y_i \qquad (11\text{–}3)$$

where y_i represents the ith possible yield on a risky security and p_i is the probability that the ith possible risky yield will be obtained.

Anticipated Loss and Default-Risk Premiums

For a risk-free security held to maturity, the expected yield equals the promised yield. However, in the case of a risky security, the promised yield may be greater than the expected yield, and the yield spread between them is usually labeled the *anticipated loss due to default*. That is,

Anticipated loss due to default on a risky security = Promised yield − Expected yield   (11–4)

The concept of anticipated loss due to default is important because it represents each investor's view of what the appropriate risk premium on a risky security should be. Let's suppose that an investor carries out a careful financial analysis of a company in preparation for purchasing its bonds and decides that the firm is a less risky borrower than perceived by the market as a whole. Perhaps the market has assigned the firm's bonds a default risk premium of 4 percent; the investor believes, however, that the true anticipated loss due to default is only 3 percent. Because the market's default risk premium exceeds this investor's anticipated loss, she would be inclined to *buy* the company's bonds. As she sees it, the risky security's yield (including its market-assigned default risk premium) is too high, and, therefore, its price is too low. To this investor, the company's bonds appear to be a bargain — a temporarily underpriced financial asset.

Consider the opposite case. An investor calculates the anticipated loss due to default on bonds issued by a state toll road project. He concludes that a default risk premium of 5 percent is justified because of a significant number of uncertainties associated with the future success of the project. However, the current yield on the risky security is only 10 percent, and the risk-free interest rate is 6 percent. Because the market has assigned only a

Exhibit 11–2

Bond-Rating Categories Employed by Moody's Investor Service and Standard & Poor's Corporation

Quality Level of Bonds	Moody's Rating Category	Standard & Poor's Rating Category	Default Risk Premium
High-quality or high-grade bonds	Aaa Aa A	AAA AA A	Lowest
Medium-quality or medium-grade bonds	Baa Ba B	BBB BB B	
Lowest grade, speculative, or poor-quality bonds	Caa Ca C	CCC CC C	
Defaulted bonds and bonds issued by bankrupt companies	— — —	DDD DD D	Highest

4 percent default risk premium, and the investor prefers a 5 percent premium, it is unlikely that he will purchase the bond. As the investor views this bond, its risky yield is too low, and, therefore, its price is too high.

Major financial institutions, especially insurance companies, banks, and pension funds, employ a large number of credit analysts for the express purpose of assessing the anticipated loss due to default on a wide range of securities they would like to acquire. These institutions believe they have a definite advantage over the average investor in assessing the true degree of default risk associated with any particular security. This high level of technical expertise may permit major institutional investors to take advantage of underpriced securities where, in their judgment, the market has overestimated the true level of default risk.

Factors Influencing Default-Risk Premiums

What factors influence the risk premiums assigned by the market to different securities? For many years, privately owned rating companies have exercised a dominant influence on investor perceptions of the riskiness of individual security issues. The two most widely consulted investment rating companies are Moody's Investor Service — a division of Dun & Bradstreet — and Standard & Poor's Corporation — a subsidiary of McGraw-Hill, Inc. Both companies rate individual security issues according to perceived probability of default (based on the borrower's financial condition and business prospects) and publish the ratings as letter grades. A summary of the letter grades used by these companies for rating corporate and municipal bonds is shown in Exhibit 11–2.[1]

Moody's investment ratings range from Aaa, for the highest-quality securities with negligible default risk, to C, for those securities deemed to be speculative and carrying a

---

[1]Although Moody's and Standard & Poor's dominate the security rating business, a number of smaller but rapidly growing rating agencies have come into prominence recently. The oldest of these is Fitch Investor Service, Inc., of New York; in 1982, Duff & Phelps, Inc., of Chicago was designated a nationally recognized statistical rating organization by the Securities and Exchange Commission (SEC). SEC recognition was also granted to McCarthy, Crisanti & Maffei, Inc., of New York in 1983. The recent growth of these smaller firms is a reflection of the increased number of corporate bankruptcies and near bankruptcies over the last few years that led many investors to seek multiple credit opinions on any given security before committing their funds.

significant prospect of borrower default. Quality ratings assigned by Standard & Poor's range from AAA, for high-grade ("gilt-edged") securities, to those financial instruments actually in default (D) or issued by bankrupt firms. Bonds falling in the four top rating categories — Aaa to Baa for Moody's and AAA to BBB for Standard & Poor's — are called *investment-grade issues*. State and federal laws frequently require commercial banks, insurance companies, and other financial institutions to purchase only those securities rated in these four categories. Lower-rated securities are referred to as *speculative issues*.

Exhibit 11–3 illustrates how the yield on bonds in two different Moody's categories — Aaa and Baa — has fluctuated in recent years, and it highlights the spread between the yields on these risky securities and those on riskless long-term U.S. government bonds. Exhibit 11–4 compares market yields on long-term U.S. Treasury bonds with those on corporate bonds in the four top rating categories, Aaa to Baa. It is interesting to note that these yield relationships are all in the direction theory would lead us to expect. For example, the yield on Aaa corporate bonds — the least risky securities rated by Moody's and Standard & Poor's — is consistently lower than yields attached to lower-rated (Baa) bonds. The graph lines representing Aaa and Baa bonds in Exhibit 11–3 never cross each other; this suggests that investors in the marketplace tend to rank securities in the same relative default-risk order as the credit rating agencies do. This seems to be an appropriate

Exhibit 11–3   **Long-Term Bond Yields** (Quarterly Averages)

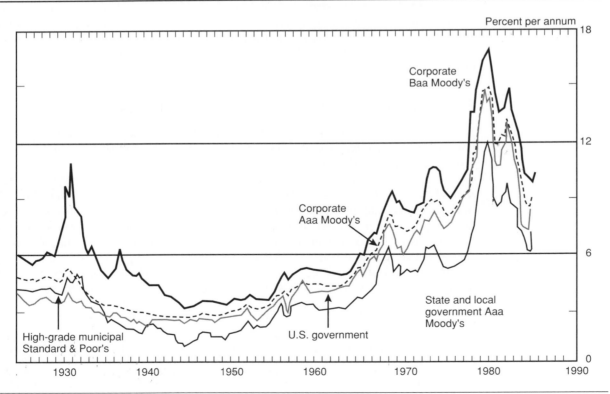

Source: Board of Governors of the Federal Reserve System, *Historical Chart Book*, 1989.

Exhibit 11–4   **Market Yields on Rated Corporate Bonds and Long-Term U.S. Treasury Bonds, 1987–1996**

| Type of Bond | Average Yields (Percent Per Annum) | | | | | | | | | |
	1987	1988	1989	1990	1991	1992	1993	1994	1995**	1996***
Long-term U.S. Treasury bonds	8.64%	8.98%	8.58%	8.74%	8.16%	7.52%	6.45%	7.41%	6.63%	6.03%
Aaa corporate bonds*	9.38	9.71	9.26	9.32	8.77	8.14	7.22	7.97	7.32	6.75
Aa corporate bonds*	9.68	9.94	9.46	9.56	9.05	8.46	7.40	8.15	7.45	6.94
A corporate bonds*	9.99	10.24	9.74	9.82	9.30	8.62	7.58	8.28	7.56	7.07
Baa corporate bonds*	10.58	10.83	10.18	10.36	9.80	8.98	7.93	8.63	7.93	7.42

*Corporate bond ratings are from Moody's Investor Service.
**1995 figures are for September.
***1996 figures are for the first week of January.

Source: Board of Governors of the Federal Reserve System, *Federal Reserve Bulletin*, selected issues.

strategy, because there appears to be a high correlation between the ratings assigned by the agencies and the actual default record of corporate bonds.

We note, however, that the spreads between yields in different rating categories vary significantly over time. There is a pronounced association between market-assigned default risk premiums and fluctuations in business activity (recessions versus expansions or boom periods). The yield spread between Aaa- and Baa-rated securities shown in Exhibit 11–3 rises during recession and decreases during periods of economic expansion. Note, for example, the marked increase in the yield spread between Aaa and Baa corporate bonds at the time of the 1969–70, 1974–75, and 1980–82 recessions and the significant decrease in that spread after these recessions ended. The correlation is not perfect, though. Fluctuations in output and income do not always influence the default risk premium on one security versus another in the same way or to the same degree. However, when economic and financial conditions suggest to investors that uncertainty has increased and that business prospects are less robust, the market translates these opinions into higher default risk premiums.[2]

Several studies in recent years have addressed the question of what factors influence default risk premiums on securities and what factors rating firms use to evaluate default risk. Among the factors identified for corporate securities are variability in company earnings, the period of time a firm has been in operation, and the amount of leverage employed (amount of debt relative to equity).[3]

---

[2]This conclusion is supported by research studies prepared by Hickman (1958) and Jaffee (1975).

[3]See especially the study by Fisher (1959). We do not know for sure what factors the security rating companies use to assign default risk ratings, but we do know that they consider at least three levels of factors: (1) condition of the economy, (2) industry conditions, and (3) borrower-specific factors, including coverage ratios (earnings before interest and taxes to interest and principal payments owed), leverage ratios (debt-to-equity ratios), liquidity indicators (such as the current ratio), and profitability measures (such as return on assets and equity). Recent studies of corporate bankruptcy, as noted by Scott (1981), have found some of these factors — especially liquidity or cash flow, earnings, debt exposure, and stock prices — to be effective discriminators between corporations eventually declaring bankruptcy and healthy firms. Moreover, a recent study by Holthausen and Leftwich (1986) finds that when Moody's or Standard & Poor's downgrades a firm's credit rating, the affected company's stock returns tend to fall immediately following the announcement.

Security Credit Ratings

Corporate and municipal debt securities sold in the financial markets generally must carry a credit rating assigned by one or more rating agencies. The two most widely respected credit-rating agencies are Moody's Investors Service and Standard & Poor's Corporation, both headquartered in New York City.

Other prominent security rating companies operating today include Fitch Investors Service, Thomson Bank Watch, and Duff and Phelps Credit Rating Co. in the U.S., as well as the Canadian Bond Rating Service, Japanese Bond Rating Institute, Dominion Bond Rating Service, IBCA, Ltd., the Japanese Credit Rating Agency, and Nippon Investor Service Inc. headquartered outside the United States. The ratings assigned by these firms are generally regarded in the investment community as an objective evaluation of the probability that a borrower will *default* on a security issue.

Each rating assigned to a security issue is a reflection of at least three factors: (1) the character and terms of the particular security being issued; (2) the ability and willingness of the issuer to make timely payments; and (3) the degree of protection afforded investors if the security issuer is liquidated, reorganized, or declares bankruptcy. The credit-rating agencies focus principally on (1) the past and probable future cash flows of the security issuer as an indication of the institution's ability to service its debt, (2) the volume and composition of outstanding debt, and (3) the stability of the issuer's cash flows over time. Other factors influencing quality ratings are the value of assets pledged as collateral and the securities' priority of claim against the issuing firm's assets.

The rating agencies stress that their evaluations of security issues are not recommendations to buy or sell or an indication of the suitability of any particular security for the investor. The agencies do not act as financial advisors to the businesses or units of government whose securities they rate, which helps to promote objectivity in assigning quality ratings. Fees are assessed for ratings based on the time and effort involved. These fees are usually paid either by the security issuer or the underwriter.

STANDARD & POOR'S CORPORATE AND MUNICIPAL BOND RATINGS

The credit ratings assigned to corporate and municipal bonds by Standard & Poor's Corporation are listed below along with the definitions used by S&P for each category:

1. AAA — Bonds rated AAA have the highest rating assigned by Standard & Poor's to a debt obligation. Capacity to pay interest and repay principal is extremely strong.

2. AA — Bonds rated AA have a very strong capacity to pay interest and repay principal and differ from the highest-rated issues only in small degree.

3. A — Bonds rated A have a strong capacity to pay interest and repay principal, although they are somewhat more susceptible to adverse changes in circumstances and economic conditions than bonds in higher-rated categories.

(continued)

4. BBB — Bonds rated BBB are regarded as having an adequate capacity to pay interest and repay principal. Adverse economic conditions or changing circumstances are more likely to lead to a weakened capacity to pay interest and repay principal for bonds in this category than for bonds in higher-rated categories.

5. BB, B, CCC, CC — Bonds in these categories are regarded as predominantly speculative with respect to capacity to pay interest and repay principal. Such bonds will likely have some quality and protective characteristics, but these are outweighed by large uncertainties or major risk exposures to adverse conditions.

6. C — the rating C is reserved for income bonds paying no interest.

7. D — Bonds rated D are in default; payment of interest and/or repayment of principal is in arrears.

The ratings from AA to B may be modified by the addition of a plus (+) or minus (−) sign to show relative standing within the major rating categories. A plus (+) sign indicates a bond of better-than-average quality in the particular rating category chosen; a minus (−) sign denotes a bond that is worse than average in that category. Provisional ratings may also be assigned, as indicated by the letter *P*, indicating that the rating assigned is heavily dependent upon the successful completion of a project being financed by the issuance of new securities. When no rating is requested or assigned, the symbol NR is assigned to the security issue in question. Each month S&P publishes a *Bond Guide* that contains a brief description of each security issue, including its yield, listing status, form, and redemption provisions.

MOODY'S INVESTORS SERVICE

Beginning in 1909, John Moody published a simple system of letter grades that indicated the relative investment quality of corporate bonds. Today, Moody's Investors Service rates thousands of issues of corporate and municipal bonds, commercial paper, short-term municipal notes, and preferred stock. These security ratings are reported in *Moody's Bond Record*, which is published monthly.

The credit ratings assigned by Moody's to corporate and state and local government (municipal) bonds are listed below with the definition of each rating category:

1. Aaa — Bonds rated Aaa are judged to be of the best quality. They carry the smallest degree of investment risk and are generally referred to as "gilt-edge." Interest payments are protected by a large or by an exceptionally stable margin and principal is secure.

2. Aa — Bonds rated Aa are judged to be of high quality by all standards. Together with the Aaa group, they compose what are generally known as high-grade bonds. They are rated lower than the best bonds because margins of protection may not be as large as in Aaa securities, fluctuation of protective elements may be of greater amplitude, or there may be other elements present that make the long-term risks appear somewhat larger than in Aaa securities.

3. A — Bonds rated A possess many favorable investment attributes and are to be considered upper-medium-grade obligations. Factors giving security to

(continued)

principal and interest are adequate, but elements may be present that suggest susceptibility to future impairment.

4. Baa — Bonds rated Baa are considered medium-grade obligations. Interest payments and principal security appear adequate, but certain protective elements may be lacking or unreliable over any great length of time. Such bonds lack outstanding investment characteristics and have speculative characteristics as well.

5. Ba — Bonds rated Ba have speculated elements; their future cannot be considered well assured. Often the protection of interest and principal payments may be very moderate and thereby not well safeguarded during both good and bad times.

6. B — Bonds rated B generally lack characteristics of a desirable investment. Assurance of interest and principal payments or maintenance of other contract terms over any long period of time may be small.

7. Caa — Bonds rated Caa are of poor standing, may be in default, and may have elements of danger with respect to principal or interest.

8. Ca — Bonds rated Ca represent obligations that are speculative in some degree, are often in default, or have marked shortcomings.

9. C — Bonds rated C are the lowest-rated class of bonds, having extremely poor prospects of ever attaining any real investment standing.

10. Con. (−) — Bonds for which the security depends on the completion of some act or the fulfillment of some condition are rated conditionally. These are bonds secured by (1) earnings of projects under construction, (2) earnings of projects unseasoned in operation experience, (3) rentals that begin when facilities are completed, or (4) payments to which some other limiting condition attaches. Parenthetical rating denotes probable credit stature on completion of construction or elimination of basis of condition.

Like Standard & Poor's Corporation, Moody's Investors Service will sometimes affix an additional symbol to its bond ratings to denote finer gradations of quality. For example, an A-rated municipal bond superior to other bonds in this category may be designated as A1.

While credit-rating agencies have a good record of correctly ranking the default-risk exposure of most security issuers, the interpretation of the ratings seems to vary across time and across different rating agencies. Because the number of credit-rating companies seems to be growing, there is some fear that security issuers in the future will "shop around" for the best ratings they can get. Fortunately, credit-rating firms have a strong incentive to keep their reputation for publishing accurate risk ratings. Otherwise, security issuers and investors would avoid agencies that lose their reputation for quality and, undoubtedly, investors who lose money from faulty ratings would seek relief in the courts.

A company with volatile earnings runs a greater risk of experiencing periods when losses will exceed the firm's ability to raise funds. The longer a firm has been operating without default, the more investors come to expect continued successful performance. Greater use of financial leverage in the capital structure of a firm offers the potential for greater earnings per share of stock, because debt is a relatively cheap source of funds (measured on an after-tax basis). However, financial leverage is a two-edged sword. As the proportion of borrowed funds rises relative to equity, the risk of significant declines in net earnings increases.[4]

The Rise and Fall of Junk Bonds

The decade of the 1980s ushered in the rapid growth and development of the market for **junk bonds** — long-term debt securities whose repayment is judged to be significantly less certain than bonds rated as investment quality, as shown in the following table:

Junk versus Investment-Quality Corporate Bonds

Investment-grade bond issues	All those debt securities rated: Aaa, Aa, A, or Baa by Moody's Investor Service AAA, AA, A, or BBB by Standard & Poor's Corporation
Junk Bonds	All those debt securities rated: Ba, B, Caa, Ca, or C by Moody's Investor Service BB, B, CCC, CC, C by Standard & Poor's Corporation

The term *junk bonds* arose years ago when several companies that were suddenly trapped in serious financial problems with low credit ratings ("fallen angels") were forced to issue inferior-quality bonds to stay alive. More recently, new companies and small established companies have also been able to reach the bond market, which previously was closed to them, by issuing these speculative-grade securities. Junk bonds have also been issued to facilitate mergers and, in the opposite situation, to prevent a corporate takeover. Many junk bonds are "zeros," which pay no interest, and others are "pics," which pay interest not in cash but in the form of new bonds — both ideal for companies with low or uncertain earning power. Such low-rated bonds often trade at interest yields of 4 or 5 percentage points or more over yields on comparable U.S. government securities. The number of individual investors and financial institutions interested in purchasing junk bonds grew rapidly during the 1980s due to the few actual defaults on these bonds. At the same time, a leading investment banking firm, Drexel Burnham Lambert, Inc., pioneered new techniques to sell junk bonds that rapidly expanded the scope of the market. Drexel provided junk bond financing for more than a thousand companies, according to Yago (1991). Many investors discovered that a diversified portfolio of junk bonds (e.g., about 12 different issues) appeared to lower overall portfolio risk to a level comparable to many higher-rated bonds. Thus, the yields offered on junk bonds appeared to be higher than their actual degree of default risk. For example, First Boston Corporation found an average loss rate of just 1.6 percent of the market value of junk bonds issued over the 1977–1987 period. Moreover, the development of an active market for junk bonds gave many small and new firms access to another source of financing besides borrowing from banks and finance companies. Certainly, the tax deductibility of interest expenses on corporate debt and the recent development of sophisticated hedging instruments (such as financial futures and options) to combat market risk encouraged private corporations to make greater use of junk securities to raise new capital.

On the negative side, however, the rapid growth of junk bonds has aroused concern among government policymakers over the declining credit quality of corporate debt. For

---

[4]A recent study by Ederington, Yawitz, and Roberts (1987) finds that *both* the ratings assigned by the credit-rating agencies and company financial reports are used by investors to assess the credit quality of bonds and derive the appropriate default risk premium.

example, insurance company regulators from New York state recently acted to limit junk bond investments by insurance firms selling policies in that state, a move soon followed by other insurance regulators across the United States. The use of junk bonds to finance hostile takeovers and the failure of hundreds of savings and loans that had purchased junk securities captured the attention of the U.S. Congress. Passage of the Financial Institutions Reform, Recovery, and Enforcement Act of 1989 outlawed further purchases of junk bonds by federally supervised depository institutions. In 1990, the king of junk bond dealers, Drexel Burnham Lambert, declared bankruptcy, as junk bond prices plummeted and federal investigators probed Drexel's dealings for possible violations of U.S. securities laws.

Moreover, a recession in the U.S. economy in 1991 resulted in a wave of defaults by firms that had issued junk bonds. However, the higher yields on junk bonds coupled with a declining supply of these securities early in the 1990s sparked a market rally in junk bond prices and an upward surge in new offerings. Much of the price gain was due to the emergence of junk bond mutual funds that often buy half or more of new junk issues. The rise in new junk bond offerings during the 1990s can be traced to more borrowing companies bypassing rigid and expensive bank loans as a source of credit and to an upward surge of corporate mergers financed by junk bond issues.

A Summary of the Default Risk, Interest Rate Relationship

In summary, careful study of the relationship between default risk and interest rates points to a fundamental principle in the field of finance: *default risk and expected return are positively related*. The investor seeking higher expected returns must also be willing to accept higher risk of ruin. Default risk is correlated with both *internal* (borrower-specific) factors associated with a loan and *external* factors, especially the state of the economy and changing demands for industry products and services.

CALL PRIVILEGES

Many corporate bonds and mortgages, most municipal revenue bonds, and some U.S. government bonds issued in today's financial markets carry a **call privilege**. This provision of the bond contract (indenture) grants the borrower the option to retire all or a portion of a bond issue by buying back the securities in advance of maturity. Bondholders usually are informed of a call through a notice in a newspaper of general circulation, while holders of record of registered bonds are notified directly. Normally, when the call privilege is exercised, the security issuer will pay the investor the *call price*, which equals the securities' face value plus a call penalty. The size of the *call penalty* is set forth in the indenture (contract) and generally varies inversely with the number of years remaining to maturity and the length of the call deferment period. In the case of a bond, one year's worth of coupon income is often the minimum call penalty required.

Calculating the Yields on Called Services

Bonds may be callable immediately, or the privilege may be deferred (postponed) for a time. In the corporate sector, bonds usually are not eligible for call for a period of 5 to 10 years after issue (known as a *call deferment*) to give investors at least some protection against early redemption. Of course, calling a security in advance of its final maturity has an impact on the investor's effective yield.

Default Risk in Action: The Failure of Orange County, California — Local Government Default on a Grand Scale

Buyers of bonds and other financial instruments must be ever watchful of *default risk* — failure to pay interest owed or to pay back the principal of a loan — which can occur in some unexpected places. A dramatic demonstration of that fact occurred in 1994 and 1995 when one of the largest county governments in the United States announced that it could no longer meet all of its debt obligations. By the summer of 1995, Orange County, California, the fifth most populous county in the U.S., had defaulted on about $800 million owed to various creditors.

The Orange County financial disaster first came to public attention in the summer of 1994. County officials announced about $2.5 billion in losses, resulting from an aggressive investment policy in which the county invested in its own mutual funds the revenues received from Orange County taxpayers and from other governmental units. In earlier years county voters had rejected most proposals to raise taxes but still wanted a full menu of government services, placing intense pressure on government officials to earn more on investments in order to supplement inadequate tax revenues.

Many Orange County investments were in risky financial derivatives, betting that interest rates would decline. For example, the county invested a substantial portion of its monies in derivatives based upon a multiple of the difference between Swiss and U.S. interest rates. When U.S. market interest rates rose, Orange County lost more than it could possibly repay, and in December of 1994, the county entered bankruptcy court. Orange County employed a *double leveraging* strategy, borrowing money by pledging securities it had bought and using that borrowed money to purchase still more securities that were also leveraged. Approximately $12 billion in funds were borrowed by Orange County to invest in additional interest-bearing securities.

Residents of the county face declines in government services and higher tax assessments as this Southern California county tries to recover its solvency and stability. To make matters worse, county residents recently voted down a proposed increase in sales taxes to help the county repay its debts. Moreover, Orange County is threatened with lawsuits from other local governments who invested in its mutual funds and claim that, under California law, they are entitled to 100 cents on the dollar. Then there are creditors who, among other claims, hold the roughly $1.3 billion in bonds that the county issued but has not yet fully repaid.

One highly questionable practice followed by some county officials was to *not* publicly disclose county reports and audits and to avoid informing other local governments that were also investing in Orange County's mutual fund. One proposed remedy for the county's problems is for the state of California to develop a new governmental structure for Orange County, placing the county in receivership and removing much of the decision-making powers of county officials (similar to what the State of New York did when New York City was in deep financial trouble during the 1970s). Complicating the problem is the unsettled nature of bankruptcy law when it comes to bankrupt governments. When a privately owned business firm fails and files for bankruptcy protection, the courts can follow fairly clear guidelines on which creditors have priority in their claims against the bankrupt firm's assets. In the case of

(continued)

a government going bankrupt, however, creditor priorities are muddled, and the bankrupt government itself plays a major role in resolving who gets paid and who loses.

In September 1995, Orange County officials, in cooperation with various local governments, business leaders, and the governor's office, appeared to have hammered out a resolution plan, which covers a 15-year pay out period. Under the proposal, tax revenues would be diverted from selected projects (such as mass transit programs) and used to repay creditors. Moreover, the cities, school districts, and other governmental units who also invested in the Orange County-managed mutual fund appear to have agreed to accept a lower priority in the race to recover their funds and have received some supplemental support from the California legislature.

The lesson of Orange County is fairly clear — default on a security issue can lead to a prolonged period of legal turmoil and huge losses. Investors must be vigilant and look for the telltale signs of impending bankruptcy, including declining earnings or revenue, rising debt, and growing liquidity problems.

To demonstrate this, we recall from Chapter 9 that the yield to maturity of any security is that discount rate, y, which equates the security's price, P, with the present value of all its future cash flows, I_i. In symbols:

$$P = \frac{I_1}{(1 + y)^1} + \frac{I_2}{(1 + y)^2} + \ldots + \frac{I_n}{(1 + y)^n} \tag{11–5}$$

where n is the number of periods until maturity. Suppose that after k periods (with $k < n$), the borrower exercises the call option and redeems the security. The investor will receive the call price (C) for the security, which can be reinvested at current market interest rate, i. If the investor's planned holding period ends in time period n, the expected holding period yield (h) can be calculated using the formula:

$$P = \frac{I_1}{(1 + h)^1} + \frac{I_2}{(1 + h)^2} + \ldots + \frac{I_k}{(1 + h)^k} + \frac{i \times C_{k+1}}{(1 + h)^{k+1}}$$
$$+ \frac{i \times C_{k+2}}{(1 + h)^{k+2}} + \ldots + \frac{i \times C_n}{(1 + h)^n} + \frac{C}{(1 + h)^n} \tag{11–6}$$

Using summation signs, this reduces to

$$P = \sum_{j=1}^{k} \frac{I_j}{(1 + h)^j} + \sum_{j=k+1}^{n} \frac{i \times C_j}{(1 + h)^j} + \frac{C}{(1 + h)^n} \tag{11–7}$$

The first term in Equation 11–7 gives the present value of all expected cash flows (I) from the security until it is called in time period k. The second term captures the present value of income received by the investor after he reinvests at interest rate i the call price (C) received from the security issuer. The third and final term in the equation shows the current discounted value of the call price the investor expects to receive when the holding period ends in time period n.

As an example, let's suppose that a corporate bond, originally offering investors an 8 percent coupon rate for 10 years and issued at $1,000 par, is called 5 years after its issue date when going market interest rates on investments of comparable risk are 6 percent.

What is this bond's 10-year holding period yield (h) if its call price equals par ($1,000) plus one year's worth of coupon income ($80)? We have

$$1,000 = \sum_{t=1}^{5} \frac{\$80}{(1+h)^t} + \sum_{t=6}^{10} \frac{\$1,080 \times .06}{(1+h)^t} + \frac{\$1,080}{(1+h)^{10}} \tag{11-8}$$

The reader, using the present value and annuity tables in the appendix, should verify that h, the 10-year holding period yield, is 7.94 percent in this example. Thus, the investor holding this bond received 0.06 percent *less* in yield than if the bond had *not* been called, but instead had been held to maturity.

Equation 11–7 shows clearly that the investor in callable securities encounters two major uncertainties:

1. The investor does not know if or when the securities might be called (i.e., the value of k).

2. The investor does not know the market yield (reinvestment rate, i) that might prevail at the time the security is called.

Therefore, how aggressively the investor chooses to bid for a callable instrument will depend upon:

1. The investor's expectations regarding future changes in interest rates, especially decreases in rates, during the term of the security.

2. The length of the deferment period before the security is eligible to be called.

3. The call price (par value plus call penalty) the issuer is willing to pay to redeem the security.

Advantages and Disadvantages of the Call Privilege

Clearly, the call privilege is an advantage to the security issuer because it grants greater financial flexibility and the potential for reducing future interest costs. On the other hand, the call privilege is a distinct disadvantage to the security buyer, who may suffer a decline in expected holding-period yield if the security is called. The issuer will call in a security if the market rate of interest falls far enough so that the savings from issuing a new security at lower interest rates more than offset the call penalty plus flotation costs of a new security issue. This means, however, that the investor who is paid off will be forced to reinvest the call price in lower-yielding securities.

Another disadvantage for the investor is that call privileges limit the potential increase in a security's market price. In general, the market price of a security will not rise significantly above its call price. The reason is that the issuer can call in a security at its call price, presenting the investor with a loss equal to the difference between the prevailing market price and the call price. Thus, callable securities have more limited potential for capital gains than noncallable securities.

The Call Premium and Interest Rate Expectations

For all these reasons, securities that carry a call privilege generally sell at lower prices and higher interest rates than noncallable securities. Moreover, there is an inverse relationship between the length of the call deferment period and the required rate of interest on callable securities. The longer the period of deferment and, therefore, the longer the investor is protected against early redemption, the lower the interest rate the borrower must pay.

Issuers of callable securities must pay a call premium in the form of a higher rate of interest for the option of early redemption and for a shorter deferment period.

The key determinant of the size of the call premium is the *interest rate expectations* of investors in the marketplace. If interest rates are expected to rise, the risk that the security will be called is low. Borrowers are highly unlikely to call in their securities and issue new ones at a higher interest rate. As a result, the yield differential between callable and noncallable securities normally will be minimal. The same conclusions apply even if interest rates are expected to decline moderately but not enough to entice borrowers to call in securities and issue new ones.

Securities are most likely to be called when interest rates are expected to fall substantially. In this instance, security issuers can save large amounts of money — more than enough to cover the call penalty plus flotation costs of new securities — by exercising the call privilege. Thus, the call premium is likely to be significant, as investors demand a higher yield on callable issues to compensate them for increased call risk. The yield spreads between bonds with long call deferments widen during such periods as investors come to value more highly the deferment feature.

Research Evidence

Is there evidence of an *inverse* relationship between interest rate expectations and the value of the call privilege? Research studies answer in the affirmative. For example, Cook (1973) finds that when interest rates are high, the call premium rises, because investors expect interest rates to fall in the future. He points out that call provisions also influence yield spreads between corporate bonds, some of which have the call privilege attached, and municipal and U.S. government bonds, which generally are *not* subject to call. For example, when interest rates are expected to fall, the spread between corporate and U.S. government bond rates tends to widen. Pye (1966, 1967) and Jen and Wert (1966, 1967, 1968) find evidence that bonds carrying a call deferment have lower rates of return than bonds that are callable immediately.

Recent research by Kraus (1973) and others suggests that calling in bonds to save on interest costs may be a "zero sum game" between the bondholders and the stockholders of a company issuing callable bonds. Gains by stockholders (due to higher earnings from savings on interest costs) may be offset by losses for the bondholders (in the form of a lower holding-period yield). Generally, a call will occur when the owners of the issuing firm believe they will benefit at the expense of the firm's creditors. In an efficient market, with all participants possessing identical interest-rate expectations, callable securities will sell at a price and yield just sufficient to compensate buyers for call risk. The management of the issuing firm should be indifferent between issuing callable or noncallable securities. Under some circumstances, however, call provisions may be beneficial to the callable security issuer where management has greater knowledge of the future course of interest rates than does the market as a whole, where a call provision prevents security holders from blocking beneficial investments that a security-issuing entity might make, or where a call privilege lowers the sensitivity of a callable security's market value to changes in interest rates. Additional research is needed to clarify more precisely who the winners and losers are likely to be from transactions involving callable securities.

Effect of Coupon Rates on Call Risk

Finally, we should note that the coupon rate on a bond is closely related to the investor's call risk. We recall from Chapter 9 that a bond's coupon rate is the rate of return against the security's par value promised by the borrower. High coupon rates mean that a bond issuer is forced to pay high interest costs as long as the bond is outstanding. Therefore, there is a strong incentive to call in such bonds and replace them with lower coupon securities.

Another problem is that bonds bearing high coupons have less opportunity for capital gains than bonds carrying lower coupon rates. This is true because the market value of a high coupon security is usually close to its call price ceiling. In contrast, bonds with more modest coupon rates sell at lower prices and carry considerably more potential for capital gains before hitting their call price. This means there is more risk of call and less potential capital gain to the investor who chooses high coupon securities. As a result, the issuer of such securities must pay a higher yield to induce investors to buy them and accept greater call risk.

In recent years, the proportion of corporate bonds issued with call privileges attached has been declining. One reason is the large number of shorter bond maturities, which means that issuing companies have less need to call in their outstanding bonds before they reach maturity. Then, too, there has been a virtual explosion in new financial instruments to hedge bond issues against interest rate risk, including financial futures, options, and swaps, also reducing the need for the interest rate protection afforded by the call privilege, as noted by Crabbe (1991). Finally, the yield premium associated with issuing callable bonds rather than noncallable bonds appears to have increased in recent years, discouraging many corporations from issuing bonds bearing a call feature.

PREPAYMENT RISK AND INTEREST RATES ON LOAN-BACKED SECURITIES

A newer form of risk affecting the relative interest rates confronting many modern investors arises when they acquire so-called *loan-backed securities*, such as mortgage pass-throughs, collateralized mortgage obligations (CMOs), auto-loan-backed securities, and credit-card-backed securities. These instruments are usually created when a lending institution, such as a bank or mortgage company, removes a group of similar loans from its balance sheet and places them with a trustee (such as a security dealer) who, using the loans as collateral, sells securities to raise new capital for the lending institution. Each of these securities derives its value from the income-earning potential of the pool of loans that backs these securities. As the loans in the pool generate interest and principal payments, these payments flow through to holders of the loan-backed securities. Unlike ordinary bonds, which usually pay nothing but interest until they finally reach maturity, loan-backed securities pay their purchasers a stream of income that includes *both* repayments of loan principal and interest. In this case, the purchaser may receive higher-than-expected repayments of principal early in the life of the pooled loans, possibly lowering his or her expected return from loan-backed securities. Investors in those loan-backed securities that carry substantial **prepayment risk** will demand higher yields to compensate them for the risk associated with early prepayment of the loans backing the securities they hold.

Prepayment risk is especially troublesome for investors purchasing securities that are backed by pools of home mortgage loans. The pool of loans serving as collateral for these securities generally consist of 25- and 30-year loans to purchase new homes. Many of these home loans will be retired early due to: (1) *refinancing of loans*, as homeowners try to get new, cheaper mortgage loans in order to lower their monthly mortgage payments as market interest rates fall; and (2) *home-owner turnover*, as families move and need to sell their homes or simply default on their loans.

The investor interested in purchasing loan-backed securities needs to make certain assumptions about the likely prepayment behavior of the loans in the pool in order to decide what the true value of the loan-backed securities must be. Each package of pooled loans would have somewhat different characteristics due to variations in loan quality and location, the condition of the economy, and other factors. The current value of a loan-backed security can be determined from:

$$
\begin{array}{c}
\text{Market value (price)} \\
\text{of Loan-backed} \\
\text{security}
\end{array}
=
\dfrac{
\begin{array}{c}
\text{Expected cash flow} \\
\text{including projected} \\
\text{prepayments of loans} \\
\text{in period 1}
\end{array}
}{(1 + y/m)^1}
+
\dfrac{
\begin{array}{c}
\text{Expected cash flow} \\
\text{including projected} \\
\text{prepayments of loans} \\
\text{in period 2}
\end{array}
}{(1 + y/m)^2}
+ \ldots +
\dfrac{
\begin{array}{c}
\text{Expected cash flow} \\
\text{including projected} \\
\text{prepayments of loans} \\
\text{in period n}
\end{array}
}{(1 + y/m)^{m \times n}}
$$

where y is the security's yield to maturity, m is the number of times during a year that interest and principal payments occur, and n is the total number of years covered by the pooled loans. Note that each expected cash flow from a loan-backed security must be adjusted to reflect the risk that some loans will pay out early, increasing cash flows to an investor in these securities in the early years and, thus, reducing an investor's expected cash flow from these securities in later years. The greater the prepayment risk, the higher the yield tends to rise and the lower the loan-backed security's price tends to go.[5]

TAXATION OF SECURITY RETURNS

Taxes imposed by federal, state, and local governments have a profound effect on the returns earned by investors on financial assets. The income from most securities — interest or dividends and capital gains — is subject to taxation at the federal level and by many state and local governments as well. Government uses its taxing power to encourage the purchase of certain financial assets and thereby redirect the flow of savings and investment toward areas of critical social need.

In 1986, the U.S. Congress enacted the Tax Reform Act, which resulted in major changes in personal and business tax rates in the United States, with major redistributive effects on the financial markets, the supply of savings, and the demand for loanable funds. Further changes were made in the federal tax code in 1990 and 1993 as the result of budget compromises between the President and the Congress. The 1986 law reduced personal and corporate tax rates; however, tax rates on high-income individuals and corporations went up again in 1993. Capital gains tax rates (previously a minimum of 20 percent) were generally increased. Capital gains are now taxable at ordinary income tax rates up to 28 percent.

The Tax Treatment of Capital Gains

Under current tax rules administered by the Internal Revenue Service, an increase in the value of a capital asset (including stocks and bonds) that the taxpayer converts into cash is

---

[5]Actually, the relationship between the value of a loan-backed security and changes in market interest rates is quite complicated. For example, when interest rates fall, investors in loan-backed securities will experience quicker recovery of their invested funds, as more borrowers repay their loans earlier and the lower interest rates increase the present value of the securities' cash flow. On the other hand, with more loans paid off early, the investor loses future interest payments which will never be received and the funds received by the security holder will have to be reinvested at lower market interest rates, reducing future earnings from the security. Generally, a loan-backed security will fall in value when lost interest payments and reduced reinvestment income offset the benefits from quicker recovery of principal and a lower discount rate applied to future cash flows.

MANAGEMENT INSIGHT:

Event Risk — Another Risk Factor Affecting Interest Rates and Security Prices

Money and capital markets research in recent years has revealed another risk factor that (at least temporarily) affects the market value of debt and equity securities issued by corporations and other units raising funds in the financial markets. This so-called **event risk** factor consists of news announcements that reflect decisions by the management of a corporation or other fund-raising unit. Examples include announcements of new stock or bond offerings, increases or decreases in corporate dividend payments, stock splits, mergers and acquisitions, replacement of old with new management, new product offerings, etc.

Financial research suggests that announcements of events like these tend to have fairly predictable impacts on security values and borrowing costs. For example,

Event	Usual Market Response
Announcement of a new security issue	The issuer's security prices usually fall, at least temporarily.
Announcement of an increased stock dividend	The issuer's security prices usually rise, at least temporarily.
Announcement of a stock split	The issuer's security prices usually rise, at least temporarily.
Debt-equity swap (a company's bonds are replaced by stock)	The company's stock price usually falls, at least temporarily.

Many financial analysts believe that events such as the foregoing trigger changes in security prices and interest rates for the affected institutions because they convey new information about the probable future performance of these institutions. For example, the management of a business firm possesses inside (asymmetric) information on the firm's true financial condition, investment prospects, and potential earnings. Presumably, management draws on this inside information when it elects to go ahead with an event such as a new security offering, increasing or decreasing dividends paid to stockholders, launching a new product, etc. Investors in the financial marketplace regard the announcements of such "events" as a revelation of how management views the firm's future prospects. (For example, management may issue new stock because it wants to increase a company's future borrowing capacity.) The result is a re-evaluation by investors of the value of a security issuer's stocks and bonds; the market prices and yields of those securities will change with the appearance of this new information.

Sources: See, for example, Stewart Myers and Nicholas Majluf, "Corporate Financing and Investment Decisions When Firms Have Information That Investors Do Not Have," *Journal of Financial Economics* XIII, No. 2 (1984); and Merton Miller and Kevin Bock, "Dividend Policy Under Asymmetric Information," *Journal of Finance*, 1985.

subject to federal income taxation. For example, if you purchased stock in XYZ Corporation for $1,900 and sold it at a later date for $3,100, you would have experienced a capital gain of $1,200. Under the Tax Reform Act of 1986, the capital gain of $1,200 is taxable as ordinary income at your current income tax rate. Thus, a $1,200 capital gain for an investor in the 28 percent tax bracket would result in a tax liability of $336 ($1,200 × 0.28).

Exhibit 11–5   **Examples of Marginal Federal Income Tax Rates (Tax Brackets)**

Single Taxpayer's Tax Brackets		Corporations Subject to Income Tax	
Taxable Income	Applicable Tax Rate	Taxable Income	Applicable Tax Rate
Up to $20,350	15%	Less than $50,000	15%
Next $28,950	28	$50,000–$75,000	25
Over $49,300	31	$75,000–$100,000	34
Over $115,000	36	$100,000–$335,000	39
		Over $335,000	34
		Over $ 10 million	35

Couples Filing Joint Returns	
Taxable Income	Applicable Tax Rate
Up to $34,000	15%
Next $48,150	28
Over $82,150	31
Over $140,000	36
Over $250,000	39.6

Treatment of Capital Losses

Net losses on security investments are deductible for tax purposes within well-defined limits. For the individual taxpayer, a net capital loss is deductible up to the amount of the capital loss, the size of ordinary income, or $3,000, whichever is smaller. For example, suppose an investor experiences a net loss on securities held and then sold of $8,000. Suppose this person receives other taxable income of $20,000. How much of the capital loss can be deducted? What is this taxpayer's total taxable income? The maximum loss deduction in this case is $3,000, and therefore the taxpayer's net taxable income is $17,000 ($20,000 minus the $3,000 in deductible losses). Current federal law allows the taxpayer to carry forward into subsequent years the remaining portion of the loss ($5,000 in this example) until all the loss has been deducted from ordinary income, but the loss cannot be carried backward.

Tax-Exempt Securities

One of the most controversial tax rules affecting securities is the tax-exemption privilege granted investors in state and local government (municipal) bonds. The interest income earned on municipal bonds is exempt from federal income taxes.[6] **Tax-exempt securities** represent a subsidy to induce investors to support local government by financing the construction of schools, highways, airports, and other needed public projects. The exemption privilege shifts the burden of federal taxation from buyers of municipal bonds to other taxpayers.

What investors benefit from buying municipals? The critical factor here is the marginal tax rate (tax bracket) of the investor, the tax rate he or she must pay on the last dollar of income received during the tax year. For individual investors, these marginal tax rates range from zero for nontaxpayers to as high as 39.6 percent for the highest income earning couples (see Exhibit 11–5 for an example of tax rates applying to individuals and corporations). The

---

[6]Although the interest income from municipals is federal income tax exempt, capital gains on municipals are generally taxable as ordinary income. In addition, most states do not tax income from their own bonds or from the bonds issued by local governments within their borders. Income from U.S. government securities is usually exempt from state and local taxes but not from federal taxes.

marginal tax rate for corporations is 15 percent on the first $50,000 in taxable profits up to as high as 35 percent on net income above $10 million. In recent years, marginal tax rates of about 27 to 28 percent have represented a break-even level for investors interested in municipal bonds. Investors carrying marginal tax rates above this range generally receive higher after-tax yields from buying tax-exempt securities instead of taxable securities. Below this range, taxable securities generally yield a better after-tax return.

The Effect of Marginal Tax Rates on After-Tax Yields. To illustrate the importance of knowing the investor's marginal tax rate in deciding whether to purchase tax-exempt securities, consider the following example. Assume the current yield to maturity on taxable corporate bonds is 12 percent, while the current tax-exempt yield on municipal bonds of comparable quality and rating is 9 percent. The after-tax yield on these two securities can be compared using the following formula:

$$\text{Before-tax yield } (1 - \text{Investor's marginal tax rate}) = \text{After-tax yield} \qquad (11\text{--}9)$$

For an investor in the 28 percent tax bracket (see Exhibit 11–5), the after-tax yields on these bonds are as follows:

Taxable Corporate Bond	Tax-Exempt Municipal Bond
12% (1 − 0.28) = 8.64%	9% before and after taxes

On the basis of yield alone, the investor in the 28 percent tax bracket would prefer the tax-exempt municipal bond.[7]

At what rate would an investor be *indifferent* as to whether securities are taxable or tax exempt? In other words, what is the break-even point between these two types of financial instruments?

This point is easily calculated from the formula

$$\text{Tax-exempt yield} = (1 - t) \times \text{Taxable yield} \qquad (11\text{--}10)$$

where t is the investor's marginal tax rate. Solving for the break-even tax rate gives

$$t = 1 - \frac{\text{tax-exempt yield}}{\text{taxable yield}} \qquad (11\text{--}11)$$

Clearly, if the current yield on tax-exempt securities is 8 percent and 10 percent on taxable issues, the break-even tax rate is $1 - 0.80$, or 20 percent. An investor in a marginal tax bracket *above* 20 percent would prefer the yield on a tax-exempt security to a taxable one at these prevailing interest rates, other factors held equal.

Comparing Taxable and Tax-Exempt Securities. The existence of both taxable and tax-exempt securities complicates the investor's task in trying to choose a suitable portfolio to buy and hold. To make valid comparisons between taxable and tax-exempt issues, the taxed investor must convert all expected yields to an *after-tax basis*.

In the case of the yield to maturity on a security, this can be done by using the following formula:

$$P_0 = \sum_{i=1}^{n} \frac{I_i(1 - t)}{(1 + a)^i} + \frac{(P_n - P_0)(1 - t)}{(1 + a)^n} + \frac{P_0}{(1 + a)^n} \qquad (11\text{--}12)$$

---

[7]The particular tax brackets favoring the purchase of municipals versus taxable securities change over time due to changes in tax laws and variations in the yield spread between taxable and tax-exempt securities.

which equates the current market value (P_0) of the security to the present value of all after-tax returns promised in the future. If the security is to be held for n years, I_i is the amount of interest or other income expected each year, and t is the marginal income tax rate of the investor. If we assume the security will be sold or redeemed for price P_n at maturity, then $(P_n - P_0)$ measures the expected capital gain on the instrument, which will be taxed at the taxpayer's ordinary income tax rate up to 28 percent under the most recent U.S. tax laws. Provided investors know their marginal income tax rate, the current price of the security, and the expected distribution of future income from the security, they can easily calculate discount rate a — the after-tax yield to maturity.

For example, consider the case of a $1,000 corporate bond selling for $900 (with par value of $1,000), maturing in 10 years, with a 10 percent coupon rate. If an investor in the 28 percent federal income tax bracket buys and holds the bond to maturity, her after-tax yield, a, could be found from evaluating the following:

$$\$900 = \sum_{i=0}^{10} \frac{\$100(1 - 0.28)}{(1 + a)^i} + \frac{(\$1{,}000 - \$900)(1 - 0.28)}{(1 + a)^{10}} + \frac{P_0}{(1 + a)^n}$$

In this instance, the reader should verify, using the annuity and present value tables at the back of this book, that the after-tax yield, a, is 8.57 percent.

Certainly, the tax-exempt privilege has lowered the interest rates at which municipals can be sold in the open market relative to taxable bonds and, therefore, the amount of interest cost borne by local taxpayers. For example, in February 1996, Aaa-rated municipal bonds carried an average yield to maturity of 5.40 percent, compared to 7.60 percent on comparable quality (taxable) corporate bonds — a yield spread of more than 2 percentage points. However, the primary beneficiaries of the exemption privilege are investors who can profitably purchase municipals and escape some portion of the federal tax burden. Other taxpayers must pay higher federal taxes in order to make up for those lost tax revenues. By limiting the municipal market to these high tax-bracket investors, the tax-exemption feature has probably increased the unpredictability of municipal bond interest rates and made the job of fiscal management for state and local government more difficult.

CONVERTIBLE SECURITIES

Another factor that affects relative rates of return on different securities is **convertibility**. Convertible securities consist of special issues of corporate bonds or preferred stock that entitle the holder to exchange these securities for a specific number of shares of the issuing firm's common stock. Convertibles are frequently called *hybrid securities* because they offer the investor the prospect of stable income in the form of interest or dividends plus capital gains on common stock once conversion occurs. The timing of a conversion is usually at the option of the investor. However, an issuing firm often can "force" conversion of its securities by either calling them in or by encouraging a rise in the price of its common stock (such as by announcing a merger offer), because conversion is most likely in a rising market.

Investors generally pay a premium for convertible securities over nonconvertible securities in the form of a higher price. Thus, convertibles will carry a lower rate of return than other securities of comparable quality and maturity issued by the same company. This occurs because the investor in convertibles is granted a hedge against future risk. If security prices fall, the investor still earns a fixed rate of return in the form of interest income from a convertible bond or dividend income from convertible preferred stock. On the other hand, if stock prices rise, the investor can exercise his or her option and share in any capital gains earned on the company's common stock.

Convertible bonds offer several significant advantages to the company that decides to issue them. Due to the conversion feature, they can be issued at a lower net interest cost than conventional (nonconvertible) bonds. Convertibles offer an alternative to issuing more common stock, which a firm may wish to avoid because additional stock could dilute the equity interest of current stockholders and reduce earnings per share. Dividends on stock are not deductible from federal income taxes, but interest on convertible bonds *is* a tax-deductible expense.

Key advantages to the investor include the fact that convertible bonds guarantee the payment of interest and generally appreciate in value when the company's common stock is also rising in price. Moreover, there is a floor under the price of a convertible bond — known as its *investment value* — below which its price normally will not fall. This is the price that would produce a yield on the convertible equal to the yield on nonconvertible bonds of the same quality. However, investors are often counseled by financial analysts not to buy convertibles unless they would be happy holding the issuing company's stock, because the issuer may call in the securities early, forcing conversion. This situation may present the investor with a substantially reduced rate of return.

THE STRUCTURE OF INTEREST RATES

As we conclude this chapter, it is important to gain some perspective on the fundamental purpose of this section of the book. In reality, Chapters 8, 9, 10, and 11 should be viewed as a unit, tied together by a common subject: what determines the level of and changes in interest rates and security yields. In Chapter 8, we argued that there is *one* interest rate that underlies all interest rates and is a component of all rates. This is the *risk-free* (or pure) rate of interest, which is a measure of the opportunity cost of holding cash and a measure of the reward for saving rather than spending all of our income on consumption. All other interest rates are scaled upward by varying degrees from the risk-free rate, depending on such factors as the term (maturity) of a loan, the risk of borrower default, the risk of prepayment, and the marketability, liquidity, convertibility, and tax status of the securities to which those rates apply.

There is, then, a structure to interest rates whose foundation is the risk-free rate (as determined by the demand and supply for loanable funds described in Chapter 8). Perhaps one picture of that **interest rate structure** is worth a thousand words. Recently, the yield to maturity on long-term U.S. Treasury bonds was reported as 7.40 percent, while corporate Baa bonds were quoted at an average yield of 8.60 percent. As Exhibit 11–6 indicates, each of these rates, like *all* interest rates, is really a summation of rewards (premiums) paid to lenders of funds to get those investors to hold a particular security. Each reward or premium is merely compensation for bearing some kind of *risk*; for example, (1) the risk of giving up liquidity and accepting greater price risk from buying a longer maturity security, (2) the risk of inflation over the term of a security, (3) the risk that the borrower will default on some or all of his promised payments, (4) the risk that some securities can be called in before they mature and the investor may have to reinvest her money at a lower interest rate, and (5) the risk of taking on a security with a weak resale market (low marketability). Each interest rate or yield that we see in today's market is the *sum* of some or all of these risk-premium factors plus the real risk-free interest rate. And when interest rates change, that change may be due to a change in the risk-free rate or to a change in any of the risk-premium factors cited above.

Exhibit 11–6   **An Example of the Structure of Interest Rates in the Financial System**

During the month of
March 1996:
The long-term
U.S. Treasury bond rate averaged 7.40% + 1.20% = 8.60%

Corporate Baa bond
rate averaged:

Estimated components of the rate on long-term U.S. Treasury bonds		
Rate premium for buying long-term security rather than short-term security	Liquidity premium	+ 1.40%
Rate premium for inflation risk	Expected inflation	+ 2.00%
Rate premium for foregoing consumption and saving money	Risk-free real-rate of interest	+ 4.00%
	Total	7.40%

Estimated components of the rate or yield spread between corporate Baa bond rate and long-term Treasury bond rate		
Rate premium for accepting less marketable security	Premium for lower marketability	+ 0.20%
Rate premium for accepting risk security might be called	Call risk premium	+ 0.25%
Rate premium for accepting risk of borrower default	Default risk premium	+ 0.75%
	Total	1.20%

Source: Bond rates derived from Federal Reserve Statistical Release H.15, March 18, 1996; interest-rate components estimated by the author.

Truly, interest rates are a complex phenomenon, affected by many factors. We need to keep this complexity in mind as we proceed to the next chapter and take on the difficult task of trying to anticipate and forecast interest rate changes and discover how to hedge against possible losses from interest rate movements.

KEY TERMS AND CONCEPTS IN THIS CHAPTER

marketability	junk bonds	tax-exempt securities
liquidity	call privilege	convertibility
default risk	prepayment risk	interest rate structure
expected yield	event risk	

STUDY QUESTIONS

1. Define the term *marketability*. Explain its importance to the securities investor and its relationship to the yield on a financial instrument.

2. Explain the meaning of the phrase *default risk*. What factors appear to influence the degree of default risk displayed by a security? In what ways are security ratings designed to reflect default risk?

3. What are *junk bonds*? Why are they issued? How does their actual yield compare to their default risk?

4. What is a *call privilege*? Why is this privilege an advantage to the security issuer and a disadvantage to the investor?

5. What types of risk are encountered by the investor in callable securities? Does the coupon rate on a bond influence its call risk?

6. Which kinds of securities are favored by current U.S. tax laws? Explain why these particular financial instruments are favored.

7. What portion of the income generated by municipal bonds is tax exempt, and what portion is taxable under federal law? Why do you think the law is structured in this way? Should it be?

8. Explain the relationship between the investor's marginal tax rate and after-tax yields on corporate and municipal bonds. Would municipal bonds be a worthwhile investment for you today? Why?

9. Define the term *convertibility*. Why are convertibles sometimes called *hybrid securities*? Convertible bonds typically carry lower yields than nonconvertible bonds of the same maturity and risk class. Explain why.

10. What is meant by the *interest rate structure*? What does the structure of rates tell us about the difficulties involved in trying to forecast interest rates?

PROBLEMS

1. In a recent Federal Reserve publication, the following market interest rates or yields were reported:

Three-month Treasury bills	7.62%
One-year Treasury bills	7.40
Five-year Treasury bonds	8.33
Long-term Treasury bonds	8.64
Corporate Baa bonds	10.20
Aaa municipal bonds	9.24

    Calculate the difference in percentage points and basis points between these rates. Explain the rate differences you derive in terms of the factors discussed in Chapters 10 and 11.

2. The market yield to maturity on a risky bond is currently listed at 14.50 percent. The risk-free interest rate is estimated to be 9.25 percent. What is the default risk premium, all other factors removed? The promised yield on this bond is 15 percent. A certain investor, looking at this bond, estimates there is a 25 percent probability the bond will pay 15 percent at maturity, a 50 percent probability it will pay a 10 percent return, and a 25 percent probability it will yield only 5 percent. What is the bond's expected yield? What is this investor's anticipated default loss? Will the investor buy this bond?

3. A 10-year corporate bond was issued on January 1, 1992, with call privilege attached. The bond was sold to investors at $1,000 par value with a 10 percent coupon rate. The bond

was called on January 1, 1995, at a price to holders of par plus one year's coupon income. At the time, the prevailing market interest rate on securities of comparable quality and term was 8 percent. If a holder of this bond reinvested the call price at 8 percent for 7 years, calculate this investor's holding-period yield for the entire period of 10 years. How much yield did the investor lose as a result of the call?

4. Aaa-rated municipal bonds are carrying a market yield today of 5.25 percent, while Aaa-rated corporate bonds have current market yields of 11.50 percent. What is the break-even tax rate that would make a taxable investor indifferent between these two types of bonds?

5. An investor purchases a 10-year U.S. government bond for $800. The bond's coupon rate is 10 percent and, at time of purchase, it still had five years remaining until maturity. If the investor holds the bond until it matures and collects the $1,000 par value from the Treasury and his marginal tax rate remains at 28 percent, what will be his after-tax yield to maturity?

6. The current market yield on U.S. Treasury bills (three-month maturities) is 5.38 percent. Investors are expecting zero inflation over the next three months, but the expected rate of long-term inflation is determined to be 2.25 percent and the long-term U.S. Treasury bond rate stands at 8.16 percent. The premium for accepting less marketability in a security is 30 basis points; the default risk premium for lower-grade (Baa) corporate bonds is 105 basis points, and the call risk premium is 29 basis points. Using this information and the concept of the structure of interest rates developed in this chapter, what is the liquidity premium? What is the yield on Baa corporate bonds?

SELECTED REFERENCES

Cook, Timothy Q. "Some Factors Affecting Long-Term Yield Spreads in Recent Years." *Monthly Review.* Federal Reserve Bank of Richmond, September 1973, pp. 2–14.

Crabbe, Lee. "Callable Corporate Bonds: A Vanishing Breed." *Finance and Economics Discussion Series #155.* Board of Governors of the Federal Reserve System, March 1991.

Ederington, L.H.; J.B. Yawitz; and B.E. Roberts. "The Informational Content of Bond Ratings." *Journal of Financial Research* 10 (Fall 1987), pp. 211–26.

Fisher, Lawrence. "Determinants of Risk Premiums on Corporate Bonds." *Journal of Political Economy,* June 1959, pp. 217–37.

Hickman, W. Braddock. *Corporate Bond Quality and Investor Experience.* New York: National Bureau of Economic Research, 1958.

Holthausen, Robert W., and Richard W. Leftwich. "The Effect of Bond Rating Changes on Common Stock Prices." *Journal of Financial Economics* 17 (1986), pp. 57–89.

Jaffe, Dwight M. "Cyclical Variations in the Risk Structure of Interest Rates." *Journal of Monetary Economics,* July 1975, pp. 309–25.

Jen, Frank C., and James E. Wert. "The Value of the Deferred Call Privilege." *The National Banking Review,* March 1966, pp. 269–78.

———. "The Effect of Call Risk on Corporate Bond Yields." *Journal of Finance,* December 1967, pp. 637–51.

———. "The Deferred Call Provision and Corporate Bond Yields." *Journal of Financial and Quantitative Analysis,* June 1968, pp. 157–69.

Kraus, Alan. "The Bond Refunding Decision in an Efficient Market." *Journal of Financial and Quantitative Analysis* VIII, No. 5 (1973).

Pye, Gordon. "The Value of the Call Option on a Bond." *Journal of Political Economy,* April 1966, pp. 200–05.

———. "The Value of Call Deferment on a Bond: Some Empirical Results." *Journal of Finance,* December 1967, pp. 623–36.

Scott, James. "The Probability of Bankruptcy: A Comparison of Empirical Predictions and Theoretical Models." *Journal of Banking and Finance* 5 (1981), pp. 317–44.

Yago, Glenn. *Junk Bonds: How High Yield Securities Restructured America.* New York and Oxford: Oxford University Press, 1991.

Chapter 12

Interest Rate Forecasting and Hedging against Interest Rate Risk

LEARNING OBJECTIVES IN THIS CHAPTER

- To examine the effect that the business cycle of expansions and recessions has on interest rates.
- To determine whether interest rates display seasonal movements.
- To review the most popular methods used to forecast interest rates in recent years.
- To examine several methods used today to hedge a borrower or a lender against the risk of loss from changes in interest rates.

In this section of the book, we have looked thus far at several of the most important factors that cause interest rates and security prices to change over time. Included in our survey have been such powerful rate- and price-determining factors as savings, investment demand, inflation, default risk, taxes, call features, and marketability. Yet even this impressive list of influential factors does not account for all of the changes in interest rates and security prices we observe daily in the real world. Political developments at home and abroad, changes in government policy, changes in corporate earnings and business conditions, announcements of new security offerings, and thousands of other bits of information flood the financial markets daily and bring about fluctuations in interest rates and security prices. In fact, for actively traded securities, demand and supply forces are continually shifting, minute by minute, so that investors interested in these securities must constantly stay abreast of the latest developments in the financial marketplace.

The Influence of the Business Cycle in Shaping Interest Rates

Amid the turmoil of daily movements in interest rates and security prices there are also long-term factors that seem to create trends or patterns in both rates and prices. One of the most obvious patterns relates to the condition of the economy — whether the economy is in a period of expansion with jobs and income rising (often accompanied by rising inflation) or in a period of recession with falling production and rising unemployment. These phases of the **business cycle** may last months or years, and interest rates tend to move with them because the demand for and supply of loanable funds responds to the business cycle. *Interest rates tend to fall* (and the prices of bonds and other debt securities rise) *during a business recession, while interest rates typically rise* (and debt security prices fall) *during a period of economic expansion.*

None of this should be particularly surprising. An expansion period encourages businesses and consumers to borrow more relative to the available supply of loanable funds,

Exhibit 12–1 **Average Yields of Long-Term Treasury, Corporate, and Municipal Bonds**

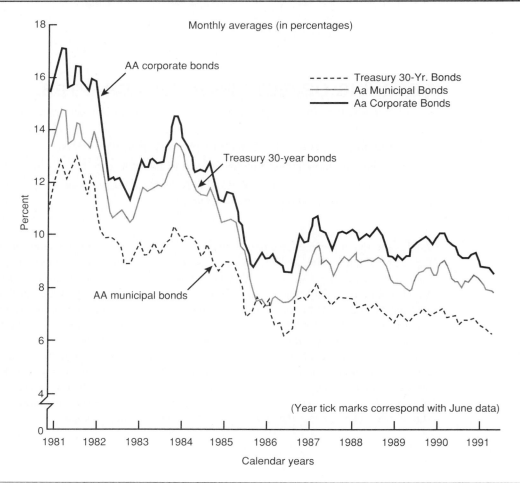

and the resulting increase in the demand for loanable funds drives up interest rates. In contrast, during recessions businesses and consumers become more cautious, reducing their borrowings relative to the available supply of loanable funds and building up their savings as a precaution against possible unemployment and loss of income. Interest rates usually fall during such periods under the combined pressure of reduced credit demands and a larger supply of savings.

The typical cyclical movement in interest rates is illustrated in Exhibit 12–1, which tracks changes in yields on long-term U.S. Treasury, corporate, and municipal bonds. For example, in 1982 the U.S. economy entered a business recession and interest rates declined sharply. Then, interest rates rose in 1983 as the economy recovered and grew rapidly. However, interest rates retreated in 1984, 1985, and the first half of 1986 as the economy's growth rate slowed, inflation moderated, and loan demand tapered off. More rapid economic growth then set in late in 1986 and into 1987, and interest rates correspondingly edged higher again, only to fall as the U.S. economy entered yet another recession early in the 1990s.

Relative Movements in Short- and Long-Term Interest Rates and Security Prices over the Business Cycle

The cyclical movements in the economy do not fall evenly across the broad spectrum of interest rates, however. In general, short-term interest rates (those attached to money market securities) are more sensitive to business cycle changes than are long-term interest rates on bonds and other capital market securities. Exhibit 12–2 depicts the typical pattern displayed by long- and short-term interest rates during the course of the business cycle.

During an expansion period, when the economy is growing at a rapid pace, all interest rates — both long- and short-term — tend to rise. However, short-term interest rates typi-

Exhibit 12–2   **Interest Rates over the Course of a Business Cycle**

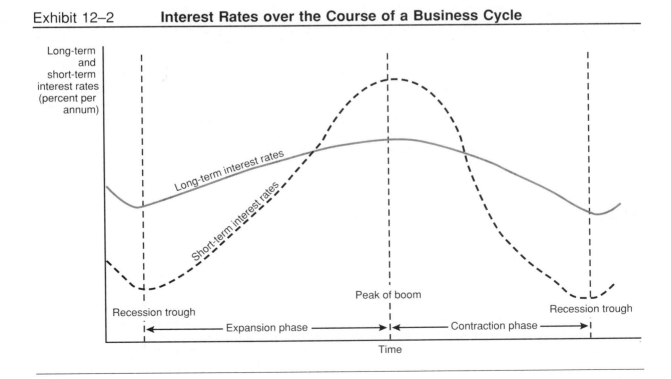

cally rise *faster* than long-term rates and, at some point in the later stages of the expansion, may climb above long-term rates. This means that at certain phases of the business cycle, especially around cyclical peaks, borrowers negotiating for a loan for, say, six months will actually pay higher annual interest rates than for the same loan stretched over 5 or 10 years. The yield curve typically has a positive slope over the expansion phase of a business cycle, probably due to expectations of rising interest rates on the part of investors. Around the cyclical peak and in the early stages of the ensuing business recession, however, yield curves usually assume a negative slope, as investors come to expect declining interest rates. Once the expansion phase of the cycle is over and the economy starts down into a recession, *all* rates begin to fall. But short-term interest rates typically drop faster than long-term rates and fall below long-term rates as the recession deepens. At some point midway in a recession, the yield curve typically assumes a *positive* slope. Once the trough (low point) of the recession is reached and recovery begins, the process is repeated, with short-term interest rates rising more rapidly than long-term rates.

Why do long-term and short-term interest rates behave in this way? Their behavior reflects another important relationship that exists between security prices and interest rates in the financial system:

Long-term security prices tend to be more volatile than the prices of short-term securities. In contrast, short-term interest rates tend to be more volatile than long-term interest rates.

Fluctuations in market *prices*, then, tend to be greater the longer the maturity of a security. This conclusion follows logically if we examine the yield-to-maturity formula discussed in Chapter 9. This formula indicates that the market price of any security equals the present value of *all* its promised future payments. With a long-term security, more future payments are affected by any given change in interest rate than is true for a short-term security. Therefore, any given increase in interest rates will bring about a greater decrease in the price (present value) of a long-term security than in the price of a short-term security. Similarly, for the same decrease in interest rates, the price of a short-term security likely will rise by less than the price of a long-term security.

The greater volatility of long-term security prices means that investors in long-term financial instruments face greater risk of capital loss (increased *principal risk*) than investors in short-term securities. Partly as a result, interest rates charged by lenders on long-term loans are usually higher than those charged for short-term credit, other factors held equal. Lenders must be compensated for the added risk of price fluctuations associated with long-term financial instruments. Of course, the long-term investor has the offsetting advantage of receiving a more stable rate of return (reduced *income risk*) than the short-term investor, because long-term interest rates are less volatile than short-term interest rates.

SEASONALITY

Just as interest rates change with cycles in business activity, there is evidence that interest rates also display **seasonality**, tending to be higher at some times of the year than at others. If seasonal rate patterns were consistent and predictable, this would be important information for both borrowers and lenders, for it would suggest the best times of the year to borrow and lend money. Although there is a diversity of opinion on the subject, most studies seem to agree that interest rates *do* display seasonal patterns. Short-term rates tend to be pushed higher through summer and fall due to rising seasonal demand for short-term funds, especially as businesses stock their shelves with inventory for the fall and for the major holidays that come late in the year. From January through May, on the other hand, slackening demand for short-term credit encourages short-term interest rates to fall, *other factors held equal.* Long-term interest rates, on the other hand, tend to experience upward pressure in the late spring through midsummer (June or July), related to heavy construction activity during this time of the year, and often approach seasonal lows in the winter months.

Several notes of caution should be added here, however. First, these seasonal patterns are easily overridden by other factors, such as changes in the economy or in government policy. For example, central banks like the Federal Reserve System frequently use their monetary policy tools to counteract seasonal changes in the supply and demand for loanable funds. Second, research evidence suggests that seasonal patterns are *not* stable over time.[1] Third, unpredictable events, such as droughts, changes in laws and regulations, and political turmoil, often create false signals of seasonal interest rate pressures. In general, we can say that seasonal interest rate patterns probably exist, but they are usually of minor importance in explaining most interest rate movements.

FORECASTING INTEREST RATES: ADVANTAGES AND PROBLEMS

The tendency of interest rates to move with the business cycle and to some extent with seasonal pressures has led some financial analysts to believe that broad interest rate movements can be predicted.[2] By using variables that reflect changing economic conditions, it has seemed logical to expect that at least longer-term movements in interest rates can be forecast (assuming, of course, that the forecaster has confidence in the forecast of the economy itself).

Advantages of Rate Forecasting

Clearly, it would be an advantage to almost everyone to be able to forecast interest rates accurately. Borrowers could plan to seek loans at those times when rates were supposed to be the lowest, saving thousands of dollars in interest costs. Banks and other lenders of funds could reduce their exposure to earnings risk and default risk by charging loan rates that are in line with their forecast of deposit interest rates. They would also be able to assess their borrowing customers' ability to meet future payments on new floating-rate loans and avoid many loan troubles in the future.

Problems in Forecasting Interest Rates

Unfortunately, while solving the problem of how to forecast interest rates would be enormously useful to almost everyone, the problem's solution is far from easy and may be impossible. For one thing, as we saw in Chapter 8, there is continuing controversy over which of several theories — loanable funds, rational expectations, and so on — explain how and why rates change. This matters greatly, because each theory suggests that we gather somewhat different information to predict which way interest rates are headed. Moreover, if the financial markets are efficient, as much research evidence suggests, all data relevant in determining security prices and interest rates should already be captured in those prices and rates. The theory of efficient markets implies that, to be consistently right, the forecaster either must have access to data the market does not now possess or must

---

[1]See, for example, Kohn (1974) and Barth and Bennett (1975).

[2]This section is based, in part, on Rose's earlier article in *Canadian Banker* (1984) and is used with the permission of that journal.

outguess the market on the implications of new information that has yet to be revealed. This is a difficult assignment!

An added problem is that current statistical forecasting tools may be too crude to generate a consistently accurate forecast of rate movements. After all, we live in an economy composed of millions of households, businesses, and units of government. Each year tens of thousands of these individuals and institutions enter the financial markets to save (supply loanable funds) or to borrow (demand loanable funds). Each and every individual financial decision affects either the demand for or supply of loanable funds and therefore influences the price of credit. To really know for sure which way interest rates are headed, we would need a working model that incorporates those thousands of individual financial decisions. Even the largest, most sophisticated econometric forecasting models, some of which contain hundreds of equations, cannot deal with the enormity of detail in today's financial markets. Perhaps as business and household computers are increasingly linked to each other and the majority of money flows are handled electronically, we may be better able to track credit demand and supply forces and anticipate future interest rate changes, but that era still lies ahead of us.

APPROACHES TO MODERN INTEREST RATE FORECASTING

The inherent difficulties in interest rate and price forecasting have not stopped financial analysts from attempting to predict the future. They are impressed by the continuing presence of broad trends in interest rates, particularly those related to the business cycle and to Federal Reserve monetary policy. A number of forecasting models have been developed in recent years; some have performed slightly better than pure chance for short periods of time. Several of the more popular forecasting approaches are reviewed below.

Money Supply Approaches

Many financial analysts attempt to forecast short-term changes in interest rates by tracking money supply figures. Each week the Federal Reserve System releases estimates of recent rates of growth in its various measures of the U.S. money supply. Among the more prominent of these measures are M1, the sum of currency and coin held by the public plus transaction (payments) deposits, and especially M2, the sum of M1 plus small-denomination savings deposits.[3]

Recall from Chapter 8 that changes in the money supply can be linked in theory to interest rate changes in several different ways. For example, the so-called **money-supply liquidity effect** suggests that an increase in money supply growth (relative to money demand) results in lower interest rates in the short run. On the other hand, slower money growth (relative to money demand) should lead to higher interest rates in the short run. A contrary force, the **money-supply expectations effect**, argues that when actual money supply growth exceeds the public's expected rate of money growth, interest rates will tend to *rise*, perhaps due to the public's fear of more inflation. Conversely, a slower than expected money growth rate may lead to *lower* interest rates, as investors come to expect less inflation or faster money growth in the future.

Recall from our discussion of interest rate theories in Chapter 8 that money supply changes can also influence interest rates through a **money-supply income effect**. An

---

[3]See Chapters 2 and 21 for a more complete discussion of the measures of the money supply.

increase in spending and income in the economy increases the public's demand for money, other factors held constant. If the money supply remains fixed or grows more slowly than money demand, the relative increase in money demand will lead to higher interest rates. Conversely, a decline or slower growth in money demand — perhaps related to slowing in the economy — will put downward pressure on interest rates, other factors being constant. Clearly, there should be a *positive* correlation between income and spending in the economy and market interest rates through income-caused changes in the demand for money, according to the money-supply income effect.

How might an interest rate forecaster use the *money-supply income effect*? Let's suppose that the government has just released an estimate that nominal gross domestic product (GDP) — a widely used barometer of spending in the economy — will increase 8 percent next year. However, the Federal Reserve System has announced that its expected growth range for money supply growth will be just 4 to 6 percent next year. If the money supply does in fact grow this slowly while the public plans to increase its aggregate spending (GDP) by 8 percent, what must happen to interest rates? Clearly, they must *rise* to bring about a faster rate of turnover (velocity) in the money supply in order to accommodate the higher volume of planned spending.

Of course, if the Fed achieves its relatively low money growth target, it is highly unlikely that GDP will be able to increase a full 8 percentage points, because the resulting higher interest rates will discourage some borrowing and spending by the public. However, the point is that we can get a clue about the *direction* of future interest rates by comparing money supply growth estimated for a future period with forecasts of economic activity for the *same* period (assuming we have confidence in both money supply and economic forecasts). Thus,

1. If projected money supply growth is greater than projected GDP income or spending growth, interest rates are likely to *fall*.

2. If projected money supply growth is less than projected GDP income or spending growth, interest rates are likely to *rise*.

Inflation and the Fisher Effect

In Chapter 10, we discussed still another approach to interest rate forecasting: the **Fisher effect**, which asserts that *the nominal (published) interest rate charged by a lender of funds must equal the lender's expected real rate of return on the loan plus the expected rate of inflation over the life of the loan.* Many economists have argued that the expected real rate is relatively constant — perhaps in the 3 to 3.5 percent range — over the long run. If so, observed changes in nominal interest rates will reflect changes in the rate of inflation expected by lenders in the financial marketplace.

The following table suggests a simple forecasting strategy using the Fisher effect:

Forecasting Interest Rates Using the Fisher Effect

If Lenders in the Marketplace Expect the Inflation Rate over the Coming Year to Average	And the Real Rate of Interest Is Expected to Be	Then the Nominal Interest Rate on a One-Year Loan According to the Fisher Effect Will Be
1%	3 to 3.5%	4 to 4.5%
2	3 to 3.5	5 to 5.5
3	3 to 3.5	6 to 6.5
4	3 to 3.5	7 to 7.5

Of course, a key problem with this approach is estimating the rate of inflation expected by lenders. Unfortunately, there is little agreement on the most accurate method for making such an estimate. One commonly used approach is to calculate a weighted average of past rates of inflation and use that average as a proxy for expected inflation. This is a crude approximation because we do not know exactly what factors the public considers in formulating its inflation forecast. More recently, periodic surveys of economists and investors have been used to represent inflationary expectations in the marketplace, but such an approach suffers from being incomplete and possibly irrelevant. Expectations can change so fast that any opinion survey could be outdated before its results are published.

Econometric Models

The four interest rate relationships we have discussed to this point — the money-supply liquidity, expectations, and income effects, and the Fisher effect — have been used in a large number of interest rate forecasting models. These so-called **econometric models** often employ current and lagged values of money, income or total spending, and past rates of inflation to predict short- and long-term interest rates through the application of statistical regression techniques. The larger models simultaneously measure changes in total spending on goods and services, business investment, inflation, employment, and a broad spectrum of interest rates, forecasting several variables simultaneously and considering interactions among both predictor and predicted variables. Among the best known models are those used by Chase Econometric Associates, Data Resources, Inc. (DRI), and Wharton Econometric Forecasting Associates, Inc. Such models are truly impressive in their complexity; for example, the Wharton model forecasts about 10,000 different variables. The complex interactions in such models between forecast variables and causal factors are illustrated in Exhibit 12–3.

An example of a relatively simple econometric model prepared by the Federal Reserve Bank of St. Louis is shown in Exhibit 12–4. This simple model contains only eight equations and generates quarterly forecasts for seven economic and financial variables, including two interest rates — the yield on Aaa corporate bonds and the short-term commercial paper rate. The type of interest rate forecasting equations used in the St. Louis model is

Exhibit 12–3	**Linking Interest Rates to the Economy in Major Econometric Models**

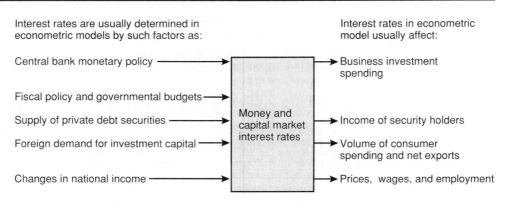

Source: Peter S. Rose, "Interest Rates, Economic Forecasting and Bank Profits," *Canadian Banker*, June 1984.

Exhibit 12–4   **Flow Diagram of the St. Louis Econometric Model**

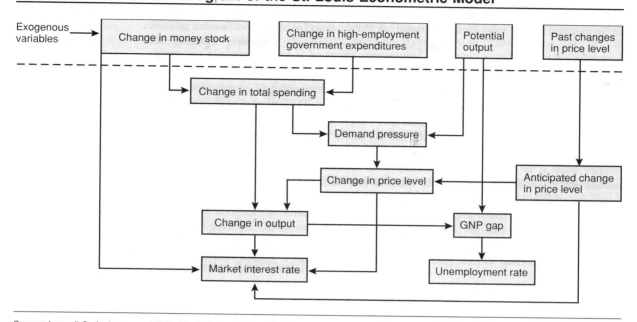

Source: Leonall C. Anderson and Keith M. Carlson, "A Monetarist Model for Economic Stabilization," *Review*, Federal Reserve Bank of St. Louis, April 1970, pp. 7–25.

illustrated by the following equation, which tracks the Aaa corporate bond rate, a key capital market interest rate:

$$
\begin{aligned}
\text{Moody's seasoned corporate Aaa bond rate in quarter } t &= 1.28 - .06 \left\{ \begin{array}{c} \text{Annual rate of} \\ \text{change in} \\ \text{money stock, } t \end{array} \right\} + 1.42 \left\{ \begin{array}{c} \text{Dummy variable} \\ \text{representing} \\ \text{specific time} \\ \text{periods} \end{array} \right\} \\
&+ \sum_{i=1}^{16} a_i \left\{ \begin{array}{c} \text{Annual rate of} \\ \text{change in total} \\ \text{output in the} \\ \text{economy, } t - i \end{array} \right\} + \sum_{i=0}^{16} b_i \left\{ \begin{array}{c} \text{Annual rate of change} \\ \text{in the U.S. price level} \\ \text{divided by the U.S.} \\ \text{unemployment rate} \\ \text{index, } t - i \end{array} \right\}
\end{aligned} \tag{12-1}
$$

Careful inspection of the preceding equation reveals the prominent roles that changes in the money stock (reflecting primarily the money-supply liquidity effect), changes in output (reflecting primarily the money-supply income effect), and changes in the price level relative to unemployment (reflecting money-supply expectations and Fisher effects) are believed to play in influencing interest rates.

The Flow of Funds Accounts as a Source of Forecasting Information

Still another forecasting approach that depends on forecasts of other variables is the Flow of Funds approach. The basic idea is to estimate the total demand for credit from different borrowing sectors in the economy, *assuming that interest rates remain at current levels.*

This might be done, for example, by extrapolating past trends in the volume of business loans, consumer loans, government borrowing, and foreign borrowing into future time periods. The Flow of Funds Accounts (discussed in Chapter 3) can be used to provide historical data with which to make such forecasts. Similarly, we can estimate the projected supply of credit from key financial institutions such as banks, insurance companies, and pension funds.

Once derived, the projected demand for credit in the economy can be compared to estimated credit supplies. If, at today's level of interest rates,

1. Projected credit demand is greater than projected credit supply, interest rates will tend to *rise*.

2. Projected credit demand is less than projected credit supply, interest rates will tend to *fall*.

3. Projected credit demand equals projected credit supply, interest rates will remain essentially *unchanged*.

This approach has been used, with variations, by such well-known institutions as Bankers Trust Company and Salomon Brothers. One obvious drawback is the numerous estimates of various sources of credit supply and credit demand that must be made, increasing the opportunities for error.

Following the Forward Calendar of New Security Offerings

One rate-determining variable often included in larger econometric models is the supply of debt securities offered in the open market at any given time. Theory suggests that an increase in offerings of *new* notes and bonds should drive interest rates higher because these offerings represent additional demand for credit. Conversely, when the volume of new debt offerings declines, lessened demand for credit should lead to lower interest rates, *ceteris paribus*.

This is the reason why many market analysts follow the announced **forward calendar** of new security offerings expected to come to market in coming weeks. Such information is regularly reported in *The Wall Street Journal* and in financial news sheets and magazines. For example, *The Wall Street Journal* might report the following:

- The Treasury will be issuing $22 billion in five-year notes this week, about $4 billion more than this time last year.

- Offerings of new state and local government bonds are scheduled to reach $3.7 billion due to heavy school and utility construction.

- In corporate issues, market offerings will top an estimated $2.5 billion, led by Textron selling a planned $175 million in notes and debentures.

Any indication that the market is becoming clogged with increased quantities of unsold notes and bonds usually triggers a forecast of rising interest rates and falling security prices in the near term.

Market Expectations and Implied Rate Forecasting

Our discussion of the rational expectations theory of interest rates in Chapter 8 and the expectations hypothesis of the yield curve in Chapter 10 suggests the critical role that public opinion, about the future, can play in influencing the financial markets. Recall from our earlier discussion of the expectations hypothesis, for example, that the slope of the yield curve itself *implies* a forecast of interest rate changes expected by the public.

For example, suppose that 30-day maturity U.S. Treasury bills are currently selling in the market to yield 10 percent, while 60-day bills carry current yields of 10.5 percent. This obvious upward slope in the short-term yield curve carries an **implied rate forecast** of what investors in the market expect Treasury bill rates to be in the next 30 days. Specific-ally, the 30-day bill rate 30 days from now is expected to be

$$\frac{\text{Current 30-day Treasury bill rate} + \text{30-day forward (expected) Treasury bill rate}}{2} = \text{Current 60-day Treasury bill rate}$$

or

$$\frac{10.0\% + \text{30-day forward (expected) Treasury bill rate}}{2} = 10.50\%$$

and thus,

$$\text{30-day forward (expected) rate on bills} = 11.00\%$$

The yield curve is projecting an 11 percent, 30-day Treasury bill rate one month from today. Why? Because, according to the unbiased expectations hypothesis, investors in an efficient market should earn the same average return over the next 60 days whether they buy a 10.5 percent, 60-day Treasury bill today or a 10 percent, 30-day Treasury bill today followed by an 11 percent, 30-day bill purchased one month from now.

A more accurate forecast of the forward rate implied by the current slope of the yield curve can be found from:

$$_{t+n}r_{kt} = \left| \frac{(1 + {}_tR_{n+kt})^{n+k}}{(1 + {}_tR_{nt})^n} \right| - 1 \tag{12-2}$$

where the security whose rate is being forecast covers k periods and the loan to the borrower begins at time $t + n$. (This formula is derived from solving Equation 10–6 in Chapter 10 for any future k-period loan rate.) For the Treasury bill whose rate we were trying to forecast in the preceding example, we have a loan period of 30 days, beginning 30 days from now. Therefore, we let $k = 1$, meaning one 30-day loan period, and $n = 1$, meaning the 30-day loan, whose rate we wish to forecast, begins one 30-day period after the current 30-day period. Thus, with a current 30-day bill rate of 10 percent and a rate at the end of the forecast period of 10.50 percent, the predicted interest rate must be

$$_{t+1}r_{1t} = \left| \frac{(1.1050)^2}{(1.10)^1} \right|^{1/1} - 1 = \frac{1.221}{1.10} - 1 = 0.11, \text{ or } 11\%$$

which matches our prediction above.

Another implied market forecast of future changes in interest rates is conveyed by current prices on financial futures contracts — a subject discussed more fully in Chapter 13. A *financial futures contract* is an agreement between a buyer and a seller to deliver a designated amount and type of securities days, weeks, or months in the future, but at a price agreed upon today. Thus, we might assume that the current prices on such contracts reflect investors' expectations about the levels of interest rates and security prices likely to prevail around the future delivery date of the securities named in the futures contract.

For example, *The Wall Street Journal* reported that contracts for the delivery of $1 million in U.S. Treasury bills in March 1996 were selling for $94.91 (assuming a $100 face value) on September 4, 1995. This price translated into an interest yield of 5.09 percent if the Treasury bills were held to maturity. In contrast, Treasury bills of comparable maturity available for immediate (cash) delivery were selling in the open market on June 14th for a yield of about 5.30 percent. Clearly, investors in Treasury bill futures contracts were signaling an expectation of falling short-term interest rates between September 1995 and March 1996.

The Consensus Forecast

Expectations models are useful barometers of current market opinion, but the financial market forecaster must recognize their inherent limitations. They give us a reading only on what the marketplace — the average investor — *expects*, not necessarily on what will happen. Expectations are often disappointed; other factors frequently intrude to upset the most convincing forecasts. Indeed, no one forecasting method has demonstrated its consistent superiority over the others. Perhaps the optimal approach is for the interest rate forecaster to use several different methods, checking to see whether a **consensus forecast** emerges. Still, the forecasting process is laden with difficulties. Many analysts today confine their forecasts to interest rate predictions only one or two months in advance, with continual reassessment and revision as new information appears.

INTEREST RATE RISK HEDGING STRATEGIES

The increasingly volatile interest rates in recent years, coupled with the inherent difficulties of rate forecasting, have led many individuals and institutions to find ways to insulate themselves from rate changes. If rate changes cannot be reliably forecast, it may be possible to *hedge* against the damaging effects of increasing or decreasing interest rates. Although several rate hedging methods have been developed, there is a price for such interest rate insurance. *Hedging lowers interest rate risk but also reduces the potential profits that could be earned by correctly anticipating the direction and magnitude of future interest rate changes.* In the paragraphs that follow we look at several popular tools for controlling interest rate risk. In Chapter 13, we look further into dealing with interest rate risk using financial futures and option contracts.

Duration

In Chapter 10, we discussed the concept of **duration**, a present value-weighted measure of the maturity of a loan or security. In that chapter, we pointed out that an investor could *immunize* his or her portfolio against interest rate changes by setting the

$$\text{Duration of a loan or security portfolio} = \text{Length of the investor's planned holding period} \qquad (12\text{--}3)$$

With this investment strategy, a rise in interest rates will reduce the market value of our investor's portfolio, but the interest return on reinvested cash flows from the portfolio will increase by an offsetting amount. The investor's *total return* will be stabilized. Similarly, falling interest rates reduce the interest return from reinvesting earnings from loans or securities, but with a duration set equal to holding-period length the market value of those financial assets will rise by a corresponding amount. Again, the total return will be stabilized.

For a financial institution (such as a bank) that both borrows and lends funds simultaneously, a good immunizing strategy is to set

$$\text{Asset duration} = \text{Liability duration} \tag{12–4}$$

In this case, changes in interest rates should affect the institution's assets and liabilities *equally*, so that changes in the market value of the institution's assets offset changes in the market value of its liabilities. The financial institution's *net worth* will be protected no matter which way interest rates move.[4]

Unfortunately, as we saw in Chapter 10, duration has limitations. It is often difficult to find desirable loans or securities with durations exactly matching the investor's holding period. Duration changes continually, and, therefore, the risk-hedging investor must continually recalculate his position. Moreover, duration models assume parallel changes in all interest rates (both short and long term). It is not clear how effective this hedging strategy will be if interest rates do not behave in such a lockstep fashion. Fortunately, other hedging devices can serve as a backstop to duration.

Stripped Securities

One innovation of the past decade that has made it easier for investors to use duration to hedge against interest rate risk is the development of **stripped securities**. In the early 1980s, several securities dealers discovered that they could separate the interest payments promised by a U.S. Treasury bond from its principal value (which is paid back to the investor at maturity) and treat each of these promised future payments as a security by itself that could be sold to the public. Each promised interest and principal payment in effect becomes a discount bond, sold for less than the amount of the payment it promises but rising in value as the date for that payment gets nearer. Each interest payment from a stripped bond is called an *interest-only security* (IO), which matures the day the Treasury makes the promised payment. The principal (or face value) of a stripped security is called a *principal-only security* (PO). Each PO is a discount bond whose market value increases over time until it equals the stripped bond's face value on the day the U.S. Treasury retires that bond.

For example, a five-year U.S. Treasury bond paying interest every six months (that is, $5 \times 2 = 10$ total interest payments) could be split into 11 discount bonds, one bond for each promised interest payment and another for the bond's principal (face) value. Each IO or PO can be bought and sold in the open market any number of times before it matures. In 1985 the U.S. Treasury decided to permit the stripping of book-entry securities kept at the Federal Reserve banks in a program called STRIPS, which significantly lowers the cost of stripping because special trust agreements are not needed. Recently, security dealers have been stripping both U.S. Treasury securities and mortgage-backed bonds.[5]

---

[4]Actually, a solvent financial institution would want to set Asset duration = Liability duration × Total liabilities/Total assets to fully protect its net worth from loss due to changing interest rates. This is true because a solvent institution's assets must total more than its liabilities; otherwise the firm is facing bankruptcy.

[5]Stripped securities can also be "unstripped" and restored to their original form — a process called *rebundling* — for those investors who prefer more conventional securities. Today many government securities are stripped and

One of the great advantages of stripped securities is that *their duration equals their maturity*. An investor concerned about hedging against interest rate risk can simply find an IO or PO with a time to maturity that matches his or her planned holding period, buy the stripped security, and hold it to maturity. No matter what changes in interest rates occur during the holding period, the rate of return and the terminal value of the investment is locked in. The stripped security's gross yield before taxes will be determined by the amount the security's price rises between day of purchase and the day it is retired.[6] There is no reinvestment risk with strips — that is, no loss from having to invest a security's periodic interest payments at lower market interest rates — because there are no interim interest payments.

GAP Management

A very popular hedging strategy among banks and other financial institutions is known as *interest-sensitivity analysis* (ISA) or **GAP management**. The basic strategy is to set

$$\frac{\text{Interest-sensitive}}{\text{asset holdings}} = \frac{\text{Interest-sensitive}}{\text{liabilities}} \qquad (12–5)$$

For example, a bank holding deposits whose interest rates rise along with increases in market rates could hold an equal volume of floating-rate loans. When the bank's deposit interest costs increase in a rising-rate period, interest revenues from floating-rate loans will increase by a similar amount, protecting the bank's net interest margin (or gap) between revenues and expenses.

To take a specific example, suppose that a bank has $100 million in loans and securities maturing or being renegotiated in the next 30 days so their attached interest rates can be adjusted to the latest market conditions. However, the bank's liabilities coming due or subject to renegotiation over the next 30 days amount to just $50 million (see Exhibit 12–5). This bank has a positive GAP between interest-sensitive assets and liabilities of $50 million ($100 million – $50 million); it is *asset sensitive*. If rates rise over the next 30 days, asset revenues should go up faster than interest expenses on bank liabilities, and profits will rise. However, if interest rates decline, the bank's profits will suffer because asset revenues will drop faster than liability costs.

A *liability-sensitive* position, in contrast, would find the bank having more interest-sensitive liabilities than rate-sensitive assets. The bank is going to experience rising profits if interest rates fall; however, rising interest rates will send liability costs soaring relative to asset revenues, and profits will decline. Only if interest-sensitive assets equal interest-sensitive liabilities is the bank fully hedged.

There are several problems with "gapping," however. In practice, it is difficult to match interest-sensitive assets with interest-sensitive liabilities exactly at every maturity. And any mismatches threaten the institution's profitability. Moreover, the choice of time horizon over which to measure the interest rate sensitivity of assets and liabilities seems to affect the measurement of each institution's exposure to interest rate risk and, therefore, management's response to the problem.

---

rebundled more than once during their term as the needs of investors for rate-hedging instruments change over time.

[6]There is evidence that the total value of all the strips derived from a bond *exceeds* the value of the original "unstripped" bond under certain circumstances. This extra value is most likely to appear when the yield curve is rising, due principally to the favorable tax treatment of stripped securities, which tends to give them higher after-tax cash flows than unstripped bonds. See especially Livingston and Gregory (1989).

Exhibit 12–5

Using GAP Management to Hedge a Bank's Cash Flows against Changing Interest Rates

The Bank Estimates That It Has	Time Periods That Assets or Liabilities Are Maturing or When Their Interest Rates Can Be Renegotiated				
	Next 24 Hours	Next 30 Days	Next 6 Months	Next Year	Beyond One Year
Loans and securities reaching maturity or whose interest rates can be renegotiated up or down of	$110 million	$100 million	$340 million	$550 million	$465 million
Deposits and other borrowings reaching maturity or whose interest rates can be renegotiated up or down of	$155 million	$50 million	$370 million	$560 million	$430 million
Interest-sensitivity GAP is	–$45 million	+$50 million	–$30 million	–$10 million	+$35 million
Bank's interest-sensitive position is	Liability sensitive	Asset sensitive	Liability sensitive	Liability sensitive	Asset sensitive
Bank's net interest margin and profitability will likely decline if	Interest rates rise	Interest rates fall	Interest rates rise	Interest rates rise	Interest rates fall
Management strategy	Use financial futures contracts, options, shifts in assets and/or liabilities, etc. to fill in the interest-sensitivity GAP in order to protect against interest rate risk				

Interest Rate Caps and Collars

A simpler approach to rate hedging is to take out a loan with an agreed-upon maximum interest rate. This so-called **rate cap** limits how far the loan rate can be adjusted upward by the lender if market interest rates rise. The lender will agree to impose a cap on the loan rate only in return for a fee to compensate for the risk that interest rates will rise above the cap. For example, the borrower may be asked to pay $2 million in fees to receive a three-year loan of $100 million whose rate is capped at 10 percent. The lender then may use financial futures or other rate-hedging techniques to offset the interest rate risk inherent in such a loan. Less common, but still widely used, are **rate collars**, which place both a rate cap and a rate floor (minimum loan rate) around the contracted loan rate. Thus, the borrower is protected against loan rates going too high and the lender is sheltered from loan rates dropping too low.

Interest Rate Insurance

Borrowers who need very large loans may seek **interest rate insurance** that protects against losses due to rising loan rates. The insurer agrees to reimburse the borrower for any additional interest expense the borrower must pay if rates climb above some maximum figure. For example, the borrower may take an insurance policy for a premium of $25,000 that reimburses the borrower for any interest costs above a 10 percent loan rate. If loan rates climb to 12 percent, the 2 percent excess interest cost will be returned to the borrower by the insurer. Banks and insurance companies often deal in such interest rate insurance policies.

Loan Options

Related to rate insurance are **loan options**, entitling a borrower to take a loan at a guaranteed interest rate over a stipulated period of time. If rates rise above the guaranteed rate and borrowing is necessary, the borrower will use the loan option and borrow at the guaranteed rate. On the other hand, if loan rates stay below the guaranteed rate, funds will be borrowed as needed at market rates and the option will not be used. An option fee is assessed by the lending institution regardless of whether the option is exercised.

Interest Rate SWAPs

Finally, early in the 1980s a new interest rate hedging tool — the **interest rate SWAP** — became popular. In an interest rate SWAP, two participating business firms independently borrow the same amount of money from two different lenders and then exchange interest payments with each other for a stipulated period of time. In effect, each company helps to pay off all or a portion of the interest cost owed by the other firm. The result is usually *lower* interest expense for both firms and a better *balance* between cash inflows and outflows for both firms. See, for example, Exhibit 12–6. SWAPs give a company a powerful tool in managing its liabilities, helping to offset any maturity mismatches that may exist between assets and liabilities.

SWAPs were first used by multinational banks in the Eurocurrency markets beginning in 1982. These huge banks generally possess excellent credit ratings. This means that, if they wish to, multinational banks can borrow at low, fixed long-term interest rates. However, these international lending institutions may decide to "sell" their ability to borrow long term at low cost in exchange for what they want most: access to low-cost, short-term funds carrying floating interest rates in order to match their short-term, floating-rate assets. The development of interest rate SWAPs has made maturity matchups like this possible. The first domestic U.S. interest rate SWAP occurred when the Student Loan Marketing Association, a federal agency that guarantees college student loans, and ITT Corporation exchanged interest rate payments on some of their debt. Most SWAPs today range from $25 to $75 million in dollar volume (usually called the *notional* amount of the SWAP because this dollar amount never changes hands). They usually cover periods ranging from about 3 years to 10 years and involve both fixed and floating-rate loans, with the floating rate often tied to the London Interbank Offer Rate on Eurodollar deposits (LIBOR), the prime rate, or the market yield on Treasury securities.

SWAPs work because the interest rate spreads related to default risk (called *quality spreads*) are generally greater in the long-term capital market than they are in the short-term money market. To see how SWAPs can simultaneously fulfill two goals — lower interest costs and better matching of the maturities of a firm's assets with the maturities of its liabilities — consider the following example. A top-rated corporation with a AAA credit rating can borrow in the long-term bond market at a 10 percent interest rate. However, this company prefers to borrow short-term money at a floating interest rate because it holds mainly short-term assets that roll over into cash just about the time its short-term borrowings come due. Because of the firm's top credit rating, it can borrow short-term funds at prime. Currently, the prime rate is 10 percent, but prime can rise or fall at any time.

A second company is interested in being the first company's SWAP partner, but this second firm has a credit rating no better than average. This firm has been told by its investment banker that it could issue long-term bonds at an interest rate of 11 percent. Alternatively, this lower credit-rated firm could borrow short-term funds at prime plus 0.50 percent (making a current short-term loan cost of 10% + 0.50%, or 10.50%). However, the

Exhibit 12–6   **Using Interest Rate SWAPs to Hedge against Fluctuating Interest Rates**

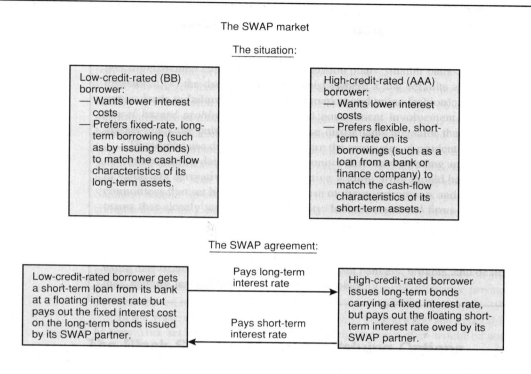

The SWAP market

The situation:

Low-credit-rated (BB) borrower:
— Wants lower interest costs
— Prefers fixed-rate, long-term borrowing (such as by issuing bonds) to match the cash-flow characteristics of its long-term assets.

High-credit-rated (AAA) borrower:
— Wants lower interest costs
— Prefers flexible, short-term rate on its borrowings (such as a loan from a bank or finance company) to match the cash-flow characteristics of its short-term assets.

The SWAP agreement:

Low-credit-rated borrower gets a short-term loan from its bank at a floating interest rate but pays out the fixed interest cost on the long-term bonds issued by its SWAP partner.

Pays long-term interest rate →

Pays short-term interest rate ←

High-credit-rated borrower issues long-term bonds carrying a fixed interest rate, but pays out the floating short-term interest rate owed by its SWAP partner.

Result: Both companies save on interest costs and better match the maturity structure of their assets and their liabilities. In reality the two parties to the SWAP exchange only the net difference in their borrowing rates, with the party owing the highest rate in the market on the payment date paying the other party the rate difference.

lower-rated firm would prefer to issue long-term bonds because it holds primarily long-term assets.

In summary, these two companies face the following situation:

The Two Parties to the SWAP:	Could Borrow in the Long-Term Bond Market at	Could Borrow in the Short-Term Loan Market at
Low credit-rated borrower	11%	Prime rate + 0.50%
High credit-rated borrower	10	Prime Rate
Quality spread	1%	0.50%

In this case, both firms can save on interest costs if each company borrows in that financial market — long-term or short-term — in which it has the greatest comparative interest cost advantage.

A bank or securities dealer might aid these two firms by helping the top-rated firm sell long-term bonds in the open market at 10 percent, while the lower-rated company agrees to make the top-rated firm's bond interest payments. In the meantime, the lower-rated firm takes out a floating-rate bank loan in the same amount at a rate of prime plus 0.50 percent.

The top-rated company agrees to pay this second firm a rate of prime less one quarter of a percentage point (25 basis points), which would cover most of the lower-rated company's interest cost. If the prime rate remains at its current level of 10 percent, each firm would owe its SWAP partner the following:

- Low credit-rated borrower pays the high-rated borrower the fixed 10 percent interest rate it owes on its long-term bonds.

- High credit-rated borrower pays the low-rated borrower prime minus one-quarter point, or 10 percent −0.25 percent.

- Low credit-rated borrower saves 11 −10, or 1 percent in long-term interest cost less 0.75 percent additional cost on the prime rate loan, or 0.25 percent.

- High credit-rated borrower saves 0.25 percent in interest cost (prime less 0.25 percent).

In this example, the two firms save the *same* amount. Often, the low credit-rated firm saves more in interest cost than does the high-rated borrower. When this happens, the firm saving the most usually agrees to help the other firm with some of its expenses (such as paying the underwriting cost of floating new bonds).

Today, borrowers often negotiate SWAP agreements with lenders at the same time they reach an agreement on a loan. For example, if a borrower is granted a floating-rate loan based on the prime rate but fears that interest rates are going up, he or she can convert that floating-rate loan into a *synthetic fixed-rate loan* through a SWAP agreement. Although the SWAP and the loan are separate agreements, together they have the *net* effect of giving the borrower a fixed borrowing cost. As the diagram below shows, when the borrower pays a floating rate to the lender, the borrower also pays a fixed interest rate to the lender under a SWAP agreement. Simultaneously under the SWAP agreement, the lender sends the borrower a floating-rate payment. Therefore, the floating-rate payment from the borrower under the loan agreement is approximately offset by the lender's floating-rate payment to the borrower under the SWAP agreement. What's left over is the borrower's fixed-rate payment to the lender under the SWAP.

The Synthetic Fixed-Rate Loan

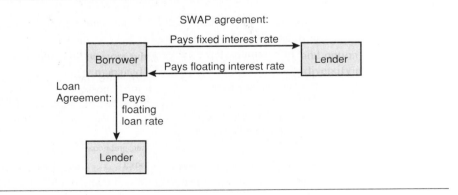

Thus, a floating-rate loan agreement has been transformed by a SWAP into a fixed-rate loan, even though the borrower remains legally committed to make all the scheduled floating interest rate payments called for by the loan agreement.

During the 1990s a new variety of SWAP contract appeared called the *index amortizing rate (IAR) SWAP*. An IAR SWAP, like most other SWAPs, is an over-the-counter contract calling for two parties to agree to exchange fixed-rate and floating-rate interest payments. However, unlike conventional ("plain vanilla") SWAPs, IARs require net interest payments that *decrease* over a SWAP's life at a rate that varies with changes in short-term interest rates. The pace at which the principal of the IAR SWAP decreases will be affected by an amortization schedule agreed upon by the two parties to the SWAP. The notional principal underlying the IAR SWAP will decline (amortize) more quickly if short-term interest rates fall and amortize more slowly if short-term interest rates rise. IARs usually defer the amortizing of the notional principal for two years (known as a "lockout" period) and then begin amortizing in the third year. Most start out at a principal value of $100 million with a five-year term and quarterly interest payments.

If short-term interest rates stay unchanged, an IAR usually lasts only about three years. But, if short-term interest rates fall significantly, IARs can run out at the end of the deferment (lock-out) period; if short-term rates rise sufficiently, the IAR may last the full five years. Thus, changes in interest rates affect the amount of future interest payments and the maturity of an IAR. As Galaif (1993–94) notes, "The amortizing feature of an IAR swap is an implicit call option that essentially gives the fixed-rate payer the right to 'call' or cancel a portion of the swap if interest rates decline substantially."[7] This feature is similar to the call privilege attached to a callable bond (discussed in Chapter 11). And, like call features on bonds, the fixed-rate payer in the IAR SWAP must pay an extra yield premium to take advantage of this implicit call option.[8]

Interest rate SWAPs have become much easier to arrange in recent years with the appearance of SWAP *brokers*. These financial firms — most often investment banks or commercial banks — usually charge a finder's fee of 25 basis points (i.e., ¼ of 1 percent of the notional amount of the swap) to bring the two parties together under the SWAP agreement. SWAP brokers charge more than this if they also are asked to administer the SWAP — that is, calculate the amount of interest owed by each party to the agreement, collect the monies owed, and distribute the required payments. The SWAP broker or another financial intermediary may also be asked to issue a *guarantee* in case either party to the SWAP cannot meet its obligations. These guarantees may cost from 1 to 15 basis points of the notional amount of the SWAP or more, depending on the credit record of each SWAP party. In recent years, SWAP dealers have developed inventories of "unmatched" SWAPs — requests from customers who are willing to enter into SWAP agreements but need a counterparty to make the SWAP complete.

SWAPs are never without risk. Either party to the agreement may go bankrupt or even steal the funds owed to its counterparty, leaving its SWAP partner exposed to as much interest rate risk as it faced before the SWAP agreement was signed. SWAPs help to cover interest rate risk but do not necessarily reduce credit (default) risk. A few SWAPs call for one or both parties to post collateral, but this is usually not done. Unfortunately, without collateral requirements, it is easy for a firm or government to overdo the use of SWAPs and get itself into trouble. One dramatic example of this occurred in March 1991, when several municipalities in

---

[7]Lisa N. Galaif, "Index Amortizing Rate Swaps," *Quarterly Review*, Federal Reserve Bank of New York, Winter 1993–94, p. 65.

[8]Another variation of the IAR swap, called a reverse index amortizing rate SWAP, or RIAR, has recently appeared, which takes the opposite position when interest rates change. In the RIAR, the notional principal amortizes more quickly if short-term rates rise and more slowly if rates fall. Thus, while the IAR swap represents an implicit call option, the RIAR is an implicit put option for the floating-rate payer in a swap contract, giving the floating-rate payer the right to reduce its floating-rate liability if short-term interest rates rise.

Great Britain took on far more SWAPs than their revenues could accommodate. In fact, one local government near London faced a SWAP interest bill so huge that, had a British court not intervened and negated its SWAP agreements, it would have had to tax each of its citizens thousands of pounds merely to pay off the interest owed on all of its SWAPs! Recently, mark-to-market swaps, essentially a sequence of shorter-term swaps and forward-rate swaps bearing a set of forward fixed rates for future rate payments, have been proposed to deal with the counterparty default risk problem, as described by Brown and Smith (1993).

Moreover, SWAPs are subject to interest rate risk due to the fact that shifts in market rates can alter the value of existing SWAP agreements and, therefore, affect a SWAP's replacement cost. As Simons (1993) shows, *rising* market interest rates result in greater risk of default on a SWAP than stable interest rates. For example, Procter & Gamble Co. lost close to $157 million in 1994 on interest rate SWAPs entered into on the assumption that interest rates would fall; they rose instead. A SWAP can be hedged against interest rate risk by entering into another SWAP agreement that is the mirror image of the first (a so-called *matched pair*). Some companies use financial futures contracts or other hedging tools to counter interest rate risk from their SWAPs rather than proliferating still more SWAPs.

One notable advantage of SWAPs is the largely unregulated character of the market. SWAPs are private agreements with minimal government interference. There is no overseer or regulatory commission to restrict the use of this interest rate hedging tool. Many firms do not even report the amount of SWAPs they have outstanding on their balance sheets. This means that investors interested in buying their bonds or their stock may not know how much risk these companies carry in the form of SWAP obligations.

Recent research suggests that SWAPs carry significant costs as well as significant benefits to their users. The benefits, as we have seen, center upon lower interest costs and better matching of the cash flows associated with assets and liabilities. The costs include the administrative burden of arranging and monitoring each party's performance under the SWAP agreement and some loss of financial flexibility. A firm that is party to a SWAP might prefer to pay off its borrowings and replace them with new sources of borrowed funds. However, it continues to be obligated to pay in interest cost what it has agreed to pay under its outstanding SWAP contracts. Thus, the benefits of SWAPs come only at a price.

SUMMARY

In this chapter, we have discussed the close relationship between changes in interest rates and the cycle of business expansion and recession in the economy. Interest rates tend to rise in periods of economic expansion, with short-term rates generally increasing faster than long-term rates. Conversely, recessions typically bring falling interest rates, with short-term rates declining more rapidly than long-term rates. This cyclical pattern in interest rates suggests to many financial analysts that interest rates can be forecast by looking at factors reflecting the state of the economy plus other determining variables. However, interest rate forecasting is at best a difficult art. The economy and its millions of individual decision-making units offer too many opportunities for the most carefully drawn assumptions to go awry.

Still, interest rate theory focuses our attention on a limited set of factors that need to be watched in conjunction with any rate forecast. These key rate-influencing factors include the *liquidity effect* of changes in the money supply, suggesting that money supply expansion may produce lower interest rates in the near term if money demand is fixed or changes slowly. The *expectations effect* contends that if money growth exceeds the public's expectations, interest rates may rise because the public may fear worsening inflation and more restrictive government policies. The *income effect* of money supply changes suggests that the growth of income and spending raises money demand and ultimately interest rates. The *supply effect* of new security offerings argues that an increase in planned new security offerings is an indicator of added credit demands and, other things being equal, tends to push interest rates higher in the short term.

Expected inflation also affects interest rates. According to the *Fisher effect*, a rise in the rate of inflation expected by lenders of funds over the life of a security causes a rise in the nominal (published) rate of interest attached to that security, especially for longer-term financial instruments. Another factor in rate forecasting is *estimated credit demands* captured by changes in consumer spending, business investment, and other measures of spending and production in the economy. Rising credit demands suggest the onset of higher interest rates unless offset by an increasing supply of credit funds. Finally, *public expectations* regarding future interest rates, security prices, spending, and government policies all exert powerful effects on the bond and stock markets and must be weighed in the forecasting process.

The great difficulties inherent in forecasting interest rates have led many borrowers and lenders of funds to practice *interest-rate hedging*, insulating themselves at least partially from the ravages of fluctuating interest rates. Among the more popular rate-hedging devices are *duration* analysis, which weights the maturity of loans and securities by the timing of their cash payments, and *GAP management*, which requires a financial institution to match the volume of its interest-sensitive assets to the volume of its liabilities that are also sensitive to interest rate changes. Still other hedging devices center around *interest rate caps*, which put ceiling rates on loans, or *collars*, which prevent rates from rising too far or falling too low. Other borrowers use *interest rate insurance* and *loan options* to avoid the highest loan rates. Finally, hedging has also been carried out in recent years through *interest rate SWAPs*, which can be used to give a borrower fixed loan rates no matter which way interest rates move and can result in lower borrowing costs. Knowledge of interest rate hedging tools is indispensable to avoid catastrophic losses in today's volatile financial marketplace. ∎

KEY TERMS AND CONCEPTS IN THIS CHAPTER

business cycle	econometric models	GAP management
seasonality	forward calendar	rate cap
money-supply liquidity effect	implied rate forecast	rate collars
	consensus forecast	interest rate insurance
money-supply expectations effect	duration	loan options
money-supply income effect	stripped securities	interest rate SWAP

STUDY QUESTIONS

1. Describe the relationship between changes in economic activity and interest rates. Why do interest rates often rise during a period of economic expansion and fall when the economy is in a recession?

2. How do long- and short-term interest rates usually behave over the course of a business cycle? Which rises or falls at a faster rate? Why?

3. Why are interest rates so difficult to forecast? What advantages can you identify from being able to forecast interest rates successfully?

4. Explain the meaning of the following terms:
   a. *Liquidity effect*   c. *Income effect*
   b. *Expectations effect*   d. *Fisher effect*

5. What variables are used more frequently to forecast interest rates in econometric models? What are some of the limitations of these models?

6. What is the *forward calendar*? Explain how it could be useful as an indicator of future security prices and interest rates.

7. How can market expectations be used as a guide to future changes in interest rates? What pitfalls are there in such an approach?

8. Explain the meaning of the term *consensus forecast*.

9. What is *hedging*? Explain briefly how each of the following rate hedging devices work:
   a. Interest rate caps   e. Rate cap
   b. Rate collars   f. GAP management
   c. Interest rate insurance   g. Interest rate SWAPs
   d. Loan options   h. Stripped securities

PROBLEMS

1. Suppose that today the one-year U.S. Treasury bond rate is 6 percent, the two-year Treasury bond rate is 7 percent, and the three-year bond rate is 8 percent. Plot a yield curve from these data. What interest rate is this yield curve forecasting on a one-year loan two years from now? What is the expected two-year bond rate one year from now?

2. Current interest rates in the corporate bond market on AAA-rated bonds are as follows: one-year bonds, 8 percent; two-year bonds, 9 percent; three-year bonds, 10 percent; four-year bonds, 11 percent; and five-year bonds, 12 percent. What is the slope of the yield curve in the one- to five-year range? Calculate the implied one-year expected rate one year from now. What one-year loan rate is expected two years from now? Three years from now? Four years from now?

3. In an interest rate SWAP transaction, a large corporation can borrow in the bond market at a current fixed rate of 9 percent and could also obtain a floating-rate loan in the short-term market at the prime bank rate. However, this firm wishes to borrow short term because it has a large block of assets that roll over into cash each month. The other party to the SWAP is a company with a lower credit rating that can borrow in the bond market at an interest rate of 11.5 percent and in the short-term market at prime plus 1.50 percent. This lower-rated company has long-term predictable cash inflows, however. The higher credit-rated company wishes to pay for its part in the SWAP an interest rate of prime less 50 basis points. The lower-rated company is willing to pay the underwriting cost associated with the higher-rated company's security issue, which is estimated to be 25 basis points. The SWAP transaction is valued at $100 million. What kind of interest rate SWAP can be arranged here? Which company will borrow short term and which long term? If the prime bank rate is currently 10 percent, who will pay what interest cost to whom? Explain what the benefit is to each party in this SWAP.

4. Suppose that a top-quality firm with an A-1 or AAA credit rating can borrow at a fixed coupon rate attached to its bonds of 12 percent. Moreover, this firm's bank is willing to extend it a LIBOR-based loan in London at a rate of 9.5 percent that will change weekly as LIBOR moves.[9] Working through its principal banker, this top-rated company makes contact with a firm whose credit rating is considerably lower (rated only BB). The lower-rated firm has been informed by its investment banker that it probably could sell bonds at a 14 percent coupon rate, and the finance company from which it receives short-term money has promised a LIBOR-based floating-rate loan of 11.25 percent. Could these two firms benefit from a SWAP under the interest rates given above? Which firm would save the most, and under what circumstances? Will the company with the lower credit rating have to offer the top-credit-quality firm an added inducement to participate in a rate SWAP? What inducement or inducements could be used to equalize the interest savings for both parties?

5. A bank is using GAP management in an attempt to control its exposure to interest rate risk. Over the next several planning periods used by management, the dollar volume of the bank's interest-sensitive assets and interest-sensitive liabilities are as follows:

Planning	Interest-Sensitive Assets (ISA) ($ Millions)	Interest-Sensitive Liabilities (ISL) ($ Millions)
Next 24 hours	$24	$31
Next 7 days	89	76
Next 30 days	214	185
Next 60 days	406	511
Next 90 days	833	762
Next year	1,019	1,542
Remaining maturities	7,660	7,318

In what period is this bank liability sensitive? Asset sensitive? Under what interest rate circumstances would the bank lose money during each of the above time periods? What could management do to mitigate the bank's current interest rate risk exposure?

6. First Security National Bank has total assets of $580 million and liabilities of $525 million. The bank finds that the average duration of its asset portfolio is 2.87 years and the average duration of its liability portfolio is 1.66 years. What would happen to the value of net worth of this bank if interest rates rise? if interest rates fall? by how much must asset duration be changed to ensure that this institution is fully hedged against interest rate risk?

SELECTED REFERENCES

Anderson, Leonall C., and Keith M. Carlson. "A Monetarist Model for Economic Stabilization." *Review*. Federal Reserve Bank of St. Louis, April 1970, pp. 7–25.

Barth, James R., and James T. Bennett. "Seasonal Variation in Interest Rates." *Review of Economics and Statistics*, February 1975, pp. 80–83.

Belongia, Michael T. "Predicting Interest Rates: A Comparison of Professional and Market-Based Forecasts." *Review*. Federal Reserve Bank of St. Louis, March 1987, pp. 9–15.

Bernanke, Ben S. "On the Predictive Power of Interest Rates and Interest-Rate Spreads." *New England Economic Review*. Federal Reserve Bank of Boston, November–December 1990, pp. 51–68.

Brown, Keith C., and Donald J. Smith. "Default Risk and Innovations in the Design of Interest Rate Swaps." *Financial Management*, Summer 1993, pp. 94–105.

---

[9]LIBOR stands for London Interbank offer rate and is the basic interest rate in the Eurodollar market, used as the basis for setting loan rates to major corporations. See Chapter 18 for a discussion of Eurodollar loan and deposit markets.

Fernald, Julia D. "The Pricing and Hedging of Index Amortizing Rate Swaps." *Quarterly Review*. Federal Reserve Bank of New York, Winter 1993–94, pp. 71–74.

Galaif, Lisa N. "Index Amortizing Rate Swaps." *Quarterly Review*. Federal Reserve Bank of New York, Winter 1993–94, pp. 63–70.

Kohn, Donald L. "Causes of Seasonal Variation in Interest Rates." *Monthly Review*. Federal Reserve Bank of Kansas City, February 1974, pp. 3–12.

Livingston, Miles, and Deborah Wright Gregory. *The Stripping of U.S. Treasury Securities*, Monograph 1989–1. New York: Salomon Brothers Center for the Study of Financial Institutions, New York University, 1989.

Rose, Peter S. "Interest Rates, Economics Forecasting, and Bank Profits." *Canadian Banker* 91, no. 3 (June 1984), pp. 38–44.

Stock, James, and Mark Watson. "New Indexes of Coincident and Leading Economic Indicators." in *National Bureau of Economic Research Macroeconomics Annual 1989*, ed. Olivier J. Blanchard and Stanley Fischer. Cambridge, Mass.: The M.I.T. Press, 1989, pp. 351–94.

Simons, Caterina. "Interest Rate Structure and the Credit Risk of Swaps." *New England Economic Review*. Federal Reserve Bank of Boston, July/August 1993.

Chapter 13

Financial Futures and Options Contracts

LEARNING OBJECTIVES IN THIS CHAPTER

- To examine the nature and characteristics of two of the most popular financial instruments — financial futures and options — used to protect against the risk of changing interest rates.
- To see how financial futures and options can be used to combat the market risks associated with making loans, purchasing and selling securities, and borrowing money.

Among the most innovative markets to be developed in recent years and also among the most rapidly growing are the markets for financial futures and options. *Futures and options trading is designed to protect the investor against interest rate risk.* In the financial futures and options markets, the risk of future changes in the market prices or yields of securities is transferred to someone — an individual or an institution — willing to bear that risk. Financial futures and options are used in both the short-term money market and the long-term capital market to protect both borrowers and lenders against changing interest rates.

Although relatively new in the field of finance, risk protection through futures and options trading is an old concept in marketing commodities. As far back as the Middle Ages, traders in farm commodities developed contracts calling for the future delivery of farm products at a guaranteed price. Trading in rice futures began in Japan in 1697. In the United States, the Chicago Board of Trade established a futures market in grains in 1848. Later, the Chicago Board developed futures and options markets for a wide range of commodities and, more recently, for financial instruments.

The Nature of Futures Trading

In the futures market, buyers and sellers enter into contracts for the delivery of commodities or securities at a specific location and time and at a price that is set when the contract is made. The principal reason for the existence of a futures market is **hedging**, the act of coordinating buying and selling of a commodity or financial claim to protect against the risk of future price fluctuations. In the futures market, investors interested in hedging trade futures contracts with investors interested in speculating (i.e., profiting from favorable market movements).

Adverse movements in prices can result in increased costs and lower profits and, in the case of financial instruments, reduced value and yield. Many investors today find that even modest changes in prices or interest rates can lead to magnified changes in their net earnings. Some investors see the futures market as a means to ensure that their profits depend more on planning and design rather than the dictates of a treacherous and volatile marketplace.

Hedging may be compared to insurance. Insurance protects an individual or business firm against risks to life and property. Hedging protects against the risk of fluctuations in market price. However, there is an important difference between insurance and hedging. Insurance rests on the principle of sharing or distributing risk over a large group of policyholders. Through an insurance policy, the risk to any one individual or institution is reduced.

In contrast, hedging does *not* reduce risk. It is a relatively low-cost method of *transferring* the risk of unanticipated changes in prices or interest rates from one investor or institution to another. Ultimately, some investor must bear the risk of fluctuations in the prices and yields of commodities or securities. Moreover, that risk is generally less predictable than would be true of most insurance claims. The hedger who successfully transfers risk through a futures contract can protect an acceptable selling price for a commodity or a desired yield on a security weeks or months ahead of the sale or purchase of that item. In the financial futures market, the length of such contracts normally ranges from three months to two years.

General Principles of Hedging

The basic principles of hedging may be described most easily through the use of a model. In this section, we examine the model of a complete, or perfect, hedge. Such a hedge contracts away *all* risk associated with fluctuations in the price of an asset. The hedger creates a situation in which any change in the market price of a commodity or security is exactly offset by a profit or loss on the futures contract. This enables the hedger to lock in the price or yield he wishes to obtain.

Opening and Closing a Hedge

Suppose an agricultural firm harvests a commodity such as wheat and is anticipating a decline in wheat prices. This unfavorable price movement can be hedged by selling futures contracts equal to the current value of the wheat. Sale of these contracts, which promise the future delivery of wheat in days, weeks, or months from now, is called "opening a hedge." When the firm does sell its wheat, it can buy back the same number of futures contracts it sold originally and "close the hedge."

Of course, the firm could deliver the wheat as specified in the original futures contract. However, this is not usually done. If the price of wheat does decline as expected, it costs the firm less to repurchase the futures contracts than the price for which it originally sold those contracts. Thus, the profit on the repurchase of wheat futures offsets the decrease in the price of wheat itself. The firm would have perfectly hedged itself against any adverse change in wheat prices over the life of the futures contracts.

What would happen if wheat rose in price instead of declined? A perfect hedge would result in a profit on the sale of the wheat itself but a loss on the futures contracts. This happens because the firm must repurchase its futures contracts at a higher price than its original cost due to the higher price for wheat. Exhibit 13–1 illustrates how a profit (or loss) on a futures contract can be used to offset a decrease (or increase) in the market price of an asset, helping the hedger achieve a desired price level.

Exhibit 13–1   **Price Changes on Assets Can Be Offset by Profits or Losses on Futures Contracts**

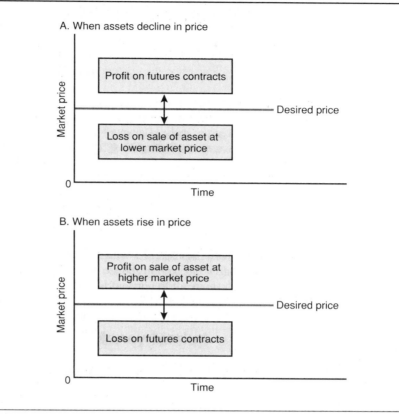

Why Hedging Can Be Effective

The hedging process can be effective in transferring risk because prices in the spot (or cash) market for commodities and securities are generally correlated with prices in the futures (or forward) market. Indeed, the price of a futures contract in today's market represents an estimate of what the spot (or cash) market price will be on the contract's delivery date (less any storage, insurance, and financing costs). *Hedging essentially means adopting equal and opposite positions in the spot and futures markets for the same assets.*

The relationship between the price of a commodity or security in the cash or spot market and its price in the futures market is captured in the concept of **basis**. Specifically,

$$\begin{array}{c} \text{Basis for a} \\ \text{futures contract} \end{array} = \begin{array}{l} \text{Spread between the cash (spot) price of a commodity} \\ \text{or security and the futures (forward) price for that} \\ \text{same commodity or security at the same point in time.} \end{array}$$

For example, if long-term Treasury bonds are selling in today's cash market for immediate delivery at a price of \$98 per bond (assuming a \$100 par value) but are selling in the futures market today for forward delivery in three months at \$88 per bond, the basis for this T-bond futures contract purchased today is \$98 − \$88, or \$10. We can also define basis in terms of interest rates; it is the difference between the interest rate attached to a security in the cash market and the interest rate on that same security in the futures market.

One important principle of futures trading is the *principle of convergence*. As the delivery date specified in a futures contract draws nearer, the gap (basis) between the futures and spot prices for the same security or commodity narrows. At the moment of delivery, the futures price and spot price on the same security or commodity must be identical (except for transactions costs), so that the basis of the futures contract becomes zero. Whether a futures trade ultimately turns out to be profitable depends on what happens to its basis now and when the contract ends. It is changes in basis that create risk in the trading of futures contracts.

Hedging through futures converts price or interest rate risk into basis risk. One useful measure of basis risk in financial futures is the *volatility ratio*:

$$\begin{array}{c}\text{Volatility ratio} \\ \text{for a} \\ \text{futures contract} \\ \text{(basis risk measure)}\end{array} = \dfrac{\begin{array}{c}\text{Percentage change in cash (spot) price of a}\\\text{commodity or security}\end{array}}{\begin{array}{c}\text{Percentage change in the price of the futures}\\\text{instrument used for hedging the commodity}\\\text{or security}\end{array}}$$

The more stable the basis associated with a given futures trade — that is, the closer the volatility ratio is to 1 — the greater the reduction of risk achieved by the futures trader. When cash and futures prices or interest rates move in parallel, basis risk is zero. The futures markets "work" to reduce risk, because the risk of changes in basis is generally *less* than the risk of changes in the price or yield from a commodity or security. However, as we will soon see, there are both risks and costs to futures trading, and losses can mount rapidly, especially for the uninformed investor. Moreover, U.S. tax laws require that income taxes be collected on any futures gains realized.

Risk Selection through Hedging

In the wheat example discussed earlier, we described a complete (perfect) hedge. In a perfect hedge, the basis remains constant throughout the contract period. Profits (losses) in the cash market *exactly* offset losses (profits) in the futures market. Such a hedge is essentially a profitless hedging position and is rare; in most futures trades, the basis fluctuates, introducing at least some degree of risk. Many investors, however, are willing to take on added risk by not fully closing a hedge, believing they can guess correctly which way prices are going. Through the futures markets, the investor can literally "dial" the degree of risk she wishes to accept. If the investor wishes to take on all the risk of price fluctuations in the hope of achieving the maximum return, no hedging will take place at all.

Financial Futures

Beginning in October 1975, the Chicago Board of Trade opened active trading in **financial futures contracts** for GNMA mortgage-backed certificates. In the ensuing months, futures contracts for U.S. Treasury securities and many other financial instruments appeared. The development of futures markets for these financial instruments was motivated by the extremely volatile interest rate movements that have characterized the financial markets for the past two decades. Repeatedly, interest rates have risen to record levels under the pressure of tight money policies and inflation, shutting out important groups of borrowers from access to credit. These high and volatile rates reduce the value of securities held by financial institutions, threatening them with a liquidity crisis and failure. Some members of the regulatory community have favored the growth of financial futures as a way to reduce the risks associated with security investments. However, as we will soon see, other regulatory authorities believe that the development of the futures markets may have encouraged speculation and increased the riskiness of those financial institutions participating in futures trading. These regulatory agencies have placed tight restrictions on the use of the futures markets, especially by the banking industry.

The Purpose of Trading in Financial Futures

The basic principle behind trading in financial futures is the same as in the commodity markets. A securities dealer, bank, or other investor may sell futures contracts on selected securities in order to protect against the risk of falling security prices (rising interest rates) and, therefore, a decline in the rate of return or yield from an investment. If the price of the security in question does fall, the investor can lock in the desired yield, because a profit on the futures contract may offset the capital loss incurred when selling the security itself. On the other hand, a rise in the market price of a security (fall in interest rates) may be offset by a loss in the futures market. Either way, the investor is able to maintain his or her desired holding period yield. (These points are illustrated in Exhibit 13–2.) Many financial institutions prefer to use the futures market to hedge against interest rate fluctuations rather than passing interest rate risk on to their customers through floating-rate loans, deposits, and other financial assets.

Under a financial futures contract, the seller agrees to deliver a specific security at a fixed price at a specific time in the future. Delivery under the shortest new contracts is

Exhibit 13–2   **Changes in the Yield on Securities Can Be Offset by Profits or Losses on Futures Contracts**

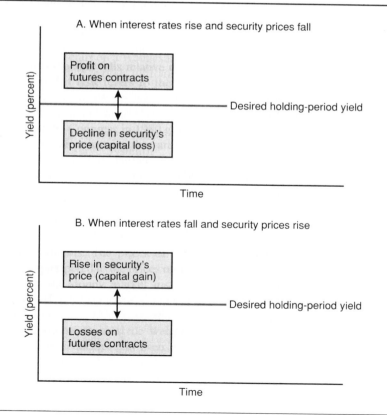

A. When interest rates rise and security prices fall

B. When interest rates fall and security prices rise

usually in 3 months from today's date; a few contracts stretch out to 18 months or even 2 years. When the delivery date arrives, the security's seller can do one of three things: (1) make delivery of the security, if he or she holds it; (2) buy the security in the spot (cash) market and deliver it as called for in the futures contract; or (3) purchase a futures contract for the same security with a delivery date exactly matching the first contract. This last option would result in a buy and sell order maturing on the same day, canceling each other out ("zeroing out") and eliminating the necessity of making delivery. In reality, settlement of contracts generally occurs in the futures market by using offsetting buy and sell orders rather than using spot (cash) transactions and making actual delivery.

Securities Used in Financial Futures Contracts

The number of futures markets and the types of securities and contracts traded in those markets have been expanding rapidly in recent years, both inside the United States and on exchanges in London, Western Europe, Japan, and around the Pacific Rim. In 1975 only one type of contract was traded at the Chicago Board of Trade. By the 1990s, many different futures contracts were being traded on several different exchanges in the United States and abroad. However, most trading in financial futures today centers on six types of securities: (1) U.S. Treasury bills, (2) Treasury bonds and notes, (3) Eurobank certificates of deposit (CDs), (4) common stock indices, (5) corporate and municipal bond indices, and (6) foreign currencies, such as the Japanese yen and the German mark.

As noted, the Chicago Board of Trade first offered interest rate futures contracts for GNMA mortgage-backed securities in October 1975. Soon other U.S. commodity exchanges — the International Monetary Market of the Chicago Mercantile Exchange (IMM); the AMEX Commodities Exchange, Inc. (ACE); and the Commodity Exchange, Inc. (Comex) — began offering futures trading in T-bills and GNMA certificates. In August 1980, the New York Stock Exchange opened its own futures floor, and in 1982, the London International Financial Futures Exchange (LIFFE) was established to offer trades in Eurodollar deposit futures. Later, LIFFE inaugurated trading in a London Financial Times Stock index, as well as contracts tied to the value of German bonds. The rapid growth of LIFFE stimulated the development of other European futures exchanges, such as the Deutsche Terminbörse (DTB) in Frankfurt and the Marché à Terme International de France (MATIF) in Paris, and the expansion of exchanges around the Pacific Rim, such as the Tokyo International Financial Futures Exchange (TIFFE), the Osaka Stock Exchange (OSE), and the Singapore International Monetary Exchange Ltd. (SIMEX).

By the early 1990s, several automated and computer-based trading systems were linking futures and options exchanges around the globe 24 hours a day. The best known of these is GLOBEX (the Global Automated Transactions System for Futures and Options) — a computer terminal network involving traders and exchanges in Chicago, London, New York, and Paris. With the GLOBEX system, a trader at a participating firm can enter bids and offers on a computer screen that is part of the network and a computer will match buy and sell orders within seconds. Other examples of the spreading internationalization, automation, and round-the-clock trading of financial futures, options, and other financial instruments include London's Automated Pit Trading System, designed to extend futures trading hours in Europe, the NASDAQ computer telephone network for automated trading between the United States and exchanges in London and Singapore, the Financial Instrument Exchange (FINEX) night trading system in New York, and the Deutsche Terminbörse trade-matching system in Frankfurt, Germany.

Each exchange controls which contracts may be offered for sale and their acceptable delivery dates, delivery methods, posting of prices, contract par values, and other essential

INTERNATIONAL FOCUS
Leading Futures and Options Exchanges Around the World

Chicago Board of Trade (CBT)

Chicago Board Options Exchange (CBOE)

London International Financial Futures Exchange (LIFFE)

New York Futures Exchange (NYFE)

New York Financial Exchange (FINEX)

Singapore International Monetary Exchange, Ltd. (SIMEX)

Sydney Futures Exchange (SFE)

Tokyo International Financial Futures Exchange (TIFFE)

Chicago Mercantile Exchange (CME)

Deutsche Terminbörse (DTB)

Marché à Terme International de France (MATIF)

Montreal Exchange (ME)

Osaka Stock Exchange (OSE)

Swedish Options and Futures Exchange (SOFE)

Toronto Futures Exchange (TFE)

Tokyo Stock Exchange (TSE)

terms of trade. Current terms of trade for several prominent futures contracts now represented on the various exchanges are summarized below.[1]

U.S. Treasury Bonds and Notes

The futures market for U.S. Treasury bonds and notes is one of the most active markets for the forward delivery of an asset to be found anywhere in the world. Treasury bonds and notes are a popular investment medium for individuals and financial institutions because of their safety and liquidity. Nevertheless, there is substantial market risk involved with longer-term Treasury bonds and notes due to their lengthy maturities and relatively thin market. Because the market for U.S. Treasury bonds is thinner than for Treasury bills and Treasury bond durations are longer, T-bond prices are more volatile, creating greater uncertainty for investors. Not surprisingly, then, U.S. Treasury bonds were among the first financial instruments for which a futures market was developed for hedging risk. Today there are parallel markets for contracts covering foreign government bonds centered on exchanges in London, Paris, Frankfurt, and Tokyo.

All U.S. Treasury bonds delivered under a futures contract must come from the same issue. The basic trading unit is a $100,000 bond (measured at par) with a theoretical maturity of 30 years and a coupon rate of 8 percent. Bonds with coupon rates above or below 8 percent are deliverable at a premium or discount from par in the months of March,

---

[1]The contract exchanges carry a heavy burden of responsibility in preserving the integrity of futures trading and the orderliness of the markets. Each exchange stands behind the transactions conducted on its floor and imposes strict rules to minimize risk to the investor. For example, daily price fluctuations are not permitted to go beyond defined limits. Qualifications of floor traders and standards for member firms are monitored on a continuing basis by management and the governing board. The U.S. government also regulates futures trading through the Commodity Futures Trading Commission and the Securities and Exchange Commission.

Exhibit 13–3   **Prices on T-Bond Futures** ($100,000, measured in points and 32nds of 100%)

TREASURY BONDS (CBT)-$100,000; pts. 32nds of 100%							
					Lifetime		Open
	Open	High	Low	Settle	Change	High	Low	Interest
June	112-23	112-29	112-05	112-22	–	3	121-23	93-06	345,064
Sept	112-06	112-08	111-20	112-06	–	3	120-29	102-06	16,747
Dec	111-16	111-22	111-09	111-21	–	4	120-15	107-25	3,192
Mr97	....	....	....	111-07	–	4	120-00	108-04	900

Est vol 275,000; vol Mn 242,510; op int 379,232, –3,846.

June, September, and December. Delivery of Treasury bonds is accomplished by book entry, and accrued interest is prorated. Price quotes in the market are expressed as a percentage of par value.

The minimum price change that is recorded on published lists or in dealer quotations is $1/32$ of a point, or $31.25 per futures contract.[2] For example, Exhibit 13–3 shows price information reported on Treasury bond contracts traded on the Chicago Board of Trade on October 11, 1995.

The first column reports the months in which each contract matures and in which delivery is to be made (in this case the first month for contracts to mature is June 1996). The next four columns show the opening price, high and low prices, and the closing (settlement) price that day. We note that Treasury bonds for delivery in June 1996 opened for trading at 112–23 (or $112 and 23/32 on a $100 par bond, or about $112,719 for a security with a $100,000 face value), and trading closed at the end of the day at a settlement price of 112–22 (or about $112,688). The price change over the last two trading sessions was nil, indicating that over this time period at least the market was relatively stable. Over the life of this particular instrument the T-bond futures price has fluctuated between a high of 121–23 (or about $121,719) and a low of 93–06 (or about $93,188). The final column, amount of open interest, shows the number of outstanding T-bond contracts not yet "zeroed out," which is usually greatest for the most recent contract to be delivered and then decreases for successive, more distant delivery dates. Total trading volume for the most recent day and the previous day appears at the bottom of the table, along with the sum of all outstanding contracts and the change in contracts over the previous two days.

Contracts on longer-term Treasury notes were subsequently developed, including a $100,000 contract (or multiples thereof) covering T-notes maturing in at least $6\frac{1}{2}$ years but not more than 10 years; T-notes maturing in not more than 5 years and 3 months and not less than 4 years and 3 months; and T-notes maturing in not more than 2 years from the last day of the delivery month. These contracts settle in March, June, September, and December and are traded at the Chicago Board of Trade. T-note contracts are priced as a percentage of their par (or face) value based upon an 8 percent coupon rate.

U.S. Treasury Bills

In January 1976, U.S. Treasury bills (which are described in Chapter 15) were declared eligible for trading in the financial futures market. The International Monetary Market (IMM), now a division of the Chicago Mercantile Exchange (CME), announced that con-

---

[2]See Chapter 9 for a discussion of the meaning of 32nds and points and how bonds and other security prices are measured.

tracts for future delivery would be written on T-bills of 90-day and one-year maturities. Ninety-day contracts are for $1 million each; single contracts on one-year bills carry denominations of $500,000. T-bill contracts mature once each quarter of the year in March, June, September, and December and are priced off of an index equal to 100 minus the highest T-bill discount rate achieved at an auction during the contract month.

Eurodollar Time Deposits

Futures trading in Eurobank dollar-denominated time deposits (which are described in Chapter 18) began in 1981 at the International Monetary Market (IMM) of the Chicago Mercantile Exchange (CME). The next year the London International Financial Futures Exchange (LIFFE) introduced a similar contract, and more recently, it introduced Eurodeposits based on leading international currencies, which have been traded on leading futures exchanges in Tokyo (TIFFE), Singapore (SIMEX), and Paris (MATIF). The Eurodollar futures market offers investors the opportunity to hedge against changing interest rates on commercial loans, bank deposits, and other money market instruments. Eurodollar futures are settled in cash with the exchange clearinghouse. Prices are expressed as an index equal to 100 minus the prevailing London Interbank Offer Rate (LIBOR) on short-term deposits that day as identified by a survey of leading banks. The minimum size trading unit is $1 million. In addition to the Eurodollar time deposit futures contract there is now a 3-month Euromark time deposit futures contract, traded at the Chicago Mercantile Exchange (CME) in million-German-mark units and settled in cash. Contracts have also been developed for the Deutsche mark, Japanese yen, Swiss franc, British pound, Canadian dollar, Australian dollar, and French franc to guard against fluctuations in the value of these currencies.

Other Money Market Futures Contracts

For money market investors, such as commercial banks, a popular financial futures contract is the 30-day Fed funds futures contract, trading in $5 million units at the Chicago Board of Trade. This device for hedging short-term money market borrowing costs and investment returns is priced at 100 minus the monthly average overnight Fed funds market interest rate for the delivery month. In the international money market, interest-rate risk associated with large commercial loans can be dealt with by using the one-month LIBOR futures contract, which trades in $3 million units at the Chicago Mercantile Exchange.

Municipal (State and Local Government) Bonds

Recently, the Chicago Board of Trade introduced a futures contract to protect rates of return for investors in state and local government bonds. The basic trading unit is $1,000 times the closing value of *The Bond Buyer's* Municipal Bond Index yield, which is settled in cash on the last day of trading for contracts that mature in March, June, September, and December.

New Foreign Bond Index Futures Contracts

Several new futures contracts involving internationally traded bonds and other debt securities have recently appeared. Examples include German government bonds, denominated in 250,000 marks, and Italian government bonds, expressed in 200 million lira, traded on the London International Futures Exchange (LIFFE). Chicago's Mercantile Exchange has introduced trading in $100,000, 10-year Canadian bonds and $1-million-denominated Canadian bankers' acceptances, while 3-year British Commonwealth Treasury bonds are traded on the Sydney Futures Exchange (SFE) and 10-year French government bond contracts are offered on the Marché à Terme International de France (MATIF) in Paris.

Stock Index Futures

In February 1982, futures contracts on the index value of those common stocks making up the Value Line Stock Index (covering 1,700 stocks) were first offered by the Kansas City Board of Trade. These contracts promised delivery of the cash value of a basket of stocks at a set price on a specified future date. Two months later, the Chicago Mercantile Exchange offered its own version of these "pin-stripe pork bellies" by opening trading in a contract tied to the Standard & Poor's (S&P) 500 Stock Index. And in May 1982, the New York Futures Exchange inaugurated trading in the New York Stock Exchange's (NYSE's) Composite Stock Price Index, which includes all stock traded on the NYSE.

The advantage of these composite contracts is that they permit an investor to participate in the "action" of the stock and bond markets without buying individual stocks. The investor merely risks his cash on whether the stock or bond index will rise or fall in value. This is accomplished by buying or selling a futures contract a few points above or below the current stock index value. For example, the popular S&P 500 contract has a value based on the level of the S&P 500 stock index multiplied by $500. If the S&P stock index rises to 400 points, the S&P futures contract would have a value of $400 \times \$500$, or $200,000. If an investor purchased the S&P index contract at 400 and then sold a similar contract later at 410 for $205,000, he would receive a trading profit of $5,000 from the exchange clearinghouse. Current exchange rules require all stock index contracts to be zeroed out so that no exchange of stock ever occurs; the difference between buying and selling prices is settled in cash only.

If the stock index gains or loses a point, the associated futures contract changes by a greater amount, presenting the investor with magnified gains or losses until he or she cancels out the trade. Buyers of stock index futures bet on rising stock prices; sellers are usually forecasting declining stock prices.

Stock index contracts have figured prominently in a form of computerized program trading call **stock index arbitrage**. Program traders seek to profit from any significant but temporary disparity between the price of a stock index (such as those stocks listed in the S&P 500 Stock Index) and the price of the associated futures contract. For example, if the stock index futures price rises above the cash value of stocks that make up that particular index by more than the net carrying cost of the futures contracts (approximated by the current rate of return on Treasury bills), program traders will spot an opportunity for profit. They will buy stocks representative of the basket of stocks in the index in the cash (spot) market and sell stock index contracts in the futures market. The result will be a profit when stock prices subsequently rise and futures contract prices fall back toward their usual positions relative to each other. On the other hand, if the stock index futures price temporarily falls below its parity with comparable stock bought in the cash (spot) market (adjusted for carrying costs and dividend yields on any stock purchased), program traders will arbitrage between the two markets, selling stock for cash and buying the momentarily underpriced futures contracts. These buy-sell pressures will quickly push cash market (spot) stock prices and futures contract prices back toward their normal relative positions.

Arbitrageurs, using these futures-related program trading strategies, can earn a hedged rate of return that tends to be higher than the return earned by simply purchasing a portfolio of riskless securities. Some analysts believe such rapid portfolio switching between stock and futures markets makes *both* markets more treacherous, especially for the small investor. Program-generated trades happen very fast — in a matter of seconds — because computers automatically place buy or sell orders. Moreover, sell orders can multiply rapidly once prices start downward. Security prices can easily fall several percentage points in minutes. Some analysts argue that stock index arbitrageurs are simply following the age-old rule to "buy cheap and sell dear," which ultimately leads to a fairer set of prices for all participants in the market. Moreover, the growth of stock index arbitrage activity has probably generated greater liquidity for *both* stocks and futures. Today the dollar value of daily trading in stock index futures contracts often outstrips the daily volume of trading on the New York Stock Exchange.

TYPES OF HEDGING IN THE FINANCIAL FUTURES MARKET

Basically *three* types of hedges are used in the financial futures market today: the long hedge, the short hedge, and the cross hedge. Cross hedges, as we will see, may be either long or short. Each type of hedge meets the unique trading needs of a particular group of investors. All three types have become popular as interest rates and security prices have become more volatile in recent years.

The Long (or Buying) Hedge

A **long hedge** involves the purchase of futures contracts today before the investor must buy the actual securities desired at a later date. The purpose of the long hedge is to guarantee (lock in) a desired yield in case interest rates decline before securities are actually purchased in the cash market.

As an example of a typical long hedge transaction, suppose that a bank or other institutional investor anticipates receiving $1 million 90 days from today. Assume that today is April 1st and funds are expected on July 2nd. The current yield to maturity on securities the investor hopes to purchase in July is 12.26 percent. We might imagine that these securities are long-term U.S. Treasury bonds, which appeal to this investor because of their high liquidity and zero default risk. Suppose, however, that interest rates are expected to decline over the next three months. If the investor waits until the $1 million in cash is available 90 days from now, the yield on Treasury bonds may well be lower than 12.26 percent. Is there a way to lock in the higher yield available now even though funds will not be available for another three months?

Yes, if a suitable long hedge can be negotiated with another trader. In this case, the investor can *purchase* ("go long") 10 September Treasury bond futures contracts at their current market price. (Recall that Treasury bond futures are sold in $100,000 denominations.) The number of bond futures contracts required can be figured as follows:

$$\frac{Value\ of\ securities\ to\ be\ hedged}{Denomination\ of\ the\ appropriate\ futures\ contract} = \frac{\$1\ million}{\$100,000} = 10\ contracts$$

Cash payment on these contracts will not be due until September.[3]

---

[3]In many practical situations, the security to be hedged and the time for risk protection will not exactly match available futures contracts. These differences introduce uncertainty into the process of determining exactly how many futures contracts will be needed. A useful formula that takes many of these problems into account is the following:

$$\begin{array}{l} Number\ of \\ futures \\ contracts \\ needed \end{array} = \begin{array}{l} Value\ of \\ securities \\ or\ loans \\ to\ be\ hedged \\ \hline denomination \\ of\ futures \\ contracts \end{array} \times \begin{array}{l} Volatility\ ratio \\ of\ price\ movements \\ in\ the\ cash\ (spot) \\ security\ relative \\ to\ the\ price\ of \\ the\ futures \\ contact \end{array} \times \begin{array}{l} Days\ exposed\ to\ risk \\ in\ the\ cash\ (spot)\ market \\ \hline Term\ of\ futures\ contracts \end{array}$$

Exhibit 13–4   **An Example of a Long Hedge Using U.S. Treasury Bonds**

Spot (or Cash) Market Transactions	Futures (or Forward) Market Transactions
April 1: A portfolio manager for a financial institution wished to "lock in" a yield of 12.26 percent on $1 million of 20-year, 8¼ percent U.S. Treasury bonds at 68–14.	**April 1:** The portfolio manager purchases 10 September Treasury bond futures contracts at 68–10.
July 2: The portfolio manager purchases $1 million of 20-year, 8¼ percent U.S. Treasury bonds at 82–13 for a yield of 10.14 percent.	**July 2:** The portfolio manager sells 10 September Treasury bond futures contracts at 80–07.
Results: Opportunity loss of $139,687.50 due to lower Treasury bond yields and higher bond prices.	**Results:** Gain of $119,062.50 on futures trading (less brokerage commissions, interest cost on funds tied up in required cash margin, and taxes).

Source: Based on an example developed by the Chicago Board of Trade in *An Introduction to Financial Futures*, February 1981. Reprinted by permission of the Chicago Board of Trade.

Suppose their price currently is 68–10, or $68,312.50 on a $100,000 face-value contract. Assume too that, as expected, bond prices rise and interest rates fall. At some later point, the investor may be able to sell the futures contracts at a profit, because their prices tend to rise along with rising bond prices in the cash market. Selling bond futures at a profit will help this investor offset the lower yields on Treasury bonds that will prevail in the cash market once the $1 million actually becomes available for investing on July 2nd.

The details of this long hedge transaction are given in Exhibit 13–4. We note that on July 2nd, the investor goes into the spot market and buys $1 million in 8¼ percent, 20-year U.S. Treasury bonds at a price of 82–13. At the same time, the investor sells 10 September Treasury bond futures at 80–07. Due to higher bond prices (lower yields) in July, the investor loses $139,687.50, because the market price of Treasury bonds has risen from 68–14 to 82–13. This represents an opportunity loss because the $1 million in investable funds was not available in April when interest rates were high and bond prices low. However, this loss is at least partially offset by a gain in the futures market of $119,062.50, because the 10 September bond futures purchased on April 1st were sold at a profit on July 2nd. Over this period, bond futures rose in price from 68–10 to 80–07. In effect, this investor will pay only $705,000 for the Treasury bonds bought in the cash market on July 2nd. The market price of these bonds will be $824,062.50 (or 82–13) per bond, but the investor's net cost is lower by $119,062.50 due to a gain in the futures market.

The Short (or Selling) Hedge

A financial device designed to deal with rising interest rates is the **short hedge**. This hedge involves the immediate sale of financial futures until the actual securities must be sold in

---

where the volatility ratio is the percentage change in market price of the cash (spot) security relative to the percentage change in price of the desired futures contract over the *most* recent period. For example, if we wish to hedge $1 million in corporate bonds for 60 days with $100,000-denominated Treasury bond futures contracts covering 90 days and recent price movements of corporate bonds and T-bond futures have displayed a volatility ratio of 0.75, then

$$\textit{Number of futures contracts needed} = \frac{\$1 \; million}{\$100,000} \times 0.75 \times \frac{60}{90} \approx 5 \; contracts$$

the cash market at some later point. Short hedges are especially useful to investors who may hold a large portfolio of securities they plan to sell in the future but, in the meantime, must be protected against the risk of declining security prices. We examine a typical situation in which a securities dealer might employ the short hedge.

Suppose the dealer holds $1 million in U.S. Treasury bonds carrying an 8¾ percent coupon and a maturity of 20 years. The current price of these bonds is 94–26 (or $948.125 per $1,000 par value), which amounts to a yield of 9.25 percent. However, the dealer is concerned that interest rates may rise. Any increase in interest rates would bring about lower bond prices and therefore reduce the value of the dealer's portfolio. A possible remedy in this case is to *sell* bond futures to counteract the anticipated decline in bond prices. For example, suppose the dealer decides to sell 10 Treasury bond futures at 86–28 and 30 days later is able to sell $1 million of 20-year, 8¾ percent Treasury bonds at a price of 86–16 for a yield of 10.29 percent. At the same time, the dealer goes into the futures market and *buys* 10 Treasury bond contracts at 79–26 to offset the previous forward sale of bond futures.

The financial consequences of these combined trades in spot and futures markets are offsetting, as shown in Exhibit 13–5. The dealer has lost $83,125 in the cash market due to the price decline in bonds. However, a gain of $70,625 (less brokerage commissions, interest on cash margins held, and any tax liability) has resulted from the gain in the futures price. This dealer has helped insulate the value of his security portfolio from the risk of price fluctuations through a short hedge.

Cross Hedging

Another approach to minimizing risk is the **cross hedge** — a combined transaction between the spot market and the futures market using different types of securities in each market. This device rests on the assumption that the prices of most financial instruments tend to move in the same direction and by roughly the same proportion. Because this is only approximately true in the real world, profits or losses in the cash market will not exactly offset losses or profits in the futures market because basis risk is greater with a cross hedge. Nevertheless, if the investor's goal is to minimize risk, cross hedging is often preferable to a completely unhedged position.

Exhibit 13–5 **An Example of a Short Hedge Using U.S. Treasury Bonds**

Spot (or Cash) Market Transactions	Futures (or Forward) Market Transactions
October 1: A securities dealer owns $1 million of 20-year, 8¾ percent U.S. Treasury bonds priced at 94–26 to yield 9.25%.	October 1: The dealer sells 10 Treasury bond futures contracts at 86–28.
October 31: The dealer sells $1 million of 20-year, 8¾ percent U.S. Treasury bonds at 86–16 to yield 10.29%.	October 31: The dealer purchases 10 Treasury bond futures contracts at 79–26.
Results: Loss of $83,125 in spot (cash) market.	Results: Gain of $70,625 on futures trading (less brokerage commissions, interest cost on cash margin maintained, and tax obligation).

Source: Based on an example developed by the Chicago Board of Trade in *An Introduction to Financial Futures*, February 1981. Reprinted by permission of the Chicago Board of Trade.

Exhibit 13–6   **An Example of a Short Cross Hedge Involving Corporate and U.S. Treasury Bonds**

Spot (or Cash) Market Transactions	**Futures (or Forward) Market Transactions**
January 2: A commercial bank holds a diversified portfolio of $5 million in high-grade corporate bonds with an average maturity of 20 years and a current market value of 73–15 per bond. The market value of the total portfolio is, therefore, $3,673,437.50.	January 2: The bank's portfolio manager sells 50 U.S. Treasury bond futures contracts at 81–20.
March 14: The market price per bond falls to 64–13, for a total value of the portfolio of $3,220,312.50 when sold.	March 14: The portfolio manager purchases 50 U.S. Treasury bond futures contracts at 69–20.
Results: The total loss in value of the corporate bonds is $453,125.	Results: Gain of $600,000 on the Treasury bond futures contracts (less brokerage commissions, interest cost on cash margins maintained, and taxes owed).

Source: Based on an example developed by the Chicago Board of Trade in *An Introduction to Financial Futures*, February 1981. Reprinted by permission of the Chicago Board of Trade.

As an example, consider the case of a bank that holds good-quality corporate bonds carrying a face value of $5 million and an average maturity of 20 years. The bank's portfolio manager anticipates a rise in interest rates, which will reduce the value of the bonds. Unfortunately, there is only a limited futures market for corporate bonds, and the portfolio manager fears that he or she cannot construct an effective hedge for these securities. However, futures contracts exist for U.S. Treasury bonds, providing a short cross hedge against the risk of a decline in the value of the corporate bonds.

To illustrate how such a cross hedge might take place, suppose that on January 2nd the total market value of the bank's corporate bonds is $3,673,437.50. This means that each $1,000 par value bond currently carries a market price of $734.69 (73–15 on a $100 basis). The portfolio manager decides to sell 50 Treasury bond futures contracts at 81–20 ($816.25 per $1,000 face value). About two months later, on March 14, interest rates have risen significantly. The value of each corporate bond has fallen to 64–13 ($644.06 per $1,000 bond). At this point, the bank's portfolio manager decides to sell these bonds, receiving $3,220,312.50 from the buyer. This represents a loss of $453,125. At the same time, however, the portfolio manager buys back 50 U.S. Treasury bond futures contracts at 69–20. The result is a gain from futures trading of $600,000. In this particular transaction, the gain from futures more than offsets the loss in the cash market. (See Exhibit 13–6 for a summary of this transaction.)

The foregoing example of a cross hedge and the preceding examples of long and short hedges are simplified considerably to make the fundamental principles of futures trading easier to understand. In the real world, placing and removing hedges is an exercise requiring detailed study of the futures market and, in most cases, substantial trading experience.

The Mechanics of Futures Trading

The mechanics of purchasing and selling futures is straightforward. The investor chooses the commodity or security he wishes to trade and the preferred maturity date for the futures contract involving that commodity or security. Then, as Exhibit 13–7 shows, the investor contacts a broker or futures commission merchant, usually through a local brokerage

Exhibit 13–7   **The Path Followed by a Futures or Options Trade on an Organized Exchange**

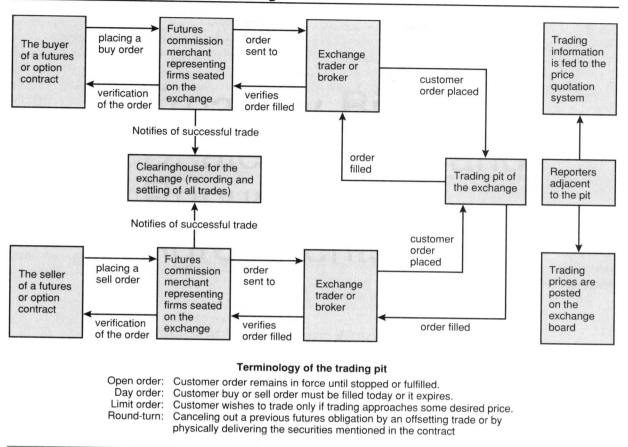

Terminology of the trading pit

Open order: Customer order remains in force until stopped or fulfilled.
Day order: Customer buy or sell order must be filled today or it expires.
Limit order: Customer wishes to trade only if trading approaches some desired price.
Round-turn: Canceling out a previous futures obligation by an offsetting trade or by physically delivering the securities mentioned in the contract

house. The broker indicates today's available price and denomination, and the investor may place an order. Such a request must be accompanied by posting with the broker a cash margin (often 5 percent or more of the contract value), which will be returned when the contract matures (less the broker's commission).

The investor's order will go from the brokerage firm to a *floor trader* working at the exchange that handles that particular kind of futures contract. All U.S. floor traders must be licensed by the Commodities Futures Trading Commission — federal regulator of the futures industry. The floor trader tries to place the investor's order through a process called *open outcry*, soliciting bids by voice and hand signals from other floor traders also trying to fulfill their customers' orders.

The open outcry technique makes each trader an auctioneer, seeking another floor trader representing a buyer willing to accept the seller's terms. When two floor traders agree on the proposed quantity and price, the contract is made. Direct entry of the contract is made into a computer record file, or each trader writes on a card the price, quantity, and delivery month of the contract and passes the card to a clerk who will turn it in to the clearinghouse for recording. Floor traders also notify observers situated around the trading pit so this information can be communicated to those outside the exchange interested in buying or selling contracts.

Once a contract is made, the seller must deliver the commodity or security specified in the invoice on the date specified. Similarly, the buyer must pay the exchange clearinghouse the invoice amount on the date spelled out in the futures contract. However, most contracts are "zeroed out" by going back through a broker with an opposite order that *cancels* the first order on or before the first contract's due date.

What is the purpose of the cash margin that each investor must post? It protects the customers, brokers, and traders against market risk. At the end of each trading day, the exchange clearinghouse is required to *mark to market* (value) each contract outstanding based on its closing price that day. The cash margin covers the loss when a futures contract falls in price. If the price decline is more than a specified percentage of the margin, the investor may get a *margin call* to post additional cash or securities for protection.

Payoff Diagrams for Long and Short Futures Contracts

We can represent losses or gains from trading in futures and from taking long or short hedging positions by using payoff diagrams of the type shown in Exhibit 13–8. In these diagrams, the different possible prices of futures (F_t) are shown along the horizontal axis. The vertical axis records any profits or losses (not including transactions costs) that result when futures prices move up or down.

A 45° line is drawn through the original purchase price (F_B) of the contract marked on both horizontal and vertical axes. Because the line through F_B has an angle of 45°, this

Exhibit 13–8   **Payoffs for Long and Short Futures Positions**

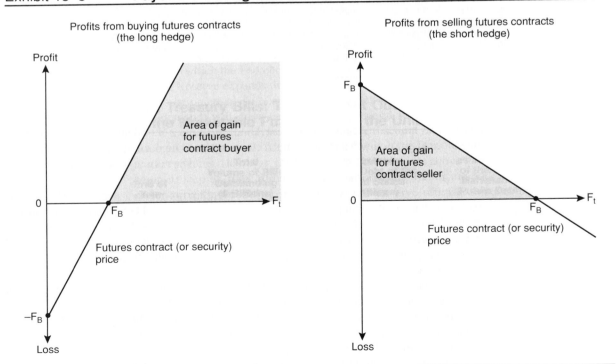

means that along this line, a change of $1 in the futures price, up or down, also results in a $1 profit or loss to the holder of the contract. Note, too, that there is no profit or loss (not counting transactions costs and taxes) when the futures contract price equals its original, or base, purchase price, F_B.

As the left-hand diagram in Exhibit 13–8 illustrates, the buyer of a long hedge in futures scores a profit if the price of the underlying security and the value of the associated futures contract rise. This happens if interest rates fall, causing subsequent futures prices to climb above their base price ($F_t > F_B$). On the other hand, suppose that futures prices fall below the original purchase price, so that $F_t < F_B$ because interest rates have risen. Then the holder of a long hedge will suffer a loss (in the absence of a hedge against the futures position itself).

The right-hand diagram in Exhibit 13–8 shows that the holder of a short futures position suffers losses when interest rates decline. In this case, the prices of the futures contract and of the securities named in that contract increase, forcing the holder of a short hedge to buy securities or futures at a higher price ($F_B > F_t$) to make delivery or to cancel out the short position. On the other hand, if interest rates rise, then the prices of futures (and the associated securities) eventually may drop below their original purchase price ($F_t < F_B$), handing the short hedger a profit (not counting brokerage fees or taxes).

Option Contracts on Financial Futures

In addition to financial futures contracts themselves, there is now also active trading in options on financial futures contracts. An **option contract** is an agreement between a buyer and seller to grant the holder of the contract the right to buy or sell a futures contract or other security at a specified price on or before the day the contract expires. Options on farm commodities and on selected common stock have been traded for decades. Recently, however, there has been an explosion of new options products, led by options on Treasury bond futures introduced in October 1982. Then, in 1985, the International Monetary Market (IMM), a division of the Chicago Mercantile Exchange, began trading option contracts on financial futures for Eurodollar deposits. In April of the following year, the IMM opened floor trading in options on U.S. Treasury bill futures. As more investors began to take an interest in options trading, the major exchanges began developing many new option contracts on stock, foreign currencies, and financial futures contracts. The options market has also spread overseas. For example, options on futures for Eurodollar deposits, British long-gilt bonds, German government bonds, and Euromarks are now traded on the London International Financial Futures Exchange (LIFFE).

Basic Types of Option Contracts

There are two basic types of option contracts. **Call options** give the contract buyer the right, but not the obligation, to buy ("call away") futures contracts or securities at a set price called the **strike price**. The seller of the contract is called the *option writer*. Under the terms of U.S. options, the buyer may exercise the option and purchase the futures or securities specified from the writer at any time on or before the expiration date of the option. European options, on the other hand, can be exercised only on their expiration date. An option that is not used by its expiration date becomes worthless.

Put options grant the contract purchaser the right, but not the obligation, to sell ("put," or deliver) futures contracts or securities to the option writer at a set (strike) price on or before the option's expiration date. Buyers of both call and put options must pay a price — known as the **option premium** — for the privilege of being able to buy or sell futures or securities at a guaranteed price. By fixing the price of a financial transaction for a stipulated period, options provide an alternative way of hedging against market risk. Their principal advantage over futures contracts is that hedging with futures contracts limits the hedger's profits. Options, in contrast, can be used to limit losses while preserving the opportunity to make substantial profits.

Most options on financial instruments are traded today on organized exchanges such as the IMM or the Chicago Board Options Exchange (CBOE). There are more options on corporate stock than on any other security; individual options on units of 100 shares cover more than 700 different stocks traded on the New York and American stock exchanges and in various over-the-counter markets. Options are also available on marketwide indexes, the most popular being Standard & Poor's 100 Index and 500 Index, the New York Stock Exchange Composite Index, and the NIKKEI 225 Stock Average.

Exchange-traded options are standardized contracts with uniform terms that control the quality of the items being traded and the permissible length of contracts and enhance the marketability of options. The options exchange sets rules for trading and pricing options; the exchange clearinghouse keeps a record of all trades and guarantees performance on all exchange-traded options. In effect, the clearinghouse becomes the ultimate seller to all option buyers and the ultimate buyer for all option sellers. Most option contracts are liquidated before they expire by each trader making an offsetting purchase or sale. For example, the buyer of a call option can "erase" his or her contract by selling a call option involving the same security with the same expiration date and strike price. Put options are liquidated in the same fashion with the buyer (seller) of the put selling (buying) a comparable put on or before the expiration date.

Option Contracts for Money Market and Capital Market Instruments

The two principal types of exchange-traded options involving short-term instruments are U.S. Treasury bill futures options and Eurodollar futures options.[4] These options call for the delivery of three-month or one-year T-bill futures on or before an expiration date that is usually three to four weeks ahead of the maturity date of the futures contracts involved. The strike price is quoted in terms of a price index equal to 100 less the bill futures' discount rate. For example, a call option on T-bill futures with a strike price of 94 means that bill futures must be delivered at an interest rate of 6 percent (100 − 94).

Eurodollar futures options, on the other hand, expire on the last day for trading the Eurodollar deposit contract that is the target of the option. This contract is somewhat unique in that an "open position" on the expiration date is settled in cash, not by delivering futures or Eurodollar deposits. Both IMM and LIFFE Eurodollar futures options trade in million-dollar units.

The Chicago Mercantile Exchange (CME) recently opened trading in options on one-month LIBOR futures contracts (traded in $3-million units) to help protect the value of international loans priced off the London Interbank Offer Rate (LIBOR). The CME also offers options on 3-month Euromark futures contracts and on Deutsche mark, Japanese yen, Swiss franc, French franc, British pound, and Australian dollar currency futures.

---

[4]U.S. Treasury bills, which are discussed at length in Chapter 15, are the most widely traded of all short-term financial instruments, having maturities ranging from a few days or weeks to one year. Each bill is a direct debt obligation of the U.S. government. Eurodollar deposits, in contrast, are large-denomination deposits in the world's largest banks with offices outside the United States. As Chapter 18 notes, they are traded daily between international banks.

For longer-term capital market securities, the most popular exchange-traded option is the Treasury bond option contract. This option is traded on the Chicago Board of Trade's Options Exchange in units of $100,000. The T-bond options' current price is quoted in points ($1 on a base of $100) and 64ths of a point. For example, on March 26, 1996, T-bond options for exercise on or before May, June, or September were quoted as follows:

Exhibit 13–9   **T-Bond Options** (CBT, $100,000; Expressed in 64ths of 100%)

Strike	Calls-Settle			Puts-Settle		
Price	May	Jun	Sep	May	Jun	Sep
111	2-14	....	....	0-34	....	....
112	1-34	2-02	2-53	0-54	1-22	2-41
113	1-00	....	....	1-20	....	....
114	0-39	1-06	1-60	1-59	2-25	3-46
115	0-22	....	....	2-42	....	....
116	0-11	0-32	1-17	3-31	3-50	5-00

T-BONDS (CBT)
$100,000; points and 64ths of 100%
Est. vol. 61,000;
Mn vol. 39,014 calls; 29,521 puts
Op. Int. Mon 385,595 calls; 259,628 puts

Source: *The Wall Street Journal,* Southwest Edition, March 27, 1996, p.C17. Reprinted by permission of *The Wall Street Journal,* © 1996 Dow Jones & Company, Inc. All Rights Reserved Worldwide.

We note that the option to call Treasury bond futures contracts in May carrying a strike price of 111 (or $111,000 on a $100,000 contract) was trading at a price of 2–14 ($2 14/64 for a $100 option or $2,219 for a $100,000 face-value contract). There are also options on 10-year and 5-year U.S. Treasury note futures having a face value of $100,000 or multiples thereof and options on 2-year T-note futures with a face value of $200,000 currently being traded at the Chicago Board of Trade (CBOT). Introduced more recently at the CBOT are options for $100,000-minimum Canadian government bond futures contracts (whose value is expressed in Canadian dollars).

As Exhibit 13–9 makes clear, the higher an option's strike price, the lower the call option's price (premium) tends to be, because there is less likelihood the call will be exercised. Moreover, call options expiring at a later date sell for higher premiums than those expiring sooner because there is more time in the case of the former options for security prices to change in a way that favors their exercise by the option buyer.

Uses of Options on Futures Contracts

Options have many uses; their two most common ones involve (1) protecting a future investment's yield against falling interest rates by using call options and (2) protecting against rising interest rates by using put options. Let's look at an example of each of these typical option transactions.

Protecting against Declining Investment Yields. A major concern of most security buyers is how to protect against falling yields and rising prices on bonds and other securities that will be purchased in the future. Options offer a way to prepare for a future investment, even if the investor doesn't yet have sufficient cash to make the investment, by carrying out a temporary transaction that helps guarantee future yields. An option contract enables an investor to set a maximum price for securities targeted for future purchase.

For example, suppose a security dealer plans to buy $100 million in U.S. Treasury bills in a few days and hopes to earn an interest yield of at least 7 percent. However, fearful of a substantial drop in interest rates before the dealer is ready to buy, he executes a call option on T-bill futures at an index (strike) price of 93 (i.e., an interest rate yield of $100 - 93$, or 7 percent). If T-bill futures rise in value above 93 (i.e., fall below 7 percent in yield), the dealer probably will exercise the option because it is now "in the money." When the market price of a futures contract or security rises above the strike price in the associated option contract, the buyer of the call option is said to be "in the money," because he can buy the futures contract or security from the option writer at the strike price (in this case, at 93) and sell at a higher price (perhaps at 93.50) in futures or cash markets. The resulting profit (after paying the option's premium, taxes, and transactions costs) offsets the loss in yield on the planned investment due to a decline in market interest rates.

If interest rates go against the dealer's forecast, however, and rise instead, the call option will be "out of the money." Its strike price will be above the market's current price for the securities or futures covered by the option. In this case, the call will *not* be exercised, and the dealer will lose the premium he paid for the option. However, the fact that interest rates rose (and, therefore, Treasury bill prices fell) means the dealer can now purchase Treasury bills at a cheaper price and a more desirable yield.

Incidentally, the profit on an exercised *call option* can be found by using the equation:

$$\text{Profit} = F - S - Pr - T$$

where F is the current futures or security price, S is the strike price agreed upon in the option contract, Pr is the premium paid by the call option buyer, and T represents any taxes owed as a result of the transaction. If the futures price, F, rises high enough, the buyer can call away futures contracts or securities from the option writer at price S and still have some profit left over after paying the premium (Pr) and any taxes incurred (T). However, if the futures price, F, declines, the option will go unexercised and the buyer's loss will equal $-Pr$. The seller of the unexercised call will then reap a profit of $+Pr$ (less taxes and transactions costs).

Protecting against Rising Interest Rates. In contrast to lenders, who worry about falling yields, borrowers' concerns usually are to keep borrowing costs from rising. Consider a bank, for example, that must borrow millions of dollars daily and fears rising money market interest rates. Perhaps market rates on deposits are currently at 8 percent and the bank fears a substantial rise in deposit rates to 9 percent. Accordingly, the bank's deposit manager purchases a put option on Eurodollar futures at a strike price of 92. If these futures fall below 92 in price due to rising interest rates, the bank's liability manager may decide to exercise the put option and sell Eurodollar futures to the option writer at the strike price. The manager will then liquidate the bank's futures position by buying equivalent futures contracts at the lower market price and profit from the spread between the strike price of 92 and the current lower market price. This profit will partially offset the bank's higher borrowing costs.

On the other hand, if interest rates do not rise, the bank's deposit manager will not exercise the put option. This will mean losing the full amount of the option premium, but the bank's borrowing costs will stay low. In this instance, it paid a premium for interest rate insurance that turned out not to be needed.

The profit to the buyer of a put option can be calculated from the following equation:

$$\text{Profit} = S - F - Pr - T$$

where S is the strike price, F the market price of the futures or securities mentioned in the option, Pr the premium paid for the option, and T taxes owed. If the futures or security price, F, falls far enough below strike price S, the put buyer will show a profit $S - F$, which will exceed the premium paid and any resulting tax liability. On the other hand, if the futures or security price rises, the put will go unexercised, and the buyer's loss will be measured by $-Pr$. The seller of the unexercised put will then experience a corresponding profit of $+Pr$ (less taxes and transactions costs).

Payoff Diagrams for Valuing Options

We can diagram how options are valued by looking first at the value of a *put* option to the investor who holds it (the option buyer) on the date or dates the option can be exercised. Exhibit 13–10 illustrates the relationship between a put option's value and the value of the underlying futures contract or security named in the option. Point S marked on the horizontal axis in Exhibit 13–10 represents the strike price, the price at which the futures contract or security can be sold by the option's holder.

Suppose the futures contract or security in question currently is selling for price F_1, which is more than its strike price, S (i.e., $F_1 > S$). In this case, the option has a current value of zero (actually less than zero because the option buyer had to pay premium Pr, which is lost if the option goes unexercised). The holder of the option obviously would prefer to sell the futures contracts she holds at current market price F_1 rather than deliver them to the option writer for a price of only S. If current price F_1 is significantly larger than S, however, the option buyer may still reap a substantial gain despite losing the option premium.

In contrast, suppose that the futures contract has a current price of F_2, where $F_2 < S$. In this instance, with a market price lower than the strike price, exercise of the option results in a profit (less taxes, brokerage commission, and option premium) for its buyer. The option buyer will deliver the futures to the option writer and receive strike price S for a net profit per contract of $S - F_2 - Pr - T$. Clearly for the holder of a put option, when $S > F_t$, the option will normally be exercised for a profit and be "in the money" as long as $S - F_t$

Exhibit 13–10   **Payoffs to the Option Buyer from Put Options**

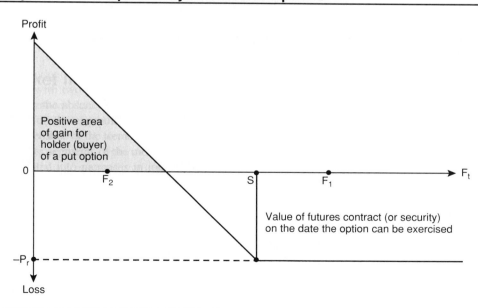

exceeds the option premium, taxes, and transaction costs. When $S < F_t$, the option will expire unexercised; the profit will be zero (or negative, if we count the premium and transactions costs) and clearly will be "out of the money." Only within the triangle in the upper left-hand corner of Exhibit 13–10 will the holder of a put option reap positive gains.

From the standpoint of the writer (seller) of a put option, the writer benefits if the option is *not* exercised. This happens if the market value of the futures contract or security remains higher than the option's strike price, as at $F_1 > S$. Exhibit 13–11 shows that the area of gain for the writer of a put option lies around and to the right of strike price S. In this region, the option currently is "out of the money" from the buyer's standpoint, and the writer pockets the premium paid by the option holder. However, if the futures price falls *below* the strike price, as at $F_2 < S$, the writer will likely be forced to accept delivery of futures contracts at their strike price despite the contract's currently depressed value. From the buyer's point of view, the put option is now "in the money."

In the case of *call* options, the writer agrees to sell securities to the buyer of the option at a stipulated strike price. If, as shown in Exhibit 13–12, the market price of the underlying futures contract or security rises above the strike price to F_1, the holder of the call option will exercise that option and call away the futures contract or security from the option writer at strike price S. Exercise of this now "in the money" call option will enable the option buyer to resell each of the newly acquired futures contracts or securities for a profit of $F_1 - S - Pr - T$. If, on the other hand, the market value of futures contracts or securities falls *below* the option's strike price, as at F_2, the option holder would be better off purchasing the futures contracts or securities in the open market rather than exercising his or her option to buy at price S. The call will expire unused ("out of the money"), and the option buyer will suffer a loss due to the premium (Pr) he or she has paid. Thus, the area of positive gain to the holder of a call option generally lies to the right of the strike price in Exhibit 13–12 and in the upper right-hand portion of that diagram.

The writer of a call option, on the other hand, gains when the market value of the futures contract or security falls below the strike price, as at $F_2 < S$ in Exhibit 13–13. At this price and at all prices below S, the call option is "out of the money" for the option buyer and will go unexercised, allowing the option writer to earn the full premium, Pr (less any

Exhibit 13–11 **Payoffs for Put Options to the Option Writer**

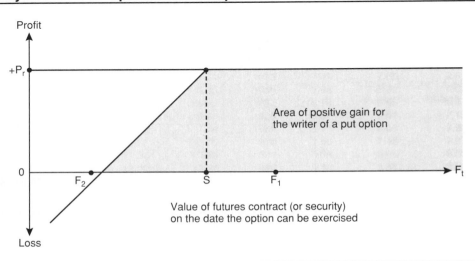

Value of futures contract (or security)
on the date the option can be exercised

Exhibit 13–12   **Payoffs to the Option Buyer from Call Options**

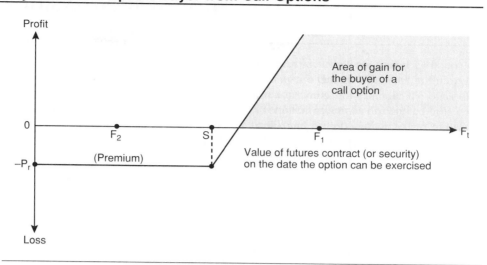

taxes and transactions costs). However, if the futures' or security's market value climbs above S, as at price F_1 in Exhibit 13–13, the writer must sell off from his portfolio currently higher-valued securities to the option buyer at the low contract price S, taking a loss equal to $F_1 - S + Pr$ on every security delivered to the buyer. The call option clearly has become "in the money" for the option buyer. As shown in Exhibit 13–13, the region of positive gain for the writer of a call option lies in the upper left-hand portion of the price diagram (including price F_2). In contrast, futures or security prices increasingly to the right of point S result in decreasing profits or increasing losses for the option writer.

Exhibit 13–13   **Payoffs to the Option Writer from Call Options**

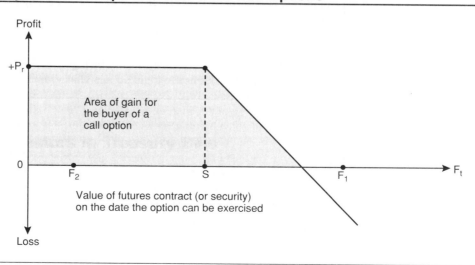

MANAGEMENT INSIGHT:
Watching Out for the "D" Word

Financial futures and option contracts belong to a broad class of financial instruments called "derivatives." (Other examples of derivatives include SWAPs, forward contracts, and loan-backed securities.) These unique instruments depend for their value on one or more underlying securities or variables, such as stock prices, interest rates, currency, or commodity prices. Recent experience has shown that "derivatives" pose their own special brand of risk for both the buyers and sellers of these instruments.

For one thing, derivatives involve at least two parties to the contract that creates them and either party may fail to deliver or pay what is agreed to, exposing the other party to loss (often referred to as *counter-party risk*). Other forms of risk associated with derivatives include *price risk* (as their market values change), *liquidity risk* (because traders may be prevented from carrying out risk-covering transactions), *settlement risk* (when securities are delivered before payment is received), *operating risk* (due to faulty internal controls on trading activity), *legal risk* (if derivative customers sue to recover their losses), and *regulatory risk* (when regulations are changed or violated). Derivatives can become so complex that it's easy for a trader to become entangled in multiple contracts and lose track of his or her firm's true position and exposure to loss. At the same time, inexperienced traders find it easy to cross the line from prudent risk management to outright speculation for profit.

Indeed, several large companies (such as Bankers Trust Company, Nippon Steel Corp., Gibson Greetings, Metallgesellschaft AG, and Proctor & Gamble) recently have reported large losses from derivatives trading. At the same time, many of the financial firms advising corporations to make heavier use of derivatives have been accused of promising too much and ignoring the welfare of their clients in pursuit of fat commissions.

Still, it's important not to overlook the potential *benefits* that properly managed derivatives trading offers users. These include saving money on interest costs or on foreign currency purchases and better balancing of a business firm's cash inflows and outflows. Moreover, with relatively low cash margins required by most brokers, it is possible to control large amounts of capital with the investment of only limited amounts of cash. And, thanks to a 1993 change in IRS regulations, losses from hedging transactions may be treated as "ordinary" losses and, therefore, are deductible from taxable income as long as the hedges and the items hedged are clearly identified up front.

Recently publicized losses in derivative trading have spawned cries for new, tougher regulation of this market. In 1992 the Commodity Futures Trading Commission (CFTC) — the chief body regulating futures and options trading in the U.S. — received broad new regulatory powers from Congress. Recently, the CFTC has moved to monitor futures and options trading more closely by developing new rules to curb insider trading in futures and options, requiring professional traders to register and undergo background checks, and keeping a close watch on "dual trading," in which exchange floor brokers simultaneously trade for themselves and their customers. U.S. futures exchanges were ordered to install new electronic trade and auditing

(continued)

equipment to improve speed and accuracy and make monitoring of trading activity easier. In the future, regulators are likely to take a close look at five issues involving the use of derivatives: (1) how adequately *users disclose their risk exposures*; (2) the *capital adequacy* maintained by both users and traders of derivatives to protect against failure; (3) how fully derivative traders *disclose the risks involved to their less sophisticated customers* (such as pension plans, smaller banks, and mutual fund investors); (4) the danger of *systemic risk* (where a few defaults among contracting parties leads to failures throughout the market in domino fashion); and (5) a possible *moral hazard problem* if ill-conceived government involvement in the derivative market leads the public to believe these instruments are safer than they really are.

Those who use derivatives must learn the principles of prudent risk management and employ up-to-date technology to monitor derivatives trading and settlements and to value any derivatives traded. Derivative-trading firms should have boards or risk committees that set boundaries on the use of these instruments and risk management teams that closely watch trading activity. Indeed, regulated firms (like commercial banks) must identify a specific risk exposure they face and tie each derivative contract to which they are a party to the particular risk exposure that contract was designed to deal with. Finally, individuals and companies using or thinking about using derivatives need professional advice from bankers, brokers, and dealers before they venture into this often volatile marketplace.

The Black-Scholes Model for Valuing Options

The diagrams presented in the foregoing section relate option prices only to the prices of the underlying futures contract or security. In the real world, we have discovered that not one, but several, variables influence the prices of options. These variables include the following:

RF = The *risk-free rate of interest* (that investors can approximately achieve by purchasing default-free government securities), which is positively related to option prices.

P = The *current market value* (price) of the futures contract or security that is the subject of the option contract, which is positively related to the option's price.

σ = The *degree of volatility* in the value of the underlying futures contract or security, measured by the variance (σ^2) or standard deviation (σ) of its rate of return, which is also positively related to the price of the option.

S = The *strike price* specified in the option contract, which is negatively related to the price of the option.

t = The *length of time* between now and the point in time when the option expires, also positively related to the option's price.

In 1973, a major breakthrough occurred in the field of finance when researchers Fisher Black and Myron Scholes developed a model that explained the price of a call option (C) using continuous-time mathematics. They determined that the call option's price could be found by solving the following differential equation:

$$C = P \times Nr\ (Y_A) - Se^{RFt} \times Nr\ (Y_B) \tag{13-1}$$

where

$$Y_A = [\ln(P/S) + RFt + \sigma^2 t/2]\sigma t^{1/2}$$

and

$$Y_B = [\ln(P/S) + RFt - \sigma^2 t/2]\sigma t^{1/2}$$

In the preceding formula, $\ln$ represents the log of a quantity relative to the base e, and Nr stands for the normal cumulative probability density function, measuring the probability that a normally distributed random variable will be equal to or less than Y. Several brokers operating today on Wall Street use high-speed computer programs that calculate the expected value of an option as figured from the above formula and then buy or sell options or securities until option prices approach their expected levels. (See the accompanying box for an example of how to use the Black-Scholes formula to calculate an option's expected value.)

Reduced to nonmathematical terms, the preceding equation suggests that option prices depend on the expected value of the underlying futures contract or security named in the option and the expected value of the strike price on the day the option expires, both expressed in present-value terms. The discount rate used is the risk-free interest rate because, Black and Scholes assumed, there are enough informed and technically sophisticated investors to effectively reduce risk close to the risk-free rate of return by constructing an adequately hedged investment portfolio. In such a portfolio, movements in the value of options, futures, and securities will offset each other, leaving the value of the investor's total portfolio fully protected against adverse price and rate movements. Subsequent testing of the Black-Scholes model suggests that it performs reasonably well at calculating the true value of European options (which can be exercised only on a single day), making significant errors only when the underlying securities have especially large or small variability in rates of return or, in the case of options on stock, when a stock's dividend payments are significant.[5]

TRADERS ACTIVE IN THE FUTURES AND OPTIONS MARKETS

A wide variety of financial institutions and individuals are active in futures and options trading today. The principal traders in futures and options are individuals, managed futures funds, and financial intermediaries. Managed futures funds are like mutual funds, offering shares to individual investors who regularly purchase futures and option contracts. These pools of professionally managed capital offer the advantage of diversifying risk by trading simultaneously in many contracts with varied maturities. The majority of these pools try to

---

[5]The Black-Scholes formula in Equation 13–1 measures the expected value of a *call* option (C). We can find the expected value of the corresponding *put* option having the same strike price and time to maturity by solving:

$$\text{Expected value of put} = C + Se^{-Rf \times t} - P$$

where P is the price of the underlying security or futures contract and S, Rf, and t are the same as defined in Equation 13–1.

The Black-Scholes option pricing model rests on some strong assumptions. It assumes that there are no transactions costs or taxes, that the underlying asset does not pay out income during the life of an option, that the standard deviation of return is constant, that security prices follow a continuous random process, homogenous expectations among investors, and that the risk-free interest rate is constant over time and the same regardless of maturity. However, repeated testing suggests that even if these assumptions are violated, the option value estimates generated by the Black-Scholes model are remarkably close to real-world values.

limit losses to the investor's original investment, liquidating holdings rather than issuing margin calls if prices drop.

Firms and individual traders representing the futures and options industries run a close second to individual investors as participants in daily trading. Many of these industry personnel speculate on interest rate movements or arbitrage between spot and futures markets. Financial institutions also play a prominent role in futures trading, led by securities dealers, commercial and mortgage banks, savings and loan associations, and insurance companies. Securities dealers are interested in risk reduction through hedging and in profitable trades arising from correctly guessing the future course of interest rates. Savings and loan associations, mortgage bankers, and insurance companies are involved in futures trading to hedge the market value and yield on their mortgage loans, mortgage-backed securities, and other longer-term investments.

Participation by commercial banks in futures trading has been quite limited to date, with only a few hundred banks active in the market on a daily basis. One major factor limiting bank participation in the futures market is federal regulation, which requires banks to limit their futures and options trading to hedging real risk-exposure situations and to receive regulatory approval before launching their hedging programs. Another problem centers on the required accounting treatment of gains and losses from futures trading. Gains or losses on futures positions must be recorded daily, even though these position changes are not realized until the contract is concluded or zeroed out. The result may be volatile fluctuations in reported income for those institutions active in futures trading. However, participation by financial institutions in the futures and options markets is expected to expand significantly as the regulatory community becomes more comfortable with the hedging concept and management becomes more knowledgeable about futures and options trading.

Potential Benefits from the Futures and Options Markets

Trading in futures and options offers several potential advantages to financial institutions and individual investors. The prospect of hedging against changes in security prices and interest rates offers the potential for reducing risk and offsetting losses, particularly for security dealers, banks, insurance companies, and other financial institutions that experience marked fluctuations in income due to changes in the differential between interest rates on borrowed funds and interest returns on assets. Moreover, if the futures and options markets do lead to a reduction of risk, this will enable many financial institutions to extend greater amounts of credit to their customers. The result could be a more efficient allocation of scarce funds within each financial institution and within the financial system as a whole.

Not all observers agree that futures and options markets result in a net gain for society by helping financial institutions reduce risk and use scarce resources more efficiently. Some analysts believe that the futures and options markets are largely speculative and not really geared for the hedging of risks per se. They see these markets as aimed principally at providing wealthy investors with a speculative outlet for their funds and as resulting in unnecessary risks due to excessive speculation. Some have argued that futures and options markets increase the price volatility of those securities whose contracts are actively traded and have played a major role in recent stock market downturns.

On balance, futures and options markets probably have resulted in a net benefit to the financial system and to the economy. They have separated the risk of changing security prices and interest rates from the lending of funds, at least for those institutions actively participating in these markets. The risk of price and yield changes is transferred to investors willing to assume such risks. The futures and options markets have helped to reduce

MANAGEMENT INSIGHT:

Pricing Options: An Example

To illustrate how to price an option on financial futures or other securities using the Black-Scholes pricing model (Equation 13–1) presented in this chapter, let's suppose that the current price of the futures contract or security in which we are interested is $100 with a standard deviation around its expected rate of return of 0.50, or 50 percent, the option on this security has a strike price of $95, and the risk-free interest rate is currently 10 percent. If the option will expire in 3 months (0.25 years), what is its expected price according to the Black-Scholes model? As Equation 13–1 in this chapter shows, the expected current price of a *call option* (C) on this security can be found from:

$$\text{Expected call option price } (C) = P \times Nr(Y_A) - Se^{-Rf \times t} \times Nr(Y_B)$$

where P is the current market price, S the strike price, Rf the risk-free rate, and t the option's time to maturity. The terms $Nr(Y_A)$ and $Nr(Y_B)$ measure the probability the option will have value to the buyer (i.e., that is the probability the option will eventually be exercised because it is "in the money"). The higher the probability that an option will be "in the money," the higher must be its price to the option buyer. Nr represents the normal distribution; the security's return is assumed to be normally distributed.

We can calculate the probability that this option will pay off from:

$$Y_A = [1n(P/S) + Rf \times t + \sigma^2 t/2]/\sigma t^{\frac{1}{2}}$$

Substituting in the figures from our example,

$$Y_A = (1n[100/95] + [0.10 \times 0.25] + 0.25 \times (0.50)^2)/0.50 \times (.25)^{1/2} = 0.43$$

We can derive the second probability estimate in the equation, Y_B, from:

$$Y_B = Y_A - \sigma t^{1/2} = (0.43) - (0.50) \times (0.25)^{1/2} = 0.18$$

Next, we find the corresponding values from the assumed normal distribution of security prices, represented by $Nr(Y_A)$ and $Nr(Y_B)$. These we can look up in a table for the cumulative normal distribution, which is contained in most statistics books. A portion of such a table is given below:

Cumulative Normal Distribution Table

Y	Nr(Y)	Y	Nr(Y)	Y	Nr(Y)	Y	Nr(Y)
−0.50	.3085	−0.20	.4207	0.12	.5478	0.20	.5793
−0.40	.3446	−0.10	.4602	0.14	.5557	0.30	.6179
−0.30	.3821	0.00	.5000	0.16	.5636	0.40	.6554
−0.25	.4013	0.10	.5398	0.18	.5714	0.50	.6915

Checking the above table for the normal probabilities associated with Y_A and Y_B gives:

(continued)

$$Nr(0.43) = .6664$$
$$Nr(0.18) = .5714$$

Then, the expected value of the call option must be:

$$\frac{\textit{Expected call option}}{\textit{price (C)}} = \$100 \times (.6664) - \$95 \times e^{-.10\times0.25} \times (.5714) = \$13.70$$

Could we also find the value of a *put* option for this same security? Assuming the same option strike price and option maturity, the expected value of the corresponding put option would be:

$$\frac{\textit{Expected put}}{\textit{option price}} = C + Se^{-Rf\times t} - P$$

Substituting in the calculated call option price (C) of $13.70, the security's price (P) of $100, the strike price ($S$) of $95, the risk-free interest rate (Rf) of 10%, and 0.25 years time to maturity (t) from the example above, we get an expected put option price of:

$$\frac{\textit{Expected put}}{\textit{option price}} = \$13.70 + \$95e^{(-.10\times0.25)} - 100$$

Checking the value of $e^{(-.10\times0.25)}$ on a pocket calculator gives:

$$\frac{\textit{Expected put}}{\textit{option price}} = \$13.7 + \$95(0.9753) - \$100 = \$6.35$$

search costs and expand the flow of information on market opportunities for those who seek risk reduction through hedging. Moreover, this developing institution has tended to unify local markets into an international forward market, overcoming geographic and institutional rigidities that tend to separate one market from another.

But futures and options trading is not without its own special risks. The risk of price and yield fluctuations is reduced through negotiating these contracts, but the investor faces the risk of changing interest rates and security prices between futures and spot markets (basis risk). It is rare that gains and losses from simultaneous trading in spot, futures, or options markets exactly offset each other, resulting in a perfect hedge. There is also the risk of broker cash margin calls on the trader due to adverse price changes (margin risk) and possible problems in liquidating an open position in futures or options (liquidity risk). Moreover, there are substantial brokerage fees for executing futures contracts and required minimum deposits for margin accounts that tie up cash in non-interest-bearing assets.[6]

---

[6]Brokerage commissions and margin requirements in contract trading are not inconsequential. For example, a so-called *round trip* — buying and selling contracts — of S&P 500 stock index futures will cost approximately $2,500. Margin accounts must be maintained above a specified minimum level. Each account is evaluated daily, and additional funds must be supplied when the account declines below the minimum level. Many traders pledge securities to their margin accounts to eliminate the necessity of repeatedly supplying new funds.

INTERNATIONAL FOCUS:

The Risk of Trading in Derivatives — The Barings Brothers' Failure

On February 26, 1995 Barings Brothers — an old-line British investment bank and security dealer — collapsed due to massive losses from trading in futures, options, and other derivative securities. At the time of its failure, Barings PLC held assets amounting to nearly 6 billion pounds and had existed for more than 230 years. However, Barings' long history and established reputation for caution and conservatism could not save the firm from huge losses stemming from its open trading position in futures and options contracts, betting on a rise in Japanese stock prices. Unfortunately for Barings, the Nikkei 225 stock market average fell rather than rose, and the old-line firm suffered over £700 million (about $1 billion) in losses.

The principal reason for Barings' collapse centered on some highly speculative trading in Nikkei-based futures contracts through its offices in Singapore. Its traders were under instructions to conduct arbitrage trading between the prices of Nikkei futures contracts on the Osaka Securities Exchange (OSE) and the Singapore Monetary Exchange (SIMEX), hoping to profit by buying contracts in the cheapest of these two markets and selling them in the most expensive market. Normally, such a trading strategy carries little risk because a long position taken in the cheaper market typically is almost fully offset by a short position adopted in the more expensive market. Even if prices don't move as expected, a loss suffered in one market should roughly offset a gain experienced in the other market under an arbitrage trading approach.

Unfortunately for Barings, one of its traders broke away from conventional arbitrage trading to adopt open (unhedged) positions, which bet that Japanese stock prices could only go one way — up. This trader soon had acquired in the neighborhood of $7 billion in Japanese stock index futures contracts. Instead of pulling back as the prospects for a Japanese stock-price rise faded, this Barings trader took on even more Nikkei futures contracts in an effort to drive Japanese stock prices higher. When the Japanese market plunged early in 1995 under the combined effects of adverse economic reports, financial problems in the Japanese banking community, and natural disasters, Barings losses exploded and overwhelmed its equity capital, forcing that storied company to fold. In March 1995, what was left of Barings was acquired by Internationale Nedevlanden Groep of the Netherlands.

Several lessons have come out of the much reported Barings case. One is the necessity of monitoring employee trading activities more closely and of building in auditing systems that allow knowledgeable employees to monitor each other's activities. In this particular case, Barings allowed the same trader to remain in charge of both its Singapore settlements department and its trading department, which made it easier for a single trader to hide losses and conceal risk exposures. Just shortly before its collapse, Barings had begun to assemble a new derivatives unit and hired a new risk manager, but these changes simply came too late.

SUMMARY

The increasingly volatile interest rates of recent years have increased the risk sensitivity of many investors. It is not surprising, therefore, that many individual and institutional investors have sought new and innovative ways to insulate their investments from fluctuations in interest rates and security prices. The financial futures market, inaugurated by the Chicago Board of Trade in 1975, and the newer markets trading in options on futures and securities have become increasingly popular forms of insulation against the risks of investing in stock and debt securities.

Futures and options markets are based on the notion of *hedging*, which is the act of contracting to buy or sell a security in the future but at a price agreed on today. By setting the price and other terms of such a contract now, the investor is at least partially insulated against the risk of future changes in interest rates and security prices. Hedging transfers risk from one investor to another willing to bear that risk. The hedger contracts away all or a portion of the risk of security price fluctuations to lock in a targeted rate of return. This is accomplished by taking equal and opposite positions in the spot (or cash) market and in the forward (or futures) market or by purchasing put or call options to deliver or to take delivery of designated securities or futures at a stipulated price on or before a specific date. If interest rates are expected to fall and the investor desires to lock in a current high yield on a security, he or she should buy a contract calling for the future delivery of the security at a set price (i.e., take on a long hedge) or purchase a call option. An opposite set of buy-sell transactions in the futures market (i.e., a short hedge) or in the options market (i.e., a put option) would generally be used if interest rates were expected to rise.

Trading in financial futures and options is limited today to a list of high-quality financial instruments, but the list is growing. Most observers expect continued growth in futures and options due to volatile conditions in global financial markets and the growing financial sophistication of investors. ∎

KEY TERMS AND CONCEPTS IN THIS CHAPTER

hedging	long hedge	call options
basis	short hedge	strike price
financial futures contracts	cross hedge	put options
stock index arbitrage	option contract	option premium

STUDY QUESTIONS

1. What is the basic purpose of futures and options trading in commodities? In securities? Where is most futures and options trading carried out?

2. Explain the similarities and differences between hedging in the futures and options markets and purchasing insurance.

3. What is a perfect or complete hedge? Define the terms *opening a hedge* and *closing a hedge*.

4. How do spot (cash) markets differ from futures (forward) markets?

5. What is *basis*? Explain how the basis for a futures contract relates to trading risk.

6. For what specific kinds of securities is there now an active futures market? Who issues these securities? Describe the restrictions imposed on trading futures contracts involving securities.

7. Define and explain the use of the following: (a) Long hedge, (b) Short hedge, (c) Cross hedge. Which works best in an environment of rising interest rates? Falling interest rates? Can you illustrate with a payoff diagram?

8. Explain carefully the uses of the following: (a) Call options, (b) Put options. Which is appropriate in an environment of rising interest rates? Of falling interest rates? Illustrate using payoff diagrams.

9. What are the principal benefits to financial institutions such as banks, securities dealers, insurance companies, and savings and loan associations from the use of the futures and options markets? Can you see any possible dangers?

10. What risks are inherent in futures and options trading? Costs?

PROBLEMS

1. An insurance company during the month of March committed itself to buy a block of home mortgages at a fixed price from a mortgage banker in September. The mortgages have a face value of $10 million. The insurer has recently prepared a forecast that indicates that mortgage interest rates will rise between now and September by a full percentage point. What kind of futures transaction would you recommend to protect the insurance company against a sizable loss on its mortgage commitment, particularly if it has to sell the mortgages shortly after they are taken into its portfolio? Indicate specifically what buy and sell transactions you would undertake in the futures market. Which futures contract would you most likely use? Why? What options contract seems best and why?

2. A large money center bank plans to offer money market CDs in substantial volume (at least $100 million) in six months due to a projected upsurge in credit deals from some of its most valued corporate customers. Unfortunately, the bank's economist has just predicted that money market interest rates should rise over the next year (with perhaps a full 1.5 percentage point increase within the next six months). Explain why the bank's management would be concerned about this development. Suppose management expects its corporate loan customers to resist any loan terms that would automatically result in loan rates being immediately adjusted upward to reflect any rate increases in the money market. What futures market transaction would you recommend? What is the best options contract alternative for the bank?

3. An investment banking firm discovers that 90 days from today it is due to receive a cash payment from one of its corporate clients of $972,500. The firm's portfolio manager is instructed to plan to invest this new cash for a horizon of three months, after which it will need to be liquidated. Interest rates are attractive today at 10 percent, but a steep decline is forecast due to a developing recession. The portfolio manager decides to try to guarantee a 9 percent rate of return today on this planned three-month investment of cash.

    a. Describe what the manager should do today in the financial futures market. Then, indicate how he will close out the futures position eventually.

    b. What are the appropriate (buy-sell) steps for the manager if options on financial futures are to be used?

4. During the month just concluded, the prices of U.S. Treasury bonds fluctuated between a price of $95 (based on a $100 par value) and a price of $93. Treasury bond futures over the same period fluctuated between $92 and $88 (based on a $100 par value). How did the *basis* for T-bond futures contracts change over this period? What was the *volatility ratio* for T-bond futures for the month just ended? Using the volatility ratio you have just calculated and assuming you wish to hedge for the next 30 days $25 million in Treasury bonds that

you currently hold with $100,000 denomination T-bond futures contracts maturing in 90 days, how many T-bond futures contracts will you need to buy to fully cover the $25 million in securities at risk?

5.   Suppose a security or financial futures contract has a current price of $36 and the call option for this security has a strike price of $40. The call option is good for three months and the risk-free rate is 5 percent per annum. The standard deviation of the continuously compounded annual return on the security is 0.50, or 50 percent. Using the Black-Scholes option pricing formula, determine the expected price of this call option.

6.   Given the figures for the call option given in Problem 5 above, determine the expected value (price) for a corresponding put option having the same maturity and strike price.

SELECTED REFERENCES

Becketti, Sean, and Dan J. Roberts. "Will Increased Regulation of Stock Index Futures Reduce Stock Market Volatility?" *Economic Review*. Federal Reserve Bank of Kansas City, November/December 1990, pp. 33–46.

Black, Fisher, and M. Scholes. "The Valuation of Option Contracts and a Test of Market Efficiency." *Journal of Finance*, May 1972.

———. "The Pricing of Options and Corporate Liabilities." *Journal of Political Economy* 81 (May–June 1973), pp. 637–54.

Board of Trade of the City of Chicago. *Hedging Interest Rate Risks*. 1st rev. ed. Chicago, 1977.

Geske, R., and Richard Roll. "On Valuing American Call Options with the Black-Scholes European Formula." *Journal of Finance* 39 (June 1984), pp. 443–55.

Scarlata, Jodi G. "Institutional Developments in the Globalization of Securities and Futures Markets." *Review*. Federal Reserve Bank of St. Louis, January/February 1992, pp. 17–30.

Chapter 14 ▰▰▰▰▰▰▰▰▰▰▰▰▰▰▰▰▰▰▰

Characteristics of the Money Market

LEARNING OBJECTIVES IN THIS CHAPTER

- To explain the many essential roles and functions performed by the money market in the financial system.
- To see who the key actors — individuals and institutions — are in the workings of the money market.
- To understand how money market loans and securities differ from other financial services and instruments in the financial marketplace.

To the casual observer, the financial markets appear to be one vast cauldron of borrowing and lending activity in which some individuals and institutions are seeking credit while others supply the funds needed to make lending possible. All transactions carried out in the financial markets seem to be basically the same: borrowers issue securities (financial assets) that lenders purchase. When the loan is repaid, the borrower retrieves the securities and returns funds to the lender. Closer examination of our financial system reveals, however, that beyond the simple act of exchanging financial assets and funds, there are major differences between one financial transaction and another. For example, an individual may borrow $100,000 for 30 years to purchase a new home, whereas another's financing need may be for a six-month loan of $3,000 to cover a federal income tax obligation. A corporation may enter the financial markets this week to offer a new issue of 20-year bonds to finance the construction of an office building, and next week find itself in need of funds for just 60 days to purchase raw materials so that production can continue.

Clearly, then, the purposes for which money is borrowed within the financial system vary greatly from person to person and transaction to transaction. And the different purposes for which money is borrowed result in the creation of different kinds of financial assets, having different maturities, risks, and other features. In this chapter and the others in Part Four, we will be focusing on a collection of financial markets that share a common purpose in their trading activity and deal in financial instruments with similar features. Our particular focus is on the *money market*, the market for short-term credit.

In the money market, loans have an original maturity of one year or less. Money market loans are used to help corporations and governments pay the wages and salaries of their workers, make repairs, purchase inventories, pay dividends and taxes, and satisfy other short-term, working capital needs. In this respect, the money market stands in sharp contrast to the capital market. The capital market deals in long-term credit, that is, loans and securities over a year to maturity typically used to finance long-term investment projects. There are important similarities between the money and capital markets, as we will see in subsequent chapters, but there are also important differences that make these two markets unique.

CHARACTERISTICS OF THE MONEY MARKET

The money market, like all financial markets, provides a channel for the exchange of financial assets for money. However, it differs from other parts of the financial system in its emphasis on loans to meet purely short-term cash needs(i.e., current account, rather than capital account, transactions). The **money market** is the mechanism through which *holders of temporary cash surpluses meet holders of temporary cash deficits*. It is designed, on the one hand, to meet the short-term cash requirements of corporations, financial institutions, and governments, providing a mechanism for granting loans as short as overnight and as long as one year to maturity. At the same time, the money market provides an investment outlet for those spending units (also principally corporations, financial institutions, and governments) that hold surplus cash for short periods of time and wish to earn at least some return on temporarily idle funds. The essential function of the money market is to bring these two groups into contact to make borrowing and lending possible.

The Need for a Money Market

Why is such a market needed? There are several reasons. First, for most individuals and institutions, inflows and outflows of cash are rarely in perfect harmony with each other. Governments, for example, collect taxes from the public only at certain times of the year, such as in April when personal and corporate income tax payments are due. Disbursements of cash must be made throughout the year, however, to cover the wages and salaries of government employees, office supplies, repairs, and fuel costs, as well as unexpected expenses. When taxes are collected, governments usually are flush with funds that far exceed their immediate cash needs. At these times, they frequently enter the money market as lenders and purchase Treasury bills, bank deposits, and other attractive financial assets. Later, however, as cash runs low relative to current expenditures, these same governmental units must once again enter the money market as borrowers of funds, issuing short-term notes attractive to money market investors.

Business firms, too, collect sales revenue from customers at one point in time and dispense cash at other points in time to cover wages and salaries, make repairs, and meet other operating expenses. The checking account of an active business firm fluctuates daily between large surpluses and low or nonexistent cash balances. A surplus cash position frequently brings such a firm into the money market as a net lender of funds, investing idle funds in the hope of earning at least a modest rate of return. Cash deficits force it onto the borrowing side of the market, however, seeking other institutions with temporary cash surpluses. Clearly, then, the money market serves to bridge the gap between receipts and expenditures of funds, covering cash deficits with short-term borrowing when current expenditures exceed receipts and providing an investment outlet to earn interest income for units whose current receipts exceed their current expenditures.

To fully appreciate the workings of the money market, we must remember that *money* is one of the most perishable of all commodities. The holding of idle surplus cash is expensive, because cash balances earn little or no income for their owners. When idle cash is not invested, the holder incurs an opportunity cost in the form of interest income that is forgone. Moreover, each day that idle funds are not invested is a day's income lost forever. When large amounts of funds are involved, the income lost from not profitably investing idle funds for even 24 hours can be substantial. For example, the interest income from a loan of $10 million for one day at a 10 percent annual rate of interest amounts to about $2,800.[1] In a week's time, nearly $20,000 in interest would be lost from not investing $10 million in idle funds. Many students of the financial system find it hard to believe that investment outlets exist for loans as short as one day. However, billions of dollars in credit are extended in the money market overnight or for only a few daylight hours to securities dealers, banks, and nonfinancial corporations to cover temporary shortfalls of cash. As we will see in Chapter 16, one important money market instrument — the federal funds loan — is designed mainly for extending credit overnight or over the weekend.

Borrowers and Lenders in the Money Market

Who are the principal lenders of funds in the money market? Who are the principal borrowers? These questions are difficult to answer, because the same institutions frequently operate on both sides of the money market. For example, a large commercial bank operating in the money market (such as Citicorp or the Bank of Montreal) will borrow funds aggressively through CDs, federal funds, and other short-term instruments while lending short-term funds to corporations that have temporary cash shortages. Frequently, large nonfinancial corporations borrow millions of dollars on a single day, only to come back into the money market later in the week as a lender of funds due to a sudden upsurge in cash receipts. Institutions that typically play both sides of the money market include large banks, finance companies, major nonfinancial corporations, and units of government. Even the central bank, such as the Federal Reserve System, the Bank of England, or the Bank of Tokyo, may be an aggressive supplier of funds to the money market on one day and reverse itself the day following, demanding funds through the sale of securities in the open market. One institution that is virtually always on the demand side of the market, however, is the government. The U.S. Treasury, for example, is the largest of all money market borrowers worldwide.

The Goals of Money Market Investors

Investors in the money market seek mainly *safety* and *liquidity*, plus the opportunity to earn some interest income. This is because funds invested in the money market represent only temporary cash surpluses and are usually needed in the near future to meet tax obligations, cover wage and salary costs, pay stockholder dividends, and so on. For this reason, money market investors are especially sensitive to risk.

The strong aversion to risk among money market investors is especially evident when there is even a hint of trouble concerning the financial condition of a major money market borrower. For example, when the huge Penn Central Transportation Company collapsed in 1970 and defaulted on its short-term commercial notes, the short-term commercial paper

---

[1]As we saw in Chapter 9, the amount of interest income from a simple interest loan may be calculated from the following formula:

$$I = P \times r \times t$$

where I is interest income, P is the principal amount loaned, r is the annual rate of interest, and t is the maturity of the loan. In the example given above, we have

$$I = (\$10,000,000)(0.10)(1/360) = \$2,777.78$$

Note that for purposes of simplifying the calculation, we have assumed a 360-day year, a common assumption in determining yields on money market instruments.

market virtually ground to a halt because many investors refused to buy even the notes offered by top-grade companies. Similarly, in 1974, when Franklin National Bank of New York, holding nearly $4 billion in assets, closed its doors, the rates on short-term certificates of deposit (CDs) issued by other big New York banks surged upward due to fears on the part of money market investors that *all* large-bank CDs had become more risky.

Types of Investment Risk

What kinds of risk do investors face in the financial markets? And how do money market instruments rank in terms of these different kinds of risk?

First, all securities, including money market instruments, carry **market risk** (sometimes called *interest rate risk*), which refers to the danger that their prices will fall (and interest rates rise), subjecting the investor to a capital loss. Even U.S. Treasury notes and bonds decline in price when interest rates rise. Not only can security prices fall, but so can interest rates. This latter development increases an investor's **reinvestment risk**, the risk that earnings from a financial asset will have to be reinvested in lower-yielding assets at some point in the future. Even government securities carry reinvestment risk.

Securities issued by private firms and state and local governments carry **default risk**. For such securities, there is always some positive probability that the borrower will fail to meet some or all of his or her promised principal and/or interest payments (as happened to Orange County, California, in 1995).

Lenders of funds face the possibility that increases in the average level of prices for all goods and services will reduce the purchasing power of their income. This is known as **inflation risk** (sometimes called *purchasing power risk*). Lenders usually attempt to offset anticipated inflation by demanding higher contract rates on their loans.

International investors also face **currency risk**: possible loss due to unfavorable changes in the value of foreign currencies. For example, if a U.S. investor purchases British Treasury bills on the London money market, the return from these bills may be severely reduced if the value of the British pound falls relative to the dollar during the life of the investment.

Finally, **political risk** refers to the possibility that changes in government laws or regulations will result in a diminished rate of return to the investor or, in the extreme case, a total loss of invested capital. For example, the windfall profits tax on U.S. petroleum companies levied by Congress in 1980 generally reduced the earnings of petroleum stockholders. Investors in industries that are closely regulated, such as banking and public utilities, continually run the risk that new price controls, output quotas, or other restrictions will be imposed, reducing their earnings potential. In some foreign countries, facilities and equipment owned by U.S. corporations have been expropriated by national governments, resulting in total loss for the investors involved. A summary of each of the foregoing kinds of risks is shown in Exhibit 14–1.

Money market instruments generally offer more protection against such risks than most other investments. The prices of money market securities tend to be remarkably stable over time compared to the prices of bonds, stocks, real estate, and commodities, such as wheat and gold. Money market instruments generally do not offer the prospect of significant capital gains for the investor, but neither do they normally raise the specter of substantial capital losses. Similarly, default risk is minimal in the money market. In fact, money market borrowers must be well-established institutions with impeccable credit ratings before their securities can even be offered for sale in this market.

Few investments today adequately protect the investor against inflation risk. Money market securities are no exception. However, they do offer superior **liquidity**, allowing the investor to quickly cash them in when a promising inflation-hedged investment opportunity comes along.

Exhibit 14–1   **Types of Risk Confronting Investors in the Money and Capital Markets**

Type of Risk	Definition
Market Risk	The risk that the market price (value) of an asset will decline, resulting in a capital loss when sold. Sometimes referred to as *interest rate risk*.
Reinvestment risk	The risk that an investor will be forced to place earnings from a loan or security into a lower-yielding investment because interest rates have fallen.
Default risk	The probability that a borrower will fail to meet one or more promised principal or interest payments on a loan or security.
Inflation risk	The risk that increases in the general price level will reduce the purchasing power of earnings from a loan or security.
Currency risk	The risk that adverse movements in the price of one national currency vis-à-vis another will reduce the net rate of return from a foreign investment.
Political risk	The probability that changes in government laws or regulations will reduce an investor's expected return from an investment.

Currency risk concerns the international investor who frequently must convert one currency into another. That risk has increased dramatically in recent years due to the advent of foreign exchange rates that float with market conditions. Investors who purchase securities in foreign markets cannot completely escape currency risk, but they are probably less prone to such losses when buying money market instruments due to the short-term nature of money market assets. These assets also provide some hedge against political risk because they are short-term investments and fewer changes in government policy are likely over brief intervals of time.

Money Market Maturities

Despite the fact that money market securities cover a narrow range of maturities — one year or less — there are maturities available within this range to meet just about every short-term investment need. We must distinguish here between original maturity and actual maturity, however. The interval of time between the issue date of a security and the date on which the borrower promises to redeem it is the security's **original maturity**. **Actual maturity**, on the other hand, refers to the number of days, months, or years between today and the date the security is actually retired.

Original maturities on money market instruments range from as short as one day on many loans to banks and security dealers to a full year on some bank deposits and Treasury bills. Obviously, once a money market instrument is issued, it grows shorter in actual maturity every day. Because there are thousands of money market securities outstanding, some of which reach maturity each day, investors have a wide menu from which to select the precise number of days they need to invest cash.

Depth and Breadth of the Money Market

The money market is extremely broad and deep, meaning it can absorb a large volume of transactions with only small effects on security prices and interest rates. Investors can easily sell most money market instruments on short notice, often in a matter of minutes. This is one of the most efficient markets in the world, containing a vast network of securities dealers, major banks, and funds brokers in constant touch with one another and alert to any bargains. The slightest hint that a security is underpriced (i.e., carries an exceptionally high yield) usually brings a flood of buy orders, but money market traders are quick to dump or avoid overpriced securities. This market is dominated by active traders who constantly search their video display screens for opportunities to arbitrage funds; that is, they move money from one corner of the market with relatively low yields to another where investments offer the highest returns available. Overseeing the whole market is the Federal Reserve System and other central banks around the globe, who try to ensure that trading is orderly and prices are reasonably stable.

There is no centralized trading arena in the money market as there is on a stock exchange, for example. The money market is a telephone and computer market, in which participants arrange trades over the phone or through computer networks and usually confirm their transactions by wire. Speed is of the essence in this market because, as we observed earlier, money is a highly perishable commodity. Each day that passes means thousands of dollars in lost interest income if newly received funds are not immediately invested. Most business between traders, therefore, is conducted in seconds or minutes, and payment is made almost instantaneously.

Federal Funds versus Clearinghouse Funds

How can funds move so fast in the money market? The reason is that money market traders usually deal in **federal funds**. These funds are mainly deposit balances of commercial banks held at the regional Federal Reserve banks and at larger correspondent banks across the nation. When a dealer firm buys securities from an investor, for example, it immediately contacts its bank and requests that funds be transferred from its account to the investor's account at another bank. Many of these transactions in the United States move through the Federal Reserve's wire transfer network. In this case, the Fed removes funds from the reserve account of the buyer's bank and transfers these reserves to the seller's bank. The transaction is so quick that the seller of securities has funds available to make new investments, pay bills, or to use for other purposes the same day a trade is carried out or a loan is made. Federal funds are often called *immediately available funds* because of the speed with which money moves from one bank's reserve account to that of another.

Contrast this method of payment with that used generally in the capital market and by most businesses and households. When most of us purchase goods and services — especially purchases involving a large amount of money — the check is the most desirable means of paying the bill. Funds transferred by check are known as **clearinghouse funds** because, once the buyer writes a check, it goes to the seller's bank, which forwards that check eventually to the bank on which it was drawn. If the two banks are in the same community, they exchange bundles of checks drawn against each other every day through the local clearinghouse — an agreed-upon location where checks and other cash items are delivered and passed from one bank to another.

Clearinghouse funds are an acceptable means of payment for most purposes, but not in the money market, where speed is of the essence. It takes at least a day to clear local checks and two to three days for checks moving between cities. For money market transactions, this is far too slow, because no interest can be earned until the check is collected. Clearinghouse funds also have an element of risk, because a check may be returned as fraudulent or for insufficient funds. Federal funds transactions, however, are both speedy and safe.

A Market for Large Borrowers and Lenders

The money market is dominated by a relatively small number of large financial institutions. No more than a hundred banks in New York, London, Tokyo, Singapore, and a handful of other money centers are at the heart of the market. These large institutions account for the bulk of federal funds trading through which many money market transactions are carried

---

INTERNATIONAL FOCUS:

Money Markets Around the World

Money markets around the world share several common characteristics. They support borrowing and lending for periods as short as a single day out to one year. They reconcile cash imbalances for public and private businesses, individuals, and institutions and do so at low levels of risk for both borrowers and lenders. Money markets also transmit government economic policies, aiding governments in financing their deficits (fiscal policy) and in managing the growth of money and credit as well as currency prices (monetary policy).

Each nation has its own money market, though some are poorly developed and others (like that of the United States) reach far beyond the boundaries of one country or continent to involve traders on many continents. There is also an *international money market* that arches over all the domestic money markets and ties them all together, trading in under-one-year credit instruments that are bought and sold all over the globe. The heart of the international money market is the Eurocurrency market, where bank deposits are traded outside the boundaries of the country where a particular currency is issued. Increasingly, domestic money markets are being integrated into the international money market; *no* nation's money market today is unaffected by movements in interest rates and security prices in the international money market.

As Dufey and Giddy (1993) have recently observed, national money markets around the globe tend to fall into one of two types — those (like the U.S. and Canada) that are *securities market dominated*, where most borrowing and lending is through open-market trading of financial instruments, and those that are *bank dominated*, where bank borrowing and lending is at the center of most transactions (as in Japan, Korea, and China). However, worldwide deregulation of many financial institutions and instruments is underway, with the probable future outcome that more money markets of the future will become more security trading oriented and less dominated by a few large banks or other financial institutions.

In contrast, in developing countries, money markets are usually dominated by banks because their securities markets usually are not well developed. In these settings, the beginnings of money market trading usually start with interbank trading of deposits. In many cases, the banks involved are government owned and at least some money market interest rates may be regulated (perhaps set arbitrarily low) so the government can issue debt more cheaply (as in Korea, for example). Moreover, the government may play a major role in allocating credit, reducing the efficiency of the financial marketplace in allocating savings and credit. Central banks like the Federal Reserve, Bank of England, and Bank of Japan are usually the single most important institution in money markets, worldwide.

---

out. In addition, securities move readily from sellers to buyers through the market-making activities of major security dealers and brokers. And, of course, governments and central banks around the world play major roles in this market as the largest borrowers and as regulators, setting the rules of the game. For example, the Federal Reserve System, operating principally through the trading desk at the Federal Reserve Bank of New York, is in the market nearly every day, either supplying funds to banks and security dealers or absorbing funds through security sales.

Individual transactions in the money market involve huge amounts of funds. Most trading occurs in multiples of a million dollars. For this reason, the money market is often referred to as a *wholesale market* for funds, as opposed to the retail market where most consumers and small businesses borrow and save.

THE VOLUME OF MONEY MARKET SECURITIES

The principal financial instruments traded in the money market are Treasury bills, federal agency securities, dealer loans, repurchase agreements, bank certificates of deposit (CDs), federal funds, commercial paper, banker's acceptances, financial futures, and Eurodollar deposits. Each of these instruments is discussed in detail in the next several chapters, but it is useful at this point to examine the relative importance, measured by the dollar volume outstanding, of each of these instruments in the U.S. portion of the money market.

In fact, the volume of money market securities has grown rapidly in recent years. One reason is the international economy's growing need for liquid, readily marketable securities. Another factor in the money market's growth has been the attractive yields offered investors. As shown in Exhibit 14–2, two of the most important money market instruments (measured by dollar volume) are Treasury bills and certificates of deposit (CDs). By 1995, well over $700 billion in U.S. Treasury bills were outstanding, representing about 15 percent of the federal government's total debt. Less in total amount but still substantial were $100,000-plus certificates of deposit issued by U.S. banks and thrift institutions. These large denomination CDs totaled nearly $400 billion in 1995. We should note, however, that the volume of CDs fluctuates with credit market conditions, corporate earnings, and changes in the interest returns available on other assets.

At least as large as Treasury bills and CDs is the total volume of securities issued by U.S. federal agencies. These high-quality securities, a substantial portion of which fall due within a year and therefore are true money market instruments, totaled more than $750 billion in 1995. Over half of all agency IOUs are issued by just three federally sponsored organizations, the Federal Home Loan banks, the Federal National Mortgage Association, and the Farm Credit banks. The remaining agency issues come from a variety of govern-

Exhibit 14–2   **Volume of Selected Money Market Instruments 1985–1995***
($ Billions at Year-End)

Financial Instruments	1985	1986	1987	1988	1989	1990	1991	1992	1993	1994	1995
U.S. Treasury bills	$400	$27	$390	$414	$431	$527	$590	$658	$715	$734	$748
Federal agency securities	294	307	341	382	412	435	443	484	571	742	758
Commercial paper	299	330	359	458	526	561	530	549	555	595	633
Bankers' acceptances	68	65	71	67	63	55	44	38	32	30	NA
Federal funds borrowings and repurchase agreements	NA	164	162	165	187	180	172	161	167	151	165
Net Eurodollar borrowings by domestic banks from their own branches	NA	31	15	9	7	37	39	71	80	76	86
Certificates of deposit ($100,000 or more)	NA	346	387	429	464	432	424	367	333	364	390

*1995 figures are for June except for commercial paper and federal agency securities, which are for March.
NA = Not available.

Source: Board of Governors of the Federal Reserve System, *Federal Reserve Bulletin*, selected issues.

ment-related enterprises and organizations, including the Department of Defense, the Export-Import Bank, the Postal Service, and the Student Loan Marketing Association.

Commercial paper issued by topflight corporations totaled more than $600 billion in 1995 and represented one of the most rapidly growing money market instruments. Many large corporations have found the commercial paper market a cheaper and more flexible place to obtain credit than borrowing from banks. Bankers' acceptances — time drafts against large multinational banks — have fluctuated with the growth of world trade and declined in recent years, but they totaled close to $30 billion in 1995.

The volume of federal funds loans — the principal means of payment in the money market — is difficult to estimate because thousands of banks are active in this market every day and not all transactions are reported. Moreover, the federal funds market is extremely volatile, reflecting wide swings in the flow of funds through the banking system. Estimates by the Federal Reserve System indicate that Fed funds loans outstanding (including repurchase agreements) amounted to nearly $170 billion in 1995.

The true size of the Eurodollar market (dollar deposits in banks abroad) is also unknown, principally because this market spans so many nations and is not regulated. The amount shown in Exhibit 14–2 of more than $80 billion in 1995 includes only the net amount of Eurodollar borrowings by U.S. banks from their foreign branches. Conservative estimates of total Eurodollar deposits worldwide place the net figure at close to $2 trillion.

THE PATTERN OF INTEREST RATES IN THE MONEY MARKET

The rates of return on money market securities vary over time and among different securities. The foundation of the market's structure is the level of yields on Treasury bills. These securities are considered to have zero default risk and minimal market value as well. The resale market for Treasury bills is the most active and deep of all securities markets, making bills readily marketable should the investor need cash in a hurry. Because of this combination of low risk and ready marketability, Treasury bills typically carry the lowest yields in the money market.

Most other yields in the money market are scaled upward from Treasury bill rates. One set of yields that hovers very close to T-bill rates is the yield on federal agency securities, considered virtually riskless by many investors. Nevertheless, agency securities are less marketable than bills, though their quantity has increased rapidly in recent years. As a result, the yield spread between agencies and bills in recent periods averages more than a quarter percentage point in favor of agency securities.

Another yield in the money market that stays close to the Treasury bill rate is the rate charged on federal funds loans. The low risk of these loans, coupled with their short maturities (usually overnight), helps to explain their relatively low yields. As shown in Exhibit 14–3, which contains a column headed "Money Rates" that appears in every issue of *The Wall Street Journal*, federal funds carried a closing interest rate at the end of the trading day on Tuesday, March 26, 1996, of 5.06 (that is 5-1/16) percent, while the shortest (13-week) U.S. Treasury bills auctioned the same day carried a yield of 4.99 percent. Thus, the federal funds rate was about one-sixteenth of a percentage point higher than the T-bill rate on this particular trading day.

The interest rates on two bank-related financial instruments — negotiable CDs and bankers' acceptances — also tend to follow changes in the market yield on Treasury bills and hover close to prevailing bill rates for the same maturities. As shown in Exhibit 14–3, the secondary market yield on three-month CDs was just slightly below the three-month T-bill rate. The spread between the Treasury bill rate and the rate of return on three-month

Exhibit 14–3   **Money Market Interest Rates**

MONEY RATES

Tuesday, March 26, 1996

The key U.S. and foreign annual interest rates below are a guide to general levels but don't always represent actual transactions.

PRIME RATE: 8.25%. The base rate on corporate loans posted by at least 75% of the nation's 30 largest banks.

DISCOUNT RATE: 5%. The charge on loans to depository institutions by the Federal Reserve Banks.

FEDERAL FUNDS: 5 5/16% high, 5 % low, 5 1/16% near closing bid, 5 1/8% offered. Reserves traded among commercial banks for overnight use in amounts of $1 million or more. Source: Prebon Yamane (U.S.A.) Inc.

CALL MONEY: 7%. The charge on loans to brokers on stock exchange collateral. Source: Dow Jones Telerate Inc.

COMMERCIAL PAPER placed directly by General Electric Capital Corp.: 5.34% 30 to 35 days; 5.32% 36 to 44 days; 5.29% 45 to 59 days; 5.24% 60 to 89 days; 5.23% 90 to 149 days; 5.19% 150 to 179 days; 5.18% 180 to 270 days.

COMMERCIAL PAPER: High-grade unsecured notes sold through dealers by major corporations: 5.46% 30 days; 5.41% 60 days; 5.36% 90 days.

CERTIFICATES OF DEPOSIT: 4.76% one month; 4.78% two months; 4.88% three months; 4.97% six months; 5.11% one year. Average of top rates paid by major New York banks on primary new issues of negotiable C.D.s, usually on amounts of $1 million and more. The minimum unit is $100,000. Typical rates in the secondary market: 5.37% one month; 5.36% three months; 5.39% six months.

BANKERS ACCEPTANCES: 5.28% 30 days; 5.20% 60 days; 5.19% 90 days; 5.16% 120 days; 5.16% 150 days; 5.15% 180 days. Offered rates of negotiable, bank-backed business credit instruments typically financing an import order.

LONDON LATE EURODOLLARS: 5 3/8% - 5 1/4% one month; 5 3/8% - 5 1/4% two months; 5 7/16% - 5 5/16% three months; 5 7/16% - 5 5/16% four months; 5 7/16% - 5 5/16% five months; 5 7/16% - 5 5/16% six months.

LONDON INTERBANK OFFERED RATES (LIBOR): 5 7/16% one month; 5 7/16% three months; 5 15/32% six months; 5 5/8% one year. The average of interbank offered rates for dollar deposits in the London market based on quotations at five major banks. Effective rate for contracts entered into two days from date appearing at top of this column.

FOREIGN PRIME RATES: Canada 6.75%; Germany 3.35%; Japan 1.625%; Switzerland 3.75%; Britain 6.25%. These rate indications aren't directly comparable; lending practices vary widely by location.

TREASURY BILLS: Results of the Monday, March 25, 1996, auction of short-term U.S. government bills, sold at a discount from face value in units of $10,000 to $1 million: 4.99% 13 weeks; 4.97% 26 weeks.

OVERNIGHT REPURCHASE RATE: 5.20%. Dealer financing rate for overnight sale and repurchase of Treasury securities. Source: Dow Jones Telerate Inc.

FEDERAL HOME LOAN MORTGAGE CORP. (Freddie Mac): Posted yields on 30-year mortgage commitments. Delivery within 30 days 7.84%, 60 days 7.89%, standard conventional fixed-rate mortgages; 5.125%, 2% rate capped one-year adjustable rate mortgages. Source: Dow Jones Telerate Inc.

FEDERAL NATIONAL MORTGAGE ASSOCIATION (Fannie Mae): Posted yields on 30 year mortgage commitments (priced at par) for delivery within 30 days 7.79%, 60 days 7.84%, standard conventional fixed rate-mortgages; 6.45%, 6/2 rate capped one-year adjustable rate mortgages. Source: Dow Jones Telerate Inc.

MERRILL LYNCH READY ASSETS TRUST: 4.80%. Annualized average rate of return after expenses for the past 30 days; not a forecast of future returns.

---

bankers' acceptances at 5.19 percent was somewhat higher than the Treasury bill-bank CD spread, lying almost a quarter of a percentage point above the 13-week T-bill rate. Bankers' acceptances also carried interest rates more than a quarter of a percentage point higher than CDs issued by large, money-center banks. CDs issued by the largest U.S. banks are rated prime and carry the lowest yields in the CD market. The same is true of prime-rated bankers' acceptances. Acceptances are considered to be a high-quality investment nearly as riskless as Treasury bills. However, the resale market for acceptances is not as active nor as deep as the T-bill market, and this difference in marketability helps to explain why acceptances must carry a slightly higher yield.

Large, well-established corporations in need of credit can, of course, draw on many different sources of funds. However, when short-term credit is needed, two of the most popular sources are borrowing from commercial banks and issuing marketable IOUs in the commercial paper market. The largest and best-known corporations generally qualify for the prime bank lending rate or for even lower loan rates. Thus, the market for prime-rated bank loans is a direct competitor with the commercial paper market. As shown in Exhibit 14–3, for those corporations able to tap either market, it is generally cheaper to borrow in the commercial paper market. This spread in rates on short-term corporate loans favoring commercial paper helps explain why the commercial paper market has been one of the most rapidly growing segments of the U.S. money market in recent years.

Another important money market interest rate shown in Exhibit 14–3 is the discount rate charged depository institutions when they borrow from the Federal Reserve banks. In contrast to the other yields discussed to this point, the discount rate is not determined by demand and supply forces in the marketplace but is set by the Federal Reserve banks with the approval of the Board of Governors of the Federal Reserve System. The level of the discount rate is governed by the Federal Reserve's assessment of the state of the economy and credit market conditions. When possible, however, the Fed tries to keep the discount rate reasonably close to market interest rates on Treasury bills. An unusually low discount rate may result in excessive borrowing at the Fed's discount window. In contrast, an excessively high discount rate forces banks to borrow heavily in the open market, increasing the volatility of interest rates and sometimes creating unstable market conditions for all borrowers.

SUMMARY

This chapter has presented a broad overview of one of the most important components of any financial system, the *money market*. By convention, money markets are defined as the collection of institutions and trading relationships that move short-term funds from lenders to borrowers. All money market loans have an original maturity of one year or less. Most loans extended in the money market are designed to provide short-term working capital to businesses and governments so they can purchase inventories, pay dividends and taxes, and deal with other immediate needs for cash. Their short-term cash needs arise from the fact that inflows and outflows of cash are not perfectly synchronized. In the real world, even with the best planning, temporary cash deficits and temporary cash surpluses are more the rule rather than the exception.

The money market at one and the same time answers the needs of borrowers for short-term credit and the needs of lenders for temporary interest-bearing outlets for their surplus funds. In a period of rapid inflation and high interest rates, it is too costly to let cash lie idle for even a few days. At the same time, however, money market investors are extremely conservative when it comes to investing their funds. They will accept little or no risk of borrower default, prefer financial instruments whose prices are stable, and usually require an investment for which funds can be recaptured quickly as the need arises. For this reason, nearly all money market instruments are of prime quality — among the safest, most liquid, and most readily marketable in the financial system. In the remaining chapters of Part Four, we examine in detail the characteristics of each of the money market's key financial instruments. ∎

KEY TERMS AND CONCEPTS IN THIS CHAPTER

money market	inflation risk	original maturity
market risk	currency risk	actual maturity
reinvestment risk	political risk	federal funds
default risk	liquidity	clearinghouse funds

STUDY QUESTIONS

1. What is the *money market*? Explain why there is a critical need for money market instruments.

2. Who are the principal lenders and borrowers active in the U.S. money market?

3. Define the following:
    a. Market risk
    b. Default risk
    c. Inflation risk
    d. Currency risk
    e. Political risk

    Which of these risks are minimized by investing in money market instruments? Does a money market investor avoid all of these risk factors?

4. What are federal funds? Clearinghouse funds? Explain which is more important in the money market and why.

5. Describe the structure of interest rates in the money market. Which instrument anchors the market and appears to be the foundation for other interest rates? Can you explain why this is so?

PROBLEMS

1. How much interest would be earned (on a simple interest basis) from a three-day money market loan for $1 million at an interest rate of 12 percent (annual rate)? Suppose the loan were extended on the third day for an additional day at the going market rate of 11 percent. How much total interest income would the money market lender receive?

2. Check the most recent issue of *The Wall Street Journal* you can find. Calculate the yield spreads in basis points between U.S. Treasury bills of varying maturity, the federal funds rate, and commercial paper, CD, and bankers' acceptance rates. How do your calculated yield spreads compare with those shown in Exhibit 14–3? Can you explain the observed differences in yield spreads using your knowledge of the factors explaining movements in interest rates discussed in Chapters 8 through 12?

3. Suppose the spread between the three-month U.S. Treasury bill rate and the three-month bank CD rate were 35 basis points. An investor has $250,000 to invest in either of these instruments for three months. How much does the investor surrender in total interest income for three months if he or she invests in Treasury bills instead of CDs? Does the investor receive any offsetting benefits by buying the bills and not the CDs?

SELECTED REFERENCES

Ahmad, Syed M., and Lee Sarver. "The International Transmission of Money Market Fluctuations." *The Financial Review* XXIX, No. 3 (August 1994), pp. 319–344.

Dufey, Gunter, and Ian H. Giddy. "Money Markets of the Pacific Basin." *Working Paper 93–10.* Mitsui Life Financial Research Center, The University of Michigan, 1993.

"Opening the Door to Japan's Short-Term Money Markets." *The Economist*, April 1, 1989, pp. 65–66.

Federal Reserve Bank of Richmond. *Instruments of the Money Market*, 1977.

Rose, Peter S. *Readings on Financial Institutions and Markets.* 1995–96 ed. Burr Ridge, Ill.: Richard D. Irwin, Inc., 1995.

Chapter 15

Treasury Bills, Dealer Loans, and Repurchase Agreements

LEARNING OBJECTIVES IN THIS CHAPTER

- To examine the nature of Treasury bills and the workings of the government securities market.
- To see how U.S. Treasury bills are auctioned each week and how their yield is determined.
- To determine why government securities dealers are so important to the functioning of the money market and how these dealers finance their operations.

As we noted in the previous chapter, the money market is an institution designed to supply the cash needs of short-term borrowers and provide investors who hold temporary cash surpluses with an interest-bearing outlet for their funds. In this chapter, we focus on one of the most important of all money market instruments, the U.S. Treasury bill. Purchases and sales of Treasury bills represent the largest volume of daily transactions in the money market. Interest rates on bills are the anchor for all other money market interest rates. Trading in T-bills, as these instruments are usually called, is one component of a vast international market for securities issued by the U.S. government and by other governments around the world. These government IOUs, which include bills, notes, and bonds, carry great weight in the financial system due to their zero default risk, ready marketability, and high liquidity. At the heart of the market for Treasury bills, notes, and bonds is a handful of securities dealers who make the market go and aid the federal government in selling billions of dollars in new securities each year. In this chapter, we examine the activities of these securities dealers and how they finance their daily trading operations in T-bills and other financial instruments.

U.S. TREASURY BILLS

U.S. Treasury bills are direct obligations of the United States government. By law, they must have an original maturity of one year or less. T-bills were first issued by the U.S. Treasury in 1929 to cover the federal government's frequent short-term cash deficits.

The federal government's fiscal year runs from October 1 to September 30. However, individual income taxes — the largest single source of federal revenue — are not fully collected until April of each year. Therefore, even in those rare years when a sizable budget surplus is expected, the government is likely to be short of cash during the fall and winter months and often in the summer as well. During the spring, personal and corporate tax collections are usually at high levels, and the resulting inflow of funds can be used to retire some portion of the securities issued earlier in the fiscal year. T-bills are suited to this seasonal ebb and flow of treasury cash because their maturities are short, they find a ready market among investors, and their prices adjust readily to changing market conditions.

Volume of Bills Outstanding

The volume of U.S. Treasury bills outstanding has grown rapidly in recent years, especially since the mid-1960s. As shown in Exhibit 15–1, the total volume of bills outstanding climbed to about $760 billion in 1995, compared to slightly over $200 billion in 1980. The major factors behind the growth of T-bills have been record federal budget deficits, occasional deep recessions that have reduced tax revenues, and the rapid expansion of certain federal programs such as national defense during the cold war, and welfare subsidies to low-income individuals and families. Moreover, the U.S. and global economies have grown rapidly at times in recent years, creating a greater need for liquid assets such as bills to aid banks and other investors in the efficient management of their cash positions. Interestingly enough, however, bills have generally declined as a percentage of the U.S. federal debt in recent years due to the more rapid growth of longer-term Treasury notes (1-year to 10-year government IOUs).

Exhibit 15–1   **U.S. Treasury Bills: Total Amount Outstanding and Their Proportion of the Marketable Public Debt of the United States, 1960–1995**

End of Year	Total Volume of Bills Outstanding ($ Billions)	Marketable Public Debt of the United States ($ Billions)	T-Bills as a Percent of the Total Marketable Public Debt
1960	$ 39.4	$ 189.0	20.8%
1965	60.2	214.6	28.1
1970	87.9	247.7	35.5
1975	157.5	263.2	43.4
1980	216.1	623.2	34.7
1985	399.9	1,437.7	27.8
1990	527.4	2,195.8	24.0
1995	760.7	3,307.2	23.0

Source: Board of Governors of the Federal Reserve System, *Federal Reserve Bulletin*, selected issues.

Types of Treasury Bills

There are several different types of Treasury bills. *Regular-series bills* are issued routinely every week or month in competitive auctions. Bills issued in regular series have original maturities of three months (13 weeks), six months (26 weeks), and one year (52 weeks). New three- and six-month bills are auctioned weekly; one-year bills normally are sold once each month. Of these three maturities, the six-month bill provides the largest amount of revenue for the U.S. Treasury.

On the other hand, *irregular-series bills* are issued only when the Treasury has a special cash need. These instruments include strip bills and cash management bills. A package offering of bills requiring investors to bid for an entire series of different bill maturities is known as a *strip bill*. Investors who bid successfully must accept bills at their bid price each week for several weeks running. *Cash-management bills*, on the other hand, consist simply of reopened issues of bills that were sold in prior weeks. The reopening of a bill issue normally occurs when there is an unusual or unexpected Treasury need for cash.

How Bills Are Sold

Treasury bills are sold using the **auction** technique. The marketplace, not the U.S. Treasury, sets bill prices and yields. A new regular bill issue is announced by the Treasury on Tuesday of each week, with bids from investors due the following Monday before 1 P.M. New York time.[1] Interested investors fill out a form tendering an offer to the Treasury for a specific bill issue at a specific price. These forms must be filed by the Monday deadline with one of the 37 regional Federal Reserve banks or branches or with the Treasury's Bureau of the Public Debt. The interested investor can appear in person at a Federal Reserve bank or branch to fill out a tender form, submit it by mail, or place an order through a security broker or depository institution.

The Treasury entertains both competitive and noncompetitive tenders for bills. *Competitive* tenders typically are submitted by large investors, including banks and securities dealers, who buy several million dollars' worth at one time. Institutions submitting competitive tenders bid aggressively for bills, trying to offer the Treasury a price high enough to win an allotment of bills but not too high, because the higher the price bid, the lower the rate of return. *Noncompetitive* tenders (normally less than $1 million each) are submitted by small investors who agree to accept the average price set in the weekly or monthly bill auction. The noncompetitive investor must pay the full par-value price of the bill at the time the tender is made and, on the issue date, receives a refund check from the Federal Reserve representing the difference between the amount paid in by the investor and the actual auction price. Generally, the Treasury fills all noncompetitive tenders for bills.

In the typical bill auction, Federal Reserve officials open all the bids at the designated time and array them from the highest price (and lowest yield) to the lowest price (and highest yield). All competitive price bids must be expressed to no more than three decimal places. For example, a typical series of bids in a Treasury auction might appear as follows:

---

[1]The foregoing schedule applies to 13-week and 26-week bills. For one-year bills a new issue is usually announced on a Friday and auctioned the following Thursday.

Hypothetical Prices and Yields Bid for Three-Month U.S. Treasury Bills

Treasury Bill Prices Bid	Equivalent Treasury Bill Yields
$99.115	3.54%
99.113	3.55
98.985	4.06
98.982	4.07
98.750	5.00
98.725	5.10
98.654	5.38

Note that all the prices bid are expressed on a $100 basis as though T-bills have a $100 par value. In fact, the minimum denomination for U.S. Treasury bills is $10,000, and they are issued in multiples of $5,000 above that minimum. The highest bidder (in this case, the one offering a price of $99.115, or a yield of 3.54 percent) receives bills, and those who bid successively lower prices also receive their bills until all available securities have been allocated.

The lowest price at which at least some bills are awarded is called the *stop-out price*. Let's suppose this is a price of $98.750 (a yield of 5.00 percent), the third price from the bottom in the array of prices shown in the table. No one bidding less than the stop-out price will receive any bills in this particular auction. However, once bills are acquired by successful bidders, many of them will be sold right away in the secondary market, giving the unsuccessful bidders a chance to add to their own T-bill portfolios. Payments for bills won in the auction must be made in federal funds, cash, cashier's check, certified personal check, by redeeming maturing Treasury securities or coupon payments, or, when permitted by the Treasury, through crediting Treasury tax and loan accounts at banks.[2] All bills today are issued only in *book-entry form* — a computerized record of ownership maintained in Washington, DC and at the Federal Reserve banks — with the owner receiving a statement of account about four to six weeks after purchase. The Treasury Department automatically sends a check to the investor the day the bill matures unless reinvestment of the maturing bill's proceeds into new Treasury securities has been requested.

Results of a Recent Bill Auction

A summary of the results from each T-bill auction is published in *The Wall Street Journal*. The results from a recent Treasury bill auction are presented in Exhibit 15–2. In this particular auction, held during March 1996, two maturities of bills — 13 and 26 weeks — were offered to the public, and both issues were heavily oversubscribed. More than $42 billion in 13-week bills and $50 billion in 26-week bills were requested by the public; however, the Treasury only awarded about $13.6 billion of the shorter-term bills and $13.5 billion of the 26-week bills.[3] Forty-five percent of the bids offering the lowest successful

---

[2]These so-called T&L accounts are Treasury deposits kept in about 10,000 of the nation's roughly 12,000 banks. The purpose of these accounts is to minimize the impact on the financial system of Treasury tax collections and debt-financing operations. As taxes are collected or securities are sold, the Treasury deposits the funds received in these T&L accounts and withdraws money from them as needed into its checking accounts held at the Federal Reserve banks.

[3]The ratio of the total amount of bids received by the Treasury over the actual amount of securities to be sold is known as the *cover*. It is a measure of the strength of the public's interest in the securities being sold.

Exhibit 15–2   **Report of Results from a Typical Weekly Auction of U.S. Treasury Bills, March 26, 1996**

Here are the details of yesterday's auction by the Treasury of 13-week and 26-week bills:

Rates are determined by the difference between the purchase price and face value. Thus, higher bidding narrows the investor's return while lower bidding widens it. The percentage rates are calculated on a 360-day year, while the coupon equivalent yield is based on a 365-day year.

	13-Week	26-Week
Applications	$42,464,780,000	$50,914,122,000
Accepted bids	$13,596,030,000	$13,519,389,000
Accepted at low price	45%	54%
Accepted noncompet'ly	$1,389,983,000	$1,258,132,000
Average price (Rate)	98.739 (4.99%)	97.487 (4.97%)
High price (Rate)	98.746 (4.96%)	97.492 (4.96%)
Low price (Rate)	98.739 (4.99%)	97.487 (4.97%)
Coupon equivalent	5.12%	5.17%
CUSIP number	912794Z56	9127943H5

Both issues are dated March 28. The 13-week bills mature June 27, 1996, and the 26-week bills mature Sept. 26, 1996.

Source: *The Wall Street Journal* Southwest Edition, March 26, 1996, p. C20. Reprinted by permission of *The Wall Street Street Journal*, © 1996 Dow Jones & Company, Inc. All Rights Reserved Worldwide.

bid (or stop-out) price on the 13-week issue received bills, and 54 percent of the bids offering the lowest successful bid (or stop-out) price on the 26-week issue were awarded some bills. Noncompetitive tenders in the amount of $1.4 billion for the 13-week issue and about $1.3 billion for the 26-week issue received their bills.

The dollar-weighted average auction price for 13-week bills was $98.739 per $100, or $9,873.90 for a $10,000 denomination bill. The 26-week issue sold for an average price of $9,748.70. This works out to a 4.99 percent return on the 13-week bill and a 4.97 percent return on the 26-week issue. On a yield-to-maturity (or coupon-equivalent) basis, the 13-week bill carried an average yield of 5.12 percent; the 26-week bill had an average yield of 5.17 percent. The highest competitive bidders paid a price of $9,874.60 for the 13-week security and $9,749.20 for the 26-week, $10,000 par value instrument. The lowest successful bidders received their 13-week bills for only $9,873.90 and their 26-week bills for $9,748.70 per $10,000 bill.[4] Those who bid less than these prices underbid in the auction and received no new bills.

Calculating the Yield on Bills

Treasury bills do not carry a promised interest rate but instead are sold at a discount from par. Thus, their yield is based on their appreciation in price between time of issue and the time they mature or are sold by the investor. Any price gain realized by the investor is treated for federal tax purposes not as a capital gain but as ordinary income received during the year the bill matures.[5] We saw in Chapter 9 that the rate or yield on most debt instruments is calculated as a yield to maturity. However, bill yields are determined by the **bank**

---

[4]An important statistic emerging from Treasury auctions that is widely followed by dealers is called the *tail*, which is the difference between the average yield established in a government security auction and the highest yield (lowest price) accepted by the government. Auctions with a greater tail than average are those in which dealers and other investors seem to have great uncertainty about where security prices and interest rates are headed and what the appropriate price should be for the securities offered in the auction.

[5]The income earned from investing in T-bills is *not* exempt from federal taxes, but it is exempt from state and local income taxes. Income from U.S. Treasury securities is subject to federal and state inheritance, gift, estate, and certain excise taxes.

discount method, which ignores the compounding of interest rates and uses a 360-day year for simplicity.

The bank discount rate (DR) on bills is given by the following formula:

$$DR = \frac{\text{Par value} - \text{Purchase price}}{\text{Par value}} \times \frac{360}{\text{Number of days to maturity}} \tag{15–1}$$

For example, suppose you purchased a Treasury bill at auction for $97 on a $100 basis (par value), and the bill matures in 180 days. Then the discount rate on this bill would be

$$DR = \frac{(100 - 97)}{100} \times \frac{360}{180} = 6\%$$

Because the rate of return on T-bills is figured in a different way than the rate of return on most other debt instruments, the investor must convert bill yields to an investment (or coupon-equivalent) yield to make realistic comparisons with other securities. The investment yield or rate (IR) on Treasury bills can be obtained from the following formula:

$$IR = \frac{365 \times DR}{360 - (DR \times \text{Days to maturity})} \tag{15–2}$$

(In leap years, 366 is used instead of 365 in this formula.) For example, the investment yield on the bill discussed above, which has a discount rate (DR) of 6 percent, would be

$$IR = \frac{365 \times 0.06}{360 - (0.06 \times 180)} = 0.0627, \text{ or } 6.27\%$$

A somewhat simpler formula for determining the investment yield or rate (IR) on Treasury bills is the following:

$$IR = \frac{\text{Par value} - \text{Purchase price}}{\text{Purchase price}} \times \frac{365}{\text{Days to maturity}} \tag{15–3}$$

The IR on the bill discussed above having a purchase price of $97 is

$$IR = \frac{100 - 97}{97} \times \frac{365}{180} \times = 0.0627, \text{ or } 6.27\%$$

Notice that this second IR formula explicitly recognizes that each bill is purchased at a discounted price, which should be used instead of par value as the basis for figuring the bill's true return. Because of the compounding of interest and the use of a 365-day year, the investment yield (IR) on a bill is always higher than its discount rate (DR).

Several other formulas have become popular among investors for calculating yields on Treasury bills when the bills are *not* held to maturity. Both equations 15–1 and 15–2 assume that the investor buys a T-bill and ultimately redeems it with the Treasury on its due date. But what if the investor needs cash right away and sells the bills to another investor in advance of their maturity? In this instance, we may use the following formulas:

$$\text{Holding-period yield on bill} = DR \text{ when purchased} \\ \pm \text{ Change in DR over the holding period} \tag{15–4}$$

where:

$$\frac{\text{Change in DR over the}}{\text{investor's holding period}} = \frac{(\text{Days to maturity when purchased} - \text{Days held})}{\text{Days held}} \\ \times \text{Difference in DR on date purchased and date sold} \tag{15–5}$$

For example, suppose the investor buys a new six-month (180-day) bill at a price that results in a discount rate (DR) of 6 percent. As is typical, the bill's price begins to rise (and

DR to fall) as it approaches maturity. Thirty days after purchase, the investor needs immediate cash and is forced to sell at a price that results in a DR of 5.80 percent. What is the investor's holding-period yield? Using Equation 15–5:

$$\text{Change in DR over the holding period} = \frac{180 - 30}{30} \times (6.00\% - 5.80\%)$$

$$= \frac{150}{30} \times 0.20\% = 1.00\%$$

Then, using Equation 15–4:

$$\text{Holding-period yield on bill} = 6.00\% + 1.00\% = 7.00\%$$

Because this T-bill rose in price, the investor experienced a gain that increased the bill's holding-period yield by 1 percent over the original discount rate of 6 percent.

Consider another problem that frequently confronts T-bill investors. Suppose a corporation has just purchased bills to serve as a temporary reserve of liquidity, but it knows that sometime in the next few weeks it will need those funds to finance a building project. However, the firm wants to hold the bills long enough to earn a specific *target yield*. How many days must the bills be held to hit the target yield? The correct formula is

$$
\begin{aligned}
&\text{Number of days to hold bill for target yield} = \\
&\frac{\begin{array}{c}\text{(Days to maturity when purchased} \times \\ \text{Difference in DR on date purchased and date sold)}\end{array}}{\begin{array}{c}\text{(Desired change in DR over holding period} \\ + \text{Difference in DR on date purchased and date sold)}\end{array}}
\end{aligned}
\tag{15–6}
$$

To illustrate the use of this formula, we can draw on the figures from the preceding example and assume the investor wants to achieve a 7 percent target yield. We have the following:

$$\begin{array}{c}\text{Numbers of days to hold bills} \\ \text{for 7 percent target yield}\end{array} = \frac{180 \times (0.20\%)}{1.00\% + 0.20\%} = \frac{36\%}{1.20\%} = 30 \text{ days}$$

Therefore, a 180-day bill purchased at a discount rate of 6 percent must be held for 30 days if the investor desires a 7 percent annual yield and expects the bill's discount rate to decline by 20 basis points.

Market Interest Rates on Treasury Bills

Due to the absence of default risk and because of the superior marketability of T-bills, the yields on these popular financial instruments are typically the lowest in the money market. And because of the tremendous size of the bill market, conditions there tend to set the tone in all other segments of the money market. A rise in T-bill rates, for example, usually is quickly translated into increases in interest rates attached to other money market instruments.

Although the prices of Treasury bills, like those attached to all money market instruments, tend to be stable, yields on bills fluctuate widely in response to changes in economic conditions, government policy, and a host of other factors. This can be seen clearly in Exhibit 15–3, which gives annual averages for the secondary market yields on 3-, 6-, and 12-month bills. T-bill rates typically fall during periods of recession and sluggish economic activity as borrowing and spending sag. Note, for example, the decline in bill yields in 1975, 1982, and 1991–1992. All of these years were periods in which the economy reached the peak of a boom period and then dropped into a recession. During periods of economic expansion, on the other hand, T-bill rates frequently surge upward, as happened between 1976 and 1981, and in 1986 and 1989. Inflationary expectations also appear to have a potent impact on bill market yields, as evidenced by the sharp run-up in T-bill rates during the late 1970s, early 1980s, and late 1980s, periods when general price increases in the economy accelerated rapidly.

It is interesting to examine the shape of the *yield curve* for bills. As Exhibit 15–3 suggests, that curve usually slopes upward, with 12-month bill maturities generally carrying the highest yields, 6-month bills the next highest, and 3-month maturities the lowest yields of all. This is not always the case, however. During certain periods — 1974, 1979–1981, and 1989–1990 are good examples — the bill yield curve seems to signal the onset of a recession by sloping downward. Occasionally, too, the yield curve for bills assumes a pronounced humped or inverted U shape, with middle maturities carrying the highest rates of return. This happened in 1974 and again early in 1991. It is difficult to assign any particular cause to this phenomenon. Sometimes the bend in the curve in the middle maturities appears to reflect heavy Treasury issues of new six-month bills or heavy bank sales of T-bills as bankers try to accommodate their customer's demand for new loans by converting their bills into loanable funds. It is noteworthy that the humped yield curve has generally appeared near the end of a boom period and shortly before the onset of a recession. During these periods, investors in the financial marketplace are especially uncertain as to which way interest rates are headed.

Recent research has found that the yield curve for Treasury bills is not determined exclusively by the expectations of investors (as implied, for example, by the unbiased expectations hypothesis of the yield curve discussed in Chapter 10). Studies by Rowe, Lawler, and Cook (1986) and by Jones and Roley (1982) indicate that Treasury bill yield curves usually slope upward because of the existence of liquidity (or term) premiums on longer-term bills — an extra yield paid to investors who buy longer-term bills to compensate them for greater price risk. Investors cannot eliminate these extra yields on longer-term bills by borrowing short and lending long, it is argued, because private investors cannot borrow at interest rates as low as the government's borrowing rate. In contrast, yield curves on private money market securities usually have much less of an upward slope than do Treasury bill yield curves and do not appear to contain significant liquidity (term) premiums. Investors can eliminate term premiums on private securities by borrowing and lending at roughly equal interest rates.

Exhibit 15–3	**Market Interest Rates on U.S. Treasury Bills, 3-, 6-, and 12-Month Maturities** (Annual Percentage Rates)

Year	3-Month	6-Month	12-Month	Year	3-Month	6-Month	12-Month
1974	7.84	7.95	7.71	1985	7.48	7.65	7.81
1975	5.80	6.11	6.30	1986	5.98	6.02	6.07
1976	4.98	5.26	5.52	1987	5.78	6.03	6.33
1977	5.27	5.53	5.71	1988	6.67	6.91	7.13
1978	7.19	7.58	7.74	1989	8.11	8.03	7.92
1979	10.07	10.06	9.75	1990	7.50	7.46	7.35
1980	11.43	11.37	10.89	1991	5.38	5.44	5.52
1981	14.03	13.80	13.14	1992	3.43	3.54	3.71
1982	10.61	11.07	11.07	1993	2.95	3.05	3.20
1983	8.61	8.73	8.80	1994	4.25	4.64	5.02
1984	9.52	9.76	9.92	1995*	5.40	5.41	5.43
				1996**	5.00	4.92	4.82

*Figures for August 1995.
**Figures for January 1996.

Source: Board of Governors of the Federal Reserve System, *Federal Reserve* Bulletin, selected monthly issues.

INTERNATIONAL FOCUS:

Treasury Bills Worldwide

U.S. Treasury bills and other U.S. government securities are traded 24 hours a day around the globe. But many people are not aware that governments in Europe, Asia, and the Americas also issue their own Treasury bills. For example, the Bank of Canada, acting as agent for the Canadian government, auctions discounted bills on Tuesday of each week to a select list of banks and dealers authorized to bid for themselves and their customers. Canadian central government bills are issued in maturities of 3-months, 6-months, and 364 days and usually trade in minimum denominations of $250,000 (Canadian dollars). In addition, Canada's provinces borrow through so-called Provincial Bills, normally issued in denominations up to $100,000 (expressed in Canadian dollars) for maturities of 3 months or less.

In Europe, Treasury bills are issued by several governments and are widely traded. Bills issued by the United Kingdom and Germany rank among the most popular in Western Europe. Both the Bank of England and the Bundesbank, Germany's central bank, trade in the bill market and monitor T-bill rates as a barometer of credit market conditions.

Treasury bills are a relatively recent government financing instrument in Japan, first appearing in 1986, but they are now sold regularly in 3- and 6-month maturities. Somewhat shorter instruments (with two-month maturities), called Financing Bills, help to cover the emergency cash needs of the Japanese government. T-bills are considered to be in short supply in Japan because the Japanese government borrows principally through longer-term bonds, and an active secondary market for T-bills has been slow to develop because of heavy taxation of T-bill returns and the diminished supply of bills. Similarly, in Korea the government issues Treasury bills irregularly without competitive bidding, and, thus, the secondary market for this money market instrument is not yet well developed. In the Philippines, the government began issuing Treasury bills in 1966, and bills now represent one of the largest components of the Philippine money market.

The Treasury bill market is one of the most important for the development of an efficient and fluid financial system in any nation. The bill market is a natural channel for government economic policy and can aid in the development of a strong central banking system. Unfortunately, many governments have not yet learned that both the oversupply and undersupply of bills can damage the development of such a market and that regulation of T-bill interest rates or restrictions on who can bid for or trade Treasury bills can be highly destructive to the development of such a market.

Investors in Treasury Bills

Principal holders of Treasury bills include commercial banks, nonfinancial corporations, state and local governments, and the Federal Reserve banks. Commercial banks and private corporations hold large quantities of bills as a reserve of liquidity until cash is needed. The most attractive feature of bills for these institutions is their ready marketability and stable price. The Federal Reserve banks conduct the bulk of their open market operations in T-bills because of the depth and volume of activity in this market. In fact, T-bills play a crucial role in the conduct of monetary policy by the Federal Reserve System. The Fed purchases and sells bills in an effort to influence other money market interest rates, alter the volume and growth of bank credit, and ultimately affect the total amount of investment spending and borrowing in the economy.[6]

PRIMARY DEALERS, DEALER LOANS, AND REPURCHASE AGREEMENTS

The money market depends heavily on the buying and selling activities of securities dealers to move funds from cash-rich units to those with cash shortages. Today, just under 40 **primary dealers** in government securities trade in both new and previously issued Treasury bills, bonds, and notes. These firms include such market leaders as Merrill Lynch, Goldman Sachs, Salomon Brothers, Inc., and Bear Stearns. About half are banks or securities affiliates of banks.

The term *primary dealer* simply means that a dealer firm is qualified to trade securities directly with the Federal Reserve Bank of New York. To join the Fed's primary dealer list, the firm must agree to be available to trade securities at all times and to post total capital of at least $50 million. Just over one third of all primary dealer firms are controlled by corporations located outside the United States, including dealers in Canada, Japan, Great Britain, Switzerland, and Hong Kong. Many customers prefer to trade only with primary dealers. Moreover, achieving primary dealership status gives foreign dealers a solid foothold in U.S. markets. Politics entered the world of the primary dealer in 1988, when the U.S. Congress passed the Primary Dealers Act, requiring the Federal Reserve to deny primary dealer designation to any foreign firm whose home country discriminates against U.S. securities firms in favor of its domestic dealers.

Until recently, the primary dealers possessed several exclusive privileges in dealing with the U.S. government. For example, they held exclusive membership on the Treasury Borrowing Advisory Committee, which helps the government decide what kinds of securities to sell at each auction. They were the only traders (along with banks) who could place bids for new government securities on behalf of themselves and their customers without posting the normally required 5 percent cash deposit on each bid amount. In contrast to nonprimary dealers, the primary dealers could bid any price and yield they chose, but other buyers were required simply to place volume orders and pay the average price established in the latest Treasury auction. In return for these privileges, a primary government securities dealer had to agree to share information regularly and freely with the Federal Reserve. The primary dealers also agreed to "meaningfully participate" in trading with the Federal Reserve at any time the Fed wishes, to make "realistic" bids, and to trade continuously in the full range of government securities.

Scandal Rocks the Market for Government Securities

Due in part to competition and the nature of Treasury auction methods, the primary dealers have had a significant incentive to attempt to "corner" the government securities market and, perhaps, to "collude" and place common bids, so that all dealers get some share of new securities in order to be able to fill their customers' orders and make a profit. In such a huge and highly competitive market, dealers can easily overbid, eliminating potential profits by either posting bid prices that are too high or by underbidding, receiving no

---

[6]We will examine Federal Reserve open market operations and the role of Treasury bills in those operations in Chapter 20.

securities from the government to meet their obligations to their customers. Thus, the dealers have an incentive to share information with each other on the size of the orders they plan to place with the government and even on the prices they hope to bid. In 1991, rumors swept through the financial markets that collusion was rampant. After several weeks of secret government investigations, officials at the Federal Reserve and the Securities and Exchange Commission alleged that they had evidence of improper trading practices on the part of the old-line primary dealer, Salomon Brothers.

It was alleged that Salomon cornered a $12-billion-plus auction of U.S. Treasury notes in May 1991, inflating the amount of its bid to the Treasury well beyond the 35 percent maximum share of a new issue normally allowed. Federal officials subpoenaed records of a New York security clearinghouse and found that, shortly after the T-note auction, several large corporate customers had been recorded as selling their new securities back to Salomon. When these customers were contacted, they reported that either they had placed no orders for new securities or that their orders were much smaller than claimed by Salomon. When Salomon wound up with nearly 90 percent of the new Treasury notes, other dealers filed complaints that they were being "squeezed" by Salomon — forced to pay exorbitant prices to purchase the new notes in order to meet their own customers' orders. Subsequently, Salomon itself, cooperating with government investigators, revealed evidence of manipulation of at least seven other government security auctions. There was also evidence that the government itself wound up paying higher borrowing costs as a result of the manipulation of the market. Ultimately, Salomon paid out close to $290 million to settle private lawsuits and government antitrust charges arising from the T-note scandal of the early 1990s.

In the wake of the Salomon scandal, the U.S. Treasury and the Federal Reserve Bank of New York set up *new* rules by which government securities would be auctioned in the future. For one thing, customers purchasing large amounts of government securities through dealers were thereafter required to *verify* in writing the amounts they bid before they could receive any allocation of new securities. In October 1991, the Treasury announced that any security dealer or broker registered with the SEC, not just primary dealers, could file bids on behalf of its customers without putting up a deposit or a guarantee. The U.S. Treasury promised that it would stop giving primary dealers an advance look at its borrowing plans before the same information was released to the public and to move swiftly to automate the bidding process for U.S. government securities rather than relying on the traditional handwritten bids.

The Federal Reserve System announced in January 1992 that it would make it possible for small dealer firms to enter the bidding for new security issues by removing a long-standing rule that a dealer must account for at least 1 percent of total Treasury market trading to qualify as a competitive bidder. At the same time, the rules of government security auctions were to be written and published for the first time and a market-surveillance committee was created, composed of representatives from the U.S. Treasury, the Securities and Exchange Commission, and the Federal Reserve System. The Treasury also pledged it would reopen previous security issues and issue more new securities if it detected that a market "squeeze" was developing with some dealers unable to find reasonably priced government securities to satisfy the needs of their customers.

Proposals for New Ways to Auction Government Securities

The scandal that rocked the government security market in 1991 gave rise to a multitude of proposals to change the way the Treasury auctions off its IOUs. The current auction method used by the U.S. Treasury to sell T-bills is called a *first-price sealed-bid auction*, or English auction. Although it has the advantage of allowing the *market* to set the prices of Treasury securities, the English auction approach has definite weaknesses, some of which result in giving security dealers significant incentive to find out what other dealers are planning to do and to share information, pool bids, and possibly collude to divide up the market.

The first-price sealed-bid, or *discriminatory-price*, auction encourages dealers to bid high to increase their probability of winning some of the auctioned securities. However, the higher the price that is bid, the lower the expected profit when any Treasury securities won in the auction are sold in the secondary market, because the highest bidders must follow through on their commitment and pay the Treasury what they have bid even though other successful bidders are paying a lower amount for the same securities. Moreover, the high bidders can sell their securities for no more later in the resale market than those who bid less. In effect, dealers bidding the highest prices face a "winner's curse," because they will incur greater probability of loss when they attempt to resell the securities won in the auction to their customers. At best, the "winner's curse" brought on by the use of the first-price sealed-bid auction method reduces the aggressiveness of competitive bidding by the dealers and probably results in the Treasury getting a lower price for its securities due to the high information costs the dealers must incur. Moreover, the use of sealed bids increases the probability that a single bidder can corner the market by submitting inflated bids.

Several experts have recently suggested remedies for this situation by making changes in the design of Treasury auctions. One popular recommendation is to set up a Dutch auction, in which bids are arrayed by price from highest to lowest but all the securities in the auction are then sold for just *one price*, the highest bid that is just sufficient to sell out the whole security issue. Thus, the price paid by every successful participant in a Dutch auction is identical (the "stop-out price") and usually comes fairly close to the market consensus price, meaning that the winner's curse has been alleviated to a certain extent. There is some fear, however, that such an approach could reduce Treasury revenues because high bidders would then pay less for their securities. However, Dutch auctions tend to incite more aggressive bidding and to encourage more individuals and institutions to participate in an auction, potentially creating more demand for Treasury securities and, possibly, lowering borrowing costs for the government.

Alternatively, the Treasury might consider using an ascending-price auction in which alternative prices are called out and bidders indicate how many securities they would take at the price announced. Treasury officials could continue to call out successively higher prices until a price is finally found that is just high enough to sell out the whole issue of securities to the assembled bidders. All bidders would then buy securities at that one price. Recent research suggests that an ascending-price auction would tend to result in the greatest revenue for the Treasury because there is less risk of a substantial winner's curse and less reason for bidders to attempt market manipulation.

However, an ascending-price Treasury auction would require a different trading mechanism than the one that prevails today. Instead of sealed bids, some form of face-to-face exchange bidding might be needed, with traders calling out their bids orally ("open outcry"). Alternatively, the government auctioneer would have to be linked through an electronic network to the bidders, perhaps using telephones and computers to convey and record the volume of bids at each proposed price. One clear advantage of such an auction system over the current sealed-bid approach is that dealers would then be able to gather important information about the distribution of bids and see how the rest of the market values the securities being offered. A key disadvantage of this auction method is the amount of time required for successive rounds of bidding to take place at each proposed price, during which time changing conditions might disrupt the market's move toward a true equilibrium that clears the market. Whatever auction procedure the Treasury uses in the future, it must appear to be fair and reasonable and inspire the public's confidence in the integrity of the government security market.

Dealers' Reliance on Borrowed Funds

Although government security dealers supply a huge volume of securities daily to the financial marketplace, these dealers depend heavily on the money market for borrowed funds. Most dealer houses invest little of their own equity in the business. Ratios of security positions held to dealer capital of 30 to 40 to 1 are not unusual. The bulk of operating capital is obtained through borrowings from commercial banks and other institutions. A major dealer firm carries hundreds of millions of dollars in securities in its trading portfolio, with 95 percent or more of that portfolio supported by short-term loans, some carrying only 24-hour maturities.

Demand Loans

The two most heavily used sources of dealer funds are demand loans from the largest banks and repurchase agreements (RPs) with banks and other lenders. Every day major banks post interest rates at which they are willing to make short-term loans to dealers. Generally, one rate is quoted on new loans and a second (lower) rate is posted for renewals of existing loans. A **demand loan** may be called in at any time if the banks need cash in a hurry. Such loans are virtually riskless, however, because they usually are collateralized by U.S. government securities, which may be transferred temporarily to the lending bank or to its agent.

Repurchase Agreements

An increasingly popular alternative to the demand loan is the **repurchase agreement (RP)**. Under this arrangement, the dealer sells securities to a lender but makes a commitment to buy back the securities at a later date at a fixed price plus interest. Thus, RPs are simply a temporary extension of credit collateralized by marketable securities. Some RPs are for a set length of time (term), while others, known as *continuing contracts*, carry no explicit maturity date but may be terminated by either party on short notice. Larger banks provide both demand loans and RPs to dealers, while nonfinancial corporations have provided a growing volume of funds to dealers through RPs in recent years. Other lenders active in the RP market include state and local governments, insurance companies, and foreign financial institutions who find the market a convenient, relatively low-risk way to invest temporary cash surpluses that may be retrieved quickly when the need arises. On some trading days, the volume of RP loans approaches $1 trillion or more.

The typical RP loan transaction can be described easily through the use of T accounts (an abbreviated balance sheet) for a dealer and for the lender of funds. Exhibit 15–4 presents a typical example of such a loan. In this case, we assume a manufacturing company has a temporary $1 million cash surplus. The company is eager to loan its temporary cash surplus right away to avoid losing even a single day's interest, while the dealer wishes to borrow at the low-cost RP loan rate to purchase interest-bearing securities. The borrowing dealer and the lending company agree on a $1 million RP loan — the minimum loan usually made in this market — collateralized by Treasury bills, with the dealer agreeing to buy back the bills within a few days and to pay the interest on the loan. Normally, the securities that form the collateral for the RP are supposed to be placed in a custodial account at a bank. When the loan is repaid, the dealer's RP liability is automatically canceled and the securities are returned to the dealer.

Exhibit 15–4   **Example of a Typical RP Loan Transaction**

	Security Dealer		Manufacturing Company	
	Assets	Liabilities	Assets	Liabilities
a. Lender of funds — a manufacturing company — has a $1 million surplus in its cash account.			Deposit at bank + $1 million	
b. A security dealer and the company settle on an RP with the dealer using the borrowed funds to buy securities.	Securities held + $1 million	RP borrowing from manufacturer + $1 million	Deposit at bank − $1 million RP loan to security dealer + $1 million	
c. The RP agreement is concluded and the funds returned (plus interest).	Dealer's cash account − $1 million	RP borrowing from manufacturer − $1 million	Deposit at bank + $1 million RP loan to security dealer − $1 million	

There is evidence that this safety device of placing securities involved in an RP agreement into a separate bank-held custodial account is not always scrupulously followed. Moreover, because the majority of outstanding RP loans are simply recorded as book entries at the Federal Reserve banks, verification of what has been done with the pledged securities can be difficult. The result is that if a government securities dealer goes out of business, a customer lending money under an RP to that dealer may have difficulty recovering the securities pledged as collateral behind the loan. Following the collapse of several dealer firms and the failure of several savings and loan associations that lost millions of dollars from inadequately collateralized security loans to those same dealers, federal authorities imposed stricter reporting requirements on the dealers. The Government Securities Act was passed in 1986, granting the U.S. Treasury oversight authority to protect the public from "unscrupulous" dealers with new rules that require written contracts between dealers and investors lending them money that describe where the securities in the RP are held, specify whether other securities can be substituted for those held as loan collateral, and clearly state that RPs are not protected by federal deposit insurance. The Securities and Exchange Commission and the federal banking agencies must enforce any rules for the government securities market that the Treasury Department writes.

Until recently, RPs were principally overnight transactions or expired in a few days. Today, however, there is a substantial volume of one- to three-month agreements, and some carry even longer maturities. Longer-term RPs are known as *term agreements.* Many recent RPs have built-in flexibility to benefit both borrower and lender. For example, *dollar repos* permit the seller of securities (borrower) to repurchase from the lender securities that are similar to, but not necessarily the same as, the securities originally sold. These so-called *flex repos,* usually involving a dealer and a state or local unit of government, are similar to deposits. In this case, the lender can withdraw part of the loan when he needs cash, and the remaining funds continue being loaned to the borrowing dealer.

The interest rate on RPs is the return that a dealer must pay a lender for the temporary use of money and is closely related to other money market interest rates. Usually, the securities pledged behind an RP are valued at their current market prices plus accrued interest (on coupon-bearing securities) less a small "haircut" (discount) to reduce the lender's exposure to market risk. The longer the term and the riskier and less liquid are the securities pledged behind an RP, the larger the "haircut" will be to protect the lender in case security prices fall. Periodically, RPs are "marked to market," and if the price of the pledged securities has dropped, the borrower may have to pledge additional collateral.

Interest income from repurchase agreements is usually determined from the formula:

$$\begin{array}{c} \text{RP interest} \\ \text{income} \end{array} = \begin{array}{c} \text{Amount} \\ \text{of loan} \end{array} \times \begin{array}{c} \text{Current} \\ \text{RP rate} \end{array} \times \frac{\text{Number of days loaned}}{\text{360 days}} \qquad (15\text{--}7)$$

For example, an overnight loan of $100 million to a dealer at a 7 percent RP rate would yield interest income of $19,444.44. That is,

$$\text{RP interest income} = \$100,000,000 \times .07 \times \frac{1}{360} = \$19,444.44$$

Under a continuing contract RP, the rate changes daily, so the calculation above would be made for each day the funds were loaned, and the total interest owed would be paid to the lender when the contract is ended by either party.

To promote a smoothly functioning market, the Federal Reserve System, through its trading desk at the New York Fed, frequently participates with the primary government security dealers in RPs. In a straight RP transaction, the Federal Reserve buys securities from a dealer on a short-term basis and then sells them back at the end of the agreed-upon period. The Fed may also enter into a reverse RP transaction with one or more dealers. In this case, the Federal Reserve Bank of New York sells securities to a dealer with an agreement to buy them back after a short period of time, thus temporarily absorbing dealer funds and reducing the ability of the dealer's bank to make loans. Whereas dealers use the RP to protect or increase their earnings from security trading, the Federal Reserve uses RPs to steady the money market and to promote national economic goals.[7]

Sources of Dealer Income

Securities dealers take substantial risks to make a market for Treasury bills and other financial instruments. To be sure, the securities they deal in are among the highest-quality instruments available in the financial marketplace. However, the prices of even top-quality securities can experience rapid declines if interest rates rise. Moreover, established dealer houses cannot run and hide but are obliged to stand ready at all times to buy and sell on customer demand, regardless of the condition of the market. In contrast to securities brokers, who merely bring buyers and sellers together, dealers take a *position of risk*, which means that they act as principals in the buying and selling of securities, adding any securities purchased to their own portfolios.

Dealers stand ready to buy specified types of securities at an announced *bid* price and to sell them at an announced *asked* price. This is called *making a market* in a particular financial instrument. The dealer hopes to earn a profit from such market-making activities in part from the positive spread between bid and asked prices for the same security. This spread varies with market activity and the outlook for interest rates but is narrow on bills (often about $50 per $1 million or less) and wider on more volatile notes and bonds (frequently in the range of about $300 per $1 million). Spreads range higher on longer-term securities, on small transactions, and on securities not actively traded due to greater risk and greater cost.[8]

---

[7]We will discuss Federal Reserve RP transactions in more detail in Chapter 20.

[8]Generally, dealers will deliver securities sold the next business day after a sale has been made (known as *regular delivery*), though smaller odd-lot transactions are usually completed within five business days — a method of delivery used for most Treasury bill trades. Large customers or dealers themselves may demand same-day settlement (known as *cash delivery*). In recent years, an increasing number of dealer transactions have been

As we have seen, the dealers' holdings of securities are financed by borrowing, so their portfolio positions are extremely sensitive to fluctuations in interest rates. For this reason, dealers frequently shift from long positions to short positions, depending on the outlook for interest rates. A **long position** means that the dealers have purchased securities outright, taken title to them, and will hold them in their portfolios as an investment or until a customer comes along. Long positions typically increase in a period of falling interest rates. A **short position**, on the other hand, means that dealers have sold securities they do not presently own to make future delivery to a customer. In so doing, they hope the prices of those securities will fall (and interest rates rise) before they must acquire the securities and make the delivery. Obviously, if interest rates fall (and security prices rise), the dealer will experience capital gains on a long position but losses on a short position. On the other hand, if interest rates rise (resulting in a drop in security prices), the dealer's long position will experience capital losses, and the short position will post a gain.

In periods when interest rates are expected to rise, dealers typically reduce their long positions and go short. Conversely, expectations of falling rates lead dealers to increase their long positions and avoid short sales. By correctly anticipating rate movements, the dealer can earn sizable *position profits*. Dealers also receive *carry income*, the difference between interest earned on securities they hold and their cost of borrowing funds. Generally, dealers earn higher rates of return on the securities they hold than the interest rates they pay for loans, but this is not always so. Because most dealer borrowings are short term, they normally are better off if the yield curve is positively sloped.

To help reduce exposure to risk, security dealers have recently diversified the revenue-generating services they offer. Some dealer firms now trade in foreign currencies, commodities (such as oil), security options, futures contracts, and SWAP contracts. Several leading dealers — for example, Merrill Lynch & Co. and Salomon Brothers — offer cash-management services in which they hold the funds of customers and invest them in securities, earning cash-management fees from those same customers. The dealers have also tried to stabilize their income by acting as financial intermediaries, simultaneously borrowing and lending money through a technique known as *matched book*, in which funds are borrowed through low-cost short-term RPs and then are loaned out through longer-term, higher-yielding RPs. The yield spread between these "matched" RPs gives the dealer a net profit unless, of course, the slope of the yield curve suddenly changes and the dealer is forced to borrow short-term money at significantly higher interest rates.

Dealer Positions in Securities

Dealer holdings of U.S. government and other securities are both huge and subject to erratic fluctuations. For example, in 1991 the dealers held a massive net long position in U.S. government securities of nearly $20 billion before falling to a sizable net short position of −$3.3 billion early in 1992. During 1995, the government security dealers held very large positions in U.S. Treasury bills, short-term T-notes, and federal agency securities but also held a huge short position in longer-term Treasury notes and bond of nearly $18 billion.

Why is there often such a tremendous difference in the size and direction of dealer portfolios from year to year? Interest rate movements and interest rate expectations explain

forward transactions — securities are purchased or sold for delivery after 5 business days from the date of the transaction if U.S. government securities are involved or after 30 days when mortgage-backed securities are the subject of the trade. Payment for all deliveries is usually made in federal funds, which can be wired into the seller's account within minutes.

a substantial proportion of the changes observed. For example, in 1991 and 1992 a deep recession drove market interest rates sharply lower, holding out the lure of higher profits if the dealers could shift their holdings into a long position. During 1995, however, short-term interest rates were falling slightly, but there was considerable fear among market participants that inflation and a more rapidly growing economy might send long-term interest rates higher, creating losses on notes and bonds held in a long position.

Dealers make heavy use of interest rate hedging tools today to further protect their portfolios from losses due to changes in interest rates. They are active participants in the *financial futures* markets and also are making increased use of *forward commitments*, in which a dealer sells securities but does not deliver those securities to the customer until more than five business days have elapsed. A dealer often does not hold the securities to be delivered under the forward commitment but waits to acquire them near the promised delivery date. This strategy minimizes the risk of loss due to interest rate changes because the dealer is exposed to risk for only a brief period before delivery is made.

Changing Sources of Dealer Financing

Where do government security dealers derive most of their funds to purchase and carry securities? The dealers make heavy use of repurchase agreements, usually collateralized by securities held in their portfolios, as we noted earlier. Commercial banks are also a major source of borrowed dealer funds. Indeed, several primary dealers are dealer departments housed in some of the world's largest banks. However, nonfinancial business corporations are the most rapidly growing source of funds for securities dealers. Many industrial corporations today find the dealer loan market a convenient, safe way to dispose of temporarily idle monies. With wire transfers of funds between banks readily available, a company can lend a dealer millions of dollars in idle cash and recover those funds in a matter of hours if a cash emergency arises.

Dealer Transactions and Government Security Brokers

Trading among dealers and between dealers and their customers amounts to billions of dollars each day. Indeed, so large is the government securities market that the volume of trading often exceeds the total volume of trading on many of the world's stock exchanges. Government securities dealers trade among themselves usually through *brokers*. Government security brokers do not take investment positions themselves but try to match bids and offers placed with them by dealers and other investors. Each broker operates a closed-circuit TV network showing dealer prices and quantities available.

Intense competition exists among government-security brokers. In 1992, for example, a "price war" broke out among leading brokerage houses, led by Liberty Brokerage, Inc., in which commissions were cut by 50 percent or more and volume discounts were offered to the largest dealers. In some cases, dealers were told that if they placed a specified minimum volume of orders each month, any subsequent trades during that same month would be handled free of charge by the advertising broker. The principal motivation for the sudden appearance of "bargain" brokerage rates was a sharp decline in trading volume, related to a slowdown in the economy.

Dealerships are a cutthroat business in which each dealer firm is out to maximize its returns from trading, even if gains must be made at the expense of competing dealers. Indeed, market analysts housed within each dealer firm study the daily price quotations of competitors. If one dealer temporarily underprices some securities (offering excessively generous yields), other dealers are likely to rush in before the offering firm has a chance to correct its mistake. It is a business with little room for the inexperienced or slow-moving trader and fraught with low margins and unstable earnings. For example, in 1982 two major firms — Drysdale Government Securities, Inc., and Lombard-Wall, Inc. — collapsed. These closings were followed by four more dealer failures: Lion Capital Group and RTD Securities in 1984, and E.S.M. Government Securities and Bevill, Bresler & Schulman Asset Management Corporation in 1985.

In 1989 and 1990, several foreign-owned dealers, including Britain's National Westminster Bank PLC, Lloyds Bank PLC, Midland Bank PLC, and L.F. Rothchilds & Co., as well as Australia's Westpac Banking Corporation, withdrew from the Fed's primary dealer list due to falling trading volume and declining profit margins. U.S. primary dealer Drexel Burnham Lambert also withdrew from that list in 1990 and filed for protection under the federal bankruptcy code. With soaring competition both at home and abroad, several primary dealers have been posting substantial net losses in recent years. Moreover, security prices and interest rates appeared to become much less volatile as the 1990s began. Unfortunately for the dealers, it is generally in periods of high price and rate volatility that these firms generate the most revenue, because the volume of security trading rises and there is more demand for interest rate risk protection at that time.

One of the most remarkable features of the dealer's business is how rapidly market conditions and the dealer's financial position can deteriorate. Large losses in the hundreds of millions of dollars can be recorded in a few hours. Moreover, dealers may buy large quantities of bonds that are not yet issued — so-called when-issued securities — without any money down and payment not due until delivery a week or so later, only to discover that within minutes the market values of these securities have dropped like a stone. Yet the government securities dealers are *essential* to the smooth functioning of the financial markets and to the successful placement of billions of dollars in new securities issued each year by the Treasury Department.

SUMMARY

In this chapter, we have examined one of the most important of all securities markets, the market for Treasury bills and other government securities. The U.S. government securities market began about 200 years ago when the first Secretary of the Treasury under the U.S. Constitution, Alexander Hamilton, organized the market and began to sell government securities to selected individuals and financial houses. This market has grown rapidly in recent years in response to huge government borrowing needs and the needs of investors for highly liquid, readily marketable financial instruments. It is difficult to overestimate the importance of the government securities market in the functioning of the global financial system. This market sets the tone for the whole financial system in terms of interest rates, security prices, and the availability of credit. It is indispensable as a tool for the government to finance its huge volume of debt, and interest rates on government securities serve as reference rates for thousands of private loan contracts. Moreover, investors all over the globe rely on government securities as a safe haven for their cash reserves. And it is in this market today that most government economic policy measures begin, in the form of Treasury issues of new securities and central bank open-market operations. A thorough knowledge of the workings of the market for government securities tells us much about the "how" and "why" of the financial system. ■

KEY TERMS AND CONCEPTS IN THIS CHAPTER

U.S. Treasury bills	demand loan	long position
auction	repurchase agreement (RP)	short position
bank discount method		
primary dealers		

STUDY QUESTIONS

1. Why has the volume of Treasury bills grown so rapidly in recent years? Explain why the T-bill is so popular with money market investors.

2. List and define the various types of Treasury bills. Why are there so many different varieties?

3. Explain how a T-bill auction works. Can you cite some advantages of this method of sale? Disadvantages?

4. How are the yields on U.S. Treasury bills calculated? How does this method differ from the method used to calculate bond yields? Why is this difference important?

5. What is the normal, or typical, slope of the yield curve for T-bills? Why? What other slopes have been observed, and why do you think these occur?

6. Who are the principal investors in U.S. Treasury bills? What factors motivate these investors to buy bills?

7. Explain why dealers are essential to the smooth functioning of the securities markets.

8. What is a demand loan? An RP? Explain their role in dealer financing.

9. In what ways do dealers earn income and possibly make a profit? To what risk is each source of dealer income subject?

10. Are the majority of government security dealers' positions in short-term or long-term securities? What causes their positions to change?

PROBLEMS

1. From the following sets of figures, (1) calculate the bank discount rate on each T-bill and (2) convert that rate to the appropriate investment (or coupon-equivalent) yield.

    a. A new three-month T-bill sells for $98.25 on a $100 basis.

    b. The investor can buy a new 12-month T-bill for $96 on a $100 basis.

    c. A 30-day bill is available from a U.S. government securities dealer at a price of $97.50 (per $100).

2. Calculate the holding-period yield for the following situations:

    a. The investor buys a new 12-month T-bill at a discount rate of $7\frac{1}{2}$ percent. Sixty days later, the bill is sold at a price that results in a discount rate of 7 percent.

b.   A large manufacturing corporation acquired a T-bill in the secondary market 30 days from its maturity but is forced to sell the bill 15 days later. At time of purchase, the bill carried a discount rate of 8 percent, but it was sold at a discount rate of 7¾ percent.

3.   A dealer in government securities currently holds $875 million in 10-year Treasury bonds and $1,410 million in six-month Treasury bills. Current yields on the T-bonds average 7.15 percent, while six-month T-bill yields average 3.28 percent. The dealer is currently borrowing $2,300 million through one-week repurchase agreements at an interest rate of 3.20 percent. What is the dealer's expected (annualized) *carry income*? Suppose that 10-year T-bond rates suddenly rise to 7.30 percent, T-bill rates climb to 5.40 percent, and interest rates on comparable maturity RPs increase to 5.55 percent. What will happen to the dealer's expected (annualized) carry income and why? Should this dealer have moved to a long position or a short position before the interest rate change just described? Should the dealer alter his or her borrowing plans in any way? Please explain your answer.

4.   A government securities dealer is currently borrowing $25 million from a money-center bank using repurchase agreements based on Treasury bills. If today's RP rate is 6.25 percent, how much in interest will the dealer owe the bank for a 24-hour loan?

5.   Suppose that a dealer borrows cash through a $40 million RP from a manufacturing corporation for one day. If the dealer will have to pay $3500 in interest on this loan, what is the current RP loan rate?

SELECTED REFERENCES

Federal Reserve Bank of New York. *Basic Information on Treasury Securities*, 1990.

Jones, David S., and V. Vance Roley. "Rational Expectations, the Expectations Hypothesis, and Treasury Bill Yields: An Econometric Analysis." *Research Working Paper 82–01*. Federal Reserve Bank of Kansas City, February 1982.

Mester, Loretta J. "There's More Than One Way to Sell a Security: The Treasury's Auction Experiment." *Business Review*, Federal Reserve Bank of Philadelphia, July–August 1995, pp. 3–17.

Reinhart, Vincent. "An Analysis of Potential Treasury Auction Techniques." *Federal Reserve Bulletin*, June 1992, pp. 403–13.

Rowe, Timothy D.; Thomas A. Lawler; and Timothy Q. Cook. "Treasury Bill Versus Private Money Market Yield Curves." *Economic Review*. Federal Reserve Bank of Richmond, July–August 1986, pp. 3–12.

Chapter 16

Federal Funds, Negotiable CDs, and Loans from the Discount Window

LEARNING OBJECTIVES IN THIS CHAPTER

- To examine the critical roles banks play in the money market.
- To illustrate three important ways that banks borrow funds in the money market: from the federal funds and certificate of deposit (CD) markets and by borrowing from the discount windows of the Federal Reserve banks.
- To see what changes the technique known as *liability management* has made in bank performance and practice.

The single most important financial institution in the money market is the *commercial bank*. Large money center banks, such as those headquartered in New York City, London, Tokyo, and a handful of other major cities around the globe, provide billions of dollars in funds daily through the money market to governments and corporations in need of cash. As we saw in the previous chapter, bank loans and repurchase agreements are a principal source of financing for dealers in government securities, while banks also make large purchases of Treasury bills and other money market securities. Commercial banks support private corporations borrowing in the money market both by purchasing their securities and by granting lines of credit to backstop a new security issue. Banks supply credit to support the movement of goods in domestic and international trade. And both large and small banks today readily lend their cash reserves to other financial institutions and to industrial corporations to cover short-term liquidity needs.

For banks to lend huge amounts of funds daily in the money market, they must also borrow heavily in that market. As we saw in Chapter 4, the owners (stockholders) supply only a minor portion of a commercial bank's total resources; the bulk of bank funds must be borrowed. The majority of borrowed funds (nearly 80 percent for most banks) comes from deposits, but a growing portion of the industry's financing needs is supplied by the *money market*. However, bank managers today are more cautious in their use of money market borrowings than was true even a few years ago. Such funds are relatively expensive to use, and their interest cost is more volatile than for most kinds of deposits. Many banks follow the strategy of maintaining a roughly equal balance between their lending and borrowing activities in the money market: The volume of short-term bank debt is counterbalanced by a nearly equal volume of short-term bank assets.[1]

In this chapter, we examine three of the most important money market sources of funds for banks and other deposit-type financial institutions: federal funds, certificates of deposit (CDs), and loans from the Federal Reserve's discount window. In Chapter 18, we discuss still another important source of funds for many of the largest depository institutions, Eurocurrency deposits.

FEDERAL FUNDS

As we saw in the introductory chapter to the money market (Chapter 14), **federal funds** are among the most important of all money market instruments for one key reason: *Fed funds are the principal means of making payments in the money market.* By definition, federal funds are any monies available for immediate payment ("same-day money"). They are generally transferred from one depository institution to another by simple bookkeeping entries requested by on-line computer, by wire, or by telephone after a purchase of securities is made or a loan is granted.

Nature of Federal Funds

The name *federal funds* came about because, early in the development of the market, the principal source of immediately available money was the reserve balance that each bank must keep at the Federal Reserve bank in its region of the United States. If one bank needs to transfer funds to another, it need only contact the Federal Reserve bank in its district, and funds are readily transferred into the appropriate reserve account — a transaction accomplished in seconds by computer.

Today, however, the Fed funds market is far broader in scope than just reserves on deposit with the Federal Reserve banks. For example, virtually all banks maintain deposits with large correspondent banks in central cities; these deposits may be transferred readily by telephone, by computer, or by wire from the account of one bank to that of another. They may also be borrowed by the institution that holds the correspondent deposit, simply by transferring funds from the correspondent deposit to an account titled "Federal funds purchased" and reversing these entries when the loan matures. Savings and loan associations, credit unions, and savings banks maintain deposits with commercial banks or with the Federal Reserve banks that also are available for immediate transfer to a customer or to another financial institution. Business corporations and state and local governments can lend federal funds by executing repurchase agreements with securities dealers, banks, and other funds traders. Securities dealers who have received payment for securities sold can turn around and make their funds immediately available to borrowers through the federal funds market.

---

[1]The idea of maintaining a roughly *equal* balance between borrowing and lending in the money market follows one of the oldest concepts in the field of finance: the *hedging principle*. As discussed in Chapter 10, in a world of uncertainty, borrowers of funds can reduce liquidity risk by matching the maturity of their assets and liabilities. This approach reduces the risk of borrowing when funds are not needed and also lowers the risk of not having sufficient cash when interest payments and other bills come due.

Borrowers of federal funds include securities dealers, corporations, state and local governments, and nonbank financial intermediaries, such as savings and loan associations and insurance companies. Without question, however, the most important of all borrowers in the Fed funds market are commercial banks, which use this instrument as the principal way to adjust their legal reserve account at the Federal Reserve bank in their district.

Use of the Federal Funds Market to Meet Deposit Reserve Requirements

Banks and other depository institutions must hold in a special reserve account liquid assets equal to a fraction of the funds deposited with them by the public. Only vault cash held on the premises and reserve balances kept with the Federal Reserve bank in the district count in meeting a U.S. bank's requirement to hold **legal reserves.** Frequently, some banks hold more legal reserves than the law requires. Because these reserves earn little or no income, most bankers active in the money market try to lend out any excess reserves in their possession, even if they only lend the funds overnight.

Banks are aided in this endeavor by the fact that their legal reserve requirement is calculated on a daily average basis over a two-week period, known as the *reserve computation period.* For example, the reserve computation period for *transaction deposits* (e.g., checking accounts and NOWs) stretches from a Tuesday through a Monday two weeks later. The Federal Reserve calculates the daily average level of transaction deposits held by each depository institution over this two-week period and then multiples that average by the required reserve percentage (3 percent for smaller banks, for example) to determine the amount of legal reserves that must be held by each institution, as we illustrated in Chapter 4. These legal reserves must average the required amount over a two-week period known as the *reserve maintenance period.* For transaction deposits, the reserve maintenance period starts on a Thursday — two days after the transaction-deposit reserve computation period begins — and ends on a Wednesday two weeks later. Thus, the reserve computation and reserve maintenance periods for transaction deposits overlap each other except for *two days.* This overlapping feature explains why this accounting system is called **contemporaneous reserve accounting.** In theory at least, contemporaneous reserve accounting promotes a closer correspondence between the growth of deposits, which reflect bank lending, and the volume of legal reserves, which can be controlled by the central bank (in the United States, the Federal Reserve System).

Legal reserves on time deposits and other nontransaction liabilities of banks are figured on the basis of the average level of these liabilities over a two-week period ending 16 days before the reserve maintenance period begins.[2] Furthermore, each depository institution is allowed to count its average vault cash holdings over the same two-week computation period as is used for transaction deposits (as shown in Exhibit 16–1) and then deduct that daily average vault cash figure from its required reserves.

---

[2]In the fall of 1990, the Federal Reserve Board lowered the percentage reserve requirement on nontransaction liabilities and Eurodollar borrowings to *zero.* However, the Fed could reimpose a reserve requirement on these sources of bank funds at any time. In April 1992 the Fed lowered the reserve requirement for all transaction deposits held by a bank over and above the first $54 million from 12 percent to 10 percent. For net transaction deposits totaling less than $54 million, the legal reserve requirement is 3 percent. These changes were designed to free up more reserves in an effort to stimulate bank lending and make U.S. banks more competitive with foreign banks with lower reserve requirements. On December 19, 1995, the Federal Reserve Board slightly increased reserve requirements for large banks by requiring that banks hold a 10 percent required reserve on total transactions accounts above $52 million. Small banks had their reserve requirements slightly lowered at the same time, as the Fed raised the amount of transaction deposits *not* subject to *any* reserve requirement from $4.2 million to $4.3 million.

Exhibit 16–1

The Contemporaneous Reserve Accounting System for Calculating Deposit Reserve Requirements of Commercial Banks and Other U.S. Depository Institutions

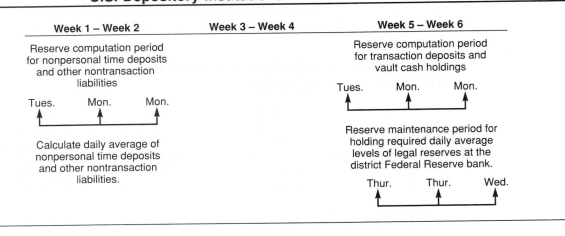

Exhibit 16–1 illustrates the reserve accounting system now in use. As this exhibit illustrates, the manager of each depository institution's money desk — the department responsible for keeping track of the depository's legal reserve position — must adjust each institution's reserve balance at the district Federal Reserve bank to the right level over the two-week reserve maintenance period.[3] The federal funds market is an indispensable tool for this kind of daily reserve management, especially for the largest and most aggressive banks, which hold few reserves of their own. Indeed, many large U.S. banks today borrow virtually all of the legal reserves behind their deposits from the federal funds market.

Mechanics of Federal Funds Trading

The mechanics of federal funds trading varies depending on the locations of the buying (borrowing) and selling (lending) institutions. For example, suppose two commercial banks involved in a federal funds transaction are located in the heart of the New York money market. These banks could simply exchange checks. The borrowing bank could be handed a check drawn on the lending bank's reserve account at the Federal Reserve Bank of New York City. This check is payable immediately ("same-day money"), and therefore Fed funds would be transferred to the borrower's reserve account before the close of business that same day. The lender, on the other hand, may be given a check drawn on the borrower. This last check is "one-day money" (payable the following day) because it must pass through the New York clearinghouse for settlement. Thus, funds flow instantly to the borrowing bank's reserve account and are automatically returned to the lending bank's reserve account the next day or whenever the loan agreement terminates. Alternatively, the lending bank can simply contact the Federal Reserve Bank of New York directly and ask it to electronically move funds from the lender's reserve account to the borrower's reserve account immediately, with the transaction usually reversed the next day. Interest on the Fed

---

[3]Actually, the money desk manager receives a little leeway under existing regulations, because each depository institution is allowed to fall up to $50,000 or 4 percent, whichever is larger, *below* its required reserve level in a given reserve maintenance period, provided it runs a corresponding excess the next maintenance period.

funds loan may be included when the funds are returned, paid by separate check, or settled by debiting and crediting the appropriate correspondent balances.

If the transacting institutions are not both located within the same Federal Reserve district, the loan transaction proceeds in much the same way except that *two* Federal Reserve banks are involved. Once borrower and lender agree on the terms of a loan, the lending institution directly, or indirectly through a correspondent bank, contacts the Federal Reserve bank in its district, requesting a wire transfer of federal funds. The Reserve bank then transfers reserves through the Fed's wire network (FEDWIRE) to the Federal Reserve bank serving the region where the borrowing institution is located. Funds travel the reverse route when the loan is terminated.

Incidentally, how do Fed funds borrowers and lenders contact each other to find out who has surplus funds to lend and who is short of funds? Computer networks and the telephone are the most common media for communicating between institutions in need of funds and those with surplus funds. In addition, a handful of *Fed funds brokers* active in the New York money market work to bring buying and selling institutions together, indicating by telephone and computer screen what funds are available and at what rate.

Volume of Borrowings in the Funds Market

Commercial banks borrow billions of dollars each day in the funds market. Total federal funds borrowings by banks in all 50 states (including security resale agreements with nonbank institutions) stood at close to $200 billion in the 1990s. The federal funds market probably extends at least $300 billion to $500 billion in credit *daily.* The large banks in New York City, by virtue of their strategic location at the heart of the domestic money market, still account for a disproportionate share of all Fed funds transactions. However, the market has broadened considerably in recent years to include both domestic and foreign banks in Atlanta, Chicago, San Francisco, and other major U.S. cities, as well as thousands of smaller banks in outlying areas.

Most federal funds loans are overnight (one-day) transactions or continuing contracts that have no specific maturity and can be terminated without advance notice by either party. One-day loans carry a fixed rate of interest, but continuing contracts often do not. There is a growing volume of loans lasting beyond one day, often arising from security repurchase agreements. These longer-maturity interbank loans are usually called *term* federal funds and are being supplied increasingly by foreign banks, savings and loan associations, insurance companies, pension funds, and finance companies as a safe and profitable way to warehouse funds until they are needed for long-term loan commitments.

Rates on Federal Funds

The federal funds interest rate is highly volatile from day to day, although on an annual basis, it tends to move roughly in line with other money market interest rates (see Exhibit 16–2). The short-term volatility of the rate arises from substantial variations in the volume of funds made available by lenders each day and the size of daily cash deficits experienced by banks and other money market participants. The funds rate tends to be most volatile toward the close of the reserve maintenance period, depending on whether larger banks are flush with or short of reserves. There are also definite seasonal patterns, with the funds rate tending to rise around holiday periods, when loan demand and deposit withdrawals are heavy. Finally, there is a "window-dressing" effect near the end of each year when many banks use Fed funds to make temporary adjustments in their balance sheets in order to "look better" in their annual reports.

Exhibit 16–2   **Effective Interest Rates on Federal Funds Transactions, 1980–1996**
(Percent per Annum)

Year	Average Daily Rate on Federal Funds	Year	Average Daily Rate on Federal Funds
1980	13.36%	1988	7.57
1981	16.38	1989	9.21
1982	12.26	1990	8.10
1983	9.09	1991	5.69
1984	10.22	1992	3.52
1985	8.10	1993	3.02
1986	6.80	1994	4.21
1987	6.66	1995	5.83
		1996*	5.22

*Average for February 1996.

Source: Board of Governors of the Federal Reserve System, *Federal Reserve Bulletin,* selected monthly issues.

Federal Funds and Government Policy

The federal funds market is an easy and riskless way to invest excess reserves for short periods and still earn some interest income. It is essential to the daily management of bank reserves, because credit can be obtained in a matter of minutes to cover emergency situations. As we have seen, the market is also critical to the whole money market, because Federal funds serve as the principal means of payment for securities and loans. Moreover, the funds market transmits the effects of Federal Reserve monetary policy quickly throughout the banking system.

Prior to 1979, the Federal Reserve routinely set target levels for the federal funds rate and raised or lowered those targets, depending on whether the Fed wished to slow down borrowing and spending in the economy or speed it up. Using daily open market operations — buying and selling securities — the Fed was able to push the funds rate in the desired direction on any given day. However, fearing accelerating inflation, the Fed announced in October 1979 that it would pay less attention to daily federal funds rates and try to control the money supply more closely. The federal funds rate then became *more volatile* from day to day, with the result that, in recent years, the Federal Reserve has once again begun to pay more attention to targeting and stabilizing the federal funds rate.

Negotiable Certificates of Deposit

One of the largest of all money market instruments, measured by dollar volume, is the **negotiable certificate of deposit (CD).** A CD is an interest-bearing receipt for funds left with a depository institution for a set period of time.[4] Banks and other deposit-type institutions issue many types of CDs, but true money market CDs are negotiable instruments that may be sold any number of times before reaching maturity and carry a minimum denomination of $100,000. The usual round-lot trading unit for money market CDs is $1 million.

The interest rate on a large negotiable CD is set by negotiation between the issuing institution and its customer and generally reflects prevailing market conditions. Therefore,

---

[4]The minimum maturity permitted for CDs under federal regulation is seven days. There is no legal upper limit on maturities, however. CDs must be issued at par and trade on an interest-bearing basis, unlike Treasury bills. Payment is made in federal funds on the day the CD matures.

INTERNATIONAL FOCUS:

The Interbank Loan Market in Russia

The federal funds market in the United States is not the only market for inter-bank loans; banks in many other countries have established a market for making loans of reserves to each other. While the U.S. Fed funds market is highly efficient and works very well, sometimes these foreign interbank markets run into trouble, and this can have serious consequences for the rest of the economy. A dramatic example of how troubles in interbank lending can send tremors through a country's financial system occurred in Russia in August 1995.

Newspaper stories and rumors spread through Russia's developing commercial banking system to the effect that several Russian banks were not sound. As this tale spread, most of Russia's more than 2,500 banks simply stopped extending loans to one another. Because there is only limited information available on any bank's true condition in Russia and their regulatory system is still rudimentary and often confus-ing, many Russian bankers indicated they could not get enough information on other banks to decide whether these banks were solvent enough to pay back their loans. As a result, the overnight market for ruble-denominated deposits literally ground to a halt, and some banks offered interest rates as high as one thousand percent in an effort to get a loan of reserves! Moreover, with bankers not trusting each other, the Russian public began to mistrust their own banks, resulting in scores of depositors demanding to retrieve their funds.

Many observers were concerned that, should such a condition continue, the Russian banking system might completely lose confidence and collapse. One possi-ble solution would be for Russia's central bank to grant loans to any banks in trouble, thus encouraging private bankers to begin lending again. Indeed, only a few days into the crisis, the country's central bank began buying government bonds held by banks and other investors in order to flood the system with liquidity. Russia's central bank appeared to have sufficient reserves to supply the liquidity needed to stabilize the banking system. However, over the longer term, reform of the Russian banking system to clarify regulations, install risk management systems, reduce past-due loans, and require banks to release more information to the public about their true financial condition seems in order. The Russian government has also recently urged larger banks to seriously consider buying out smaller and more vulnerable banking institutions.

---

like the rates on other money market securities, CD rates rise in periods of tight money, when loanable funds are scarce, and fall in periods of easy money, when loanable funds are more abundant.

The negotiable CD is one of the youngest of all U.S. money market instruments. It dates from 1961, when First National City Bank of New York (later Citicorp) began offering the instrument to its largest corporate customers. Simultaneously, a small group of securities dealers agreed to make a secondary (resale) market for CDs of $100,000 or more. Other money center banks soon entered the competition for corporate funds and began to offer their own CDs.

The decision to offer this new money market instrument was an agonizing one for banks because CDs sharply raised the average cost and the volatility of bank funds. How-ever, commercial banks had little choice but to offer the new instrument or face the loss of billions of dollars in interest-sensitive deposits. The cash management departments of major corporations have become increasingly aware of the many profitable ways available to invest their short-term funds. Prior to the introduction of the negotiable CD, many bankers found that their biggest corporate customers were reducing their deposits and buying Treasury bills, RPs, and other money market instruments. The CD was developed to attract those lost deposits back into the banking system.

Growth of CDs

Negotiable CDs are a real success story for most banks. In 1996, large ($100,000+) time deposits outstanding at banks and thrifts operating in the United States totaled more than $400 billion. This compares with only about $100 billion in large CDs 15 years earlier. Until the Penn Central crisis of 1970, large negotiable CDs were subject to legal interest rate ceilings as specified in the Federal Reserve Board's Regulation Q. However, the bankruptcy of the huge Penn Central Transportation Company rocked the money market; many large corporations, unable to sell their notes in the open market to raise short-term funds, turned to banks for help. To ease this serious liquidity crunch, the Fed suspended interest rate ceilings on large short-term CDs in June 1970 and on longer-term CDs in May 1973, enabling bankers to more easily sell their CDs and grant loans to their corporate customers. Freed from legal interest rate ceilings, the volume of large CDs soared, especially during periods of rapid economic growth.

Terms Attached to CDs

Negotiable CDs may be *registered* on the books of the issuing depository institution or issued in *bearer form* to the purchasing investor. CDs issued in bearer form are more convenient for resale in the secondary market because they are in the hands of the investors who own them. Denominations range from $25,000 to $10 million, although CDs actively traded in the money market carry a minimum denomination of $100,000. Maturities range to 18 months, depending on the customer's needs. However, most negotiable CDs have maturities of six months or less. CDs with maturities beyond one year are called *term* CDs.

Interest rates in the CD market are computed as a yield to maturity but are quoted on a 360-day basis (except in secondary market trading, in which the bank discount rate is used as a measure of CD yields). For example, if a business firm purchases a $100,000 negotiable CD for six months at an interest rate of 7.50 percent, it would receive back at the end of 180 days:

$$\$100,000 \times (1 + \frac{180}{360} \times 0.075) = \$103,750$$

To convert the yield on newly issued CDs to a coupon-equivalent (or yield-to-maturity) basis, we must multiply their yield by the ratio 365:360. The yield on CDs normally is slightly above the Treasury bill rate due to greater default risk, a thinner resale market, and the state and local government tax exemption on earnings from Treasury bills. Because investors can easily *arbitrage* between short-term markets, moving funds toward the highest yields, the CD interest rate hovers close to the average of current and future federal funds interest rates expected by investors to prevail over the life of the CD. However, as Exhibit 16–3 shows, in 1984 and again in 1988, following severe problems at some of the largest banks, risk premiums attached to CDs rose, driving them well above the federal funds rate. The yield spread between CDs and other money market instruments varies over

Exhibit 16–3   **Recent Interest Rates on Money Market CDs ($100,000 or More) versus Rates on Treasury Bills, Federal Funds, Eurodollars, and the Federal Reserve Bank of New York's Discount Rate** (Year-End)

Instrument	Period				
	1984	**1988**	**1990**	**1995**	**1996***
Certificate of deposit:					
Three month	10.37%	7.73%	8.15%	5.92%	5.15%
Six month	10.68	7.91	8.17	5.98	5.03
U.S. Treasury bills:					
Three-month	9.52	6.67	7.50	5.49	4.83
Six-month	9.76	6.91	7.46	5.56	4.77
Federal funds	10.22	7.57	8.10	5.83	5.22
Eurodollars,					
Three-month	10.73	7.85	8.16	5.93	5.14
Discount rate,					
FRB New York	8.00	6.50	6.50	5.25	5.00

Note: Based on weekly average rates as quoted by five dealers. Bill yields in the secondary market are quoted on a bank discount basis from daily closing bids.
*1996 figures are for February.

Source: Board of Governors of the Federal Reserve System, *Federal Reserve Bulletin,* selected issues.

time, depending on investor preferences, the supply of CDs and other money market instruments, and the financial condition of issuing banks.

One of the most interesting developments in recent years has been the appearance of a *multitiered* (segmented) market for CDs. Investors have grouped issuing banks into different risk categories, and yields in the market are scaled accordingly. This development is a legacy of the collapse of such banking giants as Franklin National Bank of New York in October 1974 and Continental Illinois Bank of Chicago in 1984. Faced with the spector of major bank failures, banks viewed as less stable by investors were forced to issue their CDs at significantly higher interest rates.

CDs from the largest and most financially sound banks are rated *prime;* smaller banks or those viewed as less stable issue *nonprime* CDs at higher interest rates. As is true for any depositor in a U.S. insured bank, the holder of a CD is covered against loss up to $100,000 if the issuing bank fails. Unfortunately, this insurance is of limited value to a corporation holding a million-dollar or larger CD. However, holders of large CDs do help to discipline their banks from taking on excessive risk.

Buyers of CDs

The principal buyers of negotiable CDs include corporations, state and local governments, foreign central banks and governments, wealthy individuals, and a wide variety of financial institutions. The latter include insurance companies, pension funds, investment companies, savings banks, credit unions, and money market funds. Large CDs appeal to these investors because they are readily marketable at low risk, may be issued in any desired maturity, and carry a somewhat higher yield than that on Treasury bills. However, the investor gives up some marketability in comparison with T-bills because the resale market for CDs operates well below the average daily volume of trading in bills.

Most buyers hold CDs until they mature. However, prime-rate CDs issued by billion-dollar banks are actively traded in the secondary market, centered in New York City. The purpose of the secondary market is principally to accommodate corporations that need cash quickly or see profitable opportunities from the sale of their deposits. Also, buyers of CDs who want shorter maturities or higher yields than are available on *new* CDs will enter the secondary market or redeem them in advance of maturity, except under special circumstances. Moreover, banks usually will not lend money on their own CDs as collateral because of the risk the borrower may default on the loan, in which case the bank would wind up owning its own CD and redeeming it before it matures.

CDs in Liability Management

Depository institutions use the CD as a supplement to federal funds when additional reserves are needed. A depository in need of funds simply raises the rate it is currently offering on CDs to attract new deposits. Financial institutions may also trade CDs (not their own) in the secondary market to raise funds, much as they might sell Treasury bills for cash. Today the negotiable CD plays a prominent role in the strategy of **liability management,** in which banks control the sources of their funds as well as their funds uses to achieve institutional goals.

New Types of CDs

Bankers are becoming increasingly innovative in packaging CDs to meet the needs of customers. One notable innovation occurred in 1975 when the *variable-rate CD* was introduced. Variable, or floating-rate, CDs generally carry maturities out to five years, with an interest rate that is adjusted every 30, 90, or 180 days (known as a *leg* or *roll* period). The floating interest rate is usually tied to movements in the secondary-market yield on fixed-rate CDs, the prevailing federal funds interest rate, the prime bank rate, or the going market interest rate on Eurodollar deposits. A variable-rate CD gives the investor a higher return than normally would be obtained by continually renewing shorter-term CDs and is a popular investment for money market mutual funds.

Another important innovation occurred in 1976 when Morgan Guaranty Trust in New York City introduced the *rollover* or *rolypoly CD*. Because six-month CDs are the maximum maturity traded in the secondary market, Morgan offered its customers longer-term CDs with higher rates, but in packages composed of a series of six-month CDs extending for at least two years. Thus, the rolypoly CD promised higher returns plus the ability to market some CDs in the package early to meet emergency cash needs. However, the bank's customer is still obligated to purchase the remaining certificates on each six-month anniversary date until the contract expires. Some rolypoly CDs are issued with fixed rates; others carry floating rates that change every six months.

Recent years have ushered in still more CD innovations; for example, *jumbo CDs, Yankee CDs, brokered CDs, bear and bull CDs, installment CDs, rising-rate CDs, and foreign-index CDs. Jumbo CDs* are large ($100,000+), negotiable CDs issued by nonbank thrift institutions such as savings and loan associations and savings banks. *Yankee CDs* are issued in the United States by foreign banks (mainly Japanese, Canadian, and European institutions) that usually have offices in U.S. cities. *Brokered CDs* consist of CDs sold through brokers or dealers in maximum $100,000 denominations to qualify for federal deposit insurance. Many brokers participate in exchanges in which their investing customers can purchase packages of the highest-yielding CDs issued by banks and thrifts. In the mid-1980s, *deposit notes* appeared from selected U.S. banks and from foreign banks with U.S. branches. These notes are a hybrid financial instrument, combining the features of CDs and corporate bonds with maturities reaching out beyond 1 year to as long as 10 years.

Bear and bull CDs, whose rates of return are linked to stock market performance, appeared in the mid-1980s. However, these instruments fell out of favor with the Great

---

INTERNATIONAL FOCUS:
CD Markets Around the Globe

Inside the United States, the market for bank certificates of deposit (CDs) has grown slowly at times and, in some instances, declined in recent years due to a variety of regulatory restrictions. However, an international market for CDs in the form of EuroCDs has grown rapidly, and many CD markets abroad have developed into active financial marketplaces.

In Canada, for example, the big chartered banks (such as the Bank of Montreal or Scotiabank) issue chartered bank CDs and chartered bank bearer deposit notes with maturities ranging from 30 days to 12 months in units of $100,000 and higher (though bearer CDs are available in units as small as $5,000). These instruments are sold at a discount from par and are usually obtained directly from the issuing bank. Some Canadian-bank CDs are available in both Canadian and U.S. dollars.

In Japan, bank CDs were first permitted by the Japanese Ministry of Finance at the beginning of the 1980s. Gradually, restrictions on maturities and minimum account sizes have been relaxed as the Japanese CD market has grown. Many Japanese loans today are priced on the basis of prevailing CD interest rates, though there is only a weak secondary market for these instruments due, in part, to Japanese regulation and taxation.

The Asian area of the world has also spawned *Asian* dollar CDs. These interest-sensitive bank deposits may carry fixed or floating interest yields based upon the prevailing level of the Singapore interbank offer rate (known as SIBOR). Asian CDs normally trade in $1 million units.

Half a world away in Europe, Eurodollar CDs were developed in 1966. Eurodollar CDs are negotiable, dollar-denominated time deposits issued by the foreign branches of U.S. banks and foreign-owned banks worldwide. These instruments generally carry higher yields than comparable domestic CDs due to greater perceived risk. Most Eurodollar CDs carry fixed rates, but floating-rate instruments were introduced in 1977. Eurodollar CDs can carry maturities longer than one year, and their interest rate may be adjusted every three to six months to match changes in the London Interbank Offer Rate (LIBOR). There is an active secondary market for Eurodollar CDs centered in New York City and in London.

If a country is to have a strong money market, the development of an active market for bank deposits appears to be a critical early step. Indeed, most money markets seem to owe their earliest origins to the trading of bank deposits. The key to the success of such a market seems to be a stable banking system with a minimum of government interference with interest rates and other terms on deposits sold to the public.

Global Stock Market Crash of 1987. *Installment CDs,* in contrast, allow customers to make a small initial deposit and then gradually build up the balance in the account to some target level. *Rising-rate CDs* are usually longer-term deposits whose promised yield increases over time with penalty-free withdrawals permitted on selected anniversary dates. More recently, *foreign-index CDs* have appeared, offering a return linked to economic developments abroad and to fluctuations in foreign currency values. These instruments become particularly attractive when foreign interest rates rise significantly above U.S. interest rates. Further innovations in CDs are likely in the future as banks struggle to adjust their fund-raising efforts in the face of increasingly stiff competition for funds.

LOANS FROM THE FEDERAL RESERVE'S DISCOUNT WINDOW

A money market source of funds available to banks and selected other depository institutions is the Federal Reserve's **discount window.** Each of the 12 Federal Reserve banks has a department in which banks and other qualified borrowers can come to borrow reserves for short periods.[5] Most discount window loans are short term (a maximum of 15 days), though longer-term credit can be arranged upon presentation of acceptable collateral and adequate reasons for the request. Today the Fed grants three types of loans: (1) *adjustment credit,* designed to cover short-term deficiencies in legal reserves; (2) *seasonal credit,* designed to aid institutions experiencing seasonal fluctuations in loans and deposits; and (3) *extended credit,* aimed mainly at institutions facing serious financial problems of a long-term nature. Normally, adjustment credit to cover short-term reserve deficiencies accounts for the majority of loans granted by the Federal Reserve banks.

The mechanics of borrowing from the discount window are relatively simple. A depository institution granted a loan merely receives an increase in its reserve account at the Federal Reserve bank in its district. When the loan comes due, the Fed merely removes the amount owed from the borrowing institution's legal reserve account.[6]

Causes and Effects of Borrowing from the Discount Window

Borrowing from the Fed *increases* the total volume of reserves available in the banking system until the loan is repaid. Many depository institutions come to the Federal Reserve near the end of their reserve settlement week when they find themselves short of legal reserves. Frequently, the funds available from the Federal Reserve carry a lower interest rate than the rate prevailing in the federal funds market or on other money market sources of funds. This is especially true in periods when market interest rates are changing rapidly, because the Fed changes its loan rate infrequently.

As the spread between open market rates — especially the going market interest rate on federal funds — and the Fed's loan rate widens, demands on the discount window increase. The reason is that the *spread* between the federal funds interest rate on borrowings from private depository institutions and the Federal Reserve's discount rate represents the opportunity cost for a bank in trying to raise new reserves in the open market rather than going to the Fed's discount window. The greater that spread is, the greater the opportunity cost to a bank if it chooses *not* to go to the Federal Reserve to ask for a loan. And the higher the opportunity cost, the more probable it is that more banks will turn to the Fed's discount window to obtain the reserves they need.

This last point is illustrated by the figures in Exhibit 16–4. Money market interest rates rose to record levels in 1980, spurred on by high rates of inflation. The federal funds rate averaged more than 13 percent in 1980, rising to a high of almost 20 percent in December 1980. Nevertheless, the Federal Reserve kept the rate on its loans in the 10 to 12 percent range through most of 1980. With discount window loans much cheaper than other money market sources of funds, borrowers predictably turned to the Federal Reserve banks for huge

---

[5]Until 1980, only member banks could borrow from the Federal Reserve banks except under special circumstances. However, with passage of the Monetary Control Act of 1980, nonmember commercial banks, savings banks, savings and loan associations, and credit unions offering transaction accounts or nonpersonal time deposits were authorized to borrow from the Fed's discount window on the same basis as member banks.

[6]See Chapter 20 for a more complete discussion of the methods used by depository institutions to borrow from the Federal Reserve.

Exhibit 16–4   **Volume of Borrowings from the Federal Reserve Banks, 1980–1996**
                   ($ Millions at Year-End)

Year	Discount Window Loans to Depository Institutions	Year	Discount Window Loans to Depository Institutions
1980	$1,617	1990	$ 330
1982	697	1992	120
1984	3,186	1994	210
1986	827	1995	260
1988	1,716	1996*	38

*As of February 1996.

Source: Board of Governors of the Federal Reserve System, *Federal Reserve Bulletin,* selected issues.

amounts of funds. Discount window loans climbed to almost $2 billion in 1980. Much the same pattern developed in 1984 and in 1988, when open market interest rates in the money market climbed high while the Fed kept its discount rate relatively low. The result was a sharp upsurge in borrowings from the Federal Reserve banks. On the other hand, lower market interest rates relative to the discount rate and moderate growth in bank loan demand kept Federal Reserve borrowings down in the late 1980s and for much of the 1990s.

Collateral for Discount Window Loans

Most loans granted through the Fed's discount window are secured by U.S. government securities. However, the Federal Reserve also will make loans against commercial or farm paper, bankers' acceptances, and bills of exchange. Discount window loans may be for terms as long as 90 days if the collateral used consists of U.S. government securities or other eligible paper, and up to four months on other forms of collateral. However, as we noted earlier, most loans from the discount window are for less than two weeks. To make the borrowing process as simple as possible, many depository institutions keep U.S. government securities in the vaults of the Federal Reserve banks and sign loan authorization agreements with the Fed's discount department in advance so they can borrow over the telephone. Such requests must be confirmed in writing, however.

Restrictions on Federal Reserve Credit

Large money center banks are the heaviest users of the discount window because they incur reserve deficits most frequently. However, less than 10 percent of all institutions eligible regularly borrow from the Federal Reserve despite the fact that it is often the cheapest source of reserves. In part, this is due to an uneasy feeling experienced by most bankers about being in debt to a government regulator. The Fed's own regulations discourage heavy and frequent use of the window. For example, Federal Reserve officials stress that borrowing is a "privilege, not a right" and that no depository institution should come to rely on Federal Reserve credit. Borrowing institutions are required to alternate between the discount window and other sources of funds.

In 1991, the U.S. Congress passed the Federal Deposit Insurance Corporation Improvement Act, which placed restrictions on Federal Reserve loans to troubled banks and thrifts. Undercapitalized depository institutions cannot receive discount window loans for more than 60 days in any 120-day period unless the Fed demonstrates that the borrowing institution is still a "viable entity." Fed loans to "critically undercapitalized" institutions lasting more than 60 days may make the Federal Reserve liable to the FDIC if the troubled depository fails.

The Federal Reserve's Discount Rate

The **discount rate** is the interest rate charged by the Fed on loans of reserves secured by U.S. government securities or other acceptable collateral. In reality, there are several different discount rates. The cheapest rate applies to loans (advances) for short-term liquidity adjustment or seasonal needs, secured by U.S. government securities or high-grade commercial ("eligible") paper. A slightly higher interest rate is levied against discount window loans secured by collateral of lesser quality. In times of national emergency, the Fed may also extend credit to individuals, partnerships, and even nonfinancial corporations, but the interest rate is much higher on such loans.

The individual Federal Reserve banks can recommend that the discount rate be changed; however, any change in that rate must be approved by the Federal Reserve Board in Washington, D.C. In recent years, the Fed has levied a higher interest rate for emergency borrowings when a bank is in serious financial trouble. Large, continuous borrowings over a prolonged period of time may be approved at a rate of 1 to 2 percent above the regular Federal Reserve discount rate.

As we discussed earlier, the spread between the Fed's discount rate and the market rate on federal funds has a profound effect on the amount of borrowing from the discount windows of the Federal Reserve banks. The federal funds rate usually stays *above* the discount rate because many bankers fear that making heavy use of direct loans from the Fed rather than from the impersonal federal funds market would subject them to closer scrutiny by federal authorities. The relationship between the federal funds rate and the discount rate is depicted in Exhibit 16–5. Banks cannot determine by themselves the total supply of reserves available; that supply consists of *nonborrowed reserves* (which the Fed expands or reduces through its policy tool known as open market operations) and *borrowed reserves* (which the Fed chooses to loan or not to loan through its discount window). If the Federal Reserve expands the total supply of reserves, the federal funds rate will fall, other factors being equal. In contrast, greater bank demand for reserves (due perhaps to rising loan demand) will drive the equilibrium federal funds rate higher.

If the federal funds rate drops below the discount rate, banks will not borrow from the discount window at all. All their reserves will come from federal funds and other private market sources. However, if the federal funds rate rises above the discount rate, banks will begin to step up their discount window borrowings until the added cost in the form of closer surveillance and scrutiny by Federal Reserve officials matches the net benefit of discount window borrowing (equal to the federal funds rate minus the discount rate). At that point, bank borrowing from the discount window should stop.

Research studies find the expected *positive* relationship between the interest rate spread between the federal funds rate and the Fed's discount rate and the volume of borrowing from the discount window. The higher the Fed funds rate moves, the more banks overcome their reluctance to borrow from the Fed and take advantage of the Fed's lower discount rate. There is also some evidence of greater window borrowing when the yield curve is positively sloped, perhaps reflecting expectations of higher market interest rates in the future or rising demand for bank loans. Finally, some studies find that banks borrowing heavily in one reserve settlement period are more likely to borrow heavily in the next period as well; other studies find just the opposite — heavy borrowing in one period is followed by reduced borrowing the next. This last finding appears to be consistent with the

Exhibit 16–5	**The Relationship between Discount Window Borrowing and the Interest Rates on Federal Funds and Discount Window Loans**

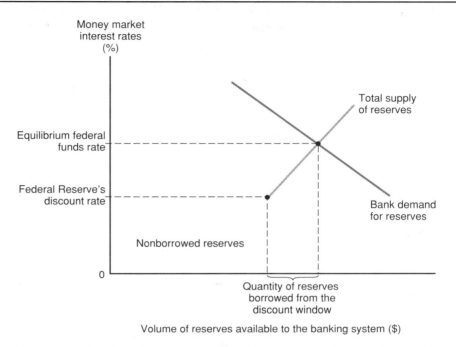

notion that borrowing from the Fed is a privilege — one that can be withdrawn at any time — not a right. Bankers may fear that borrowing too frequently wears out their welcome at the Fed.

We can illustrate how a banker evaluates the choices among federal funds, negotiable CDs, and discount window borrowings. On December 5, 1995, federal funds were trading at an annual interest rate of 5.63 percent, the discount rate charged by the New York Federal Reserve Bank was 5.25 percent, and the average rate New York money center banks were paying on large negotiable CDs (one-month maturities) was 5.13 percent. Even though reserve requirements had been set at zero on CDs several years earlier, a bank raising money by issuing CDs would have been compelled to pay deposit insurance fees to the FDIC equal to the full amount of the CD (not just the $100,000 portion that is insured). The U.S. deposit insurance fee at the time was 0.0004 cents per dollar (or four cents per $100) on any deposits received from the public.

Suppose a money center bank needed to borrow $1 million for at least one day. Its daily cost for funds derived from each of these sources would be:

$$\text{Federal funds: } \$1 \text{ million} \times .0563 \times \frac{1}{360} = \$156.39$$

$$\text{FRB discount window: } \$1 \text{ million} \times .0525 \times \frac{1}{360} = \$145.83$$

$$\text{Negotiable CDs: } \underset{\text{Deposit interest cost}}{\$1 \text{ million} \times .0513 \times \frac{1}{360}} + \underset{\text{Deposit insurance cost}}{\$1 \text{ million} \times .0004 \times \frac{1}{360}} = \$143.60$$

On this particular day, the cheapest money market funds source was issuing new negotiable CDs (even after the deposit insurance fee was taken into account). Moreover, the CDs carried a one-month maturity so that the borrowing bank would be guaranteed the relatively low CD cost rate for 30 days. However, if money market interest rates subsequently fell, pulling the Federal funds rate down below the CD rate, the bank would still be locked in to the higher CD rate for the remainder of the CD's term. Clearly, a banker must consider not only current money market interest rates but expected *future* interest rates as well when choosing a source of money market funding.

CONCLUDING COMMENT ON BANK ACTIVITY IN THE MONEY MARKET

In this chapter, we have focused on the major money market sources of funds used by banks and other depository institutions. As we have seen, banks operate on both sides of the money market, supplying billions of dollars in credit to governments, corporations, dealers, and financial intermediaries each day, while borrowing huge amounts daily from many of these same institutions.

The money market has not always been as important a source of funds for depository institutions as it is today. Prior to the 1960s, even many of the largest money center banks in the United States regarded borrowings from the money market as only a secondary source of funds. Bankers were aware that heavy dependence on money market borrowing would make their earnings more sensitive to fluctuations in interest rates. However, the force of competition intervened in the 1960s and 1970s; major corporations began to seek out alternative investments for their short-term funds rather than holding most of their money in bank deposits. Bankers were forced to turn to the money market for additional funds. As we have seen in this chapter, the banking community approached the problem in two ways. One was to offer a new financial instrument — the negotiable certificate of deposit — to compete directly for short-term corporate funds. The other approach was to draw more intensively on existing sources of money market funds, especially the federal funds market.

Prior to the 1960s and 1970s, the federal funds market was confined principally to the largest banks, which swapped reserves with each other. As bankers turned more and more to the funds market, however, it broadened tremendously. Thousands of small depository institutions in towns and rural areas across the United States began supplying their excess reserves to larger banks in the central cities, hoping to boost their earnings. In turn, the greater supply of Fed funds encouraged the largest banks to rely even more heavily on the money market and less on customer deposits as a source of reserves. The federal funds market had become an accepted institution for both the smallest and largest financial institutions.

The rapid expansion of the CD and federal funds markets was just the beginning of banking's *money market strategy.* When the Federal Reserve became concerned over the rapid growth of CDs and federal funds and clamped down with tight-money policies, innovative financial managers were forced to find new sources of reserves or face a real cutback in their lending activities. Many turned to the Eurocurrency market, borrowing deposits from abroad, or to organizing holding companies and issuing commercial paper through subsidiary corporations. Still others found innovative ways to use repurchase agreements backed by government securities to raise new funds.

All of these clever maneuvers form part of a technique called *liability management.* Bankers quickly came to realize that simply by varying the daily interest rates (yields) they were willing to offer on CDs and other funds sources, they could gain a measure of control over their liabilities. If more funds were needed on a given day to accommodate customer loan demand, a bank active in the money market would simply offer a higher yield on the particular money market instrument it desired to use. If a smaller volume of funds were required at another time, the institution could lower its offer rate on money market borrowings.

What is especially fascinating about liability management strategies is that they have had precisely the effects many analysts predicted from the start. The earnings of financial institutions *have* become more sensitive to fluctuations in interest rates; and in periods of rapidly escalating rates, profit margins have been squeezed. Whether this adverse impact on the earnings of banks will continue into the future remains to be seen. The great innovative abilities of these institutions, freed in recent years by deregulation, will do much to shape their earnings performance in the years ahead. But whatever the future holds, bankers have transformed the money market into a far larger, more dynamic, more vital institution than at any other time in history. The future rapid growth of money market transactions seems assured.

KEY TERMS AND CONCEPTS IN THIS CHAPTER

federal funds	negotiable certificate of deposit (CD)	discount window
legal reserves		discount rate
contemporaneous reserve accounting	liability management	

STUDY QUESTIONS

1. Define the term *federal funds*. Why are federal funds so important to the functioning of the money market?

2. Who are the principal borrowers in the federal fund market? Principal lenders?

3. Describe the process of reserve position adjustment for commercial banks and other depository institutions. What role does the federal funds market play in the management of depository institutions' money (reserve) position?

4. Why do you suppose the funds market is so important to the Federal Reserve in the conduct of monetary policy?

5. What is a large negotiable CD? When and why were CDs first offered in the U.S. money market?

6. What factors appear to influence the interest rate offered on the CDs issued by any particular depository institution? Explain the meaning of the term *multitiered market.*

7. What role do large negotiable CDs play in liability management?

8. What is a variable-rate CD? Rolypoly CD? Eurodollar CD? Will banks and other depositories continue to develop more innovative forms of CDs in the future? Why?

9. What is a discount window loan? What types of loans do the Federal Reserve banks make? How are those loans made and repaid?

10. What relationship exists between the discount rate and the federal funds interest rate? Can you explain why?

11. What factors influence a banker's choice among negotiable CDs, federal funds, or discount window loans as a source of borrowed reserves?

PROBLEMS

1. Security State Bank has just verified by checking with the Federal Reserve bank in its district that its daily average reserve balance for the current reserve maintenance period is $1.25 million. Today is the final day of the current reserve maintenance period, and the bank's money market officer is concerned that Security might be running a large deficit in its legal reserve account. Checking the bank's own records, the officer discovers that transaction deposits averaged $43 million and nontransaction deposits averaged $16 million over the relevant two-week reserve computation period. Vault cash holdings averaged $250,000. Currently, the Federal Reserve imposes a 3 percent reserve requirement on the total of a depository institution's transaction deposits below $41 million and 12 percent for any amount of transaction deposits over $41 million. Suppose that nontransaction deposits are subject to a 3 percent required reserve. Does Security State have a reserve deficiency? If so, is it required to cover the reserve shortfall before this current reserve maintenance period ends today? Explain your answer.

2. A money center bank is trying to decide which source of funding to rely upon to cover loans being made today. It needs to borrow $10 million in either the federal funds market, negotiable CD market, or at the Federal Reserve bank in its district. Funds are needed for at least a week, but the bank's money desk manager is most concerned about the next 24 hours. Federal funds are currently trading at 4.80 percent; rates on new negotiable CDs posted by leading banks have reached 4.70 percent. The Federal Reserve bank has posted a discount rate of 4 percent. FDIC insurance fees are currently 27 cents per $100.

    Calculate the cost to the bank for each of these three funds sources. If you were a banker facing this decision, which source would you prefer to use?

3. Glenwood National Bank is short of required legal reserves. The bank's money manager estimates it will need to raise an additional $50 million in funds to cover its reserve requirement over the next three days. Federal funds are trading today at 5.90 percent, and the bank's economist has forecast a federal funds rate of 6.15 percent tomorrow and 6.20 percent the next day. Negotiable CDs in minimum maturities of seven days have been trading in New York this morning at 5.85 percent, with a forecast of 5.90 percent tomorrow and 5.98 percent the next day. The FDIC charges 30 cents per $100 for insurance coverage. The Federal Reserve bank's discount rate is currently 5 percent, but the bank's economists expect a jump tomorrow in the Fed's discount rate to 5.50 percent.

    Please calculate the lowest-cost source of funding for Glenwood National Bank and the next cheapest source for borrowing over the next three days (today, tomorrow, and the next day). What are the relative advantages and disadvantages of each of these funding sources?

SELECTED REFERENCES

Dumitru, Diana, and E.J. Stevens. "Federal Funds Rate Volatility." *Economic Commentary.* Federal Reserve Bank of Cleveland, August 15, 1991.

Hardani, Kausorad, and Stavros Peristiani. "A Disaggregate Analysis of Discount Window Borrowing." *Quarterly Review.* Federal Reserve Bank of New York, Summer 1991, pp. 52–62.

Chapter 17

Commercial Paper and Federal Agency Securities

LEARNING OBJECTIVES IN THIS CHAPTER

- To highlight the important role that large corporations and government agencies play in the money market.
- To examine the characteristics of the oldest of all money market instruments, commercial paper.
- To see how federal agencies, by borrowing funds in the money market, help several sectors in the economy (such as agriculture, home buyers, and small businesses) to find low-cost credit.

In the previous chapter, we discussed the vital role played by banks as major borrowers and lenders in the money market. However, banks have had to share the limelight in recent years with two other groups of money market borrowers: government agencies and large corporations. Indeed, the largest of all borrowers in the money market is not a bank but a unit of government, the U.S. Treasury Department. Moreover, in the 1960s and 70s, other units within the United States government's huge structure, known as *federal agencies,* came to be major demanders of money market funds. Many of these agencies, such as the Farm Credit System, Small Business Administration, and Federal National Mortgage Association, have become familiar names to active investors worldwide, who are regularly offered a menu of attractive notes and bonds so that these agencies can carry out their mission of assisting "disadvantaged" sectors of the economy.

The ranks of private sector money market participants have also grown rapidly in recent years due to the borrowing and lending activities of some of the largest corporations. Each year, companies like American Telephone & Telegraph, Citicorp, General Motors, Marriott Corp., MCI Communications, and Philip Morris borrow billions of dollars in the money market through the sale of unsecured promissory notes known as *commercial paper.* A study at the Federal Reserve Board found that well over 1,000 corporations were regularly selling their commercial notes to money market investors.[1] Commercial paper issued by large corporations and bought principally by other large corporations has become one of the most dynamic and rapidly growing segments of the money market. In this chapter, we take a close look at both commercial paper and federal agency securities and their important roles within the financial system.

COMMERCIAL PAPER

What Is Commercial Paper?

Commercial paper is one of the oldest of all money market instruments, dating back to the 18th century in the United States. By definition, commercial paper consists of short-term, unsecured promissory notes issued by well-known companies that are financially strong and carry high credit ratings.[2] The funds raised from a paper issue normally are used for *current transactions* — to purchase inventories, pay taxes, meet payrolls, and cover other short-term obligations — rather than for *capital transactions* (long-term investments). However, a growing number of paper issues today are used to provide "bridge financing" for such long-term projects as building pipelines, office buildings, and manufacturing assembly lines. In these instances, issuing companies usually plan to convert their short-term paper into more permanent financing when the capital market is more favorable.

Commercial paper is generally issued in multiples of $1,000 and in denominations designed to meet the needs of the buyer. It is traded mainly in the primary market. Opportunities for resale in the secondary market are limited, although some dealers redeem the notes they sell in advance of maturity and others trade paper issued by large finance companies and bank holding companies. Because of the limited resale possibilities, investors are usually careful to purchase those paper issues whose maturity matches their planned holding periods.

Types of Commercial Paper

There are two major types of commercial paper — direct paper and dealer paper. The main issuers of **direct paper** are large finance companies and bank holding companies that deal directly with the investor rather than using a securities dealer as an intermediary. These companies, which regularly extend installment credit to consumers and large working capital loans and leases to business firms, announce the rates they are currently paying on various maturities of their paper. For example, not long ago, General Electric Capital Corporation, one of the largest finance company borrowers in this market, offered the following yields to interested investors:

---

[1] See Post (1992).

[2] As a further backstop to reduce investor risk, borrowers in the commercial paper market nearly always secure a line of credit at a commercial bank for a small fee or hold a compensating deposit at their bank. However, because the line of credit cannot be used to directly guarantee payment if the company goes bankrupt and the lender may renege on the credit line if the borrowing company has had a "material adverse change" in its condition, many issuers also take out irrevocable letters of credit prepared by their banks. Such a letter makes the bank unconditionally responsible for repayment if the corporation defaults on its paper. The lending institution usually charges a fee of ½ percent to 1½ percent of the amount of the guarantee it issues. Insurance companies and parent companies of paper-issuing firms also guarantee commercial paper.

Paper Maturity	Offered Yield (Percent)
30 to 33 days	5.65%
34 to 45 days	5.72
46 to 59 days	5.68
60 to 89 days	5.58
90 to 119 days	5.52

Investors select maturities that most closely approximate their expected holding periods and buy the securities directly from the issuer. Interest rates may be adjusted during the day the paper is being sold to regulate the inflow of investor funds.

Leading finance company borrowers in the direct paper market include General Motors Acceptance Corporation (GMAC), General Electric Capital Corporation (GE Capital), CIT Financial Corporation, and Commercial Credit Corporation. The leading U.S bank holding companies that issue commercial paper are centered around the largest banks in New York, Chicago, San Francisco, and other major U.S. cities.[3] Today, about 70 financially oriented U.S companies account for nearly all directly placed paper, with finance companies issuing approximately three fourths of the total. All of these firms have an ongoing need for huge amounts of short-term money, possess top credit ratings, and have established working relationships with major institutional investors in order to place new note issues rapidly.

Directly placed paper must be sold in large volume to cover the substantial costs of distribution and marketing. On average, each direct issuer will borrow at least $1 billion per month. Issuers of direct paper do not have to pay dealers' commissions, but these companies must operate a marketing division to maintain constant contact with active investors. Selected issuers, like New York's Citicorp, sell commercial paper in weekly auctions in which buyers bid and the issuing company accepts the highest prices (lowest yields) bid. Sometimes direct issuers must sell their paper even when they have no need for funds in order to maintain a good working relationship with active investor groups. These companies also cannot escape paying fees to banks for supporting lines of credit, to rating agencies that rate their paper issues, and to agents (usually bank trust departments) that dispense required payments and collect funds.

The other major variety of commercial paper is **dealer paper,** issued by security dealers on behalf of their corporate customers. Also known as *industrial paper,* dealer paper is issued mainly by nonfinancial companies (including public utilities, manufacturers, retailers, and transportation companies), as well as by smaller bank holding companies and finance companies, all of which borrow less frequently than firms issuing direct paper. The issuing company may sell the paper directly to the dealer, who buys it less discount and commission and then attempts to resell it at the highest possible price in the market. Alternatively, the issuing company may carry all the risk, with the dealer agreeing only to sell the issue at the best price available less commission, referred to as a *best efforts basis.* Finally, the open-rate method may be used in which the borrowing company receives some money in advance but the balance depends on how well the issue sells in the open market. Companies using dealers to place their paper are generally smaller, less frequent borrowers than are issuers of direct paper.

---

[3]Bank holding companies issue *both* direct and dealer paper, with the largest companies going the direct placement route. Much of this bank-related paper comes from finance company subsidiaries of large bank holding companies. Frequently, a holding company will issue paper through a nonbank subsidiary and then funnel the proceeds to one or more of its subsidiary banks by purchasing some of the banks' assets. This gives the banks additional funds to lend and may be especially helpful when a bank is having difficulty attracting deposits through normal channels.

Exhibit 17–1   **Volume of Commercial Paper Outstanding** ($ Billions, End of Period)

Instrument	1984	1986	1988	1990	1992	1994	1995*
All issuers	$237.6	$330.0	$458.5	$562.7	$545.6	$595.4	$671.1
Financial companies issuing paper:							
Dealer placed — Total	56.5	101.1	159.8	214.7	226.5	223.0	277.3
Directly placed paper — Total	110.5	151.8	194.9	200.0	171.6	207.7	214.4
Nonfinancial companies issuing paper	70.6	77.1	103.8	147.9	147.6	164.6	179.3

NA = not available
*Figures for 1995 are for the month of November.

Source: Board of Governors of the Federal Reserve System, *Federal Reserve Bulletin,* selected issues.

Exhibit 17–2   **Growth of Commercial Paper Issues in the United States**

Year	Outstanding Volume of Paper in Billions of Dollars
1960	$ 4.5
1970	33.4
1980	124.4
1990	562.7
1995*	671.1

*Figure as of November 1995.

Source: Board of Governors of the Federal Reserve System, *Federal Reserve Bulletin,* selected issues.

Recent Growth of Commercial Paper

As Exhibit 17–1 indicates, the volume of commercial paper has more than doubled since 1984. Indeed, as Exhibit 17–2 shows, commercial paper issues have tripled or quadrupled in volume in every decade since 1960. By the end of the period, more than 1200 companies had over $670 billion in commercial notes outstanding. Almost one third of the total was placed directly with investors by large finance companies and bank holding companies; the rest reached the market through the efforts of security dealers.

What factors explain the rapid growth of commercial paper? One factor is the relative cost of other sources of credit compared to interest rates prevailing on commercial paper. For the largest, best-known corporations, commercial paper is usually a cost-effective substitute for bank loans and other forms of borrowing. This is especially true for nonfinancial companies issuing paper through dealers. These firms usually come to the paper market when it is significantly cheaper to borrow there than to tap bank lines of credit. In recent years, paper has also frequently been a cheaper funds source than issuing long-term bonds or selling stock. Also, many companies use the paper market today to participate in interest rate SWAPs, which are designed to hedge against losses from fluctuating interest rates.[4]

The commercial paper market has also been propelled upward in recent years by cutbacks in bank lending. Besieged by loan-quality problems, many banks have become

[4]Chapter 12 contains an explanation of interest rate SWAPs.

more cautious, turning down many credit requests and forcing corporate borrowers to consider other funding alternatives. During periods when the economy grows slowly or declines, many corporations face severe cash shortages, which brings them into the paper market to replenish their cash positions.

Another reason for the market's rapid growth is the high quality of most commercial paper obligations. Many investors regard this instrument as a close substitute for Treasury bills and other money market instruments. As a result, market yields on commercial paper tend to move in the same direction and by similar amounts as the yields on other money market securities. This fact is shown clearly in Exhibit 17–3, which compares market yields on three-month maturities of commercial paper, Treasury bills, negotiable CDs, and bankers' acceptances. Rates on these four money market instruments tend to stay close to each other. We note that commercial paper yields are always higher than market rates on comparable maturity Treasury bills due to the greater risk and lower marketability of paper and the fact that Treasury bills are exempt from state and local taxation.

Still another key factor in the market's recent growth is the expanding use of **credit enhancements,** in the form of letters of credit and other payment guarantees. For example, a bank or other lending institution may issue a certificate that promises repayment of principal and/or interest on a customer's paper if the borrowing company fails to do so. The result is that such paper, often called *documented notes,* usually carries the higher credit rating of the guarantor rather than the lower credit rating of the issuing firm. Through these guarantees, mortgage companies, utilities, and small manufacturers in large numbers have been attracted into a market that otherwise would be closed to them, still saving on interest costs even after paying the guarantor's fee. A related development inaugurated by Merrill Lynch in 1984 allows smaller, lower-rated institutions (such as savings and loans or retail firms) to issue commercial paper collateralized by holdings of Treasury or federal agency securities or even accounts receivable.

Other groups recently entering the market include foreign banks and industrial companies, international financial conglomerates, and state and local governments (which offer *tax-exempt* commercial paper). Paper issued in the United States by foreign firms is called *Yankee paper* and frequently can be sold at lower interest costs in the United States than abroad. However, foreign borrowers in the U.S. market generally must pay higher interest costs than U.S. companies of comparable credit rating to compensate U.S. buyers for the added difficulty of gathering information on foreign borrowers and the lack of name recognition.

Exhibit 17–3	**Market Yields on Commercial Paper Compared to Yields on Other Money Market Instruments** (Average Yields on Three-Month Maturities; Percent per Annum)

Instruments	1984	1986	1988	1990	1992	1994	1996*
Commercial paper	10.10%	6.49%	7.66%	8.06%	3.75%	4.66%	5.15%
U.S. Treasury bills	9.52	5.98	6.67	7.50	3.43	4.25	4.83
Certificates of deposit	10.37	6.52	7.73	8.15	3.68	4.63	5.15
Prime bankers' acceptances	10.14	6.39	7.56	7.93	3.62	4.56	5.07

Notes: Commercial paper yields are unweighted averages of interest rates quoted by at least five dealers. Treasury bills are secondary-market yields computed from daily closing bid prices. CD rates are secondary-market yields quoted as five-day averages by five dealers. Bankers' acceptance rates are on 90-day maturities and are based on daily closing rates on domestic issues. All yields except CDs are quoted on a bank discount basis.
*Interest rates are averages for February 1996.

Source: Board of Governors of the Federal Reserve System, *Federal Reserve Bulletin,* selected issues.

INTERNATIONAL FOCUS:

The Commercial Paper Market Outside the United States

The commercial paper market in the United States, which is the largest worldwide, has been copied abroad for many years now, though other countries have added their own special features to this market for short-term, high-grade corporate IOUs. Among the leading national commercial paper markets today are those of Japan, France, Canada, and Sweden.

One of the most dramatic developments among commercial paper markets worldwide has been the recent development of the Japanese yen-denominated paper market. Yen-denominated commercial paper was first allowed to be offered in domestic Japanese markets by the Ministry of Finance in 1987. Many Japanese companies had threatened to move their short-term borrowing abroad unless the Japanese government relaxed its regulations. A year later, foreign businesses were given permission to issue "Samurai paper" inside Japan, with banks and securities companies acting as dealers to sell new issues.

With so many U.S. companies operating in Canada and many Canadian firms possessing money market access inside the United States, the Canadian commercial paper market has relatively modest dimensions. In the minds of international investors, Canadian paper must compete against paper denominated in U.S. dollars. Like U.S. paper, Canadian paper must be backed by a bank line of credit to catch the attention of money market investors. It has a broader range of maturities (usually from demand notes, cashable in 24 hours, out to about one year) than in the U.S. and also tends to be issued in larger denominations (usually $100,000 or more), suggesting that most Canadian paper is purchased by large corporations rather than by individual investors.

In the mid-1980s a new commercial paper market emerged in Europe — the *Europaper market*. Europaper soared in volume because borrowing companies were then able to tap a large reservoir of foreign investor cash. Many U.S. corporations that have had difficulty borrowing in the domestic paper market often because of declining credit quality, have turned to the Euromarket, which appears to be less quality conscious. The heaviest investors in Europaper are international banks, private corporations, and government-sponsored or government-owned central banks; in contrast, most U.S.-issued paper is bought by money market funds.

Europaper is priced below its par, or face, value and appreciates in value as maturity approaches. The interest rate quoted to investors is expressed as a discount rate (DR) like that attached to Treasury bills (see Chapter 15). For example, suppose we are interested in a $100 million Europaper issue with 90 days remaining until maturity that bears a discount rate today of 6 percent. The price the European investor must pay is:

$$\text{Price of Europaper issue} = 100 - DR \cdot \frac{\text{Days to maturity}}{360 \text{ days}}$$

$$\text{Price} = 100 - 6 \cdot \frac{90}{360} = 98.50$$

In this instance, the $100 million Europaper issue would be priced today to sell at $98.5 million.

(continued)

> There appears to be an active resale (secondary) market for Europaper, unlike the U.S. paper market, and Europaper has an average maturity almost double the average maturity of U.S. paper. U.S. commercial paper may be sold through dealers or placed directly with investors, but the bulk of Europaper is sold through international dealers with interest rates linked to prevailing Eurobank deposit interest rates.

Maturities and Rates of Return on Commercial Paper

Maturities of U.S. commercial paper range from three days ("weekend paper") to nine months. Most commercial notes carry an original maturity of 60 days or less, with an average maturity ranging from 20 to 45 days. U.S. paper is generally not issued for maturities longer than 270 days because, under the provisions of the Securities Act of 1933, any security sold in U.S. markets for a longer term must be registered with the Securities and Exchange Commission. Yields to the investor are calculated by the *bank discount method,* just like Treasury bills. As in the case of T-bills, most commercial paper is issued at a discount from par; the investor's yield arises from the price appreciation of the security between its purchase date and maturity date.

For example, if a million-dollar commercial note with a maturity of 180 days is acquired by an investor at a discounted price of $980,000, the discount rate of return (DR) is:

$$DR = \frac{\text{Par value} - \text{Purchase price}}{\text{Par value}} \times \frac{360}{\text{Days to maturity}}$$

$$= \frac{\$1,000,000 - \$980,000}{\$1,000,000} \times \frac{360}{180} = 0.04, \text{ or 4 percent}$$

If this commercial note's rate of return were figured like that of a regular bond, its coupon-equivalent yield (or investment rate of return, IR) would be

$$IR = \frac{\text{Par value} - \text{Purchase price}}{\text{Par value}} \times \frac{365}{\text{Days to maturity}}$$

$$= \frac{\$1,000,000 - \$980,000}{\$980,000} \times \frac{365}{180} = 0.0414, \text{ or 4.14 percent}$$

This second formula helps an investor compare prospective returns on paper against the returns available on other securities available for purchase. In addition to discount paper, some corporations also sell interest-bearing (coupon) paper.

The minimum denomination of commercial paper issues is usually $25,000, although among institutional investors, who dominate the market, the usual minimum denomination is $1 million. The notes typically are issued in *bearer* form, which makes their resale easier. Payment is made at maturity on presentation to the particular bank listed as agent on the note. Settlement in federal funds is usually made the same day the note is presented for payment by its holder.

Changing Yields on Paper Issues

Because yields on commercial paper are open market rates, they fluctuate with the daily ebb and flow of supply and demand forces in the marketplace. In the wide swings between easy and tight money, between depressed and resurgent economic activity in recent years, commercial paper rates have fluctuated between extreme highs and lows. For example, in

1986 and 1992–96 — years of moderate credit demands and moderate inflation — paper rates averaged less than 4 percent to only about 6.5 percent. (See again Exhibit 17–3.) In 1984, however, when intense credit demands and rapid inflation characterized the economy, paper rates averaged more than 10 percent. The commercial paper market is highly volatile and difficult to predict. This is the reason that many corporations eligible to borrow there still maintain close working relationships with banks and other institutional lenders and employ interest rate hedging techniques (such as SWAPs and financial futures contracts).

Advantages of Issuing Commercial Paper

There are several financial advantages to a company able to tap the paper market for funds. Generally, interest rates on paper are lower than on corporate loans extended by banks. This is evident from the data shown in Exhibit 17–4. In 1995 and 1996, for example, the bank prime rate averaged two to three percentage points higher than the rate on six-month dealer paper.

Moreover, the effective rate on most commercial loans granted by banks is even higher than the quoted prime rate, due to the fact that corporate borrowers usually are required to keep a percentage of their loans in a bank deposit. This *compensating balance* requirement is generally 15 to 20 percent of the amount of the loan. Suppose a corporation borrows $100,000 at a prime interest rate of 15 percent but must keep 20 percent of this amount ($20,000) on deposit with the bank granting the loan. Then the effective loan rate is 18.75 percent (or $15,000/($100,000 − $20,000)).

Another advantage of borrowing in the paper market is that interest rates there are often more flexible than bank loan rates. A company in need of funds can raise money quickly through either dealer or direct paper. Dealers maintain close contact with the market and generally know where cash may be found. Frequently, notes can be issued and funds raised the same day.

Generally, larger amounts of funds may be borrowed more conveniently through the paper market than from other sources, particularly bank loans. This situation arises due

Exhibit 17–4

Spread between the Average Prime Rate Quoted by Major U.S. Banks and the Six-Month Commercial Paper Rate, Selected Months*

Month and Year	Bank Prime Lending Rate	Six-Month Commercial Paper Rate	Rate Spread in Percentage Points
1995:			
January	8.50%	6.63%	1.87
February	9.00	6.38	2.62
March	9.00	6.30	2.70
April	9.00	6.19	2.81
May	9.00	6.07	2.93
June	9.00	5.79	3.21
1996:			
February	8.25	4.99	3.26

*The prime rate is the average of rates posted by major U.S. banks. The six-month commercial paper rate is the unweighted average of offer rates quoted by at least five dealers.

Source: Board of Governors of the Federal Reserve System, *Federal Reserve Bulletin,* selected issues.

to federal and state regulations that limit the amount of money a bank can lend to a single borrower. For national banks, the maximum unsecured loan is 15 percent of the bank's capital and surplus account. Corporate credit needs frequently exceed an individual bank's loan limit, and a group of banks (consortium) has to be assembled to make the loan. However, this takes time and often requires lengthy negotiations. The paper market is generally much faster than trying to hammer out a loan agreement among several parties.

The ability to issue commercial paper gives a corporation considerable leverage when negotiating with banks. A banker who knows that a customer can draw on the paper market for funds is more likely to offer advantageous terms on a loan and be more receptive to future customer credit needs.

Possible Disadvantages from Issuing Commercial Paper

Despite the advantages, there are some risks for corporations that choose to borrow frequently in the commercial paper market. One of these is the risk of alienating banks whose loans might be needed when a real emergency develops. The paper market is sensitive to financial and economic problems. This fact was demonstrated convincingly in 1980 when Chrysler Financial, the finance company subsidiary of Chrysler Corporation, was forced to cut back its borrowings in the paper market due to the widely publicized troubles of its parent company. At times, it is difficult even for companies in sound financial condition to raise funds in the paper market at reasonable rates of interest. It helps to have a friendly banker available to supply emergency credit when this market turns sour. Another problem lies in the fact that commercial paper cannot be paid off at the issuer's discretion, but generally must remain outstanding until maturity. In contrast, many bank loans permit early retirement without penalty.

Principal Investors

The most important investors in the commercial paper market include nonfinancial corporations, money market mutual funds, bank trust departments, small banks, pension funds, insurance companies, and state and local governments. In effect, this is a market in which corporations borrow from other corporations. These investor groups generally regard commercial paper as a low-risk outlet for their surplus funds, although recent financial problems and a few defaults among paper issuers have caused some investor groups, such as money market funds, to sharply cut back their purchases of lower-quality paper.

In 1991, the U.S. Securities and Exchange Commission (SEC) became particularly concerned about the safety of money market funds and the risk to the savings of thousands of investors who had placed nearly $500 billion with the money market fund industry. More than half the industry's assets had been invested in commercial paper, with an increasing proportion of these investments in lower-quality issues bearing higher but riskier yields. These lower-quality commercial notes are often acquired by more aggressive money fund managers interested in attracting more savings deposits by offering higher returns. Following a few defaults on paper in 1989 and 1990, the SEC ruled that, thereafter, money market funds could hold no more than 5 percent of their total assets in less than top-quality (not prime-rated) commercial paper, nor could they place any more than 1 percent of their assets in the paper of any one non-prime-rated corporate issuer. Money funds must inform investors that their shares are not insured or guaranteed by the U.S. government. The new rules appear to enhance the safety of savings held with money market funds, but they may also have placed a future restraint on the growth of the commercial paper market, making it more difficult for many companies, especially those with less-than-top credit ratings, to sell their paper.

Continuing Innovation in the Paper Market

One recent innovation in the direct paper market is the **master note,** most frequently issued to bank trust departments and other permanent money market investors by finance companies. Under a master note agreement, the investing firm agrees to take some paper each day up to an agreed-upon maximum amount. Interest owed is figured on the average daily volume of paper taken on by the investor during the current month. The prevailing interest rate on six-month commercial paper is generally used to determine the appropriate rate of return.

An extension of the paper market appeared over the past decade in the form of *medium-term notes* (MTNs). These 9-month to 10-year notes are issued by investment-grade corporations, normally carry a fixed interest rate, and are generally noncallable, unsecured obligations marketed through dealers. They are particularly suited to companies with substantial quantities of medium-term assets who wish to balance these assets with IOUs that are longer than the short maturities attached to conventional commercial paper. First sold by automobile finance companies in the 1970s, the MTN market has recently attracted industrial and utility companies in considerable numbers, and a secondary market has developed with several investment banking firms now willing to buy back these medium-length instruments. This market has become so efficient that many MTNs are sold in less than an hour after time of issue.

Beginning in 1983, a new form of paper began to appear: *asset-backed commercial paper* in which loans or credit receivables are pooled into packages and paper is then issued as claims against that pool. The loans or receivables are removed from the issuing company's balance sheet and placed in a *special-purpose entity* (SPE), which issues the paper and uses the proceeds to purchase the receivables. (See Exhibit 17–5.) Among the most popular assets pooled to back these unique commercial paper issues are credit-card receivables, installment sales contracts, and lease receivables. Participants in these programs include banks, finance companies, and retail dealers. Banks find them a handy vehicle for assisting their corporate customers to obtain financing without having to loan them money and, thereby, increase the bank's capital requirements. A bank can earn fees for advising the paper-issuing customer, reviewing the quality of the assets to be pooled, and supplying credit enhancements (usually in the form of letters of credit, surety bonds, etc.) and liquidity enhancements (to help retire maturing paper in case of temporary cash shortfalls) for outstanding paper issues.

Asset-backed commercial paper gives issuing corporations a low and stable cost of financing. For those asset-backed paper issues backed by credit and liquidity guarantees, any change of fortune at the customer's business should not appreciably affect the firm's actual funding costs. The SPE normally issues enough commercial paper to cover the discounted purchase price of the company's receivables and uses the proceeds from the paper issue to purchase the firm's receivables. The issuing customer usually services the underlying receivables, collecting interest and principal payments and passing the funds along to the SPE, or a bank chosen by the customer may service the receivables supporting the paper issue. The fact that paper is issued for less than the full nondiscounted value of the receivables generates a margin of value to protect investors who buy asset-backed paper. Asset-backed programs give corporate customers who normally would not be able to break into the high-quality paper market a chance to participate in that market as active borrowers.

Exhibit 17–5   **How Asset-Backed Commercial Paper Issues Are Usually Structured**

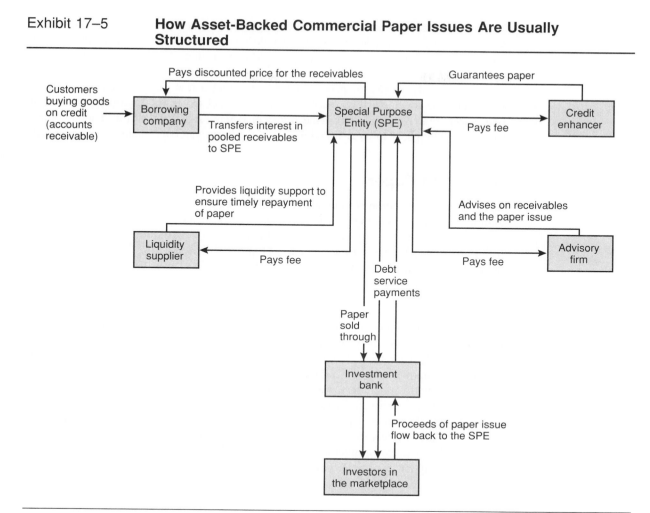

Source: Barbara Kavanagh, Thomas R. Boemio, and Gerald A. Edwards, Jr., "Asset-Backed Commercial Paper Programs," *Federal Reserve Bulletin,* February 1992, pp. 107–116.

Commercial Paper Ratings

Commercial paper is rated *prime, desirable,* or *satisfactory,* depending on the credit standing of the issuing company. Firms desiring to issue paper generally will seek a credit rating from one or more of several rating services, including such firms as Moody's Investors Service; Standard & Poor's Corporation; Fitch Investors Service; Duff and Phelps; Canadian Bond Rating Service; Japanese Bond Rating Institute; Dominion Bond Rating Service; and IBCA, Ltd. — with the first two rating companies especially prominent. Moody's assigns a rating of Prime–1 (P–1) for the highest-quality paper, with lower-quality issues designated as Prime–2 (P–2) or Prime–3 (P–3). Standard & Poor's assigns ratings of A–1, A–2, or A–3; Fitch uses F–1, F–2, or F–3. Any issue rated below P–2, A–2, or F–2 usually sells poorly or not at all.

It is extremely difficult to market unrated commercial paper. Indeed, about three quarters of the firms currently selling notes carry A–1 or P–1 ratings. Generally, commercial notes bearing credit ratings from at least two rating agencies are preferred by investors. The rating assigned to an issue often depends heavily on the liquidity position and the amount of backup lines of credit held by the issuing company. Moreover, there is evidence — for example, Crabbe and Post (1992) — that when a paper issuer's credit rating is lowered, large reductions occur in its volume of paper outstanding within a few weeks, reflecting declining demand for the downgraded issues. As Schnure (1994) observes, the ability of a company to issue paper attractive to investors in the money market is a signal of the firm's internal quality and of its willingness to incur liquidity risk in the event its credit quality is downgraded.

Dealers in Paper

The market is concentrated among a handful of dealers that account for the bulk of all trading activity. Top commercial paper dealers today include Citicorp Investment Bank; Goldman Sachs & Co.; the Credit-Suisse-First Boston Corporation; Lehman Brothers; Kuhn Loeb, Inc.; Morgan Stanley; Shearson Lehman-Swiss Banking Corporation International; Salomon Brothers; and Merrill Lynch. Dealer firms charge varying fees to borrowing companies, depending on the size of an issue and how much paper the company has issued through the dealer recently. The dealer market has become more intensely competitive in recent years as many new foreign dealers have emerged, led by Japanese firms. In 1987 and 1988, the Federal Reserve Board granted permission to several of the largest U.S. banking organizations (including Citicorp, Chase Manhattan Corporation, Chemical New York Corp., Bankers Trust, Manufacturers Hanover, and Security Pacific) to underwrite and deal in commercial paper, provided they do not allow such underwritings to become the principal part of their security marketing activities.

Dealers maintain inventories of unsold issues and repurchased paper, but they usually expect to turn over most of a new issue within 24 hours. Like dealers in government securities, paper dealers draw on repurchase agreements (RPs) and demand loans from banks to help finance their inventory positions. They generally pay interest costs only a few basis points higher than on RPs collateralized by government securities.

FEDERAL AGENCY SECURITIES

For at least 60 years, the federal government has attempted to aid certain sectors of the economy that appear to have an unusually difficult time raising funds in the money and capital markets. These "disadvantaged sectors" include agriculture, housing, small businesses, and college students. Dominated by smaller, less creditworthy borrowers, these sectors allegedly are pushed aside in the race for scarce funds by large corporations and governments, especially in periods of tight money. Beginning in the 1920s, the federal government created several agencies to make direct loans to or guarantee private loans to these disadvantaged borrowers. Several of these agencies buy selected assets from private lenders (creating a secondary market), which gives the lenders funds to make new loans to disadvantaged borrowers. Exhibit 17–6 depicts this process.

Today, federal credit agencies are large enough and, with the government's blessing, financially strong enough to compete successfully for funds in the open market and channel those funds to areas of social need. Moreover, the purposes for which these agencies were created have been sharply expanded recently. For example, several new agencies (such as the Financial Assistance Corporation) have been established merely to bail out other government agencies.

Exhibit 17–6   **Government Agencies: Performing the Roles of a Financial Intermediary**

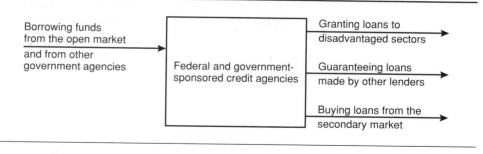

Types of Federal Credit Agencies

There are two types of federal credit agencies: government-sponsored agencies and true federal agencies. **Government-sponsored agencies** are *not* officially a part of the federal government's structure but are quasi-private institutions. They are federally chartered but privately owned; in some instances, their stock is traded on major securities exchanges. The borrowing and lending activities of government-sponsored agencies are *not* reflected in the federal government's budget. This has aroused the ire of many fiscal conservatives who regard the credit-granting operations of government-sponsored agencies as a disguised form of government spending. Some critics contend that the agencies have been used to get around limits on federal spending, such as those imposed by the Gramm-Rudman-Hollings budget law in the United States. Because these agencies are omitted from the federal government's books, annual federal deficits look considerably smaller and conceal the full extent of federal deficit financing.[5] True **federal agencies,** on the other hand, are legally a part of the government structure, and their borrowing and lending activities are included in the federal budget. Exhibit 17–7 lists the principal federal and government-sponsored agencies that borrow in the money and capital markets.

In their borrowing and lending activities, federal and government-sponsored agencies act as true **financial intermediaries.** They issue attractively packaged notes and bonds to capture funds from savers, and they direct the resulting flow of funds into loans and loan

---

[5]Public concern over the growth of federal agency activities has increased in recent years. To the extent that agency borrowing and lending increase the total amount of credit available in the economy and add to aggregate spending for goods and services, they may add to inflationary pressures. Agency borrowing is not limited by restrictions that apply to direct obligations of the U.S. government. However, bills were introduced in Congress in 1992 in an effort to impose minimum capital requirements on selected federal agencies (FNMA and FHLMC principally), but no law has yet been enacted.

Moreover, there is a tendency to create a new agency each time a new problem rears its head, increasing the cost of government activities. A prominent example is the Chrysler Corporation Loan Guarantee Board established by Congress in 1979. This board was authorized to guarantee with the "full faith and credit of the United States" notes issued by financially troubled Chrysler Corporation and other eligible borrowers. In 1987, the Financing Corporation (FICO) was established to bail out the failing Federal Savings and Loan Insurance Corporation (FSLIC), and in 1989, the Resolution Funding Corporation (REFCO) was created to support the liquidation of hundreds of failing savings and loans that the FSLIC could no longer handle. In 1988, the Financial Assistance Corporation (FAC) was created to help rescue the beleaguered Farm Credit System (FCS).

The creation of these and many other special agencies has raised a number of significant issues concerning government involvement in the private sector of the economy. How many other firms should the federal government guarantee against failure in the future? Upon what basis are such guarantees to be made? What happens to the efficiency of the market system when some firms are not allowed to fail?

Exhibit 17–7   **Principal Borrowers in the Federal Agency Market**

Agencies of the Federal Government

Export-Import Bank (EXIM)
U.S. Railway Association
Farmers Home Administration (FMHA)
General Services Administration (GSA)
Government National Mortgage Association
  (GNMA or Ginnie Mae)

Postal Service (PS)
Tennessee Valley Authority (TVA)
Federal Deposit Insurance Corporation (FDIC)

Government-Sponsored Agencies

Banks for Cooperatives (BC)
College Construction Loan Insurance
  Association (CCLIA or Connie Lee)
Federal Farm Credit Banks (FFCB)
Federal Home Loan Banks (FHLB)
Federal Home Loan Mortgage Corporation
  (FHLMC or Freddie Mac)
Federal Intermediate Credit Banks (FICB)
Federal Agricultural Mortgage Corporation
  (FAMC or Farmer Mac)

Federal Land Banks (FLB)
Federal National Mortgage Association (FNMA
  or Fannie Mae)
Student Loan Marketing Association (SLMA or
  Sallie Mae)
Financing Corporation (FICO)
Financing Assistance Corporation (FAC)
Resolution Funding Corporation (REFCO)

guarantees to farmers, small business owners, mortgage borrowers, and other sectors. The securities issued by government-sponsored agencies are usually *not* guaranteed by the federal government, but most investors believe that the government is "only a step away" in the event that any agency gets into serious trouble.[6]

Growth of the Agency Market

Armed with this implied government support, the agency market has grown rapidly, with the volume of outstanding securities climbing from about $2 billion during the 1950s to about $800 billion today (see Exhibit 17–8). Agency debt equals about one eighth of the huge U.S. public debt and is roughly one third the amount of corporate bonds outstanding.

The agency market is dominated by the government-sponsored agencies, which have restricted access to government coffers and must rely mainly on the open market to raise money. The federal agencies, in contrast, are financed through the **Federal Financing Bank (FFB),** which borrows money from the Treasury. The FFB is closely supervised by the Treasury Department and, in fact, is staffed by Treasury employees.[7]

---

[6]Government-sponsored agencies are permitted to draw on the U.S. Treasury for funds up to a specified limit with Treasury approval. However, neither the principal nor the interest on the debt of government-sponsored agencies is guaranteed by the federal government, although the issuing agency guarantees its own securities. In contrast, securities of agencies operated by the federal government are fully guaranteed by the credit of the U.S. government.

[7]Due to FFB activities, the Treasury has to add a certain amount to its regular borrowings each year to cover any FFB drawings. The FFB was created by Congress in 1973. Up to that time each federal agency did its own borrowing. As a result, the number of different agency issues was proliferating at a rapid rate, creating confusion among investors. Centralization of borrowing in one agency, it was hoped, would increase efficiency in the funding process, improve the marketability of agency securities, and give Congress a more adequate measure of the growth of agency activities. All FFB obligations are fully guaranteed by the U.S. government. The FFB, in turn, purchases only those securities fully guaranteed as to principal and interest by the issuing agency.

Terms on Agency Securities

Agency securities are generally short to medium term (out to 10 years), and about 20 percent have original maturities under one year. Money market borrowing is usually done by issuing discount notes which, like Treasury bills and commercial paper, have no promised interest rate but are sold at a price below their par value. About a dozen principal dealers sell the notes for a small fee, with banks, mutual funds, insurance companies, thrifts, and pension funds purchasing most of them. The sponsored agencies also issue short-term coupon securities and variable-rate notes. Long-term borrowing in the capital market is usually accomplished by issuing debentures, either on a monthly basis or irregularly as the need for funds arises.

Longer-term agency securities are available in denominations as small as $1,000, while the shorter-term notes traded in the money market generally come in minimum denominations of $50,000 or more. They are subject to federal income taxes, but many are exempt from state and local taxes (except for FNMA and FHLMC securities). However, state and local government estate, gift, and inheritance taxes do apply to agency obligations. Depository institutions may use agency securities as collateral for loans from the Federal Reserve's discount window and as backing for government deposits. National banks may act as dealers in agency securities.

The heaviest agency borrowers in recent years, as indicated in Exhibit 17–9, have been the Federal National Mortgage Association (FNMA), the Federal Home Loan Banks (FHLB), and the Farm Credit Banks. These three agencies account for about 70 percent of the outstanding debt issued by all federal and government-sponsored agencies, and an active secondary market exists for the short-term debt of these three agencies. Clearly, most agency borrowing goes to support, directly or indirectly, the housing market and agriculture.

The securities of all government-sponsored agencies are regarded as highly similar by investors. Comparable maturities tend to have about the same yield, regardless of the issuing agency. Each agency is able to borrow at interest rates below the average yield on its asset portfolio due to government support but pays a slightly higher interest rate than the U.S. Treasury. Most of this small difference in interest cost is due to the fact that agency securities are less marketable than Treasury IOUs. The Treasury issues a security homogeneous in quality and other characteristics, but the agency market is splintered into many pieces. The yields on agency securities are lower than yields on private debt issues, however, due to their superior credit standing. Agency yields are generally calculated on a 360-day basis like Treasury bills, with their prices quoted in 32nds of a point like corporate and U.S. government notes and bonds.

Exhibit 17–8   **Growth of the Agency Debt Market** ($ Billions)

Year-End	Total Agency Debts Outstanding
1961	$ 8.6
1971	50.7
1980	193.2
1990	434.7
1995*	811.2

*1995 figures are as of September of that year.

Source: Board of Governors of the Federal Reserve System, *Federal Reserve Bulletin,* selected issues; and U.S. Treasury Department, *Treasury Bulletin,* selected issues.

Exhibit 17–9

Total Debt Outstanding of Federal and Government-Sponsored Agencies, 1995* ($ Billions)

Agency	Total Debt Outstanding
Federal agencies:	
Export-Import Bank	$ 2.7
Federal Housing Administration	0.1
Postal Service	7.5
Tennessee Valley Authority	28.0
Other agencies	0.1
Total federal agency debt†	$ 38.4
Government-sponsored agencies:	
Federal Home Loan Banks	223.1
Federal Home Loan Mortgage Corporation	108.5
Federal National Mortgage Association	270.9
Farm Credit Banks§	53.9
Student Loan Marketing Association	51.3
Resolution Funding Corporation	30.0
Other agencies	10.7
Total government-sponsored debt†	$748.4
Total agency debt outstanding	$786.8

*Data as of June 1995.
†Figures may not add to column totals due to rounding.
§In January 1979, the Farm Credit Banks began issuing consolidated bonds to replace those securities previously issued by the Federal Land Banks, the Federal Intermediate Credit Banks, and the Banks for Cooperatives. The Resolution Funding Corporation was established by the Financial Institutions Reform, Recovery, and Enforcement Act of 1989.

Source: Board of Governors of the Federal Reserve System, *Federal Reserve Bulletin,* November 1995, Table 1.44.

The Marketing of Agency Issues

Most agency issues are sold through the **solicitation method.** A *fiscal agent* in New York City assembles a group of banks, dealers, and brokers to bring each issue to market. This solicitation group conveys to potential investors information on the size, denomination, and maturity of a new issue and asks the investors on its list to make a firm commitment to buy a certain amount of securities. Investors are not told the price of the new securities but are asked for their views on what the price should be. This pricing information is conveyed to the fiscal agent. The day after order books close, the fiscal agent prices the new securities, and delivery to committed investors occurs a few days later. Investors do not know the prices or yields on the securities they buy until after the sale but must rely on the agent's knowledge and experience to price each issue correctly.

A study by Puglisi and Vignola (1983) suggests that the fiscal agents generally are highly accurate in choosing competitive equilibrium yields on new issues of agency debt. When their pricing decisions are off the mark, they tend to err on the side of underpricing rather than overpricing a new issue. The solicitation group of dealers receives a commission from the fiscal agent for gathering investor orders.

Unfortunately, dealers in agency securities, like those who trade in Treasury securities (which includes many of the same firms), are not immune from scandal. In 1991, the scandal that rocked the government securities market (discussed in Chapter 15) spread to the agency market, where it was discovered that several dealers had falsified bids, inflating the size of their customers' orders in an effort to capture a bigger share of this market. Fines were imposed, and several dealer houses were placed on probation.

Among the most active buyers of agency securities are banks, state and local governments, government trust funds, and the Federal Reserve System. The Federal Reserve has been authorized to conduct open market operations in agency IOUs since 1966. Fed buying and selling of these securities has helped to improve their marketability and stature among private investors. Major securities dealers who handle U.S. government securities also generally trade in agency issues.

Government-sponsored agencies have become innovative borrowers in recent years. For example, FNMA and SLMA have sold securities in foreign markets, some of these denominated in foreign currencies or sold in "dual currency" form in which interest is paid in a foreign currency and the principal is repaid at maturity in U.S. dollars. These agencies have also used interest rate swaps and currency swaps to protect themselves against the risk of fluctuating interest rates and currency prices.[8]

SUMMARY

In this chapter, we have looked at two of the most rapidly growing securities markets today: commercial paper and federal agency securities. Major industrial corporations, faced with rapidly growing demands for their products and services, have turned increasingly to the market for short-term commercial notes to meet pressing cash needs. The commercial paper market offers a flexible avenue for borrowing, often at lower interest rates than those available from other lenders. At the same time, banks and finance companies, faced with burgeoning demand for credit, have found the paper market an excellent avenue for raising large amounts of short-term funds quickly with minimum inconvenience.

Equally impressive has been the growth of debt securities issued by agencies created by the U.S. government. Their extensive borrowing and lending activities in the financial markets channel billions of dollars in funds to farmers, small businesses, mortgage borrowers, and mortgage-lending institutions under more generous terms than the open market often provides. Many of these agencies, especially those aiding agriculture and the mortgage market, have been operating since the 1920s and 1930s, but their growth in recent years has been unprecedented.

All federal agencies are creatures of Congress and may be destroyed, in theory at least, at the stroke of a pen. In reality, however, with continuing rapid growth in the number of new families formed in the United States each year and the rising costs of housing, food, and fuel, the role of the federal agencies in the financial markets probably will continue to expand. Agency securities will continue to be an attractive investment for banks, corporations, and other investors who seek competitive rates of return with minimal risk. ■

KEY TERMS AND CONCEPTS IN THIS CHAPTER

commercial paper	credit enhancements	federal agencies
direct paper	master note	Federal Financing Bank (FFB)
dealer paper	government-sponsored agencies	solicitation method

---

[8]See Chapters 12 and 29 for a discussion of interest rate and currency swaps.

STUDY QUESTIONS

1. What is commercial paper? What features make it attractive to money market investors?

2. Describe the role dealers play in the functioning of the paper market.

3. How is the rate of return on commercial paper calculated?

4. What are the principal advantages accruing to a company large enough to tap the commercial paper market for funds? Are there any disadvantages?

5. Who are the principal investors in commercial paper? How is paper rated?

6. What are credit enhancements? What is asset-backed commercial paper? How have these devices aided the growth of the paper market?

7. What are disadvantaged sectors of the economy?

8. What is the difference between a government-sponsored agency and a federal agency?

9. What are the principal investment characteristics of agency securities?

10. How are agency securities marketed? What is unusual about the pricing of agency securities?

PROBLEMS

1. A new issue of 90-day commercial paper is available from a dealer in New York City at a price of $97.60 on a $100 basis. What is the bank discount yield on this note if held to maturity?

2. A note traded in the commercial paper market will mature in 15 days. The dealer will sell it to you at $98.35 on a $100 basis. What is the note's discount rate of return?

3. Commercial paper was purchased in the secondary market 30 days from maturity at a bank discount yield of 9 percent. Ten days later, it was sold to a dealer at an 8 percent discount rate. What was the investor's holding period yield?

4. What is the difference in basis points between the discount rate of return (DR) and the investment rate of return (IR) on a $10-million commercial paper note purchased at a price of $9.85 million and scheduled to mature in 25 days?

5. A commercial paper note with $1 million par value and maturing in 60 days has an expected discount return (DR) at maturity of 6 percent. What was its purchase price? What is this note's expected coupon-equivalent (investment return) yield (IR)?

6. Alamo Corporation requests a $20 million, 90-day loan from its bank, which proposes to make the requested loan at an interest rate of 6 percent and a compensating balance requirement of 20 percent of the amount of the loan. What will Alamo's effective loan rate be under these terms? Suppose 90-day commercial paper sold by dealers is currently trading at an interest rate of 6.0 percent. What is the interest rate spread between the effective loan rate quoted by the bank and the current commercial paper rate? Does the bank's proposed loan carry any advantages that borrowing through the commercial paper market won't necessarily provide Alamo Corporation?

7. What price would attach today to Europaper issued at par (100) with a maturity of 180 days and carrying a discount rate of 7 percent?

8. What is the appropriate discount rate for a 270-day Europaper issue priced at par (100) and expected to sell today at a discounted price of 96?

SELECTED REFERENCES

Crabbe, Leland. "Corporate Medium-Term Notes." *Finance and Economics Discussion Series #162.* Board of Governors of the Federal Reserve System, June 1991.

Crabbe, Leland, and Mitchell A. Post. "The Effect of SEC Amendments to Rule 2A–7 on the Commercial Paper Market." *Finance and Economics Discussion Series #199.* Board of Governors of the Federal Reserve System, May 1992.

McCauley, Robert N., and Lauren A. Hargraves. "Eurocommercial Paper and U.S. Commercial Paper: Converging Money Markets?" *Quarterly Review.* Federal Reserve Bank of New York, Autumn 1987, pp. 24–35.

Post, Mitchell A. "The Evolution of the U.S. Commercial Paper Market Since 1980." *Federal Reserve Bulletin,* December 1992, pp. 879–890.

Puglisi, Donald J., and Anthony J. Vignola, Jr. "An Examination of Federal Agency Debt Pricing Practices." *The Journal of Financial Research* 6, no. 2 (Summer 1983), pp. 83–92.

Schnure, Calvin D. "Debt Maturity Choice and Risk-Free Assets: The 'Clientele Effect' and the Commercial Paper Market." *Finance and Economics Discussion Series #944.* Board of Governors of the Federal Reserve System, April 1994.

Chapter 18

International Money Market Instruments: Bankers' Acceptances and Eurodollars

LEARNING OBJECTIVES IN THIS CHAPTER

- To see how the money market and its institutions now cover the globe, reaching across national borders to make possible global short-term borrowing and lending of funds.
- To understand how bankers' acceptances and Eurodollars are used to provide credit needed in international trade and commerce.
- To determine how the ownership of money can be transferred across international boundaries and what the effects of these funds transfers are likely to be on the domestic economy.

The money market today is not confined within the boundaries of a single nation. Money flows around the globe, seeking out those investments offering the highest expected returns for a given degree of risk. Moreover, world trade has expanded in recent years at a rapid pace, especially between the United States, the nations of Central and South America, Japan, the Pacific Basin, Europe, and the Middle East. Further increases in international commerce are expected in the decade ahead, including a significant expansion of trade between East and West. China, the nations that formerly were part of the Soviet Union, and Eastern Europe are developing close economic ties with several Western countries. The exporting of agricultural products and advanced technology by the United States, Japan, and Western Europe to Third World countries constitutes one of the major avenues for trade in the modern world.

And, of course, the growth and development of international commerce requires a concomitant expansion in both long- and short-term sources of financing. Long-term capital is needed to build new factories, transportation systems, and energy producing and refining facilities. Short-term capital from the money market is needed to finance the annual export and import of goods and to provide other working capital needs. In this chapter, we focus on two of the most widely used international money market instruments: bankers' acceptances and Eurodollars.

BANKERS' ACCEPTANCES

A **bankers' acceptance** is a *time draft* drawn on a bank by an exporter or an importer to pay for merchandise or to buy foreign currencies. If the bank honors the draft, it will stamp "Accepted" on its face and endorse the instrument. By so doing, the issuing bank has unconditionally guaranteed to pay the face value of the acceptance at maturity, shielding exporters and investors in international markets from default risk. Acceptances carry maturities ranging from 30 to 270 days (with 90 days being the most common) and are considered prime-quality money market instruments. They are actively traded among financial institutions, industrial corporations, and securities dealers as a high-quality investment and source of ready cash. An illustration of a typical bankers' acceptance, prepared at the Federal Reserve Bank of New York, is shown in Exhibit 18–1.

Why Acceptances Are Used in International Trade

Acceptances are used in the import and export trade because most exporters are uncertain of the credit standing of the importers to whom they ship goods. Exporters may also be concerned about business conditions or political developments in foreign countries. Nations experiencing terrorist violence or even civil war have serious problems in attracting financing for imports of goods and services because of the obvious risks of extending credit inside their territory. However, exporters usually are quite content to rely on acceptance financing by a domestic or foreign bank. Thus, an acceptance is a financial instrument

Exhibit 18–1   Illustration of a Bankers' Acceptance

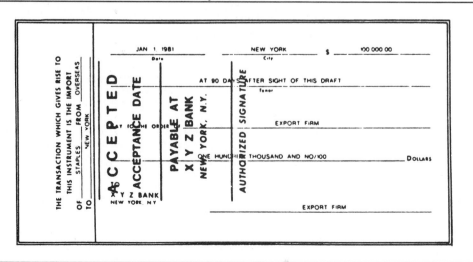

Source: Federal Reserve Bank of New York.

designed to shift the risk of international trade to a third party willing to take on that risk for a known cost. Banks are willing to take on such risk because they are specialists in assessing credit risk and spread that risk over thousands of different loans.

How Acceptances Arise

Trade acceptances usually begin when an importer goes to a bank to secure a line of credit to pay for a shipment of goods from abroad. (See Exhibit 18–2 for a flowchart illustrating how acceptances can be created.) Once the line of credit is approved, the bank issues a letter of credit in favor of the foreign exporter. This document authorizes the exporter to draw a time draft for a specified amount against the issuing bank, provided that the exporter agrees to send appropriate shipping documents giving the issuing bank temporary title to the exported goods.

Because the letter of credit authorizes the drawing of a **time draft,** not a sight draft (which is payable immediately upon presentation), the exporter must wait until the draft matures (perhaps as long as six months) to be paid. Such a delay is unacceptable for most export firms, which must meet payrolls, pay taxes, and satisfy other near-term obligations.

Moreover, the time draft generally is redeemed in the home currency of the issuing bank, and this particular currency may not be needed by the exporter. A French exporter holding a time draft from a U.S. bank, for example, would be paid in dollars on its maturity date, even though the exporter probably needs francs to pay employees and meet other local expenses. Typically, then, the exporter *discounts* the time draft in advance of maturity through his or her principal bank. The exporter then receives timely payment in local currency and avoids the risk of trading in foreign currencies.

Exhibit 18–2	**The Creation of a Bankers' Acceptance**

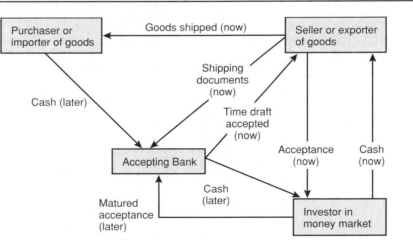

Effect of an Acceptance: Reduces risk to seller from shipping goods on credit because the purchaser has received a bank's guarantee of future payment, thus transferring risk from the seller to the accepting bank and the seller can receive his or her funds right away by discounting the acceptance before it matures.

Source: Adapted from William C. Melton and Jean M. Mahr, "Bankers' Acceptance," *Quarterly Review,* Federal Reserve Bank of New York, Summer 1981.

The foreign bank that has now acquired the time draft from the exporter forwards it (plus shipping documents if goods are being traded) to the bank issuing the original letter of credit. The issuing bank checks to see that the draft and any accompanying documents are correctly drawn and then stamps "Accepted" on its face. Two things happen as a result of this action: (1) a bankers' acceptance has been created and (2) the issuing bank has acknowledged an absolute liability, which must be paid in full at maturity. Frequently, the issuing bank discounts the new acceptance for the foreign bank that sent it and credits that bank's correspondent account for the proceeds. The acceptance may then be held by the issuing bank as an asset or sold to a dealer. Meanwhile, shipping documents for any goods that accompanied the acceptance are handed to the importer against a trust receipt, permitting the importer to pick up and market the goods. However, under the terms of the letter of credit, the importer must deposit the proceeds from selling those goods at the issuing bank in sufficient time to pay for the acceptance. When the time draft matures, the acceptance will be presented to the issuing bank for payment by its current holder.

It should be clear that all three principal parties to the acceptance transaction — the exporter, importer, and the issuing bank — benefit from this method of financing international trade. The exporter receives good funds with little or no delay. The importer may delay payment for a time until the related bank line of credit expires. The issuing bank regards the acceptance as a readily marketable financial instrument that can be sold before maturity through an acceptance dealer in order to cover short-term cash needs. In fact, nearly 90 percent of all acceptances created by U.S. banks are sold in the secondary market each year.

However, there are costs associated with all these benefits. A discount fee is charged off the face value of the acceptance whenever it is discounted in advance of maturity. The accepting bank earns a commission (usually 50 to 100 basis points of the face amount), which may be paid by either exporter or importer, in addition to the fees associated with the original line of credit.

Recent Growth of Acceptance Financing

Given the significant advantages of acceptance financing for exporters, importers, and banks, it is not surprising that the volume of bankers' acceptances outstanding grew rapidly, at least until the mid-1980s. As Exhibit 18–3 shows, the volume of U.S. dollar acceptances increased from less than $400 million in 1950 to just over $2 billion in 1960 and then tripled in 1970 to slightly more than $7 billion outstanding. However, even these rapid rates of growth look pale compared with the virtual explosion of acceptance financing during the 1970s and early 1980s. By December 1984, the volume of bankers' acceptances outstanding reached almost $80 billion — more than a tenfold increase in about 15 years.

Then the growth of acceptances leveled out and turned sharply downward. Part of the reason for the turnaround was a slowing in world trade as several leading export nations entered a recession at the beginning of the 1990s and subsequently their economies grew slowly. In addition, a wider variety of foreign currencies (including the Japanese yen) today are being readily accepted in payment for international purchases, and thus there is less need for dollar-denominated acceptances. Another factor has been greater use of direct bank loans bearing low money market interest rates for both exporters and importers. Moreover, many corporations involved in international trade have turned from banks toward the open market to borrow the funds they need, particularly through issues of bonds and commercial paper.

Exhibit 18–3   **The Growth of Bankers' Dollar Acceptances**

Year-End	Volume Outstanding at End of Period ($ Millions)
1950	$ 394
1960	2,027
1970	2,058
1980	54,744
1984	78,364
1990	54,771
1994	29,835

Source: Board of Governors of the Federal Reserve System, *Federal Reserve Bulletin* and *Monetary Statistics,* selected issues.

The majority of acceptances created by U.S. banks arise from four types of financial transactions: (1) the financing of imports into the United States; (2) the financing of exports from the United States; (3) the acquisition of dollars to add to foreign exchange reserves; and (4) the financing of goods stored in or transported between countries other than the United States. Acceptances arising from the last source are called **third-country bills.** As Exhibit 18–4 shows, third-country bills (designated as "all other uses" in the exhibit), led by dollar acceptance financing involving Japan and other nations around the Pacific Rim, are the largest acceptance category. In fact, more than half of all acceptances outstanding are accounted for by non-U.S. banks, primarily banks in Japan, France, Great Britain, Germany, Switzerland, Australia, and Canada.

Acceptances are *not* widely used inside the United States for purely domestic trade. A small amount of domestic acceptance financing is carried out to support the storage of staple commodities such as cotton and tobacco or the domestic shipment of goods. However, if a company can borrow at close to the prime interest rate, it will usually do so rather than use acceptance financing. It is usually much easier for a domestic firm to assess the financial condition of its domestic customers than to evaluate the credit standing of a foreign firm thousands of miles away. For this reason, suppliers of goods in the domestic market usually extend short-term credit (accounts receivable) directly to customers rather than insisting on the use of acceptances. Moreover, in domestic commerce, no exchange of foreign currencies is necessary, eliminating one important type of risk that motivated the growth of acceptances.

Exhibit 18–4   **Uses of Acceptance Financing** ($ Millions)

Uses of Acceptance Financing	Year				
	1975	1980	1985	1990	1994
Imports into the United States	$ 3,726	$11,536	$15,147	$13,096	$10,062
Exports from the United States	4,001	11,339	13,204	12,703	6,355
All other uses	11,000	31,480	40,062	28,973	13,417

Source: Board of Governors of the Federal Reserve System, *Federal Reserve Bulletin,* selected issues.

INTERNATIONAL FOCUS:

Trading in Bankers' Acceptances Around the World

As we saw in this section, bankers' acceptances (BAs) — the direct obligation (promise) of a bank to pay a specific amount on a certain date — have been declining in volume in the United States in recent years as substitute credit instruments have grown in popularity. The same is true in Japan, though Japanese banks are among the leading issuers of bankers' acceptances inside the United States. However, this is not necessarily the case elsewhere.

For example, in Canada, BAs have grown rapidly since their inception in the early 1960s. Canadian BAs carry maturities ranging from 30 days to a year and usually have face amounts ranging from $100,000 to $1 million. The BA market in Canada is less regulated than in the United States and has become a vehicle for trading BA-based futures and swaps. Thus, acceptances in Canada have become a significant part of interest rate risk management activities for banks and other corporations.

Where banks are freer to expand their borrowing and lending activities and represent a bigger share of money market activity and where countries are more heavily dependent on world trade, bankers acceptances still have the opportunity to play a major role in their traditional areas — financing global trade, supporting currency purchases, and dealing with credit risk.

Acceptance Rates

Acceptances do not carry a fixed rate of interest but are sold at a discount in the open market like Treasury bills. The prime borrower under an acceptance is charged a commitment fee for this line of credit, which is usually about 1½ percent (⅛ of 1 percent per month) for top-quality customers. U.S. banks are limited in the dollar amount of acceptances they can create to 150 percent of their paid-in capital and surplus (or by special permission from the Federal Reserve Board, up to 200 percent of their capital and surplus).

If the bank wishes to sell the acceptance in advance of its maturity, the rate of discount it must pay is determined by the current bid rate on acceptances of similar maturity in the open market. The yield on acceptances is usually only slightly higher than on Treasury bills because banks that issue them are among the largest and have solid international reputations (see Exhibit 18–5). Acceptance rates hover close to negotiable CD rates offered by major banks because both acceptances and CDs are unconditional obligations of the issuing bank to pay. Adding to the stature of acceptances, depository institutions are permitted to borrow reserves from the Fed's discount window using certain types of acceptances as collateral.[1]

---

[1]The bankers' acceptance is one of the safest of all financial instruments. It is an irrevocable primary debt of the bank that stamps "accepted" on its face, as well as a contingent liability of the drawing firm and of any other bank, firm, or individual who endorses the document. Moreover, domestic banks are limited in the volume of acceptances they can have outstanding relative to the size of their capital. At the same time, the customer who has requested the initiating letter of credit that gives rise to the acceptance has guaranteed payment by the maturity date. Then too, any goods shipped under the letter of credit are nearly always insured and accompanied by trust and warehouse receipts specifying value and ownership.

Exhibit 18–5

Interest Rates on Bankers' Acceptances, Bank CDs, and U.S. Treasury Bills (Average, Percent per Annum)

Instrument	1985	1987	1989	1991	1993	1995
Prime 90-day bankers' acceptances	7.92%	6.75%	8.87%	5.70%	3.13%	5.52
Three-month negotiable CDs	8.05	6.87	9.09	5.83	3.17	5.62
Three-month U.S. Treasury bills	7.48	5.78	8.11	5.38	3.00	5.14

Note: Bankers' acceptances and Treasury bill yields are quoted on a bank discount basis. Acceptance yields are averages of the midpoint of the range of daily dealer closing rates. Bill rates are auction averages.

Source: Board of Governors of the Federal Reserve System, *Federal Reserve Bulletin,* selected issues.

Investors in Acceptances

Commercial banks regard acceptances as high-grade negotiable instruments suitable for liquidity management purposes. In addition, the essential safety of acceptances is recognized by the U.S. Treasury, which permits banks to use them as collateral to back the Treasury's tax and loan accounts held in a majority of the nation's commercial banks. U.S. banks are also allowed to discount any "eligible" acceptances they hold with the Federal Reserve banks in order to borrow emergency funds. An acceptance is considered "eligible" by the Federal Reserve if it matures within six months and grows out of domestic or international trading or storage of goods. Smaller banks often participate in acceptance financing with money center banks to gain added income, spread out their risk, and accommodate their largest customers.

Other important investors in the acceptance market include industrial corporations, savings banks, money market mutual funds, foreign banks, local governments, federal agencies, and insurance companies. To many investors, acceptances are a close substitute for Treasury bills, negotiable CDs, or commercial paper in terms of quality, although the acceptance market is far smaller in volume of trading.

Only a few dealers — today there are about 20 major ones — regularly trade acceptances, usually as an adjunct to their trading activities in Treasury bills, notes, and bonds. Trading is carried out purely on a negotiated basis, with most daily volume accounted for by swaps of holdings among accepting banks. The dealers call accepting banks and place bids for acceptances on behalf of their customers. Dealers' inventories of acceptances available for purchase are small, especially of acceptances created by the 10 largest U.S. banks that are prime rated. Although a wide variety of denominations is available for both large and small investors, nonbank investors usually find the menu of fresh offerings very limited. Nevertheless, an investor who is willing to accept the odd-lot denominations in which acceptances are issued generally finds the investment rewarding in terms of a competitive rate of return, low risk, and brisk resale demand.

EURODOLLARS

Comparable to the domestic CD market, a chain of international money markets trading in deposits denominated in the world's most convertible currencies stretches around the globe. This so-called **Eurocurrency market** has arisen because of a tremendous need worldwide for funds denominated in dollars, marks, pounds, francs, yen, and other relatively stable currencies. For example, as U.S. corporations have expanded their operations in Europe, Asia, and the Middle East, they have needed huge amounts of U.S. dollars to purchase machinery and other goods in the United States and to pay federal and state taxes. The same companies have also required huge amounts of other national currencies to carry out transactions in the countries where they are represented. To meet these financial needs, international banks headquartered in the world's key financial centers began during the 1950s to accept deposits from businesses, individuals, and governments denominated in currencies other than that of the host country and to make loans in those same currencies. Thus, the Eurocurrency market was born.

What Is a Eurodollar?

Because the dollar is the chief international currency today, the market for Eurodollars dominates the Eurocurrency markets. What are **Eurodollars**? They are deposits of U.S. dollars in banks located outside the United States or in U.S.–based banking facilities free of U.S. deposit regulations.[2] The banks in question record the deposits on their books in U.S. dollars, not in the home currency. The large majority of Eurodollar (and other Eurocurrency) deposits are held in Europe, but these deposits have spread worldwide; Europe's share of the total is declining.[3]

Frequently, banks accepting Eurodollar deposits are foreign branches of U.S. banks. For example, in London, the center of the Eurocurrency market today, branches of U.S. banks outnumber British banks and bid aggressively for deposits denominated in U.S. dollars.[4] Many of these funds are then loaned to the home office in the United States to meet reserve requirements and other liquidity needs. The remaining funds are loaned to private corporations and governments abroad that need U.S. dollars. No one knows exactly how large the Eurodollar market is. One reason is that the market is unregulated. Many banks refuse to disclose publicly their deposit balances in various currencies. Another reason for the relative lack of information on market activity is that Eurocurrencies are merely bookkeeping entries on a bank's ledger and not currencies. You cannot put Eurodollars in your pocket like bank notes.

Eurodollar deposits are continually on the move in the form of loans. They are employed to finance the import and export of goods, to supplement government tax revenues, to provide working capital for the foreign operations of U.S. multinational corporations, and to provide liquid reserves for the largest banks headquartered in the United States. In total, the Eurocurrency and Eurodollar markets represent the largest of all money markets worldwide, with total funds in excess of $3 trillion.

The Creation of Eurodollars

To illustrate how Eurodollar deposits arise, we trace through a simple but typical example. Our discussion is in terms of Eurodollars, but the reader should be aware that the process being described really applies to *any* Eurocurrency.

---

[2] In 1981, the Federal Reserve Board allowed banks operating in the United States to establish international banking facilities (IBFs) — computerized record keeping centers for international transactions — which can accept deposits from nonresidents of the United States that are not subject to regulations governing the taking of domestic deposits. Thus, any deposit by a U.S. nonresident recorded in an IBF is counted as a Eurodollar deposit.

[3] Among the most important non-European centers for Eurocurrency trading are the Bahamas, Canada, the Cayman Islands, Hong Kong, Panama, and Singapore.

[4] U.S. banks are prohibited from accepting deposits or making loans in currencies other than U.S. dollars inside the United States. However, banks in other countries, branches of U.S. banks abroad, and IBFs (see note 2) can accept foreign currency-denominated accounts.

Suppose a French exporter of fine wines ships cases of champagne to a New York importer, accompanied by a bill for $10,000. The importing firm pays for the champagne by issuing a check drawn on its local bank in the requested amount. Because the French exporter deals regularly in the United States, frequently buying U.S. equipment, it is happy to accept the importer's check denominated in dollars and deposits it right away in a U.S. bank — First American Bank — where the French firm maintains a checking account. After this check clears, the results of the transaction are as follows:

French Exporter		First American Bank	
Assets	*Liabilities*	*Assets*	*Liabilities*
Demand deposit in U.S. bank +$10,000			Demand deposit owed French exporter +$10,000

Is the deposit shown above a Eurodollar deposit? *No,* because the deposit of dollars occurred in the United States, where the dollar is the official monetary unit. Suppose, however, that the French exporter is offered an attractive rate of return on its dollar deposit by its own local bank in Paris and decides to move the dollar deposit there. The Paris bank wants to loan these dollars to other customers who need them to pay bills or make purchases in the United States. After the wine exporter and its Paris bank have negotiated the terms of the deposit and the funds are transferred, the French exporter receives a receipt for a dollar-denominated time deposit in its Paris bank. That bank, in return, now holds claim to the original dollar deposit in the United States. The Paris bank has at least one U.S. correspondent bank and asks to have the original dollar deposit transferred there. We show these transactions as follows:

French Exporter		First American Bank	
Assets	*Liabilities*	*Assets*	*Liabilities*
Demand deposit in U.S. bank −$10,000		Reserves transferred to U.S. correspondent bank −$10,000	Demand deposit owed French exporter −$10,000
Time deposit in Paris bank +$10,000			

U.S. Correspondent Bank		Paris Bank	
Assets	*Liabilities*	*Assets*	*Liabilities*
Reserves received from First American Bank +$10,000	Demand deposit owed Paris bank +$10,000	Deposit with U.S. correspondent bank +$10,000	Time deposit owed French exporter +$10,000

Do we now have a Eurodollar deposit? *Yes,* in the form of a $10,000 time deposit in a Paris bank. The wine exporter's deposit has been accepted and recorded on the Paris bank's books in U.S. dollars, even though the official monetary unit in France is the franc.[5]

Let us follow this Eurodollar deposit through one more step. Assume now that the Paris bank makes a loan of $10,000 to a small oil company based in Manchester, England. The British company needs dollars to pay for a shipment of petroleum drilling equipment from Houston, Texas. By securing a dollar credit from the Paris bank, the British oil firm,

---

[5] The $10,000 time deposit is used here for illustrative purposes only. The vast majority of Eurocurrency deposits are far larger. In fact, the normal trading unit in this market is 1 million currency units.

in effect, receives a claim against dollars deposited in U.S. banks. The appropriate entries would be as follows:

Paris Bank	
Assets	*Liabilities*
Loan to British oil company +$10,000	
Deposit in U.S. correspondent bank −$10,000	

British Oil Company	
Assets	*Liabilities*
Demand deposit in U.S. correspondent bank +$10,000	Loan owed to Paris bank +$10,000

U.S. Correspondent Bank	
Assets	*Liabilities*
	Deposit owed to Paris bank −$10,000
	Deposit owed to British oil company +$10,000

Note that we have assumed that the British oil company held a deposit account in the same U.S. bank where the Paris bank held its deposits. This, of course, is often not the case, but it was done here to reduce the number of accounting entries. If another U.S. bank were involved, we would simply transfer deposits and reserves to it from the U.S. correspondent bank that held the account of the Paris bank. The result would be exactly the same as in our example: *The total amount of dollar deposits and U.S. bank reserves remains unchanged.* These funds are merely passed from U.S. bank to U.S. bank as loans are extended and deposits made in the Eurodollar market. Thus, Eurodollar activity does *not* alter the total reserves of the U.S. banking system. In fact, the workings of the Eurodollar market remind us of a fundamental principle of international finance: *Money itself usually does not leave the country where it originates; only the ownership of money is transferred across international boundaries.*

The chain of Eurodollar loans and deposits started in our example by the wine exporter's bank in Paris will go on unbroken as long as dollar loans are in demand and the funds are continually redeposited somewhere in the international banking system. Some economists believe that Eurobanks, like domestic U.S. banks, can create a multiple volume of deposits and loans for each dollar deposit they receive. However, this view has been disputed by a number of analysts (e.g., Niehaus and Hewson, 1976). They point out that major Eurobanks in their borrowing and lending activities are closer to nonbank financial institutions than to commercial banks. Eurobanks appear to closely match the maturities of their assets (principally loans) with the maturities of their liabilities (principally Eurocurrency deposits and money market borrowings); thus, funds raised in the Eurocurrency markets flow through Eurobanks back into those same markets. Rather than creating money, Eurobanks appear to function more as "efficient distributors of liquidity." If there is any actual credit or money creation in the Eurosystem, leading to a multiplication of deposits, the deposit multiplier must be close to one.[6]

---

[6]See Chapters 4 and 20 for discussions of the deposit multiplier. The granting of a Eurodollar loan to a borrower does not give the borrower "money" in a strict sense. Eurodollars are not generally acceptable as a medium of exchange to pay for goods and services. They are more like regular time deposits. The holder of a Eurodollar deposit must convert that deposit into some national currency unit before using it for spending. Thus, Eurocur-

Just as Eurodollars are created by making loans, they are also destroyed as loans are repaid. In our example, suppose the British oil company trades pounds for dollars with a foreign currency dealer and uses the dollars purchased to repay its loan from the Paris bank. At about the same time, the dollar time deposit held by the French exporter matures, and the exporter spends those dollars in the United States. As far as U.S. banks are concerned, total deposits and reserves remain unchanged. However, as a result of these transactions, all dollar deposits are now held in the United States and, therefore, have ceased to be Eurodollars.

Eurodollar Maturities and Risks

Most Eurodollar deposits are short-term time deposits (ranging from overnight to call money loaned for a few days out to one year) and therefore are true money market instruments. However, a small percentage are long-term time deposits, extending in some instances to about five years. Most Eurodollar deposits carry one-month maturities to coincide with payments for shipments of goods. Other common maturities are 2, 3, 6, and 12 months.[7] The majority are interbank liabilities that pay a fixed interest rate.

Even though Eurobanks do not issue demand deposits, funds move rapidly in the Eurocurrency market from bank to bank in response to demands for short-term liquidity from corporations, governments, and Eurobanks themselves. There is no central trading location in the market. Traders thousands of miles distant may conduct negotiations by satellite, cable, computer networks, telephone, or telex, with written confirmation coming later. Funds normally are transferred on the second business day after an agreement is reached through correspondent banks.

Eurocurrency deposits are known to be volatile and highly sensitive to fluctuations in interest rates and currency prices. A slight difference in interest rates or currency values between two countries can cause a massive flow of Eurocurrencies across national boundaries. One of the most famous examples of this phenomenon occurred in West Germany in 1971, when speculation that the German mark would be upvalued brought an inflow into Germany of billions in dollar deposits within hours, forcing the West German government to cut the mark loose from its official exchange value and allow that currency to float upward.

As Goodfriend (1981) observes, Eurodollars are not without risk. There is *political risk* because governments may restrict or prohibit the movement of funds across national borders, as the United States did for a time during the Iranian crisis. There may be disputes between nations over the legal jurisdiction and control of deposits. *Default risk* may also be a factor because banks in the Eurobank system may fail; Eurocurrency deposits usually are *not* insured. This problem is compounded by the fact that it is more costly to secure

---

rency deposits are *not* negotiable instruments. The Eurocurrency system does not create money in the traditional sense. A lender of Eurocurrency who needs liquid funds before a deposit matures must go back into the market and negotiate a separate loan.

Interest usually is paid only at maturity unless the Eurodeposit has a term of more than one year. Most deposit interest rates are tied to the London Interbank Offer Rate (LIBOR), the rate at which major international banks offer term Eurodollar deposits to each other. The rate is usually fixed for the life of the deposit, though floating rates tied to semiannual changes in LIBOR are not uncommon on longer-term deposits, with promised interest rates reset every three to six months at a spread over LIBOR.

[7]Banks active in the Eurodollar market for liquidity-adjustment purposes use *short-date* deposits. Comparable to federal funds in the domestic U.S. money market, short dates represent deposits available for as long as 14 days, though generally they are weekend or 2-day money, with some 7-day maturities as well. Short dates may carry fixed maturities or simply be payable on demand with minimal notice (such as 24 or 48 hours).

information on the financial condition of foreign banks than on domestic banks. However, on the positive side, Eurobanks are among the largest and most stable banking institutions in the world. Moreover, most foreign nations have tried to encourage the growth of Euro-currency markets through lenient regulation and taxation.

The Supply of Eurodollars

Where do Eurodollars come from? A major factor in the market's growth has been the enormous balance-of-payments deficits the United States has run since the late 1950s.[8] U.S. firms building factories and purchasing goods and services abroad have transferred ownership of dollar deposits to foreign companies and banks. Domestic shortages of oil and natural gas have forced the United States to import nearly half of its petroleum needs, generating enormous outflows of dollars to oil-producing nations. The OPEC countries, for example, accept dollars in payment for crude oil and use the dollar as a standard for valuing the oil they sell. U.S. tourists visiting Europe, Japan, and the Middle East frequently use dollar-denominated traveler's checks or take U.S. currency with them and convert it into local currency overseas. Dollar loans made by U.S. corporations and foreign-based firms have added to the vast Eurodollar pool. Many of these dollar deposits have gravitated to foreign central banks, such as the Bank of England, as these institutions have attempted to support the dollar and their own currencies in international markets.

Eurodollars in Domestic Bank Operations

Since the late 1960s, U.S. banks have drawn heavily on Eurodollar deposits as a means of adjusting their domestic reserve positions. Thus, the manager of the money desk at a large U.S. bank, knowing the bank will need extra cash reserves in a few days, can contact foreign banks holding dollar deposits and arrange a loan. The manager can also contact other U.S. banks with branches abroad and borrow Eurodollars from them. Alternatively, if the money manager's own bank operates foreign branches accepting dollar deposits, these can be placed at the disposal of the home office.

Eurodollar borrowing of bank reserves has been especially heavy during periods of rapidly rising interest rates in the United States. During the credit crunch of 1979–1980, when domestic money market rates rose to record levels, U.S. banks tapped the Eurodollar market for billions of dollars in short-term funds. Such borrowings are extremely interest-rate sensitive, however. When U.S. money market rates fell precipitously from record highs in the spring of 1980 and domestic sources of reserves became much less expensive, American banks repaid their Eurodollar borrowings nearly as fast as they borrowed these international deposits months earlier.

Eurodollars usually carry *higher* reported interest rates than many other sources of bank reserves, such as domestic certificates of deposit, due to perceptions of higher risk, although this is not always the case. (See Exhibit 18–6.) However, there are fewer legal restrictions on the borrowing of Eurodollars. For example, Eurodollar deposits have no reserve requirements or insurance fees today. In contrast, U.S. banks must pay assessments to the Federal Deposit Insurance Corporation on domestic nonbank deposits to cover the costs of deposit insurance.

In addition to meeting their own reserve needs from the Eurodollar market, U.S. banks have aided their corporate customers in acquiring Eurocurrency deposits. Direct loans in

---

[8]See Chapter 28 for a discussion of the causes and effects of U.S. balance-of-payment deficits.

Exhibit 18–6   **Interest Rates on Eurodollar Deposits and Other Money Market Instruments**

Year	Eurodollar Deposits, Three-Month Maturities	U.S.-Issued Certificates of Deposit, Three-Month Maturities	Federal Funds Interest Rate
1990	8.16%	8.15%	8.10%
1993	3.18	3.17	3.02
1995	5.93	5.92	5.83
1996*	5.14	5.15	5.22

*1996 figures are for February.

Source: U.S. Department of Commerce, *Business Statistics,* selected editions; and Board of Governors of the Federal Reserve System, *Federal Reserve Bulletin,* selected monthly issues.

Eurocurrencies are made by U.S. banks, and these banks will readily swap Eurocurrencies at the customer's request. Although most Eurocurrency loans to nonbank customers are short-term credits to provide working capital, a sizable percentage in recent years has consisted of medium-term (one- to five-year) loans for equipment purchases, frequently set up under a revolving credit agreement. Both borrowers and lenders in the Eurodollar market can more effectively hedge against interest rate risk on these international loans today due to the recent rapid growth of the Eurodollar interest-rate futures market centered in London and Chicago.

Eurodollar loan rates have two components: (1) the cost of acquiring Eurodollar deposits (usually measured by the **London Interbank Offer Rate (LIBOR)** on three- or six-month Eurodeposits) and (2) a profit margin ("spread") based on the riskiness of the loan and the intensity of competition. Profit margins are low on Eurodollar loans (often ⅛ percentage point or less) because the market is highly competitive, lending costs are low, and the risk is normally low as well. Borrowers are generally well-known institutions with substantial net worth and solid credit standing. Market transactions are usually carried out in large denominations, ranging from about $500,000 to $100 million or more.

In deciding whether to tap the Eurodollar market for funds, banks and other borrowers compare Eurodeposit interest rates with alternative borrowing costs available in their domestic financial systems. For example, U.S. banks during a recent week were looking at the following alternative borrowing costs:

Cost rate on 30-Day Eurodollar deposits (Quoted by international banks in London)	5.94%
Domestic negotiable 30-day CDs (Average yield posted by leading New York City banks)	5.13
Federal funds (Average rate quoted by brokers in New York City)	5.63

The rate spreads shown above seem to favor borrowing domestically through Federal funds or by using negotiable CDs (even though the domestic CDs carry an added insurance fee that would bring their cost up closer to that of comparable-maturity Eurodollar deposits). For a nonbank corporation borrowing money, the critical issue would be the size of the *margin* or *spread* a lender would ask for over and above the Eurodollar rate versus the domestic money market rate on Fed funds or CDs. For example, one lender might quote the borrowing company a LIBOR-based loan rate priced off the cost of 30-day Eurodollar deposits as follows:

Loan rate = 30-Day LIBOR rate + ⅛% margin = 5.94% + 0.125% = 6.07%

while another lender might ask for

$$\text{Loan rate} = \text{30-Day domestic CD rate} + \tfrac{1}{2}\% \text{ margin} = 5.13\% + 0.50\% = 5.63\%$$

or

$$\text{Loan rate} = \text{Federal funds rate} + \tfrac{3}{4}\% \text{ margin} = 5.63 + 0.75\% = 6.38\%$$

In this particular example, a loan priced off domestic CD interest rates appears to be cheaper for the borrowing corporation than a loan based on the Eurodollar deposit rate (LIBOR) or the Federal funds interest rate.

Recent Innovations in the Eurodollar Market

Since 1984, the Eurodollar market has witnessed rapid growth in medium-term credit arrangements between international banks and their corporate and governmental customers. These so-called *note issuance facilities* (NIFs) often span five to seven years and allow the customer to borrow in his or her own name by selling short-term IOUs (typically maturing in three to six months) to investors. The bank, for its part, backstops this customer paper either by purchasing any paper that remains unsold or by providing standby credit at an interest rate spread over LIBOR. The notes issued are usually denominated in U.S. dollars with par values of $100,000 or higher. With bank support, NIFs are roughly equivalent to Eurodollar CDs and compete with them for investor funds.

Benefits and Costs of the Eurodollar Market

For the most part, the development of Eurodollar trading has resulted in substantial benefits to the international community, especially to U.S. banks and multinational corporations. The market ensures a high degree of funds mobility between international capital markets and provides a true international market for bank and nonbank liquidity adjustments. It has provided a mechanism for absorbing huge amounts of U.S. dollars flowing overseas and lessened international pressure to forsake the dollar for gold and other currencies. The market reduces the cost of international trade by providing an efficient method of economizing on transactions balances.[9] Moreover, it acts as a check on domestic monetary and fiscal policies and encourages international cooperation in economic policies, because interest-sensitive traders in the market will quickly spot interest rates that are out of line and move huge amounts of funds toward any point on the globe. Central banks, such as the Bank of England and the Bundesbank, monitor the Eurodollar market continuously in order to moderate inflows or outflows of funds that may damage their domestic economies.

The capacity of the Eurocurrency market to mobilize massive amounts of funds has occasionally brought severe criticism from regulators in Europe and in the United States. They see the market as contributing to instability in currency values. Moreover, the market can wreak havoc with monetary and fiscal policies designed to cure domestic economic problems. This is especially true if a nation is experiencing severe inflation and massive inflows of Eurocurrency occur at the same time. The net effect of Eurocurrency expansion, other things being equal, is to push domestic interest rates down, stimulate credit expansion, and accelerate the rate of inflation. The ability of local authorities to deal with

---

[9]See Balbach and Resler (1980) on this point. In effect, the Eurodollar market lowers the cost of dollar-denominated financial intermediation worldwide.

inflationary problems might be overwhelmed by a Eurocurrency glut. This danger is really the price of freedom, for an unregulated market will not always conform to the plans of government policymakers.[10]

It is not surprising that certain European central banks have for more than two decades called for controls on Eurocurrency trading — for example, by imposing reserve requirements on Eurodollar deposits. (During the 1970s, France levied a 9.5 percent reserve requirement on Eurodollar loans.) But such controls have not been effective because of lack of unanimity among foreign governments and central banks. Funds tend to flow away from areas employing controls and toward free markets. The key to the future of controls in this market probably rests with the Bank of England because London is the heart of the Eurodollar market. Thus far, the Old Lady of Threadneedle Street, as that bank is often called, remains firmly against significant government restraints on Eurocurrency trading.

SUMMARY

"The world is getting smaller all the time" — a familiar and trite phrase. It is also true. Travel time between distant cities and even across oceans is measured today in hours and minutes instead of days. However, the great speed at which people can travel today is far outclassed by the velocity of funds and information transfers worldwide. Communications satellites, orbiting thousands of miles above the earth's surface, speed financial and other data to their destination in minutes, seconds, and microseconds. Telex, telephone, and microwave transmissions link large and small financial centers and permit financial transactions between traders separated by thousands of miles almost as conveniently as among those traders who meet on the floor of the New York Stock Exchange.

It is within this environment of change, which emphasizes speed and the availability of information, that the international money market instruments we have discussed in this chapter — bankers' acceptances and Eurodollars — have grown to a position of dominance. Acceptances are time drafts that represent claims against a bank for future payment and are still widely used to finance international shipments of goods. Eurodollars (or, more generically, Eurocurrencies) are time deposits placed in a foreign bank and are actively traded and exchanged from bank to bank within the international financial system.

Both of these instruments provide large amounts of credit to businesses engaged in international commerce and at the same time, offer a high-quality investment. Moreover, both acceptances and Eurodollars are traded in unregulated and efficient markets where interest rates are highly responsive to changing demand and supply forces and investor expectations. This is why thousands of corporations, including the largest banks, have entered these international markets as both borrowers and lenders. And, in the absence of government regulation, markets linking financial systems should continue to grow in size and importance, exerting an ever-widening influence on the character of economic and political relationships in the international community. ■

---

[10]There is little evidence that the rapid growth of the Eurodollar market has had any adverse effects on U.S. economic policies, however. For example, a study by Balbach and Resler (1980) concludes: "Eurodollar flows . . . have only minor effects on the U.S. money stock. This evidence warrants the conclusion that the Eurodollar market does not pose a serious threat to the ability of the Federal Reserve to control the money supply" (p. 11).

KEY TERMS AND CONCEPTS IN THIS CHAPTER

bankers' acceptance	Eurocurrency market	London Interbank Offer Rate (LIBOR)
time draft	Eurodollars	
third-country bills		

STUDY QUESTIONS

1. What is a *bankers' acceptance*? What does the word *accepted* mean?

2. Explain why acceptances are popular with exporters and importers of goods. Why are these instruments not as widely used within the United States as they are in financing international trade?

3. Evaluate bankers' acceptances as a security investment. What are their principal advantages and disadvantages from an investment point of view?

4. What is a *Eurocurrency* market? Why is it needed?

5. Define the term *Eurodollar*. Can a U.S. bank create Eurodollars? Why?

6. Describe the process by which Eurodollars are created. Explain what happens to the total volume of U.S. bank reserves and deposits in the creation process.

7. Can Eurodollars be destroyed? How?

8. List the sources and uses of Eurodollar deposits.

9. What role do Eurodollar deposits play in the reserve management operations of major U.S. banks? What are the advantages of Eurodollar borrowings over other sources of bank reserves?

10. Evaluate the Eurocurrency markets from a social point of view. What are the major benefits and costs of this rapidly growing institution? Would you support closer regulation of the Eurocurrency markets?

PROBLEMS

1. A German manufacturer of furniture sells a large order of home furnishings to an outlet store in Houston. The Houston firm pays for the shipment by wiring funds from its local bank through Fedwire to the German firm's account at Chase Manhattan Bank in New York City. Subsequently, the German manufacturer decides to invest half the funds received in a dollar deposit offered by Barclays Bank in London, where interest rates are particularly attractive. No sooner are the funds deposited in London than a Japanese auto company, shipping cars to the U.S. and Europe, asks the London bank for a loan to purchase raw materials in the United States.

    Later, when the loan falls due, the Japanese firm will go into the currency market to purchase dollars in order to retire its Eurodollar loan at Barclays Bank, receiving a dollar deposit at a U.S. bank. When the loan is repaid, Barclays gains the dollar deposit in the United States and uses the deposit to pay off the German firm when its time deposit matures. The German firm chooses to deposit the funds received from Barclays in its demand deposit account at Chase Manhattan Bank in New York City because it now needs to buy goods and services in the United States.

Construct T accounts that reflect the foregoing transactions. In particular, show the proper entries for: (1) payment by the Houston firm to the German furniture company; (2) deposit of the funds in London; (3) the loan to the Japanese automaker; (4) repayment of the loan; and (5) return of funds to the United States. Indicate which deposit is a Eurodollar deposit and if any Eurodollars are destroyed at any particular stage.

2. A company known as Standard Quality Importing ships videocassette recorders made in Japan to retail dealers in the United States and Western Europe. It decides to place an order with its Japanese supplier for 10,000 Hi-Fi VCRs at $575 each after securing a line of credit from Guaranty Security Bank in Los Angeles. Guaranty issues a credit letter to the Japanese supplier promising payment in U.S. dollars 90 days hence. However, the Japanese firm needs the promised funds within seven days from receipt of the credit letter to make purchases of technical components from an electronics firm in Phoenix, Arizona. Explain and illustrate with T accounts and diagrams how a bankers' acceptance would arise from the foregoing transactions, how the Japanese supplier could receive the dollars she needs in timely fashion, and what would happen to the acceptance at the end of the 90-day period. Use T account entries to show the movement of funds from the importer to the Japanese supplier, to the electronics firm, and to money market investors.

3. Instel Corporation has been offered a $100 million, 3-month loan at a fixed rate of 90-day LIBOR plus ⅜% margin or at the prevailing federal funds rate plus ½% margin with the loan rate adjusted every 24 hours to the federal funds rate prevailing at the close of business each day. Currently, these rates, along with prevailing yields on U.S. Treasury bills, are posted in London and New York as follows:

90-Day LIBOR rate	4.275%	3-month U.S. Treasury bill rate	4.12%
Federal funds rate	4.08	6-month U.S. Treasury bill rate	4.20
One-month (30 day) U.S. Treasury bills	4.05	1-year U.S. Treasury bill rate	4.30

Which set of loan terms would you recommend to Instel's treasurer? Why?

SELECTED REFERENCES

Balbach, Anatol B., and David H. Resler. "Eurodollars and the U.S. Money Supply." *Review.* Federal Reserve Bank of St. Louis, June–July 1980, pp. 2–12.

Goodfriend, Marvin. "Eurodollars," *Economic Review.* Federal Reserve Bank of Richmond, May–June 1981, pp. 12–18.

Jensen, Frederick H., and Patrick M. Parkinson. "Recent Developments in the Bankers' Acceptance Market." *Federal Reserve Bulletin,* January 1986, pp. 4–12.

LaRoche, Robert K. "Bankers Acceptances." *Economic Quarterly.* Federal Reserve Bank of Richmond, Vol. 79 (Winter 1993), pp. 75–85.

Niehaus, Jung, and John Hewson. "The Eurodollar Market and Monetary Theory." *Journal of Money, Credit, and Banking,* 1976, pp. 1–27.

Chapter 19

Central Banking and the Role of the Federal Reserve

LEARNING OBJECTIVES IN THIS CHAPTER

- To explore the many roles played by central banks in general (and the Federal Reserve System in particular) in the economy and financial system of a nation.
- To understand how and why the Federal Reserve System came to be established as the U.S. central bank.
- To examine how the Federal Reserve System is organized to carry out its many roles in the global economy and financial system.
- To explore the importance of central bank independence from government in carrying out effective monetary policy.

One of the most important financial institutions in any modern economy is the **central bank.** Basically, a central bank is an agency of government that has important public policy functions in monitoring the operation of the financial system and controlling the growth of its money supply. Central banks ordinarily do not deal directly with the public; rather, they are "bankers' banks," communicating with commercial banks and securities dealers in carrying out their essential policymaking functions. The central bank of the United States is the **Federal Reserve System,** a creation of Congress charged with issuing currency, regulating the banking system, and taking measures to protect the value of the dollar and promote full employment. In this and the two following chapters, we examine in detail the nature and impact of central bank operations and the major problems of policymaking faced by central bank money managers today.

THE ROLE OF CENTRAL BANKS IN THE ECONOMY
Control of the Money Supply

Central banks, including the Federal Reserve System, perform several important functions in a modern economy. The first and most important of their functions is *control of the money supply.*

What is money? Money is anything that serves as a *medium of exchange* in the purchase of goods and services. Money has another important function, however: serving as a *store of value,* for money is a financial asset that may be used to store purchasing power until it is needed by the owner. If we define money exclusively as a medium of exchange, the sum of all currency and coin held by the public plus the value of all publicly held checking accounts and other deposits against which drafts may be made (such as NOWs and money market accounts) would constitute the money supply. If we define money as a store of value, on the other hand, then time and savings accounts at banks and nonbank financial intermediaries would also be considered important components of the money supply. In Chapter 21, we will note that several different definitions of the money supply may be useful for the purpose of implementing central bank policies and monitoring their effects.

However we define money, the power to regulate its quantity and value was delegated by the U.S. Congress early in this century to the Federal Reserve System. The Fed has become not only the principal source of currency and coin (pocket money) used by the U.S. public but also the principal government agency responsible for stabilizing the value of the dollar and protecting its integrity in international markets. Why is control of the money supply so important? One reason is that changes in the money supply appear to be closely linked to changes in economic activity. A number of studies in recent years have found a statistically significant relationship between current and lagged changes in the money supply and changes in gross domestic product (GDP).[1] The implication of these studies is that, if the central bank can control the rate of growth of money, it can influence the growth rate of the economy as a whole.

Another important reason for controlling the money supply is that, in the absence of effective controls, money in the form of paper notes or bank deposits could expand virtually without limit. The marginal cost of creating additional units of money is nearly zero. Therefore, the banking system or the government or both are capable of increasing the money supply well beyond the economy's capacity to produce goods and services. Because this action would result in severe inflation and eventually bring business activity to a halt, it is not surprising that modern governments have come to rely so heavily on central banks as guardians of the quantity and value of their currencies. For example, the Federal Reserve System enters the financial markets frequently in an attempt to control domestic price inflation in order to protect the purchasing power of the dollar.

Stabilizing the Money and Capital Markets

A second vital function of central banking is *stabilization of the money and capital markets.* The financial system must transmit savings to those who require funds for investment so the economy can grow. If the system of money and capital markets is to work efficiently, however, the public must have confidence in financial institutions and be willing to commit

---

[1]See, for example, the studies by Carlson (1980) and Faust (1992).

its savings to them. If the financial markets are unruly, with volatile fluctuations in interest rates and security prices, or if financial institutions are prone to frequent collapse, public confidence in the financial system might well be lost. The flow of capital funds would dry up, resulting in a drastic slowing in the rate of economic growth and a rise in unemployment. All central banks play a vital role in fostering the mature development of financial markets and in ensuring a stable flow of funds through those markets. Pursuing this objective, a central bank will, from time to time, provide funds to major securities dealers when they have difficulty financing their portfolios so that buyers and sellers may easily acquire or sell securities. When the money supply and interest rates rise or fall more rapidly than seems consistent with economic goals, a central bank may again intervene in the financial marketplace.

Lender of Last Resort

Another essential function of central banks is to serve as a *lender of last resort*. This means providing liquid funds to those financial institutions in need, especially when alternative sources of funds have dried up. For example, through its discount window, the Federal Reserve will provide funds to selected deposit-type financial institutions to cover their short-term cash deficiencies. As we will see, before the Fed was created, one of the weaknesses in the financial system of the United States was the absence of a lender of last resort to aid financial institutions squeezed by severe liquidity pressures.

Maintaining and Improving the Payments Mechanism

Finally, central banks have a role to play in *maintaining and improving the payments mechanism*. This involves clearing checks, providing an adequate supply of currency and coin, wiring funds, and preserving confidence in the value of the fundamental monetary unit. A smoothly functioning and efficient payments mechanism is vital for business and commerce. If checks or electronic payments cannot be cleared in timely fashion or if the public cannot get the currency and coin it needs to carry out transactions, business activity will be severely curtailed. The result might well be large-scale unemployment and a decline in the rate of economic growth.

THE GOALS AND CHANNELS OF CENTRAL BANKING

Central banking is *goal oriented*. Since World War II, the United States and other industrialized nations have accepted the premise that government is responsible to its citizens for maintaining high levels of employment, combating inflation, and supporting sustained growth in the economy. This is a relatively new idea. In earlier periods, governments were assigned a much smaller role in the economic system and much less was expected of them by their citizens. It was believed that "automatic" mechanisms operated within the economy to provide stability and high employment in the long term. One of the bitter lessons of the worldwide Great Depression of the 1930s was that these mechanisms can break down and innovative government policies may be needed to restore the economy's stability and growth.

Central banking in the United States and in most other nations is directed toward four major goals:

1. Full employment of resources.
2. Reasonable stability in the general price level of all goods and services.

3. Sustained economic growth.

4. A stable balance-of-payments position for the nation vis-à-vis the rest of the world.[2]

Through its influence over interest rates and the growth of the money supply, the central bank is able to influence the economy's progress toward each of these goals. Achievement of all of these goals simultaneously has proven to be exceedingly difficult, however. One reason is that the goals often *conflict*. Pursuit of price stability and an improved balance-of-payments position, for example, may require higher interest rates and restricted credit availability — policies that tend to increase unemployment and slow economic growth. Central bank policymaking is a matter of accepting *trade-offs* (compromises) among multiple goals. For example, the central bank can pursue policies leading to a lower rate of inflation and a stronger dollar in international markets, but probably at the price of some additional unemployment and slower economic growth in the short run.

Central banking in most major nations, including the United States, operates principally through the *marketplace*. Modern central banks operate as a balance wheel in promoting and stabilizing the flow of savings from surplus-spending units to deficit-spending units. They try to ensure a smooth and orderly flow of funds through the money and capital markets so that adequate financing is available for worthwhile investment projects. This means, among other things, avoiding panics due to sudden shortages of available credit or sharp declines in security prices. However, most of the actions taken by the central bank to promote a smooth flow of funds are carried out through the marketplace rather than by government order. For example, the central bank may encourage interest rates to rise in order to reduce borrowing and spending and combat inflation, but it does not usually allocate credit to particular borrowers. The private sector, working through supply and demand forces in the marketplace, is left to make its own decisions about how much borrowing and spending will take place and who is to receive credit.

The Channels through Which Central Banks Work

Later, we will examine in some detail how the Federal Reserve System affects the economy. It is useful at this point, however, to give a brief overview of the channels through which modern central banks influence conditions in the economy and financial system. Central bank policy affects the economy as a whole by making the following changes:

1. Changes in the cost and availability of credit to businesses, consumers, and governments.

2. Changes in the volume and rate of growth of the money supply.

3. Changes in the financial wealth of investors as reflected in the market value of their security holdings.

---

[2] In the United States, two laws were passed in the 1970s in an effort to specifically define the goals to be pursued by the Federal Reserve. The Full Employment and Balanced Growth Act of 1978 listed full employment and production, increased real income, balanced growth, adequate productivity growth, an improved trade balance, and reasonable price stability as primary objectives for monetary and fiscal policy. The Federal Reserve Reform Act of 1977 amended the 1913 Federal Reserve Act to require the Fed to promote maximum employment, stable prices, and moderate long-term interest rates. Unfortunately, none of these laws contained any hint or suggestion as to how best to achieve these goals or, in the case of conflicts between the goals, which goal was to have priority. In contrast, some central banks have their priorities carefully spelled out by their governments. For example, the German Bundesbank and the proposed new European Central bank, which is currently targeted to begin operating in 1999, have been instructed to pursue *price stability* as their primary goal.

4. Changes in the relative prices of domestic and foreign currencies (currency exchange rates).

5. Changes in the public's expectations regarding future money and credit conditions and currency values (see Exhibit 19–1).

The central bank has a number of policy tools at its command to influence the cost of credit (interest rates); the value (prices) of securities; money supply volume and growth; the relative prices (exchange rates) of world currencies; and the public's expectations regarding future interest rates, currency prices, and credit conditions. In the United States, the principal policy tools used by the central bank are open market operations, changes in required reserves held by depository institutions, and changes in the discount rate on central bank loans. In turn, changes in interest rates, security prices, and bank reserves resulting from the use of the central bank's policy tools influence, first of all, the cost and availability of credit. If borrowers find that credit is less available and more expensive to obtain, they are likely to restrain their borrowing and spending for both capital and consumer goods at home and abroad. This results in a slowing in the economy's rate of growth and perhaps a reduction in inflationary pressures. Second, if the central bank can reduce the rate of growth of the money supply, this policy will eventually slow the growth of income and production in the economy due to a reduction in the public's demand for goods and services.

Third, if the central bank raises interest rates and thereby lowers security prices, this will tend to reduce the market value of the public's holdings of stocks, bonds, and other securities. The result is a decline in the value of investors' financial wealth, altering the public's borrowing and spending plans and ultimately influencing employment, prices, and the economy's rate of growth. Fourth, the central bank can make changes in domestic interest rates relative to foreign interest rates, which will affect the exchange ratios (relative prices) in world markets between domestic and foreign currencies. If the price of the home currency falls relative to foreign currency prices, the home country's exports will become cheaper and more sought after abroad, stimulating domestic production and creating more jobs.

In recent years, economic research has suggested a fifth channel for central bank policy to affect the economy: *its impact on the public's expectations* regarding future credit costs, money supply growth, the value of loans and securities, and relative currency values. If central bank operations result in shifting public expectations, businesses and consumers will alter their borrowing, spending, and investing plans (unfortunately, not always in the direction the central bank wishes), which can have profound effects on the economy's rate of growth and the creation of jobs. We will have more to say about these important channels of central bank policy in Chapters 20 and 21.

THE HISTORY OF THE FEDERAL RESERVE SYSTEM

The United States was one of the last major nations in the Western world to charter a central bank. The Bank of England was established in 1694; the Bank of France and the central banks of Switzerland and Italy were founded during the 18th century. Most major industrialized nations early in their histories recognized the need for an institution that would provide a measure of stability and control over the growth of money and credit. Public officials in the United States were hesitant to charter a central bank, for fear that it would possess great financial power and restrict the availability of credit to a growing nation. However, a series of economic and financial crises in the late 19th and early 20th centuries forced the U.S. Congress to create the Federal Reserve System.

Exhibit 19–1   The Channels of Central Bank Policy: How the Central Bank Influences the Economy

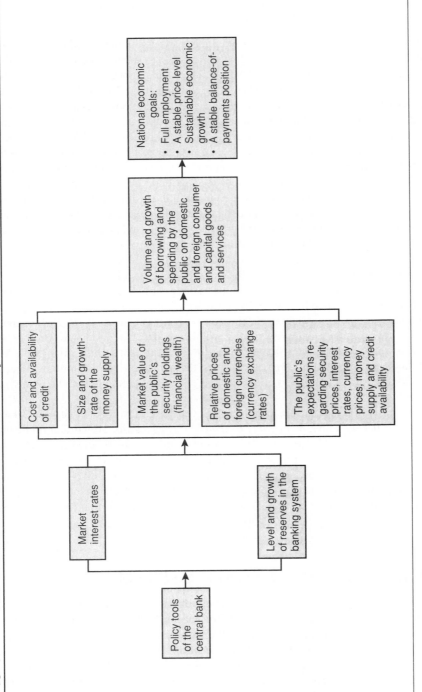

Problems in the Early U.S. Banking System

To fully understand why the Federal Reserve System was created, we must understand the problems that plagued the U.S. financial system throughout much of the nation's early history. Many of these problems were born in the years prior to the Civil War, when the states, not the federal government, controlled the nation's banking system. Unfortunately, with a few notable exceptions, the states did a poor job. Charters for new banks frequently were awarded by state legislatures and were therefore subject to political lobbying and influence peddling. If a new bank's organizers had the right political connections, a charter could be obtained by individuals with little banking experience and with minimal capital invested in the business.

Deposit banking was not as popular then as it is today. Most people preferred hard money (currency and coin) to deposits. As a result, banks made loans simply by printing and issuing their own paper notes, which circulated as currency. Because few controls existed, there was a tendency to issue these notes well beyond the financial strength of the bank making the loan. Frequently, charters were granted to "wildcat banks" that would issue a large quantity of notes and then disappear. Some banks, promising to redeem their notes in gold or silver coin, set up "redemption centers" in locations nearly impossible for the public to reach, such as in the middle of a swamp. Needless to say, there was a high failure rate among these poorly capitalized, ill-managed institutions, resulting in substantial losses to unlucky depositors.

Responding to these problems and also to the tremendous financial strain imposed by the Civil War, Congress passed the National Banking Act in 1863. This act authorized the establishment of federally licensed commercial banks, subject to regulations imposed by a newly created office, the Comptroller of the Currency, a part of the U.S. Treasury Department. Any group of businesspeople could organize a *national bank,* provided they could show that the new bank would be profitable within a reasonable period of time (usually within three years), meet the minimum equity capital requirements imposed by the Comptroller's office, and not endanger the viability of banks already operating in the local area. Under the provisions of the National Banking Act, the chartering of commercial banks was, in the main, removed from the political sphere and made subject to carefully spelled-out rules. At the same time, Congress attempted to drive state-chartered banks into the national banking system by imposing a 10 percent tax on state bank notes. It was argued that most bankers would prefer the more liberal state regulations and avoid applying for national bank charters unless they were forced to do so.

To help finance the Civil War, Congress authorized national banks to issue their own notes as circulating currency. However, these notes had to be collateralized by U.S. government securities. Under the terms of the National Banking Act, federally chartered banks could issue notes up to 90 percent of the value of Treasury securities they deposited with the Comptroller of the Currency. The result was to create a money medium under federal control to help pay for the Civil War by creating a demand from banks for U.S. government securities.

Even more important, the National Banking Act created a *dual banking system,* with both federal and state authorities having important regulatory powers over commercial banks. Unfortunately, these authorities were given overlapping powers, and in recent years competition between federal and state bank regulatory agencies has sometimes resulted in actions detrimental to the public interest. Moreover, one of the principal aims of the federal program — to drive out state-chartered banks — was *not* achieved. The state banks survived because of the growing popularity of deposit banking. Instead of issuing paper notes, commercial banks increasingly began to make loans by simply creating a deposit on their books in the borrower's name — the practice followed today. Acceptance by the public of deposits instead of notes led to the disappearance of state bank notes, making the federal government's tax on them ineffective.

Creation of the Federal Reserve System

Several festering problems (including some traceable to the provisions of the National Banking Act) resulted in the creation of the Federal Reserve System. For one thing, the new national bank notes proved to be unresponsive to the nation's growing need for a money or cash medium. The need for money and credit grew rapidly as the United States became more heavily industrialized and the Midwest and Far West opened up to immigration. Farmers and ranchers in these areas demanded an "elastic" supply of money and credit — adequate to their needs at relatively low cost. As we will soon see, the new Federal Reserve System would attempt to deal with this problem by issuing a currency of its own and by exercising closer control over the growth of money and credit.

As deposit banking and the writing of checks became increasingly popular, another serious problem appeared. The process of clearing and collecting checks was too slow and expensive. Then, as now, most checks written by the public were local in character, moving funds from the account of one local customer to that of another. These checks normally are cleared routinely through the local clearinghouse, which is simply a location where representatives of local banks meet daily to exchange bundles of checks drawn on each other's banks. For checks sent outside the local area, however, the collection process is more complicated, with some checks passing through several banks before reaching their final destination.

Before the Federal Reserve System was created, many banks charged a fee (exchange charge) for the clearing and redemption of checks. This fee was usually calculated as a percentage of the par (or face) value of each check. Banks levying the fee were called *no-par* banks because they refused to honor checks at their full face value. To avoid exchange fees, bankers would try to route the checks they received only through banks accepting and redeeming them at par. Often this meant routing a check through scores of banks in distant cities until days or weeks had elapsed before the check was finally cleared. Such a delay was not just annoying, but also served as an impediment to commercial transactions. Exchange charges resulted in needless inefficiency and increased the true cost of business transactions far above their nominal cost. A new national check-clearing system was needed that honored checks at par and moved them swiftly between payee and payer. This responsibility too was given to the Federal Reserve System, which insisted that all checks cleared through its system be honored at full face (par) value.

A third problem with the banking and financial system of that time was recurring liquidity crises. Then, as now, money and bank reserves tended to concentrate in leading financial centers, such as New York City or San Francisco, where the greatest need for loanable funds existed. Bank reserves flowed into the major cities as smaller banks in outlying areas deposited their reserves with larger banking institutions to earn greater returns. However, when the pressures for agricultural credit increased in rural areas, many country banks had to sell securities and call in their loans to city banks in the nation's financial centers to come up with the necessary funds. Thus, when the reserve demands of country banks were larger than expected, security prices in leading financial centers plummeted due to massive sell-offs of bank-held securities. Panic selling by other investors soon followed, leading to chaos in the marketplace.

The banking system clearly needed a lender of ready cash to provide liquidity to those banks with heavy cash drains and to protect the stability of the financial system. A serious financial panic in 1907 finally led to the creation of the Federal Reserve System. In 1908, Congress created the National Monetary Commission to study the financial needs of the nation. The commission's recommendations were forwarded to Congress and ultimately resulted in passage of the Federal Reserve Act, signed into law by President Wilson in December 1913. The Federal Reserve banks opened for business as World War I began in Europe.

The Early Structure of the Federal Reserve System

The first Federal Reserve System was quite different from the Fed of today. The original Federal Reserve Act reflected a mix of diverse viewpoints: an effort to reconcile competing political and economic interests. There was great fear that the Fed would have too much control over financial affairs and operate against the best interest of important segments of U.S. society. For example, small businesses, consumer groups, and farmers were concerned that the Fed might pursue restrictive credit policies, leading to high interest rates. In addition, it was recognized that the Federal Reserve would become a major financial institution wherever it was located. Any city that housed a Federal Reserve bank was likely to become a major financial center.

Responding to these various needs and interest groups, Congress created a truly "decentralized" central bank. Not 1 but 12 Federal Reserve banks were chartered, stretching across the continental United States. Each Reserve bank was assigned its own district, over which it possessed important regulatory powers. A supervisory board of seven members was set up in Washington, D.C., to promote a common monetary policy for the nation. In fact, however, the regional Federal Reserve banks possessed the essential monetary tools and made the key policy decisions during the Fed's early years.

Goals and Policy Tools of the Federal Reserve System

To deal with the financial problems of that day, the Federal Reserve Act permitted each regional Reserve bank to open a *discount window* where eligible banks could borrow reserves for short periods of time. However, borrowing banks were required to present high-quality, short-term business loans (commercial paper) to secure the loans they needed. The Fed's chief policy tool of the day was the *discount rate* charged on these loans, with each Reserve bank having the authority to set its own discount rate. By varying this rate, the Reserve banks could encourage or discourage banks' propensity to discount commercial paper and borrow reserves. Central bankers could promote easy or tight credit conditions and influence the overall volume of bank loans.

The Federal Reserve banks were given authority to issue their own paper notes to serve as a circulating currency, but these notes had to be 100 percent backed by Fed holdings of commercial paper, plus a 40 percent gold reserve. Almost as an afterthought, Congress authorized the Reserve banks to trade U.S. government securities in the open market, known as *open market operations,* the Fed's principal policy tool today. Reserve requirements were imposed on deposits held by member banks of the system, but the Fed could not change these requirements.

Slowly but surely, economic, financial, and political forces combined to amend the original Federal Reserve Act and remake the character and methods of the central bank. The leading causes of change were war, economic recessions, and, more recently, persistent inflation. For example, to combat economic recessions, fight wars, and pursue desired programs, the U.S. government issued billions of dollars in debt. As the debt began to grow, it seemed only "logical" to permit greater use of U.S. government securities in

Federal Reserve operations. Banks were authorized to use government securities as backing for loans from the Fed's discount window. The Fed itself was called on to play a major role in stabilizing the market for U.S. government securities to ensure that the Treasury would have little difficulty in refinancing its maturing debt. Government securities were made eligible as collateral for the issue of new Federal Reserve bank notes.

More than any other historical event, however, it was the Great Depression of the 1930s that changed the character of the Federal Reserve. Faced with the collapse of the banking system and unprecedented unemployment — at least a quarter of the U.S. labor force was thrown out of work during the 1930s — Congress entrusted the Fed with sweeping monetary powers as a result of the passage of the Banking Acts of 1933 and 1935. Significant changes also were made in the central bank's operating structure and lines of authority.

The seven-member Board of Governors in Washington, D.C., became the central administrative and policymaking group for the Fed. Thereafter, any changes in discount rates charged by the Reserve banks had to be approved in advance by the Board of Governors. The board was granted authority to set minimum reserve requirements on deposits and maximum interest rates that banks could pay on those deposits. To control speculative buying of stocks, the Reserve Board was empowered to set margin requirements specifying what proportion of a security's market value the investor could borrow to buy that security. Recognizing that open market operations in U.S. government securities were rapidly becoming the Fed's main policy tool, a powerful policymaking body — the Federal Open Market Committee — was created to oversee the conduct of open market operations. In summary, the Great Depression brought about a *concentration of power* within the Federal Reserve System so that the Fed could pursue unified policies and speak with one voice concerning monetary affairs.

HOW THE FED IS ORGANIZED

The Federal Reserve System today has an organizational structure that resembles a *pyramid*. As Exhibit 19–2 shows, the apex of the pyramid is the **Board of Governors,** the Federal Reserve's chief policymaking and administrative group. At the middle level of the pyramid are the Federal Reserve banks, which carry out system policy and provide essential services to banks and other depository financial institutions in their particular regions, and the Federal Open Market Committee. The bottom of the pyramid contains the member banks of the system, which the Fed supervises and regulates, and the manager of the System Open Market Account, who is responsible for buying and selling securities to achieve the goals of Fed monetary policy.

Board of Governors of the Federal Reserve System

The key administrative body within the Federal Reserve System is the Board of Governors. The board consists of seven persons appointed by the president of the United States and confirmed by the Senate for maximum 14-year terms. Terms of office are staggered, with one board member's appointment ending every even-numbered year. When a member of the Federal Reserve Board resigns or dies, the president may appoint a new person to complete the remainder of the unexpired term, and that member may be reappointed to a subsequent full term. However, no member who completes a full term can be reappointed to the Board of Governors. The president designates one member of the board as its chairperson and another as vice chairperson, and both serve four-year terms in those

Exhibit 19–2   **How the Federal Reserve System is Organized**

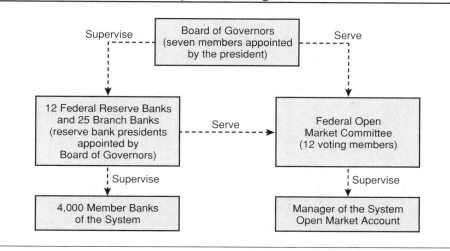

positions. In selecting new board members, the president is required to seek a fair representation of the financial, agricultural, industrial, and commercial interests and geographical divisions of the country and may not choose more than one member from any one Federal Reserve district.

The powers of the Federal Reserve Board are extensive. The board sets reserve requirements on deposits held by depository institutions subject to its rules, reviews and determines the discount rate charged on loans to depository institutions, sets margin requirements on purchases of securities, and provides leadership in the conduct of open market operations through the Federal Open Market Committee. Besides its monetary policy functions, the board supervises the activities of the 12 Reserve banks and has supervisory and regulatory control over member banks of the system. It regulates all bank holding companies, foreign banks entering the United States, and the overseas activities of U.S. banks.

In principle, the board is independent of both legislative and executive branches of the federal government. This independence is supported by terms of office much longer than the president's and by the fact that the Fed does not depend on the U.S. Congress for operating funds. The Federal Reserve supports itself from revenue generated by selling its services (such as clearing checks), making loans through the discount window, and earning interest on government securities the Fed holds. These monies are not retained by the Fed, because it is operated in the public interest and not for profit. All monies left over after expenses, dividends paid to member banks, and minimal allocations to equity reserves are transferred to the U.S. Treasury. For example, in 1995 the Fed reported operating income of $25.4 billion, of which $23.4 billion was paid to the U.S. Treasury, helping to reduce tax collections from the private sector.

The Federal Open Market Committee and Manager of the System Open Market Account

Aside from the Federal Reserve Board, the other key policymaking group within the system is the **Federal Open Market Committee (FOMC).** It has been called the most important committee of individuals in the United States because its decisions concerning the conduct of monetary policy and the cost and availability of credit affect the lives of millions of people. Membership on the FOMC consists of the seven members of the Federal Reserve Board and the presidents or first vice presidents of the Reserve banks. Only the seven members of the Board and five of the Reserve bank presidents or their representatives may vote when a final decision is reached on the future conduct of monetary policy, however. The president of the Federal Reserve Bank of New York is a permanent voting member of the FOMC, the presidents of the Chicago and Cleveland Federal Reserve banks alternate in filling one other voting seat, and the remaining three voting positions on the FOMC are rotated annually among the presidents of the nine remaining Federal Reserve banks. Each Reserve bank representative occupying a rotating seat serves a voting term of one year.

By tradition, the chairperson of the Federal Reserve Board and the president of the New York Federal Reserve bank serve as chairperson and vice chairperson of the FOMC. The law stipulates that the FOMC will meet in Washington, D.C., at least four times a year. In practice, however, the committee meets about eight times a year and more frequently if emergencies develop. Between regularly scheduled meetings, telephone conferences may occur, and the members of the FOMC may be asked to cast votes by telephone or telegram. FOMC meetings are *not* open to the public because confidential financial information frequently is discussed and also because the Fed wants to avoid sending false signals to the financial marketplace. Only Federal Reserve Board members, selected board staff, the Reserve bank presidents and their aides, and the manager and deputy manager of the System Open Market Account are permitted to attend FOMC meetings.

The name Federal Open Market Committee implies that this committee's sole concern is with the conduct of Federal Reserve open market operations in securities, a power granted to it by the Banking Act of 1935. In fact, the FOMC reviews current economic and financial conditions and considers *all* aspects of monetary policy at its meetings. It also directs Fed operations in the foreign exchange markets. Once a consensus is reached concerning the appropriate future course for monetary policy, a directive is given to the manager of the System Open Market Account (SOMA), who is a vice president of the Federal Reserve Bank of New York. The SOMA manager is told in general terms how open market operations should be conducted in the weeks ahead and what the FOMC's targets for money supply growth and interest rates are. Decisions made by the FOMC and actions of the SOMA manager at the securities trading desk in New York are binding on the entire Federal Reserve System.

The Federal Reserve Banks

When the Federal Reserve System was created in 1913, the nation was divided into 12 districts, with one **Federal Reserve bank** in each district responsible for supervising and providing services to the member banks located there. Reserve banks were established in the cities of Atlanta, Boston, Chicago, Cleveland, Dallas, Kansas City, Minneapolis, New York, Philadelphia, Richmond, San Francisco, and St. Louis. In addition, 24 branches (later expanded to 25) were created to serve particular regions within each of the 12 districts.

Using computers and high-speed sorting machines, the regional Reserve banks route checks and other cash items drawn on financial institutions in one city and deposited in another city back to the institutions on which they were drawn for proper crediting of the amounts involved. Although the Fed processes only about 40 percent of all checks written in the United States, it still handles billions of checks and other paper items that reflect billions of transactions carried out by businesses and individuals each year. The Federal Reserve maintains an electronic network (known as FEDWIRE), which transfers millions of dollars daily in money and securities among banking institutions in the United States. Approximately 30 automated clearinghouses (ACHs) are operated by the Reserve banks and their branches to handle the direct deposit of payrolls, mortgage payments, and other funds transfer requests electronically. The Reserve banks ship currency and coin to banks and other depository institutions at those times when the public needs more pocket money and store excess currency and coin in their vaults when less pocket money is needed.

The Reserve banks serve as the federal government's *fiscal agent*. This involves keeping the financial accounts of the U.S. Treasury and delivering and redeeming U.S. government securities. The Reserve banks also accept deposits for federal income, excise, and unemployment taxes. In addition to serving as the federal government's fiscal agent, the Reserve banks closely supervise the activities of member banks within their districts. They conduct field examinations of all state-chartered member banks and supervise bank holding companies headquartered in their region.

The Reserve banks play a significant role in the conduct of money and credit policy. Each Reserve bank houses a research division to study regional economic and financial developments and conveys this information to the Board of Governors and to the Federal Open Market Committee. Only 5 of the 12 Reserve banks have voting seats on the FOMC, but all 12 Reserve bank presidents or first vice presidents attend FOMC meetings to report on conditions in their region and give their views on the appropriate course for monetary policy. The Reserve banks also administer the discount windows where loans are made to financial institutions in their district.

Each Federal Reserve bank is a corporation chartered by Congress. Officially, the Reserve banks are owned by the member banks of their districts, which select a majority of each bank's board of directors. Each Reserve bank president is nominated by that Reserve bank's board of directors, and the appointment is confirmed or denied by the Federal Reserve Board. Under federal law, the board of directors of each Federal Reserve bank must consist of nine directors, six elected by bankers in the district (with three of these directors representing bankers and three the general public or nonbank interests in the same district) and three directors selected by the Federal Reserve Board. The regional Reserve banks are closely controlled by the Federal Reserve Board, which not only reviews officer appointments but also may remove any officer or director of a Federal Reserve bank and examine, reorganize, or even liquidate a Reserve bank if this appears to be necessary to serve the public interest.

Although under the terms of the original Federal Reserve Act the Reserve banks could set the discount rate on loans to depository institutions, these rate changes must now be approved by the Federal Reserve Board in Washington. The regional banks are required to participate in all open market transactions on behalf of the system. These purchases and sales are centered in the FOMC, but the Reserve banks must provide the securities needed for open market sales and must also take their *pro rata* share of any security purchases the system makes.

The Member Banks of the Federal Reserve System

The **member banks** of the Federal Reserve System consist of national banks, which are required to join the system, and state-chartered banks that agree to conform to the Fed's rules. Today, Federal Reserve member banks constitute a minority of all U.S. banks, about 40 percent of the total. In 1994, there were about 3,200 national banks and just under 1,000 state-chartered banks registered as members of the Federal Reserve System, compared to approximately 6,500 nonmember banks.

INTERNATIONAL FOCUS
The Issue of Central Bank Independence

The issue of central bank independence from governments has become a center of controversy in recent years. In the late 1980s, two studies (Alesina (1988) and Bade and Parkin (1987)) found a significant negative correlation between the inflation rate experienced by leading industrial countries and the degree of independence from the political process enjoyed by their central banks. For example, Germany and Switzerland, whose central banks operate under greater freedom from government control than most other nations, had average annual inflation rates of only about 3.5 percent between 1974 and 1990, while Italy, whose central bank appears to be closely tied to the Italian government, experienced a 12.4 percent annual inflation rate over the same time period. These researchers concluded that economies generally perform better (at least in terms of price stability) in those countries where central banks enjoy greater independence from government and greater freedom from political pressure. After all, central banks control or regulate the nation's money stock and there is often a strong political temptation to overissue money (thereby igniting inflation) in order to jump start a lagging economy or to fund extravagant government programs.

The independence from government control enjoyed by central banks varies widely around the world. In Germany, for example, the Bundesbank Act of 1957 states that the German central bank "shall be independent of instructions from the federal government." Moreover, the Bundesbank is legally obligated to follow the German government's economic policy "only insofar as this does not undermine its assigned task of preserving monetary stability." The money and credit policies of the German Bundesbank are determined by a Central Bank Council, consisting of 10 directors and the presidents of 11 Land Central Banks, representing various regions of the nation. Because each region has input into the Bundesbank's policies and because the members of the Central Bank Council are appointed for long terms of office (lasting up to eight years), the German government's control and influence over the Bundesbank is limited. Similarly, in the United States, members of the Federal Reserve's Board of Governors can serve for up to 14 years, which limits the power of Congress or the president to alter Fed policy in the short run. Moreover, the Federal Reserve does not depend upon Congress for income — it generates its own revenues through security trading and service fees. Nevertheless, the Federal Reserve is ultimately a creature of the U.S. Congress and could undergo drastic changes if a majority of the Congress decided it was unhappy with the Fed's performance.

Government involvement in central bank operations can be extensive even in nations that have had central banks for many years. For example, the Bank of England is the world's oldest central bank, dating from the late 17th Century, but it is subordinated by law to the British Treasury, which can issue directives to the central bank after consultation with its board of governors. Moreover, the British Treasury can borrow by issuing short-term IOUs to the Bank of England without legal limits. Thus, in the event of a serious policy dispute, the British government's economic

(continued)

policy preferences likely would prevail over the Bank of England's policy preferences. The Bank of England's governors and directors are appointed by the Crown, which essentially means they are selected by Britain's prime minister acting on the advice of the Chancellor of the Exchequer, who heads the British Treasury. The Governor and Deputy Governor of the Bank of England serve five-year renewable terms, while its directors serve staggered four-year renewable terms.

In Japan, the Ministry of Finance appears to exert a powerful influence on the Bank of Japan, with whom it works very closely. For example, the Ministry of Finance, not the Bank of Japan, controls bank reserve requirements and can change the central bank's bylaws or order it to take action in order to deal with a policy problem. All seven members of the Bank of Japan's Policy Board are appointed by the Japanese government, and the Ministry of Finance has a nonvoting representative on that board. The Bank of Japan is prohibited from direct purchases of new issues of long-term government securities, but it is not restricted from making short-term cash advances to the government. Moreover, the Japanese central bank, like the central banks of France and New Zealand, most obtain approval from the government for their planned budgetary expenditures. Similarly, in Russia the central bank was under the close control of the Russian parliament for many years, but it recently appears to have come under tight presidential control and shows few signs yet of real independence.

Several bills have been introduced in the U.S. Congress in recent years to restrict the freedom of action of the Federal Reserve System. One proposal would expand the authority of the Government Accounting Office (GAO) to audit *all* phases of Federal Reserve operations, including its dealings with foreign central banks and its monetary policy transactions. Another proposal would require presidential nomination and congressional approval of anyone who wishes to serve as president of a Federal Reserve Bank, thus increasing political control over key decision makers inside the Fed. Some members of Congress seem to believe that Federal Reserve bank presidents are closely tied to "banking interests" in their region, rather than serving the interests of the general public.

Still another proposed change calls for denying Federal Reserve bank presidents any voting seats on the Federal Open Market Committee (FOMC), the Fed's chief policymaking body. Moreover, some members of Congress have recently demanded that the Fed fully and immediately disclose to the public the minutes from all FOMC meetings. There has even been a call for videotaping FOMC meetings as is now done for many Congressional sessions and court trials. Within the last few years, both the Bush and Clinton administrations have proposed stripping the Fed of its bank supervision and examination functions in order to allow it to concentrate on money and credit policy. For its part, the Federal Reserve has argued that these changes would render monetary policy weak and ineffective.

One hopeful trend for the future is a recent movement in Europe, Asia, and North America to further deregulate the financial markets and relax government controls over central banks (most notably in Canada, Japan, and France). Partly as a result of this deregulation trend, central banks around the world are becoming more and more alike in terms of their powers, tools, and institutional settings. There

(continued)

is also a growing emphasis on *price stability* (avoidance of severe inflation) as the main goal of central bank operations — the goal that central banks around the world appear to have the best chance of achieving.

See, in particular, Alberto Alesina, "Macroeconomics and Politics," in *NBER Macroeconomic Annual, 1988* (Cambridge, Mass.: MIT Press, 1988); Robin Bade and Michael Parkin, "Central Bank Laws and Monetary Policy," *Unpublished Mimeograph,* Department of Economics, University of Western Ontario, 1987; and Bruce Kasman, "A Comparison of Monetary Policy Operating Procedures in Six Industrial Countries," *Quarterly Review,* Federal Reserve Bank of New York, Summer 1992, pp. 5–24.

Member banks must subscribe to the stock of the Reserve bank in their district in an amount equal to 6 percent of their paid-in capital and surplus accounts. However, only half this amount must actually be paid, with the rest payable on call. Member banks are bound by Federal Reserve rules regarding capital, deposits, loans, branch operations, formation of holding companies, and policies regarding the conduct of officers and boards of directors. These banks are subject to supervision and examination by the Federal Reserve at any time. Moreover, member banks must hold reserves behind their deposits at levels specified by the Federal Reserve Board.

A number of important privileges are granted to member banks. Legally, they are "owners" of the Federal Reserve banks because they hold the stock of these institutions and elect six of their nine directors. A 6 percent annual dividend is paid to member banks on their holdings of Federal Reserve bank stock. Member banks may borrow reserves through the discount window of the Reserve bank in their district and use the Fed's check-clearing system to process checks coming from distant cities. However, this is not an exclusive privilege, because nonmember banks and thrifts may also use the Fed's check-clearing facilities, provided that they agree to maintain a clearing account with the Reserve bank in the region. An intangible benefit of membership is the prestige that comes from belonging to the Federal Reserve System. Many bankers believe that membership in the system attracts large business deposits and correspondent accounts from smaller banks that otherwise might go elsewhere.

ROLES OF THE FEDERAL RESERVE SYSTEM TODAY

In the course of this chapter, we have talked about the many roles the Federal Reserve plays in the financial system and how these roles have changed over time. In this final section of the chapter, we attempt to pull together all of the Fed's responsibilities and roles to give a more complete view of how the central bank interfaces with the financial markets and the banking system.

The Clearing and Collection of Checks and Other Means of Payment

As we saw earlier in this chapter, one of the earliest tasks of the Federal Reserve System was to establish a nationwide system for clearing and collecting checks. When a depository institution receives a check drawn on another institution in a distant city, it can route this check directly through the Federal Reserve banks. The Fed credits an account called Deferred Availability Items on behalf of the institution sending in the check and routes that check to the institution on which it was drawn for eventual collection. At the end of a specified period, the depository institution sending in the check will receive credit in its legal reserve account for the amount of that check. Eventually, the check reaches the institution on which it was drawn and is deducted from that institution's reserve account.

Issuing Currency and Coin and Providing Other Services

The Fed helps to promote an efficient payments mechanism not just through the clearing of checks but also by issuing its own currency in response to public need. Today, nearly all of the paper money in circulation consists of Federal Reserve notes, issued by all 12 of the Reserve banks and backed mainly by Federal Reserve holdings of government securities. These notes are liabilities of the Federal Reserve bank issuing them. In fact, Federal Reserve notes are a lien against the assets of the Fed, payable to the holder in the event the Reserve banks are ever liquidated. When the public demands more currency, financial institutions request a shipment of new currency and coin from the Federal Reserve bank in the region, which maintains an ample supply in its vault. Payment for the shipment is made simply by charging the legal reserve account of the institution requesting the shipment. In the opposite situation, when depository institutions receive deposits of currency and coin from the public beyond what they wish to hold in their vaults, the surplus is shipped back to the Reserve banks. Depository institutions receive credit for these return shipments through an increase in their legal reserve accounts at the Reserve bank.

Prior to 1981, most Federal Reserve services, including the clearing of checks and shipments of currency and coin, were provided free of charge. However, the Depository Institutions Deregulation and Monetary Control Act (DIDMCA) of 1980 required the Fed to publish a set of pricing principles and to assess fees for such services as transportation of currency and coin, check clearing, wire transfer of funds, the use of Federal Reserve automated clearinghouse facilities, and the safekeeping and redemption of government securities. All fees set by the Fed are to be reviewed annually and set at levels that, over the long term, recover the total costs of providing each service.

Why did the U.S. Congress order the Fed to switch from free services to a fee basis? One reason was the rapid increase in the number of users of Federal Reserve services. DIDMCA of 1980, for the first time in U.S. history, provided for access by all nonmember depository institutions to the Fed's facilities and services, sharply increasing the Fed's operating costs. Second, Congress wanted to encourage as much competition as possible in the provision of these services so that the Fed would not be the only source of supply. (Indeed, the Fed has recently announced that it plans to turn over many of its funds-transfer services eventually to the private sector.) Still another motivating factor was a feared loss of revenue to the U.S. Treasury. All of these developments together would have substantially reduced the Fed's annual net income, most of which flows to the U.S. Treasury, if the central bank had not begun to charge for its services.

Maintaining a Sound Banking and Financial System

Another important function of the Federal Reserve System today is to maintain a sound banking and financial system. It contributes to this goal by serving as a lender of last resort, providing reserves to depository institutions through the discount window of each Reserve bank. The window represents a source of funds that can be drawn on without taking reserves away from other banks, and it helps to avoid a liquidity squeeze brought about by sudden changes in economic and financial conditions. The Fed also promotes a sound banking system by regularly examining member banks, reviewing the quality and quantity of their assets and capital, and making sure that federal and state laws are followed.

Serving as the Federal Government's Fiscal Agent

The Fed serves as the government's chief **fiscal agent.** In this role, it holds the Treasury's checking account and clears any checks written against that account. The Fed supervises the thousands of Treasury Tax and Loan Accounts (TT&L) maintained in banks across the United States, which hold the bulk of the Treasury's cash balances until the Treasury needs these monies for spending. The Fed also makes recurring payments (for example, social security benefits and salary checks for government employees) for the federal government through its electronic network of automated clearing houses. The Federal Reserve banks receive bids when new Treasury securities are offered and provide securities to the purchasers. They redeem maturing U.S. government securities as well. In general, the Fed is responsible for maintaining reasonable stability in the government securities market so that any new Treasury offerings sell quickly and the government raises the amount of money that it needs.

Carrying Out Monetary Policy

The most critical job of the Federal Reserve is to carry out **monetary policy.** Monetary policy may be defined as the use of various tools by the central bank to control the availability of loanable funds in an effort to achieve national economic goals, such as full employment and reasonable price stability. The policy tools reserved for the Federal Reserve include deposit reserve requirements, discount rates, open market operations, and margin requirements on purchases of securities. We will examine the Fed's policy tools in detail in Chapter 20.

Providing Information to the Public

Another critical function that the Federal Reserve has performed particularly well in recent years is to provide information to the public. Each Reserve bank has its own research staff, and the Board of Governors maintains a large staff of economists who follow current economic and financial developments and recommend changes in policy. The Fed makes available on a daily, weekly, and monthly basis an impressive volume of statistical releases, special reports, and studies concerning the financial markets and the condition of the economy. This information function is often overlooked in discussions of the Federal Reserve's role within the financial system, but it is one of the more important contributions of the central bank.

SUMMARY

In this chapter, we have examined the important roles played by central banks in the financial system and the economy. Central banks must function to control the money supply, maintain stable conditions in the financial markets, serve as a lender of last resort to aid financial institutions in trouble, and maintain and improve the mechanism for making payments for goods and services. In most industrialized countries, central banking is goal oriented, aimed principally at the major economic goals of full employment, reasonable price stability, sustainable economic growth, and a strong and stable balance-of-payments position with the rest of the world. In the Western world, central banks operate mainly through the marketplace, influencing credit conditions but leaving to private borrowers and lenders the basic decisions of whether to create credit, borrow, and spend.

Although there is much disagreement today as to how central banks influence the economy through their actions, economists generally agree that these institutions affect the spending, saving, and borrowing decisions of millions of individuals and businesses through at least five interrelated channels. Central bank policies influence the cost and availability of credit, the volume and rate of growth of the money supply, the market value of securities held by the public, the relative prices (exchange rates) of world currencies, and the public's expectations regarding domestic and international economic and financial conditions. Each of these policy channels ultimately affects the borrowing, consumption, and investment spending decisions of businesses, consumers, and governments all over the globe.

The central bank of the United States is the Federal Reserve System, which, compared to other central banks, has a unique organizational structure. The main administrative body within the Federal Reserve System is the Board of Governors, composed of seven persons appointed by the president of the United States and headquartered in Washington, D.C. The Federal Reserve Board controls such important policy tools as deposit reserve requirements, margin requirements on stock, and changes in the discount rate on loans to deposit-type financial institutions. However, the board's authority over the future course of economic policy and the implementation of that policy is shared with other departments within the Federal Reserve System.

For example, the Federal Open Market Committee, composed of the seven members of the Federal Reserve Board and the presidents of the Federal Reserve banks, discusses all major policy initiatives by the Fed and closely controls the system's major policy tool, open market operations. The 12 Federal Reserve banks determine which depository financial institutions can borrow from the Fed and on what terms. These regional Reserve banks also supervise banks and bank holding company activities within their districts and provide important services, including the clearing and collection of checks, shipment of currency and coin, transfer of funds by wire, and the safekeeping of securities. Moreover, each of the Reserve banks serves as the federal government's fiscal agent, dispensing and collecting government funds, selling and redeeming government securities, and helping to maintain orderly market conditions so that the federal government can borrow and refinance its debt.

Each part of the Federal Reserve System, therefore, has a key role to play in the operation of the financial system and the functioning of the economy. In the next two chapters, we explore more fully what is generally considered the Federal Reserve's most important job, *monetary policy* — the regulation of money and credit conditions in order to achieve major economic goals. ∎

KEY TERMS AND CONCEPTS IN THIS CHAPTER

central bank	Federal Open Market Committee (FOMC)	member banks
Federal Reserve System		fiscal agent
Board of Governors	Federal Reserve bank	monetary policy

STUDY QUESTIONS

1. What functions do central banks perform in a market-oriented economy? Explain why each is important to the efficient functioning of the financial and economic system.

2. What are the principal goals of the Federal Reserve System in its pursuit of monetary policy? To what extent are these goals consistent or inconsistent with each other?

3. What major problems in the late 19th and early 20th centuries led to the creation of the Federal Reserve System? How did the creation of the Fed help to solve these problems?

4. In what ways did the early Federal Reserve System differ from the Fed of today?

5. List the principal functions of the Federal Reserve System today and explain why each is important.

6. What are the principal responsibilities assigned to
   a. The Board of Governors of the Federal Reserve System?
   b. The Federal Open Market Committee?
   c. The Federal Reserve banks?
   d. The manager of the System Open Market Account?

SELECTED REFERENCES

Board of Governors of the Federal Reserve System. *The Federal Reserve and the Payments System,* rev. ed. Washington, D.C., 1990.

Carlson, Keith M. "Money, Inflation, and Economic Growth: Some Updated Reduced Form Results and Their Implications." *Review.* Federal Reserve Bank of St. Louis, April 1980.

Faust, Jon. *Whom Can We Trust to Run the Fed? Theoretical Support for the Founders' Views.* International Finance Discussion Papers, K. 7. Board of Governors of the Federal Reserve System, April 1992.

Froyen, Richard T., and Roger N. Waud. "Central Bank Independence and the Output-Inflation Tradeoff." *Journal of Economics and Business,* 47 (1995), pp. 137–149.

Manypenny, Gerald D., and Michael L. Bermudez. "The Federal Reserve Banks as Fiscal Agents and Depositories of the United States." *Federal Reserve Bulletin,* October 1992, pp. 727–742.

Mauskopf, Eileen. "The Transmission Channels of Monetary Policy: How Have They Changed?" *Federal Reserve Bulletin,* December 1990, pp. 985–1008.

Chapter 20

The Tools of Monetary Policy

LEARNING OBJECTIVES IN THIS CHAPTER

- To examine the tools available to the U.S. central bank, the Federal Reserve System, to control the growth of money and credit in the economy.
- To understand the concept of legal reserves and how actions taken by the Federal Reserve influence the level and growth of legal reserves.
- To compare the strengths and weaknesses of each of the Federal Reserve's policy tools — reserve requirements, the discount rate, open market operations, moral suasion, and margin requirements.

As we discussed in the preceding chapter, the Federal Reserve System has been given the task of regulating the money and credit system of the United States to achieve national economic goals. Prominent among these goals are the achievement of full employment, a stable price level, sustainable economic growth, and a stable balance-of-payments position with the rest of the world. As recent experience has demonstrated, these objectives are not easy to achieve and frequently conflict. Still, the central bank has powerful policy tools at its disposal with which to pursue these economic goals. Our purpose in this chapter is to examine the policy tools available to the Federal Reserve in carrying out its task of controlling the supply of money and credit.

RESERVES AND MONEY — TARGETS OF FEDERAL RESERVE POLICY

The principal immediate target of Federal Reserve policy is the *reserves of the banking system,* consisting mainly of deposits held at the Federal Reserve banks plus currency and coin held in bank vaults. These reserves are the raw material out of which banks and other depository institutions create credit and cause the money supply to grow. And because the growth of the money supply is closely linked to changes in income, production, prices, and employment, the Fed pays close attention on a daily basis to fluctuations in the quantity of reserves that depository institutions have at their disposal. The total supply of reserves can be changed directly by Federal Reserve's open market operations and by making loans to depository institutions through the Fed's discount window. The Fed can also exert a powerful effect on the growth of money and credit by changing the legal reserve requirements applicable to deposits held by depository institutions.

Although the Fed's primary concern is the volume and rate of growth of reserves held by depository institutions, all of its policy tools have an impact on *interest rates* as well. When the supply of reserves is reduced relative to the demand for reserves, interest rates tend to rise as scarce funds are rationed among competing financial institutions. Conversely, an expansion in the supply of reserves usually leads to lower interest rates because of the increased availability of loanable funds. Why do these changes occur? What are the specific links between bank reserves and the money supply?

THE COMPOSITION OF RESERVES

To answer the preceding questions, we need to look closely at what makes up the supply of reserves at depository institutions. We recall from Chapters 4 and 16 that all U.S. depository institutions offering selected kinds of deposits are required to hold a small percentage of those deposits in an asset account known as **legal reserves.** Legal reserves consist of the amount of deposits each institution keeps with the Federal Reserve bank in its district plus the amount of currency and coin held in its vault.

We noted in Chapter 4 that legal reserves may be divided into two parts: required reserves and excess reserves. In particular,

$$
\begin{aligned}
\text{Total legal reserves} &= \text{Required reserves} + \text{Excess reserves} \\
&= \text{Deposits at the Federal Reserve banks} + \\
&\quad \text{Vault cash held on the premises of depository} \\
&\quad \text{institutions}
\end{aligned} \tag{20-1}
$$

Required reserves are those holdings of cash and deposits at the Fed that a depository institution *must* hold to back the public's deposits. **Excess reserves** are the amount of reserves left over after we deduct required reserves from total legal reserves. Excess reserves may be used to make loans, purchase securities, or for other purposes. Because legal reserve assets earn little or no income, most depository institutions try to keep their excess reserves close to zero. For example, the largest banks today frequently run reserve deficits and must borrow additional legal reserves in the money market to avoid costly penalties.

The Deposit Multiplier

The distinction between excess and required reserves is important because it plays a key role in the growth of money and credit in the economy. As we observed in Chapter 4, depository institutions offering checkable deposits have the unique ability to create and destroy deposits — which are the bulk of the money supply — at the stroke of a pen. Although an individual depository institution cannot create more deposit money than the volume of excess reserves it holds, the banking system as a whole can create a multiple amount of deposit money from any given injection of reserves by using its excess reserves to make loans and purchase securities.

How much deposit money can the banking system create if it has excess reserves available? The banking system's deposit-creating potential can be estimated using a concept known as the **deposit multiplier,** or coefficient of deposit expansion. The deposit multiplier indicates how many dollars of deposits (and loans) will result from any given injection of new excess reserves into the system. If we assume the existence of a very simple financial system in which the public makes all of its payments by check and does not convert any checkbook (transaction deposit) money into savings deposits and in which depository institutions do not wish to hold any excess reserves but rather loan out immediately all the funds they receive, then the transaction deposit multiplier, or coefficient of deposit expansion, is

$$\frac{1}{\text{Reserve requirement on transaction deposits}} \qquad (20\text{–}2)$$

For example, if the Federal Reserve insists that depository institutions keep $0.12 in required reserves for each new dollar of transaction (checkbook) deposits they receive, the deposit multiplier must be 1/0.12, or 8.33.

Then how much in new deposit money can the banking system create under these circumstances? If all depository institutions continually make loans with any excess reserves they receive, the maximum amount of new deposits (and loans) that can be created by the entire banking system may be found from the following equation:

$$\text{Transaction deposit multiplier} \times \text{Excess reserves} \\ = \text{Maximum volume of new deposits and loans} \qquad (20\text{–}3)$$

If banks and other depository institutions receive additional excess reserves in the amount of $1 million and the reserve requirement behind transaction deposits is 12 percent, we have the following:

$$1/0.12 \times \$1 \text{ million} = 8.33 \times \$1 \text{ million}$$
$$= \$8.33 \text{ million in new deposits and loans}$$

A *withdrawal* of reserves from depository institutions can work in the opposite direction, destroying deposits and loans. For example, a withdrawal of deposits by the public that causes depository institutions to have a $1 million deficiency in their required reserves would eventually lead to an $8.33 million *decline* in deposits, assuming a 12 percent reserve requirement.

Of course, the real world is quite different from the simple deposit expansion model outlined above. Leakages of funds from the banking system greatly reduce the size of the deposit multiplier, so that its actual value is probably somewhat less than 2. Among the most important leakages are the public's desire to convert some portion of new checkbook money into pocket money (currency and coin) or into savings deposits, and the presence of unutilized lending capacity. Banks may choose to hold substantial excess reserves and not lend out all their excess funds because they cannot find enough qualified borrowers or wish to hold a protective "cushion" of reserves.

These various leakages of funds from transaction balances suggest the need for a slightly more complex model of the deposit and loan expansion process. In this model, the deposit multiplier would be represented by the following expression:

Transaction deposit multiplier assuming drains of funds into cash, time and savings deposits, and excess reserves

$$= \frac{1}{RR_D + CASH + EXR + (RR_T \times TIME)} \qquad (20\text{–}4)$$

In this instance, RR_D represents the required legal reserve ratio for transaction (demand) accounts, and RR_T is the required legal reserve ratio for time and savings deposits. *CASH* and *TIME* represent the amounts of additional currency and coin, and time and savings deposits the public wishes to hold for each dollar of new transaction deposits they receive, and *EXR* stands for the quantity of excess reserves depository institutions desire to hold for precautionary purposes out of each dollar of new transaction deposits. The largest amount of transaction deposits and loans that the banking system can create, assuming all of the above drains of funds occur, would be given by:

$$\frac{1}{RR_D + CASH + EXR + (RR_T \times TIME)} \times \text{Excess Reserves} = \begin{array}{l}\text{Maximum}\\ \text{volume of new}\\ \text{deposits and loans}\end{array} \qquad (20\text{--}5)$$

To illustrate the use of this formula, assume that depository institutions have just received an additional $1 million in excess reserves from some source outside the banking system. (One possible source is the Federal Reserve lowering of reserve requirements or buying securities from the public.) We further assume that, for each new dollar of transaction deposits received, the public will convert $0.25 into pocket money ($CASH = 0.25$), and $0.60 will be placed in time and savings deposits ($TIME = .60$). Further, suppose depository institutions elect to hold $0.05 of every new checkable deposit dollar received as excess reserves ($EXR = 0.05$) to protect against future contingencies. The reserve requirement on transaction deposits (RR_D) is assumed to be 10 percent, and on time and savings deposits (RR_T), 3 percent. Thus, the maximum amount of new deposits and loans that depository institutions as a group can create with $1 million in excess reserves is calculated as follows:

$$\frac{1}{0.10 + 0.25 + 0.05 + (0.03 \times 0.60)} \times \$1 \text{ million} = \frac{1}{0.418} \times \$1 \text{ million}$$

$$= 2.39 \times \$1 \text{ million}$$
$$= \$2.39 \text{ million in new deposits and loans}$$

Clearly, the deposit multiplier is far smaller when we allow for the conversion of checkable deposits into currency, coin, and savings deposits and when banks are unwilling to lend all of their excess reserves. This would appear to be good news for the central bank charged with controlling the growth of the money supply. A numerically small deposit multiplier implies that the banking system will not be able to significantly increase the size of the deposit money supply unless the supply of excess reserves is also greatly increased, and the central bank has a potent influence on the quantity of excess reserves available.

Unfortunately the existence of cash drains, time and savings deposits, and other reserve-absorbing factors, while reducing the size of the deposit multiplier, also makes forecasting deposit flows much more difficult. The central bank must be constantly alert to shifts in the public's demand for currency and coin and savings deposits as well as to the changing demands of depository institutions for excess reserves. If the central bank cannot accurately forecast changes in the public's money preferences, control of the money supply will be less precise and subject to erratic fluctuations, so that the achievement of national economic goals will be much more difficult.

The Money Multiplier

Although the concept of the deposit multiplier is useful for some purposes, central bankers are more interested in a related concept known as the **money multiplier,** which defines the relationship between the size of the money supply (including deposits, currency and coin, and other readily spendable funds) and the size of the total reserve base available to depository institutions. The money multiplier is defined as follows:

$$\text{Money multiplier} = \frac{1 + CASH}{RR_D + CASH + EXR + (RR_T \times TIME)} \qquad (20\text{--}6)$$

The terms *CASH, EXR, RR*$_D$*, RR*$_T$*,* and *TIME* are defined as they were in the deposit multiplier formula.

We note than the money multiplier differs from the deposit multiplier only in the addition of *CASH* — the proportion of new transaction deposits the public desires to hold in the form of currency and coin — to the numerator of the multiplier ratio. This change is made because currency and coin held by the public also forms an important component of the money supply and must be accounted for in measuring how fast the money supply grows over time. With the rapid spread of coin-operated machines, the amount of currency and coin outstanding has been growing faster than the volume of regular checking accounts.

Another important point to note about currency and coin is that fluctuations in the volume held by the public have a direct bearing on the reserves held by depository institutions, affecting both the size and rate of growth of demand accounts and reserves. If the public desires to hold less pocket money, the excess currency and coin typically is redeposited in transaction accounts, increasing both reserves and demand deposits. Recognizing this important link between currency and bank reserves, economists have developed the concept of the **monetary base,** which is simply the sum of legal reserves plus the amount of currency and coin held by the public.[1]

Why is the monetary base important? It is one of the principal determinants of the money supply. Specifically,

$$\text{Money multiplier} \times \text{Monetary base} = \text{Money supply} \qquad (20\text{--}7)$$

or,

$$\frac{1 + CASH}{RR_D + CASH + EXR + (RR_T \times TIME)} \times \text{Monetary base} = \text{Money supply}$$

We may use this formula as a device to estimate the size of the money multiplier. For example, in January 1996 the U.S. monetary base was about $435 billion and the sum of transaction deposits (e.g., demand deposits, NOWs, Super NOWs, and travelers checks) and currency and coin outside banks stood at $1,120 billion.[2] The money multiplier, therefore, was as follows:

$$\text{Money multiplier} = \frac{\$1,120 \text{ billion}}{\$435 \text{ billion}} = 2.57$$

On average, each $1 increase in the monetary base resulted in a rise in the U.S. money supply of about $2.57. This is one reason that the monetary base is frequently referred to as *high-powered money;* a change in the base, working through the money multiplier, produces a magnified change in the money supply.

The monetary base-money multiplier relationship identifies the most important factors that explain changes in the money supply, and it also helps us understand how a central bank like the Federal Reserve System can influence the money supply creation process.

---

[1]To be more precise, the Federal Reserve defines the *monetary base* as equal to total reserve balances plus currency and coin held outside the U.S. Treasury, Federal Reserve banks, and the vaults of commercial banks. A closely related measure of more relevance for monetary policy is called the *adjusted monetary base,* which includes all components of the regular (or source) base plus a measure of changes in reserve requirements.

[2]The definition of the money supply used in the formula above is the one labeled M1 by the Federal Reserve System. The Fed has developed several other money supply definitions, which we will examine in Chapter 21. Each concept can be linked directly to the monetary base, provided the components of the money multiplier are altered to reflect the different kinds of deposits or financial assets available to the public under each definition.

The Fed is one of the principal determinants of the size of the monetary base, along with the public and the U.S. Treasury. It can increase or decrease the total supply of reserves to change the size of the base. Alternatively, the Fed may choose merely to offset actions taken by the public or the Treasury to keep the size of the monetary base unchanged. Finally, the central bank can change the required reserve ratios behind transaction (RR_D) and time (RR_T) deposits, which will affect the magnitude of the money multiplier. Occasionally, when the central bank wishes to exert a potent impact on economic and financial conditions, it makes changes in *both* the monetary base and the money multiplier. In the next section, we take a close look at the tools the Federal Reserve System uses to influence the size of the monetary base, the money multiplier, and, ultimately, the money supply.

GENERAL VERSUS SELECTIVE CREDIT CONTROLS

To change the volume of reserves available to depository institutions for lending and investing and to influence interest rates in the economy, the Federal Reserve System uses a variety of policy tools. Some of these tools are **general credit controls,** which affect the entire banking and financial system. Included in this list are reserve requirements, the discount rate, and open market operations. A second set of policy tools may be labeled **selective credit controls** because they affect specific groups or sectors of the financial system. Moral suasion and margin requirements on the purchase of listed securities are examples of selective credit controls.

THE GENERAL CREDIT CONTROLS OF THE FED
Reserve Requirements

Since the 1930s, the Federal Reserve Board has had the power to vary the amount of required legal reserves that member banks must hold behind the deposits they receive from the public. With passage of the Depository Institutions Deregulation and Monetary Control Act (DIDMCA) of 1980, nonmember banks and other depository financial institutions (including credit unions, savings banks, savings and loan associations) were required to conform to the deposit **reserve requirements** set by the Fed. Early in the Fed's history, it was believed that the primary purpose of reserve requirements was to safeguard the public's deposits. Most recently, we have come to realize that their principal use is to give the central bank a powerful tool for emergency situations. Indeed, reserve requirements are probably the most potent policy tool the Federal Reserve System has at its disposal today. However, changes in reserve requirements are a little-used tool, as we will soon see.

Effects of a Change in Deposit Reserve Requirements. A change in deposit reserve requirements has at least *three* different effects on the financial system. First, it *changes the deposit multiplier* (or coefficient of expansion), which affects the amount of deposits and new loans the banking system can create for any given injection of new reserves. A change in reserve requirements also *affects the size of the money multiplier,* influencing the rate of increase in the money supply. If the Fed increases reserve requirements, the deposit multiplier and the money multiplier are *reduced,* slowing the growth of money, deposits, and loans. On the other hand, a decrease in reserve requirements increases the size of both the deposit multiplier and the money multiplier. In this instance, each dollar of additional reserves will lead to accelerated growth in money, deposits, and loans.

Second, a change in reserve requirements affects the *mix* between excess and required legal reserves. Suppose all depository institutions are fully loaned up and excess reserves are zero. If reserve requirements are *reduced,* a portion of what were required reserves now become excess reserves. Depository institutions will soon convert all or a portion of these newly created excess reserves into loans and investments, expanding the money supply. Similarly, if all institutions are fully loaned up, with zero excess reserves, an *increase* in reserve requirements will mean that some depository institutions will be short required legal reserves. These institutions will be forced to sell securities, cut back on loans, and borrow reserves from other financial institutions to meet their reserve requirements. The money supply will grow more slowly and may even decline.

Third, *interest rates* also respond to a change in reserve requirements. A move by the Fed toward higher deposit reserve requirements may soon lead to higher interest rates, particularly in the money market, as depository institutions scramble to cover any reserve deficiencies. Credit becomes less available and more costly. A recent study by Loungani and Rush (1994) finds that higher reserve requirements reduce aggregate investment in the economy, lower real GNP, and reduce business loans made by banks. In contrast, a lowering of reserve requirements tends to bring interest rates down and increase investment spending and incomes. Flush with excess reserves, depository institutions are willing to make more loans at lower interest rates, and fewer institutions will have to sell securities or borrow to meet their reserve requirements.[3]

An Illustration. Exhibit 20–1 illustrates the effects of changes in deposit reserve requirements. Suppose depository institutions are required to keep 10 percent of their deposits in legal reserves; $100 of legal reserves will then be needed to support each $1,000 in deposits. If there is sufficient demand for loanable funds, institutions will probably loan or invest the remaining $900. Suppose that the Federal Reserve increases reserve requirements from 10 to 15 percent. As a result, more legal reserves are necessary to support the same volume of deposits, and institutions have a $50 reserve deficit for each $1,000 of deposits. This deficit may be covered by selling loans or investment securities, borrowing funds, or reducing deposits.

On the other hand, suppose required reserves are lowered from 10 to 8 percent. There now are $20 in excess reserves for each $1,000 in deposits, and that excess can be loaned or invested, creating new deposits. We should note that *total* legal reserves available to the banking system are *not* affected by changes in reserve requirements. A shift in deposit reserve requirements affects only the *mix* of legal reserves between required and excess.

Current Levels of Reserve Requirements. Deposit reserve requirements are imposed by the Federal Reserve Board on all depository institutions that are federally insured or eligible to apply for federal insurance. Under the terms of DIDMCA of 1980, three types of deposits are, potentially at least, subject to legal reserve requirements:

1. *Transaction accounts,* which are deposits used to make payments by negotiable or transferable instruments and include regular checking accounts, NOW accounts, and any account subject to automatic transfers of funds.

[3]However, interest rates do not always move in the directions described above when reserve requirements are changed. Reserve requirements can have a "negative announcement effect" quite contrary to what the Fed has in mind. For example, in February 1992, the Federal Reserve announced that it was lowering reserve requirements on transaction deposits from 12 to 10 percent, but interest rates in the bond market immediately rose, apparently reflecting concern that the Fed might be easing money and credit conditions too quickly, generating inflation.

Exhibit 20–1   **Effects of Changes in Reserve Requirements on Deposits, Loans, and Investments**

With a 10 percent reserve requirement, $100 of reserves is needed to support each $1,000 of deposits.

Commercial Bank

Assets		Liabilities	
Loans and investments	$ 900	Deposits	$1,000
Legal reserves	100		
Required	100		
Excess	0		
	$1,000		$1,000

Increase in reserve requirements:

If required reserves are increased from 10 to 15 percent, more reserves are needed against the same volume of deposits. Any deficiencies (negative excess reserves) must be covered by liquidating loans and investments or by borrowing.

Commercial Bank

Assets		Liabilities	
Legal reserves	$ 100	Deposits	$1,000
Required	150		
Excess	–50		
Loans and investments	900		
	$1,000		$1,000

Decrease in reserve requirements:

If required reserves are reduced from 10 to 8 percent, excess reserves are created which can be loaned to the public or invested in securities.

Commercial Bank

Assets		Liabilities	
Legal reserves	$ 100	Deposits	$1,000
Required	80		
Excess	20		
Loans and investments	900		
	$1,000		$1,000

2. *Nonpersonal time deposits,* which are interest-bearing time deposits (including savings deposits and money market deposit accounts [MMDAs]) held by businesses and governmental units, but not individuals.

3. *Eurocurrency liabilities,* which are borrowings of deposits from banks and branches located outside the United States.

As shown in Exhibit 20–2, the current reserve requirement on transaction accounts of $52 million or less is 3 percent, and the net amount of transaction deposits over $52 million is subject to a 10 percent reserve requirement.[4] Time and savings deposits currently carry *no* reserve requirements, although the Federal Reserve Board could impose new reserve requirements on these deposits at any time. Average reserve requirements usually have

---

[4]The Federal Reserve Board is empowered under DIDMCA to vary reserve requirements on transaction accounts over $52 million between 8 and 14 percent. The $52 million dividing line (known as the *tranche*) is indexed and changes each calendar year by 80 percent of the percentage change in total transaction accounts of all depository institutions during the previous year ended June 30. In addition, the Garn–St Germain Depository Institutions Act of 1982 stipulated that some minimum amount of reservable liabilities (transaction accounts, nonpersonal time deposits, and Eurocurrency liabilities) of each depository institution be subject to a zero reserve requirement, adjusted by the Federal Reserve Board each year by 80 percent of the percentage increase in total reservable liabilities. By 1996, this zero reserve requirement base had been expanded to $4.3 million.

Exhibit 20–2   **Reserve Requirements of Depository Institutions**
(Percent of Deposits)

Type of Deposit and Deposit Interval	Percentage Reserve Requirement	Permissible Statutory Range
Net transaction accounts:		
$0–$52 million	3%	3%
Over $52 million	10	8-14
Nonpersonal time deposits:		
Original maturity of:		
Less than 1½ years	0	0-9
1½ years or more	0	0-9
Eurocurrency liabilities:		
All types	0	None

Note: Required reserves must be held in deposits with the Federal Reserve banks or in vault cash. Nonmember institutions may maintain reserve balances with a Federal Reserve bank indirectly on a pass-through basis with certain approved institutions. Depository institutions subject to reserve requirements include commercial banks, mutual savings banks, savings and loan associations, credit unions, agencies and branch offices of foreign banks, and Edge Act corporations.

Source: Board of Governors of the Federal Reserve System, *Federal Reserve Bulletin,* March 1996, Table 1.15.

been higher on transaction accounts than on time and savings accounts because transaction balances are considered to be less stable than time and savings deposits.

The largest depository institutions, those holding more than $52 million in net transaction balances, carry the heaviest reserve requirements. This is due to the fact that larger financial institutions hold the deposits of thousands of smaller deposit intermediaries. The failure of a large depository institution can send shock waves through the entire financial system and threaten the economic viability of many other institutions as well.

Changes in reserve requirements, can be used to carry out major shifts in government economic policy. The reserve requirement tool is exceedingly powerful, so that even a small change affects hundreds of millions of dollars in legal reserves. Moreover, it is an inflexible tool. Required reserve ratios cannot be changed frequently because this would disrupt the banking system. Not surprisingly, changes in reserve requirements do not occur very often, averaging about once every two years since World War II.

Changes in the Federal Reserve's Discount Rate

Any depository institution that accepts transaction accounts or nonpersonal time deposits may borrow reserves from the discount window of the Federal Reserve bank in its region. The Fed's Regulation A states, however, that these loans must be a *temporary* source of funds. In fact, Federal Reserve regulations require depository institutions to alternate their borrowings from the discount window with drawings from other sources, such as the federal funds market. Frequent borrowing is discouraged and may be penalized with a higher interest rate.[5]

The **discount rate** is the annual percentage interest charge levied against those institutions choosing to borrow from the Fed. The board of directors of each Federal Reserve

---

[5]For a discussion of the use of the Federal Reserve's discount window as a reserve adjustment device for banks and other depository institutions, see Chapter 16.

Exhibit 20–3   **The Discount Rates Charged by the Federal Reserve Banks on Loans to Depository Institutions** (Percent Per Annum)

Type of Loan	Short-Term Adjustment Credit	Seasonal Credit	Extended Credit Borrowing
Discount rates	5.00%	5.20%	5.70%

Note: Credit at a flexible rate somewhat above existing market rates may be extended for longer periods of time after the first 30 days of borrowing when a particular borrowing institution needs support due to exceptional circumstances. Adjustment credit is available on a short-term basis to help depository institutions meet temporary needs for funds that cannot be met through reasonable alternative sources. Seasonal credit is available to help smaller depository institutions meet seasonal needs for funds that cannot be met through other lenders. Extended credit is available when an institution is experiencing difficulties adjusting to changing market conditions over a longer period of time.

Source: Board of Governors of the Federal Reserve System, *Federal Reserve Bulletin,* April 1996, Table 1.14.

bank votes to determine what the discount rate should be in its region of the country. However, the Federal Reserve Board in Washington, D.C., must approve the rate charged in each of the 12 Federal Reserve districts. As shown in Exhibit 20–3, the basic rate on short-term loans of reserves in April 1996 was 5.00 percent. Depository institutions with marked seasonal movements in deposits or those with long-term (extended) liquidity problems could apply for extended credit at rates ranging from 5.20 percent to 5.70 percent, depending on seasonal pressures, how long funds are to be borrowed, and current market conditions.

Borrowing and Repaying Discount Window Loans. Depository institutions that borrow regularly at the discount window keep a signed loan authorization form at the Federal Reserve bank in their district and keep U.S. government securities or other acceptable collateral on deposit there. When a loan is needed, the officer responsible for managing the borrowing institution's legal reserve position contacts the district Federal Reserve bank and requests that the necessary funds be deposited in that institution's reserve account.

In Exhibit 20–4, we illustrate the borrowing process by supposing that a bank has requested a loan of $1 million and the Fed has agreed to make the loan. The borrowing bank receives an increase in its account, Reserves Held at Federal Reserve Bank, of $1 million. At the same time, the bank's liability account, Bills Payable, increases by $1 million. On the Federal Reserve bank's balance sheet, the loan is entered as an increase in Bank Reserves of $1 million — a liability of the Federal Reserve System — and also as an increase in a Fed asset account, Discounts and Advances. When the loan is repaid, the transaction is reversed.

Quite clearly, borrowings from the Fed's discount window *increase* the total reserves available to the banking system. Repayments of those borrowings cause total reserves to fall.

Effects of a Discount Rate Change. Most observers today believe that at least *three* effects follow from a change in the Federal Reserve's discount rate. One is the *cost effect*. An increase in the discount rate means that it is more costly to borrow reserves from the Federal Reserve than to use some other source of funds. Other things being equal, loans from the discount window and the total volume of borrowed reserves will decline. Conversely, a lower discount rate should result in an acceleration of borrowing from the Federal Reserve and more reserves flowing into the banking system.

Of course, the strength of the cost effect depends on the spread between the discount rate and other money market interest rates. If the Fed's rate remains below other interest

Exhibit 20–4   **Borrowing and Repaying Loans from the Fed's Discount Window**

Borrowing from a Federal Reserve Bank:

Federal Reserve		Commercial Bank or Other Depository Institution	
Assets	*Liabilities*	*Assets*	*Liabilities*
Discounts and advances +$1 million	Bank reserves +$1 million	Reserves held at Federal Reserve bank +$1 million	Bills payable +$1 million

Repayment of Borrowings from the Fed:

Federal Reserve		Commercial Bank or Other Depository Institution	
Assets	*Liabilities*		
Discounts and advances −$1 million	Bank reserves −$1 million	Reserves held at Federal Reserve bank −$1 million	Bills payable −$1 million

rates even after it is increased, then it would still be cheaper to draw on the Fed for funds. There would be little reduction in loans from the discount window. This has happened frequently in recent years, with the discount rate usually lagging well behind other interest rates in the money market.

A second consequence of changes in the discount rate is called the *substitution effect*. A change in the discount rate usually causes other interest rates to change as well. This is due to the fact that the Federal Reserve is one source of borrowed reserves, but it is certainly not the only source. An increase in the discount rate, for example, makes borrowing from the Fed less attractive, but borrowing from other sources, such as the Eurodollar market, becomes relatively more attractive. Banks and other borrowers will shift their attention to these other markets, causing interest rates there to rise as well.

A lowering of the discount rate, on the other hand, frequently causes a downward movement in market interest rates. This happens because deposit-type financial institutions will begin borrowing more from the Federal Reserve, reducing the demand for credit in other segments of the financial marketplace.

The final effect of a discount rate change is called the *announcement effect*. The discount rate has a psychological impact on the financial markets because the Fed's rate is widely regarded as an indicator of monetary policy. If, for example, the Federal Reserve raises the discount rate, many observers regard this as a signal that the Fed is pushing for tighter credit conditions. Market participants may respond by reducing their borrowings and curtailing their spending plans.

Unfortunately, the psychological impact of the discount rate may work *against* the Fed as well as *for* it. It is quite likely, for example, that if the Federal Reserve raises the discount rate, borrowers will respond by accelerating their borrowings in an effort to secure the credit they need before interest rates move even higher. Such an action would thwart the Fed's objective of slowing the growth of borrowing and spending. Because of the possibility of *negative psychological effects*, the discount rate is changed infrequently and often lags behind interest rates in the open market. The Fed, however, must often make a technical adjustment in the discount rate just to bring it closer into line with other interest rates. Even so, market participants may "read into" discount rate changes a new Fed policy position.

Open Market Operations

The limitations of the discount rate and reserve requirement policy tools have led the Federal Reserve (and many other central banks as well) to rely more heavily in recent years on **open market operations** to accomplish its goals. By definition, open market operations consist of buying and selling U.S. government and other securities by the Federal Reserve System to affect the quantity and growth of legal reserves and, ultimately, general credit conditions. Open market operations are the most flexible policy tool available to the Fed, suitable for fine-tuning the financial markets when this is necessary.

Effects of Open Market Operations on Interest Rates. The open market tool has two major effects on the banking system and credit conditions. First, it has an *interest rate effect,* because the Fed usually buys or sells a large quantity (several hundred million dollars worth) of securities in the financial marketplace at any one time. If the Fed is *purchasing* securities, this adds additional demand for these securities in the market, which tends to increase their prices and lower their yields. If the Federal Reserve is *selling* securities from its portfolio, this action increases the supply of securities available in the market, tending to depress their prices and raise their yields. The Fed has claimed for many years, however, that its principal objective is not to influence interest rates but to alter the volume of *legal reserves* available to the banking system and, through reserves, the growth of money and credit. Nevertheless, interest rate effects do follow from open market operations.

Effects of Open Market Operations on Reserves. Most authorities agree that the principal day-to-day effect of open market operations is to change the level and growth of *legal reserves.* Generally, a Federal Reserve *purchase* of securities *increases* the reserves of the banking system and expands its ability to make loans and create deposits, increasing the growth of money and credit. In contrast, a *sale* of securities by the Federal Reserve *decreases* the level of growth of reserves and reduces the growth of money and credit. The impact of Federal Reserve open market operations on the reserve positions of depository institutions is illustrated in Exhibit 20–5.

Fed Purchases. In the top portion of Exhibit 20–5, we assume that the Fed is making *purchases* of U.S. government securities in the open market from either depository institutions, which keep their reserve accounts at the Federal Reserve banks, or from other institutions and individuals. In the case of purchases from depository institutions, the Federal Reserve records the acquisition of securities in the System's asset account — U.S. securities — and pays for the securities by increasing the reserve account of the selling institution. Thus, reserves of depository institutions at the Fed *rise,* while institutional holdings of securities fall by the same amount. Note that *both* total and excess reserves rise in the wake of a Fed purchase, assuming that depository institutions have no reserve deficiencies to begin with. With these extra reserves, additional loans can be made and deposits created that will have an expansionary impact on the availability of credit in the economy.

An expansionary effect also takes place when the Federal Reserve buys securities from an institution or individual other than a depository institution. Legal reserves

Exhibit 20–5   **Federal Reserve Open Market Operations**

The Fed Buys Securities

Open Market Purchase from a Bank or Other Deposit-Type Financial Institution:

Depository Financial Institution		Federal Reserve Bank		Effects
Assets	*Liabilities*	*Assets*	*Liabilities*	Total and excess legal reserves increase.
U.S. securities −1,000		U.S. securities +1,000	Reserves +1,000	
Reserves at Fed +1,000				

Open Market Purchase not from a Depository Financial Institution.

Depository Financial Institution		Federal Reserve Bank		Effects
Assets	*Liabilities*	*Assets*	*Liabilities*	Total and excess legal reserves increase. Deposits increase.
Reserves at Fed +1,000	Deposits +1,000	U.S. securities +1,000	Reserves +1,000	

The Fed Sells Securities

Open Market Sale to a Bank or Other Deposit-Type Financial Institution:

Depository Financial Institution		Federal Reserve Bank		Effects
Assets	*Liabilities*	*Assets*	*Liabilities*	Total and excess legal reserves decrease.
U.S. securities +1,000		U.S. securities −1,000	Reserves −1,000	
Reserves at Fed −1,000				

Open Market Sale not to a Depository Financial Institution:

Depository Financial Institution		Federal Reserve Bank		Effects
Assets	*Liabilities*	*Assets*	*Liabilities*	Total and excess legal reserves decrease. Deposits decrease.
Reserves at Fed −1,000	Deposits −1,000	U.S. securities −1,000	Reserves −1,000	

increase, but total deposits — a component of the money supply — increase as well. Deposits rise because the Fed issues a check to pay for the securities it purchases, and that check will be deposited in some financial institution. Excess reserves rise, making possible an expansion of deposits and loans on the part of depository institutions. Note, however, that the rise in excess reserves is *less* in this case than would occur if the Fed bought securities only from depository institutions that maintain reserve accounts with the Federal Reserve banks. This is due to the fact that some of the new legal reserves created by the Fed purchase must be pledged as required reserves behind the newly created deposits. Therefore, Federal Reserve open market purchases of securities have *less* of an effect on total credit and deposit expansion if the Fed's transaction involves only nondeposit financial institutions and individuals.

Fed Sales. Federal Reserve *sales* of securities reduce the growth of reserves, deposits, and loans. As shown in the bottom half of Exhibit 20–5, when the Fed sells U.S. government securities from its portfolio to a depository institution, that institution must pay for those securities by letting the Fed deduct the amount of the purchase from its reserve account. Both total reserves and excess reserves *fall.* If deposit institutions were fully loaned up with no excess reserves available, the open market sale would result in a reserve deficiency. Some institutions would be forced to sell loans and securities or borrow funds, reducing the availability of credit.

The Federal Reserve may also sell securities to an individual or a nondeposit institution. As Exhibit 20–5 reveals, in this instance, *both* reserves and deposits fall. Credit becomes less available and usually more expensive.

How Open Market Operations Are Conducted. All trading in securities by the Federal Reserve is carried out through the System's Trading Desk, located at the Federal Reserve Bank of New York. The Trading Desk is supervised by the manager of the System Open Market Account (SOMA), a vice president of the New York Fed. The SOMA manager's activities are, in turn, supervised and directed by the Federal Open Market Committee. All Fed security purchases and sales are made through a select list of primary U.S. government securities dealers who agree to buy or sell in amounts called for by the Trading Desk at the time the Fed wishes to trade. Many of these dealers are commercial banks that have securities departments. The rest are exclusively dealers in U.S. government and selected private securities.[6]

The Policy Directive. How does the SOMA manager decide whether or not to buy or sell securities in the open market on a given day? The manager is guided, first of all, by a *policy directive* issued to the Federal Reserve Bank of New York following the conclusion of each meeting of the Federal Open Market Committee (FOMC). The SOMA manager attends each FOMC meeting and participates in its policy discussions. He or she listens to the views of each member of the Federal Reserve Board and the Reserve bank presidents, who describe economic conditions in their region of the country. The manager also receives the benefit of a presentation by staff economists of the Federal Reserve Board that analyzes current economic and financial developments.

An example of a recent Federal Reserve policy directive to the SOMA manager is shown in Exhibit 20–6. This directive summarizes the Federal Reserve's view of current economic developments, particularly those that pertain to the growth of output in the economy and to movements in prices and employment. In line with the Fed's concern over international affairs, especially the value of the dollar in international markets, the directive also contains a synopsis of recent developments in the international money market.

Prominently mentioned in every directive are the *monetary aggregates* — M1, M2, and M3 — all measures of the money supply.[7] The FOMC usually sets target ranges for growth in the money supply and asks the SOMA manager to use the open market policy tool in an effort to achieve those targeted growth rates. In addition, a target range for a key money market interest rate — the average rate on federal funds loans — also is specified. In the event that rates of growth in the money supply or the federal funds rate drift outside these ranges, the SOMA manager must notify the chairperson of the Federal Reserve Board for further instructions.

We note that the directive issued to the SOMA manager is extremely *general* in nature, giving specific targets or target ranges but recognizing the need for flexibility as market conditions change. This is a reflection of the crude state of the art in trying to control credit

---

[6]See Chapter 15 for a full discussion of the characteristics and activities of primary dealers.

[7]These and other money supply measures are discussed in Chapter 21.

Exhibit 20–6   **Domestic Policy Directive Issued to the Federal Reserve Bank of New York Following the Federal Open Market Committee Meetings, August 22, 1995**

At the conclusion of the meeting, the Federal Reserve Bank of New York was authorized and directed, until instructed otherwise by the Committee, to execute transactions in the System Account in accordance with the following domestic policy directive:

The information reviewed at this meeting suggests a strengthening in the expansion of economic activity in the current quarter from the weak second-quarter pace. Nonfarm payroll employment increased in June and July after declining in May; the advance was held down by continuing employment losses in manufacturing. The civilian unemployment rate in July was at its second-quarter average of 5.7 percent. Industrial production changed little in recent months after falling earlier while capacity utilization was down somewhat further. Total retail sales have risen appreciably on balance since early spring, but they edged down in July, reflecting weakness in motor vehicles. Housing starts were up sharply in July after changing little in previous months. Orders for nondefense capital goods still point to considerable further expansion of spending on business equipment over coming months; nonresidential construction has continued to trend appreciably higher. The nominal deficit on U.S. trade in goods and services widened in the second quarter from its average rate in the first quarter. After increasing at elevated rates in the early part of the year, consumer and producer prices have risen more slowly in recent months. Advances in labor compensation costs have remained subdued.

Short-term interest rates have posted mixed changes since the Committee meeting on July 5–6, while intermediate- and long-term rates have risen appreciably. In foreign exchange markets, the trade-weighted value of the dollar in terms of the other G-10 currencies appreciated substantially over the intermeeting period, with the gain occurring since the beginning of August.

M2 and M3 continued to register sizable increases in July and appeared to be expanding considerably further in August. For the year through July, M2 expanded at a rate in the upper half of its range for 1995 and M3 grew at a rate above its upwardly revised range. Total domestic nonfinancial debt has grown at a rate in the upper half of its monitoring range in recent months.

The Federal Open Market Committee seeks monetary and financial conditions that will foster price stability and promote sustainable growth in output. In furtherance of these objectives, the Committee at its meeting in July reaffirmed the range it had established on January 31–February 1 for growth of M2 of 1 to 5 percent, measured from the fourth quarter of 1994 to the fourth quarter of 1995. The Committee also retained the monitoring range of 3 to 7 percent for the year that it had set for growth of total domestic nonfinancial debt. The Committee raised the 1995 range for M3 to 2 to 6 percent as a technical adjustment to take account of changing intermediation patterns. For 1996, the Committee established on a tentative basis the same ranges as in 1995 for growth of the monetary aggregates and debt, measured from the fourth quarter of 1995 to the fourth quarter of 1996. The behavior of the monetary aggregates will continue to be evaluated in the light of progress toward price level stability, movements in their velocities, and developments in the economy and financial markets.

In the implementation of policy for the immediate future, the Committee seeks to maintain the existing degree of pressure on reserve positions. In the context of the Committee's long-run objectives for price stability and sustainable economic growth, and giving careful consideration to economic, financial, and monetary developments, slightly greater reserve restraint or slightly lesser reserve restraint would be acceptable in the intermeeting period. The contemplated reserve conditions are expected to be consistent with more moderate growth in M2 and M3 over coming months.

Votes for this action: Messrs. Greenspan, McDonough, Blinder, Hoenig, Kelley, Lindsey, Melzer, Ms. Minehan, Mr. Moskow, Mses. Phillips and Yellen. Votes against this action: None.

---

market conditions and the money supply. Many factors other than Federal Reserve operations affect interest rates and the money supply. Although the Federal Reserve can have a significant impact on the *direction* of change, it has considerable difficulty in trying to hit specific targets, especially money supply targets. The Federal Open Market Committee must be flexible and trust the SOMA manager's judgment in responding to daily conditions in the money market, which subsequently may be quite different from those anticipated when the FOMC held its last meeting.

The Conference Call. As an added check on the decisions of the SOMA manager, a conference call between staff economists at the Federal Reserve Board, a member of the FOMC, and the SOMA manager is held each day before trading occurs. The SOMA manager updates those sitting in on the conference call on current conditions in the money market and then makes a recommendation on the type and volume of securities to be bought or sold that day. At this point, the conference call participants may make alternative recommendations. Usually, however, the SOMA manager's recommendation is taken and trading proceeds.

Types of Open Market Operations. There are four basic types of Federal Reserve open market operations. (See Exhibit 20–7.) The so-called *straight,* or *outright, transaction* refers to the sale or purchase of securities in which outright title passes to the buyer on a permanent basis. In this case, a permanent change occurs in the level of legal reserves, up or down. Thus, when the Federal Reserve wants to bring about a *once-and-for-all* change in reserves, it tends to use the straight, or outright, type of transaction.

Exhibit 20–7   **Types of Open Market Transactions**

Outright or Straight Open-Market Transaction
(permanent change in the level of reserves held by depository institutions)

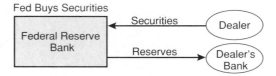

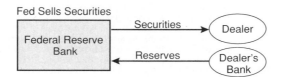

RP or Reverse RP Transaction
(temporary change in the level of reserves held by depository institutions)

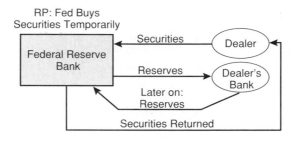

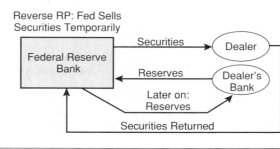

Exhibit 20–7   (Continued)

Run-Off Transaction
(permanent reduction in the level of reserves held by depository institutions)

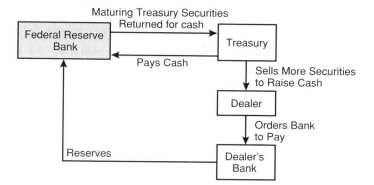

Agency Transaction
(May or may not affect the level of reserves held by depository institutions depending on the type of transaction)

A. First Type of Agency Transaction

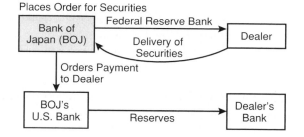

Net Effect: No change in total reserves held by all depository institutions as reserves merely shift from one bank to another; Fed acts only as a broker.

B. Second Type of Agency Transaction

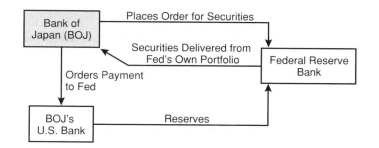

Net Effect: Total reserves of depository institutions fall in this particular transaction as payment for the securities acquired is made to the Fed; Fed acts as a dealer.

In contrast, when the Fed wishes to have a *temporary* effect on bank reserves, it employs a *repurchase agreement* with a securities dealer. Under a repurchase agreement (RP), the Fed buys securities from dealers but agrees to sell them back after a few days.[8] The result is a temporary increase in legal reserves that will be reversed when the Fed sells the securities back to the dealers. Such RPs frequently are used during holiday periods or when other temporary factors are at work that have resulted in a shortfall in reserves.

The Fed can also deal with a temporary excess quantity of reserves by using a matched-sale purchase transaction, commonly called a *reverse RP*. In this instance, the Fed agrees to sell securities to dealers for a brief period and then to buy them back. Frequently, when mail deliveries are slowed by weather or strikes, the result is a sharp increase in the volume of uncollected checks (float), giving banks and other depository institutions millions of dollars in excess reserves until the checks are cleared. The Fed can absorb these excess reserves using reverse RPs until the situation returns to normal.

The third type of open market operation is the *runoff*. The Federal Reserve may deal directly with the U.S. Treasury in acquiring and redeeming securities. Suppose the Fed has some maturing U.S. Treasury securities and wishes to replace them with new securities currently being offered by the Treasury in its latest public auction. The amount of securities that the Fed takes will *not* then be available to the public, reducing the quantity of securities sold in the marketplace. Other things being equal, this would tend to raise security prices and lower interest rates.[9]

On the other hand, the Fed may decide *not* to acquire new securities from the Treasury to replace those that are maturing. This would mean the Treasury would be forced to sell an increased volume of securities in the open market to raise cash in order to pay off the Fed. At the same time, the Treasury would draw funds from its deposits held at private banks, reducing bank reserves, to redeem the Fed's maturing securities. Other things being equal, security prices would fall and interest rates rise. Credit market conditions would tighten up. Moreover, the Federal Reserve saves on transactions costs (in the form of dealer fees) by dealing directly with the Treasury and not conducting a regular open market transaction through security dealers.

Finally, the Fed also conducts purchases and sales of securities on behalf of foreign central banks and other foreign institutions that hold accounts with the New York Federal Reserve Bank, known as *agency operations*. The Fed may buy or sell securities from its own portfolio to accommodate these foreign accounts or merely act as an intermediary between the foreign accounts and security dealers. For example, suppose that the Federal Reserve Bank in New York has just received a request from the Bank of Japan to purchase U.S. government securities. That central bank has probably built up too much cash in its U.S. accounts and decides to earn some interest on that cash by buying some Treasury bonds. To pay for the securities, the Bank of Japan transfers a portion of its deposit at a U.S. bank to its deposit account at the New York Fed. The Fed's Trading Desk may contact private dealers and make the purchase on behalf of the Bank of Japan, crediting the dealers' banks for the purchase price of the securities and reducing the Bank of Japan's Fed deposit. In this case, the total reserves of the U.S. banking system do *not change*. Reserves fall initially but then rise back to their original levels.

However, the Fed may decide to sell the Bank of Japan securities from its *own* portfolio (that is "from System account"). In this case, bank reserves fall initially, as the Bank of

---

[8]See Chapter 15 for an explanation of how these repurchase agreements are used as a source of funds for securities dealers.

[9]The Fed is prohibited by federal law from purchasing government securities directly from the Treasury Department; however, it may replace maturing U.S. Treasury securities with newly issued Treasury securities.

Japan pays for its purchase, but do not rise again. The money received from this Fed sale is "locked up" within the Federal Reserve System and does not flow out to private banks. In general, sales of Federal Reserve-held securities to foreign accounts reduce U.S. bank reserves; purchases of securities from foreign accounts for the Fed's own security account increase U.S. bank reserves.

Goals of Open Market Operations: Defensive and Dynamic. In the use of any of its policy tools, the Federal Reserve always has in mind the basic economic goals of full employment, a stable price level, sustainable economic growth, and a stable international balance-of-payments position for the United States. However, only a portion of the Federal Reserve's daily open market activity is directed toward those particular goals. The Fed is also responsible on a day-to-day basis for stabilizing the money and capital markets and avoiding sharp changes in interest rates to keep the financial markets functioning smoothly. These technical adjustments in market conditions are often referred to as *defensive* open market operations. Their basic purpose is to preserve the status quo and to keep the present pattern of interest rates and credit availability about where it is by keeping reserves of depository institutions steady.

For example, suppose that the Fed believes that the current level of reserves held by the banking system of about $50 billion is just right to hold interest rates and credit conditions where they are. However, due to changes in other factors affecting bank reserves (such as the public demanding more currency and coin from banks to spend over the holidays), total reserves in the system are expected to fall to $49 billion. The Fed is likely to buy about $1 billion in securities so that total reserves remain at $50 billion — a defensive operation.

In contrast, when the Federal Reserve is interested in the pursuit of broader economic goals, it engages in *dynamic* open market operations. These operations are designed to upset the status quo and to change money and credit conditions to a level the Fed believes to be more consistent with its economic goals. For example, if the Fed believes the economy needs to grow faster to create more jobs, it may come to the conclusion that total reserves in the banking system must increase from $50 to $55 billion. In this case, the Fed's trading desk is likely to launch an aggressive program of buying securities until reserve levels reach $55 billion. Open market operations have now become dynamic, not merely defensive.

The fact that open market operations are carried out for a wide variety of purposes makes it difficult to follow the Fed's daily transactions in the marketplace and to draw any firm conclusions about the direction of monetary policy. On any given day, the Fed may be buying or selling securities merely to defensively stabilize market conditions without any longer-term objectives in mind. The central bank is really a balance wheel in the financial system, supplying or subtracting reserves as needed on any given day. Although experienced Fed watchers find the daily pattern of open market operations meaningful, unless the investor possesses inside information on the motivation of Federal Reserve actions, it is exceedingly difficult to "read" daily open market operations. A longer-term view is usually needed to see the direction in which the central bank is trying to move the financial system.

SELECTIVE CREDIT CONTROLS USED BY THE FED

The discount rate, reserve requirements, and open market operations are often called *general credit controls* because each has an impact on the whole financial system. Another set of policy tools available to the Federal Reserve, however, is more *selective* in its impact, focusing on particular sectors of the economy. Nevertheless, use of these selective tools does contribute toward the overall objectives of the Fed to minimize unemployment, stabilize prices, and sustain economic growth.

INTERNATIONAL FOCUS:

Policy Tools Used by Central Banks Around the World

Different central banks around the world emphasize different policy tools. For example, the Bank of England (BOE) relies primarily upon purchases of Treasury and commercial bills from discount houses in the British money market to affect interest rates and the availability of credit. The BOE also may make changes in the basic lending rate that it charges borrowing banks, but the British central bank imposes no official reserve requirements on private banks operating in Great Britain.

The Bank of Canada (BOC) focuses its energies mainly on the buying and selling of short-term Treasury bills and repurchase agreements. The Canadian central bank also impacts reserves in the banking system by moving government deposits between the BOC and private banks within the Canadian system. Canada's central bank phased out its use of deposit reserve requirements in 1994.

The Bundesbank in Germany rediscounts short-term bills and employs repurchase agreements on bonds in order to produce desired credit conditions and desired levels of interest rates. The Bundesbank also sets an official loan rate on its loans to banks and on the sales of government bills. It may use currency swaps and transfers of government deposits between the Bundesbank and private banks to change the level of reserves held by the banking system and, therefore, the capacity of banks to make new loans.

The Bank of Japan (BOJ) uses security trading, primarily in commercial bills but also increasingly in Japanese government securities, to influence domestic credit conditions. The BOJ conducts active daily management of the loans it makes to banks through its discount window. Changes in discount window loans help the BOJ deal with unexpected changes in bank reserve positions. In several other Asian countries — Indonesia, Korea, Taiwan, Hong Kong, and the Phillipines — central banks issue and trade in their own IOUs in order to control money growth and influence economic conditions.

The Swiss National Bank (SNB) uses U.S.-dollar/Swiss-franc currency swaps, made with a few private banks, in order to impact domestic credit conditions and currency prices. The SNB, like the Bundesbank in Germany, may also transfer monies between government deposits that it holds and the government deposits held by private Swiss banks, thus causing reserve levels in the banking system to change.

Central banks do not change their policy tools very often. However, with deregulation of financial markets and financial institutions becoming more common all over the world, more and more central banks are choosing to work through the private marketplace to accomplish their goals, increasingly emphasizing the buying and selling of government and corporate bills or other financial instruments to change or maintain existing credit conditions. Accordingly, such arbitrary, non-market-determined tools as reserve requirements and central bank loan or discount rates are increasingly being de-emphasized or phased out. With the exception of the Bank of Japan, the discount (loan) windows of leading central banks today are more often used to relieve temporary stresses faced by individual financial institutions rather than to achieve broad policy goals.

Moral Suasion by Federal Reserve Officials

A selective policy tool that has been used more frequently in recent years is **moral suasion.** This refers to the use of "arm-twisting" or "jawboning" by central bank officials to encourage banks and other lending institutions to conform with the spirit of its policies. For example, if the Federal Reserve wishes to tighten credit controls and slow the growth of credit, Fed officials issue letters and public statements urging financial institutions to use more restraint in granting loans. These public statements may be supplemented by personal phone calls from top Federal Reserve officials to individual lending institutions, stressing the need for more conservative policies. There is evidence that the Federal Reserve has made greater use of moral suasion in recent years, perhaps (as Kane [1974] argues) because of a perception that its general policy tools have become less effective.

Margin Requirements

A selective credit control still under the exclusive control of the Federal Reserve Board is **margin requirements** on the purchase of stocks and convertible bonds and on short sales of those same securities. Margin requirements were enacted into law with passage of the Securities Exchange Act of 1934. This federal law limited the amount of credit that could be used as collateral for a loan. Regulations G, T, and U of the Federal Reserve Board prescribe a maximum loan value for marginable stocks, convertible bonds, and short sales. That maximum loan value is expressed as a specified percentage of the market value of the securities at the time they are used as loan collateral. The margin requirement on a regulated security, then, is simply the difference between its market value (100 percent) and the maximum loan value of that security.

For example, as shown in Exhibit 20–8, the current margin requirement on stock is 50 percent. This means that common and preferred stock can be purchased on credit with the stock itself used as collateral. However, the purchaser can borrow only up to a maximum of 50 percent of the stock's current market value. He or she must put up the remainder of the stock's purchase price in cash money.

As Exhibit 20–8 suggests, margin requirements are not often changed. The current margin requirements on stocks, convertible bonds, and short sales of these securities have remained unchanged since January 1974. Most observers of the financial markets believe that the imposition of margin requirements was unnecessary. These requirements arose out of the turmoil of the Great Depression, when many believed that speculative buying and selling of stocks had contributed to the economy's sudden collapse. This was probably *not* the case, but margin requirements do ensure that a substantial amount of cash will be

| Exhibit 20–8 | **Federal Reserve Margin Requirements on Stocks, Convertible Bonds, and Short Sales** (Percent of Market Value and Effective Date) |

Security	March 11, 1968	June 8, 1968	May 6, 1970	Dec. 6, 1971	Nov. 24, 1972	Jan. 3, 1974
Margin stocks	70%	80%	65%	55%	65%	50%
Convertible bonds	50	60	50	50	50	50
Short sales	70	80	65	55	65	50

Note: Regulations G, T, and U published by the Board of Governors of the Federal Reserve System, in accordance with the Securities Exchange Act of 1934, limit the amount of credit to purchase or carry margin stocks when the securities to be purchased are used as collateral. Margin requirements specify the maximum loan value of the securities expressed as a percentage of their market value at the time a loan is made.

Source: Board of Governors of the Federal Reserve System, *Federal Reserve Bulletin,* March 1996, Table 1.36.

contributed by the buyer of securities, keeping borrowing against these securities within reasonable limits. One serious limitation of this selective tool is that is does *not* cover purchases of *all* types of stocks and bonds. For this reason, its future use as a tool of Federal Reserve monetary policy is likely to remain very limited.

SUMMARY

The policy tools used by the Federal Reserve System and other central banks affect the quantity and rate of growth of legal reserves in the banking system, which, in turn, have an impact on the capacity of financial institutions to make loans and investments. Central bank policy also influences the level of and direction of change in interest rates. For example, a policy of tight money usually results in higher interest rates and a diminished supply of credit available to borrowers. An easy-money policy is usually accompanied by lower interest rates and an expanded supply of credit available. Working through both interest rates and legal reserves, the Federal Reserve has a direct impact on the size and rate of growth of the money supply. Because changes in the money supply are highly correlated with changes in economic activity, the Fed ultimately influences *both* the level of economic activity and economic growth.

Over the years, the Federal Reserve and other central banks have developed a number of tools for carrying out the objectives of monetary policy. The Fed's primary policy tool is *open market operations*, the buying and selling of securities. Open market operations are used not only to carry out major shifts in policy toward tighter or easier credit conditions (known as *dynamic* operations) but also to make technical adjustments in market conditions to preserve the status quo (known as *defensive* operations). Open market operations are carried out by the Trading Desk of the New York Federal Reserve Bank, subject to policy guidelines set by the Federal Open Market Committee.

When the Federal Reserve wishes to have a quick and powerful impact on the financial system, it may change the amount of legal reserves that depository institutions must hold behind their deposits. However, the impact of reserve requirement changes is so potent that the Fed uses this tool infrequently. A third policy tool — changes in the discount rate charged by Federal Reserve banks on loans made to depository institutions — is also used infrequently. Although this tool affects interest rates in the short run, it has a psychological impact on credit uses that often works against the aims of the Fed. Nevertheless, loans to depository institutions provide an important safety valve for the Federal Reserve in the event that its policies threaten the safety and soundness of individual financial institutions.

Other tools of monetary policy have been used by the Federal Reserve from time to time to carry out its objectives. Through public speeches and testimony before Congress, private letters, and phone calls, called *moral suasion,* the Fed frequently tries to persuade individuals and groups of the wisdom of its policies. The policy tool least used in recent years is *margin requirements* on the purchase of selected stocks and convertible bonds, which can affect the flow of credit available from financial institutions and is designed to discourage speculative borrowing. Unfortunately, margin requirements can lead to distortions in the allocation of scarce resources and discrimination in access to credit, especially for borrowers of limited means.

Although it is useful to know what tools central banks have at their disposal to deal with economic problems and what effects these policy tools are likely to have, the student of the financial system needs to know more. When is the central bank likely to use its policy tools? What factors indicate whether a change in monetary policy has occurred? How successful has the central bank been in achieving its economic goals? We address these important questions in the next and final chapter on the Federal Reserve System. ■

KEY TERMS AND CONCEPTS IN THIS CHAPTER

legal reserves	monetary base	discount rate
required reserves	general credit controls	open market operations
excess reserves	selective credit controls	moral suasion
deposit multiplier	reserve requirements	margin requirements
money multiplier		

STUDY QUESTIONS

1. What is the principal target of Federal Reserve monetary policy? Why?

2. What are legal reserves? Required reserves? Excess reserves? Explain why these concepts are important.

3. Why are deposit-type intermediaries able to create money? What factors increase the amount of deposits the banking system can create with any given injection of new reserves? What factors reduce the money-creating capabilities of the banking and financial system?

4. In what ways can the Federal Reserve influence the money creation process? The public? The U.S. Treasury?

5. How does the reserve requirement tool affect the ability of deposit-type institutions to create money? What are the principal advantages and disadvantages of the reserve-requirement tool?

6. How and why does a depository institution borrow from the Federal Reserve? Explain what happens when the Fed changes the discount rate. What are the principal advantages and disadvantages of the discount mechanism as a policy tool?

7. Why are open market operations the Fed's most popular and frequently used policy tool? What are the principal effects of open market operations on the financial system?

8. Describe the relationship between the SOMA manager and the FOMC. What is a policy directive? Why types of policy targets does the Fed use?

9. Explain the difference between an RP and a straight (or outright) open market transaction. Why is each used? What is a runoff? An agency operation?

10. Explain the difference between defensive and dynamic open market operations.

11. What is moral suasion? Do you believe this tool can be effective?

12. Explain how margin requirements affect the financial system. Why were these requirements instituted by Congress?

PROBLEMS

1. Suppose the public wishes to hold $0.40 in pocket money (currency and coin) and $0.15 in excess reserves for each new dollar of transaction money received. If reserve requirements on transaction deposits and time and savings deposits are 3 percent, what is the size of the transaction deposit multiplier? The money multiplier? Suppose $5 million in new excess

reserves appear in the banking system. How much will be created in the form of new deposits and loans?

2. Total legal reserves currently amount to $40 billion, while currency and coin in public hands total $160 billion. The narrowly defined (transaction) money supply is $525 billion. How large is the money multiplier?

3. A bank holds $130 million in the form of transaction and time and savings deposits. Its reserve deposit at the Federal Reserve bank during the current reserve maintenance period contains a daily average balance of $0.40 million for several weeks running. Calculate its required reserves and excess reserves if deposits are subject to a 5 percent legal reserve requirement. Now suppose that the bank elects to buy $1 million in Treasury bills from the Fed. Do you see any problems with this?

4. First National Bank of Elderidge borrowed $550,000 from the Federal Reserve Bank of St. Louis last Friday. The bank received short-term adjustment credit for three days and plans to repay its loan at the close of business Monday. Show the proper accounting (T account) entries for this transaction when the loan was taken out on Friday and when it is repaid Monday afternoon. How much did total bank reserves rise when this loan was made? Are reserve requirements a factor here?

5. Describe what is likely to happen to interest rates, deposits, and total bank reserves as a result of the transactions listed below:

    a. The Federal Reserve sells $50 million in securities outright to a bank.

    b. The Federal Reserve buys $85 million in securities outright from a bank.

    c. The Federal Reserve sells $93 million in securities outright to a nonbank security dealer.

    d. The Federal Reserve buys $42 million in securities outright from a nonbank security dealer.

    e. The Federal Reserve sells $21 million in securities for its own portfolio to a foreign central bank.

    f. The Federal Reserve buys $37 million in securities for its own portfolio that are being offered for sale by a foreign central bank.

    g. The Federal Reserve declines the U.S. Treasury's offer to roll over $150 million in Treasury notes that are maturing in the Fed's own portfolio in exchange for new Treasury notes; instead the Federal Reserve demands cash from the Treasury.

SELECTED REFERENCES

Emery, Robert F. "Central Banks' Use in East Asia of Money Market Instruments in the Conduct of Monetary Policy." *International Finance Discussion Papers,* No. 426. Board of Governors of the Federal Reserve System, March 1992.

Greenspan, Alan. "Commercial Banks and the Central Bank in a Market Economy." *Economic Review.* Federal Reserve Bank of Kansas City, November 1989, pp. 3–12.

Kane, Edward. "The Re-politicization of the Fed." *Journal of Financial and Quantitative Analysis,* November 1974, pp. 743–52.

Loungani, Prakash, and Mark Rush. "The Effects of Changes in Reserve Requirements on Investment and GNP." *International Finance Discussion Papers,* No. 471. Board of Governors of the Federal Reserve System, June 1994.

Meyer, Stephen A. "Non-Open-Market Monetary Policy Operations." *Business Review.* Federal Reserve Bank of Philadelphia, January–February 1988, pp. 3–16.

Roth, Howard L. "Federal Reserve Open Market Techniques." *Economic Review.* Federal Reserve Bank of Kansas City, March 1986, pp. 2–15.

Chapter 21

Indicators and Goals of Monetary Policy

LEARNING OBJECTIVES IN THIS CHAPTER

- To explain what an indicator of monetary policy is.
- To define and illustrate the most important indicators of monetary policy in use today.
- To explain how the Federal Reserve System attempts to control money supply growth.
- To examine the ways in which monetary policy actions can affect the economic goals of achieving full employment, controlling inflation, sustaining adequate economic growth, and achieving a stable balance-of-payments position.

The Federal Reserve System exerts a powerful impact on the availability and cost of credit in the financial markets. Because the Fed has a great deal to do with the broad changes that occur in interest rates, the prices of securities, and the availability of credit, economists and financial analysts spend enormous amounts of time analyzing Federal Reserve actions in an attempt to predict the future course of monetary policy. Indeed, if the experts are able to guess correctly which way the Fed is going, they can make appropriate adjustments in their security portfolios and in their borrowing and spending plans to reduce costs and maximize earnings.

It should be noted, however, that understanding the Federal Reserve's intentions and predicting the direction of monetary policy are *not* easy tasks. Many factors influence interest rates, security prices, and the flow of loanable funds in the financial markets. For example, if we see interest rates on money market instruments rising, there is often a temptation to assume that this trend reflects the actions of the Federal Reserve. In fact, interest rates are subject to all the forces of demand and supply operating in the financial marketplace. An upward surge in rates may reflect a sharp rise in borrowings by units of government and private investors, the impact of inflation, changes in the public's money-using habits, and a host of other factors. Central banks have an important influence on the financial system, but they are only one of *many* influences.

FACTORS INFLUENCING THE RESERVES OF THE BANKING SYSTEM

To fully understand the role of the Federal Reserve in the complex environment of the financial marketplace, we need to focus on the principal target of Federal Reserve policy: **legal reserves.** Recall from the previous chapter that the reserves of the banking system consist of deposits kept at the central bank plus currency and coin held in the vaults of depository institutions. These reserves are the raw material from which lenders create credit and cause the money supply to grow. This is the reason that the total supply of reserves is the main target of Federal Reserve monetary policy. However, numerous factors affect the supply of reserves available to banks and other lenders. As shown in Exhibit 21–1, these factors fall into three groups: (1) actions of the public; (2) Federal Reserve operations; and (3) operations of the U.S. Treasury Department and foreign investors.

Actions of the Public Affecting Reserves

Suppose, for example, the public desires to increase its holdings of currency and coin (pocket money). It will do so by writing checks or drafts against deposits held in banks and thrift institutions, reducing the legal reserves of these lending institutions. If these institutions were

Exhibit 21–1   **Principal Factors Affecting the Supply of Total Reserves in the Banking System**

Factor	Effect on Total Legal Reserves of the Banking System
Actions of the public:	
Increase in holdings of currency and coin	−
Decrease in holdings of currency and coin	+
Federal Reserve operations:	
Purchase of securities	+
Sale of securities	−
Loans made to depository institutions	+
Repayment of loans made to depository institutions	−
Increase in Federal Reserve float	+
Decrease in Federal Reserve float	−
Increase in other assets of the Federal Reserve banks	+
Decrease in other assets of the Federal Reserve banks	−
Increase in other liabilities of the Federal Reserve banks	−
Decrease in other liabilities of the Federal Reserve banks	+
Increase in capital accounts of the Federal Reserve banks	−
Decrease in capital accounts of the Federal Reserve banks	+
U.S. Treasury and foreign operations:	
Increase in Treasury deposits at the Federal Reserve banks	−
Decrease in Treasury deposits at the Federal Reserve banks	+
Gold purchases	+
Gold sales	−
Increase in Treasury currency outstanding	+
Decrease in Treasury currency outstanding	−
Increase in Treasury cash holdings	−
Decrease in Treasury cash holdings	+
Increase in foreign and other deposits in Federal Reserve banks	−
Decrease in foreign and other deposits in Federal Reserve banks	+

already fully loaned up, with no excess reserves, the withdrawal of currency and coin would force them to raise additional reserves by selling securities, calling loans, and borrowing. The stock of total reserves and the money supply would begin to contract. On the other hand, if the public wishes to reduce its holdings of currency and coin, pocket money will be redeposited in banks and thrift institutions, increasing the total reserves of these institutions. The volume of bank lending and investing will rise, resulting in an increase in the money supply, unless, of course, the central bank uses its policy tools to counteract the impact of the inflow of currency and coin.

Operations of the Treasury and Foreign Investors Affecting Reserves

Actions of the U.S. Treasury and foreign investors also affect the level and growth of legal reserves. The Treasury, foreign central banks, and international financial institutions keep large deposits with the Federal Reserve banks. Any increase in these deposits generally results in a decline in the reserves of depository institutions. This is due to the fact that both the Treasury and foreign institutions frequently receive payments from domestic businesses and households. These payments are nearly always made by check and drain reserves from private depository institutions as the checks are cleared at the Fed. Federal income tax payments by the public, which periodically flow out of private checkable deposits and into the Treasury's checking accounts at the Fed, are good examples of this process. Similarly, when the Treasury sells securities in the open market, investors write checks against their accounts that are eventually credited to the Treasury's deposits with the Federal Reserve banks. In both instances, the public's deposits and total reserves of the banking system fall. Conversely, whenever the Treasury or a foreign depositor writes checks against their accounts, these are normally deposited somewhere in the banking system, causing total reserves to rise.

Occasionally, the Treasury buys and sells *gold* to comply with the request of foreign governments or to hold in reserve. Payment for Treasury gold purchases is made by checks drawn on the Treasury's accounts at the Fed. Those individuals and institutions selling the gold deposit the Treasury's checks somewhere in the banking system, leading to an increase in reserves and deposits. Conversely, if the Treasury sells gold, buyers write checks against their deposits, which forces a decline in both reserves and deposits of the banking system when those checks are collected. If the decline in reserves is too great, the Federal Reserve may have to offset the impact of Treasury gold transactions through open market operations.

The Treasury's minting of new currency and coin also has an impact on reserves and deposits. Newly minted currency and coin are shipped to the vaults of the Federal Reserve banks in return for credit to the Treasury's checking accounts. When the Treasury spends these funds by issuing checks to the public, deposits and reserves in the banking system rise. Similarly, when there is a decrease in Treasury currency outstanding as currency and coin are retired, total reserves must fall. This happens because the Treasury must pay for the redeemed currency and coin by writing checks against its deposits at the Fed. To cover those checks, it must draw down its deposits kept in private banks, which reduces total reserves available to the banking system.

The Treasury does hold small amounts of currency and coin in its own vaults. When these vault deposits rise, the increase in Treasury cash holdings must have come from funds kept somewhere in the private banking system, leading to a decline in total reserves. Similarly, when Treasury cash holdings decline, the released currency and coin flow into the private banking system, and both deposits and total reserves rise.

Federal Reserve Operations Affecting Reserves

The Federal Reserve System can offset *any* of the foregoing actions by the public, foreign institutions, or the U.S. Treasury, keeping total reserves of the banking system at roughly the level it desires. As we observed in the preceding chapter, the Fed can increase total reserves by making purchases of securities in the open market, or it can reduce total reserves by selling securities. Loans made to depository institutions through the discount windows of the Reserve banks increase reserves; repayments of those loans cause reserves to fall.

The Fed often increases reserves unintentionally when the volume of float from uncollected checks rises. Banks and other depository institutions that route their checks through the Federal Reserve banks for collection receive credit in their reserve accounts after a specified period (usually within one to three days). However, many of those checks have not been collected at the time the Fed grants credit for them, due to delays in processing or transportation. Checkbook float is essentially an interest-free loan of reserves from the Fed and has the same effect on the total reserves of the banking system as a loan made through the Fed's discount window.

Finally, when the Federal Reserve banks acquire assets of any kind or issue checks to pay their debts or cover expenses, total reserves of the banking system rise. In contrast, when the Fed receives payments from banks, securities dealers, and others, total reserves fall as checks written against financial institutions are sent to the Federal Reserve banks. Similarly, when a bank joins the Federal Reserve System, it must purchase Federal Reserve stock. This action increases the Fed's capital accounts and lowers the reserves available to private banks. Generally speaking, any Federal Reserve expenditure increases reserves, and any receipt of funds by the Fed reduces the reserves available to the banking system.

The Heart of the Monetary Policy Process — Controlling Reserves to Achieve Desired Target Levels

The heart of the monetary policy process is to correctly anticipate changes in all of the foregoing factors that affect the legal reserves of the banking system. The central bank then tries to use its policy tools to *offset* or to *supplement* the various reserve-influencing factors to achieve a level and rate of growth in total reserves that is consistent with its targets for interest rates and growth in the money supply and with national economic goals.

THE FEDERAL RESERVE STATEMENT

One of the most widely followed indicators of what the Federal Reserve System is doing to influence conditions in the financial markets and the economy is known as the **Federal Reserve Statement**. It is published each week in the financial press and lists the factors that supply reserves to depository institutions and those that absorb reserves. The total amount of reserves held by depository institutions at any time equals the difference between the factors supplying reserves and the factors absorbing reserves. The Federal Reserve Statement shows levels of each reserve-supplying or reserve-absorbing factor for the current and previous month or week and any changes between the two time-periods. It is the *changes* in each reserve factor that analysts concentrate on in attempting to understand what the Federal Reserve is trying to accomplish in the financial marketplace.

Factors Supplying Reserves

A Federal Reserve Statement for the months of August and September 1995 is shown in Exhibit 21–2. The first item listed on the statement is Reserve bank credit, including Federal Reserve purchases of securities, loans from the discount windows of the Reserve banks, float, and other Federal Reserve assets. If each of these items increases, reserves available to depository institutions rise. Other factors held equal, the ability of financial institutions to make loans and investments and expand the money supply also increases, and interest rates tend to fall. A *decrease* in any component of Reserve bank credit, on the other hand, results in a decline in the reserves of depository institutions, and all else held equal, interest rates will tend to rise.

Looking more closely at the Federal Reserve Statement in Exhibit 21–2, we note that the Federal Reserve System held outright $371,068 million in U.S. government securities and $2,932 million in federal agency securities in September 1995. In addition, $4,206 million in U.S. government securities and $106 million in federal agency securities were held under repurchase agreements with securities dealers. The column marked *Change* tells us that the Fed, on balance, *bought* securities between August and September 1995. Its total security holdings rose a net $3,166 million (that is, −874+4073−87+54) during this brief interval.

Exhibit 21–2   ## Reserves of Depository Institutions ($ Millions)

Item	August 1995	September 1995	Change
Factors supplying reserve funds:			
Reserve bank credit:	$409,403	$410,884	+1,481
U.S. Government securities:			
Bought outright — system account	371,942	371,068	−874
Held under repurchase agreements	133	4,206	+4,073
Federal agency obligations:			
Bought outright	3,019	2,932	−87
Held under repurchase agreements	52	106	+54
Bankers' acceptances	0	0	0
Loans to depository institutions	371	282	−89
Float	291	408	+117
Other Federal Reserve assets	33,595	31,882	−1,713
Gold stock	11,053	11,052	−1
Special drawing rights certificate account	10,518	10,366	−152
Treasury currency outstanding	23,623	23,708	+85
Total of reserve-supplying factors	$454,597	$456,010	+1,413
Factors absorbing reserve funds:			
Currency in circulation	$410,420	$410,989	+569
Treasury cash holdings	310	322	+12
Deposits, other than reserves balances held with Federal Reserve banks, owned by the Treasury, foreign institutions, and others	10,329	12,065	+1,736
Other Federal Reserve liabilities and capital	12,758	12,176	−582
Total of reserve-absorbing factors	$433,817	$435,522	+1,735
Reserve balances held with Federal Reserve banks	$ 20,780	$ 20,458	−322

Source: Board of Governors of the Federal Reserve System, *Federal Reserve Bulletin,* December 1995, Table 1.11.

Because net Federal Reserve purchases increase the supply of reserves, other factors held equal, does this mean that the Fed was moving toward an easier, less restrictive money and credit policy in the fall of 1995? Not necessarily. We know that much central bank activity is *defensive* in nature (as explained in Chapter 20) — that is, central banks work daily to offset the effects of other factors on reserves and, thereby, preserve the *status quo* in the financial markets. In this case, were there other factors draining reserves from depository institutions that the Fed felt compelled to offset? Exhibit 21–2 suggests the answer is yes. For one thing, miscellaneous (other) Federal Reserve assets fell, and this sale of miscellaneous Fed assets would have absorbed more than $1,700 million in reserves held by the banking system if the Fed sat on its hands and did nothing.

Factors Absorbing Reserves

Moreover, the set of factors absorbing reserves were on the rise in the fall of 1995. As we can see from inspection of Exhibit 21–2, the second portion of the Federal Reserve Statement looks at those factors that reduce reserves when they are on the rise, including increases in currency in circulation, Treasury holdings of cash, miscellaneous deposits at the Fed, and the liability and capital accounts of the Federal Reserve banks. If these factors increase, reserve balances held by depository institutions must decline unless offset by reserve-supplying factors, such as Federal Reserve credit. However, a decrease in any reserve-absorbing factors results in an increase in total reserves.

Careful inspection of Exhibit 21–2 shows that a sizable change occurred in the amount of currency and coin in circulation between August and September 1995. The public had greater need for pocket money and withdrew from banks and other depositories a net of $569 million in currency and coin. Considering the currency factor alone, the supply of reserves would contract significantly as depository institutions surrendered their vault cash to meet the public's need for pocket money unless the central bank entered the market to provide more reserves. As things turned out, the Federal Reserve offset some, but not all, of the public's demand for pocket money from the banking system. If we look at the bottom of Exhibit 21–2, we see that total reserves of the banking system fell by $322 million in September 1995 — the difference between a $1,413 million increase in reserve-supplying factors and a $1,735 million advance in reserve-absorbing factors.

Why did the Federal Reserve allow the total reserves of the banking system to fall by $322 million in September 1995? One apparent reason was a fairly rapid increase in the monetary base, the U.S. money supply, and in loans granted by banks to the public. At the same time, both short-term and long-term interest rates were falling in September 1995 and the Fed appeared to be concerned that inflation might accelerate if the public continued to increase its borrowings in order to fuel new spending. Clearly, a student of the Fed needs to know not only what the numbers are but also what the conditions behind the numbers happen to be in order to fully understand what the Fed is trying to achieve.

MEASURES OF THE MONEY SUPPLY

The Federal Reserve Statement is an important indicator of monetary policy, but it is by no means the only one. Economists, business leaders, and investors look even more closely at weekly, monthly, and annual changes in various measures of the money supply. The money supply is the subject of widespread interest and attention for two reasons: (1) changes in money are highly correlated with changes in economic conditions and (2) the Federal

Exhibit 21–3   **Money Supply Measures**

Symbol	Definition	Amounts as of January 1996 ($ Billions)
M1	Demand deposits at commercial banks (except those due to other domestic banks, the U.S. government, and foreign banks and official institutions) — Cash items in the process of collection and float + NOW accounts and automatic transfer service accounts at banks and thrift institutions + Credit union share draft accounts + Demand deposits at savings banks + Currency and coin held by public outside banks and government vaults + Traveler's checks of nonbank issuers.	$ 1,119.1
M2	M1 + Savings and small-denomination time deposits at all depository institutions (except retirement accounts — IRAs and Keoghs) + Overnight and continuing contract repurchase agreements at banks + Overnight Eurodollars issued to U.S. residents by foreign branches of U.S. banks worldwide + Money market mutual funds shares not held by institutions + MMDAs	$ 3,686.0
M3	M2 + Large-denomination ($100,000 up) time deposits at all depository institutions + Term Eurodollars and term RPs + Institutional money market funds	$ 4,611.8
L	M3 + Nonbank holdings of bankers' acceptances, commercial paper, U.S. Treasury bills and other liquid Treasury Securities, and U.S. Savings Bonds	$ 5,695.1*
D	Debt of domestic nonfinancial sectors (U.S. government, state and local governments, and private nonfinancial units)	$13,841.8

*Figures for L and D are for December 1995.

Source: Board of Governors of the Federal Reserve System, *Federal Reserve Bulletin,* April 1996, Table 1.21.

Reserve has a significant impact on money supply growth through its control over the reserves of depository institutions.

Today, economists and other students of the financial system follow not just one definition of the money supply but several, each reflecting a slightly different view of what money is. (See Exhibit 21–3.) The public's money-using habits are changing rapidly, and many new financial instruments and electronic payment media have recently appeared, complicating measurement of the money supply. Continuing innovations in money-related assets force the Federal Reserve Board to revise old definitions of the money supply and, periodically, announce new ones.

Money Supply Measures

The narrowest definition of the money supply in use today is known as **M1**, the sum of checking accounts and currency and coin held by the public. This definition views money exclusively as a *medium of exchange* and includes mostly non-interest-bearing assets. Although all forms of money serve as a medium of exchange, the newer forms of money today bear interest and therefore serve partly as a *store of value,* or *temporary repository of savings.* Prominent examples include Super NOW accounts, money market deposit accounts (MMDAs), and shares in money market mutual funds held by the public that can be as accessible for making payments as conventional non-interest-bearing checking accounts, savings deposits, and small time deposits (with denominations of less than $100,000) at all depository institutions. These liquid funds plus everything in M1 make up the **M2** definition of money. The M1 definition of money is more directly related to central bank policy actions, while M2 is more closely related to growth in the economy.

An even broader measure of the money supply is **M3**, which includes all the components of M2 plus time deposits issued by depository institutions in denominations of $100,000 or more, term RPs offered by banks and thrifts, term Eurodollar deposits held by

U.S. residents at foreign banks and U.S. banks worldwide and at banking offices in Canada and Great Britain, and large-denomination institutional deposits in money market funds. Thus, M3 focuses on *liquid working balances.*

One of the broadest money supply measures is **L**, which represents total liquid assets. The critical difference between L and other measures of the money supply is the addition of various money market securities, such as short-term marketable Treasury obligations and U.S. savings bonds. The fifth and last money supply measure, **D**, or debt, serves as an approximate measure of the total supply of credit resulting from lending funds to federal, state, and local governments; private businesses; and consumers. It excludes the debt of financial institutions, however.

Federal Reserve Control of Money Supply Growth

In addition to influencing the level of short-term interest rates, the Federal Reserve attempts to regulate the growth of these measures of the money supply, particularly M2 and M3, in order to influence the economy's level of production, employment, and prices. The problem is that the Fed is not the only factor determining the size and rate of growth of the money supply. Changes in the public's money-using habits, income levels, and the credit policies of financial institutions also play key roles in money growth.

How does the Fed attempt to control the growth of the money supply? The Fed's method of money supply control has been called the *borrowed reserves operating procedure.*[1] This approach focuses on the legal reserves of the banking system, whose level and rate of growth are regulated through open market operations. Three steps are involved. First, *the Federal Open Market Committee (FOMC) sets target growth rates for selected money supply measures* (usually M2 and M3) *for the coming year and for shorter periods within the year.*[2] These targets are stated in the form of annual percentage growth rate ranges. For example, in February 1996, the Fed called for growth in M2 between 1 and 5 percent and M3 between 2 and 6 percent between fourth quarter 1995 and fourth quarter 1996.

The second step in money supply control is to *determine the growth paths for the legal reserves of the banking system necessary to achieve the targeted rates of growth in the money supply.* As we saw in Chapter 20, the total legal reserves of the banking system are linked to the money supply through the money multiplier:

$$\text{Money supply} = \text{Money multiplier} \times \text{Monetary base} \qquad (21\text{--}1)$$

where the money multiplier tells us how many dollars of money result from each dollar increase in the monetary base, and the monetary base includes total legal reserves and currency and coin held by the public. The money-multiplier relationship suggests that the growth rate of the money supply is approximately equal to the growth rate of the multiplier plus the rate of growth in the monetary base (including the growth in bank reserves). Therefore, if the Fed is to control the money supply, it must somehow control or influence the growth of the monetary base and project how the money multiplier will change over time.

[1]See especially Cacy (1980) and Heller (1988).

[2]Under the terms of the Full-Employment and Balanced Growth Act of 1978 (known also as the Humphrey-Hawkins Act), the FOMC is required to establish calendar-year growth ranges for money and credit aggregates. These ranges, which must be reported to Congress in February and July, are based on the period running from the fourth quarter of the previous year to the fourth quarter of the current year. The FOMC is at liberty to change the target growth ranges at any time, if it believes that new circumstances warrant a change.

Clearly, the Fed does not completely control either the monetary base or the size of the money multiplier. The public, by making decisions on how much currency and coin, demand deposits, and time and savings deposits it wishes to hold, and depository institutions, in deciding what excess reserves they choose to hold, exert a powerful influence on the growth of the monetary base and the money multiplier. The Federal Reserve must *estimate* what the public and depository institutions will do and try to offset those actions by manipulating the legal reserves of the banking system — the sum of reserves held on deposit at the Federal Reserve banks plus vault cash held by depository institutions — an important component of the monetary base. Unfortunately, the Fed does not fully control total legal reserves either. This is due to the fact that

$$\text{Total legal reserves} = \text{Borrowed reserves} + \text{Nonborrowed reserves} \qquad (21\text{--}2)$$

Borrowed reserves are supplied through the discount windows of the Federal Reserve banks and depend on the demand for discount window loans from depository institutions as well as Fed regulations. **Nonborrowed reserves** are all remaining total legal reserves that are *not* borrowed from the Fed.

Since October 1982, the Federal Reserve has aimed to keep the amount of borrowed reserves at or near a desired target level. The FOMC sets a borrowed reserves target that it views as consistent with its target range for the money supply and the economy. To achieve this target level of borrowed reserves, the Federal Reserve must determine what quantity of nonborrowed reserves it must provide to the banking system using its open market policy tool from this relationship:

$$\begin{array}{c} \text{Amount of} \\ \text{nonborrowed} \\ \text{reserves that} \\ \text{must be supplied} \end{array} = \begin{array}{c} \text{Estimated amount} \\ \text{of total reserves} \\ \text{that will be} \\ \text{available} \end{array} - \begin{array}{c} \text{Target level} \\ \text{of borrowed} \\ \text{reserves} \end{array} \qquad (21\text{--}3)$$

Borrowed reserves have been targeted since 1982 in order to promote more stable interest rates and to allow the Fed to take a longer-term view of money supply growth rather than making many short-term adjustments.

The third step in the money supply control process is to *undertake daily and weekly open market operations through the Trading Desk of the Federal Reserve Bank of New York to supply just enough nonborrowed reserves to achieve the desired growth path for borrowed reserves.* The Fed forecasts both required and excess reserves and then fully accommodates any changes in the demand for reserves by supplying or taking away enough nonborrowed reserves to achieve the targeted level of borrowed reserves. This means that the federal funds interest rate does *not* necessarily respond to changes in the demand for reserves, although the Fed funds interest rate may change for other reasons (such as depository institutions switching from borrowing in the federal funds market to another source of funds).

At each of its periodic meetings, the Federal Open Market Committee issues a *policy directive* to the Trading Desk specifying its desired level of restraint in controlling the growth of reserves and calling either for more, less, or unchanged restraint. The staff of the Trading Desk must interpret that policy directive as to the right amount of reserve restraint required each day in terms of the desired average level of borrowings from the Federal Reserve banks. If *more* restraint on the growth of reserves appears to be needed, the Trading Desk begins selling securities to reduce nonborrowed reserves in such a way as to cause the level of borrowings by depository institutions from the Federal Reserve banks to *increase*. If more depository institutions are in debt to the Federal Reserve in greater amounts (i.e., borrowed reserves have increased), then these institutions will begin to reduce their lending activities and impose tighter credit conditions on their borrowing customers. Money market interest rates (especially the federal funds interest rate) will begin to rise, and money supply growth will slow.

On the other hand, if *less* monetary restraint appears to be needed, the staff at the Fed's Trading Desk will begin to purchase securities from the open market until nonborrowed reserves increase enough to cause the level of borrowings from the Federal Reserve banks to *decrease*; this process continues until borrowed reserves fall to the level the Fed desires. With fewer depository institutions in debt to the Federal Reserve banks (i.e., borrowed reserves have decreased), these institutions will feel freer to expand their loans to customers. Money market interest rates (especially the federal funds interest rate) will begin to decline, and money supply growth will accelerate.

Clearly, the central bank's key focus in controlling money supply growth and changes in interest rate levels is *reserve availability.* The manager of the Federal Reserve's open market trading desk either adds more nonborrowed reserves (usually by purchasing securities) or takes some nonborrowed reserves away (usually by selling securities) until money supply growth and interest rate levels move into the range desired by the central bank.

Achieving the Fed's Money Supply Targets

How well has the Fed done in achieving its targeted growth rates for money? Overall, the Fed has held quite close to its target ranges on an *annual* basis. However, from month to month and quarter to quarter, the Fed is frequently outside its annual money supply growth targets. For example, during the third quarter of 1995, the M2 measure of money grew at an annual rate of nearly 8 percent, well outside the Fed's preferred range of 1 to 5 percent. For the year as a whole, however, M2 money growth appeared to fall within the prescribed range. Unfortunately, we don't know yet how much damage is done to the achievement of national economic goals as a result of deviations in money supply growth from its target range and the Fed's often hurried adjustments to get itself back on target.

The Fed does face a number of serious problems as it attempts to achieve its announced annual money supply targets. Continuing changes in the public's money-using habits, especially shifts from conventional bank deposits to mutual funds, distort the money supply measures and alter their relationship to the economy. Moreover, judging by the rapid pace of financial innovation and the recent development of transactions over the Internet, the Federal Reserve will eventually be forced to readjust its money supply definitions, growth targets, and its operating procedures. In addition, as we have seen earlier in this chapter, the central bank is *not* the sole determinant of what happens to the money supply or the supply of reserves in the banking system. The central bank frequently is forced to react after the fact to changes set in motion by the public, leading to sudden surges or sudden declines in money or interest rates. Adding to the central bank's problems, the relationships among money, production, employment, and prices appear to have changed in recent years, becoming somewhat less stable and less predictable due, in part, to government deregulation of the financial system. Thus, it is more difficult today for the central bank to predict how the condition of the economy will change as the Fed moves to alter money growth and the level of interest rates.

MONEY MARKET INDICATORS

While control of money growth is still an important intermediate objective of central bank policymaking, the Federal Reserve (and several other central banks around the world) has given increasing weight in recent years to targeting *the cost and availability of credit in the money market.* One reason is that central banks are charged with the responsibility of stabilizing conditions in the financial markets to assure a smooth flow of funds from savers to investors. In addition, central banks must ensure that the government securities market functions smoothly so that adequate supplies of credit are available to security dealers and that the federal government can market its billions of dollars in debt securities without serious difficulty. But to what dimension of the money market does a central bank like the Federal Reserve pay the most attention?

The Federal Funds Rate

The money market indicator that usually feels the first impact from Federal Reserve policy-moves is the *daily average interest rate on federal funds transactions.* When the Fed sells securities, the supply of reserves available to depository institutions is reduced and, other things held equal, the Fed funds rate, which is the "price" of overnight borrowings of reserves in the banking system, tends to rise. On the other hand, a Federal Reserve purchase of securities increases available reserves to depository institutions, which tends to push the Fed funds rate down.

Recently, the Federal Reserve Board adopted a new policy of "openness" when it comes to announcing its target for the federal funds interest rate. For example, in December 1995, following a meeting of the Federal Open Market Committee, the Fed announced that it was dropping its target for the federal funds interest rate from 5¾ percent to 5½ percent because the economy appeared to be slowing and inflation seemed to be under control. When the markets opened the next morning, the Fed funds rate moved quickly toward its new target level.

How is the Federal Reserve's Trading Desk able to maintain the federal funds rate at or close to its announced interest rate target? Exhibit 21–4 provides us with an illustration of the process. Suppose the Fed has targeted a Fed funds rate of 5 percent and the funds rate currently sits at the 5 percent level, where the total demand for reserves by depository

Exhibit 21–4   The Federal Reserve's Impact on the Federal Funds Rate

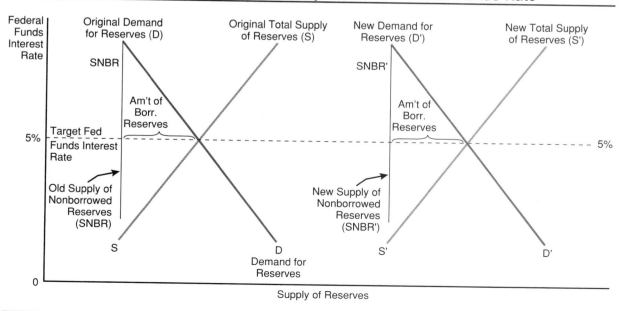

institutions, represented by schedule D in Exhibit 21–4, intersects the supply of total reserves, represented by schedule S. Note that the supply of total reserves consists of the sum of nonborrowed reserves, marked $SNBR$ in the exhibit, plus the level of borrowed reserves that depository institutions have borrowed from the Federal Reserve banks.

Now, suppose that depository institutions increase their demand for reserves to D'. If the Federal Reserve does nothing to the supply of reserves, the Fed funds rate must rise above its current 5 percent target level to accommodate the new higher level of demand for reserves. If the Fed doesn't want this to happen, it will increase the supply of nonborrowed reserves by using open market operations, changing the schedule $SNBR$ to a new schedule, $SNBR'$. This action slides the supply of total reserves over to a new schedule, S'. If the amount of borrowed reserves doesn't change, we now have a new intersection of supply and demand for reserves, but the level of the Fed funds rate stays at 5 percent. Thus, *the Federal Reserve can keep the Fed funds interest rate at or near its desired level so long as the central bank is willing to offset changes in the demand for total reserves and in the demand for borrowed reserves by making appropriate adjustments in the supply of nonborrowed reserves through open market operations*. Of course, the central bank cannot maintain the funds rate exactly at its target level every hour of every day. This is because depository institutions are constantly changing their demands for reserves and their attitudes about borrowing reserves from the Federal Reserve banks. Moreover, interest rates are impacted by the public's expectations for inflation and by the total demand and supply of credit. Nevertheless, in the short run the Fed has a powerful and rapid impact on the federal funds rate and, through that rate, on the cost of credit in other sectors of the money market.

Other Money Market Interest Rates

Other money market interest rates watched carefully by investors and financial analysts include yields on U.S. Treasury bills, rates charged securities dealers by major New York banks on short-term security loans, and the Federal Reserve's discount rate. A rise in interest rates is often regarded as an indicator of tightening credit conditions resulting from the Fed's restricting the growth of credit. When rates on T-bills and other money market securities fall, however, this may be regarded as a sign that the Fed is easing up, with perhaps even lower interest rates soon to follow.

Free Reserves

Another public indicator of money market conditions is the free reserve position of the banking system. *Free reserves* are excess reserve balances of depository institutions held at the Federal Reserve banks minus borrowings from the discount window. (Recall that excess reserves are legal reserve balances kept at the Reserve banks plus vault cash less required reserves.) Both the level and direction of changes in free reserves are thought to have meaning.

The dynamic element in free reserves is borrowing by depository institutions from the discount windows of the Federal Reserve banks. When these borrowings increase, depository institutions feel more restricted in their lending and investing until they can repay their debt to the Fed. Credit becomes more difficult to obtain and more expensive. On the other hand, when discount window borrowings fall relative to excess reserves, depository institutions feel less pressure against their reserves and may become more liberal in extending credit.

INTERNATIONAL FOCUS:

Central Banking Operating Objectives and Economic Goals Around the World

---

While central banks differ in their goals, tools, and institutional settings, the mechanism through which central banks exert their impact on the financial markets and the economy appears to be much the same on every continent. Nearly all central banks appear to work through changes in the total reserves available to the banking system. It is these reserves that affect the volume of credit that banks and other lending institutions create in order to support spending in the economy. In turn, changes in bank reserves and other central bank actions have an almost immediate impact upon short-term (money market) interest rates and on currency prices — often referred to as the *operating objectives* of central bank policy.

Central bank operating objectives vary from nation to nation. For example, the Federal Reserve System targets the overnight interbank lending rate (known as the federal funds interest rate, as we saw in Chapter 16) as do the central banks of Canada, Japan, and Switzerland. In contrast, in such nations as the United Kingdom and Germany, longer-term interest rates out to three-month maturities are used as central bank operating objectives. The Bank of Canada also intervenes in the Treasury bill market from time to time to signal its wishes concerning the future behavior of short-term interest rates.

If a central bank wants market interest rates to remain stable, it will use its tools to supply enough reserves to the banking system just to meet the demand for reserves. If it wants interest rates to rise, it will adjust reserve supplies to a level that is less than the current demand for reserves so that excess demand for reserves will drive interest rates higher. If interest rates are to be pushed lower, the central bank will employ its policy tools to increase the supply of reserves beyond the current level of reserve demands.

Generally, central banks change short-term interbank interest rates in small steps until they achieve the short-term interest rate level that each central bank desires. Then, through the forces of arbitrage and changing public expectations, longer-term interest rates eventually respond to the central bank's policy moves. This is important, because it is longer-term interest rates that appear to have the most potent effects on the public's spending decisions. For example, as interest rates change on automobile and home mortgage loans and on longer-term loans to business firms, the aggregate volume of borrowing and spending by the public changes in response to the shifting policy moves of central banks.

Free reserves can be either positive or negative, depending on whether excess reserves are larger or smaller than borrowings from the Reserve banks. When borrowings exceed excess reserves, a condition of *net borrowed reserves* prevails. On the other hand, if borrowings are less than excess reserves, the banking system has *net free reserves*. Movement from week to week toward deeper net borrowed reserves generally implies that tighter credit conditions are developing. In contrast, a change toward greater net free reserves is usually regarded as an indicator of easier credit conditions. One problem with the free reserve indicator is that many forces in addition to Federal Reserve policy affect free reserves. For example, individual depository institutions decide what volume of excess reserves they wish to hold and whether to borrow from the Federal Reserve banks. This indicator, then, is subject to much the same criticism as the other monetary policy indicators we have discussed: It is influenced by many factors other than central bank policy.

THE FEDERAL RESERVE AND ECONOMIC GOALS

For many years, the Federal Reserve System, along with other central banks around the world, has played an active role in the stabilization of the economy and the pursuit of economic goals. These goals include controlling inflation, promoting full employment and sustainable economic growth, and achieving a stable international balance-of-payments position for the United States. In recent years, these goals have proved to be extremely difficult to achieve in practice and, in fact, have often required conflicting policies. Nevertheless, the Fed remains committed to them.

The Goal of Controlling Inflation

Inflation — a rise in the general price level of all goods and services produced in the economy — has been among the more serious economic problems of the United States over the past three decades. Inflation has been a worldwide problem, with many nations experiencing far higher annual rates of inflation than those currently prevailing in the United States. Moreover, inflation is *not* new; price levels have been generally rising since the beginning of the Industrial Revolution in Europe nearly 300 years ago. There is also evidence of outbreaks of rampant inflation during the Middle Ages and in ancient times.

What is particularly alarming about inflation is its tendency to accelerate in the absence of strong efforts to control it. For example, between 1960 and 1965, the U.S. consumer price index (the CPI, or cost-of-living index) rose an average of only 1.3 percent a year. Then, between 1965 and 1970, in the middle of the Vietnam War with large federal budget deficits and rapid expansion of the money supply, the average annual growth rate of consumer prices more than tripled, climbing to a 4.2 percent annual rate. From 1970 through 1975, the CPI's average annual growth rate rose to almost 8 percent and then soared to average nearly 9 percent through 1980. Finally, large-scale unemployment and back-to-back recessions in the 1980s helped reverse the accelerating trend and significantly lowered the U.S. inflation rate, as shown in Exhibit 21–5. On the heels of a huge military buildup in the Middle East, consumer prices again rose, only to decline during a deep recession beginning in late 1990 and remain low into the 1990s, reflecting only moderate growth in the economy.

What are the *causes* of inflation? During the 1960s and 1970s, war and government spending were certainly contributing factors. Soaring energy and food costs, higher home mortgage rates, and rapid increases in labor and medical care costs also played key roles until the 1980s brought a turnaround. Another contributing factor was the decline in the value of the U.S. dollar in international markets. The dollar's weakness relative to other major currencies (particularly the German mark and the Japanese yen) raised the prices of imports into the United States and lessened the impact of foreign competition on domestic producers.

Still another causal factor is *inflationary expectations*: the anticipation of continued inflation by businesses and households. Once underway, inflation seems to develop a momentum of its own, as consumers spend more and borrow more freely to stay ahead of

Exhibit 21–5   **Measures of the Rate of Inflation in the United States**
Compound Annual Rates of Change)

	Period							
	1960–65	**1965–70**	**1970–75**	**1975–80**	**1980–85**	**1985–90**	**1990–95***	**1996****
Consumer price index (CPI)	1.3%	4.2%	7.7%	8.9%	5.5%	4.0%	2.3%	4.8%
Producer price index, finished goods (PPI)	0.4	2.9	8.6	8.6	3.5	2.6	1.4	3.8
Implicit price deflator for gross national product	1.6	4.2	6.6	7.2	5.4	3.6	2.8	—

*The changes in the consumer price index and the producer price index were measured through November 1995; the deflator is measured through the first quarter of 1995.
**1996 figures are for first month or quarter of the year.

Source: Federal Reserve Bank of St. Louis, *Annual U.S. Economic Data;* U.S. Department of Commerce; and Board of Governors of the Federal Reserve System, *Federal Reserve Bulletin,* Table 2.15, selected issues.

rising prices, sending those prices still higher. Businesses and labor unions begin to build inflation into their price and wage decisions, passing higher costs along in the form of higher prices for goods and services. The result is a wage-price spiral in which each plateau of increased costs is used as a basis for justifying further price increases.

Inflation creates distortions in the allocation of scarce resources and definitely hurts certain groups. For example, it tends to discourage saving and encourages consumption at a faster rate to stay ahead of rising prices. Moreover, the decline in the savings rate tends to discourage capital investment. Unfortunately, this means that the economy's growth in productivity (output per worker-hour) tends to slow. The fall in productivity means that the supply of new goods and services cannot keep pace with rising demands, putting further upward pressure on prices. At the same time, workers usually seek cost-of-living adjustments in wages and salaries, leading to a dramatic increase in labor costs. Some workers represented by strong unions or in growth industries usually manage to keep pace with inflation, but other groups, including many savers, retired persons, and government employees, whose income is fixed or rises slowly, often experience a decline in their real standard of living when inflation is on the rise.

The Goal of Full Employment

The Employment Act of 1946 committed the U.S. government for the first time to *minimizing unemployment* as a major national goal. The Federal Reserve, as part of the government's structure, is therefore committed to this goal as well. In recent years, the U.S. unemployment rate as determined from monthly surveys conducted by the U.S. Department of Labor has hovered in the 5 to 10 percent range. In terms of numbers of people, between 7 and 11 million workers have been actively seeking jobs but have been unable to find them. The nation's output of goods and services and its real standard of living are reduced by unemployment, which also breeds social unrest, increased crime, and higher tax burdens on those who are working.

In some years, the U.S. economy has experienced rising plateaus of unemployment. As the 1960s ended, unemployment affected less than 5 percent of the civilian labor force.

Exhibit 21–6   **U.S. Civilian Unemployment Rate** (Percent of Civilian Labor Force)

1970	4.9%	1991	6.7%
1975	8.5	1992	7.4
1980	7.1	1993	6.8
1985	7.2	1994	6.1
1990	5.5	1995	5.6
		1996*	5.8

*1996 figure is for January. Beginning in 1994, a new unemployment survey was adopted which slightly increased the unemployment rate over previous levels.

Source: *Economic Report of the President* and *Federal Reserve Bulletin,* Table 2.11, selected issues.

A recession in 1970–1971 led to substantial increases in the number of jobless workers, and there was little improvement until 1973, when the jobless rate fell below 5 percent. Following the Arab oil embargo and a deep recession in 1974–1975, the nation's unemployment rate rose to a postwar record of almost 9 percent. (See Exhibit 21–6.) The recovery of the economy between 1976 and 1979 brought the unemployment rate down to just under 6 percent midway in 1979. However, the double-dip recessions of 1980 and 1982 sent unemployment soaring again to more than 10 percent of the labor force. In the middle and late 1980s, the U.S. employment rate fell back and eventually dipped under 6 percent. During the 1990–1993 period, unemployment was on the rise again, due to a sluggish economy, increasing to around 7 percent and then falling below 6 percent as the economy grew at a faster clip later in the 1990s.

Is it possible to have zero unemployment? What is full employment? In a market-oriented economy, where workers are free to change jobs and business people are free to hire and fire, some unemployment is inevitable. There is a minimum level of unemployment, known as *frictional unemployment,* which arises from the temporary unemployment of persons who are changing jobs in response to higher wages or better working conditions. *Full employment,* therefore, refers to a situation in which the only significant amount of unemployment is frictional in nature. In a fully employed economy, everyone actively seeking work finds it in a relatively short period. During the 1960s, the President's Council of Economic Advisers defined full employment as a situation in which only 4 percent of the civilian labor force is unemployed.

In recent years, economists have raised their estimates of the amount of irreducible frictional unemployment. A key factor is the massive shifts that have occurred in the composition of the U.S. labor force in recent years, especially the rapid increase in the number of adult women seeking jobs. Women 20 years of age and older, in fact, have accounted for more than half of the net increase in the U.S. labor force in recent years. This upward surge in women's employment may be attributed to a decline in fertility rates, more varied jobs available to women, and the erosion of family incomes due to inflation. Teenage participation in the labor force also has expanded sharply under the pressure of inflation, the rising cost of college education, and the spread of vocational schools. Historically, these two groups (women and teenagers) have reported higher average unemployment rates than most other workers, moving in and out of the job market with greater fluidity than adult male workers due to family needs and schooling opportunities, thus raising the average unemployment rate.

Other groups also increasing in importance and who traditionally report high unemployment rates include nonwhite workers and unskilled laborers. One of the most conspicuous shortcomings of economic policy in recent years has been its inability to significantly lower the unemployment rate among minority workers and the unskilled. *Structural unemployment* — joblessness due to a lack of necessary skills — has not been reduced to any appreciable extent for many decades.

The Goal of Sustainable Economic Growth

The Federal Reserve has declared that one of its most important long-term goals is to *keep the economy growing at a relatively steady and stable rate*, that is, a rate high enough to absorb increases in the labor force and prevent the unemployment rate from rising but slow enough to avoid runaway inflation. Most economists believe that this implies a rate of growth in GNP or GDP of about 2 to 3 percent annually on a real (inflation-adjusted) basis. Periodically, the economy grows more slowly than this or turns down into a recession, resulting in rising unemployment. (See especially Exhibit 21–7.)

Although most recessions have been relatively brief and mild, they have averaged two each decade, or about one recession every three to five years. For example, during the 1970s, the real output of new goods and services in the United States declined in 1973–1975 and again in 1979–1980. The 1980 recession was the shortest downturn ever recorded, lasting only six months, but it was followed by a deep recession in 1982, when real GNP dropped about 2 percent. However, during the mid-1980s, a strong economic recovery produced accelerated GNP growth, up to as much as 7 percent annually, only to be followed by a significant slowdown late in the 1980s and early 1990s, when GNP grew in the 1 to 2 percent annual rate range. As the decade of the 1990s began, the United States (and several other industrialized economies) entered another recession with negative GNP growth, accompanied by increases in joblessness and a slow-down in inflationary pressures. War in the Persian Gulf seemed to deepen this recession, as consumer and business debt increased, confidence in the future sagged, and consumption spending by U.S. households (as well as business investment spending) was throttled back. By the middle of 1991, however, there were signs of a developing economic recovery, but 1992 and 1993 brought a sluggish economy and a rise in unemployment before the economy resumed moderate growth late in the 1990s.

Forecasting the actual starting point of each recession and its duration has proved to be an exceedingly difficult problem for the Federal Reserve. Each downturn in the economy springs from somewhat different causes, although most recessions involve a sharp cutback in business inventories. Fears of being caught with a large quantity of unsold goods lead to periodic cutbacks in new orders, throwing people out of work. At the same time, interest

Exhibit 21–7   **Rates of Growth in Real U.S. GNP or Real GDP**
(Compounded Annual Rates of Change)

Time Period	Annual Rate of Change in GNP	Time Period	Annual Rate of Change in GDP
1960–69	3.9%	1980–89	3.0%
1970–79	3.5	1990–95*	2.1
		1996**	2.3

*1995 figure is for first three quarters of the year.
**1996 figure is for the first quarter of the year.

Source: Federal Reserve Bank of St. Louis, *National Economic Trends* and *Annual U.S. Economic Data,* various issues; and Board of Governors of the Federal Reserve System, *Federal Reserve Bulletin,* various issues.

rates usually rise to peak levels before a recession begins, gradually choking off private investment.

Traditional economic theory suggests that a decline in the rate of economic growth should lead to a lower rate of inflation. This follows from the observation that recessions are marked by reduced demand for goods and services and falling incomes. Thus, in theory at least, a recession and slower economic growth are short-term cures for severe inflation, although for those without jobs, they are certainly high-cost cures. Interestingly enough, recent recessions have been accompanied by substantial inflation. Many observers believe the bias in the U.S. economy toward inflation, even during recessionary periods, may be due to the rapid growth of service industries relative to the manufacturing sector, welfare payments (especially unemployment compensation) that sustain money incomes, escalator clauses in wage contracts, and the expectation that government policy will always respond quickly to protect jobs whenever economic problems appear.

Equilibrium in the U.S. Balance of Payments and Protecting the Dollar

The Federal Reserve must be concerned not only with domestic economic conditions, but also with developments in the international sector. In this area, the Fed pursues two interrelated goals: (1) protecting the value of the dollar in foreign currency markets and (2) achieving an equilibrium position in the U.S. balance of payments.

When the United States buys more of the goods, services, and securities offered by other nations than those countries spend for what the United States sells, the difference must be made up by giving foreigners claims against U.S. resources. If the United States persists in purchasing or acquiring more abroad than foreigners purchase or acquire here, a disequilibrium position in the balance of payments results. This means that the United States cannot continue to draw down its reserve assets (primarily gold, foreign currencies, and special drawing rights at the International Monetary Fund) indefinitely, nor is it likely to find foreigners willing to accept unlimited amounts of dollars.[3] At some point, the federal government and the Federal Reserve must adopt policies that slow down the outflow of U.S. dollars and encourage foreigners to buy more U.S. goods, services, and securities. Failing this, the value of the dollar in international markets will begin to weaken.

In recent years, the United States has experienced some deep deficits in its merchandise trade with other nations and in its international balance-of-payments position (see Exhibit 21–8). One cause of these international deficits has been massive imports of foreign oil. Other foreign imports into the United States experiencing considerable growth include European and Japanese autos, steel products, building materials, natural gas, and crude rubber. At the same time, foreign investors have at times sharply increased their investments in the United States, making the United States a debtor nation and leading to large outflows of earnings to foreign investors. Early in the 1990s, foreign investment in the United States slowed due to economic problems and stock market crises abroad, especially in Japan, before resuming later in the 1990s.

The sizable trade deficits and current net debtor position of the United States has presented Federal Reserve policymakers with a major dilemma. Should they push up domestic interest rates and limit credit growth to protect the dollar, slow imports, and prevent future inflation? Perhaps, but this would probably slow domestic economic growth

---

[3]See Chapter 28 for a discussion of reserve assets and disequilibrium problems in the U.S. balance of payments.

Exhibit 21–8   **Merchandise Trade Balance of the United States**

Years	FOB Exports Minus CIF Imports ($ Billions)	FOB Exports Minus CIF Imports Years	($ Billions)
1965	$4.3	1987	–$159.5
1970	0.5	1989	–115.9
1975	2.2	1990	–108.1
1980	–36.2	1992	–96.1
1985	–122.1	1995*	–43.4

*Figures for third quarter 1995.

Source: U.S. Department of Commerce and Board of Governors of the Federal Reserve System, *Federal Reserve Bulletin,* Table 3.10, selected issues.

and increase unemployment. This is not an easy dilemma to solve; there are substantial costs no matter which way the central bank chooses to go.

WHAT POLICIES SHOULD WE PURSUE TO ACHIEVE NATIONAL AND INTERNATIONAL ECONOMIC GOALS?

The four key economic goals we have discussed — avoiding inflation, reducing unemployment, achieving healthy and sustainable economic growth, and achieving a strong international payments position — cannot be achieved by wishful thinking. They require carefully constructed economic policies. Unfortunately, there is a long-standing controversy over what these policies should be. Three different views have emerged over the years on what public policy strategies contribute most to low inflation, high employment, strong growth, and stable international payments. These three competing viewpoints on public policy are known as: (1) the Monetarist view, (2) the credit availability (neo-Keynesian) view, and (3) supply-side economics. We will look briefly at each one and how it proposes to solve economic problems.

Monetarist View

An approach to economic policy with varying popularity in recent years is the **Monetarist view.** Among the most important proponents of this particular approach to government policy are economists Milton Friedman, Karl Brunner, Alan Melter, David Meiselman, Anna Schwartz, Christopher Sims, and others.[4] These economists argue that the *money supply* is the dominant influence on prices, spending, production, and employment. Friedman and Schwartz (1963 p. 53), for example, after analyzing money and business cycles dating back to the Civil War, concluded that "appreciable changes in the rate of growth of the money stock are a necessary and sufficient condition for appreciable changes in the rate of growth of money income." Moreover, changes in the rate of money supply growth appear to precede changes in economic activity and inflation, suggesting that money exerts an independent causal influence on economic conditions. They believe the economy is inherently stable and tends toward full employment without inflation if left to its own

---

[4]See especially Friedman and Schwartz (1963), Anderson and Carlson (1970), and Laidler (1990) in the reference list at the end of this chapter.

devices. One of the ways in which government can aid the economy in achieving noninflationary growth and full employment is to avoid trying to fine tune the system with frequent government interference. Allegedly, attempts at fine-tuning do more harm than good, causing instability in the economy.

According to the Monetarist view, monetary policy affects the economy mainly through changes in the rate of the monetary growth. For example, if the money supply grows too rapidly, exceeding the public's expectations, an excess stock of money results. Money demand for goods and services rises rapidly and puts upward pressure on prices.[5] In contrast, when the money supply grows too slowly relative to the demand for money, the public attempts to restore its desired money balances by cutting back on spending and purchases of financial assets. The result is a drop in income and demand in the economy and a rise in interest rates so that employment and growth are slowed. The Federal Reserve can exert its most favorable effect on the economy simply by allowing the money supply to grow at a relatively constant rate (preferably about 4 to 6 percent a year), which approximates the long-term rate of growth in the economy's capacity to produce goods and services. Monetarists believe the central bank can best effect desired rates of money growth by controlling the monetary base, not by pegging interest rates (such as the federal funds rate). Unfortunately, the traditional statistical relationship between money and economic output has been so weakened over the past decade that the Monetarist view has lost much of its empirical support. Moreover, recent innovations in monetary assets and in the public's money-using habits have made it exceedingly difficult to define exactly what makes up the money supply at any moment in time.

The Credit Availability, or Neo-Keynesian, View

A more traditional approach to fighting inflation is known as the **credit availability**, or **neo-Keynesian, view**.[6] Adherents to this view believe that a wide range of factors — monetary and nonmonetary — influence employment, growth, and prices. They argue that the money supply is an important factor in generating business cycles, but it is not necessarily the most important factor. Government spending and taxation (fiscal policy) as well as money and credit policy also play critical roles in creating or reducing inflation and unemployment because of their impact on investment spending, which is the most volatile component of the total demand for goods and services in the economy. Changes in investment expenditures have a multiplier effect on total income in the economy because new investment generates income, which leads to increased consumption and still more income. Thus, even small changes in the volume and mix of investment expenditures can lead to magnified changes in income, employment, and prices.

How can government fiscal and monetary policy affect investment spending and exert an impact on inflation, employment, and growth? According to the neo-Keynesian view,

---

[5]Monetarists base this conclusion on the assumption that each unit (individual or business) in the economy desires to hold a certain quantity of money. If the money supply grows so large that it exceeds desired levels, then the cost of holding additional money exceeds its benefits. Businesses and individuals attempt to spend away their excess money balances by purchasing goods, services, and other assets. With the economy at or near full employment, prices must rise due to the added spending.

[6]The term *neo-Keynesian* is often used to describe economists who have adopted, amplified, and further refined many of the ideas of British economist John Maynard Keynes. Keynes wrote several books and many articles covering the period from World War I through World War II; his views on the causes of unemployment, inflation, and other economic problems appear in *The General Theory of Employment, Interest, and Money* (1936). Leading economists who have further refined and developed the original Keynesian theories include Patinkin (1976), Tobin (1965), and Smith (1969).

the volume of investment spending is affected directly by the cost and availability of credit, monetary growth, and total wealth. The rate of interest is especially important here, because it is a measure of the cost of financing new investment spending. A rise in interest rates, other things being equal, reduces the demand for investment funds, slowing the growth of employment, income, and prices. In contrast, lower interest rates stimulate the demand for investment, which increases income and employment and may cause more inflation (if the economy is at or near full employment). The Federal Reserve can bring about changes in interest rates, up or down, by changing the real money supply (i.e., money adjusted for changes in the price level). For example, rising inflation can be countered by slower monetary growth. If the money supply grows more slowly than the public's demand for real money balances, interest rates rise, leading to a decline in investment spending. Income in the economy grows more slowly, and inflationary pressures are reduced.

We can illustrate these hypothesized effects of changes in the money supply on interest rates and income by using a familiar methodology in economics: IS-LM analysis. This well-known tool of economic analysis is based on two key relationships: (1) the effects of changing money supply and money demand on both interest rates and income and (2) the effects of changing saving and investment decisions (including government borrowing) on both interest rates and income. IS-LM analysis assumes that there are *two* equilibrium relationships between all these factors, each represented in Exhibit 21–9. The *LM curve* is a locus (collection) of equilibrium interest rates for which money demand (*L*) equals money supply (*M*). For each level of income specified along the horizontal axis in Exhibit 21–9, the point on the LM curve directly above that level of income gives the equilibrium interest rate at which L = M. Similarly, the *IS curve* is a locus (collection) of equilibrium levels of income at which the volume of planned savings (*S*) equals the volume of planned investment (*I*), including government borrowing. For any given interest rate along the vertical axis of Exhibit 21–9, the IS curve shows that level of income at which point the economy is in equilibrium (with *S = I*). At the exact point where the IS and LM curves cross, both the economy and interest rates in the financial markets are in *equilibrium*.

Exhibit 21–9   **How Equilibrium Interest Rates and Income Change with Shifts in the Money Supply**

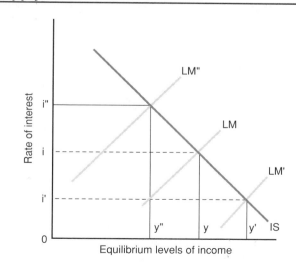

But suppose the Federal Reserve *increases the money supply.* In the short run, at least, the LM curve shifts downward and to the right to *LM'*, resulting in a *lower equilibrium interest rate (i').* Because the lower equilibrium interest rate stimulates new investment spending, there is a rise in economic activity to a new and *higher equilibrium level of income (y').* Thus, a monetary policy action by the Fed affects *both* interest rates and income (production and spending).

Suppose the Federal Reserve *decreases the money supply.* The LM curve contracts backward and to the left to *LM''*, resulting in a *higher equilibrium interest rate (i'').* With higher interest rates, some investment spending is discouraged, reducing the level of overall economic activity. A *lower equilibrium level of income (y'')* results.

Fiscal policy — government taxing and spending — also has a significant role to play in slowing inflation and promoting high employment and growth according to the neo-Keynesian view. If total spending in the private sector of the economy grows too rapidly, generating inflation, government spending can be reduced, which soon leads to less consumption spending and decreased private investment. In other words, government spending, like private spending, has a multiplier effect, up or down, on employment, income, and prices. Alternatively, private consumption and investment spending can be choked off by higher taxes. Through increased tax revenues, governments can reduce budget deficits or even run budget surpluses so that the government sector actually withdraws funds from the private spending stream. Demand for goods and services falls, leading to reduced inflationary pressures but also some increase in unemployment and slower economic growth.

Thus, the neo-Keynesian, or credit availability, view stresses the necessity of using *both* monetary and fiscal policy to achieve economic goals. Neo-Keynesians question whether merely maintaining a constant rate of growth in the money supply will, by itself, solve the twin problems of inflation and unemployment. The appropriate growth rate for money depends on economic conditions, the status of government fiscal policy, and especially the public's demand for money. Under some circumstances (especially if the demand for money were falling), a 4 percent rate of growth in the money supply could be highly inflationary. Under other circumstances (such as following a rapid rise in money demand), 4 percent money growth could lead to severe recession and higher unemployment. In either case, suggest the neo-Keynesians, the key factors to watch in gauging the direction and impact of monetary policy are interest rates and the growth of the real money supply. To fight inflation, reduce the growth rate of the real money supply and increase interest rates; to stimulate employment and economic growth, speed up real money growth and lower interest rates.

Supply-Side Economics

Shortly after President Ronald Reagan took office in January 1981, his administration announced a different approach to economic problems. It was labeled **supply-side economics**, to differentiate this strategy from methods employed during most of the postwar period that attacked inflation and unemployment from the demand side of the marketplace. Just as logically, supply-siders claimed, we could solve inflation and unemployment problems from the supply side — by increasing the output of goods and services. If the economy produces more goods and services relative to the public's demand, there is less reason for prices to rise and more jobs will open up.

How can this be done? Basically, by stimulating private investment and increasing savings to finance that investment. As Tatom (1981, p. 18) notes, "Supply-side economics is growth- and efficiency-oriented." The theory argues that economic policy has a direct impact on the rate of growth in the supply of productive resources and on technological innovation — factors that determine the economy's capacity to produce. The economy's productive capacity is lowered by government regulations that require the use of inefficient technologies or that reduce incentives to save and invest in resources. The same is true of an excessive tax burden that transfers resources from the private to the public sector. In an effort to avoid high tax rates, resource owners will divert their resources to lower-taxed, but less-efficient, equipment and spend more on consumption instead of saving. Supply-siders in recent years have recommended the following:

1. A lower and more stable rate of monetary expansion.

2. Less government regulation of business to stimulate competition and technological innovation.

3. Reduced tax rates on individual incomes and business profits to stimulate saving.

4. Accelerated depreciation of business equipment to stimulate investment.

5. A reduction in the size of the government sector in order to divert more resources into the private sector and into free markets.

Can the supply-side approach really work to simultaneously subdue inflation, bring about stable long-term economic growth with low unemployment, and improve the U.S. international payments position? The evidence from the decade of the 1980s and 1990s is decidedly mixed. The U.S. inflation rate *has* dropped significantly since its record high levels in the late 1970s, but at the price of slower economic growth. And deficits in the U.S. balance of payments have remained quite high in recent years. Much depends on the *psychological effects* of supply-side economics — its ability to persuade businesses to increase investment in plant and equipment and to convince savers to spend less on current consumption and save more. Moreover, lowering tax rates in the 1980s contributed to higher federal budget deficits that, combined with other factors, kept interest rates at relatively high levels and limited growth in private investment. Thus, it is not at all clear that supply-side economics, like Monetarism or the neo-Keynesian approach, can ensure progress toward all of society's economic goals.

THE TRADE-OFFS AMONG ECONOMIC GOALS

As we have seen in this chapter, the United States and other nations face some serious economic problems. Inflation is less severe today than in the turbulent 1970s, but unemployment and balance-of-payments problems present imposing difficulties. Does this mean that the Federal Reserve System and other government policymaking agencies have simply failed to do their jobs?

Unfortunately, the problem is not that simple. For one thing, economic goals *conflict*. For example, controlling inflation and stabilizing the U.S. international payments situation usually require the Fed to slow down the economy through restricted money supply growth and higher interest rates. However, this policy threatens to generate more unemployment and subdue economic growth. Evidence that economic goals frequently conflict was provided by British economist A. W. Phillips (1958) and U.S. economists Paul Samuelson and Robert Solow (1960) more than three decades ago. These economists uncovered an *inverse* relationship between price-level increases (inflation) and unemployment. For example, Samuelson and Solow, using data collected from the 1950s, found that stable prices could be achieved only if unemployment remained as high as 5 to 6 percent of the civilian labor force. In recent years, U.S. unemployment has hovered in the 5 to 10 percent range, while prices continue to rise about 3 to 6 percent a year. Such policy trade-offs may not be valid in the long term, as Laidler (1990) and others have recently observed; however, it is clear that the process of attaining economic stability with *both* low inflation and low unemployment can be both difficult and painful. Worse still, the government, supposedly acting in the public interest, has never prioritized the nation's economic goals so that central bank policymakers have a clear idea of which goals or goals are most important. There does appear to be a growing consensus, however, that the most feasible, long-term goal for monetary policy is probably to *control inflation* (i.e., maintain reasonable price stability).

THE LIMITATIONS OF MONETARY POLICY

In addition to conflicts among economic goals, the Federal Reserve finds that it cannot completely control financial conditions or the money supply. Changes in the economy itself feed back on the money supply and the financial markets. It becomes exceedingly difficult, especially on a weekly or monthly basis, to sort out the effects of monetary policy from the impact of broad economic forces. Moreover, the structure of the economy itself is changing — as Mauskopf (1990) observes — due to deregulation of interest rates and financial services, the abandonment of fixed exchange rates, and the increasing integration of global money and capital markets. As a result, international currency markets have begun to exert a greater impact on the domestic economy and on Federal Reserve policy-making, while changes in domestic interest rates are probably not as potent a factor affecting the economy as they were a decade ago. The Federal Reserve and other central banks must learn how to deal with these changes in fundamental economic relationships.

Finally, the Fed has received only limited cooperation from Congress in the pursuit of effective taxing and spending programs. Most economists agree that fiscal policy — the taxing and spending activities of the federal government — can have a potent impact on economic conditions. Unfortunately, changes in tax rates and federal spending programs require the cooperation of both the executive and legislative branches of the government. This kind of cooperation between Congress and the president has been difficult to achieve on a long-term basis. Frequently, the Federal Reserve System has been forced to carry the burden of economic policy almost totally alone. Under these circumstances, we should not be surprised to learn that the Fed's track record leaves much to be desired.

KEY TERMS AND CONCEPTS IN THIS CHAPTER

legal reserves	M3	nonborrowed reserves
Federal Reserve Statement	L	Monetarist view
M1	D	The credit availability, or neo-Keynesian, view
M2	borrowed reserves	supply-side economics

STUDY QUESTIONS

1. Why are indicators of Federal Reserve policy important to the Fed itself and to managers of financial institutions, corporate treasurers, and the public?

2. What is a *money market indicator*? Give examples and explain how these indicators reflect changes in credit conditions.

3. List and define the various measures of the money supply. Why do we need several different measures of money?

4. What are the principal items on the Federal Reserve Statement? Which of these items reflect Federal Reserve activities?

5. What are *borrowed reserves*? *Nonborrowed reserves*? What role does each play in current Federal Reserve strategy to regulate the growth of the money supply?

6. Define what is meant by *net free reserves* and *net borrowed reserves.* How would you interpret changes in these money market indicators?

7. Explain how the actions of the U.S. Treasury can influence the reserves of depository institutions.

8. List the principal economic goals of Federal Reserve monetary policy and define each. Which of these goals have been reasonably well achieved in recent years, and which have not? Try to explain why.

9. Explain the basic similarities and differences between the Monetarist and neo-Keynesian approaches to monetary policy. How would each deal with inflation? With unemployment?

10. What is *supply-side economics*? Do you see any problems in trying to implement the supply-side approach?

11. Outline the steps that the Federal Reserve System goes through in trying to control the growth rate of the money supply and to hit its Federal funds interest rate targets. What difficulties do you see in the Fed's approach?

12. What trade-offs appear to exist among the key economic goals? Why do you think these trade-offs exist?

PROBLEMS

1. Suppose the banking system's nonborrowed reserves total $48.3 billion, with total legal reserves standing at $51.2 billion. What must borrowed reserves be? This morning the Federal Reserve decided to undertake the sale of $500 million in government securities through open market operations. What will be the new level of nonborrowed reserves? If interest rates do not change, what will be the new level of total reserves? What must you assume to make this calculation? If interest rates do change, which way are they likely to move?

2. If the banking system has excess reserves of $410 million and a condition of net free reserves prevails in the amount of $260 million, what must the total volume of borrowings from the Federal Reserve banks be?

3. Suppose Federal Reserve Bank credit grows by $4 billion, the U.S. gold stock rises by $1 billion, special drawing rights held by the U.S. government advance by $650 million, and Treasury currency outstanding increases by $130 million. Moreover, the public increases currency and coin in circulation by $6 billion. Treasury cash holdings increase by $200 million, deposits other than reserve balances at the Reserve banks rise by $1.5 billion, and other Fed liabilities and capital grow by $100 million. By how much will reserve balances held at the Federal Reserve banks increase?

SELECTED REFERENCES

Anderson, Leonall C., and Keith Carlson. "A Monetarist Model for Economic Stabilization." *Review.* Federal Reserve Bank of St. Louis, April 1970.

Cacy, J.A. "Monetary Policy in 1980 and 1981." *Economic Review,* Federal Reserve Bank of Kansas City, December 1980, pp. 18–25.

Friedman, Milton, and Anna Jacobson Schwartz. *A Monetary History of the United States, 1867–1960.* Princeton, N.J.: Princeton University Press, 1963.

Gilbert, R. Alton. "Operating Procedures for Conducting Monetary Policy." *Review.* Federal Reserve Bank of St. Louis, February 1985, pp. 13–21.

Heller, H. Robert. "The Monetary Policy-Making Process," Speech to the Money Marketers, New York City, April 11, 1989.

———. "Implementing Monetary Policy." *Federal Reserve Bulletin,* July 1988, pp. 419–29.

Keynes, John M. *The General Theory of Employment, Interest and Money.* London: Macmillian, 1936.

Laidler, David. "The Legacy of the Monetarist Controversy." *Review.* Federal Reserve Bank of St. Louis, March–April 1990, pp. 49–64.

Long, Richard W. "The FOMC in 1979: Introducing Reserve Targeting." *Review.* Federal Reserve Bank of St. Louis, March 1980.

Mauskopf, Eileen. "The Transmission Channels of Monetary Policy: How Have They Changed?" *Federal Reserve Bulletin,* December 1990, pp. 985–1008.

Patinkin, Don. *Keynes' Monetary Thought: A Study of Its Development.* Durham, N.C: Duke University Press, 1976.

Phillips, A.W. "The Relation between Unemployment and the Rate of Change of Money Wage Rates in the United Kingdom, 1961–1957." *Economica,* November 1958.

Samuelson, Paul A., and Robert M. Solow. "The Problem of Achieving and Maintaining a Stable Price Level: Analytical Aspects of Anti-Inflation Policy." *America Economic Review,* May 1960.

Sellon, Gordon, Jr. "The Role of the Discount Rate in Monetary Policy: A Theoretical Analysis." *Economic Review.* Federal Bank of Kansas City, June 1980.

———. *The Recent Evolution of Federal Reserve Operating Procedures.* Research Working Paper 86–13, Federal Reserve Bank of Kansas City, December 1986.

Smith, Warren L. "A Neo-Keynesian View of Monetary Policy." In *Controlling Monetary Aggregates,* ed. Federal Reserve Bank of Boston, 1969.

Tatom, John A. "We Are All Supply-Siders Now!" *Review.* Federal Reserve Bank of St. Louis, May 1981, pp. 18–30.

Tobin, James. "The Monetary Interpretation of History." *American Economic Review,* June 1965.

Wallich, Henry. Member of the Board of Governors of the Federal Reserve System. "Recent Techniques of Monetary Policy." Speech to the Midwest Finance Association, Chicago, April 15, 1984.

Chapter 22

The Treasury in the Financial Markets

LEARNING OBJECTIVES IN THIS CHAPTER

- To examine the many important roles played by the Treasury Department in supporting federal government programs and pursuing the federal government's goals and objectives.

- To identify how the federal government raises funds and how it spends the funds that it raises.

- To understand how the activities of the Treasury Department affect the financial markets and the economy.

- To explore the meaning, purpose, and impact of two key government policy tools: fiscal policy and debt management policy.

One of the most important financial institutions in any economy is the government treasury. In the United States, the Treasury Department exerts a powerful impact on the financial system because of two activities that it pursues on a continuing basis. One of these is **fiscal policy,** which refers to the taxing and spending programs of the federal government designed to promote high employment, sustainable economic growth, and other worthwhile economic goals. A second area in which the Treasury exerts a potent effect on financial conditions is **debt management policy,** which involves the refunding or refinancing of the federal government's huge debt in a way that contributes to broad economic goals and minimizes the burden of the federal debt. These Treasury policymaking activities influence interest rates and the availability of credit for all sectors of the economy. In general, the Treasury pursues policies designed to achieve its economic goals but not to disturb the functioning of the financial markets or unduly interfere with the operations of the Federal Reserve System.

THE FISCAL POLICY ACTIVITIES OF THE U.S. TREASURY

Congress dictates the amount of funds the federal government will spend each year for a variety of programs ranging from welfare to national defense. Congress also determines

Exhibit 22–1   **Federal Government Revenues, Expenditures, and Net Budget Surplus or Deficit, Selected Fiscal Years, 1969–95** ($ Billions)

Fiscal Years	Total Revenues	Total Expenditures	Net Budget Surplus or Deficit
1969	$ 186.9	$ 183.6	$ 3.2
1970	192.8	195.6	–2.8
1980	517.1	590.9	–73.8
1990	1,031.3	1,251.8	–220.5
1995*	1,346.4	1,538.9	–192.5

*Estimates by the U.S. Department of the Treasury and the Office of Management and Budget.
Note: Figures based on the unified budget for fiscal years. Before 1977, fiscal years ran from July 1 through June 30. Thereafter, the federal government's fiscal year covered the October 1– September 30 period.
Source: The President's Council of Economic Advisers, *Economic Report of the President,* selected years.

the sources of tax revenue and the tax rates that must be paid by individuals and businesses. Frequently, Congress votes for a higher amount of spending than can be supported by tax revenues. Alternatively, due to a slowdown in the economy, tax revenues may fall short of projections and not be sufficient to cover planned expenditures. Either way, the result is a **budget deficit,** requiring the U.S. Treasury to borrow additional funds in the financial markets. On the other hand, government revenues may occasionally exceed expenditures, resulting in a **budget surplus,** which the Treasury may use to build up its cash balances or to retire debt previously issued.

As shown in Exhibit 22–1, U.S. Treasury budget surpluses have been *very* infrequent. In fact, the federal budget has been in surplus in only three fiscal years since 1931. The last federal budget surplus occurred during the 1969 fiscal year, when revenues exceeded expenditures by about $3 billion. Since that time, the federal budget has been continually in deficit. It seems safe to assume at this point that, even in the face of recent efforts by the administration of President Bill Clinton and a Republican-dominated Congress to reduce federal spending, federal budget deficits will continue to be a problem, forcing the Treasury to borrow a large volume of funds annually in the financial marketplace.

Sources of Federal Government Funds

It is interesting to analyze the sources of revenue the federal government draws upon to fund its activities. Exhibit 22–2 presents information on the principal sources of federal revenue and spending programs. On the revenue side, the bulk of incoming funds is derived from taxes levied against individual and family incomes. In fiscal 1995, for example, individuals were expected to pay an estimated $588 billion in income taxes, representing about 44 percent of all federal revenues that year. Social security taxes were forecast to supply $484 billion — more than a third of total federal revenue. Corporate income taxes were projected a distant third at 11 percent, and other taxes and fees for government services were expected to provide about 9 percent of all federal revenues.

During the 1970s and early 1980s, the share of federal revenues produced by personal income taxes declined. This was due to efforts by Congress to reduce withholding taxes and increase personal deductions against individual income taxes. Later, in the 1990s, personal income tax revenue rose or held steady as a proportion of all government receipts, reflecting Congress' desire to shift the tax burden more heavily onto the wealthy. At the same time, payroll taxes for social insurance increased as Congress moved to rescue the social security system from deepening deficits. Corporate taxes were increased in an effort

Exhibit 22–2   **Federal Government Revenues, Expenditures, and Net Budget Surplus or Deficit, 1995** (Estimates, $ Billions)

Budget Item	Amount	Percent of Total
On- and Off-Budget *Receipts* by Source:		
Individual income taxes	$588.5	43.7%
Corporation income taxes	150.9	11.2
Social insurance taxes & contributions	484.4	36.0
Other sources of revenue	122.7	9.1
Total revenues	$1,346.4	100.0%
On- and Off-Budget *Expenditures* by Function:		
National defense	$271.6	17.6%
International affairs	18.7	1.2
Health care	115.1	7.5
Medicare	157.3	10.2
Income security programs	223.0	14.5
Social security	336.1	21.8
Net interest payments on the federal debt	234.2	15.2
Other expenditures	182.8	11.9
Total expenditures	$1,538.9	100.0%

Note: Columns may not add to totals due to rounding.

Source: President's Council of Economic Advisers, *Economic Report of the President*, 1995.

to offset declining personal tax rates and reduce budget deficits. These changes in tax rates suggest that the federal government has attempted in recent years to make the tax structure more responsive to the nation's economic problems. When the economy headed down into a recession or inflation pushed individuals into higher tax brackets, Congress generally responded with income tax adjustments. There has also been a trend toward income tax simplification in an effort to make personal tax accounting and tax decisions fairer and less burdensome.

Federal Government Expenditures

Reflecting the effects of rising taxes and inflation, the U.S. government today collects an enormous volume of revenue from its citizens. For example, federal revenues were expected to reach more than $1.3 trillion in 1995. Where does the federal government spend this money?

Exhibit 22–2 indicates that more than half of all federal spending goes for national defense and various income security programs, including social security, Medicare, and unemployment compensation. The latter programs are designed to sustain the spending power of individuals who are retired, disabled, or temporarily unemployed. The collapse of the Warsaw Pack in Europe and economic and political problems inside the Confederation of Independent States (the former Soviet Union) stimulated the U.S. government to begin cutting back on spending for national defense (as a "peace dividend" from the end of the cold war) and to shift more resources toward social programs and environmental protection (including more funds for medical research, improved educational opportunities for children from low-income families, an upgrading of public housing and rental assistance programs, stronger antidrug programs, improved facilities for safeguarding air travel, and more aggressive efforts to clean up the environment and promote research on alternative energy sources). However, by the mid-1990s the rapid growth of Medicare and other social programs prompted Congress and the president to work toward slowing the growth of these programs.

Recent Tax and Expenditure Legislation

Confronted with inflation and deepening federal deficits, Congress and the president responded in the 1980s with major pieces of fiscal legislation that continue to affect the financial markets today. For example, in August 1981, Congress passed the Economic Recovery Tax Act, which brought about significant cuts in individual income tax rates. In addition, accelerated depreciation allowances, investment tax credits, and tax incentives for business research expenditures were included in the Economic Recovery Act in an attempt to increase investment spending and create jobs. Income tax brackets and personal exemptions were adjusted for the effects of inflation. This last provision, known as *indexing,* is designed to eliminate bracket creep, the tendency for inflation to push individual incomes into higher tax brackets. One purpose of the changes was to stimulate saving and business investment in order to reduce inflationary pressures in the economy.

Although the Economic Recovery Act may have made a significant contribution toward reducing inflation, it also contributed to deepening federal budget deficits. As Exhibit 22–1 shows, the budget deficit nearly tripled between 1980 and 1990, forcing the U.S. Treasury to borrow unprecedented amounts in the financial markets and confronting private borrowers with both higher interest rates and more limited availability of credit. The most notable legislation during this period was the Gramm-Rudman-Hollings bill (known officially as the *Balanced Budget and Emergency Deficit Control Act),* which mandated reduced budget deficits until the deficit would be completely eliminated in fiscal 1991. However, Congress soon found loopholes in Gramm-Rudman, and a more slowly growing economy generated sharply reduced tax collections. In 1992, Congress debated a balanced budget amendment to the U.S. Constitution that would have required a balance between revenues and expenditures each year, but the measure failed to pass. However, due in part to continuing public support for deficit reductions, the federal government's deficit fell as a percentage of the U.S. GDP from nearly 5 percent in 1985 to about 3 percent in 1995. At this point, President Bill Clinton and a Republican-led Congress sought out compromise legislation in an effort to eliminate federal deficits within seven years.

Effects of Federal Borrowing and Budget Deficits on the Financial System and the Economy

What are the effects of government borrowing on the economy and the financial markets? If the federal government runs a *small* budget deficit, it is possible for the Treasury to cover the shortfall in revenues by drawing on its accumulated cash balances held at the Federal Reserve banks or even by issuing new currency. In recent years, however, government deficits have been so large that substantial amounts of new debt securities have been issued. The impact of these massive borrowings on the money and capital markets and the economy depends, in part, on the *source* of borrowed funds. Exhibit 22–3 summarizes the probable effects of government borrowing designed to cover a budget deficit.

Borrowing from the Nonbank Public. For example, suppose the Treasury needs to borrow $20 billion, which it raises by selling government bonds to the nonbank public. As the public pays for these securities, it writes checks against its deposits held with depository institutions, initially reducing the size of the money supply. As these checks are deposited in the Treasury's accounts at the Federal Reserve banks, legal reserves held by depository institutions decline by $20 billion.

To gauge the full effects of government borrowing, however, we must consider the fact that the government plans to *spend* its borrowed funds. In our example, the Treasury will write checks totaling $20 billion against its Federal Reserve accounts and distribute those

Exhibit 22–3   **Effects of Government Borrowing on the Financial Markets and the Economy**

Borrowing from the Nonbank Public

	Federal Reserve Banks		Depository Financial Institutions	
	Assets	*Liabilities*	*Assets*	*Liabilities*
Sale of securities		Legal reserves of depository institutions −20	Legal reserves −20	Deposits of the public −20
		Government deposits +20		
Spending of borrowed funds		Government deposits −20	Legal reserves +20	Deposits of the public +20
		Legal reserves of depository institutions +20		

EFFECTS: No change in the money supply or total reserves; total spending in the economy and interest rates rise.

Borrowing from Depository Institutions

	Federal Reserve Banks		Depository Financial Institutions	
	Assets	*Liabilities*	*Assets*	*Liabilities*
Sale of securities		Legal reserves of depository institutions −20	Government securities +20	
		Government deposits +20	Legal reserves −20	
Spending of borrowed funds		Legal reserves of depository institutions +20	Legal reserves +20	Deposits of the public +20
		Government deposits −20		

EFFECTS: The money supply increases; total reserves are unchanged, but excess reserves fall due to increases in deposits; total spending and interest rates rise.

Borrowing from the Federal Reserve Banks

	Federal Reserve Banks		Depository Financial Institutions	
	Assets	*Liabilities*	*Assets*	*Liabilities*
Sale of secuities	Government securities +20	Government deposits +20		
Spending of borrowed funds		Government deposits −20	Legal reserves +20	Deposits of the public +20
		Legal reserves of depository institutions +20		

EFFECTS: The money supply and total reserves increase, while total spending in the economy rises and interest rates tend to fall.

checks to the public. Deposits of the public rise by $20 billion, also increasing the legal reserves held by depository institutions.

On balance, after all transactions are completed, there is *no change* in the money supply or in the total amount of reserves held by the banking system. However, there is likely to be an *increase* in total spending and income in the economy due to the fact that funds are transferred from those who purchase securities to members of the public receiving government checks. Presumably, recipients of government checks have a higher marginal propensity to spend new income than do security investors, who have a higher marginal propensity to save any new income received. Aggregate consumption spending will probably increase, and if the economy is at or near full employment, inflation may rise. Initially, the increased sale of Treasury securities should put upward pressure on interest rates. Over a longer-term period, however, it is quite possible that interest rates will eventually fall due to the higher levels of income and increased saving out of that income.

Borrowing from Depository Institutions. The effects of government borrowing are somewhat different if the borrowing takes place entirely from depository institutions. If we assume that the Treasury borrows $20 billion, deposit-type institutions pay for the securities they purchase by drafts against their legal reserve accounts held at the Federal Reserve banks. Reserves of depository institutions drop by $20 billion, as shown in Exhibit 22–3, and the Treasury's deposits rise by a like amount. However, the Treasury spends these borrowed funds, resulting in an increase in deposits held by the public and in legal reserves. The money supply rises because the public's deposits increase.

On balance, after all transactions are completed, legal reserves remain unchanged, but excess reserves fall because of the increase in deposits. There is also likely to be an increase in spending and income as the public gains additional funds. Prices may rise if unemployment is low. Interest rates may increase in the short run with the increased quantity of government securities available. However, the gain in total spending should lead eventually to a decline in interest rates due to the expansion of savings.

Borrowing from the Federal Reserve Banks. A third route for government borrowing would be to secure credit directly from the central bank. For example, in the United States, this might be done by having the Treasury issue securities directly to the Federal Reserve banks. However, this is a highly *inflationary* way for the federal government to raise money. Financially speaking, it is the equivalent of printing money. Therefore, borrowing from the Fed is restricted by law. Nevertheless, in a severe national emergency such as a serious depression, the Fed would probably be called upon to provide greater support for Treasury borrowing activities.

How would borrowing from the central bank work? The Federal Reserve banks acquire securities and increase the Treasury's deposits by the same amount. Initially, there is no withdrawal of reserves from the banking system, nor does the public lose deposits. Instead, both legal reserves and the public's deposits rise by the amount of any borrowed funds spent by the Treasury. In the example shown in Exhibit 22–3, the Treasury sells $20 billion in securities to the Federal Reserve banks, and its deposit accounts at the Fed rise by a like amount. As the Treasury spends the $20 billion, public deposits and reserves rise, causing increases in the money supply, total spending, and income. Interest rates tend to fall due to the increase in the money supply and to growth in savings over the long run.

Effects of the Retirement of Government Debt from a Budget Surplus on the Financial System and the Economy

Occasionally, the federal government runs a budget *surplus.* By definition, a budget surplus implies that the government withdraws a greater amount of funds from the economy in the form of tax collections than it puts back into the economy through government expenditures. The Treasury could save these surplus funds to cover deficits in later years. However, this is usually unpopular from a political standpoint. It is more likely that a government budget surplus would be used to retire debt previously issued. But the impact of government debt retirement on the economy and the financial system depends, in part, on who happens to hold the debt securities the government plans to retire.

Retiring Government Debt Held by the Nonbank Public. Suppose the securities scheduled for retirement are held by individuals and institutions *not* a part of the banking system. In this case, there will be little or no change in the money supply or in the reserves held by depository institutions.

This is illustrated in Exhibit 22–4, where the act of retiring government debt is separated into two steps. In the first step, we assume that the Treasury collects a surplus of $20 billion in tax revenues. This might arise, for example, if the federal government spent $100 billion, but collected $120 billion, in taxes from the public. Clearly, the public's deposits drop a *net* $20 billion. Moreover, as members of the public write checks against their transaction deposits to pay taxes, legal reserves of depository institutions also fall a net $20 billion. The Treasury's deposits at the Federal Reserve banks rise by a like amount.

Assume that the Treasury uses its surplus funds to retire securities held by the nonbank public. Security holders receive government checks totaling $20 billion, which are deposited in banks and thrifts. Legal reserves of these institutions rise by $20 billion. Of course, the Treasury loses the same amount of money from its deposits at the Federal Reserve as the government's checks are cleared. The public's deposits and money supply first decline and then rise by $20 billion, with reserves following the same path. Is there no effect, then, from retiring securities held by the nonbank public? Not likely, because the government has transferred money from the general public (taxpayers), with a high propensity to spend, to security investors who tend to be heavy savers. The net effect is probably to *reduce* total spending in the economy. Prices of goods and services may fall and unemployment may rise. It is likely, too, that interest rates will decline because the total supply of securities is being reduced, while the volume of investible savings rises in the short run.

Retiring Government Debt Held by Depository Institutions. What happens if the government uses its budget surplus to retire securities held by banks and other depository institutions? Initially, the effects are much the same. Funds are withdrawn from taxpayer deposit accounts and transferred to the Treasury's deposits at the Federal Reserve. Legal reserves of depository institutions fall by the amount of the tax surplus (in Exhibit 22–4 by $20 billion). Now, however, the surplus funds are paid to depository institutions, who turn in their securities to the Treasury. Legal reserves rise as the government spends its $20 billion deposit.

In the short term, the money supply is reduced due to the drain on taxpayer funds. Total legal reserves are unchanged, first falling and then rising. Note, however, that excess reserves increase because total legal reserves are unchanged when deposits fall. In the long term, the money supply expands due to the gain in excess reserves. With fewer taxpayer funds, however, spending in the economy should decline, which may increase unemployment. Interest rates, too, will probably decline in the short run because fewer securities are now available to investors.

Budget surpluses and the retirement of government debt tend to slow down economic activity and, therefore, could be used as a vehicle to combat inflation. If the federal government wanted to have a maximum deflationary impact on the economy, whose securities should it retire? The Treasury could have the greatest anti-inflationary impact by retiring government securities held by the Federal Reserve banks. This approach would be the equivalent of destroying money.

Exhibit 22–4   **Effects of Retiring Government Debt on the Financial Markets and the Economy**

Retiring Government Securities Held by the Nonbank Public

	Federal Reserve Banks			Depository Financial Institutions		
	Assets	*Liabilities*		*Assets*	*Liabilities*	
Collection of tax surplus		Legal reserves of depository institutions	−20	Legal reserves −20	Deposits of taxpayers	−20
		Government deposits	+20			
Retiring government securities		Government deposits	−20	Legal reserves +20	Deposits of public	+20
		Legal reserves of depository institutions	+20			

EFFECTS: No change in the money supply or in bank reserves; total spending tends to fall because funds move from active to passive spenders; interest rates tend to decline.

Retiring Government Securities Held by Depository Institutions

	Federal Reserve Banks			Depository Financial Institutions		
	Assets	*Liabilities*		*Assets*	*Liabilities*	
Collection of tax surplus		Legal reserves of depository institutions	−20	Legal reserves −20	Deposits of taxpayers	−20
		Government deposits	+20			
Retiring government securities		Legal reserves of depository institutions	+20	Government securities −20		
		Government deposits	−20	Legal reserves +20		

EFFECTS: Money supply falls in short run, while total bank reserves are unchanged. Excess reserves increase due to a fall in deposits. Total spending and interest rates decline.

Retiring Government Securities Held by the Federal Reserve Banks

	Federal Reserve Banks			Depository Financial Institutions		
	Assets	*Liabilities*		*Assets*	*Liabilities*	
Collection of tax surplus		Legal reserves of depository institutions	−20	Legal reserves −20	Deposits of taxpayers	−20
		Government deposits	+20			
Retiring government securities	Government securities −20	Government deposits	−20			

EFFECTS: Money supply and total reserves decrease by the amount of the budget surplus; total spending and interest rates decline.

Retiring Government Debt Held by the Federal Reserve Banks. As the bottom panel of Exhibit 22–4 shows, retiring government securities held by the Federal Reserve drains funds from taxpayers. However, those funds are *not* returned to the private spending stream. Instead, the government uses its increased deposits to pay off the Federal Reserve banks and retrieve the securities they hold. Legal reserves of the banking system and the money supply decline by the full amount of the budget surplus. Spending, interest rates, and the prices of goods and services are likely to fall as well.

Overall Impact of Government Borrowing and Spending

We may summarize all of these impacts of government borrowing and spending with an IS-LM diagram. We recall our earlier discussion of IS-LM analysis in Chapter 21 (see Exhibit 21–9), which links determination of equilibrium interest rates with equilibrium income (spending). In this analysis, the LM curve represents a collection of *equilibrium interest rates,* in which money demand (L) = money supply (M) for various levels of income (Y). We can also draw an IS curve, representing a collection of points at different levels of interest rates at which *income is in equilibrium;* that is, the volume of planned savings (S) by the public exactly equals the volume of planned investment plus government borrowing (I). As shown in Exhibit 22–5, the point where the IS and LM curves intersect yields *both* an equilibrium interest rate and an equilibrium level of income and spending for the economy.

What happens, then, when the government runs a deficit and increases its borrowing to finance it? As Exhibit 22–5 suggests, government borrowing adds to planned investment spending and, with money supply and money demand unchanged, equilibrium interest rates *rise* and income and production also increase. Of course, the higher interest rates discourage some additional private borrowing and spending — the so-called *crowding out effect* — even as government borrowing and spending increase. If there is substantial

Exhibit 22–5   **Effects of Additional Government Borrowing and Deficit Spending on Income and Interest Rates**

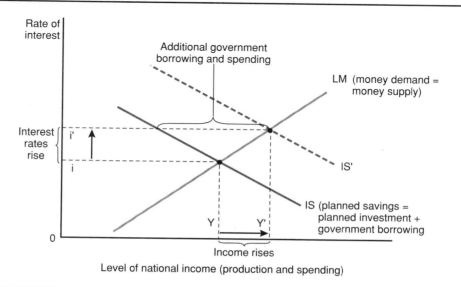

unemployment, more jobs probably will be made available and the unemployment rate will fall. If the economy is already close to full employment, the added income and spending may drive the prices of goods and services higher, generating inflation.

This conventional view of government borrowing adding to income and possibly driving up interest rates and inflation has been challenged in recent years. One counter argument is that interest rates and security prices in an *efficient* market simply may not respond to increased government borrowing, either because an equal amount of *private* borrowing and spending are crowded out of the marketplace or because the added government borrowing is already anticipated by the market and has been discounted by investors. Thus, there may be little *net* gain in terms of economic activity or change in interest rates from deficit spending.

Several recent studies support some of these arguments. For example, Aschauer (1988) produces evidence that increased government investment tends to reduce private investment, but the net decline in private investment is often less than the full amount of new government investment because some forms of public investment support and enhance private investment. Plosser (1982) and Roley (1981) find that security prices and interest rates do *not* respond significantly to the presence or absence of government deficits or to the sheer size of those deficits. Although interest rates may tend to rise as government borrowing increases, the demand for money tends to fall at the same time, which reduces the pressure of total credit demands on the financial markets. Canto and Rapp (1982) found that information on past budget deficits did *not* improve forecasts of current interest rates. Thornton (1990) looked at government deficits in 16 industrialized countries and discovered that nations with larger government deficits do *not* have higher interest rates or bigger international trade deficits than those with smaller budget deficits. By way of contrast, Cebula and Rhodd (1993) find a *positive* relationship between the size of the net U.S. budget deficit (net of interest payments) and nominal long-term interest rates, suggesting a crowding out of some private investment and slower economic growth. Finally, Dwyer (1982) found that government budget deficits did *not* appear to cause inflation in the U.S. economy. Rather, he suggests that current budget deficits appear to be more influenced by past inflation, rather than the other way around.

In total, these studies seem to provide at least weak support for what many economists call the *equivalence theorem* — changes in government borrowing and spending tend to be offset by roughly equivalent adjustments in private borrowing and spending, resulting in a relatively weak *net* effect from government fiscal policy on the economy and the financial markets. However, there is considerable controversy today about the true effects of government deficits and borrowing on the financial markets and the economy. More research on this important issue clearly is needed.

MANAGEMENT OF THE FEDERAL DEBT

As we noted at the beginning of this chapter, one of the most important activities of the Treasury is managing the huge **public debt** of the United States. The U.S. public debt is the largest single collection of securities available in the financial system today. Securities issued by the Treasury are regarded by investors as having zero *default risk* because the federal government possesses power both to tax and to create money. The government, unless it is overthrown by war or revolution, can always pay its bills.

Government securities do carry *market risk,* however, because their prices fluctuate with changes in demand and supply. In fact, the longer the term to maturity of a government security, the more market risk it possesses.

The principal role of government securities in the financial system is to provide *liquidity*. Corporations, commercial banks, and other institutional investors rely heavily on government securities as a readily marketable reserve to be drawn upon when cash is needed quickly. Although private debt securities do carry higher explicit yields than government debt of comparable maturity, the greater liquidity of government securities represents an added (implicit) return to the investor.

The Size and Growth of the Public Debt

How much money does the federal government owe? As shown in Exhibit 22–6, the gross public debt of the United States approached $5 trillion in 1995. On a per capita basis, the public debt amounts to more than $18,400 for every man, woman, and child living in the United States.

How did the federal debt become so huge? Wars, recessions, inflation, and the rapid expansion of military expenditures and social programs have been the principal causes. The federal government's debt was insignificant until the Great Depression of the 1930s, when the administration of President Franklin Roosevelt chose to borrow heavily to fund government programs and provide jobs. Even so, the public debt amounted to scarcely more than $50 billion at the beginning of World War II. The public debt multiplied five times over during the war years, approaching $260 billion by the end of World War II. (See Exhibit 22–7.) Embroiled in the most destructive and costly war in history, the U.S. government borrowed resources from the private sector to build planes, ships, and other war materials in enormous quantities.

For a brief period following World War II, it appeared that much of the public debt might be repaid. However, the Korean War intervened in the early 1950s, followed by a series of deep recessions when government tax revenues declined. The advent of the Vietnam War and rapid inflation during the late 1960s and 1970s sent the debt soaring. Between 1970 and 1980, the public debt of the United States more than doubled; it then tripled to more than $3 trillion during the 1980s. Between year-end 1990 and 1995, the federal government's gross debt increased by more than $1.5 trillion. This latest surge

Exhibit 22–6

The Public Debt of the United States, 1995*
($ Billions at End of First Quarter)

Type of Securities		Amounts
Interest-bearing public debt:		$4,950.6
Marketable debt		3,260.5
Bills	$ 742.5	
Notes	1,980.3	
Bonds	522.6	
Nonmarketable debt		1,690.2
State and local government series	113.4	
Foreign issues	41.0	
Savings bonds and notes	181.2	
Government account series	1,324.3	
Non-interest-bearing debt		23.3
Total gross public debt		$4,974.0

Note: Columns may not add to totals due to rounding.
*Figures are through the third quarter of the year.

Source: Board of Governors of the Federal Reserve and U.S. Treasury Department.

Exhibit 22–7   **The Public Debt of the United States in Selected Years, 1950–1995**
($ Billions)

Year	Total Gross Public Debt	Year	Total Gross Public Debt
1950	$225.4	1980	$ 930.2
1960	287.7	1990	3,364.8
1970	388.3	1995	4,988.7*

Source: Board of Governors of the Federal Reserve System and U.S. Treasury Department.

could be traced to the combined effects of slower economic growth that lowered tax collections, heavy government spending, and federal tax cuts.

Is this much debt simply too much? Or was Alexander Hamilton, the first U.S. Treasury secretary, accurate when he wrote: "A national debt, if it is not excessive, will be to us a national blessing"? The answer depends, in part, on the standard used to gauge the size of the public debt. Measured against the national income (the earnings of individuals and businesses that can be taxed to repay the debt), the public debt is lower now than it was a generation ago. For example, in 1995, the gross public debt amounted to about 70 percent of the U.S. GNP, compared to well over 100 percent at the end of World War II. Moreover, other forms of debt in the U.S. economy total as much or more than the public debt. For example, total mortgage debt outstanding in 1995 was about $4.7 trillion. It should be remembered that U.S. government securities are at one and the same time debt obligations *and* marketable, liquid assets to the millions of investors who hold them.

Another issue to keep in mind about today's huge federal debt and its possible burden on the economy concerns the difficulties we face in trying to accurately *measure* the true size of the debt. It turns out that the answer to the question — How big is the federal debt? — is not all that easy. For example, *inflation* increases the size of the debt because it tends to increase government deficits. In an inflationary period, the government typically must borrow more, but this does not necessarily mean that the burden of the debt has increased; government may not be exerting a greater impact on the economy. An interesting study by Eisner and Pieper (1984), for example, concludes that the real size of the U.S. federal debt (adjusted for inflation) actually *fell* between 1946 and 1980. Moreover, the size of the public debt is typically measured in terms of the *par value* of government securities outstanding. But when interest rates rise, the *market value* of government debt falls. Thus, a significant rise in interest rates will cause the value of that portion of the government's debt held by private investors to decline.

Accurate measurement of the burden imposed by government debt also means that we must consider the value of the *assets* held by government. Most national governments hold a reserve of gold and foreign currencies. We might also add the estimated value of government buildings, military hardware, highways, and airports. Thus, we may distinguish between the *gross liabilities* of the federal government — the total amount of its debt outstanding — and its *net liabilities* — government debt minus government assets. Including all of the government's assets at their fair market value would yield substantially smaller net government liabilities. Of course, to be fair, we also have to consider the amount of debt owed by off-budget federal agencies (such as the farm credit agencies or federal mortgage agencies), which amounts to about one fifth of the gross public debt. And *contingent liabilities* might be added to the government's debt total, such as deposit insurance like that offered by the FDIC to guarantee bank deposits or the Social Security Fund, which must eventually pay retirement benefits to millions of citizens. Clearly, measuring the true size of the government's debt is a difficult job. For this reason, we must be careful before jumping to any hasty conclusions about how large or significant the debt is or what its impact on the economy and financial markets might be.

The Composition of the Public Debt

The U.S. public debt as it is traditionally measured consists of a wide variety of government IOUs with differing maturities, interest rates, and other features. A small amount — less than 1 percent — carries no interest rate at all. This *non-interest-bearing public debt* consists of paper currency and coins issued by the U.S. Treasury Department, including silver certificates and greenbacks that are gradually being retired as they are turned in by the public. Virtually all paper money in circulation today is in Federal Reserve notes, which are not officially a part of the public debt but are obligations of the Federal Reserve banks.

More than 99 percent of all federal debt securities are *interest bearing* and may be divided into two broad groups: marketable securities and nonmarketable securities. By definition, *marketable securities* may be traded any number of times before they reach maturity. In contrast, *nonmarketable securities* must be held by the original purchaser until they mature or are redeemed by the Treasury. It is the marketable debt over which the Treasury exercises the greatest measure of control and has the greatest impact on the cost and availability of credit in the financial markets.

Marketable Public Debt

The marketable public debt totaled about $3.3 trillion in 1995, representing about two thirds of all interest-bearing U.S. government obligations. The marketable public debt today is composed of just three types of securities: Treasury bills, notes, and bonds. By law, a U.S. Treasury bill must mature within one year. In contrast, U.S. Treasury notes range in original maturity from 2 to 10 years, and Treasury bonds may carry any maturity, although generally they have a maturity at issue of more than 10 years.[1] With their greater liquidity and marketability, Treasury bills and notes have been especially attractive to investors in recent years. Bills and notes represented about 40 percent of all marketable government obligations in 1960; by 1995, however, these securities accounted for more than 80 percent of the marketable public debt.

Nonmarketable Public Debt

The nonmarketable public debt consists mainly of Government Account series securities issued by the Treasury to various government agencies and trust funds (see again Exhibit 22–6). These agencies and trust funds include the Social Security Administration, the Tennessee Valley Authority, and several smaller government agencies. As these governmental units accumulate funds, they turn them over to the Treasury in exchange for nonmarketable IOUs, thus reducing the federal government's borrowing activity in the open market.

---

[1] Both Treasury notes and bonds bear interest at a fixed rate payable semiannually, but bills do not carry a fixed rate. Bonds can carry a call option, allowing the Treasury to redeem them before maturity with four months' notice. Notes and bonds are issued in multiples of $1,000, or $5,000, depending upon maturity; bills are available in a minimum amount of $10,000 and in multiples of $5,000 above that minimum. Payment for purchases of Treasury securities generally must be made in cash, immediately available funds, the exchange of eligible securities, or by check to the Federal Reserve banks or to the Treasury.

Another component of the nonmarketable debt is U.S. Savings Bonds sold to the general public in small denominations, which represent only about 4 percent of the public debt.

Holdings of U.S. dollars by foreign governments and foreign investors have expanded enormously in recent years due to oil imports and the flow of U.S. capital to Europe, Asia, and the Middle East. Because large foreign holdings of dollars represent a constant threat to the value of the U.S. dollar in international markets, the Treasury periodically issues nonmarketable dollar-denominated securities to attract these overseas funds. To increase U.S. government holdings of foreign currencies that can be used to settle international claims, the Treasury can issue foreign-currency-denominated securities to investors abroad as well. The Treasury also issues special securities to state and local governments. These securities provide a temporary investment outlet for the funds raised by local governments when they borrow in the open market.

Investors in U.S. Government Securities

Who *holds* the public debt of the United States? Each month, the Treasury makes estimates of the distribution of its securities among various groups of investors, drawing on data supplied by the Federal Reserve banks, government agencies, and private trade organizations. The results from a recent Treasury ownership survey are shown in Exhibit 22–8.

It is evident from the survey that most Treasury debt — about two thirds — is held by private individuals and institutions. Rather surprising to many observers, however, is the large proportion of the public debt — a little over one third — held by the federal government itself. For example, in 1995, U.S. government agencies and trust funds, including the Social Security Trust Fund and other federal departments, held about one quarter of the total debt. The Federal Reserve banks held about 8 percent of all public debt securities outstanding.

Exhibit 22–8

Investors in the U.S. Public Debt, 1995
($ Billions at End of Second Quarter)

Investor Group	Amount Held in 1995	Percent of Total Ownership
Federal government:		
U.S. government agencies and trust funds	$1,316.6	
Federal Reserve banks	389.0	
Total for federal government investors	1,705.6	34.5%
Private investors:		
Commercial banks	$305.0	
Money market funds	58.7	
Insurance companies	260.0	
Other companies	227.7	
State and local governments	415.0	
Individuals:		
Savings bonds	182.6	
Other securities	161.6	
Foreign and international	783.7	
Other miscellaneous investors*	850.4	
Total for private investors	3,244.6	65.5
Total for all investor groups	$4,950.2	100.0%

*The miscellaneous investor group includes savings and loan associations, nonprofit institutions, credit unions, mutual savings banks, corporate pension funds, security dealers, and selected federal deposits and agencies.

Sources: Board of Governors of the Federal Reserve System and U.S. Treasury Department.

The sheer size of the government's holdings of its own debt is viewed with alarm by some analysts. A large volume of government debt held out of circulation in federal vaults tends to thin out the market for government securities, reducing the volume of trading. Other factors held constant, interest rates and security prices become more volatile and unpredictable, discouraging investment. This could be critical, because the market for government securities is the anchor of the financial system.

Among the private holders of the public debt, commercial banks and individuals are at or near the top of the list. In 1995, for example, individual investors held about 7 percent of the public debt — the majority in U.S. Savings Bonds. Commercial banks held roughly 6 percent of the total. Other financial institutions with significant holdings of U.S. government securities included money market funds, insurance companies, pension funds, savings banks and savings and loan associations, and nonfinancial corporations that hold these securities as a ready reserve of liquid funds.

The proportion of the public U.S. debt held by foreign and international investors, including foreign central banks, governments, and other international investors, has increased in recent years and totaled nearly 16 percent of all issues outstanding in 1995. Foreign holdings of government securities result, in part, from a rise in U.S. imports that lead foreign investors to build up dollar deposits in banks abroad. These investors have converted many of their dollars into purchases of Treasury securities in the money market and into foreign-currency-denominated securities purchased directly from the U.S. Treasury. Foreign holdings of U.S. Treasury securities have also increased recently due to the development of active over-the-counter markets for longer-term Treasuries in London and Tokyo. These new U.S. Treasury security markets have given Treasuries round-the-clock liquidity and are especially attractive to such investors as multinational corporations and others who find U.S. trading hours inconvenient.

A Trend toward Shorter Maturities

One of the most serious problems the Treasury has faced in the debt management field is a long-term trend toward shorter maturities of its IOUs. The percentage of marketable federal securities over five years to maturity held by private investors was a full 40 percent in 1950. By 1995, however, this long-term component of the public debt was only a little over one quarter of all marketable issues held by private investors. The average maturity of the entire marketable public debt in 1995 was about 5½ years, or about two thirds of what it was at the end of World War II. Today, roughly one third of the privately held public debt comes due each year.

A short-term public debt is a potentially serious problem because it requires the Treasury to come to market more frequently to retire or refund debt as securities pile up in shorter maturities. Moreover, in recent years, the Federal Reserve has been especially cautious about making significant changes in the posture of monetary policy at a time when the Treasury is actively in the market selling new notes and bonds. If the Treasury must refund and issue more frequently, this reduces the period of time over which the Federal Reserve can comfortably make significant changes in monetary policy. Suppose, for example, that the Fed wanted to increase interest rates and reduce the availability of credit at precisely the time the Treasury was coming to market with a new issue of bonds. Clearly, the government would have difficulty in selling its bonds in an environment of rising interest rates and falling bond prices. If maturing securities were coming due and had to be paid off, the Treasury might not be able to raise enough cash to meet its obligations.

Many analysts believe that a substantial buildup of short-term government debt contributes to inflation. Of special concern is the proportion of government securities maturing within one year — the *floating debt*. These short-term issues are the most liquid and readily marketable of all securities in the financial system. Most are held by commercial banks and other lenders of funds, who use them as an extra source of funds when reserves are scarce and credit demand is high. If the Federal Reserve wishes to reduce the growth of money and credit, it must wrestle with the problem that financial institutions can sell off their floating debt issues and generate still more credit. Nevertheless, in May of 1993, the Clinton Administration announced a policy of increased short-term borrowing in an effort to save on interest costs and reduce the size of the federal deficit.

Methods of Offering Treasury Securities

Management of the public debt is a complicated task. Treasury debt managers are called on continually to make decisions about raising new money and refunding maturing securities. They must decide what kinds of securities to issue, which maturities will appeal to investors, and the form in which an offering of securities should be made.

The Auction Method. Today, the **auction method** is the principal means of selling Treasury notes, bonds, and bills. Although several different methods have been used over time, all such techniques have a number of features in common. Both competitive and noncompetitive tenders for new securities, whose dollar amount and maturity are announced about one week in advance, are invited from the public. Competitive bidders usually include money center banks and securities houses, who usually average 75 to 85 bidders per auction. Noncompetitive bidders, including smaller financial institutions and individuals, number an average of about 20,000 per Treasury auction. Noncompetitive bidders receive an allotment of securities at the average auction price up to a maximum amount determined by the Treasury. As we have seen, federal agencies and trust funds purchase large amounts of Treasury issues. These agencies participate in virtually every auction but pay the price charged noncompetitive bidders. They receive a special allotment of securities in exchange for their maturing issues after the regular auction is concluded.

Types of Treasury Auctions. The Treasury has used three different auction methods in recent years:

1. Yield auctions
2. Dutch auctions
3. Price auctions

The auction method used most often for Treasury notes and bonds is known as a *yield auction*. The Treasury announces the amount of securities available and calls for yield bids in one basis-point increments. Investors submitting competitive bids must express their offers on an annual percentage yield basis accurate to two decimal places. For example, we might place a bid of 8.55 percent in the current bond auction. Those bidding the lowest annual percentage yield (the highest price) will be awarded their securities. Awards will continue to be made at successively higher yields (lower prices) until the issue is exhausted. (See Exhibit 22–9 for an example of an announcement of a Treasury yield auction of new bonds.)

The *price auction* is used for Treasury bills, as we saw in Chapter 15. Under this method, the Treasury accepts competitive tenders (offers) for bills on the basis of an assumed par value of 100. Competitive bidders must spell out their price offer for bills accurate to three decimal places. Thus, a dealer might bid 97.525 on a 90-day Treasury bill, which would mean that if the dealer were a successful bidder at that price and held the bill to maturity, the bank discount yield on the bill would be 9.90 percent (that is,

Exhibit 22–9   The U.S. Treasury Auctions Off Another Bond

DEPARTMENT OF THE TREASURY

Office of the Secretary
[Department Circular — Public Debt Series — No. 13–88]
Treasury Bonds of 2018
Washington, May 5, 1988.

1. INVITATION FOR TENDERS

1.1. The Secretary of the Treasury, under the authority of Chapter 31 of Title 31, United States Code, invites tenders for approximately $8,500,000,000 of United States securities, designated Treasury Bonds of 2018 (CUSIP No. 912810 EA 2), hereafter referred to as Bonds. The Bonds will be sold at auction, with bidding on the basis of yield. Payment will be required at the price equivalent of the yield of each accepted bid. The interest rate on the Bonds and the price equivalent of each accepted bid will be determined in the manner described below. Additional amounts of the Bonds may be issued to Government accounts and Federal Reserve Banks for their own account in exchange for maturing Treasury securities. Additional amounts of the Bonds may also be issued at the average price to Federal Reserve Banks, as agents for foreign and international monetary authorities.

2. DESCRIPTION OF SECURITIES

2.1. The Bonds will be dated May 15, 1988, and issued May 16, 1988. Payment for the Bonds will be based on the price equivalent to the bid yield determined in accordance with this circular, plus accrued interest from May 15, 1988, to May 16, 1988. Interest on the Bonds is payable on a semiannual basis on November 15, 1988, and each subsequent 6 months on May 15 and November 15 through the date that the principal becomes payable. They will mature May 15, 2018, and will not be subject to call for redemption prior to maturity.

2.5. A Bond may be held in its fully constituted form or it may be divided into its separate Principal and Interest Components and maintained as such on the book-entry records of the Federal Reserve Banks, acting as fiscal agents of the United States. The provisions specifically applicable to the separation, maintenance, transfer, and reconstitution of Principal and Interest Components are set forth in Section 6 of this circular. Subsections 2.1. through 2.4. of this section are descriptive of Bonds in their fully constituted form; the description of the separate Principal and Interest components is set forth in Section 6 of this circular.

3. SALE PROCEDURES

3.1. Tenders will be received at Federal Reserve Banks and Branches and at the Bureau of the Public Debt, Washington, DC 20239–1500, prior to 1:00 p.m., Eastern Daylight Saving time, Thursday, May 12, 1988. Noncompetitive tenders as defined below will be considered timely if postmarked no later than Wednesday, May 11, 1988, and received no later than Monday, May 16, 1988.

3.2. The par amount of Bonds bid for must be stated on each tender. The minimum bid is $1,000, and larger bids must be in multiples of that amount. Competitive tenders must also show the yield desired, expressed in terms of an annual yield with two decimals, e.g., 7.10%. Fractions may not be used. Noncompetitive tenders must show the term "noncompetitive" on the tender form in lieu of a specified yield.

Source: Department of the Treasury, Office of the Secretary, Department Circular — Public Debt Series — No. 13–88, Treasury Bonds of 2018, Washington, D.C., May 5, 1988.

$(100–97.525)/100×360/90)$. Dealers bidding the highest prices receive bills until all available bills are allocated in the latest auction.

The Treasury recently has been experimenting with the *uniform price,* or *Dutch auction,* method to sell new notes. After all competitive bids are in, the Treasury proceeds to award the available securities, beginning with the highest bidder, until all securities are allocated. However, the price actually paid by all bidders is the lowest accepted bid in the auction. Therefore, all investors receiving securities in a Dutch auction pay the *same* price.

Limitations of Current Treasury Auction Techniques. Unfortunately, as the scandals that rocked the government securities market in 1991 and 1992 reveal, some of the current methods used by the U.S. Treasury to auction federal securities appear to create both incentive and opportunity to manipulate and control the market, as we discussed in Chapter 15. The search is on today for new ways to auction Treasury securities that would mitigate the weaknesses in the current bidding process. Among the proposals that have recently appeared are to expand the use of uniform price (Dutch) auctions and to inaugurate an "open outcry" auction (as happens today on a stock or futures exchange) rather than sealed bids, so that all bidders know the distribution of bids and the Treasury gets the benefit of higher prices for its debt.

Marketing Techniques. The Treasury places new securities *directly* with the investing public. New Treasury bills, notes, and bonds can be bought directly from the Treasury Department or from the Treasury's agents — the Federal Reserve banks, either in person or by mail. Competitive tender offers are accepted from private and government investors at the Federal Reserve banks until 1 P.M., Eastern Standard Time, the day the new securities are sold. Individuals may also file bids for new Treasury securities with the Bureau of Public Debt in Washington, D.C. Many investors place orders for new Treasury issues through a security broker or dealer, bank, or nonbank financial institution.

Before issuing new notes and bonds, the Treasury consults Federal Reserve officials and government securities dealers as to the appropriate maturities to be offered. It also frequently is necessary to tailor the features of a new issue to appeal to investor groups that have the necessary funds to spend.

Book Entry. The marketable public debt is issued today only in **book-entry form.** This means that the investor does *not* receive an engraved certificate representing the Treasury's debt obligation but instead, receives a statement of account. The investor's name and amount of securities purchased are recorded in an Account Master Record in the automated TREAS-URY DIRECT System. Member banks of the Federal Reserve System are permitted to hold security safekeeping accounts at the Federal Reserve banks where their own security hold-ings and those of their customers are recorded. As interest is received or securities are sold or purchased, banks credit or debit their own or their customers' accounts accordingly in the TREASURY DIRECT System. Book entry is the safest form in which to hold any security because this method significantly reduces the risk of theft.

Other Services Offered Investors. To encourage greater participation in the government securities market and stimulate demand for new Treasury issues, both the Federal Reserve and the Treasury offer a number of other services to investors. For example, securities held in book-entry accounts at the Federal Reserve banks may be transferred by wire almost anywhere using the Fed's electronic wire transfer network. Interest and principal payments are electronically deposited on the due date into the deposit account each investor designates for that purpose. This device makes it easy to sell Treasury securities before maturity on a same-day basis.

Price Quotations on Treasury Securities. The widespread popularity of U.S. Treasury securities to investors around the world means that their prices and yields are closely watched everyday. Newspapers carry price and yield information for Treasury bonds, notes, and bills, which usually include the following information:

Rate	Maturity	Bid	Asked	Change	Asked Yield
6½	Aug 05n	105:16	105:18	+13	5.73
9⅜	Feb 06	127:15	127:19	+16	5.75
11¾	Nov 09–14	153:26	153:30	+22	5.92

We note from the preceding that Treasury securities are usually listed in order of the dates they will mature, from the most recent to the most distant maturities. The promised coupon rates are shown under the column marked *Rate*. Thus, in the list the first security, which matures in August 2005, promises a 6½ percent annual return, or $6.50 per year for each $100 in face value. The letter *n* next to the first entry indicates that the security in question is a Treasury note. The absence of *n* means that the security listed is a Treasury bond, as is the case with the 9⅜ and 11¾ percent bonds maturing in the years 2006 and 2009 to 2114.

The *bid* price in the next column (always expressed in dollars and 32nds of a dollar) is the price for which a dealer is willing to *buy* the security. For example, the August 2005 note has a bid price of $105¹⁶/₃₂, or $105.50 on a $100 basis. The *asked* price is the price the security's current holder (usually a security dealer) is willing to sell it for. Any investor interested in purchasing the security in question will probably seek to buy it for a price somewhere between the current bid and asked prices. The column labeled *Change* indicates the change in bid price between yesterday's closing price and the day before's closing price, expressed in 32nds of a dollar. Thus, a change of +13 indicates a price rise yesterday of 13/32 of a dollar, or $0.40625 per $100 par value security. The yield to maturity the purchaser would receive if he or she bought the security at yesterday's asked price is shown in the last column. For example, if the August 2005 note were purchased for 105:18, the investor buying at this price and holding the bond to its maturity date in August 2005 would receive a yield of 5.73 percent.

The Goals of Federal Debt Management

Over the years, the Treasury has pursued several different goals in the management of the public debt. These goals may be divided into two broad groups: (1) *housekeeping goals*, which pertain to the cost and composition of the public debt; and (2) *stabilization goals*, which have to do with the impact of the debt on the economy and the financial markets.

Minimize Interest Costs. The most important housekeeping goal is to keep the interest burden of the public debt as low as possible. The Treasury has not always been successful in the pursuit of this goal, however. Today, the interest burden on the public debt is the third largest category of federal expenditures, after welfare payments and national defense. This interest burden on the U.S. taxpayer has increased in recent years, particularly when interest rates rise or the volume of debt increases faster than the nation's income.

Reduce the Frequency of Refundings. The Treasury also tries to minimize the number of trips it must make to market to refund old securities or issue new ones. This housekeeping goal is particularly important to the Federal Reserve's conduct of monetary policy.

Frequently in the past, the Fed has followed a loosely defined policy known as *even keel* when the Treasury is in the market offering a substantial volume of notes or bonds. Even-keel policy calls for the Fed to exert a *steadying* influence on the financial markets, making sure that security trading is orderly and changes in interest rates are moderate. In principle, even-keel policy protects the Treasury's financing operations from catastrophic failure, as might occur if security prices plunged at the time of a Treasury refunding, but it can limit the Fed's freedom of action.

Economic Stabilization. A much broader goal of debt management is to stabilize the economy, promoting high employment and sustainable growth while avoiding rampant inflation. In strict terms, this would involve issuing *long-term* Treasury securities in a period of *economic expansion* and issuing *short-term* securities in a period of *recession*. The long-term securities would tend to increase long-term interest rates and therefore act as a brake on private investment spending, slowing the economy down. On the other hand, issuing short-term securities during a recession may take the pressure off long-term interest rates and avoid discouraging investment spending that is needed to provide jobs.

Unfortunately, the goal of economic stabilization often conflicts with other debt management goals, particularly the goal of minimizing the interest burden of the debt. If the Treasury sells short-term securities in a period of expansion when interest rates are high and then rolls over those short-term securities into long-term bonds during a recession when rates are low, this strategy tends to minimize the debt's average interest cost. The Treasury is able to lock in cheap long-term rates. From a stabilization point of view, however, this is exactly the wrong thing to do. The short-term debt may fuel inflation during an economic expansion; long-term debt issued during a recession may drive up interest rates and reduce private investment. Treasury debt managers are confronted with tough choices among conflicting goals.

The Impact of Federal Debt Management on the Financial Markets and the Economy

What effect do Treasury debt management activities have on the financial markets and the economy? This is a subject of heated debate among financial analysts. Most experts agree that in the short run, the financial markets become more agitated and interest rates tend to rise when the Treasury is borrowing, especially when *new money* is involved. A mere exchange of new for old securities usually has minimal effects, however, unless the offering is very large.

The longer-run impact of Treasury debt management operations is less clear. Certainly the *liquidity* of the public's portfolio of securities changes. For example, suppose $10 billion in Treasury bonds are maturing next month. Treasury debt managers decide to offer investors $10 billion in 10-year notes in exchange for the maturing bonds. The bonds, regardless of what their original maturity might have been, are now short-term securities (with one-month maturities). If investors accept the new 10-year notes in exchange for the one-month bonds, the average maturity of the public's security holdings obviously has lengthened, all else being equal. Longer-term securities, as a rule, are less liquid than shorter-term securities.

Will this reduction in public liquidity affect spending habits and interest rates? The research evidence on this question is conflicting, with many studies finding little effect from debt management activities.[2] However, there is some evidence that *lengthening debt maturities* increases the public's demand for money and *raises interest rates.* In contrast, if the Treasury offers shorter-term securities, this tends to make the public's portfolio of securities more liquid and may reduce the demand for money. The result would be an increase in spending for goods and services and, for a time, *lower* interest rates.

Still another possible debt management impact is on the *shape of the yield curve.* *Lengthening* the average maturity of the debt tends to increase long-term interest rates relative to short rates. The yield curve assumes a *steeper positive slope,* favoring short-term investment over long-term investment. On the other hand, *shortening* the debt's maturity tends to reduce longer-term interest rates and raise short-term rates. The yield curve tends to *flatten out,* if positively sloped, or even turn down, favoring long-term investment over short-term investment. The net impact on total investment spending would depend on whether private investment is more responsive to short-term interest rates or long-term interest rates.

---

[2]See especially the studies of Lang and Rasche (1977) and Smith (1960).

On balance, most authorities are convinced that the debt management activities of the Treasury do *not* have a major impact on economic conditions. The effects of debt management operations appear to be secondary compared to the powerful impact of monetary and fiscal policy on the economy and financial markets. The optimal policy is probably one that makes Treasury refunding operations as *unobtrusive* as possible, especially when these operations might interfere with the activities of the Federal Reserve System. Nevertheless, debt management represents yet another policy tool that can be used by government in the face of serious economic problems.

SUMMARY

In this chapter, we examined the many roles played by the Treasury Department in financing federal expenditures and managing the huge public debt of the United States. The federal government affects the financial system through its taxing and spending activities (fiscal policy) and through refunding the government's debt (debt management policy). Both tasks involve enormous amounts of money today. The public debt of the United States now approaches $5 trillion, and annual federal expenditures exceed the trillion dollar mark. It should certainly come as no surprise that spending and borrowing of such magnitude can have powerful effects on interest rates, security prices, and the pursuit of economic goals.

We have observed in this chapter that government borrowing tends to raise interest rates, increase the money supply, and augment total spending in the economy. The economy will grow faster, with reduced unemployment, when the government borrows and spends additional funds, but often at the price of more rapid inflation and threats to the dollar abroad. Government budget surpluses, especially when these surpluses are used to retire government debt, often lead to lower interest rates, a decline in the money supply, and reduced spending. A move toward more conservative fiscal policy and toward budget surpluses tends to dampen inflation and strengthen the dollar abroad but increases the risk of high unemployment and slower economic growth at home.

Management of the public debt can also be used to alter economic conditions. We have noted that if the Treasury refunds maturing short-term securities with longer term debt, it can reduce the liquidity of the public's security holdings. Interest rates tend to rise, credit becomes more difficult to obtain, and spending and employment tend to fall. Long-term Treasury borrowing, therefore, tends to slow down the economy's rate of growth and reduces inflationary pressures. In contrast, a debt management policy that emphasizes short-term government borrowing often leads to more rapid economic expansion and reduced unemployment, but these are sometimes purchased at the price of higher inflation.

As we discussed in the preceding chapters on the Federal Reserve System, government policymakers face few easy choices. The goals of full employment, reasonable stability in prices, and sustainable economic growth are elusive targets. Successful fiscal, monetary, and debt management policies require careful coordination among all branches of government. ■

KEY TERMS AND CONCEPTS IN THIS CHAPTER

fiscal policy	budget surplus	auction method
debt management policy	public debt	book-entry form
budget deficit		

STUDY QUESTIONS

1. What exactly is *fiscal policy*? *Debt management policy*?

2. Explain how fiscal policy and debt management policy might be used to fight inflation and unemployment.

3. List from largest to smallest the principal sources of federal government revenue. What are the principal federal spending programs?

4. Describe the effects of government borrowing on the financial system and the economy. If the federal government wished to increase total spending in the economy the most, from whom should it borrow funds?

5. Describe the effects of retiring government securities on the financial system and the economy. Whose securities should be paid off if the federal government wants to have the maximum contractionary impact on the economy?

6. What is the *crowding out effect*? What does recent research say about the link between government deficits, interest rates, and inflation?

7. Describe the principal types of securities that make up the public debt of the United States. What portions of the debt can the Treasury most closely control?

8. What problems exist in trying to measure the size of the public debt?

9. List the principal holders of the public debt. What are the most important trends in the ownership of federal securities?

10. Define the following methods of selling U.S. Treasury securities:
    a. Price auction
    b. Dutch auction
    c. Yield auction

11. List the *goals* of Treasury debt management. What is the essential difference between housekeeping goals and stabilization goals? To what extent do these goals conflict?

12. Explain how changes in the maturity structure of the public debt can affect interest rates, the yield curve, and spending in the economy.

PROBLEMS

1. Due to an unexpected decline in federal income tax collections, the Treasury is compelled to borrow an extra $40 billion to cover planned expenditures in the current government budget. Using T accounts and IS-LM analysis discussed in this chapter, trace through the likely effects of this additional borrowing on the financial markets and on the economy. Assume that 50 percent of the securities to be issued will be absorbed by nonbank institutions and private individuals and 50 percent by depository institutions. How would your analysis change if the economy were at full employment?

2. Due to drastic cuts in federal spending and strong economic growth, it now appears that the federal government will experience a $10 billion budget surplus during the current fiscal year. If the Treasury plans to retain $2 billion of this surplus in its cash account at the Federal Reserve and to use the balance to retire $5 billion in government securities held by depository institutions and $3 billion held by the general public, use T accounts to show the effects of this debt retirement operation. Using IS-LM analysis and the results from your T-account analysis, what effects do you predict for interest rates, security prices, total spending, and employment?

3.   Which type of auction for Treasury securities is described by each of the items listed below:

   a.   All bidders will pay 96.32 for the new Treasury notes being distributed today.

   b.   The highest bid in today's auction of Treasury bills was 98.250.

   c.   The Treasury has issued a circular indicating that new bonds to be offered next week will have a coupon rate of 9 percent and the lowest acceptable bid is 9.675 percent.

SELECTED REFERENCES

Aschauer, David. "Does Public Capital Crowd Out Private Capital?" *Staff Memorandum.* Federal Reserve Bank of Chicago, 1988.

Canto, Victor A., and Donald Rapp. "The 'Crowding Out' Controversy: Arguments and Evidence." *Economic Review.* Federal Reserve Bank of Atlanta, August 1982.

Cebula, Richard J., and Rupert G. Rhodd. "A Note on Budget Deficits, Debt Service Payments, and Interest Rates." *Quarterly Review of Economics and Finance,* Vol. 33, No. 4 (Winter 1993), pp. 439–455.

Dwyer, Gerald P., Jr. "Is Inflation a Consequence of Government Deficits?" *Economic Review.* Federal Reserve Bank of Atlanta, August 1982.

Eisner, Robert, and Paul J. Pieper. "A New View of the Federal Debt and Budget Deficits." *The American Economic Review,* March 1984, pp. 11–29.

Lang, Richard W., and Robert H. Rasche. "Debt Management Policy and the Own-Price Elasticity of Demand for U.S. Government Notes and Bonds." *Review.* Federal Reserve Bank of St. Louis, September 1977, pp. 8–22.

Mester, Loretta J. "There's More Than One Way to Sell a Security: The Treasury's Auction Experiment." *Business Review.* Federal Reserve Bank of Philadelphia, July/August 1995 pp. 3–17.

Plosser, Charles I. "Government Financing Decisions and Asset Returns." *Journal of Monetary Economics* 9 (1982), pp. 325–52.

Roley, V. Vance. "The Financing of Federal Deficits: An Analysis of Crowding Out." *Economic Review.* Federal Reserve Bank of Kansas City, July–August 1981, pp. 16–29.

Smith, Warren L. "Debt Management in the United States." In *Study of Employment, Growth, and Price Levels,* ed. Joint Economic Committee. Washington, D.C.: U.S. Government Printing Office, 1960.

Thornton, Daniel L. "Do Government Deficits Matter?" *Review.* Federal Reserve Bank of St. Louis, September–October 1990, pp. 25–38.

Chapter 23

State and Local Governments in the Financial Markets

LEARNING OBJECTIVES IN THIS CHAPTER

- To explore the various ways in which state, county, city, and other local units of government raise the funds they need to provide services to the public.
- To understand why state and local government borrowing has grown rapidly in recent years and to examine the financial instruments these governments use to raise money.
- To explore the marketing process by which state and local government bonds and notes are sold.

The borrowing and spending activities of state and local governments have been one of the most dynamic, rapidly growing segments of the financial system in recent years. Pressured by rising populations and inflated costs, states, counties, school districts, and other local units of government have been forced to borrow in growing numbers to meet increased demands for their services. As we will see later in this chapter, the volume of state and local government debt has more than doubled over the past decade.

Despite the rapid growth in borrowing by state and local governments, many investors consider state and local debt obligations a highly desirable investment medium due to their high quality, ready marketability, and tax exemption feature. The interest income generated by state and local securities is exempt from federal income taxes, and most states exempt their own securities from state income taxes. As a result, these high-quality debt obligations — known to investors as **municipals** — appeal to heavily taxed investors such as top-income-bracket individuals and large corporations. In addition, an active secondary market permits the early resale of many higher-quality state and local government bonds.

GROWTH OF STATE AND LOCAL GOVERNMENT BORROWING

The rapid growth of state and local government borrowing is reflected in Exhibit 23–1, which shows the total volume of municipal securities outstanding between the years of 1940 and 1995. State and local government indebtedness grew slowly until the 1950s, when it nearly tripled. The volume of municipal debt doubled again during the 1960s and more than doubled during the 1970s and 1980s. By 1995, state and local debt outstanding had climbed to more than $1 trillion.

What factors account for this strong record of growth in municipal borrowing? *Rapid population* and *income growth* are two of the most important causes. The U.S. population rose from less than 132 million in 1940 to an estimated 270 million in 1995, a gain of well over 100 million people. Rapid population growth implies that many local government services, such as schools, highways, and fire protection, must also expand rapidly. Tax revenues cannot provide all of the monies needed to fund these facilities and services.

Another factor pushing state and local borrowing higher is the *uneven distribution of population growth across the nation.* Beginning in the 1950s, a massive shift of the U.S. population out of the central cities into suburban areas began to take place. This demographic change was augmented during the 1970s, 80s, and 90s by a movement of population and industry into small towns and rural areas to escape the social and environmental problems of urban living, and toward the western and southern states in search of a warmer climate and new business opportunities. Smaller outlying communities were transformed into cities with a corresponding need for new streets, schools, airports, and freeways to commute back to the central cities for work, recreation, and shopping. The result was an upsurge in borrowing by existing local units of government and the creation of thousands of *new* borrowing units in the form of sewer and lighting districts, power and water authorities, airport and toll-road boards, and public housing authorities. Today, the United States has more than 83,000 state, county, municipal, and other units of local government. And the majority of them have the authority to issue debt, although most have constitutional prohibitions against budget deficits or limits on how much they can borrow.

Accompanying the growth and shift of the U.S. population has come an *upgrading of citizens' expectations* concerning the quality of government services. We expect much more from government today than we did a generation ago. Particularly noticeable is an increased demand for government services that directly affect the quality of life, such as better-designed schools, medical and health care facilities, and auditoriums. Instead of gravel roads and narrow highways, local citizens demand paved and guttered streets and all-weather, controlled-access highways. Many municipal governments are active in pro-

Exhibit 23–1   **Total Debt Issued by State and Local Governments in the United States, 1940–1995** ($ Billions)

Year	Debt Outstanding at Year-End	Year	Debt Outstanding at Year-End
1940	$20.3	1980	$302.8
1950	24.1	1990	848.6
1960	70.8	1995	1,063.3
1970	145.5		

Source: U.S. Department of Commerce; Board of Governors of the Federal System, *Flow of Funds: Assets and Liabilities Outstanding 1960–92;* and the *Federal Reserve Bulletin,* selected issues.

viding cultural facilities, such as libraries and museums, and are expected to play leading roles in controlling environmental pollution.

All of these public demands have had to be financed in an era of rising construction and labor costs, exacerbating the money burdens of local governments. Moreover, in the early 1990s, many local governments were faced with sluggish economic growth and loss of tax base on which to build for the future. Faced with such pressures, local governments are expected to continue borrowing heavily in future years, with the federal government, intent on reducing its deficit, able to make only limited contributions to local funding. Adding to local financial needs will be a continuing expansion of suburban communities, especially in the southern and western regions of the United States.

SOURCES OF REVENUE FOR STATE AND LOCAL GOVERNMENTS

Borrowing by state and local governments supplements their tax revenues and income from fees charged to users of government services. When tax and fee revenues fail to grow as fast as public demands, municipal borrowings rise. Moreover, when long-term capital projects are undertaken, long-term borrowing rather than taxation is the preferred method of governmental finance.

As we study state and local governmental borrowing in the financial markets, it is useful to have in mind the principal sources and uses of state and local funds. Where do the majority of state and local government revenues come from? And where does most of the money go? Exhibits 23–2 and 23–3, drawn from a recent census of state and local units of government, provide some answers to these questions.

As expected, most state and local government *revenues* are derived from *local* sources of funds: the citizens these governments serve. More than four fifths of state and local government revenues normally are derived from local sources, according to a U.S. Department of Commerce census. However, intergovernmental transfers of funds, including state aid to local schools and federal aid to the states, also provide a significant share of total revenues (about 15 percent), but such intergovernmental transfers have declined in recent years, particularly because the federal government is transferring more social programs to the states. Local governments, however, still receive about 30 percent of their revenues from state governments, on average.

Not surprisingly, *taxes* are the largest single revenue source for state and local governments. Property taxes are the mainstay of *local* government support, providing just over one quarter of general revenues, followed by sales taxes. *State* governments, in contrast, rely principally on sales and income taxes, each accounting for about 15 percent of state revenues. Selective sales taxes on alcoholic beverages, entertainment, gasoline, tobacco, and other specialized products and services are levied almost entirely at the state level and have increased significantly in recent years. User fees have also grown rapidly, with more than three quarters of U.S. cities increasing their charges and fees for city services and for access to public facilities in recent years.

Income taxes are imposed almost exclusively at the state level and are levied mainly against individuals rather than corporations. Income taxes contribute about one fifth of state government revenues but less than 5 percent of local government revenues. In the mid-1990s, many states moved to reduce taxes due to improved revenue growth and a more conservative electorate.

Not shown separately here is the growing use of lotteries and taxation of gambling that nearly half the states have either set in motion or are seriously considering. State-run

Exhibit 23–2   **Sources of Revenue and Expenditure for State and Local Governments** (Figures for Fiscal 1991–92)

Revenue Sources:	State Govt's (%)	Local Govt's (%)	Expenditures by Function:	State Govt's (%)	Local Govt's (%)
Taxes	47.0%	35.1%	Education	31.4%	37.5%
Individual income	15.0	1.6	Transportation	8.2	5.8
Corporate profits	3.1	0.3	Safety	4.6	8.6
Property	0.9	26.4	Government administration	3.2	4.7
General sales & gross receipts	15.6	3.6	Environment & housing	3.0	9.6
			Interest on debt	3.7	4.6
Selective sales	7.6	1.6	General expenditures	6.6	4.5
All other*	4.7	1.5	Utilities/liquor	1.5	11.4
User fees & misc. general revenue	14.8	20.4	Insurance trust**	10.2	1.6
Utility and liquor store revenue	1.0	8.9	Social services	27.6	11.6
Insurance trust revenues**	15.4	2.6			
Intergovernmental revenue sources:					
From federal gov't	20.4	3.1			
From state gov't	—	29.8			
From local gov't	1.3	—			
Total revenues in billions of dollars	$659.9	$612.2	Total expenditures in billions of dollars	$628.8	$622.9

*Includes death and gift taxes, severance and license taxes, and miscellaneous taxes and receipts.
**Reflect mainly taxes to provide government employee pensions and unemployment insurance on the revenue side and pension and unemployment income payments to recipients on the expenditure side.

Source: U.S. Bureau of the Census and President's Council of Economic Advisers.

lotteries often dedicate net revenues from ticket sales to the support of a specific government service, such as education, which the public seems anxious to support. Lotteries have become a popular alternative to higher taxes or to slicing government services because they are a voluntary form of taxation, but they incur high administrative costs and usually contribute only a small portion of needed funds.

State and Local Governmental Expenditures

Where do state and local governments spend most of their funds? As Exhibit 23–2 suggests, *education* is the single largest item on the budgets of local governmental units and usually ranks number one or two on state budgets. *Social services,* including public welfare and medical care, occupies a distant second place in local government spending, representing about one eighth of all outlays, but often ranks first in state budgets at about a quarter of total spending. *Transportation services,* especially highway construction and maintenance, ranked third in state spending and sixth for local governments. Overall, education, medicare and general health care, public welfare, highway construction, sanitation, and correctional facilities represent nearly two thirds of state and local government funding today.

Some of the most important government services account for only a minor share of annual public budgets. For example, the cost of ensuring public safety — police and fire protection — generally accounts for less than 10 percent of local government expenditures, although recently expenditures for police departments and jail facilities have taken an increased share of all local spending. Sewer and sanitation services, protection of the environment, and housing programs to aid the poor normally represent about 10 percent of local government costs and about 3 percent of state government spending.

State and local government expenditures have grown rapidly in recent years. In 1994, expenditures by state and local units totaled nearly $940 billion. This figure was nearly three times larger than the level of state and local government spending in 1980. Local tax revenues have simply been inadequate to handle this kind of growth in current (short-term) and capital (long-term) expenditures. Moreover, there is a growing perception that many municipal facilities need modernizing. Accordingly, borrowing in the money and capital markets against future government revenues in order to accommodate local needs for renovation, modernization, and expansion of facilities has soared. In the 1990s, several states (led by New York) began aggressive infrastructure spending programs to create more jobs, taking over a portion of the fiscal function that traditionally has been the province of the federal government, and in the late 1990s, the federal government began to pass a bigger share of welfare and social programs back to the states.

MOTIVATIONS FOR STATE AND LOCAL GOVERNMENT BORROWING

State and local governments borrow money for several reasons. The first is to *satisfy short-term cash needs;* that is, meet payrolls, make repairs, purchase supplies, cover fuel costs, and maintain adequate levels of working capital. Most state and local governments use tax-anticipation notes (to be discussed later) and other forms of short-term borrowing as a supplement to tax revenues to meet these immediate cash needs. Frequently, the construction phase of a building project is financed from short-term funds, and then permanent financing is obtained by selling long-term bonds.

The second major reason for state and local government borrowing is to *finance long-term capital investment;* that is, to build schools, highways, and similar permanent facilities. Long-term projects of this sort account for the bulk of all municipal securities issued each year. Some governmental units try to anticipate future financial needs by borrowing when interest rates are low even though project construction will not begin for a substantial period of time. Funds raised through anticipatory borrowing are then "warehoused" in various investments (such as Treasury bills) until actual construction begins.

In recent years, local governments have occasionally employed *advance refunding* of securities. Advance refundings occur when a governmental unit has been granted a higher credit rating on its bonds by a rating agency, such as Moody's Investors Service or Standard & Poor's Corporation.[1] Bonds issued previously with lower credit ratings (higher interest rates) are called in, and new securities are issued at lower cost. Any significant decline in market interest rates usually gives rise to more advance refunding activity by state and local governments.

TYPES OF SECURITIES ISSUED BY STATE AND LOCAL GOVERNMENTS

Many different types of securities are issued by state and local governments, and the variety of municipal securities available to investors is expanding rapidly. One useful

---

[1]See Chapter 11 for a discussion of security credit (default risk) ratings.

distinction is between short-term securities, which are generally issued to provide working capital, and long-term securities, used to fund capital projects.

Short-Term Securities

The most popular short-term securities issued by state and local governments are **tax anticipation notes (TANs), revenue-anticipation notes (RANs)**, and **bond-anticipation notes (BANs)**.

Tax-Anticipation and Revenue-Anticipation Notes. These notes are used to attract funds in lieu of tax receipts or other revenues expected to be received in the near future. Governments, like businesses and households, have a daily need for cash to meet payrolls and purchase supplies. However, funds raised through taxes usually flow in only at certain times of the year. To satisfy their continuing need for cash between tax dates, state and local governments issue short-term notes with maturities ranging from a few days to a few months. Most of these short-term issues are acquired by local banks. When tax funds are received, the issuing government pays off the note holders and retires any outstanding securities.

Bond-Anticipation Notes. These short-term IOUs, also called *BANs,* are used to provide temporary financing of a long-term project until the time is right to sell long-term bonds. A school district, for example, may need to start construction on new school facilities due to pressure from rising enrollments. If interest rates currently are too high to permit the issue of bonds, then construction can start from funds raised from bond-anticipation notes. Once the project is under way and interest rates decline to more modest levels, the school district then sells its long-term bonds and retires the bond-anticipation notes.

The majority of short-term notes issued by state and local governments are backed by the "full faith and credit" of the issuing government. They sell at interest rates competitive with current money market yields and reflect the credit rating of the issuer. These notes range in original maturity from one month to the more common six-month and one-year maturities, and their interest earnings are exempt from federal income taxes. Short-term tax-exempt notes are issued in marketable bearer form, with denominations ranging typically from $5,000 to $1 million. Both principal and interest are paid at maturity.[2]

Long-Term Securities

The most common type of municipal borrowing is through long-term bonds. There are two major types of municipal bonds issued today — **general obligation bonds** and **revenue bonds** — and both are used principally to finance construction.

General Obligation Bonds. These bonds, known as *GOs,* are the most secure form of municipal borrowing from the standpoint of the investor because they are backed by the "full faith and credit" of the issuing government and may be paid from *any* revenue source. State, county, and city governments, along with school districts, have the power to tax citizens to meet principal and interest payments on any debt issued. GOs are fully backed by this taxing power and usually must be approved by public referendum before

[2]Tax-exempt notes with maturities longer than a year generally bear coupons. For most tax-exempt notes, interest is computed on the basis of a 30-day month or a 360-day year, like the interest on Treasury bills.

Exhibit 23–3

New Security Issues of Tax-Exempt State and Local Governments, 1995 ($ Billions)

Types of Issue and Issuer or Use of Funds	1995	Use of Funds	1995
All issues	$146.2	Use of Proceeds from new capital issues:	
Type of issue:		Education	$24.0
General obligation	56.3	Transportation	12.6
Revenue	88.2	Utilities and conservation	11.1
Type of issue:		Social welfare	19.4
State governments	14.8	Industrial aid	6.0
Special districts	92.5	Other purposes	31.3
Municipalities, counties and townships	37.2		
Issues for new capital, total	102.8		

Note: Issues represented in the table are to raise new capital and refund outstanding debt.

Source: Board of Governors of the Federal Reserve System, *Federal Reserve Bulletin*, selected issues.

issue. The quality or level of risk of GOs depends on the economic base (income and property values) of local communities and the total amount of debt issued.

Revenue Bonds. In contrast, *revenue bonds* are payable only from a specified source of revenue, such as a toll road or a sewer project, and usually do not require a public referendum before they can be issued. These securities are not guaranteed or backed by the taxing power of government. Instead, revenue bonds depend for their value on the revenue-generating capacity of the particular project they support.[3]

As shown in Exhibit 23–3, both general obligation and revenue bonds have grown rapidly over the past decade, and there has been a virtual explosion of different types of revenue bonds. Much of the growth of revenue issues is due to welfare programs of the federal government designed to provide housing for low-income groups, improved medical facilities, and student loans, as well as efforts by local governments to modernize their facilities. The passage of Proposition 13 in California in 1978 (to be discussed later in this chapter) and the enactment of similar laws by other states has encouraged many local authorities to substitute revenue bonds for GOs.

Types of Revenue Bonds

One of the most popular revenue issues is *student-loan revenue bonds* (SLRBs), which are issued by state government agencies that lend money to college students. The federal government guarantees 100 percent of the principal and interest of an SLRB, provided the issuing agency's loan-default ratio is low. If a high percentage of students default on their

---

[3]Some municipal bonds display characteristics of *both* GO and revenue securities. For example, a *special tax bond* is payable from the revenues generated by a special tax, such as on gasoline. Many special tax bonds are backed by the full faith, credit, and taxing power of the issuing governmental unit, giving them the character of GOs. *Special assessment bonds* are payable only from assessments against property constructed or purchased from the proceeds of the bonds issued and arise from sewer and street construction or similar projects. Special assessment issues may take on the character of GOs when backed by the taxing power of the issuer. *Authority bonds* are issued by special governmental units set up by states, cities, or counties to construct and manage certain facilities, such as airports. Authority bonds may be either GOs or revenue issues.

loans, federal guarantees are limited to only a certain portion (usually 80 to 90 percent) of principal and interest payments on the bonds.

In the housing field, several new forms of state and local revenue bonds have appeared. For example, *life-care bonds,* also known as *retirement community bonds,* are issued by state and local development agencies to provide housing for the elderly. Frequently, nonprofit agencies organized by religious groups administer the property. Investor funds are secured by lease rentals and mortgages against the property.

A related security is the *Section 8 bond* issued under the terms of the Federal Housing Act. These bonds finance low- and middle-income rental housing, usually designed for elderly citizens. Section 8s are not federally guaranteed, but the U.S. Department of Housing and Urban Development (HUD) must accumulate a cash reserve for each project that protects against the failure of project residents to pay their rent. Security for Section 8s is provided by rent subsidies and a mortgage on the housing project.

Construction of hospital facilities is frequently supported by *hospital revenue bonds.* These bonds are not guaranteed but are issued by state authorities to build hospitals for lease to public or private operating agencies. Hospital revenue bonds have their principal and interest secured by lease rentals and a mortgage against hospital property.

An unusual type of municipal security that serves both public and private interests is the *industrial development bond* (IDB). These securities originally were used to finance plant construction and the purchase of land, which is then leased to a private company. More recently, IDBs have financed the construction of industrial parks, electric-generating plants, pollution control equipment, and other capital items. Their purpose is to attract industry into the local area and increase jobs and tax revenues. However, the use of public funds raised through the tax-exempt borrowing privilege for private purposes has disturbed many members of Congress. The Deficit Reduction Act of 1984 listed several prohibited uses of IDB money, placed a ceiling of $40 million on small IDBs from a single issuer, and restricted the total amount that could be issued from each state based upon its population.

Innovations in Municipal Securities

The vast majority of state and local securities promise the investor a fixed rate of return. Unfortunately, this reduces the attractiveness of GOs and revenue bonds in periods of rising interest rates and inflation. In recent years, several new municipal instruments were developed to deal with this "inflexibility" problem. For example, some tax-exempt revenue bonds have been issued as *floaters.* In one case, U.S. Steel issued $48 million in government-sponsored pollution control bonds with a flexible (floating) interest rate to protect investors against future rate changes. Buyers were so attracted by this novel idea that an additional $500 million in floating-rate bonds soon came to market, promising a yield tied to changes in rates on Treasury bills and bonds.

Still another innovation is the *option bond.* Option bonds bear a fixed rate of interest but can be sold back to the issuer or the agent at par after a specified period. One example was a $43 million issue of 9 percent, single-family mortgage bonds offered by Denton County, Texas, in December 1980. Although these bonds do not come due until 2013, a trustee has guaranteed to buy back all eligible bonds. More recently, several municipal borrowers have reduced the maturities of their bonds from 30 years to the 10- to 15-year range to improve their flexibility to investors.

Accretion, or *compound-interest,* bonds have been issued in recent years, primarily to fund the construction of new housing units. These securities defer payment of interest and, instead, reinvest the bonds' interest earnings so they will grow at a compound rate to benefit bondholders. Because compounding of interest generates a higher total yield, governments issuing these bonds are able to sell them at lower cost than conventional bonds.

These innovations in state and local government borrowing are not without costs, however. They often require more frequent borrowing by municipal governments and, in some cases, increase the average cost of government funds. In effect, many of the new financial instruments shift risk from investors to borrowers and ultimately to taxpayers. Financial planning becomes more difficult for those local governments electing to use the newer instruments.

KEY FEATURES OF MUNICIPAL DEBT
Tax Exemption

The unique feature of municipal securities is the **tax-exemption privilege**. The interest income from qualified municipal securities is exempt from federal income taxes; in addition, state law usually exempts municipals from income taxes levied by the state of issuance. This exemption feature was created so that federal, state, and local governments would not interfere with each other in raising funds and providing services to their citizens. Capital gains on municipal securities are *not* tax exempt, however, unless the security is issued at a discount from par. In that special case, any increase in price up to par value is considered part of the security's interest return and is tax exempt. However, if the security continues to rise in price, that portion of the gain above par is subject to taxation once the investor realizes the gain.

An Interest Subsidy to High-Income Investors. The tax-exempt feature has been a controversial issue for many years. It is a government subsidy to high tax-bracket investors. This is true because the value of the exemption privilege increases with the investor's marginal income tax rate. Exhibit 23–4 illustrates the impact of the investor's marginal income tax rate (or tax bracket) on the relative attractiveness of municipals compared to taxable securities. This exhibit compares the approximate after-tax yield on high-grade corporate bonds, which are fully taxable, with the yield on comparable quality municipal bonds, assuming that Aaa-rated corporate bonds are trading currently at a 10 percent before-tax yield and Aaa municipal bonds are trading at 7.75 percent. Because the 10 percent corporate bond yield is a before-tax rate of return, we must adjust it using the investor's marginal income tax rate to derive the after-tax rate of return. The before-tax corporate yield is multiplied by $(1 - t)$, where t is the investor's applicable federal tax rate.

Exhibit 23–4 illustrates the effect of this calculation for individual investors with marginal tax rates ranging from 0 to 39.6 percent and for corporations whose marginal tax rates range from 0 to 35 percent. For an individual investor in the top 39.6 percent tax bracket, the after-tax return on Aaa corporate bonds was 10 percent × (1 – 39.6), or 6.04 percent. Clearly, an investor in this high-income group would prefer to purchase municipal bonds yielding 7.75 percent rather than corporate bonds returning just 6.04 percent after taxes, other factors being equal. The same conclusion holds true for larger corporations and banks confronted with the top 35 percent corporate federal tax rate.[4] Even for

---

[4]Recent federal tax laws have sharply reduced the attractiveness of municipal securities to banks and other top tax-bracket investors. Successive tax laws have lowered the top corporate tax rate from 46 percent to 35 percent, forcing the after-tax yield on municipal bonds closer to the after-tax return on taxable securities. Federal tax reform, therefore, has made municipal bonds less attractive relative to all taxable securities. Many investors,

Exhibit 23–4   **The Impact of the Tax-Exemption Feature on the After-Tax Yields of Long-Term Corporate and Municipal Bonds**

Investor Group	Before-Tax Yield on Seasoned AAA Corporate Bonds	Appropriate Federal Income Tax Bracket for Investor Group	After-Tax Yield on Seasoned AAA Corporate Bonds	Before-Tax and After-Tax Yield on AAA Municipal Bonds
Individuals in the highest income bracket (with surcharge)	10%	39.6%	6.04%	7.75%
Large corporate investors:				
Manufacturing and industrial corporations	10	35	6.50	7.75
Property-casualty insurance companies	10	35	6.50	7.75
Commercial banks	10	35	6.50	7.75
Individuals in middle income tax brackets	10	28	7.20	7.75
Individuals and institutions in the lowest income brackets	10	15	8.50	7.75
Tax-exempt investors:				
Governments, pension funds, charities, foundations, and credit unions	10	0	10	7.75

middle-bracket investors facing a 28 percent rate, municipals often are more attractive in terms of after-tax return.

Of course, the foregoing analysis focuses exclusively on after-tax rates of return, ignoring differences in liquidity and other features of taxable and tax-exempt securities. A corporation that needs to hold securities for liquidity purposes, for example, might well hold taxable issues, such as U.S. government securities, which can be converted into cash quickly and with little risk of loss, even though their after-tax yields may be lower than the yields on municipal bonds.

For income tax brackets below the top rung, taxable securities compare more favorably with municipals. For example, many small private investors whose applicable federal income tax rate is 15 percent find taxable securities more lucrative and purchase few municipals. In effect, the tax-exempt feature limits the demand for state and local government securities to high-income individuals and mutual funds that appeal to individuals as investors, to property-casualty insurers, large nonfinancial corporations, and to other higher tax-bracket investors. This limitation may represent a serious problem in future years when many local governments must raise an enormous volume of new funds to accommodate rapidly expanding populations.

The tax exemption feature is an advantage to municipal governments because it keeps their interest cost low relative to interest rates paid by other borrowers. These savings can

especially individuals, still find municipals attractive, however, because they are one of only a few tax shelters left after federal tax reform. Banks, on the other hand, have significantly reduced their municipal holdings relative to taxable loans and U.S. government securities because federal laws have sharply reduced or eliminated, depending upon the issuer of the municipal securities, the tax deductibility of bank borrowing costs when banks purchase municipals. Overall, these tax law changes have resulted in a shift in the municipal market toward more *retail investors* — higher-income individuals and mutual funds appealing to individuals as investors — to whom the tax exemption feature of municipals is still an important tax shelter.

be passed on to local citizens in the form of lower tax rates. Of course, the U.S. Treasury is able to collect less revenue from high-bracket investors as a result of the exemption privilege and must tax low-bracket taxpayers more heavily to make up the difference. Therefore, the *total* tax bill from all levels of government is probably little affected by the tax-exempt feature of municipals.

Exemption Contributes to Market Volatility

Because the market for municipal bonds is limited by the tax-exempt privilege to top-bracket investors, prices and interest rates on municipal bonds tend to be highly volatile. Prices of tax-exempt bonds tend to rise during those periods when corporate and individual incomes are rising, because top-bracket investors have greater need to shelter their earnings from taxation at those times. However, a fall in individual or corporate earnings often leads to sharp reductions in the demand for municipal bonds. Prices of tax-exempt issues may plummet, and interest costs confronting borrowing governments may rise dramatically during those periods when corporate profits are squeezed. This makes financial planning in the state and local government sector more difficult.

A Market of "Fair Weather" Investors. Another problem that exacerbates the volatility of municipal bond prices is the limited investment horizon of many tax-exempt bond buyers. For the most part, investors active in the tax-exempt market are "fair weather" friends. Some banks, for example, may build up their state and local bond holdings when customer loan demand is weak, only to sell off substantial quantities of municipals when loan demand revives. Another major group of tax-exempt investors (high-income individuals) has finite life spans, and therefore their bonds are often sold after only a short holding period. The net result is to create an active secondary market and relatively high turnover rate for the larger, better-known municipal issues.

Credit Ratings

A feature of municipal securities that makes them especially attractive to investors is their high credit rating. About 10 percent of all municipal securities are AAA-rated by Moody's Investors Service and Standard & Poor's Corporation; about half are AA- or A-rated. A relatively small proportion of all state and local government securities are rated BA or lower or carry no published rating. This means that the majority of municipal issues are considered to be of investment quality rather than speculative buys.

Factors Behind Setting Credit Ratings. In assigning credit ratings to municipals, Moody's and other rating services consider the past repayment record of the borrowing unit of government, the quality and size of its tax base, the volume of debt outstanding, local economic conditions, and future prospects for growth in the local economy. The fact that many municipal issues are backed by taxing authority or may draw on several different sources of revenue for repayment of principal and interest helps to keep the investment quality of tax-exempt issues high. This is particularly important for one of the leading holders of municipal bonds and notes — banks. Regulations generally prohibit banks and other depository institutions from acquiring debt securities rated below BAA (so-called speculative issues). These restrictive rules encourage state and local governments to keep their credit ratings high to encourage more active participation by regulated financial institutions in bidding for new municipal bonds.

Recent Credit Quality Problems. Until recently, state and local governments possessed virtually unblemished credit records. No major defaults on municipal securities had occurred since the Great Depression. However, the turbulent economic and financial environment of the 1970s, 1980s, and 1990s caused many investors to reassess the credit standing of municipals, especially the bonds and notes issued by some of the largest cities and those associated with special local government projects, such as nuclear power production.

This problem first surfaced dramatically in the financial crisis experienced by New York in the 1970s and again early in the 1990s. Soaring costs for municipal services, excessive reliance on short-term debt, and high unemployment combined to threaten that city with record high interest costs and financial default. And in the wake of New York City's fiscal crisis, other northeastern cities — Chicago, Detroit, Philadelphia, and Washington, D.C. — also have found their credit costs rising and investor resistance to buying their securities increasing. Even though there have been few actual defaults on municipal bonds in recent years (though about 6,000 local government defaults have occurred in U.S. history) and the investors involved usually received back the principal value of their bonds (with some loss of interest), risk premiums demanded by investors purchasing lower-grade municipal bonds have at times exceeded risk premiums on comparable quality corporate bonds, setting in motion a "flight to quality" by high-tax-bracket investors.

This fundamental concern about the investment quality of municipal issues was heightened in December 1978, when Cleveland became the first major U.S. city to default on its debt since the Great Depression of the 1930s. Then, early in the 1980s, the Washington Public Power Supply System (WPPSS), a nuclear power consortium, was caught in an environmental squabble, coupled with serious project delays and cost overruns on nuclear power facilities under construction. The result, in the summer of 1983, was the largest default on a local government bond issue in American history, amounting to more than $2 billion. Since that time, utility companies with large nuclear power plants in the construction phase have frequently seen their bond interest rates rise sharply as market investors came to fear greater risk of default.

As the 1990s began, several states and cities had the credit ratings on their bonds either lowered or placed on a "credit watch" list. The most dramatic example was the state of California, which faced projected annual budget deficits in the $5 billion range. Several of California's small cities and other local governments appeared to be close to defaulting on their bonds due to defense cutbacks and falling real estate values that threaten future tax collections. During the summer of 1995, Orange County, California, one of the largest urban areas in the United States, declared bankruptcy with close to $800 million in unpaid obligations. The rapid growth in that county's population during the 1970s and 1980s put local governments in a bind due to the soaring demand for government services. However, Orange County voters rejected several proposals to raise taxes. County officials then adopted an aggressive investments policy, including heavy investments in derivative securities, which lost about $2.5 billion when interest rates rose. Faced with numerous claims from creditors (including other local governments who had invested their funds with Orange County), Orange County officials worked for nearly a year to hammer out a repayment plan to cover most of Orange County's debts.[5]

Orange County's financial collapse reminded investors in municipals that local government failures are an ever-present possibility. Government bankruptcies are more likely in areas of economic decline or in localities where growth has far outstripped the ability of

[5]See Chapter 11 for a more detailed discussion of the Orange County bankruptcy.

cities and counties to provide government services, and citizens are unwilling to levy additional taxes or authorize the issuance of new debt. Partly as a result of recent state and local government financial problems, the Securities and Exchange Commission (SEC) in 1994 and 1995 amended its Rule 15c2-12 to bar security dealers from marketing new municipal security issues unless the issuers agree to provide annual financial reports and continuing disclosure of "material events" (such as delinquencies, defaults, modification of security holders' rights, credit rating changes, or sale of property backing a security issue) to designated national data banks. At almost the same time, the SEC approved a rule to severely limit the campaign contributions that security dealers underwriting new municipal bond issues could make to local government officials and to those running for public office. The idea is to protect investors in municipals from the adverse consequences of political graft and corruption arising from state and local governments' borrowing money.

Insurance for Municipal Bonds. Investor concern over the quality of some municipal securities and the potential failure of some state and local government projects led to the creation of "sleep insurance" for selected municipal issues. First offered by Ambac Indemnity Corp. in the early 1970s and later by such companies as Municipal Bond Investors Assurance Corp. (MBIA), Financial Security Assurance, Inc., and Financial Guarantee Insurance Corporation, these insurance policies, which guarantee timely payment of principal and interest, now cover most top-rated state and local government bonds. Such insurance protection normally is requested and paid for by the bond issuer or the issuers' representative, not the investor purchasing the bonds. However, buyers of insured bonds usually receive lower yields compared to noninsured bonds. Therefore, issuers benefit from insurance policies because they can sell their bonds at lower interest cost. The rating agencies, such as Standard & Poor's Corporation and Moody's Investors Service, generally grant higher credit ratings to insured municipal securities. However, if the credit rating of the insurance company falls, the interest rates on municipal bonds insured by that particular company also tend to rise as investors become concerned about the insurer's ability to pay if the state or local government issuer cannot. Bond insurance has become more important in recent years as retail customers (individuals and mutual funds) have come to capture a larger share of purchases of new municipal securities.

Serialization

Most municipal bonds are *serial* securities. **Serialization** refers to the splitting up of a single bond issue into several different maturities. Thus, an issue of $20 million in bonds to build a municipal auditorium might include the following securities:

Amount	Due in
$1 million	1 year
$1 million	2 years
$1 million	3 years
•	•
•	•
•	•
$1 million	20 years

Splitting a single issue of municipals into multiple maturities contrasts with the practice employed by most corporate borrowers and the federal government. Corporations, for example, generally issue *term* bonds in which all securities in the same issue come due on the same date. In effect, serialization of municipal bonds is a way of *amortizing* state and local debt.

Why is serialization so popular in the municipal field? Before serial bonds were widely adopted, state and local bonds were generally term securities. A sinking fund was created at the time of issue, and annual contributions were made to the fund until sufficient monies were accumulated to pay off the bond at maturity. However, sinking funds proved irresistible to unscrupulous politicians and to governments facing financial emergencies. Accumulated funds often disappeared, leaving virtually nothing to retire municipal debt when it came due. The serial feature seemed to offer an ideal solution to this problem.

Unfortunately, serialization has created as many problems as it has solved. For one thing, splitting a security issue into a number of different maturities reduces the liquidity and marketability of municipal securities. The average-sized municipal issue sold publicly contains about $20 to $40 million in securities. Therefore, when such an issue is split into multiple maturities, there is only a small amount outstanding in any one maturity class. The potential volume of trading for particular maturities is, therefore, extremely limited. Serialization also complicates the offering of new securities, because a number of different investor groups must be attracted into the bidding. For example, banks and individuals generally prefer the shorter-term (1- to 10-year) securities, and insurance companies often want only the longest-term bonds.

HOW MUNICIPAL BONDS ARE MARKETED

The selling of municipals is usually carried out through a syndicate of banks and securities dealers. These institutions underwrite municipals by purchasing them from issuing units of government and reselling the securities in the open market at a higher price. Prices paid by the underwriting firms may be determined either by competitive bidding among several syndicates or by negotiation with a single securities dealer or syndicate. Competitive bidding normally is employed in the marketing of general obligation bonds; revenue bonds more frequently are placed through private negotiation.

In competitive bidding, syndicates (which may contain from 2 to upwards of 50 underwriters) interested in a particular bond issue will estimate its potential reoffer price in the open market and what their desired underwriting commission must be. Each syndicate wants to bid a price high enough to win the bid but low enough so that the securities later can be sold in the open market at a price sufficient to protect the syndicate's commission. That is,

$$\text{Bid price} + \text{Underwriting commission} = \text{Market reoffer price}$$

The winning bid carries the lowest *net interest cost* (NIC) to the issuing unit of government. The NIC is simply the sum of all interest payments that will be owed on the new issue divided by its principal amount.

Bidding for new issues of municipal bonds is treacherous business. Prices, interest rates, and market demand for municipals change rapidly. In fact, the tax-exempt securities market is one of the most volatile of all financial markets. This is due, in part, to the key role of banks, insurance companies, and other financial institutions in the municipal market, whose demand for municipals fluctuates with their net earnings and loan demand. Legal interest rate ceilings, which prohibit some local governments from borrowing when market interest rates climb above those ceilings, also play a significant role in the volatility of municipal trading. These combined factors render the tax-exempt market highly sensitive to the business cycle, monetary policy, and a host of other factors. The specter of high interest rates often forces postponement of hundreds of millions of dollars in new issues, and the onset of lower rates may unleash a flood of new offerings. Still another problem is federal tax reform, which has reduced the volume and attractiveness of many municipal securities to investors (commercial banks in particular).

PROBLEMS IN THE MUNICIPAL MARKET

Problems and Proposals Regarding Tax Exemption

The municipal market has been plagued by a number of problems over the years, some related to its unique tax-exempt character. Many observers question the social benefit of the tax-exemption privilege. Although state and local governments can borrow more cheaply as a result of tax exemption, the federal government must tax nonexempt groups more heavily to make up the lost revenue. Also, many important investor groups (such as pension funds) have little need for tax shelters and therefore display little interest in municipal bonds. A number of proposals have been advanced over the years for improving the depth and stability of the municipal market and eliminating the tax-exempt feature. One interesting idea calls for reimbursing state and local governments for loss of the tax-exempt privilege through federal subsidies. A related idea calls for paying a subsidy directly to investors who choose to buy municipal securities. An *Urbank* has also been proposed that, under federal sponsorship, would issue its own bonds and direct the proceeds of bond sales to municipal governments. One criticism of this approach is the danger of increased federal controls over state and local governments.

California's Proposition 13 and Taxpayer Resistance

The municipal market was rocked to its foundations in 1978 when California voters approved Proposition 13. This law set maximum real property tax rates at 1 percent of the full cash value of taxable property, except to cover those bonds already approved by voters. The state of California was prohibited from enacting a statewide property tax or property transfer tax, and any increase in state taxes required a two thirds vote of the legislature. In effect, Proposition 13 called for a 60 percent decline in real property tax collections without making provision for other sources of funds to take up the slack.

Ultimately, Proposition 13, coupled with California's deep economic problems in the 1990s, may lead to further severe financial problems among local governments in that state. Moreover, the success of Proposition 13 in California resulted in the creation of taxpayer lobby groups in other states intent on enacting similar legislation. A continuing taxpayer revolt resulted, subsequently, in more than 30 states passing legislation to limit the growth of local governments or to reduce taxes. Budget balancing was required in 49 of the 50 states. Many financial analysts have predicted dire consequences for the municipal market stemming from such laws. One hopeful sign, however, is the rejection of several drastic tax-revolt measures by voters in a number of states in the 1990s. Voters seem more aware today that tax-cutting measures can result in the elimination of important public services and in wholesale layoffs of government workers.

The Outlook for State and Local Governments

The outlook for state and local governments as the 21st century dawns is not particularly inspiring. Key areas likely to require growing financial support include housing and recreational facilities for the elderly, more equitable funding of schools, and an expanding prison population that will continue to require large-scale expenditures for correctional facilities. Unfortunately, local government revenues will struggle to keep up with these demands for funds because of projected slower growth in the economy and less generous support from the federal government. States must plan for receiving fewer federal monies in the future; on the positive side, there will be fewer federal restrictions on how local governments can spend federal money. At the same time, most states and localities are in hot pursuit of new industries to expand their economic base, which often means giving tax relief to new businesses and holding the line on the imposition of new taxes so that revenue sources are further reduced.

With slower economic growth and less federal support, more states will be under pressure to "pass the buck" to their local governments and force cities, counties, and school districts to deal with their own problems and find their own funding sources. Certainly, the need for local government services is not likely to fade, but the continued willingness of taxpayers to authorize new construction and new borrowing and the continued willingness of large numbers of investors to fund those needs in a volatile and uncertain economic environment are key issues in municipal finance for the period ahead.

KEY TERMS AND CONCEPTS IN THIS CHAPTER

municipals	bond-anticipation notes (BANs)	tax-exemption privilege
tax-anticipation notes (TANs)	general obligation bonds	serialization
revenue-anticipation notes (RANs)	revenue bonds	

STUDY QUESTIONS

1. The market for state and local government bonds has been one of the most rapidly growing financial markets in the United States since World War II. Why has this been the case? Can you foresee any serious problems on the horizon for municipals?

2. What are the principal sources of revenue for state and local governments today? Where do they spend the bulk of their incoming funds?

3. For what reasons do state and local governments borrow short- and long-term funds?

4. Give a concise definition of each of the following state and local government securities, and explain how each is used:
    a. Tax-anticipation notes
    b. Revenue-anticipation notes
    c. Bond-anticipation notes
    d. General obligation (GO) bonds
    e. Revenue bonds
    f. Special tax bonds
    g. Special assessment bonds
    h. Authority bonds

5. Revenue bonds issued by local governments and public agencies have grown more rapidly than any other type of municipal security in recent years. Several different kinds of revenue bonds are listed below. Please explain the principal purpose or function of each of these securities:
    a. SLROs
    b. Life-care bonds
    c. Section 8 bonds
    d. Hospital revenue bonds
    e. IDBs

6. What are the principal features of municipal bonds that have made them attractive to many groups of investors? What features often limit the demand for these bonds?

7. How has recent federal tax reform legislation affected the municipal market?

8. Describe how municipal bonds are marketed. What risks do syndicates face?

9. What problems do municipal and state governments face in the years ahead? What factors seem to be the principal causes of these problems?

PROBLEMS

1. Corporate bonds carrying an A rating are currently being priced to yield 8.62 percent. For an investor in the 28 percent income tax bracket, what yield must an A-rated municipal bond carry to make this investor indifferent as to yield between the corporate and the municipal bond?

2. Sandoval County issued AA-rated bonds at a net interest cost of 6.85 percent. If annual interest payments promised on these bonds amount to $12.75 million, what was the principal amount of municipal bonds issued by Sandoval County?

SELECTED REFERENCES

Aguilar, Linda M.; Richard H. Mattoon; and William A. Testa. "The Going Gets Tough: State and Local Governments Confront the Nineties." *Economic Perspectives*. Federal Reserve Bank of Chicago, April 1991.

Aronson, J. Richard, and John L. Hilley. *Financing State and Local Governments,* 4th Ed. Washington D.C.: The Brookings Institution, 1986.

Inman, Robert P. "Do You Know How Much Money Is in Your Public Purse?" *Business Review.* Federal Reserve Bank of Philadelphia, July/August 1995, pp. 19–30.

Rubin, Laura S. "State and Local Government Sector: Long-Term Trends and Recent Fiscal Pressures." *Federal Reserve Bulletin,* December 1992, pp. 892–901.

Chapter 24

Consumer Lending and Borrowing

LEARNING OBJECTIVES IN THIS CHAPTER

- To demonstrate the vital role played by consumers — individuals and families — in supplying loanable funds to the money and capital markets.
- To examine the principal characteristics of consumers as borrowers of funds in the financial system.
- To explore the principal characteristics of consumer lending institutions such as banks, credit unions, and finance companies.

Among the most important of all financial markets are the markets providing savings instruments and credit to individuals and families. Many financial analysts have referred to the period since World War II as the *age of consumer finance* because individuals and families not only are the principal source of loanable funds flowing into the financial markets today but also are one of the largest borrowing groups in the entire financial system. Moreover, the market for consumer financial services is the one market that *everyone,* regardless of profession or social status, will enter at one time or another during his or her lifetime. In this chapter, we examine the major characteristics of the consumer market for financial services, the principal lenders active in this market, and some important regulations applying to consumer borrowing and lending today.

CONSUMERS AS LENDERS OF FUNDS

Each of us is a consumer of goods and services virtually every day of our lives. Scarcely a single day passes that we do not enter the marketplace to purchase food, shelter, entertainment, and other essentials of modern living. We are also well aware, perhaps from personal experience, that consumers often borrow heavily in the financial marketplace to achieve their desired standard of living. U.S. consumers borrowed an estimated $400 billion in 1995, for example, and by the end of that year owed more than $5 trillion to various lending institutions.

What is not nearly so well known, however, is the fact that consumers as a group are also the most important **lenders** of funds in the economy. Loanable funds are supplied by consumers when they purchase financial assets from other units in the economy. In 1995, gross savings by U.S. households reached an estimated $1.1 trillion, of which about $645 billion flowed into bank deposits, bonds, stocks, and direct cash loans to others in the economy. By comparison, businesses recorded gross savings of less than $640 billion, and state and local governments racked up estimated savings of about $90 billion. Clearly, the consuming public is the chief source of the raw material — loanable funds — exchanged in the financial markets.[1]

Financial Assets Purchased by Consumers

If consumers make loanable funds available to other units in the economy by purchasing financial assets, what *kinds* of financial assets do they buy? And what are the principal sources of borrowed funds for consumers? The Federal Reserve Board's Flow of Funds Accounts provide us with a wealth of information on the borrowing and lending habits of households. Exhibit 24–1 summarizes information contained in recent Flow of Funds reports on the kinds of financial assets acquired by households. One fact immediately evident is the wide diversity of financial assets purchased by individuals and families, ranging from those of very low risk and short maturity (such as bank deposits and government securities) to long-term, high-risk investments (such as mortgages and corporate stock).

The most important household financial asset today is *pension fund reserves,* built up by individual workers to prepare for their retirement. An aging population has shown great concern in recent years that sufficient funds will be available when they retire to sustain their living standards. As a result, households increased their holdings of pension reserves between 1980 and the mid-1990s more than sixfold. In second place are holdings of *corporate stock* (equities), led by a dramatic rise in holdings of shares in mutual funds (investment companies). The recent growth in households' common stock investments appears to reflect continuing fears about inflation. Then, too, many individuals are concerned that, when they reach retirement, Social Security and other government pension programs will be inadequate to cover spiraling medical expenses and other living costs in their later years.

In third place among household holdings of financial assets are *deposits* in banks, savings and loan associations, credit unions, and other thrift institutions. These checkable demand deposits and time and savings deposits represented close to 15 percent of the total financial asset holdings of U.S. consumers in 1995. Moreover, as Exhibit 24–1 reveals, the importance of deposits in consumer financial investments generally increased until the 1980s and 1990s, when households became concerned about a rising tide of bank and thrift institution failures. At the same time, better yields appeared to be available from investments in corporate stock (including mutual funds) and government and corporate bonds.

There has also been a significant rise in household investments in small businesses, which are often owned and operated by an individual or by a member of the same family. By 1995, household investments in the equity of unincorporated business firms (included under *Other assets* in Exhibit 24–1) totaled nearly $3.6 trillion. With jobs more difficult to find in recent years, more individuals and families have attempted to organize their own businesses. At the same time, there is a trend toward early retirement and the launching of second careers by creating new businesses.

---

[1]Portions of this chapter were originally drawn from Rose (1978, June 1979, and September 1979).

Exhibit 24–1

Principal Financial Assets Held by U.S. Households, 1960, 1970, 1980, 1990, and 1995 ($ Billions)

Financial Assets Held	1960 Amount	1960 Percent	1970 Amount	1970 Percent	1980 Amount	1980 Percent	1990 Amount	1990 Percent	1995* Amount	1995* Percent
Demand deposits and currency	$ 70.2	7.3%	$ 118.2	4.7%	$ 270.7	4.1%	$ 514.0	3.7%	$ 693.6	3.5%
Time and savings accounts:	165.3	17.1	426.3	17.1	1,272.8	19.4	2,381.1	17.0	2,103.9	10.7
At commercial banks	62.1	6.4	—	—	—	—	—	—	—	—
At nonbank thrift institutions	103.3	10.7	—	—	—	—	—	—	—	—
Shares in money market mutual funds	—	—	—	—	64.9	1.0	438.6	3.1	424.0	2.2
U.S. government securities	73.5	7.6	102.8	4.1	246.9	3.8	841.1	6.0	1,080.5	5.5
State and local government securities	30.8	3.2	46.0	1.8	88.4	1.3	549.2	3.9	376.1	1.9
Open market paper	0.1	0.0	11.8	0.5	41.3	0.6	214.2	1.5	23.5	0.1
Corporate and foreign bonds	9.8	1.0	35.6	1.4	58.8	0.9	185.0	1.3	211.0	1.1
Mortgages	31.8	3.3	52.1	2.1	116.5	1.8	225.5	1.6	194.7	1.0
Corporate stock:	396.1	40.0	727.2	29.1	1,173.1	17.9	2,503.7	17.9	4,855.4	24.8
Investment companies	17.0	1.8	44.5	1.8	52.1	0.8	495.9	3.5	1,141.9	5.8
Other corporate shares	279.0	39.2	682.7	27.3	1,121.0	17.1	2,007.8	14.4	3,713.5	18.9
Life insurance reserves	85.2	8.8	130.7	5.2	216.4	3.3	373.4	2.7	501.0	3.6
Pension fund reserves	90.7	9.4	240.8	9.6	830.0	12.6	2,962.6	21.2	5,472.4	27.9
Security credit	1.1	0.1	4.4	0.2	14.8	0.2	62.4	0.4	107.6	0.5
Other assets	13.3	1.4	603.5	24.1	2,168.6	33.0	2,760.1	19.7	3,569.0	18.2
Total financial assets	$967.9	100.0%	$2,499.3	100.0%	$6,563.3	100.0%	$13,978.9	100.0%	$19,612.8	100.0%

Note: Columns may not add to totals due to rounding.
*Figures for 1995 are first quarter only.

Source: Board of Governors of the Federal Reserve System.

The Growing Menu of Savings Instruments Available to Consumers Today

One of the most important of all trends affecting consumer savings and lending today is a veritable explosion of *new* financial instruments. Banks, brokerage houses, and other financial institutions began in the 1970s to compete aggressively for consumer savings, not only by offering higher returns where the law allowed, but also by proliferating new services. Like a Baskin-Robbins' ice cream store, financial institutions began to offer household customers 31 or more flavors of savings and transaction accounts as well as credit plans to meet a wide variety of personal financial needs.

This trend toward financial service proliferation began with the introduction of the **NOW account** in New England in 1970. NOWs are checkbook deposits that, like any checking account, can be used to pay for purchases of goods and services. But NOWs also pay interest — something federal law currently prohibits with regular checking accounts. NOWs were permitted nationwide beginning in 1981 as a result of passage of the Depository Institutions Deregulation and Monetary Control Act of 1980. This law also called for the gradual phasing out of federal interest rate ceilings on all bank and thrift institution deposits so that consumers could receive competitive, market-determined interest rates on their savings.

The Depository Institutions Deregulation and Monetary Control Act of 1980 (DIDMCA) also authorized two services that compete directly with NOWs. One of these — automatic transfer service (ATS) — permits the consumer to preauthorize a bank to move funds from a savings account to a checking account to cover overdrafts. The net effect is to pay interest on transaction balances at the savings account rate. Credit unions are permitted to offer their own version of the NOW, known as the *share draft*. These interest-bearing checkbook plans give the consumer the advantage of a duplicate record system for any checks written and pay higher interest rates on liquid funds.

In 1973, money market mutual funds appeared, offering consumers *share accounts* with low denominations (most allowing accounts to be opened for as little as $1,000). Like NOWs, share accounts at money funds were developed originally to get around federal deposit interest rate ceilings and give smaller savers access to competitive rates of return on their funds. Later, several prominent brokerage houses began offering *consumer cash-management services*, in which funds could be held in an interest-bearing money market fund until transferred into stocks, bonds, or other securities, or accessed via check or credit card. Closely related to these services is the *wrap account*, for which a security broker assembles for the consumer a suitable portfolio of stocks, bonds, and other assets and actively manages that portfolio in return for an annual fee.

Life insurance firms began offering a related service known as *universal life insurance*, in which savings contributed by the policyholder are placed in a money market fund, with the life insurer making periodic preauthorized withdrawals to pay the premiums on the life insurance policy. The consumer is offered life insurance protection plus a higher return on savings.

Finally, in 1981, with passage of the Economic Recovery Tax Act of 1981, wage earners and salaried individuals were granted the right to make limited contributions each year, tax free, to an individual retirement account (IRA) offered by local banks, brokerage firms, and other financial institutions or by employers with qualified pension or profit-sharing plans. Similarly, Keogh Plan retirement accounts have been open to self-employed persons since 1962 and may be offered by the same institutions that sell IRAs.

Beginning in the late 1970s, flexible interest rate savings plans became popular as many consumers fought to stay ahead of inflation through savings instruments whose rates of return were sensitive to changes in the cost of living as well as to changing interest rates in the money and capital markets. Money market certificates of deposit were authorized by federal regulation in 1978 with interest rates that changed as market yields on U.S. government securities fluctuated. In 1982, the Garn-St Germain Depository Institutions Act allowed banks and nonbank thrift institutions to offer deposits competitive with shares offered by money market mutual funds, in the form of money market deposit accounts (MMDAs) and Super NOWs, each offering flexible interest rates but accessible via check to pay for purchases of goods and services. Finally, in 1987, several banks and savings associations, led by Chase Manhattan Bank of New York, introduced market-index certificates of deposit whose return was linked to stock market performance.

These recent innovations have been designed to bring individuals and families into the financial markets as more active lenders of funds. The newest financial services offer the consumer greater *financial flexibility* — easier access to liquid funds for transaction purposes and the ability to move funds more easily from one type of savings instrument to another. The newest savings instruments offer the potential for higher rates of return more closely tied to changing interest rates and security prices in the open market.

One interesting feature of the consumer financial services market worth remembering is that many households do *not* make a practice of purchasing all their financial services from one source. Instead, as a recent Federal Reserve Board survey by Elliehausen and Wolken (1992) reveals, households tend to *bundle,* or *cluster,* their purchases of services from certain financial firms. One typical clustering centers around the purchase of a checking account. Usually, a specific local institution will be chosen to hold a family's main checking account — in most cases, a bank, credit union, or savings and loan. Savings accounts are often placed locally as well, although increasingly households have turned to distant financial firms, such as mutual funds, to help them invest their savings at the best yields. Credit services — home mortgages and installment loans — frequently are purchased from a separate financial firm, such as a finance company, savings association, or bank. The financial service firms from which households purchase credit usually are *local* firms, but often they will search both inside and outside the local area to find a loan on the best terms. The Federal Reserve Board survey revealed that most households seem to regard checkable deposits (payments accounts), savings accounts, and credit as *separate* financial products for which they will each seek out the best terms of trade available.

CONSUMERS AS BORROWERS OF FUNDS

We have noted that consumers provide most of the savings out of which loans are made and financial assets created in the money and capital markets. However, it is also true that consumers are among the most important borrowers in the financial system. For example, in 1995, households borrowed net about $330 billion in U.S. credit markets, while nonfinancial businesses raised less than $320 billion in estimated borrowings. Equally impressive is the total amount of debt owed by households relative to other sectors of the economy. For example, total credit market debt owed by U.S. households totaled almost $5 trillion in 1995 (see Exhibit 24–2). This was only slightly less than the total amounts owed by the federal government and all state and local governments combined.

Exhibit 24–2   **The Principal Debt Obligations (Liabilities) of U.S. Households, 1960, 1970, 1980, 1990, and 1995**

Debt (Liabilities) Outstanding	1960 Amount	1960 Percent	1970 Amount	1970 Percent	1980 Amount	1980 Percent	1990 Amount	1990 Percent	1995* Amount	1995* Percent
Home mortgages	$136.8	60.5%	$290.0	57.9%	$ 943.3	62.6%	$2,714.6	67.7%	$3,245.5	65.4%
Other mortgages	9.2	4.1	19.0	3.8	31.5	2.1	133.5	3.3	198.3	4.0
Consumer installment credit	43.0	19.0	105.5	21.1	300.4	19.9	748.3	18.7	1,026.6	20.7
Other consumer credit	13.2	5.8	37.6	7.5	74.0	4.9	60.6	1.5	132.3	2.7
Bank loans n.e.c.†	7.2	3.2	6.9	1.4	29.5	2.0	42.4	1.1	31.9	0.6
Other loans	7.0	3.1	20.9	4.2	54.7	3.6	112.1	2.8	145.5	2.9
Security credit	5.4	2.4	10.4	2.1	27.2	1.8	38.8	1.0	68.0	1.4
Trade credit	2.3	0.9	5.3	1.1	17.2	1.1	54.6	1.4	93.5	1.9
Deferred and unpaid life insurance premiums	2.4	1.1	5.1	1.0	12.9	0.9	16.5	0.4	18.0	0.4
Other liabilities	—	—	0.2	—	16.6	1.1	86.1	2.1	0.1	0.0
Total liabilities	$226.2	100.0%	$500.0	100.0%	$1,507.3	100.0%	$4,007.5	100.0%	$4,959.7	100.0%

Note: Columns may not add to totals due to rounding.
*1995 figures are for second quarter only.
†Not elsewhere classified.

Source: Board of Governors of the Federal Reserve System.

Is Consumer Borrowing Excessive?

Are consumers too heavily in debt today? Certainly, the total volume of household debt outstanding is huge in both absolute terms and relative to most other sectors of the economy. However, to judge whether consumer borrowing is really excessive, that debt should be compared to the financial assets consumers hold. These assets, presumably, can be drawn on to meet any interest and principal payments that come due on consumer borrowings. Exhibit 24–3 shows that, although the volume of consumer debt has increased rapidly in recent years, the volume of household financial assets has grown even faster. For example, in 1995, financial assets held by U.S. households exceeded their estimated liabilities by nearly $15 trillion. Moreover, the absolute dollar size of that financial asset cushion has increased dramatically over the past three decades (as the third row of figures in Exhibit 24–3 demonstrates).

When we measure the ratio of consumer liabilities to financial assets, however, the picture is not quite so optimistic. As shown in Exhibit 24–3, this liability-to-asset ratio has risen from less than 20 percent in 1950 to about 25 percent in the most recent year, though the consumer debt-to-asset ratio was not as high in the mid-1990s as it was during much of the 1980s. Whether the household liability-financial asset ratio today stands at an excessive level depends, of course, on economic conditions and the educational level of consumers. If the average consumer today is better educated and more capable of managing a larger volume of debt, a relatively high ratio of liabilities to financial assets in household portfolios is probably not an alarming development. Moreover, the total wealth held by consumers includes not just their financial assets but also their real assets, such as homes, automobiles, and furniture. Although we have no really reliable measure of the value of real assets held by consumers, it is obvious that the total wealth of individuals and families (including both real and financial assets) far exceeds their current debt.

The fact that households as a group hold more financial assets than liabilities does not mean that the recent build up of consumer debt is completely innocuous, however. Recently, government policymakers have been especially concerned about a so-called *portfolio effect*

Exhibit 24–3   **The Household Sector as a Net Lender of Funds to the Rest of the Economy**

Item	1950	1960	1970	1980	1990	1995*
Total financial assets held by households	$447.5	$967.9	$2,499.3	$6,563.3	$13,978.9	$19,612.8
Total debts (financial liabilities) of households	77.4	226.2	500.9	1,507.3	4,007.5	4,959.7
Difference: Financial assets minus liabilities	$370.1	$741.7	$1,988.4	$5,056.0	$9,971.4	$14,653.1
Ratio of household liabilities to financial assets	17.3%	23.4%	20.0%	29.8%	28.7%	25.3%

Note: *1995 figures are as of the second quarter.

Source: Board of Governors of the Federal Reserve System.

that they believe has significantly slowed the growth of the U.S. economy. Consumer borrowings rose rapidly over the decade of the 1980s until, by 1990, the ratio of U.S. household debt to disposable consumer income was at a historically high 78 percent. After slackening early in the 1990s, household debt-to-income ratios rose to over 80 percent in the mid-1990s, though default rates or consumer loans declined. To the extent that U.S. households may have felt excessively burdened with this large debt accumulation and fearful about losing their jobs, they began cutting back on their rate of consumption spending in the 1990s. Because consumer spending is the largest component of the nation's GDP (production and income), the slowdown of household spending in the mid-1990s resulted in slower economic growth. This concept of a household portfolio effect argues that consumer spending is not likely to return to its former rapid trend rate until households once again feel more comfortable with the balance between their income, financial assets, and liabilities.

Categories of Consumer Borrowing

The range of consumer borrowing needs is enormous. Loans to the household sector support a more diverse group of purchases of goods and services than is true of any other sector of the economy. Consumers borrow *long term* to finance purchases of durable goods, such as single-family homes, automobiles, boats, and home appliances. They usually borrow *short term* to cover purchases of nondurable goods and services, such as medical care, vacations, food, and clothing. Financial analysts frequently divide the credit extended to consumers into three broad categories: (1) **residential mortgage credit**, used to support the purchase of new or existing homes; (2) **installment credit**, used primarily for long-term nonresidential purposes; and (3) **noninstallment credit**, used for shorter-term cash needs.

Which of these forms of consumer borrowing is most important? Exhibit 24–2 provides a clear answer. Far and away the dominant form of consumer borrowing is aimed at providing shelter for individuals and families through mortgage loans. Home mortgage indebtedness by U.S. households exceeded $3 trillion in 1995, representing about two thirds of all household debt. Moreover, the volume of home mortgage credit flowing to households has grown rapidly in recent years with the attractiveness of home ownership as a tax shelter and with recent tax reforms that favor loans secured by the borrower's home.

Installment credit is the second major component of consumer debt in the United States. Installment debt consists of all consumer liabilities other than home mortgages that are retired in two or more consecutive payments, usually monthly or quarterly. Four major types of installment credit are extended by lenders in this field: automobile credit, revolving credit, mobile homes, and other consumer installment loans. An incredibly wide variety of consumer goods and services is financed by this kind of credit, including the purchase of furniture and appliances, the payment of medical expenses, the purchase of automobiles, and the consolidation of outstanding debts. As shown in Exhibit 24–2, consumer installment debt totaled more than a trillion dollars in 1995, more than triple the amount in 1980.

The final major category of consumer debt is *noninstallment credit,* which is normally paid off in a lump sum. This form of consumer credit includes single-payment loans, charge accounts, and credit for services, such as medical care and utilities. The total amount of noninstallment loans outstanding is difficult to estimate because many such loans are made by one individual to another or by department stores, oil and gas companies, and professional service firms that do not report their lending activities. Commercial banks, however, make a substantial volume of noninstallment loans to consumers and are considered the leading lender in this field.

HOME EQUITY LOANS

One new form of consumer borrowing that is closely related to residential mortgage credit is the **home equity loan**. Like traditional home mortgages, a home equity loan is secured by a borrower's home. However, unlike traditional home mortgages, many home equity loans consist of a prearranged revolving credit line the borrower can draw on for purchases of any goods or services he or she wishes in varying amounts over the life of the credit line. Thus, the consumer can literally write himself or herself a loan simply by writing a check or presenting a credit card for purchases made up to a stipulated maximum amount, known as the *borrowing base*. The borrowing base usually equals the difference between the appraised market value of the borrower's home and the unpaid amount of the mortgage against that home multiplied by a fraction (often 0.70, or 70 percent). Thus, a home currently valued at $100,000 with an outstanding mortgage loan against it of $40,000 would give the homeowner a base amount to borrow against of about ($100,000 – $40,000) × 0.70, or $42,000. Moreover, under current U.S. tax laws, the interest owed on a loan secured by the borrower's home that qualifies under all the rules laid down in the Internal Revenue Code represents a tax-deductible expense, encouraging consumers to substitute home equity loans for other types of credit whose interest cost is not tax deductible.[2]

Most home equity loan rates are linked to the bank prime interest rate plus an extra margin for risk (i.e., a floating loan rate). Federal law requires that a maximum (ceiling) interest rate be established for all such loans made after December 9, 1987, under the terms of the Competitive Equality Banking Act. Home equity loans are allowed to cover 10 to 15 years in most cases, although a substantial proportion can be continued indefinitely. The Consumer Protection Act of 1988 prohibits a home equity lender from canceling a loan unless fraud, failure to pay, or other violations of the loan contract occur. Thus far, most home equity loans have been used to pay off other debts, make home improvements, buy automobiles, or finance an education.

Home equity credit has proved to be especially attractive to consumer lending institutions for a variety of reasons. These loans tend to have a lower rate of default because borrowers tend to feel more responsible when their home is pledged as collateral and that collateral tends to have a more stable value. Moreover, the cost of making home equity loans when amortized over the life of each loan is usually substantially lower than the cost of a series of short-term loans made to the same customer. In addition, these loans usually carry rates that adjust to the market, whereas many other consumer loans have fixed interest rates. Finally, home equity credits help the lender build a working relationship with a customer better than most other types of consumer loans, creating more opportunities for the lender to sell that customer additional services.

Because most home equity credit lines are revolving credits, the borrower can repeatedly borrow, repay, and borrow again. Moreover, most homeowners have substantial equity and, therefore, borrowing capacity in their homes — more than $3 trillion. However, if the borrower cannot make the loan payments, his or her home may be repossessed and sold to pay back the lender. Many financial experts recommend that consumers use home equity credit with caution, particularly when their future employment prospects are uncertain.

---

[2]U.S. tax laws state that the interest paid on home equity loans may still be tax deductible even if the home mortgage is taken out for reasons other than to buy or improve the borrower's principal residence, provided the loan was secured after October 13, 1987, and totals less than $100,000. There are other conditions for tax deductibility as well, so homeowners should consult IRS regulations to make sure their home loan qualifies under current tax rules.

CREDIT AND DEBIT CARDS

One of the most popular forms of installment credit available to consumers today comes through the **credit card**. Through this encoded piece of plastic, the consumer has instant access to credit for any purchase up to a prespecified limit. In the language of finance, the credit card has removed the "liquidity" constraint that restricted the spending power of millions of consumers, democratizing access to credit and spending power. More recently, another piece of plastic — the **debit card** — has made instant cash available and check cashing much easier. The growth of credit and debit cards has been truly phenomenal, and the future looks equally promising. Current estimates suggest that there are more than one trillion credit and debit cards in use worldwide, and leading nonfinancial companies (such as General Motors, General Electric, and AT&T) have recently entered in large numbers as suppliers of credit-card services.

A wide array of new consumer financial services is being offered today through plastic credit- and debit-card programs. Such services include consumer revolving credit lines and preauthorized borrowing, the purchase of medical services and entertainment, and the payment of other household bills using credit cards. In the future, customers will need to make fewer trips to their bank or other financial institution because transactions will be handled mainly over the telephone, through a conveniently located computer terminal, or through "smart cards" that have pre-encoded information (such as a pre-authorized credit line the card holder can use for making purchases). The hometown financial institution will lose much of its convenience advantage for local customers. It will be nearly as convenient for the customer to maintain a checking, savings, or loan account in a city hundreds of miles away as to keep it in a local financial institution. In short, the ticket to many consumer financial services increasingly will be a plastic credit or debit card, with the capability to process consumer financial data across great distances.

Credit Cards

Credit cards are used for very different purposes today, depending on the income and lifestyle of the user. Customers who use credit cards merely as a substitute for cash are referred to as *convenience users*. These people tend to be in upper income brackets and do not necessarily seek stores accepting their cards. Customers who purchase large items (such as furniture and appliances) and maintain large outstanding credit card balances are referred to as *installment users* because they pay only a portion of their outstanding balances each month. These individuals frequently are in lower- and middle-income brackets and tend to be the most profitable credit card customers for card-issuing firms.

For both convenience users and installment users, the principal advantage of credit cards is *convenience*. The installment loan feature of the credit card is a major attraction because it functions as a revolving line of credit, granting loans at no cost for an average of about 45 days by taking advantage of interest-free grace periods. In addition, the card itself serves to identify the customer and makes pertinent information available when the privilege of using the card is exercised. Most merchants know that charge cardholders tend to have higher incomes and better payment records than the general population. Recently, new cards have appeared that not only charge zero annual fees but also give customers rebates or discounts on purchases the more the credit card is used.

Debit Cards

Until recently, commercial banks were the only major financial institutions actively involved in the plastic card field. This situation changed rapidly during the 1970s and early 1980s, however, as nonbank financial institutions (principally credit unions, savings banks, and savings and loans) successfully invaded the plastic card market using debit cards. While a credit card permits the customer to buy now and pay later, debit cards are merely a convenient way of paying *now*. A debit card enables users to make deposits and withdrawals from an automated teller machine and also to pay for purchases by direct electronic transfer of funds from their own accounts to the merchant's account. Debit cards are also used for identification and check-clearing purposes and to access remote computer terminals for information or funds transfers.

THE DETERMINANTS OF CONSUMER BORROWING

As we noted earlier, consumers represent one of the largest groups of borrowers in the financial system. Yet individual consumers differ widely in their use of credit and in their attitudes toward borrowing money. What factors appear to influence the volume of borrowing carried out by households?

Recent research points to a number of factors that bear on the consumer's decision of when and how much to borrow.[3] Leading the list is the size of *individual or family income* and *accumulated household wealth*. Families with larger incomes and greater accumulated wealth use greater amounts of debt, both in absolute dollar amounts and relative to their income and wealth holdings. In part, the debt-income-wealth relationship reflects the high correlation between income levels and education. Families whose principal breadwinners have made a significant investment in education are most often aware of the advantages (as well as the dangers) of using debt to supplement current income. Moreover, there is a high positive correlation between education and income-earning power of the principal breadwinners in a family.

The *stage in life* in which adult income-earning members of a family find themselves is also a major influence on household borrowing. The so-called life cycle hypothesis contends that young families just starting out tend to be heavy users of debt.[4] The purchase of a new home, automobile, appliances, and furniture follow soon after a new family is formed. As children come along, living costs rise and a larger home may be necessary, resulting in additional borrowing. Later, the family's income rises, children leave home, and saving increases, while borrowing falls relative to income.

Consumer borrowing is correlated with the *business cycle*. During periods of economic expansion, the number of jobs increases, and households become more optimistic about the future. New borrowings usually outstrip repayments of outstanding loans, and the total volume of household debt rises. When an economic expansion ends and a recession begins, however, unemployment rises and many households become pessimistic about the future. Some, fearing a drop in income or loss of a job, attempt to build up savings and cut back on borrowing. Loan repayments rise relative to new borrowings, and total household debt declines.

In recent years, *price expectations* have heavily influenced consumer borrowing. This has been especially the case since the late 1960s, when the rate of inflation began to accelerate. Postponing the purchase of an automobile, a new home, furniture, or appliances usually means these goods will simply cost more in the future. If family incomes are not

---

[3]An excellent discussion of the factors influencing household borrowing is presented in the studies by Altig, Byrne, and Samolyk (1992) and Elliehausen and Wolken (1992).

[4]See especially Chen and Jensen (1985).

increasing at least as fast as consumer prices, it often pays to "buy now" through borrowing rather than postpone purchases.

Fluctuations in *interest rates* also play a role in shaping the volume and direction of consumer borrowing. Interest rates rise as the economy expands and gathers momentum. At first, the rising rates are not high enough to offset strong consumer optimism, and household borrowing continues to increase. As the period of economic expansion reaches a peak, however, the rise in interest rates becomes so significant that consumer borrowing begins to decline. The drop in borrowing leads to a decline in consumer spending, which may worsen the impending recession.

CONSUMER LENDING INSTITUTIONS

Financial intermediaries — banks, savings and loan associations, credit unions, and finance companies — account for most of the loans made to consumers in the U.S. economy. Intermediaries also dominate the market for noninstallment credit and make the bulk of home mortgage loans. Although each type of financial institution prefers to specialize in a few selected areas of consumer lending, there has been a tendency in recent years for institutions to diversify their lending operations. One important result of this diversification has been to bring all major consumer lenders into direct competition with each other.

Commercial Banks

The single most important consumer lending institution is the commercial bank. Commercial banks approach the consumer in three different ways: by direct lending, through purchases of installment paper from merchants, and by making loans to other consumer lending institutions. Roughly half of all bank loans to consumers (measured by dollar volume) consist of mortgages to support the purchase, construction, or improvement of residential dwellings; the rest consist of installment and noninstallment credit to cover purchases of goods and services. In the mortgage field, commercial banks usually prefer to provide short-term construction financing rather than to make long-term permanent loans for family housing.

Banks make a wider variety of consumer loans than any other lending institution. They grant almost half of all auto loans extended by financial institutions to consumers each year. However, most bank credit in the auto field is indirect — installment paper purchased from auto dealers — rather than being made directly to the auto-buying consumer. Moreover, banking's leadership in auto lending has been challenged in recent years by finance companies and credit unions. Indeed, in many forms of consumer installment credit today, the lead of commercial banks is threatened by challenges from aggressive nonbank lenders who see the consumer market as a key growth area for the future.

Finance Companies

Finance companies have a long history of active lending in the consumer installment field, providing funds directly to the consumer through thousands of small loan offices and indirectly by purchasing installment paper from auto and appliance dealers. These active household lenders provide auto loans and credit for home improvements and for the purchase of appliances and furniture. Finance companies often face state-imposed legal limits on the interest rates they can charge for household loans and on maximum loan size.

Other Consumer Lending Institutions

Other consumer installment lenders include credit unions, savings and loan associations, and savings banks. Credit unions make a wide variety of loans for such diverse purposes as purchases of automobiles; vacations; home repair; and, more recently, mortgage credit for the purchase of new homes. Also important in the consumer loan field in recent years have been savings and loans and savings banks, which experienced dramatic growth in consumer lending in the 1970s and early 1980s but more recently have faced much slower growth and even decline due to inadequate capital and the public's fears about the long-run soundness of some of these institutions.

Although these institutions have long been dominant in residential mortgage lending, they have moved aggressively to expand their portfolios of credit card, education, home improvement, furniture, appliance, and mobile home loans over the past decade. Much of the drive for expansion in the consumer credit field is due to recent federal deregulation of the services offered by savings institutions.

FACTORS CONSIDERED IN MAKING CONSUMER LOANS

Consumer loans are considered one of the most profitable uses of funds for most financial institutions. There is evidence, however, that such loans usually carry greater risk than most other kinds of loans, and they are more costly to make per dollar of loan. On the other hand, the lender often can offset these costs by charging higher interest rates. Consumer credit markets in many communities are less competitive than the market for business loans or for marketable securities, giving the lender an advantage.

Making consumer loans is one of the most challenging aspects of modern financial management. It requires not only a thorough knowledge of household financial statements but also an ability to assess the character of the borrower. Over the years, most loan officers have developed decision "rules of thumb" as an aid to processing and evaluating consumer loan applications. For example, many consumer loan officers insist that household debt (exclusive of housing costs) should not exceed 15 to 20 percent of a family's gross income. For younger borrowers, without substantial assets to serve as collateral for a loan, a cosigner may be sought whose assets and financial standing represent more adequate security. The duration of employment of the borrower is often a critical factor, and many institutions deny a loan request if the customer has been employed at his present job for less than a year.

The past payment record of a customer usually is the key indicator of *character* and the likelihood that the loan will be repaid in timely fashion. Many lenders refuse to make loans to consumers who evidence "pyramiding of debt," that is, borrowing from one financial institution to pay another. Evidence of sloppy money handling, such as large balances carried on charge accounts or heavy installment payments, is regarded as a negative factor in a loan application. Loan officers are particularly alert to evidence of a lack of credit integrity as reflected in frequent late payments or actual default on past loans. The character of the borrower is the single most important issue in the decision to grant or deny a consumer loan. Regardless of the strength of the borrower's financial position, if the customer lacks the willingness to repay debt, the lender has made a bad loan.

Most lenders believe that those who own valuable property, such as land or marketable securities, are a better risk than those who do not own such property. For example, homeowners are usually considered better risks than those who rent. Moreover, a borrower's chance of getting a loan usually goes up if he or she does other business (such as maintain a deposit) with the lending institution. If more than one member of the family works, this is often viewed as a more favorable factor than if the family depends on one breadwinner, who may become ill, die, or lose a job. Having a telephone at home is another positive factor in evaluating a loan application because the telephone gives the lender an inexpensive way to contact the borrower. One way to lower the cost of a loan is for the consumer to pledge a bank deposit or other liquid assets as security behind the loan. The disadvantage here is that such security ties up the asset pledged until the loan is repaid.

FINANCIAL DISCLOSURE AND CONSUMER CREDIT

Important new laws have appeared in recent years designed to protect the consumer in dealings with lending institutions. One major area of emphasis is *financial disclosure*: making all relevant information about the terms of a loan available to the borrower before a commitment is made. The assumption is that an informed borrower will be a wise user of credit. Moreover, if all important information is laid out before a loan agreement is reached, this may encourage the consumer to shop around to find the cheapest and most convenient sources of credit. However, there is considerable debate today on whether consumer protection legislation has really accomplished its goals.[5]

TRUTH IN LENDING

In 1968, Congress passed a watershed piece of legislation in the consumer credit field — the Consumer Credit Protection Act, more widely known as **Truth in Lending**. However, the Consumer Credit Protection Act covered more than just truthful disclosure by lenders of the terms of a loan. It defined and prohibited extortionate credit practices, limited garnishment of wages, and created a National Commission on Consumer Finance to oversee enforcement of the law. Shortly after the act was passed, federal regulatory agencies prepared new rules to implement and enforce the principles of Truth in Lending, such as the Federal Reserve Board's Regulation Z.

Truth in Lending simply requires banks and other lenders to provide sufficient information about a credit contract, in easily understood terms, so that the consumer can make an intelligent decision about purchasing credit. The law does not tell creditors how much to charge or to whom they may lend money. At the same time, consumers were granted certain rights. For example, they have the right to sue the lender for failure to conform to the Consumer Credit Protection Act and its supporting regulations. Consumers have the right to cancel or rescind a credit agreement within three business days if their home is included as part of the collateral for a loan. This so-called *right of rescission* usually applies to the repair or remodeling of a home or the taking out of a second mortgage on an existing home. It does *not* cover an application for a first mortgage to make the initial purchase of a home, however. And the credit requested must be intended for personal or agricultural purposes and result in a debt obligation repayable in more than four installments.

---

[5]Studies by Day and Brandt (1974) and Parker and Shay (1974) suggest that many of the goals sought by recent consumer-oriented financial legislation have *not* been achieved. Many consumers do not shop for credit and appear more concerned about the affordability of monthly payments on a loan than with how one lender's interest charge compares with that quoted by another. Survey evidence suggests that the majority of consumers are unaware of the rights and privileges granted them under recent federal financial legislation and see little practical benefit from these laws.

Financial Planning for Consumers

One of the most rapidly growing of all consumer-oriented industries is *financial planning* — rendering professional advice to the consumer on how to manage money. Although there are literally thousands of paid and volunteer financial planners available today, each offering his or her own brand of financial advice, many financial planners seem to agree on certain principles of good money management for the consumer:

1. Use borrowing cautiously, especially when your home is pledged as collateral and your income is volatile.

2. In choosing which financial assets to acquire or how much to borrow, consider the following:
   a. Decide what your personal goals are — adequate retirement income? a vacation home? a college education?
   b. Classify your goals into short term, medium term, and long term, and estimate how much money will be required for each.
   c. Target each personal investment in assets and each borrowing to match the short-, medium-, and long-term goals you have set so that the money is there exactly when you need it.
   d. Make sure any debt taken on is comfortably covered (both principal and interest) by your expected income plus financial investments.
   e. Diversify your investments — keep a roughly equal balance of funds invested in different stocks, bonds, deposits, mutual fund shares, and real estate to spread your risk.

3. Seek competent, unbiased professional advice, particularly where large purchases are to be made, large borrowings are contemplated, or when planning for retirement.

4. Make sure your liquid savings are at least equal to three months' living expenses in case of loss of a job or the need to move.

5. For the long-term protection of a family with dependents, establish a financial reserve equal to a multiple (usually 5 to 10 times) of the annual income of the family's principal breadwinner(s) through insurance policies and accumulated savings.

The most widely known provision of Truth in Lending is the requirement that a lender must tell the customer the annual percentage rate of interest (APR) charged on a loan. Lenders must disclose the total dollar cost associated with granting a loan — known as the *finance charge* — that is the sum of all charges the customer must pay as a condition for securing the loan. These charges may include credit investigation fees, insurance to protect the lender, and points on a mortgage loan. Once the finance charge is determined, it must be converted into the APR by comparing it with the amount of the loan. The APR is really the ratio of the dollar finance charge to the declining unpaid balance of a loan, determined by the actuarial method. Because all lenders must quote the APR, computed by the same method, this makes it easier for the consumer to shop around and purchase credit from the cheapest source available.

The concept of Truth in Lending has been extended in a number of directions in recent years. One important dimension concerns *advertising*. A lender that advertises one attractive feature of a credit package to consumers must also disclose other relevant credit terms. For example, a car dealer that advertises low down payments must also disclose other aspects of the loan, such as how many payments are required, what the amount of each payment is, and how many months or years are involved.

Fair Credit Billing Act

In 1974, Congress passed the **Fair Credit Billing Act** in response to a torrent of consumer complaints about credit billing errors, especially on credit cards. Many individuals found that they were being billed for items never purchased or received, that some merchants would not respond when contacted about billing errors, and that finance charges were frequently assessed even though the consumer claimed no responsibility for charges listed on the billing statement.

The Fair Credit Billing Act requires a creditor to respond to a customer's billing inquiry within 30 days. In most cases, the dispute must be resolved within 90 days. The customer may withhold payment of any amounts in dispute, although he or she must pay any portions of a bill that are not in dispute. However, no creditor can report a customer as "delinquent" over amounts of a bill that are the subject of disagreement. A creditor who fails to respond to the customer's inquiry or makes no effort to settle the dispute may forfeit the disputed sum up to $50.

Fair Credit Reporting Act

An extension of Truth in Lending occurred when the **Fair Credit Reporting Act** was passed by Congress in 1970. This law entitles consumers to have access to their credit files, which are kept by hundreds of credit bureaus active in the United States. These credit bureaus supply subscribing lenders with vital information on amounts owed and the payment records and credit ratings of individuals and families. They aid greatly in reducing the risks inherent in consumer lending. However, because the information credit bureaus supply has a substantial impact on the availability of credit to individuals and families, their activities and especially the accuracy of the information they provide have been brought under closer scrutiny in recent years.

Under the provisions of the Fair Credit Reporting Act, the consumer is entitled to review his or her credit file at any time. Moreover, he or she may challenge any items that appear in the file and demand an investigation. The credit bureau must respond, and if inaccuracies exist or if an item cannot be verified, it must be removed or the inaccuracies corrected. If the consumer determines that an item in the credit file is damaging and requires clarification, he or she may insert a statement of 100 words or less explaining the consumer's version of the matter. Data in the file are supposed to be shown only to properly identified individuals for approved purposes or on direct written request from the consumer. No information may be disclosed to anyone after a period of seven years unless the consumer is seeking a loan of $50,000 or more, purchasing life insurance, applying for a job paying $20,000 or more per year, or has declared personal bankruptcy. The consumer may sue if damaged by incorrect information in a credit file. Many financial analysts today recommend that consumers check their credit bureau report several months before applying for a major loan.

Consumer Leasing Act

In 1976, Congress passed the Consumer Leasing Act, which requires disclosure by leasing companies of the essential terms of any lease involving personal property. Short-term leases are excluded, but all those with terms over four months are covered by the law, provided the property is leased for personal, family, or household use. The customer must be told about all charges, any insurance required, the terms under which the lease may be canceled, any penalties for late payment, and any express warranties that go with the property.

Competitive Banking Equality Act

On August 10, 1987, President Ronald Reagan signed the *Competitive Banking Equality Act* into law. It requires banks and other depository institutions to more fully disclose to customers the terms on various deposit services they offer. One major change was the required disclosure of how many days a depositor must wait before a check that is deposited in an account becomes available for spending. Some depository institutions had previously delayed the granting of credit for some deposits for a week or even longer. The new law stipulated that no more than one business day usually can intervene between the day of deposit of a local check and the customer receiving credit for that deposit. Nonlocal checks must be credited to the customer's account in no more than four business days.

Truth in Savings Act

A further effort to make sure that consumers are adequately informed about the deposit accounts they purchase was made in November 1991 when Congress passed the *Truth in Savings Act*. The new law prohibits inaccurate or misleading advertising concerning deposit accounts. Each depository institution must maintain a publicly available schedule of information for each class of accounts offered and distribute that information to both new and established account holders. If depositors would be adversely affected by a change in the terms of a deposit, notice of that adverse change must be provided to the deposit holder at least 30 days before the change becomes effective. Moreover, customers must receive interest on the *full* amount of the principal deposited in an account, not on just the amount that a depository institution claims is available for investing in earning assets.

CREDIT DISCRIMINATION LAWS

The civil rights movement has had an impact on the granting of consumer loans. Among the most important civil rights laws involving consumer credit are the Equal Credit Opportunity Act of 1974 and its amendments in 1976, the Fair Housing Act of 1968, the Home Mortgage Disclosure Act of 1975, and the Community Reinvestment Act of 1977. The fundamental purpose of these laws is to *outlaw discrimination* in the granting of credit. Today, lenders must be able to justify in terms of fairness and objectivity not only the loans that are made but also those that are not made.

Community Reinvestment Act and Financial Institutions Reform, Recovery, and Enforcement Act

One of the most important and controversial pieces of financial legislation in recent years is the **Community Reinvestment Act**, signed into law by President Carter in 1977. Under its terms, financial institutions are required to make an "affirmative effort" to meet the credit needs of low- and middle-income customers. Each commercial and savings bank must define its own local "trade territory" and describe the services it offers or is planning to offer in that local area. Once a year, each institution must prepare an updated map that delineates the trade territory it will serve, without deliberately excluding low- or moderate-income neighborhoods. Customers are entitled to make written comments, which must be available for public inspection, concerning the lender's performance in meeting local credit needs. The basic purpose of the Community Reinvestment Act is to avoid gerrymandering out low-income neighborhoods and other areas that a lender may consider undesirable. In 1989, the *Financial Institutions Reform, Recovery, and Enforcement Act* was passed, requiring public disclosure of a bank's performance rating (known as a CRA rating) in meeting the credit needs of its local community under the Community Reinvestment Act. Moreover, the FDIC Improvement Act of 1991 required greater disclosure of the reasons why a depository institution received the particular community service rating that it did. The CRA ratings currently assigned to financial institutions are O (outstanding), S (satisfactory), N (needs to improve), and SN (substantial noncompliance).

Equal Credit Opportunity Act

The **Equal Credit Opportunity Act** of 1974 forbids discrimination against credit applicants on the basis of age, sex, marital status, race, color, religion, national origin, receipt of public assistance, or good-faith exercise of rights under the federal consumer credit protection laws. Women, for example, may receive credit under their own signature, based on their own personal credit record and earnings, without having their husband's joint signature. Credit applicants must be notified, in writing, of the approval or denial of a loan request within 30 days of filing a completed application. The lender may not request information on the borrower's race, color, religion, national origin, or sex, except in the case of residential mortgage loans. Under the FDIC Improvement Act of 1991, the regulatory agencies must refer loan discrimination violators to the U.S. Justice Department.

Fair Housing and Home Mortgage Disclosure Act

Two other important antidiscrimination laws are the Fair Housing Act, which forbids discrimination in lending for the purchase or renovation of residential property, and the Home Mortgage Disclosure Act (HMDA). The latter requires financial institutions to disclose to the public the amount and location of their home mortgage and home improvement loans. HMDA was designed to eliminate *redlining,* in which some lenders would mark out whole areas of a community as unsuitable for home loans. Both HMDA and the Fair Housing Act require nondiscriminatory advertising by lenders. No longer can a consumer lending institution direct its advertisements solely to high-income neighborhoods to the exclusion of other potential customers. On written advertising, the Equal Housing symbol must be attached. Clearly, then, in advertising the availability of credit and in the actual granting of credit, the principles of civil rights and nondiscrimination apply.

CONSUMER BANKRUPTCY LAWS

Over the past decade, the number of households filing for personal bankruptcy and relief from personal debts has soared. One reason for this upsurge in household bankruptcies certainly has been the rapid growth of consumer borrowing. Another reason lies in deep, periodic recessions with protracted high levels of unemployment and falling property values. However, one more reason for these record bankruptcy filings appears to be more lenient federal and state bankruptcy laws, especially the *Bankruptcy Reform Act* of 1978. This law allowed many consumers to file a bankruptcy petition even if they could pay off outstanding debts from current income, savings, or future earnings. In addition, once bankruptcy was declared, the consumer could keep substantial personal assets that could not be sold or repossessed to repay outstanding debts. These lenient provisions in federal and state statutes reduced the cost of consumer bankruptcy and encouraged more households to make a fresh start in managing their financial affairs.

Responding to the record explosion of consumer bankruptcy filings, Congress passed the Bankruptcy Amendments and Federal Judgeship Act of 1984. This new law significantly increased bankruptcy costs and restricted the amount and types of household debt that could be discharged with the filing of a bankruptcy petition. For example, federal rules now exempt no more than $4,000 in household furniture and appliances, clothing, and other personal items from forced sale to pay debts. These recent revisions in bankruptcy law serve simply as a reminder to consumers to think carefully before borrowing money and to read closely the terms of any credit agreement before signing.

SUMMARY

One of the most remarkable developments in the financial system over the past century is the awakening of the consumer as a borrower and lender of funds. Better educated and more aware of their financial opportunities today, householders have become the principal source of loanable funds flowing into the financial markets and also one of the most important borrowers. Reflecting their key influence on the financial system and financial institutions, new consumer-oriented financial services have appeared in profusion in recent years in an effort to attract and hold consumer accounts. Examples include NOWs, money market deposits, share accounts in money market mutual funds, universal life insurance, consumer cash-management services, and home equity loans.

The 1960s and 1970s ushered in landmark pieces of federal legislation to aid the consumer in borrowing and lending funds. On the borrowing side, such laws as the Consumer Credit Protection Act of 1968 (Truth in Lending), the Fair Credit Billing Act (1974), the Consumer Leasing Act (1976), and the Fair Credit Reporting Act (1970) supported the rights of consumers to know what they are being charged for credit and that their credit complaints are heard and acted upon. As a result of such laws as the Community Reinvestment Act (1977), the Equal Credit Opportunity Act (1974), the Fair Housing Act (1968), the Home Mortgage Disclosure Act (1975), the Financial Institutions Reform, Recovery, and Enforcement Act (1989), and the Federal Deposit Insurance Corporation Improvement Act (1991), lenders must make an "affirmative effort" to make credit available to all segments of their local communities without regard to age, sex, marital status, race, color, religion, or national origin of the borrower. Consumers, with the support of the federal government, are asking today not only to be told more about the cost of credit but also why credit is denied to some and granted to others.

Until the 1980s, consumers were largely neglected on the financial asset side of their ledger. Interest rate ceilings severely limited the yields that banks and other deposit-type financial institutions could pay on consumer savings deposits. Moreover, some consumers found that the credit they needed to supplement their incomes was simply not available. A rising chorus of consumer complaints led to passage of the Depository Institutions Deregulation and Monetary Control Act of 1980 and the Garn-St Germain Depository Institutions Act of 1982. These sweeping pieces of consumer-oriented financial legislation legalized interest-bearing checking accounts (NOWs), authorized automatic transfers of funds from savings to checking accounts, set up regulatory machinery for a phaseout of deposit interest rate ceilings, increased the amount of federal insurance behind the public's deposits, and expanded the number of borrowing alternatives open to consumers by granting broader consumer credit powers to thrift institutions. In 1987, the Competitive Banking Equality Act required greater disclosure of the terms surrounding checking accounts, particularly disclosure of when the customer could expect to receive credit for funds deposited in his or her checking account. Greater disclosure requirements were extended to savings accounts in 1991 when the Truth in Savings Act was passed.

Unquestionably, there is more to come. Consumers have awakened to an awareness not only of the critical role credit and savings play in determining their own well-being but also of their powerful collective influence on the whole financial system. The consumer now seems well aware that decisions made in the financial sector help to determine how many and what kinds of jobs are available, the rate of inflation and economic growth, and even the outcome of the great social issues of modern society: better housing, equality under the law, and freedom of economic opportunity. For the most part, modern governments have shown a strong determination to ensure that the individual consumer is treated fairly in the financial marketplace. Unfortunately, we cannot yet determine whether the recent plethora of consumer-oriented financial laws have brought the laudable benefits hoped for by their authors or simply threaten to mire our financial system in a debilitating swamp of red tape. On that important issue, we must await the impartial verdict afforded by time. ■

KEY TERMS AND CONCEPTS IN THIS CHAPTER

NOW account	credit card	Community Reinvestment Act
residential mortgage credit	debit card	Equal Credit Opportunity Act
installment credit	Truth in Lending	
noninstallment credit	Fair Credit Billing Act	
home equity loan	Fair Credit Reporting Act	

STUDY QUESTIONS

1. Which sector of the economy provides the largest amount of loanable funds for borrowers to draw on? Does this sector make primarily direct loans or indirect loans to borrowers?

2. What is the most important financial asset held by households? What financial asset is in second place in household portfolios?

3. Define the following terms:
    a. NOWs
    b. ATS
    c. Share drafts
    d. MMDAs
    e. Universal life
    f. Money market share accounts

g.   Home equity loans
In what ways do these financial services benefit consumers?

4.   How much money do U.S. households owe today? Do you believe consumers are too heavily in debt? Why or why not?

5.   Into what broad categories is consumer borrowing normally divided? Which is most important, and why?

6.   Discuss the factors that influence the volume of borrowing by individuals and families. What role do you believe inflation plays in the borrowing and saving decisions of households today?

7.   What factors do lending institutions usually look at when evaluating a consumer loan application? Why?

8.   What is Truth in Lending? Describe the law's major features and explain why it was enacted.

9.   What protections are offered the consumer under the Fair Credit Billing Act? Consumer Leasing Act? Fair Credit Reporting Act? Why?

10.   What are the principal purposes of the Community Reinvestment Act? Equal Credit Opportunity Act? Fair Housing Act? Home Mortgage Disclosure Act? Assess the benefits and costs of these laws.

11.   What changes in consumer rights and required disclosure of information to the consumer occurred with passage of the Financial Institutions Reform, Recovery, and Enforcement Act? With passage of the Truth in Savings Act and the FDIC Improvement Act?

PROBLEMS

1.   Home equity loans to consumers are generally based on the *residual value* of a home (i.e., market value less the remaining balance on the outstanding home mortgage loan) and the fraction of that value (known as the *loan-to-value ratio*) that the lending institution is willing to lend. The customer's borrowing base is the product of these two entities. Calculate the customer's borrowing base in the situations described below:

	Appraised Value of Borrower's Home	Mortgage Loan Balance Outstanding	Lender's Required Loan-to-Value Ratio
a.	$173,500	$ 67,800	75%
b.	64,150	23,948	70
c.	251,400	111,556	80
d.	789,000	340,722	82

2.   What consumer-oriented law or laws passed in the United States apply in each of the situations described below:

a.   Matthew Crey is discussing with a bank loan officer the terms on a loan he needs to buy a car for his family.

b.   Robert and Mary Nash believe they were discriminated against when their loan to purchase a new home was denied.

c.   Sally Ferrel was denied a loan because of an adverse report from her credit bureau, which she believes is in error.

    d.   Herbert Coleman has just received his credit card bill and finds several charges were made against his account that are not legitimate.

    e.   Mary Eacher leased an automobile from a dealer for three years, but the lease was abruptly canceled even though Mary was making all required payments on time.

    f.   First National Bank of Arden has just announced its latest CRA rating received from federal bank examiners.

    g.   Earl and Susan Tolber believe they were denied a home improvement loan because their address is in a neighborhood where the local bank does not like to make such loans.

SELECTED REFERENCES

Altig, David; Susan M. Byrne; and Katherine A. Samolyk. "Is Household Debt Inhibiting the Recovery?" *Economic Review,* Federal Reserve Bank of Cleveland, February 1, 1992, pp. 1–5.

Canner, Glenn B.; Arthur B. Kennichell; and Charles A. Luckett. "Household Sector Borrowing and the Burden of Debt." *Federal Reserve Bulletin,* April 1995, pp. 323–338.

Chen, Alexander, and Helen H. Jensen. "Home Equity Use and the Life Cycle Hypothesis." *The Journal of Consumer Affairs* 19, no. 1 (Summer 1985), pp. 37–56.

Day, George S., and William K. Brandt. "Consumer Research and the Evaluation of Information Disclosure Requirements: The Case of Truth in Lending." *Journal of Consumer Research,* June 1974, pp. 21–32.

Elliehausen, Gregory E., and John D. Wolken. "Banking Markets and the Use of Financial Services by Households." *Federal Reserve Bulletin,* March 1992, pp. 169–181.

Parker, George G. D., and Robert P. Shay. "Some Factors Affecting Awareness of Annual Percentage Rates in Consumer Installment Credit Transactions." *Journal of Finance,* March 1974, pp. 217–25.

Rose, Peter S. "Bank Cards: The Promise and the Peril." *The Canadian Banker and ICB Review,* December 1978, pp. 62–67.

————. "Social Responsibility in Banking: Pressures Intensify in the U.S." *The Canadian Banker and ICB Review,* June 1979, pp. 70–75.

————. "Credit Discrimination under Attack." *The Canadian Banker and ICB Review,* September 1979, pp. 70–75.

Chapter 25

The Residential Mortgage Market

LEARNING OBJECTIVES IN THIS CHAPTER

- To describe how the largest of all financial markets — the residential mortgage market — functions to provide credit to build and buy homes, apartments, and other dwellings.

- To understand the problems faced by individuals and families in finding credit to finance the purchase of their homes.

- To understand the problems faced by lenders of residential mortgage money in designing new loan agreements that will protect them against inflation and other risks.

- To describe the role played by the federal government and government agencies, such as Fannie Mae (FNMA) and Ginnie Mae (GNMA), in supporting the mortgage market.

One of the most important goals for many families is to own their own home. Besides the psychic benefits of privacy and a feeling of belonging to the local community, home ownership confers important financial and economic benefits on those families and individuals both able and willing to make the investment. The market value of single-family residences has risen substantially faster than the rate of inflation over the long run, offering individuals and families of even modest means one of the few available long-term hedges against inflation. Moreover, the interest cost on home mortgages is tax deductible, reducing significantly the *after-tax* interest rate levied on residential mortgage loans.

Unfortunately for families seeking home ownership, the residential mortgage market is often treacherous, swinging quickly from low interest rates and ample credit to high and rising rates with little credit available. In this highly volatile market, home ownership often becomes an impossible dream for thousands of individuals and families. Moreover, the wide swings characteristic of the residential mortgage market send reverberations throughout the economy, contributing to the cycles of "boom" and "bust" that often characterize economic activity.

RECENT TRENDS IN NEW HOME PRICES AND THE TERMS OF MORTGAGE LOANS

We can get a glimpse of the tremendous pressures buffeting the market for residential mortgages today by looking at recent trends in the prices of new homes and the cost of financing them. Exhibit 25–1 provides recent data on the average terms quoted on **conventional home mortgage loans** in the United States. A conventional mortgage loan is *not* guaranteed by the government but is purely a private contract between the home buyer and the lending institution. In this case, the lender of funds bears the risk that the home buyer will default on principal or interest payments associated with a mortgage loan, forcing foreclosure and resale of the home, although today most conventional loans are insured by private insurance companies. In contrast, mortgage loans issued through the Federal Housing Administration (FHA) or Veterans Administration (VA) are partially guaranteed as to principal and interest by the federal government and are primarily used to finance low-cost and moderately priced housing.

As shown in Exhibit 25–1, the average purchase price of a conventional single-family residence in the United States has more than quadrupled over the past two decades. With housing prices and the demand for new homes rising, sellers and lending institutions have worked to accommodate more borrowers by increasing the average percentage of a new home's purchase price they are willing to lend, to as high as 78 percent in recent years. We note from Exhibit 25–1 that mortgage lenders are also willing to extend credit for longer periods. The average maturity of conventional home mortgage loans climbed to almost 28 years in 1995. Extra fees and charges ("points") levied by lenders as a condition for making home mortgage credit available have recently fallen. The average contract interest rate on conventional mortgage loans dipped to nearly 7 percent early in 1996.

Clearly, the market prices of new homes in the United States remain at dizzying heights for many potential home buyers. With home mortgage interest rates in the vicinity of 8 percent, mortgage payments for many families now hover near $800 to $1,000 per month or more. These high home prices have simply shut out scores of families from the fulfillment of a long-standing dream: home ownership.

Several factors account for this dramatic long-term escalation in the cost of home ownership. Certainly, inflation has played a key role in driving up building costs, and this increase has been passed on to the consumer. On the demand side, a substantial rise in the number of new family formations has occurred in recent years. Children born during the great postwar

Exhibit 25–1   **Prices and Yields of Conventional Home Mortgage Loans**

Item	1974	1980	1990	1996*
Primary market:				
Conventional mortgages on new homes:				
Purchase price ($000)	$40.10	$83.50	$153.20	$179.20
Amount of loan ($000)	29.80	59.30	112.40	135.80
Loan/price ratio (percent)	74.30	73.30	74.50	77.30
Maturity (years)	26.30	28.20	27.30	27.70
Fees and charges ("points")	1.30%	2.10%	1.93%	1.07%
Contract interest rate (percent per year)	8.71	12.25	9.68	7.15
Yield on FHA mortgages (percent per year)	9.22	13.95	10.17	7.11

*As of January 1996.

Source: Board of Governors of the Federal Reserve System, *Federal Reserve Bulletin*, Table 1.53, various issues.

baby boom of the late 1940s and 1950s began to establish their own families in the 1970s and 1980s. Added to this has been a rapid increase in individuals living alone and in single-parent households. Therefore, although the U.S. birth rate dropped to the lowest levels in history, the increase in new families and in single-adult households dramatically increased the demand for housing, especially for low- and medium-priced homes.

Finally, tax reform legislation in recent years (particularly the Tax Reform Act of 1986) appears to have increased the after-tax cost of owner-occupied housing and the rents landlords are forced to charge to recover their investments in apartments and other multi-family residences. These housing costs have risen primarily because of lower personal tax rates, which make home ownership a less attractive after-tax investment, and longer required terms for full depreciation of property. The combination of tax law changes and added demand for family dwellings has sharply raised the cost of housing in the long term and diminished the financial attractiveness of investing in housing. In future years, as new family formations slow, new housing demand and increases in housing costs are likely to moderate, particularly if the rate of inflation can be restrained. Perhaps home ownership will once again become a viable option for millions of families.

THE STRUCTURE OF THE MORTGAGE MARKET
Volume of Mortgage Loans

Mortgages are among the most important securities in the financial system. The total of all mortgages outstanding in the United States is now over $4.6 trillion (see Exhibit 25–2). This total represents about two thirds of the nation's gross domestic product (GDP) and has made the mortgage market the largest primary security market in the United States. Moreover, the mortgage market has grown rapidly in recent years under the combined pressures of inflation and economic growth.

Residential versus Nonresidential Mortgage Loans

The mortgage market can be divided into two major segments: (1) **residential mortgages**, which encompass all loans secured by single-family homes and other dwelling units, and (2) **nonresidential mortgages**, which include loans secured by business and farm properties. Which of these two sectors is more important? As Exhibit 25–3 shows, loans to finance the building and purchase of homes, apartments, and other residential units domi-

Exhibit 25–2	**Total Mortgage Debt Outstanding in the United States at Year-End** ($ Billions)

Year	Amount
1950	$ 72.8
1960	206.8
1970	451.7
1980	1,451.8
1990	3,807.3
1995*	4,654.6

*Figures through third quarter of the year.

Sources: Board of Governors of the Federal Reserve System, *Annual Statistical Digest,* 1971–1975, and *Federal Reserve Bulletin,* selected issues.

Exhibit 25–3   **Mortgage Loans Outstanding, 1995*** ($ Billions)

Type of property	Amount	Percent of Total
Residential properties (one- to four-family and multifamily structures)	$3,732.5	82.4%
Nonresidential properties (commercial and farm)	794.6	17.6
All properties	$4,527.1	100.0%

*Figures are as of the second quarter of 1995.

Source: Board of Governors of the Federal Reserve System, *Federal Reserve Bulletin,* selected issues.

nate the U.S. mortgage market, accounting for about four fifths of all mortgage loans outstanding. Mortgages on commercial and farm properties accounted for less than one fifth of all mortgages issued. Because residential mortgages dominate the market, it should not be surprising that households are the leading mortgage borrower, accounting for about two thirds of outstanding mortgage debt. The next largest group of mortgage borrowers — business firms — runs a distant second.

MORTGAGE-LENDING INSTITUTIONS

In the years before World War II, mortgages were one of the most widely held securities in the financial system, comparable to stock in the great diversity of investors who chose to add these securities to their portfolios. Individuals were then the dominant mortgage investors, with financial institutions in second place. However, the rapid growth of commercial banks, savings institutions, insurance companies, and government agencies as major mortgage lenders during the past four decades has forced individual investors into the background.

Exhibit 25–4 shows the total amounts of mortgage loans held by various lender groups in 1995. Savings and loan associations, once the principal private mortgage-lending institution in the United States, have now dropped to less than a sixth of all mortgage loans outstanding. Commercial banks now rank number one among private lending institutions, holding nearly one quarter of all mortgage credit outstanding. In general, the relative share of the mortgage market accounted for by traditional private mortgage-lending institutions, such as savings and loans, savings banks, and insurance companies, has declined, while pension funds, finance companies, and government agencies have accounted for a growing share of outstanding loans. Noteworthy in this regard has been the rapidly expanding role of *mortgage pools*: continuing groups of high-quality residential mortgages insured or guaranteed by a government agency and in which investors hold shares, entitling them to a portion of any interest and principal payments generated by the pool. We will have more to say about mortgage pools later in the chapter when we discuss the expanding role of the federal government in the mortgage market.

THE ROLES PLAYED BY FINANCIAL INSTITUTIONS IN THE MORTGAGE MARKET

Mortgage lenders tend to specialize in the types of loans they grant, and some are far more important to the residential market than to commercial mortgage lending. Moreover, even within the residential lending field, different institutional lenders will favor one type of

Exhibit 25–4   **Principal Lenders in the U.S. Mortgage Market, 1995***

Lender Group	Volume of Mortgage Loans Held by Lender ($ Billions)		Percent of Total
Savings institutions (Savings and loan associations and savings banks)		$ 598.9	13.2%
Commercial banks		1,052.9	23.3
Life insurance companies		213.4	4.7
Individuals and other private lenders		609.3	13.5
Mortgage pools or trusts:		1,737.5	38.3
Government National Mortgage Association	$457.1		
Federal Home Loan Mortgage Association	496.1		
Federal National Mortgage Association	543.7		
Farmers Home Administration	0.1		
Other pools or trusts	240.6		
Federal and Related Agencies:		315.2	7.0
Government National Mortgage Association	$ 0.1		
Federal Home Loan Mortgage Corporation	44.2		
Federal National Mortgage Association	178.5		
Farmers Home Administration	41.9		
Federal Land Banks	28.0		
Federal Housing and Veterans Administration	10.1		
Other agencies	13.1		
		$4,527.1	100.0%

*Figures are for second quarter of the year.

Source: Board of Governors of the Federal Reserve System, *Federal Reserve Bulletin,* selected issues.

mortgage (e.g., conventional versus government guaranteed) over another and also desire a certain range of maturities. Some lenders are organized to deal with home mortgage borrowers one at a time, while others may prefer to acquire large packages of mortgages associated with major residential building projects.

Savings and Loan Associations

Savings and loan associations (S&Ls) are predominantly local lenders, making the majority of their mortgage loans in the communities where their offices are located. Moreover, S&Ls often service the mortgage loans they make rather than turning that task over to a mortgage bank or trust company. Servicing a mortgage involves maintaining ownership and financial records on the mortgaged property, receiving installment payments from the borrower, checking on the mortgaged property to ensure that its value is maintained, and, in the event of borrower default, foreclosing on the property to collect any unpaid balance on the loan. Historically, S&Ls have preferred single-family home mortgages, but they have diversified their portfolios in recent years to include many new kinds of mortgage-related assets, such as mobile home loans; mortgage credit for apartments and other multi-family housing units; and securities backed by pools of mortgage loans.

    The serious financial problems of the savings and loan industry in recent years and S&Ls' attempts to diversify and increase long-term capital relative to their assets in order to lower their risk of failure have brought about a substantial decline in S&Ls' share of the total mortgage market (now below 20 percent). Many S&Ls have been forced to sell off their loans, downsizing the firm, just to achieve a ratio of owner's capital to total assets acceptable to the industry's regulators. Thus, many S&Ls have few funds to devote to new mortgage loans and have lost substantial market share to other mortgage lending institutions.

Commercial Banks

In contrast to savings and loans, commercial banks have expanded their market share of nearly every type of mortgage loan. Overall, they now rank first as lenders for the purchase of homes and apartments and in the commercial mortgage field. A large share of bank mortgage credit, however, goes for shorter-term loans to finance the *construction* of new commercial and residential projects, with other lenders usually taking on the long-term mortgage loans from these projects. Commercial banks have also shown a strong interest in financing the so-called upscale home purchased by higher-income families in recent years — homes that command significantly higher prices and larger down payments.

Life Insurance Companies

Life insurance companies make substantial investments in commercial as well as residential mortgage properties. These companies search national and international markets for good mortgage investments instead of focusing only on local areas. They often prefer to purchase residential mortgages in large blocks rather than one at a time.

In the past, life insurers preferred government-guaranteed home mortgages. In recent years, however, the higher yields available on conventional mortgages have caused some shift of emphasis toward these more risky home loans. Despite the greater flexibility of conventional single-family home mortgages, however, life insurance companies have been gradually reducing their holdings of single-family home mortgages and emphasizing commercial and apartment mortgages. Commercial and apartment loans often carry "equity kickers" that permit the lending institution to receive a portion of project earnings as well as a guaranteed interest rate.

Savings Banks

Another lender of great importance in the residential mortgage market is the savings bank, headquartered mainly in the eastern United States. These institutions invest in both government-guaranteed and conventional mortgage loans. Although single-family homes constitute the bulk of savings bank mortgage loans, their loans supporting multifamily units (including large apartment projects) have grown rapidly in recent years. Like life insurance companies, savings banks often prefer to acquire residential mortgages in large blocks, such as a whole subdivision, rather than loan by loan. Like savings and loan associations, savings banks have lost mortgage market share to other private and government lenders.

Mortgage Bankers

Mortgage banking houses act as a channel through which builders or contractors in need of long-term funds can find permanent mortgage financing. In providing this service, mortgage bankers take on portfolios of mortgages from property developers, using mainly bank credit to carry their inventories of mortgages. Then, within a relatively short time span, these mortgages are placed with long-term institutional investors. Mortgage bankers supply important services to *both* institutional investors and property developers. The developers receive a commitment for permanent financing, which allows them to proceed with planned real estate projects. Institutional investors, especially life insurance companies and savings banks, receive mortgages appropriately packaged to match the timing of their cash flows and risk-return preferences. The mortgage banker often secures servicing (loan management and monitoring) fees from institutional investors who purchase the mortgages he packages and sells. Today mortgage bankers originate just under half of all home mortgages.

GOVERNMENT ACTIVITY

Adequate housing for all citizens has been a major goal of the U.S. government for many years. One of the first steps taken by Congress to achieve this goal was the establishment of the **Federal Housing Administration (FHA)** in 1934. FHA has sought to promote home ownership by reducing the risk to private lenders of residential mortgage contracts. At the same time, efforts have been made to encourage the development of an active secondary market for existing mortgage lenders to raise cash in order to make new loans and to attract new investors into the mortgage business. The combination of government guarantees and the development of a secondary market has led to greater participation in mortgage lending by *long-distance lenders,* particularly insurance companies, pension funds, and savings banks. However, government agencies today dominate the mortgage market for low- and moderate-priced loans.

The Impact of the Great Depression on Government Involvement in the Mortgage Market

Any attempt to understand how the mortgage market operates today must begin with the Great Depression and the enormous impact that economic calamity had on the market for property loans. The Great Depression generated massive, unprecedented unemployment; an estimated one quarter to one third of the civilian labor force was thrown out of work between 1929 and 1933. Few new mortgage loans were made during this period, and thousands of existing mortgages were foreclosed. With so many forced sales, property values declined precipitously, endangering the financial solvency of thousands of mortgage lenders.

The federal government elected to tackle the mortgage market's problems by moving in several directions. For example, in 1932, the Federal Home Loan Bank System (FHLB) was created to supervise the activities of savings and loan associations and make loans to those S&Ls facing liquidity crises. In 1934, the National Housing Act was passed, setting up a system of federal insurance for qualified home mortgage loans. The Federal Housing Administration (FHA) was authorized to guarantee repayment of as much as 90 percent of acceptable home loans up to a ceiling amount determined by FHA, encouraging private lenders to lend more of a home's market value, accept longer terms on home mortgages, and charge lower interest rates.

Shortly before the end of World War II, the Veterans Administration (VA) was created with passage of the Servicemen's Readjustment Act (1944). The VA was designed to aid military servicemen returning to civilian life in finding adequate housing. Like FHA, VA offered to insure residential mortgages and helped reduce the required down payment on a new home.

The Creation of Fannie Mae (FNMA)

The FHA–VA insurance program was an almost instant success, and home mortgage lending grew rapidly following its inception. Federal government efforts to create a resale (secondary) market for residential mortgages took a little longer, however. The first successful federal agency set up to buy and sell residential mortgages was Fannie Mae — the **Federal National Mortgage Association (FNMA)**. Fannie Mae was established in 1938 for the purpose of buying and selling FHA-guaranteed mortgages in the secondary market. Later, in 1948, it was authorized to trade in VA-guaranteed mortgages as well. FNMA issues commitments to buy a specific dollar amount of mortgages at a predetermined yield, significantly improving the resale potential of most home mortgage loans.

Fannie Mae raises money for its market-making activities primarily by selling short-term notes and longer-term debentures. In addition, in 1981, FNMA began to issue and guarantee securities backed by conventional mortgage loans purchased from lenders. FNMA mortgage-backed securities are marketed by lenders that deal directly with FNMA or through security dealers.[1]

The Creation of Ginnie Mae (GNMA)

Efforts by Congress to make the federal government's budget look better resulted in splitting Fannie Mae into two agencies in 1968. Fannie Mae itself became a private, shareholder-owned corporation devoted to secondary market trading. At the same time, loan programs requiring government subsidies or government credit were handed to a new corporation set up within the Department of Housing and Urban Development, known as the **Government National Mortgage Association (GNMA)**, or Ginnie Mae. In one portion of its program, Ginnie Mae purchases "assistance" mortgages to finance housing for low-income families at below-market interest rates and then sells these mortgages to FNMA or to private investors.

GNMA Mortgage-Backed Securities. Far more important for the secondary market, however, is GNMA's **mortgage-backed securities** program. Backed by the full faith and credit of the U.S. government, Ginnie Mae agrees to *guarantee* principal and interest payments on securities issued by private mortgage institutions if those securities are backed by pools of government-guaranteed mortgages. These so-called **pass-throughs** are popular with institutional lenders and even individuals as safe, readily marketable securities with attractive rates of return. Mortgage lenders raise cash to make new loans by selling the pass-throughs against mortgages that they place in a mortgage pool.

The Federal Home Loan Mortgage Corporation (FHLMC)

In 1970, the Emergency Home Finance Act gave birth to the **Federal Home Loan Mortgage Corporation (FHLMC)**, more popularly known as *Freddie Mac*. FHLMC, like Ginnie Mae, combines the mortgages it buys into pools and issues bonds against them. Securities issued by Freddie Mac are guaranteed by that agency and have been very

---

[1]Fannie Mae is the world's largest mortgage bank and for a long time had a virtual monopoly in secondary market trading activities. Early in the 1970s, however, the Mortgage Guarantee Insurance Corporation (MGIC) was organized by a private group in Milwaukee, Wisconsin. Known as Maggie Mae, this corporation pledged to insure conventional home mortgage loans carrying down payments as low as 5 percent. Today, mortgage insurance, provided by a variety of private companies, is usually required by lending institutions when the borrower makes a down payment of less than 20 percent of the purchase price of a home.

popular with investors, particularly savings and loan associations and banks. The creation of Freddie Mac reflected a desire by the federal government to develop a stronger secondary market for *conventional* home mortgages, of which it has purchased huge quantities up to a pre-specified conforming loan limit.

FHLMC Mortgage-Backed Securities. To raise funds to support these purchases, Freddie Mac sells mortgage participation certificates (PCs) and guaranteed mortgage certificates (GMCs). PCs represent an ownership interest in a pool of conventional mortgages bought and sold by Freddie Mac. FHLMC guarantees the investor's monthly interest and principal payments passed through from the mortgage pool. Guaranteed mortgage certificates (GMCs) are also claims against a pool of mortgages, but they are similar to corporate bonds in that interest is paid semiannually to investors. Repayments of principal are made once a year and are guaranteed by Freddie Mac.

Collateralized Mortgage Obligations (CMOs) and Real Estate Mortgage Investment Conduits (REMICs). Another recent innovation in fund-raising by FHLMC is the **collateralized mortgage obligation (CMO)** — a bond whose value is derived from a pool of mortgages packaged together to back (collateralize) the bond. CMOs differ from other mortgage-backed securities in that they are issued in several different maturity classes (called *tranches*) based on a projected schedule for repaying the mortgage loans in back of each CMO. A similar instrument that also partitions the principal cash flow from a pool of mortgages or mortgage-backed securities into maturity classes is called a **real estate mortgage investment conduit (REMIC).** Thus, CMOs and REMICs offer investors a range of different maturities from long-term to short-term and overcome at least some of the cash-flow uncertainty investors face when buying home mortgages themselves because a home-owner may pay off his or her loan early — known as **prepayment risk**. More recently, some mortgage-backed securities have been issued as "strips," in which the investor can receive either principal payments from a pool of home mortgages or interest payments from the pool, depending on the individual investor's preferences for maturity and risk. In 1990, CMO trusts began to appear, offering even small investors a share in pools of collateralized mortgage obligations.

Impact of Securitized Mortgages. The development of the various types of **securitized mortgages** — debt securities backed by pools of outstanding mortgage loans — by Ginnie Mae, Fannie Mae, and other lending institutions have made mortgage securities more competitive with government securities and corporate stocks and bonds, allowing many mortgage lenders to invade national and international capital markets for funds. They have also made it much easier to get old, low-yielding mortgages off lenders' books to make room for higher-yielding investments.

On the negative side, however, these new financial instruments have increased the sensitivity of mortgage interest rates to national and international market conditions. Home mortgage rates are now much more volatile than in the past. The residential mortgage market has broadened geographically, but at the price of a less predictable environment for loan rates and the availability of credit for the home buyer.

INNOVATIONS IN MORTGAGE INSTRUMENTS

Repeatedly in recent years, interest rates have climbed to high levels, only to fall back during brief recessions and then surge upward again. Each upward movement in interest rates forced mortgage lenders to cut back on the availability of funds for housing. In part, these cutbacks in mortgage funds were a response to the widespread use of **fixed-rate home mortgages (FRMs)**. FRMs return to the lender the same annual interest income (cash flow) regardless of what is happening to inflation or to interest rates. When depository institutions are forced to pay higher rates on their deposits to attract funds, their profits tend to be squeezed because the revenues from their FRMs remain unchanged. Of course, these lending institutions are able to charge higher rates on *new* mortgage loans, but new loans normally are only a small fraction of an institution's total loan portfolio. The bulk of that portfolio usually is in *old* mortgages granted during an era when interest rates often were much lower.

In short, the FRM amplifies the normal up-and-down cycle of earnings for a mortgage-lending institution, leading to low or even negative earnings in periods of rising interest rates and to positive earnings in periods of falling rates. FRMs require the *lender* to bear the risk of interest rate fluctuations. An alternative to the FRM was needed that both guaranteed lenders a satisfactory real rate of return on mortgage loans and made funds available to home buyers on reasonable terms.

Variable-Rate and Other Adjustable Mortgages

The problems created by fixed-rate mortgages led to the development of several new mortgage instruments, led by the **variable-rate mortgage (VRM)**, which permits the lender to vary the contractual interest rate on a mortgage loan as market conditions change. Generally, the VRM loan rate is linked to a reference interest rate *not* determined by the lender. For example, the yield on long-term U.S. Treasury bonds may be used as a reference rate so that, if Treasury bond yields rise, the homeowner pays a higher contractual interest rate. Alternatively, under a broader **adjustable mortgage instrument (AMI)**, the maturity of the mortgage loan may be lengthened or a combination of rate increases and maturity changes may be made as interest rates rise. In some cases, the loan principal can be increased with interest rate increases, reducing the growth of the homeowner's equity — a process known as *negative amortization*. VRMs and AMIs shift the *risk* of interest rate fluctuations, partially or wholly, from the lender to the borrower.

Under most state and federal laws, changes in the interest rates attached to VRMs are limited as to frequency and amount. However, AMIs, with their options of varying monthly payments, the maturity of a mortgage loan, or the loan principal as interest rates change, face few legal restrictions and have grown rapidly in recent years. Part of the reason for the growth of AMIs is their usually lower initial loan rate compared to FRMs, with many lenders offering *teaser rates* to attract AMI customers. Moreover, an FRM generally results in greater long-term interest cost than an AMI. In this case, the price of a more stable monthly payment is usually a higher long-term interest burden for the borrower.

Convertible Mortgages

The volatile interest rates of recent years have led to the development of a combination variable-rate, fixed-rate home mortgage loan that some home buyers find attractive today. This so-called convertible mortgage instrument (CMI) starts out with an adjustable interest rate, but later the home buyer can switch to a fixed-rate mortgage if interest rates look more favorable. However, some loan contracts carry a mandatory holding period before conversion to a fixed-rate loan is permitted and also prohibit switching after a certain length of time has elapsed (such as five years). CMIs have attracted the interest of home buyers because their initial adjustable interest rates are usually much lower than those on new fixed-rate mortgages and the switch to a fixed-rate loan in the future typically is much cheaper than refinancing an old mortgage.

Another version of the CMI now very popular is the *balloon loan*. Two types are most common: 7-year loans with an option to refinance into a 23-year fixed-rate loan and 5-year fixed-rate loans that convert to variable-rate mortgages. Borrowers under a balloon loan hope to sell their homes before refinancing their mortgage becomes necessary — sometimes a risky proposition if the housing market weakens. As the 1990s began, both FNMA and FHLMC agreed to begin buying balloon loans from lenders.

Canadian Rollover and Other Renegotiated Mortgage Loans

Recently, Canadian rollover mortgages (CRMs) have attracted some interest. These loans are usually issued for short to medium terms (5- to 10-year maturities are common). The borrower must then pay off the note or negotiate a new loan. A related variety of loan is the renegotiated rate mortgage (RRM), which carries a longer maturity, but its interest rate must be renegotiated periodically — usually every three to five years.

Still another renegotiated-type property loan is the deferred interest mortgage (DIM), by which the borrower pays a lower interest rate than with a conventional FRM and thus has lower mortgage payments. However, the borrower must eventually reimburse the lender for any accumulated interest that is postponed during the life of the loan. This reimbursement may occur through a refinancing of the loan or when the property is sold to a new owner.

Reverse-Annuity Mortgages

A mortgage-financing device that may be of help to older families and retired individuals is the reverse-annuity mortgage (RAM). This financial instrument provides income to those who may have already paid off their mortgage but intend to keep their present home. The lender determines the current value of the home and pays the borrower a monthly annuity, amounting to a percentage of the property's value. The loan is secured by a gradually increasing mortgage on the borrower's home. Repayment of the loan occurs when the annuity holder dies, with the loan being discharged against the deceased's estate, or when the home is sold.

Graduated-Payment Mortgages

A relatively new mortgage instrument developed in recent years to help lower-income families is the graduated-payment mortgage (GPM), which FHA began insuring in 1977. With the GPM, initial monthly payments on a new home are lower at first, then rise for a time before leveling off after several years. The idea is to tailor the debt service payments on a mortgage to the financial needs of the borrower. GPMs have proved popular with young families who otherwise might be stymied by high mortgage payments until their earning power improves.

Of course, the *total* amount of interest paid by the borrower will be much larger with a GPM than it would be under a conventional FRM. This occurs because the low initial payments do not cover the full amount of interest owed each month, forcing the lender to increase the size of the mortgage loan in the early years. Moreover, due to the delayed loan income, lenders generally raise the interest rate on GPMs above rates prevailing on level-payment mortgages.

Epilogue on the Fixed-Rate Mortgage

It is interesting that, with all the new mortgage instruments developed in recent years, fixed-rate mortgages (FRMs) continue to hold a substantial share of the residential loan market. This is true even though FRMs usually carry a higher interest rate than adjustable mortgages and higher origination fees and prepayment penalties. One reason appears to be public mistrust of many of the new instruments, coupled with fear of inflation, which would push up the interest rate on a variable-rate loan. Another factor is competition. It is likely, therefore, that both FRMs and VRMs will continue to exist side by side in the home mortgage market, each serving the special needs of individual lenders and homeowners.

CREATIVE FINANCING TECHNIQUES

Soaring prices of new homes and high mortgage interest rates have frequently put a damper on the demand for single-family homes in recent years. Homeowners and real estate agents have sought innovative financing techniques — *creative financing* — to make single-family homes more affordable for the average home buyer.

Second Mortgages

One of the most popular creative financing techniques is the second, or junior, mortgage. A *second mortgage* is a claim against real property that is subordinated to a first mortgage claim. Its maturity typically is much shorter than that of a first mortgage loan — 5- to 10-year terms are common. Because the second mortgage holder has a subordinated claim, the interest rate is usually higher than on a first mortgage loan.

The shorter maturities and higher interest rates attached to second mortgages have made them attractive to many lenders, particularly banks and finance companies. Historically, second mortgages have been used by homeowners to draw on the growing equity investment in their home in order to pay for improvements (such as adding an extra bedroom) or to raise cash for other needs. More recently, second mortgages have been used as a form of seller financing to speed up home sales, especially to young families lacking a down payment.

Home-Leasing Plans

In addition to second mortgages, *lease-purchase agreements* are used in which the buyer leases a home while retaining the option to buy. The seller receives lease payments plus option money, which the buyer may later apply toward a down payment on the home. The advantage of this technique is that it permits the buyer to move in right away and still have time to accumulate enough savings to make the required down payment. Meantime, the seller is receiving cash payments while still enjoying the tax advantages of renting a home.

Land-Leasing Plans and Property Exchanges

A related lease-financing option is the *land lease*. In this case, the buyer acquires title only to the house and any improvements on the land, and the seller retains title to the land on which the house stands. In return for lease payments, the buyer receives a long-term lease on the land, frequently with an option to buy. This creative technique reduces monthly payments and results in a lower initial down payment.

A simpler approach is a *property exchange* of homes between two parties. Any difference in value between the two houses exchanged can be handled by a promissory note issued by the owner of the cheaper property. Sometimes the difference in value is made up by swapping personal property, such as savings deposits or securities.

Refinancing Home Mortgages and Home Equity Loans

In recent years, many homeowners have found that it makes economic sense to convert their existing mortgage loans into *new* loans with lower interest costs because market interest rates have fallen substantially since the original loan was taken out. This happens most often to borrowers facing a fixed-rate mortgage loan, which on a long-term basis usually results in a heavier interest rate burden than is generally true with variable-rate home loans. However, many flexible-rate mortgages also allow the home buyer to convert during the early years of the loan to a fixed-rate loan bearing a lower contract rate in return for a fee.

Is refinancing an existing mortgage loan a wise move for a home buyer? The answer hinges on whether the savings outweigh the costs over a designated payback period. If mortgage interest rates have dropped at least two percentage points since the borrower took out the first mortgage loan, and the borrower plans to remain in the home long enough to fully recover the costs of refinancing (normally two to three years), then refinancing through a cheaper new loan is usually attractive. The costs of refinancing include the loss of some of the homeowner's interest deduction on federal tax returns due to the lower interest payments on the new loan and the fees that must be paid in order to set up the new loan. Moreover, loan fees on refinanced property are not immediately tax deductible but must be written off gradually over the term of a new loan.

A newer form of home mortgage financing that is growing especially rapidly today occurs when a homeowner decides to turn into usable form (liquidate) some of the built-up equity value in the home: a *home equity loan.* As discussed in Chapter 24, the homeowner contracts for a new mortgage that is larger than the outstanding balance on the existing home mortgage, generating extra cash for spending. Tax reform legislation in the 1980s granted special attractiveness to mortgage loans taken out for housing and nonhousing needs, because the home loan interest cost is often tax deductible. A recent Federal Reserve Board survey by Canner and Luckett (1990) found that about 60 percent of homeowners in the United States borrowed *additional* funds (averaging about $25,000 more) when they refinanced their old home mortgages, while about 40 percent refinanced purely to take advantage of lower prevailing interest rates and did not borrow more money than the amount owed on their original mortgage.

SUMMARY

This chapter focused on one of the most important and also one of the most troubled markets in the financial system, the residential mortgage market. Several problems have affected the performance of this market over the years. One concerns what used to be a relatively weak resale market for existing mortgages. However, federal government efforts to deal with this problem through the creation of special agencies actively buying and selling mortgages in the open market have borne fruit. An active and increasingly broad secondary market for mortgage loans has developed, with many new buyers of old mortgages, including pension funds, mutual funds, individuals, and foreign investors, entering the market.

Government and private efforts to deal with a second problem — the redesigning of the basic mortgage instrument itself — also have made progress. Lenders have turned to *new* forms of mortgage credit whose cash flows vary with market conditions. Included in this list are graduated-payment mortgages, variable-rate mortgages, Canadian rollover mortgages, renegotiated-rate mortgages, deferred-interest mortgages, and reverse-annuity mortgages.

A third problem that marks trading activity is the extreme volatility and sensitivity of this market. When the mortgage market is depressed, the building of new homes and other structures grinds to a halt, and unemployment in the construction industry soars. The federal government's response to these problems has been to create federal agencies with the power to borrow money and buy mortgages in the open market or to guarantee them against default. The buying and selling of mortgages has been carried out by such government agencies as the Federal National Mortgage Association (FNMA), the Government National Mortgage Association (GNMA), and the Federal Home Loan Mortgage Corporation (FHLMC). Government guarantees for residential mortgages are issued by the Federal Housing Administration (FHA) and the Veterans Administration (VA). The residential mortgage market is slowly being released from the many artificial constraints that have limited the free interplay of demand and supply forces and prevented an optimal allocation of scarce resources. And none too soon, for the thousands of new families formed in the United States each year and the thousands more immigrating into the U.S. are placing unprecedented pressures on this huge and volatile market. ∎

KEY TERMS AND CONCEPTS IN THIS CHAPTER

conventional home
   mortgage loans

residential mortgages

nonresidential mortgages

Federal Housing
   Administration (FHA)

Federal National
   Mortgage Association
   (FNMA)

Government National
   Mortgage Association
   (GNMA)

mortgage-backed
   securities

pass-throughs

Federal Home Loan
   Mortgage Corporation
   (FHLMC)

collateralized mortgage
   obligation (CMO)

prepayment risk

securitized mortgages

fixed-rate mortgage
   (FRM)

variable-rate mortgage
   (VRM)

adjustable mortgage
   instrument (AMI)

STUDY QUESTIONS

1.   What has happened in recent years to the prices of new homes? To interest rates and other terms on conventional home mortgage loans? What are the causes of these trends?

2.   Mortgages may be classified in several different ways. Describe the structure of the mortgage market as it relates to each of the following:
   a.   Type of mortgage contract — conventional versus government guaranteed
   b.   Residential versus nonresidential mortgages
   c.   Type of mortgage borrower

3. List the principal mortgage lending institutions in the United States. Which is most important? In what areas?

4. Identify the following federal agencies and describe their function:
    a. FHA   d. FNMA
    b. VA   e. GNMA
    c. FHLB   f. FHLMC

5. A number of new mortgage instruments have been developed in recent years to replace the conventional fixed-rate mortgage (FRM). These new financial instruments include the following:
    a. Graduated-payment mortgages (GPM)
    b. Variable-rate mortgages (VRM)
    c. Adjustable mortgage instruments (AMI)
    d. Canadian rollover mortgages (CRM)
    e. Reverse-annuity mortgages (RAM)
    Describe how each of these instruments works.

6. Explain what the following terms mean:
    a. Second mortgage
    b. Lease-purchase agreement
    c. Land lease
    d. Property exchange
    e. Refinancing

SELECTED REFERENCES

Canner, Glenn B., and Charles A. Luckett. "Mortgage Refinancing." *Federal Reserve Bulletin,* August 1990, pp. 604–12.

Canner, Glenn B.; Charles A. Luckett; and Thomas A. Durkin. "Home Equity Lending." *Federal Reserve Bulletin* 75 (May 1989), pp. 333–44.

Carlstrom, Charles T., and Katherine A. Samolyk. "Securitization: More Than Just a Regulatory Artifact." *Economic Commentary.* Federal Reserve Bank of Cleveland, May 1, 1992, pp. 1–4.

Weicher, John C. "The New Structure of the Housing Finance System." *Review.* Federal Reserve Bank of St. Louis, July/August 1994, pp. 47–65.

Chapter 26

Business Borrowing

LEARNING OBJECTIVES IN THIS CHAPTER

- To examine the different ways business firms issue securities and negotiate loans in order to borrow loanable funds in the money and capital markets.
- To explore the factors that cause business firms to increase or decrease the amount of funds they seek to borrow or raise in the money and capital markets.
- To see the powerful impact business borrowing has on interest rates and credit conditions in the economy.

Business firms draw on a wide variety of sources of funds to finance their daily operations and to carry out long-term investment. In 1995, for example, nonfinancial business firms in the United States raised nearly $740 billion in funds to carry out long-term investments, purchase inventories of goods and raw materials, and acquire financial assets. Of this total, approximately $250 billion (about one-third) was supplied from the financial markets through issues of bonds, stocks, notes, and other financial instruments. In this chapter, we look at sources of borrowed (debt) funds used by businesses today. In the next chapter, we consider the advantages and disadvantages of stock (equity) as a source of business funds.

FACTORS AFFECTING BUSINESS ACTIVITY IN THE MONEY AND CAPITAL MARKETS

The demands of businesses for funds stem from the desire of these firms to acquire new assets and to replace assets (such as plant and equipment) that are wearing out. Specifically, at any point in time

Total funding demands of business firms =

Desired increases in short-term assets (inventories of goods and raw materials, credit (receivables) extended to customers, and holdings of marketable securities and other short-term assets) +

Desired increases in long-term assets (plant and equipment, construction of new homes and other facilities for sale, and the start up or acquisition of other business firms).

These total funding demands from the business sector can be met from funds generated *inside* each firm (*internal financing*) in the form of undistributed profits and depreciation reserves and from funds generated from *outside* the individual firm (*external financing*) in the money and capital markets. Specifically,

Total business funding demands −

[Undistributed profits and depreciation reserves from inside each firm] =

Business demands for external financing from the money and capital markets.

Many factors affect the extent to which business firms draw on the money and capital markets for external funds. One prominent factor is the *condition of the economy.* A booming economy generates rapidly growing sales, encouraging business people to borrow in order to expand inventories and to issue stocks and bonds in order to purchase new plant and equipment. In contrast, a sagging economy normally is accompanied by declining sales and a reduction in inventory purchases and long-term investment. Other factors being equal, the need for external fund-raising declines when the economy grows more slowly or heads down into a recession. In contrast, rising demand for business goods and services is usually translated into rising demand for short- and long-term capital supplied from the financial markets.

Credit availability and *interest rates* also have powerful effects on business fundraising activity in the financial marketplace. Rising interest rates that typically accompany a period of economic prosperity or inflation eventually choke off business borrowing and spending plans due to the increasing cost of carrying inventories, floating new securities, and renewing credit lines. Falling interest rates, on the other hand, can stimulate business borrowing and spending, leading to a restocking of inventories and to an expansion of long-term investment financed by bonds, stocks, and direct loans.

A third factor in influencing how heavily businesses draw on the money and capital markets for financial support is the *level and expected growth of internally generated funds* (earnings and cash flow) for each firm. The financial markets are largely a *supplemental* funds source for most businesses, drawn upon to backstop internal cash flows when credit availability and economic conditions are favorable and when internally generated cash is inadequate to cover all desired business investments. Because business firms' earnings and cash flows tend to be volatile, it should not surprise us to learn that business fund-raising activity in the financial system is also highly volatile. Heavy business borrowings in one year to fill the *financing gap* between desired business capital spending and internally generated funds often are followed by a dearth of new security offerings and significant paydowns of outstanding loans the next year, particularly if internal funds have risen or if business expectations about the state of the economy have soured, reducing the volume of desired investment spending.

These marked fluctuations in business fund-raising in the financial markets result in wide swings in interest rates and security prices. Much of the volatility in stock and bond prices reported in the daily financial press may be attributed to the on-again, off-again character of financial market activity by the business sector. The key actors in this rapidly changing drama are, of course, the largest industrial corporations, which have the financial stature to tap both the open market and negotiated loan markets for debt and equity funds. Skillful analysts often can read which way the wind is blowing as far as interest rates and security prices are concerned by watching what is happening to the current earnings and investment plans of major corporations.

CHARACTERISTICS OF CORPORATE NOTES AND BONDS

If a corporation decides to use long-term funds to finance its growth, the most popular form of long-term financing is the **corporate bond** and **corporate note.** This is especially true for the largest corporations whose credit standing is so strong that they can avoid dealing directly with an institutional lender such as a bank, finance company, or insurance company and sell their long-term IOUs in the open market. Small companies without the necessary standing in the eyes of security investors usually must confine their long-term financing operations to negotiated loans with an institutional lender, an occasional stock issue, and heavy use of internally generated cash.

Principal Features of Corporate Notes and Bonds

A distinction needs to be drawn here between notes and bonds. By convention, a *note* is a corporate debt contract whose original maturity is five years or less; a *bond* carries an original maturity of more than five years. Both securities promise the investor an amount equal to the security's par value at maturity plus interest payments at specified intervals. Because both securities have similar characteristics other than maturity, we will use the word *bond* to refer to both notes and bonds in the discussion that follows.

Corporate bonds are generally issued in units of $1,000 and earn income that, in most cases, is fully taxable to the investor. Each bond is accompanied by an **indenture,** a contract listing the rights and obligations of the borrower and the investor. Indentures usually contain *restrictive covenants* designed to protect bondholders against actions by a borrowing firm or its shareholders that might weaken the value of the bonds. For example, restrictive covenants in an indenture may prohibit increases in a borrowing corporation's dividend rate (which would reduce the growth of its net worth), limit additional borrowing, restrict merger agreements, or limit the sale of the borrower's assets. These and other terms in a bond indenture are enforced by a third party — the trustee (often a bank trust department) — that represents investors holding the bonds.

Term Bonds versus Serial Bonds

The majority of corporate bonds issued today are *term bonds,* which means that all the bonds in a particular issue mature on a single date. In contrast, most bonds issued by state and local governments (municipals) and a few corporate bonds are *serial bonds,* carrying a range of maturity dates.

Recent Trends in Original Maturities of Bonds

The maturities attached to newly issued corporate bonds have fluctuated widely with changing economic conditions and shifts in interest-rate expectations and the expectations for inflation. At the beginning of the twentieth century many railroads sold bonds with 100-year-plus maturities. During the 1950s and 1960s corporations found a ready market for 20- to 30-year bonds, and telephone companies managed to sell 40-year bonds. Such long-term debt contracts are desirable from a borrowing company's point of view because they lock in low interest costs for many years and make financial planning much simpler. However, the 1970s and 1980s ushered in a trend toward much shorter-maturity corporate debt issues (many in the 5- to 15-year range), due in part to rapid inflation and interest rates that soared to record levels. The development of sophisticated interest-rate hedging tools, such as futures, options, and swaps, aided companies moving toward shorter maturity bonds because these tools help to minimize damage from more volatile short-term interest rates. Sharply lower interest rates and subdued inflation in the 1990s, however, set in motion a swing back to long-maturity bonds. For example, government agencies like the Resolution Trust Corporation and the Tennessee Valley Authority issued 40- to 50-year bonds, while such companies as Walt Disney and Coca-Cola brought 100-year issues to market.

Call Privileges

A large proportion of corporate bonds issued today carry *call privileges,* allowing early redemption (retirement) of the bonds if market conditions prove favorable. The call privilege represents a way to shorten the average maturity of corporate bonds in an era of inflation and high borrowing costs. The call feature gives the firm greater flexibility in financing its operations but can be expensive when interest rates are high and are expected to fall. Investors realize that the bond is likely to be called if interest rates fall and therefore demand a higher yield as compensation for the risk that the bond will be called and retired. However, a growing proportion of corporate bonds are issued today *without* a call privilege attached due to the trend toward shorter maturities, the added interest cost involved, and the availability of hedging instruments.

Sinking Fund Provisions

Many corporate bonds are backed by *sinking funds* designed to ensure that the issuing company will be able to pay off the bonds when they come due. Periodic payments are made into the fund on a schedule usually related to the depreciation of any assets supported by the bonds. The trustee is charged with the responsibility of making sure the user places the right amount of money in the sinking fund each time a payment is due. Periodically, a portion of the bonds may be retired from monies accumulated in the fund.

Yields and Costs of Corporate Bonds

Yields on corporate bonds tend to move in line with business conditions and respond to swings in the credit market between tight and easy money. Yields on the highest-grade corporate issues tend to move closely with yields on government bonds. In contrast, yields carried by lower-grade corporate bonds are more closely tied to conditions in the economy and to factors specifically affecting the risk position of each borrowing firm. Bonds issued by the largest U.S. companies are, with few exceptions, listed and traded on the New York or American Stock exchanges, although the largest volume of bond trading passes through dealers operating off the exchanges.

As noted in Chapter 9, there are several different ways to measure the rate of return to the investor or the cost to the firm of issuing a debt security. From the point of view of the issuing company, one widely quoted measure of the cost of a bond is its *coupon rate,* that is, the rate of interest the company promises to pay as printed on the face of the bond. However, the coupon rate may understate or overstate the true cost of a bond to the issuing company, depending on whether the bond was issued at a discount or at a premium from its par value. A better measure of the cost of issuing a bond is to compare the *net proceeds* available for the borrowing company's use from a bond sale to the present value of the stream of cash payments the firm must eventually make to bondholders.

For example, suppose a corporation issues $1,000 par bonds, but flotation costs reduce the net proceeds to the company from each bond to $950.[1] If the bonds mature in 10 years and carry a 10 percent coupon rate, the before-tax cost, k, to the issuing company is figured as follows:

---

[1] The major elements of floatation cost for a new bond issue are the underwriting spread of the securities dealer who agrees to sell the issue, registration fees, paper and printing charges, and legal fees.

$$\text{Net proceeds per bond} = \frac{\text{Interest cost in year 1}}{(1+k)^1} + \frac{\text{Interest cost in year 2}}{(1+k)^2}$$

$$+ \ldots + \frac{\text{Interest cost in year 10}}{(1+k)^{10}}$$

$$+ \frac{\text{Principal payments in year 10}}{(1+k)^{10}}$$

In this example:

$$\$950 = \frac{\$100}{(1+k)^1} + \frac{\$100}{(1+k)^2} + \ldots + \frac{\$100}{(1+k)^{10}} + \frac{\$1,000}{(1+k)^{10}}$$

A check of the present value tables in Appendix B indicates that k in this example is 10.85 percent.

However, interest charges on debt are *tax deductible,* making the after-tax cost considerably less than the before-tax cost, especially for the largest and most profitable firms. For the largest corporations with annual earnings in the top tax bracket, the marginal federal income tax rate is 35 percent. Thus, a large company issuing the bond described above would incur an after-tax cost (k') of

$$k' = k(1 - t)$$

where k is the before-tax cost and t is the firm's marginal tax rate. In this example,

$$k' = 10.85\%(1 - 0.35) = 7.05\%$$

Of course, if the firm were in a lower tax bracket, the after-tax cost of its debt would be higher. In the case of an unprofitable company (whose effective tax rate is zero), the after-tax cost of debt would equal its before-tax cost.

The before- and after-tax costs of debt vary not only with each firm's tax rate but also with conditions in the financial markets. During periods of rapid economic expansion when the supply of credit is scarce relative to the demand for credit, the cost of borrowing rises. Bonds must be marketed at lower prices and higher yields. Conversely, in periods when the economy contracts and easier credit conditions prevail, the cost of borrowing tends to decline. The prices of bonds rise and their yields fall. It should not surprise us to learn that the volume of long-term corporate borrowings often increases markedly during business recessions as companies attempt to lock in the relatively low interest rates available at that time.

The Most Common Types of Corporate Bonds

Debentures. There are many different types of corporate bonds issued in the financial markets. Among the most common is the **debenture,** which is not secured by any specific asset owned by the issuing corporation. Instead, the holder of a debenture is a general creditor of the company and looks to the earning power and reputation of the borrower as the source of the bond's value.

Subordinated Debentures. A related form of bond is the subordinated debenture, frequently called a *junior security.* If a company goes out of business and its assets are liquidated, holders of subordinated debentures are paid only after all secured and unsecured senior creditors receive the monies owed to them.

Mortgage Bonds. Debt securities representing a claim against specific assets (normally plant and equipment) owned by a corporation are known as **mortgage bonds.** These bonds may be either *closed end* or *open end.* Closed-end mortgage bonds do not permit the issuance of any additional debt against the assets already pledged under the mortgage. Open-end bonds, on the other hand, allow additional debt to be issued against pledged assets, which may dilute the position of current bondholders. For this reason, open-end mortgage bonds typically carry higher yields than closed-end bonds. Sometimes several different mortgage bonds with varying priorities of claim are issued against the same assets. For example, the initial issue of bonds against a corporation's fixed assets may be designated first mortgage bonds, and later second mortgage bonds may be issued against those same assets. If the company were liquidated, holders of second mortgage bonds would receive only those funds left over after holders of the first mortgage bonds were paid off.

Collateral Trust Bonds. A debt instrument secured by stocks and bonds issued by governments or by other corporations is called a *collateral trust bond.* Such a bond is really an interest in a pool of securities held by the bond issuer. The pledged securities are held in trust for the benefit of bondholders, although the borrowing company usually receives any interest and dividend payments generated by the pledged securities and retains voting rights on any stock pledged.

Income Bonds. Bonds often used in corporate reorganizations and in other situations when a company is in financial distress are known as *income bonds.* Interest on these bonds is paid only when income is actually earned, making an income bond similar to common stock. However, holders of income bonds do have a prior claim on earnings over both stockholders and holders of subordinated debentures. Some income bonds carry a cumulative feature under which unpaid interest accumulates and must be fully paid before the stockholders receive any dividends.

Equipment Trust Certificates. Resembling a lease in form, *equipment trust certificates* are used most frequently to acquire industrial equipment or rolling stock (such as railroad cars or airplanes). Title to the assets acquired is vested in a trustee (often a bank trust department), which leases these assets to the company issuing the certificates. Periodic lease payments are made to the trustee, who passes them along to certificate holders. Title to the assets passes to the borrowing company only after all lease payments are made.

Industrial Development Bonds. In recent years, state and local governments have become more active in aiding private corporations to meet their financial needs. One of the most controversial forms of government-aided, long-term business borrowing is the **industrial development bond (IDB).** These bonds are issued by a local government borrowing authority to provide buildings, land, or equipment to a business firm. Because governmental units can borrow more cheaply than most private companies, the lower debt costs may be passed along to the firm as an inducement to move to a new location, bringing jobs to the local economy. The business firm normally guarantees both interest and principal payments on the IDBs by renting the buildings, land, or equipment at a rental fee high enough to cover debt service costs.

Pollution Control Bonds. These debt instruments are used to aid private companies in financing the purchase of pollution control equipment. In this case, local governments purchase pollution control equipment with the proceeds of a bond issue and lease that equipment to business firms.

New Types of Corporate Notes and Bonds

Corporate bonds are traditionally called *fixed-income* securities because most pay a fixed amount of interest each year. This creates a problem for bondholders when interest rates rise, inflation increases, or both, because then the real market value of fixed-income securities falls. In recent years, repeated bouts with inflation, high interest rates, and reduced quality ratings on corporate bonds have spurred companies to develop *new* types of bonds whose return to the investor is sensitive to changing inflation and changing bond values. New bonds have appeared with deferred interest payments and variable coupon (promised) rates of return to investors, in an attempt to help issuing companies with near-term cash shortages. Among the most popular of these innovative securities are discount bonds, stock-indexed bonds, floating-rate bonds, commodity-backed bonds, warrant bonds, payment-in-kind bonds, and reset bonds.

Discount bonds, first used in 1981, are sold at a price below par and appreciate toward par as maturity approaches. Thus, the investor earns capital gains as well as interest, while the issuing corporation usually can issue discount bonds at a lower after-tax cost than conventional bonds. Some discount bonds, known as **zero coupon bonds,** pay no interest at all or carry a below-market coupon rate that later can be raised to market levels. First used by J.C. Penney in 1981, "zeros" pay a return based solely on their price appreciation as they approach maturity. However, the annual price increase is taxable as ordinary income, not as capital gains, under current IRS regulations.

Reset bonds are designed to give corporations time to strengthen their credit ratings or to deal with cash shortages. Usually these bonds start out promising a fixed rate of return to the investor. However, later the promised interest rate is changed to bring the bond's price up to some desired level. These bonds are most frequently issued by companies whose credit ratings are temporarily impaired but who hope to increase their credit quality and lower their debt costs. These lower-credit-quality bonds often carry interest rate *caps* to limit the issuing companies' exposure to interest rate risk — the danger of higher borrowing costs.

Stock-indexed bonds have an interest rate tied to stock market trends. For example, several of these bonds have had their annual interest rate tied to the annual trading volume on the New York Stock Exchange. A rise in stock trading volume raises the bond's promised rate of return to the holder.

Floating-rate bonds have their annual promised rate tied to changes in long-term or short-term interest rates, or both. *Commodity-backed bonds* carry a face value tied to the market price of an internationally traded commodity, such as gold, silver, or oil, that presumably is sensitive to inflation.

Warrant bonds permit an investor to purchase additional bonds at the same yield as the original bonds or sell detachable warrants to another investor. A related bond, called a *usable bond,* carries warrants to purchase at par the issuing company's stock, and those warrants can be traded separately from the bonds themselves. Warrant and usable bonds are most valuable when interest rates are expected to decline. Many of these new types of bonds do reasonably well in inflationary periods, but they often prove difficult to sell when inflation decreases or when investors become very risk-conscious.

Several types of bonds were developed in the 1980s and early 1990s to help issuing companies avoid early cash payments until their earnings increased. *Payment-in-kind bonds* grant the issuing firm the option of either paying the interest owed or issuing additional bonds, usually during the first five years of the bond's existence. Recent U.S. tax legislation, however, limits the tax deductibility of the interest on such bonds.

Medium-term notes (MTNs), carrying maturities of one to 10 years, have exploded onto the corporate fund-raising scene during the past decade. Although they were developed as long ago as the early 1970s, MTNs outstanding rose to nearly $100 billion in 1990 compared to less than $1 billion in 1980. Issued by nearly 300 companies, these securities are generally noncallable, unsecured, fixed-rate obligations. One advantage of MTNs for borrowing corporations is the ability to reduce exposure to interest rate risk, because MTNs give companies more opportunities to match the maturities of the assets they wish to acquire with the maturities of their liabilities.

The development of new financial instruments inside the United States has been paralleled by the growth of new corporate borrowing instruments abroad. One successful innovation is the *Euronote*, a short-term unsecured corporate IOU underwritten by a group of banks and sold to international investors. If the borrowing company cannot sell all of its notes, the banks involved buy them or provide credit at a stipulated yield spread over current interest rates. *Eurobonds* have also expanded rapidly, with many firms choosing to issue long-term bearer bonds directly to foreign investors (a subject further explored in Chapter 29).

INVESTORS IN CORPORATE NOTES AND BONDS

Today the investor market for corporate notes and bonds is dominated by insurance companies and pension funds (see Exhibit 26–1). The latter prefer buying corporate bonds in the open market; insurance companies, on the other hand, frequently purchase their corporate securities directly from the issuing company in an off-the-market transaction. The stability of cash flows experienced by pension funds and insurance companies permits them to pursue corporate bonds of long maturities and to lock in their high yields.

One of the more dynamic investor segments in U.S. corporate bonds includes *foreign* institutions, particularly leading security dealers, banks, and insurance firms, such as Credit Suisse, Deutsche Bank, Nomura Securities, and Daiwa. Many purchases of U.S. bonds have been associated with foreign takeovers of U.S. companies and the desire of foreign investors to pursue safe investments in the United States in order to escape political

Exhibit 26–1   **Principal Investors in Corporate and Foreign Bonds, 1995***

Investor Group	Amount	Percent of Total Bond Holdings
Households	$211.0	8.2%
Rest of the world (foreign investors)	339.5	13.2
Commercial banks	103.7	4.0
Savings institutions	86.2	3.4
Life insurance companies	818.5	31.9
Property-casualty insurance companies	104.2	4.1
Private pension funds	318.2	12.4
Government pension funds	280.4	10.9
Mutual funds	185.1	7.2
Security brokers and dealers	66.4	2.6
Other investors	55.7	2.2
Totals	$2,568.9	100.0%

Note: Columns may not add to totals due to rounding.
*Figures are for the second quarter of the year at annualized rates.

Source: Board of Governors of the Federal Reserve System, *Flow of Funds Accounts: Financial Assets and Liabilities,* Second Quarter 1995.

and economic turmoil abroad. Then, too, the purchase of dollar-denominated assets such as corporate bonds gives foreign investors a way to store U.S. dollars at high yield until those dollars are needed either to buy U.S. goods or to purchase commodities sold in international markets that are denominated in dollars (such as oil).

Commercial banks are *not* heavy investors in corporate bonds. Generally, bankers prefer to deal personally with a business customer and grant a loan specifically tailored to the borrower's needs rather than to enter the impersonal bond market. Increasingly in recent years, commercial banks have become direct competitors with the corporate bond market through the granting of *term loans*. A term loan has a maturity of more than one year. Responding to inflation and the soaring cost of business equipment, bankers have gradually extended the maturity of term loans, with many now falling in the 5- to 10-year maturity range. Rates on such loans generally exceed the interest cost on corporate debt sold in the open market, however, especially when banks also insist that the borrowing firm keep funds on deposit with the bank equal to a specified percentage of the loan.

One area of concern among many corporate bond investors in recent years has been an overall decline in the credit quality of corporate bonds. A substantial proportion of all corporate bonds issued over the past two decades in the United States have been "junk bonds." Significant numbers of industrial bond issuers have seen their credit ratings reduced by rating agencies during the past 15 years. As the danger of default has risen, capital market investors have demanded higher promised rates of interest on newly issued corporate bonds. Moreover, a substantial number of newly issued corporate bonds have had to carry special covenants, allowing investors to redeem their bonds with the issuing companies at a fixed price if the companies' credit ratings are lowered or if the bondholders' position is weakened by restructuring of the issuing firm's capital.

THE SECONDARY MARKET FOR CORPORATE BONDS

The resale (secondary) market for corporate bonds is relatively limited compared to the resale markets for common stock, municipal bonds, and other long-term securities. Trading volume is thin, even for some bonds issued by the largest companies. Part of the reason is the small number of individuals active as investors in this market. Individuals generally have limited investment time horizons (holding periods) and tend to turn over their portfolios rapidly when other attractive investments appear. In the past, secondary market trading in corporate bonds was also held back by the "buy and hold" strategy of institutional investors, especially insurance companies and pension funds. Many of these firms purchased corporate bonds exclusively for interest income and were content to purchase the longest-term issues and simply hold them to maturity. Today, however, under the pressure of volatile interest rates and inflation, many institutions buying corporate bonds have shifted into a more aggressive strategy labeled *total performance*. Portfolio managers are more sensitive today to changes in bond prices and look for near-term opportunities to sell bonds and make capital gains. In fact, a number of insurance companies, pension funds, and mutual funds operate their own trading departments and keep constant tabs on developments in the corporate bond market.

Unlike the stock market, no one central exchange for bond trading dominates the market. Although corporate bonds are traded on all major exchanges, including the New York (NYSE) and American (AMEX) exchanges, most secondary market trading in bonds is conducted over the telephone and through electronic networks linking customers, brokers, and dealers. Bond brokers arrange trades between dealers in return for a small commission. Dealers, on the other hand, commit themselves to take on large blocks of bonds either from other dealers or from pension funds, insurance companies, and other clients. Due to rapid and unpredictable changes in interest rates, many dealers now try to close out positions taken in individual corporate bonds in just a few days, frequently acting only as intermediaries in trades between institutional investors without committing their own capital.

THE MARKETING OF CORPORATE NOTES AND BONDS

New corporate bonds may be offered publicly in the open market to all interested buyers or sold privately to a limited number of investors. The first route, known as **public sale,** accounts for the largest proportion of corporate bond sales each year. Among smaller companies and those firms with unique financing requirements, however, the second route, known as a **private or direct placement,** has become popular.

The Public Sale of Bonds

The sale of new corporate bonds in the open market is handled principally by investment bankers. The term **investment banker** is somewhat misleading, because these firms have little or nothing to do with banking as we know it. In fact, the Glass-Steagall Act of 1933 prohibited U.S. commercial banks from underwriting most corporate securities. Japan has a similar law forbidding its banks from making greater inroads into the market for domestic corporate security offerings. This law was passed out of fear that commercial bank underwriting of corporate securities would lead to bank failures or to control of nonfinancial businesses by the banking community. Recently, however, selected commercial banks in the United States have been able to carve out a growing market share of the investment banking market, securing approval from the Federal Reserve Board for offering newly issued corporate bonds and stock through security affiliates of their holding companies. Among the leaders in this field today are Citicorp, Bankers Trust Corporation, Chemical Corporation, and J.P. Morgan.

In contrast to commercial banks, which accept deposits from the public, investment bankers underwrite new issues of corporate stocks and bonds and give advice to corporations on their financing requirements. An investment banking firm may singly take on a new issue of corporate securities or band together with other underwriters to form a *syndicate.* Either way, the investment banker's game plan is to acquire new corporate securities at the lowest possible price and sell them as quickly as possible in order to turn a profit. An investment banker may purchase the securities from the issuing company directly or merely guarantee the issuer a specific price for his securities. With either approach, it is the investment banker who carries the risk of substantial gains or losses when the securities are marked for sale in the open market.

The largest issues of corporate bonds sold in the open market are usually bid on by several groups of underwriters. Competition among these syndicates is intense. Investment bankers hope to acquire a new issue at the lowest possible bid price and place the securities with investors at a higher retail price, maximizing the *spread,* or return on invested capital. Unfortunately, each new bond issue is always somewhat different from those that have traded before and may involve hundreds of millions of dollars. Moreover, a decision on what price to bid for new securities must be made *before* the bonds are released for public trading; in the interim, the prices of bonds may change drastically. If the underwriter bids too high a price, the firm may not be able to resell the securities at a price high enough to recover the cost and secure an adequate spread. To cite an example, in October 1979, IBM Corporation offered $1 billion in notes and debentures through a collection of Wall Street underwriters.

Unfortunately, just as the IBM issue was coming to market, bond prices tumbled (due, in part, to an announcement by the Federal Reserve suggesting that credit conditions would be tightened to deal with inflation). The underwriters suffered a massive loss.

Competition in the bidding process tends to narrow the underwriter's spread between bid and asked price. If several investment banking houses band together in a syndicate, a consensus bid price must be hammered out among the participants. Disagreements frequently arise within a syndicate due to different perceptions on the probable future direction of interest rates. Because more than a hundred underwriters may be included in a single syndicate, the task of reaching a compromise and placing a unified bid for a new security issue may prove impossible. The old syndicate will break apart, with those bidders still interested in the issue hurriedly piecing together a new syndicate and a new bid.

A number of factors are considered in pricing a new corporate bond issue. Certainly the credit ratings assigned by Moody's, Standard & Poor's Corporation, or other agencies is a key item, because many investors rely on such agencies for assessing the risk carried by a new security.[2] Another factor is the "forward calendar" of security offerings, which lists new issues expected to come to market during the next few weeks. Obviously, if a heavy volume of new offerings is anticipated in the near-term, prices will decline unless additional demand appears. Changes in government policy must be anticipated because that policy can have profound effects on security prices. Other factors considered by investment bankers include the size of the issue, how aggressive other bidders are likely to be, and the strength of the "book," which consists of indications of advance investor interest in the security being offered.

Once the securities are received from the issuing company, the underwriters advertise their availability at the price agreed on by all members of the syndicate. *Delay* in selling new securities is one of the investment banker's worst enemies, because additional financing must be obtained to carry the unsold securities. Also, there is the added risk of price declines as time increases. To speed the process of selling new bonds, many investment banking firms today are affiliated with retail brokerage companies that maintain working relationships with large buyers, such as insurance companies and pension funds.

What happens to the market prices of securities sold by investment banking syndicates is the key determinant of the success or failure of the underwriting process. If the price at which a new issue can be sold falls far enough, the syndicate will disband, and individual underwriters will scramble to sell their allotments of securities at whatever price the market dictates. The spread between the selling (retail) price of corporate bonds and the proceeds paid to the issuing company (the flotation cost of a new issue) is usually less than one point ($1 for each $100 in par value). It takes only a small decline in the retail price before the underwriter's profit is eliminated. Moreover, unfavorable price movements can damage the reputation of the investment banker with investors and the client companies that issue new securities. Clearly, investment banking is both risky and highly competitive.

Private Placements of Corporate Bonds

In recent years, private placements of bonds with one or a limited group of well-informed investors have come to represent a significant proportion of public sales. For example, in 1994, private placements accounted for about 20 percent of public market sales of corporate bonds by U.S. corporations. However, the ratio of private to public sales is sensitive to the changing composition of borrowing companies and to economic conditions. Usually, periods

---

[2]See Chapter 11 for a discussion of security ratings.

of rising interest rates and reduced credit availability bring more borrowing companies into the public market, and falling rates often bring a rise in private placements. For the largest corporations, public sales and private placements are *substitutes.* When interest rates are high or credit is tight in one of these markets, the largest borrowers shift easily to the other market. Most of the borrowers in the private market are medium-sized corporations, however.

The expansion of privately placed bonds has been significantly aided by a ruling of the U.S. Securities and Exchange Commission (SEC) known as Rule 144A. The SEC eliminated restrictions on the secondary trading of private placements by large institutional investors (known as QIBs, or qualified investment buyers). This step, in effect, creates a secondary market for privately placed bonds, overcoming one of the historic barriers confronting investors who otherwise might be interested in privately placed securities. Revisions in Rule 144A have brought investment banks into the private placement arena to actively underwrite and distribute these securities. Privately placed bonds have become more liquid, bringing major new investors, such as mutual funds, into this market. The private-placement market has also been aided by the increasing presence of foreign investors and foreign issuers of private bonds in U.S. markets and by the growing number of corporate *divestitures,* which in recent years have accounted for nearly one third of all corporate acquisitions. Much of the divestiture activity reflected companies attempting to downsize their operations in order to trim operating costs or to raise scarce capital by selling marketable assets.

Who buys privately placed bonds? Life insurance companies, finance companies, and pension funds, historically, have been the principal investors in this market. These institutions hope to secure higher yields and protection against call privileges by engaging in *direct negotiation* with borrowing corporations and by using due diligence and engaging in careful monitoring of any loans they grant. The avoidance of call privileges is of special benefit to life insurance companies and pension funds because these institutions prefer the stable income that comes from purchasing long-term bonds and holding them to maturity. In fact, institutional investors active in the private-placement market frequently impose extra fees in a sales contract containing an allowance for early retirement of a security by the issuing corporation. Investors other than life insurance companies and pension funds tend to play smaller roles in the private market due to their lack of expertise, small size, and the limited resale market for privately placed securities. Actually, since 1990, life insurance companies have sharply curtailed their purchases of privately placed securities due to public pressure on life insurers to strengthen their balance sheets and because many borrowers in the private-placement market have experienced lower credit ratings, presenting more risk to life insurance companies and other interested investors.

There are several advantages to the borrower from a private placement. One is the lower cost of distribution because there are no registration fees or expenses associated with the issuance of a prospectus as there would be with a public sale. Private placements are exempt from registration with the Securities and Exchange Commission (SEC). Generally, more rapid placement of bonds takes place in the private market because only a few buyers are involved and the loan is confidential. Special concessions can often be secured, such as a commitment for future borrowing. For example, a corporate borrower may negotiate a private sale of $15 million in bonds to an insurance company but also may be granted a line of credit of $2 million a year over the next five years. This kind of commitment is not possible in the impersonal public market, where bonds are highly standardized. Moreover, lenders in the private market try to tailor the terms of a loan to match the specific cash flow and maturity needs of borrowers. This may involve a conventional fixed-rate, single-sum credit contract at the prevailing interest rate, a floating-rate loan that can be retired early if cash flows permit, or even a participating loan in which the lender charges a lower interest rate in return for a share of net income from the project financed.

One disadvantage is that interest costs generally are higher in private sales than in public sales. However, private sale bonds are less liquid and carry more risk. One indication of this is that privately placed debt issues tend to have more restrictive covenants in order to protect lenders. Still, the larger the size of a corporate issue, the smaller the cost differential between public and private placements.

THE VOLUME OF BORROWING IN THE CORPORATE BOND MARKET

The volume of borrowing through new issues of corporate notes and bonds has grown rapidly in recent years (see Exhibit 26–2). For example, annual offerings of new corporate debt securities nearly quadrupled between 1960 and 1970, nearly doubled between 1970 and 1980, and then expanded more than five times over between 1980 and 1995. Much of this growth in long-term corporate borrowing could be traced to inflation, which reduced the real cost of debt, to increased use of financial leverage to boost returns to corporate stockholders, to the development of international capital markets, and to relatively lower long-term interest rates in the 1990s. This track record suggests that the corporate debt market is very sensitive to economic conditions and to changes in the cost of long-term credit.

Another factor that has spurred the private bond market's growth is a rash of corporate takeovers and merger proposals. Targets for these corporate raids have included such well-known companies as CBS, Firestone Tire, First Interstate Banks, Crown Zellerbach, Hilton Hotels, Uniroyal, Pennzoil, Paine Webber, and National Steel Corporation, to name just a few. Many of these mergers have been motivated by deregulation of key industries in recent years, including the airlines, commercial banking, and communications; by more liberal antitrust rules followed by the U.S. government; and by the desire of many foreign investors to establish business operations inside U.S. territory. Armed with huge trade surpluses and ample national savings to draw on, Japanese firms have been particularly aggressive in acquiring U.S. firms, adding such well-known companies as CBS Records, Columbia Pictures Entertainment, Rockefeller Group, 7-Eleven Corporation, and Universal Studios to their investment list.

Frequently, these proposed mergers include plans to offer billions of dollars in *junk bonds* — high-interest-cost and low-credit-rated debt securities — as well as bank loans to

Exhibit 26–2

The Growth of Corporate Bonds and Notes Issued by U.S. Companies ($ Millions)

Year	New Issues of Corporate Bonds and Notes
1950	$ 4,920
1960	8,081
1970	30,321
1980	53,199
1990	114,500
1995*	311,500

*The 1995 figure is for the second quarter and is annualized. All figures in the exhibit represent gross proceeds of issues maturing in more than one year and are the principal amount or number of units multiplied by the offering price. Figures exclude secondary offerings, employee stock plans, mutual funds, intracorporate transactions, and Yankee bonds (sold by foreign corporations inside U.S. territory). Before 1987, the figures included only those issues that were underwritten.

Source: U.S. Department of Commerce and Board of Governors of the Federal Reserve System.

finance the transaction. With the expanded use of debt, resulting in heavier use of financial leverage and a heavier drain on company earnings due to greater borrowing costs, the credit ratings of scores of corporations have been reduced in recent years.

At the same time, low-rated (speculative) corporate bonds (rated below BBB by Standard & Poor's Corp. and below Baa3 by Moody's) have mushroomed to become a growing share of the corporate security market. The growth of this junk bond market has been spurred by corporations' desire to restructure their capital, replacing stock with debt or replacing short-term securities with long-term bonds. In fact, the volume of corporate stock retirements, replaced in most cases by debt, broke all previous records during the 1980s and 1990s. A number of these retirements were carried out to discourage "hostile" takeovers or to participate in corporate mergers and acquisitions. The federal government's antitrust policy took a turn toward ease in the 1980s and early 1990s, allowing more mergers and acquisitions without government challenge. Then, too, many companies not well known to investors have been able to tap the bond market for funds for the first time, thanks to the rapid expansion of the market for junk bonds. By the late 1980s, junk bond issues accounted for just over one third of all public bond offerings in the United States, of which about two thirds were designed for financing mergers and restructuring corporate capital.

A substantial proportion of recent corporate takeovers has been in the form of **leveraged buyouts,** in which a single investor or small group of investors (frequently including senior management of the target company) buys the publicly owned stock of a business firm by borrowing 80 to 90 percent or more of the purchase price from banks and the bond market. In many leveraged buyouts (LBOs), the assets of companies that previously were publicly owned (that is, their stock was widely dispersed among thousands of investors) were conveyed to closely held private companies and partnerships. The most famous of these LBOs was an acquisition by RJR-Nabisco in 1989, which totaled $25 billion. In these instances, the takeover group is counting on faster growth and improved profitability of the targeted company or on selling some of its assets to pay off the huge volume of acquisition debt. Because such expectations are fraught with risk, leading analysts have expressed concern over many of the buyouts, fearing they may undermine public confidence in the financial system as corporate debt continues to pile higher relative to corporate equity and profits. Indeed, in recent years, corporate profits relative to output and assets have fallen due, in part, to the pressure of higher interest payments on debt and higher taxes.

These debt-funded mergers have generated much proposed federal and state legislation to prevent "corporate raiders" from taking over some companies. Some targeted firms have developed shark repellents or poison pills, such as favorable deals for outside investors not affiliated with a corporate raider or revisions in corporate charters that make it more difficult for outsiders to take over the firm. Surprisingly, research evidence shows that stockholders of companies targeted for acquisition benefit from takeover activity, even when the planned takeover is unsuccessful. Investors apparently believe that such takeovers will improve the efficiency and profitability of the target companies beyond what their existing management has been able to do and the stock of the target firm will rise in value.

BANK LOANS TO BUSINESS FIRMS

Commercial banks are direct competitors with the corporate bond markets in making both long-term and short-term loans to business. In fact, growing numbers of corporations that once relied on banks for funds have turned instead to selling bonds in the open market, decreasing the relative importance of banks in the financial system. Still, the volume of bank credit made available to business firms remains enormous. For example, by February

1996, total commercial and industrial loans extended by commercial banks operating in the United States totaled nearly $730 billion, or about 28 percent of all U.S. commercial bank loans. Banks grant their loans to a wide variety of firms covering all major sectors of the business community. And bankers have come to play a key supporting role in the corporate debt market, issuing standby credit guarantees on behalf of borrowing companies to pay off their customers' debt if the borrowing companies cannot do so.

In recent years, the Federal Reserve Board has carried out periodic surveys of business lending practices by banks across the United States. These Federal Reserve surveys indicate that bank loans to business firms tend to be short in maturity. For example, recent surveys suggest that short-term commercial and industrial loans average less than two months to maturity, while long-term business loans average just under four years. The Federal Reserve surveys suggest that longer-term business loans carry *higher* average interest rates than short-term business loans. This is due, in part, to the greater risk associated with long-term credit. In addition, yield curves have usually sloped upward in recent years, calling for higher rates on long-term loans.[3] Moreover, the larger and longer-term a business loan is, the more likely its rate will *float* with market conditions. For example, only about a third of the short-term business loans covered in recent Federal Reserve surveys of U.S. banks carried floating interest rates, while nearly 80 percent of the long-term loans had floating rates. Clearly, banks become more determined to protect themselves against unexpected inflation and other adverse developments through floating rates as the maturity and size of a business loan increase.

The Prime, or Base, Interest Rate

One of the best known and most widely followed interest rates in the financial system is the prime bank rate, sometimes called the **base rate,** or *reference rate*.[4] The prime rate is the annual percentage rate that banks quote to their most creditworthy customers. Most prime loans are unsecured, but the borrowers often are required to keep a deposit at the lending bank equal to a specified percentage of the loan. This *compensating balance* normally is 15 to 20 percent of the amount loaned. Even for a prime borrower, therefore, the true cost of a bank loan is normally higher than the prime rate itself. Most prime loans are short term — one year or less — taken out to finance purchases of inventory and other working capital needs or to support construction projects.

Each bank must set its own prime, or base, rate, following a vote by its board of directors. Beginning in the 1930s, however, a uniform prime rate began to appear, with differences in rates from bank to bank quickly eliminated by competition. Split primes do occur for brief periods, however. A bank strapped for loanable funds may keep its prime temporarily above rates posted by other banks in order to ration the available supply of

---

[3]See Chapter 10 for a discussion of yield curves and the factors that shape them.

[4]*Base rate* is a more general term than prime, referring to that loan interest rate used as the basis for determining the current rate charged a business borrower. Most business loan rates are scaled upward from the base rate. Many commercial loans today are tied to base rates other than prime, however. This is frequently the case for large multinational companies that have ready access to credit markets abroad. For example, the London Interbank Offering Rate (LIBOR) on short-term Eurodollar deposits is often used as a base rate for large corporate loans. In some cases, the commercial paper rate, the federal funds rate, or the secondary market rate on bank CDs is also used as a loan base rate. The smaller numbers of borrowers today who remain tied to the prime rate are less mobile customers with fewer alternatives than many of the largest corporations, which have numerous alternative sources of funds and therefore can frequently demand credit at rates significantly less than prime. Such large loans are often made today at contract rates only fractions of a percentage point above a bank's cost of raising funds in the money market.

credit. Similarly, a bank with ample funds to lend may post a prime temporarily below market to encourage its best customers to borrow more frequently and in larger amounts. A relatively uniform prime rate helps corporate borrowers compare the loan offered by one bank with that offered by another bank more easily.

Traditionally, the prime rate was set by one or more of the nation's leading banks, and other banks followed the leader. However, a major innovation in the market for prime loans occurred in 1971 when Citibank of New York announced it would float its prime. Citibank's basic lending rate was pegged on a weekly basis at half a percentage point above the yield on 90-day commercial paper. Other banks soon followed, pegging their prime rates to prevailing yields on U.S. Treasury bills and other money market instruments. Linking the prime to such active money market rates as those attached to Treasury bills and commercial paper resulted in a more flexible, rapidly changing base lending rate. The prime has come to reflect somewhat more accurately the forces of shifting credit demands, fluctuations in government policy, and inflation. A more flexible prime has enabled banks to better protect their interest margins — the difference between the return on loans and the cost of bank funds — and to make credit more readily available to customers willing to pay the price.

Many business loans today are priced at *premiums* above the prime or other base rate because only the most financially sound customers qualify for prime or below-prime loans. Nevertheless, commercial loan rates typically are tied to the base rate — prime or other reference rate — through a carefully worked out formula. One popular approach, known as *prime plus,* adds on a rate premium for default risk and often an additional premium for longer maturities (term risk). Thus, the banker may quote a commercial customer "prime plus 2," with a 1 percent premium above the base rate for default risk and another 1 percent premium for term risk. Other banks use the *times-prime* method, which multiplies the base rate by a risk factor. For example, the business customer may be quoted a loan at 1.5 times prime. If the current prime is 10 percent, this customer pays 15 percent. If the loan carries a floating rate, then the interest rate in future periods can always be calculated by multiplying the base rate by 1.5.

Which of these formulas the banker uses often depends on his or her forecast of interest rates. In a period of falling rates, interest charges on floating-rate loans figured on a times-prime basis decline faster than those based on prime plus. When interest rates are on the rise, times-prime pricing results in more rapid increases in business loan rates. Therefore, times-prime financing is more sensitive to the changing cost of bank funds over the course of the business cycle.

COMMERCIAL MORTGAGES

The construction of office buildings, shopping centers, and other commercial structures is generally financed with an instrument known as the **commercial mortgage.** Short-term mortgage loans are used to finance the construction of commercial projects, and longer-term mortgages are employed to pay off short-term construction loans, purchase land, and cover property development costs. The majority of long-term commercial mortgage loans are made by life insurance companies, thrift institutions, and pension funds; commercial banks are the predominant short-term commercial mortgage lender. Banks support the construction of office buildings and other commercial projects with loans secured by land and building materials. These short-term mortgage credits fall due when construction is completed, with permanent financing of the project then passing to insurance companies and other long-term lenders. However, there is a trend for banks to make longer-term commercial mortgage loans called *mini-perms* that extend financial support of a real estate project to the five- to seven-year range.

The growth of commercial mortgages has fluctuated in recent years. The dollar volume of such loans more than tripled during the 1970s. However, the market was buffeted by severe problems in the 1980s and early 1990s due to overbuilding of commercial space and weakening demand, although lower interest rates eventually stimulated a higher volume of commercial mortgage financing. By 1990, commercial mortgages had nearly tripled again from their 1980 level, but then these mortgages fell slightly in the mid-1990s, reflecting a more slowly growing economy and the availability of other sources of funding.

In the past, most commercial real estate financing was provided through fixed-rate mortgages. Faced with inflation and a volatile economy, however, commercial mortgage lenders began searching for new financial instruments to protect their return. Many mortgage lenders today combine both debt and equity financing in the same credit package. The best-known example is the *equity kicker,* where the lending institution grants a fixed-rate mortgage but also receives a share of any net earnings from the project. For example, a life insurance company may agree to provide $10 million to finance the construction of an office building. It agrees to accept a 15-year mortgage loan bearing a 12 percent interest rate. However, as a hedge against inflation and higher interest rates, the insurance company may also insist on receiving 10 percent of any net earnings generated from office rentals over the 15-year period.

Another device used recently in commercial mortgage financing is *indexing.* In this case, the annual interest rate on a loan may be tied to prevailing yields on high-quality government or public utility bonds. Lender and borrower may agree to renegotiate the interest rate at certain intervals; every three to five years is common. There is also a trend toward shorter maturity commercial mortgage loans — many as short as five years — with the borrower paying off the debt or refinancing the unpaid principal with the same or another lending institution.

One innovation that appeared in the commercial mortgage market in the early 1990s is *securitized commercial mortgages.* Private lenders and federal agencies (especially the thrift bailout agency, the Resolution Trust Company) began seeking ways to get rid of their overburdened loan portfolios by packaging large amounts of commercial real estate loans, taking them off the balance sheet, and placing them into trust accounts or with security dealers and issuing securities against the packaged loans. Sellers of these securities (led by such firms as Goldman Sachs and Prudential Insurance Company) frequently arrange guarantees from the security issuers, resulting in many of the commercial mortgage-backed securities being rated "investment grade," attracting major financial institutions as buyers. A significant proportion of the developing commercial mortgage security market involves packaging and selling distressed real estate loans at deep discounts, thus infusing badly needed capital into this market.

SUMMARY

The majority of funds drawn on by business firms to meet their working capital and investment needs come not from the financial markets but from inside the individual firm. In most years, more than half of business capital requirements are supplied by earnings and noncash depreciation expenses — internal cash flow. However, roughly a quarter to a half of business investment needs in recent years have been met by selling securities in the financial markets. The financial system is a backstop for the operations of business firms for those periods when internally generated cash fails to increase fast enough to support the growth of sales.

The financial markets provide both short-term working capital to meet current expenses and long-term funds to support the purchase of buildings and equipment. The principal external sources of working capital include trade credit (accounts payable), bank loans and acceptances, short-term credits from nonbank financial institutions (such as finance companies), and sales of commercial paper in the open market. For businesses in need of long-term funding, the principal funds sources are the sale of bonds and notes, term loans from banks, and the issuance of common and preferred stock and commercial mortgages, with open-market borrowing generally growing and bank borrowing declining in overall importance in recent years.

Corporate bonds have original maturities of more than five years; notes carry maturities of five years or less. There is a trend today toward shorter maturities of corporate securities due to inflation, rapid changes in technology, and huge government deficits that force corporations into intense competition for funds with the government. Indexing of corporate bond rates to broader movements in the economy has also become more common. A wide variety of different bond and note issues have been developed to provide investors with varying degrees of security and risk protection, including debentures, mortgage bonds, equipment trust certificates, convertible bonds, and industrial development bonds. Each type of bond is accompanied by an indenture spelling out the rights and obligations of borrowers and investors. Corporate notes and bonds are purchased by a wide range of investors today, but the dominant buyers are life insurance companies and pension funds.

New corporate bonds may be offered publicly in the open market, where competitive bidding takes place, or in a private sale to a limited group of investors. Public sales account for the largest portion of annual long-term borrowings, but the private market appeals to many smaller firms unable to tap the open market for funds and to companies with unique financing needs or lower credit ratings. Public sales offer the advantage of competition, as investment bankers bid against each other to underwrite a new security issue. The process of competitive bidding tends to result in higher security prices and lower interest costs to corporations in need of funds.

The corporate bond market has faced competition in recent years from both domestic and foreign commercial banks making long-term business loans. These *term loans* are generally used to purchase equipment. Most such loans carry floating interest rates tied to the prime lending rate — the interest rate on loans made to a bank's most creditworthy customers. Commercial banks also are a leading financial institution in extending mortgage loans to business firms. These loans support the construction of office buildings, shopping centers, and other commercial structures. Banks generally specialize in short-term mortgages that finance construction, and long-term commercial mortgage financing is provided mainly by insurance companies, savings banks, and pension funds. Bankers' overall role in providing credit to the business sector has been declining in recent years as more firms turn to the open market to sell bonds and notes in order to raise funds. Instead, banks have increasingly come to play a supporting role in guaranteeing and monitoring corporate debt. ■

KEY TERMS AND CONCEPTS IN THIS CHAPTER

corporate bond	industrial development bond (IDB)	investment banker
corporate note	zero coupon bonds	leveraged buyouts
indenture	public sale	base rate
debenture	private or direct placement	commercial mortgage
mortgage bonds		

STUDY QUESTIONS

1. Explain what is meant by the statement, "The financial markets are a supplemental funds source for business." What factors appear to affect the volume of business fund-raising from the money and capital markets?

2. Carefully define each of the following terms:

a.	Indenture	h.	Mortgage bond
b.	Trustee	i.	Collateral trust bond
c.	Term bond	j.	Income bond
d.	Call privilege	k.	Equipment trust certificate
e.	Sinking fund	l.	Convertible bond
f.	Debenture	m.	Industrial development bond
g.	Subordinated debenture	n.	Pollution control bond

3. Explain how the true cost of a corporate bond to the issuing company may be determined.

4. Who are the principal investors in corporate bonds and notes? Why?

5. Describe the role of investment bankers in the corporate bond market. What are the principal risks encountered by these firms? Discuss the factors that must be considered in pricing a new bond issue.

6. What is a *private placement*? Who buys privately placed bonds, and why? What are the principal advantages to the borrower in a private placement of securities?

7. What is a leveraged buyout? junk bond? What are the dangers associated with these practices?

8. Provide a definition for each of the following terms:

a.	Term loan	c.	Prime rate
b.	Floating rate	d.	Compensating balance

9. For what purposes are commercial mortgages issued? What changes have occurred recently in the terms on commercial mortgages? What is an *equity kicker*?

PROBLEMS

1. A corporation sells $5,000 par-value bonds at par in the open market, bearing an 8 percent coupon rate. Costs of marketing the issue, including dealer's commission, amounted to $200 per bond. If the bonds are due to mature in 15 years, what is their before-tax cost to the corporation? If the issuing company is in the 35 percent tax bracket, what is the bonds' after-tax cost to the firm?

2. A corporation borrows $5 million from a bank at a 12 percent prime rate. If the bank requires the company to hold 15 percent of the amount of the loan on deposit as a compensating balance, what is the effective rate of interest on the loan?

3. A bank quotes one of its corporate customers a loan at prime plus four percentage points when prime is 12 percent. Another bank, posting the same prime rate, quotes this same customer a loan at 1 1/4 times prime. Which loan would you recommend the corporation take? Suppose both loans carry floating rates. Prime increases to 16 percent. Which loan is the better deal? Which would be the better deal if prime rises to 18 percent? Explain what is happening.

SELECTED REFERENCES

Booth, James. "The Persistence of the Prime Rate." *FRBSF Weekly Letter,* No. 94–20. Federal Reserve Bank of San Francisco, May 20, 1994, pp. 1–3.

Carey, Mark S.; Stephen D. Prowse; and John D. Rea. "Recent Developments in the Market for Privately Placed Debt." *Federal Reserve Bulletin,* February 1993, pp. 77–92.

Chu, J. Franklin. "The Private Placement Market Comes of Age." *The Bankers Magazine,* September 1989, pp. 56–60.

Crabbe, Leland E.; Margaret H. Pickering; and Stephen D. Prowse. "Recent Developments in Corporate Finance." *Federal Reserve Bulletin,* August 1990, pp. 593–605.

Crabbe, Leland. *Corporate Medium-Term Notes.* Finance and Economics Discussion Series No. 162. Board of Governors of the Federal Reserve System, June 1991.

Chapter 27

Corporate Stock

LEARNING OBJECTIVES IN THIS CHAPTER

- To learn about the characteristics of common and preferred corporate stock.
- To understand how the stock market operates today and what its component parts are.
- To compare and contrast the roles and functions of the organized stock exchanges and the over-the-counter market.
- To explore the question of market efficiency and examine the evidence for and against the efficiency of the stock market.

In the preceding chapters, we focused exclusively on debt securities and the extension of credit. In this chapter, we examine a unique security that is not debt but *equity*. It is a certificate representing *ownership* of a corporation, a residual claim against both the assets and earnings of a business firm. Corporate stock grants the investor no promise of return as debt does but only the right to share in the firm's net assets and net earnings, if any.

Corporate stock is unique in one other important respect. All of the securities markets we have discussed to this point are intimately bound up with the process of moving funds from ultimate savers to ultimate borrowers in order to support investment and economic growth. In the stock market, however, the bulk of trading activity involves the buying and selling of securities already issued rather than the exchange of financial claims for new capital. Thus, trading in the stock market, for the most part, is *not* closely linked to the saving and investment process in the economy unless *new* stock is involved.

A small portion of trading in corporate shares does involve the sale of *new* stock to support business investment. And that portion of the global stock market devoted to new stock issues is growing rapidly — today in nearly every nation around the world stock is replacing other ways of raising business capital. Moreover, the stock market continues to have a highly significant impact on the *expectations* of businesses when planning future investment and households when planning future consumption. Therefore, stock trading indirectly affects employment, growth, and the general health of the economy.[1] In this

---

[1] One broad index of stock market prices — Standard & Poor's Composite Index — is considered to be a *leading indicator* of subsequent changes in economic conditions, especially of future developments in industrial production, employment, and total spending (GDP). Thus, the stock market often turns in its greatest gains in the deepest

chapter, we take a close look at the basic characteristics of corporate stock and the markets where that stock is traded.

CHARACTERISTICS OF CORPORATE STOCK

All corporate stock represents an ownership interest in a corporation, conferring on the holder a number of important rights as well as risks. In this section, we examine the two types of corporate stock issued today: common and preferred shares.

Common Stock

The most important form of corporate stock is **common stock.** Like all forms of equity, common stock represents a *residual* claim against the assets of the issuing firm, entitling the owner to share in the net earnings of the firm when it is profitable and to share in the net market value (after all debts are paid) of the company's assets if it is liquidated. By owning common stock, the investor is subject to the full risks of ownership, which means that the business may fail or its earnings may fall to unacceptable levels. However, the risks of equity ownership are limited, because the stockholder is liable only for the amount of his or her investment.

If a corporation with outstanding shares of common stock is liquidated, the debts of the firm must be paid first from any assets available. The preferred stockholders then receive their share of any remaining funds. Whatever is left accrues to common stockholders on a *pro rata* basis. Unlike many debt securities, common stock is generally a registered instrument, with the holder's name recorded on the issuing company's books.

The volume of stock a corporation may issue is limited by the terms of its charter of incorporation. Additional shares beyond those authorized by the company's charter may be issued only by amending the charter with the approval of the current stockholders. Some companies have issued large amounts of corporate shares, reflecting not only their need for large amounts of equity capital but also a desire to broaden their ownership base. For example, American Telephone and Telegraph (AT&T) has more than 700 million shares of common stock listed on the New York Stock Exchange.

The *par value* of common stock is an arbitrarily assigned value printed on each stock certificate. Par is usually set low relative to the stock's current market value. In fact, some stock is issued without par value. Originally, par was supposed to represent the owner's initial investment per share in the firm. The only real significance of par today is that the firm cannot pay any dividends to stockholders that would reduce the company's net worth per share below the par value of its stock.

Common stockholders are granted a number of rights when they buy a share of equity in a business corporation. Stock ownership permits them to elect the company's board of directors, which, in turn, chooses the officers responsible for day-to-day management of the firm. Common shareholders have a *preemptive right* (unless specifically denied by the firm's charter), which gives current shareholders the right to purchase any new voting stock, convertible bonds, or preferred stock issued by the firm in order to maintain a *pro rata* share of ownership. For example, if a stockholder holds 5 percent of all shares

---

part of a recession and turns down before a boom is over. The stock market seems to provide a forecast of business capital spending plans, perhaps reflecting the fact that it captures the expectations of the business community.

outstanding and 500 new shares are issued, this stockholder has the right to subscribe to 25 new shares.

Although most common stock grants each stockholder one vote per share, nonvoting common is also issued occasionally. Some companies issue class A common, which has voting rights, and Class B common, with a prior claim on earnings but no voting power. The major stock exchanges do not encourage publicly held firms to issue classified stock, but classified shares are used extensively by privately held firms.

A right granted to all common stockholders is the right of access to the minutes of stockholder meetings and to lists of existing shareholders. This gives the stockholders some power to reorganize the company if management or the board of directors is performing poorly. Common stockholders may vote on all matters that affect the firm's property as a whole, such as a merger, liquidation, or the issuance of additional equity shares.

Preferred Stock

The other major form of stock issued today is **preferred stock.** Preferred carries a stated annual dividend expressed as a percent of the stock's par value. For example, if preferred shares carry a $100 par value with an 8 percent dividend rate, then each preferred shareholder is entitled to dividends of $8 per year on each share owned, provided the company declares a dividend. Common stockholders receive whatever dividends remain after the preferred shareholders receive their stated annual dividend.

Preferred stock occupies the middle ground between debt and equity securities, including advantages and disadvantages of both forms of raising long-term funds. Preferred stockholders have a prior claim over the firm's assets and earnings relative to the claims of common stockholders. However, bondholders and other creditors must be paid before either preferred or common stockholders. Unlike creditors of the firm, preferred stockholders cannot press for bankruptcy proceedings against a company that fails to pay them dividends. Nevertheless, preferred stock is part of a firm's equity capital and strengthens a firm's net worth, allowing it to issue more debt in the future. It also is a more flexible financing arrangement than debt because dividends may be passed if earnings are inadequate; for most preferred shares (except limited-life preferred), there is no maturity date when the securities must be retired.

Generally, preferred stockholders have no voice or vote in the selection of management unless the corporation fails to pay dividends for a stipulated period. A frequent provision in corporate charters gives preferred stockholders the right to elect some members of the board of directors if dividends are passed for a full year. Dividends on preferred stock, like those paid on common stock, are *not* a tax-deductible expense. This makes preferred shares more expensive to issue than debt for companies in the top income bracket. However, IRS regulations specify that 70 percent of the stock dividends received by corporations from unaffiliated companies are tax deductible. This deductibility feature makes preferred stock especially attractive to companies seeking to acquire ownership shares in other firms and sometimes allows preferred shares to be issued at a lower net interest cost than debt securities. In fact, corporations themselves are the principal buyers of preferred stock.

Most preferred stock is *cumulative,* which means that the passing of dividends results in an arrearage that must be paid in full before the common stockholders receive anything. A few preferred shares are *participating,* allowing the holder to share in the residual earnings normally accruing entirely to common stockholders. To illustrate how the participating feature might work, assume that an investor holds 8 percent participating preferred stock with a $100 par value. After the issuing company's board of directors votes to pay the stated annual dividend of $8 per share, the board also declares a $20 per share common stock dividend. If the formula for dividend participation calls for common and preferred shareholders to share *equally* in any net earnings, then each preferred shareholder will earn an additional $12 to bring its total dividend to $20 per share as well. Not all participating formulas are this generous, and most preferred issues are *nonparticipating,* because participation is detrimental to the interests of common stockholders.

Most corporations plan to retire their preferred stock, even though it carries no stated maturity. In fact, the bulk of preferred shares usually has call provisions. When interest rates decline, the issuing company may exercise the call privilege at the price stated in the formal agreement between the firm and its shareholders. A few preferred issues are *convertible* into shares of common stock at the investor's option. The company retires all converted preferred shares and may force conversion by simply exercising the stock's call privilege. New preferred issues are often accompanied by a sinking fund provision, whereby funds are gradually accumulated for eventual retirement of preferred shares. A trustee is appointed to collect sinking fund payments from the company and periodically to call in preferred shares or to purchase them in the open market. Although sinking fund provisions allow the issuing firm to sell preferred stock with lower dividend rates, payments into the fund drain earnings and reduce dividend payments to common stockholders.

During the 1980s and 1990s, corporations developed new types of *variable-rate preferred stock,* carrying a floating dividend rate that makes the stock a substitute for short-term debt. Many variable-rate preferred issues allow their dividend rate to be reset several times during the year, which may be accomplished by a marketing agent or via a special auction. Some companies have issued *Dutch-auction* preferred shares, a process by which stock buyers submit bids and the highest-priced bid becomes the price paid by all winning bidders. Frequently, the dividend rate has a ceiling rate based on a key market reference rate (such as the yield on commercial paper). Many preferred shares issued over the past decade have had an exchange option attached, giving the issuing company the choice of exchanging the preferred stock for debt securities. Recently another hybrid form of preferred stock appeared called "MIPS" (monthly income preferred shares) which are counted as equity but carry tax-deductible interest payments like debt.

From the standpoint of the investor, preferred stock represents an intermediate investment between bonds and common stock. Preferred shares often provide more income than bonds but also greater risk. Preferred prices fluctuate more widely than bond prices for the same change in interest rates. Compared to common stock, preferred shares generally provide less income but are, in turn, less risky.

STOCK MARKET INVESTORS

Corporate stock is one of the most widely held financial assets in the world. Only one other financial asset — government securities — is held by as large and diverse a group of individuals and institutions as are common and preferred stock. One important source of information on stockholders in the United States is the Federal Reserve Board's Flow of Funds Accounts.[2] Exhibit 27–1 gives the names of major investor groups and their total holdings of common and preferred stock for the years 1970, 1980, 1990, and 1995.

---

[2]See Chapter 3 for an explanation of the method of construction and types of information presented in the Flow of Funds Accounts.

Exhibit 27–1   **Key Investors Buying Corporate Stock in the United States**
(\$ Billions at Year-End; Market Values)

Groups of Investors	1970 Amount	1970 Percent of Total	1980 Amount	1980 Percent of Total	1990 Amount	1990 Percent of Total	1995* Amount	1995* Percent of Total
Households (individuals and families)	\$728	80.3%	\$1,165	71.3%	\$2,008	57.3%	\$3,714	50.2%
Rest of the world	27	3.0	63	3.9	228	6.5	339	4.6
Commercial banks	†	—	†	—	2	0.1	8	0.1
Savings banks	3	0.3	4	0.3	9	0.3	13	0.2
Life insurers	15	1.7	47	2.9	107	3.0	153	2.1
Property-casualty insurers	13	1.5	32	2.0	85	2.4	125	1.7
Pension funds:								
Private	68	7.5	231	14.1	537	15.3	1,209	16.4
Government	10	1.1	44	2.7	296	8.4	608	8.2
Investment-companies (mutual funds)	40	4.4	42	2.6	224	6.4	965	13.1
Security brokers and dealers	2	0.2	3	0.2	9	0.3	24	0.3
Other investors	1	0.1	2	0.1	1	0.1	235	3.2
	\$907	100.0%	\$1,633	100.0%	\$3,506	100.0%	\$7,393	100.0%

Note: Columns may not add to totals due to rounding.
*Figures are for second quarter 1995.
†Less than \$1 billion

Source: Flow of Funds Accounts, compiled quarterly by the Board of Governors of the Federal Reserve System.

Exhibit 27–1 makes clear that *households* — individuals and families — are the dominant holders of corporate stock in the United States. In 1995, for example, households held just over half of all corporate shares outstanding. Pension funds — both private and government — were a distant second, holding almost 25 percent of available shares. Mutual funds ranked third with about 13 percent of all stock holdings. Mutual funds — traditional institutional stock buyers on behalf of their customers — dramatically added to their stock holdings as a rising market in 1995 and early 1996 captured the interest of scores of individual investors. Mutual funds have been especially attractive to middle-income investors who cannot afford to buy a large number of shares and who seek the safety of professional securities management and diversification across many different stock issues that most mutual funds provide. Foreign investors ranked fourth, with about 5 percent of the total. The deposit-type financial intermediaries — commercial and savings banks — collectively held less than 1 percent of the total. State and federal laws severely limit savings bank investment in corporate stock and prohibit U.S. commercial banks themselves from purchasing or underwriting most corporate stock.

CHARACTERISTICS OF THE CORPORATE STOCK MARKET

There are two main branches of the market for trading corporate shares. One is the **organized exchanges,** which in the United States include the New York (NYSE) and American (AMEX) exchanges plus regional exchanges, including the Pacific (PSE), Midwest (MSE), Philadelphia (PHLX), Boston (BSE), and Cincinnati (CSE) exchanges. The regional exchanges historically have served to promote trading in securities of interest to investors in

Exhibit 27–2   **Leading Stock Exchanges around the World**

New York Stock Exchange	Amsterdam Exchange
American Stock Exchange	Stockholm Exchange
Tokyo Exchange	Brussels Exchange
Osaka Exchange	Sydney Exchange
London Exchange	Hong Kong Exchange
Frankfurt Exchange	Singapore Exchange
Zurich Exchange	Johannesburg Exchange
Paris Exchange	Taipei Exchange
Manila Exchange	Toronto Exchange
Milan Exchange	Wellington Exchange

their particular region of the nation. Today, however, the regional exchanges have penetrated the national market and rely to a significant degree on transactions in securities listed on both AMEX and the NYSE. The regional exchanges and the Chicago futures exchanges have captured a growing proportion of securities formerly traded on the Big Board — the New York Stock Exchange. Overseas, the Tokyo, Hong Kong, Singapore, Sydney, Frankfurt, Brussels, Paris, and London exchanges have also grown in importance as major centers for trading corporate shares worldwide, propelled in part by the privatization of many state-owned businesses and massive stock investments by U.S. investors abroad, which now exceed $7 trillion. All the exchanges around the globe (the most important of which are listed in Exhibit 27–2) use similar procedures for controlling membership and regulating purchases and sales.

Trading on the exchanges is governed by regulations and formal procedures designed to ensure competitive pricing and an active market for the stock of the largest, most financially stable companies. In contrast, the second branch of the equities market — the **over-the-counter (OTC) market** — involves trading of stock through brokers operating off the major exchanges. This "over the telephone" market is more informal and fluid than exchange trading and includes the stocks and bonds of smaller companies and of financial institutions.

The Major Organized Exchanges

American Exchanges. Among the best known organized exchanges are the Big Board — the New York Stock Exchange — and the American Stock Exchange (ASE or AMEX). The NYSE, AMEX, and the regional exchanges overlap in trading and function and are competitive markets for the most actively traded U.S. stocks. For example, about three quarters of the volume of trading on the regional exchanges is in stocks listed on the New York Stock Exchange. Thanks to an Intermarket Trading System, stock brokers and specialists on one exchange may contact traders on other exchanges to find the best prices for their customers.

Each exchange provides a physical location for trading, and trading by member firms must be carried on at that location. On the floor of the NYSE, for example, there are several counters, each containing windows, or *trading posts*. A handful of the more than 1,500 common stocks listed on the NYSE are traded from each post via the auction method as prescribed by the Exchange's Board of Governors. The exchanges permit the enforcement of formal trading rules in order to achieve an efficient and speedy allocation of equity shares.

To be eligible for trading on an organized exchange, the stock must by issued by a firm *listed* with the exchange. A substantial number of major U.S. corporations are listed on several different exchanges. The listing qualifications demanded by the New York Stock Exchange are the most comprehensive, which serves to limit NYSE trading to stocks issued by the largest companies. The basic intent of these listing rules is to ensure that the listed company has sufficient shares available to create an active market for its stock and discloses sufficient data so that investors can make informed decisions.

Even if a company meets all listing requirements, its stock must still be approved for admission by the NYSE board of directors, which includes 10 members elected by firms with seats on the exchange. Corporations that are successful in listing their stock must make an annual disclosure of their financial condition, limit trading by insiders, publish quarterly earnings reports, and help maintain an active public market for their shares. If trading interest in a particular firm's stock falls off significantly, the firm may be *delisted*. Under some circumstances, a firm may be granted "unlisted trading privileges" if its stock has been listed on another exchange. Recently, foreign firms have been admitted in large numbers to most major exchanges. For example, by 1995, the NYSE traded the securities of more than 240 firms from 40 different countries. Foreign companies with more than $5 million in assets and at least 500 shareholders whose stock is traded in the U.S. must register with the Securities and Exchange Commission, unless specifically exempted.

One of the most important advantages claimed for listing on an exchange is that it improves the *liquidity* of a corporation's stock. A relatively large volume of shares can be sold without significantly depressing the price. This feature is of special concern to large institutional investors (such as pension funds) that have come to dominate daily trading in the equities market, because these institutions trade in large blocks rather than a few shares at a time. Allegedly, a corporation can improve the market for its stock by becoming listed on a securities exchange.

Member firms of the exchange are the only ones that may trade listed securities on the exchange floor, either for their own account or for their customers. Most members own "seats" on the exchange and hold claims against the exchange's net assets. The majority of seat owners are directors or partners of brokerage firms. Member firms are allowed to sell or lease their seats with the approval of the exchange's governing board.

Member firms fulfill a wide variety of roles on an exchange. Some act as *floor traders* that buy and sell only for their own account. Floor traders are really speculators whose portfolios turn over rapidly as they drift from post to post on the exchange floor looking for profitable trading opportunities. Other members serve as *commission brokers,* employed by member brokerage firms to represent the orders of their customers, or *floor brokers,* who are usually individual entrepreneurs carrying out buy and sell orders from other brokers not present on the exchange floor. *Floor reporters* record and report transactions.

Some traders holding exchange seats are *specialists* who oversee trading in each stock. The specialist firms operating on the New York Stock Exchange act as *both* brokers and dealers, buying and selling for other brokers and for themselves when there is an imbalance between supply and demand for the stocks in which they specialize. For example, when sell orders pile up for the stocks for which a specialist firm is responsible, it moves in to buy some of the offered shares, creating a market and providing liquidity on demand by trading for their own account. Specialists help to create orderly and continuous markets and stabilize prices by agreeing to cover unfilled customer orders and by posting firm bid and ask prices to interested investors. Finally, a few *odd-lot traders,* representing large brokerage firms dealing with the public, also are active on the exchange floor. Odd lots are buy or sell orders involving fewer than 100 shares that come primarily from small individual investors. The odd-lot trader purchases 100 or more shares — a *round lot* — and retains any extra shares not needed by customers in his or her portfolio.

Japanese Exchanges. Japan has stock exchanges located in eight different cities, which lie at the heart of one of the world's largest securities markets. By far the largest Japanese exchange is the Tokyo Stock Exchange (TSE), which operates in two different sections. The First Section offers exchange services for shares of the largest corporations; the Second Section deals in the shares of smaller corporations. Most investors follow changes in Japanese stock prices by consulting the Nikkei Index, which tracks the average unweighted price of 225 shares traded each day in the TSE's First Section. A broader Japanese stock price indicator is the TOPIX, which reflects the current prices of all large-company (First Section) stocks traded on the Tokyo Exchange compared to the value of those same shares in 1968. It resembles the Standard & Poor's 500 stock index in the United States in the breadth of its coverage and the method by which the index is calculated. Rivaling the growth of the Tokyo exchange has been another exchange in Osaka, about 250 miles southwest of Tokyo. Osaka trades individual shares and recently has experienced growth in its trading of futures contracts linked to the Nikkei index of 225 stocks.

Contributions of Exchanges. Stock exchanges are among the oldest financial institutions. The New York Stock Exchange, for example, was set up following an agreement among 24 Wall Street brokers in May 1792. Stock exchanges were opened in Tokyo and Osaka, Japan, in 1878. Exchanges provide a continuous market centered in an established location with rigid rules to ensure fairness in trading. By bringing together buyers and sellers, the exchanges make stock a liquid investment, promote efficient pricing of securities, and make possible the placement of huge amounts of financial capital.

The Informal Over-the-Counter Market

The large majority of securities bought and sold around the globe are traded over-the-counter (OTC), not on organized exchanges. The customer places a buy or sell order with a broker or dealer that is relayed via telephone, wire, or computer terminal to the dealer or broker with securities to sell or an order to buy. In this system of electronically linked market-makers, brokers or dealers seek the best possible price, and the resulting competition to find the best deal brings together traders located hundreds or thousands of miles apart. The prices of actively traded securities respond almost instantly to the changing forces of demand and supply, so that security prices constantly hover at or near competitive, market-determined levels.

Many dealers in the OTC market act as *principals* instead of brokers as on the organized exchanges. That is, they take "positions of risk" by buying securities outright for their own portfolios as well as for customers. Several dealers handle the same stock so that customers can shop around. All prices are determined by negotiation with dealers acquiring securities at *bid* prices and selling them at *asked* prices. The U.S. OTC market is regulated by a code of ethics established by the National Association of Security Dealers (NASD), a private organization that encourages ethical behavior among its members. Traders who break NASD's regulations may be fined, suspended, or thrown out of the organization.

One of the most important contributions of NASD has been the development of NASDAQ (the National Association of Security Dealers Automated Quotations system). NASDAQ displays bid and asked prices for securities on video screens connected to a central computer system. All member firms report their bid-ask price quotations immediately to NASDAQ, permitting dealers and customers to determine instantly the terms currently offered on each share of stock.

THE THIRD MARKET: TRADING IN LISTED SECURITIES OFF THE EXCHANGE

The market for securities listed on a stock exchange but traded over the counter is known as the **third market.** Broker and dealer firms not members of an organized exchange are active in this market, which in the United States deals mainly in NYSE-listed stocks. The original purpose of the third market was to supply large blocks of shares to institutional investors. These investors engage mainly in *block trades,* defined as transactions involving 1,000 shares or more. Presumably, block traders possess the technical know-how to make informed investment decisions and then carry out transactions without assistance from a stock exchange and the high brokerage commissions that may entail. By trading with third-market broker and dealer firms, who, in effect, compete directly with specialists on the exchanges, a large institutional investor frequently can lower transactions costs and trade securities faster.

The third market provides additional competition for the organized exchanges. Moreover, the third market has been a catalyst in reducing brokerage fees and promoting trading efficiency, stimulating the unbundling of commissions at many U.S. broker and dealer firms, in order to more accurately reflect the true cost of each security trade. Many brokerage firms offer customers an array of peripheral services, such as research on market trends, security credit, and accounting for purchases and sales; often the customer pays for these services whether he or she uses them. The largest institutional investors have little need for such services, however, and they seek brokers and dealers offering their services at minimum cost. Recently, numerous "discount" brokerage houses have appeared, and commissions charged institutional investors have dropped substantially, leading some institutional customers to abandon the third market and return to more traditional channels for executing their security orders.

THE MARKET FOR STOCK OPTIONS

Paralleling the exchange and over-the-counter markets for stock is a market for *stock options.* As we saw in Chapter 13, an option is an agreement between two parties granting one party the right (but not the obligation) to purchase an asset from or sell an asset to the other party at a set price. The price of an option is known as the *option premium* — the cost to the option buyer of insuring against an adverse change in the price of a stock. In the stock market, both *call* and *put* options are sold, each designed to manage the risk of fluctuating security prices.

Call Options

A **call option** on stock grants the buyer the right to purchase ("call away") a specified number of shares of a given stock at a specified price up to an expiration date. Call options become attractive when the investor expects the price of a given stock to rise above the price specified in the option contract (known as the *strike price*). Thus, an option may be available to buy 500 shares of the common stock of Caledonia Manufacturing Company at $6 per share. If the stock rises to a price of $7.50 in the open market, the holder of the option can buy $3,750 worth of stock for only $3,000. Even if the option buyer does not wish to hold the stock, he or she can resell it in the open market for a short-term gain.

Another advantage of options is the financial *leverage* they grant the investor. Less money is required to control a specified number of equity shares than would be necessary if the stock were purchased outright. However, the risk of loss is greater with options. Even small changes in the price of a stock can lead to magnified changes in the value of an option.

In 1973, the Chicago Board Options Exchange initiated trading in options for selected stocks listed on the major exchanges. Today, *listed,* or exchange-traded, options are popular, along with over-the-counter or negotiated options purchased through brokers and dealers. Current holders of listed options are recorded on computerized records maintained by the Options Clearing Corporation.

Puts

The opposite of a call option is known as a **put option.** Puts grant the investor the right to *sell* a specified number of equity shares at a set price on or before the expiration date. Unlike a call, the investor in puts hopes the associated stock will *decline* in price so that he or she can sell at a price higher than currently available in the market. In this sense, puts are similar to selling a stock *short* (the sale of borrowed stock) in the hope that its price will fall. However, puts require less capital and usually result in a lower total brokerage commission than short sales of stock. Also, the investor's potential loss is limited to the price of the put plus brokerage commission, regardless of what happens to the price of the underlying stock. Like calls, puts are traded both over the counter and on organized exchanges.

Straddles

Some investors combine put and call options to establish a *straddle* on a given stock. A straddle is a combination trade in which the investor purchases a put and a call on the same stock, both carrying the same exercise price and maturing on the same date. For example, suppose the stock of Caledonia Manufacturing is selling for $7.50, but the market is so volatile that the investor is highly uncertain as to its future direction. To protect against an unexpected move, the investor buys a call option with a strike price of $8 and an $8 put option, each costing $1. Profits will be made if either the call or the put increase in value by more than $2. A rise in the market value of Caledonia's stock will cause the call option to rise in value; a fall in the stock's price will cause the put's value to increase. Sometimes, if the market fluctuates violently, *both* the put and call options will turn out to be profitable, although usually one or the other will expire without being used.

The Growth of Options Markets

Until 1982, only options for common stock were traded in organized markets. However, beginning in 1982, new options markets appeared for *stock indexes* (such as the S&P 500, the Amex Market Value Index, the Value Line Composite Index, and the New York Stock Exchange Composite Index) and for futures contracts for the S&P 500 and NYSE Composite Stock Index. Stock index options are based on a basket (collection) of common stocks that are thought to be representative of the whole market. The purpose of a stock index option is to permit investors to bet on which way the stock market as a whole is likely to go, while allowing risk-averse investors to protect against an adverse movement in the whole market. Options allow a risk-averse investor to shift market risk to someone else willing to bear that risk and hoping to profit from risk taking.

The Rise of Program Trading: Portfolio Insurance and Stock Index Arbitraging

Many analysts believe that stock markets worldwide have become more volatile due to the widespread use of computerized **program trading.** This computer-assisted investment decision-making strategy represents an attempt to shield a security investor against loss from changing prices and interest rates by making continuous changes in an investor's holdings as the relative prices between two or more financial instruments change.

There are several types of program trading today. One of the simplest types involves buying and selling stock index futures contracts. The most popular such contract is the Standard & Poor's 500 stock index contract, bought and sold on the Chicago Mercantile Exchange (CME). A buyer of this futures contract (who takes a long position in futures) promises to take delivery of the cash value of the S&P 500 index when the futures contract expires unless he or she cancels out the contract before it expires by selling a similar contract. Similarly, a seller of the S&P 500 index contract (who takes a *short* position in futures) promises to pay the contract buyer the cash value of the S&P index when the futures contract runs out. However, the contract seller can also cancel out his or her obligation by simply buying a similar contract. The clearinghouse at the futures exchange will simply "zero out" the sell and buy orders from the same trader, freeing him or her from the obligation to deliver or accept payment.

How can these futures contracts be used to protect against stock price declines? The investor could *sell* stock index futures contracts that will expire on the date he or she plans to sell the stock holdings. If stock prices decline, the loss on any shares held will be offset by a gain on the stock index futures because, in a falling market, those contracts can be bought back to "zero out" the futures position at a lower price than their original purchase price. Unfortunately, the use of pure stock index futures as just described limits profits as well as losses. For example, if stock prices rise rather than fall, the investor will suffer a loss on his or her futures position that reduces any profits earned on the stock itself.

An investor can preserve the profit potential on stock while still hedging against loss by using a *put option contract* on a stock index, such as the S&P 500 stock index. Under this arrangement, the buyer of a put option gains the right (but not the obligation) to *sell* units of the S&P stock index contract at a set price on the date the option contract expires. If stock prices fall below the strike price spelled out in the option contract, the put option goes up in value, offsetting the loss on the stock itself. However, if the stock itself goes up in value, the option contract will not be exercised and the investor will pocket a capital gain on selling the stock, minus only the small price paid for the put option. In this case, paying the price of the put option is equivalent to buying an insurance policy against declining stock prices. In essence, portfolio insurance of the type just described gives an investor protection against security price declines, with some reduction in potential gain.

More complicated portfolio insurance strategies are in use today employing so-called replicating or synthetic security portfolios. These portfolios are built using portfolio insurance techniques — that is, *dynamic hedging* strategies that continuously adjust an investor's holdings to limit exposure to adverse market developments. Dynamic hedging programs attempt to take into account the current prices of stock, options, and futures, options and futures expiration dates, interest rates, and the apparent volatility of stock prices. Replicating portfolios may consist of a basket of stocks that represent a major stock index (such as the S&P 500 stock index), index futures contracts, Treasury bills, or other financial instruments. If stock prices begin to fall, a common strategy is to sell off some stocks and move into other financial instruments that are safer, such as Treasury bills or stock index futures contracts. If the selloff of stocks makes them appear to be underpriced, stocks may then be purchased until once again all financial asset prices are aligned and there is no further reason for arbitrageurs to move funds from one market to another. Program trading systems, including portfolio insurance techniques, generally work well at limiting an investor's exposure to risk except in periods when stock prices change very rapidly, as in the great crash of October 19, 1987, or when trading is not smooth and continuous.

THE DEVELOPMENT OF A UNIFIED INTERNATIONAL MARKET FOR STOCK

The National Market System. It is clear from the foregoing discussion that the stock market is fractured into several different parts, each with its own unique collection of brokers and dealers and, in some cases, its own unique collection of customers. However, one of the most significant developments during the 1970s and 1980s was a movement to weld all parts of the equities market together into a single market for all traders. In 1975, the U.S. Congress passed the Securities Act Amendments, which instructed the Securities and Exchange Commission — the federal government's chief regulatory agency for the capital markets — to "facilitate the establishment of a national market system for securities" in order to further the development of widespread trading in equities and bring competition to stock trading, rather than confining such trading to the floor of an exchange.

Although the 1975 amendments did not specify what the proposed *national market system* would look like, the intent of Congress was to ensure that all investors would have ready access to information on security prices and transact business at the best available price. Moreover, with greater mobility of funds from one exchange to another or between the exchanges and the over-the-counter market, the resulting increase in competition in stock trading might reduce the cost to corporations of raising new capital.

After the Securities Act Amendments became law, the New York Stock Exchange announced that it would begin reporting daily trades of NYSE-listed stocks as they occurred on the exchanges. This meant that up-to-the-minute information on the latest stock trades would be reported on a *consolidated,* or *composite, tape,* available through stock ticker machines, regardless of which exchange handled the transaction. Although the invention of the consolidated tape was an important step in developing a national and, ultimately, international market system, it provided investors only with an indication of current trends in the market. No information was provided on the best bid and asked prices available. The Securities and Exchange Commission responded to this need by asking each U.S. stock exchange to make its quotations available to brokers and dealers everywhere.

The first major step in that direction occurred in April 1978 with the development of the Intermarket Trading System (ITS). Brokers and specialists could compare bid and ask prices on all the major U.S. exchanges for about 700 different stocks through a central computer system. In effect, ITS brought major U.S. equities markets into direct price competition with one another for trades in the most popular corporate stocks. Aiding the unified market's spread was a decision by the Securities and Exchange Commission, issued as Rule 19c-3. This rule states that new stock can be traded off the exchange by exchange member firms. Previously, a broker or securities dealer with membership on a particular exchange could not trade listed stocks anywhere but on the floor of that exchange. This SEC decision brought the U.S. exchanges and OTC market into direct competition for the trading of *new* stock.

The Great Stock Market Crash and Circuit Breakers

On October 19, 1987, the Dow Jones Industrial Average of stock values for 30 leading U.S. companies dropped by 508 points — the greatest one-day stock price fall in the history of the United States. The market's sudden "free fall" spread rapidly throughout the world as stock prices in Western Europe, Japan, and at other exchanges around the Pacific Rim tumbled, demonstrating how intimately tied together securities markets around the globe have become.

In order to head off future market crashes, a number of would-be "remedies" have been set in place. The most highly publicized of these are the so-called **circuit breakers.** These devices halt or slow trading during those periods when stock prices suddenly drop. In 1988, the New York Stock Exchange, in cooperation with the Chicago Mercantile Exchange, set up a device called the *sidecar.* If the Dow Jones Industrial Average declined by nearly 100 points during any trading day, all computer-driven trading orders involving stocks were to be shunted off the main market into a holding file and away from the New York Stock Exchange's DOT Trading System, which speedily executes buy and sell orders. Program-inspired traders must then post their orders manually, drastically slowing the pace of computer-driven trading orders and giving small investors a higher priority.

Later, during the summer of 1990, a market "collar" was installed, which requires coordinated stock and stock index futures program trading to move in the direction of stabilizing the market when the Dow Jones Industrial Average rises or falls by more than 50 points from its closing average the preceding day. A third circuit breaker calls for an exchange trading halt when the Industrial Average falls by 250 points and another halt if stocks, on average, fall an additional 150 points when trading is resumed. The Chicago Mercantile Exchange (CME) also imposed a daily price limit on trading financial futures of 15 index points (about a 7 percent price movement in futures) after which trading is temporarily halted. The basic idea of these circuit breakers is to prevent panic selling that can gather momentum like an avalanche, dragging all stock prices down with it.

Unfortunately, when trading is halted using circuit breakers, the *liquidity* of investors' stock holdings virtually disappears unless buyers can be found off the major exchanges in the over-the-counter market. When circuit breakers are tripped, investors may not be able to sell their shares even if they desperately need the cash. Equally important, circuit breakers could make financial markets even *more* volatile, accelerating trading whenever stock prices begin to fall. The reason is that panicky investors may rush to sell their stock out of fear that a circuit breaker will be invoked and they won't be able to sell their shares later. Indeed, a recent study by Lee, Ready, and Seguin (1993) finds that trading halts increase, rather than reduce, both volume and volatility.

It is not at all clear that shutting down a market for a brief period really prevents market crashes. For example, in the midst of the worldwide stock price tumble of 1987, several Pacific area exchanges halted trading for brief intervals and stock prices merely resumed their decline after these markets reopened. When trading is *simultaneously* halted in stock and financial futures markets, many investors have no efficient substitute for protecting themselves against interest rate risk.

(continued)

On the other hand, the tripping of circuit breakers on the stock exchange will not necessarily trigger the breakers on financial futures exchanges. The result may be that investors will rush to those markets that are still open and set off a massive selling wave there as well. Moreover, in a world with alternative trading channels for stocks and bonds, the unilateral imposition of circuit breakers and other restrictive regulations in any one nation will encourage security traders to shift their business elsewhere. Technological innovation today makes security trading possible anywhere around the globe for those traders determined to achieve their financial objectives.

Suggested references: See especially the U.S. Presidential Task Force on Market Mechanisms (1988) in the references at the end of this chapter and Charles M. C. Lee, Mark J. Ready, and Paul J. Seguin, "Volume, Volatility, and NYSE Trading Halts," Working Paper No. 93–16, Mitsui Life Financial Research Center, The University of Michigan, May 18, 1993.

NASD and Automated Price Quotations. In 1979 and 1980, the National Association of Security Dealers (NASD) moved to promote an even broader market system by further automating price quotations on over-the-counter stock. Computer terminals with expanded capacity were set up to include a wide array of information on bid and asked prices offered by traders who may be hundreds or thousands of miles apart. At the same time, NASD and representatives of the ITS moved to link quotations and trading on the six major U.S. exchanges electronically with OTC quotations and trading through NASD's automated price quotation system (NASDAQ).

In February 1980, the Securities and Exchange Commission adopted new regulations aimed at improving the flow of stock price information to brokers and investors. Previously, the NASDAQ system for securities traded over the counter had carried only "representative" bid and asked prices. Effective in 1980, however, NASDAQ was required to display on its terminals the highest bid prices and the lowest asked prices present in the market. The new rule aided investors in determining what price brokers were actually paying to execute a customer purchase order or what the true sales price is when the customer places his or her shares on the market. In theory, at least, the rule promoted competition among OTC brokers and made it easier for customers to negotiate low commission rates. Another SEC rule, which took effect in October 1980, required that the consolidated tape carrying price quotations for stock listed on the major exchanges always include the *best* price available on *any* stock, regardless of which exchange is quoting that price.

In 1982, NASD set up the National Market System to shuttle information to investors immediately on completion of stock sales. Nine years later, NASD set in motion a program for automated settlement of security trades, called the System of Automated Linkages for Private Offerings, Resales, and Trading (PORTAL). This new system has made possible purchases and sales of both unregistered domestic and foreign bonds and stocks. NASD's automated security price quotation system has also set up computer telephone connections with the International Stock Exchange and the Singapore Stock Exchange, cross-listing and executing trades among a growing list of foreign securities. For example, a New York or London trader can instruct his Tokyo office to track share prices while his home office is closed, and if stock prices reach a designated level, the overseas office will trade the securities involved according to guidelines received from the home office.

The Advent of Shelf Registration. The trend toward deregulation of the U.S. financial sector began to exert its effects on stock purchases and sales in the 1980s. On March 5, 1982, the SEC put Rule 415 — the Shelf Registration Rule — into operation. This allowed many large firms selling *new* corporate stocks and bonds to register an issue with the SEC and then sell securities from the issue at any time during the next two years. *Shelf registration* substantially reduced the cost of offering new stocks and bonds and gave offering companies greater flexibility in selecting when to enter the financial marketplace to sell new securities. Shelf registration increased competition in the underwriting of new security issues, reducing the cost of preparing and marketing new stocks and bonds.

Global Trading in Equities. These developments in the United States leading toward a unified national market for corporate stock were joined in the 1980s by movement toward a true international equities market in which the sun will never set on purchases and sales of stock. The trading of both U.S. corporate stock and shares of foreign companies on exchanges in Hong Kong, Singapore, Tokyo, and Sydney soon began to rival exchange trading in the United States and Western Europe. Satellite, cable, and wire communications networks now girdle the globe, allowing traders in distant financial centers to seek out the best prices wherever they might be. Major U.S. trading firms "pass the book" to their overseas branch offices as the sun moves west to keep abreast of the international stock and debt markets. Other traders have taken to hiring "all-nighters," who remain in the home office overnight to monitor market movements overseas and execute customer orders. Recent research by Arshanapalli and Doukas (1993), Kasa (1992) and others finds that stock markets in Europe (for example, Great Britain and Germany), Asia (especially Japan), and the United States are cointegrated, each sending shock waves to each other as price movements occur and all constantly moving toward a joint long-run equilibrium.

In September 1990, the New York Stock Exchange announced plans for after-hours trading sessions via computer without fees and with minimal disclosure rules and later announced plans to open its trading floor one-half hour earlier. These announcements represented an effort by the NYSE to lure back from overseas substantial numbers of pension funds, investment companies, and other large institutional investors that were trading in growing numbers away from the NYSE. Institutional trading of large blocks of stock inside the United States was given a boost recently when the U.S. Securities and Exchange Commission created Rule 144a, allowing financial institutions to trade large blocks of privately placed stocks and bonds without having to go through complicated disclosure procedures. The SEC also recently approved the services of Wunsch Auction Systems, Inc., which make possible the trading of stocks after U.S. exchanges and over-the-counter markets are closed.

Also in 1990, the National Association of Securities Dealers announced plans to extend the hours of operation of its automated quotations network to cover the hours when the London International Stock Exchange is open, supporting the growth of predawn stock trading inside the United States. Initially, NASDAQ International proposed to offer computer-screen trading of 400 to 500 stocks beginning at 3:30 a.m. EST in the United States. Not to be outdone, the American Stock Exchange, the Chicago Board Options Exchange, and Reuters Holdings PLC of Great Britain declared their intention in the summer of 1990 to launch a system for night trading between 6:00 p.m. and 6:00 a.m. The Chicago Mercantile Exchange and Reuters announced at the same time plans for the Globex after-hours electronic order-entry and trade-maturity trading system involving purchases and sales of financial futures contracts. Globex represents an international partnership among futures exchanges in the United States and Western Europe. The Chicago Mercantile Exchange and the Singapore International Monetary Exchange also have a trading link allowing identical futures contracts to be traded and closed out on either exchange.

One of the areas of most rapid growth in the internationalization of the equities market is the cross-listing of stocks. For example, a U.S. corporation can request to have its stock listed on the International Stock Exchange (ISE) in London. Moreover, following deregulation of London's financial markets in October 1986, several foreign firms, led by U.S. securities firms and banks, purchased seats on London exchanges. Paralleling the rapid expansion of cross-listing is global stock underwriting in which only a fraction of new stock issues may be sold in their country of origin. Today most large stock issues have underwriters from more than one nation, helping a corporate customer reach the widest possible range of international buyers.

The Development of ADRs. Further evidence of the growing links between U.S. and foreign stock markets emerged in the 1980s and 1990s with the development of new international financial instruments. For example, U.S. exchanges began trading **American depository receipts (ADRs).** These are dollar-denominated claims on foreign shares of stock that are kept in safekeeping by U.S. financial institutions (usually by commercial banks and investment banking houses). In effect, ADRs are negotiable warehouse receipts for deposits of foreign stock that U.S. investors can trade without having to assume the risks of trading in foreign currencies. Among the most popular foreign firms whose ADRs are traded in the United States are Cifra and Telefonos de Mexico, Royal Dutch Petroleum Co., British Petroleum, and Reuters Holdings in the United Kingdom.

ADRs do present some special risks of their own, however. For one thing, their underlying value is sensitive to fluctuations in foreign currency prices. A sharp decline in the value of the home country's currency, for example, can result in a significant loss of return from ADRs. Moreover, foreign stock prices tend to be more volatile than the prices of most actively traded U.S. equities. To be successful in the ADR market, U.S. investors must learn to become more aware of foreign business developments — information that often is difficult and costly to obtain. Many U.S. investors have come to prefer *sponsored* ADRs, for which the foreign firm issuing the stock hires a U.S. firm (such as a bank) to serve U.S. buyers and provide them with pertinent information. Trading in sponsored ADRs is the largest and fastest growing market for the shares of foreign companies traded in U.S. markets.

Remaining Barriers to Global Trading. Despite the recent progress toward 24-hour trading of U.S. and other nations' securities worldwide, there are still roadblocks to making trading continuous all over the globe. What we do not have yet is a uniform international settlement system so that sellers of securities, regardless of their location on the globe, are assured of receiving their funds quickly and buyers are assured of quickly receiving control of the securities they have purchased with minimal risk of nonperformance by either party. Today it takes about three days to settle the average stock transaction in the United States, and in some foreign markets, it takes even longer — a period that is long enough for substantial losses to occur.

Moreover, if we are ever to achieve a fully open and competitive global stock market, all traders must operate under similar rules so that traders in one nation with lenient regulations do not have a significant advantage over traders in a country with tougher regulations. Currently, the U.S. Securities and Exchange Commission and U.S. exchanges enforce some of the toughest rules on the planet for disclosure of relevant information to investors and for limiting speculation and computer-driven trading procedures. Until these differences in international security regulation and practice are resolved, true globally integrated capital markets with full-service round-the-clock trading will remain an abstract ideal toward which the financial markets are drawing nearer each year.

RANDOM WALK AND EFFICIENT MARKETS

Stock market behavior has figured prominently in the development of modern theories of what determines the market price and value of securities. One of the most popular of modern theories regarding the valuation of stocks and other securities is the random-walk hypothesis.

Random Walk is a term used in mathematics and statistics to describe a process in which successive elements in a data series are independent of each other and therefore are essentially random and unpredictable. The theory of random walk applied to the valuation of stocks says that the future path of individual stock prices is no more predictable than the path of a series of random numbers. Each share of stock is assumed to have an *intrinsic value* based on investor expectations of the discounted value of future cash flows generated by that stock. The market price per share is an unbiased estimator of a stock's intrinsic value and reflects the latest information available concerning the issuing company's condition and future prospects. Successive changes in the price of a stock are random fluctuations around that stock's intrinsic value, and these changes are independent of the sequence of price changes that occurred in the past. In effect, stock price changes act as though they were independent random drawings from an infinite pool of possible prices. Therefore, it is not possible to predict this week's stock price from last week's stock price. Knowledge of the sequence of past price changes prior to the current time period is of little or no help in defining the probability distribution of price changes in any current or future period.

The random walk notion is not accepted by all stock market analysts. Many analysts still subscribe to chartist, or *technical analysis,* theories, which assume that the past behavior of a security's price is rich in information concerning the future behavior of that price. Patterns of past price behavior, technical analysts argue, tend to recur in the future. For this reason, careful analysis of stock price averages and the prices of individual shares reveal important data concerning future price movements. Unfortunately, recent empirical evidence does not indicate any meaningful degree of dependence of future stock price movements on those occurring in the past. Important research studies by Fisher and Lorie (1964), Mandelbrot (1963), Fama (1965), Granger and Morgenstern (1970), and others show that recent changes in stock prices are *not* significantly related to past price changes.

Another test performed on the technical analysis theory has been to try various mechanical trading, or "filter," rules to see if the investor is better off using these rules instead of a simple buy and hold strategy. Filter rules usually require the investor to buy if a security's price goes up at least Y percent and sell when the security's price declines by Y percent or more. Research studies by Alexander (1961), Chang and Lewellen (1985), and others have found results that generally favor the simple *buy and hold* strategy, especially after brokerage commissions are considered. Average earnings generated by trading rules appear to be no better than those achieved if the investor randomly selected a group of stocks representative of the market as a whole and held them for the full holding period. Trading rules do *not* generate above-normal rates of return.

The Efficient Markets Hypothesis. The random walk notion has been supplemented in recent years by a broader theory of stock price movements known as the **efficient markets hypothesis (EMH).** As we saw in Chapter 3, a market is "efficient" if scarce resources are allocated to their most productive uses. In each case, buyers willing to pay the highest prices for each resource must receive the resources they require. In a perfectly efficient securities market, the prices of securities will fluctuate randomly around their intrinsic values and are always in equilibrium. Any temporary deviations from equilibrium prices are quickly corrected. Information relevant to the valuation of securities is simultaneously available to all investors at virtually no cost, and existing security prices fully reflect the latest information available bearing on the future profitability and risk of business firms. Moreover, security market prices adjust instantaneously to *new* information, and a new set of intrinsic values results, leading some investors to adjust their portfolios. All of this happens instantaneously, so that market price always equals intrinsic value in a state of continuous equilibrium. As a result, it is impossible in a perfectly efficient market to make economic profits by trading on the information available because an efficient market is one that quickly processes *all* relevant information.

Research Evidence on the EMH. What does available research evidence have to say about market efficiency? Research studies generally find that security prices respond promptly to new, publicly available information, but those possessing private (or inside) information or special skills do, at times, appear to earn excess returns. Prices do appear to fluctuate around a base (or intrinsic) value in an essentially random manner, as noted in excellent research reviews by Fama (1970, 1976) and Pearce (1987). Moreover, studies such as the one by Chang and Lewellen (1985) of professional portfolio management firms indicate that these firms do *not* consistently outperform randomly selected portfolios of securities bearing comparable risk.

One possible problem with the EMH: The prices of stocks often appear to overshoot their "true" values in the short run (i.e., to be excessively volatile), because some buyers react irrationally to past stock performance and not to future expected earnings, suggesting the existence of inefficiencies in using relevant information to price stocks and other securities. Eventually, stock prices may return toward their "true," or "fundamental," values based on their expected future earnings — a phenomenon called *mean reversion*. While some recent research studies seem to find evidence of mean reversion occurring in stock prices (e.g., Poterba and Summers (1988) and Fama and French (1988a and b)), other studies (e.g., Engel and Morris (1991)) either find no evidence or only weak evidence of mean reversion. Most of the observed mean-reversion tendency seems to be concentrated in the years before World War II, perhaps suggesting that the financial markets have become more efficient over time.

Summary of Findings. Overall, the securities markets must be regarded as reasonably efficient channels for directing the flow of savings into investment. Changes in security prices do appear to conform generally to some form of random-walk process in which daily price quotations cluster about a security's intrinsic value, reflecting the latest information available. Thus, above-normal profits using publicly available information as a guide for security trades are unlikely because that information is already included in current security prices. A "buy and hold" strategy coupled with random selection of securities from the *entire* market's portfolio will yield returns at least as good as those earned by professional traders, who usually turn over their portfolios rapidly. Of course, financial analysts with extraordinary ability to uncover new information may be able to achieve above-average rates of return, as least for short periods of time.

SUMMARY

The market for corporate stock is the most widely followed of all securities markets, with millions of shares changing hands each day. Though one of the oldest of the securities markets, the market for corporate shares even now is in a period of transition. Spurred by legislation and competition, electronic links between the exchanges and over-the-counter markets today help to ensure that investors, regardless of location, can transact business at competitive prices. Rapid developments in the technology of information transfer are breaking down the barriers to free and open trading posed by geography and outmoded practices and regulations. Centralized computer systems, coupled with cheaper electronic methods of data transfer and display, have paved the way for integrating existing markets into a new global market for trading in stocks and stock options. And the benefits of stronger competition and a freer flow of information to all market participants are not likely to be confined to equities alone. Ultimately, all securities markets, all investors, and the financial system as a whole will benefit from the era of change and innovation through which the stock market is now passing. ∎

KEY TERMS AND CONCEPTS IN THIS CHAPTER

common stock	call option	random walk
preferred stock	put option	efficient markets hypothesis (EMH)
organized exchanges	program trading	
over-the-counter (OTC) market	circuit breakers	
third market	American depository receipts (ADRs)	

STUDY QUESTIONS

1. In what important ways does the stock market differ from the other securities markets we have dealt with to this point?

2. What are the essential characteristics of *common stock*? What priority do common stockholders have in the event a corporation is liquidated? What limits the amount of shares a company may issue?

3. Discuss the nature of *preferred stock*. In what ways are preferred shares similar to "debt" and in what ways are they "equity" securities?

4. What are the principal differences between trading in stocks over the counter and trading on an organized exchange? How would you rate these two markets in terms of their advantages for the small investor? The large investor?

5. Explain the possible link between economic conditions and the performance of the stock market. Why do stock price movements tend to *lead* changes in general economic conditions?

6. What is the *random walk* hypothesis? Does available research evidence tend to support or deny the validity of this hypothesis?

7. What is an *efficient market*? What are the consequences of market efficiency for the behavior of security prices? Does recent research support the idea that security markets are efficient?

SELECTED REFERENCES

Alexander, S. "Price Movements in Speculative Markets: Trends or Random Walks." *Industrial Management Review,* May 1961, pp. 7–26.

Arshanapalli, Bala, and John Doukas. "International Stock Market Linkages: Evidence from the Pre- and Post-October 1987 Period," *Journal of Banking and Finance,* 1993, pp. 193–208.

Chang, Eric C., and Wilbur G. Lewellen. "An Arbitrage Pricing Approach to Evaluating Mutual Fund Performance." *The Journal of Financial Research* 8, no. 1 (Spring 1985), pp. 15–30.

Engel, Charles, and Charles S. Morris. "Challenges to Stock Market Efficiency: Evidence from Mean Reversion Studies." *Economic Review.* Federal Reserve Bank of Kansas City, September/October 1991, pp. 21–35.

Fama, Eugene F. "The Behavior of Stock Market Prices." *Journal of Business,* January 1965, pp. 34–106.

———. "Efficient Capital Markets: A Review of Theory and Empirical Work." *Journal of Finance* 25 (1970), pp. 383–416.

———. *Foundations of Finance.* New York: Basic Books, 1976.

——— Fama, Eugene F., and Kenneth R. French. "Permanent and Temporary Components of Stock Prices." *Journal of Political Economy,* 1988a, pp. 246–73.

———. "Dividend Yields and Expected Stock Returns." *Journal of Financial Economics,* 1988b, pp. 3–25.

Fisher, L., and J. Lorie. "Rates of Return on Investments in Common Stock: The Year-by-Year Record, 1926–1965." *Journal of Business,* January 1964.

Kasa, K. "Common Stochastic Trends in International Stock Markets," *Journal of Monetary Economics,* Vol. 29 (1992), pp. 95–124.

Pearce, Douglas K. "Challenges to the Concept of Stock Market Efficiency." *Economic Review.* Federal Reserve Bank of Kansas City, September–October 1987, pp. 16–23.

Poterba, James M., and Lawrence H. Summers. "Mean Reversion in Stock Prices: Evidence and Implications." *Journal of Financial Economics,* 1988, pp. 27–59.

U.S. Presidential Task Force on Market Mechanisms. *Report of the Presidential Task Force on Market Mechanisms.* Washington, D.C., January 1988.

Chapter 28

International Transactions and Currency Values

LEARNING OBJECTIVES IN THIS CHAPTER

- To explore the functions and roles of the international financial markets within the financial system.
- To see how international payments for goods and services and international lending and borrowing are tracked through the balance-of-payments accounts.
- To see how the values of national currencies (such as the dollar and the yen) are determined in the modern world.

In many ways, the world we live in is rapidly shrinking. Jet planes such as the British Concorde can race across the Atlantic between New York and London in less than four hours, about the same time it takes a Boeing 747 jetliner to travel across the United States. Fax, telephone, and cable can move financial information from one spot on the globe to another in minutes. Orbiting satellites can bring news of major international significance to home television sets the same day an event takes place and make possible direct communication between those involved in international business transactions.

Accompanying these dramatic improvements in communication and transportation is enormous growth in world trade and international investment. For example, in 1965 total exports of goods and services worldwide reached $190 billion. By the 1990s, the estimated dollar value of world trade had climbed to more than $3 trillion, or about half the U.S. gross domestic product (GDP). Moreover, the United States itself has become increasingly dependent on world trade. For example, imports into the United States represented just 4.6 percent of GDP in 1960 but had jumped to 13 percent of GDP in 1995; U.S. exports climbed from 6 percent to 11 percent of GDP over the same period. Thus, nearly one fourth of the value of production and spending in the U.S. economy stems directly from foreign trade. The international financial markets have had to grow enormously just to keep up with the expansion in world trade.

Actually, international financial markets perform the same basic functions as domestic financial markets. They bring international lenders of funds into contact with borrowers, thereby permitting an increased flow of scarce funds toward their most productive uses. The volume of capital investment worldwide is made larger because of the workings of the global financial system. And, with increased capital investment, the productivity of individual firms and nations is increased and economic growth in the international sector accelerates. The international financial markets also facilitate the flow of consumer goods and services across national boundaries, making possible an optimal allocation of resources in response to consumer demand on a global scale. With increased efficiency in resource use, the output of consumer goods and services is increased and costs of production are minimized.[1]

THE BALANCE OF PAYMENTS

One of the most widely used sources of information concerning flows of funds, goods, and services between nations is each country's **balance-of-payments (BOP) accounts.** This annual statistical report summarizes all the economic and financial transactions between residents of one nation and the rest of the world during a specific period of time. The BOP accounts reflect *changes* in the assets and liabilities of units, such as businesses, individuals, and governments, involved in international transactions, rather than the levels of their assets and liabilities. The major transactions captured in the BOP accounts include exports and imports of goods and services; income from investments made abroad; government loans and military expenditures overseas; and private capital flows between nations.

In a statistical sense, a nation's BOP accounts always "balance," because double-entry bookkeeping is used. For example, every payment made for goods and services imported from abroad simultaneously creates a claim on the home country's resources or extinguishes an existing liability. Similarly, every time a domestic business firm receives payment from overseas, either it acquires a claim against resources in a foreign country, or a claim that firm held against a foreign individual or institution is erased. In practice, however, imbalances frequently show up in the BOP accounts due to unreported transactions or inconsistencies in reporting. These errors and omissions are handled through a Statistical Discrepancy account.

The U.S. Balance of International Payments

The U.S. BOP accounts are published quarterly by the Department of Commerce. The quarterly figures are then *annualized* to permit comparisons across years. The transactions recorded in the balance of payments fall into three broad groups:

1. *Transactions on current account,* which include imports and exports of goods and services and unilateral transfers (gifts).

2. *Transactions on capital account,* which include both long- and short-term investment at home and abroad and usually involve the transfer of financial assets (bonds, deposits, etc.).

[1]These benefits from international trade and finance are most likely to occur if each nation follows the principle of *comparative advantage.* This principle argues that each country will have a higher real standard of living if it specializes in the production of those goods and services in which it has a comparative advantage in cost and imports those goods and services where it is at a comparative cost disadvantage. In simplest terms, a country should acquire goods and services from those sources — foreign or domestic — that result in the lowest cost in terms of its own resources. The principle of comparative advantage works best in an environment of free trade that permits nations to specialize in their most efficient activities.

3. *Official reserve transactions,* which are used by monetary authorities (the Treasury, central bank, etc.) to settle BOP deficits, usually through transferring the ownership of official reserve assets to countries with BOP surpluses.

Transactions that bring about an inflow of foreign currency into the home country are recorded as *credits* (+). Transactions resulting in an outflow of foreign currency from the home country are listed as *debits* (−). Thus, credit (+) items in the BOP represent an increase in a nation's buying power abroad. Debit (−) items represent decreases in a nation's buying power abroad. If a country sells goods and services or borrows abroad, these transactions are credit items because they increase external buying power. On the other hand, a purchase of goods and services abroad or a paydown of a nation's international liabilities is a debit item because that country is surrendering part of its external buying power. A summary of the major credit and debit items making up the BOP accounts is shown in Exhibit 28–1.

The actual U.S. BOP accounts for the years 1994 and 1995 as reported by the Department of Commerce are shown in Exhibit 28–2. We have subdivided these international accounts into the three major categories discussed above — the current account, capital account, and official reserve transactions account — to more fully understand how the BOP bookkeeping system operates.

The Current Account

One of the most publicized components of the U.S. BOP is the **current account,** which contains three elements:

1. The *merchandise trade balance,* comparing the volume of goods exported to those imported.
2. The *service balance,* comparing exports and imports of services.
3. *Unilateral transfers,* reflecting the amount of gifts made to foreigners by domestic citizens and government grants abroad.

The Merchandise Trade Balance.   Prior to the 1970s, the United States reported a positive *merchandise trade balance,* with exports exceeding imports in most years due to substantial demand for U.S. agricultural products and machinery overseas. However, infla-

Exhibit 28–1	**Principal Credit and Debit Items Recorded in a Nation's Balance of Payments (BOP)**

Credit Entries (Inflows of Funds, +)	Debit Entries (Outflows of Funds, −)
Exports of merchandise	Imports of merchandise
Services provided to foreign countries	Services provided to domestic citizens by foreign countries
Interest and dividends due domestic citizens from business firms abroad	Gifts of money sent abroad by domestic citizens
Remittances received from domestic citizens employed in foreign countries	Capital invested abroad by domestic citizens
Foreign purchases of securities issued by domestic firms and units of government	Dividend and interest payments to foreign countries on investments made in the domestic economy
Repayments by foreigners of funds borrowed from domestic lending institutions	

tion, U.S. government budget deficits, and other factors have turned U.S. trade surpluses into substantial deficits in recent years, as shown in Exhibit 28–2. U.S. *sources* of external buying power have generally been less than the nation's *uses* of external buying power. By mid-1995 the United States merchandise trade balance deficit was approaching an estimated $200 billion (on an annualized basis).

The Service Balance. Because Americans typically have purchased more goods from abroad in recent years than they have sold to other countries, how has this deficit (debit balance) in the merchandise trade account been paid for? Part of the needed funds have come from the service balance, which has been in surplus for many years. Services counted in the BOP accounts include insurance policies covering foreign shipments of goods, transportation services, hotel accommodations for foreigners visiting the United States, and entertainment and medical care for foreign residents. Travel by foreigners in the United States has recently accelerated, resulting in substantial increases in service income for U.S. companies accommodating foreign tourism.

Also included in the service balance are receipts of income from U.S. direct investments abroad (usually in the form of interest and dividends). These income flows are created when U.S. residents purchase foreign securities and acquire equity interests in foreign businesses. When exports of services exceed service imports, the result is a credit (+) balance in the services account. The balance in the service accounts is sometimes called the *balance in invisibles,* because services are intangible items. In 1995, the U.S. service balance, or balance in invisibles, was in surplus by more than an estimated $50 billion, helping to offset some of the U.S. merchandise trade deficit.

Balance on Goods and Services. If we combine the merchandise trade balance with the service balance, the resulting figure is labeled the *balance on goods and services.* In 1995, the United States recorded an estimated debit (−) balance on goods and services of about $145 billion.

Unilateral Transfers and U.S. Government Grants. The third category of transaction recorded in the current account, labeled *unilateral transfers,* consists of gifts from U.S. residents to foreigners. Gifts are referred to as unilateral transfers because they represent a *one-way flow* of resources to the recipient; nothing is expected in return. Of course, foreigners send gifts to U.S. recipients as well, but U.S. gift-giving abroad far exceeds the return flow. For example, gifts to foreigners from Americans were an estimated $16 billion larger than foreign gifts flowing into the United States in 1995. Each gift sent overseas represents the *use* of the nation's external buying power and therefore is recorded as a *debit* (−) item. The final item in the current account is grants made abroad by the U.S. government, which totaled an estimated $9 billion in 1995. Government grants have increased sharply of late due to debt forgiveness by the United States, which has been extended to several nations having U.S. loans.

The Balance on Current Account. When we put the four components — balance on merchandise trade, balance on services, net unilateral transfers, and government grants together — we derive the *balance on current account.* The U.S. balance on current account in 1995 was a debit balance estimated at almost $175 billion. The United States experienced this debit balance primarily because the rising value of the U.S. dollar in international markets for part of the period discouraged sales of U.S. goods abroad. Lagging economic recovery abroad added further to the nation's current account deficit.

Exhibit 28–2   **The U.S. Balance of Payments in 1994 and 1995** ($ Billions)

Credit (+) and Debit (–) Items	1994	1995*
The current account Merchandise:		
Exports of merchandise	+502.5	+570.2
Imports of merchandise	–668.6	–766.3
Balance on merchandise trade	–166.1	–196.1
Services:		
Military transactions, net	+2.1	+2.1
Investment income, net	–9.3	–11.5
Other service transactions, net	+57.7	+60.5
Service balance	+50.5	+51.1
Balance on goods and services	–115.6	–145.0
Unilateral transfers	–15.7	–16.1
U.S. government grants	–15.8	–9.4
Balance on current account	–151.2	–174.5
The Capital Account		
Change in U.S. citizens' private assets abroad (increase, –):		
Bank-reported claims	+0.9	–142.1
Nonbank-reported claims	–32.6	—
U.S. purchases of foreign securities, net	–49.8	–82.4
U.S. direct investments abroad, net	–49.4	–64.4
Private capital outflows from the United States	–130.9	–288.9
Change in foreign private assets inside the United States (increase, +):		
U.S. bank-reported liabilities	+114.4	+60.0
U.S. nonbank-reported liabilities	–4.3	—
Foreign private purchases of U.S. Treasury securities, net	+33.8	+119.9
Foreign purchases of other U.S. securities, net	+58.6	+80.8
Foreign direct investments in the United States, net	+49.4	+45.1
Private capital inflows into the United States	+252.0	+305.8
Total private capital flows, net (net capital inflow, +)	+121.9	+16.9
Change in official reserve assets		
Change in U.S. official reserve assets (increase, –):		
Gold	+0.0	+0.0
Special drawing rights (SDRs)	–0.4	–0.6
Reserve position in International Monetary Fund (IMF)	+0.5	–3.1
Foreign currencies	+5.3	–7.1
Increase (–) or decrease (+) in U.S. official reserve assets	+5.3	–10.9
Change in foreign official assets in the United States (increase, +):		
U.S. Treasury securities	+30.7	+100.7
Other U.S. government obligations	+6.0	+5.3
Other U.S. government liabilities	+2.2	+2.1
Other U.S. liabilities reported by U.S. banks	+2.9	+31.2
Other foreign official assets	–2.5	+11.8
Increase (+) or decrease (–) in foreign official reserve assets	+39.4	+151.0
Change in U.S. government assets (other than reserve assets), net (increase, –)	–0.3	–0.6
Allocation of SDRs	0.0	0.0
Statistical discrepancy	–14.3	+4.5

Note: Details may not sum to column totals due to the effects of rounding error.
*1995 figures are from the second quarter and are annualized estimates for the remainder of 1995.

Source: U.S. Department of Commerce, Bureau of Economic Analysis.

Persistent U.S. current account deficits tend to put upward pressure on domestic interest rates and place downward pressure on the value of the U.S. dollar in international markets. Correction of the U.S. current account deficit could require a slowing of domestic demand for goods and services, with resulting increases in unemployment.

The Capital Account

Flows of funds destined for investment abroad are recorded in the **capital account.** Investments abroad may be long term, as in the case of a U.S. automobile company building an assembly plant in Germany, or short term, such as the purchase of six-month British Treasury bills by U.S. citizens. Of course, capital investment flows both ways across national boundaries. For example, in 1995, U.S. citizens and private organizations invested an estimated $289 billion overseas, while foreign individuals and private institutions invested an estimated $306 billion in U.S. assets. The result was a *net private capital inflow* into the United States estimated at $17 billion. U.S. banks, hotels, energy companies, and numerous other firms have all been acquisition targets for foreign investors. In effect, foreign capital inflows have financed a substantial portion of the U.S. trade deficit.

Components of the Capital Account. The capital account in the balance of payments includes three different types of international investment: (1) short-term capital flows, (2) direct investments, and (3) portfolio investments. The latter two — direct and portfolio investments — represent a long-term commitment of funds, involving the purchase of stocks, bonds, and other financial assets having a maturity of more than one year. Short-term capital flows, on the other hand, reflect purchases of financial assets with maturities of less than one year. These short-term financial assets are mainly government notes, deposits, and foreign currencies.

What is the essential difference between *direct investment* and *portfolio investment*? The key factor is *control.* Portfolio investment merely involves purchasing securities to hold in order to receive interest, dividends, or capital gains. Direct investment, on the other hand, refers to the purchase of land or the acquisition of ownership shares in an attempt to control a foreign business firm.[2]

Claims against Foreigners. In addition to direct investment and purchases of foreign securities, the capital account also records claims against foreigners reported by domestic banks and nonbanking concerns. The bulk of the claims comprise loans extended by domestic banks to firms and governments abroad. In 1995, U.S. bank claims on foreigners fell by an estimated $140 billion. Interestingly enough, U.S. bank loans abroad have declined sharply from what they had been in earlier years. What reversed this trend? Several foreign countries, notably in South America and Eastern Europe, have been unable to service their huge loans from U.S. banks, and many international commodity loans have nosedived in value. As a result, numerous U.S. banks began to reduce their foreign lending activities. Then, too, many U.S. corporations have brought the earnings of their foreign affiliates home (known as *repatriation of funds*) to invest inside the United States.

The Basic Balance

If the current account balance is added to the long-term investment balance in the nation's international accounts, the net figure is known as the *basic balance.* We can estimate this for the United States in 1995 as follows:

---

[2]The U.S. Department of Commerce defines direct investment as ownership of 10 percent or more of the voting stock or the exercise of other means of control over a foreign business enterprise by an individual or corporation. Ownership of less than 10 percent of a foreign firm's stock is referred to as portfolio investment.

The Basic Balance

Figures in Billions of Dollars

Estimated 1995 U.S. balance on current account		−174.5
Estimated long-term capital flows:		
U.S. capital outflows	−288.9	
U.S. capital inflows	+305.8	
Net capital inflow		+16.9
Estimated 1995 basic balance		−157.6

Therefore, when merchandise trade, services, gifts, and private capital flows are taken into consideration, the United States had an estimated $157.6 billion deficit in its basic balance account. This deficit has to be covered by giving up U.S. reserves of gold, foreign currency, and other assets, or by giving foreigners larger claims (in the form of securities, etc.) against U.S. resources.

Official Reserve Transactions

When a nation has a deficit in its international payments accounts, it must settle up by surrendering assets or claims to foreign accounts. *Official reserve transactions,* involving transfer of the ownership of gold, convertible foreign currencies, deposits in the International Monetary Fund, and special drawing rights (SDRs), are usually the vehicle for settling net differences in international claims between nations.

Official reserve accounts are immediately available assets for making international payments. When these assets *increase,* this represents a source of external buying power by the nation experiencing the increase. On the other hand, a *decrease* in the official reserve accounts represents a use of external buying power by the nation experiencing the decrease. If a nation has a surplus (credit balance) in its current and capital accounts, the balance in its official reserve accounts generally rises, indicating an excess of sales abroad over foreign purchases. Conversely, a country experiencing a deficit (debit balance) in its current and capital accounts usually finds that the balance in its official reserve accounts is falling. Such a decline can be temporarily offset, however, by official borrowing by the central bank or other government agency. In 1995, foreign governments and central banks increased their holdings of gold, currencies, and other official assets in the United States by an estimated $151 billion, net. The U.S. government lost official reserve assets in the net amount of an estimated $11 billion in 1995. Most U.S. BOP deficits in recent years have not been financed primarily through changes in official reserve assets but through capital inflows from abroad, particularly purchases of U.S. stocks and bonds.

Disequilibrium in the Balance of Payments

For several years now, the United States has displayed a disequilibrium position in its balance of payments. This means that the nation has relied on foreign credit, foreign capital inflows into the U.S., and its stock of gold, foreign currencies, and other reserve assets to settle BOP deficits. However, the amount of these financial devices is limited — no nation can go on indefinitely accumulating BOP deficits, borrowing abroad, and using up its reserves. Moreover, relying on foreign capital inflows is dangerous, because the perceptions of foreign investors regarding the desirability of placing funds in the United States may change abruptly.

To this point, foreign central banks and foreign investors have regarded U.S. securities and dollar-denominated deposits as good investments and have been willing to extend an increasing volume of international credit to the United States. At some point, however, foreign governments and private investors may become satiated with dollar claims; at this point, the value of the U.S. dollar must decline in international markets. U.S. purchases of goods and services abroad would also decline because of the dollar's reduced buying power. The nation's standard of living would begin to fall until equilibrium in its balance-of-payments position is restored.

One factor that gives hope for the future lies in the capital account, in which growing investment by foreigners in the United States has helped to offset outflows of capital funds from U.S. investors. In most of the years during the past two decades, capital inflows into the United States have grown faster than U.S. investments abroad, making the United States the world's largest debtor nation. A major factor boosting foreign investment in the U.S. is the desire to avoid U.S. import restrictions by developing production facilities inside the United States. Even more significant is the political stability of the United States, offering an attractive haven for international investors concerned about instability abroad. If this capital inflow continues in the future, it will do much to alleviate the international payments problems of the United States.

THE PROBLEM OF DIFFERENT MONETARY UNITS IN INTERNATIONAL TRADE AND FINANCE

Businesses and individuals trading goods and services in international markets encounter a problem not experienced by those who buy and sell only in domestic markets. This is the problem of different monetary units used as the standard of value from country to country. Americans use the dollar as a medium of exchange and standard of value in domestic markets; the Swiss and the French rely on the franc as their basic monetary unit. There are more than 100 different monetary units around the world. As a result, when goods and services are sold or capital flows across national boundaries, it is often necessary to sell one currency and buy another.

Unfortunately, the act of trading currencies entails substantial *risk*. Exporters and importers may be forced to purchase a foreign currency when its value is rising and the home country's currency is falling in value. Any profits earned on the sale of goods and services abroad may be outweighed by losses suffered in currency exchange. Differing monetary units also complicate government monetary policy aimed at curbing inflation and ensuring economic growth. Repeatedly in recent years, massive flows of funds surged through foreign and domestic markets from speculative buying and selling of dollars, francs, and other currencies. These speculative currency flows greatly increased the problems of economic recovery and the control of inflation.

The Gold Standard

The problem of trading in different monetary units whose prices change frequently is one of the world's oldest financial problems. It has been dealt with in a wide variety of ways over the centuries. One of the most successful solutions prior to the modern era centered on *gold* as an international standard of value. During the 17th and 18th centuries, major trading nations in Western Europe made their currencies freely convertible into gold. Gold bullion could be exported and imported from one country to another without significant restriction, and each unit of currency was defined in terms of so many grains of fine gold. Nations adopting the **gold standard** agreed to exchange paper money or coins for gold bullion in unlimited amounts at predetermined prices.

One advantage of the gold standard was that it imposed a common standard of value on all national currencies. This brought a measure of stability to international trade and investment, dampened exchange rate fluctuations, and stimulated the expansion of commerce and investment abroad. A second advantage was economic discipline. Tying currencies to gold regulated the growth and stability of national economies. A nation experiencing severe inflation or excessively rapid growth in consumption of imported goods soon found itself losing gold reserves. Exports declined and unemployment rose. Eventually, the volume of imports was curtailed, and the outflow of gold slowed.

These advantages of stability and economic discipline were offset by a number of limitations inherent in the gold standard. For one thing, maintenance of that standard depended crucially on *free trade*. Nations desiring to protect their industries from foreign competition through export or import restrictions could not do so. Moreover, the growth of a nation's money supply was limited by the size of its gold stock. Problems of rising unemployment or lagging economic growth might call for rapid expansion of the domestic money supply. However, such a policy required a suspension of gold convertibility, taking the nation off the gold standard. Thus, the gold standard often conflicted with national economic goals and limited the policy alternatives open to governmental authorities.

The Gold Exchange Standard

Although government policymakers were mainly concerned about the effects of the gold standard on domestic economies, investors and commercial traders found that gold bullion was not a convenient medium of exchange. Gold is expensive to transport and risky to handle. Moreover, the world's gold supply was limited relative to the expanding volume of international trade. These problems gave rise in the 19th century to the **gold exchange standard.** Institutions actively engaged in international commerce began to hold stocks of convertible currencies. Each currency was freely convertible into gold at a fixed rate but also was freely convertible into other currencies at relatively stable prices. In practice, virtually all transactions took place in convertible currencies, and gold faded into the background as an international medium of exchange.

The gold exchange standard provided greater convenience for international traders and investors. However, this monetary standard possessed the same limitations as the original gold standard. National currencies were still tied to gold, and growth in world trade depended on growth in the international gold stock. The gold exchange standard collapsed during the economic chaos of the Great Depression in the 1930s.

The Modified Exchange Standard

Dissatisfaction with international monetary systems tied exclusively to gold resulted in a search for a new payments system following World War II. In 1944, Western countries convened an international monetary conference in Bretton Woods, New Jersey, to devise a stable money and payments system. The conference created a new mechanism for settling international payments — known as the Bretton Woods System, or **modified exchange standard** — and an agency for monitoring the exchange rate practices of member nations (known as the International Monetary Fund, or IMF, with headquarters in Washington, D.C.).[3]

---

[3]The IMF, which is headed by its Board of Governors with a representative from each member nation, establishes rules for settling international accounts between nations and grants short-term loans to member nations who lack sufficient international reserves to settle their BOP deficits. IMF balance-of-payments loans usually are accompanied by strict requirements that a member nation receiving credit must adopt stern economic measures to curtail the growth of its imports and expand its sales abroad. The IMF's credit guarantee encourages banks and other nations to grant loans to a member nation in trouble. The funds loaned by the IMF come mainly from *quotas*, which each member nation must contribute in dollars or other reserve assets. A companion organization to the IMF, the *World Bank*, also created under the Bretton Woods Agreement, makes long-term loans to speed the economic development of member nations.

The centerpiece of the Bretton Woods System was the linking of foreign currency prices to the U.S. dollar and to gold. The United States committed itself to buy and sell gold at $35 per ounce on request from foreign monetary authorities. Other IMF member nations pledged to keep their currency's price within 1 percent of its par value in terms of gold or the dollar. Central banks would use their foreign exchange reserves to buy or sell their own currency in the foreign exchange market. In practice, this usually meant that, if a foreign currency fell in value *below* par (the lower intervention point), a central bank would sell its holdings of dollars and buy that currency in the market, driving its price up toward par. If the price of a nation's currency rose more than 1 percent *above* par (the upper intervention point), the central bank involved would sell its own currency and buy dollars, driving the currency's price down toward par. If a currency fell too far in value or rose too high, resulting in market disruption and threatening a massive loss of foreign exchange reserves, the country involved would simply revalue its currency, establishing a new par value relative to gold or the dollar.

Fundamentally, the success of the Bretton Woods System depended on the ability of the United States to maintain confidence in the dollar and protect its value. One of the weaknesses of the new system was that the U.S. dollar was in short supply early in the postwar period, though the system worked well at first because the dollar was the most stable monetary medium around. Later, however, the United States began to export large amounts of capital to Western Europe and Asia. The result was sizable U.S. trade deficits that were dealt with by drains on the U.S. gold stock and by a buildup of dollar holdings abroad — an indication of fundamental problems developing in the U.S. economy. Foreign governments and investors began to lose confidence in the ability of U.S. policymakers to control the U.S. economy and subdue inflation.

Adoption of a New Managed Floating Currency Standard

Inflation and other economic problems forced the abandonment of the Bretton Woods System early in the 1970s. The first step in dismantling the old system was taken by the administration of President Richard M. Nixon in August 1971, when the U.S. dollar was devalued and the convertibility of foreign official holdings of dollars into gold suspended. Gold ceased to be an international monetary medium; it is traded today only as a commodity. Soon, the largest IMF member countries were allowing their currencies to *float* in value, responding freely to demand and supply forces in the marketplace.

In 1978, a new international payments system — **the managed floating currency standard** — was adopted by member nations of the IMF. Known as the Second Amendment to the International Monetary Fund's Articles of Agreement, the official rules under which today's international money system is supposed to operate allow *each nation to choose its own exchange rate policy, consistent with the structure of its economy and its goals*. There are, however, three principles that each member country must follow in establishing its exchange rate policy:

1. When a nation intervenes in the foreign exchange markets to protect its own currency, it must take into account the interests and welfare of other IMF member countries.

2. Government intervention in the foreign exchange markets should be carried out to correct disorderly conditions in those markets that are essentially short term in nature.

3. No member nation should intervene in the exchange markets in order to gain an unfair competitive advantage over other IMF members or to prevent necessary adjustments in a nation's BOP position.

Nations that attempt to keep the exchange value of their currencies within a fixed range around the value of some other currency or basket of currencies are known as *peggers*. The majority of pegging nations are developing countries that have strong commercial links with one or more industrialized trading partners. Examples include Korea and Venezuela, which peg the exchange rate on their currencies to the U.S. dollar. Frequently, when a developing country has strong trade relations with more than one industrialized nation, it uses a basket (group) of major currencies to set the value of its own monetary unit in order to "average out" fluctuations in the value of its exports and imports. A good example is Sweden, which pegs its krona to a basket of 15 currencies, each representing a trading partner.

Several nations peg their currency's exchange rate to a basket of currencies assembled by the International Monetary Fund, known as **special drawing rights (SDRs).** The SDR is an official monetary reserve unit designed to settle international claims arising from transactions between the IMF, governments of member nations, central banks, and various international agencies. SDRs are really "book entries" on the ledgers of the IMF, sometimes referred to as *paper gold*. Periodically, that organization issues new SDRs and credits them to the international reserve accounts of member nations based on each nation's IMF quota (contributions of currency and reserve assets to the IMF). To spend its SDRs, a nation requests the IMF to transfer some amount of SDRs from its own reserve account to the reserve account of another nation. In return, the country asking for the transfer gets deposit balances denominated in the currency of the nation receiving the SDRs. These deposit balances may then be used to make international payments. The value of SDRs today is based on a basket of currencies representing the five IMF member nations with the largest volume of exports. These five countries are the United States, Germany, France, Japan, and the United Kingdom.

Most of the developed nations *float,* rather than peg, their currencies. This means that the value of any particular currency is determined by demand and supply forces operating in the marketplace. Usually, a *managed float* is used, in which governments intervene on occasion to stabilize the value of their home currency. The United States has officially adopted a managed float policy, but in practice it often follows a "free" floating exchange rate policy, in which the open market determines the value of the dollar, with U.S. monetary authorities intervening only in emergencies.

In theory at least, a system of floating currency values should help the United States and other nations experiencing severe BOP deficits today. For example, if Americans are importing more goods from abroad than they are able to sell to overseas customers, an excess supply of U.S. dollars should build up abroad. The result should be a decline in the dollar's market value vis-à-vis other world currencies, making U.S. exports cheaper and foreign goods sold in the United States relatively more expensive. Ultimately, U.S. exports and imports should become more evenly balanced.

DETERMINING FOREIGN CURRENCY VALUES IN TODAY'S MARKETS

As we saw in the preceding section, major international currencies have floated with relative freedom since the early 1970s, their values dependent primarily on demand and supply forces in the marketplace. With this newfound freedom for currency prices and the expansion of world commerce, the volume of currency trading and the number of financial institutions participating in that trading have exploded. This is especially evident in the London and New York money markets, where exchange brokers bring in trading orders from financial institutions worldwide.

However, as the international financial system has moved increasingly toward freely floating exchange rates, currency prices have become significantly more *volatile*. The risks of buying and selling dollars and other currencies have increased markedly in recent years. Moreover, fluctuations in the prices of foreign currencies affect domestic economic conditions, international investment, and the success or failure of government economic policies. Governments, businesses, and individuals find it is more important today than ever before to understand how foreign currencies are traded and what affects their relative values.

Consider the problem faced by a corporation headquartered in the United States and selling machinery overseas. This firm frequently negotiates sales contracts with a foreign importer months before the machines are shipped. In the meantime, the value of the foreign currency the U.S. company expects to receive in payment for its products may have declined precipitously, canceling out any expected profits. Similarly, a U.S. importer bringing fine wines into domestic U.S. markets frequently must pay for incoming shipments in the currency demanded by a foreign exporter. The U.S. importer's profits could be significantly reduced if the value of the dollar declined relative to the values of foreign currencies used by the importer to pay for goods purchased abroad. The same problems confront investors in foreign securities who find that attractive interest rates available overseas must be protected from an erosion in value through suitable purchases and sales of foreign currencies. Knowledge of the foreign exchange markets is the *first step* toward successful international business and economic policy.

Essential Features of the Foreign Exchange Market

The **foreign exchange markets** are among the largest markets in the world, with annual trading volume in excess of $160 trillion. The purpose of the foreign exchange markets is to bring buyers and sellers of currencies together. It is an *over-the-counter market,* with no central trading location and no set hours of trading. Prices and other terms of trade are determined by negotiation using computer screens linked by telephone, satellite, and electronic wire all over the world. The foreign exchange market is *informal* in its operations; there are no special requirements for market participants, and trading conforms to an unwritten code of rules.

Exchange Rate Quotations

The prices of foreign currencies expressed in terms of other currencies are called **foreign exchange rates.** There are today three markets for foreign exchange: (1) the **spot market,** which deals in currency for immediate delivery; (2) the **forward market,** which involves the future delivery of foreign currency; and (3) the **currency futures and options market,** which deals in contracts to hedge against future changes in foreign exchange rates. Immediate delivery is defined as one or two business days for most transactions. Future delivery typically means one, three, or six months from today.

Exhibit 28–3 cites some recent foreign exchange rates between the U.S. dollar and other major currencies. The exhibit shows, for example, that an American importer or investor could obtain pounds sterling (£) that could be used to buy British bonds or British goods and services at a cost of about $1.5625 per pound ($1.5625/£) in November 1995. Conversely, a British investor or importer seeking to make purchases in the United States would have to pay 0.6400 pounds ($1/1.5625, or 0.6400/$) for each dollar needed. Clearly, the exchange rate between dollars and pounds is the *reciprocal* of the exchange rate between pounds and dollars, which is true as well for any other pair of currencies. Exhibit 28–4 illustrates the commonly accepted procedures for calculating exchange rates.[4]

---

[4]We note that in each quotation of a foreign exchange rate, one currency always serves as a unit of account (unit of value) and the other currency functions as the unit for which a price is stated. For example, a quote of $0.40/DM

Exhibit 28–3   **Recent Foreign Exchange Rates: The U.S. Dollar vs. Other Key Currencies** (Figures are Currency Units Per U.S. Dollar)

Country/Currency Unit	1995 Exchange Rate with U.S. Dollars ($)*	Country/Currency Unit	1995 Exchange Rate with U.S. Dollars ($)*
Canada/dollar	1.3535	Italy/lira	1,592.67
China P.R./yuan	8.3334	Japan/yen	101.94
France/franc	4.8882	Switzerland/franc	1.1437
Germany/deutsche mark	1.4173	United Kingdom/pound	156.25**

*Exchange rates are averages for November 1995.
**Exchange rate expressed in U.S. cents.

Source: Board of Governors of the Federal Reserve System, *Federal Reserve Bulletin,* January 1996, Table 3.28, p.A66.

Dealers and brokers in foreign exchange actually post not one, but *two,* exchange rates for each pair of currencies. That is, each trader sets a *bid* (buy) price and an *asked* (sell) price. For example, the dealer department in a New York bank might post a bid price for pounds sterling of £ = $1.5620US (or $1.5620/£) and an asked price of £ = $1.5625US (or $1.5625/£). This means that the dealer is willing to buy sterling at $1.5620 per pound and sell it at $1.5625. (These two exchange rates are sometimes referred to as "double-barreled" quotations.) The dealer makes a profit on the *spread* between the bid and asked price, although that spread is normally very small.[5]

Dealers and other traders in the foreign exchange market continually watch exchange rate quotations in order to take advantage of any *arbitrage* opportunities. Arbitrage in this case refers to the purchase of one currency in a certain market and the sale of that currency in another market in response to the price difference between the two markets. The force of arbitrage generally keeps foreign exchange rates from getting too far out of line in different markets around the globe.

Factors Affecting Foreign Exchange Rates

The exchange rate for any foreign currency depends on a multitude of factors reflecting economic and financial conditions in the country issuing the currency. One of the most important factors is the status of a nation's *balance-of-payments position.* When a country experiences a deficit in its balance of payments, it becomes a net demander of foreign currencies and is forced to sell substantial amounts of its own currency to pay for imports of goods and services. Therefore, balance-of-payments deficits often lead to price depreciation of a nation's currency relative to the prices of other currencies.

Exchange rates also are profoundly affected by speculation over *future* currency values. Dealers and investors in foreign exchange monitor the currency markets daily, looking

---

tells us that one deutsche mark costs $0.40. In this instance, the dollar serves as the unit of account, and the currency whose price is quoted is the mark. It is customary to place the symbol for the currency serving as the unit of account (in this case, $) in front of the stated number and the symbol of the currency whose price is being quoted (in this case, DM) following the number.

[5]Dealers will usually quote the bid price first and the asked price second and, as a rule, only the last digits in the price will be quoted to the buyer or seller. Thus, the spot bid and asked rates on pounds might be quoted by a currency dealer as 20/25 because it is assumed the customer is aware of current exchange rates and knows that the bid price being quoted is $1.5620/£ and the asked price is $1.5625/£.

Exhibit 28–4   **Methods of Calculating Foreign Exchange Rates**

Exchange Rate Conversion

Suppose the exchange rate between German Deutsche marks (DM) and the U.S. dollar ($) is DM/$ = 2.500, or DM 2.50/$.

What is the $/DM exchange rate?

Answer: 1 ÷ 2.500 = $0.40/DM

Exchange Rate Appreciation

Suppose the exchange rate between German marks and the U.S. dollar rises from DM/$ = 2.000, or DM 2.00/$, to DM 2.50/$.

How much has the dollar appreciated, in percent?

Answer: 2.500 ÷ 2.000 = 1.25, or 25%

Suppose the mark-dollar exchange rate is DM/$ = 2.5000, or DM 2.50/$. If the dollar has appreciated by 3 percent, what is the new mark-dollar exchange rate?

Answer: 2.500 × 1.03 = 2.5750, or DM 2.575/$

Exchange Rate Depreciation

Suppose the exchange rate between marks and U.S. dollars rises from DM/$ = 2.000 to DM/$ = 2.5000.

How much has the mark depreciated, in percent?

Answer: Note that the $/DM exchange rate has changed from 1 ÷ 2.000 = $0.50/DM to 1 ÷ 2.500 = $0.40/DM. The ratio of these two exchange rates is 0.4000 ÷ 0.5000, or 0.8000. Then, 1 − 0.8000 = 0.2000, or an exchange-rate depreciation of 20%

Suppose the mark-dollar exchange rate is DM/$ = 2.50 or DM 2.50/$. If the mark has depreciated 5 percent, what is the new mark-dollar exchange rate?

Answer: Because 0.4000 × 0.95 = 0.3800, the new exchange rate is 1 ÷ 0.3800 = 2.6316, or DM 2.6316/$

Suppose, once again, the mark-dollar exchange rate is DM/$ = 2.5000. If the U.S. dollar has depreciated 5 percent, what is the new mark-dollar exchange rate?

Answer: 2.5000 × 0.95 = 2.3750, or DM 2.375/$

Cross-Exchange Rates

Suppose the mark-dollar exchange rate is DM/$ = 2.5000, or DM 2.50/$, and the Swiss franc-dollar exchange rate is 2.000, or SF2.000/$. What is the SF/DM exchange rate?

Answer: 2.000 ÷ 2.500 = 0.8000, or SF 0.80/DM

Suppose the mark-dollar exchange rate is DM/$ = 2.500, or DM 2.50/$ and the dollar-Swiss franc exchange rate is $/SF = 0.5000 or 0.50/SF. What, then, is the DM/SF exchange rate?

Answer: 2.5000 ÷ (1 ÷ 0.5000) = 2.5000 ÷ 2.000 = 1.25, or DM 1.25/SF

Source: Public Information Center, Federal Reserve Bank of Chicago.

for profitable trading opportunities. A currency viewed as temporarily undervalued quickly brings forth buy orders, driving its price higher vis-à-vis other currencies. A currency considered to be overvalued is greeted by a rash of sell orders, depressing its price.

The market for a national currency is also greatly influenced by domestic conditions. Wars, revolutions, inflation, recession, and labor strikes have all been observed to have adverse effects on the currency of a nation experiencing these problems. On the other hand, signs of rapid economic growth, rising stock and bond prices, and successful economic policies to control inflation and unemployment usually lead to a stronger currency in the exchange markets. Moreover, countries with higher real interest rates generally experience an increase in the exchange value of their currencies.

Overshadowing the currency markets today is the everpresent possibility that central banks will become active participants. Major central banks around the world, including the Federal Reserve System in the United States and the Bundesbank in Germany, may decide on a given day that their national currency is declining too rapidly in value relative to other key currencies. Thus, if the dollar falls precipitously against the German mark, support operations by the Federal Reserve System in the form of heavy sales of marks and corresponding purchases of dollars may be employed to stabilize the currency markets. Usually, central bank intervention is temporary, designed to promote a smooth adjustment in currency values toward a new equilibrium level rather than to permanently prop up a weak currency.

In the United States, the Treasury Department is the agency designated to pursue market intervention in order to protect the U.S. dollar in international markets. The Treasury must decide what to do about the value of the dollar, but it is usually the Federal Reserve System that carries out the buying and selling of currencies on the Treasury's behalf through the foreign exchange desk at the Federal Reserve Bank of New York. The Fed also buys large amounts of currencies for foreign central banks and government agencies abroad. We must keep in mind that central bank intervention affects not only relative currency values but also the reserves held by private banks and the money supply. This happens because the central bank generally pays for its purchases of currency by increasing the deposit balances of private banks participating in the transaction with it. Thus, a decision by a central bank to intervene in the foreign currency markets will have *both* currency market and money supply effects unless an operation known as **currency sterilization** is carried out. For example, any increase in reserves and deposits that results from a central bank currency purchase can be "sterilized" by using monetary policy tools that absorb reserves from the banking system.

Supply and Demand for Foreign Exchange

The factors influencing a currency's rate of exchange with other currencies may be expressed in terms of the market forces of demand and supply. Exhibit 28–5, for example, illustrates a demand curve and a supply curve for dollars ($) in terms of British pounds (£). Note that the demand curve for dollars is also labeled the supply curve for pounds. This is due to the fact that an individual or institution holding pounds and demanding dollars

Exhibit 28–5   **Demand and Supply of U.S. Dollars in Terms of British Pounds**

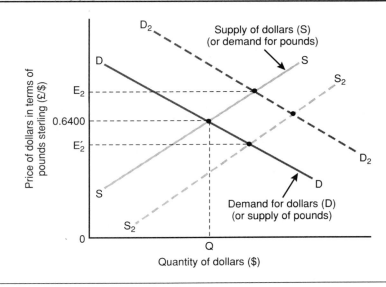

would be supplying pounds to the foreign exchange market. Similarly, the supply curve for dollars is identical to the demand curve for pounds because someone holding dollars and demanding pounds must supply dollars to the foreign currency markets in order to purchase pounds. We recall, too, that the price of dollars in terms of pounds is the reciprocal of the price of pounds in terms of dollars.

To illustrate how demand and supply forces operate in the foreign exchange markets, suppose the current exchange rate between dollars and pounds is £ = $1.5625. To purchase dollars, we have to pay 0.6400 pounds per dollar; to purchase pounds costs us $1.5625 per pound. This exchange rate between dollars and pounds is set in exchange markets by the interaction of the supply and demand for each currency. Exhibit 28–5 indicates that, at an exchange rate of 0.6400 pounds, the quantity of dollars supplied (S) is exactly equal to the quantity of dollars demanded (D).

If the price of dollars in terms of pounds were to fall temporarily *below* this exchange rate, more dollars would be demanded than supplied. Some buyers needing dollars would bid up the exchange rate toward the point where the demand for and supply of dollars are perfectly in balance. On the other hand, if the price of dollars were temporarily *above* 0.6400 pounds, more dollars would be supplied to the exchange markets. The price of dollars in terms of pounds would fall as suppliers of dollars willingly accepted a lower exchange rate to dispose of their excess dollar holdings. Only at that point where the exchange rate stood at 0.6400 pounds per dollar would quantity supplied equal quantity of dollars demanded. Only at that point would there be no reason for future changes in the exchange rate between the dollar and the pound unless changes occurred in the demand or supply of either currency.

As we noted earlier, a number of factors affect the exchange rates between currencies, including a nation's balance-of-payments position, domestic political and economic developments, and central bank intervention. Each of these factors leads to a shift in the demand for or supply of one currency vis-à-vis another, which brings about a change in their relative rates of exchange.

To illustrate the impact of shifts in currency demand and supply, suppose that consumers in Great Britain increase their demand for U.S. goods and services. As Exhibit 28–5 indicates, the demand curve for dollars would increase from D to D_2.

This is equivalent to an increase in the supply of pounds seeking dollars. The equilibrium cost of dollars in terms of pounds, therefore, will rise to E_2. British importers will be forced to surrender a greater quantity of pounds per dollar in order to satisfy the demands of British consumers for U.S. goods and services. Other things being equal, the prices of imported goods from the United States will tend to rise.

The opposite effects would occur if U.S. consumers demanded a larger quantity of British goods and services. In this case, the supply-of-dollars (demand-for-pounds) curve slides downward and to the right from S to S_2, as shown in Exhibit 28–5. Reflecting the increased demand for pounds and associated sales of dollars for pounds by U.S. importers, the dollar's price in pounds sterling falls to E'_2. The market prices of British goods and services imported into the United States tend to rise.

What happens if a central bank, such as the Bank of England or the Federal Reserve System, intervenes to stabilize the dollar-pound exchange rate at some arbitrary target level? The answer depends, among other things, on which side of the market the central bank intervenes, which currency is used as the vehicle for intervention, and the particular exchange-rate target chosen. For example, suppose that increased British demand for U.S. goods and services had driven the dollar-pound exchange rate up to E_1 as shown in Exhibit 28–6. However, this upward surge in the dollar's value had sharply reduced the purchasing power of the pound for dollar-denominated goods and services and threatened to have damaging effects on British foreign trade and industrial output. The Bank of England

Exhibit 28–6   **Effects of Central Bank Intervention to Stabilize the Dollar-Pound Exchange Rate**

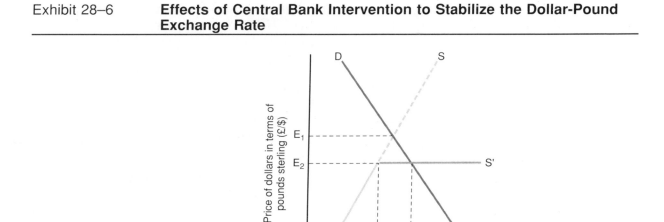

Quantity of dollars ($)

might intervene to force the dollar-pound exchange rate down to E_2 by selling dollars out of its currency reserve and demanding pounds in the foreign exchange market. In effect, the supply-of-dollars curve would be "kinked" at the stabilization price, E_2. In order to peg the dollar-pound exchange rate at E_2, the central bank would have to spend $Q'-Q$ of its dollar reserves. Otherwise, the price of dollars would again rise toward E_1 — the level dictated by demand and supply forces in the exchange markets. Conversely, if the dollar were falling to unacceptably low levels against the pound, the Bank of England or the Federal Reserve System might enter on the opposite side of the market, purchasing dollars with pounds and driving the dollar's price higher.

THE FORWARD MARKET FOR CURRENCIES

Knowledge of how the foreign exchange markets work and the ways in which currency risk can be reduced is indispensable for business managers today. Of course, the problem of fluctuating currency values is not so serious if payment for foreign goods, services, or securities must be made right away. Spot market prices of foreign currencies normally change by small amounts each day. However, if payment must be made weeks or months in the future, there is considerable uncertainty as to what the spot currency rate will be on any given future date. When substantial sums of money are involved, the rational investor or commercial trader will try to *guarantee* the future price at which currency can be purchased. This is the function of the *forward exchange market.*

Methods of Quoting Forward Exchange Rates

Trading in the spot exchange market results in agreements to deliver a specified amount of foreign currency at an agreed-upon price, usually within one or two business days and sometimes on the same day. In contrast, a **forward contract** is an agreement to deliver a specified amount of foreign currency at a set price on some future date (usually within 1, 2,

3, 6, or 12 months). The actual delivery date is referred to by traders as the *value date*. In the event customers do not know when they will need foreign currency, an *option forward contract* may be used, which gives its holder the right but not the obligation to take delivery of foreign currency in the future.

There are several different ways of measuring and quoting forward exchange rates. Suppose the spot exchange rate on German marks is $0.40US (or 0.40/DM) and that dealers in foreign exchange are selling forward contracts for delivery of marks in six months at $0.3846US. We may express the *forward* exchange rate for marks simply as $0.3846US, or $0.3846/DM — known as the *outright* rate.

Another popular method is to express the forward rate as a premium or discount from the spot rate, known as the *swap rate*. In the example above, marks are selling at a 1.54 cent *discount* in the forward market. Traders in the forward market appear to be signaling an expectation that the mark will fall in value over the next few weeks.

We may also express forward exchange rates in terms of an annualized percentage rate above or below the current spot price. To use the example above, $/DM spot = 0.4000 and $/DM forward = 0.3846. Then, the discount on forward DM for delivery in six months is figured as follows:

$$\frac{\text{Forward rate} - \text{Spot rate}}{\text{Spot rate}} \times \frac{12}{\text{Number of months forward}} \times 100$$

$$= \frac{0.3846 - 0.4000}{0.4000} \times \frac{12}{6} \times 100$$

$$= -0.0385 \times 2 \times 100$$

$$= -7.7\%$$

Marks are selling at 7.7 percent *discount* from spot in the forward market. Because marks are selling at a discount from their spot price, forward dollars must be selling at a *premium* over spot.

Suppose we know the current spot rate between two currencies and the forward premium or discount. We want to know the actual forward exchange rate. What formula should be used? The following will suffice:

$$\text{Spot rate} + \frac{\text{Spot rate} \times [\text{Premium} (+) \text{ or discount} (-) \text{ expressed as an annual rate}] \times \text{Number of months forward}}{100 \times \text{Number of months in a year}}$$

Suppose the $/DM spot = 0.4000 and forward marks for delivery in three months are selling at a 4 percent premium over spot. Using the formula above, we have:

$$0.4000 + \frac{0.4000 \times 4.0 \times 3}{1,200} = 0.4040\$/\text{DM forward}$$

This means DM/$ forward is 2.4752, or DM 2.4752/$.

FUNCTIONS OF THE FORWARD EXCHANGE MARKET

Contracts calling for the future delivery of currency are employed to cover a number of risks faced by investors and commercial traders. Some analysts group the functions or uses of forward contracts into four categories: commercial covering, hedging an investment position, speculation, and covered interest arbitrage. These four uses of the forward market are discussed below.

Commercial Covering

The export or import of goods and services usually requires someone to deliver payment in a foreign currency or to receive payment in a foreign currency. Either the payor or payee, then, is subject to currency risk, because no one knows for sure what the spot price will be for a currency at the time payment must be made. The forward exchange market can be used as a buffer against currency risk.

To illustrate, suppose that a U.S. importer of cameras has agreed to pay 5,000 marks to a German manufacturer upon receipt of a new shipment. The cameras are expected to arrive dockside in 30 days. The importer has no idea what 5,000 marks will cost in U.S. dollars 30 days from now. To reduce the risk that the price of marks in terms of dollars may rise significantly, the importer negotiates a forward contract with his or her bank for delivery of 5,000 marks at $0.30/DM in 30 days.

When payment is due, the importer takes delivery of the marks (usually by acquiring ownership of a deposit denominated in marks) at the agreed-upon price and pays the German manufacturer. Because the price is fixed in advance, the risk associated with fluctuations in foreign exchange rates has been eliminated. Today, export and import firms routinely cover their large purchases overseas with forward currency contracts or other currency risk hedging tools.

Hedging an Investment Position

Thousands of U.S. corporations have invested in long-term capital projects overseas, building manufacturing plants, warehouse and dock facilities, and office buildings. In recent years, a large return flow of long-term investments by foreign firms in the United States has occurred. Of course, the market value of these foreign investments may change drastically as the price of a foreign currency changes over time.

To illustrate, suppose a U.S. commercial bank constructed an office building in downtown London. When completed, the office facility had an estimated market value of £2 million. The current spot rate on pounds is, let us say, $1.40/£. The bank values the new building on its consolidated financial statement, therefore, at $2.8 million. However, suppose the pound has declined rapidly in value in recent months. Some market analysts expect pounds to be selling at $1.20/£ in the near future. In the absence of a hedged position, the bank would take a loss of $400,000 on its building. This is due to the fact that, at an exchange rate of $1.20/£, the office building will have a value of only $2.4 million.

Can this loss be avoided or reduced? Yes, provided the bank can negotiate a sale of pounds *forward* at a higher price. For example, the bank may be able to arrange with a dealer for the sale of £2 million for future delivery at $1.30US ($1.30/£). When this forward contract matures, if the spot price has fallen to $1.20/£, the bank can buy pounds at this rate and deliver them to the dealer at $1.30US as agreed. The result is a profit on the foreign exchange transaction of $200,000, partially offsetting the financial loss on the building due to declining currency values.

Speculation on Future Currency Prices

A third use of the forward exchange market is speculative investment based on expectations concerning future movements in currency prices. Speculators will buy currency for future delivery if they believe the future spot rate will be *higher* on the delivery date than the current forward rate. They will sell currency under a forward contract if the future spot rate appears likely to be *below* the forward rate on the day of delivery. Such speculative purchases and sales carry the advantage of requiring little or no capital in advance of the delivery date. A speculator whose forecast of future spot rates turns out to be correct makes a profit on the spread between the purchase price and the sale price.

Covered Interest Arbitrage

One of the most common transactions in the international financial system arises when an investor discovers a higher interest rate available on foreign securities and invests funds abroad. When the currency risk associated with the purchase of foreign securities is reduced by using a forward contract, this transaction is often referred to as *covered interest arbitrage.*

To illustrate the interest arbitrage process, suppose that a British auto company is selling high-grade bonds with a promised annual yield of 12 percent. Comparable bonds in the United States offer a 10 percent annual return. The bonds are of good quality and there is probably little default risk, but there *is* currency risk in this transaction. The U.S. investor must purchase pounds in order to buy the British bonds. When the bonds earn interest or reach maturity, the issuing auto company will pay foreign and domestic investors in pounds sterling. Then the pounds must be converted into dollars to allow the U.S. investor to spend the earnings in the United States. If the spot price of sterling falls, the U.S. investor's net yield from the bonds will be reduced.

Specifically, although the investor expects a spread of 2 percent a year over U.S. interest rates by purchasing British bonds, if the spot rate on pounds declines by 2 percent (on an annual basis), the interest gain will be offset by the loss on trading pounds. Clearly, a series of forward contracts is needed to sell pounds at a guaranteed price as the bonds generate a stream of cash payments. In this case, the investor will probably purchase sterling spot in order to buy the bonds and sell sterling forward to protect his or her expected income.

The Principle of Interest Rate Parity

The foregoing example suggests an important rule regarding international capital flows and foreign exchange rates: *The net rate of return to the investor from any foreign investment is equal to the interest earned plus or minus the forward premium or discount on the price of the foreign currency involved in the transaction.* The theory of forward exchange states that, under normal conditions, the forward discount or premium on one currency relative to another is directly related to the difference in interest rates between the two countries involved. More specifically, the currency of the nation experiencing higher interest rates normally sells at a forward *discount* in terms of the currency issued by the nation with lower interest rates. And the currency of the nation with relatively low interest rates normally sells at a *premium* forward relative to that of the high-rate country. A condition known as **interest rate parity** exists when the interest rate differential between two nations is exactly equal to the forward discount or premium on their two currencies. When parity exists, the currency markets are in equilibrium, and capital funds do not flow from one country to another. This is due to the fact that the gain from investing abroad at higher interest rates is fully offset by the cost of covering currency risk in the forward exchange market.

To illustrate the principle of interest rate parity, suppose interest rates in a foreign country are 3 percent above those in the United States. Then the currency of that foreign nation, in equilibrium, sells at a 3 percent discount in the forward exchange market. Similarly, if interest rates are 1 percent lower abroad than in the United States, in equilibrium, the foreign currency of the nations involved should sell at a 1 percent premium against the U.S. dollar. When such an equilibrium position is reached, movements of funds between nations, even with currency risk covered, do not generate excess returns relative to domestic investments of comparable risk. Capital funds tend to stay in the domestic market rather than flowing abroad.

It is when interest parity does *not* exist that capital tends to flow across national boundaries in response to differences in domestic and foreign interest rates. For example, suppose that interest rates in a foreign nation are 3 percent above U.S. interest rates on securities of comparable quality and the foreign currency involved is selling at a 1 percent discount against the dollar in the forward exchange market. In this case, investing abroad with exchange risks covered yields the investor a *net* added return of 2 percent per year. Clearly, there is a positive incentive to invest overseas.

Is this situation likely to persist for a long period of time? No, because the movement of funds into a country offering higher interest rates tends to increase the forward discount on its currency and lowers the net rate of return to the investor. Other factors held constant, the flow of funds abroad will subside, and capital funds will tend to stay at home until further changes in currency prices and interest rates take place.

THE MARKET FOR FOREIGN CURRENCY FUTURES

Forward contracts, as we have seen, call for the delivery of a specific currency on a specified date in the future at a set price. The intent of buyer and seller in a forward contract is to actually *deliver* the currency mentioned in the contract. In recent years, an important variation of the forward currency contract has developed — *foreign currency futures.* These too are contracts calling for the future delivery of a specific currency at a price agreed on today, *but there is usually no intent to actually deliver the currencies mentioned in the contracts.* Rather, *currency futures are traded in the majority of cases to reduce the risk associated with fluctuating currency prices.* Today, currency futures contracts are traded in the United States (for example, at the International Monetary Market (IMM) established by the Chicago Mercantile Exchange) and in a number of other world financial centers on futures exchanges (unlike forward contracts, which are traded largely in an unregulated interbank dealer market). The most popular currency futures contracts today are for the future delivery of German marks, Swiss francs, British pounds, Japanese yen, Canadian and U.S. dollars, and Eurodollars.

Currency futures are attractive to two groups: foreign exchange hedgers and foreign exchange speculators. The *hedgers,* who typically are banks, trading companies, and multinational corporations, seek to avoid damage to their profits from normal business transactions caused by unexpected changes in currency exchange rates. Usually, a hedging individual or institution seeks out a currency *speculator* who hopes to profit from changes in relative currency rates by taking on the risk the hedger seeks to minimize. Two basic transactions take place on currency futures exchanges: the buying hedge and the selling hedge.

Importers of goods typically use the *buying hedge.* In this case, a domestic importer who is committed to pay in a foreign currency when goods are received from abroad fears that currency may rise in price. He therefore *purchases* a futures contract, agreeing to take delivery of pounds at a set price as near as possible to the date on which the goods must be paid for. Because the price of this contract is fixed, the importer has "locked in" the value of the imported goods, helping to protect his potential profit on the business transaction. As a final step, near the date the goods are paid for, the importer will "zero out" his futures contract purchase by *selling* a comparable currency futures contract, perhaps through a broker trading on the floor of a currency futures exchange. The exchange's clearinghouse, which records each transaction taking place on the exchange, will automatically cancel out the importer's obligation to take delivery of or to deliver foreign currency.

How has the importer protected himself against loss due to currency risk? If a foreign currency rises in value during the life of a futures contract, the importer will experience reduced profits or increased losses on the imported goods themselves because the foreign currency has risen in value relative to his home currency. However, the market value of a currency futures contract also rises when the market value of the underlying currency increases. Therefore, the importer will be able to sell currency futures contracts at a higher price than the price for which they were originally purchased. The resulting profit in currency futures at least partially offsets the reduced gains or losses on purchase of the imported goods. On the other hand, if currency values fall, potential profits on the imported goods will increase because they can be bought more cheaply, but an offsetting loss will be recorded in futures trading because the contracts must be sold at a lower price. Cash market gains (losses) offset futures market losses (gains).

The opposite kind of hedge in currency futures is known as the *selling hedge*. This transaction is often employed by investors who purchase foreign securities and want to protect their earnings from a drop in currency values. In this instance, investors could hedge their expected earnings by *selling* futures contracts in the currency involved at the time the securities are acquired in the cash (spot) market. If contracts are sold in an amount that covers both principal and interest or dividends, investors have "locked in" their investment return regardless of which way exchange rates go. If the foreign currency involved has declined in price relative to the home currency when the security pays out cash or must be sold, a loss will be incurred in cash received, but investors will earn an offsetting futures market profit by *buying* futures contracts in an amount equivalent to those sold earlier. Conversely, if the foreign currency appreciates relative to the home currency, cash market revenues from the security will rise when the foreign currency is converted to home money, offsetting a loss from buying back futures contracts that now cost more.

OTHER INNOVATIVE METHODS FOR DEALING WITH CURRENCY RISK

The recent volatility of foreign exchange rates has given rise to an ever-widening circle of devices to deal with currency risk. For example, the *currency option* gives a buyer the right, though not the obligation, to either deliver or to take delivery of a designated currency at a set price any time before the option expires. Thus, unlike the forward market, actual delivery *may* not occur, but unlike futures trading, no follow-up purchases or sales are needed to stop delivery. The advantage of the currency option is that it limits downside risk but not upside profits.

A related hedging instrument is the *option on currency futures. Call options* on currency futures give the buyer a way to protect against rising exchange rates by buying from another investor a currency futures contract at a fixed price, thus locking in a desired currency delivery price. On the other hand, *puts* on currency futures give a hedger protection against falling exchange rates by giving him or her the right to sell currency futures at a fixed price, regardless of how market prices change. These options carry their own market price, which rises or falls based on the probability the futures option will actually be exercised by its buyer.

Another innovative device is the **currency swap.** In straight currency swaps, a company that has borrowed a foreign currency (such as yen) for a designated length of time immediately turns around and exchanges the yen for its home currency (say, dollars) with a counterparty. The counterparty may be a bank or other business firm with an exactly opposite situation, holding dollars but needing yen. As shown in Exhibit 28–7, when the loan comes due, the borrowing company reverses the transaction with the counterparty, swapping its home currency to get back the yen needed to pay off its foreign currency loan. In this case, there is no exposure to the risk of changing yen prices. The borrower has received an inflow of dollars at the beginning of the loan and experienced a dollar outflow when the loan is paid off. The currency swap has merely facilitated the borrower's ability to borrow dollars from foreign markets without currency risk. The advantage of currency swaps is that they can be arranged with longer maturities and more suitable terms of settlement than most standard currency exchange contracts. *Exchange-risk insurance* also has become popular and is available from selected government sources (such as the Export-Import Bank) and from some private insurers.

Innovative new approaches to currency risk continue to emerge each year, and many old methods have been resurrected lately. For example, many multinational firms have expanded their use of *local loans* — that is, securing credit inside the countries where they have sales or production operations. Others have resorted to issuing *dual-currency bonds* with principal and interest payments denominated in two different currencies. Some exporters now ship only if *prepayments* are made by a customer overseas that cover all or a substantial portion of the value of a shipment before it is made. Some companies simply *barter* (exchange) their goods or property directly so that no currency changes hands. *Selective currency pricing* is also employed, in which the seller invoices the buyer in a currency thought to be more stable or easier to hedge.

The ultimate economic response when other risk-reducing methods appear to be too costly or too risky is for a seller to use *risk-adjusted pricing* of goods and services traded across international boundaries. For example, goods sold to countries where currency risk is unacceptably large may be priced higher to compensate the seller for that added risk. Ultimately, individuals living in those countries where currency risk is unusually high will wind up paying higher prices for goods and services and possibly face a lower standard of

Exhibit 28–7	**The Currency Swap: Converting a Foreign Currency–Denominated Loan into a Domestic Currency Loan**

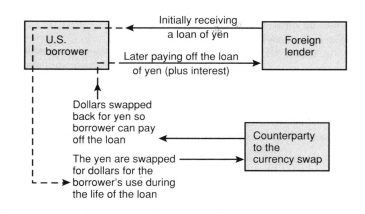

living. Currency risk, like any other form of risk in the financial system, has real consequences for the economic welfare of both individuals and nations.

GOVERNMENT INTERVENTION IN THE FOREIGN EXCHANGE MARKETS

The value of a nation's currency in the international markets has long been a source of concern to governments around the world. National pride plays a significant role in this case, because a strong currency, avidly sought by traders and investors in the international marketplace, implies the existence of a vigorous and well-managed economy at home. A strong and stable currency encourages investment in the home country, stimulating its economic development. Moreover, changes in currency values affect a nation's balance-of-payments position. A weak and declining currency makes foreign imports more expensive, lowering the standard of living at home. And a nation whose currency is not well regarded in the international marketplace will have difficulty selling its goods and services abroad, giving rise to unemployment at home.

The United States has pursued an "on-again, off-again" policy of supporting the dollar in international markets over the years, sometimes supporting the dollar vigorously and other times (as in the mid-1990s) merely "signaling" its targets for the dollar with occasional intervention. When the U.S. has intervened in the currency markets, it has done so mainly out of concern for the condition of the U.S. economy, particularly the effects of inflation. Another factor is the key role played by the U.S. dollar in the international financial system. The dollar is a **vehicle currency** that facilitates trade and investment between many nations. For example, international shipments of crude oil, regardless of their origin or destination, are usually valued in dollars. As noted in Chapter 18, the market for dollar deposits held in banks abroad — Eurodollars — is the world's largest money market, financing commercial projects and even providing operating funds for many foreign governments. For all of these reasons, the United States, as well as foreign governments and central banks, have repeatedly intervened in the foreign exchange markets to stabilize currency values and insulate domestic economic conditions from developments abroad.

Recently, the United States and other leading industrialized nations have evidenced a strong commitment to exchange rate stability, with an eye toward preventing inflation, and have displayed a consistent presence in foreign currency markets. There seems to be more acceptance among the principal trading partners of the United States today that a stronger dollar carries substantial benefits for many nations besides the United States. Accordingly, the Federal Reserve, in cooperation with the U.S. Treasury through the Treasury's Exchange Stabilization Fund, has recently made massive purchases and sales of dollars and other currencies, resulting in some of the largest holdings by the U.S. government of foreign currencies in American history. Usually, these holdings of foreign currency are invested in foreign and domestic securities to generate earnings for these agencies until needed for foreign exchange operations.

There seems little doubt that government intervention to (1) ensure smoother increases or decreases in the international market value of leading currencies and (2) coordinate more closely the economic and monetary policies of major trading nations will continue. The cost of not doing so could be extremely high. For example, a falling dollar threatens the United States with more rapid inflation because the prices of imported goods denominated in other currencies rise. Moreover, the U.S. government depends heavily on foreign investors to help finance its huge federal budget deficit. A falling dollar is a sign of declining foreign investor interest in U.S. securities. U.S. policymakers could revive foreign investor interest by pushing for sharply higher interest rates, but this step would tend to slow U.S. economic growth and create more unemployment. Clearly, government intervention in world currency markets is neither an easy nor a riskless step. However, the luxury of a single nation making economic policy decisions independent of other nations affected by those decisions now seems to be a relic of the past.

KEY TERMS AND CONCEPTS IN THIS CHAPTER

balance-of-payments
(BOP) accounts

current account

capital account

gold standard

gold exchange standard

modified exchange
standard

the managed floating
currency standard

special drawing rights
(SDRs)

managed float

foreign exchange markets

foreign exchange rates

spot market

forward market

currency futures and
options market

currency sterilization

forward contract

interest rate parity

currency swap

vehicle currency

STUDY QUESTIONS

1. What is meant by the term *balance of payments*? Describe the principal components of the balance-of-payments accounts.

2. Please supply a brief definition of each of the following terms associated with the balance of payments:
    a. Current account
    b. Merchandise trade balance
    c. Service transactions
    d. Capital account
    e. Official reserve assets
    f. Special drawing rights
    g. Direct investment
    h. Errors and omissions

3. Describe and discuss the principal trends that have occurred in the following components of the U.S. balance-of-payments accounts in recent years:
    a. Merchandise trade balance
    b. Investment in assets abroad by U.S. residents
    c. Investment in U.S. assets by foreign residents

4. What is *currency risk*? Explain how it affects exporters, importers, and securities investors active in the international markets.

5. Why was the *gold standard* developed? What problems did it solve, and what problems did it create? What is the difference between the gold standard and the gold exchange standard?

6. When and where was the modified exchange standard created? Explain how this system worked to stabilize the value of foreign currencies.

7. The international monetary system of today has been called the *managed floating currency standard*. Briefly explain what this term means. Can you foresee any problems with this approach?

8. What are SDRs? Describe their function in settling international payments and in determining exchange rates.

9. What are the principal factors affecting the value of any particular currency in the international exchange markets?

10. Distinguish between the spot and forward markets for foreign exchange. Why is it necessary to have two markets rather than one?

11. Describe the principal uses of forward exchange contracts today. Give an example of each use.

12. What is a buying hedge in currency futures? A selling hedge? Under what circumstances is each used?

13. What is *interest rate parity*? How does it influence the flow of capital funds abroad?

14. In recent years, central banks have intervened in the foreign exchange markets from time to time to support one currency or another. Why do you think central bank intervention in the market might be necessary? What impact are central bank operations likely to have?

15. What is the purpose of currency swaps? How do they work?

PROBLEMS

1. Please indicate whether each of the transactions below would represent a credit (+) or a debit (−) item in a nation's balance of payments.

    a. General Electric Corporation purchases electric switches from a supplier in Germany.

    b. Bell Helicopter sells new helicopters to a British oil field exploration company.

    c. Universal Studios makes the decision to begin building a new theme park in Singapore.

    d. Mr. and Mrs. Robert Alford of Indianapolis sent a check last month to a cousin living in Lebanon who was celebrating a wedding anniversary.

    e. George Elwin has just received a dividend check for the stock he holds in British Airways.

    f. Citicorp of New York agrees to provide insurance for goods shipped by the International Furniture Mart of Copenhagen to a London wholesale house.

2. From the figures given below calculate (a) the balance on merchandise trade, (b) the service balance, (c) the balance on goods and services, and (d) the balance on current account for the nation whose most recent balance of payments figures include the following:

Merchandise imports	$89.6 billion
Military transactions, net	7.8 billion
Unilateral transfers	1.9 billion
Investment income, net	6.2 billion
Merchandise exports	94.7 billion
U.S. government grants	0.9 billion
Other service transactions, net	2.3 billion

3. Suppose the exchange rate between British pounds (£) and U.S. dollars ($) is $1.35 per pound. What is the correct way to write this pound-dollar exchange rate? The dollar-pound exchange rate?

4.   Suppose the pound-dollar exchange rate is now 1.3500. Then, the U.S. dollar increases in value by 5 percent. What is the new pound-dollar exchange rate? What is the new exchange rate if the U.S. dollar appreciated by 10 percent?

5.   If the pound-dollar exchange rate increased from £/$ = 1.3500 to 1.4000, by what percentage amount has the pound depreciated?

6.   If the pound-dollar exchange rate is 1.4000 and the pound declines 10 percent in value, what is the new pound-dollar exchange rate?

7.   Suppose the pound-dollar exchange rate is 1.4000 and the yen-dollar exchange rate is 2.3000. What is the yen-pound exchange rate?

SELECTED REFERENCES

Carlozzi, Nicholas. "Pegs and Floats: The Changing Face of the Foreign Exchange Market." *Business Review.* Federal Reserve Bank of Philadelphia, May–June 1980, pp. 13–23.

Chrystal, K. Alec. "A Guide to Foreign Exchange Markets." *Review.* Federal Reserve Bank of St. Louis, March 1984, pp. 5–18.

Hunter, Linda C. "Europe 1992: An Overview." *Economic Review.* Federal Reserve Bank of Richmond, January 1991, pp. 17–27.

Jacobson, Kristina. "U.S. Foreign Exchange Operations," *Economic Review.* Federal Reserve Bank of Kansas City, September–October 1990.

McDonough, William T., and Robert Ennis. "Treasury and Reserve Foreign Exchange Operations." *Quarterly Review.* Federal Reserve Bank of New York, Winter 1991–92, pp. 55–60.

Chapter 29

International Banking

LEARNING OBJECTIVES IN THIS CHAPTER

- To understand the important role that large multinational banks play in both domestic and foreign markets around the world.
- To explore the different types of offices and facilities multinational banks operate overseas and to identify what financial services they offer in foreign markets.
- To understand how and why international banking is regulated.

No review of the international financial system would be complete without a discussion of the role of international banking institutions. Through these banking firms flow the majority of commercial and financial transactions that cross international borders. Along with British, Japanese, and Canadian banks, U.S. commercial banking institutions have led in the development of international banking facilities to meet the far-flung financial needs of foreign governments and multinational corporations. Until recently, the international activities of U.S. banks were concentrated principally in their foreign offices, due mainly to federal government controls over foreign lending. However, the gradual relaxation of government controls in recent decades, the high cost of maintaining a large network of foreign branches, and improvements in communications technology have encouraged many international banks to offer more international services from their *domestic* offices.

The development of multinational banking over the past century has resulted in several benefits for international trade. One benefit to the public is greater competition in international markets, reducing the prices of financial services. It also has tied together more effectively the various national money markets into a unified international financial system, permitting a more optimal allocation of scarce resources. Funds flow relatively freely today across national boundaries in response to differences in relative interest rates and currency values. Although these developments have benefited both borrowers and investors, they also have created problems for governments trying to control the volume of credit and inflation.

THE SCOPE OF INTERNATIONAL BANKING ACTIVITIES

Multinational Banking Corporations

The term **multinational corporation** usually is reserved for large nonfinancial corporations with manufacturing or trading operations in several different countries. However, this term is equally applicable to the world's leading banks, most of which have their home offices in Canada, the United States, Great Britain, Germany, France, and Japan but have established offices worldwide. These giant banks have accounted for most of the growth in multinational banking in recent decades.

Types of Facilities Operated by Banks Abroad

Major banks around the world have used many vehicles to expand their international operations. All major banks have *international departments* in their home offices to provide credit, access to foreign currencies, and other services for their international customers, and many operate *full-service branch offices* in foreign markets as well. Others maintain simple booking offices, known as **shell branches,** on such offshore islands as the Bahamas to attract Eurocurrency accounts while avoiding domestic banking regulations. **Representative offices** help find new customers and give local customers a point of contact with the home office, but they cannot take deposits. U.S. banks and foreign banks active in the United States have set up **Edge Act and Agreement Corporations** across state lines, which are special subsidiary companies that must, under Federal Reserve regulations, devote the majority of their activities to international banking. Many banking firms have also set up **international banking facilities (IBFs)** in the United States, consisting of computerized accounts maintained for international customers and subject to minimal U.S. regulations. In addition, multinational banks often make *direct equity investments* in foreign companies, either alone or as joint ventures with other financial firms.

Choosing the Right Kind of Facility to Serve Foreign Markets. Which kind of facility is adopted by a multinational bank to serve its customers depends on government regulations and the bank's size, goals, and location. Most banks begin with international departments and then, as the volume of business grows, open up representative offices, and ultimately full-service branches and investments in foreign businesses. A recent trend toward legal liberalization of foreign trade and international lending has stimulated the growth of *home-based offices* that send officers to call on customers overseas or serve clients by wire. However, many multinational banks argue that successful international operations require an institution to have a stable presence overseas in the form of agencies, branches, or representative offices.

Laws and regulations play a major role in determining the nature and location of multinational banking offices. For example, The People's Republic of China, India, and Saudi Arabia prohibit or restrict the operation of branches by foreign banks. In other areas of the world, fears of political upheaval or outright expropriation of foreign-owned facilities have limited the entry of multinational banks. For several of the largest U.S. banks, international operations yield from one third to as much as one half of their income, and a few receive more than half their earnings from international activities. Particularly noteworthy has been U.S. bank penetration of foreign consumer banking markets, such as the "money shops" operated by New York's Citibank in Great Britain. U.S. banks entered the consumer lending field in the 1920s, and they have developed considerable expertise in that field. Personal financial services represent extremely attractive opportunities in foreign markets, and U.S. banks hold a significant share of consumer loan and deposit markets abroad, especially in Europe.

SERVICES OFFERED BY INTERNATIONAL BANKS

Multinational banks offer a wide variety of international financial services to customers. These services are described briefly below. Of course, the particular services offered by each bank depend on its size, location, and the types of facilities it maintains overseas.

Issuing Letters of Credit

Most banks enter the international sector to finance trade. In most cases, credit is needed to bridge the gap between cash expenditures and cash receipts and to reduce the risks associated with long-distance trading. In these situations, a **letter of credit** is often the ideal financing instrument. A letter of credit is an international bank's future promise to pay for goods stored overseas or for goods shipped between two countries. Such letters may be issued to finance exports and imports or to provide a standby guarantee of payment behind IOUs issued by a corporate customer. Through a letter of credit, the bank substitutes its own promise to pay for the promise of one of its customers. By substituting its promise, the bank reduces the seller's risk, facilitating the flow of goods and services through international markets. Occasionally, the seller becomes concerned about the soundness of the bank issuing the letter of credit; the seller may then ask his or her own bank to issue a confirmation letter in which that bank guarantees against foreign bank default.

Buying and Selling Foreign Exchange (FOREX)

Major multinational banks have dealer departments that specialize in trading foreign currencies (FOREX). International banks buy and sell foreign currencies on a 24-hour basis to support the import and export of goods and services, the making of investments, the giving of gifts, and the financing of tourism. They also write forward contracts for the future delivery of foreign exchange.

Issuing Bankers' Acceptances

Bankers' acceptances are time drafts used mainly to finance the shipment of goods or commodities. With a bankers' acceptance, the bank agrees to pay a seller of goods when the draft expires on behalf of one of its customers who is importing goods or purchasing foreign currency. When a bank stamps "Accepted" across the face of the draft, it becomes a guarantee of future payment, and it makes the acceptance a negotiable instrument that may be traded in the open market.

Accepting Eurocurrency Deposits and Making Eurocurrency Loans

International banks accept deposits denominated in currencies other than that of their home country. These **Eurocurrency deposits** are used to pay for goods shipped between countries and serve as a source of loanable funds for banks. Eurocurrency deposits may also be loaned to corporations and other large wholesale borrowers. The majority of **Eurocurrency loans** carry floating interest rates based on the London Interbank Offer Rate

(LIBOR) for three-month and six-month Eurocurrency deposits. Eurocurrency credit normally goes to borrowers with impeccable credit ratings. One important innovation in recent years is the *syndicated Eurocurrency credit,* in which one or more multinational banks will put together a loan package accompanied by an information memorandum. Other banks can then participate in the loan without direct communication with the borrower.

Marketing and Underwriting of Both Domestic and Eurocurrency Bonds, Notes, and Equity Shares

For generations, leading international banks have assisted their domestic and foreign customers in raising capital through the issuance of new securities — bonds and other forms of debt and equity shares (stock). One of the most popular of these securities is the **Eurobond** — a debt security denominated in a currency other than that of the country or countries where most or all of the security is sold. For example, a U.S. automobile company may desire to float an issue of long-term bonds to raise capital for one of its subsidiaries operating in Greece. The company might issue bonds denominated in British pounds to be sold in Europe through an underwriting syndicate made up of banks and securities dealers.

Most Eurobonds are denominated in dollars, although substantial amounts are also denominated today in deutsche marks, guilders, pounds, yen, and francs. Eurobonds normally are straight debt offerings with maturities ranging to about 15 years, though warrants, conversion features, and adjustable interest rates and exchange rates may be attached to improve the marketability of a particular issue. The majority are callable bearer bonds with coupons attached.

Multinational banks assist the Eurobond market in several ways. Major banks such as Morgan Guaranty Trust Company of New York have established international clearing systems to expedite the delivery of Eurobonds. Banks and security brokers are the principal intermediaries through which Eurobonds find their way to the long-term investor. The borrower may contact a multinational bank and ask it to organize a syndicate to place a new Eurobond issue. At this point, a *consortium* is formed, embracing at least four or five U.S., British, Japanese, French, or German banks, and a bank located in the borrowing country. The consortium agrees to subscribe to the Eurobond issue at issue price minus commission and then organizes a large group of banks and securities dealers as underwriters. Sometimes more than 100 banks are included in the underwriting syndicate. Once formed, the underwriting group gives the borrower a firm offer for its bonds and, if accepted, works hard to place the issue with investors.

Multinational banks also assist their corporate and governmental customers with medium-term financing through note issuance facilities (NIFs). Under a standard NIF contract, a customer is authorized to periodically issue short-term notes (usually with three- to six-month maturities) to interested investors over a designated time span (perhaps five years). The bank or banks involved agree to provide backup funding (standby credit) at a spread over prevailing Euromarket interest rates. For an underwriting fee, the bank agrees to purchase any unsold notes or advance cash to the customer until sufficient market funding is obtained.

Securitizing Loans

Over the past decade, leading multinational banks have unfurled a new source of funds for themselves and their customers: securitization, or the pooling of loans having similar purposes, quality, and maturities and the selling of financial claims (securities) against the pool of loans. A good example is New York's Citicorp, which is the leading packager of consumer credit-card receivables, pooling the receivables that arise as households borrow on their credit cards and selling securities in the open market as claims against the income these receivables will ultimately bring in. International banks can earn income in several different ways from the securitization process: (1) by securitizing some of their own loans and pocketing the difference in interest earnings between the average yield on the pool of loans and the cost of issuing securities against the loan pool; (2) by agreeing to guarantee the income of investors from pools of securitized loans; (3) by retaining servicing rights on a pool of loans, collecting and recording the income received from the loans in return for a servicing fee; or (4) by acting as adviser or trustee for those customers that desire to securitize any loans or receivables they hold in order to generate new capital.

Other Services Provided by International Banks

In addition to the foregoing services, international banks offer extensive *advisory services* to their customers. These include analysis of foreign market conditions, evaluation of sales prospects and plant location sites, and advice on foreign regulations. International banks often prepare credit reports on overseas buyers for exporters of goods and services and assist domestic firms interested in entering foreign markets.

International banks offer cash management services and lease capital assets for their corporate customers. These banks frequently engage in interest rate swaps to aid multinational corporations in dealing with the risk of fluctuating market interest rates. In recent years, many international banks have added sales of insurance, credit cards, mortgage brokering services, and equity investments to their traditional service lines.

FOREIGN BANKS IN THE UNITED STATES[1]

Banks owned by foreign individuals and companies have entered the United States in great numbers in recent years. The reasons behind the expansion of foreign banking activities in the United States reflect growth in international trade and investments and the opportunity for profit in the huge U.S. market. Originally, foreign-based banks penetrated U.S. markets for the same reasons U.S. banks established facilities overseas: to follow their customers who had established operations in other countries. Once in the United States, however, foreign banks found the possibility of attracting deposits and loans from major U.S. corporations and even from U.S. households irresistible. Moreover, the U.S. economy has been more stable and prosperous than many other national economies where foreign banks are headquartered or represented.

Recent Growth of Foreign Banks in the United States

The size of foreign bank operations in the United States is impressive. By 1990, there were about 700 foreign bank offices in the United States. Japanese offices led all others, followed by France, the United Kingdom, and Canada. Data released by the Federal Reserve Board indicates that those foreign-based institutions held assets of more than $915 billion in 1994, compared to only about $200 billion in 1980. In relative terms, U.S. offices of

---

[1]This section is based in part on an earlier article by Rose (1976) in *The Canadian Banker and ICB Review* and is used with permission.

Exhibit 29–1   **The Importance of Foreign Bank Operations in the United States**

Year	Total Assets Held by Foreign Banks in the U.S. ($ Billions)	Proportion of Total U.S. Banking Assets Controlled by Foreign Banks (Percent)
1975	$ 52	5.3%
1980	201	11.9
1985	441	16.1
1990	738	21.7
1995*	960	21.8

*Figures through the end of June.

Source: Federal Reserve Board and the Federal Reserve Bank of New York.

foreign banks held about 22 percent of the total assets of all banks in the United States in June of 1995 as Exhibit 29–1 shows. The growth rate of foreign bank assets held at their U.S. offices averaged about double the growth rate of domestic bank assets during the 1980s before leveling out in the 1990s. Recent growth has made foreign banks a significant competitive factor in U.S. financial markets, especially in the markets for domestic business loans, credit guarantees, and bankers' acceptances.

Federal Regulation of Foreign Bank Activity

Until the 1970s, no federal laws regulated foreign bank activity within U.S. borders. However, Congress has been monitoring foreign bank operations since 1966, when IntraBank, a Lebanese institution, collapsed and several U.S. banks suffered severe losses. Passage of the Bank Holding Company Act Amendments of 1970 marked an initial step toward federal regulation of foreign banking. Under the terms of these amendments, any corporation controlling one or more domestic banks became subject to supervision by the Federal Reserve Board.

However, with foreign banks in the United States growing more rapidly than domestic banks, the pressure on Congress for regulation of foreign banks intensified. Proponents of restrictive legislation argued that foreign banks reduced the effectiveness of domestic monetary policy and that the lack of specific regulations applying to foreign banks was unfair to domestic banks, which must conform to an elaborate system of regulations. Perhaps more important, foreign banks could branch across state lines — a privilege denied U.S. banks until the passage of the Riegle-Neal Interstate Banking and Branching Efficiency Act in 1994.

There was also a disparity between foreign and domestic banks in the services each group of institutions was permitted to offer. U.S. banks are prohibited from offering services in domestic markets not *closely related* to traditional banking services (i.e., the extension of credit and the taking of deposits). Moreover, the Glass-Steagall Act in 1933 prohibited U.S. banks from investment underwriting of either corporate bonds or stock. Such a prohibition does not exist for most foreign-owned banks, and several foreign banking organizations moved to take advantage of this loophole.

Responding to these various arguments, Congress passed the **International Banking Act (IBA)**, which became law on September 17, 1978. Under the terms of the IBA and subsequent regulations, U.S. branches and agencies of foreign banks with worldwide assets of $1 billion or more are subject to legal reserve requirements and any federal interest rate ceilings on their deposits that might then be in force. Foreign banks that maintain U.S.

offices are required to register with the Secretary of the Treasury. Each foreign bank with an office accepting deposits from the public must select a "home state." No foreign bank may establish a federal- or a state-chartered branch outside its home state unless granted permission by the states involved. This provision of the law limited a foreign bank's ability to accept deposits across state lines, especially consumer-type deposits.

The IBA proved to be a more lenient piece of legislation than many analysts had expected. It did not attempt to punish or discriminate against foreign banks relative to their U.S. counterparts. In fact, the act set in law the principle of *mutual nondiscrimination,* used widely abroad as a regulatory standard. This principle permits foreign-owned banks to operate under the same conditions and to possess the same powers as domestic banks. It is a policy that avoids establishing two sets of banking regulations, one for domestic institutions and the other for foreign-owned banks.

Federal regulation of foreign banks was extended a step further in 1980 when the Depository Institutions Deregulation and Monetary Control Act was passed. (Please see Exhibit 29–2.) All foreign banking organizations offering services to U.S. residents became eligible for deposit insurance from the Federal Deposit Insurance Corporation and were required to conform to deposit reserve requirements set by the Federal Reserve Board. When a foreign bank opens an agency, branch, or loan production office in the United States, it must register as a bank holding company and conform with all holding company laws and regulations as administered by the Federal Reserve System. These new requirements even more firmly reflected Congress's intention to place all banks (foreign and domestic) on the same regulatory footing and in the same field of competition.

Finally, on the heels of the scandal involving the Bank of Credit and Commerce International (BCCI) of Luxembourg, the Federal Reserve Board was granted broad new powers to regulate the activities of agencies, branch offices, and subsidiaries of foreign banks inside U.S. territory. Under the terms of the Foreign Bank Supervision Enhancement Act passed by Congress in 1991, the Fed must approve any proposed agency, branch, or representative office to be set up in the United States. Because of lax regulation of BCCI by authorities in Luxembourg, the Fed was empowered to close a foreign bank office if its home country fails to subject the parent bank to comprehensive supervision and regulation, especially in monitoring its worldwide operations and ensuring the adequacy of the foreign bank's capital. Any foreign bank seeking to buy more than 5 percent of the stock of a U.S. bank or bank holding company must receive Federal Reserve Board approval. Moreover, small deposits (less than $100,000) can be accepted in the United States by foreign banks only through subsidiary companies that have FDIC insurance coverage and conform to all U.S. banking regulations.

REGULATION OF THE INTERNATIONAL BANKING ACTIVITIES OF U.S. BANKS

A far more significant problem than regulating foreign banking activities in the United States is the regulation, supervision, and control of U.S. banks offering their services overseas. What limits should be placed on U.S. banks operating overseas? Who should enforce those limits?

The first of these questions is not yet fully resolved, but the second has a ready answer. The *Federal Reserve Board* has been designated as the chief regulatory agency for international banking activities, especially where Fed member banks are involved. A member bank choosing to expand its activities abroad through the creation of foreign branches or

Exhibit 29–2   **Purposes and Provisions of the International Banking Act (IBA) of 1978 and Other Recent U.S. Banking Laws**

International Banking Act of 1978

Purpose: To promote competitive equality between domestic and foreign banking institutions operating in the United States.

Provisions: Limited the interstate branching of foreign banks.

Provided for federal licensing of branches and agencies of foreign banks.

Authorized the Federal Reserve Board to impose reserve requirements on branches and agencies of foreign banks.

Provided for foreign bank access to Federal Reserve services such as the discount window.

Provided for federal deposit insurance for branches of foreign banks.

Granted broader powers to Edge Act corporations of U.S. banks so they can compete more effectively with branches and agencies of foreign banks.

Subjected foreign banks operating branches and agencies to the prohibitions against nonbank business ventures of the U.S. Bank Holding Company Act.

Depository Institutions Deregulation and Monetary Control Act of 1980

Purpose: To further equalize deposit regulations and services that foreign banks can offer vis-à-vis domestic banks inside the United States.

Provisions: All foreign banks selling banking services to U.S. residents were made eligible for FDIC insurance coverage on their deposits but must also hold reserve requirements behind their deposits at levels specified by the Federal Reserve Board.

International Lending and Supervision Act of 1983

Purpose: To reduce the risks to international banks and their depositors from international lending.

Provisions: U.S. banks must set aside special reserves against their foreign loans.

Minimum capital requirements are imposed to protect depositors in international banks.

Foreign Bank Supervision Act of 1991

Purpose: To give U.S. authorities greater control over foreign bank activities inside the United States and to limit risk to the FDIC insurance fund from foreign bank activities.

Provisions: If foreign banks wish to accept deposits in the United States of less than $100,000, they must establish one or more U.S. banking subsidiaries and obtain FDIC insurance coverage for their deposits.

Uninsured branch offices of foreign banks cannot accept deposits under $100,000.

Prior approval of the Federal Reserve Board is required for the creation of new foreign bank branch, agency, or representative offices inside U.S. territory.

Foreign banks operating inside the United States must be subject to comprehensive supervision by their home country and must not violate U.S. law or engage in unsound banking practices. Their U.S. operations may be terminated by the Federal Reserve Board if found to be operated in an unsafe manner.

---

through investments in foreign firms must secure the approval of the Federal Reserve Board. In contrast, state laws govern the foreign operations of state-chartered banks. However, with the exception of a handful of states, state governments have exerted only nominal control over foreign banking activities.

Of prime concern to the Federal Reserve is the protection of domestic deposits and the stability of the domestic banking system. The Fed has argued that it is difficult to separate a bank's foreign operations from its domestic activities. If a foreign subsidiary gets into trouble, the danger exists that public confidence in the soundness of the controlling domestic bank will be undermined. For this reason, the Fed, in reviewing applications of U.S.

banks to expand abroad, examines closely the condition of their domestic offices to determine if their home-based operations are adequately capitalized and if the bank has sufficient management skill to support both foreign and domestic operations.

The regulatory authorities would like to develop ways to insulate the foreign activities of U.S. banks from their domestic operations. Such insulation would grant wider latitude to banking activities abroad and at the same time shield domestic banks from the hazards associated with foreign operations. Legally, one subsidiary is not liable for the debts of another. However, in practice, a domestic bank might feel compelled to aid its affiliates operating in foreign markets. The practical, if not legal, links between foreign and domestic subsidiaries of multinational banks force regulators to keep close tabs on the foreign operations of all banks.

The Fed, typically allows U.S. banks to offer a greater variety of services in foreign markets than at home, including noncontrolling equity investments in nonfinancial corporations. Although U.S. banks do not play a large direct role in our own capital markets, the broader powers available to them for international operations have brought them in as major players in capital markets overseas. The Fed argues that banking regulations in the United States reflect this nation's views on how much competition there should be in the financial system. However, competition in foreign markets depends on the policies of other nations, and Federal Reserve officials have preferred to leave such questions to the host country. The Fed tries to balance freedom against risk in deciding on the proper scope of multinational banking activities.

THE FUTURE OF INTERNATIONAL BANKING

The future of international banking is clouded at this time due to the many cross-currents of economics and politics that pervade our world. Sluggish economic growth, trade barriers, and political struggles threaten the flow of international commerce and make bank lending across national boundaries risky. In this section, we take a brief look at these problems and their implications for the future of international banking.

The Risks of International Lending

Political and Currency Risk. Lending funds in the international arena is riskier, on average, than domestic lending. *Political risk* — the risk that government laws and regulations will change to the detriment of business interests — is particularly significant in international operations. Governments are frequently overthrown and confiscation of private property is a common occurrence in many parts of the world.[2] There is also *currency risk*, that is, the risk associated with changing relative prices of foreign currencies. The value of property pledged behind an international loan falls if the currency of the home country is devalued, eroding the lender's collateral. Geography too works against the

---

[2]Many financial analysts often lump political and other risks in international lending under the general term *country risk*. This is the possibility that governments borrowing money from multinational banks may be unable or unwilling to repay and that private borrowers may, because of law and regulation, be unable to pay on their loans. For example, private borrowers may be prevented from paying due to *transfer risk*, a component of country risk in which a nation prohibits outflows of capital, dividends, or interest payments due to an internal shortage of foreign exchange. The other component of country risk — *political risk* — arises when loans cannot be repaid due to war, revolution, or changes in regulatory philosophy that adversely affect the ability of a borrower to fulfill a debt obligation.

international lender. The large distances that frequently separate lender and borrower make it difficult for a bank loan officer to see that the terms of a loan are being followed.

The risks of international lending became of much greater concern in the 1970s and 1980s because international banks became the principal source of borrowed funds for developing countries. Unfortunately, when international commodity prices declined, numerous developing countries could not meet the terms of their existing loans. Many of these debts were rescheduled by agreement between banks and debtor countries. Simultaneously, the International Monetary Fund and World Bank moved to supply more funds to give these debtor nations time to adjust their domestic economies to a harsher economic climate.

Frequently, such adjustments resulted in reduced demands for imports, slower economic growth, and increased unemployment. Some nations threatened to repudiate their international debt or unilaterally alter the terms of repayment. At the same time, some multinational banks began to withdraw or scale down their international lending operations by selling old loans at deep discounts, which limited the availability of liquidity in international markets and slowed the growth of world trade. Industrialized countries reduced their purchases of exports from developing countries, which resulted in these nations having even less spendable reserves to pay off their debts. Many multinational banks with heavy loan exposure to developing countries saw the prices of their stock and their credit ratings plummet. Some banks pioneered *debt-for-equity swaps* in which they accepted shares of stock in certain overseas projects as a substitute for holding loans. Debt-equity swaps also provided more flexible funding for developing countries.

Geographic Distribution of International Bank Lending. Beginning in the late 1970s, U.S. bank regulators inaugurated semiannual surveys of foreign lending by U.S. banking organizations. The principal concern of these regulatory agencies was that U.S. multinational banks were overly committed to foreign loans where the political and economic risks were unusually high. This might threaten the confidence of the public in the soundness of some of the world's largest banks. Recent regulatory surveys show that most loans extended by U.S. multinational banks are made to industrially developed nations and to countries in Central and South America. However, close to a third of all foreign loans are made to less-developed countries, a number of which have been in serious financial difficulty at various times.

Fortunately, the majority of loans to distant nations are short term (maturity of one year or less), and many are to banks themselves. On the whole, multinational banks appear to be relatively conservative lenders, directing their credits to large bank, corporate, and governmental borrowers situated mainly in Western Europe and in rapidly growing Asian and Latin American markets. The bulk of such loans are concentrated in the largest international banks. Nevertheless, as the peso crisis in Mexico in 1995 demonstrates, even what appear to be relatively conservative bank loans can become problem loans in a hurry when exchange rates or economic conditions change.

Public Confidence and Bank Failures

A persistent problem in international banking is the preservation of public confidence in the banking system. Essentially, this means protecting the major multinationals against failure. To avert serious financial difficulties among the world's largest banks, regulatory authorities in the United States and elsewhere look closely at the *capital positions* of multinational banks. Regulators have urged a slower expansion of international loans and avoidance of excessive credit exposure in loans to any one country, especially to non-oil-producing nations of the Third World. This is coupled with an insistence on adequate levels of equity capital, adjusted for differences in loan risk among major banks. One of the first steps in this direction occurred in 1983 when the United States Congress passed the **International Lending and Supervision Act.** This law ordered bank regulatory agencies to prepare new rules requiring U.S. banks to do the following:

1. Maintain special reserves against foreign loans in those instances where the quality of a bank's assets has been impaired by protracted borrower inability to pay out loans.
2. Limit loan rescheduling fees charged troubled foreign borrowers.
3. Disclose a bank's exposure to foreign borrowers.
4. Hold minimum levels of capital as protection for an international bank's depositors.
5. Conduct feasibility studies of foreign projects involving mining, metal, or mineral processing before approving a loan.

Then, in 1988, representatives from the Federal Reserve System, the Bank of England, the Bank of Japan, and the central banks of eight other countries signed the Basle Agreement. This historic international contract calls on central banks to monitor the capital positions of international banks under their jurisdiction and to impose minimum capital requirements on all banks. As we saw earlier in Chapter 7, the primary objective of this new international capital standard is to ensure that banks from one nation do not have a competitive advantage over banks from other nations due to more lenient capital regulations. Beginning in 1993, all banks subject to the Basle Agreement were required to hold a ratio of core capital (mainly equity funds) to total risk-adjusted assets of at least 4 percent and a ratio of total capital (core capital plus debt and other forms of capital) to total risk-adjusted assets of at least 8 percent. Thus, the Basle Agreement reduces permissible leverage for banks that may handicap the ability of bankers to meet some international credit needs in the future.

The Basle Agreement broke new ground in another way — each international bank's minimum capital requirement is to depend not only on the volume of its assets but also on the amount of risk it takes on as reflected in its balance sheet and its off-balance-sheet activities (such as the issuance of credit guarantees). Banks accepting greater credit risk must hold more capital to preserve public confidence in their long-term viability. Hopefully, the Basle Agreement represents only the first step in a new era of international cooperation among regulators of banks, securities dealers, and other financial firms aimed at promoting stability in international markets and at preserving the public's confidence in the global financial system.[3]

The Spread of Deregulation: How Fast Should We Go?

As we saw in Chapter 7, the United States began an aggressive program of deregulating domestic banking in the 1980s. Other nations — such as Great Britain with its Big Bang deregulation of banking and security dealer services in 1987 — have also made significant strides toward lifting confining rules and regulations, permitting their own banks as well as foreign banks operating within their borders to compete more equally. Unfortunately, the pattern of international banking deregulation has been spotty, with some nations (such as Japan) lowering barriers to competition slowly to protect domestic institutions. The real losers here are domestic consumers of financial services, who have fewer options and

---

[3]Increasingly, the new Basic Capital Standards have been used as a standard for approving or denying international banks to expand their activities abroad. For example, in December 1995, the Federal Reserve Board voted to allow U.S. banks to acquire foreign business interests without prior notice if no more than 2 percent of core capital is involved and if the banks involved are well capitalized and well managed.

probably pay higher prices until deregulation takes place. The key issue is how to allow deregulation of financial services on an international scale to proceed rapidly without wholesale bank failures that destroy public confidence. The Basle Agreement is a positive step in the right direction, but only a step. Finding the proper speed and scope for financial deregulation remains a challenging global issue.

An added complication was thrown into the debate over how fast and how far deregulation should go in freeing international banks when the scandal involving the Bank of Credit and Commerce International (BCCI) Holdings, S.A., broke into the headlines in the early 1990s. This far-flung international bank holding company was based in Luxembourg, which, at the time, had few rules for holding company operations. Following revelations that BCCI violated U.S. holding company law by acquiring ownership interests in U.S. banks without approval of the Federal Reserve Board, further investigation uncovered possible money-laundering activities. U.S. investigators in the Department of Justice and at the Federal Reserve began to bring indictments and levy stiff fines against principals in the BCCI case in 1992. Although it may take many years to resolve all the legal issues in the BCCI case, this incident clearly points to a broader issue for international banking in the 1990s and beyond: the necessity for regulatory cooperation and for *harmonization* of banking regulations across nations so that no bank entrusted with the public's funds can find refuge from some minimum level of public scrutiny that ensures respect for the law in its business dealings.

PROSPECTS AND ISSUES IN THE 1990s

These recent trends suggest a much different future for international banking than seemed likely in earlier years. Growth — limited by capital and the availability of experienced management — should be more gradual and loan quality more of a factor in future extensions of credit to businesses and governments abroad. However, continuing expansion of foreign banking activities in the United States, Western and Eastern Europe, the nations that emerged from the dissolution of the former Soviet Union, Asia, and Latin America can be anticipated.

Certainly, a number of critical questions must be answered for international banking. For example, to what extent will the regulatory authorities of different nations cooperate to control foreign banking activities? How can we harmonize different banking rules from one country to the next to promote competition and innovation but also public safety? What is an appropriate capital position for banks engaged in foreign lending and for those subject to significant amounts of market risk in their on-balance-sheet and off-balance-sheet activities? Where must regulation end and the free play of market forces be allowed to operate in international banking?

And, what about the rise of strong competitors in the form of nonbank firms — money market funds, security dealers and underwriters, finance companies, and the like? These firms today are offering parallel services to international banks, supplying credit, underwriting new security offerings, securitizing loans, offering savings instruments, and managing customer cash positions, but they are burdened with far fewer regulations. Leading international banks have begun to respond to these new competitors. For example, Deutsche Bank of Germany is a leading underwriter of corporate securities on the European continent; France's BNP offers savers a product that looks very much like money market fund shares; Citibank is a leading securitizer of receivables emerging from credit-card loans and other forms of lending. As the next century beckons us forward into a new era, international banks must find ways to adjust to the challenges posed by this "new competition" or suffer further erosion of their share of the international financial marketplace.

These are perplexing issues that have few clear answers. However, the importance of international banking and the penetration of domestic markets by foreign banking institutions demand that effective answers be found that strengthen the system and provide a basis for future growth and development.

KEY TERMS AND CONCEPTS IN THIS CHAPTER

multinational corporation	IBFs	Eurobond
shell branches	letter of credit	International Banking Act (IBA)
representative offices	Eurocurrency deposits	
Edge Act corporations	Eurocurrency loans	International Lending and Supervision Act

STUDY QUESTIONS

1. What are the essential differences between the following types of banking organizations?
    a. International banking departments   d. Representative offices
    b. Edge Act and Agreement Corporations   e. Full-service branches
    c. Shell branches   f. IBFs

2. What factors seem to influence the type of activities an international bank chooses to serve its customers?

3. What are the principal services offered by international banks?

4. Explain why foreign banks have entered the United States in such large numbers in recent years.

5. What federal regulations apply to foreign banks operating in the United States today? What factors motivated Congress to pass the International Banking Act of 1978? The Foreign Bank Supervision Act of 1991?

6. What federal agency is the chief regulator of international banking in the United States?

7. What is the principle of mutual nondiscrimination? What problems could it create for regulators?

8. What major problems have been encountered by the international banking community in recent years? How have these problems been dealt with?

SELECTED REFERENCES

Chrystal, K.A. "International Banking Facilities." *Review.* Federal Reserve Bank of St. Louis, April 1984, pp. 5–11.

Rose, Peter S. "Foreign Banking in the United States." *The Canadian Banker and ICB Review,* May–June 1976, pp. 58–61.

————, *Japanese Banking and Investment in the United States: An Assessment of Their Impact Upon U.S. Markets and Institutions.* New York: Quorum Books, 1991.

Rose, Peter S., and Habib G. Bassoul, "Edge Acts: Outside-In." *The Canadian Banker and ICB Review,* April 1980, pp. 52–56.

Scarlata, Jodi G. "Institutional Developments in the Globalization of Securities and Futures Markets." *Review.* Federal Reserve Bank of St. Louis, January/February 1992, pp. 17–30.

Chapter 30

The Future of the Financial System

LEARNING OBJECTIVES IN THIS CHAPTER

- To understand the economic, demographic, social, and technological forces reshaping financial institutions, financial markets, and the financial system today.

- To gain a perspective on recent trends in the financial system and to see how those trends could affect all of us personally and professionally in the future.

The system of financial markets and financial service firms is undergoing revolutionary change. New financial services and instruments are expanding rapidly in volume and variety. Home equity credit lines, international mutual funds, currency and interest rate swaps, loan securitizations, and other new services and instruments are only the vanguard of a wave of **financial innovation** sweeping through the global financial system today. A trend toward **deregulation** of the financial sector by major governments around the world has unleashed the forces of competition and innovation on a scale never seen before. Banks and insurance companies, securities dealers, mutual funds, and thrift institutions are locked in an intense struggle for the customer's business that is unparalleled in history.

The expanding competitive struggle in a deregulated financial marketplace has given rise not only to *new* services and *new* financial instruments but also to *new* types of financial institutions: large, multiproduct, multimarket, technologically sophisticated, sales-oriented organizations that are designed to weather the risks inherent in today's volatile financial marketplace. More and more, financial institutions look *alike*, offering the same services and organized in the same ways. Traditional distinctions between one type of financial institution and another are becoming hopelessly blurred. This process of **homogenization** is creating a real challenge for marketing professionals trying to convince the public that their particular financial institution is really different from its rivals.

More financial institutions are establishing interstate operations and expanding their marketing programs to cover whole regions and, in many instances, the whole globe. The results are falling geographic barriers to interinstitutional competition and strong pressure to consolidate small financial institutions into large ones. More financial institutions are becoming stockholder-owned corporations to open up new sources of capital to fund their expansion. Under intense competitive pressure and rising costs, the number of independently owned financial institutions is declining, victims of merger or failure.

Financial markets that have traditionally been local in character are expanding to become regional, national, and even international in scope. This **market broadening** reflects recent advances in communications technology. Such breakthroughs offer the prospect of reduced service delivery costs, improving employee productivity, bringing new services on line more rapidly, and expanding the effective marketing area for both old and new services. Someday most commercial and consumer loans will be traded in national and international markets, providing new sources of liquidity for financial institutions making these loans and improving the availability of credit to the public.

As new markets develop, businesses and governments will have less reason to borrow from traditional financial intermediaries and more reason to sell debt and equity securities directly to investors in the open market. Indeed, the role of the traditional financial intermediary in the channeling of savings into investment is shrinking. Moreover, the development of a market for *securitized assets* — pools of loans — allows almost any large firm with a strong market reputation to package its loans and issue new securities against them, thereby generating more cash flow to make new investments. Thus, there is less need for traditional loans from financial institutions, although many banks and insurance companies have learned that they can benefit from this trend by selling advice on how to effectively package new security offerings, by acting as agent for such offerings, and by issuing standby credit guarantees in case something goes wrong.

Of course, the trends we observe in today's financial system and among financial institutions is *not* a completely new story. Its roots lie deep in history. Today's trend toward deregulation of financial institutions counteracts the excesses of an earlier era — the Great Depression of the 1930s — when comprehensive regulation of financial institutions promised *safety* but tended to stifle both competition and innovation. Furthermore, the current emphasis in the financial sector on new product development and research, frequent technological updating, elaborate marketing programs to sell financial services, and strategic planning is a carryover from manufacturing and industrial firms that have used such techniques for decades. There is a growing awareness that the challenges and techniques of managing a financial institution are *not* fundamentally different from those of managing any other business firm. The products are different, but the methods of control and decision making are essentially the same.

SOCIAL, ECONOMIC, AND DEMOGRAPHIC FORCES AND TRENDS RESHAPING THE FINANCIAL SYSTEM

We must recognize, too, that much of what is happening in the financial system of markets and institutions today is a response to broad social, economic, and demographic trends that span generations. These trends are affecting not just financial institutions but also governments, businesses, and households in every corner of society and every nation on the globe.

For example, fundamental changes in the age makeup of the population are having profound effects on savings habits, consumption, and borrowing decisions worldwide. The population is rapidly aging, due primarily to better medical care, nutrition, and changing attitudes about childbearing. The *life-cycle hypothesis* — developed by Modigliani and Ando (1960) and others — suggests that, as individuals age, they reduce their expectations of lifetime income, mainly because their expected time in the labor force is decreasing. With retirement looming closer, personal savings rates should rise and, correspondingly, per-capita consumption spending should fall in real terms. Thus, the long-term post-World

War II boom of ever higher consumer borrowing and spending is moderating, resulting in a more slowly growing economy, lower average interest rates, and less dependence on foreign capital in the future. The challenge faced by banks, insurance companies, and other service providers will be to find better ways to accommodate the demands of older savers, including the need for retirement, tax, and estate planning.

The basic family unit is also changing, with more single-parent households, a rising age at which first marriages occur, and a declining fertility rate in most industrialized countries. However, in the United States, population growth estimates have recently been revised sharply higher due to greater-than-expected immigration, an increase in fertility, and greater longevity related to improved medical care. (The U.S. Census Bureau projects the U.S. population will rise from 255 million currently to more than 380 million by the year 2050.)

The highest divorce rate in history marks many industrialized nations, and more people are choosing to live alone. Married couples make up nearly 60 percent of all U.S. households, but less than half of these have children living in the home. People living alone make up one quarter of all households in the United States today, and their numbers appear to be rising. Also on the rise are dual-earner couples with above-average incomes, who will soon be in the majority.

More men are responsible for household chores and child care today, making them more conscious of the problems of household budgeting and the need to build savings capital. In contrast, women are entering the labor force in huge numbers and are also getting stronger educational backgrounds than at any other time in history. Today, a roughly *equal* proportion of young women and young men (ages 25 to 29) have completed at least four years of college. Moreover, in these younger age groups, the gap between the earnings of men and women has closed significantly. In general, educational levels have risen so much today that almost half of the U.S. labor force (in the 25 to 64 age group) has been enrolled in college at one time or another. High school diplomas are becoming the minimum amount of education an individual needs to avoid poverty and reliance on welfare.

Although many of these demographic trends have slowed recently, most demographers do not anticipate a significant *reversal* anytime soon, and so demands will continue to grow for new forms of housing, daycare facilities, flexible work schedules, and less expensive medical care. The result is a new matrix of financial service needs, including demands for new savings instruments and loans that support retraining, relocation, provide college educations, and supply more venture capital to support new businesses that are struggling to be born.

Added to the demographic changes are broad *economic* movements. For example, manufacturing industries are being displaced by service industries in more developed economies. The computer has transformed the economy from a system primarily reliant on manufacturing to one centered increasingly on information. The expansion of service firms is creating most of the new jobs, and these businesses have their own unique financing needs. Accelerated growth in automation, telecommunications, and biotechnology is creating the need for new kinds of credit and risk protection.

The broader and faster dissemination of information today is contributing to the internationalization of markets, which spurs competition and heightens the need for international cooperation. One of the most dramatic examples is the formation of the European Community (EC), creating a common market from 12 nations with more than 300 million household customers. Banks, insurance companies, and other financial firms licensed to operate in any one of these 12 countries will be licensed to offer their services throughout Western Europe, leading to free and open marketing of financial services. Eventually, much of Europe will have a common financial system and a common currency. These planned reforms have already set in motion a wave of mergers and joint ventures among leading European banks, insurance companies, and other firms in order to survive in a more open financial marketplace.

Similar developments loom on the horizon for Eastern Europe and the nations that make up the former Soviet Union now that the cold war has faded. Huge amounts of venture capital and funding for education are desperately needed in Russia (and the other nations that once belonged to the old Warsaw Pact) to improve their standard of living and retrain their workers in order to stem widespread unemployment and modernize.

As internationalization proceeds along with continuing advances in communications technology, there will be a whole range of benefits for the financial system and the public. More savings and investment opportunities will be opened. Investing in foreign corporations and institutions will appear to be less risky because more information will be available on their financial condition, and the markets served by these institutions will be better known and understood. The result should be a more efficient allocation of scarce resources and increases in the real output of goods and services. Arbitrage opportunities due to discrepancies in prices between markets should be less frequent and shorter in duration.

However, internationalization of the financial and economic system will not be without cost. Economic conditions within any one nation will become increasingly sensitive to foreign developments and harder for domestic policymakers to control or influence. Confirmation of security trades (known as *clearing*) and getting proper payment and timely delivery of securities bought and sold (known as *settlement*) will be more difficult and more risky in a globalized financial system, at least until advances in communications technology and international cooperation among governments and regulatory agencies catch up with rapidly advancing globalization.

So powerful are the foregoing trends that none can be ignored by the management and owners of financial service firms today. The choice now for those who work in or use the services of the financial system is either to recognize and adapt to such trends or to be swept away in their wake.

THE CHALLENGES AND OPPORTUNITIES PRESENTED BY RECENT TRENDS

There is little question now that the trends mentioned above will continue into the foreseeable future. But we must recognize that these trends have unleashed new problems of their own — great unresolved issues that must somehow be dealt with as we rush toward the future. We turn now to these critical issues for the future in the sections that follow.

Dealing with Risk in the Financial System: Ensuring the Strength and Viability of Financial Institutions

The money and capital markets and the financial institutions that operate within them depend heavily on *public confidence*. The financial system works to channel scarce loanable funds (credit) to their most productive uses only if individuals and businesses are willing to save and trust those savings to financial institutions, and only if other businesses and individuals are willing to rely on the financial system to provide credit to support their consumption and investment. When *any* financial institution develops serious problems that reach public notice, the public's confidence in other financial institutions may be damaged as well. The result can be a smaller flow of savings through *all* financial institutions and restrictions on the availability of credit. Jobs and economic growth can be adversely affected.

The Consequences of Reduced Public Confidence. There seems to be little question that the public regards financial institutions as less secure today than a generation ago. Record numbers of failed banks, S&Ls, and other financial institutions during the 1980s and early 1990s contributed to a significant decrease in public confidence. Periodic "flights to quality" by investors have become more frequent. Financial service customers are now more sensitive to the risk of losing their funds and are therefore less loyal in dealing with any *one* financial institution. Financial service *reliability* has become as important as price to many customers today.

Loss of public confidence not only produces adverse consequences for individual institutions but also damages the *efficiency* of financial market processes. A flight of funds from financial institutions reduces their operating volume, thereby making them less efficient in using resources. That portion of the public continuing to rely on the financial system is forced to pay higher prices for financial services that may be less in quantity and inferior in quality.

Ways to Promote Public Confidence. How can we ensure the continued viability of existing financial institutions and restore public confidence in them? Both government and the private sector could offer effective remedies.

Government Insurance Systems. Governments have taken major steps in recent years to ensure the safety of banks and other financial institutions in order to protect the public's funds. For example, during the 1930s, with thousands of banks failing, the U.S. Congress created the Federal Deposit Insurance Corporation (FDIC) to provide insurance coverage for small deposits. When federal deregulation of depository institutions was launched in the United States in 1980, Congress anticipated the public's concern about deposit safety and raised federal insurance maximums from $40,000 to $100,000 per depositor. In 1974, Congress created the Pension Benefit Guaranty Corporation (PBGC) to insure retirement plans promised to the employees of some private businesses. Certainly, the federal insurance idea could be extended to include other financial instruments in which the public saves its money, such as life insurance policies or annuities.

One problem with government insurance that must be resolved, however, is how to avoid distorting risk-taking decisions by the managers of private financial institutions. Federal deposit insurance, for example, has protected small depositors but led many banks and thrifts to take on greater risk because, for most of the FDIC's history, insurance premiums were the same for *all* depository institutions, resulting in riskier depository institutions being subsidized by safer institutions (known as a *moral hazard* problem).

One solution (which was mandated by Congress for the FDIC beginning in 1993) is to tie the size of government insurance premiums directly to the amount of risk taken on by each insured institution so that risk exposure to the insurance fund becomes the determinant of the cost of federal insurance to private institutions. Unfortunately, we aren't sure yet how to accurately measure the failure risk of an individual financial institution. Ideally, we would like to have a risk index that correctly *ranks* insured institutions from most risky to least risky every time. This way, we could be sure that the most risky financial service firms pay the highest insurance premiums. Our preferred risk index ought to tell us that if one financial firm is twice as risky as another, the former will pay insurance premiums twice as high as the latter. The difference in risk premiums must be significant enough to modify the behavior of riskier financial institutions. Unfortunately, no such ideal risk measure has yet been identified. Moreover, history indicates that private entrepreneurs possess great skill in finding loopholes in nearly all regulatory formulas.

Another step governments can take is to impose *minimum equity capital requirements* on financial service industries. The stockholders' equity in each financial institution provides a cushion to absorb short-term losses until management can correct weaknesses. When a financial institution has insufficient capital to cover its current and anticipated risk exposure, it faces a *capital adequacy* problem. By imposing minimum equity capital requirements on a financial institution, regulators can force a financial firm's stockholders to accept a substantial share of the risks taken on by their firm. The bigger the stockholders' share of each financial institution's total capital, presumably the more watchful the stockholders will be over the firm's risk exposure and the policies pursued by its management. In this instance, the burden of controlling risk would be vested in a financial institution's stockholders, who must supply more high-cost capital if the institution suffers so many losses that it has a capital adequacy problem.

Governments must be careful in imposing capital requirements on financial institutions, however. The international financial markets have become so competitive that if financial institutions in one nation face high minimum capital requirements while those in another nation face low or no capital requirements, the latter institutions have an unfair competitive advantage. This fact of international life led the 12 leading industrialized nations to adopt the Basle Agreement on Bank Capital Standards in July 1988. This agreement pledged bank supervisory authorities in each nation to achieve a minimum overall bank capital-to-risk-adjusted-assets ratio of 8 percent. A unique feature of this new agreement is that risk weights are to be applied to each category of assets a bank holds so that riskier banks will be forced to hold additional capital in order to protect their depositors. Important breakthroughs in cooperative international financial regulation like the Basle Agreement must continue in the future if public confidence in the broadening financial system is to be maintained.

Private Responses to the Safety Issue. Can the private financial sector satisfactorily ensure its own financial strength and stability? Is the *market* a competent police officer to control institutional risk taking? In theory at least, the private marketplace *is* its own regulator. Financial institutions choosing to accept greater risk in managing their customers' and their owners' funds must pay the penalty for risk that the market imposes: a higher cost for any funds raised and often a less reliable supply of funds, particularly in periods of economic recession when capital market investors display a heightened sensitivity to risk. Thus, the financial markets will squeeze the earnings of riskier financial institutions through the mechanism of a rising cost of capital.

One of the most important ways the private market is dealing with greater risk of failure today is by encouraging the development of *larger* financial institutions that diversify themselves geographically and by service line in order to spread risk over a greater number of markets. This development has been most evident in the rise of interstate banking in the United States and the passage of the Riegle-Neal Interstate Banking and Branching Efficiency Act of 1994. This trend toward interstate operations will encompass not only financial firms that have traditionally served broad regional and national markets (such as insurance companies and brokerage firms) but also locally oriented financial institutions (such as credit unions and savings banks).

Developing Better Tools to Deal with Risk. Another way for private financial institutions to deal with risk in the financial system is to develop and use better **risk-management tools**. Managers of successful financial institutions today must be intimately familiar with such risk-management tools as:

- *Zero coupon and stripped securities,* which can be tailored to each investor's investment horizon (discussed in Chapter 12).

- *GAP management,* which permits a financial manager to match repricing opportunities in assets with repricing opportunities in liabilities (discussed in Chapter 12).

- *Duration analysis,* which shows how a financial institution's net worth responds to interest rate changes (discussed in Chapter 10).

- *Interest rate SWAPs,* which permit institutions to trade interest payments for better matching of inflows and outflows of cash (discussed in Chapter 12).

- *Currency swaps,* which permit borrowers to switch currencies and avoid exchange risk (discussed in Chapter 28).

- *Financial futures and option contracts,* which allow setting prices today for future security purchases or sales (discussed in Chapter 13).

Although these risk-management tools are useful, *new* tools must be added to the financial manager's arsenal in the future in order to effectively hedge against the risks that will challenge tomorrow's institutions.

The Information Problem. Unfortunately, relying *exclusively* on the marketplace to ensure the strength of financial institutions is open to serious question. Given adequate information, an efficient market can correctly value individual financial institutions. But does the financial marketplace receive *all* the information it needs to generate optimal decisions? The answer is probably *no.* Depository institutions still provide only limited information to buyers of their securities. Key information regarding the quality of their loans is known in detail only to government supervisory agencies.

Capital market investors can only *approximately* price the securities of financial institutions that do not fully disclose their financial condition and prospects. Serious consideration needs to be given to greater financial disclosure of the risk exposure of individual financial institutions, especially for the protection of retirement savings. The recently passed FDIC Improvement Act of 1991 requires annual full-scope, on-site examinations of each U.S.-insured depository institution (but only once every 18 months for depositories with less than $100 million is assets). Moreover, federally insured depository institutions (except those under $150 million in assets) must supply bank regulatory agencies with annual reports, including an annual audit by an independent public accountant. The FDIC Improvement Act also calls for more public disclosure of auditor information and of the market values of institutional assets and capital. In combination with a strong, risk-adjusted insurance program, increased public information can unleash the powerful economic force of informed investing to more effectively control risk taking by financial institutions.

The Implications of Inflation for Financial Institutions

Like any business firm, a financial institution must adapt to a changing market environment if it is to survive and prosper. Perhaps nowhere in the financial marketplace has this been more evident than in dealing with inflation, which is still a serious problem for many nations around the globe (as recent events in Mexico have shown). When inflation is significant, financial institutions and the customers they serve are faced with an economic environment that favors consumption spending, penalizes saving, and presents greater risk to lenders. The declining attractiveness of financial instruments to savers, coupled with inflated credit demands, can create a serious "funding gap" for many financial institutions. Inflation also raises the cost of funds for financial institutions and can narrow their profit margins between asset yields and borrowing costs. It also can create a *capital shortage* problem for financial institutions because the squeeze on margins limits the availability of retained earnings to strengthen equity capital. With thinner capital positions, more financial institutions ultimately will fail.

A New, Reduced-Inflation Environment. The late 1980s and early 1990s have ushered in a markedly different inflation scenario in the United States: a substantially *lower* annual rate of price increases. In theory, just as financial institutions were adversely affected earlier by rapid inflation, it might be expected that the much slower inflation in recent years would be beneficial to institutions, stabilizing their profit margins and stock values.

Unfortunately, the lower average inflation rate in the most recent period has ushered in its own unique set of problems, which arose because of the fundamental *causes* of lower inflation rates. One primary cause has been a slowdown in the overall growth of the economy. Economists have known for decades that inflation could be reduced by creating idle production lines and unemployment. In the early 1990s, unemployment rose as consumer demand and production sagged and a new recession set in. Although the cost of deposits and other sources of funds has generally been significantly lower in recent years than during the 1970s and early 1980s, when inflation was higher, the demand for credit has also declined, so that the revenues of financial institutions are growing more slowly along with their costs. This limits potential earnings and makes cost control by financial institutions operating in a lower inflationary environment as important as cost control was in the severe inflationary environment of earlier years.

Will the relatively subdued inflation of the 1990s continue into the future? Many economists fear that the answer to that question is *no*, partly because the current low average inflation rate seems to rest on a comparatively narrow base and rests on public will to sustain anti-inflation policies. However, an aging population and a more slowly growing economy would seem to suggest greater price stability in the future. Recent strong investor demand for bonds and other fixed-income securities suggests a substantial degree of public confidence that inflation, in the United States at least, is more nearly under control. Nevertheless, it is difficult to argue with the broad sweep of history. The Western world has been experiencing frequent inflation since the beginning of the Industrial Revolution nearly three centuries ago. The building blocks of that inflation — expanding consumer demand, concentrations of economic power, war, and the growth of government activity in the economy — still seem to be with us.

The Importance of Financial Flexibility. If rapid inflation does rekindle, financial institutions will need to be better prepared for it than they have been in earlier periods. The key to weathering future inflationary storms is *financial flexibility*, the ability of financial institutions to shift portfolios and operating strategies in order to stay abreast of price-level changes. Investments will need to be shifted toward inflation-hedged assets such as selected common stock and real estate. Operating costs, especially wages and salaries and interest costs, will soar out of control unless they are skillfully managed with particular attention to more effective use of new technology and strategic planning.

The Effect of New Technology on the Design and Delivery of Financial Services

The Information Revolution. Providing financial services to the public involves the storage and transfer of *financial information*. A checking account, for example, conveys the information that an individual or a business firm has claim to assets managed by a bank or thrift institution. The writing of a check is a new information item, designating what amount of funds is to be removed from one account and transferred to another account. The advent of the computer has taught us that information can be transferred in microseconds via computer and through wire and satellite networks that offer more speed, lower cost, and greater accuracy.

The technological revolution in information storage and transfer is moving at an accelerating pace. Newer, smaller, and faster computer systems appear every year. Some emerging technological innovations that will have a major impact on the future of financial services include the Internet and World Wide Web, facsimile (fax) machines, smart (pre-encoded) cards, and pocket telephones.

Recent Technological Advances. One area of strong future growth will be in *networking,* or *systems integration,* in which computers are linked via communications networks. The *Internet,* or *World Wide Web,* offers banks and other financial service firms a low-cost channel through which to advertise their services. Leading financial firms (such as Bank of America) have already set up home pages on the Internet, describing their services. Moreover, once safety measures are in place to protect the customer's privacy and funds, access to financial services will be available instantly from the nearest networked computer.

Traditional communications links are increasingly being supplemented by video conferences via *satellite,* involving both managers and customers of financial institutions. Management strategy meetings and presentations to customers can be beamed into offices and homes. This medium will make it easier for financial institutions to bring in outside experts to help sell their services, using an informational approach to product advertising. Through this space-age communications channel, managers of financial service institutions will have less need to travel to conferences and face-to-face meetings with customers. Insurance agents, for example, will increasingly be computer-linked to insurance companies, resulting in faster and more efficient resolution of claims. Underwriting information and professional insurance expertise can be accessed all over the globe.

Also likely to play a larger role in the future are *facsimile machines (fax)*, which reproduce documents using signals transmitted via telephone lines. Recent advances in these instruments have improved the readability and durability of faxed documents, linked them with laser printers, and lowered their production costs. Ahead are combination machines that serve simultaneously as copiers, printers, and long-distance conveyors of information. The lower production costs made possible by these machines will open up greater access to distant markets for financial institutions. In addition, fax machines are increasingly becoming interlinked with personal computers, permitting both visual display and rapid alteration of faxed documents and the long-distance negotiation of loans and other financial services. Instead of visiting the office of a lending institution to apply for a loan, the customer can fax a loan application or use an automated teller machine to apply for a loan. Like other recent technological advances, fax technology will contribute significantly to the continuing broadening and integration of financial markets, bringing more financial institutions into direct competition and encouraging further consolidation.

Equally revolutionary will be the widespread adoption of *pocket telephones,* no bigger than a deck of playing cards, that will allow financial service customers to communicate from any location, 24 hours a day. Accompanying the development of full-service pocket telephones will be the *pocket computer.* As faster and lighter computer chips are developed, it will be possible to have pocket-size PCs that merge information storage, information retrieval, telecommunications, and computing power in one lightweight, eminently portable instrument. Pocket computers will allow both managers of financial service firms and their customers to instantly record transactions, notes, and memos; to fax documents; and to send and receive data over wireless networks. Financial decision makers will be equipped with a powerful new tool, permitting 24-hour market monitoring, decision making, and implementation.

These new technologies will also make it possible for customers to literally do away with their checkbooks. Growing numbers of depository institutions are offering telephone bill-paying services as well as home and office personal computer (PC) links to a financial institution's computer through which the customer can authorize payments from his or her account with the touch of a button. Even more significant is the spread of "smart cards" encoded with a certain amount of "digitized cash" that allow the customer to pay for goods and services at the point of sale by merely presenting a plastic card. When inserted into a suitable terminal, the amount of a purchase is automatically subtracted from the remaining balance of "digitized cash."

These and other technological advances in information technology literally make every financial service customer into a mobile "branch office." There will be less and less need to ever visit the office facilities of a financial institution. Fewer employees will be needed in the financial institutions sector and, eventually, hundreds, if not thousands, of full-service branch offices will be closed. The financial services business clearly is in transition from a labor-intensive industry to a capital-intensive one.

Public Attitudes and Cost. The adjustment of people and institutions to the unfolding technological revolution probably will be slower than the revolution itself. Many consumers and businesses still prefer the security and privacy of cash and checkbook transactions. Personal communication between financial institutions and their customers will always be important in the delivery of financial services, especially to older customers and smaller businesses. However, the cost of these traditional communications methods is rising, so their economic advantage over electronic methods is declining.

All financial institutions must be prepared for the continuing spread of new information technology. Otherwise, their competitors will wrest the "high ground" of new markets and new services away from them. But there are major challenges in this technological high ground for financial institutions, including the following:

- Customer access to financial information and the transfer of financial information must be as user friendly and as nonthreatening as possible (especially for older customers, who grew up in an era when computers and electronic processing were less in evidence).

- Operating costs and service prices must be kept low relative to more conventional paper-based or in-person information systems so that there is sufficient economic incentive for the customer to use the most cost-efficient system available.

- Adequate technological flexibility must be built in so that, as improved technologies for service production and delivery appear, they can be quickly pressed into service in order to keep each institution current and competitive. At today's rate of technological innovation, new computer systems and software packages become outdated within two to three years, on average.

- Finally, auditing and internal control programs must be strengthened to reduce the probability of loss due to computer errors or computer fraud, which can drive away customers and endanger the viability of any financial institution.

The Changing Mix of Financial-Service Suppliers

Who will offer the financial services of the future? When the customer wishes to purchase a life insurance policy or a checking account, who will be the most likely provider? One thing that is clear now is that the traditional walls between different financial industries have eroded so far that they are almost nonexistent today. For example, the cash management accounts and annuities that an insurance company sells to its customers are fully competitive with the cash-control and savings instruments offered by banks and securities firms. Most of the remaining vestiges of the traditional distinctions between one type of financial institution and another will be swept away in the years ahead — a process often called *homogenization.*

Price Sensitivity and Local Competition. Life insurance policies and other financial services will be purchased from the financial firm offering the lowest price and the best nonprice features. That low-cost supplier may differ from one market to another, depending on the level and intensity of competition.in each local financial marketplace. In smaller cities and rural communities, the local bank may turn out to be the most advantageous supplier of most financial services, as was the case in many local communities before elaborate regulatory restrictions were placed on the banking industry in the 1930s. Larger urban markets, in contrast, will continue to be characterized by multiple financial service suppliers locked in an intense competitive struggle. Moreover, financial service firms will face a customer increasingly sensitized to differing terms of sale and more ready to transfer his or her business to the cheapest source for the quality of service desired.

Importance of Established Delivery Systems. Because cost control and productivity will be key factors for the future success of financial service firms, financial institutions with extensive service delivery systems already in place will have a competitive advantage. This feature will clearly favor banking institutions with established computer and office networks. These cost and productivity advantages will lead to still more mergers and consolidations among smaller financial companies.

Banks and Insurance Companies: A Possible Alliance? Because of the superior delivery capabilities of many branch bank and holding company systems, some financial experts (such as MacDonald, 1985, and Randall, 1985) have argued that banks and insurance companies are "logical allies" for the future. Bankers can contribute an established customer base for distributing insurance services and higher retail margins; insurers can offer essential product and marketing expertise. Bankers may be in a good position to supply insurance services in their local communities because of their credibility, frequent customer contact, and conveniently located offices. Several options will be open to banks in delivering insurance products in a given local market, such as forming partnerships with insurance companies, renting lobby space to insurers, or selling lists of their customers' names to insurance firms. Some financial analysts believe that insurance will become the biggest new profit center for banks and thrift institutions by the turn of the century.

New Financial Institutions and Instruments. The future will usher in *new* financial institutions to deal with newly emerging financial service needs. For example, secondary (resale) markets for many traditionally liquid loans and securities will emerge so that lenders of funds can readily sell their older assets and gain the cash needed to make new loans. Just as high-grade common stock is traded on national exchanges, exchange trading of top-quality mortgages and other loans will eventually become a reality. These unfolding new markets will require new financial institutions and new financial services. A few of the financial instruments and services that appear to have excellent prospects for rapid growth in the future include the following:

1. Loans to remodel residential dwellings (due to the aging of existing homes and greater availability of home equity credit).

2. Home equity loans and credit lines (spurred on by changing federal tax laws).

3. New types of securitized assets, used to raise funds by issuing IOUs against pooled loans (such as small business loans).

4. Consumer cash management services (combining checking, revolving credit through credit cards, and brokerage and investment services).

5. Safety-oriented investment vehicles that allow investors to buy risky assets with greater assurance of adequate returns.

Securitization. There will be a need for new institutions to facilitate the continuing trend toward **securitization** of many of the assets held by lending institutions and by other corporations. The success of mortgage-backed securities, first offered in 1970, demonstrated that a financial institution could take some of the high-quality loans it has made and use them as collateral for borrowing money through the sale of securities. Investors purchasing the securities receive their earnings from the interest and principal payments generated by the mortgages in the pool. Today, there are loan-backed securities collateralized by such diverse assets as commercial and residential mortgage loans, credit-card receivables, auto and boat loans, mobile home loans, and computer and truck leases.

The future is likely to bring even greater use of loan-backed securities because this device opens up an additional funding source for financial institutions and for many of their customers, adding liquidity and diversification. Securitization is also likely to accelerate a shift of nonfinancial companies away from traditional types of credit obtained through a financial intermediary and toward self-financing and self-borrowing directly from investors in the open market. Banks, insurance companies, and other traditional intermediaries will have to develop new services to offset the potentially damaging effects of this trend on their future profitability.

Housing-Secured Credit. Other financial instruments that are expected to see rapid growth in the future include *home equity loans, housing-secured credit lines,* and *home remodeling loans* (stimulated by recent federal tax laws). These expanding lending opportunities will not only encourage the development of new financial firms but also spur existing institutions, especially banks and surviving savings and loans, which have accumulated years of experience in property appraisals and the revolving-type credit lines that many consumers will demand in the years ahead. Indeed, these institutions are increasingly tying home equity lending to their existing credit-card and checking account programs, giving the consumer access to instant revolving credit at lower rates and in larger volume than is currently available under conventional credit programs.

Consumer Cash Management Services. A related development will be an upsurge in the demand for *consumer cash management services.* These services are patterned after the highly successful cash management accounts (CMAs) developed by Merrill Lynch in the 1970s and combine access to a credit line, security brokerage services, and checking account privileges. Although successful consumer cash management programs have been confined largely to high-income households, the combination of advancing technology, falling geographic and legal barriers, greater interest-sensitivity of households, and the growth of larger consumer-oriented financial institutions will combine to produce low-cost cash management packages for middle-income customers. Lower-cost cash management services will also be developed for thousands of small businesses that have been overlooked by many financial service providers. The potential market in this field is enormous, but the key to tapping the market successfully will be effective cost control.

Safety-Oriented Investment Vehicles. The Great Stock Market Crash of 1987 and the volatility of security markets have substantially altered investor demand for many traditional investment vehicles. The most significant changes have been in purchases of securities by small individual investors and more risk-averse financial institutions, such as pension funds and insurance companies. Securities houses and other financial institutions must move quickly to lure these reluctant buyers back into stock and bond markets by offering financial products that appear to be safer and give investors more rapid access to the market in order to liquidate when conditions turn sour. Older savers will need investment products promising long-term income that is stable and predictable.

Management Coordination within Diversified Financial Institutions

As financial firms offer broader menus of financial services, they will become more complex businesses. The span of management control will have to increase to encompass more departments and more subsidiary firms offering different products. The difficulties of coordinating and controlling such facets of daily operations as service quality, pricing, employee benefits, recruiting, and portfolio selection will soon be evident. Failure to effectively coordinate and control these activities will weaken the diversified financial institution's performance at a time when competition in financial services is increasing. Many diversified financial firms will have difficulty attracting new capital, and some will fail, forcing the sale of some service lines ("downsizing"). Indeed, we are already seeing a trend in this direction among major financial service conglomerates, as unprofitable affiliates are spun off into the hands of new owners who may be able to manage them more efficiently.

Steps toward Better Management Coordination

The difficulties of coordination and control among larger and more diversified financial institutions will necessitate a number of key steps for the managers of financial institutions. These include the following:

- Seeking new employees better trained in coordination and control skills.
- Strengthening internal auditing procedures and improving management information systems (MIS).
- Continuing evaluation of subsidiary firms, profit centers, and service functions for their contributions to the financial firm's goals.

Not all diversified financial service companies will be successful in an intensely competitive, unforgiving financial marketplace. Not all customers will demand one-stop financial services convenience. It is not at all clear that most customers prefer to buy their financial services in bunches or that they trust all their financial affairs to a single institution. Moreover, not all customers will willingly acquiesce in the depersonalization of financial service delivery systems. There is evidence, for example, that many customers, particularly older and more financially affluent customers, actually enjoy visiting their financial institution personally and being recognized as an individual. Numerous profitable opportunities will remain for narrowly focused financial firms that do a few jobs well, recognize the economic value of sensitivity to the unique service needs of each customer, and find better methods for improving employee productivity and keeping operating costs under a tight rein.

The Future of Alternative Financial Service Distribution Systems

The channels through which financial services are distributed to the public are changing rapidly. On the one hand, there is the rapid spread of electronic delivery systems, represented by automated tellers, telephone services, home and office computers, and video shopping services, in customer-convenient locations. On the other hand, alternative service delivery systems, including traditional personalized ones, will probably exist side by side with electronic delivery methods in the years to come. Future financial services delivery and distribution systems will depend on several factors for their growth and survival:

- Their ability to keep transactions and information costs low for users.
- Their ability to protect customer privacy.
- Their ability to ease the information burden on the customer who is confronted by an ever-widening range of service options and providers.
- Their ability to deliver speed and accuracy.
- Their capacity for personalization, especially for older savers and borrowers.

The Continued Spread of Franchising. The *franchising* of financial services, with larger companies producing financial services and smaller firms delivering them to the customer, should become more popular. This will be true especially for those services dependent on high volume for profitability. Examples include security brokerage, security and insurance underwriting, credit information processing, and real estate brokerage. Franchising will allow smaller firms to update their service menus and avoid complete erosion of their market shares.

Long-Distance Service Delivery Techniques for the Future. At the same time, video conferences and holographic imaging techniques will permit even the most remote financial institutions to reach into many local markets, explaining the advantages of their particular services. Holographic (three-dimensional) images of sales personnel will eventually be capable of being transmitted over great distances, allowing managers to make a personalized sales pitch to customers without leaving home. These and other electronic sales devices will pose a growing challenge to locally oriented financial institutions, especially smaller banks, credit unions, and thrifts, forcing them to broaden their service menus, and to become more efficient and more conscious of changing customer needs.

The Future Need for Regulation of Financial Institutions

The trend toward *deregulation* of the worldwide financial sector is likely to continue. Governments will be under continuing pressure to amend and relax regulations against product-line and geographic diversification. If Congress and the states do not act to free more completely the financial institutions they supervise from today's product-line and geographic restrictions, nonregulated financial intermediaries will move in and eventually drive out the more regulated financial institutions from one market after another.

The more likely future developments in deregulation will be the following:

- Reduced barriers to geographic diversification to allow financial institutions to find new customers.

- Reduced restrictions on the portfolio choices made by financial institutions except as may be required to preserve public confidence.

- Reorganization of regulatory agencies to avoid duplication and to minimize the burden of regulation on financial institutions.

- Reduced barriers to product-line diversification (especially in securities underwriting, insurance underwriting and sales, and the ownership and management of mutual funds).

Within the United States, one of the most contentious regulatory debates will focus on the issue of what *new services* commercial banks should be allowed to offer, consistent with the public's interest in a sound banking system. During the 1980s and early 1990s, remarkably little progress was made on this key issue at the federal level, due in large part to powerful lobbies. To date, banks have most eagerly sought powers to underwrite and deal in corporate debt and equity securities, something prohibited by the National Banking (Glass-Steagall) Act of 1933. Banks' pursuit of these forbidden security powers is based on their expected profit potential as more and more corporations seek their bankers' assistance with mergers, leveraged buyouts, and the exploration of new markets.

In debating the Glass-Steagall Act, Congress expressed fears that commercial bank involvement in underwriting the stocks and bonds of corporations could lead to serious conflict-of-interest problems. For example, a bank might be able to force a corporate customer to buy some securities that it was underwriting as a condition for receiving or renewing a loan. Alternatively, a bank might be more inclined to lend money and accept the risk of inferior-quality loans simply to induce its borrowing customer to purchase the bank's underwriting service. Glass-Steagall placed securities into two classes: (1) *eligible* securities (including direct obligations of the U.S. government, federal agency securities, and general-obligation state and local government bonds) and (2) *ineligible* securities, which included corporate stocks and bonds. Federal Reserve member banks were prohibited from dealing in or underwriting any ineligible securities.

The Federal Reserve Board has gradually begun to lift these restrictions on a case-by-case basis. For example, in 1987 and 1988, several large bank holding companies (including Bankers Trust, Chase Manhattan Corp., Chemical New York Corp., Citicorp, Manufacturers Hanover, and Security Pacific Corporation) were granted authorization by the Fed to underwrite and deal in commercial paper, security-backed consumer loans, mortgage-backed securities, and municipal revenue bonds. However, these activities had to be conducted through a separate nonbank subsidiary and could not represent the principal portion (usually no more than 5 percent) of the trading firm's revenue. Late in 1988, the Federal Reserve Board indicated that it would probably respond favorably to requests from bank holding companies seeking greater underwriting powers. On the heels of this announcement, four top banking companies — Bankers Trust, Chase Manhattan, Citicorp, and J.P. Morgan & Co. — submitted applications for differing mixes of new securities powers.

In September 1989, the Federal Reserve Board decided to increase to 10 percent from 5 percent the proportion of revenues that a bank-affiliated trading company could secure from selling underwriting services for ineligible securities. In the same month, a federal circuit court confirmed a ruling made by the Comptroller of the Currency that national banks could underwrite securities issued against their own loans. Less than a year earlier, the Federal Reserve granted New York's J.P. Morgan permission to make loans to the same customers who were using its underwriting services. Then, in September 1990, J.P. Morgan became the first U.S. banking firm to receive Federal Reserve Board permission to underwrite corporate stock and the first to actually underwrite new corporate stock offerings since the 1930s. The board indicated that it was Morgan's superior capital strength that led to it receiving regulatory approval to underwrite corporate stock and that other stock underwriting applications would be approved if the applying banking organizations possessed adequate capital levels and were willing to institute safeguards to protect depositors. Subsequently more than 40 U.S. and foreign bank holding companies received debt or equity or both debt and equity underwriting powers from the Federal Reserve Board.

The desire of U.S. banks to expand their service menus and market horizons reflects the realities of the international financial marketplace. One powerful market force has been the tendency of major bank customers to bypass their banks when raising funds, working instead through dealer and merchant banks willing to float their securities and provide equity capital. Many foreign banks have been successful in providing services that U.S. banks are prohibited by regulation from offering to their biggest customers, thus shrinking U.S. banking's share of the global market. Moreover, a growing number of foreign banks have received approval from the Federal Reserve Board to underwrite corporate securities inside U.S. territory.

Nevertheless, opposition to the expansion of U.S. banking's service powers will not soon pass away. There is concern from the regulatory community over the risk implications for banks that are handed broader security underwriting, insurance, and other service powers. Because these activities typically carry greater risk and require special knowledge to manage successfully, there is fear of more bank failures. For their part, banking companies requesting new service authority point to the lack of problems with the new service powers that they have recently received. They also contend that failure to respond to the changing menu of customer financial service needs will doom U.S. banks to obsolescence and possible takeover by foreign competitors. It is argued that the new services grant banks the risk-reducing benefits of diversification. However, there is considerable conflict in the research literature on this point (see especially Rose, 1989; and Whalen, 1984), with some studies showing potential diversification benefits for banks and others none at all.

For their part, securities dealers, insurance companies, and other interested groups have argued that not only is there greater risk to the public's deposits as banks expand their service menus but also the ultimate result will be to raise failure risk for both bank and nonbank financial institutions, damaging public confidence. This is one of the most controversial issues regulators and financial institutions' management will face in the years ahead — an issue fraught with serious economic consequences for banks, nonbank financial firms, and the public they serve.

Outside the United States, the pace of financial deregulation appears to be accelerating. For example, at the recent Uruguay Round of the General Agreement on Tariffs and Trade (GATT), with 105 nations participating, both Australia and the United States proposed a global free-trade agreement in financial services. Even more recently, Mexico, Canada, and the United States crafted a free-trade agreement (NAFTA) parallel to the one signed by the United States and Canada in 1987. These moves toward freer trade in financial services have been accompanied by banking and securities deregulation in Britain; the phaseout of foreign-exchange restrictions in France, Italy, Greece, Portugal, Belgium, and Spain; recent liberalization of bank service offerings in Germany; and the licensing of European financial firms to offer their services throughout Western Europe as part of the continuing evolution of the European Economic Community.

Regulations That Could Grow

But all regulations will *not* be eliminated. Indeed, regulation of financial institutions is shifting to a different ground, with a new emphasis in some cases and a reemphasis on traditional regulatory goals in others. There will continue to be great concern over the safety of the public's savings and over maintaining public confidence in the smooth and efficient functioning of financial institutions and the markets in which they operate. Regulators are likely to be looking especially closely in the years ahead at rules applying to the adequacy of owners' equity capital, loan-loss reserves, eligibility for low-cost government insurance, and the permissible risk exposure from assets (especially loans) held by each institution.

Some key areas in which regulation of financial services and institutions is likely to continue to be important are the following:

- Financial disclosure of the condition of financial institutions to savers and borrowers in order to encourage greater market discipline.

- Social responsibility (in allocating credit and other financial services).

- Fair and equal regulatory treatment of different financial institutions (especially in the services they offer, capital requirements, tax exposure, and the mix of assets and liabilities permitted).

- Protection of "disadvantaged groups" that could be hurt by concentrated financial power and reduced competition (especially household customers, small businesses, and agriculture).

Disclosure. One important area of emphasis for the future will be **financial disclosure**. Financial institutions will be expected to divulge more completely their terms of service and their financial condition to investors and to the customers they serve in order to promote better financial decision making. Good examples of this trend are the Competitive Banking Equality Act (1987) and the Truth in Savings Act (1991) passed recently in the U.S. Both require increased public disclosure of deposit terms and withdrawal penalties as well as guaranteeing customers more rapid credit for their deposits so they will have quicker access to spendable funds.

There is potential gain here as well as risk. With greater disclosure, more financial institutions will be subject to the risk of public disfavor. Ultimately the "discipline of the market" will be more completely unleashed to help ensure prudent management and to control risk taking. However, increased disclosure will enable both investors in and customers of financial institutions to make more intelligent decisions about expected return and risk and the most economical use of available resources.

Social Responsibility. Another area of regulatory emphasis likely to grow in the future is the *social responsibility* of financial institutions. The financial services industry will find itself under increasing regulatory scrutiny concerning the fairness of its use of resources and the distribution of its services, particularly access to credit. For example, are all loan customers subjected to the same credit standards? Is there any evidence that the age, race, religion, or other irrelevant characteristics of a credit customer have entered into the decisions of what loans a financial institution has chosen to make or not make? Pressure will grow on all financial service firms to make an "affirmative effort" to serve all of their customers, consistent with sound financial practice. Indeed, the Financial Institutions Reform, Recovery, and Enforcement Act (FIRREA) of 1989 requires, for the first time, public disclosure of the community service ratings given to U.S. banks by federal examiners.

Promoting a Level Playing Field. Finally, the fair and equal regulatory treatment of all financial institutions offering essentially the same services will continue to be a burning issue in future years. Bankers, who have labeled this the *level playing field* issue, will continue to be among its strongest advocates, pressing for more equal taxation of the earnings of different financial institutions and more equal powers to expand geographically.

SUMMARY AND A LOOK FORWARD

Considerable time has been spent in this chapter exploring the broad trends that are reshaping financial markets and institutions today: service innovation and proliferation, spreading deregulation, growing competition, and the consolidation of financial institutions and financial service firms. We have also considered the broad social, economic, and demographic trends that are restructuring financial services and the institutions that produce and deliver them: a changing population that is growing older and more concerned about risk and long-term income; the expansion of service-oriented industries; advances in automation, telecommunications, and biotechnology; the information explosion; the internationalization of markets and institutions; political and business decision making by group consensus; and a growing role for market-based decisions regarding the distribution of resources and incomes.

Each of these trends must be dealt with by both management and investors in the financial sector and by the customers they serve. These trends call for new approaches and new skills: for example, greater knowledge of marketing and planning techniques and about the latest research in these fields, more sensitivity to older customers' service needs, an awareness of new technology and especially of its range of applications to management problems, and the capacity to filter a growing volume of information and to translate that information into sound business decisions.

No one knows for sure what the financial system or financial institutions of the future will look like. Only the broadest outlines seem clear at this point; the crucial details remain hidden from view. It seems a reasonable guess to predict fewer, but larger and more highly diversified financial institutions, survivors of growing competition and more capable of withstanding the fluctuations of an uncertain economy. Financial institutions will pay more attention to risk management and to the sales orientation of their managements and employees. They will need to work harder to control expenses, to improve productivity, and to retain a more price-sensitive, risk-sensitive, quality- and reliability-conscious customer. It will be an era of challenges and competition, of testing and turmoil, of openness and opportunity. There is an old Chinese curse that says, "May you live in interesting times." Financial institutions, the people they hire, and the people they serve will have many reasons to remember those words in the years that lie ahead.

KEY TERMS AND CONCEPTS IN THIS CHAPTER

financial innovation	securitization	deregulation
homogenization	market broadening	financial disclosure
risk-management tools		

STUDY QUESTIONS

1. List the principal trends in the economy, in society, and in population that you believe will affect financial institutions and financial services the most over the next five years. How about the next 10 years? For each trend listed, describe at least one response the management of a financial service firm might make to that trend.

2. If you were managing a small bank or insurance agency in your local community, what future trends in financial services and financial institutions are likely to have the greatest impact on your institution? Why? What response or responses could you make to each trend you have listed?

3. Why is cooperative international financial services regulation a necessity today?

SELECTED REFERENCES

Bhatt, Swati. "The Role of Stock Index Derivative Products in Equity Market Volatility." *Research Paper No. 8709.* Federal Reserve Bank of New York, December 1987.

MacDonald, Robert. "Bankers and Insurers: Logical Allies." *The Bankers Magazine,* January–February 1985, pp. 11–16.

Modigliani, Franco, and Albert Ando. "The Permanent Income and the Life-Cycle Hypothesis of Saving Behavior: Comparison and Tests." In *Proceedings of the Conference on Consumption and Saving,* vol. 2, ed. Irving Friend and Robert Jones. Philadelphia: University of Pennsylvania, 1960, pp. 49–174.

Randall, Ronald K. "Insurance Strategies for Profit." *The Magazine of Bank Administration,* October 1985, pp. 40, 42, and 44.

Report of the Presidential Task Force on Market Mechanisms. Washington, D.C.: U.S. Government Printing Office, January 1988.

Rose, Peter S. "Diversification of the Banking Firm: A Note." *The Financial Review* 24, no. 2 (May 1989), pp. 251–80.

Whalen, Gary. "The Nonbanking Operations of Bank Holding Companies." *Economic Review.* Federal Reserve Bank of Cleveland, Spring 1984, pp. 11–20.

Appendix: Present Value, Annuity, Compound Interest, and Annual Percentage Rate (APR) Tables

Present Value Table

Present Value of $1 to Be Received N Years in the Future

Years Hence	1%	2%	4%	6%	8%	10%	12%	14%	15%	16%	18%	20%	22%	24%	25%	26%	28%	30%	35%	40%	45%	50%
1	0.990	0.980	0.962	0.943	0.926	0.909	0.893	0.877	0.870	0.862	0.847	0.833	0.820	0.806	0.800	0.794	0.781	0.769	0.741	0.714	0.690	0.667
2	0.980	0.961	0.925	0.890	0.857	0.826	0.797	0.769	0.756	0.743	0.718	0.694	0.672	0.650	0.640	0.630	0.610	0.592	0.549	0.510	0.476	0.444
3	0.971	0.942	0.889	0.840	0.794	0.751	0.712	0.675	0.658	0.641	0.609	0.579	0.551	0.524	0.512	0.500	0.477	0.455	0.406	0.364	0.328	0.296
4	0.961	0.924	0.855	0.792	0.735	0.683	0.636	0.592	0.572	0.552	0.516	0.482	0.451	0.423	0.410	0.397	0.373	0.350	0.301	0.260	0.226	0.198
5	0.951	0.906	0.822	0.747	0.681	0.621	0.567	0.519	0.497	0.476	0.437	0.402	0.370	0.341	0.328	0.315	0.291	0.269	0.223	0.186	0.156	0.132
6	0.942	0.888	0.790	0.705	0.630	0.564	0.507	0.456	0.432	0.410	0.370	0.335	0.303	0.275	0.262	0.250	0.227	0.207	0.165	0.133	0.108	0.088
7	0.933	0.871	0.760	0.665	0.583	0.513	0.452	0.400	0.376	0.354	0.314	0.279	0.249	0.222	0.210	0.198	0.178	0.159	0.122	0.095	0.074	0.059
8	0.923	0.853	0.731	0.627	0.540	0.467	0.404	0.351	0.327	0.305	0.266	0.233	0.204	0.179	0.168	0.157	0.139	0.123	0.091	0.068	0.051	0.039
9	0.914	0.837	0.703	0.592	0.500	0.424	0.361	0.308	0.284	0.263	0.225	0.194	0.167	0.144	0.134	0.125	0.108	0.094	0.067	0.048	0.035	0.026
10	0.905	0.820	0.676	0.558	0.463	0.386	0.322	0.270	0.247	0.227	0.191	0.162	0.137	0.116	0.107	0.099	0.085	0.073	0.050	0.035	0.024	0.017
11	0.896	0.804	0.650	0.527	0.429	0.350	0.287	0.237	0.215	0.195	0.162	0.135	0.112	0.094	0.086	0.079	0.066	0.056	0.037	0.025	0.017	0.012
12	0.887	0.788	0.625	0.497	0.397	0.319	0.257	0.208	0.187	0.168	0.137	0.112	0.092	0.076	0.069	0.062	0.052	0.043	0.027	0.018	0.012	0.008
13	0.879	0.773	0.601	0.469	0.368	0.290	0.229	0.182	0.163	0.145	0.116	0.093	0.075	0.061	0.055	0.050	0.040	0.033	0.020	0.013	0.008	0.005
14	0.870	0.758	0.577	0.442	0.340	0.263	0.205	0.160	0.141	0.125	0.099	0.078	0.062	0.049	0.044	0.039	0.032	0.025	0.015	0.009	0.006	0.003
15	0.861	0.743	0.555	0.417	0.315	0.239	0.183	0.140	0.123	0.108	0.084	0.065	0.051	0.040	0.035	0.031	0.025	0.020	0.011	0.006	0.004	0.002
16	0.853	0.728	0.534	0.394	0.292	0.218	0.163	0.123	0.107	0.093	0.071	0.054	0.042	0.032	0.028	0.025	0.019	0.015	0.008	0.005	0.003	0.002
17	0.844	0.714	0.513	0.371	0.270	0.198	0.146	0.108	0.093	0.080	0.060	0.045	0.034	0.026	0.023	0.020	0.015	0.012	0.006	0.003	0.002	0.001
18	0.836	0.700	0.494	0.350	0.250	0.180	0.130	0.095	0.081	0.069	0.051	0.038	0.028	0.021	0.018	0.016	0.012	0.009	0.005	0.002	0.001	0.001
19	0.828	0.686	0.475	0.331	0.232	0.164	0.116	0.083	0.070	0.060	0.043	0.031	0.023	0.017	0.014	0.012	0.009	0.007	0.003	0.002	0.001	0.001
20	0.820	0.673	0.456	0.312	0.215	0.149	0.104	0.073	0.061	0.051	0.037	0.026	0.019	0.014	0.012	0.010	0.007	0.005	0.002	0.001	0.001	
21	0.811	0.660	0.439	0.294	0.199	0.135	0.093	0.064	0.053	0.044	0.031	0.022	0.015	0.011	0.009	0.008	0.006	0.004	0.002	0.001		
22	0.803	0.647	0.422	0.278	0.184	0.123	0.083	0.056	0.046	0.038	0.026	0.018	0.013	0.009	0.007	0.006	0.004	0.003	0.001	0.001		
23	0.795	0.634	0.406	0.262	0.170	0.112	0.074	0.049	0.040	0.033	0.022	0.015	0.010	0.007	0.006	0.005	0.003	0.002	0.001			
24	0.788	0.622	0.390	0.247	0.158	0.102	0.066	0.043	0.035	0.028	0.019	0.013	0.008	0.006	0.005	0.004	0.003	0.002	0.001			
25	0.780	0.610	0.375	0.233	0.146	0.092	0.059	0.038	0.030	0.024	0.016	0.010	0.007	0.005	0.004	0.003	0.002	0.001	0.001			
26	0.772	0.598	0.361	0.220	0.135	0.084	0.053	0.033	0.026	0.021	0.014	0.009	0.006	0.004	0.003	0.002	0.002	0.001				
27	0.764	0.586	0.347	0.207	0.125	0.076	0.047	0.029	0.023	0.018	0.011	0.007	0.005	0.003	0.002	0.002	0.001	0.001				
28	0.757	0.574	0.333	0.196	0.116	0.069	0.042	0.026	0.020	0.016	0.010	0.006	0.004	0.002	0.002	0.001	0.001	0.001				
29	0.749	0.563	0.321	0.185	0.107	0.063	0.037	0.022	0.017	0.014	0.008	0.005	0.003	0.002	0.002	0.001	0.001	0.001				
30	0.742	0.552	0.308	0.174	0.099	0.057	0.033	0.020	0.015	0.012	0.007	0.004	0.003	0.001	0.001	0.001	0.001	0.001				
40	0.672	0.453	0.208	0.097	0.046	0.022	0.011	0.005	0.004	0.003	0.001	0.001										
50	0.608	0.372	0.141	0.054	0.021	0.009	0.003	0.001	0.001	0.001												

Source: Robert N. Anthony and James S. Reece, *Accounting Principles*, 4th ed. (Homewood, IL: Richard D. Irwin, 1979).

Annuity Table

Present Value of $1 Received Annually for N Years Running

Years (N)	1%	2%	4%	6%	8%	10%	12%	14%	15%	16%	18%	20%	22%	24%	25%	26%	28%	30%	35%	40%	45%	50%
1	0.990	0.980	0.962	0.943	0.926	0.909	0.893	0.877	0.870	0.862	0.847	0.833	0.820	0.806	0.800	0.794	0.781	0.769	0.741	0.714	0.690	0.667
2	1.970	1.942	1.886	1.833	1.783	1.736	1.690	1.647	1.626	1.605	1.566	1.528	1.492	1.457	1.440	1.424	1.392	1.361	1.289	1.224	1.165	1.111
3	2.941	2.884	2.775	2.673	2.577	2.487	2.402	2.322	2.283	2.246	2.174	2.106	2.042	1.981	1.952	1.923	1.868	1.816	1.696	1.589	1.493	1.407
4	3.902	3.808	3.630	3.465	3.312	3.170	3.037	2.914	2.855	2.798	2.690	2.589	2.494	2.404	2.362	2.320	2.241	2.166	1.997	1.849	1.720	1.605
5	4.853	4.713	4.452	4.212	3.993	3.791	3.605	3.433	3.352	3.274	3.127	2.991	2.864	2.745	2.689	2.635	2.532	2.436	2.220	2.035	1.876	1.737
6	5.795	5.601	5.242	4.917	4.623	4.355	4.111	3.889	3.784	3.685	3.498	3.326	3.167	3.020	2.951	2.885	2.759	2.643	2.385	2.168	1.983	1.824
7	6.728	6.472	6.002	5.582	5.206	4.868	4.564	4.288	4.160	4.039	3.812	3.605	3.416	3.242	3.161	3.083	2.937	2.802	2.508	2.263	2.057	1.883
8	7.652	7.325	6.733	6.210	5.747	5.335	4.968	4.639	4.487	4.344	4.078	3.837	3.619	3.421	3.329	3.241	3.076	2.925	2.598	2.331	2.108	1.922
9	8.566	8.162	7.435	6.802	6.247	5.759	5.328	4.946	4.772	4.607	4.303	4.031	3.786	3.566	3.463	3.366	3.184	3.019	2.665	2.379	2.144	1.948
10	9.471	8.983	8.111	7.360	6.710	6.145	5.650	5.216	5.019	4.833	4.494	4.192	3.923	3.682	3.571	3.465	3.269	3.092	2.715	2.414	2.168	1.965
11	10.368	9.787	8.760	7.887	7.139	6.495	5.937	5.453	5.234	5.029	4.656	4.327	4.035	3.776	3.656	3.544	3.335	3.147	2.752	2.438	2.185	1.977
12	11.255	10.575	9.385	8.384	7.536	6.814	6.194	5.660	5.421	5.197	4.793	4.439	4.127	3.851	3.725	3.606	3.387	3.190	2.779	2.456	2.196	1.985
13	12.134	11.343	9.986	8.853	7.904	7.103	6.424	5.842	5.583	5.342	4.910	4.533	4.203	3.912	3.780	3.656	3.427	3.223	2.799	2.468	2.204	1.990
14	13.004	12.106	10.563	9.295	8.244	7.367	6.628	6.002	5.724	5.468	5.008	4.611	4.265	3.962	3.824	3.695	3.459	3.249	2.814	2.477	2.210	1.993
15	13.865	12.849	11.118	9.712	8.559	7.606	6.811	6.142	5.847	5.575	5.092	4.675	4.315	4.001	3.859	3.726	3.483	3.268	2.825	2.484	2.214	1.995
16	14.718	13.578	11.652	10.106	8.851	7.824	6.974	6.265	5.954	5.669	5.162	4.730	4.357	4.033	3.887	3.751	3.503	3.283	2.834	2.489	2.216	1.997
17	15.562	14.292	12.166	10.477	9.122	8.022	7.120	6.373	6.047	5.749	5.222	4.775	4.391	4.059	3.910	3.771	3.518	3.295	2.840	2.492	2.218	1.998
18	16.398	14.992	12.659	10.828	9.372	8.201	7.250	6.467	6.128	5.818	5.273	4.812	4.419	4.080	3.928	3.786	3.529	3.304	2.844	2.494	2.219	1.999
19	17.226	15.678	13.134	11.158	9.604	8.365	7.366	6.550	6.198	5.877	5.316	4.844	4.442	4.097	3.942	3.799	3.539	3.311	2.848	2.496	2.220	1.999
20	18.046	16.351	13.590	11.470	9.818	8.514	7.469	6.623	6.259	5.929	5.353	4.870	4.460	4.110	3.954	3.808	3.546	3.316	2.850	2.497	2.221	1.999
21	18.857	17.011	14.029	11.764	10.017	8.649	7.562	6.687	6.312	5.973	5.384	4.891	4.476	4.121	3.963	3.816	3.551	3.320	2.852	2.498	2.221	2.000
22	19.660	17.658	14.451	12.042	10.201	8.772	7.645	6.743	6.359	6.011	5.410	4.909	4.488	4.130	3.970	3.822	3.556	3.323	2.853	2.498	2.222	2.000
23	20.456	18.292	14.857	12.303	10.371	8.883	7.718	6.792	6.399	6.044	5.432	4.925	4.499	4.137	3.976	3.827	3.559	3.325	2.854	2.499	2.222	2.000
24	21.243	18.914	15.247	12.550	10.529	8.985	7.784	6.835	6.434	6.073	5.451	4.937	4.507	4.143	3.981	3.831	3.562	3.327	2.855	2.499	2.222	2.000
25	22.023	19.523	15.622	12.783	10.675	9.077	7.843	6.873	6.464	6.097	5.467	4.948	4.514	4.147	3.985	3.834	3.564	3.329	2.856	2.499	2.222	2.000
26	22.795	20.121	15.983	13.003	10.810	9.161	7.896	6.906	6.491	6.118	5.480	4.956	4.520	4.151	3.988	3.837	3.566	3.330	2.856	2.500	2.222	2.000
27	23.560	20.707	16.330	13.211	10.935	9.237	7.943	6.935	6.514	6.136	5.492	4.964	4.524	4.154	3.990	3.839	3.567	3.331	2.856	2.500	2.222	2.000
28	24.316	21.281	16.663	13.406	11.051	9.307	7.984	6.961	6.534	6.152	5.502	4.970	4.528	4.157	3.992	3.840	3.568	3.331	2.857	2.500	2.222	2.000
29	25.066	21.844	16.984	13.591	11.158	9.370	8.022	6.983	6.551	6.166	5.510	4.975	4.531	4.159	3.994	3.841	3.569	3.332	2.857	2.500	2.222	2.000
30	25.808	22.396	17.292	13.765	11.258	9.427	8.055	7.003	6.566	6.177	5.517	4.979	4.534	4.160	3.995	3.842	3.569	3.332	2.857	2.500	2.222	2.000
40	32.835	27.355	19.793	15.046	11.925	9.779	8.244	7.105	6.642	6.234	5.548	4.997	4.544	4.166	3.999	3.846	3.571	3.333	2.857	2.500	2.222	2.000
50	39.196	31.424	21.482	15.762	12.234	9.915	8.304	7.133	6.661	6.246	5.554	4.999	4.545	4.167	4.000	3.846	3.571	3.333	2.857	2.500	2.222	2.000

Source: Robert N. Anthony and James S. Reece, *Accounting Principles*, 4th ed. (Homewood, IL: Richard D. Irwin, 1979).

Compound Interest Rate Table

Annual Percentage Rate

(Future Value of $1—Principal Plus Accumulated Interest)

Number of Periods	1.00%	1.50%	2.00%	2.50%	3.00%	3.50%	4.00%	4.50%	5.00%	6.00%	7.00%	8.00%	9.00%	10.00%	12.00%	14.00%	16.00%	18.00%
1	1.010	1.015	1.020	1.025	1.030	1.035	1.040	1.045	1.050	1.060	1.070	1.080	1.090	1.100	1.120	1.140	1.160	1.180
2	1.020	1.030	1.040	1.051	1.061	1.071	1.082	1.092	1.103	1.124	1.145	1.166	1.188	1.210	1.254	1.300	1.346	1.392
3	1.030	1.046	1.061	1.077	1.093	1.109	1.125	1.141	1.158	1.191	1.225	1.260	1.295	1.331	1.405	1.482	1.561	1.643
4	1.041	1.061	1.082	1.104	1.126	1.148	1.170	1.193	1.216	1.262	1.311	1.360	1.412	1.464	1.574	1.689	1.811	1.939
5	1.051	1.077	1.104	1.131	1.159	1.188	1.217	1.246	1.276	1.338	1.403	1.469	1.539	1.611	1.762	1.925	2.100	2.288
6	1.062	1.093	1.126	1.160	1.194	1.229	1.265	1.302	1.340	1.419	1.501	1.587	1.677	1.772	1.974	2.195	2.436	2.700
7	1.072	1.110	1.149	1.189	1.230	1.272	1.316	1.361	1.407	1.504	1.606	1.714	1.828	1.949	2.211	2.502	2.826	3.185
8	1.083	1.126	1.172	1.218	1.267	1.317	1.369	1.422	1.477	1.594	1.718	1.851	1.993	2.144	2.476	2.853	3.278	3.759
9	1.094	1.143	1.195	1.249	1.305	1.363	1.423	1.486	1.551	1.689	1.838	1.999	2.172	2.358	2.773	3.252	3.803	4.435
10	1.105	1.161	1.219	1.280	1.344	1.411	1.480	1.553	1.629	1.791	1.967	2.159	2.367	2.594	3.106	3.707	4.411	5.234
11	1.116	1.178	1.243	1.312	1.384	1.460	1.539	1.623	1.710	1.898	2.105	2.332	2.580	2.853	3.479	4.226	5.117	6.176
12	1.127	1.196	1.268	1.345	1.426	1.511	1.601	1.696	1.796	2.012	2.252	2.518	2.813	3.138	3.896	4.818	5.936	7.288
14	1.149	1.232	1.319	1.413	1.513	1.619	1.732	1.852	1.980	2.261	2.579	2.937	3.342	3.797	4.887	6.261	7.988	10.147
16	1.173	1.269	1.373	1.485	1.605	1.734	1.873	2.022	2.183	2.540	2.952	3.426	3.970	4.595	6.130	8.137	10.748	14.129
18	1.196	1.307	1.428	1.560	1.702	1.857	2.026	2.208	2.407	2.854	3.380	3.996	4.717	5.560	7.690	10.575	14.463	19.673

Compound Interest Rate Table (continued)

Annual Percentage Rate

(Future Value of $1—Principal Plus Accumulated Interest)

Number of Periods	1.00%	1.50%	2.00%	2.50%	3.00%	3.50%	4.00%	4.50%	5.00%	6.00%	7.00%	8.00%	9.00%	10.00%	12.00%	14.00%	16.00%	18.00%
20	1.220	1.347	1.486	1.639	1.806	1.990	2.191	2.412	2.653	3.207	3.870	4.661	5.604	6.727	9.646	13.743	19.461	27.393
22	1.245	1.388	1.546	1.722	1.916	2.132	2.370	2.634	2.925	3.604	4.430	5.437	6.659	8.140	12.100	17.861	26.186	38.142
24	1.270	1.430	1.608	1.809	2.033	2.283	2.563	2.876	3.225	4.049	5.072	6.341	7.911	9.850	15.179	23.212	35.236	53.109
26	1.295	1.473	1.673	1.900	2.157	2.446	2.772	3.141	3.556	4.549	5.807	7.396	9.399	11.918	19.040	30.167	47.414	73.949
28	1.321	1.517	1.741	1.996	2.288	2.620	2.999	3.430	3.920	5.112	6.649	8.627	11.167	14.421	23.884	39.204	63.800	102.967
30	1.348	1.563	1.811	2.098	2.427	2.807	3.243	3.745	4.322	5.743	7.612	10.063	13.268	17.449	29.960	50.950	85.850	143.371
32	1.375	1.610	1.884	2.204	2.575	3.007	3.508	4.090	4.765	6.453	8.715	11.737	15.763	21.114	37.582	66.215	115.520	199.629
34	1.403	1.659	1.961	2.315	2.732	3.221	3.794	4.466	5.253	7.251	9.978	13.690	18.728	25.548	47.143	86.053	155.443	277.964
36	1.431	1.709	2.040	2.433	2.898	3.450	4.104	4.877	5.792	8.147	11.424	15.968	22.251	30.913	59.136	111.834	209.164	387.037
38	1.460	1.761	2.122	2.556	3.075	3.696	4.439	5.326	6.385	9.154	13.079	18.625	26.437	37.404	74.180	145.340	281.452	538.910
40	1.489	1.814	2.208	2.685	3.262	3.959	4.801	5.816	7.040	10.286	14.974	21.725	31.409	45.259	93.051	188.884	378.721	750.378
42	1.519	1.869	2.297	2.821	3.461	4.241	5.193	6.352	7.762	11.557	17.144	25.339	37.318	54.764	116.723	245.473	509.607	1044.827
44	1.549	1.925	2.390	2.964	3.671	4.543	5.617	6.936	8.557	12.985	19.628	29.556	44.337	66.264	146.418	319.017	685.727	1454.817
46	1.580	1.984	2.487	3.114	3.895	4.867	6.075	7.574	9.434	14.590	22.473	34.474	52.677	80.180	183.666	414.594	922.715	2025.687
48	1.612	2.043	2.587	3.271	4.132	5.214	6.571	8.271	10.401	16.394	25.729	40.211	62.585	97.017	230.391	538.807	1241.605	2820.567
50	1.645	2.105	2.692	3.437	4.384	5.585	7.107	9.033	11.467	18.420	29.457	46.902	74.357	117.391	289.002	700.233	1670.704	3927.357
52	1.678	2.169	2.800	3.611	4.651	5.983	7.687	9.864	12.643	20.697	33.725	54.706	88.344	142.043	362.524	910.023	2248.099	5468.452
54	1.711	2.234	2.913	3.794	4.934	6.409	8.314	10.771	13.939	23.255	38.612	63.809	104.962	171.872	454.751	1182.666	3025.042	7614.272
56	1.746	2.302	3.031	3.986	5.235	6.865	8.992	11.763	15.367	26.129	44.207	74.427	124.705	207.965	570.439	1536.992	4070.497	10602.113
58	1.781	2.372	3.154	4.188	5.553	7.354	9.726	12.845	16.943	29.359	50.613	86.812	148.162	251.638	715.559	1997.475	5477.260	14762.381
60	1.817	2.443	3.281	4.400	5.892	7.878	10.520	14.027	18.679	32.988	57.946	101.257	176.031	304.482	897.597	2595.919	7370.201	20555.140

Source: Federal Reserve Bank of New York, *The Arithmetic of Interest Rates*, pp. 26–27.

Interest Rate Table for Daily Compounding (360-Day Basis Year)

Number of Years	Annual Percentage Rate					
	5.00%	5.25%	5.50%	5.75%	6.00%	6.25%
	(What a $1 Deposit Will Grow to in the Future)					
1	1.0520	1.0547	1.0573	1.0600	1.0627	1.0654
2	1.1067	1.1123	1.1180	1.1237	1.1294	1.1351
3	1.1642	1.1731	1.1821	1.1911	1.2002	1.2094
4	1.2248	1.2373	1.2499	1.2626	1.2755	1.2885
5	1.2885	1.3049	1.3215	1.3384	1.3555	1.3727
6	1.3555	1.3762	1.3973	1.4187	1.4405	1.4625
7	1.4259	1.4515	1.4774	1.5039	1.5308	1.5582
8	1.5001	1.5308	1.5622	1.5942	1.6268	1.6601
9	1.5781	1.6145	1.6518	1.6899	1.7288	1.7687
10	1.6602	1.7028	1.7465	1.7913	1.8373	1.8844
15	2.1391	2.2219	2.3080	2.3975	2.4904	2.5868
20	2.7561	2.8994	3.0502	3.2087	3.3756	3.5511
25	3.5512	3.7834	4.0309	4.2946	4.5755	4.8747
30	4.5756	4.9370	5.3270	5.7478	6.2019	6.6918

Number of Years	Annual Percentage Rate					
	8.25%	8.50%	8.75%	9.00%	9.25%	9.50%
	(What a $1 Deposit Will Grow to in the Future)					
1	1.0872	1.0900	1.0928	1.0955	1.0983	1.1011
2	1.1821	1.1881	1.1941	1.2002	1.2063	1.2124
3	1.2852	1.2950	1.3049	1.3148	1.3249	1.3350
4	1.3973	1.4115	1.4259	1.4404	1.4551	1.4699
5	1.5192	1.5386	1.5582	1.5781	1.5982	1.6186
6	1.6517	1.6770	1.7027	1.7288	1.7553	1.7822
7	1.7958	1.8279	1.8607	1.8940	1.9279	1.9624
8	1.9525	1.9924	2.0333	2.0749	2.1174	2.1607
9	2.1228	2.1718	2.2219	2.2731	2.3255	2.3792
10	2.3080	2.3672	2.4279	2.4903	2.5542	2.6197
15	3.5062	3.6421	3.7832	3.9298	4.0820	4.2402
20	5.3267	5.6036	5.8949	6.2014	6.5238	6.8629
25	8.0922	8.6215	9.1854	9.7861	10.4261	11.1080
30	12.2937	13.2648	14.3125	15.4430	16.6628	17.9790

Source: Federal Reserve Bank of New York.

Interest Rate Table for Daily Compounding (360-Day Basis Year) (continued)

6.50%	6.75%	7.00%	7.25%	7.50%	7.75%	8.00%

Annual Percentage Rate

(What a $1 Deposit Will Grow to in the Future)

6.50%	6.75%	7.00%	7.25%	7.50%	7.75%	8.00%
1.0681	1.0708	1.0735	1.0763	1.0790	1.0817	1.0845
1.1409	1.1467	1.1525	1.1584	1.1642	1.1702	1.1761
1.2186	1.2279	1.2373	1.2467	1.2562	1.2658	1.2755
1.3016	1.3149	1.3282	1.3418	1.3555	1.3693	1.3832
1.3903	1.4080	1.4259	1.4441	1.4625	1.4812	1.5001
1.4850	1.5077	1.5308	1.5543	1.5781	1.6022	1.6268
1.5861	1.6145	1.6434	1.6728	1.7027	1.7332	1.7642
1.6941	1.7288	1.7642	1.8004	1.8373	1.8749	1.9133
1.8095	1.8513	1.8940	1.9377	1.9824	2.0281	2.0749
1.9328	1.9824	2.0333	2.0855	2.1390	2.1939	2.2502
2.6871	2.7912	2.8993	3.0117	3.1284	3.2496	3.3755
3.7357	3.9299	4.1343	4.3492	4.5753	4.8132	5.0634
5.1936	5.5333	5.8952	6.2807	6.6915	7.1292	7.5955
7.2204	7.7907	8.4061	9.0701	9.7866	10.5596	11.3937

Annual Percentage Rate

9.75%	10.00%	10.25%	10.50%	11.00%	12.00%	13.00%

(What a $1 Deposit Will Grow to in the Future)

9.75%	10.00%	10.25%	10.50%	11.00%	12.00%	13.00%
1.1039	1.1067	1.1095	1.1123	1.1180	1.1294	1.1409
1.2186	1.2248	1.2310	1.2372	1.2498	1.2754	1.3016
1.3452	1.3554	1.3658	1.3762	1.3973	1.4404	1.4849
1.4849	1.5001	1.5153	1.5308	1.5621	1.6268	1.6941
1.6392	1.6601	1.6813	1.7027	1.7464	1.8372	1.9327
1.8095	1.8372	1.8654	1.8939	1.9524	2.0748	2.2049
1.9975	2.0332	2.0696	2.1067	2.1827	2.3432	2.5155
2.2050	2.2502	2.2962	2.3433	2.4402	2.6463	2.8698
2.4341	2.4902	2.5477	2.6064	2.7281	2.9886	3.2741
2.6870	2.7559	2.8266	2.8992	3.0499	3.3752	3.7353
4.4044	4.5751	4.7523	4.9364	5.3263	6.2009	7.2191
7.2197	7.5950	7.9899	8.4053	9.3019	11.3922	13.9522
11.8345	12.6085	13.4331	14.3116	16.2447	20.9295	26.9651
19.3990	20.9313	22.5845	24.3683	28.3697	38.4513	52.1150

Annual Percentage Rate Table for Monthly Payment Plans

Number of Payments	Annual Percentage Rate							
	10.00%	10.50%	11.00%	11.50%	12.00%	12.50%	13.00%	13.50%
	(Finance Charge Per $100 of Amount Financed)							
1	0.83	0.87	0.92	0.96	1.00	1.04	1.08	1.12
2	1.25	1.31	1.38	1.44	1.50	1.57	1.63	1.69
3	1.67	1.76	1.84	1.92	2.01	2.09	2.17	2.26
4	2.09	2.20	2.30	2.41	2.51	2.62	2.72	2.83
5	2.51	2.64	2.77	2.89	3.02	3.15	3.27	3.40
6	2.94	3.08	3.23	3.38	3.53	3.68	3.83	3.97
7	3.36	3.53	3.70	3.87	4.04	4.21	4.38	4.55
8	3.79	3.98	4.17	4.36	4.55	4.74	4.94	5.13
9	4.21	4.43	4.64	4.85	5.07	5.28	5.49	5.71
10	4.64	4.88	5.11	5.35	5.58	5.82	6.05	6.29
11	5.07	5.33	5.58	5.84	6.10	6.36	6.62	6.88
12	5.50	5.78	6.06	6.34	6.62	6.90	7.18	7.46
18	8.10	8.52	8.93	9.35	9.77	10.19	10.61	11.03
24	10.75	11.30	11.86	12.42	12.98	13.54	14.10	14.66
30	13.43	14.13	14.83	15.54	16.24	16.95	17.66	18.38
36	16.16	17.01	17.86	18.71	19.57	20.43	21.30	22.17
42	18.93	19.93	20.93	21.94	22.96	23.98	25.00	26.03
48	21.74	22.90	24.06	25.23	26.40	27.58	28.77	29.97
54	24.59	25.91	27.23	28.56	29.91	31.25	32.61	33.98
60	27.48	28.96	30.45	31.96	33.47	34.99	36.52	38.06
66	30.41	32.06	33.73	35.40	37.09	38.78	40.49	42.21
72	33.39	35.21	37.05	38.90	40.76	42.64	44.53	46.44
78	36.40	38.40	40.41	42.45	44.49	46.45	48.64	50.74
84	39.45	41.63	43.83	46.05	48.28	50.54	52.81	55.11
90	42.54	44.91	47.29	49.70	52.13	54.58	57.05	59.54
96	45.67	48.22	50.80	53.40	56.03	58.68	61.35	64.05
102	48.84	51.59	54.36	57.16	59.98	62.83	65.71	68.62
108	52.05	54.99	57.96	60.96	63.99	67.05	70.14	73.26
114	55.30	58.43	61.61	64.81	68.05	71.32	74.63	77.96
120	58.58	61.92	65.30	68.71	72.17	75.65	79.17	82.73
180	93.43	98.97	104.59	110.27	116.03	121.85	127.74	133.70
240	131.61	139.61	147.73	155.94	164.26	172.67	181.18	189.77
300	172.61	183.25	194.03	204.94	215.97	227.11	238.35	249.69
360	215.93	229.31	242.84	256.50	270.30	284.21	298.23	312.35

Source: Federal Reserve Bank of New York.

Annual Percentage Rate Table for Monthly Payment Plans (continued)

			Annual Percentage Rate					
14.00%	**14.50%**	**15.00%**	**15.50%**	**16.00%**	**16.50%**	**17.00%**	**17.50%**	**18.00%**
			(Finance Charge Per $100 of Amount Financed)					
1.17	1.21	1.25	1.29	1.33	1.37	1.42	1.46	1.50
1.75	1.82	1.88	1.94	2.00	2.07	2.13	2.19	2.26
2.34	2.43	2.51	2.59	2.68	2.76	2.85	2.93	3.01
2.93	3.04	3.14	3.25	3.36	3.46	3.57	3.67	3.78
3.53	3.65	3.78	3.91	4.04	4.16	4.29	4.42	4.54
4.12	4.27	4.42	4.57	4.72	4.87	5.02	5.17	5.32
4.72	4.89	5.06	5.23	5.40	5.58	5.75	5.92	6.09
5.32	5.51	5.71	5.90	6.09	6.29	6.48	6.67	6.87
5.92	6.14	6.35	6.57	6.78	7.00	7.22	7.43	7.65
6.53	6.77	7.00	7.24	7.48	7.72	7.96	8.19	8.43
7.14	7.40	7.66	7.92	8.18	8.44	8.70	8.96	9.22
7.74	8.03	8.31	8.59	8.88	9.16	9.45	9.73	10.02
11.45	11.87	12.29	12.72	13.14	13.57	13.99	14.42	14.85
15.23	15.80	16.37	16.94	17.51	18.09	18.66	19.24	19.82
19.10	19.81	20.54	21.26	21.99	22.72	23.45	24.18	24.92
23.04	23.92	24.80	25.68	26.57	27.46	28.35	29.25	30.15
27.06	28.10	29.15	30.19	31.25	32.31	33.37	34.44	35.51
31.17	32.37	33.59	34.81	36.03	37.27	38.50	39.75	41.00
35.35	36.73	38.12	39.52	40.92	42.33	43.75	45.18	46.62
39.61	41.17	42.74	44.32	45.91	47.51	49.12	50.73	52.36
43.95	45.69	47.45	49.22	51.00	52.79	54.59	56.40	58.23
48.36	50.30	52.24	54.21	56.18	58.17	60.17	62.19	64.22
52.85	54.98	57.13	59.29	61.46	63.66	65.86	68.09	70.32
57.42	59.75	62.09	64.46	66.84	69.24	71.66	74.10	76.55
62.05	64.59	67.14	69.72	72.31	74.93	77.56	80.22	82.89
66.77	69.51	72.28	75.06	77.88	80.71	83.57	86.44	89.34
71.55	74.51	77.49	80.50	83.53	86.59	89.67	92.78	95.91
76.40	79.58	82.78	86.01	89.27	92.56	95.87	99.21	102.57
81.33	84.73	88.15	91.61	95.10	98.62	102.17	105.74	109.35
86.32	89.94	93.60	97.29	101.02	104.77	108.56	112.37	116.22
139.71	145.79	151.93	158.12	164.37	170.67	177.02	183.42	189.88
198.44	207.20	216.03	224.93	233.90	242.94	252.03	261.19	270.39
216.13	272.65	284.25	295.92	307.67	319.47	331.34	343.26	355.23
326.55	340.84	355.20	369.63	384.11	398.65	413.24	427.88	442.55

Money and Capital Markets Dictionary ▬▬▬

actual maturity The number of days, months, or years between today and the date a loan or security is redeemed or retired. (*Chapter 14*)

add-on rate A method for calculating the interest charge on a loan when the interest bill is added to the principal amount of the loan. That sum is then divided by the number of installment payments required to determine the amount of each payment needed to eventually pay off the loan. (*Chapter 9*)

adjustable mortgage instrument (AMI) A home mortgage loan under which some of the terms of the loan, such as the loan rate or the maturity of loan, will vary as market conditions change. (*Chapter 25*)

American depository receipts (ADRs) Dollar-denominated claims on specific foreign shares of stock that are held in safekeeping by U.S. financial institutions, giving U.S. investors access to selected foreign stock without having to accept or make payments in foreign currencies. (*Chapter 27*)

annual percentage rate (APR) The actuarially determined rate on a consumer loan that the federal Truth-in-Lending law requires lenders to communicate to borrowers. (*Chapter 9*)

arbitrage The purchase of a security or currency in one market and the sale of that security or currency in another market in response to differences in price or yield between the two markets. (*Chapters 1 and 28*)

asked price The price at which a securities dealer is willing to sell securities to the public. (*Chapter 3*)

asymmetric information The concept that different participants in the financial markets often operate with different sets of information, some possessing special or inside information that others do not possess. (*Chapter 1*)

asymmetry The financial marketplace contains pockets of inefficiency in the availability and use of information relevant to the value (*price*) of assets. (*Chapter 3*)

auction A method used to sell securities in which buyers file bids and the highest bidders receive securities. (*Chapter 15*)

auction method The principal means by which U.S. Treasury securities are sold to the public. (*Chapter 22*)

balance-of-payments (BOP) accounts A double-entry bookkeeping system recording a nation's transactions with other nations, including exports, imports, and capital flows. (*Chapter 28*)

bank discount method The procedure by which yields on U.S. Treasury bills, commercial paper, and bankers' acceptances are calculated; a 360-day year is assumed, and there is no compounding of interest income. (*Chapter 15*)

bankers' acceptance A time draft against a bank that the bank has agreed to pay unconditionally on the date the draft matures. (*Chapter 18*)

bank holding company A corporation that owns stock in one or more commercial banks. (*Chapter 4*)

banking structure The number, relative sizes, and types of banks in a given market or in the industry as a whole. (*Chapter 4*)

base rate A loan rate used as the basis or foundation for determining the size of the current interest rate to be charged a borrower, such as the prime rate or LIBOR. (*Chapter 26*)

basis The spread between the cash (spot) price of a commodity or security and its futures (forward) price at any given point in time. (*Chapter 13*)

Basle Agreement An agreement among the central banks of leading industrialized nations, including the nations of Western Europe, Canada, the United States, and Japan, to impose common capital requirements on all their banks in order to control bank risk exposure and avoid giving one nation's banks an unfair advantage over another nation's banks. (*Chapter 7*)

bid price The price a securities dealer is willing to pay to buy securities from the public. (*Chapter 3*)

Board of Governors The chief policymaking and administrative body of the Federal Reserve System, composed of seven persons appointed by the president of the United States and confirmed by the Senate for maximum 14-year terms. (*Chapter 19*)

bond A debt obligation issued by a business firm or unit of government that covers several years, usually over five years. (*Chapter 3*)

bond anticipation notes Short-term securities issued by a state or local government to raise funds to begin a project that eventually will be funded using long-term bonds. (*Chapter 23*)

book-entry form The method by which marketable U.S. Treasury securities are issued, with the buyer receiving only a receipt, rather than an engraved certificate, indicating that the purchase is recorded on the Treasury's books or recorded in another approved location. (*Chapter 22*)

borrowed reserves Legal reserves loaned to depository institutions through the discount windows of the Federal Reserve banks. (*Chapter 21*)

borrowing The change in liabilities outstanding reported by a sector or unit in the economy over a specified time period. (*Chapter 3*)

branch banking A type of banking organization in which services are sold through multiple offices, all owned and operated by the same corporation. (*Chapter 4*)

budget deficit A government's financial position in which current expenditures exceed current revenues. (*Chapter 22*)

budget surplus A government's financial position in which current revenues exceed current expenditures. (*Chapter 22*)

business cycle Fluctuations in economic activity, with the economy passing alternately through expansionary (*boom*) and recessionary (depressed) periods. (*Chapter 12*)

call options Grant the buyer the right to purchase a specified number of shares of a given stock or volume of debt securities at a specified price up to an expiration date. (*Chapters 13 and 27*)

call privilege The provision often found in a bond's contract (indenture) that permits the borrower to retire all or a portion of a bond issue by buying back the securities in advance of their maturity. (*Chapter 11*)

capital account A record of flows of short-term and long-term funds into and out of a nation and included in its balance-of-payments accounts. (*Chapter 28*)

capital market The institution that provides a channel for the borrowing and lending of long-term funds (over one year). (*Chapter 1*)

central bank An agency of government that has public policy functions such as monitoring the operation of the financial system and controlling the growth of the money supply. (*Chapter 19*)

circuit breakers Rules for trading on a securities exchange that bring a halt to trading or that slow certain kinds of trades when security prices decline beyond a prespecified limit. (*Chapter 27*)

classical theory of interest rates An explanation of the level of and changes in interest rates that relies on the interaction of the supply of savings and the demand for investment capital. (*Chapter 8*)

clearinghouse funds Money transferred by writing a check and presenting it for collection. (*Chapter 14*)

collaterized mortgage obligation (CMOs) A type of mortgage-backed security offered in more than one maturity class in order to reduce prepayment risk to investors. (*Chapter 25*)

commercial paper A short-term debt security issued by a corporation that is not tied to any specific collateral but is secured only by the general earning power of the issuing corporation. (*Chapter 17*)

Community Reinvestment Act A federal law passed in 1977 that requires depository institutions to designate the market areas they will serve and to provide services without discrimination to all neighborhoods within their designated market areas. (*Chapter 24*)

common stock A residual claim against the assets and earnings of the issuing corporation evidencing a share of ownership in that company. (*Chapter 27*)

compound interest The payment of additional interest earnings on previously earned interest income. (*Chapter 9*)

Comptroller of the Currency Federal regulatory agency that charters national banks in the United States. (*Chapter 7*)

consensus forecast A prediction of interest rates or economic conditions based on a variety of projections derived from several different forecasting methods. (*Chapter 12*)

consolidation A trend among banks and other financial institutions in which smaller institutions are being combined through merger and acquisition into larger institutions. (*Chapter 4*)

contemporaneous reserve accounting The method of determining the amount of legal reserves a bank or other depository institution must hold behind its deposits and other reservable liabilities in which the reserve computation and reserve maintenance periods overlap. (*Chapter 16*)

contractual institutions Financial institutions that attract savings from the public by offering contracts that protect the saver against risk in the future, such as insurance policies and pension plans. (*Chapter 2*)

conventional home mortgage loan Credit funds extended to a home buyer by a private lender without a government guarantee behind the loan. (*Chapter 25*)

convertibility A feature of some preferred stocks and bonds that entitles the holder to exchange those securities for a specific number of shares of common stock. (*Chapter 11*)

corporate bond A debt contract (IOU) of a corporation whose original maturity is more than five years. (*Chapter 26*)

corporate note A debt contract (IOU) of a corporation whose original maturity is five years or less. (*Chapter 26*)

coupon effect The size of a debt security's promised interest rate (coupon) influences how rapidly its price moves with changes in market interest rates. (*Chapter 10*)

coupon rate The promised interest rate on a bond or note consisting of the ratio of the annual interest income promised by the security issuer to the security's face (par) value. (*Chapter 9*)

credit A loan of funds in return for a promise of future payment. (*Chapter 1*)

credit availability (neo-Keynesian) view A view of economic policy that contends that both fiscal policy (government spending and taxation) and monetary policy (activities of the central bank) are needed to achieve a nation's economic goals. (*Chapter 21*)

credit card A plastic card that allows the holder to borrow cash or to pay for goods and services with credit. (*Chapter 24*)

credit enhancements Financial devices, such as letters of credit from a bank, that upgrade the credit rating of a borrower and allow that borrower to obtain credit at lower cost. (*Chapter 17*)

credit unions Nonprofit associations accepting deposits from and making loans to their members. (*Chapter 5*)

cross hedge The purchase of a futures contract for a different financial instrument than is being traded in the cash market. (*Chapter 13*)

currency futures and options market Agreements that allow businesses or individuals acquiring or selling foreign currencies to protect themselves against future fluctuations in currency prices by shifting currency risk to someone else willing to bear that risk. (*Chapter 28*)

currency risk Possible losses to a borrower or lender in foreign markets or to a holder of assets in foreign markets due to adverse changes in currency prices. (*Chapter 14*)

currency sterilization An action taken by a central bank to offset the impact from government purchases or sales of currencies on bank reserves and deposits through the use of central bank policy tools. (*Chapter 28*)

currency swap A contract designed to reduce the risk of loss due to changes in currency prices by exchanging one nation's currency for another that is of more use to a borrower. (*Chapter 28*)

current account A component of a nation's balance-of-payments accounts that tracks purchases and sales of goods and services (trade) and gifts made to foreigners. (*Chapter 28*)

current savings The change in net worth recorded by a sector or unit in the economy over the current time period. (*Chapter 3*)

current yield The ratio of a security's promised or expected annual income to its current market price. (*Chapter 9*)

D Definition of the U.S. money supply that includes the total debt of domestic nonfinancial sectors. (*Chapter 21*)

dealer paper Short-term commercial notes sold by borrowing corporations and issued through security dealers who contact interested investors to determine whether they will buy the notes. (*Chapter 17*)

debenture Long-term debt instruments secured only by the earning power of the issuing corporation and not by any specific assets pledged by the issuing firm. (*Chapter 26*)

debit card A plastic card that is used to identify the owner of the card or to make immediate payments for goods and services. (*Chapter 24*)

debt management policy The refunding or refinancing of the federal government's debt in a way that contributes to broad national goals and minimizes the burden of the debt. (*Chapter 22*)

debt securities Financial claims against the assets of a business firm, individual, or unit of government, represented by bonds and other contracts evidencing a loan of money. (*Chapter 2*)

default risk The risk to the holder of debt securities that a borrower will not meet all promised payments at the times agreed upon. (*Chapters 11 and 14*)

deficit-budget unit An individual, business firm, or unit of government whose current expenditures exceed its current receipts of income, forcing it to become a net borrower of funds in the money and capital markets. (*Chapter 2*)

demand loan A borrowing of funds (usually by a security dealer) subject to recall of those funds on demand by the lender. (*Chapter 15*)

deposit multiplier A number that indicates how many dollars of new deposits will result from an injection of one more dollar of excess reserves into the banking system. (*Chapter 20*)

depository institutions Financial institutions that raise loanable funds by selling deposits to the public. (*Chapter 2*)

Depository Institutions Deregulation and Monetary Control Act (DIDMCA) Law passed in 1980 by the U.S. Congress to deregulate interest rate ceilings on deposits and grant new services to nonbank thrift institutions as well as to impose common reserve requirements on all depository institutions. (*Chapter 5*)

deregulation The lifting or liberalization of government rules that restrict what private businesses can do to serve their customers. (*Chapters 4, 7, and 30*)

direct finance Any financial transaction in which a borrower and a lender of funds communicate directly and mutually agree on the terms of a loan. (*Chapter 2*)

direct paper Short-term commercial notes issued directly to investors by borrowing companies without the aid of a broker or dealer. (*Chapter 17*)

discount method A method for calculating the interest charge on a loan that deducts the interest owed from the face amount of the loan, with the borrower receiving only the net proceeds after interest is deducted. (*Chapter 9*)

discount rate The interest charge (in annual percentage terms) set by the Federal Reserve banks for borrowing by depository institutions from the Reserve banks. (*Chapters 16 and 20*)

discount window The department in a Federal Reserve bank that grants credit to banks and other depository institutions in need of short-term loans of legal reserves. (*Chapter 16*)

disintermediation The withdrawal of funds from a financial intermediary by ultimate lenders (savers) and the lending of those funds directly to ultimate borrowers. (*Chapter 2*)

duration A weighted average measure of the maturity of a loan or security that takes into account the amount and timing of all promised interest and principal payments associated with that loan or security. (*Chapters 10 and 12*)

econometric models The use of systems of equations and statistical estimation methods to explain or forecast changes in interest rates or other variables. (*Chapter 12*)

Edge Act corporations Special subsidiaries of U.S. banking organizations authorized by federal law to offer international banking services. (*Chapter 29*)

efficient market A competitive market in which the prices of financial instruments traded there fully reflect all the latest information available. (*Chapter 1*)

efficient markets hypothesis A theory of the financial markets that argues that security prices tend to fluctuate randomly around their intrinsic values, return quickly to equilibrium, and fully reflect the latest information available. (*Chapters 3 and 27*)

Equal Credit Opportunity Act A federal law passed in 1974 forbidding lending institutions from discriminating in the granting of credit based on the age, race, ethnic origin, religion, or receipt of public assistance of the borrowing customer. (*Chapter 24*)

equities Shares of common or preferred stock, with each share representing a certificate of ownership in a business corporation. (*Chapter 2*)

Eurobond A long-term debt security denominated in a currency other than that of the country or countries where most or all of the security is sold. (*Chapter 29*)

Eurocurrency deposits Deposits of funds in a bank denominated in a currency foreign to the bank's home country. (*Chapter 29*)

Eurocurrency loans Loans made by a multinational bank in a currency other than that of the bank's home country. (*Chapter 29*)

Eurocurrency market An international money market where bank deposits denominated in the world's most convertible currencies are traded. (*Chapter 18*)

Eurodollars Deposits of U.S. dollars in foreign banks abroad or in foreign branch offices of U.S. banks or U.S. international banking facilities (IBFs). (*Chapter 18*)

event risk The probability that changes inside a firm or other security-issuing individual or institution or external happenings will affect the value of the securities involved. (*Chapter 11*)

excess reserves Cash and deposits at the Federal Reserve banks held by depository institutions that are in excess of their legal reserve requirements. (*Chapter 20*)

expected yield The weighted average return on a risky security composed of all possible yields from the security multiplied by the probability that each possible yield will occur. (*Chapter 11*)

Fair Credit Billing Act A federal law giving customers the right to question entries on bills sent to them for goods and services purchased on credit and giving them the right to expect that billing errors will be corrected as quickly as possible. (*Chapter 24*)

Fair Credit Reporting Act A federal law that gives credit customers the right to view their credit record held by a credit bureau and to secure quick correction of any errors in that record. (*Chapter 24*)

federal agencies Departments or divisional units of the federal government empowered to borrow funds in the open market in order to make loans to private businesses and individuals or otherwise subsidize private lending or borrowing. (*Chapter 17*)

Federal Deposit Insurance Corporation Federal agency established in 1934 to insure the deposits of commercial banks and later expanded in 1989 to insure the deposits of savings and loan associations as well. (*Chapters 5 and 7*)

Federal Deposit Insurance Corporation Improvement Act (FDICIA) Passed by the U.S. Congress in 1991, this federal law provided additional capital and borrowing authority for the Federal Deposit Insurance Corporation (FDIC) and permitted the regulatory authorities to restrict the activities of and even close undercapitalized banks. (*Chapter 5*)

federal financing bank A unit of the federal government created in 1973 that borrows money through the U.S. Treasury Department and channels these funds to federal agencies. (*Chapter 17*)

federal funds Funds that can be transferred immediately from their holder to another party for immediate payment for purchases of securities, goods, or services. (*Chapters 14 and 16*)

Federal Home Loan Mortgage Corporation (FHLMC) A federal agency created in 1970 to improve the resale (secondary) market for home mortgages. (*Chapter 25*)

Federal Housing Administration (FHA) An agency of the federal government established in 1934 to guarantee mortgage loans for low-priced and medium-priced homes, thereby reducing the risks of lending by financial institutions making qualified home loans. (*Chapter 25*)

Federal National Mortgage Association (FNMA) A federal agency created in 1938 to buy and sell selected residential mortgages in the secondary market and encourage the development of a resale market for home loans. (*Chapter 25*)

Federal Open Market Committee (FOMC) The chief body for setting money and credit policy within the Federal Reserve System, consisting of the seven members of the Federal Reserve Board and the presidents of the 12 Federal Reserve banks, only 5 of whom may vote. (*Chapter 19*)

Federal Reserve bank One of 12 regional banks chartered by the U.S. Congress to provide central banking services to a specific region of the nation. (*Chapter 19*)

Federal Reserve Statement A listing of the factors supplying reserves to and absorbing the reserves of depository institutions. (*Chapter 21*)

Federal Reserve System The central bank of the United States, created by Congress to issue currency and coin, regulate the banking system, protect the value of the dollar, and promote full employment. (*Chapters 7, 19, and 24*)

finance companies Financial-service firms that provide both business and consumer credit. (*Chapter 6*)

financial asset A claim against the income or wealth of a business firm, household, or unit of government usually represented by a certificate, receipt, or other legal document. (*Chapter 2*)

financial disclosure The provision of relevant information to the public to aid individuals and institutions in making sound financial decisions. (*Chapter 30*)

financial futures contracts Contracts that call for the future delivery or sale of designated securities at a price agreed upon the day the contract is made. (*Chapter 13*)

financial innovation A trend in the financial system toward developing new services and new service delivery methods. (*Chapter 30*)

Financial Institutions Reform, Recovery, and Enforcement Act (FIRREA) Federal law passed in 1989 to bail out the U.S. savings and loan industry, strengthen the federal deposit insurance program, and liquidate the assets of failed thrift institutions. (*Chapter 5*)

financial investment The net change in financial assets held by a sector or unit in the economy over a specified time period. (*Chapter 3*)

financial market An institutional mechanism created by society to channel savings and other financial services to those individuals and institutions willing to pay for them. (*Chapter 1*)

financial system The collection of markets, individuals, institutions, laws, regulations, and techniques through which bonds, stocks, and other securities are traded, financial services produced and delivered, and interest rates determined. (*Chapter 1*)

fiscal agent A role of the Federal Reserve System in which it provides services to the federal government, such as clearing and collecting checks on behalf of the U.S. Treasury and conducting auctions for the sale of new Treasury securities. (*Chapter 19*)

fiscal policy The taxing and spending programs carried out by government in order to promote high employment, price stability, and other economic goals. (*Chapter 22*)

Fisher effect The theory of inflation and interest rates that argues that nominal interest rates respond one-for-one to changes in the expected rate of inflation over the life of a loan. (*Chapter 10*)

Fixed-rate mortgage (FRM) Mortgage loan that carries an unchanging loan rate. (*Chapter 25*)

Flow of Funds Accounts A system of social accounts prepared quarterly by the Board of Governors of the Federal Reserve System that reports the amount of saving and borrowing in the U.S. economy by major sectors. (*Chapter 3*)

foreign exchange markets Channels for trading national currencies and determining relative currency prices. (*Chapter 28*)

foreign exchange rates The prices of foreign currencies expressed in terms of other currencies. (*Chapter 28*)

forward calendar The anticipated supply of new bonds or other securities expected to come to market over the next week, month, or other period. (*Chapter 12*)

forward contract An agreement to deliver a specified amount of currency, securities, or other goods or services at a set price on some future date. (*Chapter 28*)

forward market Channel through which currencies, securities, goods, and services are traded for future delivery to the buyer with the terms of trade set in advance of delivery. (*Chapter 28*)

GAP management A technique for protecting a financial institution's earnings from losses due to changes in interest rates by matching the volume of interest-sensitive assets held to the volume of interest-sensitive liabilities taken on. (*Chapter 12*)

Garn–St Germain Depository Institutions Act A law passed by the U.S. Congress in 1982 to further deregulate the depository institutions sector and to give federal deposit insurance agencies additional tools to deal with failing institutions. (*Chapter 5*)

general credit controls Monetary policy tools that affect the entire banking and financial system, such as open market operations or changes in the Federal Reserve's discount rate. (*Chapter 20*)

general obligation bonds Debt obligations issued by state and local governments and backed by the "full faith and credit" of the issuing government (i.e., may be repaid from any available revenue source). (*Chapter 23*)

Glass-Steagall Act The national bank act of 1933 that created the federal deposit insurance system and separated commercial from investment banking. (*Chapter 7*)

gold exchange standard A system for making international payments in which each national currency is freely convertible into gold bullion at a fixed price and also freely convertible into other currencies at relatively stable prices. (*Chapter 28*)

gold standard A system of payments for purchases of goods and services in which nations agree to exchange paper money or coins for gold bullion at predetermined prices and allow gold to be exported or imported freely from one nation to another. (*Chapter 28*)

Government National Mortgage Association (GNMA) A federal government agency created in 1968 to assist the home mortgage market through such activities as purchasing mortgages to finance low-income family housing projects and guaranteeing principal and interest payments on securities issued by private mortgage lenders that are backed by pools of home mortgages. (*Chapter 25*)

government-sponsored agencies Institutions originally owned by the federal government but now privately owned with the authority to borrow from and lend money to private businesses and individuals or to issue loan guarantees. (*Chapter 17*)

hedging The act of buying and selling financial claims or using other financial tools in order to protect against the risk of fluctuations in market prices or interest rates. (*Chapter 13*)

holding-period yield The rate of return received or expected from a loan or security over the period the investor actually holds it, including the price for which the instrument is sold to another investor. (*Chapter 9*)

home equity loan Extension of credit to individuals who own their homes in which the borrowers' homes are pledged as collateral to support the loans and the amount of the loan is based on the difference between the market value of the home and the amount of any home mortgage debt outstanding (i.e., the owner's equity in a home). (*Chapter 24*)

homogenization The tendency of different financial institutions to offer the same services. (*Chapter 30*)

implied rate forecast The market's expectation about future interest rates as indicated by the shape of the yield curve or by financial futures prices. (*Chapter 12*)

income effect The relationship between interest rate levels and the volume of saving in the economy that argues that the advent of higher interest rates may induce savers to save *less* because each dollar saved now earns a higher rate of return. (*Chapter 8*)

indenture A contract accompanying the issue of a bond or note by a corporation or other borrower that lists the rights, privileges, and obligations of the borrower and of the investor who has purchased the bond or note. (*Chapter 26*)

indirect finance Also known as financial intermediation, in which financial transactions (especially the borrowing and lending of money) are carried on through a financial intermediary. (*Chapter 2*)

industrial development bond Debt security issued by a local government to aid a private company in the construction of a plant and/or the purchase of equipment or land. (*Chapter 26*)

inflation A rise in the average level of all prices of goods and services traded in the economy over any given period of time. (*Chapter 10*)

inflation-caused depreciation effect Changes in the expected inflation rate may not lead to equivalent increases in nominal interest rates due to the tendency of depreciation charges on existing plant and equipment to lag behind the rising cost of replacement plant and equipment, discouraging business investment and credit demand. (*Chapter 10*)

inflation-caused income effect The relationship between changes in the rate of inflation and shifts in income (including consumption and saving) that lead to changes in real and nominal interest rates. (*Chapter 10*)

inflation-caused income tax effect The presence of a progressive income tax structure tends to cause nominal interest rates to increase by more than the expected increase in inflation. (*Chapter 10*)

inflation-caused wealth effect Changes in inflation may alter the value of wealth held in financial assets by individuals and institutions, causing a change in their savings plans and leading to offsetting movements in real and nominal interest rates. (*Chapter 10*)

inflation premium The expected rate of price inflation that, when added to the real interest rate, equals the nominal interest rate on a loan. (*Chapter 10*)

inflation risk (or purchasing power risk) The probability that increases in the average level of prices for all goods and services sold in the economy will reduce the purchasing power of an investor's income from loans or securities. (*Chapter 14*)

installment credit All liabilities of a borrowing customer other than home mortgages that are retired in two or more consecutive loan payments. (*Chapter 24*)

interest rate The price of credit, or ratio of the fees charged to secure credit from a lender to the amount borrowed, usually expressed on an annual percentage basis. (*Chapter 9*)

interest rate insurance An insurer agreeing to reimburse a borrower for additional interest expense if the borrower's loan rate climbs above some specified maximum loan rate. (*Chapter 12*)

interest rate parity A condition prevailing in international markets where the interest rate differential between two nations matches the forward discount or premium on their two currencies. (*Chapter 28*)

interest rate structure The concept that the interest rate or yield attached to any loan or security consists of the risk-free (*or pure*) rate of interest plus risk premiums for the security holder's exposure to various forms of risk. (*Chapter 11*)

interest rate SWAP A contract between two or more firms in which interest payments are exchanged so that each participating firm saves on interest costs and gets a better balance between its cash inflows and outflows. (*Chapter 12*)

internal financing The use of saving by an economic unit, rather than debt, to support the acquisition of real and/or financial assets. (*Chapter 2*)

International Banking Act A U.S. law passed in 1978 to bring foreign banks operating in the United States under regulation. (*Chapter 29*)

international banking facilities (IBFs) A domestically based set of computerized accounts recording transactions of a U.S. bank with its foreign customers. (*Chapter 29*)

International Lending and Supervision Act A federal law passed in 1983 requiring U.S. banks to increase their capital and to pursue more prudent international loan policies. (*Chapter 29*)

investment Expenditures on capital goods or on inventories of goods or raw materials that are used to produce other goods and services, causing future production and income to rise. (*Chapter 1*)

investment banker Financial institution that assists corporations and units of government in raising funds by underwriting their security offerings and rendering financial advice. (*Chapters 6 and 26*)

investment companies Financial intermediaries that sell shares to the public to raise funds and invest the proceeds in stocks, bonds, and other securities. (*Chapter 6*)

investment institutions Financial intermediaries selling their customers securities and other financial assets in order to build up savings for retirement or for other customer uses. (*Chapter 2*)

junk bonds Corporate debt securities with low credit ratings (below investment grade). (*Chapter 11*)

L The definition of the U.S. money supply that includes the M3 definition of money plus nonbank public holdings of U.S. Savings Bonds, short-term Treasury securities, commercial paper and bankers' acceptances, net of money market mutual funds' holdings of these same assets. (*Chapter 21*)

leasing companies Financial service firms that provide businesses and consumers access to equipment, motor vehicles, and other assets for a stipulated period of time at an agreed-upon leasing rate. (*Chapter 6*)

legal reserves Deposits held at the Federal Reserve banks by depository institutions plus currency and coin held in the vaults of these institutions. (*Chapters 4, 16, 20, and 21*)

letter of credit An authorization to draft funds from a bank provided stipulated conditions are met. (*Chapter 29*)

leveraged buyouts A form of corporate takeover in which the management of a company or other small group of investors buys the publicly owned stock of the firm, financing the transaction mainly with new debt that will be repaid from planned increases in company earnings. (*Chapter 26*)

liability management The techniques used by banks to control the amount and composition of their borrowed funds by changing the interest rates they offer to reflect competition and the intensity of the bank's borrowing requirements. (*Chapter 16*)

life insurance companies Financial service firms selling contracts to customers that promise to reduce the financial loss to an individual or family associated with death, disability, or old age. (*Chapter 6*)

liquidity The quality or capability of any asset to be sold quickly with little risk of loss and possessing a relatively stable price over time. (*Chapters 11 and 14*)

liquidity preference theory of interest rates An explanation of the level of and change in interest rates that focuses on the interaction of the supply of and demand for money. (*Chapter 8*)

liquidity premium The added yield (*interest return*) that must be paid to investors to get them to buy and hold long-term instead of short-term securities. (*Chapter 10*)

loanable funds theory of interest rates The credit view of what determines the level of and changes in interest rates that focuses on the interaction of the demand for and the supply of loanable funds (*credit*). (*Chapter 8*)

loan options Contracts entitling a borrower to take out a loan at a guaranteed interest rate over a stipulated time period. (*Chapter 12*)

London interbank offer rate (LIBOR) Short-term interest rate attached to Eurocurrency deposits traded between banks. (*Chapter 18*)

long hedge The purchase of futures contracts calling for the delivery of securities or commodities to the hedger on a specific future date at a set price. (*Chapter 13*)

long position The purchase of securities outright from the seller in order to hold them until they mature or must be sold. (*Chapter 15*)

M1 The narrowest definition of the U.S. money supply consisting of currency outside the Treasury, Federal Reserve banks, and the vaults of banks, plus checking accounts and other checkable deposits held by the nonbank public. (*Chapter 21*)

M2 The definition of the U.S. money supply that includes M1 plus savings and small-denomination (under $100,000) time deposits, money market fund shares not held by institutions, money market deposit accounts (MMDAs), overnight Eurodollar deposits issued to U.S. residents by foreign branches of U.S. banks worldwide, and overnight and continuing-contract repurchase agreements issued by commercial banks. (*Chapter 21*)

M3 The definition of the U.S. money supply that includes M2 plus large-denomination ($100,000-plus) time deposits and term repurchase agreements issued by commercial banks and thrift institutions, term Eurodollars held by U.S. residents at foreign branches of U.S. banks worldwide and at all banking offices in the United Kingdom and Canada, and institution-owned balances in money market mutual funds. (*Chapter 21*)

managed float An international monetary and payments system in which the value of any currency is determined by demand and supply forces in the marketplace, but governments intervene on occasion in an effort to stabilize the value of their own currencies. (*Chapter 28*)

managed float currency standard System of currency valuation in which each nation chooses its own currency exchange rate policy. (*Chapter 28*)

margin requirements The difference between the market value of a security and its maximum loan value as specified by a regulation enforced by the Federal Reserve Board. (*Chapter 20*)

market An institutional mechanism for trading goods and services. (*Chapter 1*)

marketability The feature of a loan or security that reflects its ability to be sold quickly to recover the purchaser's funds. (*Chapter 11*)

market broadening A tendency for financial service markets to expand geographically over time due to advances in technology and increased customer mobility. (*Chapter 30*)

market risk (or interest rate risk) The probability that the prices of securities or other assets will fall (due to rising interest rates), confronting the investor with a capital loss. (*Chapter 14*)

market segmentation argument A theory of the yield curve in which the financial markets are thought to be separated into several distinct markets by the maturity preferences of various investors so that demand and supply for loans and securities in each market determine relative interest rates on long-term versus short-term securities. (*Chapter 10*)

master note A borrowing arrangement between a corporation issuing commercial paper and an institution buying the paper in which the buying institution agrees to accept new paper each day up to a specified maximum amount. (*Chapter 17*)

maturity Length of calendar time in days, weeks, months, and years before a security or loan comes due and must be paid off. (*Chapter 10*)

member banks Banks that have joined the Federal Reserve System, consisting of all federally chartered (*national*) banks and any state-chartered U.S. banks that meet the Federal Reserve's requirements for membership. (*Chapter 19*)

modified exchange standard A system of currency exchanges and international payments in which foreign currencies are linked to gold and the U.S. dollar, with the price of gold in terms of U.S. dollars remaining fixed. (*Chapter 28*)

monetarist view An approach to economic policy that contends that the money supply is a dominant influence on the price level, spending, production, and employment in the economy. (*Chapter 21*)

monetary base The sum of legal reserves in the banking system plus the amount of currency and coin held by the public. (*Chapter 20*)

monetary policy The use of various tools by central banks to control the cost and availability of loanable funds in an effort to achieve national economic goals. (*Chapter 19*)

money A financial asset that serves as a medium of exchange and standard of value for purchases of goods and services. (*Chapter 2*)

money creation The ability of banks and other depository institutions to create a deposit, such as a checking account, that can be used as a medium of exchange (to make payments for purchases of goods and services). (*Chapter 4*)

money market The institution set up by society to channel temporary surpluses of cash into temporary loans of funds, one year or less to maturity. (*Chapters 1 and 14*)

money market deposit accounts (MMDAs) Deposits whose interest yields vary with market conditions and are subject to withdrawal by check. (*Chapter 5*)

money market mutual fund An investment company selling shares to the public and investing the proceeds in short-term securities, such as Treasury bills and other money market instruments. (*Chapter 5*)

money multiplier The ratio of the size of the money supply to the total reserve base available to depository institutions. (*Chapter 20*)

money-supply expectations effect A method for forecasting interest rates that compares actual growth of the money supply with the market's expectation for money supply growth. (*Chapter 12*)

money-supply income effect Increases and decreases in income and spending resulting in changes in the demand for money, and leading to corresponding increases or decreases in interest rates. (*Chapter 12*)

money-supply liquidity effect Increases or decreases in the money supply causing interest rates to move in the opposite direction (assuming money demand is unchanged). (*Chapter 12*)

moral suasion A monetary policy tool of the central bank in which its officers and staff try to persuade bankers and the public through speeches and written communications to conform more closely to the central bank's goals. (*Chapter 20*)

mortgage-backed securities Debt obligations issued by private mortgage-lending institutions using selected residential mortgage loans they hold as collateral; the mortgage loans generate principal and interest payments to repay holders of the mortgage-backed securities. (*Chapter 25*)

mortgage bank A financial service firm that works with property developers to provide real estate financing and then places the long-term loans with long-term lenders such as insurance companies and savings banks. (*Chapter 6*)

mortgage bonds Long-term debt secured by a lien on specific assets, usually plant and equipment, held by the issuing corporation. (*Chapter 26*)

multinational corporation A large company with manufacturing, trading, or service operations in several different countries. (*Chapter 29*)

municipals Debt securities issued by states, counties, cities, school districts, and other local units of government. (*Chapter 23*)

mutuals Depository institutions owned by their depositors, such as savings banks and many savings and loan associations. (*Chapter 5*)

national banks U.S. banking institutions that received their charter of incorporation from the Comptroller of the Currency, an agency of the U.S. government. (*Chapter 4*)

National Credit Union Administration (NCUA) Federal regulatory agency that oversees the activities of federally chartered credit unions. (*Chapter 7*)

National Income Accounts A system of social accounts compiled and released quarterly by the U.S. Department of Commerce that presents data on the nation's production of goods and services, income flows, spending, and saving. (*Chapter 3*)

negotiable certificate of deposit (CD) A marketable receipt issued by a bank of other depository institution to a customer acknowledging the deposit of customer funds for a designated period at a specified interest rate formula. (*Chapter 16*)

negotiated markets Institutional mechanisms set up by society to make loans and trade securities in which the terms of trade are set by direct bargaining between a lender and a borrower. (*Chapter 1*)

nominal interest rate The published rate of interest attached to a loan or security that includes both a real interest rate component and the inflation rate (inflation premium) expected over the life of the loan or security. (*Chapter 10*)

nonborrowed reserves The largest component of the total legal reserves of depository institutions, consisting of all those legal reserves owned by depository institutions themselves and not borrowed from the Federal Reserve banks. (*Chapter 21*)

noninstallment credit A loan that is normally paid off in a lump sum rather than in a series of installment payments. (*Chapters 9 and 24*)

nonresidential mortgages Loans secured by business and farm properties. (*Chapter 25*)

note A shorter-term debt obligation issued by a business firm, individual, or unit of government to borrow money with a time to maturity that usually does not exceed five years. (*Chapter 3*)

NOW account An interest-bearing checking account available to individuals and nonprofit institutions from banks and other depository institutions. (*Chapters 22 and 24*)

Office of Thrift Supervision Federal agency that charters and supervises savings and loans. (*Chapter 7*)

open market operations The buying and selling of securities by a central bank to affect the quantity and growth of the legal reserves of depository institutions and general credit conditions in order to achieve the nation's economic goals. (*Chapter 20*)

open markets Institutional mechanisms created by society to make loans and trade securities in which any individual or institution can participate. (*Chapter 1*)

option contract An agreement between contract writers and contract buyers to accept delivery of ("call") securities or place with buyers ("put") securities at a specified price on or before the date the contracts expire. (*Chapters 13 and 21*)

option premium The fee that the buyer of an option contract must pay to the writer of the contract for the right to deliver or accept delivery of securities at a set price. (*Chapter 13*)

organized exchanges Locations where stocks, bonds, and other securities are traded according to the rules and regulations for trading established by members of the exchange. (*Chapter 27*)

original maturity The interval of time between the issue date of a security and the date on which the borrower promises to redeem it. (*Chapter 14*)

over-the-counter market A mechanism for trading stocks and other securities through brokers or dealers operating off the major securities exchanges. (*Chapter 27*)

pass-throughs Securities issued against a pool of mortgage loans held by a financial institution. (*Chapter 25*)

pension funds Financial service firms selling retirement plans to their customers in which savings are set aside in accounts established in the customers' names and allowed to accumulate at interest until those customers reach retirement age. (*Chapter 6*)

perfect market A market in which all available information affecting the value of financial instruments is freely available to everyone, transactions costs are minimal, and all participants in the market are price takers rather than price setters. (*Chapter 1*)

political risk The probability that changes in government laws or regulations will result in a lower rate of return to the investor or, in the extreme case, a total loss of invested capital. (*Chapters 14 and 29*)

portfolio immunization An investment strategy that tries to protect the expected yield from a security or portfolio of securities by acquiring those securities whose duration equals the length of the investor's planned holding period. (*Chapter 10*)

preferred habitat The theory of the yield curve that holds that investors prefer certain maturities of securities over other maturities due to differences in liquidity needs, risk, tax exposure, and other factors. (*Chapter 10*)

preferred stock A share of ownership in a business corporation that promises a stated annual dividend. (*Chapter 27*)

prepayment risk The probability that a loan or security (especially securities that draw their earnings from pools of loans) will be paid off ahead of schedule, lowering the investor's expected yield from the instrument. (*Chapters 11 and 25*)

price elasticity The ratio of changes in the price of a debt security to changes in its yield. (*Chapter 10*)

price of credit The rate of interest that must be paid to secure the use of borrowed funds. (*Chapter 8*)

primary dealers Security firms that are recognized by the Federal Reserve System to buy and sell securities with the Fed. (*Chapter 15*)

primary markets Institutional mechanisms set up by society to trade newly issued loans and securities. (*Chapter 1*)

primary securities The IOUs issued by borrowers from a financial intermediary and held by the intermediary as interest-bearing assets. (*Chapter 2*)

private (or direct) placement Placing securities with one or a limited number of investors rather than trying to sell them in the open market. (*Chapter 26*)

program trading Computer-assisted decisions about security purchases and sales in an effort to take advantage of temporary price differences between securities or security price indexes in different markets in order to earn above-average returns or to protect against excessive market risk. (*Chapter 27*)

property-casualty insurers Financial service firms selling contracts to protect their customers against losses to person or property due to negligence, crime, adverse weather changes, fire, and other hazards. (*Chapter 6*)

public debt The volume of debt obligations that are the responsibility of the federal government and therefore of its taxpayers. (*Chapter 22*)

public sale When securities are sold in the open market to any individual or institution willing to pay the price, usually through investment bankers. (*Chapter 26*)

put options Contracts granting the buyer the right to sell a specified number of equity shares or debt securities at a set price on or before the expiration date. (*Chapters 13 and 27*)

random walk A theory of security price movements that argues that the future path of individual security prices is no more predictable than is the path of a series of random numbers. (*Chapter 27*)

rate cap A maximum interest rate inserted into a loan agreement that limits how far the loan rate can rise over the term of the loan. (*Chapter 12*)

rate collars Loan agreements containing both a minimum and a maximum loan rate to protect both borrower and lender against excessive interest rate risk. (*Chapter 12*)

rate of interest The price of acquiring credit, usually expressed as a ratio of the cost of securing credit to the total amount of credit obtained. (*Chapter 8*)

rational expectations theory of interest rates An explanation of the level of and changes in interest rates based on changes in investor expectations regarding future security prices and returns. (*Chapter 8*)

real estate investment trusts (REITs) Tax-exempt corporations that receive at least three quarters of their gross income from real estate transactions and devote a high percentage of their assets to real property loans. (*Chapter 6*)

real interest rate The rate of return from a financial asset expressed in terms of its purchasing power (adjusted for inflation). (*Chapter 10*)

real investment The net change in real assets held by a sector or unit in the economy over a specified time period. (*Chapter 3*)

reinvestment risk Probability that earnings from a loan or security will have to be reinvested in lower-yielding assets in the future. (*Chapter 14*)

representative offices Facilities established in distant markets by a bank in order to sell the bank's services and assist its clients; these offices usually cannot accept deposits or make loans. (*Chapter 29*)

repurchase agreement (RP) A loan (usually granted to a bank or security dealer) that is collateralized by high-quality securities (usually government securities). (*Chapter 15*)

required reserves Holdings of cash and funds on deposit with the Federal Reserve banks by depository institutions that are required by law to backstop the public's deposits held by these same institutions. (*Chapter 20*)

reserve requirements The percentage of various liabilities (such as deposits received from the public) that must be held by depository institutions, either in vault cash or on deposit at the Federal Reserve banks. (*Chapter 20*)

residential mortgage credit Loans provided to support the purchase of new or existing single-family homes and other permanent dwellings. (*Chapter 24*)

residential mortgages Loans secured by single-family homes and other dwellings. (*Chapter 25*)

revenue-anticipation notes (RANs) Short-term debt obligations issued by state and local units of government in lieu of expected future governmental revenues in order to meet near-term cash needs. (*Chapter 23*)

revenue bonds Debt obligations issued by state and local governments that are repayable only from a particular source of funds, such as revenues generated by a toll road or toll bridge or from user fees derived by selling water or electric power. (*Chapter 23*)

risk-free rate of interest The rate of return on a riskless security, often called the *pure rate of interest* or the *opportunity cost of money*. (*Chapter 8*)

risk management tools Financial devices (*such as futures and options*) that permit a borrower or lender of funds to protect against the risks of changing prices and interest rates. (*Chapter 30*)

savings The amount of funds left over out of current income after current consumption expenditures are made or, for a business firm, the current net earnings retained in the business instead of paid out to the owners. (*Chapter 1*)

savings and loan associations A leading home mortgage lender in the United States, making predominantly local loans to finance the purchase of housing for individuals and families. (*Chapter 5*)

savings banks Depository institutions that are owned by their depositors and can be chartered by the federal government and by some states. (*Chapter 5*)

seasonality Patterns in the behavior of interest rates, with rate increases during certain seasons of the year and decreases during other seasons. (*Chapter 12*)

secondary markets Institutional mechanisms set up by society to trade or exchange loans and securities that have already been issued. (*Chapter 1*)

secondary securities Financial claims, such as deposits, issued by a financial intermediary to raise loanable funds. (*Chapter 2*)

Securities and Exchange Commission Regulatory body of the federal government charged with monitoring the behavior of security brokers, dealers, and investment institutions. (*Chapter 7*)

securitization The selling of shares or certificates representing an interest in a pool of income-generating assets (such as mortgage loans) as a method for raising funds by a financial institution. (*Chapters 5 and 30*)

securitized assets Loans packaged together in a pool and securities representing claims to the income generated by the pooled loans are sold to investors (*Chapter 4*)

securitized mortgages Securities issued against a pool of mortgage loans whose interest and principal payments are paid to the security holders. (*Chapter 25*)

security dealers Financial firms that provide a conduit for buyers and sellers of marketable securities by holding a portfolio of these securities and standing ready to buy and sell these securities at an announced price. (*Chapter 6*)

selective credit controls Monetary policy tools that affect specific groups or sectors in the financial system. (*Chapter 20*)

semidirect finance Any financial transaction (especially the borrowing and lending of money) that is assisted by a security broker or dealer. (*Chapter 2*)

serialization The splitting up of a single bond issue into several different maturities (used most often for state and local government bonds). (*Chapter 23*)

share draft Interest-bearing checking account offered by a credit union. (*Chapter 5*)

shell branches Booking offices of multinational banks, usually set up offshore to attract deposits and avoid certain domestic banking regulations. (*Chapter 29*)

short hedge The sale of futures contracts promising the delivery of securities or commodities to another party on a specific future date at a set price. (*Chapter 13*)

short position Dealers and other investors promise to sell and deliver in the future securities they do not currently own, hoping security prices will fall in the interim. (*Chapter 15*)

simple interest method A method of figuring the interest on a loan that charges interest only for the period of time the borrower actually has use of the borrowed funds. (*Chapter 9*)

social accounting A system of record keeping that reports economic and financial activity for the whole economy and/ or between the principal sectors of the economy. (*Chapter 3*)

solicitation method A method for selling federal agency securities in which orders are taken from buyers and the securities are priced and delivered to investors after the order book is closed. (*Chapter 17*)

sources and uses of funds statements A financial report prepared for each sector of the economy in the Federal Reserve Board's Flow of Fund Accounts that shows changes in net worth and changes in holdings of financial assets and liabilities over a specific time period. (*Chapter 3*)

special drawing rights (SDRs) An official monetary reserve unit developed by the International Monetary Fund to settle international claims between nations. (*Chapter 28*)

spot market Channel through which currencies, securities, commodities, or other goods and services are traded for immediate delivery to the buyer once buyer and seller agree on the terms of trade. (*Chapter 28*)

State Banking Commissions Government boards that charter and supervise banks headquartered in a given state. (*Chapter 7*)

stock-index arbitrage The program trading strategy in which professional traders look for temporary underpricing or overpricing of stock-index financial futures contracts compared to the cash market (spot) prices of comparable stocks, simultaneously buying (selling) stocks and selling (buying) futures contracts to profit from any temporary relative mispricing of these two financial instruments. (*Chapter 13*)

stocks Ownership shares in a corporation, giving the holder claim to any dividends distributed from current earnings. (*Chapter 3*)

strike price The price for securities specified in an option contract; also called the *exercise price*. (*Chapter 13*)

stripped securities Interest-bearing financial instruments (usually bonds) that have been split up into multiple discount securities, each composed of one interest payment (known as an *IO*) or one promised principal payment (known as a *PO*). (*Chapter 12*)

substitution effect Positive relationship between rate of interest and volume of savings in the economy. (*Chapter 8*)

supply-side economics An approach to economic policy that argues that the nation's economic policy should be directed toward increasing productivity and the supply of goods and services in order to combat inflation. (*Chapter 21*)

surplus-budget unit An individual, business firm, or unit of government whose current income receipts exceed its current expenditures and therefore is a net lender of funds to the money and capital markets. (*Chapter 2*)

symbiotic A conglomerate financial firm that frequently merges insurance sales, security brokerage, real estate brokerage, financial counseling, and credit services within the same organization. (*Chapter 6*)

tax-anticipation notes (TANs) Short-term debt obligations issued by state and local governments to provide for immediate cash needs until tax revenues come in. (*Chapter 23*)

tax-exemption privilege A feature bestowed by law on some financial assets (such as state and local government bonds) that makes the income they generate free of taxation at federal or state and local government levels, or both. (*Chapter 23*)

tax-exempt securities Debt securities issued by state, city, county, and other local units of government or by other qualified borrowers whose interest income is exempt from federal taxation and from most state taxes as well. (*Chapter 14*)

third-country bills Bankers' acceptances issued by banks in one country that finance the transport or storage of goods traded between two other countries. (*Chapter 18*)

third market Mechanism through which securities listed on a stock exchange are traded off the exchange in the over-the-counter market. (*Chapter 27*)

time draft A bank's promise to pay a stipulated amount of funds upon presentation of the draft on a specific future date. (*Chapter 18*)

transaction accounts Deposits (such as a checking account or other accounts offered by financial institutions) that can be used to make payments for purchases of goods and services. (*Chapters 4 and 20*)

Truth in Lending A law passed by the U.S. Congress in 1968 that requires covered lenders to disclose fully all the relevant terms of a personal loan to the borrower and to report a standardized loan rate (known as the APR, or annual percentage rate). (*Chapters 9 and 24*)

unbiased expectations hypothesis A theory of the yield curve which contends that the curve's shape is determined exclusively by investor expectations regarding future interest rate movements. (*Chapter 10*)

U.S. Treasury bills A debt obligation, one year or less to maturity, issued by the United States government. (*Chapter 15*)

variable-rate mortgage (VRM) Home mortgage loans carrying an interest rate that varies during the term of a loan, generally depending on the movement of interest rates in the open market. (*Chapter 25*)

vehicle currency A monetary unit of a nation that is not only the standard of value (unit of account) for domestic transactions but is also used to express the prices of many goods and services traded between other nations as well. (*Chapter 28*)

wealth Accumulated assets held by an economic unit as a result of saving. (*Chapter 1*)

wealth effect (of saving and interest rates) The relationship between the volume of saving and interest rates that contends that the net wealth position of savers (the balance in their portfolios between debt and financial assets) determines how their desired levels of saving will change as interest rates change. (*Chapter 8*)

yield curve Relationship between short-term interest rates and long-term interest rates (that is, between yield to maturity and time to maturity of a debt security) as reflected in a smooth curve with an upward, downward, or horizontal slope. (*Chapter 10*)

yield to maturity The interest rate on a debt security that equates the purchase price of the security to the present value of all its expected annual net cash inflows (income) from now until its maturity date. (*Chapter 9*)

zero coupon bonds Long-term debt obligations that are sold at a price well below their par (or face) value and without any promised interest payments; the buyer's gain is in the form of price appreciation over time toward the debt securities' par (or face) value. (*Chapter 26*)

Index